# Twentieth-Century Literary Criticism

# Guide to Gale Literary Criticism Series

| For criticism on | Consult these Gale series |
|---|---|
| Authors now living or who died after December 31, 1959 | *CONTEMPORARY LITERARY CRITICISM (CLC)* |
| Authors who died between 1900 and 1959 | *TWENTIETH-CENTURY LITERARY CRITICISM (TCLC)* |
| Authors who died between 1800 and 1899 | *NINETEENTH-CENTURY LITERATURE CRITICISM (NCLC)* |
| Authors who died between 1400 and 1799 | *LITERATURE CRITICISM FROM 1400 TO 1800 (LC)*  *SHAKESPEAREAN CRITICISM (SC)* |
| Authors who died before 1400 | *CLASSICAL AND MEDIEVAL LITERATURE CRITICISM (CMLC)* |
| Authors of books for children and young adults | *CHILDREN'S LITERATURE REVIEW (CLR)* |
| Dramatists | *DRAMA CRITICISM (DC)* |
| Poets | *POETRY CRITICISM (PC)* |
| Short story writers | *SHORT STORY CRITICISM (SSC)* |
| Black writers of the past two hundred years | *BLACK LITERATURE CRITICISM (BLC)* |
| Hispanic writers of the late nineteenth and twentieth centuries | *HISPANIC LITERATURE CRITICISM (HLC)* |
| Native North American writers and orators of the eighteenth, nineteenth, and twentieth centuries | *NATIVE NORTH AMERICAN LITERATURE (NNAL)* |
| Major authors from the Renaissance to the present | *WORLD LITERATURE CRITICISM, 1500 TO THE PRESENT (WLC)* |

ISSN 0276-8178

*R*

# Volume 85

# Twentieth-Century Literary Criticism

**Criticism of the
Works of Novelists, Poets, Playwrights,
Short Story Writers, and Other Creative Writers
Who Lived between 1900 and 1960,
from the First Published Critical
Appraisals to Current Evaluations**

**Jennifer Baise**
*Editor*

**Thomas Ligotti**
*Associate Editor*

*Detroit*
*San Francisco*
*London*
*Boston*
*Woodbridge, CT*

**STAFF**

Jennifer Baise, *Editor*

Thomas Ligotti, *Associate Editor*

Maria Franklin, *Permissions Manager*
Kimberly F. Smilay, *Permissions Specialist*
Kelly A. Quin, *Permissions Associates*
Sandy Gore, *Permissions Assistant*

Victoria B. Cariappa, *Research Manager*
Andrew Guy Malonis, Barbara McNeil, Gary J. Oudersluys, Maureen Richards, Cheryl L. Warnock, *Research Specialists*
Patricia T. Ballard, Tamara C. Nott, Tracie A. Richardson, *Research Associates*
Phyllis Blackman, Corrine Stocker, *Research Assistant*

Mary Beth Trimper, *Production Director*
Cindy Range, *Buyer*

Gary Leach, *Graphic Artist*
Randy Bassett, *Image Database Supervisor*
Robert Duncan, Michael Logusz, *Imaging Specialists*
Pamela Reed, *Imaging Coordinator*

Library of Congress Catalog Card Number 76-46132
ISBN 0-7876-2743-7
ISSN 0276-8178

Printed in the United States of America
10 9 8 7 6 5 4 3 2 1

# Contents

Preface  vii

Acknowledgments  xi

# Preface

Since its inception more than fifteen years ago, *Twentieth-Century Literary Criticism* has been purchased and used by nearly 10,000 school, public, and college or university libraries. *TCLC* has covered more than 500 authors, representing 58 nationalities, and over 25,000 titles. No other reference source has surveyed the critical response to twentieth-century authors and literature as thoroughly as *TCLC*. In the words of one reviewer, "there is nothing comparable available." *TCLC* "is a gold mine of information—dates, pseudonyms, biographical information, and criticism from books and periodicals—which many libraries would have difficulty assembling on their own."

## Scope of the Series

*TCLC* is designed to serve as an introduction to authors who died between 1900 and 1960 and to the most significant interpretations of these author's works. The great poets, novelists, short story writers, playwrights, and philosophers of this period are frequently studied in high school and college literature courses. In organizing and reprinting the vast amount of critical material written on these authors, *TCLC* helps students develop valuable insight into literary history, promotes a better understanding of the texts, and sparks ideas for papers and assignments. Each entry in *TCLC* presents a comprehensive survey of an author's career or an individual work of literature and provides the user with a multiplicity of interpretations and assessments. Such variety allows students to pursue their own interests; furthermore, it fosters an awareness that literature is dynamic and responsive to many different opinions.

Every fourth volume of *TCLC* is devoted to literary topics. These topic entries widen the focus of the series from individual authors to such broader subjects as literary movements, prominent themes in twentieth-century literature, literary reaction to political and historical events, significant eras in literary history, prominent literary anniversaries, and the literatures of cultures that are often overlooked by English-speaking readers.

*TCLC* is designed as a companion series to Gale's *Contemporary Literary Criticism*, which reprints commentary on authors now living or who have died since 1960. Because of the different periods under consideration, there is no duplication of material between *CLC* and *TCLC*. For additional information about *CLC* and Gale's other criticism titles, users should consult the Guide to Gale Literary Criticism Series preceding the title page in this volume.

## Coverage

Each volume of *TCLC* is carefully compiled to present:

- criticism of authors, or literary topics, representing a variety of genres and nationalities

- both major and lesser-known writers and literary works of the period

- 6-12 authors or 3-6 topics per volume

- individual entries that survey critical response to each author's work or each topic in literary history, including early criticism to reflect initial reactions; later criticism to represent any rise or decline in reputation; and current retrospective analyses.

## Organization of This Book

An author entry consists of the following elements: author heading, biographical and critical introduction, list of principal works, reprints of criticism (each preceded by an annotation and a bibliographic citation), and a bibliography of further reading.

- The **Author Heading** consists of the name under which the author most commonly wrote, followed by birth and death dates. If an author wrote consistently under a pseudonym, the pseudonym will be listed in the author heading and the real name given in parentheses on the first line of the biographical and critical introduction. Also located at the beginning of the introduction to the author entry are any name variations under which an author wrote, including transliterated forms for authors whose languages use nonroman alphabets.

● The **Biographical and Critical Introduction** outlines the author's life and career, as well as the critical issues surrounding his or her work. References to past volumes of *TCLC* are provided at the beginning of the introduction. Additional sources of information in other biographical and critical reference series published by Gale, including *Short Story Criticism, Children's Literature Review, Contemporary Authors, Dictionary of Literary Biography,* and *Something about the Author,* are listed in a box at the end of the entry.

● Some *TCLC* entries include **Portraits** of the author. Entries also may contain reproductions of materials pertinent to an author's career, including manuscript pages, title pages, dust jackets, letters, and drawings, as well as photographs of important people, places, and events in an author's life.

● The **List of Principal Works** is chronological by date of first book publication and identifies the genre of each work. In the case of foreign authors with both foreign-language publications and English translations, the title and date of the first English-language edition are given in brackets. Unless otherwise indicated, dramas are dated by first performance, not first publication.

● Critical essays are prefaced by **Annotations** providing the reader with information about both the critic and the criticism that follows. Included are the critic's reputation, individual approach to literary criticism, and particular expertise in an author's works. Also noted are the relative importance of a work of criticism, the scope of the essay, and the growth of critical controversy or changes in critical trends regarding an author. In some cases, these annotations cross-reference essays by critics who discuss each other's commentary.

● A complete **Bibliographic Citation** designed to facilitate location of the original essay or book precedes each piece of criticism.

● Criticism is arranged chronologically in each author entry to provide a perspective on changes in critical evaluation over the years. All titles of works by the author featured in the entry are printed in boldface type to enable the user to easily locate discussion of particular works. Also for purposes of easier identification, the critic's name and the publication date of the essay are given at the beginning of each piece of criticism. Unsigned criticism is preceded by the title of the journal in which it appeared. Some of the essays in *TCLC* also contain translated material. Unless otherwise noted, translations in brackets are by the editors; translations in parentheses or continuous with the text are by the critic. Publication information (such as footnotes or page and line references to specific editions of works) have been deleted at the editor's discretion to provide smoother reading of the text.

● An annotated list of **Further Reading** appearing at the end of each author entry suggests secondary sources on the author. In some cases it includes essays for which the editors could not obtain reprint rights.

# Cumulative Indexes

● Each volume of *TCLC* contains a cumulative **Author Index** listing all authors who have appeared in Gale's Literary Criticism Series, along with cross references to such biographical series as *Contemporary Authors* and *Dictionary of Literary Biography.* For readers' convenience, a complete list of Gale titles included appears on the first page of the author index. Useful for locating authors within the various series, this index is particularly valuable for those authors who are identified by a certain period but who, because of their death dates, are placed in another, or for those authors whose careers span two periods. For example, F. Scott Fitzgerald is found in *TCLC,* yet a writer often associated with him, Ernest Hemingway, is found in *CLC.*

- Each *TCLC* volume includes a cumulative **Nationality Index** which lists all authors who have appeared in *TCLC* volumes, arranged alphabetically under their respective nationalities, as well as Topics volume entries devoted to particular national literatures.

- Each new volume in Gale's Literary Criticism Series includes a cumulative **Topic Index,** which lists all literary topics treated in *NCLC, TCLC, LC 1400-1800,* and the *CLC* yearbook.

- Each new volume of *TCLC,* with the exception of the Topics volumes, includes a **Title Index** listing the titles of all literary works discussed in the volume. In response to numerous suggestions from librarians, Gale has also produced a **Special Paperbound Edition** of the *TCLC* title index. This annual cumulation lists all titles discussed in the series since its inception and is issued with the first volume of *TCLC* published each year. Additional copies of the index are available on request. Librarians and patrons will welcome this separate index; it saves shelf space, is easy to use, and is recyclable upon receipt of the following year's cumulation. Titles discussed in the Topics volume entries are not included *TCLC* cumulative index.

# Citing Twentieth-Century Literary Criticism

When writing papers, students who quote directly from any volume in Gale's literary Criticism Series may use the following general forms to footnote reprinted criticism. The first example pertains to materials drawn from periodicals, the second to material reprinted from books.

[1]William H. Slavick, "Going to School to DuBose Heyward," *The Harlem Renaissance Re-examined,* (AMS Press, 1987); reprinted in *Twentieth-Century Literary Criticism,* Vol. 59, ed. Jennifer Gariepy (Detroit: Gale Research, 1995), pp. 94-105.

[2]George Orwell, "Reflections on Gandhi," *Partisan Review,* 6 (Winter 1949), pp. 85-92; reprinted in *Twentieth-Century Literary Criticism,* Vol. 59, ed. Jennifer Gariepy (Detroit: Gale Research, 1995), pp. 40-3.

# Suggestions Are Welcome

In response to suggestions, several features have been added to *TCLC* since the series began, including annotations to critical essays, a cumulative index to authors in all Gale literary criticism series, entries devoted to criticism on a single work by a major author, more extensive illustrations, and a title index listing all literary works discussed in the series since its inception.

Readers who wish to suggest authors or topics to appear in future volumes, or who have other suggestions, are cordially invited to write the editors.

# Acknowledgments

The editors wish to thank the copyright holders of the excerpted criticism included in this volume and the permissions managers of many book and magazine publishing companies for assisting us in securing reproduction rights. We are also grateful to the staffs of the Detroit Public Library, the Library of Congress, the University of Detroit Mercy Library, Wayne State University Purdy/Kresge Library Complex, and the University of Michigan Libraries for making their resources available to us. Following is a list of the copyright holders who have granted us permission to reproduce material in this volume of *TCLC*. Every effort has been made to trace copyright, but if omissions have been made, please let us know.

# Caradoc Evans

## 1878-1945

(Full name David Caradoc Evans) Welsh short story writer, novelist, and playwright

## INTRODUCTION

Although he gave his first collection the apparently sentimental title *My People,* Welsh short-story writer Caradoc Evans is known for his caustic portrayals of his homeland and his neighbors. So fierce was Welsh sentiment against him that two galleries in Wales refused his portrait, and while it was on display in London, Evans's visage was slashed across the throat. In his origins at the fringes of Great Britain, his antipathy toward the land of his birth, and his inventive use of language, Evans has been compared to a more famous contemporary, James Joyce. Like Joyce, he effectively burned his bridges to his Celtic past, but won over an English audience—and ultimately a younger generation of compatriots, a group that in Evans's case included Dylan Thomas.

### Biographical Information

Evans's background is closely tied to the tradition of Welsh Nonconformism, the Protestant movement which rebelled against the Church of England as the Anglican Church had rebelled against Rome. In Wales, adherence to the Church of England was seen as adherence to England. Hence the terms "Tory" and "Anglican" went together, as did "Liberal" and "Nonconformist," and the union of Evans's Anglican father with his Liberal mother constituted a mixed marriage. When Williams Evans, a farmer, became involved with the sale of land that had belonged to a Nonconformist tenant evicted for disobeying his Anglican landlord, his wife's family disowned her. Evans was four years old when his father died, leaving the boy's mother with limited means for raising Evans and his four siblings. She ultimately became a tenant farmer herself, and Evan's childhood was one of extreme poverty—a factor which influenced the bitterness of his later writing. The Welsh village, as Evans would later portray it in *My People* and other works, was a rigid society controlled by the minister, who inhabited the chapel or "capel," and the schoolmaster or "schoolin." In Evans's view, it was a world rife with hypocrisy, an opinion shaped in part by the high esteem with which the community viewed his pusillanimous uncle Joshua Powell. The latter's refusal to fund Evans's secondary schooling, a small gesture for Powell which would have immeasurably helped the young boy, served to engender in Evans an abiding bitterness reflected in his later portrayals of hypocritical figures such as Sadrach in *Capel Sion.* At age fourteen,

Evans was forced to go to work as an apprentice draper, a position equivalent to that of a clerk in an American dry-goods store of the era. Evans remained employed thus, in Wales and later London, from 1893 to 1906, when the sale of two sketches to a newspaper convinced him that he could make a living in journalism. In 1907 he married Rose Jesse Sewell. During the next decade, he wrote for a variety of publications, including *T. P.'s Weekly* and *Ideas.* He served as editor of the latter from 1915 to 1917 and published his first two collections of stories during World War I. *My People* and *Capel Sion* brought him instant notoriety in Britain. Critics compared him to ancient Greek dramatists, Jonathan Swift, and Maksim Gorky; on the other side of the Atlantic, H. L. Mencken, who saw in Evans's Wales a mirror of the American South that he had often excoriated, echoed the praise accorded him by British critics. In Wales, Evans's unflattering portraits of his homeland brought on an anger that bordered on hatred. A group of Welsh students protested the premiere of Evans's one play, *Taffy,* but the ruckus only heightened Evans's celebrity. Evans continued to work as a journalist, becoming editor of *T. P.'s Weekly* in 1923 while he worked on his first novel, *Nothing to Pay.* He lost his job when *T. P.'s Weekly* folded in 1929, and the onset of the Depression reduced his opportunities as a journalist; meanwhile, he had met and begun an affair with an aristocratic romance novelist, Marguerite Barczinsky. Marguerite persuaded him to leave Rose, and in the early 1930s he broke completely with his past, divorcing his wife and cutting off his ties among Fleet Street journalists. Evans, who married Marguerite in 1933 and moved with her to the country, intended to become a full-time novelist, but his writing suffered, and his novels *Wasps, This Way to Heaven,* and *Mother's Marvel* were unremarkable compared to his earlier work. Except for a period in the late 1930s when he experienced a brief surge of creativity, most of his last twelve years were unhappy ones as Evans, regretting his haste in leaving his former life behind, resigned himself to the fact that he would thenceforth live off of Marguerite's wealth. Though his work improved during World War II, as *Pilgrims in a Foreign Land* proved, his mood did not. By the latter part of 1943 Evans became irresponsible with regard to his health, for instance spending a great deal of time in the cold and wet outdoors without a coat. He caught pneumonia, and in 1945 he was hospitalized for heart trouble. He died on 11 January 1945.

### Major Works

Evans's most noted works are his first two collections, *My People* and *Capel Sion.* Formerly, rural Wales had been known chiefly to literature through Allen Raine, who idealized it as Dylan Thomas, Richard Llewellyn, and others would do to a lesser extent in later years. Evans's fictional town of Manteg offered a portrait so fiercely sardonic that Welsh policemen harassed booksellers daring enough to offer the book for sale. Evan Rhiw in the story "Lamentations," from *My People,* is not atypical of the characters. Engaging in an incestuous relationship with his daughter Matilda, he gains absolution from the village minister, who announces that God ("The Big Man" in the Welsh argot of Evans's stories) has told him who is truly to blame: Matilda, the "adder in his house." The tales are written in a spare style, largely devoid of authorial comment or attempts to influence the readers' opinion; and Evans uses an unusual amalgam of Welsh and English—both modern English and the English of the King James Bible. The stories in *My Neighbours* offer similar characterizations, with the chief distinction being the fact that they take place in London and feature a character named Ben Lloyd, a vicious sycophant through whom Evans meant to parody David Lloyd George, Britain's Welsh-born Prime Minister. The play *Taffy* is more lighthearted, centering on the love affair between the free-spirited Marged and the reforming minister Spurgeon. However, with his first novel, *Nothing to Pay,* Evans returned to bleak themes; his presentation of the miser Amos Morgan offers little of the implied humor—as acerbic as it is—which alleviates the negativity of his first three collections. Twelve years elapsed between the publication of *Nothing to Pay* and that of *Pilgrims in a Foreign Land,* years that would see turmoil in Evans's personal life and a downward turn in his work as a writer. Whereas his earlier writing had been notable in part for its clean style and the absence of authorial intrusion, *Wasps* and the other novels he wrote after marrying Marguerite Barczinsky were characterized by a tendency toward aphorisms and toward telling rather than showing. In the stories collected in *Pilgrims* and *The Earth Gives All and Takes All,* however, Evans seemed to have found his voice again, albeit in a slightly mellowed form: there are glimmers of goodness among the characters in these later collections.

---

# PRINCIPAL WORKS

*My People: Stories of the Peasantry of West Wales* (short stories) 1915
*Capel Sion* (short stories) 1916
*My Neighbours* (short stories) 1919; enlarged edition published as *My Neighbors: Stories of the Welsh People,* 1920
*Taffy: A Play of Welsh Village Life* (drama) 1923
*Nothing to Pay* (novel) 1930
*Pilgrims in a Foreign Land* (short stories) 1942
*The Earth Gives All and Takes All* (short stories) 1946

# CRITICISM

**Edwin Pugh (essay date 1917)**

SOURCE: "The Welsh Peasant," in *The Bookman,* London, Vol. LI, No. 306, March, 1917, pp. 191-2.

[*In the following essay, a review of* Capel Sion, *a countryman gives cautious praise to Evans's literary ability, but questions his view of the Welsh people.*]

"Art for Art's sake" was one of the war cries of the 'nineties, and curiously enough it was heard loudest and most often in literary circles. I cannot recall one painter, actor, or musician who echoed that cry. Yet we have had since all manner of revolutionary movements in painting, music, and drama, whilst our authors seem to be carrying on in very much the same way now as twenty-five years ago. It is significant, too, that of all the "Art for Art's sake" young lions of those roaring times hardly one is to be counted, with the possible exception of Mr. George Moore, among the foremost writers of to-day. The reason is, of course, that "Art for Art's sake" is a motto with as little to recommend it as "Eating for eating's sake." One might almost say, with slight reservations, that all the most notable books written in our time, from "Alice in Wonderland" to "The Heavenly Twins," were written with a purpose.

And so it is with Mr. Caradoc Evans's *Capel Sion.*

If there were no high moral purpose underlying the stark realism of this book it would lack all justification. Even its fine artistic merits would not redeem it from condemnation. As it stands, however—and I say this in all reverence—it is as moral as the Bible, whose style it adopts with consummate effect, and whose lessons it inculcates with the same impersonal force and sincerity.

Speaking as a man of Welsh blood and temperament I am bound to accept the authenticity of these studies of the Welsh peasantry, their character and habits, though I have little first hand knowledge of that particular class of Celt. But, during my sojourns in Wales, I have caught glimpses, suggestions, indications—call them what you will—of the way of life there in the more obscure and lesser known districts, sufficient in themselves to enable me to recognise that Mr. Evans is stating no more and no less than the truth in these amazing stories and sketches.

And that is the only word for them: Amazing! They are amazing as the discovery of a race of heathen people living in our very midst: a race eaten up by all manner of superstition, cruel and lustful, covetous and grasping. No stories of pioneer exploration or missionary travel have ever revealed among naked painted savages a more horrible state of things than this book reveals. It is neither better nor worse than its predecessor *My People*: it is merely a continuation of it, or rather an elaboration. It exhibits the same high qualities of simplicity and strength, wrought into a style which is as distinctive as the style of Bunyan, with whom Mr. Evans in certain aspects might be compared, if it were not that he is content to let the reader draw his own moral from the narrative instead of stating it in so many words.

It would be impossible to outline any of these stories, because of the author's economy of means. Not a word or a stroke is wasted. The very backgrounds seem to evolve themselves out of the incidents; they are never described. We have no full-length portraits of any of the people, and yet we visualise them as clearly as if we beheld them in the flesh. They talk, and we hear their voices. They weep, they rave, they laugh—and again we hear them, we recognise the force and picturesqueness of their everyday speech, their common idiom, with its strange commingling of poetry, symbolism, and blasphemy. And there again is the hand of the master; for it is always the most primitive folk who in their ordinary converse one with another, are most often at once poetic, symbolic, and blasphemous.

And yet. . . . Is Mr. Evans's view of his own people a comprehensive view? I cannot believe it. I cannot but think that something of bitter passion and revolt has blurred his sight a little and limited his range of vision, blinded him almost wholly to their virtues, however few and rare. For a race cannot be utterly wicked and vicious, and endure. That way lies racial suicide, and the Welsh, even the Welsh peasantry, are very much alive.

Therefore, before parting from Mr. Evans with the utmost gratitude for the artistic delight he has given me, I would entreat him, in his next book, to try to get a little more light and shade into his pictures, to portray something, at least, of these Welsh peasants' more kindly and worthy traits: of their hospitality, for instance, which I have personally experienced. Mr. Evans has given us so much. That is why we want so much more. And that he can give us much more is as plain to see as the genius of his writing.

### *The Nation* (essay date 1918)

SOURCE: "Phases of the Short Story," in *The Nation,* New York, Vol. 107, No. 2790, December 21, 1918, p. 779.

[*In the following excerpt, a review of* Capel Sion, *a critic questions the authenticity of Evans's bitter portraits.*]

Not long ago a young Welshman signing himself Caradoc Evans electrified England, or at least the reviewers of England, by issuing a little "first book" called **My People.** It was a book of sketches about the peasantry of West Wales, a people who had not been used in fiction before. It possessed the prime asset, therefore, of a new local color, an atmosphere, which is a matter no longer easily to be discovered even in patchwork Britain. But it had something better than that, for purposes of electrification, namely, an absolutely God-forsaken view of human nature and an utterly unscrupulous tongue. Here is a combination "hard to beat." Nobody but a reviewer can understand how refreshing a book like this *[Capel Sion]* may be, now and then, to professional palates which are simply tired of the usual thing. It has not only the fresh flavor (or smell) of an unexploited localism, but the ancient lure of a new window opened towards reality. We cannot know whether the smell is true, or whether the window really is a new one, or really opens on reality, but—perhaps! For the moment at least we feel ourselves shaking clear of the bogs of convention and the fogs of sentiment with which our way is compassed. Disagreeable, yes, but the real thing? Why not? Let us give it a hand, anyhow, "on the chance." Hence our chorus of British reviewers greeting the **My People** of young Mr. Caradoc Evans as a book of genius and vision and high art. Of course (they say) it is "grim," "frank," "merciless," even "ugly"; but that is because it is "stark," "powerful," "strong meat for strong men." Mr. Clement Shorter is outraged that the libraries should exclude such a book. The *Westminster Gazette* doesn't relish its matter, but finds refuge in praise of its manner: "Nothing but artistic purpose, and the rarer endowment of artistic capacity, could have carried a writer triumphantly through his welter of meanness and brutality and hypocritical depravity." In brief, he has wallowed well, but what if the welter be of his own making? What is his "triumph"—to have achieved tragic beauty, or to have fillipped our jaded senses with the uncommonly "high" flavor of an otherwise homely dish? Perhaps the answer is suggested by a noticeable tendency among the reviewers to value this "new" writer chiefly, after all, as one who has out-Hardied Hardy and taught the shade of Dostoievsky a thing or two. *Capel Sion* is of exactly the same substance and quality. We beg leave to question its sincerity as a document or as art. Its sketches of these Welsh people have a dreadful effectiveness because of their unrestrained cruelty. You can always get a literary effect, like any other object, by going straight for it without eyes or heart for anything else. No doubt there are Welsh peasants as blasphemous, as lustful, as selfish, as filthy, as utterly contemptible as the people in this book. That there are whole communities of them, in Wales or anywhere else, for whom nothing better can be said, it is impossible to believe.

### *The Dial* (essay date 1919)

SOURCE: A review of *My People* and *Capel Sion,* in *The Dial,* Vol. LXVI, February 8, 1919, pp. 154-6.

[*In the following essay, a review of* My People *and* Capel Sion, *a critic cautiously accepts Evans's negative view of humanity.*]

Is this revelation or fiction? Such uniform squalor and bestiality scarcely seems consistent with truth. The author [of **My People** and **Capel Sion**] appears to have used up his literary faculties on variations of the general themes of sexual degradation and avarice. It is not to be denied that he has made excellent literary material out of these unpleasant themes, but it is the excellence of his handling which makes it so difficult to suppress a question concerning the truth of his tales and sketches. It is not at all impossible that these peasants of West Wales may be violent distortions of our correct selves, to whom the veiling of emotion and desire has become like a sixth sense. But whether the tales and sketches are faithful transcriptions of truth or merely fiction, they possess force and vitality. If Mr. Evans has not written of the people of West Wales, then he has created a new type of peasant and, in any event, his work is literary creation which our moral prejudices or preconceptions should not permit us to neglect. He has told us of a people who live their lives on a non-moral basis and who are yet so conscious of sin and of their moral responsibility to the Big Man and the "little white Jesus" that what might easily have been indifferent non-morality becomes gross and repulsive immorality. These peasants, in spite of their anthropomorphic religiosity, seem naively unconscious that filth is dirty. Their God is a primitive patriarch, between whom and themselves there is hardly any barrier of ritual, though at the same time there is no beauty in the communion. The Big Man speaks in the vulgar language of the commonest peasant—being, one supposes, in common with all gods, a reflection of his worshipers. He doesn't hedge himself about with any symbols of divinity—though he does insist on being invisible to mortal eyes—and may be induced to wink at any subversion of the moral laws, provided that the Respected, or the minister, intercedes (for a consideration) on behalf of the sinner. "Ianto opened his Bible and read. Afterwards he removed the tobacco from his mouth and laid it on the table and he reported to God with a clean mouth."

The tales and sketches have at least the sound of truth. And perhaps it is only our desire to have people live cleanly that makes it so very easy for us to believe that the peasants of these books are nothing more than creatures of the author's imagination.

### *The English Review* (essay date 1923)

SOURCE: "The Little Spoon," and "Taffy," in *The English Review,* Vol. 36, April, 1923, pp. 344-50.

[*In the following essay, a review of* Taffy, *a critic lauds Evans's play as a refreshing change from most current offerings for the stage.*]

Mr. Caradoc Evans bounded into fame shortly before the war as the discoverer of a new literary method. Once more the Bible was the source, but he had another, Wales, and the idiom of Wales transcribed into English, which he used as a searchlight upon the insular idiosyncrasies of his people. Wales was virgin soil for literature and Mr. Evans was fiercely regional. He sovietised (before Lenin) the King's English. The stories he wrote (published mostly in this REVIEW struck a new theme and a new note. Their quality, of daring and incisive re-creation, staggered. They were at once tragic and comic. He was of course pilloried, denounced by his "Fathers," and damned, but he held his course, and in time the stories appeared in book form, when literary London recognised an "original" and a new force. Then came the war and the transvaluation of values that have succeeded war, in which all that went before was forgotten, barred and banned to make room for the new values which were to give us a new world and what not, where indeed we stand to-day still re-valuing, still seeking the de-morphinisation of art and society. Into this knock-about flux Mr. Evans tipped out a play, *Taffy,* thanks to the largeness of Mr. Dennis Bradley, who not only produced the piece, but really presented it to the edification of a representative art-caring audience.

After the trash which has graced the boards since the Armistice, *Taffy* naturally puzzled. To begin with, Mr. Evans refuses compromise. Though no one can call him a highbrow, whatever the tag may mean, he is a high-kicker with a message. He wallows in that long-lost article—sincerity, out-Heroding any revivalist, withering all politicians, scorning the conventionalities of the box-office theatre, too proud to pander to the commonness, rottenness, vulgarity, and clap-trap of the machine-made play that has reduced our stage to the lowest in Europe; and such a man starts with a heavy handicap, for the London Theatre is a purely commercial business, and the man who thinks otherwise is not a "patriot." This was made evident during the production. A Welsh chorus punctuated his sallies with antiphonal chants, culminating in a rally for "Lloyd George," which, however, fell flat, as the audience was a cultured one, far from the madding crowd of the hustings. In short, *Taffy* hit, hurt, and heartened.

It was a stimulating afternoon. The parochial quarrelling about zinc or tiles for the chapel, who is to pay for it, who not to profiteer out of it, how to do in this "big head" or that preacher, and all that kind of thing reminiscent of the terrific rows, intrigues, enthusiasms, and squabbles that used to go on years ago over the building of Cathedrals—such was the theme, infinitely minute and localised, represented by three "big heads," a pair of rival preachers, a sweet Welsh maid and her farmer father, ending in a little love episode which took the boy preacher from the Church and led the venerable preacher, "tearful Ben"—a great scream of a type—to take unto himself his fifth wife. Not much movement, perhaps. No slop, no brandy-balls for the pit, no bawd or catch or penny-whistle tintinnabulation for the ladies—just hard, inexorable, caustic life as it is, or as the author sees it.

To our jaded theatre-mind, steeped in the artificialities of the commercial play, which bears no relation to psychology at all, the thing seemed preposterously over-emphasised, over-laden, over-keyed. Many could not stand this showing-up of a village mentality; all shook their heads at the notion of trying so brilliant a spate of satire, wit, fun, and human analysis upon the people. No doubt Mr. Evans is a phenomenon. He has the single-track mind. He cannot portray his people with char-rm, as Sir J. M. Barrie portrays the Scot, and he lacks the poetry of Synge, who Biblified his people. He stands between Bernard Shaw and Synge. His weakness is partly technical, partly the weakness of his race—he himself is a preacher. *Taffy* is a sermon in sermons. A little bit too homilectic for the Theatre, which demands light and shade and that indefinable something which leaves some things to the imagination.

Refusing hypocrisy himself, he seems to have forgotten that hypocrisy is the world's social weapon, and so in uncloaking his characters he deprives them, protests, too much. They are too revealed, too undifferentiated, too bare. Not as real men, perhaps, but as theatre men certainly, the result being a sameness of character and procedure which detracts from the illusion so essential to the footlights. His village is one of Iagos all the way; call it realism. Yet it hummed, held, and was a joyous performance. There were great scenes, one superb moment handled by Miss Evans with mastery, a delicate love-passage, and innumerable unexpected scintillations of bathos, drama, and antithesis. Mr. Evans reached heights and plumbed depths. He has written himself into his work, which has the great merit of vitality. We saw live men. We heard live words. We left more alive than when we entered the theatre.

What is to be done with *Taffy?* Will it die because it is so alive? Presumably. Any bidders? I wonder. Anyhow, *Taffy* was a little event, an Ark in theatre-land. It has reinstated Mr. Caradoc Evans, thus promoting the slow process of de-morphinisation. Those who saw it will not forget Ben and his sermons, or the Elders, or the wench who drew the young preacher back to the land, or the pithy, racy, quaint dialogue, or the hen, in place of a close-up. Theatrical managers may cry cock-a-doodle-doo to it, but Mr. Evans may yet, with management and manipulation, be able to say "hey cockalorum" to the great public, when *Chu-Chin-Chow* and Co. have gone to the land of their Fathers.

**Glyn Jones (essay date 1968)**

SOURCE: "Three Prose Writers: Caradoc Evans, 1878-1945," in *The Dragon Has Two Tongues: Essays on Anglo-Welsh Writers and Writing,* J. M. Dent & Sons Ltd., 1968, pp. 64-80.

[*In the following excerpt, Jones offers his personal reminiscences of Evans.*]

I first met Caradoc Evans in the company of Dylan Thomas in, I think, 1934. It seems to me strange now that I should at that time have sought him out, because, at fifty-six, he had been, for many years, a hated and notorious figure in Wales, the author of such works of calculated provocation as *My People, Capel Sion, My*

*Neighbours, Nothing to Pay, Wasps* and *Taffy.* (I wonder if Caradoc's early books would have aroused such fury and attracted so much publicity if they had been given titles less jeering and inflammatory, say *Tales of Bygone Wales,* or *Remembering Aberteifi.*) He was regarded in Wales as the enemy of everything people of my upbringing and generation had been taught to revere, a blasphemer and mocker, a derider of our religion, one who by the distortions of his paraphrasings and his wilful mistranslations had made our language and ourselves appear ridiculous and contemptible in the eyes of the world outside Wales. But he was also one of the very few Welshmen at that time who had made a name for himself by writing in English, and in spite of everything commonly urged against them I read his strange stories almost always with curiosity and respect, often with considerable admiration.

In reply to my letter asking for permission to visit him, I received from Caradoc a cordial invitation to tea, written in a minute and rather spiky script in the central two or three square inches of a large sheet of writing-paper which had a list of Caradoc's books printed down the side. He was living then in a pleasant house called Queen's Square House, near the centre of Aberystwyth, in Cardiganshire, with his second wife Oliver Sandys (Countess Barcynska) and her son Nicholas.

I do not know enough about the nobility of Poland to judge whether Mrs Evans's title was genuine, or *soi-disant* on the part of her first husband. Did the Poles have counts, and were some of them Jewish? Certainly Mrs Evans was a fine and generous Englishwoman whom I always liked and admired very much, warm-hearted, merciful, tireless in her concern for the young, for outcasts and misfits, and bountiful towards her friends and dependants. Also she was an industrious and highly successful writer, the author, one of her publishers claims, of more than seventy best-selling novels. Caradoc's nickname for her was the sentimentalist.

On the day of our visit Dylan and I were shown into a spacious drawing-room furnished with splendid antiques of varying periods and styles, the sort of place that, although roomy, seems overcrowded with too many exotic ornaments and large vases of fancy grass, and Buddhas, and icons with scarlet lamps burning under them, and too many damask curtains. Caradoc was sitting in the middle of this profusion, in the process of being interviewed by a local newspaper man. Mrs Evans was also present, looking like an ex-actress, or what I thought an ex-actress would look like; that is, her face was very much made up, she wore unusual and highly coloured clothing and a good deal of conspicuous jewellery, including shoulder-length ear droppers. Her welcome to us, two complete strangers, was extremely cordial. I thought by the loudness and brusqueness of Caradoc's Cardiganshire English, and the violent pipe-brandishing, that he was quarrelling with his inter·viewer. I feel sure now that the truculence and the wrangling and the pontificating upon the absurdities of our

National Eisteddfod were no more than an act. He knew well from his own considerable experience of journalism that his outrageous remarks and behaviour were good copy and good publicity for himself. Soon after our arrival the reporter departed and Caradoc's manner changed immediately, and he turned upon us the full blaze of his blarneying charm. His courtesy, simplicity and gentle manners have been remarked upon by many who knew him. He was not by any means a good-looking man. He had a large, ill-shaped nose and a too-long upper lip, and his face was at once very bony and flabby, with thin hanging skin. His lower lip pouted, and the hood-like lids, which he often slid forward and held down over his eyes, were of reptilian thinness. Mrs Evans talks in one of her books about his 'shaggy goat's hair', and that is a perfect description of the coarse, wiry, dirty-grey covering rising thick and upright on top of his head. In conversation he was a great encourager, a concentrated and smiling listener, an enthusiastic nodder and agree-er. And of course to a young and inexperienced writer like myself—I cannot speak for Dylan—much of his fascination was his familiarity with the literary life of the capital,[1] his references to people like Norman Douglas, Mary Webb and Arthur Machen, whom he had known in Fleet Street. I recall little of our conversation apart from the goodwill of it. A few months later, early in 1935, having seen a story of mine in print, he wrote to tell me how much he had enjoyed it. After that I was prepared to listen very sympathetically to whatever was said in defence or praise of Caradoc and his work.

Caradoc's life began in 1878 at Pantycroy, a farm in Carmarthenshire, but his boyhood was spent in Rhydlewis in the next county, on a small farm called Lanlas-uchaf, to which the family had moved. The people of Cardiganshire, the Cardis, have in Wales a name for thrift, even meanness and parsimony, similar to the reputation of the Scots in England, and many stories are told, often by Cardis themselves, about what Caradoc calls their 'close-handedness'. Several tales are based on the allegation that the London water supply—pionereed incidentally by a Welshman, Sir Hugh Myddelton—is often unlawfully diverted by some of the numerous Cardigan dairymen of the capital into the metropolitan milk; and it is alleged that the wreath which appears annually on the Myddelton statue has been subscribed for by these same grateful tradesmen. One story says that the charge against a passer of dud cheques in Carmarthenshire stated that he had obtained credit by false pretences; when he crossed the county boundary and faced a similar accusation in Cardiganshire, the charge had to be reduced to *attempting* to obtain credit by false pretences. Many of Caradoc's short stories concern a peasant greed for money and possessions, but humour of this sort enters hardly at all into his treatment of this obsessive theme.

Caradoc's memories of his schooldays, his friends tell us, were painful, and embittered for many years by a deep sense of failure. But towards the end of his life he could depict his time in Rhydlewis elementary school like this:

'One of my schoolins[2] used to stand sadly in front of me, cut a bit of spanish, pop it into his mouth, scratch his back head,[3] and say: "There will be whiskers on eggs before the twelve times in your head." He was short and slim and had whiskers all over his face and in his nostrils and ears, and he produced a child a year without outside help.

'Another was a whipper-snapper who claimed to be able to count with his eyes shut and sing louder than any other man in the district. He said if there was a twp[4] more twp than me he would rather be Son Prodigal.

'Though I never brought home a certificate merit or moved higher than the second from the bottom of my class and the porridge in the bottomer's head was not done, I knew one thing: schoolins got their jobs because they were religious Independents and the Independents were stronger than the Methodists.'[5]

In spite of the teachers' alleged low opinion of him, Caradoc was invited to remain at school when his leaving time arrived, as a 'monitor' or apprentice schoolteacher. Instead, like many youths of his time and situation, he left home to serve in a shop, in his case the Market Hall in Carmarthen town, a drapery store belonging to an uncle. He was fourteen at the time. Later, doing the same sort of job, he moved to Cardiff, and then at twenty-two he left Wales for London.[6] The management of the Holborn drapers where, after a period in Kentish Town, he found work, handed him a four-page brochure of the house rules governing shop assistants in their employment who 'lived in'. Caradoc's comment on this production was that he found Moses's ten commandments hard enough to keep, and Wallis's two hundred had him 'whacked'. 'Whacked' meant eventually sacked. At the end of two years he got a more congenial job in the drapery department of Whiteley's 'the universal provider', at thirty-five pounds a year all found, 'living in' with about five hundred other men in a sort of civilian barracks. By this time Caradoc was beginning to feel a desperate need for privacy to read and write. While at Whiteley's he read Jerome K. Jerome and such books as Forster's *Life of Dickens* and Besant's *All Sorts and Conditions of Men,* but a cubicle shared with two or three other shop assistants made serious study impossible, and he determined to find a room for himself and live out. He got a job in an Oxford Street store and rented a room in Marylebone, in a street in which Trollope had once lived. He saved up ten pounds, applied for a job on a periodical called *Chat,* at three guineas a week, and got it, solely, he thought himself, because he turned up in his shop assistant's frock-coat and pin-striped trousers for the interview. Unfortunately *Chat's* proprietor was an eccentric who used to burn the linoleum to keep the office warm, and before long his paper folded. But Caradoc was now a journalist, at twenty-six he had finished with his hated shop-keeping for good, and he became in turn a sub-editor on the *Daily Mirror,* an assistant to Sir John Hammerton in his work on the Harmsworth Encyclopaedia, editorial assistant on *T.P.'s Weekly,* editor of *Ideas* and *The Sunday Companion.* Thomas Burke, who worked in Fleet Street at the same time as Caradoc, says that he was 'everywhere popular', and that he made a deep impression upon the place.[7] A sharp distinction seemed to have existed between Caradoc's attitude to his journalism and to the writing of his short stories, which went on concurrently. His preference in journalism was for what was popular, of the widest possible appeal; he laughed at the *Sunday Times* and thought the *News of the World* a splendid job. His taste was in fact unaccountable. Although we know he owned a copy of Johnson's Dictionary, and read Dickens, Chekhov, Tolstoy, Balzac and Renan, and greatly esteemed the fastidious Arthur Machen, he yet admired some lady novelists 'several degrees inferior to Marie Corelli'.[8]

It has been suggested that the twelve-year-long shop-keeping period of Caradoc's life, with its poverty and its humiliations, and its agonizing consciousness of wasted powers, explains the savagery of his writing, the sombre skill with which he exposes the sham and corruption of the human heart, especially the Welsh human heart. I think it possible that these things did increase a bitterness and a sense of injustice already present, but it is perhaps worth remarking that the people he satirized most cruelly and most frequently were not the snubbing ribbon-and-button-buyers, and the vindictive shopwalkers of Cardiff and London, but the peasants of west Wales, at whose hands, as far as we know, he had suffered no injustice. Caradoc was a man who, as we have seen, had been a failure at school. And yet like many failures conscious of great powers within them, he probably knew that his teachers' estimate of him was mistaken and undeserved; that his defeat had occurred in the particular type of education he was unlucky enough to have to endure because it happened to be in vogue in a certain place at a certain time. The mechanical, uncreative, arid, mock-English education of Rhydlewis at the end of the last century was almost bound to send someone like Caradoc to the bottom of his class.

In her book *Unbroken Thread* Caradoc's widow hints at another cause of bitterness. His mother's brother, a country doctor, died leaving £60,000, an enormous sum at that time, but it would appear that he never did anything towards the education of his nephew. Mrs Evans quotes Caradoc as saying: 'My mother never asked him [for financial help]. She didn't realize the value of education. But when I became a young man I did—and it was from then the rankle festered and was never healed. It became a running sore like all the root causes of my angers.' This message was received by Mrs Evans from beyond the veil, after her husband's death. Whether it is satisfactory explanation of Caradoc's famous bitterness I do not know. It certainly suggests that the journey to the other side has a debilitating effect on a man's expression. Professor George Green[9] thinks that the appearance of several satirical books in the early years of this century, *The Unspeakable Scot, The Egregious Englishman,* and

so on, might have helped to create an atmosphere in which Caradoc's stories could be appreciated. They might have suggested to him the possibility of satirizing the Welsh.[10] We know that early in his career he had written stories of a very different sort from those he is usually associated with. 'I wrote Cockney stories', he says, 'after the manner of Edwin Pugh and Arthur Morrison. I showed them to my friend and he said: "You don't know what you're writing about. Tell stories about people you know—the Welsh." I filled a penny exercise book, both sides, with a Welsh love-story. "This doesn't sound true," I said to myself. "Any Welsh preacher could have written it." I let the years go by.'[11] His first story to be published appeared in *Reynolds News,* which paid him fifteen shillings. In 1915 the *English Review* under Frank Harris gave him five guineas for a story, and the same year his first book, ***My People,*** was published. He was thirty-seven years of age at the time.

Caradoc, after his period of journalism, was certainly not unaware of the value to a writer of shock and publicity. But whatever lay behind his work—personal bitterness, a sense of grievance or injustice, an ambition to do something out of the ordinary, the journalist's knowledge that wickedness is more sensational than virtue, the desire to attract attention to his gifts by methods of shock and sensation—his stories certainly could not be ignored. Thomas Burke called him the English Gorki, Hugh Walpole the most striking thing in English letters, Stephen Graham the *sans-culotte* of English literature and Naomi Royde-Smith the most savage satirist since Swift.[12] To many of his fellow countrymen, after the publication of *My People,* he became 'the best-hated man in Wales'.

He says this of his early life in London:

'Now I came across a young man preaching the Shop Assistants' Union at shop doors and street corners. He said a shop-assistant lives without honour and dies as unhonoured as an ass. He came from Lampeter and named Evan Sydney Duncan Davies; and he was a very argumentative young man. But he could argue many subjects and was never hackneyed. He took me to the Poets' Corner in Westminster Abbey, the Cheshire Cheese, where I sat in Dr Johnson's chair, old City churches, Dickens' landmarks, Carlyle's house in Chelsea, and the houses where lived Irving and Ellen Terry and Mrs Patrick Campbell. He showed me the London he loved and seemed to be part of; and there was born in me a deep and abiding love of London. He introduced me to Hardy's novels, Ragget's stout in a pub in Oxford Street, cod cutlets in a restaurant off Ludgate Circus, Defoe's *Plague, The Pilgrim's Progress,* and to Robert Blatchford's writings in the *Clarion.* It was Blatchford's simple grandeur that led me to discover the English Bible. So what schoolins failed to do this young shop-assistant from Lampeter did: educate me.

'I joined a grammar class at Toynbee Hall, but I gave it up for grammar is the study of a lifetime. Then I joined a composition class at the Workingmen's College . . . Somehow I came to read Genesis again and when I was about the middle of it "Jiw-Jiw this is English writing" I said to me. On a Saturday night I went to the Hammersmith Palace and there I saw Marie Lloyd, and "Jiw-Jiw," I said to me, "she tells a story not by what she says but by what she does not". I kept up Genesis and Marie Lloyd.'[13]

One of the features of Caradoc's work which seems to attract critical attention and cause sharp controversy, is this famous literary style whose origins he has just indicated. I am prepared to believe on the evidence of the stories themselves that in the above account he is giving—as he might himself have translated *calon y gwir*—the heart of the truth. The rhythms and the vocabulary of Genesis in the Authorized Version are everywhere in his work. 'In the foolishness of her vanity she curled her yellow hair like a Jezebel, and she fashioned the front of her hair into a fringe which she wore over her forehead.' 'These things Martha did; and Danyrefail prospered exceedingly: its possessions spread even to the other side of Avon Bern.' 'The night of the Hiring Fair Evan drank in the inn, and the ale made him drunk, and he cried a ribald song; the men with whom he drank mocked him, and they carried him into the stable and laid him in a manger, and covered him with hay; and in the stall they put a horse, thinking the animal would eat Evan's hair and beard. But the Big Man watched over Evan, and the horse did not eat his beard.' This is Caradoc's normal narrative style, direct, strong, unencumbered, biblical. Perhaps the only non-biblical words in these three quotations are 'its' and 'ribald'. But Caradoc's world is not the nomadic and pastoral one of the book of Genesis, but a modern society, settled, agricultural, even in some cases urban and industrial, and this means that his seventeenth-century masterpiece is an inadequate model, at least where vocabulary is concerned, for his purpose. Even in his earliest work he is forced to use words like 'materialism', 'surgery', 'fripperies', 'ogled', 'trickish', 'tall-hatted', 'credited', 'India-rubber', 'song-like', 'shuddered', 'middle-class', and 'sapidness', and phrases like 'spirit laden eloquence' and 'togged in black gowns'. When Caradoc is writing about rural Cardiganshire he is naturally under less pressure to employ a non-biblical vocabulary than when he is writing about the Cardis of London.

Another feature of Caradoc's narrative style which has its parallel, if not its origin, in the Bible is the infrequency of extended passages of description, whether of scenery, weather or of persons. He rejects the detailed set scene as Genesis does. He lived much of his life in his native Cardiganshire, a country of quite outstanding natural beauty, of clear seas, bays, cliffs, green hills, magnificent rivers, but very little of this appears in his work. 'The sense of the beautiful or the curious in Nature', he says, 'is slow to awake in the mind of the Welsh peasant'; and I sometimes wonder whether this might not have been true of Caradoc himself, who confesses in his journal that 'God never meant me to live in the country'. Or his exclusion of natural beauty from his stories may have been for a reason I shall touch on presently. If a person is to be described in his work at all, which is uncommon, a sentence or two has usually to do the job. ' . . . as they stood up in their pew you saw that . . . Lisbeth's body was as a billhook.' ' . . . this short man with a large head, broad shoulders, billowy belly, bandy legs, and a smile that nothing drove from his face.' 'His face, school-slate in shape, was grey and pale yellow like cornland after harvest, and it was flat other than that his nose was like a sickle stuck into the ground. In season his hat stood on a scarecrow.' Seldom indeed does consecutive description reach the dimensions of this last, or of the following: 'He wore whipcord leggings over his short legs, and a preacher's coat over his long trunk, a white and red patterned celluloid collar about his neck and a bowler hat on the back of his head; and his side-whiskers were trimmed in the shape of a spade.' Scene setting he avoids too, although with his compactness of style he can make this vivid and effective when he does undertake it. 'The transparent china lamp on the tinsel-draped mantelpiece lit up the group on the hearth: Bern-Davydd, a loosely woven rope of whitish hair like a coil of sheep's wool which has been caught in a barbed wire, and exposed many days to the weather, extended from ear to ear; Lamech, the ball of his small nose glittering against swarthy skin and bushy black beard and moustache: Puah, her feet resting on the fender, and the tuft of red hair on the right side of her mouth shivering like boar's hairs between the fingers of an ancient cobbler as she turned over the leaves of the book she was not reading.'

Caradoc bases his style, as we have seen, on that of the English Bible. This raises the question why he, a Welsh-speaking Welshman, chose the English language to write in at all in preference to his own. English was for him, at least at the level of art, laborious; but was the fascination of what's difficult part of its attraction for him? Or was his choice the result of a sort of pride, or even arrogance, a desire to make a name for himself, to be somebody, and respected, among the rich, powerful and really literary English, rather than among the Welsh, a small, culturally negligible nation with, so in his ignorance he thought, insufficiently exacting literary standards. ('Any Welsh preacher could have written it.') Or was it that his scorn expressed in English sounded more devastating than when expressed in Welsh? I cannot help feeling that part of the answer lies in Caradoc's education, which, whether in elementary school in Cardiganshire, or in adult class in London, was entirely in English. It seems unquestionable that the language of his awakening, as we have seen, and of whatever literature he was acquainted with—the Bible, Hardy's novels, Defoe's *Plague,* the *Pilgrim's Progress,* Dickens, etc.— was English.

Although Caradoc's descriptive passages have a biblical infrequency and almost always a biblical brevity, he is a copious employer of dialogue, and an element of this part of his practice has given very great offence to many of his countrymen. Anyone ignorant of Welsh, the argument goes, would assume that the conversations of Caradoc's monoglot Welsh characters are, as rendered by him, direct translations of their words into English. Certainly he has the problem, unknown to those Anglo-Welsh authors like Jack Jones and Gwyn Thomas who write about the anglicized industrial valleys of Wales, of rendering the Welsh speech of his farm labourers and shopkeepers as effective English dialogue. But it would be a mistake to assume, as is commonly done, that what Caradoc did was to translate Welsh speech into English. He does indeed sometimes translate—and even unintentionally mistranslate—some Welsh idioms into English. When he writes phrases like 'head-stiff', 'large money', 'red penny', 'kill your hay', 'rob me pure', 'forehead of a house' and 'one hundred and a half', we can assume he had in mind the Welsh phrases of which these are literal translations—*penstiff, arian mawr, ceiniog goch, lladd eich gwair, fy nhwyllo'n lan, talcen tŷ* and *cant a hanner.* But for the large majority of those notorious and outrageous sayings which he puts, in story after story, into the mouths of his characters, there are no parallels, not even remote ones, in Welsh. Nothing in Welsh, I would say, corresponds to *Big Man's Palace,* meaning, presumably, heaven, to *Dear Little Big Man,* meaning God, to *Little Holy Respected,* or to such monstrous locutions as 'Sober serious, mouth not that you . . . ', or 'Glad day to you, Evan the son of Hannah', or 'old boy ugly', 'you wicked spider', 'Hold thy chin, little Dinah', 'What iobish do you spout?', 'the Great Male', 'Shut your chins, you dirty cows', 'move your tongue about Sara . . . ' and so on. Why then did Caradoc use them, knowing them, as we may be sure he did, to be false? I think he saw in the necessity to translate his characters' Welsh speech into English a splendid artistic opportunity. What he did was to invent a whole language for them, and he invented it with one purpose, which was to create in his stories a certain atmosphere, an atmosphere of hypocrisy, stupidity, cunning and sham religion. This grotesque speech plays a large part in bringing about the powerful impression of universal falsity and uncouthness, which is the one he almost always wishes for, and for that purpose it is admirably chosen.

The second, and more serious, of the counts against Caradoc concerns the *matter* of his stories rather than the manner. The picture of our country he confronts his readers with, particularly in his early books, gave great offence in Wales and was of course indignantly repudiated. His play *Taffy* almost wrecked a London theatre. There was talk in Wales of publicly burning his books, and threats of physical attacks upon him were made from time to time. Is Caradoc's vision of Wales a true one? Only a non-Welsh writer, I feel sure, would regard this question as irrelevant.

An artist like Caradoc Evans does not concern himself with large and impersonal entities like nations. He deals only with a relatively small area of Wales during a short period and with only a handful of characters drawn from one social section of that area. He makes no Balzacian

claims that these characters are chosen with deliberation as being the most significant and representative in the society depicted by him. On the other hand, when people laughed to scorn the more repulsive and squalid events of his stories as crude and malicious inventions, and declared they could not have happened in enlightened, nonconformist Cardiganshire, Caradoc replied that almost every incident narrated in his work was something he had seen, and known, in his own life in the county. They are, he maintains, authentic, and chapter and verse could be given for almost every one. But this, to me, does not in any way prove that he is therefore giving an accurate picture of the life and the community of this part of west Wales. For one thing, at this point, the second of the two influences which he claims formed his style must be taken into account. The first was his reading of Genesis. This was the other, which I mentioned earlier. 'On a Saturday night I went to the Hammersmith Palace and there I saw Marie Lloyd, and "Jiw-Jiw," I said to me, "she tells a story not by what she says but by what she does not". I kept up Genesis and Marie Lloyd.'

What exactly did Caradoc mean by this? The statement is open to more than one interpretation, and I think Caradoc may have begun by having one meaning in mind, and that then he went on to another. I never heard Marie Lloyd, but Rob Wilton the comedian, it seems to me, was a master in his act of probably a similar sort of 'leaving out', the sort that in the first sentence of a story tells us that Charlie Evans has been having an argument and presently reveals that Rob is visiting Charlie in hospital. Caradoc may have employed a leap something like this at times, but his technique of omission goes much deeper. It is in fact the basis of his method. All authors inevitably 'leave out'; even the famous 'all-including chronicle' is necessarily highly selective. What Caradoc did was deliberately to suppress, beginning with the really marvellous beauty of Cardigan's natural scenery, everything he knew to be admirable in the life and circumstances of the people he was writing about, their hospitality and sense of community, their self-sacrifice, their devotion to their religion, their reckless and stubborn courage. Caradoc was brought up near one of the centres of Rebecca, and as a boy might easily have spoken to men who had taken part in those courageous, imaginative and effective disturbances; only nine years before he was born the radical nonconformist farmers of his county were being evicted from their farms for having the guts to vote—there was no secret ballot—openly against their own Tory landowners, although they knew the consequences would inevitably be eviction. Obviously the man who showed his courage and defiance in this way would find no place in a Caradoc story, not before *Pilgrims in a Foreign Land* at least. The point need not be laboured historically, but may be effectively illustrated from Mrs Evans's record of three small events which took place during her life in Cardiganshire during the last war.[14] 'Big Head'[15] Cabbages tows his vegetable produce to town with an ancient car to the peril of every other vehicle and every pedestrian. Cabbages he sells at a price a cabbage should be ashamed to fetch even in wartime, and for onions no bigger than tennis balls he used to get fourpence each before they were controlled. He is childless and has taken into his house an evacuee little girl whom he clothes and educates and hopes to make a teacher and to whom he has willed his house and his land. Will not God take this into account?

'There is Big Head Whimey Moustache. He has a pretty tenor voice and when he sings he blows his moustache about as if they were fine strands of silk. He sold an old emaciated cow at an enormous price to a young Englishman who took up farming to dodge the Army. The day he did that he was marrying his servant girl who was going to have a baby by a sweetheart who never came back from Dunkirk. He made her respectable and the child of the man who died for his country has his name. He was turned sixty on the day of his wedding, and since the infant has come the clock of ages has taken him back twenty years.

'There is Holyman Shon who used to sell—and would now if he could—dairy-cake with as much baked clay in it as cake. He gives his ration of butter to a soldier's wife. Two sons he lost in the Great War and if you ask him where his third and last son is he will tell you, "I sent him after Hitler and told him not to come back till he has found him." '

Here, in these three accounts by Mrs Evans, we have, obviously, Caradoc material, mixed up with matter which he would almost certainly reject. For most of his writing life he would have used approximately only the first half of these stories in every case, the unscrupulous money-grubber, the swindler who cheats the poltroon, the fraudulent Holy Joe. He would have regarded the elements of generosity in these anecdotes, the kindliness, the joy, the tenderness, as *what was to be left out*—the little evacuee transformed into a humble heiress, the unmarried mother married and her child given a name, the soldier's wife with her rations gratuitously doubled. This, it seems to me, is the way in which Caradoc employed the 'leaving out' technique whose beginnings he heard hinted at in the act of Marie Lloyd. A remarkable aspect of his achievement was that he managed to convince so many, by his art, that his small piece of the picture was really the whole.

It was both a strength and a limitation of Caradoc's art that his deliberate narrowness of vision enabled him to deal thus with only a very small sector of the life about him. His peasants he represents as being largely without politics, which in the area he writes about they certainly were not, and without culture, which they might have been, although I doubt it. (I do not wish to be more dogmatic because I know that there are pockets in Wales, in spite of what I have said about a widespread culture, which are intellectually and culturally arid. I remember staying as a boy on the farm of relatives in Carmarthenshire. There, although my uncle was a dead

shot and kept a hunter in the stable, the only books I ever saw were the Bible and the ready reckoner, and the second of these was in use much oftener than the first. And the farms around that I visited seemed to be at the same cultural level.) Religion Caradoc grants his people, but far from being life-giving it is stunting and hypocritical. 'The Capels', he says in his self-portrait,[16] 'keep the people down and chase the living God away'. Surely the things that were keeping the people of rural Wales down were, as they thought themselves, not the capels, but the lack of education, and the oppressive and brutal landlordismand its resultant poverty, which drove thousands into the squireless but amply chapelled industrial valleys, and to the United States, and into the Welsh 'colony' in the Argentine. Caradoc's complete ignorance of history, or his disregard of it, intensifies his vision, but it also helps to restrict it and to make its expression monotonous and predictable.

Every artist's understanding is partial, but Caradoc's is surely much more intentionally circumscribed than is usual. Hypocrisy, lust, double dealing, he sees with great clarity, but to tenderness, nobility, idealism, joy, he is as a writer, as we have seen, indifferent; not entirely so, because by the time he has reached *Pilgrims in a Foreign Land,* published in 1942, he has mellowed somewhat, he has become freer and more fanciful and he writes in this volume stories which have elements of grotesque or amusing fairy tales. But the characters he shows us in, say, *My People* are, it seems to me, too grim even for his own artistic purpose. Because often in Caradoc's stories, when one is likely to experience stirrings of compassion for some brow-beaten, wronged or cheated creature, Caradoc will underline the corruption of this victim also, or show us his physical repulsiveness, swindled and outraged though he may be. Variety, contrast or counterpoint there must be in any work of art, but Caradoc does not achieve this by presenting us with themes of moral tension, or contrasts of beauty and ugliness, or even variations of social or intellectual background. His world is almost universally joyless, a vision of physical and moral squalor, and the only variety in it arises from two things: first, the biblical dignity of the narrative passages in contrast with the idiotic and ludicrous buffoonery of the dialogue; second, urbane language of dead-pan solemnity used to describe situations of complete absurdity or farce like the drunken man in the manger whose hair might have been eaten by a horse, in the passage I have already quoted. But these devices have never been for me sufficient to dispel tedium from an extended reading of his stories, especially when the strain upon him of maintaining the rather artificial idiom becomes apparent in the writing.

Caradoc, so often in anger and journalism called a 'realist', does not seem to me to have created a realistic world at all. If we go to a *petit maître* like him for a 'true picture of Wales', whatever that might mean, we won't find one. He shows us not Wales but Welshmen; not even Welshmen, but a few peasants only in a restricted area. T. S. Eliot has a phrase somewhere: 'the desert of the exact likeness to the reality which is perceived by the most commonplace mind'. Caradoc's vision, which sees certain sins of flesh and spirit with blinding clarity, is too narrow, too partial, to present us with a lifelike and realistic picture of Wales. The world he shows us is not lifelike, but it is very much alive, and quite homogeneous; and this organic vitality of a work of art itself is surely what we should judge the work by, and not its resemblance to what we conceive to be the 'exact likeness to the reality'. Of course unless fantasy is intended,17 common sense tells us that there should be some correspondence between the description and the thing described. But Caradoc's work is not documentary. In the world of statistics and sociology his stories are valueless. Not in the world of the imagination and knowledge of the depravity of the human heart. Do we read *Anna Karenina* for a true picture of Tsarist Russia, or *Scarlet and Black* for a true picture of 1830 France, or *Bleak House* for a true picture of Victorian England? Do not these great works engage and enliven and fill out and occupy our imaginations, and deeply satisfy our inner life, our feelings, what is still left to us of our childhood, rather than give us information about foreign countries? Isn't this the reason for their greatness? Much of the adverse criticism of Caradoc has come about because Wales is a small nation fighting desperately for her life, and Caradoc, because of his scurrilous portrait of her, and his guiding principle of never writing anything that could be construed as praise, was seen as a traitor, joining in the attack upon what was held dear, and was being desperately defended. This is understandable, at least to a Welshman. It is all very well for still great, assured and confident England to laugh at those plays and books by Englishmen that deride her, to join in the self-mockery and to make pets of her satirists. Wales, her language, her national identity threatened with extinction, feels herself unable to afford such tolerance. Art may be the lie which reveals to us the truth, but when the 'lie' is uttered by a Welshman about his own country, it is the lie itself for many which will have overwhelming power and not the truth which it is intended to demonstrate.

But all this obviously does not mean that in a few stories like **'Be This her Memorial'**, and **'The Way of the Earth'**, Caradoc is not a master of this form. Here is part of the first of these stories[18] which tells of Nanni, a desperately poor and very old woman, crooked, wrinkled, toothless, who lives alone in a mud-walled hovel. The minister of her chapel, Josiah Bryn-Bevan, is soon to leave for a bigger church, and Nanni decides to present him with a large and ornate Bible. To pay for this she, a pauper, starves herself of normal food. Such is her devotion to him that instead of giving her customary help at hay harvest, she hammers hob-nails into her boots and tramps the countryside to wherever he is preaching. This angers the farmers who want her cheap labour.

'One night Sadrach Danyrefail called at her cottage to commandeer her services for the next day. His crop had been on the ground for a fortnight, and now that there was a prospect of fair weather he was anxious to gather it in. Sadrach was going to say hard things to Nanni, but the appearance of the gleaming-eyed creature that drew back the bolts of the door frightened him and tied his tongue. He was glad that the old woman did not invite him inside, for from within there issued an abominable smell such as might have come from the boiler of the witch who one time lived on the moor. . . .

'Two Sabbaths before the farewell sermon was to be preached, Nanni came to Capel Sion with an ugly sore at the side of her mouth; repulsive matter oozed slowly from it, forming into a head, and then coursing thickly down her chin on to the shoulder of her black cape, where it glistened among the beads. On occasions her lips tightened, and she swished a hand angrily across her face.

' "Old Nanni", folk remarked while discussing her over their dinner-tables, "is getting as dirty as an old sow."

'During the week two more sores appeared; the next Sabbath Nanni had a strip of calico drawn over her face. . . .

'At the end of his farewell sermon the Respected Josiah Bryn-Bevan made reference to the giver of the Bible, and grieved that she was not in the Capel. He dwelt on her sacrifice. Here was a Book to be treasured, and he could think of no one who would treasure it better than Sadrach Danyrefail, to whom he would hand it in recognition of his work in the School of the Sabbath.

'In the morning the Respected Josiah Bryn-Bevan, making a tour of his congregation, bethought himself of Nanni. The thought came to him on leaving Danyrefail, the distance betwixt which and Nanni's cottage is two fields. He opened the door and called out:

' "Nanni."

'None answered.

'He entered the room. Nanni was on the floor.

' "Nanni, Nanni!" he said. "Why for you do not reply to me? Am I not your shepherd?"

'There was no movement from Nanni. Mishtir Bryn-Bevan went on his knees and peered at her. Her hands were clasped tightly together, as though guarding some great treasure. The minister raised himself and prised them apart with the ferrule of his walking-stick. A roasted rat revealed itself. Mishtir Bryn-Bevan stood for several moments spell-bound and silent; and in the stillness the rats crept boldly out of their hiding places and resumed their attack on Nanni's face. The minister, startled and horrified, fled from the house of sacrifice.' The last time I saw Caradoc was in the summer of 1944, a few months before he died. Professor Gwyn Jones, with whom my wife and I were staying in

Aberystwyth, invited him and Mrs Evans to tea from their home at New Cross, a hamlet outside the town, where they had been living since 1940. How Caradoc, in the ten intervening years since my first sight of him, had changed! His clothes were as outlandish and colourful as ever; he was wearing black corduroy jacket and trousers, a magenta shirt, a cable-stitch cricket sweater and a brimless straw hat shaped like a smallish beehive. But his body at sixty-seven was old, and his face, with the droop-lidded eyes and the blunt, bulby, long-nostrilled nose, seemed gnarled and scooped out, the cheekbones in particular standing forth with prominence under the thin skin. But the day of this last meeting he set himself out to win us, he used all the Welsh charm and blarney he was master of, he listened with a concentrated pleasure that suggested he wanted to do nothing else, he acted, he told us scandalous tales about the literary eminent, and mixing in the most comical way the accents of Aberteifi and London clubland, described encounters with Frank Harris, W. H. Davies, Sean O'Casey and others. When we left Gwyn Jones's house for a stroll I had the chance to tell Caradoc I thought his character sketches of Mary Webb and W. H. Davies, then appearing in the *Welsh Review,* among the most interesting things he had written. He grinned through his pipe-smoke, rugged and momentarily bright-eyed, he seemed glad I had said that. Five months later I felt glad myself I had said it, because going to my job by train one cold winter's morning in 1945 I read in the newspaper that he was dead.

NOTES

[1] The literary capital of Wales for the Anglo-Welsh then was of course London.

[2] Schoolmasters.

[3] Caradoc is here at his game of literal translation from Welsh; he means his backside.

[4] Dunce, dullard, blockhead.

[5] From *Self-portrait* by Caradoc Evans, *Wales,* January, February, March 1944.

[6] See Caradoc's autobiographical novel *Nothing to Pay* (Faber, 1930).

[7] *Caradoc Evans.* Oliver Sandys (Hurst and Blackett, 1946).

[8] *Caradoc Evans.* R. B. Marriott. *Wales,* summer, 1945.

[9] *The Earth Gives All and Takes All.* Caradoc Evans (Dakers, 1946). Introduction by Professor George Green.

[10] The novel *Madge Carrington and her Welsh Neighbours* (Stanley Paul, 1911), also gives an unflattering picture of Welsh people. Its author, 'Draig Glas' (Arthur Tyssilio Johnson), was said to be the author of *The Perfidious Welshman* (Stanley Paul, 1910).

[11] *Wales,* January, February, March 1944.

[12] One personal characteristic that Caradoc shared with Swift was bodily fastidiousness. Micturators who omitted to pull the chain after them aroused his ire.

[13] *Wales,* January, February, March 1944.

[14] *Full and Frank* by Oliver Sandys (Hurst and Blackett, pp. 133-4).

[15] Chapel elder or deacon presumably.

[16] *Wales,* January, February, March 1944.

[17] But even the authors of *Mortmere* felt there should be some connection between life and their description of it.

[18] Included in *My People* (Andrew Melrose, 1915).

## T. L. Williams (essay date 1970)

SOURCE: "Taffy at Home: The Humour and Pathos of Welsh Village Life," in *Caradoc Evans,* edited by T. L. Williams, University of Wales Press, 1970, pp. 29-99.

[*In the following excerpt, Williams provides an extensive study of Evans's work—including the text of an early story in its entirety—and examines aspects of his psychohistory.*]

Caradoc quite possibly gained great psychological relief from the publication of **My People,** but thenceforth he had the mark of Cain upon him, and however much he might protest his love for Wales (and nothing better illustrates the "love" half of his relationship with Wales than his regular "sermon-tasting" at New Cross chapel— here, if anywhere, was the compulsive attraction towards the thing rejected), he would never again be trusted. Rather than attempt to make amends, therefore, he was almost compelled to produce more of the same.

Thus Caradoc's recantation was made with **My People.** There is a sense in which the book vitiated any development towards sweetness and light, for these outpourings were no juvenilia, but the finished and highly polished artefacts of a mature man. (The book was published just before his thirty-sixth birthday.) If this was his considered view of his countrymen. it would be difficult to retract it in a later work, however magnanimous he wished to be. Besides, who would believe him? This is how he saw the situation himself: "I made a literary sensation that surprised me. I was the shocking Welshman, the traitor to his country, so I had to keep it up by saying shocking things at every given opportunity—at lectures and in public . . ." He had to "keep it up," and it is significant that the only novels in which the characters begin to approach (though they never reach) normality are those with English settings and characters, **This Way to Heaven** and **Mother's Marvel,** and parts of **Nothing to Pay** and **Wasps.** After **My**

*People,* the only literary development discernible is towards a more and more minute paring of the substance of the story, even to the point where the meaning becomes obscured. Thus we should take the opportunity of looking at one of Caradoc's first attempts at a story with a Welsh theme (published in *London Chat,* 21 September, 1907), not only for its intrinsic interest, but for the comparison and contrast it provides with the style and themes of the later work.

## TAFFY AT HOME

*The Humour and Pathos of Welsh Village Life*

by

D. Evans-Emmott

We in Manteg contend that the importance of London is greatly exaggerated, and that the importance of Manteg is underestimated. London is represented on the map by a black mark, which is, to quote Jack teilwr, as big as your head, while Manteg does not even figure on the home-made map which hangs on the schoolroom wall. But Manteg is of great consequence, nevertheless, and we are all agreed that were London not London, then Manteg would be the Metropolis.

The word Manteg implies a calm place. The name is a distinct libel, for there is life in the village, and, on occasions, life of the most tumultuous order, too. We still remember how Ianto railed in a bit of land along the riverside with spiked wire, and how the neighbours swooped down in the dead of night armed with pickaxes and shovels, and broke down the citadel; Ianto and his supporters retreating to Sally's hen-house. We have vivid recollections of the consternation caused when Mr. Adams denounced Howell Powell from the pulpit for blacking his face on a New Year's Eve. Any child can tell you of the memorable Saturday night when Dan and Sarah Anne found that the pigs were dead because they had been sitting on them; and every child is taught to lisp the words of wisdom that the minister sorrowfully told Dai Lanlas when he caught him red-handed reading an English book.

At present the village is an irregular collection of houses on the banks of the River Teify. Sheltering the village from the cold winds that blow across the moors, is a steep ascent, and the nearest railway station is a distance of ten miles.

Shoni Shenkins tells me that he remembers the first house in the neighbourhood, and that that was, as it still is, the shop. Over the door, says Shoni, was the simple inscription, "Jane Watkins, Licensed to Sell Tobacco." For six days in the week packets of starch and soap were placed on the floor of the small window, but before the seventh dawned these gave way to a huge Bible, with brass clasps, on which rested a framed picture of Davydd Charles o'r Bala.

Shan, as she was known, religiously observed the Sabbath. On that day no one ever induced her to transact business. The minister tried on one occasion, but it afterwards transpired that he was only testing Shan's principles.

Now the thatched old cottage has been pulled down; Jane Watkins long since has been gathered to her forefathers in the Methodist graveyard, where her name, carved with fantastic flourishes on her tombstone, remains to this day. And where "shop Shan" once stood, now stands a red-brick building, with large bow windows and grey Carnarvon tiles. On the wall facing the roadway appears the name of the proprietor, a grandson of Shan, "Josiah Watkins, General Dealer."

Mr. Watkins makes periodical visits to London and Bristol, and brings to Manteg the very latest things in fashion. Travellers, in carriages hired in the town, drive to the shop, and talk with him in English, greatly to our disgust. It should be said that Josiah speaks that language with a fluency that staggers one. There was once a rumour that while in London he was seen coming out of a theatre. However, after a masterly examination at the hands of Thomas Gôf, nothing was proved. Before this, Josiah was in the running for a deaconship, but his chances diminished hopelessly. The next Sunday, Mr. Vaughan, of the Methodist Chapel, preached a powerful sermon dealing with the evils attendant upon playacting.

Mr. Watkins is also the registrar of births, deaths, and marriages, and he performs the duties of which office with exemplary discretion. He very wisely stipulates that all couples who intend to get married shall show that they possess sufficient means whereby to purchase household linen, which, incidentally, J. Watkins will supply at a trifle over cost prices. There is a legend of a godless, dare-devil fellow, one Will Ty'r Avon, who, on the pretext of going to town to buy a suckling, induced Watkins to lend him his cart. It was a mean thing to do. Will did not bring home a pig, but brought a wife, a common wench from Pembrokeshire somewhere. The insolent fellow had the audacity to jest about it afterwards, but Josiah had his revenge—he very properly mentioned Will in no favourable terms at the next prayer-meeting. Shortly afterwards Will fell down a quarry, and was killed. "Providence," declared the righteous Josiah Watkins, when he heard of the fatality, "cannot be outwitted." With that, he hastened to Will's widow and got the order for mourning.

It is marvellous the progress the village is making—there are twenty-eight houses, not counting the two chapels, the schoolroom, and the parish church. In spite of this, we remain constant to the habits and customs which characterised the Welsh people a hundred years ago. There is Shemmi, the sodiwr, an old Crimean veteran, who boasts that in his days of active service he shot more people than he has since seen, still wearing the same clothes on Sundays as he wore the day he married Nani. They are a primitive kind of modern evening dress, with large gilt buttons, so brightly polished as to enable Mali Evans's boy, who sits in the pew behind, to see his face in them.

Gloomily he looks upon any new-fangled idea that is introduced into the village, and straightway predicts for us the fate of Sodom and Gomorrah. The last time I saw Shemmi he was seated on a low, three-legged stool, breaking stones on the roadside. I asked after his son. For a moment, he went on smoking vigorously, blowing out clouds of smoke. Then suddenly he threw his pipe on the ground, and, with tightened lips, brought down his hammer furiously upon the stones. I could swear that I saw something suspiciously like a tear dropping from one of his small, blinking eyes. His son, it appears, had died, and had been buried far away—far away among the heathen English. "I should have liked," said Shemmi, the soldier, "to have had the boy at my side on the Resurrection morning to salute at the sound of the Trumpet."

The relative merits of the chapels are subjects which receive much discussion in the village. That the Methodists are unquestionably the better singers, is a point upon which we are all agreed. On the other hand, as Jack teilwr argues, there is no mention in the Bible of the vocal powers of any of the saints. Moses did not sing, neither did Jacob, nor Paul, nor John. Solomon might have done, but then he was a doubtful character. It reflects greatly upon the credit of the Dissenters (Congregationalists are known as Dissenters in the rural districts of Wales) that the irreverent argument is only used in extreme cases.

Again, we the Dissenters, like sermons to be short and sweet, lasting thirty or thirty-five minutes, while an hour and a half is the average time in the Methodist chapel.

During the Revival there was much competition as to which of the sects should display the more fervour. In this the other side was victorious; their meetings often went on until the small hours of the morning. But it was the Dissenters that converted Robert, the pig-dealer. Robert was a rank atheist and blasphemer. He never wore his best clothes on the Sabbath. He had been known to whistle "The Black Pig" outside the chapel door while Mr. Adams was preaching. The Methodists said that Robert was only shamming, but when he commenced to pay off his debts—most of which had been put down as bad, and by which even Mr. Vaughan himself benefited—the most sceptical came to agree that it was a famous victory. There is one person who does not even now believe in Robert's conversion. I allude to Mrs. Bowen, of the Red Cow. In the bar-parlour is a slate, both sides of which are covered with figures, testifying to his insincerity.

We in Manteg have no respect whatsoever for the preacher who reads his sermons. It is an open secret that Mr. Rhys Lewis, of the English Church, conceals his manuscript between the leaves of the Bible, and rumour has it that he buys his sermons ready-made. Essec Griffiths, the postman, himself a Dissenter, and therefore a prejudiced person, has, after a most exhaustive inquiry, failed to discover incriminating evidence. Objections are also taken to the facts that Mr. Rhys Lewis prays from a book with his eyes open, and that he reads the first lesson in English. Welsh, we contend, was spoken in the Garden of Eden; Welsh is the language of Holy Writ; Welsh will be spoken in Heaven. As regards prayer, I cannot do better than quote Josi Davies. "Prayer," he said one day in his workshop, where we were discussing the parson, "should be spontaneous and fiery. It should make us miserable sinners feel the flames of hell coiling round our putrid bodies."

Josi is an authority, for he presides over the weekly prayer-meetings held in the Congregational chapel. It is grand to hear Josi pray. He begins in a low, hesitating voice. Little by little he grows eloquent. His voice swells like mighty waters rushing over rocks at one moment, to fall again into soft, pleading cadences like the running of a brooklet. "One word more," he cries. Josi's one word takes half an hour to say. Once, while he was praying, Bettws fell asleep, and snored. Josi took it to be the groan of a wicked soul in anguish. We had no conception of the enormity of our sins until that night. Each of us was mentioned by name, including the minister. Mr. Adams took for his text the next Sunday, "The mote in your brother's eye."

It is on prayer-meeting nights that the devil hangs around Manteg. Few have seen him, many have felt his pernicious presence. Nancy Bargoed one dark December night was pushed violently into the ditch. In vain she struggled to regain the roadway. All that she could see were the outlines of a pair of horns, the roots of which were set in sockets, throwing out green lights. "Devil!" shrieked Nancy, "get thee gone!" And she went her way in peace. Nancy rose to the heights of a popular heroine after that. A young man from London came down and photographed her for a newspaper.

Not long afterwards, on the night that Deio's little girl died, she actually saw the corpse candle dancing across the fields towards the house long before death took place.

But the event that caused most consternation was the appearance of the "ladi wen" (white lady). Dai John was the man who saw her. He was coming home late in the night from the "Red Cow," when he noticed, standing on the top of a gate, a figure clothed in a long, loose, white robe. Dai tried to talk to her, not realising that she was a spectre, and for a reply heard the chattering of teeth. Some said that she was the ghost of a woman murdered in the dim, distant ages; others declared she was an angel weeping over the iniquities of Manteg. Dai, at the first opportunity, stood up in chapel and announced himself a converted sinner. The landlady of the Red Cow still says that she lost a good customer in Dai.

Undoubtedly the greatest honour that can befal [*sic*] anyone in Manteg is to possess a corpse. Tightly over windows blinds are drawn. Relatives of a deceased person, however distant, clothe themselves in sombre black. Neighbours bring offerings of tea and sugar and biscuits. Not until the hour of the funeral is the lid of the coffin screwed down, because visitors like to gaze upon the passive features of the dead.

Woe be unto they who fail to weep at the graveside. "It was a dry funeral," is a remark one seldom hears. For a whole year the mourners must sit in chapel, their heads bowed, black-bordered handkerchiefs closely applied to eyes. Godly folk have a death in their houses at least once every two or three years.

Preparations for death always anticipate the coming of the dark angel. When Shacki Rees was ill, and expected to die, I called at his house and found Marged, his wife, putting on the fire the kettle which contained the water with which to shave the dead Shacki. She then stropped the razor. Shacki heard the ominous jingling noise the blade made upon the leather. Slowly he opened his eyes, one at a time. He ran white fingers through the stubby beard that had grown during his illness. "I think Marget," said he, stepping on to the floor, "that I'll keep my beard, whateffer."

We then had tea with the boiling water, because, as Shacki said, it was a pity to waste it. And Shacki lived for five years and three months after that.

It is tempting to describe this piece as embryonic, but those familiar with Caradoc's work will recognise that growth, growth of vision, of theme, of humanity even, was arrested at this point. Certainly it would be difficult to deduce from the style and the language that this account of Welsh life had come from the author of *My People*—there is a hint here of the school essay on a set theme, of too much deliberation, belied by phrases like "The name is a distinct libel," "the village is an irregular collection of houses," "greatly to our disgust" and "new-fangled idea," phrases which would be sedulously excluded from his later work. The Caradoc of 1915 would probably express the word "idea" as "thinks," and he certainly would not write: "I could swear that I saw something suspiciously like a tear dropping from one of his small, blinking eyes." But there is a more familiar ring about this sentence: "Shortly afterwards Will fell down a quarry, and was killed." The later stories were to see the perfection of this method of succinctly expressing the most horrendous violence in the space of half a dozen words. In addition, all the themes and character-types would reappear in *My People.* Josiah (the name occurs frequently) Watkins, with his supplies at "a trifle over cost price," will be reincarnated as the unspeakable Rhys Shop; the preacher and the divided Nonconformists are already there, along with their prejudices ("the heathen English") and their superstitions and taboos ("He never wore his best clothes on the Sabbath," "He had been known to whistle 'The Black Pig'

outside the chapel door while Mr. Adams was preaching," "We . . . have no respect . . . for the preacher who reads his sermons," "Welsh is the language of Holy Writ"); and to complete the survey of rural superstitions, we have the Corpse Candle and the White Lady. Finally, the story of Shacki and Marged Rees becomes, almost word for word, the story of Madlen and Twm in **"The Glory That Was Sion's"** (*My People*).

Hardly a story then,—more a collection of anecdotes, bearing a close relation to his later work. But the differences are also worth noting. Caradoc is here describing "his people," but in this instance he sets himself in their midst, the effect of which is to personalise the anecdotes, to make the characters real and their prejudices and superstitions almost endearing, the opposite of the revulsion one sometimes feels when, in *My People,* these characters have been depersonalised into puppets on a string. On the other hand, even without a knowledge of *My People* and *Capel Sion,* it is difficult to detect any genuine humour behind the irony. Caradoc seems, rather, to be writing as elegantly as possible about his home community, and, even at this early stage, to be repudiating it as some form of prehistoric primitivism. But he had not yet developed that oblique narrative style which so perfectly expressed his rejection of these people.

How that style evolved was first revealed in the magazine *Wales,* and it is worth repeating Caradoc's words here:

> Somehow I came to read Genesis again and when I was about the middle of it "Jiw-Jiw this is English writing", I said to me. On a Saturday night I went to the Hammersmith Palace and there I saw Marie Lloyd, and "Jiw-Jiw," I said to me, "she tells a story not by what she says but by what she does not." I kept up Genesis and Marie Lloyd.

Elsewhere he is reported as saying that he "evolved the idea of a basis of Old Testament diction coupled with a translation of the Welsh idiom" (*Caradoc Evans,* by Oliver Sandys, p. 78). The plots for the stories came, he said, "through [Duncan] Davies and myself talking of the Welsh country people and telling each other true tales that were stranger than fiction . . ." (Sandys, p. 77). It should be asked what Caradoc means when he says that the language of his stories is partly a "translation of the Welsh idiom," for when he makes a character say something like "How you are?" this does not translate the word order of the Welsh sentence, "Sut ydych chwi?" (verb preceding subject). The early reviewers of Caradoc's books pointed out, quite correctly, that his allegedly literal translations from the Welsh were, by virtue of their literalness, mistranslations, and therefore grotesque. Glyn Jones, however, whose bilingualism is decisive here, argues in his essay on Caradoc in *The Dragon Has Two Tongues* that he is not translating at all: "for the large majority of those notorious and outrageous sayings which he puts . . . into the mouths of his characters, there are no parallels, not even remote ones, in Welsh"

(p. 73). Only a few phrases seem to Glyn Jones to be direct translations: "When he writes phrases like 'head-stiff,' 'large money,' 'red penny,' 'kill your hay,' 'rob me pure,' 'forehead of a house' and 'one hundred and a half,' we can assume he had in mind the Welsh phrases of which these are literal translations—*penstiff, arian mawr, ceiniog goch, lladd eich gwair, fy nhwyllo'n lân, talcen tŷ,* and *cant a hanner*" (p. 73).

When the stories were first published it was of course the language which drew the most comment from the critics, for it not only drew attention to itself but served also to intensify the horror aroused by the matter of the story. Form and content, in other words, were perfectly matched. Thus English critics might ask: "Is this what the Welshman really sounds like when he speaks his native language?" while the Welsh critics were justifiably angry and quick to deny that any Welshman could speak "iobish" like that. But both sides missed the point. Despite Caradoc's use of the word "translation," his language is entirely his own creation for his own artistic purposes. If we must look for the source of his distortions, it is my own tentative opinion that it can be traced to the sound, not of his peasants' Welsh, but of their halting English. When, for example, Caradoc spells Davies as "Daviss," and has one of his characters say "Mistarr Eevanss," it should be possible to hear the English accents of West and North-West Wales. Nor is it surprising that the man who spent fifty-one weeks of the year in the metropolis should be sensitive, during his annual visit home, to the accents of the people he had left behind.

The Welshman who is also an artist is doubly sensitive to the sounds of words. Most Welshmen, whether they speak Welsh or not, are *aware,* however dimly, of their native language. It beckons to them in place names, street and shop signs, it is taught in the schools, and even the most anglicised Welshman has probably sung in Welsh at one time or another. Aneirin Talfan Davies, in his essay "Llenydda yn Gymraeg—Pam?" has some interesting remarks about the Celtic artist's sensitivity to language. He quotes Gwyn Thomas, whose parents and elder brothers spoke Welsh, on this question of the Anglo-Welsh artist's awareness of the native language: "Everything I have ever written . . . has had at the back of my idiom the language of people who have been talking a language for 2,000 years that I never knew . . . This is rather uncanny and weird, but it is something to be accepted because I will never get rid of it all." Mr. Davies suggests that one of the consequences of this awareness is the mangling of English by Welsh, Scots and Irish writers in a vain attempt to fashion a language which will be suitable to convey the inheritance of the racial memory ("etifeddiaeth côf cenedl") which has been transmitted in a language now alien to men like Gwyn Thomas. Theories based on notions of racial memory tend, despite Freud, to be difficult to substantiate, and it seems to me improbable that any of the Anglo-Welsh writers (apart from Caradoc) have delib-erately set out to create a medium of expression which will convey something called "Welshness" or the "Welsh tradition." But it does seem reasonable to suppose that they have inherited the traditional Welsh concern with the word itself, the sound of the word, and the way it fits into the rhythm of a line of poetry or a sentence of prose. This is reflected in the precision of language of Anglo-Welsh writers, and in their fascination with language as a source of beauty in itself. The language of Shakespeare's Glendower ("I can call forth spirits from the vasty deep") might be advanced as an example of the characteristic achievement of Anglo-Welsh literature—fascination with the unusual word, combined with high flights of the imagination. That is, as far back as the sixteenth century, Welshmen were being portrayed as speaking a distinctive kind of English, but I believe we can say no more than this. This distinctive English is not an attempt to create an approximation to the older language; it is the result of living in a country where poetry, with its attention to the single word, has been an integral part of life, and of living in a bilingual culture, with the constant awareness of the differences in words and in the sounds they make.

Aneirin Talfan Davies is a Welsh-language critic sympathetic to the artistic intentions of Caradoc Evans, and in his essay he sees similarities between Caradoc's linguistic manipulations and those of James Joyce and J. M. Synge. Joyce, as we know, took infinite pains over each word that he wrote, and in *Portrait of the Artist as a Young Man* we follow his developing awareness of the sounds and meanings of words and his consciousness that the language he spoke was not standard English. In their search for a language which is not standard English but which must nevertheless make use of English words, writers like Joyce and Caradoc Evans end up by forging their own private language and style, though Talfan Davies disapproves of this in Caradoc's case. My reason for referring to Mr. Davies's essay is to refute what I take to be its underlying assumption, namely that Anglo-Welsh writers are searching for a linguistic medium with which to express the "Welshness," as I called it, of their sensibility. This was certainly the theme of one of Mr. Davies's earlier essays on the subject (in *Welsh Anvil*) in which he noted that Anglo-Welsh writers fail to find "a universal medium within their own prescribed world" *because* the Welsh language exists as the perfect medium of literary expression within Wales. Thus he says, the Anglo-Welsh must rely on a "faithful idiomatic translation from the Welsh" (in the case of Caradoc Evans), or else they produce "the sublimation . . . of a local dialect, or rather linguistic oddities, which derive from the close proximity of two languages within one society." For so perceptive a critic of the Anglo-Welsh, these statements are puzzling. "Linguistic oddities" hardly does justice to the artistic intentions of the Anglo-Welsh writers, while my quotations from Glyn Jones should have shown that Caradoc for the most part was not translating from Welsh at all.

The language of Caradoc's stories achieves its grotesque effects not because it is a (mis-) translation from the Welsh, but because he went out of his way to search for the archaic or unusual word, working always with the precision of a poet. Having established biblical diction as the basis of his language, he then pored over his dictionary looking for the archaic or literary word which might serve to reinforce the impressions of primitiveness aroused by that diction. And where he found no suitable word he would invent one or use Welsh slang. The effect of this is to endow his peasant society with a claustrophobic, prison-cell atmosphere in which the inmates act and react upon each other as in some Dantesque horror in the depths of hell. Here is a list of the more unusual words, taken at random from the whole range of his published work: *gruntled* 'grunted'; *fulbert* (Welsh, Anglo-Welsh slang for "fool," possibly deriving from Welsh *ffwlbart* 'pole-cat'); *diffiding* (=concealing or overcoming—meaning not clear); "*snaggled* teeth" *baston;* "*crumped* shoulders"; *shonk* (from the Welsh *sionc* 'smart,' 'agile'); *clonk* (slang for "gossip"); *sponer* (man who goes courting); *gustless* (she "stared at this man who was as gustless as skimmed milk and unsatisfying as water"—'gust' of course is an archaism for 'taste'); *vilipended* and *quobbed* ("So much was he vilipended and poked fun at that his heart quobbed for means to punish her"); "his stomach wambled"; *maffled* (stuttered); *pugil* (a small dose); *scimia;* "*nousling* her into the sacredness of cash"; *slipthrift* ("Ap Reuben, who was a slipthrift in patriotic speech . . ."—it seems to be parallel with "spendthrift"); *cribbed* 'cheated'; *coggery* 'cheating'; *suspired* (a poeticism); *drumblish* humour; *dunning;* "*roytish* thicket of streets"; *hogcote;* "*braky* thickets"; *rabbling; menseless;* "she *wonder-gaped*"; *solifidian; prossing* over; *dwale* (=deadly nightshade); "a *softling* spark"; "*roscid* lips"; *whimwham* (another archaism); *shogged; mopsical* (humour); *complane* 'level with'; *growtheaded clodderer; spact* 'clever'; *data* 'father'; *merrybegotten* 'illegitimate'; *grumptious; wejen* 'woman'; *stutted* (for "stuttered"); *love-piffle; dablen* (from Welsh *tablen* 'beer'); *baglor* (Welsh for "bachelor"); *stablanning* (with the meaning of "stuttering"); *sombreous;* "a *drumly* liver."

This (selective) list of words can be roughly divided into two groups. There are the archaic, poetic and otherwise obscure words like *dwale, dunning, pugil, scimia,* etc., which Caradoc seems to have discovered on his journey through his dictionary. Then a second group can be formed from the Welsh words (*dablen, shonk, baglor,* etc.) and from Caradoc's adaptations of English words (*sombreous, slipthrift, grumptious,* etc.). In thus bestowing his own suffixes and spellings upon existing English words he is being faithful to the spirit of compromise of some Welsh people in their use of the English language. It is not unusual for example, to hear a Welsh person, unable immediately to find the English word that best fits the emotion or thing he wants to describe, invent on the spur of the moment a word whose sound approximates to the thing described. But Caradoc goes no further than this "Welshification" of certain English words.

He never attempts to reproduce that remarkable tendency of some Welsh people to speak both English and Welsh within the same sentence, switching from one language to the other and back again with fluent ease and no sense of incongruity. (Incidentally, one of the most famous examples of this sort of bilingualism occurs in *Wil Brydydd y Coed* by the nineteenth century satirist Brutus, the pseudonym of David Owen.) In distorting the English language and deliberately seeking out the archaic or obscure word, Caradoc was always striving for one artistic effect, which was to hem the reader into the constricted and claustrophobic society he describes, and the list of words above gives some indication, in microcosm, of that claustrophobia. His ability to achieve the effect intended, to develop a language that exactly matches the spiritual and intellectual horizons of his sub-human peasants, is the mark of his artistic success. Words like "roytish", "shogged," "quobbed" and so on, with their heaps of consonants and closed vowels, help to convey the idea of stunted intellect. Similarly, lips are not "rosy" but "roscid"—in other words, the very sound of his carefully chosen language seems designed to cut off whole areas of human experience. Feelings of romance, sentiment, good humour or love are all dispensed with as he pursues his single, nihilistic effect. The same is true even of Caradoc's many variations on the verb "to say" and its opposite. They are: *mouth, voice, speak you, word to, speech to, open my lips, clap your lips, clap your throat, clap your teeth, waggle your wild tongue, shake your tongue, rein your tongue, move your tongue, hold thy chin, make utterance.* Many of Caradoc's most vehement early critics used these variations as proof of the man's charlatanism. Where on earth, never mind in Wales, ran the argument, could you hear people talking like that? Caradoc never attempted to defend the style of his stories as he did their content, nor did he need to, since phrases like "waggle your wild tongue" and "clap your teeth," while obviously false to the speech of peasants in West Wales, are true to his artistic purposes. That is, they not only have a vaguely biblical ring, in keeping with his closeness to the Book of Genesis, but they are also sharp, mean, warped words, true, once again, to the type of mind laid bare in the stories.

Before considering Caradoc's work in more detail, we should look briefly at some of the social, political and literary conditions in the years immediately preceding and following the publication of **My People.** It was of course the period that saw Lloyd George's rise to supreme power, a rags to riches story that brought immense pride to the Welsh people. Kenneth O. Morgan, in his monograph on Lloyd George, stresses the almost fairy-tale quality of his life story and at the same time explicitly identifies Lloyd George's role in the creation of a new national pride in Wales:

> The spectacle (writes Dr. Morgan) of a Welsh country boy, bred in the home of a village shoemaker, rising to the highest office in the land, talking with kings and dominating international conferences, while still retaining his unmistakable national identity, did more than any other single factor to restore the confidence of the Welsh

people in their own capacities. After centuries of isolation and contempt, Welshmen in 1916 felt themselves to be in the limelight of world events.

In 1909 Lloyd George presented his "People's Budget," which proposed, amongst many revolutionary tax changes, to levy a tax on land. This particular tax proposal succeeded in arousing the wrath of the Tory opposition in the Commons, loud bellowings of fury in the House of Lords, and outrage in all those sections of the community most likely to be affected by the measure. After his famous Limehouse speech, in which he heralded the end of the old aristocratic order, the clamour against this "contumacious Welsh demagogue" became deafening. Malcolm Thomson, Lloyd George's official biographer, has brought together some of the choicer epithets hurled against him:

> He was a liar, a thief, a mountebank, a Communist, an Anarchist, a blatant blusterer, a dangerous demagogue, a fomentor of revolution, a Pecksniff and a Perkin Warbeck, a bravo, a traitor, a devil's advocate, a Socialist wolf in Liberal clothing, and a Welsh poacher. "I would like," announced the Duke of Beaufort, "to see Winston Churchill [who consented to act as President of the Budget League, a propaganda forum in support of the budget] and Lloyd George in the middle of twenty couple of dog hounds." Children in the nurseries of Mayfair and Belgravia were hushed to sleep with the warning, 'If you aren't good, Lloyd George will get you." If he had faced contumely during the Boer War, Lloyd George was now the object of a reviling far more savage and bitter, because rooted in fear.

Naturally, reactions to the budget in Wales were altogether different, since its proposals promised to bring an element of democracy into the Welsh countryside after a century of squirearchical repression. Thus, the more L.G. was attacked, the more he was supported in Wales.

But in 1910 there appeared *The Perfidious Welshman* by "Draig Glas" (presumed later to be a certain Arthur Tyssilio Johnson), a book frankly designed to puncture Welsh pride and stoke up the fires of controversy. It had much in common with Caradoc's work, except that it had no artistic pretensions and was more systematic in its denunciation. The author, "a slim and malignant sneak" according to Sir Marchant Williams, who reviewed the offending book in the *Western Mail,* identified himself with that thorn of Welsh Nonconformist life, the High Church-squirearchy axis, but, excellent credentials these, he was able to speak Welsh, that "dialect" as he called it. Here are a few of his more inflammatory opinions:

> Few people can tell a lie to your face with such perfect composure as a Welshman.

> Wales is the most priest-ridden country in the world ... The Nonconformist minister—an ill conditioned, illiterate and ill-mannered tag of humanity, with a smug, self-satisfied expression—is a veritable

genius for keeping his flock within the grip of his extortionate power.

> ... the supreme indifference with which Taffy's conscience estimates a breach of etiquette, or decency, or morality, so long as it is hidden from other people's eyes. In easygoing Wales ... you are never a sinner until you are found out.

> The world has never produced a more unscrupulous and self-interested hypocrite than the Welsh M.P. who springs from Nonconformist stock. He has all the wiles of a serpent and the slipperiness of an eel.

In 1912 T. W. H. Crosland entered the fray with *Taffy Was a Welshman.* It is a companion volume to his earlier satire *The Unspeakable Scot,* except that in addition to the common aim of deflating the pretensions of the Celtic minorities, there is here the added incentive to stick pins in Lloyd George, who crops up constantly in the narrative as "Davy Bach." Crosland was anxious also to scotch any rumours that he might be "Draig Glas," or, as he puts it, "the blue Welshman." In fact, he was so contemptuous of "Draig Glas's" achievement and angered at the unwarranted linking of his name with *The Perfidious Welshman* that he was ready to present *Taffy Was a Welshman* as the only legitimate attack on the irredeemable Welsh. Whereas "Draig Glas" was sarcastic and Caradoc Evans was the savage satirist, Crosland is more the gentle ironist. "What right (he seems to be saying) has a presumptuous Welshman from the wilds of the Nonconformist countryside to meddle in our (English) affairs? Let us, therefore, check to see what skeletons are concealed in his cupboard." And so he ambled through the usual platitudes about the Welsh character. Inevitably the book was attacked by the *Western Mail* reviewer, who concluded thus:

> The Welshman is forging ahead. England is beginning to feel the pinch. In Parliament, in the pulpit, in the university, in the slop, in the newspaper office, the "glittering, alert little Welshman" (quoting Crosland) is coming more and more to the front, and John Bull and the rest of the firm have all their work cut out to mind their number. Well, the Cymro is going to have his place in the sun, and all the Croslands in the kingdom or out of it cannot stop him in his march.

And how the reviewer's complacent smile must have broadened when, in 1916, his words were triumphantly vindicated: the archetypal Welshman had indeed "forged ahead", to become the first Welsh Prime Minister of Great Britain. We need only recall Kenneth Morgan's words to reconstruct that sense of vindication and complacency: "After centuries of isolation and contempt, Welshmen in 1916 felt themselves to be in the limelight of world events." The English may continue to sneer at Welsh pride and self-confidence—sneers from outside are easy to deal with—but woe betide the Welshman who now struck a wrong note on the harp during the national festivities. Caradoc Evans was just such a man.

In the space available here it is obviously impossible to examine the whole of Caradoc's work in the depth it deserves, but since he shows no fundamental change of direction, either stylistically or in terms of theme, throughout his literary career, we need not feel we are doing him an injustice by looking closely at only a few of his stories, all of them representative of his best achievement and some of them fairly accessible in anthologies of the short story, notably in *Welsh Short Stories,* selected by Gwyn Jones, (O.U.P.). The first story in *My People* is **"A Father in Sion."** It begins thus:

> On the banks of Avon Bern there lived a man who was a Father in Sion. His name was Sadrach, and the name of the farmhouse in which he dwelt was Danyrefail. He was a man whose thoughts were continually employed upon sacred subjects. He began the day and ended the day with the words of a chapter from the Book and a prayer on his lips.

It is fitting that this should be (part of) the opening paragraph of *My People,* for we are here introduced to much that is common to the whole book. Like the majority of Caradoc's leading characters, Sadrach Danyrefail is a pillar of chapel society, his thoughts are employed only on "sacred subjects," a prayer is never far from his lips, and he observes the Sabbath and attends the "Seiat." Sadrach has eight children, an early hint that we can expect something unusual about his wife Achsah. One night he "lacked the heavenly symmetry of the mind of the godly," and the reason emerges in this summary of his prayer, in which there is a hint of the language of the Parables:

> Would the all-powerful Big Man, the Big Man who delivered the Children of Israel from the hold of the Egyptians, give him a morsel of strength to bear his cross? Sadrach reminded God of his loneliness. Man was born to be mated, even as the animals in the fields. Without mate man was like an estate without an overseer, or a field of ripe corn rotting for the reaping-hook.

In the inflated grandeur of his prayer he postures as a Welsh Job, and cries out, "Let me weep in my solitude. Oh, what sin have I committed, that God should visit this affliction on me?" The utterance of such a prayer is sufficient, as usual in Capel Sion, to sanction all the ensuing barbarity, directed in this case against Achsah, the woman, ten years older than himself, whom Sadrach married for money. She is mad, he declares to the children, and because "it is not respectable to let her out" and it is "not Christian" to send her to the asylum, he will lock her in the harness loft. "Respectable" and "Christian" are interchangeable words in this society, and when they fall from the lips of the pious of Sion we always have to make the necessary reversal of meaning. And why is Achsah alleged to be mad?

> "Rachel, Rachel, dry your eyes. It is not your fault that Achsah is mad. Nor do I blame Sadrach the Small, nor Esau, nor Simon, nor Sarah, nor Daniel, nor Samuel, nor Miriam. Goodly names have I given you all. Live you up to them. Still, my sons and daughters, are you not all responsible for Achsah's condition? With the birth of each of you she has got worse and worse. Child-bearing has made her foolish. Yet it is un-Christian to blame you."

Achsah the prisoner now only emerges at night with a cow's halter over her shoulders, and once a week Sadrach drives her out into the fields "for an airing." The narrative recalls their precipitate wedding and the accompanying whispers, along with Sadrach's explanation (an important detail of the plot) of how Sadrach the Small came to be born six months after the wedding. "Achsah, dear me, was frightened by the old bull . . . She was running away from him, and as she crossed the threshold of Danyrefail, did she not give birth to Sadrach the Small?"

Three months after he had locked Achsah up, Sadrach returned one night with a new wife, Martha. Rachel, the eldest daughter, objects that she has been supplanted by Martha:

> "People are whispering," said Rachel. "They do even say that you will not be among the First Men of the Big Seat."
>
> "Martha is a gift from the Big Man," answered Sadrach. "She has been sent to comfort me in my tribulation, and to mother you, my children."
>
> "Mother!"
>
> "Tut, tut, Rachel," said Sadrach, "Martha is only a servant in my house."

This snatch of conversation illustrates well several of the themes running through Caradoc's work: there is first of all the ubiquitous "whispering" in this kind of small community with its emphasis upon "not being seen" to do something; there is obeisance to the power of the Big Seat, or diaconate; the sentence, "Martha is a gift from the Big Man," brings out their superstition and anthropomorphism; there is the peasant craftiness of Sadrach's recovery from the mistake of "to mother you" to the more consolatory "only a servant," and that last phrase sums up well the depersonalisation of human relationships under the Capel Sion regime.

Under the influence of Martha, Danyrefail "prospered exceedingly," but then "vexation" followed: six of the children died inside two years. Slight relief from the vexation comes when Sadrach the Small announces his intention to marry the economically valuable SaraAnn, daughter of Old Shemmi. On the eve of the wedding "Sadrach drove Achsah into the fields" and informed her of the happy event. The next day she manages to escape from her loft and, concealed behind a hedge, she watches the wedding procession pass by. As they pass, she counts the number of people in the procession and finds what seems to be "a large mistake." She hides behind another hedge and counts a second time.

"Sadrach the Small and Miriam!" she said, spreading out her doubled-up fingers. "Two. Others? Esau. Simon. Rachel. Sarah, Daniel. Samuel. Dear me, where shall I say they are? Six. Six of my children. Mad, mad am I?" . . . She laughed. "They had grown, and I didn't know them."

Achsah waited the third time for the wedding procession. This time she scanned each face, but only in the faces of Sadrach the Small and Miriam did she recognise the faces of her own children. She threw herself on the grass. Esau and Simon and Rachel, and Sarah and Daniel and Samuel. She remembered the circumstances attending the birth of each . . . And she had been a good wife. Never once did she deny Sadrach his rights. So long as she lasted she was a woman to him.

"Sadrach the Small and Miriam," she said.

She rose and went to the graveyard. She came to the earth under which are Essec and Shan, Sadrach's father and mother, and at a distance of the space of one grave from theirs were the graves of six of the children born of Sadrach and Achsah. She parted the hair that had fallen over her face, and traced with her fingers the letters which formed the names of each of her six children.

. . . . .

As Sara Ann crossed the threshold of Danyrefail, and as she set her feet on the flagstone on which Sadrach the Small is said to have been born, the door of the parlour was opened and a lunatic embraced her.

It is a story of hypocrisy and vicious cruelty, in which the complacency of Sadrach is never for a moment undermined by the various mishaps that befall him. He sums up the typical Caradoc Evans character: hypocritical, pious, grasping, cruel, and a monumental liar. Sadrach is also a bigamist. But the story is just as much about the masochistic Achsah as about the sadistic Sadrach. The last few paragraphs of the story are as near as Caradoc comes in his stories to bestowing compassion upon one of his suffering characters. In her painful counting of the procession, her bewildered reiteration of the children's names, her rapid flash-back to the moment of birth and her illiterate scratching on the gravestones, we experience all her anguish and uncomprehending despair, and feel the life draining away from her body and then from her mind as she plunges into insanity. It is on this last savage irony that the whole story is based: the woman who, in order to ease (unwittingly) the course of her husband's sexual desires, consents to be labelled mad, but who nevertheless manages to preserve her sanity for two years in her "asylum," finally succumbs to insanity as the truth dawns.

There can be no doubt that Caradoc meant us to feel the deepest pity for Achsah; but what are the facts? She is mindless—or, to put a better colouring on it, fatalistic. Her consciousness cannot be touched—only the primitive in-

stincts of motherhood can energise her, and then, unhappily, only into insanity. In her cow's halter she is less than human, and she shares this degradation with many of Caradoc's women characters. Women indeed are frequently the chief victims of chapel bigotry and male idleness, but invariably the sympathy he obviously feels for these characters is dissipated by his loathing of them. Similarly, the feelings of pity induced by Achsah's suffering are dispelled (for me) at the last moment, for she is now a genuine threat to other people's happiness. It is this latter reaction that I carry away from the story, rather than one of increased pity for her new condition, and this is possibly a tribute to Caradoc's art: such women, he seems to say, deserve our sympathy, but we must also remember that though this is a patriarchal society, the women acquiesce too easily in the prevailing ethos, and therefore deserve to be scourged as much as the men. Achsah, it should also be pointed out, was a willing accessory to Sadrach's blasphemous avowal in chapel about the circumstances of his son's birth.

The ending, true to the highest standards of the short story form, is hardly an ending: the story reverberates in the mind, leaving behind an atmosphere of fear and foreboding, and raising all sorts of questions. Is Achsah's reappearance at this moment meant as retribution upon the males of Danyrefail? Is she perhaps reclaiming her rightful position in the house? Probably not. More fascinating is Achsah's symbolic greeting of Sara Ann on the very threshold which had led to all her troubles (if, that is, we are to believe the detail about Sadrach the Small's birth). This patterning of events possibly implies that Sara Ann will go on to experience the same kind of wretched life as Achsah's. But the deeper meaning of the story lies in Caradoc's attitude to his characters. **"A Father in Sion"** contains one of the most lyrical and moving passages that he ever wrote. It is the description of Rachel's death:

Rachel developed fits; while hoeing turnips in the twilight of an afternoon she shivered and fell, her head resting in the water ditch that is alongside the hedge. In the morning Sadrach came that way with a load of manure.

"Rachel fach," he said, "wake you up now. What will Martha say if you get ill?"

He passed on.

When he came back Rachel had not moved, and Sadrach drove away, without noticing the small pool of water which had gathered over the girl's head. Within an hour he came again, and said:

"Rachel, Rachel, wake you up. There's lazy you are."

Rachel was silent. Death had come before the milking of the cows.

The counterpoint is perfect between the quiet peacefulness of the pastoral landscape (and although he rarely devotes many words in his stories to the pastoral background, it is always there as a silent force) and the unremitting callousness and brutality being enacted within that landscape. The scene is a savage satire on the pastoral life, as are all Caradoc's stories and novels with a Welsh setting. All spark of humanity has been eroded from the lives of these characters. They do not *question* life, they are puppets designed to illustrate Caradoc's overriding theme that Welsh life and religion have exacted this penalty from the people. Given this determinist theme, it is questionable whether, for example, he could have made Achsah, or any of his suffering characters, into a truly tragic figure. As it is, Achsah is only a dumb victim, too inarticulate to protest. Nor is there much protest from Caradoc the narrator, and this is his weakness—he sees the cruelty as evil, but revels in it and turns the screw a little tighter.

The fifteenth story in *My People,* "The Blast of God," has similar themes: the fate of the downtrodden woman and the contrast between the pastoral scene and the human beings within it. Here are the opening paragraphs, which are quoted for their relevance to Caradoc's view of pastoralism:

> Owen Tygwyn—Tygwyn is the zinc-roofed house that is in a group of trees at the back of Capel Sion—was ploughing when his wife Shan came to the break in the hedge, crying:
>
> "For what you think, little man? Dai is hanging in the cowhouse. Come you now and see to him."
>
> Owen ended the furrow and unharnessed the horse, which he led into the stable and fed with hay. Then he unravelled the knot in the rope which had choked the breath out of his son Dai. When he was finished and Dai was laid on the floor of the cowhouse, Shan said to him:
>
> "Eat you your middle-of-the-day morsel now, before you go back to the old plough."
>
> Having eaten to his liking of the beaten potatoes and buttermilk, Owen resumed his labour, and while he was labouring he rehearsed a prayer he would make for a male child, and that prayer he said to the Big Husband at the far end of the light. His petition reached the ears of God, and after twenty months it was answered: the cry of the infant woke him, and he got out of bed and lit a tallow candle, and read his Bible, because he was very glad. With the rising of the sun he brought his three cows into the close.

Many critics have noted that Caradoc shows no awareness of the beautiful scenery of rural Cardiganshire, and it is certainly true that he has none of the city-dweller's nostalgia for the countryside, that place of virtue, innocence and cornucopia. The simple answer to this is that the countryside of Caradoc's childhood, though a pleasant enough holiday spot then and now, is unspectacular and isolated. Moreover, Caradoc was brought up in an age when the Sunday School trip was the only (and

annual) means that children had of escaping the home environment. The inhabitants of Manteg ("Beautiful Place"—the location of Capel Sion) are restricted to visiting Morfa, the seaside-resort destination of the Sunday School trip; Castellybryn (Newcastle Emlyn) on market days or as Grammar School pupils; and Carmarthen, more particularly "College Carmarthen," where the future administrators of Capel Sion are trained. In Caradoc's country there are no hills for the eye to focus on in preference to the daily round, and it is thus hardly surprising that in such a restricted universe the minutiae of people's lives should assume such importance. That is one point. Another is the fact that this land is agriculturally poor and unyielding; in Caradoc's stories (and this is probably a close reflection of the actual situation in those times) the land is a destructive force: in its service bodies waste away, while it gives little in return, except death. There is a paragraph in **"The Blast of God"** which sums up this destructive quality:

> As their souls rejoiced, the weariness which follows heavy toil made their bones stiff. Shan was flat and unlovely, and of the colour of earth. Except on the Sabbath she covered her bosom with many shawls and a discarded waistcoat, and in the wrinkles of her face there was much dirt.

These people know what it means to toil, the sort of toil that can never be conducive to uplifting thoughts; on the contrary, the sort of toil that narrows horizons and turns the human spirit back upon itself. The earth is ugly, the body dirty—the people are, as Richard Vaughan, another Anglo-Welsh writer, has put it, "moulded in earth," but there are no potentialities in this rural setting for growth into ripeness and maturity. Rather, Caradoc comes closer to the Lawrentian indictment of *industrial* life of a writer like Rhys Davies. In the opening paragraphs of **"The Blast of God"** the rhythmic plod of the prose seems to express the monotonous daily round of pastoral life, where the act of ploughing has a deadening effect upon the mind, making it impossible for these peasants to respond to the extraordinary in life. In the story, Owen Tygwyn continues mechanically on his way until he has finished his task, and *then* he sees to his hanged son. In this kind of pastoral life, Owen has got his priorities right: a dead son has no economic value; a completed furrow has.

There is no love in Caradoc's countryside, least of all romantic love. One of the best stories in *Capel Sion,* **"A Keeper of the Doors,"** bears this out. The victim in this story is Leisa, a spirited woman, hard-working and, at twenty-three, one would expect, in the flower of womanhood; the oppressor is her husband Michael, indolent, bed-loving and bald, a man whom life has passed by, whose one day of energy and activity is the Sabbath, the only day on which he rises before dusk, since it is then that he renews the weekly task of preserving his soul, as well as his position as an important member of Sion. His married life (like the majority of Caradoc's fictional marriages) is a nullity, and the only thing that arouses his interest in his spouse is the possibility of her death, for death brings glory to the deceased's relatives. His laziness, however, means that she is working herself into the grave, and one hot summer's day she collapses in the field and dies. What we have, in other words, is a denial of all that the pastoral tradition stands for, since here in the countryside, according to that tradition, love should flourish. One reason, in Caradoc's view, why the women suffer is that they are not *men,* or, to put it in terms relevant to Capel Sion, they are not "photographs" of the Big Man. From birth, therefore, they are automatically degraded because of their unlikeness to the divine image. The only women who do seem to survive unscathed, albeit in some shadowy, limboesque existence, are the wives of preachers, partaking by reflection, as they do, in the glory of God. Or else, they are women like Bertha Daviss, respected as the village gossip, whose right to spread malice, while manifestly culpable herself sexually, is unquestioned.

As a footnote to this consideration of Caradoc's sceptical view of the pastoral life this passage also is worth quoting:

> By the sweat of his limbs he kept profitable the twenty acres of gorse land attached to Tyhen; he tilled and digged and drained, and his body was become crooked and the roots of his beard caked with some of the earth that had enabled him to gather much wealth, even seventy sovereigns.

Capel Sion's sole competitor, therefore, in the race to destroy these people is the land, the one taking care of their spiritual destruction, the other their physical destruction. When Caradoc describes the effects of their long agricultural toil, he drops his satirical smile and strives with maximum effect, as here, to capture the fatigue of their struggle. But these peasants are turning in a vicious circle, for the end of their struggle is to contribute to the coffers of Sion. He who contributes most will rise the highest, both in Sion and in heaven. Also, in their anxiety to ensure their place in the Palace of White Shirts after death, they forget to live and, not surprisingly, they fail to respect life. Thus characters like Achsah and Leisa undergo the most vicious suffering at the hands of the people of Sion—hardly people, but crude, insensitive morons, rather, for whom religion is the ultimate sanction for all kinds of barbarity. And yet another woman Nell Blaenffos, in the ironically-titled (most of Caradoc's short story titles are ironic) **"A Heifer Without Blemish,"** agrees to be debased to animal level: she turns out to *be* the "heifer without blemish" whom Tomos has journeyed to market to buy. She, like a host of other characters, is physically gross, and always this physical grossness is the image of an *inner* deformity, the sort of mental deformity that can assent to the brutalisation of society implied in, for example, Nell's "heifer" status. His vision, in other words, belongs to the twentieth century at its bleakest: here, long before the television age, we have a society unable to communicate articulately: a society without meaning except for the coherence of its materialist philosophy; a society alienated from the deeper springs of

human experience, and certainly from the beauty in religion. But at the same time this vision is too consistently negative. He sees the irony, the absurdity, even the cruelty, of portraying a woman symbolically as a heifer, but no sympathy for the woman emerges, because she is intimately a part of this society and, like Achsah, gives assent to its values.

Similarly, even those officially proscribed by Sion, like Simon and Beca and their daughter Sara Jane in **"The Way of the Earth"** *(My People),* readily give their assent to the tyrannous values of Sion. **"The Way of the Earth"** begins in the present, moves into the past and then forward again as it describes the career of Sara Jane, a flighty, wanton, vain woman, who is yet another victim of the patriarchal society. But despite her misfortunes, which are the wages of her wantonness, this is really the story of Simon and Beca:

> Simon and Beca are waiting for Death. The ten acres of land over Penrhos—their peat-thatched cottage under the edge of the moor—grows wilder and weedier. For Simon and Beca can do nothing now. Often the mood comes on the broken, helpless old man to speak to his daughter of the only thing that troubles him.
>
> "When the time comes, Sara Jane fach," he says, "don't you hire the old hearse. Go you down to Dai the son of Mali, and Isaac the Cobbler, and Dennis the larger servant of Dan, and Twm Tybach, and mouth you like this to them: 'Jasto, now, my little father Simon has gone to wear the White Shirt in the Palace. Come you then and carry him on your shoulders nice into Sion.'"
>
> "Yea, Sara fach," Beca says, "and speak you to Lias the Carpenter that you will give no more than ten over twenty shillings for the coffin."
>
> Simon adds: "If we perish together, make you one coffin serve."
>
> Neither Simon nor Beca has further use for life. Paralysis shattered the old man the day of Sara Jane's wedding; the right side of his face sags, and he is lame on both feet. Beca is blind, and she gropes her way about. Worse than all, they stand without the gates of Capel Sion—the living sin of all the land: they were married after the birth of Sara Jane, and though in the years of their passion they were all that a man and a woman can be to each other, they begat no children. But Sion, jealous that not even his errant sheep shall lie in the parish graveyard and swell in appearance those who have worshipped the fripperies of the heathen Church, will embrace them in Death.
>
> The land attached to Penrhos was changed from sterile moorland into a fertile garden by Simon and Beca. Great toil went to the taming of these ten acres of heather into the most fruitful soil in the district. Sometimes now Simon drags himself out into the open and complains when he sees his garden; and he calls Beca to look

how the fields are going back to heatherland. And Beca will rise from her chair and feel her way past the bed which stands against the wooden partition, and as she touches with her right hand the ashen post that holds up the forehead of the house she knows she is facing the fields, and she too will groan, for her strength and pride are mixed with the soil.

"Sober serious, little Simon," she says, "this is the way of the earth, man bach."

But she means that it is the way of mortal flesh . . . of her daughter Sara Jane, who will no longer give the land the labour it requires to keep it clean and good. Sara Jane has more than she can do in tending to her five-year-old twins and her dying parents, and she lets the fields pass back into wild moorland.

The slow unwinding of this strong language with its biblical intonations might suggest that Caradoc is taking a quasi-Romantic view of Simon and Beca's toil against the backdrop of Nature, for he does seem to sympathise with their changed fortunes and to find a value in their devotion to the soil. But then the other details of the narrative begin to obtrude and to emphasise the utter desolation of their lives, while the dialogue reveals all their loathesome avarice. As the story proceeds we can see that their present physical desolation is the complement of their lifelong spiritual desolation. Whether the blame for their condition is laid upon Sara Jane or upon "the way of the earth," it is a fact that they have spent all their married life dedicated to the kind of avarice that will ensure their return within "the gates of Sion." Here is how Caradoc describes their life together in a passage, the rhythm of which tends to enact the sense of their effort-laden skimping over the years:

> He and Beca saved; oil lamp nor candle never lit up their house, and they did not spend money on coal because peat was to be lifted just beyond their threshold. They stinted themselves in halfpennies, gathered the pennies till they amounted to shillings, put the silver in a box till they had five sovereigns' worth of it, and this sum Simon took to the bank in Castellybryn on his next carrier's journey.

And the end of their relentless exercise was to be "the time their riches would triumph over even Sion and so open for them the gates of the temple." The association of religion and money is a regular theme in Caradoc's work, but more important here is the stranglehold of the Capel Sion ethos upon these two stunted creatures, even after decades of being "without the gates."

The rest of the story is soon told. Sara Jane had grown conceited when "farm servants ogled her in public places" and when "men spoke to her frankly, and with counterfeit smiles in their faces." She had even used that ultimate symbol of vanity in this society: scented soap. At last, she was courted by William Jenkins, whom Simon deemed to be a "godly man" because he owned a "Shop General" and wore a white collar. In due course, Sara Jane became pregnant: "'Concubine!' cried Beca; 'Harlot! cried Simon," both of them too old perhaps to recall their own hasty wedding. In the bargaining that followed, William Jenkins held out for, and obtained, the highest price. He says:

> "Simon Penrhos, one hundred of pounds you've got in the bank, man. Give me that one hundred this morning before the wedding. If you don't do that you shall see."

> Simon shivered. He was parting with his life. It was his life and Beca's life. She had made it, turning over the heather, and wringing it penny by penny from the stubborn earth. He too, had helped her. He had served his neighbours and thieved from them. He wept.

> "He asks too much," he cried. "Too much."

> "Come, now, indeed," said William Jenkins. "Do you act religious by the wench fach."

Even in the thoroughgoing examination of hypocrisy which *My People* is, that last remark still manages to stand out. Simon acquiesced, Jenkins paid off his debts, and lived with Sara Jane for twelve months, after which his creditors began to press once more, "wherefore William Jenkins gave over the fight and fled out of the land."

The themes of avarice, hypocrisy and lust are fully explored in this story, in which, along with all Caradoc's early stories, one will look in vain for the character who is not a mentally and physically stunted subhuman. However, the satirist is the last kind of writer to feel obliged to draw rounded characters with a normal mixture of good and evil, especially if his vision is as narrow and his passion as intense as Caradoc's although even the most Juvenalian of satirists might recognise that the granting of some merit to one's opponent is one of the most effective devices of satire. But one of the distinguishing features of Caradoc's satire is its concentration upon and cauterising of the *man* as well as the man's vice, the deviation from the norm of civilised behaviour. Admittedly, it is often difficult to dissociate the vice from the man, but most satirists do manage to maintain the distinction, usually by ascribing some minimal virtue to the man, just enough for us to retain some sympathy for him. But Caradoc withdraws the least trace of virtue from his characters, and thus the least vestige of sympathy. In **"The Way of the Earth"** Simon and Beca have stored money for many painful years, and now they are shattered by its loss, but we cannot feel much sympathy, and may even smile, because they have had their comeuppance after years of petty thieving.

Caradoc's satiric methods and victims never varied throughout his literary career (except fleetingly in *The Earth Gives All and Takes All*), a fact which intrigues me and leads me to speculate about the three unusually candid statements from the Sandys biography: to his wife he says, "There was a rankle in me that I couldn't get rid of and the rankle was my bank balance or the lack of it . . ."; "Caradoc wanted my maternal affection as well as my woman's love"— in her autobiography, Full and Frank (Hurst and Blackett, 1941); Mrs. Evans (Oliver Sandys) had earlier written: "I had not been able to understand why he, who is in awe of no one, should be in such awe of [his mother], but now I know it was his childhood's awe of her and his reverence for her . . . Caradoc does not remember being kissed by his mother, but his regard for her was the strongest thing in him . . ." Thirdly: "he hated and abominated deception and would not stand for it, and I am sure that in his right moments he hated and spurned his own kink in that direction." And in one of the postscripts to the biography Hannen Swaffer refers to Caradoc's inferiority complex. If we also remember Caradoc's early loss of his father, his ambition to be a preacher and the puritanism of rural Nonconformist Wales, we have a basis for making some psychoanalytic deductions from the stories.

If Swaffer is correct about the inferiority complex, we need not look much further for an explanation of the irrational hatreds displayed in the stories. He probably felt inferior to those London Welsh drapers, dairymen and preachers whom he attacks so vehemently and so insistently, genuinely hating them, but also envying their position perhaps. Then, the pennypinching of his childhood and youth should be borne in mind when we read seemingly endless studies of avarice and its debasement of the mind and body. Avarice is the *main* theme of eight of the stories in *My People,* three in *Capel Sion,* five in *My Neighbours,* the whole of *Taffy,* and the whole of the autobiographical *Nothing to Pay,* where, suitably, the treatment is exhaustive and final. (Avarice appears in later books, but more often as a source of comedy—in fact, it is more than likely that in writing *Nothing to Pay* he succeeded in purging himself of his neurotic concern for money.) "He hated and abominated deception," says Mrs. Evans, and yet he had his own "kink" in that direction, an observation which further helps to explain some of the hatred he poured upon his characters. When Caradoc is painting the full horror of mental cruelty, avarice, hypocrisy, lust and covetousness, and lashing the characters responsible for those vices, he is, so the psychoanalyst might argue, fighting against those tendencies in himself. He pillories himself by making his characters suffer the sins he is guilty of in his subconscious, although the *artist,* or the conscious mind, has the final word by allowing the major sinners of Capel Sion (the preacher and the deacons) to remain unscathed. We might also speculate how much the loss of his father contributed to his rejection of religion and the kind of patriarchal society depicted in the stories.

The salient characteristic of Caradoc's childhood society, as we have seen, was its puritanism. It seems to me that the two most extreme, and diametrically opposed, reactions to sexual puritanism are represented, on the one hand, by the private life of Lloyd George, and, on the other, by the stories and novels of Caradoc Evans. Nor is it surprising that Caradoc should have satirised Lloyd George in *My Neighbours.* Lloyd George's extravagant sexuality has been well documented by his son, Richard, who writes: "It must be remembered that even in Victorian days fear and guilt about sex were mainly characteristic of urban and middle-class morality. Lloyd George had almost no inhibitions about these things—his religious beliefs were superficial, even though he could throw up a smoke screen of quotations from the scriptures . . . to conceal the paganism of his soul." If we can accept the report of his son, we can safely assume that Lloyd George never knew the reality of sexual repression. Which is just as unhealthy a state as the variety of sexual repressions we find exhibited in Caradoc's work, although, for good measure, Caradoc finds space to include a few characters of Lloyd George vintage. But for the most part Caradoc presents sex in terms of sadism, masochism and voyeurism, the first two especially in the early stories, the latter, repulsive at best, in his post-1930 work. It is the voyeurism, the keyhole-peeping, that causes the suffocating eroticism of some of the later work, the kind of eroticism that led his publisher to reject Kitty Shore's Magic Cake. Readers may draw their own conclusions about Caradoc's sexual proclivities or repressions, as the case may be. My own view, based on a reading of the books and on what is known of his life, is that something in his psychological make-up (a combination of the loss of his father, an obsession about money, the stifling of his personality while in the drapery trade, his roots in a puritan society, and, perhaps above all, his "reverence" and "awe" for his mother) disqualified him for fulfilment in love. If this view of him is anywhere near the truth, it will account for the frustration and cynicism everywhere evident in his books.

**"Greater Than Love"** *(My People)* illustrates Caradoc's handling of sex in his work, although I should hasten to add that with its seaside setting and its emphasis on the physicality of the characters (as opposed to their hypocrisy, avarice, etc.) it is not a representative story. Sam is passionately in love with Esther, but he is too much of a clod ever to satisfy her ambition to be a "ladi." On a community trip to the seaside, Esther is seduced by Hws Morris, a theological student. Sam kills them both, savagely—a genuine *crime passionnel.* It can be fairly objected that Caradoc's range of emotions is extremely narrow, but his examination of the more negative emotions, as this study of jealousy should remind us, can be more than adequate. The story contains this passage:

> Esther passed beyond the stones, and in a cave she cast off her clothes and walked into the sea; and having cleansed herself, she dried her skin in the heat of the sun. When she got out from the cave, Hws Morris came up to her.

> "Hungry you are," he said to her. "Return you into the cave and eat a little of this cake."

He led her far inside, so far that they could not see anything that was outside. Hws Morris placed his arm over Esther's shoulders, and his white fingers moved lightly over her breast to her thing. He stole her heart.

Although, as I have noted, lust is a strong theme in his work, it is unusual to have the physical side of sex described so openly, it being more often presented at secondhand through the medium of gossip. Other indirect methods are to refer to gravel being thrown at a girl's window and to the fact that a girl's waistline begins to alter its shape. However, the description of Esther's seduction raises the question of what I have referred to as Caradoc's voyeurist tendencies. When, as in this story, he describes sex directly, he concludes by writing an unhealthy kind of prose of titillation, in which sex becomes dark, unclean and furtive. And although the above passage seems to offer a perfect illustration of the Freudian back-to-the-womb complex, it seems to me more a straight-forward example of the way Caradoc always succeeds in making sex repellent, something to be experienced, animal-like, in a corner. Even when his sex is not furtive it is still repellent, as the two quotations below should reveal. They are from **"For Better"** (*My Neighbours*) and depict the amorous pursuits of Ben Lloyd (a pseudonym, I think, for Lloyd George):

> Though Ben and Gwen were left at peace they could not satisfy nor crush their lust.
>
> . . . . .
>
> Unknown to her husband Gwen stood before Ben; and at the sight of her Ben longed to wanton with her. Gwen stretched out her arms to be clear of him and to speak to him; her speech was stopped with kisses and her breasts swelled out. Again she found pleasure in Ben's strength.

Apart from the fact that they were portraying the most famous of all London Welshmen as a rampant and hypo-critical satyr, it is not too difficult to see why passages such as these should have given offence. There is noth-ing obscene or pornographic about them, but they are prurient, and prurience is the main characteristic of all Caradoc's writing about sex. When he writes some such sentence as "He was frank with her," we might well wish that *he* (Caradoc) could have been more frank, or else that he had left the subject alone.

If Caradoc had written nothing else after **"Be This Her Memorial"** *(My People),* this story would nevertheless have been sufficient to put him in the front rank of European short story writers. From first to last it is a story that evokes extremes of horror and revulsion, and the conclusion is almost literally hair-raising. It has its origins, according to Caradoc, in a true incident, which he describes in his **"Self-Portrait"** in Wales:

> At the time of his leaving us Davydd Adams [not Thomas as this article has it—he was, we should recall, "minister Capel Independents" and chief model for the Respecteds Bern-Davydd and Bryn-

Bevan] worked a money collection for himself and an old woman roasted rats and ate them to save a pound for this collection. Years later I wrote a story about this and Davydd Adams heard of it, and he said: "True-true, the pound is in collection plate Heaven."

The story begins, unusually for **My People**, in the first person, but quickly turns to concentrate on the ancient figure of Nanni, a "crooked, wrinkled, toothless old woman" with "blackened gums," who in her "search for God . . . fell down and worshipped at the feet of a god" in the person of the Respected Josiah Bryn-Bevan. "She helped to bring Josiah into the world; she swaddled him in her own flannel petticoat," and when eventually he became minister of Capel Sion "even Josiah's mother was not more vain than old Nanni." Throughout the story the emphasis is on Nanni's sacrifice, both material (she gives "a tenth of her income to the treasury of the Capel," her income being three and ninepence of poor-house relief) and, at the end, physical. Nanni is "broken with grief" when she hears that her god has discerned the finger of God in a "wealthy" sister church in Aberystwyth. For the first time in years she prays to the "living God" (instead of her god in Sion) that she may live long enough to hear Bryn-Bevan's final words. A "Seller of Bibles" visits her cottage and offers her "one copy—one copy only—at cost price." How kind, she exclaims, but when told the price she replies: "Dear, dear; the Word of the little Big Man for a sovereign!" But she goes ahead and orders a Bible and asks the Seller to bring it the next week, inscribed to the effect "that it was a gift from the least worthy of his flock to the Respected Josiah Bryn-Bevan, D.D." Now she spends all her remaining time following Bryn-Bevan around the countryside to hear his farewell sermons in the chapels under his care. But her labour, for which the parish pays her, is required in the hay-fields, and one night Sadrach Danyrefail calls to re-mind her of her obligations:

> Sadrach was going to say hard things to Nanni, but the appearance of the gleaming-eyed creature that drew back the bolts of the door frightened him and tied his tongue. He was glad that the old woman did not invite him inside, for from within there issued an abominable smell such as might have come from the boiler of the witch who one time lived on the moor. In the morning he saw Nanni trudging towards a distant capel where the Respected Josiah Bryn-Bevan was delivering a sermon in the evening. She looked less bent and not so shrivelled up as she did the night before. Clearly, sleep had given her fresh vitality. [This last detail seems particularly macabre when we finally learn what it really is that revitalises her so.]

On the eve of the farewell Sabbath she packs the Bible up "reverently" and entrusts it to Sadrach, unable her-self to attend the presentation. Here is the conclusion of Nanni's story:

> At the end of his sermon the Respected Josiah Bryn-Bevan made reference to the giver of the Bible, and grieved that she was not in the Capel.

He dwelt on her sacrifice. Here was a Book to be treasured, and he could think of no one who would treasure it better than Sadrach Danyrefail, to whom he would hand it in recognition of his work in the School of the Sabbath.

In the morning the Respected Josiah Bryn-Bevan, making a tour of his congregation, bethought himself of Nanni. The thought came to him on leaving Danyrefail, the distance betwixt which and Nanni's cottage is two fields. He opened the door and called out:

"Nanni."

None answered.

He entered the room. Nanni was on the floor.

"Nanni, Nanni?" he said. "Why for you do not reply to me? Am I not your shepherd?"

There was no movement from Nanni. Mishtir Bryn-Bevan went on his knees and peered at her. Her hands were clasped tightly together, as though guarding some great treasure. The minister raised himself and prised them apart with the ferrule of his walking-stick. A roasted rat revealed itself. Mishtir Bryn-Bevan stood for several moments spellbound and silent; and in the stillness the rats crept boldly out of their hiding places and resumed their attack on Nanni's face. The minister, startled and horrified, fled from the house of sacrifice.

**"Be This Her Memorial"** sums up the achievement and the message of *My People*. In some stories the farcical elements may detract from the effect of the satire, but here everything is subordinated to the construction of a complex symbol of the evil Caradoc saw in this society. Thus the Seller of Bibles, the man, as Caradoc called him, who defrauds servant girls (and old women on poor relief), and the Respected Bryn-Bevan, whose ingratitude and insensitivity are the outward manifestations of his massive egocentricity, are peripheral figures in the story. Nanni is a symbol of all the dark inner forces that Caradoc imagined he saw at work in this rural Welsh society. She contains the meaning of Sion, she epitomises the Sionites, she represents their superstitiousness, she has met the Bad Man and has nursed their god, Bryn-Bevan. This latter fact elevates her into something greater than he, and makes her sacrifice, likewise a symbolic gesture, all the more ironic. The story reveals both Caradoc's own horror at the darkness within her soul, a horror typified by Sadrach's reaction to the gleaming eyes that stare out of the gloom, and his fascination with the soullessness of her sacrifice, a blind sacrifice so typical of the Sionites. It is a story about the absence of love and the lack of meaningful communication between people.

But the symbol has an opposite aspect, equally bad. Nanni is also a representative of the ordinary chapel-goer, blind herself, who is preyed upon by the rats (the elders of Sion perhaps). Or again, she represents reli-

gion eating away at the soul of these people, tearing them up and converting them into monsters—the true religion of darkness. Her character withstands these differing interpretations in which she both preys and is preyed upon because there is no *good* and evil in Sion, no light and shade, only a uniform evil. The chapel may give the lead in evil, but its acolytes need no prompting to supersede it in viciousness—it is a matter of constant interaction. Nowhere does Caradoc Evans show such controlled satire and bitterness as here. The pride, vanity and avarice of the preacher eats up "her memorial"—her Bible is given away, her body is eaten away. The hideous monstrosity of the symbol is Caradoc's most powerful expression of his hatred. Hatred of what, though? Not of real Welsh society, it hardly needs to be said. But he does hate intensely this *model* of Welsh society that he has created, which in turn stands for all the things in *himself* that he despised. This perhaps is Caradoc's supreme achievement as a man: he was able to come to terms with the evil in himself and write about it—his book is a confession almost, and as such an indictment of the Protestant faith.

The main and most frequent (literary) criticism to be levelled against the stories is their lack of chiaroscuro but, as I have tried to indicate, the consistency of his vision demands that uniform darkness and oppressiveness. For aspiring young writers in the Wales of the interwar period Caradoc's success with the themes and the linguistic medium of *My People* was an inspiration, but from the point of view of his literary career as a whole we may have some reason to regret his success and the controversy surrounding it, for the judgement pronounced in *My People* was final enough to militate against further development; while any relenting, any movement towards the light, might have been construed as capitulation to the views of his critics. *Capel Sion*, however, demonstrated that capitulation was not a word to be found in Caradoc Evans's dictionary.

One of the greatest problems confronting the writer who achieves wide success with his first published work is the writing of his second book. Indeed, for Caradoc the problem might have seemed insuperable, for had he not already presented fifteen satirical studies of the hypocrisy of Sion, each of which might have been developed into a novel? But whether Caradoc had not yet exhausted his supply of real-life incidents, or whether his imagination had grown extra fertile, he was now in *Capel Sion* able to produce fifteen more stories, many of them measuring up to the highest standards of *My People* (especially **"The Tree of Knowledge," "The Pillars of Sion," "Judges,"** and **"A Keeper of the Doors"**). To adapt Gwyn Jones's metaphor, here were fifteen splashes of petrol on to the flames of *My People* After the success of the latter it was logical that Caradoc should turn, in the new book, to examine the real cause of the illness that afflicts the society in his first book. The stories in *Capel Sion* do not differ greatly in theme from *My People,* except that here the source of evil in society is more consistently diagnosed as **Capel Sion.** It stands as a central symbol, never described in detail, though there is no need for description since most chapels are alike architecturally (and not only in Wales— both Matthew Arnold and D. H. Lawrence winced over the ugliness of the ubiquitous chapel, that product of nineteenth century philistinism). Capel Sion is, we can imagine, a commonplace little bethel, stark, severely puritan in design, uncomfortable and, since it has no aesthetic pretensions, often a blight on the landscape. And inside this unlovely building is preserved the most rigid of hierarchical structures—below the pulpit, and sharing in its autocratic power, sit the men of the Big Seat, the wealthy men of Sion; below them are the middling wealthy (the term is relative) on the floor of the chapel; and, outcasts almost, there are the people of the loft or gallery, labourers and the like, whose contributions to Sion are minimal.

Such, then, is the architecture of this shrine of Hypocrisy, dedicated to the Nonconformist cause, the overseer of an arbitrary and oppressive conformity. As we see in *Capel Sion,* it turns a blind eye to the vices of wrongdoers at their death, so long as their bodies can be claimed for Sion's burial ground for the greater glory of Sion; the vilest of sins can be atoned with the sacrifice of produce to the Respected; the most hideous crimes can be exonerated since it is not logically possible for a prominent member of Sion to be sinful, especially if he is rich. The people of Sion genuinely believe in the position of their Respected as God's chosen representative on earth, while for them the photographs in their Bibles are true likenesses of the biblical characters. It is this elementary ignorance, coupled with an unquestioning belief in their own religious superiority, that goes to make up their hypocrisy, the greatest of their vices, but only the antecedent of many others, the most prominent of which are covetousness and avarice. Avarice is necessarily a prominent vice because of Sion's rapacious and consuming material/financial demands upon its members, demands that set the standards for the conduct of society as a whole. All humane impulses are made subordinate to these materialistic demands, and that Caradoc attaches great importance to this is evident from the relatively high number of stories that contain (as we have seen) virtually the same incident, namely the death or collapse of a character which will be ignored until the task in hand has been completed, maybe hours later. This incredible suffering, we must infer, derives from the stranglehold of the Capel Sion ethos. The demands of Sion are also reflected in ordinary business transactions, where everybody is on the make, and swindling has divine sanction. In addition, there is, as a farcical sub-theme, the conventional hostility towards the Church—indeed, there never enters into the consciousness of Sion the possibility that Truth may have several shades. All these themes in the stories are woven around the central theme of the authoritarian power of Sion. Its power, in modern terms, may be likened to that of some vast industrial corporation, geared to productive efficiency, which rejects pitilessly those who do not make the grade, or else to a Communist bureaucracy, in which there is no place for the nonconformist. In fact, one often has the impression that the preacher's function is to be the sales manager in charge of a certain product (the religion of Sion) whose marketability is to be measured by the number of graves in the graveyard or by the number of occupied seats in the chapel.

One final detail about *Capel Sion*: the twelfth story, **"Judges,"** ends with the central character slicing the family cat in two (in front of the children), and rather like an avenging angel, hanging one piece on the door of his brother's house and the other on the door of the Shepherd's Abode. In 1917 Caradoc published in Volume XXIV of The English Review a story called **"The Day of Judgment,"** which was never re-published, though it belongs in subject matter with **"Judges"** and seems to be a continuation of the latter story. There are two possible explanations: **"Judges"** and **"The Day of Judgment"** may originally have formed one story which was conveniently split into two. Or else, Caradoc may have been pressed by friends, after the publication of *Capel Sion,* to reveal in another story what happened after the tantalising conclusion of **"Judges."**

*My Neighbours* was published, according to the titlepage, in 1919, but seems not to have been released for sale until some time around St. David's Day, 1920, presumably so that the book could have the maximum possible effect upon the London Welsh, to whom it is primarily addressed. The picture of the London Welsh here is as unflattering and vitriolic as that of the peasants in his first two books, but it is also noticeable (and this is true of his career as a whole) that once Caradoc moves away from the Welsh setting (ten of the thirteen stories are set in London), there is a falling off in the level of achievement. The main criticism to be levelled against the London Welsh stories is their lack of moral satire, the sort of satire provoked by an author's rage against a specific abuse. Instead, many of the stories seem to have been motivated by nothing higher than personal dislike of certain luminaries in the firmament of the Cymmrodorion, the chapels and the drapery shops. Above all he seems to have despised Lloyd George, who appears as I have previously noted, under the very thin disguise of Ben Lloyd, the leading character in **"According to the Pattern"** and **"For Better."** These two stories do not merit detailed analysis, but it is worth quoting from them if only for their historical importance and for the intriguing way they manage to steer clear of the laws of libel.

It will be helpful to refer once again to Richard Lloyd George's biography of his father to try to link some of the description there with elements in the character of Ben Lloyd. "He was (says Richard Lloyd George) the greatest Bible-thumping pagan of his generation . . . His speeches, which sometimes slipped into Welsh when he got carried away, were freely embellished with analogies about valleys and mountain summits, or woods and storms . . . Religion had to be a potent, a living thing . . . its mystery had to excite the mind and the emotions.

He loved a good sermon, much in the way he enjoyed a brilliant speech or a fine piece of choral singing . . ." What he has to say in the following passage about his father's courtship of a certain Mrs. D. seems to approximate very closely to the story of Ben Lloyd and Gwen, the wife of the dull, impotent draper, Enoch Harries, in **"For Better."** *Any* kind of woman, apparently, satisfied Lloyd George, representing "a challenge, like the nun to Don Juan." "My parents' friends amongst the Welsh colony included a successful draper and his wife . . . She was a lively, attractive creature, rather loquacious, very stylish, perhaps a little flamboyant as I recall. There were Sunday outings . . . and I remember father taking me for long walks in the country around Walham Green [with Mrs. D.]. The affair continued for a long time . . . Mr. D., although quite a good business man and tradesman, was a colourless personality. He had, however, certain ambitions which I think would have remained unfulfilled were it not for father's assistance." Mrs. D., we are told, had one child by Lloyd George, and there was "a lot of gossip about it at the time." Caradoc, as a Fleet Street journalist, was in an ideal position to pick up all the details of the gossip, and Richard Lloyd George's description of the affair almost amounts to a synopsis of Caradoc's story **"For Better."**

**"According to the Pattern"** is the story of Ben Lloyd's rise from lowly origins to the heights of the London preaching world. He is therefore much in demand as a speaker at public functions, and the following is an extract from his St. David's Day speech at the Queen's Hall. The spelling of certain words in these quotations probably imitates what must have been the Caernarvonshire accent of Lloyd George:

> "Half an hour ago we were privileged to listen to the voice of a lovely lady [Gwen]—a voice as clear as a diamond ring. It inspired us one and all with a hiraeth for the dear old homeland—for dear Wales, for the land of our fathers and mothers too, for the land that is our heritage not by Act of Parliament but by the Act of God. . . .

> "Who owns this land to-day? The squaire and the parshon. By what right? By the same right as the thief who steals your silk and your laces, and your milk and your butter, and your reddy-made blousis. I know a farm of one hundred acres, each rod having been tamed from heatherland into a manna of abundance. Tamed by human bones and muscles—God's invested capital in His chosen children. Six months ago this land—this fertile and rich land—was wrestled [sic] away from the owners. The bones of the living and the dead were wrestled away. I saw it three months ago—a wylderness. The land belonged to my father, and his father, and his father back to countless generations . . .

> "I am proud to be among my people to-night. How sorry I am for any one who are not Welsh. We have a language as ancient as the hills that shelter us, and the rivers that never weery of refreshing us . . ."

He goes on to defend the system of living-in and fines in drapers' shops, arguing that "the man who tries to destroy them is like the swimmer who plunges among the water lilies to be dragged into destruction . . ." After this, Ben goes from strength to strength until a safe entry into Parliament seems guaranteed, except that he has one compulsive weakness which may yet cramp his ambitions:

> He trembled from head to foot to ravish every comely woman on whom his ogling eyes dwelt. His greed made him faithless to those whom he professed to serve: in his eagerness to lift himself he planned, plotted, and trafficked with the foes of his officers. Hearing that an account of his misdeeds was spoken abroad, he called the high London Welshmen into a room, and he said to them:

> "These cruel slanderers have all but broken my spirit. They are the wicked inventions of fiends incarnate. It is not my fall that is required—if that were so I would gladly make the sacrifise—the zupreme sacrifise, if wanted—but it is the fall of the Party that these men are after. He who repeats one foul thing is doing his level best to destroy the fabric of this magnificent organization that has been reared by your brains. It has no walls of stone and mortar, yet it is a sity builded by men. We must have no more bickerings. We have work to do. The seeds are springing forth, and a goodly harvest is promised: let us sharpen our blades and clear our barn floors. Cymru fydd—Wales for the Walsh—is here. At home and at Westminster our kith and kin are occupying prominent positions. Disestablishment is at hand. We have closed public houses and erected chapels, each chapel being a factor in the education of the masses in ideas of righteous government. You, my friends, have secured much of the land, around which you have made walls, and in which you have set water fountains, and have planted rare plants and flowers. And you have put up your warning signs on it—'Trespassers will be prosecuted.'

> . . . . .

> "But we must do more. I must do more. And you must help me. We must stand together. Slander never creates; it shackles and kills. We must be solid. Midway off the Cardigan coast—in beautiful Morfa—there is a rock—Birds' Rock. As a boy I used to climb to the top of it, and watch the waters swirling and tumbling about it, and around it and against it. But I was unafraid. For I knew that the rock was old when man was young, and that it had braved all the washings of the sea."

I can do no more than mention, in the space available here, two of the best stories not only in *My Neighbours* but in Caradoc's work as a whole—**"A Widow Woman"** and **"Joseph's House,"** both with Welsh settings. They are more personal and painful than most of his stories, and **"Joseph's House"** contains in embryo many of the details that were later to be developed in *Nothing to Pay.* The theme of personal sacrifice is strong, and the basic relation-ship in both stories is that between mother and son. It seems quite probable, therefore, that in the Mali of **"A Widow Woman"** and the Madlen of **"Joseph's House"** Caradoc is trying, amongst other things, to say something about his own mother (whose name was Mary).

By 1920, therefore, with three volumes of short stories behind him, Caradoc Evans was a notoriety, the mere mention of whose name would provoke the most passionate argument. Nor was Caradoc slow to stoke up the fires of controversy, as the columns of the *Western Mail* during that time will readily bear out. His many letters to that newspaper and his public talks (the drafts of which are deposited in the National Library of Wales) are all variations on the theme of Wales's spiritual blight at the hands of Nonconformity. One of these letters, published in the *Western* Mail of 22 December, 1915, will suffice to indicate just how vehement was Caradoc's response to his critics:

> Mr. Davies does not like this book because of its awful truths. Were I regardless of truth and were I anxious to become rich in money I would have written an indictment against the Church in Wales. The Welsh preachers would then report well of me, and the praying men and the singing men and women would lift up their voices in my praise. As it is, the leaders of Welsh Nonconformity are uneasy that word of their tyranny will get into England. They and their members of Parliament have lied to the English how the heart of rural Wales is very beautiful; the pastors are fathers in Sion, and the peasants have neither spot nor blemish; and of all the sects that will seek to go into the Palace, none from Capel Sion will stay without the gates. There is none like us in wisdom and understanding.
>
> The rulers of Sion know that this book is true, hence they terrorised the booksellers of Wales to boycott it and the libraries to ban it. They revile me and close their doors against me, and they are forgetful of a saying from a book in which they have no faith: 'Am I become your enemy because I tell you the truth?' And truth is always violent. When Jesus cleared the Temple of the money-changers He used scornful words. I am astonished that Sion of the period did not suppress Him.
>
> 'Give me all that you have' is the command of the preacher. When he sits at our table we must place before him our fattest fowl, though the taste of fresh meat is unfamiliar to our lips. We must sacrifice to him continually, and our offerings must be the best we possess. We leave at his door our first and whitest-hearted cabbage and our sweetest potatoes. We toil on our unproductive land until the earth chokes the lines in our flesh that he may live as befits a God. He is Aaron and Nero. He is a spiritual hypocrite. He will steal your food, and when he is filled he will weep forth words that you are hungry. With his hand he has broken our people. The oil of Christianity he has changed into vitriol. And when one murmurs against him

> his spite is horrible: he will go forth and make mischief in the offender's family.
>
> Someone has said how the Welsh hills sing with joy that the Sabbath has come. I have heard no song. I have heard men and women conversing lewdly on their way home from Sion, and I have heard young servant girls screaming frightfully in the arms of praying men.
>
> Wales knows that *My People* is true. The libraries know that it is true. They banned it in accordance with the command of Welsh Nonconformity, which is exceedingly strong in our government. The Rev. T. Eynon Davies knows it is true, as he knows that not one person of any consequence has told him that it is 'all rot.'

There were "noisy protestants" in the gallery, remarked *The Times* drama critic, when *Taffy* received its first performance on 26 February, 1923. Dylan Thomas (who refers, in *Portrait of The Artist as a Young Dog,* to "the great Caradoc Evans") read the play and was so deeply impressed that he was able to recite whole portions of it, and it is more than likely that he still remembered *Taffy* when he came to write *Under Milk Wood*. The characters in the play are: Twmi and his daughter Marged (played at the first performance by Edith Evans); Josi, Essec, and Rhys (all, like Twmi, Big Heads in Sion); Ben Watkin, a case-hardened preacher who competes with Spurgeon, a young preacher, just out of college, for the control of the Sion machine; and finally Captain Shacob, a sea-faring farmer. The climax of the play comes when Spurgeon relinquishes his hold over Sion, lyrically declares his love for Marged, and returns to the land, where, he says, he will "seek God in the ploughshares." This pantheistic statement, together with Spurgeon's avowal of love for Marged, is the nearest we come in Caradoc's work to the positive affirmation of a philosophy. Although the London critics responded well to the play, seeing it as a welcome change from the conventionalities of the "box-office theatre," it contains many *longueurs*. Already there are signs of the laboriousness with which, in his later work, he sought epigrammatic perfection in the sentence. The result of such striving is a lack of fluidity, so that one rarely experiences in reading Caradoc the desire to read inexorably on from chapter to chapter. But there is no lack of fluidity in the racy nautical language of Captain Shacob and the lyricism of Marged. Here is the angry speech Marged delivers to the three hypocritical deacons:

> Your prayers will build you nothing. You are men of speech and your sorrow is dry. You have no regard for the first Capel Sion that was Bensha's mud-walled hut on the moor. Every night a candle burnt at the window to guide the folk who came on the narrow path to read the Beybile in Welsh or to seek Bensha to go and read the Beybile to the dying. And however black and stormy the night no one lost his way or went in vain. The Sion that you want to pull down was built by love. Short is the fame of Love. After their day's work women brought timber down the hill and over

the valley to make this Sion. And in the night men opened gravel pits and brought upstones from the quarry by the light of a flaming fire of twigs and furze. All worked in the sure belief of another God than the God of the English-speaking parson who shot calves and lambs for sport and whose horses trod the corn and tore the hedges. Their love and sacrifice are nothing to you. Do not the moments of their labour taunt you with shame? You pule and whine and pluck your garments like a man waiting for a feast for which he has made no provision.

The play ends with the ironic contrast between Marged and Spurgeon embracing in love and Rhys Shop coming on stage with his hens, saying, "Off now, hungry hens. Off and gobble the lot of the wedding rice." Despite all the positives in the play, nothing much has changed in Capel Sion. And this is the play's weakness as comedy. The function of comedy should be to satisfy, at the end of the play, our outraged sense of virtue—we want to see the villains exposed and punished before we can be certain that things have returned to normal. The hypocrites of Sion are denounced loudly enough but they are not "exposed" in the sense that henceforth they will live altered lives, while their "punishment" is to be deprived of the profits that would have accrued from building a new chapel. We must also ask whether it is possible for romantic love to flower in a community that we have hitherto been led to believe is a nest of imbeciles, hypocrites and incipient rapists.

Caradoc had originally written *Taffy* in the form of a novel, but his first published venture in this genre was *Nothing to Pay*. A leading article (no less) in the WESTERN MAIL condemned the book as "frankly obscene 'realism'." "It is called 'realism' in the jargon of the modern school. We prefer to call it filth. *Nothing to Pay* is a dirty book, and we are surprised at its publication." This is nonsense, but it is not difficult to see what the newspaper found so objectionable.

There are over fifty characters in the book, over a score of whom have some sexual exploit attributed to them; there are two or three abortions, and one woman is slowly murdered with powdered glass for imprudently becoming pregnant; and over all there hangs the odour of Amos, the central character, whose dark, twisted and thoroughly evil personality makes the atmosphere of the novel so nauseous. But in the first hundred pages or so Caradoc brings great zest to the description of his peasants' physicality, and there are many passages describing the landscape which reveal the poet that was always latent in him. In the following passage the beauty of nature is contrasted with the spiritual desolation of man:

> The morning and evening mists lifted and the sun washed away the frost which gleamed on the grass and the ploughed earth. Yet Ianto found no joy. His heart was as lonely as a dead man's heart. In Moriah and at eisteddfod and in mart and fair he was forlorn. The inhabited places were desolate, for he merged his mind in no one's. God's promise was unfulfilled, and he was discontented with the

discontent which is begotten of money and which nothing can lull to sleep.

*Nothing to Pay,* to put a label on it, is a picaresque novel, though with the most dismal of anti-heroes in Amos. Here is the main character journeying from the country to the city, but not, in this instance, from rural innocence to urban vice, rather from rural corruption to city squalor. There is no sense of an initiation into experience, since Amos is evil from his earliest days, and though he is constantly on the scene, he is often not the active protagonist, but merely the passive receiver of impressions. I suspect that Amos represents a nightmare vision of what Caradoc might have become if he had not had the spirit and imagination to rebel against his drapery chains. Since so many of the events in the novel derive from autobiographical recollection, it seems inescapable that the hateful Amos is a sort of self-flagellation, a catharsis, for Caradoc. After this novel he was able to remove *himself* from his fiction.

The result is to be seen in his next novel, *Wasps,* where there is some distancing of perspective and a more objective moral criticism. Despite the conventional declaration that "All the incidents and characters of this tale are entirely fictitious," the novel had to be withdrawn before publication because the novelist Edith Nepean had seen herself libelled in the character of Dame Edith. Caradoc deleted the character and somehow managed to satisfy the lawyers by substituting the homosexual Ernie Brown, who was given the same role and almost the same language that had previously been assigned to Dame Edith. He also had to find a new publisher for the book. The title comes from the pet theory of John Honeybone, one of the many wizened and impotent characters in the novel, that all mankind are wasps, having, that is, some prominent vice that controls all their actions. "Greed (he says) is our controlling wasp and by it shall mankind perish." There are three other kinds of wasp: "faith by which we are robbed, hope by which we are tortured, and charity by which we are demeaned." And then the novel goes on to offer us a vast panorama of all the vices that flesh is heir to. The characters here, however, are more recognisable as human beings than are the caricatures in *My People,* but they are nevertheless unlovely and unloveable, although sometimes the writing achieves a comic gusto which allows us to overcome our dislike of what is being presented. The rapid succession of scenes, each a short story in itself illustrating the central theme of waspishness, gives the impression of formlessness, and certainly we miss that gradual sense of growth associated with the developmental structure of the novel. Both *Nothing to Pay* and *Wasps* prove that Caradoc was most at home in the short story.

The same is true of *Morgan Bible* (1943)—I prefer to say nothing about the two disastrous novels of 1934, *This Way to Heaven* and (what came to be called) *Mother's Marvel. Morgan Bible,* in its unities of time, place and character, has the structure of classical drama.

Not that this has any significance, any more than the fact that the action takes place on Sunday, 3 September, 1939. The novel, a rampant and hilarious comedy, shows Caradoc's tendency in these last years of his life to strive with painstaking care for the perfect aphorism. Thus we progress from clever sentence to clever sentence, like this: "A happy Welshman is as rare as a bee in the snow"; "A ram on his rambles finds out the brambles"; "Sermons are like women. Peep underneath and they are all the same. Sooner you can put a new udder on a cow than a new sermon in the mouth of a preacher." Morgan Bible himself is a grotesquely comic character, towering with Falstaffian aplomb over the whole story, but grotesque because he has murdered his bigamous second wife and will not scruple to eliminate his first wife when she inconveniently appears on the scene, and, with unflagging energy, he is now planning to marry the widow whose husband he poisoned earlier in the day. Much of the comedy centres around the elaborate schemes the characters propose for removing the body of the dead husband, Josh, from Capel Salem, the scene of the action, to Penlan, a distance of some twenty miles. All the characters want the honour (and profit) of transporting the corpse back home, but while they argue amongst themselves Josh is carried out of the chapel house in a sitting position by his widow and Bowen, B.A., placed on a Crosville bus (passed off as a very sick man) and so carried in the cheapest possible way to Penlan, for the corpse is able to use the return ticket he had bought that morning. But mixed in with the comedy there are some nasty examples of human cruelty. The overall effect of the novel is similar to that produced by the films of Ingmar Bergman, in which there is the feeling of the absurd in human nature and the presence of strong fantasies beneath otherwise calm exteriors. (I think, incidentally, that Caradoc was fascinated by cinematic techniques.)

In 1942 Caradoc had published another volume of short stories, *Pilgrims in a Foreign Land.* Many of these stories are fables, some of them are pointlessly obscure, but all of them have greater range than his early short stories. But there is also a loss of intensity because Caradoc the moralist is not under the same pressure of passion that he formerly felt. He is more detached now, the savage indignation has gone, and there is now the hint of the leisured writer setting himself a "theme" and writing to it—it's a challenge to his inventiveness, but it does not involve his heart. In the last two years of his life, after the publication of *Morgan Bible,* he continued to write short stories, and these were collected by his wife and published posthumously as *The Earth Gives All and Takes All,* stories, as she labelled them, "without bitterness." All the same, his domestic life during the war years seems to have been filled, so recent evidence suggests, with extreme bitterness and frustration, which spilled over into irrational fury and hatred against those around him, so much so that Mrs. Evans contemplated divorce on several occasions. But Caradoc Evans was consistent, for just as many of the early stories were, as I have suggested, a form of self-flag-ellation, so at the end of his life he was still prepared to come to terms with his inner self. The result was the title story **"The Earth Gives All and Takes All."**

It concerns a lazy farmer who travelled around spouting his wise "sayings" while his wife Silah and the labourer Ianto keep the farm going. The farmer dies and the story ends with Silah and Ianto, a year later, supervising the birth of a calf. According to Mrs. Evans in her Preface to the book, Caradoc identified himself with the farmer, whose heart (like Caradoc's, we must imagine) "tumbled about and about in its hole." And when the farmer has a vision of truth—"he looked into his loft and all his sayings were dry dust on the floor"—it is Caradoc's vision, too. "I have looked into my head (says Caradoc) and all my book writings and all my thinks are dry dust." It is a brave confession, even if it has about it a tinge of disillusion and despair. But at least these last stories show that he can write with love and humanity. He also rejects his "sayings," and thus the need to hold up the flow of the prose with an unlimited series of perfectly executed aphorisms. The greater fluency of this volume is directly attributable to his abandonment of his epigrammatic style. Even so, his characteristically "claustrophobic" style remains, mainly because he cannot abandon the short sentence which had once served him so effectively in flaying the spiritual poverty of Sionism.

All Caradoc's critics since 1915, both hostile and friendly, have lamented the fact that he did not use his unquestioned genius for more positive ends. But there are other things to lament than this lack of light amongst the shade. He witnessed two world wars, the Depression, the disintegration of the Liberal Party, the rise of socialism and the birth of political nationalism in Wales, but, fundamental as all these events were, there are *less than ten* references in the whole of Caradoc's work to contemporary affairs. When there were momentous changes afoot in literature, music, painting, pyschology and politics, and when most writers, after 1915, were struck by the spiritual and physical dissolution of society in Britain and Europe, Caradoc continued to stick rigidly to his vision of a static, nineteenth century Welsh society. But there were compensations, especially for those young Welshmen who saw the dangers of complacency in Welsh society. Perhaps only a Welshman could understand *emotionally* the significance of those early stories in which Caradoc was opening, for the very first time in the literature of Nonconformist Wales, a new window on to Welsh life. Here was a man who brought a sense of freedom, the sense that it was possible, after all, to give expression to those innermost thoughts which the piety of rural Wales seemed to have permanently bottled up, and to cock a snook at the Nonconformist world which for so long had managed to tie art inextricably to religion. Here was someone to untie the knots, and it was thus Caradoc who set the style and tone for much that was to follow in Anglo-Welsh writing. Not that the Anglo-Welsh writers needed a "model" to copy, since they were all excellent writers anyway, besides being products of a later generation and different (for the most part) social conditions. But at least he showed his successors what could be done, and what achieved. It is fair to add, however, that Caradoc's notoriety probably made it more difficult for the other Anglo-Welsh writers to be readily accepted by the people of Wales.

One last point: I complained above about Caradoc's lack of political awareness, but the writer who (like Jane Austen) lives through a revolutionary period in history and chooses not to comment on it directly is not therefore parochial or shirking his social duty. What matters is the universality of the author's theme and the moral relevance of his vision. Caradoc Evans was not an intellectual writer with a strong philosophy to propound, but he nevertheless left behind a literature which, for all that it is steeped in late nineteenth century Wales, belongs peculiarly to the twentieth century in its fierce questioning of man's motives, its rejection of religion and its bleak vision of an alienated society. He will disturb us for some time yet.

## Mary Jones (essay date 1982)

SOURCE: "The Satire of Caradoc Evans," in *The Anglo-Welsh Review,* Vol. 72, 1982, pp. 58-65.

[*In the following essay, Jones discusses the pastoral qualities of Evans's satire.*]

"Satyr is a sort of Glass", writes Swift, "wherein Beholders do generally discover everybody's Face but their Own; which is the chief Reason for that kind Reception it meets in the world, and that so very few are offended with it".[1] Swift might have been amazed at the reception of Caradoc Evans' work. Perhaps no event has made the Welsh public react so like the savage caricatures of them portrayed in *My People* as the publication of that volume of short stories in 1915. Contemporary reviews, articles and letters express disgust and outrage. And neither was the abuse any less upon the publication, the following year, of *Capel Sion.* "They called in the police when he wrote *My People*", wrote a reviewer in the Sketch, "*Capel Sion* should bring out the troops".[2] (The allusion is to a police raid on Cardiff bookshops to forfeit all copies of *My People*—an unauthorised act that led to a question in the House of Commons). Though, as a corollary of Swift's comment, one might surmise that offence is taken at satire when the reader discovers his own face, the objection of Caradoc Evans' readers was, on the contrary, that not only could they not see their own faces, they couldn't see anyone else's either. It is indeed noticeable that nearly all the vicious criticism is directed at the stories' lack of 'realism'; the fact that they paint a distorted picture of Welsh life was enough for them to be condemned out of hand; hardly anyone in all those letters and articles mentions satire, the entire controversy raging over the literal truth of the stories.

As they are so obviously satirical, with all the distortion, caricature and parody of satire, this reaction to them makes curious reading, but it is understandable. The stories purport to reveal a people, a nation, a race, and that people objected to the grotesque image of itself partly because it would be taken by others to be the literal truth (which indeed proved to be the case, as English reviews show). Moreover, taken literally, the stories foster a traditional racial scorn—they promote, for instance, the view of national depravity contained in the 'Taffy was a Welshman' jingle—the only effect of which is to harden prejudice. For however much the stories might aim at insight through attack, with regard to their Welsh readers, they are written, too, for English readers. Indeed, the position of the author writing in English about Welsh-speaking Wales is akin to the writer of pastoral; both represent one people and way of life through the eyes of, and in the language of, another. And when one community sees itself being misrepresented to a larger and more powerful one (whether derogatively in satire or idyllically in pastoral) the literary convention that is employed seems unacceptable. A rural reaction to pastoral is perhaps as likely to focus on indignation about factual inaccuracy as the Welsh reaction to Evans' satire did.

This satire has more affinity with pastoral than simply that Evans' position, as an Anglo-Welsh writer, parallels the position of the writer of pastoral. The conventions of the two forms are sufficiently close for the one mode to allow scope for the other. Though the focus of pastoral, in exaggerating the virtue of unsophisticated life, is on remedy, while the focus of satire, in exaggerating the vice of sophisticated life, is on attack, both tend to the one moral aim of reforming a corrupt society. From Skelton to Salinger writing in English has made use of the pastoral mode for satiric ends, and Caradoc Evans' stories belong with this tradition of pastoral satire, in which the simplicity of the unsophisticated shows up the corruption of those in power, to which they are victim and of which they are judge.

The centre of the village society with which the stories deal is the Nonconformist chapel. It is seen to dictate the structure and nature of that society and to control the behaviour of its members. And it is seen to be morally corrupt, to judge human worth in economic terms (the most religious is he who supplies the greatest wealth to the chapel, the sinner is he who fails to give). Thus greed, selfishness, cheating and theft are sanctioned by the criterion of wealth, while the second criterion of preserving appearances (there is no sin without evidence) sanctions duplicity, cunning, hypocrisy.

The corrupt rulers within this social hierarchy—the minister and deacons—are seen as thoroughly evil; the poor, who are usually peasant farmers, are the exploited victims. In **'Be This Her Memorial'** Nanni, victim of the Chapel's demands, saves the 3/9 a week she gets on poor relief to purchase a bible for the departing minister, by eating rats: she is found by the minister, dead, clutching a roasted rat and half eaten herself by rats. She is a victim of the society her fate judges. Women are often such victims; indeed, in his reply to the *Weekly Dispatch's* enquiry about the authenticity of the events in the stories of *Capel Sion*, Evans, while stressing their authenticity, twice admits he has altered the events, both times to bring about the death of the woman victim.[3] However they react to their victimisation, whether passively like Acsah, or rebelliously, like Betti, the women or peasant farmers are driven to death or insanity. In passages such as the following from **'The Way of the Earth'**, the inhumanity, crippling humiliation, and petty productivity politics (in terms of corpses) of Capel Sion are seen in relation to peasant life—a life which is grim and hard, but which gives human dignity.

> Simon and Beca "stand without the gates of Capel Sion—the living sin of all the land . . . But Sion, jealous that not even his errant sheep shall lie in the parish graveyard and swell in appearance those who have worshipped the fripperies of the heathen Church, will embrace them in Death.
>
> The land attached to Penrhos was changed from sterile moorland into a fertile garden by Simon and Beca. Great toil went to the taming of these ten acres of heather into the most fruitful soil in the district. Sometimes now Simon drags himself out into the open and complains when he sees his garden; and he calls Beca to look how the fields are going back to heatherland. And Beca will rise from her chair and feel her way past the bed which stands against the wooden partition, and as she touches with her right hand the ashen post that holds up the forehead of the house, she knows she is facing the field, and she too will groan, for her strength and pride are mixed with the soil.
>
> 'Sober serious, little Simon", she says, "this is the way of the earth, man bach."
>
> But she means that it is the way of mortal flesh . . . of her daughter Sara Jane, who will no longer give the land the labour it requires to keep it clean and good."[4]

Simon and Beca's identity is bound up with the earth, and nature and human life are seen to move according to the same pattern. The earth is the true reflection of their lives; its assessment of them does not accord with that of the Chapel, and is a judgement on the Chapel's treatment of them. Where the Chapel humiliates them, the earth makes them proud; their dignity arises from turning 'sterile moorland' into 'fertile garden', and the terms in which this activity is spoken of—making the land 'clean and good'—imply there is a moral worth in their life-work, and so in their lives, that is denied by the Chapel. Similarly Ianto in **'The Earth Gives All and Takes All'**, is felt to have a gentle goodness born of his close contact with the earth. "He walked on the earth with his eyes on the earth. For sure and for sure

he spoke to the earth with the tongues of his boots."[5] "He was like a pillar of good earth."[6] His happy, mild, 'harmless' nature springs from his way of life. The earth is a basis for moral judgement; the act that 'makes it good' is a good act. It holds the balance of life; it 'gives all and takes all'. As a controlling force in the lives of the peasants it stands in opposition to the other controlling force, the Chapel (and the God of the Chapel). The contrast of victimiser and victim in the stories is often expressed in their different attitudes to the earth; the victimiser is lazy, refusing to work on the land, concentrating his energies on scheming and cheating, while the victim toils ceaselessly on the land. The earth is a hard master, stern and dominating, but it is not partisan. It is not subject to cunning or fawning; it is incorruptible. By contrast, the God of the Chapel, as stern and dominating, is seen as savagely partisan, revengeful and vindictive. He is the God of the Old Testament, just where that figure differs from the New Testament of God. He works on the principle of revenge, he supports racial superiority and male superiority. He is on the side of the wealthy, through whom and in league with whom he works. God enlightens the minister, Bern-Davydd, regarding suitable revenge schemes, and Bern-Davydd in turn "informed God of a just punishment for those who rebel."[7] The Chapel God is made, by the ministers and deacons, in their own image.

The earth, on the other hand, is aloof, separate, entirely neutral. The immorality of the way of the Chapel God and the morality of the way of the earth is often suggested by the language of the stories. God is spoken of in grossly sexual terms; Heaven and Hell are very physically drawn: the Hobbesian view of religion as a perversion of sexuality is believable in the village of Manteg. The purposes and manifestations of the Chapel God are revealed in crude, repulsive terms, while man's relationship with the earth is expressed in a lyrical manner. For instance, in **'According to the Pattern'**, the terms in which God's presence in the minister is spoken of ("Of him this was said: 'White Jesus bach is as plain on his lips as the snout of a big sow."[8]) contrasts in tone and effect with his step-sisters' description of their rural life ("'We wake at the caw of the crows', they said, 'and weary in the young of the day'"[9]). The Chapel and its God are the object of satire; the way of life close to the earth is never satirically treated.

In this way, then, the author adopts the position of moral satirist, deploring the stranglehold of the Chapel upon the lives of Welsh villagers, and using the simple dignity of life close to the earth to throw into relief the corruption of the Chapel. To the extent that he does this he is writing pastoral satire.

In most of the stories, however, much of this effect is obscured because the 'way of the earth' does not consistently show up the corruption of the Chapel. Indeed, the way of life of the peasant is more often seen to breed the slave-mentality which makes him vulnerable to the Chapel's corruption. In **'The Way of the Earth'**, after the passage quoted, Simon is seen to have been thieving from his neighbours (to gain enough wealth to defy Capel Sion's ban) and he and Beca attack their pregnant daughter in the very terms in which they were attacked for the same 'sin' by the Chapel. They are victims who take on the identity of their victimiser towards others (even their daughter). And though when she marries Jenkins (a draper in debt who marries for Simon and Beca's money) he is seen as thoroughly disreputable, the wrangling over the dowry is pretty equally scheming on both sides. Simon has made his money from two sources, making good the earth and thieving:

> "Simon shivered. He was parting with his life. It was his life and Beca's life. She had made it, turning over the heather, and wringing it penny by penny from the stubborn born earth. He, too, had helped her. He had served his neighbours, and thieved from them. He wept."[10]

There is sympathy and satire, it seems, in this passage. The narrator's position is not clear; he no longer seems to be advocating freeing the helpless peasants from the power of the Chapel, so much as saying that human nature is like this, that this moral corruption is innate in humankind, from the humblest peasant to the richest minister. The story **'Earthbred'** seems to go further—a story of London-Welsh society, dealing with cheating and hypocrisy, it suggests that these vices are bred of life close to the earth, are characteristic of rural life. The corruption of the city is not redeemable by the goodness of rural life, as it is in traditional pastoral; on the contrary, the city has been corrupted by the country. Indeed, except for one very early story, the stories of the Cardiganshire farmer going to London are stories recording the easy transition from rural to urban corruption. They attack the assumptions about rural life which are implicit in pastoralism rather than expose corruption through the use of pastoral convention, and this is not pastoral satire but satirical pastoral.

The earth is seen to exert an influence upon the farmer which is parallel to, rather than opposed to, that of the Chapel. It is bent on the exploitation of the farm-worker. It no longer gives and takes equally, it is destructive. It gave Leisa "little and robbed her of herself."[11] "Hard is the earth and foolish are we to be her slaves. She takes us in life and marries us in death",[12] comments Katrin. Mankind's slavery to the land brings about physical sickness and dehumanisation. The tiller of the land is reduced by constant toil to infertility or to a passive vegetable state: Peggi seemed "like a sapless tree which harbours every refuse that the wind blows"[13] (an image significantly repeated of the Chapel in another story[14]— slavery to the Chapel or to the land produces the same kind of vulnerability).

Although such a story as **'Be This Her Memorial'** is pure pastoral satire, most of the stories blend pastoral satire and satirical pastoral. Three that well illustrate the difference in effect when pastoral satire domi-

nates, on the one hand, and when satirical pastoral dominates, on the other, are, respectively **'The Talent Thou Gavest'** and **'A Just Man in Sodom'** (continued in **'Calvary'**), for they deal with rather similar situations. Eben of the first is off-set by Pedr of the latter two. Both youths, after the manner of the wise fool, reveal to the self-deceived villagers truths about the kind of lives they lead, and both have a view of the Christian ideal which leads them to a rejection of the Chapel society. They are the outcast victims whose solitary existence on the moors leads them to an insight into the corruption of the village society. When they impart their wisdom to the villagers they are reviled and rejected. They are forced to renounce their 'talent' if they want to be accepted in the village (as Eben does) or to retreat into their solitude with sheep (as Pedr does). To this extent the three stories make use of a pastoral framework, but the first uses it to satirize Chapel morality, the other two to satirize the outcast and his moorland 'wisdom'. For Eben's Christian ideal, unlike Pedr's, is an acceptable ideal; he rejects the extremes of the Old Testament which the Chapel has accepted as dogma, for reasons of conscience.

> "I have not preached to you at all the real religion,"

he says, rejecting his traditional Nonconformist preaching,

> "I offered you the White Palace or the Fiery Pool. Men, Men, that is not right."[15]

Driven out of the Chapel, he asks: "How could I preach against my conscience?"[16] To redeem himself in that society, he sacrifices conscience and moral principles for money and duplicity:

> "God has told me to resume my labours in Capel Salem . . . Let not the matter of the little sovereigns engage your minds at this joyful time. Has not our dear brother Ben Shop Draper arranged all that?"[17]

The insight, conscience and vision of an ideal that he gains as a shepherd are overcome by village pressure, but the goodness he sacrifices is a real goodness. Pedr, on the other hand, is only a 'just' man in Sodom ironically: his 'justice' is a crude Old Testament form of justice—he punishes the villagers for their sins by stealing one of Sadrach's calves and sacrificing it on an alter he calls Calvary. In **'The Talent Thou Gavest'** there is opposition between the moral religion that life on the moor can bring and the immoral religion of the Chapel; in **'A Just Man in Sodom'** and **'Calvary'** Pedr's religion is a parody of the Chapel religion. If he exposes the real sins of the villagers which their cunning and duplicity conceal, he does it from arrogance and ambition; this 'wise fool' is revealed to be really foolish. When the villagers judge Eben to be mad, it becomes a judgement upon them; when they judge Pedr to be mad, they are right. The story of Eben develops the idea that a moorland life imparts a goodness to the shepherd, and is primarily pastoral satire; the story of Pedr implies that such a life only encourages insanity, and is primarily satirical pastoral.

Because pastoral satire and satirical pastoral are incompatible (the first implies an acceptance of the pastoral convention, the latter its rejection) the use of both together means that often the stories have a profoundly negative effect, in denying any sense of good or worth. Taken as a whole they present an inconsistency of attitude and a jarring of optimism and pessimism. It is an inconsistency which is well brought out in Evans' comments in reply to criticism of *My People*. Again and again he states that his purpose is to destroy the influence of Nonconformism in Wales and free his people; again and again he states that it is impossible for anyone or anything to do the Welsh any good.

> "I write because I believe that the cesspools of Wales should be stirred up, because I want to see my people freed from religious tyranny, because I love my country so much that I would exhibit her sores that they may be healed,"[18]

he says, and again explicitly states:

> "Our faults are not of our own making. They have been foisted upon us by Liberal Nonconfirmity."[19]

In statements like these, which attribute the social vices of West Wales to Nonconformity, he seems to be taking upon himself the role of moral satirist, writing to stir opinion with a view to social reform. But elsewhere, and still during the same period of controversy, he seems to withdraw from that position:

> "I did not create hypocrites, cheats, thieves, murderers, immoral men and women. They came to me, as they will come to you if you go and live in West Wales . . . It is not for me to convert these people; it is for the preachers, and they do not want to."[20]

Here, it seems, he is saying that the Chapel makes use of, rather than reforms, the vices it finds, not creates, in society—vices that seem to be innate in the breed of man in West Wales. Again he says:

> "There are three things beyond God's repair: the fury of an abandoned woman, the deeds of a drunken man, and the mind of a Welshman,"[21]

and in the same vein:

> "I do not think my stuff has done Wales any good. It is not in me to do that. It is not in anyone."[22]

So, as a satirist, Evans wavers between faith in the Welsh freed from Nonconformity, and despair about the possibility of change. Highet, in *The Anatomy of Satire* speaks of two kinds of satire, the kind that aims at improvement, correcting ignorance, and the kind that aims to wound, despising people. Evans' stories waver between the two types; the first is found in the pastoral satire, the second in the satirical pastoral.

NOTES

[1] Swift, Jonathan, A Tale of A Tub and Other Early Works 1696-1707. Oxford, Basil Blackwell, 1965, p. 140.

[2] *The Daily Sketch,* 16th December, 1916.

[3] *The Weekly Dispatch,* 14th December, 1916.

[4] Evans, Caradoc, *My People,* London, Melrose, 1915, pp. 32-33.

[5] Evans, Caradoc, *The Earth Gives All and Takes All,* London, Dakers, 1946, p. 10.

[6] Ibid, p. 4.

[7] Evans, Caradoc, *My People,* London, Melrose, 1915, pp. 107-108.

[8] Evans, Caradoc, *My Neighbours,* London, Melrose, 1919, p. 33.

[9] Ibid p. 40

[10] Evans, Caradoc, *My People,* London, Melrose, 1915, p. 43.

[11] Evans, Caradoc, *Chapel Sion,* London, Melrose, 1916, p. 185.

[12] Evans, Caradoc, *Pilgrims in a Foreign Land,* London, Dakers, 1942, p. 106.

[13] Evans, Caradoc, *Capel Sion,* London, Melrose, 1916, p. 149.

[14] Evans, Caradoc, *My People,* London, Melrose, 1915, p. 50.

[15] Ibid. p. 51.

[16] Ibid. p. 53.

[17] Ibid. p. 55.

[18] Evans, Caradoc, Letter in *The Western Mail,* 23rd January, 1917.

[19] Evans, Caradoc, Ms. in the National Library of Wales, MS. 20033C, p. 14.

[20] Evans, Caradoc, Letter in *The Western Mail,* 26th December, 1916.

[21] Evans, Caradoc, Ms. in the National Library of Wales, MS. 29933C, p. 3.

[22] Sandys, Oliver, *Caradoc Evans 1879-1945,* London, Hurst & Blackett Ltd., 1945, p. 71.

## Mary Jones (essay date 1985)

SOURCE: "A Changing Myth: The Projection of the Welsh in the Short Stories of Caradoc Evans," in *The Anglo-Welsh Review*, No. 81, 1985, pp. 90-5.

[*In the following essay, Jones explores varieties of structure, archetype, and emplotment as they developed in Evans's fiction.*]

When reviewers of Caradoc Evans' first volume of short stories [*My People*] claimed it revealed "primeval beings who still live within a six hour railway journey of London,"[1] and "ferocious primitives"[2] whose "sacrifices are made to that which is older than Paganism and as old as human sin,"[3] they were reacting in a way that must have delighted Caradoc Evans. For he responded to the storm of protest that followed the publication of his book, by stressing, in defence of his portrayal of the Welsh, their primitive nature and their mythical origin. But where the reviewers tended to look to the African continent for parallels of folk-custom, seeing little difference "between the candidly savage hlobonga of the Zulu and the bed courtship of West Wales,"[1] and finding the book valuable "for the light (it) has shed on the psychology of the Obi Man,"[3] Evans looked rather to the pre-historic East to trace the origin and identity of the Welsh. Claiming they were too strange and contradictory to 'explain',[4] he accounted for them in outrageous mythical terms:

> We have not travelled very far from Eden. Our features suggest Jew and Egyptian. Our place of origin is somewhere in the East. During our period there we led disorderly lives. It is likely that the orgies that take place in our chapels and at our eisteddfodau are survivals of that distant day. We fought with Jew against Egyptian and with Egyptian against Jew, and we taught new vices to loose women of both races. But we could not hoodwink God. He got weary of us and He folded us in a cloud and dropped us in a corner called Wales because he would forget us.[5]

Two mythical identities merge here: one of creatures who are the embodiment of vice, who account for the evil in the world, and the other of original man, turned out of Eden, wandering in search of a lost identity in an alien world ("We are the lost tribe—a tribe that has lost its soul,"[6] he claims elsewhere.) In his first three volumes of short stories it is the first of these mythical views that dominates; in the last two volumes it is the second (as indicated by the title '**Pilgrims in a Foreign Land**'). And this change of focus occasions a change of form in the stories. From being a savage attack on the Welsh, they become folk-tales that probe the nature of fallen man.

The change is fundamental, yet Evans' narrative style remains the same—strongly Biblical. It is a style which instantly suggests that the Welsh are a lost tribe of Israel, or at any rate a forgotten survival of some ancient race, at once oriental and occidental, which has mysteriously escaped the evolution of Western civilisation. But whereas in the satirical stories the style is powerful and effective, in the later more tolerant tales it loses force, the Biblical archaisms doing little more than heightening a sense of the quaintness of fable and folk-tale.

The style is effective in the early stories because it gives rise to a two-fold irony. On the one hand, the Biblical tone exposes the villagers' lives as a travesty of Christianity, for it evokes values that are contrary to the vice, unprincipled behaviour, pettiness and crime being described. On the other hand, these corrupt carryings-on are seen to be actually akin to events in the Bible—the characters do act like 'the children of Isaac' (the title of an intended novel about them), Betti is like Jezebel and Potiphar's wife[7], and so on. Thus the ironic discrepancy between the New Testament and the Old is exploited to reveal the discrepancy between the Christian spirit and life in rural Wales, and both the Old Testament and rural Wales are degraded. The Welsh see the God they have made in their own image in the same light as he is seen in the Old Testament. "Look you at God of the Bible. He commanded and threatened and dictated. And is he not a Welshman?"[8] berated Evans. The Old Testament and Capel Sion are locked together in a way that reduces both to barbarity.

The contrast between the effect of the style and the impression gained of the characters in these early stories, is enhanced by the distinction between the narrative and the dialogue. For the former has a loftiness which the latter, drawing heavily on mistranslations of Welsh idiom, lacks. The characters' speech is crude and elementary, conveying an impression of subnormality, and suggesting again the primeval minds of the speakers. Professor George H. Green quotes Evans as saying, in defence of his rendering of 'Bod Mawr' as 'Big Man' rather than 'Great being': "I know very well what *bod mawr* means in the dictionary or to a Welsh scholar. But I know very well what it means to the man I am writing about. He is quite incapable of thinking of a great being . . . I am trying to represent that man's mind and how it works. If he does not really say 'Big Man', he thinks it, and his imagination will go no further."[9] Evans is conveying a mentality bound by the immediate physical world, incapable of imagination or abstract thought; for Bern-Davydd a heavenly robe is Sunday's white shirt, just as Mog Edwards' love of Myfanwy Price in *Under Milk Wood* is inseparable from the wares with which he is surrounded in his draper's shop. There is no imaginative projection beyond day-to-day village life either in Llaregyb or around Capel Sion: in Llaregyb this indicates a child's viewpoint, while around Capel Sion it indicates warped, brutish man, but in both cases the villagers are enclosed in their own remote, impregnable world. Dylan Thomas treats it amorally, using it to claim a funny-sad innocence: to Caradoc Evans it is an immoral world, and through it he attacks inhumanity.

And yet an early account by Evans of Welsh village life (written when he was twenty-eight) has all the charm of *Under Milk Wood* and none of the viciousness that characterises his first three volumes of stories. **'Taffy at Home'** fondly depicts a community that is farcical, child-like, engagingly outrageous. Subtitled 'The Humour and Pathos of Welsh Village Life,' it is, like the Scottish stories of J. M. Barrie that Evans sought to emulate, sentimental. The village folk are shown as simple and innocent, but these qualities are the outcome of an undeveloped moral sense rather than moral purity. Their actions are in fact materialistic, hypocritical, intolerant and vengeful, but the moral judgements implied in such terms are as out of place in Manteg as they are in Llaregyb: the spite and cunning is harmless idiosyncrasy, a source of comedy not of anguish. There are no victims.

How different is this sympathetic, if patronising, enjoyment of eccentrics, from Evans' bitter satire a few years later on the same characters, who are the repulsive grotesques of *My People, Capel Sion* and *My Neighbours.* The guile and greed are same; it is the humour and pathos' that have gone, and with them the narrator's affectionate tone, his comic irony, and his personal involvement. The villagers deliberately and pitilessly cause suffering. T. L. Williams points out that the ending of **'Taffy at Home'** is repeated almost word for word in the ending of **'The Glory that was Sion's.'**[10] But how noticeably, too, do they differ. In the first, Shacki outwits the preparations for his death comically, and then, along with the narrator, cosily joins in the joke—"We then had tea with the boiling water, because, as Shacki said, it was a pity to waste it."[11] In the second, though, the preparations for Twm's death are inspired by hatred and they cause fear, and then Twm outwits them, hostility remains— "'Madlen!' he cried. 'Little Madlen, is not the old kettle boiling then? There's slow mule you are! Come, make you a cup of tea now.'"[12]

Only in one respect is Evans' treatment of the Welsh in **'Taffy at Home'** and the later stories consistent: in all they are an anachronistic people, immersed in ancient ways, in an isolated, extreme place, surviving the progress and change in the world almost untouched.

This mythicizing of the Welsh is particularly striking when the five volumes of stories are contrasted to the realistic stories of Londoners that Evans wrote before beginning *My People.* It is interesting, too, to see the sense of social victimisation which develops in these realistic stories—several of them highlight the plight of social outcasts, such as a condemned prisoner's mother and wife, and an unemployed ex-prisoner and his abused girl—for it is precisely this awareness of social victims which intrudes into this depiction of Welsh village life after **'Taffy at Home'.** Indeed, the first story of *My People* that he wrote (it was also the first in which he adopted a Biblical style), **'Be This Her Memorial',** is one in which society's abuse of the poor and vulnerable is keenly realised. Nanni is a victim of economic exploitation and moral blackmail, pressurised into a sacrifice that is as sickening morally as it is physically, and the narrator takes a severe, explicit moral stand.

Increasingly, though, the victims of the stories (usually women, but sometimes children and old people) become less unequivocally innocent than Nanni, and the narrator's moral position becomes correspondingly less stark. It is revealing, in this respect, to contrast the stories of Nanni and of Griffi (in **'A Sacrifice Unto Sion'**). They have a comparably horrific climax: Nanni is eaten by the rats she is forced to live on and Griffi is eaten by the pig he has not the strength to feed. In both cases the story exposes the inhuman economic priorities of the Chapel. But Griffi has spent his youth living by those very economic standards, and when in turn his son Dewi turns him off the farm because of his economic uselessness, and drives him to the poverty he dies in, he is treated according to the standards by which he himself has lived. No such retribution occurs in Nanni's fate; she is, throughout, an innocent victim.

The growing complexity of the narrator's moral position is seen in the greater use he makes of the ironic possibilities afforded by his style. The harsh, righteous tone of **'Be This Her Memorial'** is replaced by ironic assertions in which the narrator affects to fail to see through his characters' hypocrisy by conveying it to the reader. When Joshua weeps and prays for revenge upon his rebellious sister the narrator comments: "Thus the Lord comforts His children: when Joshua arose, lo, his eyes were dry,"[13] as though a miracle has occurred, rather than the insincerity of his sorrow been exposed. Again, "Presently Dewi reached an age of knowledge,"[14] sounds approving, while alerting the reader to the dawning of a cunning scheme. In the first three volumes such irony is satirical in effect, and leads to moral condemnation of the characters, but in the last stories there is sometimes a moral ambiguity in the irony, which holds the characters in a nice balance of sympathy and censure. In "Other farmers would repent their marriage, but there is no repentance in a man who carries a heavy crop of wisdom,"[15] for instance, there is a praise of fortitude as well as criticism of the arrogance that lies behind it. The effect is made morally complex by the confusion of the notions of repentance and regret.

This change from satirical irony to an irony of real moral ambiguity accords with the change in the nature of the mythicizing that occurs between the first three and the last two volumes of stories. It is a change as radical as that between **'Taffy at Home'** and *My People,* although of course it occurs over a longer period, for more than twenty years separate the appearance of the third and fourth collections. The Welsh no longer epitomise evil in their social interaction; they have become more mysterious beings, lone travellers tested by a stony wilderness (rather than peasants toiling on the land) and their encounters, often allegorical, often supernatural, lead them to wisdom and understanding. The stories are, that is, predominantly myths, rather than being satires based on a mythical view of a race. They now have universal application and seek to make order, in simple terms, of a chaotic world—'Bliss is in the mist,' for instance, explores the nature of happiness through a re-working of the Proserpina myth, and 'Do not borrow your brother's head,' shows human nature to be half divine, half foxy.

These two stories exploit a common feature of folktales—the exploring of sayings and proverbs, and increasingly Evans uses such features in a central way in his stories. The narrator in the early **'Be This Her Memorial'** might declare that the story contradicts the saying that "Mice and rats . . . frequent neither churches nor poor man's homes,"[16] but this is a purely incidental effect of the events related; in 'Do not borrow your brother's head', on the other hand, the contradiction of the saying that 'two heads are better than one' is the central irony of the story.

It is, indeed, in his use of a motif common in folktales—namely the battle of wits or of wills—that Evans' development as a short story writer can be most clearly seen. For this battle of wits features at all points of his career. In **'Taffy at Home'** it takes the form of ingenious tit-for-tat that affords humour and makes moral concern seem unsporting. But in the satirical stories, instead of allaying a moral response, the battles have a morally disquieting effect, because they are desperate and because they proceed to an overthrow of justice. The triumph of wrong, moreover, comes with the relief of resolution when it ends the tension that is built up through a battle of wits, and this, too, is disquieting.

**'The Woman who Sowed Iniquity'** is a good example of a story centred on such a battle. Betti and Joshua are locked in strife; the devious scheming is equal on both sides; Betti as easily shifts her tactics from defiance to fawning as Joshua moves from pious pose to anger; they are a good match for each other. But in that the society in which they struggle sanctions male superiority, they cannot compete on equal terms. It is the teasing of victim by victimiser, and, as in a bullfight, the spectator's suspense is aroused by the devious techniques of the victimiser and the devious wriggling of the victim, rather than by any serious doubt about the outcome. The victim cannot win, but she can give the victimiser a good run for his money.

The battle of wits is a game, therefore, in which the characters play parts. They assume masks, which take in even themselves and the narrator. "She was moved to step away," we read of Sara Jane, "for she had heard read that the corners of streets are places of great temptation,"[17] but this, of course, is why she is there at all. The reader's interest in the skill of the game is at odds with his moral response to the unequal rules for the players and to the criminal outcome. Evans enhances the disturbing effect of this when he ends the stories at the close of the battle of wits, before the climax of the action. In **'Redemption',** for instance, Evan's first two

attempts to get rid of his servant and mistress, Hannah, before marrying the wealthy Jane Pant, fail; he plans the third more thoroughly, sets the trap, and entices Hannah into it. It is about to spring when the story ends. Similarly, in **'The Woman who Sowed Iniquity'** Joshua, finding that all his scheming to oust his sister from her farm fails, plans her death to look like an accident. His plan becomes clear in the last sentence—the climax of the story is the climax of his schemes, not of events. By focussing on the battle of wits, not their outcome, Evans satirically warps the moral focus of the stories.

In the last two volumes, however, the battle of wits has no such disconcerting effect: it upholds, rather than flouts, a just outcome of the story. Indeed, it is in the first story in *Pilgrims in a Foreign Land* that, for the first time, the victim turns the table on her victimiser. Adah, recognising Pilgrim Whiskers as the father of her illegitimate child, holds a scythe poised against his neck while each argues his case with God; then Adah beheads him. But this story is not typical: most of the battles of wits in both *Pilgrims in a Foreign Land* and *The Earth Gives All and Takes All* read like folk-tale accounts of outwitting the trolls, where wit and intelligence are used to overcome brawn and stupidity (there is in fact an adaptation of a troll story, where the protagonist, challenging the squire to an eating contest, persuades him to slit his stomach by himself slitting the pouch into which he has stuffed all his food[18]). But such battles have none of the power or poignancy of the earlier ones.

As the social opposition between Nonconformist minister and peasant gives way to that between squire and gypsy, the rational and magical merge; spells are cast, curses are laid; there are love-potions, gypsies capable of metamorphosis, and supernatural creatures which harm or protect, or even make flat land hilly. It is the stuff of myth and folk-tale, but too often the effect is ludicrous—the stories seem almost to mock myths and folk-tales as series of absurd tricks. It is doubtful, though, whether this can have been the intention of a man who took such exception to the way Nonconformism had deliberately obliterated the folklore of Wales.[19]

That Evans persisted in a mythical view of the Welsh, which gives his best work much of its strength, was finally his limitation as a writer, too. For while his vision of villagers who epitomise evil lends itself to the satirical treatment of the early stories, which are hard-hitting, fervent, grimly controlled, his later, more humane stories are weakened by his lack of control over his vision of lost pilgrims. And inasmuch as it is a mythical race that is projected throughout, one wonders whether this portrayal of the Welsh is any less distorting than the romantic or sentimental portrayal that is ousted; and whether, in destroying "the sandcastle dynasty of Allen Raine",[20] Caradoc Evans has really given Anglo-Welsh literature any firmer foundation on which to build.

REFERENCES

[1] Rees, R.F.W., 'The Celt and Realism', *The Globe,* 23rd October 1915.

[2] Anon., Review of *My People, The English Review,* December 1915.

[3] Prothero, J.K., 'Wales and the Obi Man', *New Witness,* 13th June 1916.

[4] Evans, Caradoc, Ms 4. 'Articles', National Library of Wales, Ms 20033C, p. 1.

[5] Ibid., p. 23.

[6] Ibid., p. 52.

[7] Evans, Caradoc, *My People,* London, Melrose, 1915, pp. 75-6.

[8] Evans, Caradoc, Ms 4. 'Articles', National Library of Wales, Ms 20033C, p. 25.

[9] Evans, Caradoc, *The Earth Gives All and Takes All,* London, Dakers, 1946, p. xxvii.

[10] Williams, T.L., *Caradoc Evans,* University of Wales Press, 1970, p. 38.

[11] Evans, Caradoc, 'Taffy at Home', *London Chat,* 21st September 1907.

[12] Evans, Caradoc, *My People,* London, Melrose, 1915, p. 65.

[13] Ibid., p. 78.

[14] Evans, Caradoc, *Capel Sion,* London, Melrose, 1916, p. 135.

[15] Evans, Caradoc, *The Earth Gives All and Takes All,* London, Dakers, 1946, p. 3.

[16] Evans, Caradoc, *My People,* London, Melrose, 1915, p. 95.

[17] Ibid., p. 36.

[18] Asbjørnsen, P.C. and Moe, J. (ed.), *Norwegian Folk Tales,* Oslo, Dreyers Forlag, 1960, p. 83. and Evans, Caradoc, *Pilgrims in a Foreign Land,* London, Dakers, 1942, pp. 31-4.

[19] Evans, Caradoc, Letters in the *South Wales Daily News,* 21st April 1915.

[20] Jones, Gwyn, *The First Forty Years,* Cardiff, University of Wales Press, 1957, p. 9.

## D. Z. Phillips (essay date 1991)

SOURCE: "Distorting Truth," in *From Fantasy to Faith: The Philosophy of Religion and Twentieth-Century Literature,* Macmillan, 1991, pp. 84-94.

[*In the following excerpt, Phillips provides a religious context for the portrayal of Welsh Nonconformism in Evans's stories.*]

[The] words in our lives reveal who we are. Of course, those lives do not conform to a neat pattern, but are, rather, a mixed bag. People's perspectives vary, so that the aspects under which they see the world cannot be taken for granted. One of the most difficult things is to see ourselves. We may not appreciate the distortions in our midst. We may not be ready to have them pointed out, least of all by one of our own kind.

In 1932, the painter, Evan Walters, offered to lend his fine portrait of the writer, Caradoc Evans, to the National Museum of Wales. The offer was declined on the grounds that the Museum already possessed a recent example of his portraiture. Everyone knew how to read this coded reply. The vast majority of letters sent to the newspaper the *Western Mail* supported the decision. One lady concluded her letter with the words: '*Câs gŵr na charo y wlad a'i magodd*'—'Hateful is the man who does not love the land of his birth'. Evans was accused of distorting Welsh life: its people, its language and its religion. Here is the *Western Mail*'s critical reaction to his second volume of short stories **Capel Sion,** which it saw as carrying on the pattern established in his first collection, **My People.**

> It may be that Mr Evans spent his early days among some people of the kind he depicts; if so, he seems to have lived in a sort of moral sewer. For all his characters are repulsive, and designedly so. They are certainly not Welsh; they are certainly not Welsh peasants; and the language they speak is not to be found anywhere in the world outside Mr Evans's books. It is charitable to believe that his knowledge of the language is of the slightest; if his idiotic representation of the talk of the peasantry is not due to ignorance, then may the Lord forgive him. For his offence is rank—as rank as the book itself. The stories are gross in tone, in intent, and in effect, and the reviewer's final feeling on finishing the work is to go and have a bath.

**My People** was published in 1915 and **Capel Sion** in 1916. Since then, Welsh Nonconformity and its political connections have ceased to be the power they once were. Nevertheless, even now, we have only to scratch the surface to find this attitude to Evans re-emerging. On attempting, without much hope of success, to get hold of T. L. Williams' useful study, *Caradoc Evans* in the University of Wales Press *Writers of Wales* series, in a Welsh bookshop I was told, 'I'll have a look for it, but we didn't think much of him, mind'. Notice the confident use of 'we'. For her,

Evans was the outsider, the betrayer, a man alienated from his people and from his roots in Wales.

It is often said that Wales, a small country, struggling to retain its language and its cultural distinctiveness, cannot afford to be critical of itself. There are plenty all too ready to deride it. Yet, understandable though that reaction may be, it will not do. Protectiveness kills the very culture it seeks to preserve. Furthermore, criticism of others and of oneself can manifest the distinctiveness of a culture just as much as praise of it.

In order to understand the reaction which faced Caradoc Evans, we have to understand that it is not one which is confined to Nonconformist Wales and its parochialism. Not at all. It is a reaction to be found, for example, in the most powerful country in the world. Flannery O'Connor refers to a challenge thrown out by an editorial in *Life* magazine. It asked, 'Who speaks for America today?' Commenting on this challenge in 1957, Flannery O'Connor said:

> The gist of the editorial was that in the last ten years this country had enjoyed an unparalleled prosperity, that it had come nearer to producing a classless society than any other nation, and that it was the most powerful country in the world, but that our novelists were writing as if they lived in packing boxes on the edge of the dump while they awaited admission to the poorhouse.[1]

The editorial went on to say that what was needed in literature was a 'redeeming quality of spiritual purpose' which would express 'the joy of life itself'. Literature was to be uplifting; it should feed *Life*'s image of America. It is a far cry from America to Nonconformist Wales, but in its essence, the demand is the same. What differs, of necessity, is the social and cultural milieu through which it is expressed. In Wales, that milieu prided itself on being religious. Literature, then, should give a spiritual uplift. Its humour should be 'healthy' humour and its criticisms reserved for the enemies of religion. Evans was held to have sinned against all these requirements. So far from giving spiritual uplift, his work indulged in savage satire. Its humour, if it can be called that, was black humour and the object of his criticisms was the very religion which literature should aim to sustain.

Flannery O'Connor often alluded to the challenge of *Life* magazine. Once, she said:

> What these editorial writers fail to realise is that the writer who emphasises spiritual values is very likely to take the darkest view of all of what he sees in this country today. For him, the fact that we are the most powerful and the wealthiest nation in the world doesn't mean a thing in any positive sense. The sharper the light of faith, the more glaring are apt to be the distortions the writer sees in the life around him.[2]

Here, the contrast is between secular materialism and religion. What made Evans so hard to take for many Welsh people was that the distortions he attacked were within religion itself. Little can be found in his work, if anything, about the spirituality of Welsh Nonconformity. His emphasis is almost entirely on the narrow code of do's and don'ts that Nonconformity can become. As T. L. Williams says:

> The code was nowhere more powerful than in its draconian enforcement of that sabbatarianism which came to be synonymous with the 'Welsh Sunday', but at the same time this strict Sunday observance was probably the most vulnerable point in the whole puritan ethic, for it encouraged secrecy, furtiveness and, above all, hypocrisy. In short, it tended to produce a situation in which one's 'sin' was less important than the *discovery* of one's sin, and in which there could be a great discrepancy between the ideals of Nonconformist behaviour and the actual behaviour of those who professed to subscribe to the code. There is of course nothing shocking in this very ordinary human failure to live up to ideals; it is just that in rural Welsh society the clamour of public (chapel) censure against the wrongdoer (for example, the formal ceremony of 'breaking out' from the chapel the girl who was expecting an illegitimate baby) was such as to reinforce and perpetuate the tendency to cover things up hypocritically. A natural corollary to this situation was the paradox by which the worst offence against this Nonconformist (and politically radical) society was to be nonconformist, to be the outsider, who preferred his own moral, or immoral, code.[3]

Yet, it must be remembered, if Welsh Nonconformity can be the subject of strong satire, so can Roman Catholicism. The fitting comparison is not with the criticisms of James Joyce and others from a liberal, humanistic perspective, but with criticisms from within the fold by writers such as J. F. Powers. Speaking of him Flannery O'Connor says:

> Catholic life as seen by a Catholic doesn't always make comfortable reading for Catholics . . . In this country we have J. F. Powers, for example, a very fine writer and a born Catholic who writes about Catholics. The Catholics that Mr Powers writes about are seen by him with a terrible accuracy. They are vulgar, ignorant, greedy, and fearfully drab, and all these qualities have an unmistakeable Catholic social flavour. Mr Powers doesn't write about such Catholics because he wants to embarrass the Church; he writes about them because, by the grace of God, he can't write about any other kind. A writer writes about what he is able to make believable.[4]

When Evans, a Welshman, wrote about Welsh Nonconformists, it did not make comfortable reading for them either. But what he saw, he too saw with a terrible accuracy: hypocrisy, greed, lust. He too gave these vices an unmistakeable Welsh Nonconformist flavour. It will be objected that all Nonconformists were not of this kind. True enough, but, like Powers, Evans wrote about this kind of Nonconformist because he couldn't write about any other kind. It cannot be said that he did not want to embarrass the Chapel. He did. But what he wanted to embarrass was its respectability rather than its religion. It must be remembered that all his life he had a love-hate relationship with the Nonconformity he vilified. Drawing back from it in revulsion and disgust, nevertheless, he could not leave it alone, but was drawn to it again, aware of other things it had to offer, but which he could not write about. There were times when he regretted that he had not trained for its ministry, and to the end he was a great sermon-taster. When he died in 1945, the letters of condolence showed how much he was liked by ordinary people all over Wales. He was a kind-hearted man whom the community of New Cross, near Aberystwyth, came to know as such. George H. Green says:

> This was the Caradoc the neighbours came to know—the man whose body six of them carried on their shoulders up the steep hill behind his New Cross home, behind the little chapel where his friend, Tom Beynon, preached the simple sincere sermons that Caradoc admired and liked. He liked and admired them, not because they dealt with points of theology, but because they were free of the humbug and hypocrisy he saw about him, and hated and attacked consistently. If through hating hypocrisy he became hated by some, so much the worse for them. It is by themselves—not Caradoc—that they are condemned.[5]

But, it may be said, the issue of distortion has been ducked. Did not Evans distort what he saw about him, a distortion highlighted in the curious language in which he chose to express himself? Without a doubt, Evans used a distorted language in which to write, but the character of the distortion involved has been badly misunderstood by Welsh and English readers alike. Both shared a common assumption, namely, that Evans was translating straightforwardly from Welsh into English. For their part, the English concluded that his was how Welsh people spoke and were duly amused. The Welsh, on the other hand, saw nothing but grotesque failure on Evans' part and were duly infuriated. But since Evans was not attempting to translate in the first place, both reactions are ridiculously wide of the mark. Evans' language is a special creation on his part to bring about a desired artistic effect. The sources of the language are numerous: some literal translations from Welsh, some outlandish translation, use of stumbling efforts to speak English by predominantly Welsh speakers, use of Welsh slang, the coining of English words based on Welsh slang, and so on. But all these sources are blended together as befits the occasion, answering to no preordained pattern. One other essential element in Evans' use of language must be mentioned, namely, the enormous influence on it of the Authorised Version of the English Bible. According to Evans' own testimony, before writing one of his stories he would read from the Old Testament. From this he took the rhythm, economy and grandeur of its language. Combining this with the Welsh sources we have mentioned, the result was a brilliant parody, through distortion, of the Welsh religious discourse of a people who lived by the Book.

The distortion, then, has to be admitted, but it is a distortion intimately connected with truth. The Welsh were perfectly correct to say that they did not speak and behave in the extreme ways Evans depicted. But why should they assume that he was involved in straightforward description? Flannery O'Connor was amused at critics who said that she had convinced them that people in Georgia actually behaved in the ways she depicted and were duly horrified. They failed to understand her use of distortion as we may fail to understand Evans'. Speaking of Kafka's *Metamorphosis* which begins with a man waking up to find that he has turned into a cockroach, Flannery O'Connor says: 'The truth is not distorted here, but rather, a certain distortion is used to get at the truth'.[6]

The same is true with O'Connor and Evans. She said that in a world in which religion was not understood, the writer is forced to employ shock tactics. She said that for the deaf we have to shout, and that for the almost blind we have to draw large and startling figures. Evans found the deaf and the almost blind, not outside religious circles, but within them. He wanted to forge a language which would shock them into realising something about themselves they would not see otherwise. The measure of his success can be seen from the fact that many who expressed public outrage, admitted in private that much of what he said was true. To those who matched public outrage with private outrage, respectability had penetrated the soul to recesses which even Evans' brilliance could not reach.

One of the most savage short stories in *My People* is "**Be This Her Memorial.**"[7] It is the story of Nanni, by far the oldest member of Capel Sion. Her income is three shillings and ninepence a week which she receives from the Poor Relief Officer. It keeps her out of the poorhouse and thus grants her the freedom to listen to Respected Josiah Bryn-Bevan the minister of Capel Sion whom she idolises. She helped to bring him into the world, knitted socks for him when he was a farm servant, and, when he entered the ministry, gave a tenth of her income to support him in Capel Sion. 'Unconsciously she came to regard Josiah as greater than God: God was abstract; Josiah was real'.

A rumour comes to her that the Respected Josiah Bryn-Bevan had received a call from a wealthy sister church in Aberystwyth. Notice, 'Respected' not 'Reverend' which would be the normal translation of the Welsh 'Parchedig'. The use of 'Respected' helps him to play against it the fact that respect is the last thing this minister deserves. Notice too that the minister gets a *call* (presumed to be from God), rather than an invitation from another church. Evans slyly implies that God always calls his ministers to chapels which will increase their salaries. 'Is it a good call?' one minister will ask another, the salary featuring prominently in the reply. With present salary structures, this has ceased to be a telling point. Nanni prays to God: '"Dear little Big Man", she prayed, "let not your son bach religious depart"'. Then she recalled how good God had been to her, how He had permitted her to listen to His son's voice; and another fear struck her heart. ' "Dear little Big Man", she muttered between her blackened gums, "do you now let me live to hear the boy's farewell words".'

She is visited by a Bible salesman from whom she buys a large brass-clasped gaudy illustrated Bible as a farewell gift for the minister who has announced his departure. She is absent from Capel Sion for many Sundays, following Josiah Bryn-Bevan wherever he happened to be preaching. She was absent from the hay-making too, but when Sadrach Danyrefail goes to remonstrate with her, he is frightened by the gleaming-eyed creature who confronts him and repulsed by the abominable smell from inside her cottage. She begins to appear in chapel with oozing sores at the side of her mouth. ' "Old Nanni," folk remarked while discussing her over their dinner-tables, "is getting as dirty as an old sow".'

She makes the final payment on the Bible and asks Sadrach Danyrefail to present it to the minister on her behalf when he delivers his last sermon. But she is absent from the service. After his sermon, the Respected Josiah Bryn-Bevan referred to her Bible and dwelt on her sacrifice. But he then thoughtlessly presents the Bible to Sadrach Danyrefail in recognition of his work with the Sunday School. The next morning, making a tour of his flock, the minister calls on Nanni. He finds her on the floor:

> There was no movement from Nanni. Mishtir Bryn-Bevan went on his knees and peered at her. Her hands were clasped tightly together, as though guarding some great treasure. The minister raised himself and prised them apart with the ferrule of his walking-stick. A roasted rat revealed itself. Mishtir Bryn-Bevan stood for several moments spellbound and silent; and in the stillness the rats crept boldly out of their hiding places and resumed their attack on Nanni's face. The minister, startled and horrified, fled from the house of sacrifice.

What was he horrified by? Well, the rats presumably, the half-eaten face and the stench. That is why many readers called the story a horror-story. That is what the protests were about—associating Nonconformity with such horrors. Is that what we are horrified at and protest against? Flannery O'Connor has said: 'I believe that there are many rough beasts now slouching towards Bethlehem to be born and that I have reported the progress of a few of them, and when I see these stories described as horror stories I am always amused because the reviewer always has hold of the wrong horror.'[8]

The real horror in Evans' story is the horror latent in Nonconformity which could allow Nanni's fate to befall her. Further, there is the horror of the way in which her incredible capacity for sacrifice is corrupted and distorted in the chapel and in herself. True religion and sacrifice are being eaten away. The story is based on a true incident of a woman who roasted rats to save a pound for the chapel collection. Speaking of the ruins of Nanni's cottage, Evans says: 'If you happen to be travelling that way you may still see the roofless walls which were silent witnesses to Nanni's great sacrifice—a sacrifice surely counted unto her for righteousness, though in her search for God she fell down and worshipped at the feet of a god'.

Evans has compassion and pity for those who suffer, but he is ruthless in his exposure of hypocrisy and respectability. Such exposure characterises what many regard as a second horror story in *My People,* namely, **"A Father in Sion."**[9] The main character, Sadrach is described as follows:

> He was a man whose thoughts were continually employed upon sacred subjects. He began the day and ended the day with the words of a chapter from the Book and a prayer on his lips. The Sabbath he observed from first to last; he neither laboured himself nor allowed any in his household to labour.

In other words, Sadrach conforms to the Nonconformist sabbatarian code. But what of his conduct in other respects? He has eight children, a man of rampant sexuality. He tells the children that their mother Achsah, who brought the farm as a gift to the bridegroom, has gone mad, though this is not the case. She is 10 years older than him. To get rest from him she accepts the situation. Sadrach keeps her locked up. Her condition is said to be a disgrace and no one is allowed to see her. Occasionally, he gives her an airing in the fields with a cow's halter over her shoulders. He brings another woman, Martha, to the farm, in marrying whom he has committed bigamy. Because he is prosperous and eloquent all this is tolerated in Sion:

> Sadrach declared in the Seiat that the Lord was heaping blessings on the head of His servant. Of all who worshipped in Sion none was stronger than the male of Danyrefail; none more respected. The congregation elected him to the Big Seat. Sadrach was a tower of strength unto Sion.

But affliction follows in the wake of prosperity. Six of the eight children die. His one remaining son Sadrach the Small is to marry Sara Ann with whose family a prosperous arrangement has been made. He tells Achsah of the wedding and, somehow or other, she frees herself in order to see it. In an extremely moving part of the story, Evans describes her looking furtively at the wedding procession, searching for the faces of her children. When she cannot find them, she begins to think that she really is going mad. She then realises that they must be grown-up by now and thinks that is the reason she cannot find them. She looks again, but has to accept that only Miriam and Sadrach the Small remain. She remembers the circumstances of the birth of all her children; how she had never refused her husband his rights; been a woman to him as long as she lasted. She goes to the graveyard and finds the graves of her six children, tracing with her fingers the letters of their names. This is how the story ends: 'As Sara Ann crossed the threshold of Danyrefail, and as she set her feet on the flagstone on which Sadrach the Small is said to have been born, the door of the parlour was opened and a lunatic embraced her.'

Arranged madness ends in real madness. This is horror enough, along with the deaths of the children. But presiding over it all is the unspoken horror of the order and life imposed on his family by Sadrach the most respected of chapel deacons. Evans is not simply emphasising the gap between religion and respectability, but pointing out how, for many, respectability was the essence of their religion.

A final example from *My People,* is the story "**The Way of the Earth.**"[10] Simon and Beca, he paralysed and she blind are simply waiting for death. Their daughter Sara Jane had been born out of wedlock and so they were outcasts from Capel Sion. But they had not always been in this state of destitution. Their farm had flourished and Simon and Beca had saved their money confident in the knowledge that when they had enough the doors of Sion would open to them. Their avarice is in unison with the chapel's avarice. They are anxious to get their 24-year-old daughter respectably married and are ready to drive a hard bargain when William Jenkins of the General Shop courts her. The people of Capel Sion look on with interest. But William Jenkins has made her pregnant. Simon's and Beca's bargaining power is utterly destroyed. William Jenkins takes everything they have. They will never enter Capel Sion now. He pays off his creditors. He lives with Sara Jane for a year, but when the creditors return, he flees from the land. Notice the key line in the bargaining between Simon and William Jenkins:

> Simon shivered. He was parting with his life. It was his life and Beca's life. She had made it, turning over the heather, and wringing it penny by penny from the stubborn earth. He, too, had helped her. He had served his neighbours, and thieved from them. He wept.
>
> 'He asks too much,' he cried. 'Too much.'
>
> 'Come, now, indeed,' said William Jenkins. 'Do you act religious by the wench fach.'

As T. L. Williams says, 'Even in the thoroughgoing examination of hypocrisy which *My People* is, that last remark still manages to stand out'.[11] *Act religious*—that equation of scheming avarice and respectability with religion says it all. A limited picture? Certainly. A complete picture? Certainly not. But a true picture nevertheless, even when what is shown employs distortion to reveal a truth.

In the 1985 miscellany of Caradoc Evans' work, *Fury Never Leaves Us,* a miscellany made up, in the main, of hitherto unpublished material, the editor John Harris, who is engaged on a Life of Caradoc Evans, writes: 'You simply cannot get a Caradoc Evans book these days', complained Rhys Davies in 1962, "you don't see them in libraries and certainly never in bookshops".'[12] That position remained unchanged until very recently.[13] His literary reputation still depends on one or two contributions in anthologies of Welsh short stories or horror stories. In the latter, as usual, he is included for the wrong horror.

In a world of grants and subsidised publishing, respectable Wales had a subtler way of responding to attack than with counter-attack—the way of silence. But that silence is testimony to something we have every reason to be ashamed of: the ways we have, not only in Wales, of creating, in the very name or religion, life under a godless heaven.

NOTES

[1] Flannery O'Connor, 'The Fiction Writer and His Country' in *Mystery and Manners* (Farrar, Straus & Giroux, 1969), pp. 25-6.

[2] Ibid., p. 26.

[3] T. L. Williams, *Caradoc Evans* (University of Wales Press, 1970), pp. 5-6.

[4] Flannery O'Connor, 'Catholic Novelists and their Readers' in *Mystery and Manners,* p. 173.

[5] George H. Green in *Caradoc Evans* by Oliver Sandys, (Hurst & Blackett, 1946), p. 157.

[6] Flannery O'Connor, 'Writing Short Stories' in *Mystery and Manners,* pp. 97-8.

[7] Caradoc Evans, all quotations from *Be This her Memorial* in *My People* (Andrew Melrose, 1919).

[8] Flannery O'Connor, 'Writing Short Stories' in *Mystery and Manners,* pp. 97-8.

[9] Caradoc Evans, all quotations from *A Father in Sion* in *My People.*

[10] Caradoc Evans, *The Way of the Earth* in *My People.*

[11] T. L. Williams, op. cit., ר. 67.

[12] John Harris, 'Preface' in John Harris (ed.), *Fury Never Leaves Us: A Miscellany of Caradoc Evans* (Poetry Wales Press, 1985), p. 7.

[13] *My People* was finally reprinted by Poetry Wales Press in 1988.

**Nicholas Wroe (essay date 1993)**

SOURCE: "A Welsh Joyce," in *The Times Literary Supplement,* No. 4701, May 7, 1993, p. 20.

[*In the following essay, a review of* Selected Stories, *Wroe offers a favorable assessment of the book—in spite of Evans's negative portrayals of his characters.*]

Caradoc Evans, who died in 1945 after a career as a draper, writer and journalist, gloried in his own description of himself as "the most hated man in Wales". John Harris, in his excellent introduction to this collection [*Selected Stories*] illustrates some of the ways this entirely accurate assessment manifested itself. He had, "his books suppressed, a play howled down in the West End, a radio talk banned by the BBC and a portrait on public display knife-slashed across the throat". It seems strange that someone who, comparatively recently, could arouse such strong feelings should today be virtually unknown. But his work leaves no doubt as to why he elicited these reactions.

Evans's first collection of stories, *My People* (1915), is subtitled *Stories of the peasantry of West Wales.* Calling his subjects "peasantry" was shocking enough to the Welsh establishment at home, while London preferred to present, and probably to believe in, a rather more idealized notion of rural Wales. The stories are devastating.

The depiction of the utter venality of his society, the appalling cruelty, hypocrisy and immorality of his characters and the entirely corrupting influence of the clergy and organized religion, is delivered in an unrelenting stream of visceral exposure. In both *My People* and *Capel Sion* (1916), he writes as an insider, turning a spotlight on to his own backyard. The opening story, **"A Father in Sion",** tells of a husband who declares his wife mad, makes her live in a loft and takes her out once a week in a cow-halter. In **"The Way of the Earth",** an old couple, blind and paralysed, are relieved of their life savings by a feckless shopkeeper who agrees to marry their pregnant daughter. After spending a lifetime turning "sterile moorland into a fertile garden", they are left, penniless and incapable of work, on the deteriorating farm. Evans does not lard his brutal tales with any sympathy for the many victims. The most dreadful histories are told without any authorial comment. Several stories in his early collections simply conclude with a bald account of a violent death. The killer of a preacher who seduces Esther, in **"Greater Than Love",** "had difficulty in drawing away the blade, because it had entered the man's skull. Then he returned to the place Esther was, and her he killed also." Other dénouements include the corpse of an old woman being attacked by rats, a man killing a cat, splitting it in two and nailing half to his brother's door, and a woman being pitch-forked to death.

In *My Neighbours* (1920), Evans turned on the drapers and dairymen of the London Welsh, whom he had joined as a draper's assistant. It also gave him an opportunity to lambast the old charlatan David Lloyd George through the character of Ben Lloyd. Although clearly a duplicitous and adulterous politician on the make, Ben Lloyd, like Lloyd George, retains enough vile charm to placate even those he betrayed. The cuckolded husband of Gwen, bought off with a safe Welsh constituency, ends by saying: "'Ben's kindness is more than I expected. Much that I have I owe to him.' 'Even your son,' said Gwen."

While Evans generally makes use of a straightforward narrative, his language is far from conventional. His blend of Welsh syntax with an exuberant mock-biblical style ("Easier for you to thread a camel with large horns and three humps through the eye of a stocking needle than for a bastard slip to pass into the Palace of White Shirts") is sometimes difficult but always highly emotive. Allied to searing abuse ("Why don't you clap up the blackhead of your neck"), his writing jumps from the page to match in force the horrors of the society revealed. Evans has been compared to Irish writers in this respect; on the publication of *A Portrait of the Artist as a Young Man,* Joyce was described as the Irish Caradoc Evans: "astonishingly powerful and extraordinarily dirty". Despite offering no solutions, little hope and a vision of almost unremitting bleakness, these stories remain vibrant and are curiously refreshing.

### Chris Hopkins (essay date 1996)

SOURCE: "Translating Caradoc Evans's Welsh English," in *Style*, Vol. 30, No. 3, Fall, 1996, pp. 433-44.

[*In the following essay, Hopkins examines Evans's transliteration of Welsh words, along with other aspects of his interpretation of his native language and culture.*]

Though the Welsh writer Caradoc Evans has not achieved the same worldwide recognition as his Irish contemporary James Joyce, he is a writer who resembles his more famous counterpart in a number of ways. Like Joyce he wrote a first book about his own nation that caused much offense and public controversy, making its author immediately notorious. Like Joyce he drew on naturalist techniques to create a highly critical portrait of his own people in the first decade of the twentieth century. Like Joyce he published a collection of linked short stories that seemed intended to represent in a hostile way the nation of their author. Where Joyce wrote about the citizens of Dublin, Evans wrote about the values of a fictional village called Manteg. An association was made between the two writers by a reviewer of Joyce's *Portrait of the Artist as a Young Man,* who called Joyce "an Irish edition of Mr. Caradoc Evans" (qtd. in Deming 85; discussed in Hopkins, "James Joyce" 23-26). Clearly, Evans's fame (and indeed the comparison to Joyce) has now faded outside Wales itself, so that he needs some introduction before the extremely interesting variety of English that he invented can be discussed. Evans was born in the village of Rhydlewis in an agricultural area of Cardiganshire in West Wales in 1877. In 1891, at the age of 14, he went to work as a draper's apprentice in the shop of a distant relation in the comparatively large town of Carmarthen. He remained a draper (or rather a draper's assistant) for the next fifteen years, working in shops in Barry

Docks, Cardiff, and, finally, London. In London he attended evening classes at The Working Men's College at St. Pancras, and by 1906 he had changed his trade from that of draper to the more congenial one of journalist. He worked first as an editor (on papers owned by Northcliffe) and then as a writer for a popular weekly journal called *Ideas*. He published his first book-length work, *My People,* in 1915, and instantly became famous. In England the book was generally favorably reviewed, but in Wales Evans was referred to as a "renegade" and his narratives were said to be "a farrago of filth and debased verbal coinage" and "the literature of the sewer" (Harris 38).

The virulence of this reception had very much to do with Wales's self-image. Evans's stories suggested little of value in the national culture; moreover, they criticized the national religion of Wales, Non-Conformity, as well as Welsh mores in general. The portrayal of Welsh-speaking peasants as morally vicious people and religious hypocrites was particularly likely to cause offense since, as Irish authors like J. M. Synge similarly found, most Welsh people regarded peasant culture as the last bastion of a true Welshness unpolluted by English, urban influence. John Harris suggests that some of the points made by Evans had already been made in Welsh language periodicals (though in safer discursive forms), and that Evans's most offensive act was to write his stories in English and thus expose Wales to English ridicule (44-45). Evans himself characteristically shows an awareness of this possibility in a letter to the leading Welsh newspaper, *The Western Mail*. In it he claims that "the leaders of Welsh Nonconformity are uneasy that word of their tyranny will get into England" (William 153). It is notable that in Evans's version, the English are identified with the "truth," which transcends mere questions of national pride. Additionally, it might be said that even to "translate" these Welsh speakers into English is an act of betrayal, since it implies an (superior) English-speaking viewpoint on them.

It is the English that Evans uses in *My People* that is the subject of this article. Though it is an invented rather than an "actual" variety of English, it is produced from a particular language situation that is of interest in its own right, and it reflects interestingly on how narratives and their readers can use varieties of "non-standard English." Moreover, Evans's use of notions of language variety and translation also suggest that these linguistic issues profoundly influence the meaning of his stories and therefore serve as an obvious stylistic starting point for his portrait of Wales. Evans's style is so striking that virtually all critics of his work refer to it, but surprisingly few have made a systematic study of how that style translates Welshness for English readers. This article builds on earlier discussions of Evans's style (Davies and Harris 79-80, 83-84; Jones 90-91; Williams, *Caradoc Evans* 39-42; Williams, "Birth" 158-59, 161-64, 168), but introduces new ideas about translation and language variety as fundamental factors in his writing.

An invented variety of English would seem to be an anomaly in that we normally assume language varieties to be distinctive usages of particular communities. This assumption is exactly what Evans exploits when he invents an English variety to "translate" the peasant community of Manteg. The particular perceptions and habits of mind of his speakers are encoded in their language, which he "translates" for the English (language) reader into a variety that will act as an equivalent to the particular idiolect of this Welsh-language community.

The central importance of this method in Evans's representation of Wales is suggested by the discussion of translation as a key issue by contemporary reviewers and correspondents. Many of Evans's critics highlighted his method of "translation" as the most basic source of his unflattering representation of Welsh peasantry. The Reverend Arthur Sturdy commented that "the [English critics who know nothing about the peasants of West Wales] have complimented him upon his unique-style, little thinking that it is simply due to unidiomatic translation from the Welsh" (qtd. in Williams, "Birth" 158). In his view the fault stems from Evans's failure to translate the original language of his subjects into proper English. The overall effect, he says, is to falsify the image of Welsh peasantry. Other correspondents also objected to the translations, similarly arguing that they did not accurately represent the original utterance. Challenged one critic: "we defy him . . . to find Welsh equivalents for them" (qtd. in Williams, "Birth" 161). Another said that "literal translations of the idioms of the French peasantry into the kind of English for which Mr. Evans makes himself responsible would be sheer rubbish" (qtd. in Williams, "Birth" 163). One correspondent takes a neutral phrase as an example of an Evans-like mistranslation:

> Mr. Evans seems to suggest that there can be two opinions of his English rendering of the Welsh language. There cannot be. A man who translated, say, "ceffyl du John" into "horse black John" instead of "John's black horse" is either an ignoramus or—a Caradoc Evans. And every page of his two books teems with clotted idiocies.
>
> (qtd. in Williams, "Birth" 161)

The "clotted idiocies" may refer particularly to words grouped together without any indication of their usual (English) grammatical relationships. Interestingly, Evans replied quite specifically, saying:

> Of course, I would not render "ceffyl du John" into "horse black John." In the rendering of the idiom you must also create atmosphere. If the Bible or Tolstoy or Maupassant were done into straight English none of us would get any nearer to the life and conditions with which these authors deal.
>
> (qtd. in Williams, "Birth" 161)

This reply is notably ambiguous. While denying that he would translate the example as suggested, he acknowledges that his translation is not Standard English. He thus admits that his translation is interpretative rather than simply mimetic. Though Evans's taste for provocative replies to critics has led him to be characterized as *deliberately* literal-minded in this arena (Williams, "Birth" 147), he argues here for a notion of truth that is not simply a matter of literal detail: "I know that my vision is true" (qtd. in Williams, "Birth" 161). Evans's various explanations of his methods suggest some of the complexity that his acts of translation raise. On one occasion he argued that his unidiomatic translation preserved precisely the actual conceptual experience of the Welsh original:

> I know very well what *Bod Mawr* means in the dictionary or to a Welsh scholar [i.e., "Great Being" or God]. But I know very well what it means to the man I am writing about. He is quite incapable of thinking of a great being. A white robe means to him his Sunday shirt, complete with celluloid collar. I am trying to represent that man's mind and how it works. If he really does not say "Big Man" [i.e., for *Bod Mawr*], he thinks it, and his imagination will go no further. It is what he ought to say if he were telling the truth about his thoughts, which is what I am trying to do.

> (qtd. in Harris, *My People* 11)

His claim here is for a kind of translation that, though not perhaps literally accurate, is nonetheless ultimately true. An unusual letter from one of Evans's few Welsh supporters suggests that this truth was all too recognizable:

> As a West Wales Welshman, I resent the tone of the criticism . . . passed upon Mr Caradoc Evans's stories. . . . This is not so much on the grounds that scanty justice has been accorded to the great literary value of his work, but that its truth has been disputed.

> I was born in West Wales, and until the age of fifteen I spoke no tongue other than the debased dialect which was then, and still is, the method of communication. I was initiated into the slimy, oleaginous sham-piety so fiercely satirised by Caradoc Evans, and well know the truth of his contention that "the hand of the Nonconformist minister in Wales is heavier than that of the priest is supposed to be in Ireland."

> As to the manner in which Caradoc Evans has conveyed the Welsh idiom, it seems to me that he alone of all authors who have assayed this difficult task has been rewarded with any measure of success. The artist is perfectly justified in his means, provided he creates the desired effect. . . . To me—one with a perfect knowledge of the Welsh idiom—he conveys in a magical way the very "gesture" . . . of the West Wales vernacular.

> (qtd. in Williams, "Birth" 163)

The complexity of this plaudit equals that of Evans's own justifications. On the one hand, the writer claims authentic biographical knowledge, while on the other he speaks of "means" and "effect" and of an inner essence of meaning (the very "gesture"). This testimony is again witness to the centrality of the act of translation to Evans's work. It may be significant, as Trevor Williams suggests, that this correspondent (Mr. E. D. Davies) wrote from an English address. His reference to a "debased dialect" certainly suggests a sense of himself as having progressed from "primitive" origins to his present position as a "sophisticated" user of the English language. Moreover, he implies that it is from this position of sophistication outside West Wales that he can understand the truth of Evans's fiction.

Evans's "translation," then—a fictionalization built on certain assumptions—is what needs to be examined in detail. One must assume the translation itself to be literal to account for its oddities. This assumption implies that the "translator" has made little attempt to homogenize the discontinuities that result from translation—that is, the translator gives us access only to what has been said. A non-interventionist translator of this kind would accord with naturalist aesthetics, which rejects the idea of an arranging, moralizing author or narrator and calls instead for the objective presentation of "facts." At the same time, the unadjusted discontinuities of register and discourse give ample space for comparative judgments against implied norms. Evans thus clearly but covertly assumes that the Standard English of most written language represents not only a linguistic but also a value norm. His "translation" is into a kind of Standard English, but one that falls short of standard norms in that it tries to reproduce exactly what was said and thus preserves nonstandard features and deviant value systems. Moreover, where the "translation" itself uses different registers or discourses of English, these must be assumed to reproduce similar contrasts in the original Welsh. While acknowledging and reproducing difference, this assumption in turn may nevertheless suggest that the relation between different registers and discourses is a natural one, having the same effect in different languages. The possibility that Welsh could, for example, mix formal and informal registers in different ways from English is not entertained, since when it does so the effect is always most easily understood as comic or ironic.

Bearing these assumptions in mind, we can now look in detail at how Evans's *My People* uses its translated English variety and to what effect. I have chosen one story to look at in detail, **"The Talent Thou Gavest,"** the fourth in the collection. Though like each story in the collection it has its own distinctive features, the story is fairly representative of Evans's techniques. The narrative concerns Eben, a shepherd boy who becomes a preacher. It starts with Eben's last day at school:

> Eben the son of Hannah held up his right arm and displayed the palm of his hand.

> Mishtir Lloyd the Schoolin said: "Put your old hand down now," and, gaping his mouth, proceeded to call out the register; when he came to the end, he said:

"What for was your right hand up just now, man, Eben the son of Hannah?"

"Did I not want to tell him, little Mishtir, that I am not coming to school any more then?" replied Eben.

"Dear me, dear me, now indeed you are not coming for why?"

"Mishtir bach, does he not know that I am going to the moor to mind the sheep of Shames?"

"Ho, and you say that?"

(73)

Immediately, the reader knows that this narrative does not follow the rules of Standard English. Though it uses no particularly unusual words or unexpected word order, the first sentence does not correspond to normal expectations about the connectedness of a commonly understood gesture and its meaning. A more normal and concise description of Eben's gesture would require only the first part of the phrase: "Eben . . . held up his right arm" (though "hand" would be more common). Given the context of the following speech (which makes it clear that the scene is set in a school), the meaning of this sentence would usually be taken to be that Eben has made the customary sign of a student to ask permission to speak to a teacher. The additional description, though, by specifying more detail about the action, undermines its customary nature and meaning, apparently signaling that the manner of Eben's gesture is more important than its simple performance. This implication is an illusory one, however, for it is not followed up, and we must therefore reread the description as being motivated not by a wish to differentiate this performance of the gesture from others, but rather as a description by one who does not appreciate the gesture as commonly understood. We probably do not assign this defamiliarizing description to the narrator as author, however, but instead read it as an account of the perception of the gesture either by Eben or by Mishtir Lloyd. This suggests that the gesture, so commonly understood from an English normative point of view, is performed clumsily and without a "natural," internalized understanding of its meaning. Even with this first sentence, then, a sense of these characters as "foreign" thinkers is established.

This effect is continued by slightly different means in the next sentence, involving the name of the subject, "Mishtir Lloyd the Schoolin'." "Mishtir" is meant to represent a Welsh pronunciation of "Mister" (though an English speaker cannot tell whether this orthography represents a translation of a Welsh word with "local color" or whether it represents the pronunciation of a loan word). "Schoolin'" as a title is clearly unusual since it uses an abbreviated participle form as if it were a noun, instead of the standard noun, "the Schoolmaster." This "translation" might be seen as relatively neutral in effect (though such "mispronunciations" and "misformed" words traditionally function in

English fiction as indicators of low social status and/or intelligence and as a source of humor). However, the next clause is clearly prejudicial: "gaping his mouth." Except in a context of astonishment, "gaping" suggests vacancy and yokeldom, a facial expression revealing either mental vacuity or an inability to suit external gesture to any purposeful inner meaning. On the one hand, the word "gaping" reproduces a sense of an original Welsh word that has a different range of meaning, but on the other hand it also judges such different usage by normative English standards.

This "translation," in fact, is the fundamental device of *My People*—a dual standard that appears to allow a different language and culture to retain its difference, but that in fact constantly reads those differences as if they are culpable failures of understanding. This "translated" Welsh English variety always suggests the presence of two languages: the original intentions of a different language system and the stilted translation. This duality, however, is never an equally weighted one: the dominance of the norm in the hierarchy is always clear. Though stilted, the translation is seen not as a "misleading" or poor analogy for the original utterances, but as a true account of original clumsiness and inarticulateness. The duality becomes, in fact, not only a way of rendering "foreignness," but also a strategy for implying ironic readings. Readers see the failures that every speech and description make evident to them, and that *apparently* ought to be evident even to the characters, but are not.

The remainder of the passage quoted above continues the application of this device through different aspects of language. Word order is particularly important as an indicator of a "foreign" speaker and it is used here to show a cultural difference that is nevertheless judged as a lack of articulacy: "now indeed you are not coming for why?" It is notable that this different word-order is not simply invented: it does bear a relation to the different word order of Welsh and the carrying over of this into English by primarily Welsh speakers. This element of authenticity appears in two other features here, the use of the diminutive and Eben's addressing of Mishtir Lloyd in the third person. The diminutive is used very frequently by Evans throughout *My People,* either in its original Welsh form *bach* (one of the few actual Welsh words he uses) or in a "translated" form, as in this instance: "little Mishtir." The joke here is the traditional one of inappropriateness in "peasant" language—a formal term of address is compromised by an informal term of endearment. The use of the third person to an addressee who is in fact present is a respectful form of address (a usage that becomes clear in *My People*), but here it reads as if Eben really does not know that Lloyd is there. This (ab)use of actual language habits is frequent, and not only does it provide a source of humor and prove the reader's superiority, but it also appears to mark actual Welsh ("mis")conceptions about social relationships. Finally, in this passage, the mismatch between mode of expression and intended meaning can be seen in the odd use of interrogative sentences. Each of the final five speeches by Eben and Lloyd is interrogative in form, and two seem to be genuine questions. The remaining three, however, are really statements (or at least need not be questions), including the final, "Ho, and you say that?" The last example is particularly confusing since the redundancy of the question seems to suggest that it must mean something more. In fact, it closes the conversation, and therefore the question must be merely a redundant exclamation.

Eben thus becomes a shepherd, and, interestingly, a Standard English narrator briefly emerges to comment on his state:

> His life was lonely; books were closed to him, because he had not been taught to read; and the sense of the beautiful or curious in nature is slow to wake in the Welsh peasant. After a time Eben began to hold whispered conversations with himself. (74)

The obvious narratorial nature of this comment suggests that Eben cannot himself reflect clearly on his own condition. Moreover, there is a rare flash of sympathy for his deprivation, a deprivation caused partly by his early departure from school, yet not seen as such by either teacher or pupil. It is not incidental that this narratorial intervention should come in a passage that is not in "translated" Welsh: that language is always a sign of deprivation, as Standard English is the light that could lighten the darkness. The narrator's account is soon replaced by Eben's own ways of thinking about himself—ways seen as actions and speeches rather than thought in the usual sense:

> One afternoon he fell asleep, and in his dream the Big Man . . . came to him saying:
>
> "Eben, bach, why for you now do you waste your time in sleep? Go you little son, and dig a hole in the place where stood old Shaci's hut."
>
> "It'll be a big hole, little Big Man," answered Eben, "if I must make it the size of old Shaci's hut."
>
> The Big Man replied: "There's a boy you are for pleading! . . ."
>
> That night the God of capel Sion came to Eben again.
>
> "Now that you have got the talent, Eben bach, do you use it," he said.
>
> "Dear little Big Man," answered Eben, "there's foolish you talk. Did I not dig till my old hands were covered with blisters provokeful you are."
>
> The Big Man spoke: "Eben bach, here is the talent. . . . "
>
> Weeks passed and months passed, and each night Eben said this prayer . . .

> "God did promise me a talent: let him show me what he meant."
>
> (74-75)

This passage presents another very characteristic kind of exchange in *My People:* a conversation with God. These exchanges reveal an obviously comic element, one dependent on register switches. The first oddity is the term "the Big Man," which lacks the gravitas of more usual terms of address for God; it is a joke much used in the conversation. Sometimes Eben seems to use comically informal terms ("there's foolish you talk"), sometimes God seems much inclined to the idiomatic ("there's a boy you are for pleading!").

Usually in *My People* the Big Man tells you what you want to hear, especially if you are already powerful. Thus in the final story, **"Lamentations,"** the Ruler (minister) of Capel Sion, Bern-Davydd receives (?) the following (welcome) command:

> The Big Man despised Evan Rhiw, and said to the respected Davydd Bern-Davydd, . . .
>
> "Bern-Davydd oppress Evan Rhiw. Go you up and down the land now and say to the people 'Lo, you animals in the image of the Big Man, God's blast is on the old male of Rhiw.'"
>
> (140)

The unstated assumption here seems to be that God's commands are translated by men into their own wishes. This logic remains wholly subtextual and depends on the creation of a scepticism in the reader about the goals that God sets himself and on the odd identity of these goals to the (likely) wishes of the channel through which they are communicated. But this assumption is not presented as conscious hypocrisy. Rather, those who are powerful and respectable in Manteg articulate such desires instinctively in this way, without any need or ability to reflect on their origin. In one way, this practice would appear to represent a genuine appreciation of difference (this *is* how people in Manteg think), but in another way it suggests a deviousness so deep that its thinkers cannot reveal it even to themselves. They are thus utterly protected from guilt or responsibility, whited sepulchres who can never have any possibility of penetrating to the truth within since this truth really has no linguistic existence for them.

This technique also corresponds with the general absence of stated norms within the text. Evans said that he was partly inspired by the music-hall star Marie Lloyd, who would tell "a story not by what she says but by what she does not" (Harris 12). Given the obvious deviancy of the language and particularly its contradictions in *My People,* the filling in of gaps will tend to be strongly normative. Thus the messages of the Big Man are like the messages of the narratives themselves: they will be judged against normal expectations. The status of God's commands is like that of all the speech of Manteg: they are "true" in that they reflect how these people think, and they are untrue because the people of Manteg cannot understand why assigning these ideas to God may not be the most obvious explanation of their origins. The language of the characters and the representation of God as originator of meaning suggest that these Welsh peasants are doubly (but culpably) deprived. They cannot think of meanings other than the most obvious, but they also know that in some way unspeakable to them, these meanings are not "facts," but merely their own manipulations. They are thus to be blamed not only for their language habits, but also for their failure to develop a language that could truthfully explain the logic behind these habits. This reading hierarchy leaves the reader's Standard English as the unspoken language of truthful explanation.

Eben's dream and subsequent conversations with the Big Man work in a way similar to Bern-Davydd's exchange with God, but the meaning or content of his desire is less easily located than in Bern-Davydd's case. This difference implies more complexity to Eben than to Bern-Davydd, and any such suggestion is unusual in *My People*. It is as if Eben is searching for replacements for the books that only the English narrator knows about. In Manteg, he cannot think through his lack except through religion, and religion also provides the only outlet for Eben's unnamed urge for something different and more fulfilling. Thus Eben has to wait until God's notably unspecific message achieves a meaning in his own mind. He decides to become a preacher, and thereby assume the only role that will allow him to make social use of his liking for talking to himself. The implication of Eben's decision may be that this is the only way in which someone from Manteg could achieve a position analogous to that of the writer in "less deprived" cultures.

This reading seems possible, given the career of Eben. Just as he has an unusually complex (because unspecified) message from God, so he is unusual as a "ruler in Sion" in experiencing a complex religious conversion. At first, he finds fulfillment in giving the Capel members what they wish to hear:

> Beautiful and song-like was the supplication that Eben offered: he sang mournfully for those at sea, for sinners that worshipped in places other than capel Sion; he sang joyously for the First men who occupied the high places.
>
> (76)

In terms of the content of his sermons, he is like the Big Man himself, supporting what the Capel already know—that they are the chosen. But his style is also important, for it too corresponds to what the Capel expect from a preacher: an experience that is aesthetic and soothing.

Both style and content alter when Eben has his religious experience:

> But in the high day of his spiritual prosperity Eben's power decreased: his discourses got to be less songlike, he conversed with rather than preached to his congregation, and he wrote out his sermons. Men and women murmured: "there's pity, now, dear me, about Eben bach the Singer."

> The men of the Big Seat reproached him.
>
> "Well-well, Eben bach, no one wept again the last Sunday," said Ben Shop Draper. . . .
>
> "For what he say that life is more than religion?" asked Ben.
>
> (77)

Appropriately the deacons (the men of the Big Seat) are much more interested in the style than they are in the content, even though his sermons have now become radically challenging to the Capel. Together with the congregation they lament Eben's lack of emotional effect (in terms suggesting the failure of a star turn). They come to the content only afterwards, and Eben is much more interested in telling them about it than they are in listening:

> "Listen you to me now," said Eben. "I have not preached to you at all the real religion. I offered you the White Palace or the Fiery Pool. Men, men, that is not right. If you don't live in Heaven here you won't live in Heaven when you perish. Look you at Roberts of the Shop Grocer. Did he not make his servant Mari very full barely a year after he stood up in the Seiet and said that he prayed each night to be taken to Mistress Roberts? . . .
>
> "Man, man, wrong you are to speak so about Roberts of the Shop Grocer," said Ben. "Poor Roberts bach was sorely tempted, and he is forgiven. And has he not sent the bad bitch about her business? Now think you over these things, and do not you be a blockhead to throw away your house and one hundred of sovereigns a year."
>
> (77)

Eben wants to translate what are mere stories (of heaven and hell) into actual codes of conduct. Hence he moves from an emphasis on style and performance to one on the message itself. This shift has a noticeable effect on the patterns of his speech. Though his explanation of his message has several markers of "Welshness," it is nevertheless much more readily understood than much of the dialogue in the story. Despite the superficial signs of being like that other dialogue, it is in fact much more like (an implied) Standard English in that it represents a normal seeming logic. One notes how much more fluent and articulate Eben seems to have become here compared with his speech to the Big Man (the last time we witnessed his direct speech). It is as if he has escaped the values of Manteg and thus discovered the articulacy of English.

This effect is brought out by the markedly odd logic of the leaders of Manteg, who reverse the "normal" reading of Mari and Roberts to make him the victim and her the villain and who automatically consider the 100 sovereigns as the religious issue that should be of primary importance to Eben. Ironically, they do fulfill Eben's sense that religion should be more practical, but not quite in the way he intends.

Eben cannot preach against his conscience, and so he leaves the Capel. It is notable that in arguments with the people of Manteg (all of whom maintain that it is foolish and irreligious to give up 100 sovereigns), Eben becomes even more like a Standard English speaker: "'But I want to use it,'" retorted Eben. "'The congregation won't let me, Lloyd bach. So long as I employed half a talent all went well'" (78). He never loses this "educated" voice, even when he decides to give up his principled stand. He has grown much more articulate since he was Eben the shepherd boy, but his fluency must only be used as a specific kind of licensed escape from the linguistic deprivation and unreality of Manteg. He cannot try to bring about a real escape from its entrapment. Thus he ends the story writing a letter to a new chapel seeking appointment; the letter employs his fluent preaching style, together with Ben Shop Draper's sense of the practical: "Pray, my beloved, that my labours will be very fruitful among you. Let not the matter of the little sovereigns engage your minds at this joyful time, has not our brother Ben Shop Draper arranged all that?" (79-80).

Before he writes the letter that both attests to his linguistic development and shows that he will still be imprisoned by the general linguistic limitations of Manteg, he returns to the ways of thinking through which he embarked upon his career:

> "What are you waiting for, man?"
>
> "For the Angel of the Lord. . . . "
>
> Taking off his coat and waistcoat . . . he dug a hole in the ground. . . .
>
> "Big Lord . . . the talent Thou gavest me brought a great deal of woe with it. Let thy angel here, O Big Man, bear witness now that I return to Thee Thy talent. And do thou let me depart in peace, to make the best use of the half-talent which is mine . . .
>                                                                                (79)

This exchange between man and God differs from the earlier one, because it is experienced by a different and more articulate Eben, one whom we have seen thinking aloud in more conventional ways. It is as if he is now playing at this representation of thought as a sign of his reabsorption into Capel Sion and Manteg.

It is clear that the use that Evans makes of his invented and "translated" Welsh English is very complex. The way in which the reader is maneuvered into reading the (imaginary) language variety is based in part on general assumptions about language varieties and the communities that use them, on assumptions about translation, and on the irony and other patterns within the narratives. But this description only covers the most literal sense in which translation and language variety is at the center of *My People*. Notions of language, variety, translation, and meaning seem also to form much of the content of narratives, which constantly foreground not only how the people of Manteg speak, but also how they mean (and do not mean) for themselves and for the reader whose viewpoint is constructed as normal and natural.

The early review that compared Joyce to Evans still remains virtually unique in its comparisons between the two writers, but the common ground to which it briefly (and unfavorably) alluded is substantial. Where Joyce's relation to Ireland has been much discussed, outside Ireland as well as within, Evans's relation to Wales and what it can tell us about both Welsh and English conceptions of nation still deserves more, and more widespread, critical attention.

WORKS CITED

Deming, R., ed. *James Joyce: The Critical Heritage.* London: Routledge, 1970.

Evans, Caradoc. *My People.* Ed. John Harris. Bridgend: Seren (Poetry Wales Press), 1987.

Harris, John, ed. *My People.* By Caradoc Evans. Bridgend: Seren (Poetry Wales Press), 1987.

———, and John Davies. "Caradoc Evans and the Forcers of Conscience: A Reading of 'A Father in Sion.'" *The Anglo-Welsh Review* 81 (1985): 79-89.

Hopkins, Chris. "'James Joyce is an Irish edition of Mr Caradoc Evans': Two Celtic Naturalists." *Irish Studies Review* 12 (Autumn 1995): 23-26.

———. "Peasant Languages and Celtic Nations: The Englishes of J. M Synge and Caradoc Evans." *English and the Other Languages.* Ed. Ton Haanselaas and Marius Buning. Amsterdam: Rodopi, 1996 (forthcoming).

Jones, Mary. "A Changing Myth: The Projection of the Welsh in the Short Stories of Caradoc Evans." *The Anglo-Welsh Review* 81 (1985): 90-96

Williams, Trevor. "The Birth of a Reputation: Early Welsh Reaction to the Work of Caradoc Evans." *The Anglo-Welsh Review* 19 (1971): 147-71.

———. *Caradoc Evans.* Cardiff: U of Wales P. 1970.

---

# FURTHER READING

## Biography

Green, George H. "Caradoc." In *The Earth Gives All and Takes All,* pp. vii-xxxiv. London: Andrew Dakers, 1946.

In a preface to Evans's last collection, Professor Green combines personal reminiscences of Evans with a biographical sketch.

Harris, John. "Caradoc Evans: A Biographical Introduction." In *Fury Never Leaves Us: A Miscellany of Caradoc Evans,* edited by John Harris, pp. 9-45. Bridgend, Mid Glamorgan, Wales: Poetry Wales Press, 1985.

> An illustrated overview of Evans's career, including details on his childhood and circumstances that informed his later work.

Jenkins, David. "Community and Kin: Caradoc Evans 'At Home.'" *Anglo-Welsh Review* 24, No. 53 (Winter 1974): 43-57.

> A study of the embittering events of Evans's childhood, and of their influence on his writing.

## Criticism

Jones, Gwyn. "Let My People Go." *Times Literary Supplement* No. 3489 (9 January 1964): 33-34.

> An overview of *My People,* and its impact on Welsh literature, by a Welsh writer who knew Evans.

Review of *My People. Times Literary Supplement*, No. 3390 (16 February 1967): 132.

> A laudatory review on the occasion of the reissue of Evans's first book, in which, the reviewer observes, the author portrays "a fabulous hell" among the green hills of rural Wales.

Olson, Ray. Review of *My People. Booklist* 84, No. 17 (1 May 1988): 1476.

> Praises *My People,* which in Olson's view inaugurated the modern history of Anglo-Welsh literature.

# Eric Gill

## 1882-1940

(Full name Arthur Eric Rowton Gill) British essayist and autobiographer; sculptor and typographer

## INTRODUCTION

Eric Gill is known as much for his essays as for the fruits of his primary careers in sculpture, engraving, and typographic design. In *Art-Nonsense and Other Essays,* as well as numerous other works, Gill commented on issues of aesthetics, politics, religion, and other subjects, in each case building a detailed and highly structured argument from first principles. After an initial interest in socialism, Gill in 1913 adopted Catholicism, and thereafter was an enthusiastic proponent of that faith. In his writing he promoted his spiritual views, which carried with them a strongly anti-materialist attitude which put him as much at odds with communism as with capitalism.

### Biographical Information

Gill was born on 22 February 1882 in Sussex, the son of a minister. When he was fifteen, he went to study at Chichester Technical and Art School, where he developed an interest in calligraphy; he left Chichester in 1899 to work as an apprentice architect with W. H. Caroe in London. Gill was drawn to Fabian socialism, and his reading of H. G. Wells inspired him to abandon religious faith. Perhaps influenced by the utilitarian emphasis of most socialist thought, Gill opted to become a stone-carver, a less prestigious but in his view more authentic profession than that of architect. He studied lettering at the Central School of Arts and Crafts under Edward Johnston, whose holistic approach to the lettering craft had a profound impact on Gill's emerging vision of art as primarily an expression of integrity. In 1904 Gill married Ethel Moore, with whom he would father three daughters and adopt a son. Having taken on an apprentice, Joseph Cribb, in 1906, Gill moved his family to Ditchling, in Sussex, the following year. There he began to draw around him a group of artists and intellectuals who joined him in rejecting capitalist materialism, and engaged in a brief extramarital affair with another young Fabian socialist. But as his circle grew and he came into contact with scholars interested in religion, such as the Hindu writer Ananda Coomaraswamy, Gill became drawn to spiritual subjects. In 1913 he converted to Catholicism, a watershed event in his life. Gill's involvement in the Church increased, and he fulfilled one of his most important commissions as a sculptor, the Stations of the Cross at Westminster Ca-

thedral. In 1924, following a financial dispute with a colleague, Gill left Ditchling for Capel-y-ffin in Wales. The remoteness of his new locale forced him to spend a great deal of time traveling, so in 1928 he moved his family to Pigotts, near High Wycombe in England. At Pigotts, where he would live for the remainder of his life, Gill began to gather around him a new group of fellow artists, and published *Art-Nonsense and Other Essays,* which brought together twelve years' worth of published writings. During the 1930s, a decade in which he brought out numerous books, Gill carved the figures of Prospero and Ariel for the BBC's London headquarters, a panel depicting the creation of Adam for the League of Nations Assembly Hall in Geneva, and a monument to the recently deceased G. K. Chesterton. Gill himself died of lung cancer on 17 November 1940.

### Major Works

In *Art-Nonsense and Other Essays, Beauty Looks After Herself, Trousers & the Most Precious Ornament,* and other essay collections, Gill approached a number of subjects. He usually relied on a formula that emphasized structure and logic. Like the Roman Catholic catechism, which starts from first principles about the nature of God and creation, a typical Gill essay, regardless of its subject matter, begins with a statement of its author's underlying beliefs regarding fundamental human nature and humans' relationship to their creator. The essay steadily builds from those bedrock principles toward the subject at hand, be it fashion, typography, or capitalism, making an apparently incontrovertible case for Gill's point of view, which usually reflected strict Catholicism mixed with unorthodoxies, particularly in near-total renunciation of the capitalist economic system. Capitalism, Gill believed, placed a wedge between man and God, between man and man, and between man and himself. "[I]n a world devoted to commerce," he wrote, ". . . the male creature is under eclipse." His integrity, and thus his manhood, has been taken from him by a system in which, for instance, "the baker bak[es] inferior commercial bread in order to make money to buy the inferior bread of other commercial bakers." Nor did Gill embrace the "answer" to capitalism offered in Stalin's Russia: in *The Necessity of Belief,* he condemned communism for rejecting "the god whom capitalists profess to worship and do not" while keeping the "servitude" of the capitalist system. Gill retraced the steps of his conversion from socialism to Catholicism in his *Autobiography,* which was published shortly after his death.

## PRINCIPAL WORKS

*Art-Nonsense, and Other Essays* (essays) 1929
*Beauty Looks After Herself* (essays) 1933
*The Necessity of Belief* (nonfiction) 1936
*Trousers & the Most Precious Ornament* (essays) 1937
*Autobiography* (autobiography) 1940

---

## CRITICISM

### Rene Hague (essay date 1930)

SOURCE: A review of 'Art-Nonsense and Other Essays', in *The Criterion,* Vol. IX, No. XXXVI, April, 1930, pp. 550-53.

[*In the following essay, a review of* Art-Nonsense, *Hague takes issue with Gill's approach to his subject matter.*]

There are probably few artists who do not suffer from the inspiration of the critics, and by this time, no doubt Mr. Gill has had a bellyfull. His collection of essays and lectures written between the years 1918 and 1929 comes accordingly as the counter-attack to which the defence is driven. *Art-Nonsense* is certainly a work of defence, and, I believe, moreover, that the defence is two-fold, at once conscious and unconscious; conscious, in as much as Mr. Gill has deliberately chosen a simplification, both in the use of words and in his manner of approach to the problems with which he deals, which makes it possible for him to establish with greater ease his main idea that art is simply the normal earthly human activity. When Mr. Chesterton said that art was 'the signature of mankind' he was speaking in a different sense (and wider of the mark), but he appropriated the words which were more fitted to Mr. Gill's belief. By 'simplification' I mean that the reader will look in vain in *Art-Nonsense* for any clue to 'the mystery of the beautiful'; and I have used the word 'earthly' with deliberation to indicate that the arts are regarded not least as practical affairs, and that if you accept Mr. Gill's description of art as 'deliberate human skill' you must forgo any semi-Platonic notion that the incarnation in material media of some higher reality (—call it, with Mr. Oliver W. F. Lodge, The Kingdom of Heaven, if you can stomach his metaphor—) is in any way *essential* to all the arts. You must, in fact, break down the idea that there is any difference in kind between the fine and the servile arts. This is not, I hope, a misrepresentation of Mr. Gill's first principle that 'art is simply the well making of what needs to be made.'

This does not mean that the artist is not concerned with the beautiful; two essays in particular, *Id Quod Visum Placet* and *The Criterion in Art,* make this sufficiently clear. But there are numerous protests against the assumption that because some of the arts minister to mental delight therefore the name of art should be denied to those works of human skill which have only a practical utility.

I have taken the liberty of saying that this line of approach is consciously adopted towards a certain end, because it is obvious that it is largely a practical measure, and because the insistence on the kinship between all kinds of skill is essential to the safeguarding of Mr. Gill's belief that art is always continuous and present, that however different may be the forms which it may take, yet is it always to be found when the human being is busy about his ordinary activities. Moreover, before it can be at all fruitful to discuss the nature of the fine arts, it would appear to be as well to rid the vulgar mind of the notion that the 'professional artist' either exercises a superhuman function or has a monopoly of the only human faculty which approaches the supernatural. Even the phrase 'Collaboration with God in creating' (which comes from Mr. Gill) may be open to this abuse. This phrase which has just been quoted contains the second main principle which runs through *Art-Nonsense.* It shares the field so fairly with the notion of well-making that it is quite apparent that Mr. Gill is no more going to deny the existence and rightness of the arts which are ordered to no practical end than he is going to suffer the exclusion of all but those arts. He insists, however, that they are all of the one family. To the products of the finer arts different names may be given, and the naming is probably the chief source of annoyance and disagreement. If Mr. Herbert Read, for example, cares to write of symbols or phantasms, I believe that Mr. Gill (though grimacing at the phrase) would admit that their production is indeed a legitimate form of art. He would find the *non-sequitur* in the assumption that to the manufacture of motor-cars, for example, should be denied the title of art.

There may be more impertinence—I hope that there is not—in referring to the second aspect of Mr. Gill's defence, the unconscious. In this the defence becomes more personal, being directed not so much against the destruction of current forms of art-nonsense as towards an apology for the particular form of art which Mr. Gill practises himself. It is in the first place significant that both the arts of sculpture and engraving are ones in which the steps from those branches which have a practical utility to those which have a mental utility may be the most readily observed. It is only natural, accordingly, that Mr. Gill should insist that there is a steady and continuous progression from the one extreme to the other; and still more natural that he should feel that only the artist himself can see clearly how his practice stands. In painting the progression becomes less easy to trace, though it is still observed. In music and letters it may be completely lost to sight, for what can hold the same position with relation to those arts which map-engraving and the work of a mason hold to the arts of engraving and sculpture? Before reading the final essay from which the book derives its title, I was convinced that Mr. Gill was so devoted to his thesis for reasons which were personal. It seemed obvious that he insisted on the hierarchy of the arts so strongly because he was a certain sort of artist himself. Wherefore his remarks on this very point are the more striking. Writing of the servile arts and the fine arts he says 'There is not only a large number of things which are difficult to place in either category, but, and this is the fertile field for art-nonsense, things which are labelled "fine" art are often made in the same spirit and with the same intention as things labelled servile art, and vice versa.' It might be thought that the discovery of a personal motive, that is the discovery that a certain line of argument had been adopted because it was so obviously illustrated by the actual practice of the man who used the argument, might invalidate the conclusions. It is not so. It must on the contrary be insisted that Mr. Gill's work clinches his argument, for it illustrates that it is indeed the same spirit and intention, the same man, which directs the making of a tombstone and of the Belle Sauvage who decorates his title-page.

## Rayner Heppenstall (essay date 1936)

SOURCE: A review of 'The Necessity of Belief', in *The Criterion,* Vol. XV, No. LXI, July, 1936, pp. 718-21.

[*In the following essay, a review of* The Necessity of Belief, *Heppenstall treats Gill primarily as a one-man phenomenon rather than as a thinker.*]

Outside his engraving, his sculpture and his lettering, Mr. Gill has to be regarded, I fancy, rather as a personal legend than as a true teacher. He is important as the creator rather of an important phantasy than of as important intellectual structure. He expounds a way of life. It is the way of pre-Tridentine Christianity, under post-War Capitalism, generated by William Morris and adapted to a generation which knows its D. H. Lawrence by the superaddition of a great deal of manly-tender paganism. And Mr. Gill's ability to sustain this phantasy with far more conviction than all the other contemporary mediævalists is due, precisely, to the fact that his own basic trade, that of letter-cutting, is circumstantially unchanged by Capitalism, *is* pre-Tridentine, and so involves Mr. Gill himself in no serious inconsistencies.

The followers are also provided with ideas. And the few that the phantasy necessarily calls for, though rather too simple to be the whole truth, are importantly good ideas, good viable ideas, good slogans. There is the basic conception of work all done to the glory of God. It resolves into:

'All art is propaganda.'

This is prose. Rather more lyrically, we have:

'Look after truth and goodness,
And beauty takes care of herself.'

Or, in graver rhythm (from Ananda Coomaraswamy):

'The artist is not a special kind of man,
But every man is a special kind of artist.'

Or:

'Art is the right making
Of things that require to be made.'

There are others, in prose. There is the prose distinction between the man of prudence and the man of art (the point of the structure at which Mr. Gill's paganism properly enters). There is the critique of Industrialism on the two grounds that it has 'released man the artist from the necessity of making anything useful' and that it 'reduces man the worker'—which is to say, the special kind of artist who does not practise, the lapsed artist—'to a subhuman condition of intellectual irresponsibility'. There is, finally, a definition of political salvation as 'the re-integration of work and pleasure, use and beauty'. And all these are, as I say, such immediately vital half-truths that Mr. Gill's whimsically vigorous reiteration and heroic embodiment of them is important, even intellectually.

The whole structure is a personal legend, none the less, and phantasy, a way of life valid ultimately only for Mr. Gill himself. It is, perhaps, an unimportant observation that to cancel five centuries, though Mr. Gill explicitly disclaims any wish to do that, is his only consistently practical politics, that, in fact, there is only a psychological difference between the validity of Mr. Gill and that of G. K. Chesterton. But I do not think it has yet been pointed out that, for instance, Mr. Gill's affirmations of the incompatibility of art and Industrialism depend, from first to last for their plausibility, on our granting him a definition of art which already contains the statement. For Mr. Gill's art stopped at the Renaissance. No creative activity of the modern world falls seriously within the scope of Mr. Gill's consideration. And contemporary Industrialism is the natural product of all the energies released at the Renaissance, without which, though no Woolworth, yet, also, no Leonardo, no Shakespeare, no Beethoven.

For that matter, no Eric Gill, no anti-Industrialism, no intellectual stock-in-trade. . . . And, if all this seems too general for the review of a particular book, so, I protest, does Mr. Gill's particular book.

Opening a disquisition called ***The Necessity of Belief,*** the reader cannot help fancying that he is about to have demonstrated the necessity of believing *in* something, probably a God. And, if the writer is a notorious Catholic, he will probably fancy that it is a question of the truth, as compelling belief, of the Incarnation. But there is nothing so unsubtle as that about Mr. Gill. He begins by examining the word 'belief', argues that it properly means 'the affirmation of certainty' (which is not so bright, at least, as Bernard Shaw's 'affirmation of what you know to be untrue, for the purposes of emotional satisfaction') and concludes that 'all belief is religious belief'. And then we begin to think that we see what Mr. Gill is up to. He turns to the topic of 'The Ability to Believe', and we think we see that this book is more exactly entitled than we had thought. Believing, itself, is blessed. This is going to be a book about the psychology of belief, in general. 'It is more blessed to receive than to reject.' There are two kinds of temperament, the believing and the unbelieving. And the unbelieving are the wicked. Why? Because the erotic analogies of mystical experience are not going to be wasted, because Mr. Gill's Christian is also a pagan, because:

'If they can reject what you have to give they will do so. They expect to be convinced by force or not at all. They cannot see that they must collaborate. They refuse to collaborate. They are like those virgins who can only be raped.'

But even this, though a characteristic, is not the crucial statement. We are not, after all, to be regaled with the pagan psychology of a Christian phantasy. Mr. Gill goes on, next, to a demonstration of the fact that even Communists, with all their protestations, *believe,* to a Fabian analysis of contemporary society, to a discussion of the relations of belief and personality, to yet another 'dissolution or liquidation of the problem of evil'—when will Christian intellectuals understand that 'the problem of evil' is a specifically Christian problem, that it does not exist for non-Christians except in moments when they are incapable, anyhow, of 'listening to reason' and that its 'dissolution or liquidation' is, therefore, a piece of scholastic tautology?—and then—oh, dear!—to yet more Fabian sociology, though this lot is far more lively, until, after some three hundred pages, the reader thinks, once again, that he sees what Mr. Gill is up to. Not only is this less a book about something than a book by Eric Gill. Not only is it not a serious, but a vibrantly emotional book. It is not a book at all. It is a collection of essays.

And, once again, we are wrong. For Mr. Gill suddenly announces the theme, thesis and purpose of his book, on page 326.

'Man accepts the notion of being because he experiences being in himself.'

Which is *very* unfair. . . . For everything that Mr. Gill has been saying, these last three hundred and twenty-six pages, has rested on that assumption. It has been because Mr. Gill is unable to conceive of man as other than a person, as individual being, that he horridly misrepresents the Marxians, for instance, the Freudians and Nietzsche. It was his inability to conceive of man except as an unique and accomplished soul in the face of no less unique and accomplished inanimate things that let him treat as he did 'the problem of evil'. If this is what he was out to prove, then, at least, he should have taken into account the notion, common to Marxian, Freudian and indeed all specifically modern thought, that personality is potential, that the individual is defined in his relations to others, diffuse in solitude, that 'being' is not behind but inherent in 'doing' and that things are not considered, but only the relations between things, in what replaces, for non-Christians, 'the problem of evil'. Still, after this revelation, the remaining thirty pages are easy. And the second reading is unmixed pleasure.

For, when we have taken in the fact that this book is a phenomenon for which its author has not been formally (nor anything finally) responsible, it is possible to enjoy, without worrying, its innumerable grand patches. It is unlikely that Mr. Gill will approve of this attitude. He has no doctrine of virtuosity. Although, among his own work, a great many of us prefer the erotic and useless even to the devotional and useful imagery,[1] yet his view of art is grimly utilitarian. And he is not, he claims, maliciously, a man of letters. None the less, Mr. Gill has an alarmingly vivid literary eye. His descriptions of complicated situations, the virtuoso effects of his understatement (in this book, at least) and his flair for manipulating crowded instances are no less admirable for being beside the purpose. And I fancy that some of the prose, for clarity, nerve and movement (nearly all the last hundred pages, but it works up with the emotional work-up, notably in a fine Landorian paragraph on page 329), is as good as any that is now being written.

[1] This is not the only gap between Mr. Gill's critical theory and creative practice. Using the distinction as it is made by Adrian Stokes, although his sculptural work is unmistakable 'carving', his theory is 'plastic'. His practical concernment is material, superbly so, his theoretical concernment functional.

**Cyril F. Hudson (essay date 1936)**

SOURCE: A review of 'Work and Leisure', in *The Criterion*, Vol. XV, No. LIX, January, 1936, pp. 352-53.

[*In the following essay, Hudson offers* Work and Leisure *as an antidote to the totalitarian madness taking hold of Europe.*]

[**Work and Leisure**] consists of three lectures delivered at University College Bangor, a year ago. The casual reader may be surprised to find that in the titles of the individual lectures 'art' has been substituted for 'work'. This is because Mr. Gill uses the word 'art' in the scholastic sense of making things—any thing—with skill; 'all things made are works of art', and to suppose that 'the word Art itself means something to do with beauty is a very great mistake'. An artist is an artisan, the master of an art. The conventional modern view that art and commerce have nothing to do with each other is therefore wholly mistaken; on the contrary, since the end of art is consumption and enjoyment, it cannot exist without commerce—that is, the exchange of works of human skill. Not commerce, but commercialism, is the enemy: the making of things, not for consumption and enjoyment and delight, but for sale; and the making of them, moreover, not by artisans, but by machines, tended by men and women whose task, by its very nature, is without responsibility, without interest—since its purpose is not to satisfy the consumer but to enrich the employer—and without joy. In an industrialized community men can only be artisans in the true sense when they are not at 'work', and even then their 'art', their creative activities, must be directed towards the making of things of no use to anybody, since useful things—the things people want, or can be hypnotized by high-powered salesmanship into thinking that they want—are made, increasingly, by machinery. The 'problem of leisure' is the problem of how to find satisfaction in occupations which cannot be allowed to satisfy anybody, since the machines must at any cost be kept going, and markets found for their products, in order to provide profits for their owners and 'employment' (without which those who own nothing but their labour must starve) for their minders. All this is not to say that machine-made things are evil; on the contrary, they 'exhibit all the goodness that is possible to them, being what they are'. But their goodness is no more than that of 'functional suitability'; gaiety, grace, love and holiness are excluded from the making of such things, and therefore from the things themselves. They can never be beautiful, since beauty is *id quod visum placet,* and man, who is a spiritual being, can only find real and enduring pleasure in the contemplation of that which expresses his true nature. Modern man, the victim of industrialism's separation of art ('making things') from beauty and holiness, has achieved a perverted vindication of his spirituality by attaching these values to special kinds of 'artist', so that holiness is now regarded as the concern only of the priest and the saint, and beauty that of the painter, the musician and the poet: the factory is the sphere in which functionalism can operate, while the altar and the studio are given over to holiness and æsthetics. Beyond these, 'fretwork and fretfulness' rule.

Such is the Termite State. Mr. Gill's is a notable addition to the literature of diagnosis and criticism concerning it. The tragedy of contemporary politics is that the blind are leading the blind. None of the programmes suggested for the rescue of civilization—no single Plan, whether Fascist or Nazi or Communist or National Government—betrays the slightest awareness that, though the symptoms of disease are manifested in the body and structure of society, it is the soul of man that is sick. To our politicians and bankers and journalists, man is an economic animal and no more. Such a view is atheistic, and political philosophies based upon it are doomed to futility because they ignore truth: they leave reality out of account. There are two lies at the heart of society. The first is that man can leave God out of his calculations and yet live a fully human life. The second, implicit rather than expressed in Mr. Gill's diagnosis, is

that natural conditions are other than they are: that the energies of men must still be devoted, not to living, but to creating the material means of life, and that the earthly existence of vast numbers of 'workers' must, necessarily and unavoidably and for ever, be a foretaste of hell. To the theist, a society with such falsehoods at its heart, unnecessarily substituting nightmare for reality, and preferring darkness to light, is a society living in sin: the object of God's Judgment—and of His Redemption.

## Olaf Stapledon (essay date 1936)

SOURCE: "The Credo of Mr. Gill," in *The London Mercury,* Vol. XXXIV, No. 200, June, 1936, p. 183.

[*In the following essay, Stapledon presents* The Necessity of Belief *as an accurate treatment of contemporary issues, but faults Gill for his tendency to proselytize.*]

Delightful yet exasperating, lucid yet confused, in some respects salutary yet in others pernicious, [*The Necessity of Belief*] strikingly illustrates at once the promise and the danger of the disposition not to be hypnotized by modern scientific culture. Delight is afforded by Mr. Gill's direct and even racy style, by his blend of gaiety and seriousness, by his relish of the life both of body and of spirit, above all by his insistence on values which in our day are apt to be over-looked. Exasperation, on the other hand, is sometimes aroused by his light-hearted neglect of the philosophical difficulties of his position, and also by his failure to distinguish between the basic experiences of value and the doctrines with which these have been overlaid. He may be justified when he charges the Russians with having "emptied out the Baby of Bethlehem only to swallow the foul and befouling bath water of London and Manchester"; but we should feel more confidence in his own apprehension of the bare essentials of the spirit if he did not try to reinstate, along with the Baby, the holy water of Rome, and the priests and all Rome's theories.

There is much truth in Mr. Gill's analysis of the sickness of the modern world, and much to applaud in his indignant protest against the injustice and vulgarity of our social order. We have lost faith, he says, in human personality. Industrialism was founded on the immoral expropriation of the peasants. It thrived by the immoral enslavement of the growing landless population. It has imposed on nearly all of us a mode of life in which we cannot be persons but only robots. At the same time, materialistic science, by putting man under the microscope, has missed all that is most characteristic in him, and conceives him as nothing but a mechanism of electric charges. Mr. Gill seeks to rehabilitate the common-sense view of a man as no mere sequence of mechanical events but a real being capable of real love and hate, righteousness and sin, wisdom and folly. Every one of us, when he is not bemused by theories, knows himself to be an enduring and responsible person, and knows personality to be intrinsically good, both in himself and others. No microscopic view of the mechanism of body and of instinctive mind should be allowed to obscure this intuition.

All this is salutary. But Mr. Gill is not content to make a gay affirmation of the worth of personality and of the intuitions of truth, beauty and goodness, and of the felt ultimate rightness of the universe. Though he disclaims the intention of writing a Roman Catholic tract, he does in effect do so. It is possible to be just as sure as Mr. Gill himself of the intrinsic goodness of personality, and even of the felt, though unintelligible, ultimate rightness of the universe without craving the support of any metaphysical doctrines whatever.

Mr. Gill would apparently have us go back to the age of universal hand-work and universal acceptance of the Catholic faith. It may well be that both in respect of work and in respect of faith that age has much to teach us. It may be that civilization will never find health till by some means or other the joy of craftsmanship is reinstated. It may be, also, that no real peace can occur till the world community becomes what Mr. Gill calls a "unanimous society," dominated by a common "faith." But it seems very improbable that salvation should lie simply in reinstating the life and the faith of a vanished world.

## Holbrook Jackson (essay date 1938)

SOURCE: "Eric Gill," in *The Printing of Books,* Cassell & Company Ltd., 1938, pp. 140-54.

[*In the following excerpt, Jackson discusses Gill's aesthetic in lettering with reference to his notions of ethics.*]

Eric Gill is not content with being an artist. He wants to know what he is about, and in his essays he seems to be reasoning as much with himself as with his reader. He is superlatively honest in the process despite a dialectical ingenuity which recalls that of a medieval schoolman, or John Ruskin. A reference to the panels of the Stations of the Cross which he carved for Westminster Cathedral as 'furniture, not decorations', is indicative of his attitude towards the arts. The remark appears in a defence of the architecture of the cathedral, or of as much of it as he can tolerate. Bentley, it seems, dreamed of a brick building encrusted with marble and carved ornaments, and where he went his own decorative way he was commonplace or even ridiculous. 'The outside of the building is almost entirely ruined by this absurd pandering to the appetite for ornamentation.' Gill likes the exterior 'as a piece of brick and concrete work' just as well as 'the great interior' before its pure architecture was smothered in coloured marbles and mosaics.

His career as well as his attitude towards the arts and crafts recall William Morris, but not always in the same way or for the same reasons. Like Morris, he began life in an architect's office, and, in addition to his distin-

guished achievement in sculpture (one of the few arts Morris did not practise), he is a letterer, a writer, a social reformer, and a typographer. But here the resemblance ends. Gill is never Gothic, least of all when designing letters or types. 'Lettering is for us the Roman alphabet and the Roman alphabet is lettering', he says.[1] His craftsmanship remains architectural although he never became an architect. His sculptures look as though they ought to have grown out of buildings rather than been stuck on to them, just as his book decorations intend to be typographic, that is, to grow out of the printed text. Neither his work nor his ideas are quite happy when standing alone. They must be related to something—a book or a building, a church, or God. Whatever reasons Morris gave for making beautiful things his real reason was to delight the senses. Eric Gill also believes that it is the business of art to please the senses, but he does not stop there. Sensibility is not enough. The art and the pleasure must be good: 'That is good art which pleases the senses as they ought to be pleased and the mind as it ought to be pleased.'[2] Neither is he content with an ethical generalization, however apposite. The moral conception of goodness is not enough. Goodness must be religious. 'God alone is good',[3] he says. And he resolves the problems of art by referring them back to moral or religious principles. Printing is put to the same test. In practice, however, it is not possible, at least in these times, to be consistently good in that strict sense.

> 'There are', he says, 'two typographies, as there are two worlds; and apart from God or profits, the test of one is mechanical perfection, and of the other sanctity—the commercial article at its best is simply physically serviceable and, *per accidens,* beautiful in its efficiency; the work of art at its best is beautiful in its very substance and, *per accidens,* as serviceable as an article of commerce.'[4]

There is no doubt which of these two typographies he prefers and, although he is primarily out to serve God, he is prepared to serve Mammon in the form of the commercialism he abhors, on approved terms, namely by designing books and types which are serviceable in the commercial sense as distinct from the books and types which he designs to please the mind and the senses as they ought to be pleased. He will, in fact, remain in the world but not of it. And he is able to do so without serious hurt to his work or his conscience because he realizes that works of commerce and works of sanctity are destined to go on side by side (for long if not for ever), and that having two distinct objects and methods there is no reason why we should not help to cleanse the one whilst clinging to the other, industry 'becoming nobly utilitarian as it recognises its inherent limitations, and the world of human labour, ceasing any longer to compete with it, becoming more strictly and soberly humane'. It is a beneficent compromise born of a sense of fact. Eric Gill makes the best of two worlds by giving of his best to each, which is consistent with his belief that 'there is no happiness in a world in which things are not as good as they can be', and there can be few well-wishers of craftsmanship, and especially of typography, who do not welcome the honesty and clarity of the rules he has evolved for himself and applied so fastidiously.

Sometimes, however, he is a little hard on even a corrupt industrialism. There can be no serious complaint when he says that 'Commercial printing, machine printing, industrial printing would have its own proper goodness if it were studiously plain and starkly efficient.' But his conditions begin to assume questionable shape when he pushes his logic so far as to demand that 'the typography of Industrialism' when it is 'not deliberately diabolical and designed to deceive', should not only be plain but that it should 'be wholly free from exuberance and fancy', because 'ornament is a kind of exuberance' and 'you cannot be exuberant by proxy'. Every sort of ornament, therefore, is to be renounced, for, he says, 'printers' flowers will not spring in an industrial soil, and fancy lettering is nauseating when it is not the fancy of type-founders and printers but simply of those who desire to make something appear better than it is'. It is obviously a counsel of perfection and therefore respectable, especially where it vetoes the use of devices to make things look better than they are. But Francis Meynell has proved that printers' flowers can show a pleasing and healthy growth both as books and advertisements 'in such a soil', and 'fancy lettering', even when it is the expression of a typefounder's or a printer's ebullience, irrespective of a desire for increased turnover, should not be encouraged, except in carefully chosen circumstances, and, as a matter of fact, it rarely is encouraged by Eric Gill, who has shown his sense of the value of simplicity in printing, and holds the commendable and courageous opinion that 'commonplace and normality' are 'essential to a good book-type'.[5]

On the other hand, he has many aphorisms which, if observed by industrialists, might conceivably help a mechanical commerce to behave itself. In the first place, as it is the aim of industry in a commercial age to be mechanical, all compromises are doomed to failure. 'It is not a question whether machine work be better than hand work—both have their proper goodness—it is simply a matter of difference . . . not all things made by machinery are bad things', nor is it true that 'the handicraftsman is the only kind of man that merits salvation. The industrialist is very welcome to all the credit he can get as a servant of humanity. The time has come when the handicraftsman should cease to rail at him or envy him. Let each go his own road.' He even goes so far as to say that, although the industrialist makes no claim to produce works of art, 'he does so nevertheless—when he is not imitating the works of the past'. And finally, whilst favouring simplicity in printing, Gill tolerantly leaves the door open for reasoning according to taste by the use of the concept 'pleasant'. After distinctiveness is achieved, 'pleasant reading is the compositor's main object'. What is pleasant is not stated, because perhaps so subjective a term is not amenable to definition. For him, characteristically, 'it involves first and last a consideration of what is holy'. But for the printer it means the discovery of the 'bounds of the virtue of haste . . . the bounds of the virtue of fancifulness . . . and above all they must collaborate to discover what is really pleasant in human life'. Even a convinced upholder of *laissez-faire* could face such principles with fortitude.

That being his attitude towards printing, how does he behave? The answer is, of course, to be found in his work. It is not what an artist says that matters so much as what he does, and what Eric Gill does as a craftsman or an artist is convincing, even though his dialectics and his theology may irritate or repel. His art is something more than a challenge: it is an achievement which manages to be both original and traditional, and, in so far as it is purposeful, and most of it has a purpose, it succeeds in being something as well as in doing something.

Gill left architecture for lettering. He carved letters in stone and drew them on paper and painted them on wood. It is a natural progress from lettering to printing. There are inherent relationships. In his case the recognition of those relationships was inevitable, for printing was the extension of an early passion for lettering, which he pursued as a child and perfected as a young man under the guidance of Edward Johnston; and the designing of type was a natural evolution for a printer who was also a letterer of genius. Twenty years ago he and a few friends started and operated the St. Dominic's Press at Ditchling in Sussex, from which issued many curious pamphlets and a small magazine, called *The Game* (1916-23), and his interest in printing continues professionally at the office of Hague & Gill in High Wycombe. His work as a typographer is also to be seen in the title-pages and books issued by a number of publishers in England and abroad, and notably in those produced in collaboration with Robert Gibbings at the Golden Cockerel Press. But whatever the operation or purpose, his attitude towards typography is predominatingly that of a letterer.

Gill never forgets that he is a letterer, and his typefaces, even after they have passed through the ordeal of mechanization, retain some of the sensitive qualities of that craft. He always goes back to first principles and first causes, and his typography begins with the designing of the letter. Thus his printing is inclined to assert its lettered origins, as might be expected from one who is convinced that 'a good piece of lettering is as beautiful a thing to see as any sculpture or painted picture'.[6] He has got this enthusiasm into the pages of his books with the result that the type is sometimes disconcertingly self-important. Gill's lay-out is often restless, but it is possible to forget it; it is possible also (rather surprisingly) to forget his unregistered right-hand margins, but it is difficult to become unconscious of his types.

He is so enamoured of lettering and so conscious of its origin and purposes that he has lately come to the conclusion that it should no longer be associated with printing. 'Lettering', he says, 'has had its day. Spelling, and philology, and all such pedantries have no place in our world. The only way to reform modern lettering is to abolish it.'[7] He argues that the book of the future should be printed in shorthand, which he considers to be more suitable for modern mechanical conditions.

This, however, is a dip into a future where eccentricity has plenty of room to flap its wings, and in the mean-time it may be presumed that typography will have his more normal services in the old tradition, for it is as a designer of types rather than of books that Gill has most influenced modern typography. His habit of innovation by throwing back to the primitive and the archaic has not as yet been imitated, nor is there any likelihood of such individual preferences as no title-page (as in the first edition of the *Essay on Typography*), or a combined title and contents page (as in the second edition), or the unregistered right-hand edges of his lines, being widely adopted, any more than there is an indication that a specially designed text italic, such as Joanna, will be demanded by readers of poetry.[8]

His aim both as a letterer and a typographer is always 'to discover the norm', and this consistent throwing back, or digging down, has been of great value especially in the realm of type-faces,[9] where, with the intelligent cooperation of the Monotype Corporation, he has had a good influence more widespread than could otherwise have been possible. As a designer of types he has been an adapter rather than an inventor, the invention of a new type being next to impossible. But there is distinct originality in his treatment of a text italic in his Joanna, and he has made Perpetua his own much as Edward FitzGerald added *Omar Khayyám* to the treasury of English poetry; whilst he has given grace and proportion to the most bleakly functional of all types. The Gill Sans types are an inevitable consequence of functionalism or mechanical design, and quite naturally they have become the predominant modern commercial typographical characters. It is one of Gill's most emphatic rules that design for mechanical production must be free from ornamentation, and he has successfully pushed this idea to its logical conclusion in the Sans series. 'Mechanised man', he says, 'knows no fancy and curved serifs and such like refinements, dependent as they must be upon the sensibilities of the man who makes them, are rightly to be eschewed by those who design things for machine facture.'[10] He believes, however, that serifs are a useful adjunct to letters, and it might be argued that he designed the Sans series to put mechanized printing in its proper place. He blames machine printing for still being medieval and incapable of

supplying 'a plain job'. The master printer is not a printer but a salesman who refuses to do a plain job of work because it is not good business. 'It won't sell because it won't tickle any buyer's fancy', but this, he is careful to point out, is not a peculiarity of the printing trade. 'To get anything really plain is very difficult, but in the trade of book printing it is as yet impossible.' But his objection is only to mechanical ornamentation and faked fancifulness. Decoration and ornament are the province of the artist not of the gadget-ruled business man.

He has contributed definite characteristics to typographical design, as well as to the designing of types, and, exotic as some of his designs seem to be, they have not only a firm link with the past but a reasoned relationship with the present. He has courageously faced the problem of the mass-production of books and hammered out for himself and others rules which are logically derived from the needs of the reader. He does not set out to make a book beautiful but a book useful, believing that beauty will take care of itself if the rules of honest and considerate production are followed. 'The things which should form the shape and proportion of the page', he says, 'are the hand and the eye.'[11] The ordinary commercial editions of his own essays, particularly the second edition of the *Essay on Typography,* and the new *Temple Shakespeare,* show how distinction and convenience can meet even on business grounds if there is good taste and honesty on both sides.

NOTES

[1] *An Essay on Typography* (2nd ed. 1936), 24.

[2] *Beauty Looks After Herself* (1933), 27.

[3] Ib. 15.

[4] *An Essay on Typography* (1931).

[5] Introd. to 'SS. Perpetua and Felicity', *The Fleuron,* vii (1930).

[6] *An Essay on Typography* (2nd ed. 1936), 122.

[7] *An Essay on Typography* (2nd ed. 1936), 133.

[8] Gill's Joanna italic was first used for an entire book in Margaret Flower's edition of Shakespeare's Sonnets (Cassell & Co., Ltd., 1933).

[9] Eric Gill is responsible for four new (or newly designed) type-faces: Joanna Roman, Joanna Italic, Perpetua, Gill Sans.

[10] *A Specimen of Three Book Types designed by Eric Gill: Joanna, Joanna Italic, Perpetua* (1934), Preface.

[11] *An Essay on Typography* (1936), 108.

## Walter Shewring (essay date 1944)

SOURCE: "Considerations on Eric Gill," in *The Dublin Review,* No. 431, October, 1944, pp. 118-34.

*[In the following essay, Shewring reconsiders Gill's work in light of the relationship between the beautiful and the useful.]*

Two new books by Eric Gill[1] have heartened his disciples by their mature reaffirmation of characteristic principles and their reinforcement of many familiar positions; they have also interested many who before his death knew little of him but were won to some allegiance by his *Autobiography.* At the same time they have called forth a number of criticisms—voiced in reviews of the books themselves and in general discussions of his work, in print or in conversation—which since they repeat similar criticisms in the past may be taken to spring from difficulties sincerely and widely felt. Given the importance of his teaching, these misunderstandings of it deserve attention, and I therefore propose to examine a few controverted points with such amplification or illustration as experience shows to be desirable.

There is first of all the matter of "fine arts" and common arts, or of art and the crafts. Most of our contemporaries abruptly disjoin them; Eric Gill always refused to do so, and it has sometimes been imagined that he blinded himself to a real difference between two species of things. This is certainly not the case; he often made the distinction, and in one form or another it may be found in most of his books—necessary arts, ministering formally to physical needs, and arts of "recreation" (in a strong sense of the word), ministering formally to intellectual needs. But in the first place he subordinated this distinction to the fundamental character common to all the arts ("the well-making of what needs making", "the skill of man in doing and making"); in the second place he gave the warning that the line between art and craft, between liberal or recreative arts and servile or necessary arts, is in practice hard to draw. Does this mean that picture-painting, for instance, is obviously a "fine art" and house-painting obviously a craft, but that it is difficult to decide whether carpentry and calligraphy are "arts" or are "merely" crafts? Yes, with some reservations; but it also means more than that. It means that the necessary and the recreative, the servile and the liberal, are by no means exclusive of each other; the intellectual interacts with the physical, the spiritual is not unnecessary, and objects of household use may embody a metaphysical symbolism. And in application to concrete instances, it means that for all ages to some extent, and for ours to a great extent, a particular human work lies often outside the category conveniently assigned it—perhaps below, perhaps above.

Let me example two actual works. One is a carving by Brancusi, reproduced in the *Encyclopaedia Britannica* with the article "Sculpture Technique". For the modern critic, it belongs pre-eminently to the category of "fine art". It is entitled "Bird in Space", and its appraiser in the *Encyclopaedia* calls it "a simple form so subjective that it has no aesthetic meaning except to the artist". The worth of the carving is unrelated to birds or flight; it consists in the subtleties of visible shape which please us by correspondence with the symmetries of the mind and which ultimately imply (though the sculptor might not acknowledge this) a patterned, ordered and God-created universe. My second example comes from the Pacific Islands and is in the possession of Dr. Coomaraswamy.[2] For the modern critic, it certainly belongs to the category of "applied art"; it is a harpoon head of whalebone, completely adapted to its purpose, though making a theological point by the introduction of a little carved face to signify "Death, or God as the ender as well as the beginner of life". This carving is unquestionably a "useful" object; yet viewed as a shaped and patterned thing, it has the same subtleties, the same appeal and implications, as Brancusi's "pure sculpture". As W. R. Lethaby once remarked, "Artificer and artist seem to be two forms of the same word. One has gone up in the world, the other down. Which is which?"

To illustrate the same thesis from a somewhat different point of view—if we look at a reasonably well-made vase by a modern craftsman, then at a reasonably good Post-Impressionist painting, we may easily acknowledge the painting as of a higher order of things than the vase; if in visiting the British Museum we look first at Sung vases, then at the *Three Bodhisattvas* of the same period, the pre-eminence of the painting is still more easily acknowledged. But what if we turn our contrast to ancient vases and modern picture? The scale of comparison has ceased to be obvious, and it might indeed be maintained that everything of value which the modern painter has done has also been done by the Chinese potter. Or again, a modern small crucifix, a modern page of calligraphy, may be quite remarkably good and undeniably works of art without breaking free from a certain circumscription; but St. Cuthbert's Cross at Durham, a page of the *Codex Sinaiticus*—these are things which we are bound to view otherwise; looking at them, we think to ourselves, "After that, there is nothing more to be said."

From such examples it seems fair to conclude that while every age has its own more or less consistent scale of the arts, comparison between various ages may reveal some intersection, and that this is due to the relative greatness or decadence, normality or abnormality, of the ages themselves. If one holds (and Eric Gill very strongly held it) that ours is a decadent and abnormal age, it will appear as inevitable that no art in it can reach its full scope; and it is by their scope, not by their essential nature, that traditional thought divides the higher and lower arts. Hence on the one hand we have the modern craftsman, working often most admirably but against the grain of his time, and unable to achieve in his isolation what was achieved in his own craft when it was "a thousand men thick".[3] And we have on the other hand the self-conscious modern painter, developing refinements of pure pattern and shape which after all seem scarcely to go beyond the best examples of ancient craftsmanship, so that one sometimes wonders whether the admitted gifts of such persons might not be better employed in following and raising the arts of common life.[4] And in the painter's case as against the craftsman's we may say that there is a *deliberate* limitation of scope; for one of the most evident things in the painting of great and normal ages is that it provides a direct intellectual content as well as the indirect implications of pattern which it shares with the lower degrees of art. Thus the particular greatness of the *Three Bodhisattvas* as compared with the Sung vases lies in the communication of the Buddhist idea of sanctity—a communication effected not by a catalogue title but by the painting as a whole. Again, there are Chinese paintings of musicians which imply and impart an understanding of the whole nature of music—something which simply does not enter into the paintings of recent centuries, where persons and instruments are means to the imitation of textures, to experiments with light and shade, or merely to "abstract design", according to date and fashion. It is precisely this kind of intellectual content which modern painters characteristically[5] disown in their fear of the anecdotal; and the lack of anything like it in typical works of our time is a major cause of that alienation of the common man which marks the present relations of art and society. For the common man, however untrained in the matter of art and however prone to equate catalogue titles with real content, is reasonable at least in his expectation that a painted picture should normally be "about something"—an expectation once satisfied in the caves of Ajanta or the Camposanto of Pisa. Baulked of it now, he comes to agree with the "artist" himself that art is an affair for a handful of exceptional persons sundered from ordinary society; and in spite of the wish of a few artists to elevate the lay mind, the wish of a few laymen that art would come down within their reach, the main antithesis grows meanwhile. Like the Stylite in Gibbon, the artist has ascended a pedestal whose height has been raised with passing years. The crowd below may be envious or indifferent; the hermit has reached his "last and lofty station", and may almost at any moment now "expire without descending".

The divorce of the fine arts from workaday life—by now an evident fact—is deplored by some, welcomed by others. To these latter—to those artists and critics and connoisseurs who hold that now for the first time art has won its true status—the position taken by Eric Gill is of course antipathetic, but should not therefore be unintelligible. That artists should actually pride themselves on isolation from the community was a thing naturally repugnant to one who remembered that every artist is also a man, and that every man in his life's work has duties to the community. The claim that fine art has beauty as its private prerogative was a patent absurdity to one who had philosophical foundations; it is easy to show that beauty inheres in anything that is what it should be; that it is to be found in the works of nature and in the truths

of metaphysics (though many critics of Eric Gill have little use for either[6]); and that as far as the arts are concerned, it is one of a number of qualities which belong to all alike. "Every artist," says St. Bonaventure,[7] "intends the work made to be beautiful, useful, and lasting, and a work is prized and welcomed when it answers these three conditions"—a dictum as true of a chair as of an altarpiece. As for the actual achievement of modern painters, sculptors and architects, Eric Gill was very far from despising it. In his earlier days particularly, he went out of his way to defend such work against misguided criticism, and to the end of his life there were individual artists for whom he reserved the warmest admiration—one may mention especially David Jones. But as he entered more deeply into the work of other times and the principles that informed it—as he studied the Middle Ages in the light of St. Thomas and the great Eastern cultures in the light of their own traditional thought—he saw with increasing clearness the difference dividing such civilizations from our own. The best minds of the modern movement did indeed attain a kind of greatness, and to compare them with mere academicians was to compare the living with the dead; but though it is much to be alive, there are after all degrees of life, and what were these modern masters to those of the past? Sienese primitives, the Church of the Holy Wisdom, the colossal Buddha and rock-cut Kapila of Anurādhapura—must we not acknowledge these things not only as greater than anything of our own age but as great in a higher mode? So too with the "new sensibilities" which modern artists so often claimed; the claim might be just in its degree, but then every age has its own sensibilities—not to speak of things which are supreme, Rajput paintings, early Japanese prints, even some Greek vases have refinements of sensibility which are manifestly denied to us, and if in works of the truly great ages such qualities may be less remarked, it is not that they are absent but that they are subordinated to spiritual depth and intellectual power.

There is a further and strangely neglected consideration which bears directly on all this matter of fine and useful arts. This is that the useful arts themselves—what in one sense of the word may be called the *common* crafts—are in fact so far from common in our industrialized world that it is rare to find any understanding of their nature and implications. There are many corollaries to this; the immediate point is that those who most emphasize the division of art and the crafts—whether popular critics or academic philosophizers—are usually ignorant of one of the two classes of things they so confidently compare. I do not complain of this ignorance in itself (it is natural in any of us today and for many reasons is hard to overcome); my complaint is that much argument on this matter—conducted not from first principles but by induction from specified instances—is stultified by the contrast of something familiar to the writer with something else which is really quite unfamiliar but is not recognized to be such. "Here is art," says the reasoner in effect—and he quotes examples from modern painting and sculpture and architecture, perhaps from novels and music too. This is ground he knows thoroughly; he has seen hundreds of works by Matisse and Chirico and Picasso and Epstein and Le Corbusier; he probably lives among modern artists; he has seen them at work and discussed with them; he is well acquainted with all their points of view. But he then proceeds with "Here is craft", for which he produces perhaps three instances (a table, a cup, a knife and fork), faintly praising the hand-made object, then dismissing it as a thing scarcely more beautiful (if at all) than the best machine-made substitute, and in any case incommensurable with a painting or sculpture on which highly individual genius has lavished its sensibilities. Comparison in these terms is fallacious on many counts, though some of them need not concern us now (for instance, its probable disregard of household objects from China and Peru which in other circumstances might be more flatteringly appraised). The chief points are three: that it is likely the critic understands far less than he supposes of the actual examples given; that he forgets the whole multitude of crafts of which he knows nothing; and that he ignores the cumulative effect of the sum of the crafts.

I suspect the critic's understanding of even the works he chooses; this because he commonly speaks of them in words which would be as applicable to quite different things. He will talk about a table as if it were a would-be painting or sculpture, something therefore which a modern may adequately appreciate in terms of lines and masses; he prescinds from its material, its making, its maker. Criticism of one thing as if it were another is usually bad criticism[8]; and to consider a work of art apart from its making is not to consider it as a work of art. When he praises a given picture, the critic is conscious of it as a communication of one man to other men; his words may be limited to the thing before him, but he makes his judgement not merely in the light of genuine understanding of a piece of human workmanship, but in a penumbra of general sympathy with the aims and way of life of this painter and other painters. There is little comparable in the case of the table. Carpentry may be known to the critic as a hobby practised by an acquaintance, as something once casually discussed with genteel purveyors of "arts-and-crafts"; but is it known to him, is it present to his judgement, as the work of a man's life, with traditional rules and with social implications? Probably not; hence on his part a superficial aesthetic judgement (toying, it may be, with the "pattern" of nails which ought simply never to have been used), a lack of insight which prompts him to ask why anyone achieving so little as this should care to use his hands at all. Precisely; were there in carpentry no more than the critic sees, there would be every reason for leaving it to machines.

But suppose the critic really to have an intimate knowledge of the two or three crafts referred to; there are countless others outside his province, each a possible subject for well-informed appraisal, each with its title to be considered before judgement is pronounced on the whole body of crafts. Dyeing, spinning, weaving; print-ing and paper-making; metalwork of all kinds; lettering in stone and paint and ink; hedging and thatching and gardening—these are a mere few of numberless crafts whose products environ us but whose nature and processes seldom awake enquiring interest. Yet every one of them has its due manner of practice, its rights and wrongs, its subtleties of achievement, its ambushes for the unwary. And ignorance of such things, however trivial in this or that example, has a cumulative effect unnoticed by its victims but acutely marked to a man like Eric Gill, possessing unusual knowledge of many crafts and analogical sympathy extending to all. When Mr. Smith the connoisseur[9] was displaying his private collection of Braque and Derain, it was no great matter that he should take for cotton the scarf of unpolished silk worn by his guest; we all have our blind spots. But when one must face in turn the bogus modernity of his house, the pathetic furniture (visibly wilting in framework as in fashion), the ignoble and ill-assorted rugs, the frankly vulgar tea-service—it became clear that Mr. Smith's discernment did not penetrate far even in visual things which might have been thought to be well within his scope.[10] Besides, it was difficult to forget that the kindly "invitation to view" had been couched in an uncouth hand under a barbarous letter-heading on meretricious paper (it was to be followed by an unbelievable Christmas card). And here were the daughters of the house, apportioning their attention between illustrated weeklies, a lush recording of harmonized folk-songs, and uncritical reminiscences of last evening's jazz; here were the children, playing with toys of revolting shape and worse material—all to the evident satisfaction of the connoisseur himself. Well—as far as kindness and family virtues went, Mr. Smith might be the salt of the earth, but it was out of the question to give the name of "culture" to an outlook and way of life where sensibility and intelligence were at one point hypertrophied and were utterly atrophied at a hundred others. Contrariwise, it was possible to recall certain other households—in Southern France, elsewhere in Europe, even in some sequestered parts of England—where there was no "fine art" about but where everything that was there was good—house, furniture, pottery; talk and music; dress and food and garden—where everything made and done was well made and well done, was one with itself and its surroundings and with a whole view of things; for a way of life so integrated, culture was not an idle word.

It should not be hard to see that understanding of any craft has in most times and places been closely linked with proximity—physical proximity to the exercise of the craft, spiritual proximity to the craftsman's aims and ideas. In the English villages and small towns of a century ago it was natural and usual to see the craftsman at work and to assimilate by direct experience the principles of his making and the qualities of its product. Every man to his trade (though trade did not mean trading[11]), and a hundred trades, all different but analogous, could teach one what good workmanship was, what tests would reveal slipshod and bungled work, what was meant by the maker's responsibility, what standards would be expected of oneself when one chose one's own trade. And though there are some refinements of workmanship whose perfect appraisal belongs to the workman himself and to the most enlightened patron ("Who but the Rāja and the goldsmith should know the value of the jewel?"), yet a society such as this provided at least those indispensable grounds of good judgement which so sadly are lacking now; the intelligent maker was also the intelligent user and buyer, and the general interchange fostered that sympathy which draws "the good singer to the good scribe"[12]. But the community of a hundred years ago was already in social decadence and was soon to decay further. The children crowding about the blacksmith then had had ancestors who had crowded about the builders, painters and glassmakers of the village church, makers whose way of making was strange enough to the nineteenth century; and the next generation might see the blacksmith go. Once begun, such disintegration spreads insensibly. The Cotswold farmer whose house was traditionally well tiled has sons who have never seen a tiler at work; for them or their sons again the old tiles are no more than a curiosity which may be left to dilapidate or sold to a collector. What the village loses from its inheritance is something more than the visible and material; another sermon has gone with the stones, and kinship with crafts and craftsmen has faded further towards extinction.[13]

Our own generation has reached the last limits of remoteness from everything that is meant by the crafts. To the mass of the population village life is unknown, and if through necessity or for pleasure some numbers return to the countryside, the chances are now against their finding the vestiges of a working tradition. Few country places have kept a mason or smith, a wheelwright or carpenter; and where will one find them all together? Some purely agricultural crafts—hedging, for instance, and rick-making—are still everywhere practised, but they pass unrecognized by the townsman, who as likely as not mistakes their operations for those of nature. As for the crafts of the town, in the nature of things they still exist—in traditional or in untraditional fashion, the things we use must all be made somewhere—but who in a great town of today is likely to know the whereabouts of the silversmiths and the carpet-makers, the printers, the saddlers, the potters? Or suppose their workshops found; how could one summon courage to go inside and talk with the men, to see them using their hands and hear from the elders what changes in their manner of work had been brought by the machine? Modern customs forbid so human a proceeding; the small workshop is as a rule inaccessible, and with it a fund of knowledge which neither the studio nor the factory can supply. For those who seriously wish to understand the crafts it remains to glean what experience they can from such direct contact as it is possible to make; to approach the matter respectfully, aware that the principles which they see applied in one or two crafts have been and are applied with characteristic differences in a multitude of others; and to supplement these slender resources by studying authentic records of traditional craftsmanship in its natural environment—such things as Sturt's *Wheelwright's Shop,* Rose's *Village Carpenter,* Benfield's *Purbeck Shop,* the chapter on craftsmen in Massingham's *English Countryman* and (further afield and with ampler background), Coomaraswamy's *Indian Craftsman,* Marco Pallis' *Peaks and Lamas,* and Firth's *Art and Life in New Guinea.* Without some such preamble it is hard indeed for the great number of men today—for the intelligentsia no less than the laity—to enter far into the thought of Eric Gill and to reconcile as he did the notions of artist and workman, art and work.

Work—the whole doctrine of it is central to his philosophy, a stumbling-block to the doubter, a growing illumination to those who once accept it. What I have said already has touched the arts in a merely external way; I have been concerned with the spectator's point of view. But true art, in Lethaby's words, "is *the evidence of the workman's joy in his work.* Art should be looked on not as enjoyment and luxury to the buyer, but as life and breath to the maker—and extend the idea to cover everything of quality and goodness in things made by hands, and further to beautiful care of the tilled earth." When the nature of work is misunderstood, the nature of art is also misunderstood.

"As an indispensable means towards gaining over the world that mastery which God wishes for his glory, all work has an inherent dignity and at the same time a close connection with the perfection of the person. This is the noble dignity and privilege of work, which is not in any way cheapened by the fatigue and the burden which has to be borne, as the effect of original sin, in obedience and submission to the will of God." This pronouncement of Pius XII[14] applies without exception to all kinds of work which it naturally falls to man to perform. To use human powers to impose order on things, to transform existing material in accordance with human will, to shape what is outside oneself to something determined by oneself—that is work, Adam's privilege, the privilege of the human person, without which the person is incomplete. To suffer fatigue in so doing, to be able to do less than one would, to feel continually the weariness of the flesh—that is Adam's curse, though it too has lost its sting through the labour of Christ in the workshop and Mary in the home.

Work, in general—the humblest as well as the highest kind—has in traditional teaching been regarded as a means to asserting human dignity and to the collaboration of man with Heaven. This is signified by Christopher Smart in his symbolism of the third pillar of knowledge for the third day of creation.

> Eta with living sculpture breathes,
> With verdant carvings, flow'ry wreathes
>  Of never-wasting bloom;
> In strong relief his goodly base
> All instruments of labour grace,
>  The trowel, spade, and loom.

In ancient civilizations outside our own tradition the same view of things has been explicitly held—above all in regard to agriculture, as the most fundamental and primary kind of work. Hence those solemn inaugurations of ploughing or harvesting by a traditional ruler—the most famous example comes from China, but there are others elsewhere.[15] In contrast with this is the opinion—characteristic of decadent civilizations and therefore of ours—that work with one's hands is a degrading necessity and that man is ennobled by its avoidance.

This hostility to the notion of work comes partly of course from softness and partly from snobbishness; it was so in ancient Greece, it is so today.[16] But deeper than this is a Manichaean attitude to the world, reluctance to view the physical universe as good and holy in all its parts, distrust of common things and of common men. Those who honour the man of genius at the expense of mankind may be expected to behave similarly towards material things. To certain men a mountain is venerable, but the soil is merely dirt; the sculptor's stone, the engraver's wood are materials to be respected, but not so other stone or wood. For them it is unbelievable that a lifetime may be well and happily spent in learning, in mastering and in using the qualities of these common things, in leaving on them the mark of one's own mind and will. Yet that is the privilege of the responsible workman, who knows that each thing, like each person, has its own nature, and that this nature must be "humoured, not drove". That is why things made by men's hands have the character of humanity—something otherwise unobtainable, something which, more than beauty, is the endearing property of true art.

It follows that much in men's labour which to those outside may appear monotonously repetitive is to the workman himself the continuance of an intimacy which he has no desire to break off—much like a conversation in French, uncomprehendingly overheard. Here are reflections by a quarryman on a parson's remark to a fellow-worker ("You must find it *very* monotonous work, eh?"). "Not only was the parson seeing the successful result of lifelong training, there was the knowledge of centuries behind it. The quarry itself was the planning of one man's life. Slowly yet surely he had lengthened his workings until he had surrounded an area of stone so that no other quarry should be able to cut in on it. Not one block came out of it without bringing a sense of satisfaction because it was in proper order and according to plan. Yet because a stranger saw a man punching away at a square stone for half an hour he had to suggest it was boring work. Evidently he did not know the interest in making something permanent; a stone that will go into a building and there outlast many generations can hardly be without some interest to the producer."[17]

Observe that the parson would have remained within his rights had he said that *he* would have found the work unbearable; and a farmer or sailor might reasonably have said the same thing, and as reasonably have been told by the quarryman that a parson's or farmer's or sailor's work would have been so to him. No one suggests that any and every man should find any and every sort of work congenial; on the contrary, every man to his trade, on the understanding that every other trade in its proper and natural conditions is fit for someone and is consonant with human dignity. But this draws implications with it. It implies in the first place every man's right to the free choice of a way of life, to the exercise of that function which he has natural ability to fulfil. This point has been urged by the present Pope, and it rests on the teaching of St. Thomas[18]: "The principles of government would be flouted if men were kept by their ruler from exercising their proper functions (unless, it may be, exceptionally, in temporary crisis)." But in our present society—in peace as in war—this is just the fate of masses of men; supposing them to find work at all, and supposing it to be good in itself, it is still not their own choice, and one man's work is another's drudgery.

There is a further implication. Work which in itself and in its natural conditions is good and honourable and rational may become the contrary of all this through perversion of the conditions. This may be so if some task which in a normal society would be a brief incident in a day's varied work is made by unnatural specialization to become a life's employment, which it never was meant to be. It may be so if for penal or economic reasons potentially useful labour is deliberately made useless.[19] And again it may be so if the nature and purpose of certain work is distorted by the use of machines.

With this mention of machines we come to the "last wave" of controversy. It is widely thought that Eric Gill was simply "against machinery", and that there the matter ends. Let me reply with one quotation. "Obviously machinery as such is consistent with Christianity, though many machines may be used for objects which are inconsistent with Christianity." That sentence from one of his earliest essays[20] expresses a view which he found no occasion to withdraw, though he returned to it continually with amplifications and distinctions. I will summarize the results.

Clear thought on the matter of machines requires a preliminary distinction between their invention and their use. It is as inventions that they make their most plausible appeal—as proofs of the ingenuity of the human mind; and it is commonly said that it would be foolish or sinful not to use these visible triumphs of man's peculiar faculties. But that is an illegitimate leap in argument. It is only for its speculative achievement that any invention is good in itself. When the inventor can say "The nature of physical forces being such, mathematical relations being such, these materials being such, a thing so made will act thus and thus"—he has brought an accession to human knowledge which, great or small, is independent of any practical application. But in this sense, and other things being equal, a new and more deadly poison gas is as creditable to its inventor as a new and more potently healing drug; and here the least thinking mind begins to discriminate. The principle is the same for machines. Granting them all to be more or less ingenious, it is still an open question whether a given machine is worth using, whether what it does is worth doing, whether it works more good or harm.

What then do machines do? What are they for? Some do things worth doing which otherwise could not be done at all. Such is a clock—it is not an improved sundial but something really different; and though the provision of mechanical time has had some effects of doubtful good, it would be unreasonable to deprecate the invention. Eric Gill certainly did not. Some machines, again, do things which might be done otherwise, but do them with an increase of speed which for some reason may be thought specially valuable. To this class belong, perhaps, some kinds of medical apparatus, and more obviously machines of transport. Approval of these is subject to one's considering the necessity for the speed; speed is far from a good in itself, and the exploitation of rapid travel has been principally disastrous; nevertheless one might admit exceptionally what one disapproved as a rule. With such machines Eric Gill was not particularly concerned. But there is another class of them—probably the largest—which was very much his concern: those which supplant the human hand in the making of things. Their defenders call them more perfect and more developed tools; to which he replied with an irreproachable distinction.[21] Tools, he said, were means of helping a man to make a thing; machines were means of making which had to be helped by the man. "If you are responsible for the form and quality of the thing made, then whatever apparatus you use is a tool rather than a machine. And as that responsibility diminishes, so the apparatus becomes more and more a machine until the point is reached when, as with the latest automatic machinery, the machinist has no responsibility whatever." To put it another way—a tool is an instrument of precision because it enables the user of it to do precisely what he intends with the particular work in hand; it serves, as his bare hands could not, his idea of the thing to be made; it can be adapted to the individuality of the material. A machine may seem an instrument of precision; it is not one, for it cannot enable its user to approach more closely his own idea; it can only force on the material a shape invented by someone else without reference to the work in hand.

Consider this in the light of an example—that of a wheelwright making felloes half a century since.[22] "The tools were axe and adze and sometimes hand-saw, and the implements (besides a square) a chopping-block and a felloe-horse. Yet it is vain to go into details at this point; for when the simple apparatus had all been got together, a never-ending series of variations was introduced by the material. . . . Knots here, shakes there, rind-galls, waney edges (edges with more or less of the bark in them), thicknesses, thinnesses, were for ever affording new chances or forbidding previous solutions, whereby a fresh problem confronted the

workman's ingenuity every few minutes. He had no band-saw (as now) to drive, with ruthless unintelligence, through every resistance. The timber was far from being a prey, a helpless victim, to a machine. Rather it would lend its own subtle virtues to the man who knew how to humour it. . . . At the bench you learn where a hard knot may be even helpful and a wind-shake a source of strength in a felloe. . . . " Contrast with such work as this the processes of a modern factory where the "ruthless unintelligence" of the band-saw has in fact ousted the intelligence of ten or twenty or fifty men. It is clear in the first place that the work done on the timber is not the same work. The machine does not and cannot do the work of so many wheelwrights or carpenters; it supplants them without replacing them; its products are essentially makeshifts. Secondly it is clear that the workmen at the machine are not the same kind of men as those who had used their hands and tools. The work is no longer "life and breath to the maker", the core of a human vocation sufficient to itself; the slight moral responsibility left to the machine-minder is no substitute for the full moral and full intellectual responsibility of the true workman; and if in some cases the machinist may still seem to "rejoice in his labour", this is either because of the human intercourse which accidentally accompanies it, or at best because of a schoolboy pleasure in handling big machines which rests on sheer ignorance of the scope and nature of adult human work. Who then, or what, has gained by the change? Not the timber itself, which has been clumsily maltreated. Not the user, who must accept less suitable and less lasting goods. Not the worker, whose personality has been stunted. Only the factory owner, who has lessened his costs by the degradation of men and material; and even he has not much advanced towards gaining his own soul.

What is true of this example would seem to be true of most, and the plea of Eric Gill was not for the indiscriminate abolition of machines but against their indiscriminate acceptance. Granted that certain things which are called machines have something left of the qualities of a tool; granted that a particular machine may have very special advantages to set against disadvantages; let this and let every case be considered on its merits. Is the use of this or that machine compatible with good workmanship, with the real benefit of the consumer, with the dignity and responsibility of the workman? Are the things made things worth making? What of this "labour-saving device"? The urban housewife who uses it escapes an hour of rational work, but are not the makers of it condemned to a lifetime of irrational drudgery? These are fundamental questions, and they are not answered by the comfortable assertion that "the machine has come to stay". In a reasonable and humane society machines—and inventions generally—would not be allowed to stay if their use ran counter to the real interests of the community. And there is nothing intrinsically impossible in the control of such things. The Chinese invented gunpowder without an immediate sequel of irresponsible destruction; they invented printing but did not uproot calligraphy; they invented the tempered scale and yet retained the traditional modes. In the modern world a number of inventions have been temporarily or permanently suppressed through commercial covetousness. Is all restriction unthinkable in the cause of good work, social justice and the dignity of the human person?

Such in brief was Eric Gill's attitude to our industrial society. Apart from misapprehensions of detail, it often evoked the general criticism that one who thus viewed the modern world was so remote from the practical and the practicable that his message could but be vain; that he himself could not possibly live in accordance with his principles; and that his greatness was after all of the kind he so often depreciated, that of a genius in the fine arts, to be remembered for certain sculptures, engravings, drawings, and for lettering in stone which was the best for centuries. To this the most general answer is that if a man is a prophet at all, he is to be judged primarily by the truth of what he says, not by the numbers of those who act upon it. He addresses himself to human beings possessed of free-will; he says: "The state of things is not as you think but is thus and thus; if you do not change, your fate will be this or that." He knows the truth and is bound to speak it; what ensues must rest with others. The city to which he speaks may perhaps repent in sackcloth and ashes; perhaps it may perish utterly; perhaps a few will escape from the burning. The prophet's greatness, the prophet's duty, remain the same. And it is important to note that though Eric Gill's ideas were counter to modern customs and assumptions, they were never counter to human nature; he did not suppose that man could be naturally perfect or that malice and original sin would somehow be outgrown. The kind of society he believed in was something that had existed historically in many times and places; and however unlikely an early return to it might be, an eventual return (with whatever modifications) was a possibility which could only be denied by those who denied free-will.

On such likelihood or unlikelihood he took different views at different times—in his last years he had little hope indeed. Meanwhile he was always eager to find a palliative for particular evils, to propose a second best as possible here and now, though it must be inevitably on a lower plane of things than the real best. This was in accord with his practice in the immediate work of engraving or type-designing; if a client rejected what he thought best himself, he would patiently listen to suggestions and use them if he could. They might do much less than justice to the true nature of the work, but provided they were not quite absurd, provided they left to be done something at least worth doing, he would submit to them with a cheerful resignation. In a like spirit he advocated some social measures which in a really Christian society would not be called for—workmen's ownership when there seemed little expectation of widely diffused private property, monetary reform when Christian poverty seemed too distant a goal.

Possessing such practical tolerance, he found no great difficulty about consistent living within an alien society. The first thing was to see and accept the truth; the next, if society allowed one (and it allowed him) to do one's own work in a human and responsible way; after that, to encourage others to see and work in the same manner; finally, in supplying one's needs, to rely as much as possible on those of like thinking, but where reasonable possibility failed, to look elsewhere without superstitious scruple. If one's own friends and the local small tradesmen could meet one's ordinary necessities, it would be unjust and foolish to disregard their claims. But if something one needed was to be had now only from towns, only from the big shops, only as made by machines, one saw to it that it was good of its kind and bought it without ado. "What about travelling by train?" innocent undergraduates would ask, and could scarcely believe it was not a poser.

To those who knew him, to those who followed him, the greatness of Eric Gill must be essentially different from that of those whom the world calls artists. He made indeed more things of beauty than it is often given to men to make, but to understand him one has to pass through art and beyond. When I think of Eric Gill, I think of the words of Christopher Smart: "In my nature I quested for beauty, but God, God hath sent me to sea for pearls."

NOTES

[1] *Last Essays* (1942): *In a Strange Land* (1944). Jonathan Cape. 5s. and 6s.

[2] It is reproduced in Graham Carey's *Pattern* (John Steven's Pamphlets, Rhode Island, 1938).

[3] "Art must be everywhere. It cannot exist in isolation, or only one man thick. It must be a thousand men thick." (W. R. Lethaby.)

[4] "This is, in fact, the diagnosis of the shortcoming of all our modern individualistic art, that seven-eighths of it is the work of men who ought to be servants, and not masters; while the work of the one-eighth (if there be so large a proportion of genius) is necessarily intelligible only to a very small audience." (Coomaraswamy, *Arts and Crafts of India and Ceylon* (1913), p. 24.)

[5] Even today, there remain some painters who stand outside the heresy of "pure form" and who do communicate intellectual content as understood above; they therefore escape the circumscription which other painters impose on themselves, but not that imposed by the character of the age itself.

[6] In the welter of modern aesthetic schools it is difficult to generalize, but contempt of natural beauty is fashionable in places. "Real flowers!" said an eminent French engraver to an otherwise "modern" hostess. "How vulgar! I will make you some in mother-of-pearl." On the

other hand, there are those who collect mineral and vegetable formations of suitably "significant form" to range with their Henry Moores. As for metaphysics among the devotees of fine art, it is better to be silent.

[7] *De reductione artium.*

[8] Some women in judging pictures appear to see the colours as those of dress materials, deploring "clashes" which do not exist in the paints as such. On the other hand, some aesthetes criticize colours in nature, supposing them to be would-be paints.

[9] I should perhaps make it clear that what follows is a composite picture, not a particular portrait.

[10] A reviewer of *Last Essays* reproved its author for "his failure to distinguish between the useful and the fine arts", but praised the accompanying engravings under the designation of "woodcuts".

[11] Cf. Pepys: "At home practising to sing, which is now my great trade" (*Diary,* 12 June, 1661).

[12] St. Thomas, *S.T.,* I-II, 27, 3, ad. 2.

[13] I find that Dr. Coomaraswamy has given a similar instance from Ceylon. "The capacity for good work in making and laying tiles is dying out, so that it is increasingly difficult to get it, and a majority of persons scarcely are aware that good work was ever done, or can recognize it when they see it." (*Mediaeval Sinhalese Art* (1908), p. 228.)

[14] Allocution of Christmas Eve, 1942. Cf. Ecclesiasticus vii, 16: "Hate not laborious works, or husbandry ordained by the Most High."

[15] The classic passage for China is from the *Record of Rites.* "The Son of Heaven in his own person, taking the plough in his carriage of state, leads the Three Dukes, the Nine Ministers, the great Lords and the high officers of state to plough the field of God. Three furrows the Son of Heaven turns up, five furrows the Dukes, nine furrows the ministers and lords. They return, and in the great chamber with the dukes, ministers, lords, and officers all in waiting, the goblet is lifted and the word given, 'The wine of labour'." (Hughes' translation.) Compare the following for Ceylon: "Great chiefs were not ashamed to hold the plough in their own hands, and it was thought becoming for the young men to reap at least a part of the harvest every year; for which damascened and ivory-handled sickles were sometimes used." (Coomaraswamy, *Mediaeval Sinhalese Art,* p. 29.)

[16] Physical softness may go quite well with the cult of athletics, as Socrates was aware.

[17] Eric Benfield, *Purbeck Shop* (1940), pp. 88-9.

[18] *C.G.,* III, 71.

[19] "The workers from the National Workshops who were set the task of wheeling about soil on the Champ de Mars just to keep them employed, were not slow to become the rioters of June. Dostoevsky's convict, compelled to move tree trunks in the morning and in the evening put them back in their original positions, underwent the tortures of hell itself. Work of which the worker knows the futility and which deprives effort of its normal purpose is nothing more than slavery. (Borne and Henry, *A Philosophy of Work,* chap. 3.)

[20] "The Factory System and Christianity", *The Game,* Advent 1918.

[21] Cf. *Sacred and Secular* (1940), pp. 102-6.

[22] George Sturt, *The Wheelwright's Shop* (1934), p. 45.

### Donald Attwater (essay date 1947)

SOURCE: "Eric Gill," in *Modern Christian Revolutionaries: An Introduction to the Lives and Thought of Kierkegaard, Eric Gill, G.K. Chesterton, C.F. Andrews, Berdyaev,* The Devin-Adair Company, 1947, pp. 161-228.

[*In the following excerpt, Attwater discusses Gill's life and beliefs, and delineates his unique brand of socialism.*]

Arthur Eric Rowton Gill was born on February 22nd, 1882, at Brighton, and his first home was in a suburban street of this town which he afterwards characterized as a shapeless and meaningless mess. He was the second of thirteen children. His father was a minister of that small sect, "connection," called after its foundress, Selina, Countess of Huntingdon, and he was a man of earnestness, culture and probity, of a type very common in nineteenth-century England. Eric had other ecclesiastical associations: not only did he marry the daughter of the sacristan of Chichester cathedral, but his paternal grandfather and great-uncle were missionaries in the South Seas, as were two of his brothers and one sister. When the present writer first knew him, after the war of 1914-18, he would often disclaim any missionary enterprise for his own convictions, but as the years passed he became in fact more and more of a missionary, "publicist," and would sometimes with a wry smile refer to his family tradition in playful extenuation.

But this was not the only, or the most important, thing concerning which early influences persisted. Unlike so many "rebels" from the English middle and professional class, Eric Gill never (except possibly for a brief period in his youth) deliberately cut himself off from his origins; particularly did he never foul the nest of his own family and upbringing. I have said that his father was a typical Victorian, and it has been acutely noted by David Jones that Eric himself was, in a way, a Victorian person—not least in his solid sincerity and high seriousness, combined with a gay frolicsomeness such as is found in the mathematician Dodgson or in Lear (Edward, not the Shakespearian king). The Gill household was a happy one, and it was poor, really poor, from the point of view of ways and means; so far was this from having an embittering effect on Eric (or, I believe, on any of them) that it was the practical starting-point of his own repudiation of worldly wealth and his attachment to a decent poverty as a fundamental necessity for any good revolution, personal or social. It was a cultured family—the father had some skill as a painter, the mother as a singer, and a glance at their children's names shows their literary interests (Eric, "or Little by Little," Kingsley, Carlyle, Maurice, MacDonald, Roberston, Enid from Tennyson). But above all it was a religious family: "We took religion for granted just as we took the roof over our heads. . . . But taking things for granted doesn't mean you aren't interested in them or that, on occasion, you won't be very interested indeed" (*Auto.*, p. 59). And the religion was that combination of evangelical doctrine and upright conduct, combined both with strict domestic discipline and dissenting independence, that at its best has been so valuable a factor in making the modern English character: the "nonconformist conscience" is despicable only in its decay. The young Gills were brought up on virtuous principles, and "these principles were put before us in such a way as to win our assent to them—assent both notional and affective" (*Auto.*, p. 56).

Eric's schooling lasted some half-dozen years, in a private school at Brighton, and consisted solely of "learning things out of little books and being able to remember enough to answer questions." It made no particular impression on him, and he showed no special aptitude for book-learning: his real enthusiasms were cricket and football, not as competitive contests but as things worth doing for their own sake—games, and drawing locomotive engines. In later life he made no complaints against the sort of teaching he had received: rather was he thankful that his schoolmasters had been too timid or too uninterested to try to coerce his mind or to mould him against his proper nature. Naturally he came to have ideas on schooling: these he never had the opportunity to work out and develop (though he used them with startlingly good effect in bringing up his own family), but their foundation was that children should be given a good comprehensive view of the world in general, showing the growth and decay of peoples and nations in the light of man's spiritual nature and eternal destiny; and that the amount of formal learning to be done should be kept down to the lowest possible minimum, for we are educated, not by learning, but by *doing*—"that is, in my mind, the whole secret of education, whether in schools or in workshops or in life." He did not think it really matters much whether a person can read and write, and it seemed to him unreasonable "to burden the budding mind of a child with too much high intellectual stuff" about duty and culture and all that sort of thing. Mathematics was the school subject that most appealed to him: it called

for that accuracy and precision that had already been inculcated at home, it ministered to an appetite for orderliness that was to increase with his years. The *Autobiography* gives a strong impression that the young Eric was an intelligent, observant, sensitive boy, in no way "freakish," healthy in mind and body, whose favourite author was G. A. Henty.

> "The children of large families, especially when the parents are poor, do not complain with bitterness because they go short of clothes, firing or food. Unless their minds are poisoned by jealousy or covetousness, they regard all such hardships as being part of the game of life, and, as is well known, no people are happier than the children of the large families of poor parents when those parents are engaged in humane occupations, even under hard conditions, provided that the parents are examples of justice and charity" (*Belief*, p. 222).

When he wrote those lines Eric Gill certainly had his own early home in mind. "The shepherd boy who helps his father in the cold nights of the lambing season does not curse the physical universe and refuse to attend church or chapel on Sunday." During the past couple of generations many comfortably-circumstanced (and other) people have refused to attend church or chapel—"abandoning institutional religion" it is called—for various reasons, often cogent, often not; parallel with this phenomenon has been another, much smaller, less picturesque and fashionable and therefore less talked about, of people abandoning unbelief or an elastic undogmatic form of religion for one more vigorous, exacting and authoritative, in other words, seeking for a teaching church. When Eric Gill became a Roman Catholic in 1913 he went on from where his father had left off. Mr. Gill senior had resigned from the Congregationalists because he, the shepherd, would not have his religious message dictated to him by his flock; the Countess of Huntingdon's Connection received its doctrine "from above" ("which is the proper place for doctrine to come from"), embodied in the Anglican Book of Common Prayer; then, in 1897, he took the next step in the same direction and joined the Church of England, taking his family with him. This was an important date in his eldest son's life, not simply because Eric was taken away from school, at the age of fifteen, but because they all went to live at Chichester, and the effect of this city on the growing boy's mind was profound. Not because it was old (which it is) or "picturesque" (which it isn't) but because it was an ordered human thing: not a disorderly mess made by the speculative builder, like the Brighton suburb, but "a place, the product of reason and love. . . . Here was no dead product of mathematical calculation, no merely sanitary and convenient arrangement. Here was something as human as home and as lovely as Heaven. That was how it seemed to me. . . . " (*Auto.*, p. 77). For a time he studied drawing and lettering at the local art-school, but got considerably more out of his own drawing and exploration in the cathedral and from the wise friendship of one of its prebendaries, Doctor Robert Codrington. It was a time compounded of "rapture and rebellion"; the mental and physical surge of adolescence was disturbing him. So he became dissatisfied and unhappy, and after two years he was sent off to London to be apprenticed in the large drawing-office of an ecclesiastical architect.

The first three of the next five years was a period of disillusionment, disintegration and revolt, first against religious mugwumpery, then against social and political perversions, lastly against the fatuity and play-acting that passed for architecture. Eric Gill began to be interested in "revolution." "Religion in St. Saviour's, Clapham, and irreligion in the architect's office were unequally matched. Nothing in the outward show of that Christianity could possibly hold me—the frightful church, the frightful music, the apparently empty conventionality of the congregation. And nothing that the parson ever said seemed to imply any realization that the Church of England was in any way responsible for the intellectual and moral and physical state of London" (*Auto.*, p. 108). So he slid out of Anglicanism into a vague and hungry agnosticism, and seeing that most professional politics was as much a sham as a great deal of professional religion, that Parliament did not represent the people and laws were really made in boardrooms and private gatherings, he became in an equally nebulous way a socialist. But he kept his head. Youthful "emancipation" not seldom dissolves into licence, liberty is made a cloak for malice: young Gill did not take that easy path, if only, as he modestly implies, it did not look all that easy to him. As for architecture—and here too he owed much to the sensitive conscience and clear mind of a fellow draughtsman, George Carter—he soon saw that it was not the same thing as building and that the tyranny of the architect in his office had reduced the working mason and builder to the mere copying of things designed on paper in the smallest detail by other people. Such irrational and inhuman division of labour was not for him: he wanted to be a workman, with a workman's rights and duties, to design what was to be made and make what he had designed. What work that he could do was wanted? He soon found it—letter-cutting in stone. In the evenings he went to the writing-classes of that great man Edward Johnston; after twelve months he got his first small commission, and from that day forth was never out of a job. He just walked out of the architect's office.

In 1904, at the age of twenty-two, Eric Gill married, and set up house in a block of workmen's dwellings in Battersea. Before very long, after the birth of two daughters, they removed to Ditchling in their native county. There was no "back-to-the-land" sentiment behind this, though Eric always loved the life of the earth—and especially "the earth that man has loved, for his daily work and the pathos of his plight"—and Mary his wife was a farmwife by second nature. What was behind it was the conviction from experience that a big city was no place in which to bring up children.

" . . . we were not only able to marry young . . . but also . . . I was subjected to the influence of marriage without the complications of suburban snobbery and domestic indignity. . . . Marriage meant babies—if it weren't for babies there wouldn't be marriage. . . . But the consequences are momentous. You are no longer simply concerned to discover what conditions are best for your work (that which you do for your living—*i.e.*, in return for the bread and butter you eat) and what conditions are best for your comfort, you are concerned to discover what conditions are best for a growing family" (*Auto.*, pp. 132-34).

Meanwhile the inscription-cutting and tombstone business was prospering, and Gill's skill brought him to the notice of such as Roger Fry and found him a friend and customer in Count Kessler, of Weimar. In 1909, with much diffidence and trepidation, he made his first essay in stone-carving, a female figure, and this new venture at once drew more attention to him. Sculptors nowadays mostly *model* their statuary, building it up in clay, and then have this model reproduced in stone by a professional carver with various machines and gadgets: here was a man who carved his thing himself directly out of the stone; one, moreover, who thought in terms of stone (not of clay) and of carving (not of modelling). "So all without knowing it I was making a little revolution. I was reuniting what should never have been separated: the artist as man of imagination and the artist as workman . . . I really was like the child who said 'first I think and then I draw my think'—in contrast with the art-student who must say, 'First I look and then I draw my look.' Of course the art critics didn't believe it. How could they? They thought I was putting up a stunt—being archaic on purpose. Whereas the real and complete truth was that I was completely ignorant of all their art stuff and was childishly doing my utmost to copy accurately in stone what I saw in my head. . . . " (*Auto.*, p. 162). Despite this misunderstanding the "art world" opened its doors to receive him; Epstein and John, Ambrose McEvoy and William Rothenstein were among his friends; he was "given the opportunity to become acquainted at close quarters with the leading intellectual and artistic folk of our great empire"—and then, not for the first or last time, Gill saw himself standing at the edge of a yawning pit of danger, and drew back: or rather, not scorning the tactics of the Desert Fathers or St. Benedict, he ran away, "escaped."

> Among the artists "there was no smell of burning boats—burning boats was the one thing no fellow should do. I think it might not unfairly be said that they all believed in beauty, were interested in truth and had doubts about the good. . . . I was so very much not the artist as they were artists, and though I was an agnostic in those days I was so very much not the sceptic as they were sceptics. . . . They most certainly believed in something called Art and I most certainly did not, and I came more and more to detest the whole art world. I believed in religion and was desperately trying to find it, and they seemed to regard religion as being essentially nonsense but valuable as a spur

to aesthetic experience and activity. . . . I say I did not believe in Art or the art world. But of course I believed very much in the arts—with a small a and an s—whether it be the art of cooking or that of painting portraits or church pictures. But that's a very different matter and puts the 'artist' under the obligation of knowing *what* he is making and *why*. It ranks him with the world of workmen doing useful jobs. And as for the art *world,* well, that is even more sickening, especially when all the snobbery of intellectual distinction comes in. . . . Everybody was extremely kind and refined—and distinguished, but 'I'd rather be a heathen suckled in a creed outworn. . . . ' On the other hand, in yet another sense, I believed in art very much indeed. The artist as prophet and seer, the artist as priest—art as man's act of collaboration with God in creating, art as *ritual*—these things I believed very earnestly. But here again I was generally at variance with my high-art friends. Their views were both more simple and more mysterious than mine. They were essentially aesthetes: that was the awful truth. They played about with religion and philosophy and labour politics, but that was all very superficial; what they really believed in and worked for was aesthetic emotion as understood by the art critics. But art as the ritual expression of religion I did indeed believe in and they did not. . . . So I gradually escaped from the high-art world which for a time seemed to be closing round me. Doubtless I never was a serious artist as serious art was understood in that world. I was the son of a nonconformist parson, the grandson of a missionary. Life was more than art" (*Auto.,* pp. 172-74).

The last two sentences are among the most significant pieces of self-revelation in all Gill's *Autobiography*. But before that repudiation could be complete, before he could become a citizen of a new and whole world, another and final crisis—"the end is the beginning"—had to be passed.

．．．．．

Gill was in process of solving—*solvitur ambulando*—the problem of work; but he was also faced with the problem of social injustice, and that depended on religion. There was the evil of having too little material goods and the evil of having too much, of bossing and of being bossed: where did this evil arise and what was the remedy? He knew that socialism could answer neither question correctly, but was convinced that somewhere, somehow, religion could. But he had cut himself off from the religion of his childhood, and had no reason to suppose that Christianity could be the cure for the world's sickness.

"The churches seemed to be concerned solely with their sectarian games—they hardly seemed to be interested even in feeding the hungry. And if you could not count on the parsons to help to redress even common cruelties and injustices, how much less could you count on them in deeper matters? For that was how it struck me, and that was why

eventually I had to leave the Fabian Society also, for I could not believe that charity was the flowering of justice, but, on the contrary it seemed to me, all inarticulate though I was and quite utterly unable to express the matter, that justice was the flowering of charity." Hunt's Abu ben Adhem was all wrong. "You couldn't profess to love your fellow men and know no more. It was damned impudence to start with—damned pharisaism too. I give tithes of all I possess; I give alms—see, boys, in short, how I love my fellow men. That was not at all what was meant when it was said: How can you love God whom you have not seen, if you do not love your neighbour whom you have seen? It means that you must *start* by loving God and, in the light of that love, in that light of love—for God *is* love—and as its necessary and inevitable fruit, you must love your neighbour. But you must love God first. Otherwise your neighbour-love would be a wrong kind of love; it would turn out to be no love at all or simply self-love" (*Auto.,* pp. 151-52).

The churches "seemed to be doing precisely what was forbidden—professing to love God whom they had not seen and yet bearing no fruit in love of neighbours. Their God-love was suspect. Their God himself was suspect. But, on the other hand, my friends, the socialists, were in no better case." They professed love of their neighbour and nescience of God's existence, so how could their love be well founded? Their concrete demands were endless, from higher wages to higher studies, from baths to abolition of privilege; and this conception of a "soup-kitchen world" was opposed, not because it was godless, but because it would cut down profits.

"You can't just demand justice for the poor and leave it at that. You must find out who are the poor and what is 'who,' and what is justice that the poor should be given it." It's no good agitating for municipal housing till you have made up your mind what sort of a being it is that has got to be housed. "Is it conceivable that he is a temple of the Holy Ghost? But what the devil is that? And what kind of housing can possibly be his suitable shrine?" (*Auto.,* p. 154). Religion is the first thing necessary; without it there is no answer to the primary and fundamental questions, What is man, and why? But Gill had no religion, and all the ready-made ones were wrangling among themselves, so that even of the Christian churches no two seemed to answer the questions alike. There was therefore nothing for it but for him to make up a religion for himself, or rather a metaphysic, a preamble to religion (considering it schematically).[1] And then he began to discover, very slowly and gradually, that his new invention was an old one. "To invent" means to come upon, to find, to uncover; and what Gill was inventing was, to his surprise and indeed alarm, stripped of all real or assumed irrelevancies, Roman Catholicism.

"I did not think so to start with. In fact I thought I was doing quite the opposite. I thought the Christianity of the churches was dead and finished, and surely one can be forgiven for thinking so. The effect of Christianity in the world seemed non-existent, and I knew of Roman Catholicism only by repute. I did not know any Roman Catholics and I hardly ever went into any Roman Catholic churches or even read Roman Catholic books; moreover what little I knew of Roman Catholicism from outward appearances was, in a general way, revolting. . . . I suppose nothing on earth is more completely and efficiently camouflaged than Peter's 'barque,' which, from a short distance, looks exactly like the Ritz Palace Hotel." But "I found a thing in my mind and I opened my eyes and found it in front of me. You don't become a Catholic by joining the Church; you join the Church because you are a Catholic" (*Auto.,* 166, 93, 170).

And so in 1913, on his thirty-first birthday, Eric Gill and his wife and three children were received into the Roman Catholic Church.

I am not writing an *apologia pro vita sua* in the sense of that phrase canonized by John Henry Newman (or, for that matter, in any sense). But Gill's becoming a Catholic (or as I, writing as a Roman Catholic, would prefer to put it, his coming into visible fellowship with the Church) was certainly the most important, the most formative, the most integrating and creative factor in his life:[2] and I say this not as a pious *cliché* or expression of sectarian partiality, but as a plain fact which must be patent to anyone who knew him or who studies his work. Moreover his action in this regard has at times been misunderstood or even, in perfect good faith, misrepresented. A little more must therefore be said about it, and first, that Gill was never, at any time of his life, an ecclesiastically-minded layman, in the depreciatory sense of that expression; I would even dare to say, at the risk of being misunderstood, that he was not "interested in religion"—but he was passionately in love with God.

"I was never interested in all the stuff my high-church brothers and their friends went in for—synods and councils and the thirty-nine articles of religion, and ritual and vestments and the episcopal succession. That all seemed twaddle to me, and I wasn't interested in the anti-catholic stuff either—Pope Joan and Maria Monk and the Spanish Inquisition, medieval corruption, cardinals' mistresses, superstition and pious frauds. I knew, surely everyone knows, that a man can be a holy man, a good man and an intelligent man, and yet be covered with sores, have a shocking temper and be subject to all the temptations of the flesh" (*Auto.,* p. 170). Religion means the rule of God, and Gill had a vision of a holy church ruling the world in the name of God—not a theocracy in a political but in a personal sense; speaking as one having authority—not authoritarian in principle (whatever the appearance and practice to the contrary), not answering every difficult or tom-fool question, but saying quietly and firmly "*This* is the way of the Lord," and putting the responsibility on her children to walk in it. So it was not professional apologetics or intellectual wrestling or that mythical[3] "aesthetic appeal" or that desire to "escape into an imposed

certainty" (of which so much is heard) that persuaded Gill he had found the Church of God: like many another, he found as many problems to cope with after he became a Catholic as before, only they were different problems; as for books, "if any mere book did do anything to make me a Catholic, it is *Bishop Blougram's Apology,*" which had been put before him as an anti-Catholic tract. How then did he become convinced? His own account tells us little and that little is not very clear—as is to be expected, for faith and the coming of faith are little more "patient of dialectial exposition" than is God himself. "I would not have anyone think that I became a Catholic because I was *convinced* of the truth, though I *was* convinced of the truth. I became a Catholic because I fell *in love* with the truth, and love is an experience. I saw. I heard. I felt. I tasted. I touched. And that is what lovers do" (*Auto.,* p. 247). Certainly he was deeply impressed by the fruits that Christianity had borne amid the corruptions of the dark and middle ages—and there was the Gospel.

> "I had been brought up on the Gospel, so of course I can't say what effect that book would have had on me if it had been possible to approach it entirely from outside. It might be more impressive or it might be less. It is impossible to tell. But the mere fact that you've been brought up with a thing doesn't necessarily give it an unfair pull over your mind. I don't see why it should. It might work just the other way. All I know is that I felt like the prodigal son. I had been away, squandering my substance in riotous living—not with women and wine, though that would have been nice, but with riotous young minds and the wine of strong words—and now I was, in a manner of speaking, coming home. . . . 'The Church proceeds confidently in her doctrine of God'—and not only that, but her doctrine of God inspires confidence. Perhaps the reader doesn't think so. To me it was obvious. The Christ of the Gospel was the Christ of the Church in spite of all the funny stuff—Vatican paraphernalia, 'respository art,' and heathen superstition masquerading as Christian revelation. I boasted to myself that I could see the wood quite plainly in spite of the trees" (*Auto.,* pp. 182-3).

But on pages 193-4 of the *Autobiography,* in the course of an account of a visit to the Benedictine monastery of Mont César at Louvain, there is what seems to this writer a most significant passage. Eric attended one of the conventual offices in the church.

> "At the first impact I was so moved by the chant, which you must remember I had never heard a note of in my life before, as to be almost frightened. . . . This was something alive, living, coming from the hearts and minds and bodies of living men. It was as though God were continuing the work of creation here and now, and I was there to hear, to see—even almost to touch. . . . There, at Louvain, after the slow procession of incoming monks and the following short silence when I first, all unprepared and innocent, heard 'Deus in adjutorium . . .' I knew, infallibly, that God existed and was a living God—just as I knew him in the answering smile of a child or in the living words of Christ."

Many would set this down simply as emotionalism, therefore unreliable and of uncertain value, if not valueless: especially might this be said by those who do not know the timeless, "unearthly" quality of the chant of the Roman church—had it been the "Gloria" of the B-minor Mass or the "Credo" of Gretchaninov the objection would be weightier. And Gill seems to have anticipated the objection, for he goes on: "There is a palpable righteousness in the things that God has made and that man is God's instrument for making. Emotion follows—of course, inevitably, naturally, but emotion is that which is suffered. It is the suffering that follows knowledge. We may, and often do, forget the knowing and wallow only in the emotion. It is better to forget the emotion. And when I got home from Louvain I did forget it and I remembered only that Christianity was 'pas symbolique.'"

I know the man; I know the music; I know the occasion: I do not believe that that was emotionalism. The Spirit bloweth where and how he listeth; God is not bound by his own sacraments, he can make a sacrament, an outward vehicle of inward grace, of any created thing: and surely Eric Gill received a sacrament, a "charismatic sacrament," if such an expression be allowable, bearing the grace of light and faith, there in the abbey church of Mont César; the bodiless finger of God, clothed in the materiality of public corporate worship, touched him.

It has been said that all of the "denominational" disagreements of Christians flow from one fundamental disagreement about the nature of the Church. It seems that they can indeed be reduced to that and it is therefore worth looking at how the Church appeared to Eric Gill, a man whose convictions attracted people of widely differing views.

> "It has been said that the Church exists in order that words may have a meaning. That, in its ultimate essence, is what a church is, that by which how, when and why cease to be pragmatical catcalls and become intelligible symbols, symbols patient of interpretation" (**Belief,** p. 310). The Church is "a perfectly human institution, matter and spirit, and the primacy is of the spirit, therefore guided by the Holy Ghost, therefore the bride of Christ, therefore a divine institution also. . . . Just as, in my mind, the Christianity enunciated by St John and St Paul is the necessary complement of the Christianity enunciated by the other evangelists, so the Church as sacrificing priest is the necessary complement of the Church as the living voice. And just as Calvary was the necessary consummation of Christ's life, so the Eucharist is the necessary consummation of our life in him. . . . Our earthly life is symbolized by the bread and wine. Under the appearance of bread and wine God gives himself to us. Thus are we made sharers of his divinity who saw fit to share our humanity. Thus man, who was made in the beginning with the dignity of God's image, is yet more wonderfully renewed" (**Auto.,** pp. 190, 246).

Gill was the last man to confound things that should not be mixed up, to confuse the Church of God with the life and opinions of people, clerical or lay, who profess her membership. None saw more clearly than he the sectarianism (historically explainable) of many Roman Catholics in England, their obsession with such secondary issues as the "schools question," the efforts of their politics to convince an unnecessarily unbelieving generation that Catholics were as keen on the British Empire, mass-production, money-making and wireless culture as anybody else; their shocking complacency: "We alone were good and intelligent, and everyone else was in outer darkness: Protestants, heretics, and either fools or knaves. It was assumed that the Church was hated and Catholics absolutely basked in that hatred, wallowed in it."[4] But he saw no less clearly that the Roman church in England is "a living member of the Universal Church and knows a greatness and a wisdom and a holiness which is entirely unknown to the majority of English people" (**Auto.,** 209, 198).

The Church for Gill, then, was the church of the oldest Christian tradition—something which teaches the necessary truths about man's first beginning and last end, wherein fallen and divided man is united, restored and divinized, particularly in the sacramental meal which commemorates and continues the redeeming sacrifice of her Master and Lord.[5] No simply human assembly can do these things; she is divine. Her members on earth, members not in the sense of members of a club, but as a hand of the body or a branch of the tree, visibly or hiddenly united with her, are human: she is human.

Of what can be said against the Roman Catholic Church on her human side he was only too well aware—but "the world" was painfully apparent, even to the length of apostasy and betrayal, among the first Twelve themselves, yet who now would choose the alternative of following Herod and Pilate?

> "When you think of St Peter's and the toy soldiery, and the purple and lace of its fat wordly-looking prelates, and when you think of the subtle intangibilities and intransigencies of its diplomacy, it is not difficult to understand why people run away in a panic—what's it all got to do with the Man on the Ass, anyway? But to me the alternative was too clear to be missed or to be run away from. In fact both alternatives were too clear. The frightful, the truly frightful, horror of the corruption of the ancient Church was as nothing to the essential dirtiness, dirtiness in its very being and nature, of the industrial-capitalist world" (**Auto.,** p. 189).

So he answered the question, the "all-inclusive and final question," "Do you believe all that the holy Church teaches?" with an unhesitating "Yes." "But as to *what* she teaches on all the multiplication of funny subjects that we worry ourselves about, well, at the great risk, or rather, certainty of being thought both lazy and unscrupulous, I made up my mind to confine my attention to things that seemed fundamentally important and things that intimately concerned me" (*Auto.,* p. 191). Not for him to trouble his head about whether Jonah really lived inside a fish or whether Pope Honorius I taught heresy or whether Anglican orders are valid—or what "valid" means in that connection.

He had a strong glowing faith, but it was not the faith of a child or of the proverbial Breton peasant—because he was not a child or a Breton peasant. His was the faith of a man of more than common fineness of spirit and intellectual ability, and he had put away childish things. But his understanding of what are and what are not childish things differed greatly from that of the more complacent or unimaginative who quote St. Paul on that head—with the result that he was childlike in the sense of Christ's admonition. Playfulness was a trait in his character, "play" was one of his sacred words, and he loved to think of children—and grownups—playing before their Father in the streets of the Heavenly Jerusalem. But he would tolerate no prettifying of or toying with the majestic mysteries of the Christian faith and life: in his *Sacred and Secular* can be read a manly and adult application of the "little way" of St Teresa of Lisieux, and a book about the same simple young nun provoked him to a blistering review that was probably as near vituperation as he ever got.

. . . . .

For the next four years Gill was principally engaged in carving the fourteen panels called stations of the cross for Westminster Cathedral, the work which put him definitely in the front rank of contemporary English sculptors. Then—it was September, 1918—he was conscripted for the army. He was, of course, by now under no illusions about politics, but he had paid no particular attention to the causes and conduct of war or to the congruity or otherwise of Christians engaging in organized violence at the behest of the civil power: his attitude was that warfare and fighting was not his line of business, that if he were really wanted he would be fetched, and then he would go quietly. So he was drafted into the mechanical-transport section of the R.A.F. His military service lasted under four months, but it was a "monstrous and momentous experience." After four years of war the "people's army," especially on home-stations, had been thoroughly militarized and dehumanized, the recruits were unwilling and fed-up from the start (at one camp at which he was stationed there were several suicides a week), and Gill found himself, not with young rustics or tradesmen (in the proper sense of that word) or others with whom he had common interests, but with men from the suburbs of industrial towns, under the worst sort of n.c.o. "If I had not had that brief taste of army life I should never have known what it is like to be one of the 'submerged tenth,' an under-dog, a person of no use to anyone but as an instrument, a unit on a pay-sheet . . ." (*Auto.,* p. 205).

After his release Gill returned to work at Ditchling Common, where with friends and their families living in neighbouring houses there was in process of formation a society of Roman Catholics, a gild, bound by their common faith and common ideas about work and society: printing, stonecarving and carpentry were among their trades. The six years that followed are passed over in a very few pages of the *Autobiography,* but they were important in that they saw the beginning and development of Eric's association with the Order of Preachers. The members of the Ditchling gild, though living in independent households, soon found the need of some limited rule of life to be followed by all, and one or other of the third-orders, founded by the friars in the middle ages, was obviously indicated: their choice fell on that one which forms part of the Order of Preachers, "Black Friars," founded by St Dominic in 1215.[6] The principal work of this order is sufficiently indicated by its name: the Dominicans are essentially teachers, and in particular they are exponents of the philosophical and theological teaching and method of St Thomas Aquinas, himself a Dominican, the fine flower of the colossal Christian and intellectual rebirth of the thirteenth century.

Eric became an enthusiastic disciple of Aquinas. This must not be misunderstood. He was never an accomplished thomist, he was not even deeply read in St Thomas's works; he learned his teaching principally in the old way, by word of mouth, from the several Dominican friars who were his lifelong friends and admirers. "The starting-point of human progress," says Christopher Dawson, "is to be found in the highest type of knowledge—the intuition of pure being . . . man's development is not so much from the lower to the higher as from the confused to the distinct." The first need of our time, says Jacques Maritain, is an intellectual need, the need for clarity of understanding. "Good will is not so obviously wanting as good sense," glossed Gill, and agreed with Dawson and Maritain with passionate intensity. St Thomas as the philosopher of being, as pre-eminently the philosopher of common sense, as a mind of almost unearthly clarity, with a method to match it—that was what first attracted him; and then he found in St Thomas, stated and argued clearly and succinctly as nowhere else, the principles of God and man which Eric used with such devastating force (but not, alas! with corresponding effect) against the politico-industrial set-up of contemporary society. That, I think, both in life and teaching, was the principal preoccupation of the Ditchling days, to show Catholics in particular that the material basis of what is called twentieth-century civilization is fundamentally incompatible not simply with Christianity but with man's natural good: the groundwork was laid of that social teaching which for the rest of his life he put tirelessly, not only before his co-religionists, but before all who were willing to listen. And while Aquinas helped him with metaphysical and psychological principles, he found masterly statements of principles of practice and analyses of the evils of the day in the social pronouncements of two popes, Leo XIII and Pius XI, notably the encyclical-letters "Rerum novarum" and "Quadragesimo anno"; documents which, translated into turgid italianate English, explained and explained away time and again, used as slogans and stamping-ground for study clubs instead of springs of action, have lacked the influence they ought to have had in this country.

When his vigorous and mathematically-inclined mind first came under the influence of the presentation of Christianity which owes so much to Western medieval rationalism and Counter-reformation juridicism, when he was first entranced by St Thomas's use of aristotelian logic and categories of thought, Gill ran some danger of becoming too exclusively engrossed in man's rational powers,[7] of believing that all truth can be expressed in syllogistic terms, even of ultimately bogging-down in the morass of legalism:[8] he was in violent revolt from the confused thinking and aesthetic emotionalism of the "art world," from the relativist opportunism of socialist politics, from excessive dependence on religious experience that was not necessarily religious. And he was now coming into contact with people many of whom, with sneers at the alleged muddleheadedness, illogicality and compromise of their fellow Englishmen, continually lauded the alleged realism and logical consistency of Frenchmen and Italians and Roman Catholics in general. But Gill was too fearless, too widespirited, too mentally alert to succumb to the danger; if he had too much good sense to confuse prejudice or arbitrary judgement, wishful thinking or emotion, with intuition, so was he too whole a character to underrate the intuitive, the charismatic, the prophetic. This became more pronounced as he got older, and in the year before he died he wrote:

> "The best and the most perfect way is the way of love. This applies not only to life but also to teaching. The best and most perfect way to inculcate, for example, the virtue of honesty is to shew that love implies it. It is probable that no other method can ever be successful; for though we are rational beings, inasmuch as we are persons . . . yet we use our reason so rarely and fitfully and with so rash a carelessness, without training or discipline; we follow our prejudices and predilections with such confidence and impudence that any appeal based upon rational argument is unlikely to be successful. Moreover the lovely has a wider reference than the reasonable: what we love we do not merely desire—it is something that, whether consciously or not, we recognize to be right as well as good, not only desirable but also as it ought to be; and the fact that this recognition is arrived at by that leap of the intelligence that we call intuition, and not by discursive reasoning and the painful process of thinking it out step by step by logical argument, seems to show that reasoning is both unnecessary and absurd . . ." *Seems to be*, not *is; and*, not *or*.

And, as Walter Shewring has emphasized (*Blackfriars*, February 1941, pp. 87-89), Eric increasingly disassociated himself from that strong obscurantist party that refuses to look outside the Roman Catholic Church for any assistance whatever in the pursuit of truth. "He accepted every consequence of the Ambrosian principle embraced

by St Thomas, that *all* truth is from the Holy Ghost." No one was to think that "when I affirm the truth of Christianity I am therefore denying the truth of other faiths—at the most I am only denying their denials" (*Machine Age*, p. 19). There was no question of minimizing Christian doctrine: "Of all truths, the truth dearest to Eric Gill was that of the Incarnation. . . . But he responded eagerly to the call of such exponents of Eastern wisdom as Ananda Coomaraswamy (a venerated friend) and René Guénon"; and the present writer can testify to his eagerness to learn from the Eastern Christian tradition and mentality, with which, indeed, he came to have some close affinities.

Gill and his family left Ditchling Common in 1924[9] for a more remote and undisturbed home in a valley of the Black Mountains in Breconshire. Two other families accompanied them from Ditchling and there was another of friends already there, but no attempt was made at any organization or communal living beyond what is necessarily involved by common interests and close contiguity. Here, at Capel-y-ffin, he did little stone-carving but a lot of lettering and wood-engraving and there was the beginning of his great work as a designer of printing-types, work which brought him into association with that "business-world" he so often attacked: it is an appreciative reference to the Monotype Corporation in the *Autobiography* that brings forth his disclaimer (often repeated elsewhere) of any intention to impute malice and wickedness to any individual man of business, so many of whom he had met were "more than nice," men with inherited traditions of honesty and good service trying to maintain those traditions within a system that must prove fatal to them sooner or later. However strongly he spoke of the business world or "the rich" or the sufferings of the workers, what he really had his eye on was not the iniquities of individual persons but an organization of society in which they are all unavoidably tied up, which, whether he knows it or not, bears in its way as hardly on Henry Ford as on Bill Jones: there must be justice for dukes (if there be any) as much as for dustmen—and in either case justice is due to them precisely as men, human beings. In another section of this book F. A. Lea writes of G. K. Chesterton that, "What he beheld was not the calculated exploitation of one class by another, but an all-pervading injustice accepted as a matter of course nearly as much by the 'proletarian' as the capitalist. What he strove to create was a general consciousness of its existence, equal to his own, so that it must either become deliberate and challenging, or else be rectified, by the substitution of co-operation for competition." This is exactly true of Gill (though he would not refer to his "revolution" in such equivocal terms: competition is sometimes good, and there can be co-operation for evil).

·  ·  ·  ·  ·

As he grew older Eric Gill gave more and more attention to the problem of man in society, the question both social and religious of how persons can lead a whole, and therefore at least potentially holy, life on this earth. He was always a most strenuous and fully-occupied worker, but latterly screwed out ever more time for books, articles and lectures directly or indirectly concerned with this theme. With, I believe, very little conscious missionary purpose, this son of missionaries and brother of the Friars Preachers expounded Christian principles and practice in places where they would otherwise hardly, or never, have been heard.[10] He accepted invitations to speak or write, on this or that aspect of work and art or on social problems or on peace and war, indifferently for Catholics and Quakers, capitalists and communists, official bodies and obscure groups. This high-tide of lecturing came later, but it was at Capel-y-ffin that writing began to have a notable part in his activities, his pamphleteering, as he called it. His earlier publications were single essays; then came collections of articles reprinted from numerous periodical publications, many of them little known; and then longer single essays, *e.g.,* on clothes, on typography, culminating in two full-length books, *The Necessity of Belief*[11] and the *Autobiography.*

These writings give a very clear and, on the whole, adequate account of Gill's ideas and arguments; and they are remarkable not only for their internal consistency but for their consistency and correlation as a whole: from the few paragraphs on Slavery and Freedom written in 1918 down to the posthumously published autobiography he was "telling the same story," often in the same words. He was not afraid of repeating himself: "It has been said that I am one of those writers who can only keep to the point by returning to it. I may say in self-defense that there are many readers who can only remember the point if it is repeated often enough" (*Beauty,* p. 5); in particular, certain pregnant "sayings" and quotations with which every reader of Eric Gill is familiar occur in the earliest writings as in the latest: such, for example, are "Look after goodness and truth, and beauty will look after herself," "Man is made up of body and spirit, both real and both good," St Augustine's "Love, and do what you will." The same basic ideas are always there—the nature of man and his relation to God, the Christian revelation, human responsibility and therefore the necessity of freedom, human sin and divine grace, man's work as a calling to collaborate with God in creation—and it seems to me that in general their application underwent but little real development: what did develop was Eric Gill himself; he saw the same things but saw deeper into them, he saw farther and he saw more clearly, and in that vision he wrote about the same things again.

There can also be found in Gill's writings, especially the *Autobiography,* about as good a picture of what a man was like as can be got without knowing him in person—except in one particular (and here I except the *Autobiography* and, in a measure, *The Necessity of Belief*): his actual style of writing and expressing himself was not always *l'homme même,* it was often misleading. It is sometimes said by those who did not know him personally that Gill was intolerant, dogmatic (in the vulgar sense) and contemptuous of those who disagreed

with him: an obituary-writer who ought to have known better attributed to him a mythical "rich flow of invective." It is easy to see how hasty readers formed this misconception: as he often admitted, in and out of print, his manner of writing could give an impression of cocksureness, of laying down the law. But it was a laughably wrong impression, for not the least remarkable thing about Eric was his humility and a diffidence that was sometimes staggering. While never deferring to an opinion, by whomever expressed, unless and until he came to agree with it, he would ask and listen to the opinion of all and sundry on whatever topic turned up, even on technical matters of his own work. I have seen him bring a handful of engraving proofs in to the evening meal and ask for the criticism of all present—the family, visitors, servants: and next morning some of the suggestions of those inexpert critics were carried out. This humbleness of mind is well illustrated by the following passage from a letter written only a few weeks before his death.

> "I've been in bed off and on since April 15 and never anything very serious . . . Old age coming on I guess. Anyway it gave me time and opportunity to write book for Cape as ordered—100,000 words about my so-called 'life.' He asked for an autobiography but I told him it couldn't be done: it would have to be an 'autopsychography,' and that's what it is. . . . Really it amounts to a 'search for the City of God,' but of course I can't give it a fine title like that. . . . It feels to me as though I ought really to die now. I don't know how I shall be able to face the world after stripping myself more or less naked as I have done."

Since the publication of that 'autopsychography' there is no longer any excuse for thinking Eric Gill bumptious and intolerant.

Gill had hammered out in his mind and tested by practice certain principles, and these he put forward tirelessly for consideration and debate. But he hated to appear to be taking upon himself what he regarded as an office primarily of the clergy, and for that reason, as well as for the sake of first principles and of those who do not accept Christianity, he would appeal to natural reason as often as, or more often than, to divine revelation, to justice rather than to charity: charity he lived, his passion for justice was a fruit of his intense lovingness, and in more intimate private talk he would speak of God and of love more often than of either justice or reason. His intellectual judgements were downright ("We are told not to cast pearls before swine," he said, "And to adjudge persons swine in this sense necessitates making an intellectual judgement of them"), but he was always scrupulous to try to avoid making, or seeming to make, moral judgements of persons. I do not recollect ever hearing him utter a word intended to wound, and time and again I have watched him trying to find a worthy explanation of someone's apparently indefensible action, or gently changing the conversation when another's character or deeds were coming in for rough handling. Some years ago he and I were invited to speak in support of the war-resisters' candidate for the lord-rectorship of Glasgow University. The audience was extremely disorderly and Gill (who had a poor delivery) was hardly heard: I, by hardening my heart and being rude, forced some sort of hearing. "The difference between the two speakers," commented a Presbyterian minister afterwards, "was that Gill was forgiving those hooligans all the time, whereas Attwater did not forgive them till he had finished." Very characteristic of Gill; so, too, was his bewilderment that intelligent young people (he was extremely sympathetic towards the young, but without a trace of the "Youth" ramp) could come to a serious meeting only in order to make a din.

The last twelve years of his life Gill lived in Buckinghamshire, twelve full and fruitful years in which, by unflagging work and perfect order in the conduct of his affairs, his thought, writing and lecturing were enabled to keep pace with his stone carving and typography.[12] One of the carving jobs was ten panels for the new museum at Jerusalem, which involved two longish visits to Palestine, which must be spoken of here because his stay there was the last of several things in his life that he regarded as "revelations."

Many people go to Palestine and come back having apparently seen nothing but flies and touts, dirt and "backwardness," the rivalries of religions and the quarrels, emulations and meannesses of their sects. All these things are there and in good measure, and Eric saw them, but there are other things to be seen, and he saw them too. "In the Holy Land I saw a holy land indeed; I also saw, as it were eye to eye, the sweating face of Christ. . . . To me it was like living with the Apostles. It was like living in the Bible." And the beauty he saw was of people, of the Palestinian "Arabs" living without pride and with dignity in their poverty, sinful but humanly sinful; of places, Galilee and the Jordan wilderness; of the work of men's hands, above all of that Moslem shrine, the Haram as-Sharif at Jerusalem, which he declared to be the most beautiful place he had ever seen, the most spiritually pervaded. "Tell me where there is another. Is it in London, in Trafalgar Square? Is it the Place de la Concorde? Is it on the Acropolis at Athens? They tell me that is very lovely, but at Jerusalem living men worship the living God; at Athens there is but a memory of what was. Is it even in the piazza of St. Peter's? No, not there. . . . "

As for the shrines of Christendom, the basilica of Bethlehem, reminder also of the pride and glory of blood-stained Byzantium, the church of the Holy Sepulchre, reminder also of the brutalities and arrogance of Western Europe breaking in on Asia—these he would rather have as they were, half-ruinous, cluttered with the ecclesiastical junk of half a dozen churches, dirty and profaned, than restored and polished up by Caesar's building-contractors. "By the inscrutable decree of God the sweat is not thus to be wiped from His face"; the squabblings of Catholics and Orthodox, Armenians and Greeks, do less dishonour to Christ than if they should abandon his cross entirely and "hand the whole notion of salvation to the sanitary authority," as our civilization seeks to do. Jerusalem has "not yet rendered to Caesar the things that are God's" (*Auto.,* pp. 281, 257).

Blessed are the poor, for theirs is the Kingdom of God: that truth was first taught in the Holy Land and Gill found that it can still be learned there to-day, and he came back with his mind made up. "Henceforward I must take up a position even more antagonistic to my contemporaries than that of a mere critic of the mechanistic system. I must take a position antagonistic to the very basis of their civilization. And I must appear antagonistic even to the Church itself. Of course that is all nonsense but that is how it must appear. For the Christians everywhere have committed themselves to the support of capitalist industrialism and therefore to the wars in its defence, mechanized war to preserve mechanized living, while I believe that capitalism is robbery, industrialism is blasphemy and war is murder" (*Auto.,* p. 257). It was with these convictions, more or less clearly envisaged, that Eric Gill had lived most of his life; and with them thus reinforced, seen as it were from a Pisgah height between the hill of redemptive Death and the tomb of bodily and spiritual Resurrection—the spot in which Palestinian folk-wisdom so aptly recognized the centre of the world—he worked out his few remaining earthly years.

He died in a hospital close to London, in the night of November 17-18, 1940. An air raid was going on.

2

*Christian revolutionary.* It was characteristic of Eric Gill that when something came up for discussion he would seek at once a definition of terms, and that as a starting-point for such definition he would consult the dictionary for the etymology and current meanings of the words concerned— the "Concise Oxford" was always kept handy. Turning, then, to the "Shorter Oxford," I find under *Christian,* "one who follows the precepts and example of Christ"; this, with the addition of "tries to" before "follow," is very suitable for my purpose. Under *revolutionary* I find "[one who works for or advocates] the complete overthrow of the established government in any country or state by those who were previously subject to it: a forcible substitution of a new ruler or form of government."

That Gill was a sincere and fervent *Christian* in the above wide sense needs no demonstration, nor that he was one in a more strict sense; for he voluntarily united himself with the Roman Catholic Church: and, whatever may be thought of some passages in her history, of some of her teaching and still more of the teaching of some of her theologians, of some of her practice and still more of the practice of many of her members, that church as a whole must be recognized as an unflinching upholder throughout the centuries of the traditional fundamental truths of Christian faith and life. Gill, therefore, professed no eclectic or dilettante Christianity: he sought to follow Christ, not, for example, as the world's most attractive or convincing ethical teacher, but because he believed him to be the One God, clothed in human flesh, with all that follows from that stupendous concept.

Two possible misunderstandings may here be cleared up. On the one hand, he was no doctrinaire religionist, no sectarian peddler of the beliefs of his church as a sort of spiritual and religious patent-medicine which would cure all ills by the simple swallowing; he never flourished the Catholic faith like a tomahawk. He believed that faith with all his heart and soul, and he never forgot it is part of that faith that its dogmas must be lived as well as assented to before they can bear fruit. "To be religious means to believe in order, and order implies a person ordering"—God: and "a great religious period is one in which men proceed confidently in a doctrine of God." He believed ("We do not claim that what we believe is true because we believe it, but simply that what we believe is what we hold to be certain"), he believed that God ordained a teaching church on earth—but that does not involve belief in every word that proceeds from the mouth of her theologians (who in any case not seldom contradict one another): "theologians have not infrequently made confusion where their job was to clear things up. They have collected the butterfly only to kill it and pin it down, and the meaning they have pinned down has turned out to be not the real meaning but only that one which was suitable for such pinning."

On the other hand, neither was Gill "anti-clerical." In the continental sense of the expression, which involves opposition to a given church or even to Christianity itself, obviously he was not: in the English sense, which seems ultimately to convey the idea that clergymen necessarily know less about true religion than anybody else, his words sometimes appear to be strongly imbued with it. I do not refer to such good-humoured digs as that "[the problem of evil is such that] even theologians have been humble before it," but to harder sayings: for instance, that the swagger, human prowess and greatness implied by the church architecture of Renaissance Rome is more defiling to the face of Christ than our contemptuous spittle. "The nonsensical and illusory grandeurs of Rome, Rome, the Holy City, decked out in the finery of ballrooms and banks, the soul-ensnaring magnificence of statistical display, the grand appearance of doctrinal and ethical unity . . . it seemed to me that we should do better to eschew our grandeurs and forget our numbers—and brag less about unity while, to the heathen and the pagans and the infidels, the most conspicuous thing about Christians is their sectarian disunity. . . . For while we fight among ourselves about doctrine, we are united in the common worship of money and material success. Here I do not exaggerate. That is the awful thing" (*Auto.*, p. 254). "The clergy are in the position of men standing on the brink of a frozen pool and shouting to men drowning under the ice that they should take good deep breaths if they want to be healthy" (*M. & M.*, p. 36). "The clergy are everywhere acknowledged to be

custodians of faith and morals—the faith is what you more or less blindly believe because your school-teachers taught it during 'religious instruction,' and morals are little more than a list of things you mustn't do. Man as an intelligent and intellectual being is hardly mentioned, and never expected to function" (*W. & P.*, p. 100). "It must be a commonplace of our experience that the widespread scepticism of our time is as much the consequence of loss of respect for the preachers of Christ as it is of the writings and teachings of unbelievers, and that that loss of respect is a necessary preliminary" (*Auto.*, p. 104). Many clergy (and others) don't like people to say that sort of thing: the fact that it is true makes it worse.

For the teaching office of the Church, for the priestly office of its ministers, Gill had the profoundest reverence and respect, because it is a special participation in the one true universal priesthood of Jesus Christ (and he was very alive to the truth that every Christian in his measure shares in that priesthood). But this is not to say that the mistakes, exaggerations, deficiencies of persons exercising authority in holy orders should be extenuated or ignored, that as a matter of discipline it is good to treat clergy as outside criticism: that is obscurantism, weakness, laziness, and produces that "clericalism" of which a French archbishop has recently declared, "the Church disapproves of it and we don't want any of it at any price." Moreover, accusations against churches and ecclesiastical authorities can be substantiated only by Christian doctrine. "If you are amazed by the policeman-like frame of mind of many of the clergy and their apparent conviction that the spirit killeth but the letter quickeneth (so that you would think getting to Heaven was a business of going by the book!) you must still remember that the opposite doctrine is Christian teaching, and that it is the authority to which they themselves appeal who is the judge" (*Auto.*, p. 255).

The above-quoted definition of *revolutionary* would certainly never fit so gentle and unpolitically-minded a person as Gill, but in our day the scope of the word has been much extended, to include those who seriously oppose any widely-accepted and well-established state of affairs or social or other system and the principles and philosophy pertinent to it. I suspect that the word started life as a term of abuse, which would account for its definition in negative terms: now that it has become domesticated it is better defined positively, as, say, "an advocate of principles and policies which involve the overthrow or reversal of established systems, etc." And in this wider sense Gill was unquestionably a revolutionary. Not that he used the word much or thought of himself in such terms: in *Work and Property* is an essay called **"Art and Revolution"** which would be extremely puzzling to most revolutionaries: only at the end does he refer to them at all—and then to dismiss them as mere "progressives"! His reference to his own "little revolution" has already been quoted (p. 166); nevertheless to bring that about would mean "the complete destruction of a civilization in which money is god and men of commerce are our rulers." But "this destruction will come about without any need for 'revolutionary' activity. Let no one suppose I propose to wave a red flag. The present civilization is founded upon an unnatural condition and will come to a natural end. If there are battles, murders and sudden deaths it will not be the fault of"[13]—men like Eric Gill. "A kingdom not of this world"; "Poverty, chastity and obedience"—such were the slogans on the banners of *his* revolt. "These may sound strange watchwords for revolutionists. Consider then the alternatives: Riches, pleasure and irresponsibility, and a kingdom not founded in Heaven!" (*Art Nonsense,* p. 108).

The word "revolution" as commonly used connotes physical violence, and both those who fear and those who welcome the thing like to think of it in terms of the barricades. But the dictionary gives also a more fundamental meaning, "The action of turning over in the mind; consideration; reflection." And it is here that Gill really belongs: "the spirit has the primacy." What he fought for was a "unanimous society," one in which there is unity of *mind* among the people, "who know the same truth and will the same good": what he fought against was the evil *frame of mind* in contemporary society, one that is radically unchristian and antichristian, therefore contrary to nature and to nature's God, "as anti-God as any atheist could wish."

Yes, a Christian revolutionary. And not a revolutionary who happened to be a Christian, or in spite of being a Christian, but revolutionary *because* Christian.

. . . . .

Gill being so many-sided a person (each side marvellously correlated with each other), and we humans having a boundless capacity to misunderstand and misinterpret one another, it may clear the picture somewhat to state and explain some of the things that he was *not,* or that he was not in the usual sense of the terms used. The use of labels, especially of ill-defined labels, to tag on to people, whether to express a judgement, favourable or unfavourable, or to pigeonhole them away in what are assumed to be meaningful categories, is one of the minor pernicious diseases endemic in our time.

"The individual rebel, however unspotted from the world he may keep himself, is bound to be tainted by idiosyncrasy and eccentricity; he is likely to be both a prig and a faddist. He will set up for himself a standard of his own making, unless he first ally himself to truth, and truth is a 'who' and not a 'what'!" (*Art Nonsense,* p. 123). Eric did not "ally" but submitted himself to Him who is Truth, and thus was his mind kept purged of idiosyncrasy and eccentricity, priggery and faddism— he was no individualistic crank (certain peculiarities of dress and the like to the contrary notwithstanding). But more of this will be said when I come to speak of his ordinariness and feeling for the "common man," as also then of his freedom from that lop-sided mental superiority that we call "being highbrow" and the fidgety self-conscious "culture" that goes with it.[14] We are all," he

said, "so many sweethearts to God. Are we going to fob him off with borrowed kisses—with even the best Elizabethan love-songs? Would he not rather have the vulgar endearments which are our own?" Gill mixed much and sympathetically with cranks and highbrows and *exaltés* of all kinds, and it is not surprising that he has been labelled (sometimes mutually exclusively) with some of their enthusiasms.

He is, for example, commonly regarded as a back-to-the-lander, and it is true that he lived by choice in the country, had the deepest regard for its people and their work, and said, not once but repeatedly, that "The salvation of England cannot be brought about by town improvement; it can only come by the land." But precisely because "the town, the holy city, is nourished upon elements drawn from the soil. The modern towns of our industrial England have no such nourishment."

> "It *is* a lot of nonsense, all this cackle about the beauty of the country. And the cackle would never have been heard if the towns had not become such monsters of indecency and indignity. The town properly thought of is the very crown and summit of man's creativeness. . . . The countryside exists to support and uphold and nourish and maintain the city. . . . Thus the call to the land, to the earth, is the necessary first call. We must be born again, and we must be born again on the land, to dig the earth, to plant and cultivate, to be shepherds and swineherds, to hew wood and draw water, to build simple dwellings and simple places of prayer. But we need not therefore be blinded to what is the truth. Because Babylon is vile it does not follow that Jerusalem is vile also" (*Auto.,* pp. 230-8).

That is not the language of that often rather sentimental state of mind that has earned the contemptuous epithet "back-to-the-landery"; and Gill, while sympathizing with and admiring the heroism of those who follow a call to undertake an agricultural "simple life" in groups and associations, refused the gross over-simplification of regarding this as a cure-all to be urged on people indiscriminately: in particular did he protest against any "attempt to make out that a certain kind of simple, self-supporting country life is the only life for good Christian people" (*Beauty,* p. 34).

Gill had a great appreciation of "that most manly of great men," William Morris (as for Ruskin, who spoke the truth "more eloquently than Cobbett or Disraeli, and more solemnly"), and he was inevitably mixed up in the arts-and-crafts movement. But he had to repudiate it—and was told by the late W. R. Lethaby ("Who shall measure the greatness of this man?") that he was "crabbing his mother." But Gill was not begotten of that movement, and he saw unerringly its two great weaknesses: being unable to compete with mass-production, its products were luxury articles, bought only by the well-to-do; and it positively helped the industrial producers, who copied its designs in their factories and thus started a flood of shams that still further corrupted people's judgement of the times. So Gill escaped from arts-and-crafts: "I'm no gentleman and I don't understand loyalty to lost causes when the causes deserve to be lost."

And he was no medievalist, in the common sense of an uncritical admirer who sees in the middle ages an ideal of life and achievement—Merrie England and all that—which we should in some mysterious way seek to restore or at least approximate to. He associated himself with a religious order medieval in its origin and some of its existing customs—but it is also one of the most up-to-date; he sat at the feet of Aquinas—but Aquinas was a man of universal and timeless mind; he often referred to medieval conditions and practice for illustration, contrast and commendation—but there was nothing specifically medieval about his own dominating ideas. "I do not cite the middle ages because they were good ages or because, in those ages, a certain set of ideas were held to be just and seemly. I do not 'cite' them at all. I am merely describing. . . . " (*Art,* p. 37). Christianity teaches that the enemies of peace and good order are self-seeking and injustice, and for centuries that teaching bore fruit in the subordination of commerce, the outlawry of usury, the upholding of law that defended persons and families as such and evolved the noble concept of the *liber et legalis homo,* "free and lawful man" (now being rapidly superseded, as Richard O'Sullivan, K.C., pertinently remarks, by that of the "insured (or insurable) person"). Gill did not say that that teaching never failed in its effect or that its fruit was always plentiful; but it was after, and with the help of, the Renaissance and the Reformation that commerce and mercantile imperialism became insubordinate and the results of money-lending were honoured, poverty became a disgrace and the rich man as such was esteemed, the workman became on the one hand the artisan and on the other the artist, men gave God's glory to man. Nevertheless, "I am not advocating any indiscriminate praise of pre-Renaissance or pre-industrial works. The seeds of our worship of riches were sown long before Luther or James Watt. A great deal of medieval cathedral-building was no more than human swank and aggrandizement" (*W. & P.,* p. 136), and the religion and law of the middle ages were disfigured by any amount of wickedness, superstition and violent tyranny.

There was a time when Gill could hardly bring himself to use the word "artist," otherwise than as a term of opprobrium; the artist as a special kind of man, the lapdog of the rich and great, the aesthetician ("relations of masses" and all that), the exploiter of temperament and sensibility, the beauty-wallah—he was certainly not that kind of artist; he was a workman, a carver of stone. The beauty of God is the cause of the being of all that is, said St Thomas, and earthly beauty is no mere delightfulness, or its perception a matter of emotion: it is "that order in things which we perceive to be in itself and at once both right and good. It is perceived by intuition and the knowledge of it is developed by contemplation" (*Art Nonsense,* p. 102); it is the splendour or radiance by which being is manifest, the shiningness perceived in

things which are made as they should be; all well-made things are beautiful. "A beautiful thing is that which, being seen, pleases," and there is a whole essay in *Art Nonsense* (pp. 143-158) expounding this apparently simple, if not jejune, definition of Aquinas. "Beauty cannot be taught, and it is best not talked about. It must be spontaneous. It cannot be imposed. . . . Its enemies are irreligion and the offspring of irreligion—commercialism and the rule of the trader" (*Art Nonsense,* p. 94). To recognize it we must use our minds: just as a good life is a mortified life, so "good taste" (as we say) is mortified taste, that is, "taste in which the stupid, the sentimental, the irrelevant is *killed.*"

This is not the beauty, this is not the culture, talked about in the "art world" and the welfare departments of philanthropic industrialists and the caverns of the B.B.C. Human culture is the product of necessary work, not of formal education or the activities of leisure hours ("hobbies"): it cannot be plastered on to mankind like an "ornament" glued on to a Woolworth mirror. "To hell with culture, culture as a thing added like a sauce to otherwise unpalatable stale fish! The only culture worth having is that which is the natural and inevitable product of an honourable life of honourable work" (*S. & S.,* p. 173). The divorce of beauty from usefulness and work from culture is an achievement of the bourgeois mind "and there will never be an end of the bourgeois until we have abolished Art," the art of the "art world."

It has been said (*Blackfriars,* February 1941, p. 26) that "one of the difficulties of Eric Gill's position (it was also his strength) was that in his social writings, and increasingly in the later works, his preoccupation was moral, and, if we understand his metaphysics rightly, exclusively moral." That is perfectly true; and yet Gill was emphatically not a moralist in the vulgar sense. He did not go around telling people what they should or should not do, deciding what was right or wrong, sinful or good; he did not identify religion with personal rectitude alone. He knew perfectly well that they cannot be separated, that his own teaching on this, that and the other had immediate and far-reaching implications for personal morality; but his shyness, his humility and his fear lest he trespass on another man's job made him time and again repudiate any intention of talking about morals: his appeal was to good sense rather than to good will, and it was not till comparatively late that he found himself unable to keep silent when silliness, culpable ignorance, falsity or unlovingness had to be identified with sin and that he would refer boldly to the pertinent words of St James or St Paul of our Lord himself.

"'Patriotism is not enough'—morality is not enough. Man is not merely a moral being. He is not merely moral or immoral. He does not merely will good or evil. He also knows true or false: at least he is capable of doing so. And not only does man know and will, he also loves" (*W. & L.,* p. 115). That was a common approach. In one of his attacks on the idea of the "leisure state" he declared: "It is not a moral problem. Leisure is not a problem because people are not good enough to use it properly"; it is an intellectual problem, of what to do that is worth doing. He deprecated the moral fervour that was mixed up with the arts-and-crafts and land movements: morally the handicraftsman or farm-labourer is in precisely the same position as any responsible chemist or engineer. When he deplored the deceits and shams of gothic-revival architecture he was accusing nobody of sin; his appeal was to reason—such things are foolish: "My indignation is not so much a product of moral rectitude as of intellectual exasperation." Nor did he fail to note the weak ineffectiveness of religiose moralism: "Instead of doing anything about economics the moralists fulminate against the murder of unborn children and the selfishness of modern young people [in the practice of birth-prevention]. As somebody said: 'The drains are smelling—let's have a day of intercession.' And as another said: 'The economic depression is a good thing—it is sent to try us'" (*M. & M.,* p. 28). No wonder Pope Pius XI had to mourn that the people at large are estranged from the Church. It is not by moralism or formalist dogmatism, any more than by socialism or the "first-aid" of humanitarianism, that a sick world can be brought to health: "No 'welfare-work' in East London slums will supply religion with a reason of being otherwise lacking. No distribution of property or nationalization of the means of production, distribution and exchange will produce Jerusalem in England's green and pleasant land if the earthly paradise have no City of God for its model. No truth, no good, no beauty will shine out of human handiwork unless the truth that 'whosoever will lose his life shall save it' be known, willed and loved" (*Belief,* p. 304).

Repeatedly from 1936 onwards Eric Gill spoke and wrote against war, on the platforms and in the publications of the Peace Pledge Union, of Pax and of other associations of war-resisters—yet, though he freely used the term of himself for convenience, he was no pacifist as the word is currently understood. He held that taking part in warfare is not of itself and essentially at variance with a profession of Christianity, that the concept of the possible just war is a valid one, in the conditions commonly received (and usually very imperfectly examined) by Roman Catholics and others: this position Gill held *ex animo,* it appealed to him as traditional, authoritative, reasonable and true. But the more he saw of the contemporary world, the more he learned about political and economic forces, the more that "scientific" means of warfare developed, so much the more he became disturbed in mind. Gradually he began to realize that, as Lord Grey had said, "War is the same word as it was a century ago, but it is no longer the same thing"; the spiritual insight and logic of the medieval and seventeenth-century theologians had been applied to a quite different thing: is it possible to fulfil their conditions for a justifiable war in the new conditions? Gill decided that it is not (and here he parted company from the great majority among those of his co-religionists who have given the matter a moment's thought). He still did not

say that no war has ever been justified, that the use of military force is always wrong: he said that war as we know it to-day is such that no human being, much less a Christian, should take part in it; it has become bestial, inhuman, and to talk of patriotism and the defence of civilization by such means is irrelevant. "Modern war is a remedy worse than any conceivable disease"; it is no remedy at all for the congeries of diseases which at present afflict the world: it is an extension and amplification of them. Whatever high-minded, great-souled, public-spirited combatants may intend or do, war is supremely harmful to man's love of God and his fellows, to the spirit of truth and righteousness and justice, to human responsibility and to creative work: depersonalization is at its height and at no other time are men so stirred to undiscriminating hate and abandoned to irrational processes.

"What is the alternative of which we are so afraid? . . . Are we afraid of national humiliation, are we afraid to be humbled? But it is written 'Blessed are the meek, for they shall inherit the earth.' Are we afraid of poverty? But it is precisely poverty which as Christians we should welcome. There will be no peace, there can be no peace, while wealth, comfort, riches are the ideal we set before ourselves" (*Peace,* p. 11). This had been a foremost idea in his mind when he came back from Palestine: "It became clear that it is no use renouncing war unless we first of all renounce riches. That is the awful job before us. . . . A whole world doomed to perpetual fighting—and no remedy but to persuade it to renounce riches. What a forlorn hope!" (*Auto.,* p. 256). Indeed, Gill was more interested in the causes of war than in the strictly moral problem of war itself: all over his later writings are scattered references showing the inevitability of the sort of wars we have in the sort of world we live in—and we all help to make that world.

"Let peacemakers remember above all that it is no manner of good preaching peace unless we preach the things that make for peace—that even the love of our fellow men is no good unless it means giving rather than taking, yielding rather than holding, sharing rather than exclusive possession, confederation rather than sovereignty, use rather than profit. And it means the subordination of the man of business and the dealer and moneylender, both in the world and even more in our own hearts" (in *The Christian Pacifist,* January 1940).

Gill's thought on war, coming later in life, is set out with less system and detail than his other dominant ideas. His insistence on the foulness and shameful vulgarity in all departments of war as waged to-day laid him open to the charge that he was letting his feelings of disgust run away with him, and he was sometimes misunderstood in this way: it is therefore necessary to emphasize that he did not condemn modern war simply because it is horrible. It is a question of means: he denied that spiritual goods can be obtained by killing and hate and destruction, and he vindicated the right of any man to refuse to take part in such an undertaking.

"Could not Christ have called on twelve legions of angels to fight for him? And he did not. And shall we think to make a Christian triumph by calling up twelve armies equipped with all the products of our commercialism?—guns, bombs, poisons! (We can only obtain such things by calling in the financiers and borrowing their money.) Shall we thus 'make the world safe for Christianity'?" (*Stations,* p. 5.)

In this context, of the horrors of war, it may be noted in passing that Gill's treatment of the problem of evil is far from satisfactory. He devotes a special chapter to it in *The Necessity of Belief,* and it contains some most valuable analysis and observations, especially the emphasis on the necessity of the distinction between moral and physical evil. There is also a third kind, which may be called spiritual evil, but to treat them, as he seems to do, as being in watertight compartments is bad psychology (and incidentally weakens his own arguments against modern war). The whole thing is badly oversimplified. "There is no problem of evil," he concludes, "There is only the intellectual difficulty of understanding the physical universe and the moral difficulty of withstanding our own appetites and lusts." But surely that precisely is the problem of evil.

. . . . .

Having, I hope, cleared up a few possible misunderstandings by this brief reference to some negatives, I turn to a single, and more persuasive and significant, positive: Eric Gill was an "ordinary man," a man-in-the-street, both in his estimate of himself and in fact. "I am," he said, "an ordinary person who refuses to be bamboozled. . . . What concerns me first of all is what man, the common man, the man in the street, the man in the workshop, the man on the farm, claims for himself. After all, I believe it is true to say that the philosopher and the prophet do not claim for man what he does not claim for himself" (*Belief,* p. 227). He assumed no authority to teach: "The most I claim is to speak as one of the people, and as one for whom *vox populi* is *vox Dei.* It is not my voice, it is the people's voice. I claim that what I say is what mankind says. It is no little flock that proclaims man's free will. It is no minority of peculiar persons that asserts man's being" (*Belief,* p. 331). Worms are apt to get the best view of the roots of things, and the important criticism of things as they are to-day comes not from princes and bishops, poets and politicians, but from "man the worm, man the proletarian, man the delectable whore." Early in 1939 the Royal Institution of Great Britain invited four well-known people, of whom Gill was one, to address its members on the relations of art and industry; and he told the assembly that it was a pity that a labourer from a factory had not been asked to speak as well (the address is reprinted in *Sacred and Secular*). On all sides we see men in revolt, and the principal instigators of rebellion in our time have been, not the professed revolutionaries, however important, but those "little men" who "wrote, in cheap books and parish magazines, or preached, in nonconformist chapels, country churches or inconspicuous papist pulpits, the humane doctrine of responsibility for sin and the dual but individual nature of man."

> They were not conscious agitators, "but they did in fact prevent the entire submergence of the proletariat in the non-human system of industrialism. They did preserve as matters of common knowledge and common belief the common man's idea of himself: that he is a unique individual and uniquely valuable. If this idea persists as a commonplace of Christian doctrine, if Christianity persists as a commonplace profession, it is not due to the splendid writings, great speeches or heroic behaviour of one or more magnificent Christians—though such there were and such played their part—but to the widespread unheroic efforts of little men, little pastors, little sheep. There can be no rebellion without grounds of rebellion. It is the grounds of rebellion of which the little men have preserved the knowledge. There can be no rebellion except against wrong. It is the idea of right and wrong which the little ministers have kept alive" (*Belief,* p. 267).

All this did not arise from any doctrinaire democracy, any sentimental regard for "the masses," any invertedly snobbish contempt for learning and experience; the human perfectibility of man was a heresy that had no attraction for Gill, and his comments on "the suburbs" were exceeded in pungency only by his comments on workers' ambitions to emulate the suburbs. No. Just as man's chief means to culture, worship and the contemplation of being have from the beginning been the necessity of providing himself with food, clothing and shelter—ordinary things—so wisdom, knowledge and understanding derive and ramify from fundamental truths discernable, whether through reason or revelation, by the ordinary man, man the tool-using animal, such a man as Eric Gill. In England at the end of the nineteenth-century there were thousands of obscure families like the Brighton Gills; Eric's schooling was rather below the average in such families; he had no advantage of upbringing and the rest that he did not share with thousands of other young men; he was for years no more than a letter-cutter and stone-mason, living as such; when he found himself in a so-called superior environment for example, among artists and literary people, he did not like it and cleared out; he had no high and over-mastering ambition; he was not endowed by nature with any abnormal intellectual ability, he read widely, but enthusiastically or critically rather than studiously: in a word, he was quite an ordinary man—but one who used to the utmost his mind, his will and his heart.

This is one of the reasons why Gill's criticism is so important. He was not like so many philosophers who argue from the abstract to the concrete without any practical experience of the concrete. In the order of time, Gill started with the concrete; like the carpenter in Miss Sackville-West's poem (I quote from memory and perhaps inaccurately), he knew what it was to "hold down Reality, struggling, to a bench": when he expounded a philosophy of work and art, it was, for once, a working artist speaking. He slowly worked from the concrete back to the abstract and, used to dealing with real things, he found that abstractions too are realities (in the measure of their truth)—and he handled them accordingly. It is sometimes necessary to screw a piece of wood tightly in a vice to keep it still: Gill found it is sometimes necessary metaphorically to screw an idea in a vice, for a similar reason and however impatient it may be of the treatment.

Eric lived for, worked for and spoke for and to his own kind. I have heard it said that, if he begins at the beginning, reads with attention and does not skip, any person of ordinary intelligence can understand the dozen volumes of St. Thomas Aquinas's monumental *Summa,* but that no one without special training and knowledge can understand the works of Descartes and Comte, Kant and Berkeley. I have not attempted either exercise, so I do not know if this be true. But I do know that any simple fellow can read the writings of Eric Gill and find intelligible and convincing exposition of such daily and practical problems as God and man, matter and spirit, belief and science, personality, free will and responsibility, art, work and industry—all those things that are, whether we know it or not, of the first importance to every man jack of us. Gill wrote and spoke deliberately "on the level of ordinary human speech and thought," and so for the man Jack and the woman Jill, with no long words or technical jargon, no vague uplift or recondite notions, no metaphysical flights beyond the range of the kitchen and the bar (if only the kitchen and the bar would turn off the radio and pay attention thoughtfully for a bit): not these, but a straightforward examination of what are really everyman's problems, in language that everyman can understand, usually with illustrations that are at once familiar to him. And not only did Gill write what the ordinary person can read: he wrote what the ordinary person knows—but does not always know that he knows.

### 3

Nicholas Berdyaev has said somewhere that Christian theology needs to be complemented by a Christian anthropology. He does not, I suppose, imply that there is no such thing, but that it needs to be studied more deeply and intensively and (especially in view of current theories and practice) brought before the people at large, non-Christian as well as Christian, with the earnestness and perseverance that has hitherto been reserved for theology. Eric Gill was in explicit agreement. His own most outstanding characteristic was integrality and completeness: he was a whole man, and every aspect of himself, his work and his beliefs, was integrated and interdependent, fused into one shining personality. He was a living and amazingly successful example of what he was always trying to do, what he called "my difficulty and my enthusiasm"—"to discover how things are related and to discover a right relation where a wrong one exists." It appeared to him that lack of integralness is *the* disease, the master disease, from which civilized mankind is suffering: we are not simply uprooted, we are torn to pieces.

The God of Christianity is the source of all being, Being itself, He Who Is, the God of Abraham, Isaac and Jacob. But this conception has been weakened and watered down till he is thought of merely as the Author of Nature or the Supreme Lawgiver or even—Heaven help us!—the Great Artificer who "made my mate": that is, if he is not simply the Unknown God. Just so with the Christian concept of man. He has been almost lost in a Heraclitan flux, become a creature who does, acts, becomes: "the doing is all." The concept of being has to be recovered also in relation to man. To-day it is no longer the personality of God alone that has to be upheld, but the personality of man as well. Each and every man and woman is an individual person to start with, who takes on communal functions; he is not a "functional unit which may or may not end up by developing individual idiosyncrasies." As an object of God's love his value is, as we say, absolute: he is an end, not a means. The state is a means to an end—man's good life and convenience: the Bible is a means, to the end that man may know and live the truth; Christ's resurrection was a means, to "our rebirth into the living hope." But man is, like the daisy in its eternal quality, or Dame Julian's nut, "a thing, a being in itself. It is not a means to an end. 'It lasteth and for ever shall, for God loveth it.'" And it is not only in the face of such philosophies as fascism, nazism and communism that these things have to be maintained, that we have to uphold that man is "a creature who knows and wills and loves: a rational being, responsible for his acts and the intended consequences of his acts . . . made in the image of God (child of God and, if he will, heir also), a creature who loves" (*Machine Age,* p. 26).

Eric Gill based himself ultimately on man's consciousness; that consciousness testifies to his personality, and divine revelation enlarges and infinitely enriches that truth. And fundamental to the Christian idea of man is the further truth that he is made up of matter and spirit, both real and both good, manifestations of the same one reality, a figure of our theandric life with all its glories and trials that Eric constantly returned to. And in his thirst for right relations he never allows us to forget that "though there is a distinction of category between matter and mind, and though the mind is the ruling partner, the body and mind do not act separately. . . . And so in man's history it is not possible to think that this or that was simply the product of environment, economic circumstance or material force, nor is it possible to think that such and such was simply the product of his spirit. The two parts or principles of man's being are inextricably intertwined and death for man is precisely the disintegration of matter and spirit" (*Belief,* p. 273).

Throughout Christian history there has been a tendency to belittle, or worse, the material side of human life, a tendency varying in strength from the formal heresies of encratic gnostics and manicheans, catharists and puritans, to the sometimes hardly less mischievous exaggerations of those orthodox people, of all denominations, who seek to keep themselves or others from sin, or to answer the question of evil, or to ensure a godly detachment from this world, by an attitude that seems to imply the essential evil of created matter, especially of the human body: so widespread and continuing is this manichean dualism (by no means confined to Christians) with its corollary of seeing asceticism as an end and not simply a means, that it looks as if it is a specific result of that spoiling of human nature that Christians call The Fall. Against it Gill struck hard and often, directly or indirectly, sometimes so regardlessly of contemporary convention that some were shocked to silence and others provoked to calling him names, from "pelagian" and "antinomian" to less "polite" expressions. But he went deeper than his critics, he saw the ultimate term of the false mysticism that would have us behave as pure spirits while yet inhabiting bodies: "The 'degradation' of making anything useful—the 'sordidness' of child-bearing—the 'mere animality' of digestion: such are the phrases of Sodom and Gomorrah. Such are the phrases of aesthetes, and they disclose the root ideas of puritanism. Matter is not good enough for man" (**Beauty,** p. 107). He was far from oblivious of the disorders that so properly alarm the moralist, but he did not trust for their remedy, humanly speaking, in mere negation, "Thou shalt not." God is the source of all enjoyment, and when we enjoy his creation in the way he intended we share his enjoyment.

"Adam could not see the Wood for the Tree. Adam sinned when he fell from contemplation (as the theologian says): that is to say when he saw himself as self-satisfactory, when, like Herod, 'he gave not God the honour.' There is indeed this danger. It is of course, and obviously, man's besetting sin. It is pride, the root of all sin. But the remedy is not the denial of enjoyment but the giving of thanks. The remedy is not the denial of material goods, but the recognition of material goods as gifts, and not only as gifts, but as gifts which signify the Giver" (**W. & L.,** p. 112).

And many of Gill's critics on this head failed to notice that, if he emphasized the goodness of material things strongly and often, he emphasized the primacy of spirit more strongly and more often. Sensual pleasures are called enthralling because they can make slaves of men, "and the worse slavery is the subjection of mind to matter, of the spiritual to the material, of the immeasurable to the measurable, of the infinite to the finite . . . Materialism spells slavery. Freedom, they say with one voice (Italian, German or Russian) 'freedom is a concession of the state.'" Other tongues besides Italian, German and Russian go to make up that ghastly voice. Man is enslaved thus to-day to a terrifying degree, and this success of the materialist philosophers and propagandists has depended upon a monstrous suppression of truth, the truth about man's real nature and significance among created things.

> "No religion has ever been such a 'dope.' Priests have endeavoured to make men think themselves worms before God. They have exploited men's sense of responsibility and their consequent sense

of sin. But those who in their enthusiasm oppose religion have gone further still. Men are no longer worms before God. There is no God who could desire the death of a sinner. Man is of no importance to God, because he is of no importance at all. Man's appetite for abasement cannot be further exploited. However much Christian men have been taught to grovel before their Creator, they were at least taught as a dogma that God died for their redemption—they had that much intrinsic importance. The materialist does not grovel before his Creator; he just simply grovels, because grovelling is all he can do. He is a worm and no man. . . . We crawl on the face of the earth because our presence here has no other significance" (**Belief,** p. 150).

Nevertheless, materialism too is a philosophy—without a metaphysic, and a religion—without the infinite. The fact that more attention is paid in England to-day to banks and insurance-offices than to churches shows, not a loss, but a change of religion—ultimate reality is sought in material things rather than in things of the spirit; the productions of modern Europe are as much an index to dominant religious ideas as are those of the middle ages or of India; an aeroplane is no less the work and expresses the genius of a whole people than the cathedral at Chartres. And a decisive factor in riveting Gill's attention on Christianity in general and the Roman Catholic Church in particular was her age-long struggle against these two excesses, belief that the material life is all and belief that it is nothing; whatever the aberrations of some of her members and of unorthodox sects, she has been unwavering in her affirmation that matter and spirit are both real and both good, and that spirit has the primacy. Thus the Church rejects both Western materialism and Eastern idealism, and emerges as "the arbiter of East and West because she refuses the denials of either."

The principal connotation of the word "revolution" to-day is a drastic change in socio-economic organization and conditions; and Eric Gill's social principles can be summed up in these words: responsibility, poverty, love of God. On the last I need not dwell: if what I have already said does not persuade the reader that to Gill the one thing necessary is love of God and his Christ and a humble listening to the promptings of the Holy Spirit, then that reader must turn to Gill's own writings (as I hope he will in any case). Let him read the essay on art and holiness in **Work and Leisure:** I quote at random, from page 121: "Man is a creature who loves. Ultimately he can only love the holy. . . . Is the word 'holy' a stumbling-block (to the Jews a stumbling-block, to the Gentiles foolishness)? Why be afraid or shy of the word? Primarily it means hale and hearty, whole, unsullied, perfect and therefore of God—godly, sanctified, sacred; and therefore gay and light and sweet and cheerful and gracious. 'Oh taste and see how *gracious* the Lord is.' But gay—above all things gay. . . . "

Man has free will. "The freedom of the will, whether proved by argument or not, is a fact of human experience, and to be accepted as such. . . . Pathological states of mind apart—and let the psychologists enlarge the sphere of pathology as much as they can—the free will remains and man is master, captain of his soul." To have free will involves having responsibility, being responsible for what one chooses to do: "We know, we affirm, I know and I affirm that at the very core of our being, of my being, there is the fact of responsibility." Gill did not say much about freedom or liberty but was constantly referring to responsibility, and the one involves the other: responsibility cannot be used unless there be freedom. He quotes Aquinas: "The free man is responsible for himself, but for the slave another is responsible. . . . The highest manifestation of life consists in this: that a being governs its own actions. A thing which is always subject to the direction of another is somewhat of a dead thing. . . . Hence a man in so far as he is a slave is a veritable image of death." Christianity imperatively demands responsibility: profession of it must be freely chosen by a free act, it must be lived equally freely. The Church and slavery could not permanently co-exist, and this was a major factor in eventually bringing formal slavery to an end; where there is a diminished responsibility there Christianity cannot be fully developed or fully effective.

Gill was sometimes criticized for apparently making too sweeping generalizations about "the rich." The same objection can be (and has been) raised against many good Christians, such as St. Basil and St. John Chrysostom, and for that matter against the gospels themselves. In speaking of the hidden power of liturgical Latin, Gill says he does not believe that the words *Divites dimisit inanes* can in their English form, "The rich he hath sent empty away," convey "such a stupendously revolutionary threat as that which they do in fact convey." Obviously he did not take upon himself to make moral judgements on rich people, whether individually or collectively; he was concerned with what St. Paul was concerned with, that revolutionary threat and the truth which lies behind it, which Gill stated in as forcible a half-dozen lines as he ever wrote: "There is no idolatry so destructive of charity, so desolating, there is nothing which so certainly obscures the face of God, as the desire of money—the root of all evil. 'The root of all evil!' Did I make up that phrase? No; it is the word of God to man. The root of all evil, the *root*. The root of all *evil*" (*Auto.*, p. 194).

"The principle of poverty," he declared, "is the only one consonant with the nature and destiny of man and his material environment and condition." What is meant by this poverty? Not, of course, indigence, destitution, evil poverty; but good poverty, that spiritual thing, explicit in Christian teaching, which bears fruit in human life and works. "To go without, to give up, to lose rather than gain, to have little rather than much—that is its positive teaching. Blessed are the poor in spirit; the humble, the common man, the common woman, simple women, mothers of children—'How hard is it for a rich man to enter Heaven'. . . . But it is only in love that

this poverty can be embraced" (*S. & S.*, p. 56). "Is it not clear, beyond any possibility of doubt, that whatever other things may or must be said of the teaching of Christ and of the witness of his saints, it is the blessing of poverty which is the central fact of Christian sociology?" (*Machine Age*, p. 13). And our present organization, while it keeps many in dire want, insufficiency or grinding insecurity, holds up for our admiration and effort the pursuit of wealth and luxury; while many are ill-clad and ill-fed and ill-housed, many (and not only, or even principally, "the rich") have a standard of living that is absurdly high. It was this, the standard of living which the middle class and the emulators of the middle class consider their due, that specially outraged Eric's doctrine of poverty: when a trade-union might be expected to be discussing work it is found trying to shove or bolster up the standard of living, however much too high it may be already (see *Belief*, p. 61 *et seq.*).

If "money" is the ruling influence in the state, if production for profit rather than for use rules in industry, the fault is ultimately ours, because "money" is the ruling power in our hearts.

. . . . .

Responsibility is of two kinds. There is moral responsibility for what we do and intend or refrain from doing, and there is intellectual responsibility for the kind and quality of what we make, "make" being understood in no narrow sense. Gill constantly returned to the theme of how deeply the idea of "making" enters properly into man's life and informs his work (*cf.*, the popular "What has he *made* of his life?"). "Deeds done, when viewed in themselves and not simply as means to ends, are also to be regarded as things made."

Work, says the dictionary, is "the exertion of energy, physical and mental" otherwise than for purposes of recreation. God has made the world and man such that work is necessary for life and, since nothing that truly subserves our life can be bad, there can be no form of necessary work which is in itself degrading. Nevertheless, an idea is now very prevalent that physical labour is bad, a thing to be avoided so far as possible, though even in the most mechanized conditions there must be a basic element of such labour. In a Christian society there should be no kind whatever of physical work which is either derogatory to human beings or incapable of being ennobled and hallowed; therefore, said Gill, "at every turn our object must be to sanctify rather than to exclude physical labour, to honour it rather than to degrade it, to discover how to make it pleasant rather than onerous, a source of pride rather than of shame. . . . There is no kind of physical labour which is at one and the same time truly necessary to human life and necessarily either unduly onerous or unpleasant."

Our industrial civilization fosters and encourages the notion that much manual work is, of itself, sub-human drudgery; when the working life of thousands of factory "hands," shop-assistants, clerks, domestics, navvies and transport workers and labourers on our pitiful farms is considered, this seems to be true; and it appears obviously a good thing that, by the use of more machinery, more of this drudgery should be got rid of. Thus it has come about that people have come to believe that all physical labour is in itself bad. We seek to reduce it to a minimum and we look to our leisure time for all enjoyable exercise of our bodies. (The contradiction has been overlooked that if physical exercise be bad in work, then it is bad in play also.)

> "It should be obvious that it is not the physical labour which is bad but the proletarianism by which men and women have become simply 'hands,' simple instruments for the making of money by those who own the means of production, distribution and exchange. And those who argue in favour of the still further elimination of physical labour on the ground that much manual labour is, of itself, sub-human drudgery are playing into the hands either of those for whose profit the mechanical organization of industry has been developed or of the communists and others who look to the 'leisure state' as the *summum bonum.* We must return again and again to the simple doctrine: physical work, manual labour, is *not* in itself bad. It is the necessary basis of all human production and, in the most strict sense of the words, physical labour directed to the production of things needed for human life is both honourable and holy."

Having through our cupidity and indolence degraded most forms of work, domestic and other, so that they are no longer to be viewed as pleasant, still less as sacred, having made men and women into "hands" and profit-making instruments, herded together in monstrous cities, "we turn round and curse the very idea of labour. To use the body, our arms and legs and backs, is now held to be derogatory to our human dignity. . . . It is at the very base of the Christian reform for which we stand that we return to the honouring of bodily work."

The contempt shown for manual work has not been extended to those activities which in modern times are distinguished as the "fine arts"; on the contrary, their practitioners are excessively honoured, and a kind of mythology or mystagogy has grown up which Eric Gill castigated under the name of "art nonsense": he devoted a whole book, *Art and a Changing Civilization,* to what he called "the debunking of art." The isolation of something called Art (with a big A), especially pictorial art and the aesthetic chatter that goes therewith, the putting of the artist on a pedestal as someone apart from and above other men, the cultivation of an absurd artificiality called the "artistic temperament," such things, he said, imply "a bourgeois frame of mind, and are a notable product of a bourgeois society."

All the arts, whether "useful" or "fine," have their origin in man's fundamental needs, to supply himself with food,

clothing and shelter, to pray to and praise God, to recreate himself; and accordingly Eric, putting aside all irrelevancies about emotion, self-expression, and the like, defined art simply by its earlier meaning, as "the well-making of what needs making," thus vastly extending its scope as commonly understood to-day. Time and again he quoted the words of Ananda Coomaraswamy: "An artist is not a special kind of man, but every man is a special kind of artist"; it was on the artist as workman, as a "collaborator with God in creating," that his thought on this matter was centred, the objective approach to work that was destroyed in so many arts by the Renaissance. "I would rather have brick-laying and turnip-hoeing done well and properly and high art go to the devil (if it must), than have high art flourishing and brick-laying and turnip-hoeing be the work of slaves" (*Auto.,* p. 177). It was again to the common man that he looked; his revolution was again away from the specialist, the expert, professionalism, towards the ordinary person and his needs.

> "I have no use at all for 'Art' as commonly understood to-day. . . . I would abolish the fine arts altogether. Music—let us sing in church and at work and at harvest-festivals and wedding parties and all such times and places. But let us abolish the concert-hall. Painting and sculpture—let us paint and carve our houses and churches and town-halls and places of business. But let us abolish art-galleries and royal academies and picture-dealers. Architecture—let us employ builders and engineers, and let them be imbued with human enthusiasms and not be moved merely by the desire for money or by merely utilitarian standards. Poetry—let those who can, write our hymns and songs and prayers. Let them write dirges for funerals and songs for weddings, and let them go about and sing to us or read to us in our houses. But let us abolish all this high nonsense about poets who are 'not as other men.' And let us abolish all the art-schools and museums and picture-galleries" (*W. & P.,* p. 87).

Fountain-pens, motor-cars and the like are as much works of art as pictures and carvings, the bridge across the Saint Lawrence river at Quebec would stand comparison with any medieval cathedral or castle; the difference between them is that the pictures and castles are the work of an individual artist—responsible workman—or a number of them working together, whereas the only artist concerned with the production of the motor-car or the bridge is the *designer,* architect, thereof, the others concerned being mostly willing or unwilling proletarian "hands." And each method faithfully reflects the philosophy and religion and life of a society: Chartres cathedral, simply as a building, could arise from none other than an ultimately spiritual background, the Canadian bridge is as clearly a product of the materialistic enthusiasms of the times in which we live.[15]

> "Work itself becomes a game, and the curse of Adam—'in the sweat of thy brow thou shalt eat

bread'—is turned to blessing, for man has found joy in his labour and that that is his portion. Thus, while the necessity remains and use is neither denied nor condemned, all things made become works of love, all deeds become things in themselves, all means become ends. This is the basis, the concreted and untrembling foundation of human art. This is man's response to his responsibility—that he freely wills what is necessary, he makes what must be into a thing he has chosen.

"These are the things which the materialism of our time denies and derides. By its separation of work from pleasure, its divorce of use from beauty and of beauty from meaning, it has produced a real disintegration of humanity, and on the basis of its materialism there is no remedy for its sufferings but a more efficient organization of material. Let there be plenty for all and no parasites. Let all the milk be sterilized. They say: Let thought be free and let all work be commanded. We say: There is no such thing as free thought and let all works be free offerings. Materialism spells slavery. . . . 'Freedom is a concession of the state'" (*Belief*, pp. 330-1).

And the ultimate slavery and degradation of the artist is to be "freed from the necessity of making anything useful."

4

Some Christians made it a matter of reproach against Gill that *apparently* he did not pay enough attention to the cruelties and injustices of communists and their implacable persecution of all religion or to the cruelties and injustices of fascists and nazis and their subtle efforts to nullify the Church's influence.[16] They overlooked that in his writing and public speaking he was concerned more with diseases than with symptoms; and they were incredulous when assured that he did not believe that fundamentally and potentially the societies of Great Britain and the United States and France were much better than those of Russia and Italy and Germany; that, in effect, respectable" democratic" capitalist-industrialism is as atheistic, as destructive of responsibility and liberty, of holy poverty and the human person, of hope and love, as is communism itself; that its practical materialism has precisely the same effects as the dialectical materialism with which marxists oppose metaphysical and spiritual truth; that, in fact, totalitarian stateism, particularly in its communist form, is a logical development of the civilization of "the democracies."[17] No wonder communism seems the only just politics for the "beehive state" that most people seem to want and few try to prevent, for if all things are to be made by machines within a "rationalized" system there must naturally be more and more standardization.[18]

Fascism and socialism and marxism do not offer holiness: they offer more physical convenience and psychological satisfaction (by flattering human sensibility) in return for the obedience of their citizenry. They tell us they are going to cure a disease—by aggravating it.

"Had it not been for the spur which trade-unionism gave to human inventiveness and the consequent development of machinery it would very certainly have been necessary either to repeal the Factory Acts, and all acts designed to protect the animal classes, or else to abandon the ambition of being a first-class multiple-store and shop-keeping nation." The socialist movement "offered nothing in the way of divine inspiration, nothing beyond the ideal of a world in which all should be hygienically and warmly clad—with a sort of B.B.C. 'culture park' looming in the background; as though to say: When we've properly got going with the love of our fellow men, then we'll see what we can do about culture and, well, you know, religion and art and stuff" (*Auto.*, pp. 141, 163). The marxists go one worse. "They have thrown away the God whom the capitalists profess to worship and do not, and have accepted the servitude which capitalism has developed and perfected but whose existence the capitalists deny. Thus they have not emptied out the baby with the bath water. They have retained the bath water while emptying out the baby. They have emptied out the Baby of Bethlehem only to swallow the foul and befouling bath water of London and Manchester" (*Belief*, p. 271). And not simply the slums and misery of those cities, which are accidental to our materialism (Are we not getting rid of them?), but its substance—its philosophy, its reversal of human and spiritual values. If capitalism is as irreligious as socialism, socialism is as inhuman and enslaving as capitalism. For all its lip-service to the spirit, its church on Sundays, and museums and art-galleries and "Shakespeare for the workers," "business" is materialist. "For all their real devotion to pure art, pure science, or pure what-not, the reformers are as much materialists as the men of business. The communists among them are clearheaded enough to recognize this; they are honest enough to proclaim it and glory in it."

"Workers, throw off your chains!"—and then put them on again. No revolution that accepts materialism and its modern social incarnation, industrialism, can really be a revolution.

It was, then, central to the social-revolutionary aspect of Eric Gill's teaching that industrial capitalism implies a way of life and work that is inconsistent with man's nature and with the Christian religion. Capitalism is a social theory based on the profit-motive, and its essence and object is production for profit; both "labour" and "products" must be looked at primarily from the point of view of saleability, and not from that of their intrinsic quality and man's real needs. Its method is that of industrialism, which had three main processes, viz., the proletarianization of the craftsman, of the agricultural worker, and of the "small man" generally, the concentration of production in factories, and the use of machines, leading to mass-production by the division and sub-division of labour.

"Eric Gill," wrote Father Kenelm Foster, O.P., "holds things together. He is our great *pontifex*, bridge-builder. Spirit and matter, body and mind, knowing and loving:

he distinguished them with exquisite clarity, and then held them together. He did it *in practice;* wherever he went he made matter alive with rational beauty. Why did he loathe industrialism?—fundamentally because he thought that *in practice* it separates what God has joined together, the body and the mind." That was indeed the main point among his many serious charges against industrialism: not its cruelty (for it is now realized that too obvious unkindness "does not pay"), but "the change which it has brought about in the nature of the work to be done and therefore in the minds of the men who do it"; it produces a world wherein "on the one hand we have the artist concerned solely to express himself; on the other is the workman deprived of any self to express." He did not assert that this was anything new in the world's history: the attempt to divorce art from work and use from beauty has been made—and resisted—from the beginning. But industrialism leads so clearly to the separation of mind and matter, which spells death to man, that death may be said to be its very object.

"It is only as persons that we serve one another, and when personal control is divorced from ownership it is only with great difficulty that men retain responsibility for the form and quality of what is done or produced . . . the men have no responsibility whatever, except a moral responsibility to obey the terms of their contract, *i.e.,* to do what they are told. Thus the craftsman is finally degraded—he ceases to be a person who in any way designs what he makes and makes what he designs; he is no longer even a hand: he has become a tool, a sentient part of the machine" (*Machine Age,* pp. 34, 38)—and this without overlooking the real love of machines and the great skill and craftsmanship displayed both by machine-makers and machine-minders. "Our industrial system does not enslave the workers in any legal or technical or political sense. It does not necessarily maltreat their bodies or coerce their minds. It simply reduces the workman to a subhuman condition of intellectual irresponsibility.[19] It simply separates, divorces, the material and the spiritual." More and more workmen are being deprived of intellectual responsibility, becoming automatons in their work, prevented from being artists.

> "And in their leisure, the time when they are not working they must be content to be amused; for industrialism has deprived them of the necessity of making anything useful." "The value of the creative faculty derives from the fact that that faculty is the primary mark of man. To deprive man of its exercise is to reduce him to subhumanity. . . . A man is as out of place in a factory as in a lightless dungeon. . . . If the populations of our factory-towns were not constantly recruited from the country they would wither intellectually as certainly as they wither morally and physically" (*W. & P.,* pp. 84-85).

Intellectual responsibility the concern of a few, or one; for the rest, obedience: the idea has become painfully familiar in other spheres besides industry.

It is more horrible, wrote Gill, that men of business should rule us through the profit-making system they have perfected, and impose their foul view on the world, "than it would be if the whole race of men and women should rot their bodies with lechery and drunkenness." It produces things which, in their nature, because of the manner of their production, are unsuitable for the use of human beings: "We are making a bee-hive when we should have a house. We are making an apiary when we should have a motherland." The thing and its results have been summed up in words that might have been spoken by Eric Gill but, in fact, came from Pope Pius XII: "In this age of mechanization the human person becomes merely a more perfect tool in industrial production and . . . a perfected tool for mechanized warfare."

Eric did not deny the impressiveness of the powers which industrialism has helped to confer on us, or seek to decry them. He had no romantic ideas about the "immorality" of using machinery, nor did he suppose its use was likely to be noticeably lessened in any foreseeable future. "It is art-nonsense to say that because the Forth Bridge is made of iron it is not a work of art. . . . It is no more immoral to make things by machinery than by hand. It is immoral to make things badly and pretend that they are good, and no amount of 'hand' is an excuse for stupidity or inefficiency" (*Art Nonsense,* pp. 313-14). The trouble is that machines are not simply complicated tools designed by workmen to help them in their work. "They are things designed to enable their owners to make things in great quantities in order to make great quantities of money. No definition of machinery and no description of machine industry can neglect these facts. . . . The real distinction between tools and machines is discovered in the sphere of control and responsibility. Who is responsible for the thing made or the deed done?" (*Belief,* pp. 103, 88).

It was characteristic of his all-roundness and freedom from "teetotalism" that Gill was interested in machines (*e.g.,* the internal-combustion engines of the lorries he drove in the R.A.F.) and appreciative of their beauty—so like the beauty of bones and crystals and insects' wings; I have seen him stand entranced before a shop-window full of useful gadgets and neatly-fitting boxes and files. It was not for nothing that for ten youthful years he drew nothing but locomotive engines, held by the "character and meaning that were manifest in their shape." Need it be said there is no inconsistency here? On one occasion, asked by the proud owner of a sham-gothic residence how he liked the building, Eric replied that he liked the electrical switchboard in the hall. His questioner expressed surprise. "Oh, I like anything reasonable," explained Eric, to which his host replied, "That's too abstruse for me." When it is added that the owner was a scientist that anecdote becomes even more significant.

Eric Gill's indictment of industrialism has been widely misunderstood, and his sweeping generalizations of its evil effects sometimes gave understandable offence. When he said time and again that it reduces the workers to a subhuman condition of intellectual irresponsibility, the word "intellectual" was not always heard; when he said so often that the industrial population is dehumanized he did not always add that he meant dehumanized as workmen, as makers of things: machine-minding is often very skilful work and many mechanics are highly skilled and responsible workmen, but they are so in relation to the machine and not to the thing which the machine turns out. It would have been well had he more frequently and clearly stated his recognition of "the many men, and women, who in spite of the inhuman nature of their employment, retain the notions which properly belong to private and personal enterprise" (*Machine Age,* p. 35). Even so, from our own personal experience of people, we may think that he exaggerated, and in respect to present actuality perhaps he did: but he was looking also to the future—and he was a far-seeing man.

Again, when in answer to the oft-made objection that "A man can be a good Christian in a factory," he replied, "Yes; and St. Agnes was a good Christian in a brothel—but that was no reason why she should stay there!" it is not surprising that the objector should not be silenced, for the analogy between a factory and a brothel does not go very far. Of course he knew perfectly well, he never forgot, that Christianity can enable us to lead godly, righteous and sober lives amid any conditions: his point was that some conditions are more favourable than others. "A social order cannot in itself force any one to do anything, but it can be such as to place many obstacles in the way" of those who would live in a human and Christian manner: in a score of places (*e.g., Art Nonsense,* p. 132), he sets out briefly, clearly and cogently why the conditions of industrialism are so bad in this respect, and it is only common prudence to remove removable handicaps. His case is most forcibly and brilliantly set out in *Money and Morals,* but its presentation there also showed most manifestly an element of exaggeration. It is gravely false, it is shocking, to say that "It is waste of time teaching Christian morals in the present condition of things," as he himself at once goes on to admit; but his admission is too reserved. It is true that the exercise of heroic virtue can't be counted on—but the grace of God can. He is on surer ground when he declares that "truth and error cannot permanently lie down together and Christian morals cannot *permanently flourish* in the same bed with a life contrary to nature" (*italics mine*).

That just as right thinking precedes right faith, so a certain way of living is the necessary preamble to Christian morals, is quite true if rightly understood; but it can be distorted, and it is easy to overlook that if Eric set that "certain way of living" very high it was because he was also looking at a very high and enlightened and unrestricted standard of life and conduct. And why should he not? Are we not bound to? "Be ye perfect. . . . " Moreover, on the psychological side, there was the factor of reaction. In his dealings with his fellow Christians he was met on all sides by clergy, the shepherds of the flock, who seemed to seek every excuse to avoid finding fault with industrial capitalism: among Catholics, in spite of the outspoken social encyclical-letters of Pope Leo XIII and Pope Pius XI, he did not find "clergy and laity all agog for social or any other reform, and in general the clergy seem to regard it as their job to support a social order which, so far as it is possible, forces us to commit all the sins they denounce" (*Auto.,* p. 214). What seemed to him so unbelievable, shocking and blasphemous was the complacency of apparently the majority of Christians, not only about the purity of their faith and practice, but also about the *kind* of world in which they live and which they have co-operated in making.

In any case, it seemed to Gill, the Christians who ask the question, "Is communism (or capitalism or nazism or whatnot) compatible with Christianity?" are approaching the matter from the wrong end. The proper question is, "Is Christianity compatible with the industrial and authoritarian development of society?" And the answer is certainly, "No"; for at the root of Christianity is the doctrine of individual personal responsibility. "Man is man all the time, and not only in his spare time."

In *The Problem of Pain* C. S. Lewis has given us a timely warning against "making use of the idea of corporate guilt to distract our attention from those humdrum, old-fashioned guilts of our own which have nothing to do with 'the system' and which can be dealt with without waiting for the millennium." In *Christianity and Crisis* Reinhold Niebuhr writes: "We do not find it particularly impressive to celebrate one's sensitive conscience by enlarging upon all the well-known evils of our Western world and equating them with the evils of the totalitarian systems." Substituting" capitalist-industrial" for "totalitarian" in the second quotation, no one who knew him or attentively reads his writings will imagine for a moment that Eric Gill stood in need of such warnings: but they do indicate very real dangers for those of us who share his thought. He was a man of peculiarly well-balanced mind and sensitive conscience, and all those of us who would follow him are not similarly well equipped: it was said by a friend precisely of Gill and a third party that "God sends disciples to geniuses to keep them humble." It is not given to everyone who sees the evils and abuses of industrial capitalism to see them in their setting so clearly or to examine them and their possible remedies with such precision as did Eric Gill; and very few of us are enabled more or less to escape them (though we shall be wise to do so if we get the chance, as St. Benedict escaped from the evils of sixth-century Rome).[20] But we can safely and surely do what Eric writes of so movingly and delicately in quite another context on pages 223-27 of the *Autobiography,* we can take the delights and dangers and evils of the society in which we live and, following the words of that same St. Benedict in the prologue to his *Rule,* "cast them on the rock which is Christ."

In face of industrialism, as of every other similar question, we have to beware of the exaggeration contrary to the excessively moralistic interpretation of Christianity:

it must not be obscured that the Christian religion has directly to do with only two problems—sin and virtue. It can be applied to ploughing up pasture or to poetry only through being effectively applied to the problem of sin and virtue in farmers and poets. It can be applied to society only through the individual members of society: the disappearance of industrial capitalism, the establishment of one of these "Christian orders" we hear so much about, could by themselves effect little for the kingdom of God. "The holiness of God is something more and other than moral perfection"—but without moral goodness there can be no holiness at all, no wholeness. Eric Gill tried to live in the light of "Seek first the kingdom of God, and his righteousness"[21] and, as has been said before, he more and more found the way to that kingdom to be through the word of St. James, "pure religion and undefiled is this, to visit the fatherless and widows in their affliction and to keep unspotted from the world."

. . . . .

"No individual Christian in our society is to be condemned except in so far as he approves or promotes the evil thing. And, again, no individual, in relation to our society, is to be praised except in so far as he promotes the Christian revolution (*i.e.*, 'turning round') by which once more a Christian society may be revived" (*W. & P.*, p. 6). In his article in *Blackfriars* already referred to, Bernard Kelly remarks that: "The categories in which Gill lived, worked, and wrote were absolute: religious, moral, metaphysical. They were not the categories of political expediency. Thus he was eminently qualified in the critique of social programmes, Catholic and not, put forward to restore a tolerably Christian social structure, but he was not qualified to judge them precisely as politically feasible." Or, as Eric put it, politics are not my line of business; if he agreed with the Reverend F. H. Drinkwater that "the economic problem fills the whole sky," yet the only socio-economic reform he put forward (apart from his insistence on production for use and not for profit, and with one notable exception to be mentioned later) was the abolition of the middleman and the financier.

Way back as an architect's pupil in London he had realized that "it was not so much the working *class* that concerned me as the working man—not so much what he *got* from working as what he *did* by working," and had got hold of the notion that "a good life wasn't only a matter of good politics and good buildings and well-ordered towns and justice in economic relations." Social reform is the business of those who know the nature and destiny of man, he declared, and "the trouble with the present age is that it is just the knowledge of those things which it is most uncertain about, and consequently politics and social guidance are left to a crowd of amateurs—novelists, multiple-storekeepers, manufacturers of motor-cars or chemicals—whose profession of disinterestedness is only slightly more credible than that of thieves and robbers" (*Art Nonsense*, p. 315); and in the first essay of **Work and Property** he conveniently summarized some of the things that these amateurs ought to know.

As for the professional politicians—"Liberals and Conservatives—Labour! All these parties wish to preserve the *status quo*. But it is just the *status quo* which is in question." People of all kinds toy with communism both because it seems better politics than *that* and because it seems to offer an approximation to absolutes in a world wherein religion has grown cold: afraid to face Love, too tired to rebuild his house, they "fall back on an 'economic interpretation of history,' and are satisfied to live by bread alone." It was in Palestine that Gill fully realized in all their beastliness the materialism, exploiting imperialism and mechanized labour in which England has been a pathfinder and pioneer, and he came back determined to keep clear of all politics and politicians.

> "For . . . politics is beyond me. Politics is . . . outside my scope, something I can't do. Moreover I do not believe political arrangements and rearrangements are real. It is all a confused business of ramps and rackets—pretended quarrels and dishonest schemings, having no relation to the real interests of peoples. . . . The prestige of Parliament is an empty fraud. It is not too much to say that [parliamentarians] are not and never have been anything but agents for the defence of monetary interests. Such was the origin of parliamentary representation, such is its very soul. . . . And, particularly, do not believe politicians. By the nature of their trade they have no professional pride and can have none. The phrase 'professional politician' has brought the very notion of professionalism to dirt" (*Auto.*, pp. 259, 148).

Again there is an element of exaggeration, but it would be pharisaical to stress it. Years before Eric had been strongly impressed by Julien Benda's book, *La Trahison des Clercs* (called in the English version *The Great Betrayal*); he came to see even more clearly that the poet, the artist, the scholar, the "clerk," who should be a disinterested[22] man, is indeed a traitor if he puts himself almost unreservedly at the service of the relative and contingent: and if it be a question of professional politics, he will be buried under a mountain of mud, "whereas it is necessary that he should keep his feet on the earth and his head above ground." In the words of The Preacher, without the craftsmen and the husbandmen the city cannot be built or flourish, "but they shall not dwell or go up and down therein; nor shall they go up into the assembly or sit among the judges." In other words, let them keep out of politics. "Nevertheless they shall strengthen the state of the world, and their prayer shall be in the work of their craft. . . . "

The increasing "politicization" of people in these latter days was very grievous to Gill; for himself he hardly ever adverted of his own accord to such concepts as democracy, dictatorship and the like. A man who was about to address a meeting of war-resisters asked him for a message to them. "Tell them to keep clear of politics," was the reply.

Politics even at its best is quite insignificant beside Christian doctrine and its implications. The "Magnificat" is irrelevant in our dirty struggles between "interests" and classes and nations and political programmes—so it must be the struggles themselves that are really irrelevant. "Religion is politics, and politics is brotherhood," said William Blake—"and brotherhood is poverty," added Eric Gill.

> "All our politics," he wrote in a publication of the Cotswold Bruderhof, "are based on a denial of the Gospels. Our capitalist society is founded solely upon the notion that those who have money have the duty to get more, and that those who have none must be enslaved or exploited or 'employed'—until machines make their existence unnecessary. The fascist societies want to create empires and become as rich and great as the others. The communist societies want to make the rich poor in order that the poor may become rich. But the Church of God wants to make the rich poor and the poor holy.

> "This is the circle of human politics: When we have accepted poverty there will be peace among men. Only when we make peace shall we become the children of God. Only when we love God shall we love our fellow men. Only when we love our fellow men shall we have peace. When we have peace we shall have poverty, and when we have poverty we shall have the kingdom of Heaven."

. . . . .

Remembering that by poverty Gill meant, where material goods are concerned, not less than a reasonable sufficiency for decent human life, it need occasion no surprise that he saw the chief "practical" means to the restoration of the dignity of physical work, and of the quality of things made, in the ownership of property; and he came to advocate as a practicable necessary reform the ownership of the means of production by the workers (*not* by the state; "workers" means all who work in a given enterprise, including the managing director if he works and if there is a job for him to do). This can be found set out in the essay on Work and Property in the book of that name and in another, "Ownership and Industrialism," in *Sacred and Secular;* but here I follow mainly a letter to the *Catholic Herald* newspaper in which he summarized his argument.

The right to property, he said, is not primarily a moral right, one due to man on account of his free will, but is, so to say, an intellectual right, due on account of his intelligence: it follows from man's material necessities and intellectual nature, deriving not from his need to *use* things but from his need to *make* things. As a moral being purely as such, man has no right of private ownership; he quotes Pope Leo XIII and Aquinas on the duty to possess things not as one's own but as common. (Incidentally, Christians, especially the Catholic clergy, have made a big mistake in presenting the right to private property as apparently simply a matter of morals, "a thing good men believe in and bad men deny, and that's all about it." We have sought to defend the institution of private property by the very arguments which are our opponents' strongest line of attack: "the earth is the Lord's," his gift to us is for our "individual appropriation and public use"—and we have done our best to destroy both, and so allowed such miseries to be heaped upon man that the socialist says, "Destroy private property!" to which the communist adds, "And religion with it," for it has been made to look as if the Church herself were on the side of big business and exploitation.)

It is, then, to man as workman, as an intelligent being who must manipulate things in order to make them serviceable, that private ownership is both necessary and a natural right, and only when there is full control of the means of production can there be proper and efficient manipulation. Unless the farmer own the fields (or have a tenancy on terms nearly equivalent to ownership) he cannot exercise his best skill and intelligence upon them; unless the carver own the tools and stone he cannot properly exercise his skill and intelligence therewith; unless the miner own the mine, individually or jointly with others, he or they cannot properly control the job of mining. This necessity of manipulation it is which gives the right of private property in the means of production: "The exercise of art or work, whether it be that of a craftsman or a manual labourer, is the formal reason of individual appropriation," as Maritain observes.

It is obvious that, as things are, the ground upon which alone a claim to private property in productive goods can be validly made has to a considerable extent been destroyed. The factory "hand" can make no claim to private ownership in his work and the big-machine industries and transport are no longer in any true sense private enterprises: they are (as their directors boast) public services. Hence the moral force of communism: what are public services should be publicly owned for the profit of all. There no longer remains any rational and Christian objection to communal ownership, since the only reason for private ownership, the intellectual operation of the workman by which he imprints on matter the mark of rational being, has been destroyed by the development of machine industry.

The conclusion is inescapable. We cannot have any right to private property in the means of production unless we are prepared to abandon industrialism; most people are not so prepared, and even if they were, it would be impossible to return immediately to pre-industrial methods.

> "Let us resolutely put away all dreams of that sort. Let us abandon the coteries of vegetarians and nut-eaters and artist-craftsmen. . . . Politics deals with things as they are. . . . Ownership is necessary to human happiness, to human dignity and virtue, and ownership means control. A share in profits is not ownership. Money in the savings-bank is not control of the means of production.

The only desirable and at the same time the only possible reform of 'our world' is distribution of ownership" (*S. & S.,* p. 168).

Capitalist organization implicitly and communist organization explicitly lead to public ownership for private use. This is the exact opposite of Christian society, where there should be private ownership for the sake of common use. In our existing society we have degraded nearly all production and transport to being huge impersonal and therefore sub-human enterprises—and yet we have the insolence or folly to endeavour to maintain private ownership in the use of productive things and to declare that this sort of "private property" is a principle of Christianity which must be defended against ravening "reds" and subversive "leftists." "The newspapers and politicians and big-businessmen talk as though everybody in England had private property, and enough private property to make complete human beings of themselves, and as though it was only in wicked Russia that no one was allowed to own anything privately" (*Unemployment,* p. 27).

Workers' ownership of the means of production, then, was what Gill put forward as a practicable, perhaps the only practicable, step towards the Christian society in which there shall be private ownership for the sake of public use, a private ownership not asked for "on the selfish ground of private enjoyment, but for the sake of the good of things to be made and in order that the public use which morality demands may be a use of good things." The alternative we shall have to accept is in all probability some form of communistic industrialism and the "leisure state," wherein man's intelligence will wither away in highbrow snobbery or mob vulgarity.

> But "that alternative is no revolution, it is simply *progress.* In fact so-called revolutionaries are simply 'progressives.' They want, instead of the present world, the world which the present one *implies.* They want the same thing only more so—the same things only more of them. . . . Merely to transfer ownership from private persons to the state is no revolution; it is only a natural development. Government by the proletariat is no revolution; it is only the natural sequel to the enfranchisement of lodgers. But to abolish the proletariat and make all men owners— and to abolish mass-production and return to a state of affairs wherein 'the artist is not a special kind of man but every man is a special kind of artist'—that would be a revolution in the proper sense of the word. And merely to proclaim an atheist government is no revolution—for that would be to make explicit what is already implicit in capitalist commercialism; but to return to Christianity would be truly revolutionary" (*W. & P.,* pp. 53-54).

. . . . .

Meanwhile—let us lift up our hearts to the Lord.

"I am quite perfectly certain that the ultimate truth of the created universe is that which is implied in the saying of Julian of Norwich: 'It lasteth and forever shall, for God loveth it,' and that as the actuality of everything is dependent upon God's will, so everything is sustained in being by his love."

In that belief Eric Gill lived, and in that belief he died.

NOTES

[1] For more particulars of these conclusions the *Autobiography* gives a reference to *The Highway,* organ of the Workers' Educational Association, November 1910 to February 1911.

[2] Gill ends his autobiography with it: the remaining ninety-one pages, one third of the whole book, are labelled "postscript."

[3] As will be seen in a subsequent paragraph, this epithet does not call in question the beauty of Roman Catholic services, which with the liturgies of worship of other ancient churches form a supreme work of art. But in the average Roman Catholic church they come in for some rough handling, and are disguised by a layer of commercial fripperies, "devotional" externals, and a lack of really corporate approach that faithfully reflect the contemporary world.

[4] It must in fairness be recognized, as Gill recognized, that these things have been considerably modified in the past twenty years.

[5] To discourage individualistic devotion and to emphasize the corporate nature of this act, Gill advocated the putting of the altar in the middle of the church with the congregation all around. See "Mass for the Masses" in *Sacred and Secular.*

[6] A third-order, whose members are called "tertiaries," is an association of lay people, not normally living in community, who follow a private rule of life under the direction of an order of mendicant friars. To-day they hardly differ in practice from any other similar religious society; in the middle ages their obligations and significance were more serious.

[7] But, as Gill often pointed out, the use of reason is not to be identified with the process of ratiocination. And "the senses are a kind of reason" (he did not invent that saying, he found it in St. Thomas).

[8] Early in our friendship he surprised me by saying of the Church's condemnation of a certain action as sinful in essence that "I can't understand *why.* I'm always rebelling against it. Now if it were merely a disciplinary rule, imposed for reasons of expediency, I'd be quite happy about it." Years later he told me that his attitude had become quite the opposite: he had learned to be critical of the desirability and efficacy of rules and regulations and the ingenuities of casuists and canon lawyers. "The more canon law, the less religion" (it was not Gill but an ecclesiastic who said that).

[9] The Ditchling gild still exists. Its press published the first work in English of that great Frenchman Jacques Maritain, viz., *Art et Scolastique,* translated by the Reverend John O'Connor under the title "The Philosophy of Art."

[10] "The deep religion of his teaching has been to me literally the revelation of a new gospel," wrote Dr. Mulk Raj Anand in his *Hindu View of Art.*

[11] He disliked this title as pretentious, and wanted to call it "Believe It or Not." His publishers, Messrs. Faber & Faber, would not agree, but he had his way with the subtitle. *See* bibliography.

[12] Among his stone works (not all at this time) were stations of the cross in churches at Bradford and Leatherhead, the Leeds University war memorial, and carvings for the underground station at St. James's Park, at Broadcasting House, and for the League of Nations building at Geneva. He was also commissioned for work on the new Anglican cathedral at Guildford. He designed eleven faces of printing type, including a Greek, a Hebrew and an Arabic face. He engraved (on wood) many decorations for the books of the Golden Cockerel, Count Kessler's, and other presses. He was made an associate of the Royal Academy, an honorary member of the Royal Institute of British Architects, an L.L.D., *honoris causa* of Edinburgh University, and was one of the original recipients of the new designer-for-industry honour (!). Some even of his friends did not know of these recognitions, which he regarded simply as manifestations of the uncritical kindness of the public bodies concerned.

[13] He wrote this in 1928 (*Art Nonsense,* p. 291); I quote it in 1941.

[14] Gill might well have echoed Göring's famous remark about culture and a revolver. But whereas Göring would shoot down the good men, Gill would shoot down the bogus things. *See* again later.

[15] It may be noted in passing that Gill did not entertain the delusion that the culture of the past was Christian in the sense that it was in any way a direct product of the Church or of ecclesiastics. Medieval bishops, priests and monks were clergy and customers, not workmen and producers (with individual exceptions, of course). "In fact, the civilizing power of man is a lay power—fostered, encouraged, nursed, petted by the Church but, in its own sphere, independent. . . . [The Church] takes what she is given" (*Beauty,* p. 32). Strictly speaking, there is no such thing as a Christian or Catholic or Protestant culture: there are the various cultures which grow up in societies of people who are Catholics or Protestants or what not, which reflect the corresponding ideas more or less faithfully.

[16] It is true that for a long time he held the view that militant godlessness is only an accident of marx-leninist communism, provoked by the insufficiency of and support of bourgeois exploitation by so many Christians. Later, I think, he came to realize that the destruction of spiritual religion is essential to marxist theory. In any case, it may be questioned whether stoning the prophets is worse than ignoring them altogether.

[17] He did not of course, as some fanatics do, claim that in the present war there is nothing to choose between the combatants. He saw many reasons why a victory for Great Britain and the United States and the defeat of the Axis powers offers hope for a desperate world, whereas the reverse would increase the desperation of our state. But that is little enough without a real "revolution."

[18] But, like so large a number of people of very different views, Gill tended, I think, to exaggerate the popularity of communist views (even as vague aspirations) in England.

[19] Gill quoted this aphorism so often that he made it his own. It originated, I believe, with Father Martin d'Arcy, S.J.

[20] Eric defined the chief aim of his life's work to be "to make a cell of good living in the chaos of our world"; to do something towards "reintegrating bed and board, the small farm and the workshop, the home and the school, the earth and Heaven."

[21] In reading Gill it must be borne in mind that the Rheims-Douay version of the Bible translates δικαιοσύνη, *iustitia,* not by "righteousness" but "justice." This is rather misleading, since in current use the connotation of the word "justice" is almost entirely rational and juridical.

[22] In view of an increasing misuse of this word it seems desirable to point out that it is *not* a synonym for "uninterested." I think Eric himself defined the saint as "the wholly disinterested man."

## Frances Spalding (essay date 1981)

SOURCE: "Making Things Well," in *The Times Literary Supplement,* No. 4107, December 18, 1981, p. 1460.

[*In the following essay, a review of a biography, Spalding critiques Gill's sexual attitudes and other aspects of his thinking.*]

The revival of craft in the high-tech age proves that William Morris's battle with the machine was not as finally lost as it once seemed. Eric Gill argued that handicraft methods would not die out because they met an inherent, indestructible need in human nature. In the last decade a craftsman emerging from the Royal College was more likely to disappear into the Cotswolds than into industry. But if the craft revival is here to stay, so too are the often invidious effects of the machine.

Goods of high quality may be more widely available but Morris's wish is still an ideal: "We are waiting for what must be the work, not the leisure and taste of a few scholars, authors and artists, but of the necessities and aspirations of the workmen throughout the civilized world." Gill hoped and laboured for the same. Michael Yorke, in his excellent reassessment of the artist, [*Eric Gill: Man of Flesh and Spirit*] constantly reminds us that the issues which exercised Gill are still unresolved today.

It is tempting to regard Gill as an anachronism, a throwback to the twelfth century in the unholy era of the first machine age. He looked like a medieval craftsman crossed with a monk for he never wore trousers but dressed in a loose-fitting, belted smock. Beneath this protruded his knee-length silk underpants, which matched in colour his scarlet socks. As he intended, his garb marked him out from the drab uniform representative of an anonymous society. He despised the "Daily-Mail mind" and much else in twentieth-century Britain, and though he executed sculpture for BBC's Broadcasting House, he forbade the wireless in his own home. Like Pugin, he looked back admiringly to the Catholic Middle Ages through, as Dr Yorke points out, a pre-Raphaelite or Tennysonian haze, forgetting medieval corruption and censorship and finding its life "Christian, normal and human". He observed that art was then the making well of whatever needed making. By contrast the artist in the twentieth century, with its rabid commercialism and self-expression, had become either a mere lap-dog to the rich or an indulgent recluse, cultivating private eccentricities.

In Gill's one-eyed view, two things had begun this decline: capitalism and the Renaissance, "that glorious attack of high fever". For him, Giotto was an end not a beginning, and the logical outcome of increasing verisimilitude was the devaluation of art into the picture postcard or photograph. He regretted the separation of the artist from the artisan and thought it degrading for the artist to be released from all necessity of producing something useful. Yet what the artist does retain, which the man at the conveyor belt does not, is total responsibility for the making. The artist is therefore envied, the individuality of his work over valued. It becomes rare or extreme, while its audience dwindles to an educated or cultured elite. Yorke, pursuing Gill's line of thought, argues:

> Museums are now the only places an artist and a workman might meet, and there are no shortages of museums as the capitalists and governments of our industrial nations are willing to finance any amount of this kind of cultural charity to salve their consciences for robbing the worker of any outlet for his sense of beauty in the course of his daily work. If you are to regard a nation's culture as something made and consumed in leisure time, then, wrote Gill, "to hell with culture as a thing added like a sauce to otherwise unpalatable stale fish".

Gill called himself a stone-cutter, emphasizing his usefulness in the art with which he first made his reputation. His stone inscriptions, or those made to his directions by assistants, can be found all over England. He never lacked work, though he shunned the London art world, moving to Ditchling in Sussex in 1907 after the birth of his second daughter. There he and his wife rediscovered certain domestic traditions and adopted the rule "never buy what you can make". He was eventually joined by the calligrapher Edward Johnston, the sculpture Desmond Chute and the printer Hilary Pepler and the "Ditchling community" began. In 1918 Gill, Pepler and Chute were invested as novices in the Third Order of St Dominic, and from then on work and worship intermingled. Gill's religion (he had been converted to Catholicism in 1913) further deepened his artistic beliefs. "Work is sacred, leisure is secular", he declared, believing like Morris that a thing made should be a joy to both the maker and the user. He hoped others would abandon "individualistic domesticity" for the dignified poverty of a community like his. As Dr Yorke astutely remarks: "That the majority of workmen actually wanted a life more like that of their capitalist masters did not occur to Gill (who knew no factory workers at all) until towards the end of his life."

An enthusiast, he was easily led but congratulated himself on the choice of his leaders. One of these was Edward Johnston, whose calligraphy classes at the Central School had first awakened Gill's interest in lettering. Johnston devoted a series of lectures to the inscription on Trajan's Column, and after twelve talks had reached the letter "C". In 1906, Gill travelled to Rome to study the inscription at first hand but never slavishly copied its example, adding to his Roman letters the serifs which are a distinguishing mark of a chisel-formed letter. But with Edward Johnston he also helped popularize the "sans serif" or block-letter form, today ubiquitously used on railway stations or wherever there is a need for maximum clarity: Gill later transferred this style into typography which, since its invention, had imitated writing, maintaining the variation in thickness produced by the pen. Certain of Gill's sans serif printing types adopt a line of unvarying thickness. These are best suited for captions, as in lengthy texts the absence of serifs, which help the eye across the page, creates "vertical slip".

His eleven type designs prove that he was not opposed to the machine in itself, which could, he said, produce "the beauty of bones", but to the way it enslaved and demeaned workers. He was attracted to wood-engraving because the artist was responsible for the entire production; there was no division of labour between designer and engraver. He could do anything he wanted in this medium, controlling the lights and darks with dazzling skill, the discipline of the technique sharpening his designs. Nor are they emotionally cold, as certain of Gill's critics declared, for the quaint poses, reminiscent of medieval art, are both elegant and affecting. Moreover in his work for Pepler's St Dominic's Press and for the Golden Cockerel Press he blended image and text with great invention.

These engravings also represent an outpouring of his religious and sexual beliefs. Introduced by Ananda Coomaraswamy to Hindu art and to its frank portrayal of sexual acts, Gill afterwards aimed at a synthesis of "Ajanta and Chartres". He used an image of naked copulation to symbolize Christ's love for his Church, and his literal illustration of *The Song of Songs* aroused a Catholic controversy. In his own character, capricious lusts warred with his love of order and precision. The man who declared that a workman's bench should be kept as neat as an altar suddenly absconded to Chartres with his mistress and periodically resorted to prostitutes. "Man is matter and spirit", he wrote, "both real and both good." But the spirit was not always infused into the matter. Gill carved a pair of lovers for Roger Fry who regretted that, "till we're much more civilized in the real sense", it could not be publicly exhibited. He thought the sculpture "noble" but criticized Gill's gilding of the necklace, finding in that detail a hint of pornography.

Gill's strong sexuality was one of the two forces that formed the content of his art. Michael Yorke deals frankly with the artist's erotica. Fascinated by pubic hair and genitals, Gill left a whole folder of drawings in which the male organ is shown from front, side view and in elevation, its measurements recorded and the owner's initials pencilled in. He drew female nudes in poses that exposed their pudenda, and when he showed a series of these to some friends, John Rothenstein broke the shocked silence by asking who the sitter had been: "The Deputy Librarian of High Wycombe", Gill replied. Like Stanley Spencer, he wanted to believe that all sexual desire is holy and was prepared to misread, over-select or ignore aspects of Catholic teaching in order to prove it. It was said of him that after conversion he thought of everything in terms of sex, even religion. "The excess of amorous nature fertilizes the spiritual field", he declared. He saw that all freedoms are interconnected and therefore related the Puritan oppression of sex to the oppression caused by industrialism. By portraying sexual matters, he saw himself helping "to destroy the morality which is corrupting us all".

Gill's nude drawings, with their fringe of shadow suggesting shallow relief, are as finely chiselled as his sculptures and stone inscriptions. Like Blake, he sought the bounding line that banishes chaos. All the parts had to be round, firm, flowing, clear and clean (his epithets). Dr Yorke finds these nudes some of the finest drawings produced this century, but with this few critics in the past have agreed. One irritating mannerism is Gill's emphatic retouching of the nude's outline, the black mark lingering on parts like an obsessive caress. Yorke remarks that Gill, despite his medieval view of women as creatures entirely subservient to men (creativity being equated with male virility),

is here "obeisant" before the sex he despised. But the drawings suggest otherwise. The woman's head is often left vacant or cut off by the edge of the paper, her body licked into position by an unfaltering line. These drawings are surely as much about possession as the erotic photographs that Gill collected. They bleakly expose his want of human sympathy, in the same way his autobiography exposes his lack of respect for his wife. ("I had £15 in hand, a bed, a table, some chairs and a few knives and forks and the top hat I was married in. I also had a wife . . .") Yorke does not extend our knowledge of Mary Gill, who remains a silent, unusually patient background figure.

Much else about Gill can irritate. Lady Rothenstein regretted his "hard and unsubtle clarity" and his "abrasively opinionated and aggressive intellect". His prose is turgid and repetitive and his argument often over-simplistic. His ideas were drawn from others, chiefly from Carlyle, Ruskin, Morris and Blake. As he himself admitted, his knowledge of history was poor and, as Yorke demonstrates, his political thinking was impractical and naive. He wrote fifty-five books and pamphlets, yet as a writer struck D. H. Lawrence as a crass, crude amateur, "maddening like a tiresome, uneducated workman arguing in a pub". Yet respect for what Gill achieved and tried to achieve continues to grow. In 1980, Manchester's Whitworth Art Gallery mounted the show "Strict Delight" which looked at all aspects of his work, and several of his rarely seen sculptures were shown more recently at the Whitechapel Art Gallery. This book warms interest into liking, perhaps because Michael Yorke's broad and humorous impartiality mellows Gill's fanaticism and egocentricity. One is also seduced by the book's layout and presentation, which even Gill could surely not have faulted.

Herbert Read was of the opinion that Gill's life and philosophy would outlive his work. He aspired towards integration, of matter with spirit, of the artist with society, moving towards Blake's Gates of Paradise through "Mutual Forgiveness of each vice". He hoped communities like those he started at Ditchling, then at Capel-y-ffin, and finally at Piggotts, would mushroom; and that the workers would rise up and demand the right to make fewer but better goods. But as Yorke wryly comments, "the slow deliberate making of a thing to last for generations seems irrelevant to people who may have no future". Gill, however, thought he was only a beginning, that it would take several generations to effect "a reasonable, decent, holy tradition of working". He told this to David Jones who, Yorke concludes, "thought he did not sound very hopeful".

**Maureen Corrigan (essay date 1983)**

SOURCE: "Gill, Chesterton and Ruskin: Mediaevalism in the Twentieth Century," in *The Chesterton Review*, Vol. IX, No. 1, February, 1983, pp. 15-30.

[*In the following essay, Corrigan traces the connection between Gill and G. K. Chesterton, both Catholic, and John Ruskin, who distanced himself from Catholicism.*]

G.K. Chesterton's ready talent for perceiving life in terms of paradox had at least one remarkable lapse. When he and fellow Catholic, Eric Gill, became the most outspoken disciples of Ruskinian mediævalism in the twentieth century, Chesterton failed to see the joke. Perhaps, in this instance, he saw not a contradiction but a cure. Ruskin, after all, had suffered from what Chesterton once termed a "splitting headache" which distorted his vision to the extent that he recognised all parts of a Gothic cathedral except the altar.[1] Through a sustained series of historical contortions, Ruskin managed more successfully than any of his contemporaries to pry mediævalism away from its Catholic underpinnings. The fact that many of the aesthetic and social programmes Ruskin popularised were derived, quietly, from Catholic sources—the writings of A.W.N. Pugin and French art historian, Alexis Rio[2]—makes his achievement even more impressive. It remained for the two converts, Chesterton and Gill, to reverse his argument in order to reinvest the wholeness of the mediæval ideal with the holiness of its integral religion. Consequently, their shared insistence on the necessity of Catholicism to the mediæval movement represents a return to certain origins of Ruskin's thought, rather than a distortion of that thought. Indeed, by the close of the nineteenth century such a spiritual revitalisation seemed essential. The efficacy of mediævalism as a metaphysical programme had always been endangered by the sensational aspects of the revival: a hundred years' encrustation of Gothic facades, ornaments, and sentimental historical fiction nearly had obliterated the deeper impulses of the movement. Ruskin's line of ethical mediævalism, in particular, was threatened by the eccentricities of its offspring, Aestheticism and the Arts-and-Crafts Movement. In an odd twist of intellectual history, however, the substance of Ruskin's mediævalist thought was salvaged by a reunion with its Catholic foundations—this time in the form of the social and aesthetic philosophy of G.K. Chesterton and Eric Gill.

The particular vision of the past that Chesterton and Gill inherited from Ruskin sanctioned such essential tamperings. In fact, the serious contribution of the various revival movements in the nineteenth century was not their conflicting and static idealisations of the mediæval, classical, and Renaissance periods, but their motivating assumption that the spirit of a culture was somehow separable from its traditional forms of expression. Taken to its logical consequences, the revivalist formula actually encouraged the destruction of those older forms in order to carry forward more effectively the values of the past. Thus, Ruskin's argument that nineteenth-century Protestantism more truly embodied the mediæval religious spirit accorded with a familiar revivalist line of reasoning. Escape into an utopian past, then, was not the final aim; rather, revivalism was part of the larger Romantic attempt to overcome man's estrangement from his own natural and historical context. Ruskin's mentor, Carlyle, presented the hope of revivalism in *Heroes and Hero Worship*: "the whole Past is the possession of the Present. To know it consciously brings us into a closer and clearer relationship with the past."[3] From Coleridge to Gill, revivalists sought to make the significance of the Middle Ages a conscious influence in the contemporary culture. More than any single aspect of his thought, Ruskin's vision of the vital continuity of history was deeply influential for his followers. Chesterton's restatement of this perspective in *The Victorian Age* represents such a familiar way of viewing history that it is no longer identified as an exclusively revivalist notion: "Roman Britain and Mediæval England are still not only alive but lively: for real development is not leaving things behind, as on a road, but drawing life from them as from a root."[4]

Ruskin, Chesterton, and Gill were understandably anxious to distinguish this important concept of revival in which the animate spirit of the past was somehow embodied anew in later forms, from the notion of mere, imitative restoration. Ruskin set the tone for future debate in *The Seven Lamps of Architecture*: "Do not let us talk then of restoration. The thing is a Lie from beginning to end. You may make a model of a building as you may of a corpse."[5] In turn, Chesterton and Gill both echo this central concept of revival as continuance, rather than as an artificial adoption of past modes. Chesterton employs the definition of "right revival" to distinguish his mediævalism from the colourful fancies of William Morris:

> The men of the time of Chaucer had many evil qualities, but there was at least one exhibition of moral weakness they did not give. They would have laughed at the idea of dressing themselves in the manner of the bowmen at the battle of Senlac, or painting themselves an aesthetic blue, after the custom of the ancient Britons. . . . Any real advance in the beauty of modern dress must spring honestly and naturally out of the life we lead.[6]

Gill's letters to the *Chichester Observer* in 1901 protested the folly of restoring the Chichester Cross as a monument to Queen Victoria. His outrage and his ethics were reminiscent of Ruskin:

> If it be found necessary to replace carved stones let us cut them into our own design so that they will harmonise with and carry on the old weathered stones on either side. Such work would be no deception. . . . But do not let us pretend to be Gothic workmen when we are not.[7]

Implementing Ruskin's distinction between a revival of the mediæval spirit and a restoration of its time-bound appearances, Chesterton and Gill could justify radical modern reform on the grounds that it was essentially true to their mediæval ideal. Ironically, this myth of revival that Ruskin provided for Chesterton and Gill also served as the basis for their Catholic reconversion of his conception of the Middle Ages as well as his social and aesthetic thought.

Disagreement focused, primarily, on Ruskin's historical schema. Although all three revivalists endorsed a conservative, rather than a progressive, view of history, they differed greatly in their arguments for the grounds of mediæval coherency. The question was of particular importance to Chesterton and Gill, for in the hierarchy of values implicit within their critical writings "coherency" represents the paramount virtue. Interestingly, the association of the Middle Ages with coherency seems to have been forged early in the personal development of the two men. In their respective biographies, Chesterton and Gill link a childhood sense of wholeness with the unity of their mediæval surroundings. Chesterton's North Kensington suburb which originally impressed him with its self-sufficient completion (a block of shops contained "the essentials of a civilisation")[8] would be transfigured into a feudal city-state in *The Napoleon of Notting Hill.* Similarly, Gill devotes much space in his autobiography to a contrast between the orderliness of Chichester, a city of mediæval origins, and the chaos of his first home, Brighton. Coherency also figures not only as an attribute of an historical time or place but as the highest human moral attribute. In Chesterton's study, *William Cobbett,* he praises the father of Distributism for his ability to "see life steadily, and see it whole."[9] Eight years later, Gill echoed the compliment in an address to the English-Speaking Union on John Ruskin. He ascribed Ruskin's unpopularity to a similar inclination to see "life more or less whole," to see "the roots of human action, and therefore of human art, [as] moral roots."[10] Ruskin's unified discussions of art and society presented a powerful alternative to the modern sense of disintegration (what Gill termed "a long word for death").[11] Certainly, Ruskin's arguments on architecture must have held a special poignancy, upon first encounter, for Gill. As a young architect's apprentice to the Office of the Ecclesiastical Commissioners, Gill would fortify himself with breakfast readings of *The Seven Lamps of Architecture* and *Unto This Last,* and then venture out to encounter the architectural abominations that so provoked Ruskin. During subsequent study under William Lethaby and Edward Johnston at the London County Council Central School of Art and Design, he applied Ruskin's aesthetics to the practical realm of lettering and stone-carving. Although his vision of the Middle Ages as an ideal and coherent society permanently won Ruskin two disciples, Chesterton and Gill were compelled to reject his explanation for the break-up of the mediæval world.

In many ways, Chesterton and Gill had the easier task: the Renaissance and the Reformation simply composed one movement during which, as Gill said, "man first glimpsed the face of man and fell down and worshipped."[12] In Gill's words:

in the fourteenth century, or thereabouts, a change took place—gradually. The mediaeval conception of life decayed. The rule of the Church and of princes gave way to the rule of merchants. In the sixteenth century (1500 onwards) the merchant class, which had been subordinate and even despised, gradually emerged and become the ruling class. . . . By the fifteenth century rich merchants were already building churches out of their own money—out of their profits. (As Carnegie and Lord Nuffield build libraries and picture galleries to-day.) By the sixteenth century they had ceased to build churches and were building themselves country mansions.[13]

In Ruskin's synthesis, however, the fall into modernity was more problematical. He faced the dilemma of charting the dissolution of the mediæval world without blaming Protestantism. Moreover, he had to account for the decline of architecture, painting, and sculpture without conceding what Pugin claimed, that "the excellence of art was only to be found in Catholicism."[14] Ruskin's solution does not lend itself to a convincing summary, largely because it rests on the penetrating eloquence of his own prose. In *Stones of Venice,* for example, he traces the decay of mediæval society to a weakened relationship with Nature, Nature's God, and One's Own Truth.[15] His use of these ideal terms was not intended to be evasive; indeed, their significance painstakingly develops throughout his work. More specifically, the rise of the commercial spirit is held responsible, in *Stones of Venice,* for creating the new basis for social relationships. Gothic architecture (which Ruskin divorces from its "Romanist" associations and instead praises for its functionalism) mirrored this disintegration of social affection. In the absence of higher imperatives, the mentality of the marketplace corrupted Gothic architecture by demanding luxury and a surface perfection. Although Chesterton and Gill continue Ruskin's condemnation of commercialism, they most directly echo one of his sources—A.W.N. Pugin—in their Catholic version of the fall. Pugin contended that the widespread adoption of Gothic architecture prefigured an eventual Catholic re-conversion of England. Naturally, this view of architecture as mystical inspiration led some critics to question the basis of Pugin's own faith: notably, Ruskin maintained that Pugin was "jangled into a change of religion by the chimes of a belfry."[16] Pugin's Catholicism, however attained, is evident in the controversial *Contrasts* where he identifies Protestantism as the "destructive principle" which tore apart the unified fabric of mediæval society, its art and architecture:

When the Common Prayer and Articles had been set forth, heavy fines were imposed, and even death was inflicted, on those who did not receive them as the only rule of faith or form of religious worship; and by such means as these, men had been driven for a short time into an outward show of uniformity. But where was the inward unity of soul—where that faith that had anciently bound men together? Alas! that was utterly fled.[17]

By adopting Pugin's argument that Catholicism represented the foundation of order in the Middle Ages, Chesterton and Gill refocused Ruskin's call for a "finer moral perception" to mend the modern fragmentation. This essential change in perspective directed the Catholic correctives which Chesterton and Gill proposed to two descendants of Ruskin's thought: the Arts-and-Crafts Movement and Aestheticism.

The diagram of history shared by Ruskin, Chesterton, and Gill plunges abruptly downward at the point labelled "Industrialism." Not, as all three men would explain, because machines themselves are inherently evil, but because the ethics and economics of industry encourage the complete divorce of art from life. In his lecture on Ruskin, Gill describes this schism that Ruskin foresaw and the twentieth century realised:

> On the one hand there are the artists (painters, sculptors, poets, musicians), more and more concerned with introspection, more and more concerned with digging about in their own souls to discover peculiar emotions, the special emotions of special people—eccentric people necessarily become more and more eccentric as they become more and more isolated—eventually having the museum as their resting place.

> On the other hand we see all the ordinary needs of life produced by commercial production—the machine, mass production. All things are thought of by their makers simply as things to be sold. The ordinary workman is reduced to a subhuman condition of intellectual irresponsibility. The man is now a tool, a tooth on a wheel, depending for his amusement on what is served out to him in his spare time.[18]

Ruskin recognised that under commercial conditions where labour was motivated by profit, rather than by pride in one's own work, the ordinary workman was destined to become a mere tool, an extension of the machinery around him. His diagnosis in the "Nature of Gothic" essay makes even Gill's prose seem restrained:

> Men may be beaten, chained, tormented, yoked like cattle, slaughtered like summer flies, and yet remain in one sense, and the best sense, free. But to smother their souls with them, to blight and hew into rotting pollards the suckling branches of their human intelligence, to make the flesh and skin which, after the worm's work on it, is to see God, into leathern thongs to yoke machinery with—this is to be slave-masters indeed.[19]

Sadly, the solutions Ruskin proposed in *Stones of Venice* had, by the end of the nineteenth century, only aggravated the problem. Ruskin had concluded that the divisions could be healed if all men would once again embrace craft work, discourage the manufacture of luxury items, and reject an imitative work or an exact finish. Finally, he recommended that Gothic architecture be universally adopted because of its imperfection (which at least signified that its builders

were thinking and acting freely). His concepts eventually translated into the Arts-and-Crafts Movement.

The Movement's neat reversal of Ruskin's aims is a familiar, if rueful tale: in short, the terms "craft" and "craftsman" became connotative of a self-conscious, overpriced archaism. The betrayal, however, also occurred on a deeper level. Ruskin's insistence on craft work represented a means toward recovery of many of the interior values missing in modern culture. Many of his disciples among the Aesthetes and in the Arts-and-Crafts Movement (and often there is little important distinction) misread *Modern Painters* and *Stones of Venice* as sanctioning the cultivation of the asocial inwardness of their own special, artistic natures. Chesterton and Gill, confronted with this drastic split between the artist and society, saw Catholicism as offering, in part, a means of socialising an impulse toward interiority which had become increasingly eccentric.

Gill moved, inevitably, in Arts-and-Crafts circles during his apprenticeship period in London, but he soon came to share H.G. Wells's sense of the "fungoid growths which encumber the floor of the Arts-and-Crafts exhibitions."[20] Along with Chesterton, Gill felt that the Movement mistakenly focused on the surface effects of the division between art and society; meanwhile, the root cause of that division, the rise of the commercial spirit, was tactfully ignored. The emphatic solutions proposed by Chesterton and Gill represented nothing less than a comprehensive reordering of society on a religious basis.[21] Oddly, by reinvesting art with a "universal" religious significance, Chesterton and Gill found themselves in the same isolated cultural position as the rarified artists they denounced.

An absolute insistence upon the First Cause underlying all relationships emerges in the collected essays of Chesterton and Gill in topics as diverse as "On Sandals and Simplicity," "Pope and the Art of Satire," and "Five Hundred Years of Printing"; but the articles which the two men wrote on the sculptor, Jacob Epstein, will serve to telescope the Catholic alterations they made in Ruskin's thought. Chesterton's article, "On Mr. Epstein," reviews his sculpture, "Night," and discusses the dilemma of public art in the modern world. Monuments, argues Chesterton, demand a community of feeling between the sculptor and the spectator and are, consequently, survivals from a time when men did not feel an immense distance between the craftsman and the crowd. In a rhetorical leap familiar to regular readers of Chesterton or Gill, Chesterton specifies the nature of this "community of feeling": "All art is religious art; and all public art should really be of the religion of the people."[22] The implicit solution appears obvious; since the people have no shared religion they must rediscover one before art can return to its former excellence. Chesterton remains content to illuminate the issue and trusts his readers to draw carefully directed conclusions. In contrast, Gill loudly hammers his point home. In an article for *G.K.'s Weekly* entitled,

**"What's It All Bloomin' Well For?"** Gill prefaces his remarks on the Hudson Memorial by Jacob Epstein by establishing the context of the modern situation—this time in distinctly Ruskinian terms:

> Here we have a world in which nine men out of ten are, by the circumstances of their employment, turned into irresponsible idiots, instead of being responsible workmen. . . . Big business, large scale industry!—big money rather and large scale slavery!—that's the truth of them.[23]

After this characteristic outburst, Gill identifies, by omission, the Catholic crux of the problem:

> There is a committee to decide about the monument—very mixed committee; mixed in mind. There's no harm in a mixed committee if the mixing is merely due to the variety of trades or professions followed by its members (one king, one bishop, one hairdresser, one journalist . . . but all of one faith), but there's every harm if the mixing is due to the variety of misbeliefs held by its members (one agnostic, one C of E, one Jew . . . but all of middle class).[24]

Chesterton and Gill rejected escape into the pre-industrial past as fanciful, but they unabashedly professed the need for a pre-Reformation religion to rebuild the foundations for a modern art.

Considering that Gill had once collaborated with Jacob Epstein, as well as William Rothenstein, and Augustus John in plans for creating a modern Stonehenge, his comment in the essay cited above that the Hudson sculpture looked as "though Epstein had gnawed it with his teeth"[25] was rather stern stuff. Gill, however, did not remain long in the high art world. The commonsense attitude that both he and Chesterton cultivated toward art represented a conscious reaction against the aesthetic legacy of the 'Nineties and its claim of a special sensibility for the artist. Simplicity, instead was applauded by the two men and defended as a hallmark of the mediæval world. In the essay, "Chaucer and the Renaissance," Chesterton suggests that "the mediæval mind did not really believe that truth was to be found by going to extremes. And the Elizabethan mind already had a sort of hint that it might be found there; at the extreme edges of existence and precipices of the human imagination."[26] The distinction also describes the difference between the perspective of Chesterton and Gill, and that of their friends in the high art world. More importantly, by ascribing a taste for the simple and commonplace as characteristic of the Middle Ages, Chesterton wrestled mediævalism away from the Aesthetes and reasserted its value as a programme for social change.

The quest for mediæval simplicity extended into the two men's choice of livelihood. Gill especially took pride in his image as a workman. Explaining the advantages of manual labour in a letter of 1912 to William Rothenstein, Gill reasoned: "I have got the fly wheel safety-valve of letter-cutting to hearten me when sculpture and the

modern world seem equally bloody."[27] In this context, Chesterton's decision to continue the demanding routine of newspaper work long after his literary reputation was established seems less a personal quirk than a determination to remain firmly planted in a practical realm. A direct, journalistic style, moreover, characterised the prose style of both men. By writing plainly, Chesterton and Gill proclaimed themselves in opposition to the baroque sensibilities of their immediate predecessors. Accordingly, the virtue of simple speech was a compliment Chesterton awarded to the men whose ideas he particularly admired. In his study of Cobbett, Chesterton asserts: "It is possible to speak much too plainly to be understood,"[28] and he adds that this was Cobbett's downfall. Four years later the phrase reoccurs when Chesterton, in a review of Gill's *Art Nonsense* (1930), defends him against charges of being a religious mystogogue. Instead, Chesterton argues, Gill's integral vision made him a member of "the great company of those who talk too plainly to be understood."[29] Undoubtedly, Chesterton included himself in this company.

Not everyone found the style refreshing. D.H. Lawrence who declared that "Gill is more profound than Karl Marx or Whitehead or a dozen other philosophers"[30] rankled at the unassuming style of his essays:

> Mr. Gill is bad at the mere craft of language; he sets a writer's nerves on edge all the time. . . . His style is irritating like an uneducated workman in a pub holding forth and showing off and making a great deal of noise with a lot of cliches.[31]

Admittedly, Gill, in particular, perfected his simple prose style to the point of affectation. The distinctive rhetoric, however, was essential to the presentation of the aesthetic position he shared with Chesterton. Life, they insisted, was more than art; and by discussing it in a commonsense manner perhaps art could be put in its place—the accessible place it had occupied in the mediæval world. Gill makes their hierarchy of values explicit in a 1925 letter accepting Chesterton's request for an article on the Hudson Memorial:

> What is wanted is the attitude of mind of that decent person who says "he doesn't know anything about art but he knows what he likes," but . . . in our case it's to be because what we like is what we *know* to be likeable—because we know in Whom we believe. I am sure that the two ground notions for us "Distributists" (I say, it is an awful word though!) are the ones I've put into the article herewith—viz: "a work of art is simply a thing well made" & "Look after Goodness & Truth & Beauty will take care of itself." We can push those notions in all departments & rescue art from the snobbery & worse which kills it—i.e. kills all good workmanship.
>
> Well, please forgive me for thus rushing at you.[32]

The split between the artist and society could be healed when a common faith was once again adopted. Ruskin's successful excision of Catholicism from the mediæval ideal had unintentionally fostered the secular, private inwardness of Aestheticism and the Arts-and-Crafts Movement. As Chesterton notes in *The Victorian Age,*

> Ruskin's dark and doubtful decision to accept Catholic art but not Catholic ethics had bourne rapid or even flagrant fruit by the time that Swinburne, writing about a harlot, composed a learned and sympathetic and indecent parody on the Litany of the Blessed Virgin.[33]

The Catholic mediævalism of Chesterton and Gill, instead, stressed the responsibility of art to society and, thus, endorsed a programme of social reform more faithful to Ruskin's original design.

In 1916, Cobbett's *Cottage Economy* was reprinted by Hilary Pepler for his St. Dominic's Press. This collection of lectures dealt with ordinary topics such as the proper care of pigs, bees, and goats, the brewing of beer, and the abuse of candles. Cobbett's denunciation of tea is especially energetic—tea, he claims, is a "weaker kind of laudanaum," and for little girls "the gossip of the tea table is no bad preparatory school for the brothel."[34] This edition of *Cottage Economy,* however, was distinctive for its introduction by G.K. Chesterton and accompanying woodcuts by Eric Gill. The two men were attracted to this seemingly incongruous project because Cobbett's pragmatic lectures were inspired by principles they admired: the right of the common man to own private property and to be self-sufficient—the same principles which formed the foundations of Distributism. Actually, the term, "Distributism" can be misleading, for it implies a political philosophy distinct from the aesthetic and social programmes of Chesterton and Gill. Distributism, however, was integrally connected with the two men's larger, mediævalist vision: their familiar ideas of simplicity, the reunion of the artist and society, and the necessary right of private responsibility, simply resurfaced, through Distributism, in a more decidedly political forum.

If Cobbett provided the practical basis for Distributism (indeed, *Cottage Economy* became an indispensible manual for living at Gill's agrarian crafts commune at Ditchling), Ruskin's philosophy of political economy furnished its ideological structure. In *Unto This Last,* Ruskin defines wealth as the possession of the valuable by the valiant, and proceeds to prove that the acquisition is possible only under certain moral conditions of society. He also firmly defends the right of private ownership: "whereas it has long been known and declared that the poor have no right to the property of the rich, I wish it also to be known and declared that the rich have no right to the property of the poor."[35] Once again, Chesterton and Gill were in the position of resurrecting Ruskin's thought with a Catholic bias; their respective visions of the correct set of "moral conditions" necessary to a healthy society predictably differed. Eventually, the Catholics' demands for an encompassing, religious re-organisation of society surpassed the political solutions offered by Distributism. Gill, in particular, felt impatient with Distributism, Fabian Socialism, and other political and economic reform movements which, he felt, merely called for the redivision of goods when more fundamental changes were essential. In line with his Catholic perspective on history, Gill traced the problems of capitalist society to the usurpation of a vital religious order by the rule of the marketplace which could not be redeemed. Although he came to avoid the "Distributist" label, Gill realised the idea of the paternalistic society Ruskin envisioned in *Unto This Last* in his religious crafts communities at Ditchling, Capel-y-ffin, and Pigotts. Perhaps reform was only feasible in these self-contained "cells of good living."[36]

By integrating Ruskin's ideas on art and society into their own Catholic perspective, Chesterton and Gill effectively reversed the critical achievement of Ruskin's Protestant interpretation of mediævalism. The revision was justified, however, for Ruskin's thought urgently needed salvaging from the failures of Aestheticism and the Arts-and-Crafts Movement, as well as from the modern tendency to dismiss all things Victorian. As Gill recognised:

> I believe that though Ruskin's ideas on religion were full of prejudices and full of pruderies, and though his ideas on art were full of pedantry and false reasoning—as, for instance when he described architecture as being that kind of building, to which some sort of sculpture was added, as though architecture could not exist without sculpture (that is putting it rather crudely, I know, but that was the gist of his ideas)—though such were his ideas upon religion and art, his ideas on justice and equity, founded less upon idiosyncrasy, are unshakeable and permanent.[37]

Thus Ruskin's mediævalism, converted by Chesterton and Gill, extended well into the twentieth century.

NOTES

[1] G.K. Chesterton, *The Victorian Age in Literature* (New York, 1930), pp. 63, 65.

[2] Ruskin's complex debt to Pugin and Rio exceeds the present confines of discussion. See: Graham Hough, *The Last Romantics* (London, 1949), p. 90; Francis G. Townsend, "Ruskin and the Landscape Feeling," *Illinois Studies in Language and Literature,* 35, No. 3 (Urbana, Illinois, 1951); and David J. DeLaura, "The Context of Browning's Painter Poems," *PMLA,* 95 (1980), pp. 367-388.

[3] Thomas Carlyle, *On Heroes, Hero-Worship and the Heroic in History* in *The Collected Works of Thomas Carlyle* (London, 1870), p. 47.

[4] G.K. Chesterton, *Victorian Age,* p. 12.

[5] John Ruskin, *The Works of John Ruskin,* ed. E.T. Cook and Alexander Wedderburn, Library edition, 39 vols. (London, 1903-1912), VIII, 244.

[6] G.K. Chesterton, "William Morris" in *Twelve Types* (London, 1906, rpt. 1976), pp. 23-24.

[7] Walter Shewring (ed.), *The Letters of Eric Gill* (New York, 1944), pp. 18-19.

[8] G.K. Chesterton, *Autobiography,* (London, 1936, rpt. 1969), p. 110.

[9] G.K. Chesterton, *William Cobbett* (New York, 1926), p. 246.

[10] Eric Gill, "John Ruskin" in *It All Goes Together* (New York, 1944), pp. 46-47.

[11] Eric Gill, "Secular and Sacred in Modern History," in *It All Goes Together,* p. 173.

[12] Eric Gill, *Art and a Changing Civilisation* (London, 1934), p. 79.

[13] Eric Gill, "Sculpture on Machine-Made Buildings" in *It All Goes Together,* pp. 62-63.

[14] A.W.N. Pugin, *Contrasts* [1836] (New York, 1969), p. 15.

[15] John Ruskin, *Works,* ed. Cook and Wedderburn, XI, 267.

[16] John Ruskin, *The Works of John Ruskin,* IX, p. 438 as cited in Alice Chandler, *A Dream of Order: The Medieval Ideal in Nineteenth-Century Literature* (Lincoln, Nebraska, 1970), p. 188.

[17] A.W.N. Pugin, *Contrasts,* p. 33.

[18] Eric Gill, "John Ruskin," p. 46.

[19] John Ruskin, *Works,* ed. Cook and Wedderburn, X, 193.

[20] Eric Gill, "The Failure of the Arts and Crafts Movement," *The Socialist Review,* (December, 1909), p 289.

[21] Graham Greene in "Eric Gill," in *The Lost Childhood* (New York, 1953), 133, has argued that the drawback of this perspective was its threatened absorption into the "overpowering tradition of eccentricity."

[22] G.K. Chesterton, "On Mr. Epstein," in *Come to Think of It* (New York, 1931), p. 72.

[23] Eric Gill, "What's It All Bloomin' Well For?" in *G.K.'s: A Miscellany of the First Five Hundred Issues of G.K.'s Weekly* (London, 1934), pp. 177-178.

[24] Eric Gill, "What's It All Bloomin' Well For?" in *G.K.'s Weekly* (London, 1934), pp. 179-180.

[25] Eric Gill, "What's It All Bloomin' Well For?" in *G.K.'s Weekly* (London, 1934), pp. 181.

[26] G.K. Chesterton, "Chaucer and the Renaissance" in W.H. Auden (ed.) *G.K. Chesterton: A Selection From His Non-Fictional Prose* (London, 1970), p. 31.

[27] Walter Shewring, *Letters* p. 38.

[28] G.K. Chesterton, *Cobbett,* p. 163.

[29] G.K. Chesterton, "Eric Gill and No Nonsense," in *A Handful of Authors* (New York, 1953), p. 187.

[30] D.H. Lawrence, "Eric Gill's *Art Nonsense,*" *The Book Collector's Quarterly,* XII (October, 1933), 4.

[31] D.H. Lawrence, "Eric Gill's *Art Nonsense,*" *The Book Collector's Quarterly,* XII, 3-4.

[32] Walter Shewring, *Letters,* p. 190.

[33] G.K. Chesterton, *Victorian Age,* p. 69.

[34] William Cobbett, *Cottage Economy* (London, 1822), p. 20.

[35] John Ruskin, *Unto This Last* (New York, 1967), p. 61.

[36] Walter Shewring, *Letters,* pp. 458-459.

[37] Eric Gill, "John Ruskin," p. 47.

## Peter Redgrove (essay date 1984)

SOURCE: "Scribing-out Inscape," in *The Times Literary Supplement,* No. 4222, March 2, 1984, p. 214.

[*In the following essay, a review of two books—one a selection from Gill's writing, another a collection of his engravings—Redgrove faults Gill for his tendency to over-analyze, but praises the simple beauty of his artwork.*]

In his *Autobiography* Eric Gill tells us about his sensations as he watched Edward Johnston, his calligraphy teacher, for the first time. When he

> saw the writing that came as he wrote, I had that thrill and tremble of the heart which otherwise I can only remember having had when first I touched her body or saw her hair down for the first time . . . or when I first heard the plain-chant of the Church . . . or first saw the North Transept of Chartres from the little alley between the houses . . . I was struck as by lightning, as by a sort of enlightenment . . . sometimes, when you are drawing the human body, even the turn of a shoulder or the firmness of a waist, it seems to shine with the radiance of righteousness . . . it was no mere dexterity, that transported me; it was as though a secret of heaven were being revealed.

When a man's art is mixed up not only with his political and religious beliefs but with his sexuality as well, and he sees all this as a whole, and says it plainly, the Establishment tends to draw its skirts aside. Eric Gill has dwelt under something of a cloud for many years. He did not fit in with the art for art's sake School of Paris ideologies, and was partially eclipsed by his great contemporaries Moore, Hepworth and Nicholson. Moreover, he was not just a sculptor, or solely a typographer, he was an engraver and trenchant writer too. He would not confine himself within specialisms, and always did his best to demolish the distinctions between fine and applied art.

Moreover, either the Catholicism or the sensuality seemed problematic, depending on your viewpoint. Gill was undoubtedly a very sexual man, as his painstakingly kept diaries and journals recording details of masturbation and infidelity show, and such sexual-mystical experiences as the above-quoted were at the heart of his art. He describes his carvings for the London Underground headquarters as "attempts at 'love-making'" in one letter, and in another he says "the best route to Heaven is via Elephanta and Elura and Ajanta".

One would hope that testimony to such an important "determining influence" would be represented in an anthology of Gill's writings. Brian Keeble [in *A Holy Tradition of Working: Passages from the Writings of Eric Gill*] says that he has not attempted to represent every nuance of Gill's thinking on "the nature of art, beauty and workmanship", but he has in fact selected for the celibate angle and the scholastic manner. It is the side of Gill's writing that Lawrence hated, calling it "argufying"; it is the "dry legalistic element" that John Rothenstein deplored in Gill's mind that existed "in spite of his Nonconformist origins". The allegiances that should arise for the artist through the experience of holiness are painfully teased out in logical propositions, but the foundation is missing, the lightning-strike, the "radiance of righteousness"; and therefore the "holy tradition" is incomplete. One can see that the book might very well serve as a severe catechism for the serious artist questioning his place in the modern world; but he would need the inspiration of Gill's visual works as well. I am not sure that a reissue of the *Autobiography*, at one time very popular but now out of print, wouldn't have served better. "Man is matter and spirit, both real and both good", says Gill, but not here, "and the funny is certainly part of the good."

Gill was, I believe, theologically very close to Hopkins. The latter's declaration of God's grandeur, "like shining from shook foil" in the Thisness or *haecceitas* of anything, once its inscape had been grasped, seems to me like true Gill, while scholastic logic-chopping by itself is not. "About all the turns of the scaping from the break and flooding of the wave to its run out again I have not yet satisfied myself" says Hopkins in diary notes that any sculptor might be proud of: "to make out how the comb is morselled so fine into string and tassel . . . saw big smooth flinty waves, carved and scuppled . . .". Such scribing-out of inscape is immediately present on opening Gill's *Engravings* [*The Engravings of Eric Gill*]. Often the "bounding lines" are like waves of pleasure in a kind of visual echo-sounding that explores posed face or figure. There is much wit, too, and explicitly sexual joy—and here the *Engravings* tend to contradict the Selection. For example, Brian Keeble cites the following from *Beauty Looks After Herself*: "But the lovely and the beautiful are mixed because man is matter as well as mind. Hence man's work is concerned with both the *beautiful* and the *lovely*. But art is specifically concerned with the beautiful . . .". Unfortunately for Gill's written thesis, the engravings are both beautiful *and* lovely.

### Harry Remde (essay date 1984)

SOURCE: A review of 'A Holy Tradition of Working: Passages from the Writings of Eric Gill', edited by Brian Keeble, *Parabola*, Vol. IX, No. 2, April, 1984, pp. 102-4.

[*In the following essay, Remde describes Gill as a flawed—and thus deeply human—writer.*]

This extraordinary book [*A Holy Tradition of Working: Passages from the Writings of Eric Gill*] is a selection of Eric Gill's writings representing his thought over a period of many years. That the book may be called extraordinary is due to man's present situation. In a normal (traditional) society, i.e., a society in which human actions conform to spiritual needs, this book would not have been written; Gill would be an ordinary man. But all around us, now as in Gill's lifetime, an empty knowledge accumulates—empty not in itself, but in the way that we receive it.

The compiler of this book has selected sentences, paragraphs, and entire sections of Gill's writings and arranged them under headings appropriate to his work as a noted sculptor, designer, and craftsman of the late nineteenth and early twentieth centuries. The result is pure Gill. Containing some of the most intense portions of his thought, the chapters have an almost aphoristic strength, although they are occasionally tedious to read. They show that Gill was a socially radical, intensely religious, extraordinarily perceptive man. Inevitably, there is repetition and overlapping of ideas within and between the chapters. The temper of the writing varies from psychological to aesthetic theorizing, from protest to religious assertion. Yet central to each chapter is Gill's belief that man's daily work, done properly and well, is the means by which he can look heavenward. Man must look here for his salvation. Through his working, he can become a man. "The working life is the contemplative life," said Gill. "Perfection . . . is the house of God to which [what is made] bears witness." Man's *need to work* is given to him, to be used for his becoming. This is the seed of tradition.

Gill lived and worked during a period of intensive industrialization in England. People had yet to lose faith in the notion that everything important to them could be brought under their control. Gill's indignation at what he saw happening was no mere resentment of change but a conviction that what was needful for human beings was systematically being destroyed. While his contemporaries looked to the outside for the source of their well-being, Gill looked to his work. Like Blake, he foresaw a condition of industry in which man the maker would have a smaller and smaller part, and perhaps no part at all.

Gill was as opposed to distinctions in the importance of different kinds of work as he was to the spreading of industrialism. He denied a line between fine art and art, between art and craft, between these and other forms of making. To him, all work was worthy. "Every man is a special kind of artist," said Coomaraswamy. What was made well, i.e., wholly, was art. Every good workman could recognize it as such. "By . . . common sense . . . men appreciate what is in accordance with right conduct." "By . . . a common sensibility . . . men appreciate what is in accordance with right making, that is to say, with art."

But, we ask, what is the *method* of this sensibility? How does *right making* come about? What method of working produces the seed? Here the book disappoints us. Gill replies, but not precisely. (To reply otherwise may be impossible.) He says that "man is matter and spirit." "Man is a bridge connecting the material and the spiritual." "Art is a translation into material of something seen inwardly." "The imagination is the faculty by which what the eye sees and what the mind thinks about it is re-created into what the man loves." And again: "Art abides entirely on the side of the mind." But what is the process? What is the method, the *way* of working? Each workman no doubt must find it for himself.

Perhaps it may be permitted to one workman to try to say, in his own words, what he believes it to be. Simply this: we cannot know what our work can tell us until we are ready. To arrive at this moment is difficult. We must *know* that we do not know. Not until man the learner stands unknowing and without regret in front of his work does he become man the maker. The work of man the maker is art. Gill says: "The good workman works well without knowing that he is wise."

What is given in this moment of becoming? Something is known within the body, it turns the heart, is transformed into an intelligence. Perhaps in this way we pay for our own existence. Gill says: "It is the result of the mind's recognition of what is after its own kind." From Romans 1:20, he quotes: "The invisible things of God may be clearly seen, being understood by the things which are made."

More than with other authors, the reader must recognize his own experience in Gill's, knowing that a common weakness unites us. The moment of perception seems so full of possibility that, without noticing, we allow it to slip into our ordinary thought or feeling. The effect is immediate: pride, theorizing, assertion, even naiveté. For example, I cannot agree with Gill's insistence that man is a thoroughly responsible creature, that he has a free will. At a moment of knowing, yes. At all other times, no. One has only to look around!

Gill's writings shift back and forth between strength and weakness, between dogma and what deeply moves the reader. There is a humbleness that reminds us that he, as he urges us all to be, was a maker of things.

Man the maker can remain independent of, but exert an influence on, whatever social system is present. "Let man rediscover his norm and he will re-create . . . a normal society." "It is the abnormal that must be planned beforehand—the bureaucracy, corporative or communist; the tyranny, military or capitalist." "In . . . a [normal] society the binding and informing power is a spiritual one."

Finally, like all naive and trusting men, Gill says that "the best will be made when all agree to start with sheer reasonableness, continue with honesty, and let the end be what it may."

---

# FURTHER READING

## Biography

Greene, Graham. "Eric Gill." In *Collected Essays*, pp. 347-50. New York: Viking, 1951.
    In this 1941 essay, Greene profiles Gill as a peculiarly English type of Catholic "eccentric."

Heppenstall, Rayner. *Four Absentees*. London: Barrie and Rockliff, 1960, 206 p.
    The author's reminiscences of Gill, George Orwell, Dylan Thomas, and J. Middleton Murry.

Oldenburg, Peter. "Eric Gill." In *Heritage of the Graphic Arts: A Selection of Lectures Delivered at Gallery 303, New York City, Under the Direction of Dr. Robert L. Leslie,* edited by Chandler B. Grannis, pp. 131-37. New York: R. R. Bowker, 1972.
    The author recalls how, as a refugee from Hitler's Germany in 1933, he joined Gill's community of craftsmen. The memoir is illustrated with photographs of Gill's sculpture and examples of his typography.

Speaight, Robert. *The Life of Eric Gill*. London: Methuen, 1966, 323 p.
    Illustrated biography composed of four chapters based on phases of Gill's life: "London, Brighton and South

Coast 1882-1907," "Ditchling 1907-24," "Capel-y-ffin 1924-28," and "Pigotts 1928-40", which includes a special appendix, a short bibliography, and an index of Gill's life and works.

## Criticism

Mellquist, Jerome. "The New Art Books." *Kenyon Review* III, No. 1 (Winter 1941): 521-24.

Maintains that Gill's *Autobiography* is a book whose "make-up . . . worthily recalls everything that he stood for."

Reich, Ronny and Ayala Sussman. "The Hebrew Episode in the Typography of Eric Gill." *Gutenberg Jahrbuch* 67 (1992): 305-8.

A study of Hebrew-language directory inscriptions designed by Gill for the Palestine Archaeological Museum in Jerusalem.

Russell, Richard F. "Belles-Lettres." *London Mercury* XXII, No. 127 (May 1930): 79-81.

Favorable review of *Art-Nonsense and Other Essays* which argues that "Mr. Eric Gill is an art critic in the true sense of the word."

---

**The following sources published by Gale include further information on the life and work of Eric Gill:** *Contemporary Authors,* **Vol. 120, and** *Dictionary of Literary Biography,* **Vol. 98.**

---

# Herman Mankiewicz

## 1897-1953

(Full name Herman Jacob Mankiewicz) American screenwriter

## INTRODUCTION

Best known for his collaboration with Orson Welles on the screenplay for *Citizen Kane,* Mankiewicz authored the screenplays for many of Hollywood's most critically praised early sound comedies. His work is credited with helping to formulate a new standard for early sound films, which relied on dialogue, banter, and repartee rather than action to further the film's plot. His urbane wit as adaptor, sole writer, collaborator, or script doctor is exemplified in director George Cukor's *Dinner at Eight,* the Marx Brothers's early films, *Monkey Business* and *Horse Feathers,* and W. C. Fields's *Million Dollar Legs.* In these primarily dialogue-driven films, the characters engage in such wordplay as double entendres, puns, and allusions to poke fun at upper-class pretentiousness and snobbery. These rhetorical techniques also served to circumvent Hollywood censors' concerns over explicit sexual references. Alienation from Hollywood's most influential producers and directors due to heavy drinking and excessive gambling resulted in his removal from several projects and loss of recognition in the film credits for his other cinematic accomplishments. However, he shared an Academy Award with Orson Welles for his work on *Citizen Kane,* another nomination for *The Pride of the Yankees,* and critical accolades for *The Pride of St. Louis* and the comedies *It's a Wonderful World* and *Rise and Shine.*

### Biographical Information

Mankiewicz was born in New York City and attended Columbia University. He continuously sought favor from his domineering and critically abusive father, Franz Mankiewicz, a German-language newspaper editor. The two men were highly competitive, as was the later relationship between Mankiewicz and his younger brother, Joseph. Joseph also enjoyed a distinguished career in film, most notably as screenwriter and director of the dramas *A Letter to Three Wives* and *All about Eve.* Similar to the later controversy over authorship of *Citizen Kane,* the brothers engaged in a bitter dispute over who actually wrote the screenplay for *Million Dollar Legs,* an issue that the two men never resolved although Joseph ultimately received the film credit. While attending Columbia, Mankiewicz began writing revues for college audiences. A brief stint as a newspaper reporter in Germany brought him into contact with dancer Isadora Duncan, who employed him as a publicity man. When he returned to New York in

the early 1920s, he worked as George S. Kaufman's assistant on theater coverage for *The New York Times.* This tenure brought Mankiewicz into contact with several of the era's most preeminent humorists of the Algonquin Round Table, including Robert Benchley, Dorothy Parker, and Ben Hecht. After writing several unsuccessful plays, Mankiewicz moved to Hollywood, where he quickly gained recognition as a clever and witty writer of title cards for silent films, as well as for co-writing with director Tod Browning *The Road to Mandalay.* Through Mankiewicz's urging, several other members of the Algonquin Round Table emigrated to Hollywood, where they joined him in revolutionizing cinematic dialogue and creating the archetype of the hard-living, heavy-drinking screenwriter who enjoyed Hollywood's excesses while loathing the town's reputation for creating low art at high wages. Mankiewicz's increasingly heavy drinking and gambling cost him many screenwriting credits, including the Marx Brothers's *A Night at the Opera,* which was credited to George S. Kaufman and Mollie Ryskind. He briefly resuscitated his career with three films, *Citizen Kane, The Pride of the Yankees,* and *The Pride of St. Louis,* before succumbing to edema in 1953.

### Major Works

Because of Mankiewicz's erratic behavior and Hollywood's system of denying screen credit to out-of-favor individuals, the extent of Mankiewicz's actual contribution to the films for which he is best known is continuously debated. The most notable of these debates concerns *Citizen Kane.* Although he shared credit with Orson Welles, Mankiewicz claimed, "There is hardly a comma that I did not write," while Welles asserted that Mankiewicz merely doctored the script. Although Mankiewicz enjoyed a close relationship with William Randolph Hearst, the ostensible inspiration for the character Charles Foster Kane, the screenwriter's collaboration on the film resulted in a long, personal vendetta against Mankiewicz in Hearst's newspapers. Much of the film closely resembles Preston Sturges's 1931 screenplay for *The Power and the Glory* and Edwin Arlington Robinson's poem *Richard Cory*; large portions are derived directly from Hearst's public speeches and personal life. However, Mankiewicz, Welles, and critics divided bitterly over actual responsibility for authorship of the screenplay. Two of Mankiewicz's later dramas, *The Pride of the Yankees* and *The Pride of St. Louis,* concern, respectively, baseball greats Lou Gehrig and Dizzy Dean. These films are noted for their downplaying of the baseball element in favor of sensitive character depictions. *Dinner at Eight* and the comedy work he did for the Marx Brothers typifies Mankiewicz's satirical skewering of the wealthy.

## PRINCIPAL WORKS

*The Road to Mandalay* (screenplay) 1926
*\*The Dummy* (screenplay) 1929
*The Man I Love* (screenplay) 1929
*Thunderbolt* (screenplay) 1929
*Men Are Like That* (screenplay) 1930
*Honey* (screenplay) 1930
*Ladies Love Brutes* [with Waldemar Young] (screenplay) 1930
*Love among the Millionaires* (screenplay) 1930
*The Vagabond King* (screenplay) 1930
*Monkey Business* [with S. J. Perelman] (screenplay) 1931
*The Royal Family of Broadway* [with Gertrude Purcell] (screenplay) 1931
*Man of the World* (screenplay) 1931
*Horse Feathers* [with Will B. Johnstone and Bert Kalmar] (screenplay) 1932
*Million Dollar Legs* [with Joseph Mankiewicz] (screenplay) 1932
*Girl Crazy* [with Tim Whelan] (screenplay) 1932
*Dinner at Eight* [with Frances Marion] (screenplay) 1933
*Stamboul Quest* (screenplay) 1934
*A Night at the Opera* [with George S. Kaufman and Mollie Ryskind] (screenplay) 1935
*It's a Wonderful World* [with Ben Hecht] (screenplay) 1939
*Citizen Kane* [with Orson Welles] (screenplay) 1941
*Rise and Shine* (screenplay) 1941
*Pride of the Yankees* [with Jo Swerling] (screenplay) 1942
*The Spanish Main* [with George Worthing Yates] (screenplay) 1945
*The Pride of St. Louis* (screenplay) 1952

\*This work is an adaptation of the short story "The Ransom of Red Chief," by O. Henry.

---

# CRITICISM

**Pauline Kael (essay date 1971)**

SOURCE: "Raising Kane," in *The Citizen Kane Book*, Little, Brown and Company, 1971, pp. 3-84.

[*In the following essay, Kael examines the film* Citizen Kane, *the cinematic milieu in which it was made, the film's biographical sources, and the careers of Orson Welles and Herman Mankiewicz to support her controversial hypothesis that authorship of the film's Academy Award-winning screenplay belongs mainly to Mankiewicz.*]

*Citizen Kane* is perhaps the one American talking picture that seems as fresh now as the day it opened. It may seem even fresher. A great deal in the movie that was conventional and almost banal in 1941 is so far in the past as to have been forgotten and become new. The Pop characterizations look modern, and rather better than they did at the time. New audiences may enjoy Orson Welles' theatrical flamboyance even more than earlier generations did, be-

cause they're so unfamiliar with the traditions it came out of. When Welles was young—he was twenty-five when the film opened—he used to be accused of "excessive showmanship," but the same young audiences who now reject "theatre" respond innocently and wholeheartedly to the most unabashed tricks of theatre—and of early radio plays—in *Citizen Kane.* At some campus showings, they react so gullibly that when Kane makes a demagogic speech about "the underprivileged," stray students will applaud enthusiastically, and a shout of "Right on!" may be heard. Though the political ironies are not clear to young audiences, and though young audiences don't know much about the subject—William Randolph Hearst, the master jingo journalist, being to them a stock villain, like Joe McCarthy; that is, a villain without the contours of his particular villainy—they nevertheless respond to the effrontery, the audacity, and the risks. Hearst's career and his power provided a dangerous subject that stimulated and energized all those connected with the picture—they felt they were *doing* something instead of just working on one more cooked-up story that didn't relate to anything that mattered. And to the particular kinds of people who shaped this enterprise the dangers involved made the subject irresistible.

*Citizen Kane,* the film that, as Truffaut said, is "probably the one that has started the largest number of filmmakers on their careers," was not an ordinary assignment. It is one of the few films ever made inside a major studio in the United States *in freedom*—not merely in freedom from interference but in freedom from the routine methods of experienced directors. George J. Schaefer, who, with the help of Nelson Rockefeller, had become president of R.K.O. late in 1938, when it was struggling to avert bankruptcy, needed a miracle to save the company, and after the national uproar over Orson Welles' *The War of the Worlds* broadcast Rockefeller apparently thought that Welles—"the wonder boy"—might come up with one, and urged Schaefer to get him. But Welles, who was committed to the theatre and wasn't especially enthusiastic about making movies, rejected the first offers; he held out until Schaefer offered him complete control over his productions. Then Welles brought out to Hollywood from New York his own production unit—the Mercury Theatre company, a group of actors and associates he could count on—and, because he was inexperienced in movies and was smart and had freedom, he was able to find in Hollywood people who had been waiting all their lives to try out new ideas. So a miracle did come about, though it was not the kind of miracle R.K.O. needed.

*Kane* does something so well, and with such spirit, that the fullness and completeness of it continue to satisfy us. The formal elements themselves produce elation; we are kept aware of how marvellously worked out the ideas are. It would be high-toned to call this method of keeping the audience aware "Brechtian," and it would be wrong. It comes out of a different tradition—the same commercial-comedy tradition that Walter Kerr analyzed so beautifully in his review of the 1969 Broadway revival of *The Front Page*, the 1928 play by Ben

Hecht and Charles MacArthur, when he said, "A play was held to be something of a machine in those days. . . . It was a machine for surprising and delighting the audience, regularly, logically, insanely, but accountably. A play was like a watch that laughed." The mechanics of movies are rarely as entertaining as they are in *Citizen Kane,* as cleverly designed to be the kind of fun that keeps one alert and conscious of the enjoyment of the artifices themselves.

Walter Kerr goes on to describe the second-act entrance prepared for Walter Burns, the scheming, ruthless managing editor of *The Front Page:*

> He can't just come on and declare himself. . . . He's got to walk into a tough situation in order to be brutally nonchalant, which is what we think is funny about him. The machinery has not only given him and the play the right punctuation, the change of pace that refreshes even as it moves on. It has also covered him, kept him from being obvious while exploiting the one most obvious thing about him. You might say that the machinery has covered itself, perfectly squared itself. We are delighted to have the man on, we are delighted to have him on at this time, we are aware that it is sleight-of-hand that has got him on, and we are as delighted by the sleight-of-hand as by the man.

*Citizen Kane* is made up of an astonishing number of such bits of technique, and of sequences built to make their points and get their laughs and hit climax just before a fast cut takes us to the next. It is practically a collection of blackout sketches, but blackout sketches arranged to comment on each other, and it was planned that way right in the shooting script.

It is difficult to explain what makes any great work great, and particularly difficult with movies, and maybe more so with *Citizen Kane* than with other great movies, because it isn't a work of special depth or a work of subtle beauty. It is a shallow work, a *shallow* masterpiece. Those who try to account for its stature as a film by claiming it to be profound are simply dodging the problem—or maybe they don't recognize that there is one. Like most of the films of the sound era that are called masterpieces, *Citizen Kane* has reached its audience gradually over the years rather than at the time of release. Yet, unlike the others, it is conceived and acted as entertainment in a popular style (unlike, say, *Rules of the Game* or *Rashomon* or *Man of Aran,* which one does not think of in crowd-pleasing terms). Apparently, the easiest thing for people to do when they recognize that something is a work of art is to trot out the proper schoolbook terms for works of art, and there are articles on *Citizen Kane* that call it a tragedy in fugal form and articles that explain that the hero of *Citizen Kane* is time—time being a proper sort of modern hero for an important picture. But to use the conventional schoolbook explanations for greatness, and pretend that it's profound, is to miss what makes it such an American triumph—that it manages to create something aesthetically exciting and durable out of the playfulness of

American muckraking satire. *Kane* is closer to comedy than to tragedy, though so overwrought in style as to be almost a Gothic comedy. What might possibly be considered tragic in it has such a Daddy Warbucks quality that if it's tragic at all it's comic-strip tragic. The mystery in *Kane* is largely fake, and the Gothic-thriller atmosphere and the Rosebud gimmickry (though fun) are such obvious penny-dreadful popular theatrics that they're not so very different from the fake mysteries that Hearst's *American Weekly* used to whip up—the haunted castles and the curses fulfilled. *Citizen Kane* is a "popular" masterpiece—not in terms of actual popularity but in terms of its conceptions and the way it gets its laughs and makes its points. Possibly it was too complexly told to be one of the greatest commercial successes, but we can't really tell whether it might have become even a modest success, because it didn't get a fair chance.

2.

Orson Welles brought forth a miracle, but he couldn't get by with it. Though Hearst made some direct attempts to interfere with the film, it wasn't so much what he did that hurt the film commercially as what others feared he might do, to them and to the movie industry. They knew he was contemplating action, so they did the picture in for him; it was as if they decided whom the king might want killed, and, eager to oblige, performed the murder without waiting to be asked. Before *Kane* opened, George J. Schaefer was summoned to New York by Nicholas Schenck, the chairman of the board of Loew's International, the M-G-M affiliate that controlled the distribution of M-G-M pictures. Schaefer had staked just about everything on Welles, and the picture looked like a winner, but now Schenck made Schaefer a cash offer from Louis B. Mayer, the head of production at M-G-M, of $842,000 if Schaefer would destroy the negative and all the prints. The picture had actually cost only $686,033; the offer handsomely included a fair amount for the post-production costs.

Mayer's motive may have been partly friendship and loyalty to Hearst, even though Hearst, who had formerly been associated with M-G-M, had, some years earlier, after a dispute with Irving Thalberg, taken his investment out of M-G-M and moved his star, Marion Davies, and his money to Warner Brothers. M-G-M had lost money on a string of costume clinkers starring Miss Davies (*Beverly of Graustark,* et al.), and had even lost money on some of her good pictures, but Mayer had got free publicity for M-G-M releases out of the connection with Hearst, and had also got what might be called deep personal satisfaction. In 1929, when Herbert Hoover invited the Mayers to the White House—they were the first "informal" guests after his inauguration—Hearst's *New York American* gave the visit a full column. Mayer enjoyed fraternizing with Hearst and his eminent guests; photographs show Mayer with Hearst and Lindbergh, Mayer with Hearst and Winston Churchill, Mayer at lunch with Bernard Shaw and Marion Davies—but they never, of course, show Mayer with both Hearst and Miss Davies. Candid cameramen sometimes caught the two together, but Hearst, presumably out of respect for his wife, did not pose in groups that included Miss Davies. Despite the publicity showered on her in the Hearst papers, the forms were carefully observed. She quietly packed and left for her own house on the rare occasions when Mrs. Hearst, who lived in the East, was expected to be in residence at San Simeon. Kane's infatuation for the singer Susan Alexander in the movie was thus a public flaunting of matters that Hearst was careful and considerate about. Because of this, Mayer's longtime friendship for Hearst was probably a lesser factor than the fear that the Hearst press would reveal some sordid stories about the movie moguls and join in one of those recurrent crusades against movie immorality, like the one that had destroyed Fatty Arbuckle's career. The movie industry was frightened of reprisals. (The movie industry is always frightened, and is always proudest of films that celebrate courage.) As one of the trade papers phrased it in those nervous weeks when no one knew whether the picture would be released, "the industry could ill afford to be made the object of counterattack by the Hearst newspapers."

There were rumors that Hearst was mounting a general campaign; his legal staff had seen the script, and Louella Parsons, the Hearst movie columnist, who had attended a screening of the film flanked by lawyers, was agitated and had swung into action. The whole industry, it was feared, would take the rap for R.K.O.'s indiscretion, and, according to the trade press at the time (and Schaefer confirms this report), Mayer was not putting up the $842,000 all by himself. It was a joint offer from the top movie magnates, who were combining for common protection. The offer was presented to Schaefer on the ground that it was in the best interests of everybody concerned—which was considered to be the entire, threatened industry—for *Citizen Kane* to be destroyed. Rather astonishingly, Schaefer refused. He didn't confer with his board of directors, because, he says, he had good reason to think they would tell him to accept. He refused even though R.K.O., having few theatres of its own, was dependent on the other companies and he had been warned that the big theatre circuits—controlled by the men who wanted the picture destroyed—would refuse to show it.

Schaefer knew the spot he was in. The première had been tentatively set for February 14th at the Radio City Music Hall—usually the showcase for big R.K.O. pictures, because R.K.O. was partly owned by the Rockefellers and the Chase National Bank, who owned the Music Hall. The manager of the theatre had been enthusiastic about the picture. Then, suddenly, the Music Hall turned it down. Schaefer phoned Nelson Rockefeller to find out why, and, he says, "Rockefeller told me that Louella Parsons had warned him off it, that she had asked him, 'How would you like to have the *American Weekly* magazine section run a double-page spread on John D. Rockefeller?'" According to Schaefer, she had also

called David Sarnoff, another large investor in R.K.O., and similarly threatened him. In mid-February, with a minor contract dispute serving as pretext, the Hearst papers blasted R.K.O. and Schaefer in front-page stories; it was an unmistakable public warning. Schaefer was stranded; he had to scrounge for theatres, and, amid the general fear that Hearst might sue and would almost certainly remove advertising for any houses that showed *Citizen Kane,* he couldn't get bookings. The solution was for R.K.O. to take the risks of any lawsuits, but when the company leased an independent theatre in Los Angeles and refurbished the Palace (then a vaudeville house), which R.K.O. owned, for the New York opening, and did the same for a theatre R.K.O. owned in Chicago, Schaefer had trouble launching an advertising campaign. (Schenck, not surprisingly, owned a piece of the biggest movie-advertising agency.) Even after the early rave reviews and the initial enthusiasm, Schaefer couldn't get bookings except in the theatres that R.K.O. itself owned and in a few small art houses that were willing to take the risk. Eventually, in order to get the picture into theatres, Schaefer threatened to sue Warners', Fox, Paramount, and Loew's on a charge of conspiracy. (There was reason to believe the company heads had promised Hearst they wouldn't show it in their theatres.) Warners' (perhaps afraid of exposure and the troubles with their stockholders that might result from a lawsuit) gave in and booked the picture, and the others followed, halfheartedly—in some cases, theatres paid for the picture but didn't play it.

By then, just about everybody in the industry was scared, or mad, or tired of the whole thing, and though the feared general reprisals against the industry did not take place, R.K.O. was getting bruised. The Hearst papers banned publicity on R.K.O. pictures and dropped an announced serialization of the novel *Kitty Foyle* which had been timed for the release of the R.K.O. film version. Some R.K.O. films didn't get reviewed and others got bad publicity. It was all petty harassment, of a kind that could be blamed on the overzealous Miss Parsons and other Hearst employees, but it was obviously sanctioned by Hearst, and it was steady enough to keep the industry uneasy.

By the time *Citizen Kane* got into Warners' theatres, the picture had acquired such an odd reputation that people seemed to distrust it, and it didn't do very well. It was subsequently withdrawn from circulation, perhaps because of the vicissitudes of R.K.O., and until the late fifties, when it was reissued and began to play in the art houses and to attract a new audience, it was seen only in pirated versions in 16 mm. Even after Mayer had succeeded in destroying the picture commercially, he went on planning vengeance on Schaefer for refusing his offer. Stockholders in R.K.O. began to hear that the company wasn't prospering because Schaefer was anti-Semitic and was therefore having trouble getting proper distribution for R.K.O. pictures. Schaefer says that Mayer wanted to get control of R.K.O. and that the rumor was created to drive down the price of the stock—that Mayer hoped to scare out Floyd Odlum, a major stockholder, and buy his shares. Instead, Odlum, who had opposed Nelson Rockefeller's choice of Schaefer to run the company, bought enough of Sarnoff's stock to have a controlling interest, and by mid-1942 Schaefer was finished at R.K.O. Two weeks after he left, Welles' unit was evicted from its offices on the lot and given a few hours to move out, and the R.K.O. employees who had worked with Welles were punished with degrading assignments on B pictures. Mayer's friendship with Hearst was not ruffled. A few years later, when Mayer left his wife of forty years, he rented Marion Davies' Beverly Hills mansion. Eventually, he was one of Hearst's honorary pallbearers. *Citizen Kane* didn't actually lose money, but in Hollywood bookkeeping it wasn't a big enough money-maker to balance the scandal.

### 3.

Welles was recently quoted as saying, "Theatre is a collective experience; cinema is the work of one single person." This is an extraordinary remark from the man who brought his own Mercury Theatre players to Hollywood (fifteen of them appeared in *Citizen Kane*), and also the Mercury coproducer John Houseman, the Mercury composer Bernard Herrmann, and various assistants, such as Richard Wilson, William Alland, and Richard Barr. He not only brought his whole supportive group—his family, he called them then—but found people in Hollywood, such as the cinematographer Gregg Toland, to contribute their knowledge and gifts to *Citizen Kane*. Orson Welles has done some marvellous things in his later movies—some great things—and there is more depth in the somewhat botched *The Magnificent Ambersons*, of 1942 (which also used many of the Mercury players), than in *Citizen Kane*, but his principal career in the movies has been in adaptation, as it was earlier on the stage. He has never again worked on a subject with the immediacy and impact of *Kane*. His later films—even those he has so painfully struggled to finance out of his earnings as an actor—haven't been *conceived* in terms of daring modern subjects that excite us, as the very idea of *Kane* excited us. This particular kind of journalist's sense of what would be a scandal as well as a great subject, and the ability to write it, belonged not to Welles but to his now almost forgotten associate Herman J. Mankiewicz, who wrote the script, and who inadvertently destroyed the picture's chances. There is a theme that is submerged in much of *Citizen Kane* but that comes to the surface now and then, and it's the linking life story of Hearst and of Mankiewicz and of Welles—the story of how brilliantly gifted men who seem to have everything it takes to do what they want to do are defeated. It's the story of how heroes become comedians and con artists.

The Hearst papers ignored Welles—Hearst may have considered this a fit punishment for an actor—though they attacked him indirectly with sneak attacks on those associated with him, and Hearst would frequently activate his secular arm, the American Legion, against him. But the Hearst papers worked Mankiewicz over in headlines; they persecuted him so long that he finally appealed to the American Civil Liberties Union for help. There was some primitive justice in this. Hearst had never met Welles, and, besides, Welles was a kid, a twenty-five-year-old prodigy (whose daughter Marion Davies' nephew was bringing up)—hardly the sort of person one held responsible. But Mankiewicz was a friend of both Marion Davies and Hearst, and had been a frequent guest at her beach house and at San Simeon. There, in the great baronial banquet hall, Hearst liked to seat Mankiewicz on his left, so that Mankiewicz, with all his worldliness and wit (the Central Park West Voltaire, Ben Hecht had called him a few years earlier), could entertain the guest of honor and Hearst wouldn't miss any of it. Mankiewicz betrayed their hospitality, even though he liked them both. They must have presented an irresistible target. And so Hearst, the yellow-press lord who had trained Mankiewicz's generation of reporters to betray *anyone* for a story, became at last the victim of his own style of journalism.

### 4.

In the first Academy Award ceremony, for 1927-28, Warner Brothers, which had just produced *The Jazz Singer,* was honored for "Marking an Epoch in Motion Picture History." If the first decade of talkies—roughly, the thirties—has never been rivalled in wit and exuberance, this is very largely because there was already in Hollywood in the late silent period a nucleus of the best American writers, and they either lured their friends West or were joined by them. Unlike the novelists who were drawn to Hollywood later, most of the best Hollywood writers of the thirties had a shared background; they had been reporters and critics, and they knew each other from their early days on newspapers and magazines.

In his autobiography, Ben Hecht tells of being broke in New York—it was probably the winter of 1926—and of getting a telegram from Herman Mankiewicz in Hollywood:

> WILL YOU ACCEPT THREE HUNDRED PER WEEK TO WORK FOR PARAMOUNT PICTURES? ALL EXPENSES PAID. THE THREE HUNDRED IS PEANUTS. MILLIONS ARE TO BE GRABBED OUT HERE AND YOUR ONLY COMPETITION IS IDIOTS. DON'T LET THIS GET AROUND.

A newspaper photograph shows Mankiewicz greeting Hecht, "noted author, dramatist, and former newspaperman," upon his arrival. After Hecht had begun work at Paramount, he discovered that the studio chief, B. P. Schulberg—who at that time considered writers a waste of money—had been persuaded to hire him by a gambler's ploy: Mankiewicz had offered to tear up his own two-year contract if Hecht failed to write a successful movie. Hecht, that phenomenal fast hack who was to become one of the most prolific of all motion-picture writers (and one of the most frivolously cynical about the results), worked for a week and turned out the script that became Josef von Sternberg's great hit *Underworld.* That script brought Hecht the first Academy Award for an original story, and a few years later he initiated the practice of using Oscars as doorstops. The studio heads knew what they had in Hecht as soon as they read the script, and they showed their gratitude. Hecht has recorded:

> I was given a ten-thousand-dollar check as a bonus for the week's work, a check which my sponsor Mankiewicz snatched out of my hand as I was bowing my thanks.
>
> "You'll have it back in a week," Manky said. "I just want it for a few days to get me out of a little hole."
>
> He gambled valiantly, tossing a coin in the air with Eddie Cantor and calling heads or tails for a thousand dollars. He lost constantly. He tried to get himself secretly insured behind his good wife Sara's back, planning to hock the policy and thus meet his obligation. This plan collapsed when the insurance-company doctor refused to accept him as a risk.
>
> I finally solved the situation by taking Manky into the Front Office and informing the studio bosses of our joint dilemma. I asked that my talented friend be given a five-hundred-a-week raise. The studio could then deduct this raise from his salary. . . .
>
> I left . . . with another full bonus check in my hand; and Manky, with his new raise, became the highest paid writer for Paramount Pictures, Inc.

The bait that brought the writers in was money, but those writers who, like Mankiewicz, helped set the traps had their own reason: conviviality. Mankiewicz's small joke "Don't let this get around" came from a man who lived for talk, a man who saw movie making as too crazy, too profitable, and too *easy* not to share with one's friends. By the early thirties, the writers who lived in Hollywood or commuted there included not only Mankiewicz and Hecht and Charles MacArthur but George S. Kaufman and Marc Connelly, and Nathanael West and his brother-in-law S. J. Perelman, and Preston Sturges, Dorothy Parker, Arthur Kober, Alice Duer Miller, John O'Hara, Donald Ogden Stewart, Samson Raphaelson (the *New York Times* reporter who wrote the play *The Jazz Singer*), Gene Fowler, and Nunnally Johnson, and such already famous playwrights as Philip Barry, S. N. Behrman, Maxwell Anderson, Robert E. Sherwood, and Sidney Howard. Scott Fitzgerald had already been there for his first stretch, in 1927, along with Edwin Justus Mayer, and by 1932 William Faulkner began coming and going, and from time to time Ring Lardner and Moss Hart would turn up. In earlier periods, American writers made a living on newspapers and magazines; in the forties and fifties, they went into the academies (or, once they got to col-

lege, never left). But in the late twenties and the thirties they went to Hollywood. And though, apparently, they one and all experienced it as prostitution of their talents—joyous prostitution in some cases—and though more than one fell in love with movies and thus suffered not only from personal frustration but from the corruption of the great, still new art, they nonetheless as a group were responsible for that sustained feat of careless magic we call "thirties comedy." **Citizen Kane** was, I think, its culmination.

5.

Herman J. Mankiewicz, born in New York City in 1897, was the first son of a professor of education, who then took a teaching position in Wilkes-Barre, where his second son, Joseph L. Mankiewicz, was born in 1909, and where the boys and a sister grew up. Herman Mankiewicz graduated from Columbia in 1916, and after a period as managing editor of the *American Jewish Chronicle* he became a flying cadet with the United States Army in 1917 and, in 1918, a private first class with the Fifth Marines, 2nd Division, A.E.F. In 1919 and 1920, he was the director of the American Red Cross News Service in Paris, and after returning to this country to marry a great beauty, Miss Sara Aaronson, of Baltimore, he took his bride overseas with him while he worked as a foreign correspondent in Berlin from 1920 to 1922, doing political reporting for George Seldes on the *Chicago Tribune.* During that time, he also sent pieces on drama and books to the *New York Times* and *Women's Wear.* Hired in Berlin by Isadora Duncan, he became her publicity man for her return to America. At home again, he took a job as a reporter for the *New York World.* He was a gifted, prodigious writer, who contributed to *Vanity Fair,* the *Saturday Evening Post,* and many other magazines, and, while still in his twenties, collaborated with Heywood Broun, Dorothy Parker, Robert E. Sherwood, and others on a revue *(Round the Town),* and collaborated with George S. Kaufman on a play *(The Good Fellow)* and with Marc Connelly on another play *(The Wild Man of Borneo).* From 1923 to 1926, he was at the *Times,* backing up George S. Kaufman in the drama department; while he was there, he also became the first regular theatre critic for *The New Yorker,* writing weekly from June, 1925, until January, 1926, when Walter Wanger offered him a motion-picture contract and he left for Hollywood. The first picture he wrote was the Lon Chaney success **The Road to Mandalay.** In all, he worked on over seventy movies. He went on living and working in Los Angeles until his death, in 1953. He left three children: Don, born in Berlin in 1922, who is a novelist *(Trial)* and a writer for the movies (co-scenarist of *I Want to Live!)* and television ("Marcus Welby, M.D."); Frank, born in New York in 1924, who became a lawyer, a journalist, a Peace Corps worker, and Robert Kennedy's press assistant, and is now a columnist and television commentator; and Johanna, born in Los Angeles in 1937, who is a journalist (on *Time)* and is married to Peter Davis, the writer-producer of *The Selling of the Pentagon.*

Told this way, Herman Mankiewicz's career sounds exemplary, but these are just the bare bones of the truth. Even though it would be easy to document this official life of the apparently rising young man with photographs of Mankiewicz in his Berlin days dining with the Chancellor, Mankiewicz in his newspaperman days outside the *Chicago Tribune* with Jack Dempsey, and so on, it would be hard to explain his sudden, early aging and the thickening of his features and the transparently cynical look on his face in later photographs.

It was a lucky thing for Mankiewicz that he got the movie job when he did, because he would never have risen at the *Times,* and though he wrote regularly for *The New Yorker* (and remarked of those of the Algonquin group who didn't, "The part-time help of wits is no better than the full-time help of half-wits"), *The New Yorker,* despite his pleas for cash, was paying him partly in stock, which wasn't worth much at the time. Mankiewicz drank heavily, and the drinking newspaperman was in the style of the *World* but not in the style of the *Times.* In October, 1925, he was almost fired. The drama critic then was Brooks Atkinson, and the drama editor was George S. Kaufman, with Mankiewicz second in line and Sam Zolotow third. Mankiewicz was sent to cover the performance of Gladys Wallis, who was the wife of the utilities magnate Samuel Insull, as Lady Teazle in *School for Scandal.* Mrs. Insull, who had abandoned her theatrical career over a quarter of a century before, was, according to biographers, bored with being a nobody when her husband was such a big somebody. She was fifty-six when she resumed her career, as Lady Teazle, who is meant to be about eighteen. The play had opened in Chicago, where, perhaps astutely, she performed for charity (St. Luke's Hospital), and the press had described her as brilliant. The night of the New York opening, Mankiewicz came back to the office drunk, started panning Mrs. Insull's performance, and then fell asleep over his typewriter. As Zolotow recalls it, "Kaufman began to read the review, and it was so venomous he was outraged. That was the only time I ever saw Kaufman lose his temper." The review wasn't printed. The *Times* suffered the humiliation of running this item on October 23, 1925:

### A NEW SCHOOL FOR SCANDAL

The *School for Scandal,* with Mrs. Insull as Lady Teazle, was produced at the Little Theatre last night. It will be reviewed in tomorrow's *Times.*

Mankiewicz was in such bad shape that night that Kaufman told Zolotow to call Sara Mankiewicz and have her come get him and take him home. Mrs. Mankiewicz recalls that he still had his head down on his typewriter when she arrived, with a friend, to remove him. She says he took it for granted that he was fired, but nevertheless went to work promptly the next day. Zolotow recalls, "In the morning, Herman came down to the office and asked me to talk to Mr. Birchall, the assistant managing editor, on his behalf. Herman had brought a peace offering of a bottle of Scotch and

I took it to Birchall. He had a red beard, and he tugged at it and he stabbed the air a few times with his index finger and said, 'Herman is a bad boy, a bad boy.' But he took the bottle and Herman kept his job until he got the movie offer."

The review—unsigned—that the *Times* printed on October 24, 1925, was a small masterpiece of tact:

As Lady Teazle, Mrs. Insull is as pretty as she is diminutive, with a clear smile and dainty gestures. There is a charming grace in her bearing that makes for excellent deportment. But this Lady Teazle seems much too innocent, too thoroughly the country lass that Joseph terms her, to lend credit to her part in the play.

Scattered through various books, and in the stories that are still told of him in Hollywood, are clues that begin to give one a picture of Herman Mankiewicz, a giant of a man who mongered his own talent, a man who got a head start in the race to "sell out" to Hollywood. The pay was fantastic. After a month in the movie business, Mankiewicz—though his Broadway shows had not been hits, and though this was in 1926, when movies were still silent—signed a year's contract giving him $400 a week and a bonus of $5,000 for each story that was accepted, with an option for a second year at $500 a week and $7,500 per accepted story, the company guaranteeing to accept at least four stories per year. In other words, his base pay was $40,800 his first year and $56,000 his second; actually, he wrote so many stories that he made much more. By the end of 1927, he was head of Paramount's scenario department, and in January, 1928, there was a newspaper item reporting that he was in New York "lining up a new set of newspaper feature writers and playwrights to bring to Hollywood," and that "most of the newer writers on Paramount's staff who contributed the most successful stories of the past year were selected by 'Mank.'" One reason that Herman Mankiewicz is so little known today is, ironically, that he went to Hollywood so early, before he had gained a big enough reputation in the literary and theatrical worlds. Screenwriters don't make names for themselves; the most famous ones are the ones whose names were famous before they went to Hollywood, or who made names later in the theatre or from books, or who, like Preston Sturges, became directors.

Mankiewicz and other *New Yorker* writers in the twenties and the early thirties were very close to the world of the theatre; many of them were writing plays, writing about theatre people, reviewing plays. It's not surprising that within a few years the magazine's most celebrated contributors were in Hollywood writing movies. Of the ten friends of the editor Harold Ross who were in the original prospectus as advisory editors, six became screenwriters. When Mankiewicz gave up the drama critic's spot, in 1926, he was replaced by Charles Brackett, and when Brackett headed West, Robert Benchley filled it while commuting, and then followed. Dorothy Parker, the book reviewer Constant Reader, went West, too. Nunnally Johnson, who was to work on over a hundred movies, was a close friend of Harold Ross's and had volunteered to do the movie reviewing in 1926 but had been told that that job was for "old ladies and fairies." Others in the group didn't agree: Benchley had written on movies for the old *Life* as early as 1920, and John O'Hara later took time out from screenwriting to become the movie critic for *Newsweek*—where he was to review *Citizen Kane.* The whole group were interested in the theatre and the movies, and they were fast, witty writers, used to regarding their work not as deathless prose but as stories written to order for the market, used also to the newspaperman's pretense of putting a light value on what they did—the "Look, no hands" attitude. Thus, they were well prepared to become the scenarists and gag writers of the talkies.

6.

The comic muse of the most popular "daring" late silents was a carefree, wisecracking flapper. Beginning in 1926, Herman Mankiewicz worked on an astounding number of films in that spirit. In 1927 and 1928, he did the titles (the printed dialogue and explanations) for at least twenty-five films that starred Clara Bow, Bebe Daniels, Nancy Carroll, Esther Ralston, George Bancroft, Thomas Meighan, Jack Holt, Richard Dix, Wallace Beery, and other public favorites. He worked on the titles for Jules Furthman's script of *Abie's Irish Rose,* collaborated with Anita Loos on the wisecracks for *Gentlemen Prefer Blondes,* and did the immensely successful *The Barker* and *The Canary Murder Case,* with William Powell, Louise Brooks, James Hall, and Jean Arthur. By then, sound had come in, and in 1929 he did the script as well as the dialogue for *The Dummy,* with Ruth Chatterton and Fredric March (making his screen début), wrote William Wellman's *The Man I Love,* with Richard Arlen, Pat O'Brien, and Mary Brian, and worked for Josef von Sternberg and many other directors.

Other screenwriters made large contributions, too, but probably none larger than Mankiewicz's at the beginning of the sound era, and if he was at that time one of the highest-paid writers in the world, it was because he wrote the kind of movies that were disapproved of as "fast" and immoral. His heroes weren't soft-eyed and bucolic; he brought good-humored toughness to the movies, and energy and astringency. And the public responded, because it was eager for modern American subjects. Even those of us who were children at the time loved the fast-moving modern-city stories. The commonplaceness—even tawdriness—of the imagery was such a relief from all that silent "poetry." The talkies were a great step down. It's hard to make clear to people who didn't live through the transition how sickly and unpleasant many of those "artistic" silent pictures were—how you wanted to scrape off all that mist and sentiment.

Almost from the time the motion-picture camera was invented, there had been experiments with sound and attempts at synchronizatiion, and the public was more than ready for talking pictures. Many of the late silents, if one looks at them now, seem to be trying to talk to us, crying out for sound. Despite the legend of paralysis of the medium when sound first came in, there was a burst of inventiveness. In musicals, directors like René Clair and, over here, Ernst Lubitsch and, to a lesser degree, Rouben Mamoulian didn't use sound just for lip synchronization; they played with sound as they had played with images, and they tried to use sound without losing the movement of silents or the daring of silent editing. Some of the early talkies were static and inept; newly imported stage directors literally staged the action, as if the space were stage space, and the technicians had to learn to handle the microphones. But movies didn't suddenly become stagebound because of the microphone. Many of the silents had always been stagebound, for the sufficient reason that they had been adapted from plays—from the war-horses of the repertory, because they had proved their popularity, and from the latest Broadway hits, because the whole country wanted to see them. The silent adaptations were frequently deadly, not just because of construction based on the classical unities, with all those entrances and exits and that painful emptiness on the screen of plays worked out in terms of absolutely essential characters only, but because everything kept stopping for the explanatory titles and the dialogue titles.

Even in the movies adapted from novels or written directly for the screen, the action rarely went on for long; silents were choked with titles, which were perhaps, on the average, between ten and twenty times as frequent as the interruptions for TV commercials. The printed dialogue was often witty, and often it was essential to an understanding of the action, but it broke up the rhythm of performances and the visual flow, and the titles were generally held for the slowest readers, so that one lost the mood of the film while staring at the dialogue for the third scanning. (It seems to me, thinking back on it, that we were so eager for the movie to go on that we gulped the words down and then were always left with them for what, to our impatience, seemed an eternity, and that the better the movie, the more quickly we tried to absorb and leap past the printed words, and the more frustrating the delays became.) The plain fact that many silent movies were plays without the spoken dialogue, plays deprived of their very substance, was what made the theatre-going audience—and the Broadway crowd of writers—so contemptuous of them. Filmed plays without the actors' voices, and with the deadening delays for the heterogeneous audience to read the dialogue, were an abomination. Many of the journalists and playwrights and wits of the Algonquin Round Table had written perceptively about motion pictures (Alexander Woollcott, who managed to pan some of the greatest films, was an exception); they had, in general, been cynical only about the slop and the silent filmed plays. But though they had been active in the theatre, there had been no real place for them in movies; now, with the introduction of sound, they could bring to the screen the impudence that had given Broadway its flavor in the twenties—and bring it there before the satirical references were out of date. Sound made it possible for them to liberate movies into a new kind of contemporaneity.

7.

There is an elaborate body of theory that treats film as "the nocturnal voyage into the unconscious," as Luis Buñuel called it, and for a director such as Buñuel "the cinema seems to have been invented to express the life of the subconscious." Some of the greatest work of D. W. Griffith and other masters of the silent film has a magical, fairy-tale appeal, and certainly Surrealists like Buñuel, and other experimental and avant-garde filmmakers as well, have drawn upon this dreamlike vein of film. But these artists were the exceptions; much of the dreamy appeal to the "subconscious" and to "universal" or "primitive" fantasies was an appeal to the most backward, not to say reactionary, elements of illiterate and semiliterate mass society. There was a steady load of calendar-art guck that patronized "the deserving poor" and idealized "purity" (i.e., virginity) and "morality" (i.e., virginity plus charity). And all that is only one kind of movie anyway. Most of the dream theory of film, which takes the audience for passive dreamers, doesn't apply to the way one responded to silent comedies— which, when they were good, kept the audience in a heightened state of consciousness. When we join in laughter, it's as if the lights were on in the theatre. And not just the Mack Sennett comedies and Keaton and Chaplin kept us fully awake but the spirited, bouncy comediennes, like Colleen Moore and Marion Davies, and the romantic comedy "teams," and the suave, "polished" villains, like William Powell. My favorite movies as a child were the Bebe Daniels comedies—I suppose they were the movie equivalent of the series books one reads at that age. During 1927 and 1928, Paramount brought a new one out every few months; Bebe, the athletic madcap, would fence like Douglas Fairbanks, or she would parody Valentino by kidnapping and taming a man, or she might be a daredevil newsreel camera-woman or a cub reporter.

I did not know until I started to look into the writing of *Citizen Kane* that the man who wrote *Kane* had worked on some of those pictures, too—that Mankiewicz had, in fact, written (alone or with others) about forty of the films I remember best from the twenties and thirties (as well as many I didn't see or don't remember). Mankiewicz didn't work on *every* kind of picture, though. He didn't do Westerns, and once, when a studio attempted to punish him for his customary misbehavior by assigning him to a Rin Tin Tin picture, he turned in a script that began with the craven Rin Tin Tin frightened by a mouse and reached its climax with a house on fire and the dog taking a baby *into* the flames. I had known about Mankiewicz's contribution to *Kane* and a few other films, but I hadn't realized how extensive his career was. I had known that he was the producer of *Million Dollar Legs* (with W. C. Fields and Jack Oakie and Lyda Roberti) and *Laughter* (with Fredric March

and Nancy Carroll), but I hadn't known, for example, that he had produced two of the Marx Brothers films that I've always especially liked, the first two made in Hollywood and written directly for the screen—*Monkey Business* and *Horse Feathers*—and part of *Duck Soup* as well. A few years ago, some college students asked me what films I would like to see again just for my own pleasure, and without a second's thought I replied *Duck Soup* and *Million Dollar Legs,* though at that time I had no idea there was any connection between them. Yet surely there is a comic spirit that links them—even the settings, Freedonia and Klopstokia, with Groucho as Prime Minister of one and Fields as President of the other—and now that I have looked into Herman Mankiewicz's career it's apparent that he was a key linking figure in just the kind of movies my friends and I loved best.

When the period of the great silent comedians, with their international audience, was over, a new style of American comedy developed. One couldn't really call a colloquial, skeptical comedy a "masterpiece," as one could sometimes call a silent comedy a masterpiece, especially if the talkie looked quite banal and was so topical it felt transient. But I think that many of us enjoyed these comedies more, even though we may not have felt very secure about the aesthetic grounds for our enjoyment. The talking comedies weren't as aesthetically pure as the silents, yet they felt liberating in a way that even great silents didn't. The elements to which we could respond were multiplied; now there were vocal nuances, new kinds of timing, and wonderful new tricks, like the infectious way Claudette Colbert used to break up while listening to someone. It's easy to see why Europeans, who couldn't follow the slang and the jokes and didn't understand the whole satirical frame of reference, should prefer our action films and Westerns. But it's a bad joke on our good jokes that film enthusiasts here often take their cues on the American movie past from Europe, and so they ignore the tradition of comic irreverence and become connoisseurs of the "visuals" and "mises en scène" of action pictures, which are usually too silly even to be called reactionary. They're sub-reactionary—the antique melodramas of silent days with noise added—a mass art better suited, one might think, to Fascism, or even feudalism, than to democracy.

There is another reason the American talking comedies, despite their popularity, are so seldom valued highly by film aestheticians. The dream-art kind of film, which lends itself to beautiful visual imagery, is generally the creation of the "artist" director, while the astringent film is more often directed by a competent, unpretentious craftsman who can be made to look very good by a good script and can be turned into a bum by a bad script. And this competent craftsman may be too worldly and too practical to do the "imaginative" bits that sometimes helped make thereputations of "artist" directors. Ben Hecht said he shuddered at the touches von Sternberg introduced into *Underworld:* "My head villain, Bull Weed, after robbing a bank, emerged with a suitcase full of money and paused in the crowded street to notice a blind beggar and give him a coin—before making his getaway." That's exactly the sort of thing that quantities of people react to emotionally as "deep" and as "art," and that many film enthusiasts treasure—the inflated sentimental with a mystical drip. The thirties, though they had their own load of sentimentality, were the hardest-headed period of American movies, and their plainness of style, with its absence of false "cultural" overtones, has never got its due aesthetically. Film students—and their teachers—often become interested in movies just because they are the kind of people who are emotionally affected by the blind-beggar bits, and they are indifferent by temperament to the emancipation of American movies in the thirties and the role that writers played in it.

I once jotted down the names of some movies that I didn't associate with any celebrated director but that had nevertheless stayed in my memory over the years, because something in them had especially delighted me—such rather obscure movies as *The Moon's Our Home* (Margaret Sullavan and Henry Fonda) and *He Married His Wife* (Nancy Kelly, Joel McCrea, and Mary Boland). When I looked them up, I discovered that Dorothy Parker's name was in the credits of *The Moon's Our Home* and John O'Hara's in the credits of *He Married His Wife*. Other writers worked on those films, too, and perhaps they were the ones who were responsible for what I responded to, but the recurrence of the names of that group of writers, not just on rather obscure remembered films but on almost *all* the films that are generally cited as proof of the vision and style of the most highly acclaimed directors of that period, suggests that the writers—and a particular group of them, at that—may for a brief period, a little more than a decade, have given American talkies their character.

8.

There is always a time lag in the way movies take over (and broaden and emasculate) material from the other arts—whether it is last season's stage success or the novels of the preceding decade or a style or an idea that has run its course in its original medium. (This does not apply to a man like Jean-Luc Godard, who is not a mass-medium movie director.) In most productions of the big studios, the time lag is enormous. In the thirties, after the great age of musical comedy and burlesque, Hollywood, except for Paramount, was just discovering huge operettas. After the Broadway days of Clifton Webb, Fred Astaire, the Marx Brothers, Fanny Brice, W. C. Fields, and all the rest, M-G-M gave us Nelson Eddy and Jeanette MacDonald, and Universal gave us Deanna Durbin. This is the history of movies. J. D. Salinger has finally come to the screen through his imitators, and Philip Roth's fifties romance arrived at the end of the sixties. It may be that for new ideas to be successful in movies, the way must be prepared by success in other media, and the audience must have grown tired of what it's been getting and be ready for something new.

There are always a few people in Hollywood who are considered mad dreamers for trying to do in movies things that have already been done in the other arts. But once one of them breaks through and has a hit, he's called a genius and everybody starts copying him.

The new spirit of the talkies was the twenties moved West in the thirties. George S. Kaufman was writing the Marx Brothers stage shows when he and Mankiewicz worked together at the Times; a little later, Kaufman directed the first Broadway production of *The Front Page.* Kaufman's collaborators on Broadway plays in the twenties and the early thirties included Marc Connelly, Edna Ferber, Ring Lardner, Morrie Ryskind, and Moss Hart as well as Mankiewicz—the nucleus of the Algonquin-to-Hollywood group. Nunnally Johnson says that the two most brilliant men he has ever known were George S. Kaufman and Herman Mankiewicz, and that, on the whole, Mankiewicz was the more brilliant of the two. I think that what Mankiewicz did in movies was an offshoot of the gag comedy that Kaufman had initiated on Broadway; Mankiewicz spearheaded the movement of that whole Broadway style of wisecracking, fast-talking, cynical-sentimental entertainment onto the national scene. Kaufman's kind of impersonal, visionless comedy, with its single goal of getting the audience to laugh, led to the degeneration of the Broadway theatre, to its play doctors and gimmickry and scattershot jokes at defenseless targets, and so it would be easy to look down on the movie style that came out of it. But I don't think the results were the same when this type of comedy was transplanted to movies; the only bad long-range consequences were to the writers themselves.

Kaufman fathered a movement that is so unmistakably the bastard child of the arts as to seem fatherless; the gag comedy was perfectly suited to the commercial mass art of the movies, so that it appears to be an almost inevitable development. It suited the low common denominator of the movies even better than it suited the needs of the relatively selective theatre audience, and the basic irresponsibility of this kind of theatre combined with the screenwriters' lack of control over their own writing to produce what one might call the brothel period of American letters. It was a gold rush, and Mankiewicz and his friends had exactly the skills to turn a trick. The journalists' style of working fast and easy and working to order and not caring too much how it was butchered was the best kind of apprenticeship for a Hollywood hack, and they had loved to gather, to joke and play games, to lead the histrionic forms of the glamorous literary life. Now they were gathered in cribs on each studio lot, working in teams side by side, meeting for lunch at the commissary and for dinner at Chassen's, which their old friend and editor Harold Ross had helped finance, and all over town for drinks. They adapted each other's out-of-date plays and novels, and rewrote each other's scripts. Even in their youth in New York, most of them had indulged in what for them proved a vice: they were "collaborators"—dependent on the fun and companionship of joint authorship, which usually means a shared shallowness. Now they collaborated all over the place and backward in time; they collaborated promiscuously, and within a few years were rewriting the remakes of their own or somebody else's rewrites. Mankiewicz adapted Kaufman and Ferber's *The Royal Family* and *Dinner at Eight,* turned Alice Duer Miller's *Come Out of the Kitchen* into *Honey,* and adapted George Kelly's *The Show-Off* and James Thurber's *My Life and Hard Times* and works by Laurence Stallings and other old friends while Ben Hecht or Preston Sturges or Arthur Kober was working over something of his. They escaped the cold, and they didn't suffer from the Depression. They were a colony—expatriates without leaving the country—and their individual contributions to the scripts that emerged after the various rewrites were almost impossible to assess, because their attitudes were so similar; they made the same kind of jokes, because they had been making them to each other for so long. In Hollywood, they sat around building on to each other's gags, covering up implausibilities and dull spots, throwing new wisecracks on top of jokes they had laughed at in New York. Screenwriting was an extension of what they used to do for fun, and now they got paid for it. They had liked to talk more than to write, and this weakness became their way of life. As far as the official literary culture was concerned, they dropped from sight. To quote a classic bit of dialogue from Budd Schulberg's *The Disenchanted:*

> "Bane had two hits running on Broadway at the same time. Even Nathan liked 'em. Popular 'n satirical. Like Barry, only better. The critics kept waiting for him to write that great American play."

> "What happened to him?"

> "Hollywood."

Hollywood destroyed them, but they did wonders for the movies. In New York, they may have valued their own urbanity too highly; faced with the target Hollywood presented, they became cruder and tougher, less tidy, less stylistically elegant, and more iconoclastic, and in the eyes of Hollywood they were slaphappy cynics, they were "crazies." They were too talented and too sophisticated to put a high value on what they did, too amused at the spectacle of what they were doing and what they were part of to be respected the way a writer of "integrity," like Lillian Hellman, was later to be respected—or, still later, Arthur Miller. Though their style was often flippant and their attitude toward form casual to the point of contempt, they brought movies the subversive gift of sanity. They changed movies by raking the old moralistic muck with derision. Those sickly Graustarkian romances with beautiful, pure high-born girls and pathetic lame girls and dashing princes in love with commoners, and all the Dumas and Sabatini and Blasco-Ibáñez, now had to compete with the freedom and wildness of American comedy. Once American films had their voice and the Algonquin group was turned loose on the scripts, the revolting worship of European aristocracy faded so fast that movie stars even stopped bringing home Georgian princes. In the silents, the heroes were often simpletons. In the talkies, the heroes were to be the men who weren't fooled, who were smart and learned their way around. The new heroes of the screen were created in the image of their authors: they were fast-talking newspaper reporters.

That Walter Burns whose entrance in *The Front Page* Kerr described was based on Walter Howey, who was the city editor of the *Chicago Tribune,* at $8,000 a year, until Hearst lured him away by an offer of $35,000 a year. Howey is generally considered the "greatest" of all Hearst editors—by those who mean one thing by it, and by those who mean the other. He edited Hearst's *New York Mirror* at a time when it *claimed* to be ten per cent news and ninety per cent entertainment. The epitome of Hearstian journalism, and a favorite of Hearst's until the end, he was one of the executors of Hearst's will. At one time or another, just about all the Hollywood writers had worked for Walter Howey and/or spent their drinking hours with friends who did. He was the legend: the classic model of the amoral, irresponsible, irrepressible newsman who cares about nothing but scoops and circulation. He had lost an eye (supposedly in actual fighting of circulation wars), and Ben Hecht is quoted as saying you could tell which was the glass eye because it was the warmer one. Hecht used him again in *Nothing Sacred,* as Fredric March's editor—"a cross between a Ferris wheel and a werewolf"—and he turns up under other names in other plays and movies. In a sense, all those newspaper plays and movies were already about Hearst's kind of corrupt, manic journalism.

The toughest-minded, the most satirical of the thirties pictures often featured newspaper settings, or, at least, reporters—especially the "screwball" comedies, which had some resemblances to later "black" comedy and current "freaky" comedy but had a very different spirit. A newspaper picture meant a contemporary picture in an American setting, usually a melodrama with crime and political corruption and suspense and comedy and romance. In 1931, a title like *Five Star Final* or *Scandal Sheet* signalled the public that the movie would be a tough modern talkie, not a tear-jerker with sound. Just to touch a few bases, there was *The Front Page* itself, in 1931, with Pat O'Brien as the reporter and Adolphe Menjou as Walter Burns; Lee Tracy as the gossip columnist in *Blessed Event* and as the press agent in *Bombshell;* Clark Gable as the reporter in *It Happened One Night;* Paul Muni giving advice to the lovelorn in *Hi, Nellie;* Spencer Tracy as the editor in *Libeled Lady;* Stuart Erwin as the correspondent in *Viva Villa!;* Jean Harlow stealing the affections of a newspaperman from girl reporter Loretta Young in *Platinum Blonde;* Jean Arthur as the girl reporter in *Mr. Deeds Goes to Town;* a dozen pictures, at least, with George Bancroft as a Walter Howey-style bullying editor; all those half-forgotten pictures with reporter "teams"—Fredric March and Virginia Bruce, or Joel McCrea and Jean Arthur, or Loretta Young and Tyrone Power (*Love Is News*); Cary Grant as the editor and Joan Bennett as the reporter in

*Wedding Present;* and then Cary Grant as Walter Burns in *His Girl Friday,* with Rosalind Russell as the reporter; and then Cary Grant and James Stewart (who had been a foreign correspondent in *Next Time We Love*) both involved with a news magazine in *The Philadelphia Story,* in 1940. Which takes us right up to **Citizen Kane,** the biggest newspaper picture of them all—the picture that ends with the introduction of the cast and a reprise of the line "I think it would be fun to run a newspaper."

### 9.

After years of swapping stories about Howey and the other werewolves and the crooked, dirty press, Mankiewicz found himself on story-swapping terms with the power behind it all, Hearst himself. When he had been in Hollywood only a short time, he met Marion Davies and Hearst through his friendship with Charles Lederer, a writer, then in his early twenties, whom Ben Hecht had met and greatly admired in New York when Lederer was still in his teens. Lederer, a child prodigy, who had entered college at thirteen, got to know Mankiewicz, the MacArthurs, Moss Hart, Benchley, and their friends at about the same time or shortly after he met Hecht, and was immediately accepted into a group considerably older than he was. Lederer was Marion Davies' nephew—the son of her sister Reine, who had been in operetta and musical comedy. In Hollywood, Charles Lederer's life seems to have revolved around his aunt, whom he adored. (Many others adored her also, though **Citizen Kane** was to give the world a different—and false—impression.) She was childless, and Lederer was very close to her; he spent a great deal of his time at her various dwelling places, and took his friends to meet both her and Hearst. The world of letters being small and surprising, Charles Lederer was among those who worked on the adaptation of *The Front Page* to the screen in 1931 and again when it was remade as *His Girl Friday* in 1940, and, the world being even smaller than that, Lederer married Orson Welles' ex-wife, Virginia Nicholson Welles, in 1940, at San Simeon. (She married two prodigies in succession; the marriage to Welles had lasted five years and produced a daughter.)

Hearst was so fond of Lederer that on the evening of the nuptials he broke his rule of one cocktail to guests before dinner and no hard liquor thereafter. A guest who gulped the cocktail down was sometimes able to swindle another, but this is the only occasion that I can find recorded on which Hearst dropped the rule—a rule that Marion Davies customarily eased by slipping drinks to desperate guests before Hearst joined them but that nevertheless made it possible for Hearst to receive, and see at their best, some of the most talented alcoholics this country has ever produced. Not all writers are attracted to the rich and powerful, but it's a defining characteristic of journalists to be drawn to those who live at the center of power. Even compulsive drinkers like Mankiewicz and Dorothy Parker were so fascinated by the great ménage of Hearst and his consort—and the guest lists of the world-famous—that they managed to

stay relatively sober for the evenings at Marion Davies' beach house (Colleen Moore described it as "the largest house on the beach—and I mean the beach from San Diego to the Canadian border") and the weekends at San Simeon.

If **Kane** has the same love-hate as *The Front Page,* the same joyous infatuation with the antics of the unprincipled press, it's because Mankiewicz, like Hecht and MacArthur, revelled in the complexities of corruption. And Hearst's life was a *spectacle.* For short periods, this was intoxication enough. A man like Hearst seems to embody more history than other people do; in his company a writer may feel that he has been living in the past and on the outskirts and now he's living in the dangerous present, right where the decisions are really made.

Hearst represented a new type of power. He got his first newspaper in 1887, when he was twenty-four, by asking his father for it, and, in the next three decades, when, for the first time, great masses of people became literate, he added more and more papers, until, with his empire of thirty newspapers and fifteen magazines, he was the most powerful journalist and publisher in the world. He had brought the first comic strips to America in 1892, and his battling with Pulitzer a few years later over a cartoon character named the Yellow Kid revived the term "yellow journalism." Because there was no tradition of responsibility in this new kind of popular journalism, which was almost a branch of show business, Hearst knew no restraints; perhaps fortunately, he was unguided. Ultimately, he was as purposeless about his power as the craziest of the Roman emperors. His looting of the treasures of the world for his castle at San Simeon symbolized his imperial status. Being at his table was being at court, and the activities of the notables who were invited there were slavishly chronicled in the Hearst papers.

The new social eminence of the Mankiewiczes, who sometimes visited San Simeon for as long as ten days at a time, can be charted from Louella Parsons' columns. By the end of 1928, Louella was announcing Mankiewicz's writing assignments with a big bold headline at the top of the column, and was printing such items as:

> One of the few scenario writers in Hollywood who didn't have to unlearn much that he had learned is Herman Mankiewicz. Herman came to Paramount directly from the stage, and naturally he knows the technique just as well as if he hadn't written movies in the interval.

It was worth another item in the same column that Herman Mankiewicz had been observed "taking his son down Hollywood Boulevard to see the lighted Christmas trees." In 1931, the Mankiewiczes were so prominent that they were among those who gave Marion Davies a homecoming party at the Hotel Ambassador; the other hosts were Mr. and Mrs. Irving Thalberg, Mr. and Mrs.

King Vidor, Mr. and Mrs. Samuel Goldwyn, John Gilbert, Lewis Milestone, Hedda Hopper, and so on. Hedda Hopper, who worked as a movie columnist for a rival newspaper chain but was a close friend of Marion Davies (to whom, it is said, she owed her job), was also an enthusiastic reporter of Mankiewicz's activities during the years when he and his ravishing Sara were part of the Hearst-Davies social set.

When writers begin to see the powerful men operating in terms of available alternatives, while they have been judging them in terms of ideals, they often develop "personal" admiration for the great bastards whom they have always condemned and still condemn. Hearst was to Mankiewicz, I suspect, what Welles was to be to him a little later—a dangerous new toy. And he needed new toys constantly to keep off the booze. Mankiewicz could control himself at San Simeon in the late twenties and the very early thirties, as, in those days, he could control himself when he was in charge of a movie. Producing the Marx Brothers comedies kept him busy and entertained for a while. With the title of "supervisor" (a term for the actual working producer, as distinguished from the studio executive whose name might appear above or below the name of the movie), he worked on their pictures from the inception of the ideas through the months of writing and then the shooting. But he got bored easily, and when he started cutting up in the middle of preparing *Duck Soup,* in 1933, he was taken off the picture. When the Marx Brothers left Paramount and went to M-G-M, he joined them again, in the preparation of *A Night at the Opera,* in 1935, and the same thing happened; he was replaced as supervisor by his old boss George S. Kaufman.

His credits began to taper off after 1933, and in 1936 Mankiewicz didn't get a single credit. That year, he published an article called **"On Approaching Forty,"** a brief satirical account of what had happened to him as a writer. It began:

> Right before me, as I write, is a folder in which my wife keeps the blotters from Mr. Eschner, the insurance man, Don's first report card, the letter from the income tax people about the gambling loss at Tia Juana, the press photograph of me greeting Helen Kane (in behalf of the studio) at the Pasadena Station and my literary output. There are four separate pieces of this output and they are all excellent. I hope some friend will gather them into a little book after my death. There is plenty of ninety point Marathon in the world, and wide margins can't be hard to find.

He includes those tiny pieces in their entirety, and after one of them—the first three sentences of a short story—he comments:

> I moved to Hollywood soon after I had made this notation and was kept so busy with one thing and another—getting the pool filled, playing the Cadillac and Buick salesmen against each other, only to compromise on a Cadillac and a Buick,

after all, and locating the finance company's downtown office—that the first thing I knew, a story, a good deal like the one I had in mind, appeared in the *Saturday Evening Post,* and in *Collier's,* too.

This is the end of his article:

> The fourth note looks rather naked now, all by itself on the desk. It says, simply:
>
> "Write piece for *New Yorker* on reaching thirty-fifth birthday. No central idea. Just flit from paragraph to paragraph."
>
> People who complain that my work is slipshod would be a little surprised to find that I just am *not* always satisfied with the first thing I put down. I'm changing that thirty-fifth to fortieth right now.

**"On Approaching Forty"** didn't come out in *The New Yorker;* it appeared in the *Hollywood Reporter.*

Ambivalence was the most common "literary" emotion of the screenwriters of the thirties, as alienation was to become the most common "literary" emotion of the screenwriters of the sixties. The thirties writers were ambivalently nostalgic about their youth as reporters, journalists, critics, or playwrights, and they glorified the hard-drinking, cynical newspaperman. They were ambivalent about Hollywood, which they savaged and satirized whenever possible. Hollywood paid them so much more money than they had ever earned before, and the movies reached so many more people than they had ever reached before, that they were contemptuous of those who hadn't made it on their scale at the same time that they hated themselves for selling out. They had gone to Hollywood as a paid vacation from their playwriting or journalism, and screenwriting became their only writing. The vacation became an extended drunken party, and while they were there in the debris of the long morning after, American letters passed them by. They were never to catch up; nor were American movies ever again to have in their midst a whole school of the richest talents of a generation.

We in the audience didn't have to wake up *afterward* to how good those films of the thirties were; in common with millions of people, I enjoyed them while they were coming out. They were immensely popular. But I did take them for granted. There was such a steady flow of bright comedy that it appeared to be a Hollywood staple, and it didn't occur to me that those films wouldn't go on being made. It didn't occur to me that it required a special gathering of people in a special atmosphere to produce that flow, and that when those people stopped enjoying themselves those pictures couldn't be made. And I guess it didn't occur to older, more experienced people, either, because for decades everybody went on asking why Hollywood wasn't turning out those good, entertaining comedies anymore.

By the end of the thirties, the jokes had soured. The comedies of the forties were heavy and pushy, straining for humor, and the comic impulse was misplaced or lost;

they came out of a different atmosphere, a different *feeling.* The comic spirit of the thirties had been happily self-critical about America, the happiness born of the knowledge that in no other country were movies so free to be self-critical. It was the comedy of a country that didn't yet hate itself. Though it wasn't until the sixties that the self-hatred became overt in American life and American movies, it started to show, I think, in the phony, excessive, duplicit use of patriotism by the rich, guilty liberals of Hollywood in the war years.

## 10.

In the forties, a socially conscious film historian said to me, "You know, Paramount never made a good movie," and I brought up the names of some Paramount movies—*Easy Living* and *Trouble in Paradise* and lovely trifles like *Midnight*—and, of course, I couldn't make my point, because those movies weren't what was thought of in the forties as a good movie. I knew I wouldn't get anywhere at all if I tried to cite **Million Dollar Legs** or *Mississippi,* or pictures with the Marx Brothers or Mae West; I would be told they weren't even movies. Though Paramount made some elegant comedies in the "Continental" style, many of the best Paramount pictures were like revues—which was pretty much the style of the Broadway theatre they'd come out of, and was what I liked about them. They entertained you without trying to change your life, yet didn't congratulate you for being a slobbering bag of mush, either. But by the forties these were considered "escapist entertainment," and that was supposed to be *bad.* Many of the thirties comedies, especially the Paramount ones, weren't even "artistic" or "visual" movies—which is why they look so good on television now. They also sound good, because what that historian thought of as their irresponsibility is so much more modern than the sentimentalities of the war years. What was believed in was implicit in the styles of the heroes and heroines and in the comedy targets; the writers had an almost aristocratic disdain for putting beliefs into words. In the forties, the writers convinced themselves that they believed in everything, and they kept putting it all into so many bad words. It's no wonder the movies had no further use for a Groucho or a Mae West; one can imagine what either of them might have done to those words.

It's common to blame the McCarthyism of the fifties and the removal of blacklisted writers for the terrible, flat writing in American movies of recent years, but the writers might have recovered from McCarthyism (they might even have stood up to it) if they hadn't been destroyed as writers long before. The writing that had given American talkies their special flavor died in the war, killed not in battle but in the politics of Stalinist "anti-Fascism." For the writers, Hollywood was just one big crackup, and for most of them it took a political turn. The lost-in-Hollywood generation of writers, trying to clean themselves of guilt for their wasted years and their irresponsibility as *writers,* became political in the worst way—became a special breed of anti-Fascists.

The talented writers, the major ones as well as the lightweight yet entertaining ones, went down the same drain as the clods—drawn into it, often, by bored wives, less successful brothers. They became naïvely, hysterically pro-Soviet; they ignored Stalin's actual policies, because they so badly needed to believe in something. They had been so smart, so gifted, and yet they hadn't been able to beat Hollywood's contempt for the writer. (Walter Wanger had put twenty-seven of them to work in groups in succession on the script of Vincent Sheean's *Personal History.*) They lived in the city where Irving Thalberg was enshrined; Thalberg, the saint of M-G-M, had rationalized Mayer's system of putting teams of writers to work simultaneously and in relays on the same project. It had been lunatic before, but Thalberg made it seem mature and responsible to fit writers into an assembly-line method that totally alienated them and took away their last shreds of pride. And most of the Algonquin group had been in Hollywood so long they weren't even famous anymore.

Talented people have rarely had the self-control to flourish in the Hollywood atmosphere of big money and conflicting pressures. The talented—especially those who weren't using their talents to full capacity—have become desperate, impatient, unreliable, self-destructive, and also destructive, and so there has always been some validity in the businessman's argument that he couldn't afford to take chances on "geniuses." Thalberg didn't play around with a man like Mankiewicz; after throwing him off *A Night at the Opera,* he didn't use him again.

The writers who had become accustomed to being assembly-line workers were ready to believe it when, in the forties, they were told that, like factory workers, they were "part of the team on the assembly line" and needed "that strengthening of the spirit which comes from identity with the labor of others." Like the producers, the Screen Writers Guild respected discipline and responsibility, but though the businessmen had never been able to organize people of talent—producers like Thalberg just kept discarding them—the union ideologues knew how. The talented rarely become bureaucrats, but the mediocre had put down roots in Hollywood—it doesn't take long in Los Angeles, the only great city that is purely modern, that hasn't even an architectural past in the nineteenth century. In the forties, the talented merged with the untalented and became almost indistinguishable from them, and the mediocre have been writing movies ever since. When the good writers tried to regain their self-respect by becoming political activists in the Stalinist style, it was calamitous to talent; the Algonquin group's own style was lost as their voice blended into the preachy, self-righteous chorus.

The comedy writers who had laughed at cant now learned to write it and were rehabilitated as useful citizens of the community of mediocrity. It was just what the newly political congratulated themselves on—their constructive, uplifting approach—that killed comedy.

When they had written frivolously, knowing that they had no control over how their writing would be used, or buried, or rewritten, they may have failed their own gifts and the dreams of their youth, but the work they turned out had human dimensions; they were working at less than full capacity, but they were still honest entertainers. Their humor was the humor of those trapped by human weakness as well as by "the system," and this was basic comedy—like the jokes and camaraderie of Army men. But when they became political in that morally superior way of people who are doing something for themselves but pretending it's for others, their self-righteousness was insufferable. They may have told lies in the themes and plots of the thirties comedies, but they didn't take their own lies seriously, they didn't *believe* their own lies, the way they did in the forties. In the forties, the Screen Writers Guild and the Hollywood Writers Mobilization (for wartime morale-building) held conferences at which "responsible" writers brought the irresponsibles into line. The irresponsibles were told they were part of an army and must "dedicate their creative abilities to the winning of the war." And, in case they failed to understand the necessity for didactic, "positive" humor, there were panels and seminars that analyzed jokes and pointed out which ones might do harm. It was explained to the writers that "catch-as-catch-can," "no-holds-barred" comedy was a thing of the past. "A very funny line may make black-market dealings seem innocent and attractive," they were told, and "Respect for officers must be maintained at all times, in any scene, in any situation."

Show-business people are both giddy and desperately, sincerely intense. When Stalinism was fashionable, movie people became Stalinists, the way they later became witches and warlocks. Apparently, many of the Hollywood Stalinists didn't realize they were taking any risks; they performed propaganda services for the various shifts in Russia's foreign policy and, as long as the needs of American and Russian policy coincided, this took the form of super-patriotism. When the war was over and the Cold War began, history left them stranded, and McCarthy moved in on them. The shame of McCarthyism was not only "the shame of America" but the shame of a bunch of newly rich people who were eager to advise the world on moral and political matters and who, faced with a test, informed on their friends—and, as Orson Welles put it, not even to save their lives but to save their swimming pools. One might think that whatever they had gained emotionally from their activity they would have lost when they informed on each other, but it doesn't seem to have always worked that way. They didn't change their ideas when they recanted before the House Un-American Activities Committee; they merely gave in and then were restored to themselves. And they often seem to regard it not as their weakness but as their martyrdom. Show-business-Stalinism is basically not political but psychological; it's a fashionable form of hysteria and guilt that is by now not so much pro-Soviet as just abusively anti-American. America is their image of Hell (once again,

because of Vietnam, they're in a popular position), and they go on being "political" in the same way, holding the same faith, and for the same reasons, as in the late thirties and the forties. The restoration there is fairly general. In Hollywood recently, a man who used to be "involved" told me he wanted to become more active again, and added, "But, you know, I'm scared. The people who are urging me to do more are the same ones who ratted on me last time."

Mankiewicz was too well informed politically to become a Communist Party-liner. Because he didn't support this line, he was—and only in part jokingly—considered a "reactionary" by the activists of the Screen Writers Guild. Yet he went on to write the movie they point to with pride in Hollywood, the movie they all seem to feel demonstrates what *can* be done and what movies should be doing, and it's their all-time favorite because they understand it—and correctly—as a leftist film. Its leftism is, however, the leftism of the twenties and early thirties, before the left became moralistic. There were other expressions of the tough spirit of the thirties that came after the thirties were over. There may be a little of it in the newspaper film of the fifties *Sweet Smell of Success,* but the ambivalence there is harsher, grimmer, more artistically "serious" than it was in the thirties; there's some in the happy mockery of Hollywood in *Singin' in the Rain,* which takes off from Kaufman and Hart's *Once in a Lifetime,* and in the films of Preston Sturges, who alone somehow managed to stay funny and tart. The only writer of this whole group who became a director with an individual style, Sturges kept American comedy alive singlehanded through the mawkish forties. Maybe he was able to because he was a cynic and so politically baroque that he wasn't torn by doubts and guilts. The political show in Hollywood in the forties was just one more crazy scene to him; he'd grown up rich and eccentric in Europe, the son of that expatriate lady (called Mary in *The Loves of Isadora*) who gave Isadora Duncan the fatal scarf.

But Mankiewicz climaxed an era in **Kane.** He wrote a big movie that is untarnished by sentimentality, and it may be the only big biographical movie ever made in this country of which that can be said. **Kane** is unsanctimonious; it is without scenes of piety, masochism, or remorse, without "truths"—in that period when the screenwriters were becoming so politically "responsible" that they were using all the primitive devices to sell their messages, and movies once again became full of blind beggars, and omens of doom, and accidental death as punishment for moral and sexual infractions, and, of course, Maria Ouspenskaya seeing into people's hearts—the crone as guru.

## 11.

Orson Welles wasn't around when **Citizen Kane** was written, early in 1940. Mankiewicz, hobbling about on a broken leg in a huge cast, was packed off—away from temptation—to Mrs. Campbell's Guest Ranch, in

Victorville, California, sixty-five miles from Los Angeles, to do the script. He had a nurse and a secretary to watch over him and John Houseman to keep him working, and they all lived there for about three months—in a combination dude ranch and rest home, where liquor was forbidden and unavailable—until the first draft of *Citizen Kane,* called simply and formidably *American,* was completed.

That insurance-company doctor who refused to accept Mankiewicz as a risk back in 1927 had no need to be prophetic. Ben Hecht once described a summer earlier in the twenties when he and his wife and Charles MacArthur were living in a borrowed house near Woodstock, New York, with no money, and Harpo, Groucho, Chico, and Zeppo Marx and their wives, sweethearts, and children came to stay, and then Herman Mankiewicz arrived, carrying two suitcases. "He had decided to spend his vacation from the *New York Times* drama section with us," Hecht wrote. "He had not been allowed to bring any money with him because of Sara's certainty that he would spend it on liquor, and thus impair the influence of country air and sunshine. . . . Herman's larger suitcase contained sixteen bottles of Scotch and nothing else." A few weeks later, Hecht and MacArthur went in to New York to try to sell a play they'd just written, and encountered Mankiewicz, who, having sent his wife and children out of town to escape the heat, was "occupying Prince Bibesco's grand suite in the Plaza Hotel while His Highness capered in Long Island."

Hecht went on, "We moved in with him, there being no rent to pay. We discovered, while helping Herman to undress the first night, that his torso was bound with yards of adhesive tape. He had slipped while trying to get out of the bathtub and lamed his back. When Herman was asleep, MacArthur and I rolled him on his stomach and with an indelible pencil wrote ardent and obscene love messages on his taping. We signed them Gladys and chuckled over the impending moment in Far Rockaway when Herman would undress before his keen-eyed Sara."

Not only was Mankiewicz alcoholic and maniacally accident-prone; he was a gambler, constantly in debt. There was a sequence in a thirties movie about a gambling newspaperman that was based on the way the other writers at Paramount used to line up with him when he got his check on Friday afternoon and walk with him to the bank so they could get back some of the money he'd borrowed from them during the week. His old friends say that he would bet from sheer boredom; when he ran out of big sporting events, he would bet on anything—on high-school football games or whether it would rain. He got to the point where he was bored with just betting; he wanted the stakes to be dangerously high. He once explained, "It's not fun gambling if I lose two thousand and just write a check for it. What's thrilling is to make out a check for fifteen thousand dollars knowing there's not a penny in the bank." James Thurber referred to him as an "incurable compulsive

gambler." He described how Mankiewicz went to a psychiatrist to see if anything could be done about it. "I can't cure you of gambling," the analyst told him on his last visit, "but I can tell you why you do it."

By the late thirties, Mankiewicz had just about run out of studios to get fired from. Scott Fitzgerald described him in those years as "a ruined man." His friends would get him jobs and he would lose them—sometimes in spectacular ways that became part of Hollywood legend. Perhaps the best-known is his exit from Columbia Pictures. In his biography of Harry Cohn, who was then the head of the studio, Bob Thomas describes it this way:

> The most famous incident in the Columbia dining room concerned an erratic genius named Herman J. Mankiewicz. . . . The free-wheeling world of journalism seemed better suited to his temperament than did Hollywood. He possessed two failings that were inimical to the autocratic studio domains: he drank, and he was scornful of his bosses.

> These faculties tumbled him from the position of a major screenwriter, and he had difficulty finding jobs. His agent, Charles Feldman, proposed a post at Columbia. Cohn was interested, since he enjoyed hiring bargain talent discarded by the major studios. . . . Cohn agreed to employ him at $750 a week.

> "I want to make good," said Mankiewicz when he reported to William Perlberg, then Columbia's executive producer.

> "Fine," said the producer. . . . "But . . . don't go in the executive dining room. You know what will happen if you tangle with Cohn."

> Mankiewicz concurred. . . . His work habits were exemplary, and he produced many pages a day. But . . . his office was on the third floor, near the door to the executive dining room. As Riskin, Swerling, and other fellow-writers emerged after lunch, he could hear them laughing over wisecracks and jokes that had been told inside. Mankiewicz himself was considered one of Hollywood's premier wits and raconteurs, and he rankled over his banishment.

> One day Perlberg entered the dining room and was startled to find Mankiewicz sitting at the end of the table. The writer held a napkin to his mouth and promised, "I won't say a word."

> When Cohn entered the room, he gave Mankiewicz a warm greeting, then assumed his monarchial position at the head of the table.

> Cohn began the conversation: "Last night I saw the lousiest picture I've seen in years."

> He mentioned the title, and one of the more courageous of his producers spoke up: "Why, I saw that picture at the Downtown Paramount, and the audience howled over it. Maybe you should have seen it with an audience."

"That doesn't make any difference," Cohn replied. "When I'm alone in a projection room, I have a foolproof device for judging whether a picture is good or bad. If my fanny squirms, it's bad. If my fanny doesn't squirm, it's good. It's as simple as that."

There was a momentary silence, which was filled by Mankiewicz at the end of the table:" Imagine—the whole world wired to Harry Cohn's ass!"

Mankiewicz's attitude toward himself and his work is summed up in one very short, very famous story. A friend who hadn't seen him for a while asked, "How's Sara?"

Mankiewicz, puzzled: "Who?"

"Sara. Your wife, Sara."

"Oh, you mean Poor Sara."

The only evidence of an instinct for self-preservation in the life of Herman Mankiewicz is his choice of keen-eyed Sara. He was in bad shape by 1939, but Mayer kept him on the payroll—some said so that top people at M-G-M could collect their gambling winnings from him. But Mayer also seems to have had some affection for him, and Sara had become a close friend of Mayer's daughter Irene. Mayer became concerned about Mankiewicz's gambling debts, and, assuming that Mankiewicz was also concerned about them, he concluded that if he got the debts straightened out, Mankiewicz would pull himself together. Mayer called him in and asked him how much money he needed to get financially clear. Mankiewicz came up with the figure of $30,000, and Mayer offered to advance him that sum on a new contract if he would swear a solemn vow never to gamble again. Mankiewicz went through an elaborate ritual of giving Mayer his sacred word, and walked out with the $30,000. The very next day, it is said, Mankiewicz was playing poker on the lot, and he had just raised the stakes to $10,000 when he looked up and saw Mayer standing there. Mankiewicz left the studio and didn't return. A few days after that—early in September of 1939—Thomas Phipps, a nephew of Lady Astor's, who was also employed as a writer at M-G-M, was driving to New York to court a lady there, and, with nothing better to do, Mankiewicz decided to go along. As Mankiewicz described the trip some months later, in a guest column he wrote, filling in for Hedda Hopper on vacation, it was fairly giddy right from the start. Mankiewicz said that each song on the car radio sent Phipps swooning, because either he had heard it while he was with his lady or he had heard it while he was not with her. On the outskirts of Albuquerque, the car skidded and turned over. Mankiewicz's jocular account included as the climax "thirty-four weeks in a cast in bed and thirty-two weeks in a brace." Phipps had a broken collarbone; when it healed, he proceeded on his romantic way to New York. Mankiewicz had a compound fracture of the left leg, which, together with further injuries suffered while the fracture was healing, left him with a limp for the rest of his life.

During the long recuperation—very long, because on his first night out on the town after his cast was removed, he went on crutches to Chasen's, got drunk, slipped and broke more bones, and had to be put in another cast—Mankiewicz, bedridden and in exile from the studios, began to write the Mercury Theatre's "Campbell Playhouse" radio shows, with the actors often gathered around his bed for story conferences, and even rehearsals. Welles, having come to Hollywood in July to fulfill his contract with Schaefer, had been flying to and from New York for the series; in October he arranged to have the shows originate in Los Angeles, and in November he hired Mankiewicz to write five of them. Welles had met Mankiewicz sometime earlier in New York. This is John Houseman's recollection of those events, set down in a letter to Sara Mankiewicz after her husband's death:

> I remember so well the day Orson came back to the theatre from 21, telling me he had met this amazingly civilized and charming man. I can just see them there at lunch together—magicians and highbinders at work on each other, vying with each other in wit and savoir-faire and mutual appreciation. Both came away enchanted and convinced that, between them, they were the two most dashing and gallantly intelligent gentlemen in the Western world. And they were not so far wrong! Soon after that I met Herman myself, but I didn't get to know him until . . . he lay in bed at Tower Road, his leg in a monstrous plaster cast . . . and we started to do those peculiar collaborative radio shows in the beginning of our long conspiracy of love and hate for Maestro, the Dog-Faced Boy. Then came *Kane* and Victorville and those enchanted months of inhabiting Mrs. Campbell's ranch with our retinue of nurse and secretary and our store of Mickey Finns!

Tower Road was where the Mankiewiczes lived and the Mercury group gathered. The Dog-Faced Boy is, of course, Orson Welles (Cocteau once described him as "a dog who has broken loose from his chain and gone to sleep on the flower bed"), and the Mickey Finns were a medical concoction that was supposed to make Mankiewicz hate alcohol. It failed. The secretary, Mrs. Rita Alexander (she lent her name to the character of Susan Alexander), recalls that during her first week, before Sara Mankiewicz had had a chance to give her a briefing, Mankiewicz persuaded her to take him in to the town of Victorville, where he could get a drink. She withstood his wiles after that. He really wasn't in condition to do much drinking; the broken bones included a hip break, and he was in such poor condition that even eating presented problems. Mrs. Alexander recalls spoon-feeding him bicarbonate of soda, and recalls his courtly, formal apologies for the belches that rocked the room.

## 12.

There are monsters, and there are also sacred monsters; both Welles and Mankiewicz deserve places in the sacred-monster category. Some writers on film—particularly in

England—blithely say that Kane wasn't based on Hearst, using as evidence statements that Welles made to the press in early 1941, when he was trying to get the picture released. But those who think Louella Parsons got the *mistaken* idea that the picture was about Hearst don't understand what kind of man the young Welles was. Welles and Mankiewicz wanted to do something startling, something that would cap the invasion of the Martians—which had, after all, panicked only the boobs, and inadvertently at that, though Welles now makes it sound deliberate. This time, he and Mankiewicz *meant* to raise cain. The pun is surely theirs, and Hearst had walked right into it; he was so fond of a story called *Cain and Mabel,* which he'd bought and produced as a Cosmopolitan Picture back in 1924, that he remade it late in 1936, at Warners', starring Clark Gable and Marion Davies. It had been one of her last pictures before her retirement. Cain and Mabel—it was a perfect description of Hearst and Marion. In 1960, when Welles was interviewed on British television, he said, "Kane isn't really founded on Hearst in particular." I suppose he was feeling rather expansive at that moment, and it may have seemed to limit his importance if his Kane had been based on anyone "in particular." In the same interview, he said, "You asked me did Mr. Hearst try to stop it. *He* didn't. . . . He was like Kane in that he wouldn't have stooped to such a thing." This was rather droll, but Welles seemed to mean it. He didn't seem to know much about Hearst anymore; probably he'd forgotten. One may also fairly conclude that Welles, with that grandeur which he seems to have taken over from the theatre into his personal life, was elevating Hearst, lending Hearst some of his own magnitude. More characteristically, however, his grandeur is double-edged, as in this typical statement on Gregg Toland:

> I had a great advantage not only in the real genius of my cameraman but in the fact that he, like all men who are masters of a craft, told me at the outset that there was nothing about camera work that any intelligent being couldn't learn in half a day. And he was right.

Welles was thus telling us that he learned all there was to know about camera work in half a day. What, one wonders, was the craft that Toland needed to master? Welles, like Hearst, and like most very big men, is capable of some very small gestures. And so was Mankiewicz, who brought his younger, more stable brother, Joe, out to Hollywood and helped him get started, but, as soon as Joe had some success, began behaving atrociously, referring to him as "my idiot brother."

Mankiewicz's ambivalence was generally on a higher level, however. There are many different kinds of senses of humor, and the one that sometimes comes through Mankiewicz anecdotes is the perverse soul of Kane himself. There is, for example, the story that Ezra Goodman tells in *The Fifty Year Decline and Fall of Hollywood.* Hollywood was not often elegant and correct, but the producer Arthur Hornblow, Jr., was known for the

punctiliousness of his social functions. At a dinner party that he gave for Hollywood notables, Herman Mankiewicz drank too much and threw up on the table. "A deadly hush descended over the assembled guests. . . . Mankiewicz broke the silence himself: 'It's all right, Arthur; the white wine came up with the fish.'"

The man who in those circumstances could put his host down was a fit companion for Welles. They were big eaters, big talkers, big spenders, big talents; they were not men of what is ordinarily called "good character." They were out to get not only Hearst but each other. The only religious remark that has ever been attributed to Mankiewicz was recorded on the set of *Citizen Kane:* Welles walked by, and Mankiewicz muttered, "There, but for the grace of God, goes God."

## 13.

Herman Mankiewicz didn't—to be exact—write *Citizen Kane;* he dictated it. The screenwriters may have felt like whores and they may have been justified in that feeling, but they were certainly well-paid whores. In New York, they hadn't had secretaries, but the movie business was mass culture's great joke on talent. The affectation of "Look, no hands" became the literal truth. Mankiewicz dictated the script while the nurse watched over him and John Houseman stood by in attendance. This was a cut-rate job—Mankiewicz was getting $500 a week for his ghostly labors—but it was still in the royal tradition of screenwriting. Outside the movie business, there has probably never been a writer in the history of the world who got this kind of treatment. There was an urgency about it: Welles and most of the Mercury Theatre company were in Hollywood doing their weekly radio shows and waiting while this odd little group spent the spring of 1940 in Victorville preparing the script for Orson Welles' début in films.

Welles had come to Hollywood the previous July in a burst of publicity, but his first two film projects hadn't got under way. Within a few months of his arrival, he was being jeered at because nothing had happened. Although his contract with R.K.O. gave him freedom from interference, Schaefer and his legal staff had to approve the project and clear the shooting script and, of course, the budget. It had been agreed that his first project would be Conrad's *Heart of Darkness,* which he had already done as a radio drama. He was to play both Marlow and Kurtz, the two leading roles, and it was reported in the trade press that he was working on the script with John Houseman and Herbert Drake, who was the Mercury's press agent. In the latter part of 1939, Welles brought actors out from New York and shot long test sequences, but the budget looked too high to the poverty-stricken studio, and the production was repeatedly postponed. He decided to do something while he was waiting—something that he could start on right away, to get the Mercury actors on the R.K.O. payroll—and he hit on a spy thriller with a political theme: *The*

*Smiler with the Knife,* from the novel by Nicholas Blake (C. Day Lewis). Welles adapted the book himself—"in seven days," according to the trade press—but this project was abandoned almost at once because of differences with Schaefer over casting. (Welles wanted to use Lucille Ball, then a contract player at R.K.O., in the lead, and Schaefer didn't think she could carry the picture. As the whole world knows, she wound up owning the studio, but Schaefer wasn't necessarily wrong; she never did carry a picture.) There was still hope for *Heart of Darkness*—and a lot of money had already been spent on it—but things seemed to be falling apart for the Mercury group. By the end of 1939, Welles was desperate for a subject that would be acceptable to R.K.O. The movie plans were up in the air, and there was dissension within the Mercury group about staying on in Hollywood with nothing definite in sight to work on. Some of the actors left to take jobs elsewhere, and some were beginning to get film roles—a development that upset Welles, because he wanted them to be "new faces" in his first film.

A policy meeting was arranged to discuss the failing fortunes of the group and to decide whether to keep them all in Los Angeles or send some of them back to New York. The more or less administrative heads of the Mercury Theatre met for dinner in an upper room at Chasen's. The group included Welles; Houseman, who had founded the Mercury Theatre with him; two all-purpose assistants, Richard Wilson and William Alland; the press agent, Drake; and several others. Houseman argued that the actors should return to New York, but nothing had been settled by the time the coffee and brandy arrived, and then Welles, in a sudden access of rage, shouted that Houseman wanted to desert him, that Houseman had always been against him, and he threw the coffee warmers—full of Sterno canned heat—at Houseman. He did not throw them very precisely, it seems; he threw them not so much with intent to hit as in Houseman's general direction. Dave Chasen, having been summoned by a waiter, opened the door, and, with the aplomb he had used back in the thirties in vaudeville, when he was the stooge of the comedian Joe Cook, he took one look—a curtain was on fire by then—and closed the door. The men in the room stamped out the fire, and Houseman went home and sent Welles a letter of resignation. The partnership was ended, and a week later Houseman left for New York.

Welles' tantrum and how it ended the partnership that had created the Mercury Theatre was the talk of the actors who gathered around Mankiewicz's bed, and it must have registered on Mankiewicz in a special way: it must have practically thrust on him the recognition of an emotional link between Welles and William Randolph Hearst, whose tantrums had been the stuff of legend among newspapermen for half a century, and whose occasional demonstrations of childishness were the gossip of guests at San Simeon. A week or two after the Chasen's dinner party, Mankiewicz proposed to Welles that they make a "prismatic" movie about the life of a man seen from several different points of view. Even before he went to work in Hollywood and met Hearst, when he was still at the *New York Times,* Mankiewicz was already caught up in the idea of a movie about Hearst. Marion Fisher, the Mankiewicz baby-sitter, whose family lived in the same Central Park West building, was learning to type in high school and Mankiewicz offered to "test her typing." He dictated a screenplay, organized in flashbacks. She recalls that he had barely started on the dictation, which went on for several weeks, when she remarked that it seemed to be about William Randolph Hearst, and he said, "You're a smart girl." Mankiewicz couldn't pay her but she and her parents saw about fifty shows on the theatre tickets he gave them, and it was a great year for Broadway—1925. Although in the intervening years Mankiewicz had often talked to friends about what a movie Hearst's life would make, his first suggestions to Welles for the "prismatic" movie were Dillinger and, when Welles was cool to that, Aimee Semple McPherson. Only after Welles had rejected that, too, and after they had discussed the possibilities in the life of Dumas, did he propose Hearst. Mankiewicz must have been stalling and playing games to lead Welles on, because although he was interested in both Dillinger and Aimee Semple McPherson, and subsequently did prepare scripts on them, this movie had to be a starring vehicle for Welles, and what major role could Welles play in the life of either Dillinger or Aimee? From what Mankiewicz told friends at the time, when he sprang the name Hearst, Welles leaped at it.

Welles had grown up hearing stories about Hearst from Dr. Maurice Bernstein, who was his guardian after his parents died. Dr. Bernstein was a good friend of Ashton Stevens, who had originally been the drama critic on Hearst's flagship paper, the *San Francisco Examiner,* and had gone on to work for Hearst in Chicago. Welles himself was a Hearst-press "discovery"; it was Ashton Stevens, whom Dr. Bernstein got in touch with, who had publicized the nineteen-year-old Orson Welles when he produced *Hamlet* on a vacant second floor in Illinois. But Welles, being a knowledgeable young man, would have known a great deal about Hearst even without this personal connection, for Hearst was the unifying hatred of all liberals and leftists. Welles, with his sense of the dramatic, would have known at once what a sensational idea a movie about Hearst was. Aimee and Dillinger just didn't have the dimensions that Hearst had; Hearst was even right for Welles *physically.* Welles and Mankiewicz must have enjoyed thinking what a scandal a movie about him would make. Mankiewicz didn't need to have misgivings about repercussions, because the risks would all be Welles'. Schaefer had signed Welles up to a widely publicized four-way contract as producer, director, writer, and actor. It was understood that he would take the credit for the script, just as he did for the scripts of the radio plays. His R.K.O. contract stated that "the screenplay for each picture shall be written by Mr. Orson Welles," and Welles probably took this stipulation as no more than his due—a necessity of his station. He probably accepted the work that others did for him the way modern Presidents accept the work of speech-writers.

The title *American* suggests how Mankiewicz felt about the project. Several years before, in 1933, his friend and drinking companion Preston Sturges had written a big one, an original called *The Power and the Glory,* which, when it was produced, with Spencer Tracy and Colleen Moore in the leading roles, made Tracy a star. *The Power and the Glory* was about a ruthless railroad tycoon who fails in his personal life, and it was told in flashbacks and narration from his funeral. It was an impressive picture, and it was lauded in terms similar to those later used about *Kane.* "Its subject," William Troy wrote in the *Nation,* "is the great American Myth, and its theme is futility." The ballyhoo included putting a bronze tablet in the New York theatre where it opened to commemorate "the first motion picture in which narratage was used as a method of telling a dramatic story." (Hollywood, big on ballyhoo but short on real self-respect, failed to transfer the nitrate negative to safety stock, and modern prints of *The Power and the Glory* are tattered remnants.) Not only is the tycoon treated ambivalently by Sturges but in the boyhood sequence he is injured through his own arrogance, so that he acquires a jagged, lightning-like scar on his hand—the mark of Cain. The idea of the big-businessman as a Cain figure was basic to this genre, which had become popular in the Depression thirties, when many business giants of the twenties were revealed to be swindlers, or, at the very least, ruthless. In another 1933 film, *I Loved a Woman,* a tycoon's mistress sang at the Chicago Opera House. (It was where the tycoons' mistresses did sing in the twenties.) In 1937, Mankiewicz himself had done a trial run on the tycoon theme (with Edward Arnold as a lumber baron) in *John Meade's Woman.* To do Hearst, a much more dangerous man—the only tycoon who was also a demagogue—in a technique similar to Sturges's but from several different points of view would make a really big picture.

But there was a sizable hurdle: How could they get R.K.O. to approve this project? Welles and Mankiewicz went on talking about it for a couple of weeks, while Mankiewicz continued writing the weekly radio shows. When they decided to go ahead and try to slip it over on the studio somehow, Welles still had to find a way to get Mankiewicz to do the writing; the Mercury company couldn't be kept waiting in Los Angeles indefinitely while Mankiewicz wandered loose. Mankiewicz had had to be hauled off to sanatoriums to be dried out too many times for Welles to take chances, and the screenwriters who had worked with Mankiewicz at Metro told too many stories about his losing interest in the scripts he was assigned to and drinking so much during working hours that the other writers would load him into a studio car in mid-afternoon and have the driver haul him home, where Sara would unload him and put him to bed, and he would sleep it off before dinner and be ready for the night's drinking. He had just injured himself

again, in his fall at Chasen's, and his bones were being reset, but soon he would be off on the town once more, despite cast or crutches, and there would be no way to hold him down to work. Welles hit on the scheme of packing Mankiewicz off to the country to recuperate. In early January, 1940, Welles flew to New York, and over lunch at "21" the young magician prevailed on Houseman to return to the Coast and do him and the Mercury one last service by running herd on Mankiewicz; only a month had passed since the fiery scene at Chasen's. (It was to be not the last but the next-to-last collaborative project of Welles and Houseman. A week after *American* was done and the troupe had left Victorville, Houseman and Welles were on bad terms again, but Mankiewicz, who was said to have read every new book by publication date, even when he was in the worst possible shape, told them that they'd be crazy if they didn't buy a new book that was just coming out, and dramatize it. Houseman went to work on it, and as a result Richard Wright's *Native Son* was adapted for the stage and produced so quickly that Welles had it playing in New York by the time *Citizen Kane* opened.)

Both Houseman and Mankiewicz unquestionably had mixed feelings about Welles by the time they found themselves at the guest ranch. Houseman admits that right from the beginning, when Mankiewicz started on the script, they planned to have Welles re-enact his tantrum. It was set for the scene in which Susan leaves Kane (Welles' wife, Virginia, had brought suit for divorce during the month Welles had his tantrum), and Mankiewicz wrote it up rather floridly and with explicit directions, in a passage beginning, "Kane, in a truly terrible and absolutely silent rage . . . " When it was time to shoot the scene, the various members of the group who had been at Chasen's—or had heard about what happened there—and everybody *had*—encouraged Welles to do what he had done that night. Last year, William Alland, describing the making of the film in an interview printed in the magazine of the Directors Guild of America, said:

> There was one scene which stands out above all others in my memory; that was the one in which Orson broke up the roomful of furniture in a rage. Orson never liked himself as an actor. He had the idea that he should have been feeling more, that he intellectualized too much and never achieved the emotion of losing himself in a part.
>
> When he came to the furniture-breaking scene, he set up four cameras, because he obviously couldn't do the scene many times. He did the scene just twice, and each time he threw himself into the action with a fervor I had never seen in him. It was absolutely electric; you felt as if you were in the presence of a man coming apart.
>
> Orson staggered out of the set with his hands bleeding and his face flushed. He almost swooned, yet he was exultant. "I really felt it," he exclaimed. "I really felt it!"

Strangely, that scene didn't have the same power when it appeared on the screen. It might have been how it was cut, or because there hadn't been close-in shots to depict his rage. The scene in the picture was only a mild reflection of what I had witnessed on that movie stage.

Writing that scene into the movie was a cruel trick on Welles, designed to make him squirm. He had been built up so much that he was by then the white hope (as it used to be called) of the theatre. In 1938, even George S. Kaufman and Moss Hart had taken him to be that; they had written one of their worst maudlin "serious" plays (and a flop)—*The Fabulous Invalid,* a cavalcade-of-the-American-theatre sort of play—and had modelled its hero on Welles. The hero—the leader of a new acting company—made a classic final curtain speech to his actors:

> We haven't got very much money, but we've got youth and, I think, talent. They'll tell you the theatre is dying. I don't believe it. Anything that can bring us together like this, and hold us to this one ideal in spite of everything, isn't going to die. They'll tell you it isn't important, putting makeup on your face and playacting. I don't believe it. It's important to keep alive a thing that can lift men's spirits above the everyday reality of their lives. We mustn't let that die. Remember—you're going to be kicked around, and a lot of the time you're not going to have enough to eat, but you're going to get one thing in return. The chance to write, and act, say the things you want to say, and do the things you want to do. And I think that's enough.

For the people who did much of the work on Welles' projects, the temptation must have been strong to expose what they considered this savior's feet of clay.

The menagerie at Mrs. Campbell's being scarcely a secret, they had many visitors (Welles himself came to dinner once or twice), and several of these visitors, as well as Houseman and Mrs. Alexander, describe how Herman Mankiewicz turned out the script that became *Citizen Kane.* Mankiewicz couldn't go anywhere without help; he sat up, in the cast that covered one leg and went up to his middle, and played cribbage with Mrs. Alexander during the day, while telling her stories about Hearst and Marion Davies and San Simeon. Then, at night, from about eight-thirty to eleven-thirty or twelve, he dictated, and she would type it out so he could have it the next day. Mrs. Alexander recalls that during the first days on the job, when she was fascinated by the romantic significance of "Rosebud" and asked him how the story would turn out, he said, "My dear Mrs. Alexander, I don't know. I'm making it up as I go along." Welles was so deeply entangled in the radio shows and other activities and a romance with Dolores Del Rio at the time the script was being prepared that even when he came to dinner at Victorville, it was mainly a social visit; the secretary didn't meet him until after Mankiewicz had finished dictating the long first draft. Welles probably made suggestions in his early

conversations with Mankiewicz, and since he received copies of the work weekly while it was in progress at Victorville, he may have given advice by phone or letter. Later, he almost certainly made suggestions for cuts that helped Mankiewicz hammer the script into tighter form, and he is known to have made a few changes on the set. But Mrs. Alexander, who took the dictation from Mankiewicz, from the first paragraph to the last, and then, when the first draft was completed and they all went back to Los Angeles, did the secretarial work at Mankiewicz's house on the rewriting and the cuts, and who then handled the script at the studio until after the film was shot, says that Welles didn't write (or dictate) one line of the shooting script of *Citizen Kane.*

Toward the end of the period at the ranch, Mankiewicz began to realize that he'd made a very bad financial deal, and that the credit might be more important than he'd anticipated. After talks with Mrs. Alexander and the Mercury people who visited on weekends, he decided he was going to get screen credit, no matter what his bargain with Welles had been. Meanwhile, Houseman, who says that according to his original agreement to go off to the ranch he was supposed to get some kind of credit, discovered once again, and as so many others had, that it wasn't easy to get your name on anything Orson Welles was involved in. Houseman was apparently fed up with arguments, and he says he waived his claim when he saw how determined Welles was; he left for New York and got started on the preparations for *Native Son.* But Mankiewicz was an experienced Hollywood hand and veteran of credit brawls who kept all his drafts and materials, and a man who relished trouble. He had ample proof of his authorship, and he took his evidence to the Screen Writers Guild and raised so much hell that Welles was forced to split the credit and take second place in the listing.

At the time the movie came out, Mankiewicz's contribution to the film was generally known. The screen credit was to Herman J. Mankiewicz and Orson Welles. The *Hollywood Reporter* simplified the credit to "Written by Herman Mankiewicz"; Burns Mantle, in his newspaper column, referred to Mankiewicz's having written it; and, of course, Ben Hecht explained to the readers of *PM,* "This movie was not written by Orson Welles. It is the work of Herman J. Mankiewicz." In that period, it was well known that if the producer of a film wanted a screenplay credit it was almost impossible to prevent him from getting it. So many producers took a writing credit as a *droit du seigneur* for a few consultations or suggestions that the Screen Writers Guild later instituted a rule calling for compulsory arbitration whenever a producer sought a credit. Under the present rules of the Guild, Welles' name would probably not have appeared. And so it was by an awful fluke of justice that when Academy Awards night came, and Welles should have got the awards he deserved as director and actor, the award he got (the only Academy Award he has ever got) was as co-author of the Best Original Screenplay.

14.

The Mercury group weren't surprised at Welles' taking a script credit; they'd had experience with this foible of his. Very early in his life as a prodigy, Welles seems to have fallen into the trap that has caught so many lesser men—believing his own publicity, believing that he really was the whole creative works, producer-director-writer-actor. Because he *could* do all these things, he imagined that he *did* do them. (A Profile of him that appeared in *The New Yorker* two years before *Citizen Kane* was made said that "outside the theatre . . . Welles is exactly twenty-three years old.") In the days before the Mercury Theatre's weekly radio shows got a sponsor, it was considered a good publicity technique to build up public identification with Welles' name, so he was credited with just about everything, and was named on the air as the writer of the Mercury shows. Probably no one but Welles believed it. He had written some of the shows when the program first started, and had also worked on some with Houseman, but soon he had become much too busy even to collaborate; for a while Houseman wrote them, and then they were farmed out. By the time of the *War of the Worlds* broadcast, on Halloween, 1938, Welles wasn't doing any of the writing. He was so busy with his various other activities that he didn't always direct the rehearsals himself, either—William Alland or Richard Wilson or one of the other Mercury assistants did it. Welles might not come in until the last day, but somehow, all agree, he would pull the show together "with a magic touch." Yet when the Martian broadcast became accidentally famous, Welles seemed to forget that Howard Koch had written it. (In all the furor over the broadcast, with front-page stories everywhere, the name of the author of the radio play wasn't mentioned.) Koch had been writing the shows for some time. He lasted for six months, writing about twenty-five shows altogether—working six and a half days a week, and frantically, on each one, he says, with no more than half a day off to see his family. The weekly broadcasts were a "studio presentation" until after the *War of the Worlds* (Campbell's Soup picked them up then), and Koch, a young writer, who was to make his name with the film *The Letter* in 1940 and win an Academy Award for his share in the script of the 1942 *Casablanca,* was writing them for $75 apiece. Koch's understanding of the agreement was that Welles would get the writing credit on the air for publicity purposes but that Koch would have any later benefit, and the copyright was in Koch's name. (He says that it was, however, Welles' idea that he do the Martian show in the form of radio bulletins.) Some years later, when C.B.S. did a program about the broadcast and the panic it had caused, the network re-created parts of the original broadcast and paid Koch $300 for the use of his material. Welles sued C.B.S. for $375,000, claiming that he was the author and that the material had been used without his permission. He lost, of course, but he may still think he wrote it. (He frequently indicates as much in interviews and on television.)

"Foible" is the word that Welles' former associates tend to apply to his assertions of authorship. Welles could do so many different things in those days that it must have seemed almost accidental when he didn't do things he claimed to. Directors, in the theatre and in movies, are by function (and often by character, or, at least, disposition) cavalier toward other people's work, and Welles was so much more talented and magnetic than most directors—and so much younger, too—that people he robbed of credit went on working with him for years, as Koch went on writing more of the radio programs after Welles failed to mention him during the national publicity about the panic. Welles was dedicated to the company, and he was exciting to work with, so the company stuck together, working for love, and even a little bit more money (Koch was raised to $125 a show) when they got a sponsor and, also as a result of the *War of the Worlds* broadcast, the movie contract that took them to Hollywood.

If there was ever a young man who didn't need unearned credits, it was Orson Welles, yet though he was already too big, he must have felt he needed to dazzle the world. Welles was hated in Hollywood long before he'd made a movie; he was hated almost upon his arrival. From time to time, Hollywood used to work up considerable puerile resentment against "outsiders" who dared to make movies. The scope of Welles' reputation seems to have infuriated Hollywood; it was a cultural reproach from the East, and the Hollywood people tried to protect themselves by closing ranks and making Welles a butt of their humor. Gene Lockhart composed a stupid, nasty ditty called "Little Orson Annie," which was sung at Hollywood parties; the name stuck and was used by the columnists, though Hedda Hopper supported him and suggested that Hollywood reserve judgment, and Louella Parsons, on December 31st, selected him as "the most discussed personality to come to the films in 1939." Yet for Welles, with his beard (he was growing it for the Shakespearean production he intended to stage as soon as he could pick up his Hollywood loot), to be ensconced in the Mary Pickford-Buddy Rogers estate, right next door to Shirley Temple, was too much for Hollywood. Welles became the victim of practical jokers. One night when he was dining at Chasen's, an actor cut off his tie with a table knife. Not all the jokes were so Freudian, but they were mostly ugly. Welles had come with an unprecedented contract. Probably the old Hollywoodians not only expected him to fall on his face but hoped he would, so that their mediocrity and prosperity would be vindicated. But Welles was the braggart who makes good. And, despite their resentment, they *were* dazzled by *Citizen Kane.*

15.

The picture got a thunderous reception, even in the Hollywood press. In recent years, the rumor has spread that *Citizen Kane* opened to bad reviews—presumably on the theory that it was so far ahead of its time that it wasn't understood—and this is now recorded in many film histories. But it was very well understood by the press (who would understand a newspaper picture better?), and it got smashing reviews. It isn't, after all, a difficult picture. In some ways, it was probably better understood then than it is now, and, as far as I can determine, it was more highly praised by the American press than any other movie in history. The New York opening of *Citizen Kane,* which had been scheduled for February 14, 1941, finally took place on May 1st, and a week later it opened in Los Angeles. In January, Hedda Hopper had "doubted" whether the picture would ever be released, and some of the trade press had predicted that it wouldn't be. Possibly it wouldn't have been except for the screenings that Welles arranged and the publicity that he got.

The whole industry was already involved in the picture. Although technically Welles had the right of final cut, the editor, Robert Wise, was instructed by the studio, with Welles' consent, to take a print to New York in January. Wise ran it for the heads of all the major companies and their lawyers, and for six weeks he and his then assistant, Mark Robson, who was on the Coast, fussed over the movie, making tiny, nervous changes— mostly a word here or there—that the executives and lawyers hoped would render the picture less objectionable to Hearst. Meanwhile, Schaefer had engaged Time, Inc.'s legal specialist on invasion-of-privacy suits; the lawyer instructed Schaefer that if he made one small cut in the film, no one could win such a suit. The dangerous section was a bit of dialogue by Raymond, the butler, suggesting that the old man was senile. Schaefer says he had no difficulty persuading Welles to agree to the cut. However, at the beginning of March, Hearst sent for Walter Howey, and no one was sure what they might be poking into. "Nor are private lives to be overlooked," Hedda Hopper predicted; and her predictions were the same as threats. Hearst's maneuvers were in the true Kane spirit: In January, Hedda Hopper had warned that "the refugee situation would be looked into," which meant that there would be pressure for a legal review of whether various imported stars and directors should be allowed to remain in the country, and the industry would be attacked for employing foreigners; that is, refugees from Hitler. Three days after the press previews, the Hearst newspapers, the American Legion, the Veterans of Foreign Wars, and other patriotic organizations went into action to rid radio of "subversives." The "subversives" they were after were William Saroyan, Maxwell Anderson, Marc Connelly, Robert E. Sherwood, Stephen Vincent Benét, Paul Green, Sherwood Anderson, and James Boyd, who were involved with Welles in a series of C.B.S. radio plays on the general theme of freedom, which, although it had been encouraged by the Justice Department, was now condemned as un-American and as tending to promote Communism. Before *Citizen Kane* was released, *PM* reported that Hearst photographers were following Welles "in G-man style," trying to get something on him, while *Variety* reported "persistent inquiries at the draft board as to why Welles hadn't been drafted." It was along about this time that

Hearst himself saw the picture. Schaefer says, "Hearst personally sent to me at the studio and asked to see a print, and we let him have it. This was before it opened. There was no response, no comment. Orson knew this." Welles may have feared that Schaefer would buckle unless he squeezed him from the other side, or, as Schaefer claims, it may have been Welles' way of getting more publicity, but, for whatever reason, Welles began to issue threats: he gave R.K.O. the deadline of March 30th for releasing the picture or facing a lawsuit. On March 11th, Welles called a press conference to alert the press to the danger that the film might be suppressed, and gave out this statement:

> I believe that the public is entitled to see *Citizen Kane.* For me to stand by while this picture was being suppressed would constitute a breach of faith with the public on my part as producer. I have at this moment sufficient financial backing to buy *Citizen Kane* from R.K.O. and to release it myself. Under my contract with R.K.O. I have the right to demand that the picture be released and to bring legal action to force its release. R.K.O. must release *Citizen Kane.* If it does not do so immediately, I have instructed my attorney to commence proceedings.
>
> I have been advised that strong pressure is being brought to bear in certain quarters to cause the withdrawal of my picture *Citizen Kane* because of an alleged resemblance between incidents in the picture and incidents in the life of Mr. William Randolph Hearst.
>
> Any such attempts at suppression would involve a serious interference with freedom of speech and with the integrity of the moving picture industry as the foremost medium of artistic expression in the country.
>
> There is nothing in the facts to warrant the situation that has arisen. *Citizen Kane* was not intended to have nor has it any reference to Mr. Hearst or to any other living person. No statement to the contrary has ever been authorized by me. *Citizen Kane* is the story of a wholly fictitious character.
>
> The script for *Citizen Kane* was scrutinized and approved by both R.K.O. Radio Pictures and the Hays office. No one in those organizations nor anyone associated with me in the production of the picture believed that it represented anything but psychological analysis of an imaginary individual. I regret exceedingly that anyone should interpret *Citizen Kane* to have a bearing upon any living person, or should impugn the artistic purposes of its producers.

Several of the magazines responded to his plea for the pressure of publicity by reviewing the picture before it opened, obviously with the intention of helping to get it released. A review in *Time* on March 17, 1941, began:

> As in some grotesque fable, it appeared last week that Hollywood was about to turn upon and destroy its greatest creation.

It continued:

> To most of the several hundred people who have seen the film at private showings, *Citizen Kane* is the most sensational product of the U.S. movie industry. It has found important new techniques in picture-making and story telling. . . . It is as psychiatrically sound as a fine novel. . . . It is a work of art created by grown people for grown people.

In *Newsweek,* also on March 17, 1941, John O'Hara began his review with

> It is with exceeding regret that your faithful bystander reports that he has just seen a picture which he thinks must be the best picture he ever saw.
>
> With no less regret he reports that he has just seen the best actor in the history of acting.
>
> Name of picture: *Citizen Kane.*
>
> Name of actor: Orson Welles.
>
> Reason for regret: you, my dear, may never see the picture.
>
> I saw *Citizen Kane* the other night. I am told that my name was crossed off a list of persons who were invited to look at the picture, my name being crossed off because some big shot remembered I had been a newspaperman. So, for the first time in my life, I indignantly denied I was a newspaperman. Nevertheless, I had to be snuck into the showing of *Citizen Kane* under a phony name. That's what's going on about this wonderful picture. Intrigue.
>
> Why intrigue? Well, because. A few obsequious and/or bulbous middle-aged ladies think the picture ought not to be shown, owing to the fact that the picture is rumored to have something to do with a certain publisher, who, for the first time in his life, or maybe the second, shall be nameless. That the nameless publisher might be astute enough to realize that for the first time in his rowdy life he had been made a human being did not worry the loyal ladies. Sycophancy of that kind, like curtseying, is deliberate. The ladies merely wait for a chance to show they can still do it, even if it means cracking a femur. This time I think they may have cracked off more than they can chew. I hope.

Along the way, O'Hara said such things as

> My intention is to make you want to see the picture; if possible, to make you wonder why you are not seeing what I think is as good a picture as was ever made. . . . And aside from what it does not lack, *Citizen Kane* has Orson Welles. It is traditional that if you are a great artist, no one gives a damn about you while you're still alive. Welles has had plenty of that. He got a tag put to his name through the Mars thing, just as Scott Fitzgerald, who wrote better than any man in our

time, got a Jazz Age tag put to his name. I say, if you plan to have any grandchildren to see and to bore, see Orson Welles so that you can bore your grandchildren with some honesty. There never has been a better actor than Orson Welles. I just got finished saying there never has been a better actor than Orson Welles, and I don't want any of your lip.

> Do yourself a favor. Go to your neighborhood exhibitor and ask him why he isn't showing *Citizen Kane.*

The same day—March 17, 1941—*Life,* which was to run several more features on the movie in the following months, came out with four pages of pictures and a review:

> Few movies have ever come from Hollywood with such powerful narrative, such original technique, such exciting photography. Director Welles and Cameraman Gregg Toland do brilliantly with a camera everything Hollywood has always said you couldn't do. They shoot into bright lights, they shoot into the dark and against low ceilings, till every scene comes with the impact of something never seen before. Even the sound track is new. And for narrative Welles has tapped a segment of life fearfully skirted by the U.S. cinema: the swift and brutal biography of a power-mad newspaper tycoon, a man of twisted greatness who buys or bullies his way into everything but friends' love and his nation's respect. To a film industry floundering in a rut, *Citizen Kane* offers enough new channels to explore for five years to come.

Hearst must have known he would be in for a bad time if the picture should be withheld; the Luce magazines—*Time* and *Life*—had always been eager to embarrass him, and certainly wouldn't let the subject drop. (The financial backing that Welles said he had to buy the picture was probably from Henry Luce.) One surmises that Hearst decided not to try to block its release—though the petty harassment of R.K.O. and others involved went on, like a reflex to a blow.

Here is a representative selection from the reviews:

> *Variety:* A film possessing the sure dollar mark.
>
> *Times* (Bosley Crowther): Suppression of this film would have been a crime. . . . *Citizen Kane* is far and away the most surprising and cinematically exciting motion picture to be seen here in many a moon. . . . It comes close to being the most sensational film ever made in Hollywood.
>
> *Herald Tribune* (Howard Barnes): A young man named Orson Welles has shaken the medium wide-awake with his magnificent film, *Citizen Kane.* His biography of an American dynast is not only a great picture; it is something of a revolutionary screen achievement. . . . From any standpoint *Citizen Kane* is truly a great motion picture.
>
> *Post* (Archer Winsten): It goes without saying this is the picture that wins the majority of 1941's

movie prizes in a walk, for it is inconceivable that another will come along to challenge it. . . . Orson Welles with this one film establishes himself as the most exciting director now working. . . . Technically the result marks a new epoch.

*PM* (Cecelia Ager): Before *Citizen Kane,* it's as if the motion picture was a slumbering monster, a mighty force stupidly sleeping, lying there sleek, torpid, complacent—awaiting a fierce young man to come kick it to life, to rouse it, shake it, awaken it to its potentialities, to show it what it's got. Seeing it, it's as if you never really saw a movie before: no movie has ever grabbed you, pummelled you, socked you on the button with the vitality, the accuracy, the impact, the professional aim, that this one does.

*Esquire* (Gilbert Seldes): Welles has shown Hollywood how to make movies. . . . He has made the movies young again, by filling them with life.

*Cue* (Jesse Zunser): It is an astounding experience to watch Orson Welles, 25-year-old Boy Genius of the Western World, in the process of creating on the screen one of the awesome products of his fertile imagination. You come away limp, much as if you had turned into Broadway and suddenly beheld Niagara Falls towering behind the Paramount Building, the Matterhorn looming over Bryant Park, and the Grand Canyon yawning down the middle of Times Square.

*Hollywood Reporter:* A great motion picture. . . . A few steps ahead of anything that has been made in pictures before.

*Chicago Journal of Commerce* (Claudia Cassidy): Anyone who has eyes in his head and ears to hear with will enjoy *Citizen Kane* for the unleashed power of its stature on the screen.

Even Kate Cameron, in the *Daily News,* gave it four stars, and on Sunday, May 4th, Bosley Crowther (though he had some second thoughts of his own) wrote in the *Times,* "The returns are in from most of the local journalistic precincts and Orson Welles' *Citizen Kane* has been overwhelmingly selected as one of the great (if not the greatest) motion pictures of all time. . . . " The *Film Daily* said, "Welles can prepare his mantel for a couple of Oscars."

16.

Had it not been for the delays and the nervous atmosphere that made the picture *seem* unpopular and so *become* unpopular, it might have swept the Academy Awards. It had taken the New York Film Critics Award with ease, but early in 1942, when the 1941 Academy Awards were given, the picture had the aroma of box-office failure—an aroma that frightens off awards in Hollywood. The picture had been nominated in nine categories, and at the ceremony, each time the title or Orson Welles' name was read, there were hisses and loud boos. The prize for the Original Screenplay was perhaps partly a love gesture to Herman Mankiewicz, one of their own; the film community had closed ranks against Orson Welles.

While the picture was being shot, Welles, like a good showman, had done his best to preserve the element of surprise, and he had been smart about keeping a tight, closed set. He didn't want interference from anybody, and even though the R.K.O. executives had read the script, when one of them "dropped in" once to see what was going on, Welles coolly called a halt in the shooting, and the Mercury players went outside and played baseball until he left. There were visitors, of course. Invitations to attend the first official day of shooting were sent to the press, and Welles was simply careful about what he shot that day. And the crew didn't go out to play baseball when Louella Parsons visited the set a few weeks later; they were just very careful, so that even though she had heard rumors that the picture was about Hearst, everything looked so innocent and Welles denied the rumors so disarmingly that she went on giving him an enthusiastic press. (She later described his outfoxing her on this occasion as "one of the classic double crosses of Hollywood.") But Mankiewicz, with his "Don't let this get around," was practically incapable of keeping a secret. He was so proud of his script that he lent a copy to Charles Lederer. In some crazily naïve way, Mankiewicz seems to have imagined that Lederer would be pleased by how good it was. But Lederer, apparently, was deeply upset and took the script to his aunt and Hearst. It went from them to Hearst's lawyers (who marked various passages) before it was returned to Mankiewicz, and thus Hearst and his associates were alerted early to the content of the film. It was probably as a result of Mankiewicz's idiotic indiscretion that the various forces were set in motion that resulted in the cancellation of the première at the Radio City Music Hall, the commercial failure of *Citizen Kane,* and the subsequent failure of Orson Welles. This was how, even before the film was finished, Hearst's minions were in action, and how there was time for Mayer and his people to set about their attempt to suppress the film, and, having failed in that, to destroy it commercially.

In the aftermath of the pressures, and of the disappointing returns on the film, the members of the Academy could feel very courageous about the writing award. Mankiewicz had become a foolhardy hero in taking on Hearst; *Kane* was Mankiewicz's finest moment. They wanted him to have a prize; he deserved it and he needed it. Hollywood loves the luxury of show-business sentimentality, and Hollywood loves a comeback. The members of the Academy destroyed Orson Welles that night, but they probably felt good because their hearts had gone out to crazy, reckless Mank, their own resident loser-genius, the has-been who was washed up in the big studios, who was so far down he had been reduced to writing Welles' radio shows. At the beginning of the thirties, he had been earning $4,000 a week; at the end of the thirties, he was a ghost. What they couldn't know was that *Kane* was Welles' finest moment, too; the reason they couldn't know it was that their failure to back him that night was the turning point. Welles had made *Citizen Kane* at twenty-five, and he seemed to have the world before him. They'd had time to get used to Mank's self-destructiveness, and he'd been down on his luck so long he was easy to love; besides, they admired the pranks that had got him thrown out of one studio after another. Welles was self-destructive in a style they weren't yet accustomed to.

One may speculate that if the members of the Academy had supported Welles and voted *Citizen Kane* Best Picture of the Year, if they had backed the nation's press and their own honest judgment, the picture might have got into the big theatrical showcases despite the pressures against it. If they had, *Kane* might have made money, and things might have gone differently for Welles—and for American movies. The Academy had plenty of sentiment but not enough guts. And so Orson Welles peaked early. Later, as his situation changed and his fortunes sank and *Kane* became the golden opportunity of his youth, his one great chance of freedom to accomplish something, then, when he looked back, he may really have needed to believe what he was quoted as saying in France: "Le seul film que j'aie jamais écrit du premier au dernier mot et pu mener à bien est *Citizen Kane*." The literal translation is "The only film that I ever wrote from first word to last and was able to bring to a successful issue is *Citizen Kane*," but I think that what it means is "The picture came out well." What else can it mean when one considers the contributions of Mankiewicz and Toland and all the rest? Men cheated of their due are notoriously given to claiming more than their due. The Academy members had made their token gesture to *Citizen Kane* with the screenplay award. They failed what they believed in; they gave in to the scandal and to the business pressures. They couldn't yet know how much guilt they *should* feel: guilt that by their failure to support *Citizen Kane* at this crucial time—the last chance to make *Kane* a financial success—they had started the downward spiral of Orson Welles, who was to become perhaps the greatest loser in Hollywood history.

### 17.

Like D. W. Griffith, Orson Welles came into the movies in order to make money so that he could continue in the theatre, and, like Griffith, he discovered that movies were the medium in which he could do what he had barely dreamed of doing in the theatre. Soon—even before he started on *Citizen Kane*—Welles was desperate for money to make movies. It took guile to get *Kane* approved. Robert Wise, whom the head of the R.K.O. editing department had assigned to the picture because he was close to Welles' age, says, "Orson sneaked the project onto R.K.O. He told the studio that he was merely shooting tests." Sets were built, and shooting began on June 29, 1940; the "test shots" were fully produced. The Mercury actors and associates were there

anyway, most of them under personal contract to Welles, as Mankiewicz was. But Dorothy Comingore, not a member of the Mercury Theatre but a Hollywood bit player (who, as Linda Winters, had worked in Westerns and with the Three Stooges and in Blondie and Charlie Chan pictures), says that she lived on unemployment checks of $18 a week while she "tested for one month" for the role of Susan Alexander. She adds, "All these tests were incorporated into the film; they were never retaken." After a month, with the studio buzzing about how brilliant the footage was, the movie was practically a *fait accompli,* and Welles was able to bulldoze Schaefer into approving the project. All the people who were already at work on *Citizen Kane*—the cameraman, the grips, the composer, the assistants, and the actors—met at Herman Mankiewicz's house for breakfast, and Welles announced that the picture had been approved and could formally begin. They officially started on July 30, 1940, and they finished "principal photography" eighty-two shooting days later, on October 23, 1940, even though Welles—almost as accident-prone as Mankiewicz—broke his ankle during the scene when he ran down the stairs from Susan's room while yelling that he'd get Boss Gettys.

Yet it took more than guile to function in the motion-picture business at that time. It helped to be mercenary, of course, but what really counted then was not to care *too* much about your work. After *Citizen Kane,* the contract that gave Welles the right of final cut was cancelled, so he did not have control of *The Magnificent Ambersons,* and it was shortened and mangled. The industry was suspicious of him, and not just because of the scandal of *Kane,* and the general fear of Hearst, and *Kane*'s unsatisfactory financial returns. Alva Johnston described the Hollywood attitude toward Welles in an article in the *Saturday Evening Post* in 1942, the year after *Kane* came out:

> Big agents soon lost interest in the boy genius. They learned that he wasn't interested in money. Welles became known as a dangerous Red because, when his first picture project was shelved after the studio had wasted a good deal of money on it, he offered to make another picture for nothing.

> Genius got a bad name on account of Welles. It was brought into complete disrepute by Saroyan. The gifted Armenian came to Hollywood with a small agent and insisted on working without a salary, leaving it to M-G-M to set a value on his services after his work was completed. He said, "I'll trust the studio." The $10,000,000-a-year agency business is wholly based on the motto "Don't trust the studio." Since the Welles and Saroyan affairs, it has been practically impossible to interest a big agent in an intellectual giant.

When you write straight reporting about the motion-picture business, you're writing satire. Motion-picture executives prefer to do business with men whose values they understand. It's very easy for these executives—businessmen running an art—to begin to fancy that they are creative artists themselves, because they are indeed very much like the "artists" who work for them, because the "artists" who work for them are, or have become, businessmen. Those who aren't businessmen are the Hollywood unreliables—the ones whom, it is always explained to you, the studios can't hire, because they're crazy. As soon as movies became Welles' passion, and he was willing to work on any terms, he was finished in the big studios—they didn't trust him. And so, somehow, Welles aged before he matured—and not just physically. He went from child prodigy to defeated old man, though today, at fifty-five, he is younger by a decade or two than most of the big American directors.

In later years, Welles, a brilliant talker, was to give many interviews, and as his power in the studios diminished, his role in past movies grew larger. Sometimes it seems that his only power is over the interviewers who believe him. He is a masterful subject. The new generation of film historians have their own version of "Look, no hands": they tape-record interviews. Young interviewers, particularly, don't bother to check the statements of their subjects—they seem to regard that as outside their province—and thus leave the impression that the self-aggrandizing stories they record are history. And so, as the years go on, if one trusts what appears in print, Welles wrote not only *Kane* but just about everything halfway good in any picture he ever acted in, and in interviews he's beginning to have directed anything good in them, too. Directors are now the most interviewed group of people since the stars in the forties, and they have told the same stories so many times that not only they believe them, whether they're true or false, but everybody is beginning to.

This worship of the director is cyclical—Welles or Fellini is probably adored no more than von Stroheim or von Sternberg or De Mille was in his heyday—but such worship generally doesn't help in sorting out what went into the making of good pictures and bad pictures. The directors try to please the interviewers by telling them the anecdotes that have got a good response before. The anecdotes are sometimes charming and superficial, like the famous one—now taken for motion-picture history—about how Howard Hawks supposedly discovered that *The Front Page* would be better if a girl played the reporter Hildy, and thus transformed the play into *His Girl Friday* in 1940. ("I was going to prove to somebody that *The Front Page* had the finest modern dialogue that had been written, and I asked a girl to read Hildy's part and I read the editor, and I stopped and I said, 'Hell, it's better between a girl and a man than between two men.'") Now, a charming story is not nothing. Still, this is nothing but a charming and superficial story. *His Girl Friday* turned out joyously, but if such an accident did cause Hawks to see how easy it was to alter the play, he still must have done it rather cynically, in order to make it conform to the box-office patterns then current. By the mid-thirties—after the surprise success of *It Happened One Night*—the new independent, wisecracking girl was very popular, especially in a whole cycle of newspaper pictures with rival girl and boy reporters. Newspaper pictures were now "romantic comedies," and, just as the movies about lady fliers were almost all based on Amelia Earhart, the criminal-mouthpiece movies on William Fallon, and the gossip-column movies on Walter Winchell, the movies about girl reporters were almost all based on the most highly publicized girl reporter—Hearst's Adela Rogers St. Johns. Everybody had already been stealing from and unofficially adapting *The Front Page* in the "wacky" romantic newspaper comedies, and one of these rewrites, *Wedding Present,* in 1936 (by Adela Rogers St. Johns' then son-in-law Paul Gallico), had tough editor (Cary Grant) and smart girl reporter (Joan Bennett) with square fiancé (Conrad Nagel). This was the mold that *The Front Page* was then squeezed into to become *His Girl Friday,* with Cary Grant, Rosalind Russell, and Ralph Bellamy (already a favorite square from *The Awful Truth*) in the same roles, and Rosalind Russell was so obviously playing Adela Rogers St. Johns that she was dressed in an imitation of the St. Johns girl-reporter striped suit.

Some things that students now, seeing films out of the context of the cycles they were part of, may take to be brilliant inventions were fairly standard; in fact, the public at the time was so familiar with the conventions of the popular comedies that the clichés were frequently spoofed within the pictures. But today, because of the problems peculiar to writing the history of modern mass-art forms, and because of the jumbled circumstances in which movies survive, with knowledge of them acquired in haphazard fashion from television, and from screenings here and there, film enthusiasts find it simpler to explain movies in terms of the genius-artist-director, the schoolbook hero—the man who did it all. Those who admire *Citizen Kane,* which is constructed to present different perspectives on a man's life, seem naïvely willing to accept Welles' view of its making; namely, that it is his sole creation.

Howard Hawks must wonder what the admiration of the young is worth when he learns from them that he invented overlapping dialogue in *His Girl Friday,* since it means that they have never bothered to look at the text of the original Hecht and MacArthur play. Welles, too, has been said to have invented overlapping dialogue, and just about everything else in *Kane.* But unearned praise is insulting, and a burden; Welles sometimes says, "I drag my myth around with me." His true achievements are heavy enough to weigh him down. Welles is a great figure in motion-picture history: he directed what is almost universally acclaimed as the greatest American film of the sound era; he might have become the greatest all-around American director of that era; and in his inability to realize all his artistic potentialities he is the greatest symbolic figure in American film history since Griffith.

18.

In the past few years, I have heard two famous "artist" directors, after showings of their early films, explain how it happened that in the screen credits there was someone else listed for the script. It seems there was this poor guy on the lot who needed a credit desperately, and the company asked the director if he'd give the stumblebum a break; the incompetent turned in some material, but the director couldn't use any of it. Some listeners must swallow this, because in the latest incense-burning book on Josef von Sternberg the screen credits are simply ignored, and he, rather than Ben Hecht, is listed as the author of *Underworld.* Herman J. Mankiewicz has been similarly dropped from one film after another. The directors' generosity to those poor credit-hungry guys seems to have cut-off points in time (the directors' creative roles get bigger when the writers are dead) and in space (when the directors are interviewed abroad). Orson Welles, however, didn't need time or distance; he omitted any mention of his writer right from the start. (This custom is now being followed by many directors.) In later years, when he has been specifically asked by interviewers whether Mankiewicz wrote the scenario for *Citizen Kane,* he has had a set reply. "Everything concerning Rosebud belongs to him," he has said. Rosebud is what was most frequently criticized in the movie, and Gilbert Seldes, in one of the most solid and intelligent reviews of *Kane* (in *Esquire*), called it "a phony" and "the only bit of stale stuff in the picture." Welles himself has said, "The Rosebud gimmick is what I like least about the movie. It's a gimmick, really, and rather dollar-book Freud."

Welles may have been goaded into malice; he had probably never come up against a man so well equipped to deal with him as Mankiewicz. Welles, who used to tell stories about how when he was seventeen he became a *torero* in Seville and entered several *corridas* and was billed on the posters as "The American," may have got a few welts, starting with Mankiewicz's original title— *American.* When Welles read the script, he must certainly have recognized what he was caught in. There's no doubt that Welles—the fabulous Orson Welles— wasn't accustomed to sharing credit. However, his persistent lack of generosity toward Mankiewicz started at the time the movie came out, and it may have its basis in a very specific grievance. Mankiewicz may have outsmarted Welles on the credits more than once. Nunnally Johnson says that while *Citizen Kane* was being shot, Mankiewicz told him that he had received an offer of a ten-thousand-dollar bonus from Welles (through Welles' "chums") to hold to the original understanding and keep his name off the picture. Mankiewicz said that Welles had been brooding over the credits, that he could see how beautiful they would be: "Produced by Orson Welles. Directed by Orson Welles. Starring Orson Welles." It was perfect until he got to "Herman J. Mankiewicz" in the writing credit, which spoiled everything. Mankiewicz said he was tempted by Welles' offer. As usual, he needed money, and, besides, he was fearful of what would happen when the picture came out—he might be black-balled forever. William Randolph Hearst, like Stalin, was known to be fairly Byzantine in his punishments. At the same time, Mankiewicz knew that *Citizen Kane* was his best work, and he was

proud of it. He told Johnson that he went to Ben Hecht with his dilemma, and that Hecht, as prompt with advice as with scripts, said, "Take the ten grand and double-cross the son of a bitch."

I asked Nunnally Johnson if he thought Mankiewicz's story was true, and Mankiewicz actually had got the offer and had taken Hecht's advice. Johnson replied, "I like to believe he did." It's not unlikely. Mankiewicz wrote the first draft in about three months and tightened and polished it into the final shooting script of *Citizen Kane* in a few more weeks, and he probably didn't get more than eight or nine thousand dollars for the whole job; according to the cost sheets for the movie, the screenplay cost was $34,195.24, which wasn't much, even for that day, and the figure probably includes the salary and expenses of John Houseman and the others at Victorville. Mankiewicz may easily have felt he deserved an extra ten thousand. "An Irish bum," Johnson calls him—and if that makes him sound lovable, the operative word is still "bum." If Mankiewicz made up the story he told Johnson—and he was probably capable of such juicy slander—this kind of invention may be a clue to why Welles tries to turn the credit into blame. And if Mankiewicz did get the offer, did take the money, and did double-cross Welles, this might equally well explain why Welles doesn't want Mankiewicz to get any honor.

But Welles needed Mankiewicz. Since sound came in, almost every time an actor has scored in a role and become a "star," it has been because the role provided a realistic base for contradictory elements. Welles has never been able to write this kind of vehicle for himself. *Kane* may be a study of egotism and a movie about money and love, but it isn't just another movie about a rich man who isn't loved; it's a scandalously unauthorized, muckraking biography of a man who was still alive and—though past his peak influence—still powerful, so it conveyed shock and danger, and it drew its strength from its reverberations in the life of the period. Mankiewicz brought to the film the force of journalism. The thirties had been full of movie biographies of tycoons and robber barons, and some, like *The Power and the Glory,* were complexly told, but even Preston Sturges, as if in awe of the material, had taken a solemn, almost lachrymose approach to the money-doesn't-bring-happiness theme. Mankiewicz did it better: the prismatic technique turned into a masterly juggling act. There's an almost palpable sense of enjoyment in the script itself; Mankiewicz was skillful at making his points through comedy, and frequently it's higher, blacker comedy than was customary in the thirties pictures. Welles is a different kind of writer—theatrical and Gothic, not journalistic, and not *organized.* His later thrillers are portentous without having anything to portend, sensational in a void, entertaining thrillers, often, but *mere* thrillers.

Lacking the realistic base and the beautifully engineered structure that Mankiewicz provided, Welles has never again been able to release that charming, wicked rapport with the audience that he brought to *Kane* both as actor and as director (or has been able to release it only in distorted form, in self-satire and self-humiliation). He has brought many qualities to film—and there was perhaps a new, mellowed vitality in his work in the flawed *Falstaff* of a few years ago—but he has brought no more great original characters. In his movies, he can create an atmosphere but not a base. And without that the spirit that makes Kane so likable a bastard is missing. Kane, that mass of living contradictions, was conceived by Mankiewicz, an atheist who was proud of his kosher home, a man who was ambivalent about *both* Hearst and Welles.

However, things that get printed often enough begin to seep into the general consciousness of the past, so there is a widespread impression that Welles wrote *Citizen Kane.* And even if one hadn't heard that he wrote it, and despite the presence in the film of so many elements and interests that are unrelated to Welles' other work (mundane activities and social content are not his forte), Kane and Welles are identified in our minds. This is not only a tribute to Welles as an actor but a backhanded tribute to Mankiewicz, who wrote the role for Welles the actor and wrote Welles the capricious, talented, domineering prodigy into the role, combining Welles' personality and character traits with Hearst's life in publishing and politics and acquisition.

If one asks how it is that Herman J. Mankiewicz, who wrote the film that many people think is the greatest film they've ever seen, is almost unknown, the answer must surely be not just that he died too soon but that he outsmarted himself. As a result of his wicked sense of humor in drawing upon Welles' character for Kane's, his own authorship was obscured. Sensing the unity of Kane and Welles, audiences assume that Kane is Welles' creation, that Welles is playing "the role he was born to play," while film scholars, seeing the material from Welles' life in the movie, interpret the film as Welles working out autobiographical themes. It is a commonplace in theatre talk to say that Olivier *is* Archie Rice or Olivier *is* Macbeth without assuming that the actor has conceived the role, but in movies we don't see other actors in the same role (except in remakes, which are usually very different in style), and film is so vivid and the actor so large and so close that it is a common primitive response to assume that the actor invented his lines. In this case, the primitive response is combined with the circumstances that Welles' name had been heavily featured for years, that the role was a new creation, that the movie audience's image of Welles was set by this overpowering role, in which they saw him for the first time, and that not only was the role partly based on him but he began to live up to it. Herman Mankiewicz died, and his share faded from knowledge, but Welles carries on in a baronial style that always reminds us of Kane. Kane seems an emanation of Welles, and if

Mankiewicz didn't take the ten thousand, he might just as well have, because he helped stamp Welles all over the film.

### 19.

James Agee, who didn't begin reviewing until later in 1941, wrote several years afterward that Welles had been "fatuously overrated as a 'genius,'" and that he himself, annoyed by all the talk, had for a while underrated him. At the time the film was released, the most perceptive movie critic in the United States was Otis Ferguson (an early volunteer and early casualty in the Second World War), on the *New Republic.* Ferguson saw more clearly than anybody else what was specifically good and bad in *Kane,* and though he was wrong, I think, in maintaining that unobtrusive technique is the only good technique, he did perceive that *Citizen Kane* challenged this concept.

One of the games that film students sometimes play is to judge a director on whether you have the illusion that the people on the screen will go on doing what they're doing after the camera leaves them. Directors are rated by how much time you think elapsed before the actors grabbed their coats or ordered a sandwich. The longer the time, the more of a film man the director is said to be; when a director is stage-oriented, you can practically see the actors walking off the set. This game doesn't help in judging a film's content, but it's a fairly reliable test of a director's film technique; one could call it a test of movie believability. However, it isn't applicable to *Citizen Kane.* You're perfectly well aware that the people won't go on doing what they're doing—that they have, indeed, completed their actions on the screen. *Kane* depends not on naturalistic believability but on our enjoyment of the very fact that those actions *are* completed, and that they all fit into place. This bravura is, I think, the picture's only true originality, and it wasn't an intentional challenge to the concept of unobtrusive technique but was (mainly) the result of Welles' discovery of—and his delight in—the fun of making movies.

The best American directors in the thirties had been developing an unpretentious American naturalism; modern subjects and the advent of sound had freed them from the heavy dead hand of Germanic stage lighting and design. And so Ferguson was dismayed to see this all come back, and it *was* depressing that the critics who had always fallen for the synthetic serious were bowing and scraping and calling the picture "deep" and "realistic." Probably so many people called it realistic because the social satire made contact with what they felt about Hearst and the country; when they used the term, they were referring to the content rather than the style. But it was the "retrogressive" style that upset Ferguson— because it was when Orson Welles, an "artist" director, joined the toughness and cynicism and the verbal skills of the thirties to that incomparable, faintly absurd, wonderfully overblown style of his that people said "art."

Where Ferguson went wrong was in not recognizing one crucial element: that the unconcealed—even flaunted—pleasure that Welles took in all that clap-trap made it new.

And it has kept it new. Even a number of those who worked on *Kane,* such as Houseman and Dorothy Comingore, have observed that the film seems to improve with the years. At the time, I got more simple, frivolous pleasure from Preston Sturges's *The Lady Eve,* which had come out a few months earlier, and I found more excitement in John Huston's *The Maltese Falcon,* which came out a few months later. At the time (I was twenty-one), I enjoyed *Kane* for the performances and the wit, but I was very conscious of how shallow the iconoclasm was. I don't think I was wrong, exactly, but now the movie seems marvellous to me. It's an *exuberant* shallow iconoclasm, and that youthful zest for shock and for the Expressionist theatricality seems to transform the shallowness. Now the movie sums up and preserves a period, and the youthful iconoclasm is preserved in all its freshness—even the freshness of its callowness. Now that the political theme (in its specific form, that is) is part of the past, the naïveté and obviousness fade, and what remains is a great American archetype and a popular legend—and so it has a strength that makes the artificially created comic world of a movie like *The Lady Eve* disappear by comparison. *Citizen Kane* has such energy it drives the viewer along. Though Mankiewicz provided the basic apparatus for it, that magical exuberance which fused the whole scandalous enterprise was Welles'. Works of art are enjoyed for different reasons in different periods; it may even be one of the defining characteristics of a lasting work of art that it yields up different qualities for admiration at different times. Welles' "magic," his extraordinary pleasure in playacting and illusion and in impressing an audience—what seems so charming about the movie now—was what seemed silly to me then. It was bouncy Pop Gothic in a period when the term "comic strip" applied to works of art was still a term of abuse. Now Welles' discovery of movie making—and the boyishness and excitement of that discovery—is preserved in *Kane* the way the snow scene is preserved in the glass ball.

Seeing the movie again recently, I liked the way it looked; now that the style no longer boded a return to the aestheticism of sets and the rigidly arranged figures of the German silents, I could enjoy it without misgivings. In the thirties, Jean Renoir had been using deep focus (that is, keeping the middle range and the background as clear as the foreground) in a naturalistic way. The light seemed (and often was) "natural." You looked at a scene, and the drama that you saw going on in it was just part of that scene, and so you had the sense of discovering it for yourself, of seeing drama in the midst of life. This was a tremendous relief from the usual studio lighting, which forced your attention to the dramatic action in the frame, blurred the rest, and rarely gave you a chance to feel that the action was part of anything larger or anything continuous. In Welles' far

more extreme use of deep focus, and in his arrangement of the actors in the compositions, he swung back to the most coercive use of artificial, theatrical lighting. He used light like a spotlight on the stage, darkening or blacking out the irrelevant. He used deep focus not for a naturalistic effect but for the startling dramatic effect of having crucial action going on in the background (as when Kane appears in a distant doorway). The difference between Renoir's style and Welles' style seems almost literally the difference between day and night. Welles didn't have (nor did he, at that time, need) the kind of freedom Renoir needed and couldn't get in Hollywood—the freedom to shoot outside the studio and to depart from the script and improvise. *Kane* is a studio-made film—much of it was shot in that large room at R.K.O. where, a few years earlier, Ginger Rogers and Fred Astaire had danced their big numbers. However, Welles had the freedom to try out new solutions to technical problems, and he made his theatrical technique work spectacularly. Probably it was the first time in American movies that Expressionism had ever worked for comic and satiric effects (except in bits of some of the early spoof horror films), and probably it would have been impossible to tell the *Kane* story another way without spending a fortune on crowds and set construction. Welles' method is a triumph of ingenuity in that the pinpoints of light in the darkness conceal the absence of detailed sets (a chair or two and a huge fireplace, and one thinks one is seeing a great room), and the almost treacherously brilliant use of sound conceals the absence of crowds. We see Susan at the *deserted* cabaret; we see her from the back on the opera-house stage and we imagine that she is facing an audience; we get a sense of crowds at the political rally without seeing them. It was Welles' experience both in the theatre and in radio that enabled him to produce a huge historical film on a shoestring; he produced the *illusion* of a huge historical film.

But, seeing *Kane* now, I winced, as I did the first time, at the empty virtuosity of the shot near the beginning when Kane, dying, drops the glass ball and we see the nurse's entrance reflected in the glass. I noticed once again, though without being bothered by it this time, either, that there was no one in the room to hear the dying Kane say "Rosebud." I was much more disturbed by little picky defects, like the obtrusive shot up to the bridge before the reporter goes into the hospital. What is strange about reseeing a movie that one reacted to fairly intensely many years ago is that one may respond exactly the same way to so many details and *be aware* each time of having responded that way before. I was disappointed once again by the clumsily staged "cute" meeting of Kane and Susan, which seemed to belong to a routine comedy, and I thought the early scenes with Susan were weak not just because while listening to her dull, sentimental singing Welles is in a passive position and so can't animate the scenes but—and mainly—because the man of simple pleasures who would find a dumb girl deeply appealing does not tie in with the personality projected by Orson Welles. (And as Welles doesn't project any sexual interest in either Kane's first wife, Emily, or in Susan, his second wife, we don't know how to interpret Susan's claim that he just likes her voice.) Most of the newspaper-office scenes looked as clumsily staged as ever, and the first appearance of Bernstein, Kane's business manager, arriving with a load of furniture, was still confusing. (He seems to be a junk dealer—probably because an earlier scene in *American* introducing him was eliminated.) I disliked again the attempt to wring humor out of the sputtering confusion of Carter, the old Dickensian editor. It's a scene like the ones Mankiewicz helped prepare for the Marx Brothers, but what was probably intended to make fun of a stuffed shirt turned into making fun of a helpless old man trying to keep his dignity, which is mean and barbarous. I still thought Susan became too thin a conception, and more shrill and shrewish than necessary, and, as Emily, Ruth Warrick was all pursed lips—a stereotype of refinement. I was still uncomfortable during the visit to Jed Leland in the hospital; Leland's character throughout is dependent on Joseph Cotten's obvious charm, and the sentimental-old-codger bit in this sequence is really a disgrace. The sequence plays all too well at a low conventional level—pulling out easy stops. I still didn't see the function of the sequence about Kane's being broke and losing control of his empire, since nothing followed from it. (I subsequently discovered that things weren't going well on the set at one point, and Welles decided to go back to this scene, which had been in an earlier draft and had then been eliminated. What it coördinated with was, unfortunately, not restored.) This sequence also has the most grating bad line in the movie, when Kane says, "You know, Mr. Bernstein, if I hadn't been very rich, I might have been a really great man."

What's still surprising is how well a novice movie director handled so many of the standard thirties tricks and caricatures—the device of the alternative newspaper headlines, for example, and the stock explosive, hand-waving Italian opera coach (well played by Fortunio Bonanova). The engineering—the way the sequences are prepared for and commented on by preceding sequences, the way the five accounts tie together to tell the story—seems as ingenious as ever; though one is aware that the narrators are telling things they couldn't have witnessed, one accepts this as part of the convention. The cutting (which a reading of the script reveals to have been carried out almost exactly as it was planned) is elegantly precise, and some sequences have a good, sophomoric musical-comedy buoyancy.

What had changed for me—what I had once enjoyed but now found almost mysteriously beautiful—was Orson Welles' performance. An additional quality that old movies acquire is that people can be seen as they once were. It is a pleasure we can't get in theatre; we can only hear and read descriptions of past fabulous performances. But here in *Kane* is the young Welles, and he seems almost embarrassed to be exposed as so young. Perhaps he *was* embarrassed, and that's why he so often

hid in extravagant roles and behind those old-man false faces. He seems unsure of himself as the young Kane, and there's something very engaging (and surprisingly *human*) about Welles unsure of himself; he's a big, overgrown, heavy boy, and rather sheepish, one suspects, at being seen as he is. Many years later, Welles remarked, "Like most performers, I naturally prefer a live audience to that lie-detector full of celluloid." Maybe his spoiled-baby face was just too nearly perfect for the role, and he knew it, and knew the hostile humor that lay behind Mankiewicz's putting so much of him in the role of Hearst the braggart self-publicist and making Kane so infantile. That statement of principles that Jed sends back to Kane and that Kane then tears up must surely refer to the principles behind the co-founding of the Mercury Theatre by Welles and Houseman. Lines like Susan's "You're not a professional magician, are you?" may have made Welles flinch. And it wasn't just the writer who played games on him. There's the scene of Welles eating in the newspaper office, which was obviously caught by the camera crew, and which, to be "a good sport," he had to use. Welles is one of the most self-conscious of actors—it's part of his rapport with the audience—and this is what is so nakedly revealed in this role, in which he's playing a young man his own age and he's insecure (and with some reason) about what's coming through. Something of the young, unmasked man is revealed in these scenes—to be closed off forever after.

Welles picks up assurance and flair as Kane in his thirties, and he's also good when Kane is just a little older and jowly. I think there's no doubt that he's more sure of himself when he's playing this somewhat older Kane, and this is the Kane we remember best from the first viewing—the brash, confident Kane of the pre-election-disaster period. He's so fully—classically—American a show-off one almost regrets the change of title. But when I saw the movie again it was the younger Kane who stayed with me—as if I had been looking through a photograph album and had come upon a group of pictures of an old friend, long dead, as he had been when I first met him. I had almost forgotten Welles in his youth, and here he is, smiling, eager, looking forward to the magnificent career that everyone expected him to have.

20.

Just as Welles suggested the radio-bulletin approach to the H. G. Welles landing-of-the-Martians material to Howard Koch, he may very well have suggested the "March of Time" summary of Hearst's career in his early talks with Mankiewicz. Welles had worked as an actor for the "March of Time" radio program in 1934 and 1935, and he had worked steadily as a narrator and radio actor (his most famous role was the lead in the popular weekly mystery show "The Shadow") until he went to Hollywood. The "March of Time" is exactly the kind of idea the young Welles *would* have suggested. It's the sort of technique that was being used in the experimental theatre of the late thirties—when the Federal Theatre Project (in which Welles and Houseman had worked together) staged the documentary series "The Living Newspaper," and when members of the Group Theatre and other actors were performing anti-Fascist political cabaret. The imitation "March of Time" was not a new device, even in movies; it had already been used, though humorlessly, to convey the fact that a theme was current, part of "today's news," and to provide background information—as in *Confessions of a Nazi Spy*, of 1939. What was needed to transform that device and make it the basis for the memorable parody in **Citizen Kane** was not only Welles' experience and not only his "touch" but the great sense of mischief that he and Mankiewicz shared. The smug manner of the "March of Time" was already a joke to many people; when I was a student at Berkeley in the late thirties, there was always laughter in the theatres when the "March of Time" came on, with its racy neo-conservatism and its ritual pomposity—with that impersonal tone, as if God above were narrating. There was an element of unconscious self-parody in the important tone of the "March of Time," as in all the Luce enterprises, and, in his script, Mankiewicz pushed it further. He used consciously those elements which part of the public already found funny, bringing into a mass medium what was already a subject for satire among the knowledgeable.

Mankiewicz's "On Approaching Forty" had not appeared in *The New Yorker,* but a few weeks after it was printed, in 1936, Wolcott Gibbs, who was to take Mankiewicz's old chair as *The New Yorker*'s drama critic (and who was the first occupant of that chair not to emigrate to Hollywood), published the celebrated Profile "Time—Fortune—Life—Luce," which was written in mock Timese ("Backward ran sentences until reeled the mind," and so on, concluding with "Where it all will end, knows God!"), and this was probably not merely the spur to Mankiewicz but the competition. Mankiewicz's pastiche was fully worked out in the first long draft of the script, the processed prose and epigrams already honed to perfection ("For forty years appeared in Kane newsprint no public issue on which Kane papers took no stand. No public man whom Kane himself did not support or denounce—often support, then denounce"). And even on paper—without Welles' realization of the plan—the section is good enough to invite the comparison that I suspect Mankiewicz sought with the Gibbs parody. (Mankiewicz's widow keeps the Oscar statuette for **Citizen Kane** on the mantel, along with the latest *Who's Who in America* with the marker set at her sons' listing, and on the shelf next to the mantel are the bound volumes of *The New Yorker* in which her husband's reviews appeared.)

Part of the fun of the "March of Time" parody for the audiences back in 1941 was that, of course, we kept *recognizing* things about Hearst in it, and its daring meant great suspense about what was to follow in the picture. But Mankiewicz tried to do more with this parody than is completely evident either in the final script or in the film itself. He tried to use the "March of Time" as a historical framing device to close one era and open the next, with Hearstian journalism giving way to the new Luce empire. In the movie, it seems a structural gimmick—though a very cleverly *used* gimmick, which is enjoyable in itself. In Mankiewicz's original conception, in the long first-draft *American,* which ran three hundred and twenty-five pages, that device is more clearly integral to the theme. In Mankiewicz's conception, the Hearst-Kane empire is doomed: Kane's own death is being "sent" to the world by the filmed "March of Time" (called "News on the March" in the movie), which means the end of the newspaper business as Hearst knew it. The funny thing is that Mankiewicz, in commenting on Hearst's lack of vision, overestimated Luce's vision. After Luce took news coverage from newspapers into news magazines, he moved into photo-journalism and then into news documentaries, but he didn't follow through on what he had started, and he failed to get into television production. Now, after *his* death, the Luce organization is trying to get back into film activities.

In Mankiewicz's original conception, the historical line of succession was laid out as in a chronicle play. Hearst supplanted the old-style quiet upper-class journalism with his penny-dreadful treatment of crime and sex and disasters, his attacks on the rich, his phony lawsuits against the big corporations that he called "predators," his screaming patriotism, his faked photographs, and his exploitation of superstition, plus puzzles, comics, contests, sheet music, and medical quackery. His youthful dedication to the cause of the common people declined into the cheap chauvinism that infected everything and helped to turn the readers into a political mob. The irony built into the structure was that his own demise should be treated in the new, lofty style of Luce.

And it was in terms of this framework that the elements of admiration in the ambivalent portrait of Kane made sense. Hearst represented a colorful kind of journalism that was already going out. Mankiewicz was summing up the era of *The Front Page* at the end of it, and was treating it right at its source in the American system that made it possible for a rich boy to inherit the power to control public opinion as his own personal plaything. *American* (and, to a lesser degree, **Citizen Kane**) was a there-were-giants-in-those-days valedictory to the old-style big scoundrels. The word had been used straight by Mrs. Fremont Older in 1936 when she published the authorized biography, *William Randolph Hearst, American.* "American" was Hearst's shibboleth; his Sunday magazine section was the *American Weekly,* and he had been changing his newspaper titles to include the word "American" whenever possible ever since Senator Henry Cabot Lodge accused him of being un-American in those days after the McKinley assassination when Hearst was hanged in effigy. Hearst's attacks on McKinley as "the most despised and hated creature in the hemisphere" had culminated in an editorial that said "Killing must be done" shortly before it was. When the storm died down, Hearst became super-American. For Mankiewicz, Hearst's Americanism was the refuge of a scoundrel, though by no means his last refuge; *that*, in the first draft, was clearly blackmail. What the title was meant to signify was indicated by Kane in the "News on the March" segment when he said, "I am, have been, and will be only one thing—an American." That was pure flag-waving Pop before we had a name for it: "American" as it was used by the American Legion and the Daughters of the American Revolution. In addition, Mankiewicz may have wanted to score off his movie friends who since the middle thirties—the period of the Popular Front—had also been draping themselves in the flag. In that period, the Communist left had become insistent about its Americanism, in its rather embarrassing effort to tout American democracy, which it had called "imperialism" until the U.S.S.R. sought the United States as an ally against Hitler. In the later title, "Citizen" is similarly ironic; Hearst, the offspring of an economic baron, and himself a press lord and the master of San Simeon, was a "citizen" the way Louis XIV at Versailles was a citizen. And joining the word to "Kane" (Cain) made its own point.

Both the parodistic use of Timese and the facelessness of Luce's company men served a historical purpose in the first script. But *American* was much too long and inclusive and loose, and much too ambitious, and Mankiewicz rapidly cut it down (copies of these gradually shorter drafts were saved) until it reached the hundred and fifty-six pages of the final shooting script—which still made for a then unusually long picture, of a hundred and nineteen minutes. In the trimming, dialogue that was crucial to the original dramatic conception of the Hearst-Luce succession was cut. (In terms of the final conception, though, it's perfectly clear why.) This deleted exchange between Thompson, the investigating reporter for the Rawlston (Luce) organization, and Raymond, Kane's butler, makes the point about the line of succession from Hearst to Luce all too explicitly:

THOMPSON

Well, if you get around to your memoirs—don't forget, Mr. Rawlston wants to be sure of getting first chance. We pay awful well for long excerpts.

RAYMOND

Maybe he'd like to buy the excerpts of what Mr. Kane said about him.

THOMPSON

Huh?

RAYMOND

He thought Rawlston would break his neck sooner or later. He gave that weekly magazine of yours three years.

THOMPSON

(*Smugly*) He made a bit of a mistake.

RAYMOND

He made a lot of mistakes.

Welles, who did such memorable casting in the rest of the movie, used a number of his own faceless executive assistants in the vapid roles of the Luce men. They are the performers in *Citizen Kane* that nobody remembers, and they didn't go on to become actors. William Alland, whose voice was fine as the voice of "News on the March" but who was a vacuum as Thompson, the reporter, became a producer and investment broker; another of Welles' assistants, Richard Wilson, who also played a reporter, is now a director (*Three in the Attic*); still another, Richard Barr, is the well-known New York theatrical producer. Among the "News on the March" men, there were some bit players who did have potential faces (Alan Ladd was one of them), but they weren't presented as personalities. Nevertheless, in a movie as verbally explicit as *Citizen Kane* the faceless idea doesn't really come across. You probably don't get the intention behind it in *Kane* unless you start thinking about the unusual feebleness of the scenes with the "News on the March" people and about the fact that though Thompson is a principal in the movie in terms of how much he appears, there isn't a shred of characterization in his lines or in his performance; he is such a shadowy presence that you may even have a hard time remembering whether you ever saw his face, though this movie introduced to the screen a large group of performers who made strong, astonishingly distinct impressions, sometimes in very brief roles. Perhaps the acting and the group movement of the faceless men needed to be more stylized, the dialogue more satirical; as it was done, it's just dull rather than purposefully blank. Welles probably thought it didn't matter how bad these actors were, because they should be colorless anyway; after R.K.O. gave him the go-ahead on the project, he didn't reshoot the test scene he had made of the projection-room sequence. But the movie misses on the attitudes *behind* Luce's new journalism. It's true that for the practitioners of Timese impersonality becomes their personal style and reporters become bureaucrats, but there's also a particular aura of programmed self-importance and of awareness of power—the ambitiousness of colorless people.

Among the minor absurdities of the script is that the "News on the March" men never think of sending a cameraman along with the inquiring reporter, though Gable had just played a newsreel cameraman in *Too Hot to Handle*, in 1938, and though in *The Philadelphia Story*, which had opened on Broadway in 1939, and which Mankiewicz's brother Joe produced for the screen in 1940, while *Kane* was being shot, the magazine team, also obviously from Luce, includes a photographer. There's something rather pathetic—almost as if *Kane* were a Grade B movie that didn't have a big enough budget for a few extra players—about that one lonely sleuthing reporter travelling around the country while a big organization delays the release of an important newsreel documentary on the head of a rival news chain. Maybe Mankiewicz, despite his attempt to place Hearst historically through the "March of Time" framework, still thought in terms of the older journalism and of all the gimmicky movies about detective-reporters. And Mankiewicz was by temperament a reckless, colorful newspaperman. That deleted material about the Luce organization's wanting Raymond's memoirs, with Raymond's teaser "He made a lot of mistakes," is part of an elaborate series of scandalous subplots, closely paralleling scandals in Hearst's life, that were cut out in the final script. In the movie, Susan says to Thompson, "Look, if you're smart, you'll get in touch with Raymond. He's the butler. You'll learn a lot from him. He knows where all the bodies are buried." It's an odd, cryptic speech. In the first draft, Raymond *literally* knew where the bodies were buried: Mankiewicz had dished up a nasty version of the scandal sometimes referred to as the Strange Death of Thomas Ince. Even with this kind of material cut down to the barest allusions, Mankiewicz, in **Citizen Kane,** treated the material of Hearst's life in Hearstian yellow-journalism style.

## 21.

Welles is right, of course, about Rosebud—it *is* dollar-book Freud. But it is such a primitive kind of Freudianism that, like some of the movie derivations from Freud later in the forties—in *The Seventh Veil,* for instance—it hardly seems Freudian at all now. Looking for "the secret" of a famous man's last words is about as phony as the blind-beggar-for-luck bit, yet it does "work" for some people; they go for the idea that Rosebud represents lost maternal bliss and somehow symbolizes Kane's loss of the power to love or be loved. The one significant change from Hearst's life—Kane's separation from his parents—seems to be used to explain Kane, though there is an explicit disavowal of any such intention toward the end. Someone says to Thompson, "If you could have found out what Rosebud meant, I bet that would've explained everything." Thompson replies, "No, I don't think so. No. Mr. Kane was a man who got everything he wanted, and then lost it. Maybe Rosebud was something he couldn't get or something he lost. Anyway, it wouldn't have explained anything. I don't think any word can explain a man's life. No. I guess Rosebud is just a piece in a jigsaw puzzle, a missing piece."

Nevertheless, the structure of the picture—searching for the solution to a mystery—and the exaggerated style make it appear that Rosebud *is* the key to Kane's life, and the public responds to what is presented dramatically, not to the reservations of the moviemakers. Rosebud has become part of popular culture, and people remember it who have forgotten just about everything else in **Citizen Kane;** the jokes started a week before the movie opened, with a child's sled marked "Rosebud"

dragged onstage in the first act of *Native Son,* and a couple of years ago, in *Peanuts,* Snoopy walked in the snow pulling a sled and Charlie Brown said, "Rosebud?" The Rosebud of Rosebud is as banal as Rosebud itself. It seems that as a child Herman Mankiewicz had had a sled, which may or may not have carried the label "Rosebud" (his family doesn't remember); he wasn't dramatically parted from the sled, but he once had a bicycle that was stolen, and he mourned that all his life. He simply put the emotion of the one onto the other.

Though Rosebud was in the long first draft, it didn't carry the same weight there, because the newspaper business itself undermined Kane's idealism. In that draft, Kane, like Hearst, in order to reach the masses he thought he wanted to serve and protect, built circulation by turning the newspapers into pulp magazines, and, in order to stay in business and expand, squeezed non-advertisers. The long script went as far as to show that, in the process of becoming one of the mighty, Kane-Hearst, like Louis B. Mayer and so many other tycoons, developed close ties to the underworld. Mankiewicz was trying to give a comprehensive view of the contradictions that emerge when an idealist attempts to succeed in business and politics. Fragments of this are left, but their meaning is no longer clear. For example, the point of the sequence of Kane's buying up the staff of the *Chronicle,* the paper that was outselling his *Inquirer* by featuring crime and sex, was that the *Chronicle*'s staff would change him by deflecting him from an idealistic course (and Jed tries to point this out to Bernstein), but as it appears in the film it almost seems that in buying the *Chronicle*'s staff Kane is corrupting *them.*

It is just a fragment, too, that Kane's first wife, Emily, is the niece of the President of the United States. Hearst's only wife, Millicent, the daughter of a vaudeville hoofer, was a teen-age member of a group called The Merry Maidens when he met her. Emily was probably made the niece of the President in order to link Kane with the rich and to make a breach in the marriage when Kane was held responsible for the assassination of the President (as Hearst was accused of having incited the death of President McKinley).

In the condensation, the whole direction was, for commercial reasons, away from the newspaper business that dominated the early script, and, for obvious reasons, away from factual resemblances to Hearst's life. This was generally accomplished by making things funny. For example, Hearst had actually been cheated out of the office of mayor of New York by fraud at the polls, and this incident was included in *American.* In **Citizen Kane** it became, instead, a joke: when Kane loses the election for governor, the Kane papers automatically claim "FRAUD AT POLLS." This version is, of course, a quick way of dramatizing the spirit of yellow journalism, and it's useful and comic, but the tendency of this change, as of many others, was, whether deliberately or unconsciously, to make things easier for the audience by playing down material on how wealth and the power it buys can also buy the love of the voters. Hearst (the son of a senator whose money had got him into the Senate) did buy his way into public office; as a young man, he was twice elected to Congress, and he had tried to get the Democratic nomination for President just before he decided to run for mayor of New York. The movie flatters the audience by saying that Kane couldn't buy the people's love—that he "was never granted elective office by the voters of his country."

Actually, it wasn't the voters but crooked politicians who defeated Hearst. When the Tammany boss Charles F. Murphy refused to help Hearst get the Democratic nomination for mayor, he ran as an independent, campaigning against the corrupt Tammany "boodlers," and he printed a cartoon of Murphy in prison stripes. Kane gives Boss Jim Gettys this treatment. Murphy was so deeply wounded by the cartoon that he arranged for Hearst's ballots to be stolen, and, it is said, even managed to rig the recount. That reckless cartoon was the turning point in Hearst's political career. The movie gives Gettys a different revenge; namely, exposing Kane's "love nest"—which was something that also happened to Hearst, but on another occasion, long after he had abandoned his political ambitions, when his *Los Angeles Examiner* was attacking the *Los Angeles Times,* and the *Times* used his own tactics against him by bringing up his "double life" and his "love nest" with Marion Davies. The movie ultimately plays the same game. *Citizen Kane* becomes a movie about the private life of a public figure—the scandals and tidbits and splashy sensations that the Hearst press always preferred to issues. The assumption of the movie was much like that of the yellow press: that the mass audience wasn't interested in issues, that all it wanted was to get "behind the scenes" and find out the dirt.

## 22.

As the newspaper business and the political maneuvering were pared away, the personal material took on the weight and the shape of the solution to a mystery. Even so, if the movie had been directed in a more matter-of-fact, naturalistic style, Thompson's explanation that Rosebud was just a piece in a jigsaw puzzle would have seemed quite sensible. Instead, Welles' heavily theatrical style overemphasized the psychological explanation to such a point that when we finally glimpse the name on the sled we in the audience are made to feel that we're in on a big secret—a revelation that the world missed out on. However, Rosebud is so cleverly worked into the structure that, like the entrance that Hecht and MacArthur prepared for Walter Burns, it is enjoyable as beautiful tomfoolery even while we are conscious of it as "commercial" mechanics. I think what makes Welles' directorial style so satisfying in this movie is that we are constantly aware of the mechanics—that the pleasure *Kane* gives doesn't come from illusion but comes from our enjoyment of the dexterity of the illusionists and the working of the machinery. *Kane,* too, is a clock that laughs. *Citizen Kane* is a film made by a very young

man of enormous spirit; he took the Mankiewicz material and he played with it, he turned it into a magic show. It is Welles' distinctive quality as a movie director—I think it is his genius—that he never hides his cleverness, that he makes it possible for us not only to enjoy what he does but to share his enjoyment in doing it. Welles' showmanship is right there on the surface, just as it was when, as a stage director, he set *Julius Caesar* among the Nazis, and set *Macbeth* in Haiti with a black cast and, during the banquet scene, blasted the audience with a recording of the "Blue Danube Waltz"— an effect that Kubrick was to echo (perhaps unknowingly?) in *2001.* There is something childlike—and great, too—about his pleasure in the magic of theatre and movies. No other director in the history of movies has been so open in his delight, so eager to share with us the game of pretending, and Welles' silly pretense of having done everything himself is just another part of the game.

Welles' magic as a director (at this time) was that he could put his finger right on the dramatic fun of each scene. Mankiewicz had built the scenes to end at ironic, dramatic high points, and Welles probably had a more innocently brazen sense of melodramatic timing than any other movie director. Welles also had a special magic beyond this: he could give *élan* to scenes that were confused in intention, so that the movie seems to go from dramatic highlight to highlight without lagging in between. There doesn't appear to be any waste material in *Kane,* because he charges right through the weak spots as if they were bright, and he almost convinces you (or *does* convince you) that they're shining jewels. Perhaps these different kinds of magic can be suggested by two examples. There's the famous sequence in which Kane's first marriage is summarized by a series of breakfasts, with overlapping dialogue. The method was not new, and it's used here on a standard marriage joke, but the joke is a basic good joke, and the method is honestly used to sum up as speedily as possible the banality of what goes wrong with the marriage. This sequence is adroit, and Welles brings out the fun in the material, but there's no *special* Wellesian magic in it— except, perhaps, in his own acting. But in the cutting from the sequence of Kane's first meeting with Susan (where the writing supplies almost no clue to why he's drawn to this particular twerp of a girl beyond his finding her relaxing) to the political rally, Welles' special talent comes into play. Welles directs the individual scenes with such flourish and such *enjoyment of flourish* that the audience reacts as if the leap into the rally were clever and funny and logical, too, although the connection between the scenes isn't established until later, when Boss Jim Gettys uses Susan to wreck Kane's political career. As a director, Welles is so ebullient that we go along with the way he wants us to feel; we're happy to let him "put it over on us." Given the subject of Hearst and the witty script, the effect is of complicity, of a shared knowingness between Welles and the audience about what the movie is about. Kane's big smile at the rally seals the pact between him and us. Until

Kane's later years, Welles, in the role, has an almost total empathy with the audience. It's the same kind of empathy we're likely to feel for smart kids who grin at us when they're showing off in the school play. It's a beautiful kind of emotional nakedness—ingenuously exposing the sheer love of playacting—that most actors lose long before they become "professional." If an older actor—even a very good one—had played the role, faking youth for the young Kane the way Edward Arnold, say, sometimes faked it, I think the picture might have been routine. Some people used to say that Welles might be a great director but he was a bad actor, and his performances wrecked his pictures. I think just the opposite—that his directing style is such an emanation of his adolescent love of theatre that his films lack a vital unifying element when he's not in them or when he plays only a small part in them. He needs to be at the center. *The Magnificent Ambersons* is a work of feeling and imagination and of obvious effort—and the milieu is much closer to Welles' own background than the milieu of *Kane* is—but Welles isn't in it, and it's too bland. It feels empty, uninhabited. Without Orson Welles' physical presence—the pudgy, big prodigy, who incarnates egotism—*Citizen Kane* might (as Otis Ferguson suggested) have disintegrated into vignettes. We feel that he's making it all happen. Like the actor-managers of the old theatre, he's the man onstage running the show, pulling it all together.

23.

Mankiewicz's script, though nominally an "original"—and in the best sense original—was in large part an adaptation of the material (much of it published) of Hearst's life. Hearst's life was so full of knavery and perversity that Mankiewicz simply sorted out the plums. Mankiewicz had been a reporter on the *New York World,* the Pulitzer paper, where Hearst himself had worked for a time before he persuaded his father to give him the *San Francisco Examiner.* When Hearst got the *Examiner,* he changed it in imitation of the *World,* and then expanded to New York, where he bought a paper and started raiding and decimating the *World*'s staff. One of his favorite tactics was to hire away men he didn't actually want at double or treble what Pulitzer was paying them, then fire them, leaving them stranded (a tactic memorialized in *The Front Page* when Walter Burns hires and fires the poetic reporter Bensinger). Kane's business practices are so closely patterned on Hearst's that in reading about Hearst one seems to be reading the script. Descriptions—like the one in the *Atlantic Monthly* in 1931—of how Hearst cynically bought away the whole of Pulitzer's Sunday staff might be descriptions of Kane's maneuver. In 1935, *Fortune* described Hearst's warehouse in the Bronx in terms that might have been the specifications for the warehouse in the film, and by 1938 even the *Reader's Digest* was reprinting, from the *Saturday Evening Post,* a description of Hearst's empire in phrases that might be part of the script:

All his life Mr. Hearst bought, bought, bought—whatever touched his fancy. He purchased newspapers, Egyptian mummies, a California mountain range, herds of Tibetan yaks. He picked up a Spanish abbey, had it knocked down, crated, shipped to New York, and never has seen it since.

To his shares in the Homestake, largest gold producer in the United States, his Peruvian copper mines, his 900,000 acre Mexican cattle ranch, and his other inherited properties, he added 28 daily newspapers, 14 magazines here and in England, eight radio stations, wire services, a Hollywood producing unit, a newsreel, a castle in Wales, and one of the world's largest collections of objects d'art, gathered at a toll of $40,000,000.

Kane's dialogue is often almost Hearst verbatim; in the margin of the script that Mankiewicz lent to Charles Lederer one of Hearst's lawyers annotated Kane's speech beginning, "Young man, there'll be no war. I have talked with the responsible leaders," with the words "This happens to be the gist of an authentic interview with WRH—occasion, his last trip from Europe." Some of the dialogue was legendary long before the movie was made. When Hearst was spending a fortune in his circulation war with Pulitzer, someone told his mother that Willie was losing money at the rate of a million dollars a year, and she equably replied, "Is he? Then he will only last about thirty years." This is no more than slightly transposed in the film, though it's really milked:

THATCHER

Tell me, honestly, my boy, don't you think it's rather unwise to continue this philanthropic enterprise . . . this "Inquirer" that is costing you a million dollars a year?

KANE

You're right, Mr. Thatcher. I did lose a million dollars last year. I expect to lose a million dollars this year. I expect to lose a million dollars next year. You know, Mr. Thatcher, at the rate of a million dollars a year . . . I'll have to close this place in sixty years.

(To audiences in 1941, Thatcher, appearing at the congressional-committee hearing, was obviously J. P. Morgan the younger, and the Thatcher Library was, of course, the Pierpont Morgan Library.)

Mankiewicz could hardly improve on the most famous of all Hearst stories, so he merely touched it up a trifle. According to many accounts, Hearst, trying to foment war with Spain, had sent Richard Harding Davis to Havana to write about the Spanish atrocities and Frederic Remington to sketch them. Remington grew restless there and sent Hearst a telegram:

EVERYTHING IS QUIET. THERE IS NO TROUBLE HERE. THERE WILL BE NO WAR. I WISH TO RETURN.—REMINGTON.

Hearst replied,

> PLEASE REMAIN. YOU FURNISH THE
> PICTURES AND I'LL FURNISH THE WAR.—
> W. R. HEARST.

In the movie, Bernstein reads Kane a telegram from a reporter named Wheeler:

> GIRLS DELIGHTFUL IN CUBA, STOP. COULD
> SEND YOU PROSE POEMS ABOUT SCENERY
> BUT DON'T FEEL RIGHT SPENDING YOUR
> MONEY, STOP. THERE IS NO WAR IN CUBA.
> SIGNED WHEELER.

And Bernstein asks, "Any answer?"

Kane replies:

> DEAR WHEELER, YOU PROVIDE THE PROSE
> POEMS, I'LL PROVIDE THE WAR.

These stories were so well known at the time of the movie's release that in the picture spread on the movie in *Life* (with captions in the very style that Mankiewicz had parodied in his "News on the March") the magazine—unconsciously, no doubt—returned to the Hearst original, and flubbed even that:

> Kane buys a newspaper in New York and sets
> out to be a great social reformer. But even at
> 25 he is unscrupulous and wangles the U.S. into
> war by fake news dispatches. To a cartoonist in
> Cuba he wires: "You get the pictures and I'll
> make the war."

One passage of dialogue that is bad because it sounds slanted to make an ideological point is almost a straight steal (and that's probably why Mankiewicz didn't realize how fraudulent it would sound), and was especially familiar because John Dos Passos had quoted it in *U.S.A.,* in his section on Hearst, "Poor Little Rich Boy." (That title might be the theme of the movie.) Dos Passos quotes Hearst's answer to fellow-millionaires who thought he was a traitor to his class:

> You know I believe in property, and you know where
> I stand on personal fortunes, but isn't it better that
> I should represent in this country the dissatisfied
> than have somebody else do it who might not have
> the same real property relations that I may have?

Hearst apparently did say it, but even though it's made more conversational in the movie, it's unconvincing—it sounds like left-wing paranoia.

### KANE

I'll let you in on another little secret, Mr. Thatcher. I think I'm the man to do it. You see, I have money and property. If I don't look after the interests of the under-privileged maybe somebody else will . . . maybe somebody without any money or property.

Despite the fake childhood events, Kane's life story follows Hearst's much more closely than most movie biographies follow acknowledged and named subjects. Kane is burned in effigy, as Hearst was, and there is even a reference to Kane's expulsion from Harvard; one of the best-known stories in America was how young Willie Hearst had been expelled from Harvard after sending each of his instructors a chamber pot with the recipient's name handsomely lettered on the inside bottom. Even many of the subsidiary characters are replicas of Hearst's associates. For example, Bernstein (given the name of Welles' old guardian) is obviously Solomon S. Carvalho, the business manager of Pulitzer's *World,* whom Hearst hired away, and who became the watchdog of the *Journal's* exchequer and Hearst's devoted business manager. There was no special significance in the use of Mankiewicz's secretary's last name for Susan Alexander, or in naming Jed Leland for Leland Hayward (Mankiewicz's agent, whose wife, Margaret Sullavan, spent a weekend visiting at Victorville), just as there was no significance in the fact that the actor Whitford Kane had been part of the nucleus of the Mercury Theatre, but the use of the name Bernstein for Kane's devoted, uncritical friend had some significance in relation not only to Welles but to Hearst, and it was Mankiewicz's way of giving Hearst points (he did it in the breakfast scene when Emily is snobbish about Bernstein) because, whatever else Hearst was, he was not a snob or an anti-Semite. (For one thing, Marion's brother-in-law—Charles Lederer's father—was Jewish.) No doubt Mankiewicz also meant to give Kane points when he had him finish Jed's negative review of Susan's singing in the same negative spirit—which was more than George S. Kaufman had done for Mankiewicz's review back at the *New York Times.* This episode is perversely entertaining but not convincing. *Kane* used so much of Hearst's already legendary life that for liberals it was like a new kind of folk art; we knew all this about Hearst from books and magazines but gasped when we saw it on the big movie screen, and so defiantly—almost contemptuously—undisguised.

The departure from Hearst's life represented by Susan Alexander's opera career, which is a composite of the loves and scandals of several Chicago tycoons, didn't weaken the attack on Hearst—it strengthened it. Attaching the other scandals to him made him seem the epitome of the powerful and spoiled, and thus stand for them all. Opera—which used to be called "grand opera"—was a ritual target of American comedy. It was an easier target for the public to respond to than Hearst's own folly—motion pictures—because the public already connected opera with wealth and temperament, tycoons in opera hats and women in jewels, imported prima donnas, and all the affectations of "culture." It was a world the movie public didn't share, and it was already absurd in American movies—the way valets and effete English butlers and the high-toned Americans putting on airs who kept them were absurd. George S. Kaufman and Morrie Ryskind had worked opera over in two of the Marx Brothers pictures; Mankiewicz had been taken off *A Night at the Opera,* but what he and Welles—with the assistance of Bernard Herrmann—did to opera in *Citizen Kane* was in almost exactly the same style, and as funny.

Mankiewicz was working overseas for the *Chicago Tribune* when Harold McCormick and his wife, Edith Rockefeller McCormick, were divorced, in 1921. The McCormicks had been the leading patrons of opera in Chicago; they had made up the Chicago Opera Company's deficits, which were awe-inspiring during the time the company was under the management of Mary Garden (she chose to be called the "directa"), rising to a million dollars one great, lavish season. After the divorce, McCormick married Ganna Walska, the preëminent temperamental mediocre soprano of her day. Mankiewicz combined this scandal with a far more widely publicized event that occurred a few years later, replacing Hearst and Cosmopolitan Pictures with Samuel Insull and his building of the Chicago Civic Opera House. Insull didn't build the opera house for his wife (dainty little Gladys Wallis didn't sing), but there was a story to it, and it was the biggest opera story of the decade. After the McCormick-Rockefeller divorce, their joint largesse to opera ended, and the deficits were a big problem. Insull, "the Czar of Commonwealth Edison," who also loved opera (and dallied with divas), wanted to put it on a self-supporting business basis. He concluded that if an opera house should be built in a skyscraper, the rental of the upper regions would eventually cover the opera's deficits. The building was started in 1928; it had forty-five stories, with the opera company occupying the first six, and with Insull's office-lair on top. The structure was known as "Insull's throne," and it cost twenty million dollars. The opening of the new opera house was scheduled for November 4, 1929; six days before, on October 29th, the stock market crashed. The opening took place during the panic, with plainclothesmen and eight detective-bureau squads guarding the bejewelled patrons against robbers, rioters, and the mobsters who more or less ran the city. (The former Mrs. McCormick attended, wearing, according to one newspaper report, "her gorgeous diamond necklace, almost an inch wide and reaching practically to her waist"; Mrs. Insull wore pearls and "a wide diamond bracelet.") Mankiewicz must have placed the episode of the opera house in Chicago in order to give it roots—to make it connect with what the public already knew about Chicago and robber barons and opera. (Chicago was big on opera; it was there that the infant Orson Welles played Madame Butterfly's love child.) Insull's opera house never really had a chance to prove or disprove his financial theories. Mary Garden quit after one year there, calling it "that long black hole," and in 1932, when Insull's mammoth interlocking directorate of power plants collapsed and he fled to Greece, the opera house was closed. Insull was extradited, and in the mid-thirties he stood trial for fraud and embezzlement; he died two years before *Citizen Kane* was written.

The fretful banality of Susan Alexander is clearly derived from Mankiewicz's hated old adversary Mrs.

Insull—notorious for her "discordant twitter" and her petty dissatisfaction with everything. The Insulls had been called the least popular couple who had ever lived in Chicago, and there was ample evidence that they hadn't even liked each other. Opera and the Insulls provided cover for Mankiewicz and Welles. George J. Schaefer, who is quite open about this, says that when he couldn't get an opening for *Kane,* because the theatres were frightened off by the stories in the Hearst press about injunctions and lawsuits, he went to see Hearst's lawyers in Los Angeles and took the position that Kane could be Insull. No one was expected to be fooled; it was simply a legal maneuver.

There was also an actual (and malicious) scrap of Hearst's past in the opera idea in the first draft. As Mankiewicz planned it, Susan was to make her début in Massenet's *Thaïs.* As a very young man, Hearst had been briefly engaged to the San Francisco singer Sybil Sanderson. In order to break the engagement, Miss Sanderson's parents had sent her to study in Paris, where she became well known in opera and as the "constant companion" of Massenet, who wrote *Thaïs* for her. But to use *Thaïs* would have cost a fee, so Bernard Herrmann wrote choice excerpts of a fake French-Oriental opera—*Salammbô.* (Dorothy Comingore did her own singing in the movie except for the opera-house sequence; that was dubbed by a professional singer who deliberately sang badly.) The Kane amalgam may also contain a dab or two from the lives of other magnates, such as Frank Munsey and Pulitzer, and more than a dab from the life of Jules Brulatour, who got his start in business by selling Eastman Kodak film. Hope Hampton, his blond protégée and later his wife, had a career even more ridiculous than Susan Alexander's. After she failed as a movie actress, Brulatour financed her career at the Chicago Opera Company at the end of the twenties, and then, using his power to extend credit to movie companies for film stock, he pushed the near-bankrupt Universal to star her in a 1937 disaster, in which she sang eight songs.

The only other major addition to Hearst's actual history comes near the beginning of the movie. The latter days of Susan Alexander as a tawdry-looking drunken singer at El Rancho in Atlantic City, where she is billed as "Susan Alexander Kane"—which tells us at once that she is so poor an entertainer that she must resort to this cheap attempt to exploit her connection with Kane—may have been lifted from the frayed end of Evelyn Nesbit's life. After her divorce from Harry K. Thaw—the rich socialite who murdered Stanford White on her account—she drifted down to appearing in honky-tonks, and was periodically denounced in the press for "capitalizing her shame."

24.

Dorothy Comingore says, "When I read for Orson, Herman was in the room, with a broken leg and a crutch, and Orson turned to him and said, 'What do you think? And Herman said, 'Yes, she looks precisely like the image of a kitten we've been looking for.'"

The handling of Susan Alexander is a classic of duplicity. By diversifying the material and combining several careers, Mankiewicz could protect himself. He could claim that Susan wasn't meant to be Marion Davies—that she was nothing at all like Marion, whom he called a darling and a minx. He could point out that Marion wasn't a singer and that Hearst had never built an opera house for her—and it was true, she wasn't and he hadn't, but she was an actress and he did run Cosmopolitan Pictures for her. Right at the beginning of the movie, Kane was said to be the greatest newspaper tycoon of this or any other generation, so he was obviously Hearst; Xanadu was transparently San Simeon; and Susan's fake stardom and the role she played in Kane's life spelled Marion Davies to practically everybody in the Western world. And even though Mankiewicz *liked* Marion Davies, he was the same Mankiewicz who couldn't resist the disastrous "Imagine—the whole world wired to Harry Cohn's ass!" He skewered her with certain identifying details that were just too good to resist, such as her love of jigsaw puzzles. They were a feature of San Simeon; the puzzles, which sometimes took two weeks to complete, were set out on tables in the salon, and the guests would work at them before lunch. And when Kane destroys Susan's room in a rage after she leaves him, he turns up a hidden bottle of booze, which was a vicious touch, coming from Mankiewicz, who had often been the beneficiary of Marion's secret cache. He provided bits that had a special *frisson* for those in the know.

One can sometimes hurt one's enemies, but that's nothing compared to what one can do to one's friends. Marion Davies, living in the style of the royal courtesans with a man who couldn't marry her without messes and scandal (his wife, Millicent, had become a Catholic, and she had also given him five sons), was an easy target. Hearst and Louella Parsons had set her up for it, and she became the victim of **Citizen Kane.** In her best roles, Marion Davies was a spunky, funny, beautiful girl, and that's apparently what she *was* and why Hearst adored her. But, in his adoration, he insisted that the Hearst press overpublicize her and overpraise her constantly, and the public in general got wise. A typical Davies film would open with the theatre ventilating system pouring attar of roses at the audience, or the theatre would be specially redecorated, sometimes featuring posters that famous popular artists had done of her in the costumes of the picture. Charity functions of which she was the queen would be splashed all over the society pages, and the movie would be reviewed under eight-column headlines. In the news section, Mayor Hylan of New York would be saying, "When Knighthood Was in Flower is unquestionably the greatest picture I have ever seen. . . . No person can afford to miss this great screen masterpiece," or "Little Old New York is unquestionably the greatest screen epic I have ever looked upon, and Marion Davies is the most versatile screen star ever cast in any part. The wide range of her stellar acting is something to marvel at. . . . Every man, woman and child in New York City ought to see this splendid picture. . . . I must pay my tribute to the geniuses in all lines who created such a masterpiece."

When the toadying and praise were already sickening, Hearst fell for one of the dumbest smart con tricks of all time: A young movie reviewer named Louella O. Parsons, working for the *New York Telegraph* for $110 a week, wrote a column saying that although Marion Davies' movies were properly publicized, the star herself wasn't publicized *enough.* Hearst fell for it and hired Parsons at $250 a week, and she began her profitable lifework of praising (and destroying) Marion Davies. Some of Davies' costume spectacles weren't bad—and she was generally charming in them—but the pictures didn't have to be bad for all the corrupt drumbeaters to turn the public's stomach. Other actresses were pushed to stardom and were accepted. (The flapper heroine Colleen Moore was Walter Howey's niece, and she was started on her career when she was fifteen. D. W. Griffith owed Howey a favor for getting *The Birth of a Nation* and *Intolerance* past the Chicago censors, and her movie contract was the payoff. She says that many of the Griffith stars were "payoffs.") Marion Davies had more talent than most of the reigning queens, but Hearst and Louella were too ostentatious, and they never let up. There was a steady march of headlines ("Marion Davies' Greatest Film Opens Tonight"); there were too many charity balls. The public can swallow just so much: her seventy-five-thousand-dollar fourteen-room mobile "bungalow" on the M-G-M lot, O.K.; the special carpet for alighting, no. Her pictures had to be forced on exhibitors, and Hearst spent so much on them that even when they did well, the cost frequently couldn't be recovered. One of his biographers reports a friend's saying to Hearst, "There's money in the movies," and Hearst's replying, "Yes. Mine."

Marion Davies was born in 1897, and, as a teen-ager, went right from the convent to the musical-comedy stage, where she put in two years as a dancer before Ziegfeld "glorified" her in the "Ziegfeld Follies of 1916." That was where William Randolph Hearst, already in his mid-fifties, spotted her. It is said, and may even be true, that he attended the "Follies" every night for eight weeks, buying two tickets—one for himself and the other for his hat—just "to gaze upon her." It is almost certainly true that from then "to the day of his death," as Adela Rogers St. Johns put it, "he wanted to know every minute where she was." Marion Davies entered movies in 1917, with *Runaway Romany,* which she also wrote, and then she began that really strange, unparalleled movie career. She had starred in about fifty pictures by the time she retired, in 1937—all under Hearst's aegis, and under his close personal supervision. (Leading men were afraid to kiss her; Hearst was always watching.) The pictures were all expensively produced, and most of them were financial failures. Marion Davies was a mimic and a parodist and a very original sort of comedienne, but though Hearst liked her to make him laugh at home, he wanted her to be a romantic maiden in the movies, and—what was irreconcilable with her talent—dignified. Like Susan, she was tutored, and he spent incredible sums on movies that would be the perfect setting for her. He appears to have been sincerely infatuated with her in old-fashioned, sentimental, lady-like roles; he loved to see her in ruffles on garden swings. But actresses didn't become public favorites in roles like those, and even if they could get by with them sometimes, they needed startling changes of pace to stay in public favor, and Hearst wouldn't let Marion Davies do anything "sordid."

To judge by what those who worked with her have said, she was thoroughly unpretentious, and was depressed by Hearst's taste in roles for her. She finally broke out of the costume cycle in the late twenties and did some funny pictures: *The Red Mill* (which Fatty Arbuckle, whom Hearst the moralizer had helped ruin, directed, under his new, satirical pseudonym, Will B. Goodrich), *The Fair Coed,* my childhood favorite *The Patsy,* and others. But even when she played in a slapstick parody of Gloria Swanson's career (*Show People,* in 1928), Hearst wouldn't let her do a custard-pie sequence, despite her own pleas and those of the director, King Vidor, and the writer, Laurence Stallings. (King Vidor has described the conference that Louis B. Mayer called so that Vidor could make his case to Hearst for the plot necessity of the pie. "Presently, the great man rose and in a high-pitched voice said, 'King's right. But I'm right, too—because I'm not going to let Marion be hit in the face with a pie.'") She wanted to play Sadie Thompson in *Rain,* but he wouldn't hear of it, and the role went to Gloria Swanson (and made her a star all over again). When Marion Davies should have been playing hard-boiled, good-hearted blondes, Hearst's idea of a role for her was Elizabeth Barrett Browning in *The Barretts of Wimpole Street,* and when Thalberg reserved that one for *his* lady, Norma Shearer, Hearst, in 1934, indignantly left M-G-Mand took his money and his "Cosmopolitan Pictures" label over to Warner Brothers. (The editors of his newspapers were instructed never again to mention Norma Shearer in print.) It was a long blighted career for an actress who might very well have become a big star on her own, and she finally recognized that with Hearst's help it was hopeless. By the time *Citizen Kane* came out, she had been in retirement for four years, but the sickening publicity had gone grinding on relentlessly, and, among the audiences at *Kane,* probably even those who remembered her as the charming, giddy comedienne of the late twenties no longer trusted their memories.

Mankiewicz, catering to the public, gave it the empty, stupid, no-talent blonde it wanted—the "confidential" backstairs view of the great gracious lady featured in the Hearst press. It was, though perhaps partly inadvertently, a much worse betrayal than if he'd made Susan more like Davies, because movie audiences assumed that Davies was a pathetic whiner like Susan Alexander, and Marion Davies was nailed to the cross of harmless stupidity and nothingness, which in high places is the worst joke of all.

25.

Right from the start of movies, it was a convention that the rich were vulgarly acquisitive but were lonely and miserable and incapable of giving or receiving love. As a mass medium, movies have always soothed and consoled the public with the theme that the rich can buy everything except what counts—love. (The convention remains, having absorbed the *Dolce Vita* variation that the rich use each other sexually because they are incapable of love.) It was consistent with this popular view of the emptiness of the lives of the rich to make Susan Alexander a cartoon character; the movie reduces Hearst's love affair to an infatuation for a silly, ordinary nothing of a girl, as if everything in his life were synthetic, his passion vacuous, and the object of it a cipher. What happened in Hearst's life was far more interesting: he took a beautiful, warm-hearted girl and made her the best-known kept woman in America and the butt of an infinity of dirty jokes, and he did it out of love and the blindness of love.

*Citizen Kane,* however, employs the simplification, so convenient to melodrama, that there is a unity between a man's private life and his public one. This simplification has enabled ambitious bad writers to make reputations as thinkers, and in the movies of the forties it was given a superficial plausibility by popular Freudianism. Hideous character defects traceable to childhood traumas explained just about anything the authors disapproved of. Mankiewicz certainly knew better, but as a screenwriter he dealt in ideas that had popular appeal. Hearst was a notorious anti-union, pro-Nazi Red-baiter, so Kane must have a miserable, deformed childhood. He must be *wrecked* in infancy. It was a movie convention going back to silents that when you did a bio or a thesis picture you started with the principal characters as children and showed them to be miniature versions of their later characters. This convention almost invariably pleased audiences, because it also demonstrated the magic of movies—the kids so extraordinarily resembled the adult actors they would turn into. And it wasn't just makeup—they really did, having been searched out for that resemblance. (This is *possible* in theatre, but it's rarely feasible.) That rather old-fashioned view of the predestination of character from childhood needed only a small injection of popular Freudianism to pass for new, and if you tucked in a trauma, you took care of the motivation for the later events. Since nothing very bad had happened to Hearst, Mankiewicz drew upon Little Orson Annie. He *orphaned* Kane, and used that to explain Hearst's career. (And, as Welles directed it, there's more real emotion and pain in the childhood separation sequence than in all the rest of the movie.)

Thus Kane was emotionally stunted. Offering personal emptiness as the explanation of Hearst's career really doesn't do much but feed the complacency of those liberals who are eager to believe that conservatives are "sick" (which is also how conservatives tend to see liberals). Liberals were willing to see this hollow-man explanation of Hearst as something much deeper than a cliché of popular melodrama, though the film's explaining his attempts to win public office and his empire-building and his art collecting by the childhood loss of maternal love is as unilluminating as the conservative conceit that Marx was a revolutionary because he hated his father. The point of the film becomes the cliché irony that although Hearst has everything materially, he has nothing humanly.

Quite by chance, I saw William Randolph Hearst once, when I was about nineteen. It was Father's Day, which sometimes falls on my birthday, and my escort bumped me into him on the dance floor. I can't remember whether it was at the Palace Hotel in San Francisco or at the St. Francis, and I can't remember the year, though it was probably 1938. But I remember Hearst in almost terrifying detail, with the kind of memory I generally have only for movies. He was dinner-dancing, just like us, except that his table was a large one. He was seated with Marion Davies and his sons with their wives or dates; obviously, it was a kind of family celebration. I had read the then current *Hearst, Lord of San Simeon* and Ferdinand Lundberg's *Imperial Hearst,* and probably almost everything else that was available about him, and I remember thinking, as I watched him, of Charles A. Beard's preface to the Lundberg book—that deliberately cruel premature "Farewell to William Randolph Hearst," with its tone of "He will depart loved by few and respected by none whose respect is worthy of respect. . . . None will be proud to do honor to his memory," and so on. You don't expect to bump into a man on the dance floor after you've been reading that sort of thing about him. It was like stumbling onto Caligula, and Hearst looked like a Roman emperor mixing with the commoners on a night out. He was a huge man—six feet four or five—and he was old and heavy, and he moved slowly about the dance floor with *her.* He seemed like some prehistoric monster gliding among the couples, quietly majestic, towering over everyone; he had little, odd eyes, like a whale's, and they looked pulled down, sinking into his cheeks. Maybe I had just never seen anybody so massive and dignified and old *dancing,* and maybe it was that plus who he was, but I've never seen anyone else who seemed to incarnate power and solemnity as he did; he was frightening and he was impressive, almost as if he were wearing ceremonial robes of office. When he danced with Marion Davies, he was indifferent to everything else. They looked isolated and entranced together; this slow, huge dinosaur clung to the frowzy-looking aging blonde in what seemed to be a ritual performance. Joined together, they were as alone as the young dancing couple in the sky with diamonds in *Yellow Submarine.* Maybe they *were* that couple a few decades later, for they had an extraordinary romance—one that lasted thirty-two years—and they certainly had the diamonds (or *had* had

them). He seemed unbelievably old to me that night, when he was probably about seventy-five; they were still together when he died, in 1951, at the age of eighty-eight.

The private pattern that was devised as a correlative (and possible explanation) of Hearst's public role was false. Hearst didn't have any (recorded) early traumas, Marion Davies did have talent, and they were an extraordinarily devoted pair; far from leaving him, when he faced bankruptcy she gave him her money and jewels and real estate, and even borrowed money to enable him to keep his newspapers. He was well loved, and *still* he was a dangerous demagogue. And, despite what Charles A. Beard said and what Dos Passos said, and despite the way Mankiewicz presented him in *Citizen Kane,* and all the rest, Hearst and his consort were hardly lonely, with all those writers around, and movie stars and directors, and Shaw, and Winston Churchill, and weekend parties with Marion Davies spiking teetotaller Calvin Coolidge's fruit punch (though only with liquor that came from fruit). Even Mrs. Luce came; the pictures of Hearst on the walls at Time-Life might show him as an octopus, but who could resist an invitation? Nor did Hearst lose his attraction or his friends after he lost his *big* money. After San Simeon was stripped of its silver treasures, which were sold at auction in the thirties, the regal-party weekends were finished, but he still entertained, if less lavishly, at his smaller houses. Dos Passos played the same game as *Citizen Kane* when he wrote of Hearst "amid the relaxing adulations of screenstars, admen, screenwriters, publicitymen, columnists, millionaire editors"—suggesting that Hearst was surrounded by third-raters and sycophantic hirelings. But the lists and the photographs of Hearst's guests tell another story. He had the one great, dazzling court of the first half of the twentieth century, and the statesmen and kings, the queens and duchesses at his table were as authentic as the writers and wits and great movie stars and directors. When one considers who even those screenwriters were, it's not surprising that Hearst wanted their company. Harold Ross must have wondered what drew his old friends there, for he came, too, escorted by Robert Benchley.

It is both a limitation and *in the nature of the appeal* of popular art that it constructs false, easy patterns. Like the blind-beggar-for-luck, *Kane* has a primitive appeal that is implicit in the conception. It tells the audience that fate or destiny or God or childhood trauma has already taken revenge on the wicked—that if the rich man had a good time he has suffered remorse, or, better still, that he hasn't really enjoyed himself at all. Before Mankiewicz began writing the script, he talked about what a great love story it would be—but who would buy tickets for a movie about a rich, powerful tycoon who also found true love? In popular art, riches and power destroy people, and so the secret of Kane is that he longs for the simple pleasures of his childhood before wealth tore him away from his mother—he longs for what is available to the mass audience.

26.

Even when Hearst's speeches, or facsimiles of them, were used in **Kane,** their character was transformed. If one looks at his actual remarks on property and then at Mankiewicz's adaptation of them, one can see how. Hearst's remarks are tight and slightly oblique, and it takes one an instant to realize what he's saying. Mankiewicz makes them easier to grasp (and rather florid) but kills some of their almost sinister double edge by making them consciously flip. He turns them into a joke. And when Mankiewicz didn't make the speeches flip, Welles' delivery did. When you hear Kane dictate the telegram to Cuba, you don't really think for a minute that it's *acted* on. And so the movie becomes a comic strip about Hearst, without much resonance, and certainly without much tragic resonance. Hearst, who compared himself to an elephant, *looked like* a great man. I don't think he actually was great in any sense, but he was *extraordinary,* and his power and wealth, plus his enormous size, made him a phenomenally commanding presence. Mankiewicz, like Dos Passos, may have believed that Hearst fell from greatness, or (as I suspect) Mankiewicz may have liked the facile dramatic possibilities of that approach. But he couldn't carry it out. He couldn't write the character as a tragic fallen hero, because he couldn't resist making him funny. Mankiewicz had been hacking out popular comedies and melodramas for too long to write drama; one does not *dictate* tragedy to a stenotypist. He automatically, because of his own temperament and his writing habits, turned out a bitchy satirical melodrama. Inside the three hundred and twenty-five pages of his long, ambitious first draft was the crowd-pleasing material waiting to be carved out. When one reads the long version, it's obvious what must go; if I had been doing the cutting I might have cut just about the same material. *And yet* that fat to be cut away is everything that tends to make it a political and historical drama, and what is left is the private scandals of a poor little rich boy. The scandals in the long draft—some of it, set in Italy during Kane's youth, startlingly like material that came to the screen twenty years later in *La Dolce Vita*—served a purpose beyond crowd pleasing: to show what a powerful man could cover up and get away with. Yet this, of course, went out, for reasons similar to the ones that kept Kane, unlike Hearst, from winning elected office—to reassure the public that the rich *don't* get away with it.

Welles now has a lumbering grace and a gliding, whale-like motion not unlike Hearst's, but when he played the role he became stiff and crusty as the older Kane, and something went blank in the aging process—not just because the makeup was erratic and waxy (especially in the baldheaded scenes, such as the one in the picnic tent) but because the character lost his connection with business and politics and became a fancy theatrical notion, an Expressionist puppet. Also, there are times when the magic of movies fails. The camera comes so close that it can reveal too much: Kane as an old man

was an actor trying to look old, and Welles had as yet only a schoolboy's perception of how age weighs one down. On a popular level, however, his limitations worked to his advantage; they tied in with the myth of the soulless rich.

The conceptions are basically *kitsch;* basically, **Kane** is popular melodrama—Freud plus scandal, a comic strip about Hearst. Yet, partly because of the resonance of what was left of the historical context, partly because of the juiciness of Welles' young talent and of the varied gifts and personalities others brought to the film, partly because of the daring of the attack on the most powerful and dangerous press lord known to that time, the picture has great richness and flair; it's *kitsch* redeemed. I would argue that this is what is remarkable about movies—that shallow conceptions in one area can be offset by elements playing against them or altering them or affecting the texture. If a movie is good, there is a general tendency to believe that everything in it was conceived and worked out according to a beautiful master plan, or that it is the result of the creative imagination of the director, but in movies things rarely happen that way—even more rarely than they do in opera or the theatre. There are so many variables; imagine how different the whole feeling of *Kane* would be if the film had been shot in a naturalistic style, or even if it had been made at M-G-M instead of at R.K.O. Extraordinary movies are the result of the "right" people's getting together on the "right" project at the "right" time—in their lives and in history. I don't mean to suggest that a good movie is just a mess that happens to work (although there have been such cases)—only that a good movie is not always the result of a single artistic intelligence. It can be the result of a fortunate collaboration, of cross-fertilizing accidents. And I would argue that what redeems movies in general, what makes them so much easier to take than other arts, is that many talents in interaction in a work can produce something more enjoyable than one talent that is not of the highest. Because of the collaborative nature of most movies, masterpieces are rare, and even masterpieces may, like **Kane,** be full of flaws, but the interaction frequently results in special pleasures and surprises.

27.

The director should be in control not because he is the sole creative intelligence but because only if he is in control can he liberate and utilize the talents of his coworkers, who languish (as directors do) in studio-factory productions. The best interpretation to put on it when a director says that a movie is totally his is not that he did it all himself but that he wasn't interfered with, that he made the choices and the ultimate decisions, that the whole thing isn't an unhappy compromise for which no one is responsible; not that he was the sole creator but almost the reverse—that he was free to use all the best ideas offered him.

Welles had a vitalizing, spellbinding talent; he was the man who brought out the best in others and knew how to use it. What keeps *Citizen Kane* alive is that Welles wasn't prevented (as so many directors are) from trying things out. He was young and *open,* and, as the members of that crew tell it—and they remember it very well, because it was the only time it ever happened for many of them—they could always talk to him and make suggestions, as long as they didn't make the suggestions publicly. Most big-studio movies were made in such a restrictive way that the crews were hostile and bored and the atmosphere was oppressive. The worst aspect of the factory system was that almost everyone worked beneath his capacity. Working on *Kane,* in an atmosphere of freedom, the designers and technicians came forth with ideas they'd been bottling up for years; they were all in on the creative process. Welles was so eager to try out new ideas that even the tough, hardened studio craftsmen were caught up by his spirit, just as his co-workers in the theatre and in radio had been. *Citizen Kane* is not a great work that suddenly burst out of a young prodigy's head. There are such works in the arts (though few, if any, in movies), but this is not one of them. It is a superb example of collaboration; everyone connected with it seems to have had the time of his life because he was able to contribute something.

Welles had just the right background for the sound era. He used sound not just as an inexpensive method of creating the illusion of halls and crowds but to create an American environment. He knew how to convey the way people feel about each other by the way they sound; he knew how they sounded in different rooms, in different situations. The directors who had been most imaginative in the use of sound in the early talkies were not Americans, and when they worked in America, as Ernst Lubitsch did, they didn't have the ear for American life that Welles had. And the good American movie directors in that period (men like Howard Hawks and John Ford and William Wellman) didn't have the background in theatre or—that key element—the background in radio. Hawks handled the dialogue expertly in *His Girl Friday,* but the other sounds are not much more imaginative than those in a first-rate stage production. When Welles came to Hollywood, at the age of twenty-four, his previous movie experience had not been on a professional level, but he already knew more about the dramatic possibilities of sound than most veteran directors, and the sound engineers responded to his inventiveness by giving him extraordinary new effects. At every point along the way, the studio craftsmen tried something out. Nearly all the thirty-five members of the R.K.O. special-effects department worked on *Kane;* roughly eighty per cent of the film was not merely printed but reprinted, in order to add trick effects and blend in painted sets and bits of stock footage. The view up from Susan singing on the opera stage to the stagehands high above on the catwalk, as one of them puts two fingers to his nose— which looks like a tilt (or vertical pan)—is actually made up of three shots, the middle one a miniature. When the camera seems to pass through a rooftop sky-light into the El Rancho night club where Susan works, the sign, the rooftop, and the skylight are miniatures, with a flash of lightning to conceal the cut to the full-

scale interior. The craftsmen were so ingenious about giving Welles the effects he wanted that even now audiences aren't aware of how cheaply made *Citizen Kane* was.

In the case of the cinematographer, Gregg Toland, the contribution goes far beyond suggestions and technical solutions. I think he not only provided much of the visual style of *Citizen Kane* but was responsible for affecting the conception, and even for introducing a few elements that are not in the script. It's always a little risky to assign credit for ideas in movies; somebody is bound to turn up a film that used whatever it is—a detail, a device, a technique—earlier. The most one can hope for, generally, is to catch on to a few late links in the chain. It was clear that *Kane* had visual links to James Wong Howe's cinematography in *Transatlantic* (Howe, coincidentally, had also shot *The Power and the Glory*), but I had always been puzzled by the fact that *Kane* seemed to draw not only on the Expressionist theatrical style of Welles' stage productions but on the German Expressionist and Gothic movies of the silent period. In *Kane,* as in the German silents, depth was used like stage depth, and attention was frequently moved from one figure to another within a fixed frame by essentially the same techniques as on the stage—by the actors' moving into light or by a shift of the light to other actors (rather than by the fluid camera of a Renoir, which follows the actors, or the fragmentation and quick cutting of the early Russians). There were frames in *Kane* that seemed so close to the exaggerations in German films like *Pandora's Box* and *The Last Laugh* and *Secrets of a Soul* that I wondered what Welles was talking about when he said he had prepared for *Kane* by running John Ford's *Stagecoach* forty times. Even allowing for the hyperbole of the forty times, why should Orson Welles have studied *Stagecoach* and come up with a film that looked more like *The Cabinet of Dr. Caligari?* I wondered if there might be a link between Gregg Toland and the German tradition, though most of Toland's other films didn't suggest much German influence. When I looked up his credits as a cameraman, the name *Mad Love* rang a bell; I closed my eyes and visualized it, and there was the Gothic atmosphere, and the huge, dark rooms with lighted figures, and Peter Lorre, bald, with a spoiled-baby face, looking astoundingly like a miniature Orson Welles.

*Mad Love,* made in Hollywood in 1935, was a dismal, static horror movie—an American version of a German film directed by the same man who had directed *The Cabinet of Dr. Caligari.* The American remake, remarkable only for its photography, was directed by Karl Freund, who had been head cinematographer at Ufa, in Germany. He had worked with such great directors as Fritz Lang and F. W. Murnau and G. W. Pabst, and, by his technical innovations, had helped create their styles; he had shot many of the German silent classics (*The Last Laugh, Variety, Metropolis, Tartuffe*). I recently looked at a print of *Mad Love,* and the resemblances to *Citizen Kane* are even greater than my memories of it suggested. Not only is the large room with the fireplace at Xanadu similar to Lorre's domain as a mad doctor, with similar lighting and similar placement of figures, but Kane's appearance and makeup in some sequences might be a facsimile of Lorre's. Lorre, who had come out of the German theatre and German films, played in a stylized manner that is visually imitated in **Kane.** And, amusingly, that screeching white cockatoo, which isn't in the script of **Kane** but appeared out of nowhere in the movie to provide an extra "touch," is a regular member of Lorre's household.

Gregg Toland was the "hottest" photographer in Hollywood at the time he called Welles and asked to work with him; in March he had won the Academy Award for *Wuthering Heights,* and his other recent credits included *The Grapes of Wrath* and the film in which he had experimented with deep focus, *The Long Voyage Home.* He brought along his own four-man camera crew, who had recently celebrated their fifteenth year of working together. This picture was made with love; the year before his death, in 1948, Toland said that he had wanted to work with Welles because he was miserable and felt like a whore when he was on run-of-the-mill assignments, and that "photographing **Citizen Kane** was the most exciting professional adventure of my career." I surmise that part of the adventure was his finding a way to use and develop what the great Karl Freund had taught him.

Like the German cinematographers in the silent period, Toland took a more active role than the usual Hollywood cinematographer. For some years, whenever it was possible, he had been supervising the set construction of his films, so that he could plan the lighting. He probably responded to Welles' penchant for tales of terror and his desire for a portentous, mythic look, and since Welles didn't have enough financing for full-scale sets and was more than willing to try the unconventional, Toland suggested many of the Expressionist solutions. When a director is new to films, he is, of course, extremely dependent on his cameraman, and he is particularly so if he is also the star of the film, and is thus in front of the camera. Toland was a disciplined man, and those who worked on the set say he was a steadying influence on Welles; it is generally agreed that the two planned and discussed every shot together. With Welles, Toland was free to make suggestions that went beyond lighting techniques. Seeing Welles' facial resemblance to the tiny Lorre—even to the bulging eyes and the dimpled, sad expression—Toland probably suggested the makeup and the doll-like, jerky use of the body for Kane in his rage and as a lonely old man, and, having enjoyed the flamboyant photographic effect of the cockatoo in *Mad Love,* suggested that, too. When Toland provided Welles with the silent-picture setups that had been moribund under Karl Freund's direction, Welles used them in a childlike spirit that made them playful and witty. There's nothing static or Germanic in Welles' *direction,* and he had such unifying energy that just a couple of years ago an eminent movie critic cited the cockatoo in **Citizen Kane** as "an unforced metaphor arising naturally out of the action."

It's the Gothic atmosphere, partly derived from Toland's work on *Mad Love,* that inflates **Citizen Kane** and puts it in a different tradition from the newspaper comedies and the big bios of the thirties. **Citizen Kane** is, in some ways, a freak of art. Toland, although he used deep focus again later, reverted to a more conventional look for the films following **Kane,** directed by men who rejected technique "for its own sake," but he had passed on Freund's techniques to Welles. The dark, Gothic horror style, with looming figures, and with vast interiors that suggested castles rather than houses, formed the basis for much of Welles' later visual style. It suited Welles; it was the visual equivalent of The Shadow's voice—a gigantic echo chamber. Welles, too big for ordinary roles, too overpowering for normal characters, is stylized by nature—is by nature an Expressionist actor.

### 28.

Two years after the release of **Citizen Kane,** when Herman Mankiewicz had become respectable—his career had taken a leap after **Kane,** and he had had several major credits later in 1941 and had just won another Academy nomination, for his work on **Pride of the Yankees**—he stumbled right into Hearst's waiting arms. He managed to have an accident that involved so many of the elements of his life that it sounds like a made-up surreal joke. Though some of his other calamities are lost in an alcoholic fog—people remember only the bandages and Mankiewicz's stories about how he got them, and maybe even he didn't always know the facts—this one is all too well documented.

Driving home after a few drinks at Romanoff's, he was only a block and a half from his house when he hit a tiny car right at the gates of the Marion Davies residence. And it wasn't just any little car he hit; it was one driven by Lee Gershwin—Ira Gershwin's wife, Lenore, a woman Mankiewicz had known for years. He had adapted the Gershwins' musical **Girl Crazy** to the screen in 1932, and he had known the Gershwins before that, in the twenties, in New York; they were part of the same group. It was a gruesomely comic accident: Hearst was living on the grounds of the Marion Davies estate at the time, in that bungalow that Marion had used at M-G-M and then at Warners, and he was conferring with the publisher of his *New York Journal-American* when he heard the crash. Hearst sent the publisher down to investigate, and as soon as the man reported who was involved, Hearst went into action. Lee Gershwin had had two passengers—her secretary, who wasn't hurt, and her laundress, whom she was taking home, and who just got a bump. Mrs. Gershwin herself wasn't badly hurt, though she had a head injury that required some stitches. It was a minor accident, but Mankiewicz was taken to the police station, and he apparently behaved noisily and badly there. When he got home, a few hours later, his wife, Sara, sobered him up, and, having ascertained that Lee Gershwin had been treated at the hospital and had already been discharged, she sent him over to the Gershwins' with a couple of dozen roses. Marc Connelly, who was at the Gershwins' that night, says that when Mankiewicz arrived the house was full of reporters, and Ira Gershwin was serving them drinks and trying to keep things affable. Mankiewicz went upstairs to see Lee, who was lying in bed with her head bandaged. Amiable madman that he was, he noticed a painting on the bedroom wall, and his first remark was that he had a picture by the same artist. He apparently didn't have any idea that he was in serious trouble.

Hearst's persistent vindictiveness was one of his least attractive traits. Mankiewicz was charged with a felony, and the minor accident became a major front-page story in the Hearst papers across the country for four successive days, with headlines more appropriate to a declaration of war. It became the excuse for another Hearst campaign against the orgies and dissolute lives of the movie colony, and Hearst dragged it on for months. By then, the Hearst press was on its way to becoming the crank press, and Hearst had so many enemies that Mankiewicz had many friends. When Mankiewicz appealed to the American Civil Liberties Union, there had already been stories in *Time, Newsweek, Variety,* and elsewhere pointing out that the persecution in the Hearst papers was a reprisal for his having written the script of *Citizen Kane.* Mankiewicz, however, had to stand trial on a felony charge. And although he got through the mess of the trial all right, the hounding by the Hearst papers took its toll, and his reputation was permanently damaged.

In a letter to Harold Ross after the trial, Mankiewicz asked to write a Profile of Hearst that Ross was considering. "Honestly," he wrote, "I know more about Hearst than any other man alive. (There are a couple of deaders before their time who knew more, I think.) I studied his career like a scholar before I wrote *Citizen Kane.*" And then, in a paragraph that suggests his admiration, despite everything, for both Hearst and Welles, he wrote, "Shortly after I had been dragged from the obscurity of the police blotter and—a middle-aged, flat-footed, stylish-stout scenario writer—been promoted by the International News Service into Cary Grant, who, with a tank, had just drunkenly ploughed into a baby carriage occupied by the Dionne quintuplets, the Duchess of Kent, Mrs. Franklin D. Roosevelt (the President's wife), and the favorite niece of the Pope, with retouched art combining the more unflattering features of Goering and Dillinger, I happened to be discussing Our Hero with Orson. With the fair-mindedness that I have always recognized as my outstanding trait, I said to Orson that, despite this and that, Mr. Hearst was, in many ways, a great man. He was, and is, said Orson, a horse's ass, no more nor less, who has been wrong, without exception, on everything he's ever touched. For instance, for fifty years, said Orson, Hearst did nothing but scream about the Yellow Peril, and then he gave up his seat and hopped off two months before Pearl Harbor."

29.

In 1947, Ferdinand Lundberg sued Orson Welles, Herman J. Mankiewicz, and R.K.O. Radio Pictures, Inc., for two hundred and fifty thousand dollars for copyright infringement, charging that *Citizen Kane* had plagiarized his book *Imperial Hearst.* On the face of it, the suit looked ridiculous. No doubt (as Houseman admits) Mankiewicz had drawn upon everything available about Hearst, in addition to his own knowledge, and no doubt the Lundberg book, which brought a great deal of Hearst material together and printed some things that had not been printed before, was especially useful, but John Dos Passos might have sued on similar grounds, since material that was in *U.S.A.* was also in the movie, and so might dozens of magazine writers. Hearst himself might have sued, on the basis that he hadn't been credited with the dialogue. The defense would obviously be that the material was in the public domain, and the suit looked like the usual nuisance-value suit that Hollywood is plagued by—especially since Lundberg offered to settle for a flat payment of $18,000. But R.K.O. had become one of Howard Hughes' toys in the late forties, and a crew of expensive lawyers was hired. When the suit came to trial, in 1950, Welles was out of the country; he had given his testimony earlier, in the form of a deposition taken before the American vice-consul at Casablanca, Morocco. This deposition is a curious document, full of pontification and evasion and some bluffing so outrageous that one wonders whether the legal stenographer was able to keep a straight face. *Citizen Kane* had already begun to take over and change the public image of Hearst; Hearst and Kane had become inseparable, as Welles and Kane were, but Welles possibly didn't really know in detail—or, more likely, simply didn't remember—how close the movie was to Hearst's life. He seemed more concerned with continuing the old pretense that the movie was not about Hearst than with refuting Lundberg's charge of plagiarism, and his attempts to explain specific incidents in the movie as if their relationship to Hearst were a mere coincidence are fairly funny. He stated that "I have done no research into the life of William Randolph Hearst at any time," and that "in writing the screenplay of *Citizen Kane* I drew entirely upon my own observations of life," and then was helpless to explain how there were so many episodes from Hearst's life in the movie. When he was cornered with specific details, such as the picture of Jim Gettys in prison clothes, he gave up and said, "The dialogue for the scene in question was written in its first and second draftings exclusively by my colleague Mr. Mankiewicz. I worked on the third draft." When he was read a long list of events in the film that parallel Hearst's life as it is recorded in *Imperial Hearst,* he tried to use the Insull cover story and came up with the surprising information that the film dealt "quite as fully with the world of grand opera as with the world of newspaper publishing."

Mankiewicz, in a preparatory statement, freely admitted that many of the incidents and details came from

Hearst's life but said that he knew them from personal acquaintance and from a lifetime of reading. He was called to testify at the trial, and John Houseman was called as a witness to Mankiewicz's labor on the script. Mankiewicz was indignant that anyone could suggest that a man of his knowledge would need to crib, and he paraded his credentials. It was pointed out that John Gunther had said Mankiewicz made better sense than all the politicians and diplomats put together, and that he was widely known to have a passionate interest in contemporary history, particularly as it related to power, and to have an enormous library. And, of course, he had known Hearst in the years of his full imperial glory, and his friends knew of his absorption in everything to do with Hearst. According to Houseman, he and Mankiewicz thought they were both brilliant in court; they treated the whole suit as an insult, and enjoyed themselves so much while testifying that they spent the time between appearances on the stand congratulating each other. Mankiewicz, in a final gesture of contempt for the charge, brought an inventory of his library and tossed it to the R.K.O. lawyers to demonstrate the width and depth of his culture. It was an inventory that Sara had prepared some years before, when (during a stretch of hard times) they had rented out their house on Tower Road; no one had bothered to look at the inventory—not even the R.K.O. attorneys before they put it into evidence. But Lundberg's lawyers did; they turned to "L," and there, neatly listed under "Lundberg," were three copies of *Imperial Hearst*. During Mankiewicz's long recuperation, his friends had sent him many books, and since his friends knew of his admiration for many sides of the man he called "the outstanding whirling pagoda of our times," he had been showered with copies of this particular book. The inventory apparently made quite an impression in court, and the tide turned. The jury had been cordial to Mankiewicz's explanation of how it was that he knew details that were in the Lundberg book and were unpublished elsewhere, but now the width and depth of his culture became suspect. After thirty days, the trial resulted in a hung jury, and rather than go through another trial, R.K.O. settled for $15,000—and also paid an estimated couple of hundred thousand dollars in lawyers' fees and court costs.

Mankiewicz went on writing scripts, but his work in the middle and late forties is not in the same spirit as *Kane*. It's rather embarrassing to look at his later credits, because they are yea-saying movies—decrepit "family pictures" like *The Enchanted Cottage*. The booze and the accidents finally added up, and he declined into the forties sentimental slop. He tried to rise above it. He wrote the script he had proposed earlier on Aimee Semple McPherson, and he started the one on Dillinger, but he had squandered his health as well as his talents. I have read the McPherson script; it is called *Woman of the Rock*, and it's a tired, persevering-to-the-end, burned-out script. He uses a bit of newspaper atmosphere, and Jed again, this time as a reporter, and relies on a flashback structure from Aimee's death to her childhood; there are "modern" touches—a semi-lesbian

lady who manages the evangelist, for instance—and the script comes to life whenever he introduces sophisticated characters, but he can't write simple people, and even the central character is out of his best range. The one device that is interesting is the heroine's love of bright scarves, starting in childhood with one her father gives her and ending with one that strangles her when it catches on a car wheel, but this is stolen from Isadora Duncan's death, and to give the death of one world-famous lady to another is depressingly poverty-stricken. Mankiewicz's character hadn't changed. He had written friends that he bore the scars of his mistake with Charlie Lederer, but just as he had lent the script of *Kane* to Lederer, Marion Davies' nephew, he proudly showed *Woman of the Rock* to Aimee Semple McPherson's daughter, Roberta Semple, and that ended the project. His behavior probably wasn't deliberately self-destructive as much as it was a form of innocence inside the worldly, cynical man—I visualize him as so *pleased* with what he was doing that he wanted to share his delight with others. I haven't read the unfinished Dillinger; the title, *As the Twig Is Bent*, tells too hoary much.

In his drama column in *The New Yorker* in 1925, Mankiewicz parodied those who thought the Marx Brothers had invented all their own material in *The Cocoanuts* and who failed to recognize George S. Kaufman's contribution. It has been Mankiewicz's fate to be totally ignored in the books on the Marx Brothers movies; though his name is large in the original ads, and though Groucho Marx and Harry Ruby and S. J. Perelman all confirm the fact that he functioned as the producer of *Monkey Business* and *Horse Feathers,* the last reference I can find to this in print is in *Who's Who in America* for 1953, the year of his death. Many of the thirties movies he wrote are popular on television and at college showings, but when they have been discussed in film books his name has never, to my knowledge, appeared. He is never mentioned in connection with *Duck Soup,* though Groucho confirms the fact that he worked on it. He is now all but ignored even in many accounts of *Citizen Kane*. By the fifties, his brother Joe—with *A Letter to Three Wives* and *All About Eve*—had become the famous wit in Hollywood, and there wasn't room for two Mankiewiczes in movie history; Herman became a parenthesis in the listings for Joe.

### 30.

Welles has offered his semi-defiant apologia for his own notoriously self-destructive conduct in the form of the old fable that he tells as Arkadin in *Confidential Report,* of 1955—an "original screenplay" that, from internal evidence, he may very well have written. A scorpion wants to get across a lake and asks a frog to carry him on his back. The frog obliges, but midway the scorpion stings him. As they both sink, the frog asks the scorpion why he did it, pointing out that now he, too, will die, and the scorpion answers, "I know, but I can't help it; it's my character." The fable is inserted conspicuously, as a personal statement, almost as if it were a confession, and it's a bad story for a man to use as a parable of his life, since it's a disclaimer of responsibility. It's as if Welles believed in predestination and were saying that he was helpless. Yet Welles' characterization of himself seems rather odd. Whom, after all, has he fatally stung? He was the catalyst for the only moments of triumph that most of his associates ever achieved.

Every time someone in the theatre or in movies breaks through and does something good, people expect the moon of him and hold it against him personally when he doesn't deliver it. That windy speech Kaufman and Hart gave their hero in *The Fabulous Invalid* indicates the enormous burden of people's hopes that Welles carried. He has a long history of disappointing people. In the *Saturday Evening Post* of January 20, 1940, Alva Johnston and Fred Smith wrote:

> Orson was an old war horse in the infant prodigy line by the time he was ten. He had already seen eight years' service as a child genius. . . . Some of the oldest acquaintances of Welles have been disappointed in his career. They see the twenty-four-year-old boy of today as a mere shadow of the two-year-old man they used to know.

A decade after *Citizen Kane,* the gibes were no longer so good-natured; the terms "wonder boy" and "boy genius" were thrown in Welles' face. When Welles was only thirty-six, the normally gracious Walter Kerr referred to him as "an international joke, and possibly the youngest living has-been." Welles had the special problems of fame without commercial success. Because of the moderate financial returns on *Kane,* he lost the freedom to control his own productions; after *Kane,* he never had complete control of a movie in America. And he lost the collaborative partnerships that he needed. For whatever reasons, neither Mankiewicz nor Houseman nor Toland ever worked on another Welles movie. He had been advertised as a one-man show; it was not altogether his own fault when he became one. He was alone, trying to be "Orson Welles," though "Orson Welles" had stood for the activities of a group. But he needed the family to hold him together on a project and to take over for him when his energies became scattered. With them, he was a prodigy of accomplishments; without them, he flew apart, became disorderly. Welles lost his magic touch, and as his films began to be diffuse he acquired the reputation of being an intellectual, difficult-to-understand artist. When he appears on television to recite from Shakespeare or the Bible, he is introduced as if he were the epitome of the high-brow; it's television's more polite way of cutting off his necktie.

The Mercury players had scored their separate successes in *Kane,* and they went on to conventional careers; they had hoped to revolutionize theatre and films, and they became part of the industry. Turn on the TV and there they are, dispersed, each in old movies or his new series or his reruns. Away from Welles and each other, they were neither revolutionaries nor great originals, and so

Welles became a scapegoat—the man who "let everyone down." He has lived all his life in a cloud of failure because he hasn't lived up to what was unrealistically expected of him. No one has ever been able to do what was expected of Welles—to create a new radical theatre and to make one movie masterpiece after another—but Welles' "figurehead" publicity had snowballed to the point where all his actual and considerable achievements looked puny compared to what his destiny was supposed to be. In a less confused world, his glory would be greater than his guilt.

**Michael Wood (essay date 1973)**

SOURCE: A review of *The Shooting Script,* in *The New York Review of Books,* Vol. 20, November 29, 1973, pp. 6-10.

[*In the following omnibus review of several books on film, including Pauline Kael's essay excerpted above and the published screenplay for* Citizen Kane, *Wood identifies the contradictory nature of Charles Foster Kane as the source of the film's greatness.*]

Broken empires, scattered dynasties. Hollywood always loved nostalgia, and *Gone With The Wind* was a better title than anyone knew. Early Egypt, ancient Rome, the gracious old American South cropped up so often and so appealingly in Hollywood movies because they were all *gone,* taken by Time's fell hand. The flashback in the Forties and Fifties was not really a narrative device at all but a compulsion, the instrument of a constant, eager plunging into the past. A slow, misty dissolve, and off we went into the day before yesterday, when things were different; into a time before all this (whatever *all this* might be in any given movie) happened to us.

It looks now as if there was plenty of prophecy there; premature symbolic mourning for the time when Hollywood itself would also be gone. Certainly Selznick, producer and only begetter of *Gone With The Wind,* came to think so. "Hollywood's like Egypt," he told Ben Hecht. "Full of crumbled pyramids. It'll never come back. It'll just keep on crumbling until finally the wind blows the last studio props across the sand." Hollywood, in spite of daily rumors of its death, is probably livelier than such an elegy implies; but a glance at a stack of recent books about American movies suggests that Selznick ought to have been right, even if he wasn't.

Here are books about the making of *Gone With The Wind* itself (1939); about the making of *Citizen Kane* (1940); a book to celebrate the thirtieth anniversary of *Casablanca* (1943); an assortment of Mankiewicz's recollections about the making of *All About Eve* (1950); a collection of interviews with people involved in the making of *An American in Paris* (1951). The *Kane, Casablanca,* and *All About Eve* books have screenplays of those movies for good measure. Every now and again an editor or a writer in one of these texts will murmur something about scholarship and history and the study of film, but the heart isn't in it. Good old soupy nostalgia is what these books are about, and of them all only Arlene Croce's brilliant essay on Fred Astaire and Ginger Rogers is entirely free from it; and that is only because nostalgia is the wrong word for the confused, haunted longings that Fred and Ginger provoke in us. Fred and Ginger were too crisp and casual and stylish for us to be simply nostalgic about them, so we have to shift our nostalgia to the brittle dancing world they seemed to inhabit.

*Citizen Kane,* of course, remains an unsafe, unsure, unsettling movie, and Pauline Kael escapes nostalgia at least some of the time because she is serious and intelligent about the film. The other four books, though, are really serious and intelligent only about the pastness of the past, or rather about nostalgia's curious paradox: here we are, talking about films gone by, *because* they are gone; but they are *not* gone, since here we are, talking about them. We meet to celebrate the miracle: *Gone With The Wind* has not gone with the wind.

Reality, Gavin Lambert tells us elegantly but obscurely, has conferred a lasting relevance on *Gone With The Wind.* He speaks of popular art, of legend and archetype, of "situations deeply woven into the fabric of American life." "It becomes," he says, "like watching mythology performed in public." Pauline Kael talks about *Citizen Kane* as a popular work ("not in terms of actual popularity but in terms of its conceptions and the way it gets its laughs and makes its points") and also throws in a remark or two about archetype and legend. All these comments point in the right direction, but they don't do much more than point. Even Pauline Kael's wonderful phrase for *Citizen Kane*—"it isn't a work of special depth or a work of subtle beauty. It is a shallow work, a *shallow* masterpiece"—doesn't take us as far as it seems to. She tells us all about the movie's attractive, sloppy, slightly cheap shallowness, but leaves us just as much in the dark as ever about why it *is* a masterpiece.

Popular art of any kind is a genuine puzzle, since our critical vocabularies were not made for it. Even if we don't take to the *auteur* theory of cinema, we do like the idea of an intention behind a work; yet legends and archetypes can hardly be entirely the fruit of any kind of intention, still less of an *artistic* intention. There is too much accident in such matters, and popular art is not the expression of an individual talent but a reading of the mind of its audience. Characteristic moments in popular movies, for example, provide not the shock of originality but the illuminating sense of life and style being given to something we half knew already. They have the flavor of old jokes told well. They are full-blown, as Gavin Lambert says of a sunset in *Gone With The Wind,* but not over-blown—although I think he is wrong about that sunset, it *is* overblown.

The point of popular art is not to defeat our expectations but to outdo them, to fulfill them overwhelmingly.

Think of Welles's abuse of long, raking camera angles; of Hitchcock's taste for naturally overproduced locations like Mount Rushmore; of the high crane shot of the Civil War dead and dying at the railroad station in *Gone With The Wind;* of the voices visiting Vivien Leigh at the end of that movie, urging her to go back to Tara. Think of the smart, weary wit of the dialogue in *Citizen Kane;* of Bogart in *Casablanca* telling Ingrid Bergman what he remembers of their last day in Paris ("I remember every detail. The Germans wore gray, you wore blue"); or of Bogart again, telling Claude Rains that he came to Casablanca for the waters ("Waters?" Rains says. "What waters? We're in the desert." Bogart: "I was misinformed").

And so on and on, through hundreds of famous, unforgettable shots, lines, set-ups, cuts, compositions. All too much; all distinctly hammed up; all fine where they are, in movies. They just *sound* overdone when you describe them. André Bazin once wrote that Chaplin was not sentimental, he just seemed sentimental to literary people because in a book he *would be* sentimental. This is not always true, since *Limelight* is mawkish by non-literary standards too. But it is true for *Modern Times,* which feels sentimental when you think about it but isn't when you see it. The same argument can be applied to many great moments in movies: they would be overdone in another medium. I don't mean to suggest, of course, that one can't overdo things in the movies, merely that different standards apply for telling how much is enough.

What all this means is that the most interesting of these books about the making of famous movies are also, ultimately, the most disappointing. Lucid and informative as they are, Gavin Lambert's *GWTW* and Pauline Kael's *Raising Kane* can't overcome the central fallacy of looking for the authors of legends, and Miss Kael is even reduced to throwing the whole thing into the lap of chance: "Extraordinary movies are the result of the 'right' people's getting together on the 'right' project at the 'right' time." Well, well. One can't quarrel with that. But once we have admitted our helplessness in this way, all we can look for from such studies is a kind of historical justice about credits for a film, a means of setting the record straight about who did what. A deserving cause, to be sure; and it is good to see Herman J. Mankiewicz (Joseph L.'s elder brother) win posthumous glory for his dazzling screenplay for *Citizen Kane;* interesting to learn how much Cameron Menzies, production designer on *Gone With The Wind,* was responsible for the lush, glossy appearance of the movie, and for the fact that it doesn't *look* as if it was shot by three different directors. But what about the movies themselves? When we know who made them, and how, what is it that has been made, and why do these expensively photographed hallucinations matter to us?

*The Magic Factory* and *All About Eve* stay fairly safely within the limits of studio gossip, or oral history, as it's called these days; although the first has some useful technical information about *An American in Paris,* and the second has some very good gags ("My films," Mankiewicz says, "seem to lose something in the original English," and he is very funny about a much admired Antonioni wall—"The plaster shop at Cinecittà turns out that particular wall, in that particular texture, by the mile"). Howard Koch's *Casablanca* is really just a screenplay squeezed between fatuous essays by Koch and others, and concerns not the making of the film but Koch's delight in the kids who keep on digging it. Still, *Casablanca* is Koch's immortality, and the man whose credit for the celebrated *War of the Worlds* radio broadcast was stolen from him by Orson Welles is understandably edgy about posterity's memory of him.

Arlene Croce is very much concerned with how the films of Fred Astaire and Ginger Rogers, from *Flying Down to Rio* (1933) to *The Barkleys of Broadway* (1949), were put together, but the finished films themselves remain firmly at the center of her interest, and she writes extraordinarily well about them. She describes an Astaire solo in *Roberta,* for example, as "full of stork-legged steps on toe, wheeling pirouettes, in which he seems to be winding one leg around the other, and those ratcheting tap clusters that fall like loose change from his pockets"; she writes a whole historical and sociological essay in a few mildly facetious sentences:

> In the class-conscious Thirties, it was possible to imagine characters who spent their lives in evening dress—to imagine them as faintly preposterous holdovers from the Twenties, slipping from their satin beds at twilight, dancing the night away and then stumbling, top-hatted and ermine-tangled, out of speakeasies at dawn. It was a dead image, a faded cartoon of the pre-Crash, pre-Roosevelt Prohibition era, but it was the only image of luxury that most people believed in, and *Top Hat* revived it as a corrected vision of elegance. . . . *Top Hat* is a Thirties' romance of the Twenties. . . .

Miss Croce underlines what I take to be the secret of Fred and Ginger's enduring success: their apparent ordinariness, their almost severe abstinence from emphasis. Astaire seems to sing like a person who can't sing; like the rest of us. Only he sings with such intelligence and restraint and precision that he has lasted longer, *as a singer,* than people like Nelson Eddy, who really had voices but now sound like parodies of themselves. The same goes for Ginger Rogers, especially as an actress. Her performances are so persistently offhand, low-keyed, that she becomes an island of calm surrounded by a frenzy of overacting from everyone except Fred. Yet she *is* acting, there is nothing wooden or insufficient about her style.

"They were the two most divinely *usual* people in the history of movies," Miss Croce writes—that *divinely* being one of her very rare false notes. Their dancing, she says, "had none of the excesses, nothing of the sweet tooth of its period." Precisely. Their style was so personal that it was clearly a work of art; but it was also

a style that played at not being a style at all, and thus became a continuing myth of ease and natural grace. Their dances, as Miss Croce says, were their love scenes, and they made no declarations other than those. They danced out a dream that was both tough and tender, they created a world in which talent and skill were all the eloquence you needed. As Miss Croce reminds us, when Fred falls for Ginger by looking at a flip-book of her dancing, he has not just fallen in love with a girl, he has fallen in love with a girl who dances like *that.*

By implication, then, Arlene Croce shows us how individual talents and public longings can meet up in a myth, and how movies can matter to us. But to get beyond implication, we need some kind of hypothesis about the relation between the movies and the public longings they incorporate, some sense of the social function of movie mythologies.

Pauline Kael gives us a clue when she writes that a star is created when a starring role provides "a realistic base for contradictory elements." Welles as Charles Foster Kane incarnates the contradictions spelled out by Herman Mankiewicz. But there is more than this. *Citizen Kane* is *about* contradiction itself, defining Kane as an American only to define an American as a creature of conflicting impulses, perpetually at liberty because no one knows what to make of him, ultimately ruined because he himself can't pull those opposing urges together.

"It's become a very clear picture," Mankiewicz wrote in a speech that didn't survive into the final film. "He was the most honest man who ever lived, with a streak of crookedness a yard wide. He was a liberal and a reactionary. He was a loving husband—and both his wives left him. He had a gift for friendship such as few men have—and he broke his oldest friend's heart like you'd throw away a cigarette you were through with. . . . " In the film Kane is described as a communist by some, as a fascist by others. A title card then tells us that Kane himself thinks he is only one thing: an American. Kane is accused of having his newspapers attack companies in which he himself holds large amounts of stock. He admits this, says Kane is a scoundrel who should be boycotted, and offers a thousand dollars in support of such a boycott. On the other hand, as the publisher of a newspaper, it is his duty, he says, to protect the people of the city from "money-mad pirates"— like Kane in his alternative avatar.

In one of the movie's most famous sequences, Kane comes across his old friend Leland asleep across his hostile notice of the opera début of Kane's protégée. Kane finishes the notice in accord with Leland's obvious intentions, then fires Leland for writing a bad notice. We can see this as a triumph for Kane's tolerance, or as merely an attempt to buy Leland off, to convince him, as Leland himself puts it, that he is an honest man. We have to recognize a certain amount of charm and generosity in the gesture in any case, since Welles plays it that way. But there is childishness beneath it all, a belief that truth and integrity will be upheld if you support both sides of everything, that radical contradictions can be lived with as long as you let both competing teams run free. If Kane ceased to inhabit these contradictions, he would cease, in the movie's terms, to be an American. Kane, the movie suggests, is not merely a man like the rest of us (Americans are not merely people like the rest of us), who often want to have our cake and eat it. Having his cake and eating it is a passion and a neurosis with Kane; it is his life.

The greatness of the movie, it seems to me, lies in its failure to focus this theme as well as it tries to, in its failure to present us with a coherent view of Kane. Kane, like his model Hearst, was too horrible to be admired and too attractive to be rejected, a genuine, full-scale, mythological American, a mass of self-love and self-hatred, of benevolence and barbarism. Kane is so baffling to us because we are baffled by our own attitudes toward him, and while the movie is orderly enough to let us see the man, it is also disorderly enough to be true to our bafflement, faithful to our puzzled, foiled understanding of his life. In the light of all this, of the film's splendid, disquieting lack of an angle on Kane, the neatness of the Rosebud ending, the finally discovered suggestion that all Kane really needed was motherly love, strikes me as a wonderfully sharp, savage joke on us all, Welles and Mankiewicz included, no doubt.

I should say at once that I don't think Americans are really any more caught up in contradictions than anyone else. But they do seem to like to see themselves that way, and *Citizen Kane* catches and inflames this liking. The larger point, though, is that we can read *Citizen Kane* as merely doing very plainly and very forcefully, almost schematically, what all movies that matter to us do in one form or another. What it does is dramatize contradictions which are scattered about in the national life, which bother us enough for us to want them acknowledged, but which really *are* irreducible contradictions, and therefore can be acknowledged only in play, only as shadows. This is more or less how Lévi-Strauss defines the function of myth in primitive societies: the reconciliation of the irreconcilable within a fictional narrative. The reconciliation takes place in fiction because it can't take place in reality.

One needs to add, for an advanced society, more adept at self-deception, that even a full acknowledgment that there *is* a contradiction can hardly take place in reality. We work out in movies (and in jokes and plays and novels and television shows and nightclub acts and elsewhere) threats which beckon to us from just off the edges of our consciousness, which haunt us without ever quite appearing in daylight. I would want to say too, going beyond Lévi-Strauss in this, or perhaps stepping back from his position, that it is not at all necessary for the narrative to reconcile its irreconcilable elements at the level of the story. It is enough that those elements should live together for the space of the tale, and

thereby prove that the contradiction, while possibly tragic and destructive, is not totally and terminally debilitating. Life goes on in the story, and the story, by sympathetic magic, may induce life to go on outside it.

A simple example. Westerns regularly set a homeless, wandering hero against a sheeplike community which needs his help: the lonely aristocrat confronts the huddled mob. The aristocrat gives the mob a lecture about how they should try to get along without heroes like himself and should gang up and get the bad guys, not just sit around waiting for Randolph Scott to ride in. The films are officially democratic, but secretly elitist, since we are all with the hero rather than with the cowardly townsfolk. Or rather we are on both sides, but more on one than on the other. We have spent two hours in the cinema thinking about democracy and the individual without even being aware that we were thinking at all, and one of the contradictions of our culture has been tired out and laid to rest, temporarily, by the exercise.

But if most films are myths in Lévi-Strauss's sense, not all myths are alike in their treatment of contradictions. *Citizen Kane* lays them bare, leaves them dangling, and thereby corresponds very closely to a definition Richard Chase once gave of American, as distinct from European, fiction. Fred Astaire, on the other hand, transcends all those paradoxes about his style seeming not to be a style in the same way that a good poet can always get a poem—out of not being able to write—he is thus an artist in a perfectly simple, old-fashioned, "European" sense. But there are films which neither transcend nor expose contradictions but exploit them sentimentally, turn untidy bewilderment into comforting, even inspiring disaster. What we ask of such films is not that they should take us out of our confused lives but that they should, obliquely, lend our confusion a bit of dignity and grandeur.

*Casablanca,* for example, beneath its topical allusions and its wry repartee, is a movie about the ambivalent charms of being alone. If you're alone you're not loved; if you're loved you're ensnared. The film allows Bogart to end up loved *and* alone, or at least discreetly partnered by Claude Rains instead of engulfed in the love of Ingrid Bergman. Yet he is letting her go for her sake, and for the sake of the free world. Like Kane, only far more successfully, he has his cake and eats it.

I must emphasize that this is not a *psychological* reading of *Casablanca,* a guess at why the Bogart character does what he does. I think he does what he does for heroic, sentimental, and entirely admirable reasons. But the *mythology* shows him, and us, winning on all fronts, and some of the topical remarks in the movie reinforce this reading in a curious way. "I stick my neck out for nobody," Bogart says more than once, bitterly. Claude Rains tells him that that is a "wise foreign policy," and later comments that Bogart is "completely neutral about everything." Sidney Greenstreet drives home the point by jokingly saying that isolationism is no longer a practical policy—he is referring to his own deals in

Casablanca, not to the war. The year is 1941 in the movie, 1943 in the cinema. The effect of all this is not to give political overtones to a romantic movie but to give political isolationism a strong romantic and personal flavor. We might listen to some of the echoes, political and otherwise, of a phrase of our own like "I don't want to get involved"—it is the private corollary to Jefferson's thesis about foreign entanglements. The myth in *Casablanca* concerns getting involved without getting involved.

The myth in *Gone With The Wind,* as Gavin Lambert suggests, concerns survival; or more precisely, the price of survival; or more precisely still, survival while paying something less than the full price for it. The film celebrates the victory of the ruthless, irrepressible lovers of life (Clark Gable, Vivien Leigh) over the genteel bearers of the old civilized values (Leslie Howard, Olivia de Havilland). But the cost of this victory is beautifully masked by an abundance of sympathy for the losers, embodiments of the Gallant South after all, and by the dramatic sufferings of the winners, who lose their child and each other. Clark Gable and Vivien Leigh thus win *and* lose in a way that satisfies every greedy moral instinct we have, because they engage and then placate an abiding American worry, a contradiction that appears again and again in American movies, although it is not often as grandly drawn as it is in *Gone With The Wind.* It is a worry about selfishness, which we try to think of as a vice but which we all know to be a major American virtue.

Would we then condone *anything* done in the name of self? Of course not, but we have a terrible time drawing the line. There are countless movies, starring Bogart or Robert Mitchum or William Holden or Alan Ladd, in which the hero's selfishness is felt to be unanswerably attractive. The movies deal with this, usually, by a twist in the plot which lets these egoists in for a spot of selfless, redeeming heroism—or by having them, as in *Gone With The Wind,* appear to expiate their selfishness by suffering a lot. Yet the attraction of their original position, of their defense of their prime duty to themselves, remains long after the rest of the movie has slipped from the mind. Selfishness in American movies is as baffling as Charles Foster Kane, and for much the same reasons. Indeed Kane's selfishness is part of his charm and part of the problem. But where *Citizen Kane* won't let us rest even when we feel sorry for Kane, *Gone With The Wind* asks us to settle back and savor the joys of doublethink, continuing primly to believe that selfishness doesn't pay, as we sit and watch the payments come rolling in.

"A country that no longer had any legends, the poet says, is doomed to die of cold. That is possible. But a people that had no myths would already be dead." Thus Georges Dumézil, the great comparative mythologist. A myth is the working out of contemporary preoccupations in a story. We live among myths, and to some extent by our myths. A legend is a myth which has faded, it is the working out of yesterday's worries, now seen to belong to yesterday, now taken up as a harmless fiction. It is the narrative form of nostalgia. So we look back at old movies, and nostalgia's paradox takes another turn. These films are gone; not gone; and they allow us to contemplate problems we used to have as if we still had them. They were good old problems, we fondly think. They were problems with familiar faces. They don't make them like that any more.

## Stephen Farber and Marc Green (essay date 1984)

SOURCE: "Family Plots: Writing and the Mankiewicz Clan," in *Film Comment,* Vol. 20, No. 4, July-August, 1984, pp. 68-77.

[*In the following excerpt, Farber and Green trace the history of the Mankiewicz family in the film industry.*]

> For people who have never learned to communicate to each other, it's curious that we love communication so much. Other families who are far more taciturn and less verbal succeed in communicating love and more basic emotions better than we ever did.
>
> —Christopher Mankiewicz

.  .  .  .  .

A fixture in Hollywood since the silent days, the Mankiewicz clan has been a family of wits and intellectuals in an industry overrun with dunces and boors. Herman Mankiewicz won a screenwriting Oscar for co-authoring *Citizen Kane.* His brother, Joseph, has the unprecedented distinction of winning four Academy Awards in the space of two years—for writing and directing *A Letter to Three Wives* and *All About Eve.* Joseph's son Tom contributed to *Superman* as well as to several of the stylish James Bond movies of the 1970s. Herman's son Don wrote a prize-winning novel, *Trial,* was nominated for an Academy Award for co-writing *I Want To Live!,* and created several long-running TV series. His brother Frank was Robert Kennedy's press secretary, campaign manager for George McGovern, a syndicated columnist, and head of National Public Radio. Their sister Johanna was a novelist and a writer for *Time* magazine until her accidental death in 1974, and Johanna's husband, Peter Davis, produced and directed *Hearts and Minds* and *The Selling of the Pentagon.* Frank's son Josh is an ABC correspondent, while Don's daughter Jane is a *New Yorker* writer and his son John is a young screenwriter. Even a distant cousin from the Canadian branch of the family, Francis Mankiewicz, won the Canadian equivalent of the Oscar for directing the film *Les Bons Debarras.*

Of course, other families of writers have worked in the movies—the Benchleys, the Kanins, the Goldmans. But the Mankiewiczes may be unique for the number of writers they have produced and for the sophistication of their best work. Another second-generation writer, Dore Schary's daughter, Jill Schary, succinctly defined the Mankiewiczes' special status: "The family was wonderful to know and impossible to compete with. . . . They did not have the money of the other major Hollywood families and the kind of power that such money brings, but they had the power that comes from quality and class and style."

The family patriarch, Franz Mankiewicz, immigrated to New York in 1892. A newspaper reporter and editor, Franz went back to school in his forties, eventually earned his Ph.D., and became a professor at New York's City College. He edited the *Modern Language Quarterly* and founded a luncheon round table for German-born intellectuals, including Albert Einstein. Through their father, the Mankiewicz children were exposed at an early age to academics, artists, scientists, and politicians. Professor Mankiewicz was a brilliant man but an unyielding, tyrannical father. He was especially hard on Herman, who was 12 years older than Joseph. Although Herman was an "A" student, nothing he ever did seemed to satisfy his father. If he scored 92 on a test, the Professor wanted to know about the eight points.

Herman and Joseph each entered Columbia at age 15 and graduated before the age of 20. In 1920, Herman went to work as a foreign correspondent in Berlin, then was hired as a publicist for Isadora Duncan. A few years later, he returned to New York, wrote theater reviews for the *New York Times* and *The New Yorker,* and co-authored two Broadway plays.

After graduating from Columbia, Joseph was sent off to Europe to attend the University of Berlin, with the understanding that he would return to Columbia to teach literature. "That was my father's idea, but not mine," Joseph says. "When I hit Berlin in 1928, I was dazzled by the theater." Although he vowed then and there to pursue a career in the arts, Joseph always felt a pang of guilt for having abandoned his father's profession. In one of his early triumphs, *A Letter to Three Wives,* Joseph made a hero of the learned, cynical schoolteacher, played by Kirk Douglas, who despises the hack writing that his wife (Ann Sothern) does for radio soap operas. A strict grammarian, Douglas chides Sothern in one scene for saying "those kind" instead of "this kind." Exasperated, she shoots back, "There are men who say 'those kind' who make $100,000 a year."

"There are men who say 'stick 'em up' who make a lot more," Douglas counters wryly. "I don't intend to do either."

That was Joseph's homage to his father.

. . . . .

If some East Coast intellectuals scorned the hedonism of Hollywood in the Twenties, Herman Mankiewicz surrendered to it instantly. Upon arriving in Los Angeles in 1926, he purchased a big Cadillac and promptly joined a country club. Herman lived high, drank heavily, gambled recklessly. A year after he came to Hollywood, Herman was named head of Paramount's scenario department, earning $1250 a week. A bon vivant, Herman was renowned for his scabrous wit—Ben Hecht called him the Central Park West Voltaire. One wisecrack has become legendary. During a dinner party at the home of Arthur Hornblow, Jr., a stickler for the niceties of etiquette, Herman imbibed a bit too much and threw up at the table. Though still green around the gills, Herman promptly reassured the host, "Don't worry, Arthur, the white wine came up with the fish."

Herman worked on dozens of movies at Paramount, including several of the early Marx Brothers classics—*Monkey Business, Horse Feathers,* and *Duck Soup.* Before long, Herman sent for his brother Joe, arranging a job for him as junior writer at Paramount. The atmosphere was definitely that of a boom town. When Joseph Mankiewicz looks back on those early days, a sense of wonder fills his voice. "As a young writer, I used to wander around the studio at night," he says. "That's when the sets were built. There was all this activity, lights blazing. It was fantastic. The commissary was open 24 hours a day. Every day at 5:00, the barber shop was locked, and only executives could use it. You went in if you were one of the privileged. Louis B. Mayer had a manicure every day, and had the blackheads squeezed out of his forehead. The ministering that went on at that barber shop!"

"You never left the lot for anything," Joseph adds. "When you were at the studio, you were not only safe from the outside world, you could participate in any part of the outside world you wanted to. If you wanted to register to vote or renew your driver's license, they came on the lot. Once I wanted some toys, and I had my secretary call Robinson's downtown. They said they couldn't bring the toys over, but they told her, 'If Mr. Mankiewicz would like to come down some evening, we'll keep the toy department open for him and have a saleslady there.' I went downtown, and we were the only two people in Robinson's department store. That's beyond belief now, but that's the way it was."

When Joseph first came to work in Hollywood, he was often confused around town with his older brother, which he resented. "I now know what they will put on my tombstone," he once commented. "'Here lies Herm—I mean Joe—Mankiewicz!'" Fiercely protective of his own ego, Joseph was especially sensitive on the issue of screen credits. When the *Los Angeles Record* mentioned that Herman, not he, had written the dialogue for *The Social Lion,* Joseph demanded a printed retraction. Another controversy developed over the 1932 comedy classic *Million Dollar Legs,* starring W. C. Fields. Herman was producer of the film and supervised Joseph and his co-writer, Henry Myers. The authorship is still contested. In 1978, Joseph told his biographer,

Kenneth Geist, "I don't think Herman, throughout his entire life, mentioned *Million Dollar Legs* as something he'd been connected with." Herman's widow, Sara Mankiewicz, disputes this and says, "Herman always boasted about *Million Dollar Legs* and regarded it as one of his happiest and most delightful pictures."

The pettiness of this credit dispute suggests the rivalry that was to consume the Mankiewicz brothers throughout most of their careers. Joseph once remarked, "Everyone else has a mother or father complex, but I have a Herman complex!" He knew that Herman was always better liked than he was. Herman was generous to a fault and adored by a galaxy of friends. By contrast, Joseph is known to this day as a tightwad. His son Christopher refers to him as "miserly."

Money was a particular source of tension between the brothers. In his first year in Hollywood, when Joseph's salary reached the then-respectable figure of $125 a week, Herman made him put a fifth of it into a savings account; six months later, Herman "borrowed" all the money to pay off one of his gambling debts. Some years later, Joseph refused to borrow on his life insurance to meet more of Herman's debts. Furious, Herman ordered Joseph to come to screenwriter Charles Lederer's office. When Joseph got there, Herman turned to Lederer and fumed, "Now will you kindly tell this little SOB what a brother is—that everything he has is mine."

As Joseph's career ascended and Herman's started to wane, the relations between them grew increasingly strained. The roles the Mankiewicz brothers had played in their first days in Hollywood were reversed, and Herman was galled by Joseph's success. He began referring to Joseph as "my idiot brother." For his part, Joseph denigrated Herman's abilities as a writer, arguing that he was essentially a raconteur who did not always succeed in committing his wit to paper.

. . . . .

Herman, by contrast, was continually in conflict with producers and studio executives, who had scant patience for his irrespressible sarcasm. In a fit of pique, Irving Thalberg threw him off the Marx Brothers comedy *A Night at the Opera,* though L.B. Mayer continued to believe in Herman's talent and kept him on the payroll. It was Herman's gambling, rather than his impudence, that troubled Mayer. He advanced Herman $30,000 on a new contract if Herman would never gamble again. The very next day, Mayer found Herman engaged in a high-stakes poker game on the MGM lot. Herman was gone that afternoon. Herman's impudence, however, cost him his job at Columbia, when he responded to Harry Cohn's method of detecting a film of poor quality (when his fanny twitched) with, "Imagine the whole world wired to Harry Cohn's ass."

Herman's son Frank once said, "There was something self-defeating about his being in Hollywood. I guess that's why he drank too much and insulted people who could help him. He was a gambler, and he probably was an alcoholic, but those are not sins. He never stole from the poor, he never fired anybody on Christmas."

In 1941, Herman pulled himself together for one last blaze of glory. A decade earlier, he had been a frequent guest of William Randolph Hearst at San Simeon. Since Hearst allowed his guests only one cocktail before dinner, his mistress, Marion Davies, had a secret cache of booze for heavy drinkers. But Herman kept himself reasonably sober, and when the company sat down to dinner, Hearst would always place Mankiewicz to his immediate left so that he wouldn't miss a single one of his guest's witty ripostes. What Hearst did not realize was that Herman was taking his own mental notes of everything he observed at those glittering dinner parties. Later, Herman suggested to Orson Welles the idea for a movie to be called *American*—an exposé of a powerful American press lord over a period of 50 years—that became *Citizen Kane,* and earned Herman an Oscar as well as the undying wrath of his former host. And his brother Joseph lamented to his wife, "I don't think I'll ever win an Oscar. . . . He's got the Oscar and I'm a producer at Metro, goddamn it!"

At one point in the movie, Charles Foster Kane says to his childhood guardian, "If I hadn't been very rich, I might have been a really great man." One would guess that line was written by Herman. He continued to fantasize about pursing the serious writing of which he believed himself capable. Though he completed an epic-length screenplay about evangelist Aimee Semple McPherson, the project never came to fruition, and he hated himself for accepting yet more hackwork assignments.

His downfall was abetted by Hearst, who viewed *Citizen Kane* as a personal betrayal. Hearst's attorneys unsuccessfully sought legal grounds for an injunction. Hearst columnist Louella Parsons denounced the film repeatedly before its release, and Hearst's friend Louis B. Mayer offered $842,000 to RKO president George J. Shaefer if he would destroy the negative. All of these tactics failed, and Hearst waited to find some other means of avenging himself.

Hearst's opportunity came in 1943, when Herman, on the way home from a late-night binge, smashed into another car just outside Marion Davies' residence in Beverly Hills, where Hearst was staying at the time. Two passengers in the other car were slightly injured. Mankiewicz was charged with a felony and had to stand trial. Worse, Hearst saw to it that the accident was trumpeted as front-page news in all his papers across the country, and on March 14, the *L.A. Examiner* ran a major page one story—"Felony Charge Filed Against Mankiewicz"—about an accident resulting in nothing more serious than a bruised knee. Inside was a full-page spread of photographs, including a "diagram of Beverly Hills Collision—Film Writer Accused." Hearst refused to let the story die. He flogged Mankiewicz several times a week; he also used the incident as a pretext for launching a series of follow-up stories about the degenerate lifestyle of Hollywood. Eventually, Mankiewicz appealed to the American Civil Liberties Union for help in putting a halt to the harassment. But the studio brass, always sensitive to bad publicity regardless of its merits, were quick to disavow him.

Herman's screenwriting output dwindled over the course of the decade, and by the end of the 1940s he could barely find work at all. As his politics shifted to the right during the last years of his life, he became even more of a pariah. His son Don believes that his ideological conversion was motivated mainly by his distaste for the knee-jerk liberalism that masqueraded as political conviction in Hollywood. "He resented not so much the idiocy of the political points of view that were being pressed on him, but the liberals' unwillingness to *do* anything in support of their values," says Don.

Don remembers the simmering rage his father felt as he reached the end of his life: "There is a celebrated story of his breaking into tears, drunken tears, and being able to say nothing but 'Goddamn it, I am a better writer than Bernie Hyman.' Bernie Hyman was a script supervisor of some sort who was sitting in judgment on him. My father was out of work almost all the time in those last years. He was totally overqualified not only for the work he was doing, but for the conversations that went around the dinner table. He told me once that one of the most important aspects of American policy was the influence of Thomas Marshall during Woodrow Wilson's illness. And he said, 'I have to discuss this with people who think Thomas Marshall's the fellow who started a high school in Burbank.'"

No doubt Herman's bitterness during those last years was magnified by Joseph's growing success and status. Joseph showed promise in his early directing efforts at Twentieth Century-Fox, such as *The Ghost and Mrs. Muir,* a supernatural comedy with Gene Tierney and Rex Harrison; and *House of Strangers,* starring Edward G. Robinson and Susan Hayward, about the conflict within an Italian banking family (supposedly based on the Gianninis, founders of the Bank of America and major financiers of the movie industry). After collecting his four Oscars for *A Letter to Three Wives* and *All About Eve,* Joseph was universally recognized as the premier writer-director in Hollywood.

*All About Eve* remains Joseph L. Mankiewicz's masterpiece, probably because it touched deeply personal chords. Sexual jealousy is a common theme in movies, but only a very few films have dealt with professional jealousy and rivalry, and that is what makes *All About Eve* so distinctive and provocative. It was the kind of drama Joseph understood from firsthand experience and was in a position to illuminate. He drew on his unresolved feelings about his relationship with Herman in framing the story of the aging star Margo Channing

(Bette Davis), who is betrayed by her protégée, the treacherous young upstart Eve Harrington (Anne Baxter). "You gather I don't like Eve?" Joseph once asked in an interview. "You're right," he confessed, "I've been there."

According to Herman's biographer, Richard Meryman, "In Herman's mind the successful Joe had become self-important, ruthless, and somehow fraudulent." As Joseph won more and more kudos, Herman took satisfaction in reminding himself that almost all of Joseph's triumphs (including *A Letter to Three Wives* and *All About Eve*) were adaptations of other writers' stories and that Joseph had never written an original screenplay that could hold a candle to **Citizen Kane.**

. . . . .

For all the intellectual qualities they may have shared, Herman and Joseph were polar opposites in their personal lives. Despite his heavy drinking and reckless gambling, Herman seems to have been a devoted husband and father. In fact, Joseph used to tease Herman for his prudishness; he claims that, while working at MGM, he was frequently called upon to rewrite the stiff, unconvincing love scenes in Herman's screenplays. Joseph was much more disciplined than Herman in every area but sex. Joseph is known for his series of love affairs with well-known actresses, including Joan Crawford, Linda Darnell, Gene Tierney, and Judy Garland.

Joseph thought of himself as something of an amateur psychologist—he had a lifelong infatuation with psychoanalysis—and his biographer Kenneth Geist reports that he frequently used psychoanalytic techniques on women, an approach that drew many insecure young actresses to him. His son Christopher says, "When I got married, my father said to me, 'You know, of course, you're marrying your mother.' This is a guy who really wanted to be a shrink, and I guess he had great success with women, particularly movie stars, by dealing with them on a psychological level. Rather than saying, 'You have great tits, my dear,' like everybody else was saying, he found a new tactic."

Joseph's first marriage, to actress Elizabeth Young, quickly ended in divorce. His second marriage, in 1934, was to Rosa Stradner, a gifted actress who came from Max Reinhardt's theater in Vienna. It was Louis B. Mayer who brought her to Hollywood, where she made her American film debut playing James Stewart's wife in *The Last Gangster.* Joseph wanted her to abandon her acting and devote herself to being a homemaker, probably the one role she was least capable of playing well. The Hollywood social scene did not stimulate her, and she was far too intelligent for the mindless activities to which Hollywood wives were being consigned. "My mother was terrifically frustrated," Chris says. "She always felt cheated that my father had said to her, 'You're going to give up your career.'"

According to Dr. Frederick Hacker, a psychiatrist and a friend of the family, Rosa believed that she had the potential to be a Garbo or a Bergman, and that she had forsaken a promising career to marry Joseph. She drank heavily whenever her husband was working. In 1942, Rosa fell into a catatonic state and spent nine months at the Menninger Clinic. When she recovered, Joseph did cast her as the mother superior in his production of *The Keys of the Kingdom,* a sanctimonious religious drama starring Gregory Peck. It was to be Rosa's last movie role. In 1948, she tried to resume her stage career in a play called *Bravo!* She traveled East, full of excitement. But she was replaced during the Boston tryout, and her acting career was over.

In 1951, Joseph moved his family to New York, feeling that the atmosphere there would be healthier for all of them. "I never could stand the city of Los Angeles," he explains. "At birthday parties, as you came through the door, the kids would say, `What movie are you going to show? How many clowns you got? Only *one* clown? We had a tightrope walker at *my* birthday party.' I had seen too much of that going on. I did not want my kids growing up in that environment. And I felt if I didn't get out then, when I had just won four Oscars in two years, I'd never get out. Nobody was going to say that I left because I couldn't get a job."

•

From the time he moved back East, Joseph saw less of Herman, and relations between the brothers remained fairly distant for the rest of Herman's life. In his last years, Herman had only two screen credits—*A Woman's Secret,* a forgotten melodrama adapted from a trashy novel by Vicki Baum, and *The Pride of St. Louis,* a biography of Dizzy Dean that is a pale imitation of his earlier tribute to Lou Gehrig, *The Pride of the Yankees.* Herman's career was washed up; the drinking and the disappointments had taken a physical as well as an emotional toll. In 1953, he succumbed to a series of ailments—heart trouble, uremic poisoning, and liver infection—brought on in part by his heavy drinking. Shortly before his death, he said, "I don't know how it is that you start working at something you don't like, and before you know it, you're an old man."

When Herman died, Joe and Rosa flew out from New York for the funeral. On the day of the funeral, the couple had one of their ugliest quarrels, and Joe stormed out of Herman's house. The strained relationship between Joseph and his wife did not improve. They spent more and more time apart. Their quarrels grew more violent, and Rosa's hold on reality became more tenuous. In 1958, Rosa Mankiewicz committed suicide by swallowing an overdose of sedatives. "The night my mother died," Chris recalls, "I was at the all-night movies in Times Square. It was my freshman year at Columbia. I rushed over to the apartment when I finally got the message, at three or four o'clock in the morning. Later on, as we were going down the elevator, the family

psychiatrist said to me, 'What are your feelings at this moment?' I said, 'This may seem strange to you, but I feel intensely happy, that a great weight has been lifted off my shoulder. The agony of my mother is finally over, and at least there will no longer be that terrible tension.' He said, `That's the first honest emotion I heard expressed here tonight.'"

•

Although not all of Joseph L. Mankiewicz's films succeeded at the box office, he was still regarded as one of America's most prestigious movie-makers throughout the decade of the 1950s. His Waterloo came when he started work on *Cleopatra* in 1961. It was a project that he reluctantly took over in mid-course and foolishly believed he could salvage. The financial temptations were overpowering. In addition to an extravagant salary, Fox paid Mankiewicz a $1.5 million fee to purchase his production company. At the time, it was the highest sum ever paid to a movie director.

In other respects, this misbegotten project was an unfortunate harbinger—the first example of a film that came into existence because of an irresistible "deal." Elizabeth Taylor never wanted to star in the movie, so she made a salary demand that she was certain would be rejected—a $1 million fee, against 10% of the gross. To her astonishment, Twentieth Century-Fox, then under the management of Spyros Skouras and Peter Levathes, accepted her terms.

Shortly after production began under director Rouben Mamoulian, Taylor was hospitalized with influenza; her health deteriorated rapidly, and she came close to dying. When Mankiewicz was hired to replace Mamoulian, Fox had already poured $6 million into the picture without producing a foot of usable film. Fox kept shifting the location from Hollywood to London to Rome and back to Hollywood again. The studio's European representative was described by Mankiewicz as "only capable, with difficulty, of ordering a ham sandwich." But Mankiewicz plunged in, telling himself that this monumental mess could be transformed into an artistic masterpiece. He tried to write dialogue in the style of Shakespeare and Shaw, but he was waging a losing battle. There was simply not enough time to get the screenplay in shape, and with costs rising every day, Mankiewicz had to write as he filmed, depending on drugs to keep up the pace.

By the time *Cleopatra* limped to completion in 1963, Twentieth Century-Fox was under a new commander. Darryl F. Zanuck had returned to Hollywood, seizing power from Spyros Skouras, Zanuck insisting on recutting the film over the director's protests, defiantly stating, "I would rather go back to another job than leave picture making totally in the hands of an artist."

"Zanuck rode over the movie with a bulldozer," Mankiewicz recalls 20 years later. Mankiewicz's four-hour cut was chopped to three hours soon after its release; crucial plot points and evocative scenes were left on the cutting room floor.

In a state of exhaustion after the ordeal of *Cleopatra,* Mankiewicz did not work on another feature film for three years. He returned with *The Honey Pot,* an ingenious contemporary variation on Ben Jonson's *Volpone.* Despite some wonderfully urbane repartee between Rex Harrison and Maggie Smith, *The Honey Pot* was coolly received by both critics and audiences. Mankiewicz's next picture, a slyly cynical Western, *There Was a Crooked Man* (starring Kirk Douglas and Henry Fonda), fared no better.

Mankiewicz recouped somewhat with *Sleuth,* released in 1972. Although it was no more than a faithful transcription of Anthony Shaffer's hit play about the deadly battle of wits between a jaded mystery writer and his wife's lover, Mankiewicz won an Academy Award nomination for his stylish direction, and both Laurence Olivier and Michael Caine were nominated for their performances. It remains Joseph L. Mankiewicz's last film. His son Tom believes that, since *Sleuth* was a commercial as well as a critical success, Joseph may have wanted to leave well enough alone rather than risk another failure. "He's a man filled with immense pride," Tom suggests. "I think he's very concerned about ending his career on a good note."

. . . . .

Many of the conflicts and patterns played out between Herman and Joseph Mankiewicz were reenacted by their children. Just as Herman and Joseph had been opposite types as youngsters, so were Herman's sons, Don and Frank. While Frank was highly competitive as a boy and always a diligent, vigorous achiever, Don was overweight, deeply introverted, sloppy, and given to bouts of indolence.

The older of the two, Don first enrolled in law school but dropped out during World War II to join the army. "During the war," Don recalls, "I wrote in about an hour and a half a very short piece, which I sent to *The New Yorker,* and I believe they gave me $185. I calculated what that would be for a 40-hour week, and I said, 'My father was right. This had got to be the easiest business that ever was!' Then I went for many years without a sale of any kind." When his Harper Prize-winning novel, *Trial,* a McCarthy-era melodrama about a well-meaning liberal lawyer duped into becoming a pawn of the Russians, was bought by MGM in 1955, Don moved back to Hollywood to write the screenplay. Later, Don rewrote *I Want To Live!*—a strong tract against capital punishment—for his Uncle Joe's company, Figaro Productions; the film brought him an Oscar nomination and won an Academy Award for its star, Susan Hayward.

During the 1950s, Don began writing for such television series as *Studio One* and *Playhouse 90.* Later, he created pilots for *Marcus Welby, M.D.* and *Ironside.* But there were problems: "After we did the pilot for that show," Mankiewicz remembers, "NBC called and said, 'We're ordering the series, but we want to know one thing: When does Chief Ironside walk?'"

In 1982, Don took a job as story editor on *Hart to Hart* the suspense-adventure series starring Robert Wagner and Stephanie Powers, which his cousin, Tom, helped to create. "When you write a book," Don says, "what finally goes on the page with your name is what you wrote. Here in Hollywood, that's not the case. On *Hart to Hart,* the actors say what they goddamn please, and it quickly infects the day players and the director, and there's total anarchy. I want my name on the series to establish that I worked there, but I sure as hell don't want my English teacher to know what I was doing. Television is a trash medium. You can't get away from it."

Today, Don seems to keep feeling some of the same bitterness that tortured his father, Herman Mankiewicz, during his last years. "My father kept saying that it is not a good business and it will destroy you," Don remarks. "But he always said that he had never in his life succeeded in talking anybody out of it, and he did not expect to talk me out of it, either. He did warn me, 'Try to understand that whatever they pay you, A) you will earn it five times over, and B) it will not suffice to pay your psychiatrist bills.' And he was basically right."

. . . . .

Joseph's sons, like Herman's, were opposites. Tom, the younger, was more affable and sociable, dubbed "fun-loving Tom" by his father, though he was subject to psychosomatic asthma attacks as a result of the pressures he felt at home. Christopher, the older, was more moody and withdrawn. Chris and Tom responded to their father's influence in opposite ways. "Tom went out to seek approval, love, and attention by excelling," Chris says. "I went out to do the opposite. I wanted to hurt my father by being the worst kid. The more I fucked up, the more I figured I was giving him pain and hardship. And I guess that's what I wanted to do."

Joseph Mankiewicz was a very demanding father, much as his own father had been. Chris remembers the evening his father picked up two Academy Awards for *All About Eve.* His parents came home from a post-Oscar party, and his mother told him of what had transpired. A guest had come up to them and burbled, "Joe, congratulations!"

Mankiewicz looked at him quizzically and asked, "Do I know you?"

The man said, "No, actually we've never met."

"Then why do you call me Joe? Please call me Mr. Mankiewicz."

Chris says, "That was a moment, a flash, which reminded me of how intimidating my father was to me as well, and I guess that's why I've never forgotten it. I remember a couple of years later, when he was shooting

*Julius Caesar,* we were out in California for the summer and were staying in Norma Shearer's beach house. I'd gotten some bad grades. My father berated me, and I started to cry. When he saw me crying, he really heaped on the abuse. I realized that I had opened myself up, and he was just merciless. Right then, I made a determination that I would never break in front of him again."

Because Joseph had little time for his son's problems, Christopher was shunted off to psychiatrists from the time he was 13 until he graduated high school. Chris remembers the experience as one of the rites of growing up in Hollywood: "What all of us seemed to have in common was constantly going to the shrink. Most of us progressed from nannies to nurses to housekeepers to psychiatrists. There was always a surrogate parent around. The attitude of my father and others was, 'I'm too involved. You and I could never talk these things out. I think it would be a good idea if you had somebody you could talk to freely and openly.' So that they didn't have to interrupt their careers and their lives and deal with the issues that fathers and mothers should be confronting with their children, we were shipped out to professionals. That has got to be somewhat unique to the Hollywood experience. I can't think of a group of kids who more frequently were going to shrinks in the Forties and Fifties. The idea of just sitting down and rapping with your parents was inconceivable in my family. But the shrinks were always there."

Both Chris and Tom found the lure of show business irresistible when it came time to carve out their own careers. "You grew up as a kind of aristocracy," Chris explains. "You knew that everybody was interested in you. It made you something special because what your folks did was special. I don't know if that's a good thing. In retrospect, I feel some of us are as useless as the czar's children. Anything that seems to suggest routine, although it might be clinically quite healthy for us, seemed repellent. So when you get out of high school and start to think of what to do with your life, you look around and most things look pretty dull in comparison to show business. Even if you have no particular talent for writing or directing, that's what you gravitate toward."

For a time, Tom thought of being an actor. But his father quashed that ambition after going to see Tom perform in a summer stock production.

Tom heeded his father's advice. After working briefly as a production assistant, he wrote a few TV shows and films, as well as the book for a short-lived musical called *Georgy,* based on the hit film *Georgy Girl.* Writing intimidated Tom at first because of the inevitable comparisons he knew he would face. "For me," Tom admits, "there was something terribly frightening about writing a screenplay when you have the last name of Mankiewicz. You say to yourself, 'Oh, shit, no matter what I write, it sure ain't any *All About Eve,* is it?' It takes a long time to get over that. When I first came out here, everybody said, 'Give my regards to your old man,

will you, and by the way, if there's anything I can do for you. . . . ' On the one hand, all of that is very nice and tremendously advantageous. On the other hand, it sort of robs you of any sense of achievement. It's a real double-edged sword. And it wasn't until I had been asked back several times and, as awful as it sounds, for a lot of money, that I could finally convince myself that these people really want *me* because they think that I'm the best person to write the script."

When Tom was hired to do a rewrite of the James Bond movie *Diamonds Are Forever,* the direction of his career was set. He was on the path to phenomenal success, even if it was not the kind of success he had once envisioned for himself. He worked on several more Bond movies—*Live and Let Die, The Man with the Golden Gun, The Spy Who Loved Me*—and a couple of pictures for the English mogul Sir Lew Grade (whom some refer to as Sir Low Grade), *The Cassandra Crossing* and *The Eagle Has Landed.* Tom became known as a reliable script doctor and rewrite man, though he found that role increasingly thankless. When director Richard Donner called him from Paris and begged him to rewrite the script of *Superman,* Mankiewicz initially declined. Donner was dissatisfied with the earlier drafts by Mario Puzo, Robert Benton, and David and Leslie Newman, and he desperately needed Mankiewicz's help to get the script in order. He sent two massive screenplays to Mankiewicz's home. Tom read through the scripts and again decided to turn the project down. As he tells it, "The doorbell rang the very next night. I opened the door, and there was Dick Donner in a Superman suit. He said, 'You've got to do the picture.' He was very persuasive. I rewrote both those scripts from top to bottom, and I've never worked so hard in my life."

After *Superman,* Tom's friend TV producer Leonard Goldberg asked him to rewrite the pilot for *Hart to Hart.* In return, Tom was given the chance to direct the two-hour pilot as well as several of the episodes of the long-running series. He was credited as creative consultant and has a piece of all the syndication sales. Tom created another TV series—the short-lived *Gavilan,* with Robert Urich—and has written the script for an expensive new screen version of *Batman.* Tom Mankiewicz is Hollywood's reigning king of the comic strips and capers; he has made his reputation writing special-effects spectacles and featherweight adventures.

Ironically, this is exactly the sort of product his father always detested. Chris comments pointedly on Tom's success: "For years, my father has predicted that special effects would take over and movies would become circuses. What he predicted has happened, and the fact that my brother is so successful in writing *Superman* and James Bond movies must confirm to him pitifully that Tom is an exponent of what he regards as the mindless entertainment that passes for films. If my brother were a more open kind of person—he isn't, unfortunately—he would admit that he's had real problems in terms of competing with his father. I don't think in a million years that he would conceive that he has ever written anything or even could write anything as good as *All About Eve*. But he's extraordinarily successful. He just signed an incredible deal with Warner Brothers for an unbelievable amount of money, at a time when most people are out of work, including me. For whatever reason, he's the flavor of the month or the flavor of the year."

Tom insists that he needed to establish financial independence from his family as a first step toward artistic maturity. He felt he could achieve that independence best by mastering a genre that was as far removed as possible from the typical "Mankiewicz movie." He elaborates, "I wanted to be able to say to my father, 'Listen, I've got my own area over here. This is my part of the yard, and you don't do this kind of thing. Maybe I'll do one of yours someday, but I don't need any money, thank you very much. I'm standing right here on my own.' That gives you a kind of confidence and security. I think I've got my own identity, and I've established a good base camp." Nevertheless, Tom recognizes what he has achieved and what he may have sacrificed along the way. "I'm under no illusions when I walk into Warner Brothers that they're saying, 'Here comes another Noel Coward.' They say, 'Dollars and cents, here he comes.'"

"I think Dad is probably disappointed that I have not worked up to what he considers to be, and I must say I consider to be, my creative potential," Tom admits. "He's never said he's disappointed, but I know he is, and I know that come Oscar night some year, he would love to see some wonderful film that I wrote and directed being honored."

"I do share Tom's disappointment," Joseph L. Mankiewicz affirms when talking about his son's career. "Or put it this way. He came to share my disappointment. On the other hand, I understand completely. I wrote for W.C. Fields." "I wrote Westerns. I wrote anything when I started out. The point is, Tom sold his stuff. Now I happen to think he's better than that. Tom found it a little too easy. Instead of shooting the fourth draft of his screenplay, they shot the second. I have said to him, 'I don't think the second draft is good enough, Tom. You can do better.' But he didn't have to do better, and that was a pity. You see, Tom didn't have sitting on his tail half a dozen very good producers."

"Maybe I wasn't hungry enough in the past," Tom admits. "When things are going well, you can get lazy with the best of intentions. If you can make a very good living writing James Bond—and God knows there's nothing wrong with it, people love the pictures and the money is good—then when somebody asks if you want to do another one, the easy thing to do is to take it. When I started out, I sort of thought of myself as an enormously sensitive young writer who wanted to do these deeply personal films. I don't know how many years ago that was. But I still intend to be."

Tom's brother, Christopher, has faced a more difficult passage, perhaps because he is one of the rare Mankiewiczes who is not a writer. His father helped him to get his first job in the business at Columbia Pictures, and he subsequently pursued the executive route, working for various independent producers, as well as at middle management jobs for United Artists and Columbia. He has also tried to direct and produce films on his own, so far without much success.

In discussing his career choices, Chris admits that he has been inhibited by the fear of competing with his father. "When the opening and the opportunity presented itself," he says, "I went into being what we laughably call an executive, rather than perceiving myself to be a writer and working in an area where I could be in a direct *mano-a-mano* competition with my father. I tried to write a couple of things, and I thought they were terrible. I didn't want to give up my right to criticize other people's work. Or maybe it's simply because it's much easier not to compete and not to write. I hope that isn't the case. I've gotten to an age and to a point where the fact that I will be a footnote in the history of the cinema doesn't bother me at all. I just don't have the drive."

His father, however, dismisses the notion that a family name creates some sort of paralyzing obstacle to success. "That's a problem that's as old as the hills, isn't it?" asks Joseph. "I felt the same thing. When I was 17 years old and a student at Columbia, my brother was getting known around New York City. He was an Algonquin wit. And he was George Kaufman's assistant at the *New York Times* drama department. Well, I wanted to write. I started writing things and sending them off to magazines under the name of Joe Mason. And I remember when I got my first check for 17 bucks. I sold something I had written. I don't think it's a valid point that Chris makes. I've encouraged him in the sense that I've gotten him positions. I got him all sorts of jobs, and he didn't keep them. He fought a lot. Chris is very opinionated. I have always told Chris he should strike out and work in the area in which he has the greatest knowledge. Chris has the most incredible knowledge of recorded music, which he's never used really. I told him there's a lot of money to be made in musicology and a lot of prestige. But suddenly, he got the bug to make movies. I don't know how or why. Unfortunately, he wanted to start off at the top, as a director. Chris has been trying to make it; he's having a rough time. I hope he gets his act together."

"If you're a Mankiewicz who doesn't know what you want to do, especially if you're in the film business," Tom observes, "you're kind of an eyesore. Chris is still searching for a base camp. He is at a lower level on the mountain, not as a human being or not with his intelligence. And so I think it still gnaws at him. I always thought how hard it would be to be Lorna Luft. Not only is Judy Garland her mother, but Liza Minnelli's her sister. Chris isn't saddled with that with me, because I'm not the most famous guy in the business. He's saddled with it a little bit in that I *am* successful in the business. God, I wish Chris could get that picture to direct. I wish he could get that one big score that's always eluded him. If he got it, I think he'd be damn good. I have no competitive feelings with him at all. I wish to Christ he'd win the Oscar next year. It would make his life a lot easier. It would make our relationship a lot easier, too. I think he feels the family pressure much more than I do right now."

Echoing his father's criticism, Tom feels that his brother's only difficulty is his lack of diplomacy. Chris once had a position with producer Martin Ransohoff, and Tom has told an amusing story of how he asked Ransohoff what it was like working with Chris. "Chris was easily the most intelligent man I've ever had working for me," Ransohoff replied. "Then why did you fire him?" Tom asked. Ransohoff chuckled slyly. "Why should I pay a guy $2000 a week to look at me like I'm an idiot?"

That story sums up an essential truth about this remarkable Hollywood family. Whether successful or not, the Mankiewiczes are clearly far more intelligent than most of the people who have worked in the movie industry. No doubt most of them have been "overqualified" for their jobs, as Don Mankiewicz said of his father. Their travails are typical of those experienced by other intellectuals in Hollywood down through the years. Their love-hate relationship to Hollywood parallels the ambivalence expressed by many other gifted writers, from Dorothy Parker and F. Scott Fitzgerald to Joan Didion and John Gregory Dunne. Even as they are seduced by the money and the glamour of the film capital, they feel the need to apologize compulsively for their movie work. Joseph Mankiewicz often has referred to himself as "the oldest whore on the beat." "I was never committed to Hollywood," he insists. "I was never committed to film, either. Nor was Herman, for that matter. My brother's greatest talent was his knowledge of the American political scene. If he had written a political column, Herman would have been far greater than Walter Lippmann ever was. As for me, yes, I've worked in films, but I also directed for the Metropolitan Opera. I'm writing a book on the history of the performing woman, the actress, how women came into the theater. I'm working on a play. I'm a writer, not a Hollywood writer. There's a difference between families in the film business like the Goldwyns and the Selznicks, and our family. If there were no film business, you wouldn't have those other families, but you would still have the Mankiewiczes. We'd still be writers."

Over the last decade, Joseph has felt a mounting frustration in contemplating his own place in the film business. "I've turned down a lot of crap," Joseph asserts. "But on the other hand, my name just doesn't come up out in Hollywood any more. Maybe they think I'm too old. Over the years the characters at the studios change, so no matter who you are, you have to manufacture a certain amount of personal hype, and that is something I've never done. I never had a press agent. It's very easy if you're not there for your name to be forgotten. I'm on the public mailing list for Filmex (the Los Angeles International Film Exposition). They send me mimeographed handouts addressed 'Dear Friend of the Film' or 'Dear Film Buff.' I once got an invitation from the American Film Institute, when they voted on the best films of all time. *All About Eve* was in the top ten. And I got a mimeographed letter inviting me to buy a ticket for $350 and come and mingle with the men who had made those films. I had made one of them! I called Elia Kazan because *On the Waterfront* was also among the top ten, and I asked him, 'Did you get this same form letter and the $350 request?' He said, 'Are you out of your mind? I got free tickets.' I said to him, 'I'm on the public mailing list!'"

That comment reveals Mankiewicz's confusion. At the same time that he scoffs at Hollywood and mocks its values, he still craves obeisance from the town that once revered him. He remembers a time when his intellect won him the respect of his inferiors. In a more melancholy, reflective mood, Joseph comments: "I don't think there are that many good writers in Hollywood today because the demand for good writing isn't there. What they want today is quick writing. I have a screenplay that was aborted simply because I took too much time in writing it. You have to understand that none of my films were ever blockbusters. Never. I was the kind of filmmaker whom studios could afford. Most of the films I wrote and directed made a profit—not through the roof, but they got their money back and some profit. I don't think I could get *All About Eve* financed today. First of all, it takes longer to write. And it takes good acting and careful direction, not of lenses but of the actors. The big films today are like cartoon strips, and the dialogue is the kind that you read in balloons. I don't think they'd be impressed by a Faulkner in Hollywood today."

Tom Mankiewicz recalls the one time, in 1972, when he and his father both happened to be working on the same lot, Pinewood Studios outside London. Joseph L. Mankiewicz was directing *Sleuth,* his last film to date. Tom was working on his second James Bond movie, *Live and Let Die.*

"The Bond movie had eleven sound stages," Tom says, "and my father had one. Of course, it was the classiest stage you would ever want to see, with Olivier and Michael Caine and Ken Adam designing the sets and Ozzie Morris photographing. My father used to come out at night after finishing shooting. The Bond picture would be going late, and he used to open the door to E Stage and there were girls in bikinis and machine guns and underwater battles. It seemed so crazy to him. He'd say, 'What are you doing in here all day long? I don't understand any of this. I'm working with two guys and a camera.' Sometimes he and I would walk part of the way back to the Connaught Hotel. And he would say to me, 'You know, I don't think I'm ever going to do another picture.'"

**Michael Buckley (essay date 1984)**

SOURCE: "The Regency Salutes The Brothers Mankiewicz," in *Films in Review,* Vol. XXXV, No. 10, October, 1984, pp. 490-91.

[*In the following excerpt, Buckley discusses a revival of the films of brothers Herman and Joseph Mankiewicz.*]

At the Regency, Manhattan's leading revival house, the old stars never die . . . or fade away. They shine in mint condition, in 35 mm. prints, dazzling us with right moves and bright lines. Its most recent series (August 12-September 22) presented highlights from the careers of the Brothers Mankiewicz: Herman J., best-remembered for his extensive work on *Citizen Kane,* and Joseph L., who enjoys the distinction of being the only winner of successive Oscars for writing and direction—*A Letter to Three Wives* (1949) and *All About Eve* (1950), the film that holds the record for Academy Award nominations (14).

It marked the first time that the theatre (on Broadway between 67th & 68th Streets) has honored screenwriters. "We wanted to do something a little different," explains Frank Rowley, who designs the double bills. Once a theme has been chosen, Rowley determines which movies "are unlikely to draw an audience." he then arranges the remaining pieces into the mosaic of a series—pairing stylish entries (*Dinner at Eight* and *Citizen Kane*) and others that intrigue: *Another Language* and *Stamboul Quest.* A particular regret, says Rowley, "is not being able to play *The Late George Apley.*" Unavailable, it's one of six features (of 20) directed by Joseph L. Mankiewicz that were excluded. The others: *Somewhere in the Night, Escape, The Barefoot Contessa, The Quiet American,* and *There Was a Crooked Man.* A form common to many JLM pictures (and also prominent in *Citizen Kane*) is the flashback, which shows the effect of the past upon the present (and how) the past *exists* in the present."

Herman (1897-1953), an established writer by the time Joseph, born in 1909, arrived on the Hollywood scene, has had his life and career detailed in (among other books) *Mank,* by Richard Meryman and Pauline Kael's *The Citizen Kane Book.* The Regency showed nine films that he wrote, solely or in collaboration. Of these, three are well-known to film buffs: *Citizen Kane,* for which he and Orson Welles won Oscars for the Best Original Screenplay of 1941; *Dinner at Eight* (1933), with its all-star cast and classic fade-out repartee between Jean Harlow and Marie Dressler; and *The Pride of the Yankees,* the 1942 biopic of baseball great Lou Gehrig (Gary Cooper) for which Mankiewicz (with Jo Swerling) received his only other Academy Award nomination.

The other six HJM pictures on view were more obscure: *Another Language* (1933): Helen Hayes weds Robert Montgomery, but falls in love with his nephew (John Beal); *Stamboul Quest* (1934): Fraulein Doktor (Myrna Loy), Germany's most successful spy, whispers "Ich liebe dich" to American medical student George Brent; *The Show Off* (1934): Spencer Tracy plays a dreamer who ultimately succeeds; *After Office Hours* (1935): Clark Gable and Constance Bennett solve a murder and discover love; *It's A Wonderful World* (1939): James Stewart, trying to prove himself innocent of a murder charge, kidnaps poet Claudette Colbert and gets Cupid on his case; *My Dear Miss Aldrich* (1937): Maureen O'Sullivan inherits a newspaper and makes editor Walter her Pidgeon.

In the new book, *Hollywood Dynasties* by Stephen Farber and Marc Green, Joseph Mankiewicz is quoted: "I don't think there are that many good writers in Hollywood today because the demand for good writing isn't there . . . I don't think I could get *All About Eve* financed today."

The retrospective included six of the 19 films (none of which he wrote) that Joseph produced at MGM, where Louis B. Mayer refused him the opportunity to direct. He's been quoted as having hated his years as a producer. Chosen were: *Fury* (1936), wherein Spencer Tracy seeks revenge on vigilantes; *Double Wedding* (1937), a farce starring William Powell and Myrna Loy; *Mannequin* (1938), where Joan Crawford marries Spencer Tracy for his money and gains interest; *Three Comrades* (1938), an appealing tear-jerker that finds Roberts Taylor and Young and Franchot Tone in love with terminally ill Margaret Sullavan; *Shopworn Angel* (1938), one of sentiment's finest hours with showgirl Margaret Sullavan (her singing dubbed by Mary Martin) marrying naive soldier Jimmy Stewart; and *The Philadelphia Story* (1940), the privileged class enjoying its privileges" via a radiant Hepburn as Tracy, Cary Grant and James Stewart (in his Oscar-winning role).

Also shown was *The Keys of the Kingdom* (1945), which JLM produced for 20th Century Fox and co-wrote with Nunnally Johnson. The picture features Rosa Stradner (Mankiewicz's second wife) as the Mother Superior; in *Pictures Will Talk* by Kenneth L. Geist, their son, Christopher, claimed that she was the prototype for much of the Margo Channing character in *All About Eve.* In addition, the series included the following, on which Joseph had a writing credit: *Manhattan Melodrama* (1934), which starred Gable, William Powell and Myrna Loy in the story of childhood friends who grow up on opposite sides of the law; *If I Had A Million* (1932), an all-star tale about people acquiring sudden wealth; and *Million Dollar Legs* (1932), a W.C. Fields comedy concerning the Olympics.

The last named was the only film on which the brothers worked together: Herman (uncredited) as Producer and Joseph as co-writer; however, much controversy exists over the former's participation. In her book, Pauline Kael supports the belief that Herman wrote the screenplay, a claim that his brother has vehemently denied.

JLM's life and career are dealt with in the Geist book (which its subject is said to dislike), and others such as

Gary Carey's *More About All About Eve* and *Joseph L. Mankiewicz* by Bernard F. Dick. Fourteen features that he directed and wrote (occasionally sans credit) completed the salute. They included his—and Brando's—only excursions into Shakespeare (*Julius Caesar,* 1953) and musicals (*Guys and Dolls,* 1955), the aforementioned *All About Eve* and *A Letter to Three Wives* (a great double bill that began the series), and the film which Mankiewicz disowns: *Cleopatra* (1963), which the studio edited. He thinks that the picture has been cut so much it may become "the world's most expensive and beautifully photographed banjo picks."

Seldom seen items were: *Dragonwyck* (1946), his directorial debut; *The Ghost and Mrs. Muir* (1947), a charming romantic fantasy; *House of Strangers* (1949), which won Edward G. Robinson the Best Actor Award at Cannes; *No Way Out* (1950), a searing study of bigotry with a venomous Richard Widmark and introducing Sidney Poitier; and *People Will Talk* (1951), a delightful and unappreciated picture (one of Mankiewicz's favorites), with Cary Grant and Jeanne Crain. The latter, incidentally, appears to be the director's least liked leading lady. According to the Geist book, he named her characters (in *A Letter to Three Wives* and *People Will Talk*) Deborah because, "I don't like the name . . . and I don't like Jeanne Crain." She was Darryl F. Zanuck's choice to play Eve in *All About Eve* but lost the role—at JLM's insistence—to Anne Baxter, whom she would later replace (due to pregnancy) in *People Will Talk.*

### Robert L. Carringer (essay date 1985)

SOURCE: "Scripting," in *The Making of Citizen Kane,* University of California Press, 1985, pp. 16-35.

[*In the following excerpt, much of which reiterates factual information uncovered by Carringer in a Winter 1978 essay in* Critical Inquiry, *Carringer examines Mankiewicz's script* American, *which was the original draft of* Citizen Kane, *to support his thesis that Welles and Mankiewicz deserve equal credit for the screenplay.*]

Welles's first step toward the realization of *Citizen Kane* was to seek the assistance of a screenwriting professional. Fortunately, help was near at hand. Writing talent had always been in short supply in the Mercury operation because of the inexorable demands of the weekly radio shows. When Welles moved to Hollywood, it happened that a veteran screenwriter, Herman J. Mankiewicz, was recuperating from an automobile accident and between jobs. Mankiewicz was signed to write scripts for the Mercury's "Campbell Playhouse" radio program. When the opportunity to work on a screenplay for the Mercury presented itself, Mankiewicz was still available, and he took on this additional assignment as well.

Mankiewicz was an expatriate from Broadway who had been writing for films for almost fifteen years. He had anticipated a trend in 1926 when, as an aspiring young writer, critic, and playwright, he had answered Hollywood's call. Unlike others who took seasonal contracts and used their lucrative screenwriting salaries to support what they regarded as their real work back East, Mankiewicz stayed on and worked almost exclusively in films until his death in 1953. In the early years, he mainly wrote intertitles for silent films. After sound came in, he did his best work in comedy. His credits include select specimens of sophisticated dialogue comedy (*Laughter,* **Royal Family of Broadway, Dinner at Eight**) and of the anarchic farce associated especially with the Marx Brothers (***Monkey Business, Horse Feathers***) and W.C. Fields (***Million Dollar Legs***). In his film work, Mankiewicz was never known as a distance runner; in all the examples just cited, he received either screenplay co-credit or some special form of billing, such as associate producer. In contrast, writers like Ben Hecht and Samson Raphaelson were getting sole or top screenwriting billing on their best comedy scripts. Mankiewicz hit his peak in 1934 and 1935, when he received sole screenwriter credit on four films at MGM—**The Show-off** (with Spencer Tracy), **Stamboul Quest** (with Myrna Loy and George Brent), **After Office Hours** (with Clark Gable), and **Escapade** (with Luise Rainer, who was making her American debut). After that, his output fell dramatically. Between 1935 and the time when he was assigned to *Citizen Kane,* he received screenplay credit on only two films. Not that this state of affairs was really disadvantageous to Welles. He lacked the patience that original story construction requires. He preferred to start with a rough diamond and do just the cutting and polishing himself. Besides, a more secure and better-established writer would almost certainly insist on prerogatives. As things stood, Mankiewicz was hardly in a position to make demands.

Whether Welles or Mankiewicz came up with the idea for a send-up of William Randolph Hearst is a matter of dispute. Welles claims he did. The Mankiewicz partisans—chiefly Pauline Kael (and through her Mankiewicz's widow Sara) and John Houseman—say it was the other way around. Kael maintains that Mankiewicz had been toying with the idea for years. She reports the testimony of a former Mankiewicz baby-sitter that she took dictation from Mankiewicz on a flashback screenplay involving Hearst even before he went to Hollywood. Houseman, who had broken with Welles and the Mercury by this time, writes in his memoirs that Welles sought him out in New York and pleaded with him to come back and help with a screenplay idea that, Welles said, had been proposed by Mankiewicz. The conversation is said to have taken place at "21" shortly after the first of the year in 1940. But in an affidavit taken at the time of the film's release, Mercury assistant Richard Baer swore that the original idea was first broached by Welles at the "21" luncheon and that Welles and Houseman, who agreed to sign on, approached Mankiewicz about it back in California. We will probably never know for sure, but in any case Welles had at last found a subject with the right combination of monumentality, timeliness, and audacity. Lampooning Hearst was nothing new; he had been at the center of controversy for his entire public life. But in the 1930s it became commonplace to question or even attack the older ideal of America and the system of values that Hearst represented. (Even FDR spoke out against the possessors of "self-serving wealth," such as Hearst, branding them enemies of the republic and obstacles to social reform.) Nor was the tabloid angle on Hearst's personal life as original a stroke as it has been made out to be. In his 1939 novel *After Many a Summer Dies the Swan,* Aldous Huxley had been far nastier in his insinuations about Hearst and Marion Davies than anything in the **Citizen Kane** scripts. What was new was to take on Hearst from within Hollywood, where he had enormous influence and power to retaliate and was almost universally feared.

For obvious reasons, the project needed to be kept as quiet as possible. Consequently, it was decided that Mankiewicz would do his work away from Hollywood. There was another motive for this, too: Mankiewicz had a drinking problem (the main cause of his career decline). Houseman would go along to provide assistance but also to keep Mankiewicz out of trouble and on course. Mankiewicz went on the RKO payroll on February 19, 1940. He was to receive $1,000 a week, with a bonus of $5,000 on delivery of the script. During the last week in February or the first week in March, he and Houseman, together with a secretary, Rita Alexander, went into seclusion at a guest ranch in the desert at Victorville, California, several hours' drive from Hollywood. There, during March, April, and early May 1940, the first installments of the **Citizen Kane** script were written. First and second drafts were completed during this period. Alexander took them down from Mankiewicz's dictation; Houseman served as editor. In his lengthy account of the Victorville interlude, Houseman gives the impression that Mankiewicz started out with a clean slate and that virtually everything in the Victorville drafts is Mankiewicz's original invention. Kael made the same assumption. In arguing the case for Mankiewicz's authorship, she placed a great deal of emphasis on prior activities that were circumstantially parallel—for instance, that he had written unproduced screenplays based on Aimee Semple McPherson and John Dillinger that employed the device of multiple narration. For his part, Welles says he had lengthy discussions with Mankiewicz about the story before Mankiewicz left for Victorville. (He concludes that Mankiewicz never admitted this to Houseman or anyone else involved.) Welles gave Bogdanovich some examples of story incidents in the script he said originated with him. By looking into Welles's past for evidence, as Kael did into Mankiewicz's, we come up with other possibilities that would seem to substantiate his claim. For instance, the unmade *Smiler With the Knife* would also have been an attack on a controversial contemporary figure. In fact, in Welles's script, the Howard Hughes figure would have been introduced to an audience in the film by means of a "March of Time" newsreel feature. There is another set of tantalizing parallels:

A 1936 "March of Time" radio broadcast included an obituary of munitions tycoon Sir Basil Zaharoff, with invented dramatic episodes. In the opening scene, secretaries are burning Zaharoff's papers in the immense fireplace in the great hall of his chateau—the secret records (the narrator tells us) of a lifetime's involvement in wars, plots, revolutions, and assassinations. Other scenes present witnesses who testify to Zaharoff's ruthlessness. Finally, Zaharoff himself appears—an old man nearing death, alone except for servants in the gigantic palace in Monte Carlo that he had acquired for his longtime mistress. His dying wish is to be wheeled out "in the sun by that rosebush." Welles played Zaharoff.

THE VICTORVILLE SCRIPTS

In mid April, after six weeks of work, Mankiewicz and Houseman sent down a first rough draft. More than 250 pages long, *American,* as it was called, was what rough drafts usually are—excessive in content and lacking in focus. But nevertheless it provided what was most needed at this stage: a firm story structure on which to build.

*American* is the biography of a publishing tycoon and public figure told in retrospect after his death by the persons who had known him best. A similar plot premise had been used in *The Power and the Glory* (1933), directed by William K. Howard from a script by Preston Sturges, in which Spencer Tracy portrayed a controversial railroad magnate who was revered by a faithful few but detested by the many. One of the main weaknesses of that film is the cumbrousness of its flashback structure. To compensate for this tendency of multiple flashback plots, Mankiewicz came up with an ingeniously simple plot device—a mysterious deathbed utterance that is presumed to be the key to everything. Rosebud is a rather shameless piece of melodramatic gimmickry, but it is arguably a more effective narrative device than Welles's original idea of making the object of mystery something literary, such as a line from a Romantic poem. (Welles has always ceded the Rosebud gimmick to Mankiewicz.)

Equally as important as Rosebud is the cast of supporting characters, a gallery of stereotypes, admittedly, but an interesting and very serviceable variety: parents of humble origin from the West, a Wall Street tycoon, a pragmatic business manager, a stuffy first wife of enormous social standing, a somewhat dandified closest friend, and a shopgirl mistress.

About two-thirds of the way through *American,* there is a large story gap—probably an indication that the draft sent down at someone's insistence was incomplete. The missing portion would come to include all of Kane's early relationship with Susan—their meeting, the love nest, their marriage, her singing career. But after the gap, *American* resumes with another firm plot situation, the elderly Kane withdrawn with Susan to Xanadu, and it concludes with the identification of the rosebud clue for the audience.

Structurally, *American* has roughly the narrative order that the final *Kane* shooting script will have, and some of the material (especially in the first third) will remain substantially the same. But there are also some serious problems. To begin with, considerable paring is needed. Many scenes are undeveloped, superfluous, or merely dull. Among the most expendable material in *American* are scenes of Thatcher visiting Kane at his Renaissance palace in Rome on his twenty-fifth birthday to discuss the future management of Kane's interest; of Kane's honeymoon with Emily in the remote Wisconsin woods, with an army of chefs and servants in attendance (Kane's yacht, which had to be shipped up piece by piece and reassembled, is anchored in a small lake nearby); of a subplot involving Kane and the president, an oil scandal, and an inflammatory editorial that leads to an assassination attempt; of a chance meeting between Kane and his father at the theater one evening, the latter in the company of a "young tart" who turns out to be his new wife; of Kane's discovery of an affair between Susan and a young lover at Xanadu (Kane has him killed); and of the funeral of Kane's son (he was shot when he and other members of a fascist movement staged a raid on an armory in Washington). For another thing, much of the material in *American* lacks convincing dramatic motivation. Several key events are still early in gestation. Since most of the Susan material has not been written, there is no love nest to expose, and Kane's crooked opponents conspire to steal the election from him. Leland goes to Chicago not because of the election but because of an affront to his integrity as drama critic: a new policy, apparently instituted with Kane's blessing, to guarantee favorable notices to producers for their shows in exchange for advertising considerations. When Susan sings in Chicago, Leland passes out at his typewriter before finishing the review, but instead of having Kane finish it for him (an inspired touch), a box is run on the theatrical page saying the review will be a day late (the way it really happened to Mankiewicz once when he was a second-stringer on the *New York Times*). There are also internal inconsistencies. For instance, Emily is still alive in 1940, but she refuses to be interviewed; yet her part of the story appears at the appropriate place anyway, without a narrator. By far the most serious dramatic problem in *American* is its portrait of Kane. Mankiewicz drew a good deal of his material directly from Hearst without really assimilating it to dramatic need. There is a large amount of Hearst material in *Citizen Kane*—for instance, his scandalmongering, his ideological inconsistencies, San Simeon, the vast collections of everything under the sun, the awkwardness of his May—December romance with Marion Davies, even some of his memorable lines—but this is nothing approaching what is in the Mankiewicz script. *American* is by and large a literal reworking of specific incidents and details from Hearst's life. Much of it Mankiewicz knew on his own. As a former newspaper reporter, he had the professional's familiarity with all the great legends of journalism's most colorful era. As a privileged visitor to San Simeon, Mankiewicz would have observed firsthand such things

as Marion Davies's tippling, her passion for jigsaw puzzles, Hearst's fondness for arranging elaborate picnic outings, and so on.

But it is clear that Mankiewicz also borrowed from published accounts of Hearst. He always denied it, claiming all his information was firsthand, but coincidences between *American* and Ferdinand Lundberg's *Imperial Hearst* are hard to explain. Lundberg reports that Hearst's father acquired the *San Francisco Examiner* in 1880 for a bad debt of $100,000—precisely the amount Thatcher is offered for the *Enquirer* (thus spelled in *American*) after he acquires it in a foreclosure proceeding. Lundberg describes Hearst's phenomenal success in his first years in newspaper publishing and offers as a landmark the fact that by 1889 the *Examiner* had reached a Sunday circulation of 62,000. In *American,* when the *Enquirer*'s circulation reaches the 62,000 figure, Kane has it painted on a huge sign outside his rival's window. Lundberg reports that Hearst actually won his 1905 campaign for mayor of New York City:

> *Hearst won the election.* He was the victor by several thousand votes, it has since been established, but the Tammany bruisers, heeding their instructions from Murphy, went berserk. Hearst's campaign people were assaulted and ballot boxes were stolen from the Hearst wards and dumped into the East River.

Identical details appear in dramatized form in *American:*

> Narrator:
>
> On election day A LITTLE MAN, in an overcoat, with a card in his hat reading, "Watcher," is being given the bum's rush out of a laundry. (Sign in the window of the laundry reads "Polling Booth.") A line of about twenty people is stretched outside the door, with a policeman guarding the head of the line. As the Watcher is dragged through the door, he stands his ground firmly and turns to the policeman. The policeman deliberately turns his back on him. The Watcher is dragged along.
>
> SMALL BACK ROOM. Three men in overcoats and hats are sitting around the table. One has in front of him a huge pile of unfolded ballots.
>
> MOONLIGHT. A row-boat in the East River. A man reaches into the bottom of the boat, brings up a ballot box, and, helped by another man, throws the box into the river.

To have played the material in *American* as written would have involved some serious problems of copyright infringement. Strictly from a legal standpoint, *American* would be unusable without massive revision. The problem also has a dramatic side. Hearst was too free and easy a source of information for an unsteady writer like Mankiewicz. Most of *American* is quite simply *à clef* plotting with only the barest effort at characterization. Kane himself at this stage is more an unfocused composite than a character portrait, a stand-in mouthing dialogue manufactured for some imaginary Hearst. In this sense, Hearst is one of the principal obstacles to the script's further development. Before any real progress with the characterization could be made, the ties to his life had to be cut. That process began immediately after *American* and continued to the end of scripting. A lot of Hearst material survives in the film, but it is far less than was there at the beginning. (Lundberg eventually brought suit anyway.) One reason why Welles could later maintain so confidently that Kane was not Hearst may be that he had eliminated so much of Mankiewicz's Hearst material from the script that he imagined he had somehow eliminated Hearst in the process.

On April 28, less than two weeks after *American,* forty-four pages of revisions emanated from Victorville. Three very important changes appear in these pages. A decision has been made about the part of the story Emily might have told—most of it is to be assigned to Leland—and the framing segments with Bernstein and Leland have been rewritten to reflect this change. The stolen election has been abandoned; now Kane actually loses. The cause is presented in two important new scenes—one in which Emily insists Kane pay a certain call with her after the Madison Square Garden rally and its sequel, the encounter in Kane and Susan's love nest.

On or about May 9, Mankiewicz and Houseman completed their work at Victorville and returned to Hollywood with a second draft. Mankiewicz immediately went off to MGM on another assignment. Though he attempted to keep up with the revisions in the following weeks, he ceased to be a guiding hand in the *Citizen Kane* scripting process at this point. For this reason, it is important to look at the second draft carefully.

The most striking changes in the second draft involve Kane himself. Large chunks of material obviously based on Hearst have been removed. The stolen election is one example. Another involves Kane's educational history—how he was thrown out of college on account of a prank. Only one scene showing Kane with his publishing rivals remains. *American* had several tiresomely repetitive scenes intended to illustrate the libertine aspect of Kane's nature—Kane and Leland accompanied by women of questionable character at an expensive restaurant, Rector's, at the theater, and so on. This material has been considerably reduced in the second draft. The business of Susan's lover has also disappeared. Interesting scenes for Kane have been added—for instance, when Kane finds Leland passed out at his typewriter, he finishes the review himself, and when Susan leaves him, he smashes up her room. Other new scenes are not so fortunate—one, for instance, involving the burial of Kane's son in the chapel at Xanadu. Kane is overcome with grief. As he stares at the row of crypts, he begins to prattle about his mother, who also is buried there. He recalls how she loved poetry and begins to read the verse inscription on the wall.

Some individual narratives have been restructured, but the effect is more to bring out problems in the original

material than to provide solutions. When what would have been Emily's story is shifted to Leland, one result is that he is now responsible for a disproportionate share of major episodes in Kane's life—the human side of Kane's early years as a crusading publisher, the entire story of Kane's marriage and its deterioration and breakup, Leland's growing disillusionment with Kane's compromise of his values, and their final break over the opera review. But there is an even more serious problem. Leland's narration is now loaded with dramatic crises—not only the two that were originally his, the shady promotional scheme and the opera debut, but three of Emily's—the assassination attempt, Susan, and the lost election. The difficulty stems from the nature of *American,* which is essentially a string of discrete events lifted from a colorful biography. Once the necessary process of rearranging begins, the dramatic unmanageability of such material becomes apparent. One of the main problems that subsequent revisions will face is how to deal with a large surplus of crisis moments.

A related difficulty appears in the new version of Bernstein's story. Several episodes are newly assigned to him, including Thatcher's angry encounter with Kane in the *Enquirer* office, the first installment of the opera review incident with Leland passed out at his typewriter (Leland later tells the sequel of Kane's finishing the review), scenes of Bernstein as an uncomfortable social guest at Xanadu, and the divestiture sequence in which Thatcher and company take control of Kane's newspapers. Apparently, the writers are considering whether a narrator ought to have firsthand knowledge of what he relates. If the answer is yes, serious structural imbalances will be created elsewhere (there are now no scenes between Thatcher and the adult Kane), and the pacing of events will be seriously disrupted (as when a dramatic tour de force like the opera review is broken up and shared between two narrators). Even partial fidelity to such a principle would create difficult problems for other parts of the story (Kane's intimate life with Emily, for instance). Eventually, it is sacrificed to the general principle that we ought to see a developing chronological view of Kane's life.

Elimination of redundant material, the addition of several new scenes between Kane and Susan, the inspired touch of the opera review, and the improvement of many passages of dialogue are among the main accomplishments of the second draft. But numerous difficulties still remain, especially with the portrait of Kane, and on balance the second draft might most justly be characterized as a much-improved rough draft.

### WELLES AND THE LATER DRAFTS

Amalia Kent reworked the May 9 script into accepted continuity form, as she had done with the scripts for *Heart of Darkness* and *The Smiler With the Knife.* Copies were sent to Schaefer in New York, whose assent was needed to proceed, and to department heads so that planning could begin. Kent then prepared a breakdown script. This document contains only the scene designations and their physical descriptions. It allows the architectural values of a script to be separated from its literary values and formally stated for the purposes of budgeting the production. Once such information went into wider circulation, special precaution was needed to keep the secret under wraps. An informal conspiracy of silence began to be resolutely observed by all those immediately involved. Although it was obvious they were dealing with Hearst, no one spoke of this or acknowledged it unless it was strictly necessary in the course of work. There is one good reason why the silence worked so well despite the number of people involved: There were horror stories of how things that happened on sets somehow got back to Hearst and how even an unintentional offense could cost someone a career. Schaefer was unfazed by the potential complications (he probably saw another "War of the Worlds" in the making, and his lawyers did not object to the script) and gave his approval. Welles's contracts were redrawn. The new agreement formalized the postponement of both *Heart of Darkness* and *Smiler With the Knife* and allowed Welles to proceed with this unnamed project first. It was to be completed by October 1, 1940, after which he would still owe the two pictures called for in the two-for-one compromise worked out on *Heart of Darkness*.

Schaefer brought Welles East for an RKO sales meeting to assure skeptical distributors and exhibitors that he had something under way. Revisions on the Mankiewicz script resumed with great intensity after Welles returned to Hollywood on June 1. During the first two weeks of June alone, around 140 pages were revised—more than half of the total script. When the budget estimate based on the Mankiewicz script came out in mid June, the working script with changes in progress was consolidated and identified as a new draft, the third. Altogether, more than 170 pages in this script had been added or revised since Welles had taken over the script in mid May.

The new draft eliminates around 75 pages of the Victorville scenes. Some had been intended to enhance character—Kane and Leland at Rector's with their girls, for instance. Others had been intended to foreshadow—scenes of Kane and Susan in Chicago for her opera debut, for instance, give privileged glimpses into their private relationship. Others were merely redundant—Kane and family and a group of politicians gathered to announce his entry into politics, Bernstein's appearances at Xanadu, and (perhaps the most outrageous episode in *American*) the appearance of Kane Senior and his young wife. The most dramatic changes made by Welles involved the collapsing of lengthy expository sequences played as straight dramatic interchanges into snappy and arresting montages. The circulation buildup, which originally had been played in encounters between rivals and in expository discussions between Kane and his associates, is now given in a montage: the composing room, the Declaration of Principles on a front page,

a wagon with a sign "Enquirer: Circulation 26,000," various shots of the paper being delivered, a new number (62,000) being painted on the wall of a building, and Kane, Bernstein, and Leland looking at a *Chronicle* window display that includes a photograph of the rival paper's staff and a sign with its circulation figures. The scenes showing how Kane checkmated Thatcher and his cronies with pilfered documents have been eliminated, to be replaced by a three-and-a-half-page montage (expanded from a suggestion in *American*) of the *Enquirer*'s growing impact on the American scene in the 1890s. This montage ends with a close-up of Kane's passport (it reads: "Occupation—Journalist"), which provides a bridge to the scene of Kane's departure for Europe on a Cunard liner. The assassination material has been condensed in much the same fashion. The scenes showing how Kane's home life suffers as he becomes more deeply involved in the oil scandal story are eliminated. After Kane's encounter with the president, a rapid montage showing cartoon and editorial attacks on the president ends with a close-up of the word *TREASON*, then the assassination itself—a hand firing a gun, hands and uniformed arms struggling with the first hand, the White House in the background, a ticker tape spelling out the news.

The Welles revisions address two of the most glaring dramatic problems in the Victorville material, though still not conclusively. The first involves Emily. While it is possible to eliminate her as a narrator, she is still a necessary presence and force in Kane's life. The story of their marriage has to be accounted for, even if not by her. The Victorville script recognized this by retaining a series of conventional expository scenes chronologically depicting the disintegration of the marriage. Welles threw out the first of these scenes—the couple on their honeymoon—and substituted a much brisker treatment: two brief glimpses of their courtship. In the first, Kane introduces himself to Emily on board a ship bound for Europe and brashly declares his intentions; in the second, a short time later, they are making wedding plans. Welles eliminated a domestic scene that showed Kane doting over his young son but obviously preoccupied with his work and substantially revised a turgid scene after the assassination when Emily makes known her true feelings toward Kane. It is clear that Welles was dissatisfied with the Victorville treatment. In each successive draft of the script, he rewrites the material heavily, until he arrives at a totally appropriate way of playing it—the breakfast table montage.

The second problem involves the surplus of crises in the Leland narration. Most of this section has been rewritten as a kind of extended inquisitorial, in which Leland confronts Kane with the main issues and calls on him for an accounting—his complicity in the assassination attempt, the promotional scheme, his unfairness to Emily, his irresponsibility to others in general. That most of the result is either unfathomable or incoherent is hardly surprising. Welles is simply having Leland do with Kane the same thing *he* was doing with Kane. We do not move very far toward a solution to the problem of crises at this stage. But as a starting point in the necessary process of transforming Kane from Mankiewicz's cardboard portrait into the complex and enigmatic figure we see in the film, this set of revisions has significance well beyond their actual achievement.

Finally, some new material of special interest is added. Georgie, madame of a high-class brothel, makes her first appearance in the story. The party that Kane gives for his staff eventually adjourns to Georgie's Place. On the day of the assassination attempt, Kane is at Georgie's when one of his editors calls with the news. Whether these additions enhance the story or not, Welles himself was very keen on them. The first one remained in the script despite Hays Office objections to it, and although the scenes do not appear in the finished film, they were actually shot. A more durable addition is the lengthy direction that we are to see Susan's debut a second time, from her point of view—unquestionably one of the most inspired touches in the film.

On June 14, the preliminary budget estimate based on the Victorville script was ready. It showed a total picture cost of $1,082,798—more than twice the amount specified in Welles's contract as the limit above which special approval was required. It waved another red flag as well: A million dollars was a kind of magic number at RKO. Department heads worked under a standing rule of thumb never to exceed that amount except in the most extraordinary circumstances. In a similar situation, *Heart of Darkness* had been abandoned. Inconceivable as it now seems, the same thing could have happened to **Citizen Kane** even at this late stage. From June 14 to July 2, when the matter was finally resolved, the film was not actually shut down, but its future was definitely in doubt. During that period, the estimate was reduced by more than $300,000. Budgetary realities led to sweeping changes in all areas of the film's production. These areas will be dealt with in successive chapters. Insofar as the scripting is concerned, there were two major consequences: the need for immediate and drastic reductions and the reenlistment of Mankiewicz (because Welles now had to take charge of the overall problem) to assist in accomplishing them.

Welles's initial response was that the changes he had made in the Victorville material had almost surely brought down the cost already. A new draft incorporating all changes was prepared. Before submitting it, he eliminated the sequences set in Rome. Not only did this remove several costly sets from the budget, but it was also a sound decision for the story. The Rome sequences gave us our first view of the adult Kane at a very wrong moment dramatically, where he was living it up in Europe as a young man who had yet to take on any important responsibility. Instead of advancing the story, the Rome sequences tended to slow it down. With this material removed, Kane could now be introduced with one of those sudden and stunning, impulsive strokes that were to become his trademark—just a single sharp

line in a letter: "I think it would be fun to run a newspaper." The new draft was the fourth. Called Final (the usual name for the draft first mimeographed), it is the first on which the title **Citizen Kane** appears. It was ready from the stenographic service on June 18. The prognosis of the production estimators was gloomy— "any cuts so far made will not effect major savings," and it is still "fifty to sixty pages longer than the longest script we have ever shot in this studio."

On June 18, Mankiewicz went back on the payroll. He stayed on until July 27, around the time a regular shooting schedule began. During this period, three new drafts of the script were mimeographed. Up until this point, it has been possible to be relatively precise about who wrote what. After June 18, the identification process becomes much more difficult. The problem is not so much that Welles and Mankiewicz are both involved at the same time but rather the unusual production circumstances. Welles was preoccupied with other things now, so we can be sure it was Mankiewicz who was literally making the changes in the script. But to what degree was he determining or even influencing them? During the first week after Mankiewicz's return, the script was reduced by more than twenty-five pages. As we shall see, Welles, art director Perry Ferguson, and Gregg Toland jointly managed the budgetary crisis. Did the changes mainly involve adjusting the script to decisions that they had already made? Meanwhile, rehearsals began. To circumvent a rule against uncompensated rehearsing, the cast assembled each day at the Mankiewicz home. How many of the changes came about in rehearsal, with Mankiewicz serving in effect as a transcribing secretary? The records themselves do not provide the answers, but it seems clear that Mankiewicz's creative role was considerably diminished by this time.

The Revised Final draft, the fifth in all, is dated June 24. There are four principal changes, each one entailing an appreciable reduction in playing time or set costs. A long discussion between Leland and Emily after the election disaster is eliminated. In two other places, the action is telescoped: The early romance of Kane and Emily is now dealt with in a single shot—a closeup of a diamond ring on a hand, from which the camera pulls back to reveal the lovers kissing; the deterioration of the marriage is presented in a single scene; and the dockside scene of Kane's departure for Europe is removed, which eliminates the need for another set.

By July 2, severe cutting in all categories had made possible a revised estimate of $737,740. At this point, Schaefer gave final approval to proceed. One week later, a new draft, the sixth, the Second Revised Final, was ready for the Hays Office. It was fourteen pages shorter than the preceding draft, almost entirely as a result of one fundamental change—the removal of the assassination attempt on the president and its long, talky aftermath. The account of Kane's first meeting with Susan, originally a part of her narration, has been moved to Leland's story to replace the assassination material. In this position, their meeting is followed by the political campaign; now there is only one political crisis to be dealt with. Two of the film's most important conceptions also appear for the first time in this draft. One resolves the problem posed by Kane's first marriage, which has been reduced to the celebrated breakfast table montage: "NOTE: The following scenes cover a period of nine years—and played in the same set with only changes in lighting, special effects outside the window, and wardrobe." The second provides what may be the film's most striking, and is certainly one of its most resonant, images. The previous draft called for an unidentified scene "still being written" after Kane leaves Susan's smashed-up room; it appears in the new draft as the instruction to walk down the corridor between facing mirrors.

The seventh draft, the Third Revised Final—the shooting script—is dated July 16. It contains two very important structural changes. In the preceding draft, the newspaper party had been played in two separate segments—the first half in Bernstein's story, the second in Leland's—and Kane's European trip and engagement had been placed in between. The original justification for this was that the second part of the sequence centered on Leland's objections to Kane's behavior over Cuba. The incident of the opera review was to be broken up in the same way— Leland is found passed out at his typewriter in Bernstein's story; Kane is seen finishing the review in a continuation many pages later—so that each narrator reported only what he could have known firsthand. In the new draft, both sequences are rewritten to be played continuously. This decision smoothes out some rough edges, and it was to have an enormous impact on the effect of these scenes in the film.

THE CONTROVERSY OVER WRITER CREDIT

Although Welles denies it, the conclusion seems inescapable that he originally intended to take sole credit for the *Citizen Kane* script. The principal evidence is in letters written by Arnold Weissberger, New York attorney for Welles and the Mercury Theatre, to Welles and RKO in September and October 1940. The precedent for such an action had been established on the radio shows. The contractual agreements in radio were similar to those with RKO—Welles, on behalf of the Mercury, signed the primary contract with the sponsor. Writers were engaged under subsidiary contracts with the Mercury, and they assigned all claims of authorship to the corporation. In this way, a legal basis was created for Welles to claim script authorship regardless of the nature or extent of his actual contribution to the writing. He freely asserted the privilege: On the great majority of the radio broadcasts, either Welles was given sole writing credit on the air or no credit was given. Only rarely was another writer mentioned in this connection, and seldom if ever was the writer a member of the regular Mercury Theatre writing staff.

Mankiewicz's contract for work on the *Citizen Kane* script was with the Mercury Theatre, not with RKO. It contained the standard waiver of rights of authorship:

All material composed, submitted, added or interpolated by you under this employment agreement, and all results and proceeds of all services rendered or to be rendered by you under this employment agreement, are now and shall forever be the property of Mercury Productions, Inc., who, for this purpose, shall be deemed the author and creator thereof, you having acted entirely as its employee.

Apparently Welles believed that this agreement gave him unqualified right to decide the *Citizen Kane* scripting credit as he saw fit, as he had done in radio. In Hollywood, however, writers had been able to secure certain countervailing privileges. By industry custom, authorship and screen credit were treated as separate issues. Though a screenwriter signed away all claim to ownership of his work, he could still assert a right to public acknowledgment of his authorship of it. A set of guidelines had been worked out to ensure that those who deserved screen credit got it, and these guidelines were subscribed to by all the major studios. In certain circumstances, a writer who felt unjustly treated could submit his case to arbitration. There were unusual complications surrounding *Citizen Kane,* but the force of accepted practice was strongly in Mankiewicz's favor.

Mankiewicz received his last paycheck on August 3, bringing his total pay for work on *Citizen Kane* to $22,833.35. A letter from Weissberger to Welles on September 6 reveals the course of action they intended to pursue in regard to credits. Weissberger says he has learned that Mankiewicz will probably try to make trouble over the matter of screen credit. He does not want to go into details in writing; an intermediary who is returning to Hollywood soon will explain. He quotes the authorship waiver in Mankiewicz's contract and concludes from it that Mankiewicz has no claim to any credit whatever. He is looking into the situation further, and in the meantime Welles should say nothing. When the time comes, he can confront Mankiewicz with his contract. (Weissberger also explains that he has just learned of possible complications with the Screen Writers' Guild. This and his interpretation of the authorship waiver both indicate how thoroughly unfamiliar he was with the inner workings of Hollywood.) On September 17, the Mercury office drew up a preliminary billing sheet on *Citizen Kane* for review by RKO's legal department. The column for the writer credit contains this curious notation: "It has not been determined if there is to be a credit given for story or screenplay." This probably indicates that they were following Weissberger's instructions to keep quiet pending further advice. Another possibility is that they were preparing a fallback position in case Weissberger's preliminary opinion failed to hold up: to omit the writer credit altogether, as was sometimes done on the radio scripts. (Better no credit at all than to share credit—that way at least no attention would be drawn.) If so, they were not aware that such a course would have been equally problematic: A request for waiver of screenplay credit would come under a process of review similar to that for credit assignment.

On October 1, Weissberger raised the credits issue in a letter to RKO's West Coast legal department. He begins by repeating his contention that "Mercury's legal right to deny credit can be established." He acknowledges, however, that Mankiewicz may have recourse within the industry, and he asks for details on how similar complaints have been handled in the past. He is particularly concerned, he says, about whether the matter is likely to result in arbitration proceedings and "unpleasant publicity." The reply was guarded but clear in its implications: There are no agreements currently in effect under which Mankiewicz could force an arbitration. A new agreement with the Screen Writers' Guild containing a provision for arbitration has just been executed and will soon go into effect. Since Mercury is not a signatory to this agreement, it is not contractually bound to observe it. Nevertheless, RKO would not want to use this technicality to take advantage of the situation. And, to confirm Weissberger's suspicion, yes, disputes over writer credits generate a lot of publicity.

If Mankiewicz originally had some kind of understanding with Welles on the credits, the course of events can only have made him have second thoughts. As *Citizen Kane* moved along in production, rumors began to leak out that the early footage was sensational. It appeared that what some had predicted might turn out to be true—*Citizen Kane* would be a high point in everyone's career. Mankiewicz began to complain openly. With the general feeling for Welles in Hollywood what it was, support was not hard to line up. In a short time, Mankiewicz was able to build a full-scale word-of-mouth campaign in his behalf. On October 3, *Hollywood Reporter* rated his prospects high: "The writer credit won't be solo for Welles, if Herman Mankiewicz can keep talking." Faced with a combined threat of public exposure and further ostracism from the industry, Welles relented. In a gesture reminiscent of Kane, he put Mankiewicz's name first. The proposed credit read:

ORIGINAL SCREENPLAY

Herman J. Mankiewicz

Orson Welles

When this proposal was submitted to the Screen Writers' Guild for review, an ironic reversal occurred. The Guild pointed out that the credit proposed violated a provision in the writer-producer agreement that a producer could not take screenplay credit "unless he does the screen play writing entirely without the collaboration of any other writer." At this point, Mankiewicz joined Welles in an appeal, whereupon the Guild disclaimed jurisdiction because of the nature of the original contract between Welles and Mankiewicz, and the co-credit was allowed to stand.

Mankiewicz also received a form of public satisfaction. On Academy Awards night, Welles watched in humiliation as *Citizen Kane* lost in category after category and finally won only a shared Oscar for screenwriting. However, that was Mankiewicz's last moment in the limelight. After a temporary upsurge following *Citizen Kane,* his career trailed off again. Welles eventually got vindication of his own. By the time *Citizen Kane* was revived in the 1950s, Mankiewicz's name had been forgotten, along with the dispute over screen credit. Not that the details would have been of much interest: Directors were the prevailing critical interest, and films were being considered strictly as directors' creations. As a result, everyone but Welles was shut out of a share of the newfound glory for *Citizen Kane.* It was against this background that Pauline Kael undertook to rehabilitate Mankiewicz's reputation.

He could not have wished for a more sympathetic biographer. *Raising Kane* is a colorful biography of Mankiewicz as a Dickensian character—a good-hearted loser, undisciplined and always in some kind of hot water, but with a wit that serves as his saving grace. (Consoling his hosts just after he had thrown up on their formal dinner table, he assured them that the white wine had come up with the fish.) It is also a classic piece of journalistic exposé. Kael brought two principal charges: that Welles conspired to deprive Mankiewicz of screen credit and that Mankiewicz wrote the entire script. The second charge made the first seem all the more heinous. Her principal evidence was hearsay testimony from witnesses and participants who were openly sympathetic to Mankiewicz. The first charge seems to be true. Concerning the second, Kael wrote:

> Welles probably made suggestions in his early conversations with Mankiewicz, and since he received copies of the work weekly while it was in progress at Victorville, he may have given advice by phone or letter. Later, he almost certainly made suggestions for cuts that helped Mankiewicz hammer the script into tighter form, and he is known to have made a few changes on the set. But Mrs. Alexander, who took the dictation from Mankiewicz, from the first paragraph to the last, and then, when the first draft was completed and they all went back to Los Angeles, did the secretarial work at Mankiewicz's house on the rewriting and the cuts, and who then handled the script at the studio until after the film was shot, says that Welles didn't write (or dictate) one line of the shooting script of Citizen Kane.

This, as we now know, is a flagrant misrepresentation.

Welles attempted a point-by-point rebuttal of Kael in his interviews with Peter Bogdanovich. He also made a brief direct reply in a letter to the editor of the London *Times.*

> The initial ideas for this film and its basic structure were the result of direct collaboration between us; after this we separated and there were two screenplays: one written by Mr. Mankiewicz, in Victorville, and the other, in Beverly Hills, by myself. . . . The final version of the screenplay . . . was drawn from both sources.

Concerning Kael's treatment of the arbitration matter with the Screen Writers' Guild, Welles claims that Mankiewicz's motive was not to guarantee himself co-credit. "Quite the opposite. What he wanted was sole credit." Both Welles's contentions have a degree of factual basis, but each requires careful qualification. There *were* two separate drafts going for a time, as we have seen, but this was *after* Victorville; Mankiewicz's Victorville script was the foundation for all subsequent development. At one point, the arbitration matter did involve a question of sole screenplay credit for Mankiewicz, as we have also seen, but this came along very late, rather than being the issue all along, as Welles implies.

Welles had given a much more accurate summation in his testimony in the Lundberg copyright infringement case. In response to a question about the authorship of a specific scene, he said that it "was written in its first and second draftings exclusively by my colleague Mr. Mankiewicz. I worked on the third draft and participated all along in conversations concerning the structure of the scenes." To summarize: Mankiewicz (with assistance from Houseman and with input from Welles) wrote the first two drafts. His principal contributions were the story frame, a cast of characters, various individual scenes, and a good share of the dialogue. Certain parts were already in close to final form in the Victorville script, in particular the beginning and end, the newsreel, the projection room sequence, the first visit to Susan, and Colorado. Welles added the narrative brilliance—the visual and verbal wit, the stylistic fluidity, and such stunningly original strokes as the newspaper montages and the breakfast table sequence. He also transformed Kane from a cardboard fictionalization of Hearst into a figure of mystery and epic magnificence. *Citizen Kane* is the only major Welles film on which the writing credit is shared. Not coincidentally, it is also the Welles film that has the strongest story, the most fully realized characters, and the most carefully sculpted dialogue. Mankiewicz made the difference. While his efforts may seem plodding next to Welles's flashy touches of genius, they are of fundamental importance nonetheless.

### James Naremore (essay date 1989)

SOURCE: "Citizen Kane," in *The Magic World of Orson Welles,* Southern Methodist University Press, 1989, pp. 52-83.

[*In the following excerpt originally published in 1978, Naremore sides with Carringer as to the authorship of* Citizen Kane, *and suggests the script was as much concerned with Mankiewicz's and John Houseman's perception of Orson Welles as it was based on the life of William Randolph Hearst.*]

*Citizen Kane* is the product of an individual artist (and a company of his associates) working at a particular movie studio at a particular historical moment. This fact ought to be self-evident, but one needs to state it because the question of the "authorship" of *Kane* has become the oldest, worst-tempered, and most confused argument in

movie history. The debate has been revived in recent years by Pauline Kael, whose long essay for *The Citizen Kane Book* forced numerous angry replies from movie historians eager to defend Welles's contribution to the script. For those readers interested in a more complete, authoritative account of exactly who wrote what and when on *Citizen Kane,* I recommend Robert Carringer's study of the production history of the film. Carringer, who researched the RKO archives, examined all seven revisions of the script, and spoke to most of the people concerned, found documentary proof that Welles was one of the principal authors of the screenplay. In other words, the credits as they appear on the screen are fairly accurate: *Kane* was produced by Welles's company, co-authored by Herman Mankiewicz and Welles (John Houseman was offered screen credit, but declined), and directed by Welles, who also played the leading character.

Notice, however, that there are *two* sets of credits for the movie: at the beginning we are told that *Kane* is a Mercury production "by Orson Welles," and at the end, after the coat-grabbing finale, we are given a complete list of contributors, in which Welles's name plays a subsidiary role. Interestingly, both of these views of the film's authorship are correct—the first does not cancel out the second, and the truth of the film's origins can be understood only by keeping both in mind simultaneously.

Actually, the entire film works according to an identical principle, so that everything evokes its opposite and all statements about the protagonist are true in some sense. There are, to choose one minor example of the method, two snow-sleds. The first, as everyone knows, is named "Rosebud"; the second is given to Kane as a Christmas present by Thatcher, and is seen only briefly—so briefly that audiences are unaware that it, too, has a name. If you study the film through a movieola or an analyzing projector, you will discover that for a few frames sled number two is presented fully to the camera, its legend clearly visible. It is named "Crusader," and where the original has a flower, this one is embossed with the helmet of a knight.

Welles was probably unconcerned when his symbolism did not show on the screen. "Crusader" was a tiny joke he could throw away in a film that bristles with clever asides. I mention it not only because I am foolishly proud of knowing such esoterica, but also because it is a convenient way to point up the split in Kane's character and in the very conception of the film. In many ways it is appropriate that Thatcher should try to win the boy over with a sled named "Crusader." Kane will repay this gift by growing up to be a crusading, trust-busting newspaperman, out to slay the dragon Wall Street. (Hearst, his counterpart, had been known for the way he embarked on crusades, and in his earlier days, when it suited him, had been the enemy of the traction trust.) On another level, the two sleds can be interpreted as emblems of a sentimental tragedy: Kane has lost the innocence suggested by "Rosebud" and has been transformed into a phony champion of the people, an overreacher who dies like a medieval knight amid the empty Gothic splendor of Xanadu.

The essence of the film, in other words, is its structure of alternating attitudes. It is an impure mixture of ideas, forms, and feelings—part magic show, part tragedy; part satire, part sentiment—as divided as Kane himself. In fact the contrast between "Crusader" and "Rosebud" is only the most superficial instance of the way the film deliberately sets images, characters, and ideas against one another, as if it were trying to illustrate Coleridge's notion that good art always reconciles discordant elements. Thus the Freudian aspects of the screenplay create an ironic, almost playful effect, whereas the imagery of "Rosebud" tries to pull the audience's emotions back in the direction of mystery, demonic energy, and pathos. Nearly everything in the story is based on this sort of duality or ambiguity, so that we are constantly made aware of the two sides to Kane. He has not only two snow-sleds but two wives and two friends. The camera makes two visits to Susan Alexander and two journeys to Xanadu; it even shows two closeups of "Rosebud," once as it is being obliterated by the snows of Colorado at Mrs. Kane's boardinghouse, and then again as it is incinerated in the basement of Kane's Florida estate. Finally, in the most vivid clash of all, we are given two endings: first the reporter Thompson quietly tells his colleagues that a single word can't sum up a man's life, and the camera moves away from him, lingering over the jigsaw pieces of Xanadu's artwork; after Thompson's exit, however, the same camera begins tracking toward a furnace, where it reveals the meaning of "Rosebud" after all. The film has shifted from a darkened, intellectual irony to a spectacular dramatic irony, from apparent wisdom to apparent revelation.

Such perfect contrasts keep our feelings qualified, in suspension, leaving most audiences unsure whether to regard *Kane* as high seriousness or as some kind of brilliant conjuring trick. At every level the movie is a paradox: Kane himself is both a villain and a romantic, Faustian rebel, as much like Welles as he is like Hearst. The style of the film—and under this rubric may be included the various contributions of script, acting, and camera—is both derivative of earlier Hollywood models and self-consciously critical of them. The leftist political implications of the project adversely affected Welles's entire career, and yet in many ways *Kane* evades the concrete issues; it does, of course, mount a powerful attack on Hearst, but the attack is somewhat oblique— actually, *Kane* is almost as deeply concerned with the movies themselves, and with the potentially deceptive, myth-making qualities of the media, which are linked by extension to the deceptions of the Hearst press. Hence it produces a certain ambivalence not only toward its subject but toward the very methods which are used to disclose the subject.

Some of these tensions and internal divisions may be seen in the following close descriptive analysis. Taken together, they help make *Kane* not only a rich psychological portrait but a subtle commentary on its own text—a film that reveals all the paradoxes and contradictions of the Welles myth in general.

I

The movie opens with an act of violation. The dark screen slowly lightens to show a "No Trespassing" sign which the camera promptly ignores. To the strains of Bernard Hermann's haunting, funeral "power" music, we rise up a chain link fence toward a misty, bleak, studio-manufactured sky. The camera movement is accompanied by a series of dissolves which takes us first to a new pattern of barbed-wire, elongated chain links and then to an arrangement of iron oak leaves, presumably adorning a gate. I say "presumably" because the opening montage is meant to captivate and confuse the audience, leaving them slightly unsure of where they are at any given moment. The point here is not to reveal Kane's private world but to provide fascinating glimpses, frustrating the viewer with a baffling subjectivity. Thus, as we are taken beyond the gigantic "K" atop the fence and progressively nearer to a lighted window in a castle, we encounter a surreal combination of images: monkeys in a cage, gondolas in a stream, a golf course. Only the window provides continuity; in fact it seems to defy the logic of space by remaining at exactly the same point on the screen in each shot, growing portentously larger with every dissolve.

Kane's castle looks a bit like the home of a sorcerer, chiefly because of the stereoptic, *Snow White*-like effect of the RKO art work. Welles has to be credited for the way he allowed the talents of Perry Ferguson, Van Nest Polglase, Vernon Walker, and the Disney animators to come into play throughout the film. He had the wisdom to turn the rough cut of "News on the March" over to the newsreel department for editing, since they could best duplicate the style, and here he is able to use the art department with equal intelligence. Who else but Hollywood designers could have created such a spooky, compelling, vulgar design, a brilliant mixture of kitsch and idealism, satire and mystery? Except for the crepuscular lighting, their vision of Xanadu compares with the architecture of a Hearst-like estate which had recently been described by Aldous Huxley in *After Many a Summer Dies the Swan* (1939):

> On the summit of a bluff and as though growing out of it in a kind of stony efflorescence, stood a castle. But what a castle! The donjon was like a skyscraper, the bastions plunged headlong with effortless swoop of concrete dams. The thing was Gothic, mediaeval, baronial—doubly baronial, Gothic with a Gothicity raised, so to speak, to a higher power, more mediaeval than any building of the thirteenth century. . . . It was mediaeval, not out of vulgar historical necessity, like Coucy, say, or Alnwick, but out of pure fun and wantonness, platonically, one might say. It

was mediaeval as only a witty and irresponsible modern architect would wish to be mediaeval, as only the most competent modern engineers are technically equipped to be.

Our approach to this bizarre domain is as voyeuristic as anything in Hitchcock. The camera is drawn like a moth to the lighted window, where its journey is frustrated; the light immediately clicks out. Notice that the same forward movement of the camera, usually accompanied by dissolves, will be used throughout the film, until it becomes a stylistic motif. One thinks, for example, of the way the camera twice crawls up the walls of the El Rancho nightclub and moves toward a broken skylight; a dissolve takes us through the broken glass, enabling us to peer at Susan Alexander. There are a number of less obvious instances of the same technique, and some of them are worth listing here:

1) When Thompson (William Alland) enters the vaults of the Thatcher Memorial Library, the camera starts moving forward toward him, only to have a great iron door close in its face; a dissolve takes us beyond the door, the camera peering over Thompson's shoulder at the pages of Thatcher's diary.

2) When the flustered editor Carter (Erskine Sandford) leaves the offices of the *Inquirer,* sent by Kane to drum up sensational news, the camera stands looking at an artist's rendering of the building; a slow forward movement begins, a dissolve taking us closer to a window where Kane is writing his declaration of principles; another dissolve takes us through the window and inside the room.

3) When Kane first meets Susan and goes up to her apartment, the camera stand quietly in the hallway looking through an open door; Kane shuts the door and the camera rushes forward impetuously, almost anxiously, stopping only when Susan opens it again.

4) Near the end of the film, Kane walks out of Susan's bedroom at Xanadu, going past a mirrored hallway that casts reflections of his aging body off into infinity; after he passes, the camera zooms slightly forward toward the darkness of the empty glass.

5) In the climactic moments, the camera glides forward over Kane's possessions, a collection that looks like an aerial view of a metropolis. A dissolve takes us closer, the camera moving past the flotsam of Kane's life: a symbolic toy-box, a set of old newspapers bound in twine, a photo of Kane circa his first marriage, an iron bedstead from an earlier scene, another photo of Kane as a boy with his mother, and finally the snow-sled. Just as the camera draws near this final object, and before we can read the inscription, a workman enters and carries the sled away; another dissolve takes us to the furnaces, where the camera continues moving forward directly into the flames, at last coming to rest on the burning "Rosebud."

The constant forward movement of the camera through windows and doors and into dark corners is of course perfectly in keeping with the film's attempt to probe Kane's sexual unconscious, and it creates an appropriately eerie effect. Moreover, the ultimate revelation of the burning sled produces a vivid feeling of entropy—as if the camera had pushed as far as possible and the source of Kane's mystery were being consumed at the very moment when it is being discovered. There is still another sense, however, in which the technique of the opening segment becomes a part of the film's structure and meaning. It establishes the camera as a restless, ghostly observer, more silent and discreet than the journalists who poke about among Kane's belongings, but linked to them in certain ways. Like Kane's own newspapers, the camera has become an "inquirer," its search implicating the audience in a desire to find Kane's private rather than his public meaning.

The periodic frustrations the camera encounters—a door closing, a light clicking out—are like affronts to the audience's curiosity. They also create a sense of mystery and subtle anxiety which is enhanced by other elements in the opening of the film; consider, for example, the fascinating but confusing imagery we encounter inside Xanadu. When the camera reaches Kane's window only to have the light turned out, we dissolve to an equivalent reverse angle inside the bedroom. All we see, however, is a deeply shadowed figure lying as if in state. Throughout this sequence Kane will be photographed in expressionist shadow, or else the camera will be placed so near his figure that we can barely read the image. A gigantic closeup of the dying man's lips is the largest single shot, but until the lips move and whisper the crucial word, we have no idea what we are looking at. Even when they do move, they create a slightly ludicrous impression: a big mustachioed mouth seen from so close it looks like the mountains of a strange planet.

Nearly everything in Kane's bedroom is presented in this dreamlike, subjective, slightly confusing way. The inexplicable closeup of a cottage (a still photo superimposed with moving snow) turns out to be a paperweight, and when the camera pulls back to reveal this fact some confusion lingers, because everything—Kane's hand, the paperweight, and the background—is covered with snowflakes. From this shot we cut to another view of the hand, this time shown on the opposite side of the screen—a deliberately chaotic and "bad" editing style that does not allow the audience to orient itself inside the room. When the paperweight rolls down the steps and crashes (another piece of trickery created by several images spliced together) we cut to the most confusing shot of all: a reflection in a convex piece of broken glass, creating an elaborate fish-eye effect which is virtually a parody of the lens Toland will use to photograph the movie. We can barely make out a nurse opening a strange ornamental doorway and entering; another cut, to a low angle near the head of Kane's bed, shows the nurse placing a sheet over a body.

These fragmentary glimpses of Kane's world have been so fantastic, so enshrouded with darkness and mystery, that they hide more than they reveal. They tantalize the audience, only to cap the effect suddenly, without warning, by introducing the "News on the March" title card. The newsreel, once it gets under way, allows viewers to settle momentarily into a new, more logical narrative mode, grounded in presumably objective, documentary facts. It illustrates the dramatic curve of Kane's public life, explaining the origins of the strange castle we have just seen, and providing a general map for the various local instances which will be developed later in the film. Thus, as David Bordwell has pointed out, the two opening segments are like *hommages* to the fountainheads of cinematic "perception"—the fantasy of Méliès and the documentary realism of Lumière. Nevertheless these two modes do not achieve a synthesis. The newsreel, as much as the opening scenes, tends to remind the audience of the voyeurism inherent in the medium, and leaves Kane as much an enigma as ever. If the private Kane was seen too subjectively, too close up, the public Kane is seen too objectively and usually from too far away.

"News on the March" is a wonderfully funny parody of the hyped-up journalism that Hearst and Luce had helped to create; in fact Welles and about a fourth of the Mercury players had previously worked in the radio version of "The March of Time," and had borrowed freely some of its famous catch-phrases, such as "this week, as it must to all men, death came to . . . " But for all its self-important tone, the newsreel offers mainly a compilation of Kane's public appearances, usually filled with scratches and photographed from awkward vantage points. Repeatedly Kane is shown alongside politicians, allying himself first with the progressives and then with the fascists; in his early career he is shown waving and smiling at the public in awkward gaiety, but in the later pictures he becomes somber and camera-shy. We are told that "few private lives were more public," but actually we have only disturbing glimpses into Kane's domestic habits: a doctored photo of one of his Xanadu parties; a shot of him sitting beside an empty swimming pool, swathed in towels and going over a manuscript; a peep through a latticed gate, as a hand-held camera with a telephoto lens tries to show the old man being pushed in a wheelchair. The newsreel gives the impression that Kane was always being interviewed, investigated, or eavesdropped upon, but it leaves little sense of what the man was like and only a superficial notion of his influence on public affairs. Even "1941's biggest, strangest funeral" is shown only as a brief shot outside a pseudo-Gothic pile; the image is grainy (Toland's imitation of newsreel stock is always perfectly accurate) and the sky is a giant diffuser of light, so that we can see only a few rich mourners from a distance, over the massed heads of reporters.

Throughout this "documentary" there is a comic disparity between the awesomeness of Kane's possessions and the stilted old codger we actually see, as if the newsreel were trying to establish him both as a mythical character like Noah or Kubla Khan and as something of a joke. Kane consistently supports the wrong politicians; he marries a president's daughter and then gets caught in a sex scandal with Susan Alexander; he drops wet concrete over his Edwardian coat at a public ceremony; he vouches for the peaceful intentions of Hitler. He is so bumbling and foolish that little remains of him but his wealth, and even that is treated as a believe-it-or-not curiosity. But if we are awed at Kane's money and contemptuous of his behavior, we also begin to dislike the reporters who poke microphones in his face. This feeling is reinforced when Welles detaches us from the newsreel, suddenly breaking the illusion by cutting to a side view of the screen and the projection lights, then making an aural joke: the projector clicks off and the pompous musical fanfare groans to a stop, as if somebody were giving "News on the March" a raspberry.

The ensuing conversation among reporters is derived from a colorful presentation of a scene inside a movie theatre in the 1937 Theatre Guild production of Sidney Kingsley's *Ten Million Ghosts;* it is also one of the most self-reflexive moments in the film—shot in an actual RKO screening room which has been made to look more like a region of the underworld. The air is smoky and the reporters are sinister shadows; indeed they remain shadows throughout, even in the closing scenes, when a group of them tour the bric-a-brac of Kane's estate. The corners of forties-style suits are outlined against a blank white movie screen, and the editor (Philip Van Zandt) is shown from a radically low angle, gesturing against a "Nuremberg" light beaming down from the projection booth. Rawlston and his yes-men correctly perceive the emptiness and inconclusiveness of the newsreel, but their solution is to find an "angle." "It isn't enough to tell us what a man did," Rawlston says, "you've got to tell us who he was." The solution to this problem is the dying word "Rosebud," a gimmick worthy of Hearst himself, a device that will unify the story and give the newsreel viewers a sentimental insight into Kane's character.

Rawlston gives Thompson a tap on the shoulder and a shark's smile, ordering him to go out and get "Rosebud" "dead or alive." Notice, however, that the audience is not allowed to feel comfortably superior to this scene. We have already been made curious about "Rosebud," which, after all, has exactly the same function for Welles and Mankiewicz as it does for Rawlston. Indeed, Welles indirectly admitted this fact in one of his interviews with Peter Bogdanovich, where he talked about his discomfort with the sled idea: "Rosebud remained, because it was the only way we could get off, as they say in vaudeville." In other words, without "Rosebud" the movie would lack a neatly rounded plot and a nicely punctuated ending, in much the same way as Rawlston's newsreel lacks the proper impact until some oversimplified "key" has been concocted to explain Kane's life.

The projection room segment therefore serves to criticize the script and the whole process of filling a blank movie screen; it becomes ironically appropriate to have

Herman Mankiewicz, Joseph Cotten, and Erskine Sandford barely visible in the shadows of the room, playing the roles of reporters who scoff at Kane's dying words. Everybody, the audience included, has been involved in a dubious pursuit; Welles has stimulated our curiosity only to make us feel cautious. The three opening sections of the film have helped initiate the search for "Rosebud," but they are filled with so many ironies and opacities that they threaten to undermine the search before it has started.

The story now becomes a series of reminiscences by the witnesses to Kane's life, who create a "rounded" picture of the man. And here it is important to note that the script is fundamentally different from a movie like *Rashomon:* it does not becloud events by presenting separate versions of an unknowable reality, but instead gives different facets of a single personality—a method similar to the one Herman Mankiewicz's brother Joseph was later to use successfully in such pictures as *All About Eve* and *The Barefoot Contessa.* Kane's life is depicted more or less chronologically, through the memories of five characters who knew him at progressively later stages in his life. We never have the feeling that these characters are distorting the truth (even though Leland recounts domestic events he could not possibly have seen), and if we discount the opening and closing moments of the film, and the details of Thompson's search, the private life of Kane is shown in nearly as straightforward a fashion as the public facts of the newsreel. For all its juggling of time, therefore, *Kane* has a logical, rational structure; it is a film about complexity, not about relativity.

Thompson's quest is initiated with a thunderclap and a Gothic rainstorm, in a scary but comic contrast to Rawlston's last words ("It'll probably turn out to be a very simple thing."). We see a garish, dripping poster of a blonde woman, and the camera moves upward, sliding over the roof of the El Rancho and down through the skylight. (The name of the club is significant: El Rancho was the name Hearst gave his California ranch in the days before he built San Simeon.) Here again we are made to feel that the search for "Rosebud" is tawdry and sensational, notably so in a deep-focus shot that concludes Thompson's abortive interview with Susan. Thompson steps into a phone booth and his hat brim is silhouetted at the right corner of the screen; he closes the door and the headwaiter (Gus Schilling) moves just a fraction to the left so that he is framed by one of the rectangular glass panels; in the distance, her head bowed drunkenly over a table, is Susan. We are made aware of her sordid life, and we see a chain of predators arrayed in front of her. The waiter is trying to spy on Thompson, who has been trying to learn about Kane; Thompson, in turn, has to convey information to his boss at the other end of the line. "Hello, Mr. Rawlston," he says. "She won't talk." The composition of the shot is all the more troubling because the extreme depth of perspective makes the chain of predators seem to extend out into the audience, bringing the viewers by implication into the film's corrupt world.

The El Rancho scene ends with still another kind of self-conscious flourish, a blackout joke. Thompson tries bribing John, the headwaiter, who comments innocently, "Thank you . . . thanks. As a matter of fact, just the other day, when the papers were full of it, I asked her. She never heard of Rosebud." Fade out, with an ironic, playful chord of Herrmann's music. Nearly all the fragments of the narrative have been structured this way, with a mild shock or a witty image at the beginning and a joke or an ironic twist at the end. It is exactly this quality which made Pauline Kael describe *Kane* as the epitome of "thirties comedy," a genre which she points out was fathered on Broadway by George S. Kaufman in the twenties; Kael is particularly good at describing the "fullness and completeness" with which the film manipulates this tradition, becoming, at least in its opening parts, a collection of sketches "arranged to comment on each other." The striking thing about *Kane,* however, is that the cynical, wisecracking style of the Kaufmans and Hechts has been put to the service of something more difficult, the movie achieving a rare commingling of brittle artifice, tough social realism, and romantic tragedy. The "thirties comedy" is there, of course, especially in the early scenes, but the ultimate feeling is different, affected by Welles's and Toland's Germanic staging, by the unsentimental acting of players like Dorothy Comingore (whose voice bears a prophetic resemblance to Marilyn Monroe's), and by the indirect influence of impressionist novelists like Conrad and Fitzgerald. To call *Kane* essentially a comedy or a "newspaper" yarn is therefore to place the main emphasis on certain features in the first third of the story, and to oversimplify its scope and tone.

Just how complex this tone is may be seen in the next sequence—Thompson's visit to the Thatcher Library—which begins with another joke. Herrmann plays his "power" motif with a flat, stale brass; the camera tilts down from the model of a huge, ugly statue of Thatcher and locates Thompson speaking with a prototypical lady librarian, who reminds him of the rules pertaining to all manuscripts. Obviously the library has been designed to emphasize Thatcher's vanity and coldness: the inner vault seems as long as a football field, and at the far end is a small safe from which an armed guard extracts a volume of a diary, bringing it forward as if he were bearing the Eucharist. The whole ridiculous edifice appears to have been constructed to house Thatcher's tiny memoirs, but the effect of the imagery is more than simple invective.

The mannish librarian stands at military attention while the guard, caught in the beam of a "Nuremberg" light, brings forth a glowing book. Thompson is closer to the foreground, so that he looks a bit like Kafka's Joseph K. come before the Courts of Law. The Gothic lighting is meant partly to create a comic irony, yet at the same time it produces an awesome scene, an effect of wonder coexisting with the satire. Lawrence Goldstein and Jay Kauffman, in their book *Into Film,* have described the vault as a "way station between heaven and hell . . . the guard becomes a divine messenger bringing the fiercely glowing documents out of the darkness [like] the tablets offered Moses; and the hard mahogany table that will receive the documents burns with the glint of a sacred altar." Throughout *Kane,* this aura of sacredness is mixed with elements of hokum and profanity, so that we are aware of banal material goods being mystified into a spiritual netherworld. The lighting style, like nearly everything in the movie, resists being described either as pure satire, as seriousness, or as old-fashioned "movie magic"; instead it is carefully designed to underscore one of the film's leading themes—the transformation of money into myth.

The principle of contrast which guides the film is repeated when, from one of the darkest moments, we move to one of the lightest. The "Thatcher" portion of the film, which grows out of Thompson's reading of the diary, is at first somewhat Dickensian in mood, as befits Thatcher's generation. Thatcher himself is a cold-hearted moneybag, and his story tells how a poor child rises suddenly to great expectations. Within a few moments we see Charles Foster Kane being lifted from a snowy playground in front of his mother's boardinghouse and set down at a richly Victorian Christmas celebration, although in both places the atmosphere is chilly, the boy surrounded by menacing adult figures. George Coulouris (made up to look rather like John D. Rockefeller) plays Thatcher in broad caricature, delivering his lines at top speed; in a charmingly exuberant and altogether anti-realistic montage which foreshadows the opening of *The Magnificent Ambersons,* he constantly turns to face the camera, muttering in disgust as the young Kane grows up, founds a newspaper, and then attacks Wall Street. But Kane rises only to have an ignominious fall; the narrative as a whole covers the period between the winter of 1871 and the winter of 1929, when Kane, ironically forced to turn part of the control of his newspapers over to his former guardian, broods on his failure, telling Thatcher that he would like to have been "everything you hate." By the end, we are made to feel that Capital has always been in charge of Kane's life, and that the market crash has done little more than solidify the power of America's major bankers by placing the *Inquirer* in Thatcher's hands. At the same time a nostalgic evocation of the nineteenth century has given way to a somber present; indeed the deep-focus shot of the room where Kane signs part of his rights away bears a vague resemblance to the tomb-like Thatcher Library.

The portrait of Kane which emerges from these memoirs contains as many ironies and ambiguities as the plot. In the boarding-house scene, where for once we might expect to see Kane as the innocent victim of social determinism, he is depicted as something of a brat; in fact, the closeup of Mrs. Kane hovering protectively over her child is almost comic because he looks like such a mean kid. By contrast, he is at his most charming and sympathetic during the early scene in the newspaper office, where his potential danger is underlined, but where he

is shown as a darkly handsome, confident young man, loyal to his friends and passionate about his work. This is, in fact, the point of Welles's full-scale entry into the film, and it is predictably stunning: Thatcher, who has been reading a succession of *Inquirer* headlines, lowers a paper ("Galleons of Spain off Jersey Coast") to reveal Kane sitting at his editorial desk. Here at last, greeted by a triumphal note of Herrmann's music, is the young Welles of Mars panic fame, propped easily in a swivel chair, clad in shirt sleeves, sipping coffee. He has been made up to look casually rich and beautiful, and he glances at Thatcher with a bemused, Machiavellian glint in his eye. In the same shot Leland and Bernstein enter the frame, Leland calmly taking a cigar from the desk (he is an addict, as we see later), and Bernstein scurrying past on official business. Throughout the scene, Welles makes himself a calm figure at the center of a storm, blithely dictating a telegram which echoes one of Hearst's most famous comments to a reporter ("Dear Wheeler, you provide the prose poems and I'll provide the war"), and, in a large, climactic closeup, thumbing his nose at Thatcher's warnings ("You know, Mr. Thatcher, at the rate of a million dollars a year I'll have to close this place—in sixty years").

In this scene, as in other episodes from the same period in his life, Kane seems generous with money and disrespectful toward stuffy Victorian authority; perhaps most importantly, he says he is committed to the "people" as opposed to the "trusts." Thatcher and the elderly editor Carter—a harrumphing old banker and a genteel incompetent—are perfect foils to his rebelliousness. They behave like outraged schoolmasters, making Kane's yellow journalism and his attempt to start a war in Cuba seem like a combination of boyish pranksterism and creative energy. But Kane's bullying attitude and what he actually says tend to suggest a totally different sort of character. He himself offers an explanation for our mixed emotions: "The trouble is," he tells Thatcher, "you don't realize you're talking to two people." On the one hand is the Kane we see, the pretty young man who claims to represent the interests of the public; on the other hand is the Kane who has investments in Wall Street and who knows down to the penny the amount of his holdings ("eighty-two thousand, three hundred and sixty-four shares of Public Transit Preferred"). "If I don't look after the interests of the underprivileged," he remarks, in one of the places where contradictions are reconciled, "maybe somebody will—maybe somebody without money or property."

When Thompson closes the diary and exits the library ("Thanks for the use of the hall"), he goes to interview Bernstein, who maintains the spell of Kane's charm. Bernstein talks mainly about the period between the founding of the newspaper and Kane's marriage to Emily Norton, a woman who "was no Rosebud." The only real apologist for Kane in the film, Bernstein is basically a likeable character, and evokes sympathy. Except for the reporters, he is the only person who has remembered Susan after Kane's death ("I called her myself the day he died. I thought maybe somebody ought to"). He is also completely free of self-importance and moral superiority, and even his reactionary comment on the Panama Canal arises more from a defense of his dead friend than from any self-serving motive. He is realistic about old age and death (old age is the "only disease you don't look forward to being cured of"), as well as about his position in life ("Me? I'm chairman of the board. I got nothing but time"); nevertheless he seems spry and at peace with himself. Even the setting for his interview is conducive of a melancholy serenity: shadows fill the room, but rain falls outside the high windows and a fire burns in the hearth. Bernstein sits in a big leather chair, his face reflected in the polished surface of his desk as if in a quiet pool. Here, photographed in a long take which contains some of the most discreet camera movements in the film, he tells the little story about seeing a girl in a white dress on the Jersey Ferry (Welles's favorite moment, beautifully acted by Everett Sloane, whose voice and manner come dangerously close to suggesting an old crone) and he reminds us that he is the only character who has been with Kane until "after the end."

And yet the kindness and the cozy atmosphere do not conceal the fact that Bernstein's friendship has been compromised. We soon learn that he has been more like a devoted child, and his devotion has had sinister consequences. All his judgments rise logically out of his character as an over-faithful associate, from a different social class than Kane, who has become a kind of stooge. The furthest removed from the patrician Leland, he is described, in a scene that was dropped from the completed film, as having once been in the "wholesale jewelry business"; his talents, Kane says wryly, "seemed to be what I was looking for." Thus even though Kane will tell Emily in no uncertain terms that Bernstein may pay a visit to the family nursery, there remains a discreet distance between the two men; we see Leland and Kane arrive together at the *Inquirer* offices in a hansom cab, dressed in the height of New York fashion, while Bernstein tags along atop a delivery wagon, fulfilling his purpose as the guardian of Kane's possessions. Later, at the political rally and at Susan's concert, Bernstein will be photographed in the company of Kane's goons; as Kane's financial agent and unquestioning companion, he has been responsible for whatever dirty work needed doing, and it is clear that he has always placed loyalty above principle. Hence there is a deep irony in the comfortable serenity of his old age, a luxury which has come to him like a "tip" from his employer.

Bernstein's reminiscences are chiefly about adventure and male camaraderie; even so, further ironies are obvious. Kane sweeps into the *Inquirer* and turns it overnight into a twentieth-century paper, flamboyantly promising to be a knight-errant for the people, "a fighting and tireless champion of their rights as citizens." Only a few moments before, however, he has cynically concocted a lurid news item about sex and murder, during which he tells Carter, "if the headline is big enough, it makes the news

big enough." Bernstein himself acknowledges these warts on Kane's character, but interprets them as ingredients of a tragic flaw. "I guess Mr. Leland was right about the Spanish-American War," he says, but he defends Kane anyway, describing him as a man connected with the destiny of the country.

During Bernstein's flashback, the sense of manifest destiny and the exhilaration of seeking Kane in action give the film most of its feel as a "newspaper" picture, although it is a picture of such ambition and intelligence that it makes others of the type seem shallow. It manages to show all the contradictions in liberal democracy through a single editorial desk, the newsroom literally becoming a focal point of social history, where we see the country moving through various stages of democratization—each attempt at progress generating new conflicts and new evils. Here, as later in *The Magnificent Ambersons,* Welles found a way to combine the chronology of individual characters with the chronology of the nation at large; America moves from the age of the Tycoon, through the period of populist muckraking, and into the era of "mass communications," with turn-of-the-century types like Kane being destroyed by the very process they have set in motion. Perhaps in this respect Bernstein's defense of Kane has a historical validity. Kane is in fact the quintessential "American" that Mankiewicz's original title for the film *(American)* had called him—a man designed to embody all the strengths and failings of capitalist democracy.

As I have already suggested, the film's ambiguity and ironic detachment about Kane, its acute sense of the relation between character and history, spills over into the portraits of the minor players. Bernstein and Leland, for example, are marvelously paired, the tensions and contrasts between them becoming indistinguishable from the separate aspects of Kane's own personality. Leland, whom Thompson now visits in a geriatric ward, is often regarded as the spokesman for the "moral" of the film, but while it is true that he serves as a sort of conscience for Kane, he is as flawed and human as the doggedly loyal Bernstein. Like everyone else, he has been placed in a social and psychological context: the last member, the ultimate refinement, of a fading and effete New England aristocracy ("one of those old families where the father is worth ten million bucks and then one day he shoots himself and it turns out there's nothing but debts"), he is an aesthete who despises the capitalists but who seems out of place among the workers. Clearly he lacks Kane's vitality, and is fascinated with Kane for that very reason. A dandy and a puritan, he is very much the "New England schoolmarm" Kane has named him; in fact, the film may be hinting that his involvement with Kane is partly a displacement for sexual feelings. Mankiewicz and Welles were prohibited from showing a scene in a bordello where Kane unsuccessfully tries to interest Leland in a woman, but even without this scene Leland seems to have no active sex life. As a young man in the Bernstein section he barely conceals his admiration for Kane, who has been his benefactor and who apparently shares his idealism.

When he grows disillusioned, there is inevitably a "loose" woman involved: at the big *Inquirer* party, his frowns of disapproval and complaints about the war with Spain are intercut with images of Kane making time with one of the chorus girls, and when the "love nest" with Susan Alexander brings an end to Kane's political career it is Leland, not Emily Kane, who behaves like a jilted lover.

In his old age, Leland suggests an idealist who has degenerated into a cynic. (Joseph Cotten's makeup here has always seemed to me a bit overdone, but he has been perfectly cast in the role, his voice suggesting a "weak" version of the slightly genteel, upperclass Southern lilt one hears in Welles's own speech.) He has grown a bit smug, but his mock senility and his bitter jokes do not completely hold off despair. He tells Thompson that "a lot of us check out with no special conviction about death. But we do know what we're leaving . . . we believe in something." These words, which can be taken as a valid criticism of Kane, are relatively small comfort. Leland himself is so lacerated with age and disillusionment that he now has only cigars to sustain him. He is charming of course, but his wit has a hollow, grotesque quality, resembling nothing so much as a dried-out Hollywood script writer. The setting itself emphasizes sterility and death—a purgatorial hospital sunroof where a few ghostly figures in wheelchairs are attended by ugly nurses, and where even the sunlight seems cold.

The atmosphere of Leland's interview is particularly ironic in view of the story he tells. Although Bernstein has suggested that "Rosebud" might be a woman, it is Leland who talks about Kane's love life; a more intimate friend than Bernstein, he recounts the period between Kane's first marriage and his attempt to turn Susan Alexander into an opera star. From a sociopolitical study of Kane, the script now begins to shift toward straightforward, though rather simplified, psychoanalysis.

At this point in his history, Kane is a greater public figure than ever, his politics constantly being played off against the crisis of his personal life. The two women he meets are as much physical and social opposites as Leland and Bernstein have been, yet in their own way both are connected to his desire to assert mastery, his need to find what Leland calls "love." The celebrated breakfast-table montage showing the disintegration of Kane's marriage to Emily (Ruth Warrick, whom Leland describes aptly as "like all the girls I knew in dancing school") is followed by the comic toothache scene in Susan Alexander's apartment, the allegro pace dissolving into a sweet, intimate rendezvous. Aided by what is surely the least ostentatious, most persuasive makeup job in the film, Welles turns rapidly from an ardent husband wooing a president's niece into a tired businessman courting a salesgirl.

Susan's toothache is a typical Hollywood "meet-cute" device, and as if he were acknowledging his own cleverness Welles casts shadow pictures on the wall to amuse her: "Gee," she says, "you know an awful lot of tricks. You're not a professional magician are you?"

Kane, however, is as much the victim of illusions as their creator. He sentimentally imagines that Susan has a mother like his own, and the scene where he presides quietly over her "recital" is followed immediately by the opening of his campaign for governor—the sexual conquest linked to a hubristic attempt to dominate the populace. In fact, the closing line of Susan's song concerns the theme of power: it comes from *The Barber of Seville,* and roughly translates "I have sworn it, I will conquer."

The ensuing political rally is almost pure expressionism, and is a good example of how the film creates large-scale effects with a modest budget and the optical printer. In place of a crowd of Hollywood extras, the figures in the audience are obviously painted and abstracted, revealing both Kane's delusions of grandeur and the crowd's lack of individuality. Everything is dominated by Kane's ego, from the initial "K" he wears as a stickpin, to the huge blowup of his jowly face on a poster, to the incessant "I" in his public speech; now and then, however, we cut away to the back of the hall, the oratory becoming slightly distant, Kane suddenly looking like a fanatical puppet gesticulating on a toy stage. He talks about "the workingman and the slum child," and meanwhile the frock-coated men behind him are arranged to resemble the bloated rich of a Thomas Nast cartoon, one of them leaning on a polished walking stick while his silk top hat lies casually on the floor. The atmosphere is somehow both Germanic and purely American, Kane's stem-winding campaign speech taking place in a setting that subtly evokes newsreel shots of Hitler's harangues to his political hacks.

Throughout the rally Kane's supporters—Leland, Bernstein, Emily, and his young son—have been isolated in ironic, individual closeups, but his political rival, Boss Jim Gettys (Ray Collins), stands high above the action, the stage viewed over his shoulder, so that he dominates the frame like a sinister power. It is Gettys who is truly in control of this campaign, and the showdown he subsequently arranges between himself, Kane, Emily, and Susan—a private conversation in perfect contrast to the rally—is one of the most emotionally effective scenes in the film. There are over a dozen shots in the sequence, one of them a rather long take, but no closeups; the characters are dynamically blocked, with Kane, Susan, and Gettys alternately stepping into complete shadow as the tide of the conversation changes. On the whole, however, the scene is as much a triumph of ensemble acting as of direction. The evil Gettys, who is surely as much a monster as Kane, is underplayed by Collins, who suggests a nice family man with just a touch of crudeness; knowing his power, he behaves courteously to Emily, even though he tells Kane that he is "not a gentleman." "You see, my idea of a gentleman . . . Well, Mr. Kane, if I owned a newspaper and didn't like the way somebody was doing things . . . I wouldn't show him in a convict suit with stripes, so his children could see him in the paper, or his mother."

One mamma's boy has taken revenge on the other, and as a result Kane explodes. "I can fight this all alone," he shouts, and then screams, "Don't worry about me. I'm Charles Foster Kane! I'm no cheap, crooked politician trying to save himself from the consequences of his crimes. Gettys! I'm going to send you to Sing Sing!" What makes the scene even more powerful are the voices of the two women, who provide a virtually musical counterpart to the male contest. Emily's voice is quiet, determined, and formal: "There seems to be only one choice for you to make, Charles. I'd say that it's been made for you." Meanwhile Susan, who is completely ignored by everyone, pipes shrilly, "What about me? Charlie, he said my name'd be dragged through the mud."

Here, at the same moment as the political issues are about to be brought forward, the film has shifted almost completely into its examination of Kane's sexual life. In fact the only concrete evidence we are given of Kane's tyranny, the only person we will actually see being damaged by his actions, is Susan Alexander. The issue seems to warrant a brief digression, because in this respect *Kane* contrasts vividly with the usual muckraking accounts of William Randolph Hearst's career. Although Mankiewicz and Welles alluded to many of the deceptions described by writers like Ferdinand Lundberg, they underplayed the violence associated with the real Hearst empire, suggesting it only through occasional asides and the imagery of the political rally. Thus Hecht and MacArthur's *The Front Page,* for all its amoral, rover-boys comedy, actually does a good deal more to convey the seamy side of Hearst's endeavors. For example, during the newspaper wars of early twentieth-century Chicago, Hearst had employed gangsters to rout his competitors; gunmen like Dion O'Bannion had beaten up rival newsboys and even shot innocent civilians, while Hearst's editors blamed the trouble on "labor agitators." Through most of the century Hearst was a vigorous opponent of unions and child labor legislation, and his mining interests in Peru were more or less forced labor camps. Lundberg had charged that Hearst's employees were not merely the victims of sweat shops: "they have, in many instances, been literally enslaved, indentured for long periods, and kept in employment against their will, under the muzzles of guns." *Citizen Kane*'s only apparent reference to such crimes is to show Bernstein in the company of hired toughs, and to have Leland berate Kane for his paternalistic attitude toward workers. Just when Leland meets the politically broken Kane in the abandoned newsroom and accuses him of swindling the public, the film veers off into the most intimate details of Kane's love affair with Susan.

Such a phenomenon is all the more interesting if we look back at some of the previous Hollywood movies about capitalists—*The Power and the Glory* (Fox, 1933), for example, or *I Loved a Woman* (Warner Brothers, 1933)—where, as in *Kane,* the treatment of the tycoon's public life gives way to a preoccupation with his private affairs. Several critics have already stressed the similarity between *The Power and the Glory* and *Kane;* the earlier film is not especially liberal in tone—in fact it contains a vicious and even racist scene in which the protagonist, Spencer Tracy, heroically puts down a mob by insulting a thickly accented labor organizer. Nevertheless, screenwriter Preston Sturges's flashback technique and certain of his characterizations were undoubtedly known to Mankiewicz and Welles. Spencer Tracy's floozy mistress, for example, slightly resembles Susan Alexander, and the scene in a child's nursery where the love affair is brought to an end is reminiscent of the climactic moments in Susan's bedroom at Xanadu. Equally influential, it seems to me, is *I Loved a Woman,* which not only suggests certain features of Kane's character, but also foreshadows the whole Emily-Susan side of the plot. *I Loved a Woman* concerns John Hayden (Edward G. Robinson), a Chicago meat packer's son who begins life as an aesthete and becomes a monopolist and profiteer. "I'm a human puzzle," he says at one point, referring to his penchant for art collecting. Hayden marries a cold, ambitious socialite, a scheming woman who gradually changes him from a fop into a ruthless meat baron. Miserable in this loveless marriage, he is attracted to a young opera singer (Kay Francis), who needs his financial backing. Midway through the film she invites him up to her apartment; there, in a scene remarkable for its parallels with *Kane,* the aspiring singer plays "Home on the Range" on an old piano, while the tycoon sits back in a cozy chair and remarks that the song reminds him of his mother.

Although *I Loved a Woman* contains some veiled references to the career of Samuel Insull, it, like *The Power and the Glory,* is a mediocre and sentimental film, interesting chiefly for its possible relationship to *Kane.* And what both of these earlier works show is that Mankiewicz and Welles were using one of the oldest and most effective ploys of Hollywood melodrama: they were disguising, condensing, and displacing the social issues—using a love story to illustrate the character flaws that would presumably make the tycoon a danger to the public. The only difference at this level between *Kane* and previous films is the degree to which its politics are tilted to the left.

But even though the shift into sexual themes results in a kind of evasion, the basic issues are not entirely subverted. Susan Alexander is only roughly similar to Marion Davies, but that is obviously not because Welles and Mankiewicz feared Davies's wrath or wanted to protect her. Susan serves as a reminder to the audience of Hearst's domineering patronage of his mistress, and more importantly she becomes a symbol for his treatment of the society at large. As Leland tells us, she represents for Kane a "cross-section of the American public." She has had a middle-class mother who gave her music lessons, and when Kane meets her she is also a working girl, undereducated and relatively innocent. (Like most of the characters in the film, Susan has mixed motives; she is not the addle-brained gold digger some critics have made her seem.) She comes from a social level similar to that of Kane's own parents, and his relationship with her is comparable to his relationship with the masses who read his papers. It is true that Kane showers her with wealth, but this merely confirms Leland's remark in the desolated, post-election newspaper office: 'You just want to persuade people that you love them so much that they ought to love you back." In fact, all of Leland's accusations and prophecies about Kane's relationship to his readers are fulfilled in Susan's part of the film. "You talk about the people as though you owned them," Leland says. Kane's treatment of Susan is a confirmation of this charge, and it also reminds us of the violence he is willing to use to have his way; thus in the last reels, which show Kane retreating more and more from public life, Susan is reduced from a pleasant, attractive girl to a harpy, and then to a near-suicide.

The film emphasizes the fact that Susan sings unwillingly, at the command of her master. During the election campaign, Kane establishes his "love nest" and the relationship is summarized in a single shot: in the foreground Susan is poised awkwardly at a grand piano; farther back in the room, Kane is enthroned in a wicker chair, applauding slowly and grinning in satisfaction; still farther back in the frame, visible through the archway to another room, is a sumptuous double bed. After his marriage to Susan, Kane tells the reporters, "We're going to become an opera star," and he hires Matisi to begin the arduous, comically inappropriate series of music lessons. The backgrounds in this part of the film grow more and more opulent, while Susan becomes increasingly driven and humiliated. Her singing becomes not only a painful form of work but a kind of involuntary servitude. As a result, her resemblance to Marion Davies fades. She looks more like those Peruvians toiling at gunpoint in Hearst's copper mines, even though she is certainly getting better pay.

The choice of opera rather than movies for Susan's career is also significant. It not only brings references to Welles's boyhood, to Insull, McCormack, and Sybil Sanderson into the film, but it also highlights the difference in social class between Susan and the patrons for whom she works. We see her kneeling on satin pillows, pitifully frightened and garishly made up, singing "Ah! Cruel" to a dozing, tuxedoed audience, while up in the rafters a laborer holds his nose and shakes his head sadly. "I'm not high-class like you," Susan tells Kane in an even shriller voice when she kneels again on the floor and reads the Leland-Kane review, "and I never went to any swell schools." She attempts to quit the opera, reminding Kane that "I never wanted to do it in the first place." Kane, however, orders her to continue because "I don't propose to have myself made ridiculous." In a scene remarkable for the way it shows the pain of both people, his shadow falls over her face—just as he will later tower over her in the "party" scene, when a woman's scream is heard on the soundtrack.

Leland has warned that the workingman will not always tolerate Kane's patronage: "you're not going to like that one little bit when you find out it means your working-man expects something as his right and not your gift." This, of course, is one reason why Susan leaves Kane. Naturally we sympathize with Kane when he recalls "Rosebud" and when the camera reveals his secret in the closing moments; in some ways the Susan Alexander plot has clouded the issues, replacing political with personal concerns, but in other ways it shows how the public and sexual concerns are interrelated. Rather like the symbols in a dream, Susan helps to censor the content even while she preserves its underlying significance.

But if concrete political issues are somehow present in the film, Kane himself continues to be depicted as a mystery to be unraveled. The wide-angle, deep-focus photography in the later sections enhances the mystery by frustrating Welles's inquisitive camera, setting up a feeling of space that can never be crossed no matter how many "No Trespassing" signs are disregarded. Throughout, Kane has been presented with a mixture of awe, satiric invective, and sympathy. He has provoked widely different responses from the people around him: in the newsreel he has been attacked for different reasons by both capital and labor; at his death, the *Inquirer* has shown a distinguished-looking photo with the banner headline, "CHARLES FOSTER KANE DIES AFTER A LIFETIME OF SERVICE," while the rival *Chronicle* has pictured him glowering under a dark hat brim, with the headline reading "C. F. KANE DIES AT XANADU ESTATE." To Thatcher, Kane was a spoiled do-gooder who was a menace to business; to Bernstein, he was a hero who helped build the country; to Leland, he was an egomaniac who wanted everybody to love him but who left only "a tip in return." Ultimately the audience has been made to feel that no single response is adequate, and near the end, the disparate judgments take the form of a single, complex emotion. Thompson, functioning as the audience's surrogate, remarks to Susan Alexander, "You know, all the same I feel sorry for Mr. Kane." Susan, the only character we've actually seen Kane victimize, the only person who could condemn the man outright, gives Thompson a harsh look and a terse reply: "Don't you think I do?"

Susan's comment crystallizes the film's divided attitude. In the later sequences where Kane nearly destroys Susan, the images of his massive form towering over the submissive woman are more than simple evocations of tyranny: we fear along with Susan, but we also feel sympathy for Kane, who is pained by age and thwarted desire. This feeling of pity is especially strong toward the end, where the most powerful and intense moments, the enraged breaking up of Susan's room and the discovery of the paperweight, are played off against the predatory Raymond (Paul Stewart) and the vast, chilly labyrinth of Xanadu. As the inquiry has deepened, the tone of the film has shifted subtly; the comic blackout sketches that characterize the Thatcher and Bernstein sections have been replaced by a darker, more grotesque mingling of comedy and tragedy that belongs to Leland and Susan—the scenes near the big Xanadu fireplace, for example, with Susan's voice echoing, "A person could go crazy in this dump"; or the gaudy picnic, with a stream of black cars driving morosely down a beach toward a swampy encampment, where a jazz band plays "This Can't Be Love" against a matted background of sinister RKO bats. Each phase of the movie becomes more painful than the one before, until we arrive at the most cynical of the witnesses, Raymond, who is ironically responsible for the most intimate part of the story: Susan leaves, her image receding down a corridor into infinity (another brilliant use of optical printing), and Kane blindly destroys her room, the crisis bringing back memories of childhood loss and rejection.

As Kane has grown increasingly isolated, the camera has stressed the space between him and other people; Thompson never emerges from the shadows, but by the end of Raymond's story he has become less like a reporter and more like a sympathetic, slightly troubled onlooker. (It seems to me a mistake to speak of him as a fully developed character, as some commentators do. Even the acting of the role is clumsy—William Alland being in fact an amateur who suggests a man wandering into the fiction from outside.) Finally he gives up his search, knowing too much to expect a simple answer. We, of course, are in a more privileged position, and are given, if not a rational explanation, a vision of "Rosebud," an image which both transcends and unifies the various witnesses to Kane's life.

Of course Welles was uneasy about the whole snow-sled idea. He dismissed "Rosebud" in a famous remark, calling it "dollarbook Freud" and emphasizing that Herman Mankiewicz thought it up. Pauline Kael has said that it is "such a primitive kind of Freudianism that it . . . hardly seems Freudian at all." It should be noted, however, that some of the psychoanalytic ideas in *Kane* might indeed have come straight from a textbook. According to Freudian terminology, Kane can be typed as a regressive, anal-sadistic personality. His lumpen-bourgeois family is composed of a weak, untrustworthy father and a loving, albeit puritanical mother; he is taken away from this family at a pre-pubescent stage and reared by a bank; as an adult he "returns" to what Freud describes as a pregenital form of sexuality in which "not the genital component instincts, but the *sadistic* and *anal* are most prominent" (*General Introduction to Psychoanalysis,* 1917). Thus, throughout his adult life Kane is partly a sadist who wants to obtain power over others, and partly an anal type, who obsessively collects zoo animals and museum pieces. His childhood, as Joseph McBride has pointed out, seems far from idyllic; nevertheless, it is a childhood toward which he has been compulsively drawn.

The burning sled, whether it is classically Freudian or not, contributes to a coherent and, it seems to me, a psychologically valid characterization. The closing scenes also provide a fascinating commentary on the limits of human power; more specifically, they are a statement about the disparity between the world as it is and the world as imagination would have it be. Throughout the film, Mankiewicz and Welles have underlined the fact that Kane is essentially child-like, a man who, for all his power, can never be completely in control of his life; just as he is not a "self-made" tycoon, so he is not the creator of his private destiny. All of his energies are spent in trying to create his own world, or in rebelling against anyone who asserts authority over his will. He despises Thatcher of course, and when he can no longer "look after" the little people he begins to hate them. He tries to maintain a dangerous but awe-inspiring daydream, of which Xanadu is only the most obvious manifestation. Whenever the dream world is threatened, he responds with a child's rage. For example, when Thatcher interrupts Kane's play in the snow, the boy defends himself by striking out with his sled; when Jim Gettys interrupts the political game, Kane breaks into a terrifying but pathetic fury, his enraged voice cut off as Gettys exits and calmly closes a door; when Leland and Susan assert their independence, Kane retaliates with all the force of his pent-up anger. When we last see him he throws a literal tantrum, regressing to the state of a child destroying a nursery.

Whatever his influence in other spheres, Kane cannot control his own fate. (In 1941, with the New Deal in ascendance and the United States entering a war against fascism, it must have seemed to Welles that Hearst was in a similar position.) He is forever imprisoned by his childhood egotism, living out power fantasies and converting everything into toys. The film is full of these toys: first there is the sled, then the newspaper, then the Spanish-American War. (Notice, in fact, how the war has been depicted as a child's game, with the *Inquirer* reporters sporting little wooden rifles and funny hats.) Toward the end there is Susan, with her marionette-style opera makeup and her dollhouse room in a fantasy castle. The final toy, the paperweight Kane discovers after his tantrum, is probably the most satisfactory image of them all; it represents not so much a lost innocence as a striving after an imaginary, "adult" autonomy. It symbolizes an ideal—a self-enclosed realm, immune from change, where Kane can feel he has control over his life. The sled burning at the heart of the furnace therefore becomes less a purely Freudian explanation than the logical conclusion to Kane's tortured romantic idealism. It is one of those images, known to passion and the imagination, that Yeats called "self-born mockers of Man's enterprise."

After our discovery of this sled, *Citizen Kane* concludes with still another reminder of the camera's inquisitiveness, a near complete reversal of the process with which it began. The camera retreats from the magic castle, staring at the awesome smoke of corruption in the sky, settling at last on the "No Trespassing" sign outside the gate. Even the title has been a contradiction in terms.

II

As an aesthetic object and as a psychological portrait, *Kane* becomes a highly satisfying film, representing what is probably the limit to which a story could move toward self-conscious "art" and "significance" while still remaining within the codes of the studio system. As a portrait of an archetypal tycoon, it is so effective that it has become part of American folklore. And its central images keep returning in contemporary life—Nixon secluding himself in San Clemente, or Howard Hughes, before his death, owning a retreat in the Bahamas which he called the "Hotel Xanadu." For all its evasiveness about Hearst's crimes, *Kane* is also a deliberately political film, growing directly out of the ethos of the Popular Front. As we have seen, it continually reminds the viewer of things outside itself—either the movies, or Hearst, or the "Welles phenomenon." Before leaving it, therefore, one needs at least briefly to shift discussion away from formalist analysis and closer to the *auteur* and the audience. In this way, one can see that *Kane*'s biographical, autobiographical, and political complexities are logical extensions of the aesthetic and psychological tensions I have been describing.

We may begin by noting that *Kane*'s splendidly artful ambivalence toward its central character is not shared by the major biographies of Hearst written during the thirties: in fact these books are as much in conflict as Thatcher and the labor spokesman in the *Kane* newsreel. The authorized portrait, Mrs. Freemont Older's *William Randolph Hearst, American* (1936), makes Hearst a paragon of civic virtue, a sort of philosopher-king. Ferdinand Lundberg's *Imperial Hearst* (1937), which I have already mentioned and which was cited in an absurd plagiarism case against Mankiewicz and Welles, is a muckraking journalist's account of Hearst's crimes. Interestingly, W. A. Swanberg's "definitive" *Citizen Hearst,* which appeared in 1961, takes a middle-of-the-road view; although Swanberg does not acknowledge it, his title and the structure of his narrative clearly were influenced by the movie.

All this data about Hearst is valuable to students of *Kane,* not only for its own sake, but because it shows how the film delights in making references to its primary source. Even the *New York Inquirer* is significant. In real life a paper with that title, which was published by the Griffin brothers, was owned by Hearst. "From the legal standpoint," Irving Hoffman wrote, "they might as well have referred to the paper in the picture as the *Journal-American.*" Nevertheless, it is important to remember that Kane and Hearst are not identical. Welles was at least technically correct when he said that Kane was a fictional character partly based on several turn-of-the-century tycoons. In translating the yellow journalist into a creature of fiction, he and Mankiewicz had borrowed freely from other lives. They had departed from biographical fact in a number of crucial ways, each of them important to the dramatic and perhaps also the ideological effect of the film.

Unlike the biographers, Welles and Mankiewicz chose to concentrate on a private life rather than the public structuring of an empire. They also gave Kane a humble birth, which was not true of any of his possible models; it was certainly not true of Hearst (the whole point of Dos Passos's famous sketch had been that W. R., born into Phoebe Hearst's "richly feathered nest," could never understand his public), and it was not true of McCormack or Insull or Welles or Mankiewicz. Last, and in some ways most significant because more than anything else it aroused the ire of the Hearst press, they made Susan Alexander into a tormented, unhappy creature who walks out on her supposed benefactor—this in contrast to the Hearst-Davies relationship, which was generally happy. Indeed when death finally came to Hearst, it was very different from Kane's death in the film. Hearst did not spend his last days alone in the caverns of his estate; several years earlier he had moved to the less resplendent Beverly Hills mansion of his mistress, and he died with her close at hand. His last words were unrecorded.

These changes imply that Welles and Mankiewicz were trying to create sympathy for Kane by playing down his menace. As a tycoon in the grip of a psychological compulsion, as a poor boy suddenly given wealth, he becomes less, not more, representative of his class. To some viewers he has looked like a great man doomed by his own good fortune, an embodiment of the same "American Dream" myth that is often applied to Welles. When the script is summarized, Welles's and Mankiewicz's sense of melodrama appears to have displaced their politics.

Of course Hearst's life *was* in some sense melodramatic, and writers of the left in the thirties took relish in giving his career the structure of a Hollywood-style morality play. Dos Passos saw Hearst as a "spent Caesar grown old with spending," and Charles Beard, in his introduction to the Lundberg biography, predicted that the old man would die lonely and unloved. By showing Kane as a tragicomic failure, Mankiewicz and Welles were doing no more than what these writers had done, and when they changed the facts to suit the demands of melodrama they were, in principle at least, entirely justified; after all, they were conveying political attitudes through fiction, not through biography. Thus *Citizen Kane* might have been an answer to the plea made toward the end of *Imperial Hearst:*

> Down through the years [Hearst] has played a great and ghastly part in shaping the American mind. He could, more truthfully than any other man, say, "The American mentality is my mentality." This is not because Hearst has become "the voice of the people," speaking their unformulated thoughts and desires. It has been because adequate, widespread and *popularized* criticism of his innumerable deceptions has been lacking.

The italics here are Lundberg's, and they convey his feelings of urgency. *Kane,* however, emphasizes the failures of Hearst more than the deceptions; as Charles Eckert has remarked, the hero dies on a "mystified bed of capital." Harry Wasserman has been more explicit: "It is safe and reassuring," he writes, "to think of Citizen Kane and his sled . . . but unsettling and dangerous to discover the sometimes insidious results of such innocent obsessions. What is more important to remember about a character like Kane is not how the loss of a sled influenced his life, but how the newspapers published by his real-life counterpart Hearst might have influenced a war."

One response to such comments is to say that the film clearly does satirize Kane's public life, and that its "mystifications" are at least partly ironic. It exposes Kane's manipulative interest in the Spanish-American War, it reveals his exploitative "philosophy" of journalism, and it makes several references to his attacks on organized labor. In the election scenes it depicts the corruption of machine politics with the force of a great editorial cartoon. Moreover, it links the press to the politicians themselves, showing Kane hoist on his own petard. In regard to Kane's so-called "progressive" youth, the film is explicit in its denunciation; his democratic aspirations are seen as in reality a desire for power, a means to extend paternalistic benevolence to the "people." We even see Kane on a balcony conferring with Hitler, an image that colors the audience's reaction to everything the character does. What is more radical and more interesting, however, is that *Citizen Kane* brings its own workings under scrutiny, questioning the whole process of popular entertainment, including the "image making" of the movies. From the beginning, when "Rosebud" is introduced as a cheap means of spicing up a newsreel, until the end, when Thompson confesses the futility of searching out the meaning for a single word, *Kane* casts doubt on its own conclusions. Moreover, Welles's brilliant manipulation of cinematic technique keeps reminding us that we are watching a movie, an exceedingly clever and entertaining manipulation of reality, rather than reality itself. This is not, of course, to say that Welles hated Hollywood movies; on the contrary, it was precisely his delight in the conventions of the medium that gave his self-consciousness and self-criticism such poetic force.

Even so, the film is primarily about Kane's private life. It shows that the characters are determined by their material existence, and yet it seems fatalistic about this condition, suggesting that there is no way to radically transform human consciousness. It treats the political issues allusively, aiming relentlessly at "Rosebud" and making Kane a sympathetic, if frightening, character, a tragic failure rather than a living threat. Because of its all-inclusive ironies, its sentimental mythology, and the sheer gusto of its Hollywood craftsmanship, it has always been open to a certain amount of justifiable criticism from the left; indeed the most doctrinaire critics have suggested that *Kane* is a pernicious influence on its audience, leaving us complacently and ignorantly believing that money can't buy happiness.

There are, of course, several possible reasons why the film takes a personal and psychological approach and loads itself with plot conventions from earlier movies—Welles's own ambivalence about the Kane type, for example, or

Mankiewicz's methods of working, or the simple wish to stay within the realm of fantasy and entertainment. Doubtless one of the more important reasons why *Kane* is not a more didactic film is that from the time of the modern-dress *Julius Caesar* Welles had contended that the problem with left-wing melodrama was its "cardboard, Simon-Legree villains." But a still deeper reason is suggested by the fact that *Kane* often seems to be very much about Orson Welles himself. It was Welles, after all, who was known as the *enfant terrible,* and this may account for *Kane*'s emphasis on infantile rage. It was Welles, not Hearst, who was raised by a guardian, and the guardian's name has been given to a character in the film. It was Welles who made a famous comment comparing the movies to his own personal electric train set, almost like Kane remarking that it would be "fun" to run a newspaper. According to John Houseman, who worked on an early version of the script, "the deeper we penetrated beyond the public events into the heart of Charles Foster Kane, the closer we seemed to come to the identity of Orson Welles." Houseman, Mankiewicz, and Welles himself deliberately set about filling the script with parallels and private jokes about the film's director; even Raymond the butler was modeled on a suspicious servant who used to lurk around Welles's big Hollywood house. Bernard Herrmann once summed up all the evidence when he noted that the film is "in a way . . . a dream-like autobiography of Welles"; hence, it is no surprise that the film should have been more about psychology than about the structure of an empire, more sympathetic than purely destructive to the central character.

And yet, certainly, the political and even the personal significance of the film was not lost on the man who was the other chief model for Kane. For all its rich poetic sentiment and its mixing of Hollywood convention with iconoclastic social commentary, the most important fact about Welles's first film is that it proved to be a fundamentally dangerous project. Unlike films of the previous decade, it was at least loosely based on a live and kicking subject, a proto-fascist demagogue whose power in Hollywood was second only to his power over a newspaper empire. The dimensions of that power can be assessed by simply glancing through *Variety* for the ten years or so before *Kane* was produced. In November 1928, for example, one reads that "any time the Hearst paper gets in back of a picture it is a box office natural. . . . They did it last week on Marion Davies *(Show People)* and the gross jumped to $33,000." In February 1932, one finds a note on Hearst's interest in movie content: "To avoid trouble with the Hearst papers as in the case of *Five Star Final,* Warners sent a script of its new newspaper story, 'The Ferguson Case,' to William Randolph Hearst."

In this atmosphere *Kane* was remarkable, and the results were about what could have been expected. Hearst was rumored to have taken it lightly, but the reprisals taken by his press are a matter of record; he even sent a personal note to columnist John Chapman suggesting that anyone who admired the film unreservedly was a "treasonable Communist" and not a "loyal American." As is widely known, the critical response was adulatory, but RKO had difficulty finding bookings. If L. B. Mayer had been successful in buying the rights, the film would never have been shown at all. *Kane* got sensational publicity from Hearst's rivals (probably this was part of Welles's strategy), but not enough to calm the fears of distributors, who began to grumble ominously that Welles was more interested in courting critics than in selling the picture where it counted. In 1941, *Motion Picture Herald* wrote that "Mr. Welles is showing the picture to almost anyone who might be interested except the showmen who might have to deal with it. . . . It is possible that he has not yet, in his preoccupations, heard about the exhibitor." The condescension in these remarks does not conceal the fact that theatre managers were concerned about Hearst's wrath, to say nothing of what they regarded as the potential artiness of the film. Ultimately, *Kane* was recognized by the reviewers, by certain Hollywood professionals, and even, somewhat reluctantly, by the Motion Picture Academy. It established Welles as a major talent, but at the same time it made his future in American movies problematic.

The paradox—and one of the biggest contradictions of them all—is that Welles had no desire to wreck the motion picture industry. He was a devoted worker who had studied the Hollywood masters and whose film, despite its complexity, was in the best tradition of American popular entertainment. As he himself put it, he was never inclined to "joke with other people's money." *Kane* was held to a relatively modest budget ($749,000) and was praised by journals like the *Hollywood Reporter* for its frugality. Nevertheless, various Hollywood bosses had perceived Welles as an "artist" and a left-wing ideologue who *might* bring trouble. *Kane*

may not have been a thoroughgoing anti-capitalist attack, but it was close enough to insure that Welles would never again be allowed such freedom at RKO.

NOTES

See David Bordwell's essay on *Kane,* mentioned in the notes to chapter 2. See also Robert Carringer's "Rosebud, Dead or Alive," *PMLA* (March 1976), and *"Citizen Kane, The Great Gatsby,* and Some Conventions of American Narrative," *Critical Inquiry* (Winter 1975). Carringer's research into the scripts of *Kane* was not yet published as this book went to print, but I am grateful to him for allowing me to see his conclusions. For a useful discussion of self-reflexive narrative in *Kane,* I recommend Kenneth Hope's unpublished thesis, "Film and Meta-Narrative" (Bloomington, Indiana University, 1975). The various biographies of W. R. Hearst include Mrs. Freemont Older, *William Randolph Hearst, American* (New York: Appleton-Century, 1936); Ferdinand Lundberg, *Imperial Hearst* (New York: Modern Library, 1937); W. A. Swanberg, *Citizen Hearst* (New York: Scribner, 1961). For comments on the politics of *Kane,* see Charles Eckert, "Anatomy of a Proletarian Film," *Film Quarterly* (Spring 1975), pp. 65-76. See also Harry Wasserman, "Ideological Gunfight at the OK Corral," *The Velvet Light Trap,* No. 11, pp. 22-31.

---

# FURTHER READING

### Biography

Meryman, Richard. *Mank: The Wit, World, and Life of Herman Mankiewicz.* New York: William Morrow, 1978, 351 p.

  Depicts Mankiewicz as a tragic figure who never wrote to his own high level of expectations.

The following sources published by Gale include further information on the life and work of Herman Mankiewicz: *Contemporary Authors,* Vol. 120, and *Dictionary of Literary Biography,* Vol. 26.

# Florence Nightingale

## 1820-1910

English public health reformer and nurse.

## INTRODUCTION

Florence Nightingale is recognized as the outstanding nineteenth-century proponent of public health reform and the originator of modern nursing methods. As an administrator, Nightingale drafted a considerable sum of documents on matters of preventive medicine. She proposed the analysis of medical statistics in an innovative attempt to further modernize medicine. Nightingale's efforts also brought about drastic improvements in hospital hygiene and brought nurses professional respect never before known. Driven by faith throughout her life, Nightingale is additionally remembered for her *Suggestions for Thought to Searchers after Religious Truth,* which contains the essay "Cassandra"—a work embraced by contemporary feminists for its radical suggestions concerning the importance of women in spiritual and secular life.

### Biographical Information

Nightingale was born to well-to-do English parents in Florence, Italy. She and her elder sister Parthenope were tutored at the family home in Derbyshire and at their winter estate in Hampshire by their father, William Edward Nightingale, in languages, history, literature, and philosophy. They also received instruction from a governess in music and art, the remaining subjects considered suitable for women in Victorian society. As an upper middle-class young woman in nineteenth-century England, Nightingale was expected to socialize daily in the drawing rooms of the wealthy and forbidden to pursue a career. At the age of sixteen, however, Nightingale experienced what she believed to be a call from God that would lead her to look beyond polite English society for self-fulfillment. A tour of the European continent between 1837 and 1839 temporarily satisfied Nightingale's craving for experience, and introduced her to hospitals and nursing. Nevertheless, she continued to feel constrained by her idle life in England for another decade. In 1849 she refused the marriage proposal of Richard Monckton Milnes, and in the fall of that year embarked on a trip to Egypt, which she documented in her *Letters from Egypt.* Before returning to England, Nightingale made her way through Germany. In Kaiserwerth she visited the Institute for the Training of Protestant Deaconesses, where the sisterhood nursed the ill and cared for orphaned children. By 1853 Nightingale had embarked upon her own career in nursing, despite the protests of her parents, at London's Establishment for Gentlewomen during Illness. The English declaration of war on Russia in 1854 prompted Nightingale to volunteer for service. Then

British Secretary of War Sidney Herbert accepted and asked her to lead a group of nurses to Scutari during the conflict. The Crimean War lasted two years, during which time Nightingale succeeded in rectifying the atrocious conditions she found in the British war hospital where she was stationed. Upon her return to England in 1856, Nightingale was hailed as a heroine. Though she had contracted an illness abroad that left her bed-ridden, sometimes for long periods, she set about a process of hospital reform. Later she created the Nightingale School of Nursing at St. Thomas Hospital using a public endowment. Increasingly suffering from ill health, Nightingale continued her work, expanding her interests into, among other areas, sanitation projects in British India. Nightingale died on 13 August 1910.

### Major Works

The vast majority of Nightingale's writings and her voluminous correspondence concern public health reform in England and abroad. The most widely known of these, *Notes on Nursing: What It Is and What It Is Not*, contains her thoughts on the necessity of strict hygiene in public hospitals and on the importance of professional nursing. *Proposal for Improved Statistics of Surgical Operations* reflects Nightingale's innovative ideas on the efficacy of statistical analysis in medicine. Other works, such as *Suggestions in Regard to Sanitary Works Required for Improving Indian Stations*, detail her observations of the worldwide improvements made possible by her theories. In the three volumes of *Suggestions for Thought to Searchers after Religious Truth* Nightingale departs from her public health studies to consider several theological questions. This work contains the essay "Cassandra," in which Nightingale voices her protest against the stultifying atmosphere in Victorian England which prevented women from entering professional life and relegated them to the nation's drawing rooms, where they were expected to engage in polite conversation and other trivial pastimes.

## Critical Reception

Nightingale's vast influence and seemingly indefatigable efforts as a public health reformer earned her near mythic status during her lifetime. Her legend was further enhanced by William Wordsworth's celebratory poem "The Lady of the Lamp" and by many other literary accolades of the time. After her death, the Nightingale myth was likewise advanced by several of her biographers, who made Nightingale a symbol of heroic womanhood. Later critics, however, have shifted their focus toward such subjects as Nightingale's theological writings, her personal psychology, and the feminist implications of her work in order to derive a wider understanding of her contributions to modern life.

---

# PRINCIPAL WORKS

*The Institution of Kaiserwerth on the Rhine, for the Practical Training of Deaconesses, under the Direction of the Rev. Pastor Fliedner, Embracing the Support and Care of a Hospital, Infant and Industrial Schools, and a Female Penitentiary* (nonfiction) 1851

*Letters from Egypt* (letters) 1854

*Female Nursing in Military Hospitals: Presented by Request to the Secretary of State for War* (nonfiction) 1857

*Statements Exhibiting the Voluntary Contributions Received by Miss Nightingale for the Use of the British War Hospitals in the East, with the Mode of Their Distribution, in 1854, 1855, 1856* (nonfiction) 1857

*Mortality of the British Army, at Home and Abroad, and during the Russian War, as Compared with the Mortality of the Civil Population in England. Illustrated by Tables and Diagrams* (nonfiction) 1858

*Notes on the Matters Affecting the Health, Efficiency, and Hospital Administration of the British Army, Founded Chiefly on the Experience of the Late War: Presented by Request of the Secretary of State for War* (nonfiction) 1858

*Notes on Hospitals: Being Two Papers Read before the National Association for the Promotion of Social Science, Liverpool, in October 1858. With Evidence Given to the Royal Commissioners on the State of the Army in 1857* (nonfiction) 1859

*Notes on Causes of Deterioration of Race* (nonfiction) 1860

*Notes on Nursing: What It Is and What It Is Not* (nonfiction) 1860

*Suggestions for Thought to Searchers after Religious Truth. 3 vols.* (nonfiction) 1860

*Sidney Herbert* [enlarged edition published as *Army Sanitary Administration, and Its Reform under the Late Lord Herbert*] (nonfiction) 1861

*Deaconesses' Work in Syria: Appeal on Behalf of the Kaiserwerth Deaconesses' Orphanage at Beyrout* (nonfiction) 1862

*How People May Live and Not Die in India* (nonfiction) 1863

*Note on the Supposed Protection Afforded against Venereal Disease by Recognizing Prostitution and Putting It under Police Regulation* (nonfiction) 1863

*Observations on the Evidence Contained in the Stational Reports Submitted to Her by the Royal Commission on the Sanitary State of the Army in India* (nonfiction) 1863

*Proposal for Improved Statistics of Surgical Operations* (nonfiction) 1863

*Sanitary Statistics of Native Colonial Schools and Hospitals* (nonfiction) 1863

*Death of Pastor Fliedner, of Kaiserwerth* (nonfiction) 1864

*Suggestions in Regard to Sanitary Works Required for Improving Indian Stations, Prepared by the Barrack and Hospital Improvement Commission, in Accordance with Letters from the Secretary of State for India in Council, Dated 8th December, 1863 and 20th May, 1864 (nonfiction) 1864*

*Note on the Aboriginal Races of Australia* (nonfiction) 1865

*Suggestions on a System of Nursing for Hospitals in India* (nonfiction) 1865

*Suggestions on the Subject of Providing, Training, and Organizing Nurses for the Sick Poor in Workhouse Infirmaries* [enlarged edition published as *Suggestions for Improving the Nursing Service of Hospitals and on the Method of Training Nurses for the Sick Poor*] (nonfiction) 1867

*Memorandum on Measures Adopted for Sanitary Improvements in India up to the End of 1867; Together with Abstracts of the Sanitary Reports Hitherto Forwarded from Bengal, Madras, and Bombay* (nonfiction) 1868

*Introductory Notes on Lying-in Institutions. Together with a Proposal for Organising an Institution for Training Midwives and Midwifery Nurses* (nonfiction) 1871

*Address from Miss Nightingale to the Probationer-Nurses in the "Nightingale Fund" School, at St. Thomas's Hospital, and the Nurses Who Were Formerly Trained There* (nonfiction) 1872

*Notes on the New St. Thomas's Hospital* (nonfiction) 1873

*Life or Death in India: A Paper Read at the Meeting of the National Association for the Promotion of Social Science, Norwich, 1873. With an Appendix on Life or Death by Irrigation* (nonfiction) 1874
*Metropolitan and National Nursing Association for Providing Trained Nurses for the Sick Poor: On Trained Nursing for the Sick Poor* (nonfiction) 1876
*In Remembrance of John Gerry, Who Fell Asleep in Jesus, at Lea Hurst, July 17, 1877; Aged 22 Years* (nonfiction) 1877
*Health and Local Government* (nonfiction) 1894
*Health Teaching in Towns and Villages: Rural Hygiene* (nonfiction) 1894
*Village Sanitation in India* (nonfiction) 1894
*A Letter from Florence Nightingale about the Victorian Order of Nurses in Canada* (nonfiction) 1898
*Florence Nightingale to Her Nurses: A Selection from Miss Nightingale's Addresses to Probationers and Nurses of the Nightingale School at St. Thomas's Hospital* (nonfiction) 1914
*Selected Writings of Florence Nightingale* (nonfiction) 1954

---

# CRITICISM

## Joseph H. Choate (speech date 1910)

SOURCE: "Florence Nightingale," in *American Addresses,* The Century Co., 1911, pp. 341-60.

[*In the following speech, originally delivered in 1910, Choate describes Nightingale's career as a war nurse.*]

I consider it a very great privilege to be permitted to stand here for a few minutes to speak about Florence Nightingale. How could this great convention of the nurses of America, gathered from all parts of the country, representing a thousand schools of trained nurses; representing more than fifty thousand graduates of those schools, and more than twenty-five thousand pupils of those schools to-day—how could they better close their conference than by coming here to-night, to celebrate the foundation, by that great woman, of the one first great training school for nurses, which was the model of them all? And how could she, that venerable woman, be more highly honored than by this gathering, in a distant land, of these representatives of the profession which she really founded and created, to do her homage? I hope that before we close our proceedings this evening, we shall authorize our presiding officer to send her a cable of affection and gratitude for all the great work she has done, not only from all the nurses of America, but to testify the admiration of the entire American people for her great record, and her noble life.

One word as to the place and date of her birth. She was born in the beautiful city of Florence, where the steps of Americans always love to linger, in the very first year of the reign of George the Fourth. She lived in honor and triumph through the succeeding reigns of William the Fourth, of Victoria, and of Edward the Seventh, and at last united with the rest of her countrymen to hail the accession of George the Fifth who, I am sure, values her among his subjects quite as highly as he does the most renowned statesmen and greatest soldiers among them.

She was born in the first administration of James Monroe, the fifth president of the United States—before the Monroe doctrine had ever yet been thought of. She has lived through the entire terms of the twenty succeeding presidents, and is now cherished in the hearts of the American people as one of the great heroines of the race.

As there were great heroes before Agamemnon, so she would be the last to wish us to deny or ignore the fact that there were splendid nurses engaged in the work, even before she was born. Not trained nurses, nursing according to the modern school of the Nightingale system, but women, ladies, refined, delicate, accomplished, giving themselves to the service of the sick and suffering. And I believe we ought always to acknowledge the debt of gratitude that the world owes to the great Roman Catholic Church for the Sisters of Mercy whom for centuries it was sending out for the relief and succor of the sick and suffering in all parts of the world. It has been truly said that for centuries the Roman Catholic community was training and setting apart holy women to minister to the sick and poor in their own homes, and had hospitals supplied with the same type of nurses. A large number of these women were ladies of birth and breeding, who worked for the good of their souls and the welfare of their church; while all received proper education and training, and abjured the world for the religious life. Now all you have to add to that character is the discipline and special training and organization which Florence Nightingale contributed to this great profession, to bring into view the trained nurse as she is to-day.

This woman of great brains, of large heart, of wonderfully comprehensive faculties, appears to have been born a nurse. If the stories we hear of her in the nursery are true, that was literally so; because they tell us that her dolls were always in very delicate health, and had to be daily put to bed and nursed and petted, with all possible care; and that the next morning they were restored to health, only to become ill again for her service the next night. And her sister's dolls—she was less careful of them—suffered all kinds of broken limbs, and were subjected to amputation and splinting and decapitation; and Florence was on hand always to restore those broken fragments to their original integrity.

She had every possible advantage to make her what she afterwards came to be. She was born in that most interesting phase of English society—in English country life—where for centuries it has been the rule that the lord of the manor, the squire in his mansion, the leading person of the region and his family, have the responsibility always upon them to take care of the sick and suffering among all their neighbors. She was trained in that school; and one of her first experiences was to visit with her mother the poor and the sick of all the neighboring region.

And she had a magnificent education. She was not averse to the pleasures of society; but she fortunately had a father who believed in discipline, and he gave her the finest education known to that day. Not only was she thoroughly trained in Greek and Latin and mathematics, but in French and German and Italian, and I do not suppose there was any young woman of her time who was better or more brilliantly educated than this woman, who was to become the leading nurse of the world.

She was brought up to believe in work and training. And would you know the secret of her success; would you realize the rule of her life? Let me give it to you in her own words. "I would say," she says, "I would say to all young ladies who are called to any particular vocation, qualify yourself for it, as a man does for his work. Don't think you can undertake it otherwise. Submit yourself to the rules of business, as men do, by which alone you can make God's business succeed." And again she says: "Three-fourths of the whole mischief in women's lives arises from their excepting themselves from the rules of training considered needful for men."

Besides this, she had every possible advantage in the way of association. Early in life, as a very young girl, or young woman, she made the intimate acquaintance of Elizabeth Frye, who had already for many years been visiting the sick in the prisons and had established, under her old-fashioned Quaker garb, such an immense reputation as a reformer of prison life. And through Elizabeth Frye, she fell in, fortunately, with the Fliedners, Theodore and Fredericka Fliedner, who had established at Kaiserwerth in Germany a real training school for nurses; and it was the delight of her life, that she, an accomplished lady, went to that training school of the Fliedners, on the banks of the Rhine, and labored hard, adopting the garb, following the habits, and associating on terms of absolute equality with the nurses who were there being trained, all of whom, but herself, I believe, were of the peasant class; and came out of it, after a few months, knowing as much about nursing as it was possible for any woman then to know.

Then she visited the hospitals of all the great countries of Europe, and among others, she spent some weeks, or months, with the Sisters of St. Vincent De Paul, that splendid Catholic institution where some of those nurses, such as I have described to you, were already gathered, and there she added to her wealth of knowledge and richness of experience.

She recognized no religious differences. Catholic and Protestant were both alike to her. The real object of her life; the real object that she had in view in influencing other women was how best she might help them to benefit mankind.

The English hospitals of that day could not, by any chance, be compared with those upon the continent which she had visited. The character of the nurses was absolutely beneath contempt. Let me read you from a very authoritative statement what was the truth about them: "The nursing in our hospitals was largely in the hands of the coarsest type of women; not only in training, but coarse in feeling, and even coarser morally. There was little to counteract their baneful influence, and the atmosphere of the institutions, which as the abode of the sick and dying had special need of spiritual and elevating influences, was of a degrading character. The habitual drunkenness of these women was then proverbial, while the dirt and disorder rampant in the ward were calculated to breed disease. The profession— if the nursing of that day can claim a title so dignified— had such a stigma attached to it, no decent woman cared to enter it; and if she did, it was more than likely she would lose her character."

Now, she had to contrast with this the splendid discipline and training that was maintained at Kaiserwerth, and the very fine character of the nurses whom she had seen in these Catholic institutions abroad. She had acquired a thorough training and was ready to become a true pioneer in the profession to which she was to give her life. She wrote a book about her experiences at Kaiserwerth. It shows that she was a woman in every sense of the word, full of sensibility. She never married; but although she never married herself, she approved of it. Let me read you a few words from her own book. In her description and reminiscences of Kaiserwerth, she says: "It has become the fashion of late to cry up old maids, and inveigh against marriage as the vocation of all women; to declare that a single life is as happy as a married one, if people would but think so; so is the air as good a medium for fish as water, if they did but know how to live in it. So she could be single and well content. But hitherto we have not found that young English women have been convinced, and we must confess that in the present state of things their horror of being old maids seems justified."

So you see, it was not without a full appreciation of all that goes to make home life tender and happy that she turned her back upon matrimony, and gave it up to nursing and caring for the sick and suffering.

She was fortunate at every step of her career. She was the immediate neighbor, down there on the borders of Wiltshire, of the famous Sydney Herbert, who afterwards became the war minister of the day, at the time of the Crimean war, and at his splendid ancestral home, Wilton House, she was a frequent visitor; she was well liked by that household and by all who knew her. Her training told; her education told; her character told. Let me read you a wonderful prophecy that was made about her, long before the Crimean war broke out, long before she had shown the world what was in her, and what she could do. This verse is by Ada, Countess of Lovelace, the daughter of Byron; and I call it a wonderful prophecy:

In future years, in distant climes,
  Should war's dread strife its victims claim;
Should pestilence unchecked, betimes,
  Strike more than swords, than cannon maim;
Then readers of these truthful rhymes
  Will trace her progress through undying fame.

It is not often that you will find in history such a prophecy as that, so absolutely realized within a few short years.

Then came the breaking out of the Crimean war. As Colonel Hoff told you, twenty-five thousand English soldiers landed at Scutari. And such a state of things, I won't say never has been heard of, because it is often heard of in the outbreak of many a war. War often finds a nation utterly unprepared to engage in it. There were no ambulances, no nurses, no means provided for caring for the wounded and suffering soldiers as they were brought in from the fields of battle.

Fortunately we had a great war correspondent at the Crimea in those days—we afterwards knew him here, when he wrote the dispatches about our battle of Bull Run—Mr. William Howard Russell, as he was then called, who spoke in clarion notes to the men, and especially to the women of England, making an appeal which reached the ears of this wonderful woman, and made her the heroine of her age. Let me read you one sentence of Russell's appeal. After describing the horrible state of things that existed at the Crimea, and the shameful want of preparation for the care of the soldiers, he says: "Are there no devoted women amongst our people, willing to go forth to minister to the sick and suffering soldiers of the east, in the hospitals of Scutari? Are there none of the daughters of England, at this stormy hour of night, ready for such a work? France has sent forth her Sisters of Mercy unsparingly, and they are even now by the bedsides of the wounded and dying, giving what woman's hand alone can give of comfort and relief. Must we fall far below the French in self-sacrifice and devotedness in a work which Christ so signally blessed, as done to Himself, 'I was sick and ye visited me'?"

And a lady, the wife of an officer, wrote from the seat of war: "Could you see the scenes that we are daily witnessing, you would indeed be distressed. Every corner is filled with the sick and wounded. If I am able to do some little good I hope I shall not be obliged to leave. Just now my time is occupied in cooking for the wounded. Three doors from me is an officer's wife who devotes herself to cooking for the sick. There are no female nurses here, which decidedly there should be. The French have sent fifty Sisters of Mercy, who, I need hardly say, are devoted to the work. We are glad to hear that some efforts are being made at home."

Miss Nightingale was one of the first to respond to that appeal. And yet there was hostile objection from many quarters: from official quarters, where it was thought that the present regimen, the present organization, was good enough, and could do all the work; from social sources, for whom Mrs. Grundy spoke, "Why, certainly it cannot be proper for young women—young ladies—to go as nurses in a soldiers' hospital, of all things in the world! Too horrible to think of!"

There was a great deal of that sort of opposition; and there was religious opposition, too. When she made up the band of thirty-seven nurses, which Colonel Hoff has spoken of as her first contingent with whom she went to the Crimea, there were ten Catholic Sisters of Mercy, twelve Church of England Sisters, I believe, and then there were some who belonged to neither organization; and the religious people took it up, and they said, "She is evidently going to the Crimea to convert the soldiers to the Roman Catholic Church;" and others said, "No, that isn't so; don't you see she is taking some that are neither Catholic nor Episcopalian? We really believe that she belongs to that horrible sect, the Unitarians!"

Even *Punch,* who always represents the current feeling of the day, made a little light of her, with mingled admiration and raillery. Let me read you two of his verses, in honor of "The Lady Birds," as they were called in London, before they started for the seat of war.

THE NIGHTINGALE'S SONG TO A SICK
SOLDIER

Listen, soldier, to the tale of the tender nightingale;
  It is a charm that soon will ease your wounds
    so cruel.
Singing my song for your pain, in a
    sympathetic strain,
  With a jug of lemonade and gruel,
Singing succor to the brave, and a rescue from
    the grave;
  Hear the Nightingale sing that goes to the Crimea.
'Tis a Nightingale as tender in her heart as in
    her song,
  To carry out her golden idea.

When this terrible state of things was disclosed by the letters of Russell and other news that came from the seat of war, the government was as horror-stricken as the people, and so were Mr. Sydney Herbert, the life-long friend of Florence Nightingale, and Mrs. Herbert, who was also one of her friends. Mr. Herbert, who was responsible for the administration of military affairs, said to his wife, "We must send for Florence!" And then a most singular coincidence happened. He wrote her a most serious and dignified letter, pointing out the necessity of sending a band of nurses, composed of capable and courageous women; and he said to her, "It all depends upon you; if our plan is to succeed, you must lead it." And without pressing her unduly, he put it before her as a matter of conscience and duty. I believe that letter was written on the fifteenth of October, 1854, when the first horrible news came from the front. What I call the remarkable coincidence was that on the same day, without knowing anything about the writing of that letter, Florence Nightingale was writing unsolicited, to Sydney Herbert, the Secretary of War, offering her services to lead a band of nurses to the front.

Time would fail me if I undertook to tell you the frightful condition of things she found when she got there. Doubtless you have all read of it. The great Barracks Hospital of Scutari was filled with thousands and thousands of sick and wounded men who had been brought from the seat of war, without nurses, without suitable food, without a laundry, without the possibility of a change of clothes, without a kitchen for the preparation of proper food, with no possible conveniences or appliances for the care of the sick and the wounded. The descriptions are too horrible to realize or to repeat. She found these three or four thousand men in this great hospital, which had been a barracks and had been converted, off-hand, into a hospital—a place for the deposit of these poor bodies of the sick and wounded; and that was about all that had been done for them before Miss Nightingale arrived. They had had no medical attendance from the time they left the front, many days before; they had had no change of clothing, nor the possibility of a bath or a clean shirt.

And this woman, with her thirty-seven nurses, came among them. It was chaos! confusion, worse—confounded! She put to use her wonderful powers of organization, and in two months she had that hospital in absolute control. A kitchen was established and a laundry, and she provided ten thousand clean shirts for these sufferers, and had taken absolute command of the whole establishment, as the government had given her authority to do. In six months, great resources being sent to her from home, great numbers of recruits to her nurses arriving, every soldier, to the number of six thousand in the Barracks Hospital and in the General Hospital at Scutari, was being well and comfortably taken care of and provided for.

Then came all the other horrors that attend war. Fever broke out, and the frost-bitten men who had lain in the trenches before Sebastopol were brought in, after spending five days out of seven in those horrible trenches, exposed to the Crimean frost, with nothing but the linen clothes that they had worn in Malta. All these ghastly things she had to take care of and provide for, but her genius was equal to the emergency. Her powers of organization, her powers of endurance seem to me to surpass those of any other woman on record. They tell us that for twenty hours at a time she would stand when the ships arrived—twenty hours at a time—receiving those broken fragments of men that came from the front, seeing that they were properly handled and cared for. And when all the work of the day was done and others rested she made her rounds, visiting the worst cases, the most frightful cases. They weren't safe, she thought, unless she personally visited them. She, the Lady in Chief, as she was ordinarily called, and "The Lady of the Lamp," as she became known in poetry and history, visited the bedsides of the suffering, soothed the wounded and dying. She wrote letters to their friends at home, and did everything that one woman could do to restore life and light to the suffering. Let me read you Longfellow's tribute to her:

> On England's annals, through the long
> Hereafter of her speech and song,
>   That light its rays shall cast
>   From the portals of the past.
>
> A lady with a lamp shall stand
> In the great history of the land,
>   A noble type of good,
>   Heroic Womanhood.

Then she went on from Scutari to the Crimea. She went so far as to visit Sebastopol itself, going to the very front, and not only looked into the trenches, but entered the great crater of that vast volcano of war; and on her way back she was stricken with the Crimean fever and very nearly lost her life. They carried her to the hospital—one of those improvised hospitals on the heights of Balaklava, five hundred feet above the sea. She was nursed for weeks and weeks, and finally brought back to life. They tell us of the Six Hundred at Balaklava: that "into the jaws of death rode the six hundred!" Why, this woman was in the jaws of death from the time she landed at Scutari until she was stricken down, eight months afterwards.

Then they said, "You must go home to England; that is the only way for you to get well." "I will not go home," she replied, "I will not leave these soldiers;" and she continued her heroic duties of nursing and supervising. She was a great genius in every sense of the word. She would not go home, and did not go, until not only the war had closed, but until long after; until every soldier had been shipped home to England, and every hospital was cleared.

And then, how do you think she went home? she, the foremost woman in the world now! to whom all mankind and womankind looked with reverence and honor. How do you think she went home? Did she go with a flare of trumpets? Did she expect or wait for a grand demonstration on her return? Did she notify everybody or anybody that she was coming? Not at all. She had such a horror of publicity, she was so modest, so meek—one of those that are going to inherit the earth—that she went home incognito. She arrived in England without letting anybody know it. She managed somehow or other to get into the back door of her father's house in Derbyshire, and the first that was known of her having returned to England was when the neighbors heard that Miss Florence was really sleeping in her father's house. *Punch,* always quick to respond to public feeling, reflected the sentiment of the hour with respect to her return. *Punch* says this:

> Then leave her to the guide she has chosen;
> She demands no greeting from our brazen throats
>   and vulgar clapping hands.
> Leave her to the sole comfort the saints know that
>   have striven;
> What are our earthly honors: her honors are
>   in heaven!

Earthly honors awaited her. In truth the whole nation was up in arms to do her honor, to pay homage to her, and to make some reward for her wonderful sacrifice and services. Subscriptions were opened, not only in all parts of England, but in all the English dominions, extending all around the British Empire. Subscriptions were actually opened among the English residents at Hong Kong, and fifty thousand pounds was poured out by the English people into her lap. England is full of generosity to her heroes and heroines. She rewards her great generals with munificent sums; and so her people in this case wanted in like manner to honor this heroine of their own.

What did she say? She said, "Not for me; not one penny for me. I will not take a penny. But it has been the ambition of my life to establish a training school for nurses—the first of its kind to be conducted on high and broad and pure methods and principles. Let it all be devoted to that, and I accept the gift. Otherwise, not." And so it came about that the first great nurse's training school was established at St. Thomas's Hospital, which bears her name. It is still supported by "The Nightingale Fund," and is a model and example for all the training schools of the world.

Colonel Hoff has told you of her subsequent life. Practically her health was ruined. She has been fifty-five years an invalid, often confined to her bed, and yet always working for the good of humanity, always for the relief of the sick and wounded, the sanitation of camps and the relief and succor of the soldiers.

But she has had her reward; through all ranks of mankind, wherever there is a heart to beat in response to such noble deed as hers, there has been a glorious answer.

I will only speak for a few minutes of those things in which we are especially interested and first of the Red Cross. The convention that met in Geneva, in 1863, founded it, and it has from time to time since been the subject of subsequent amendment. Our Hague Conference, in 1907, had representatives from forty-four nations, and there for the first time all the nations of the world became parties to the Red Cross movement, which meant the saving of the sick and wounded, and hospital and ambulance corps to rescue them from all the perils of war and of battle; which meant preparation for war while yet there is peace, so that these horrible sufferings that have been witnessed at the outbreak of almost every war may not be repeated. At the meeting of the Congress of Red Cross Societies, held in London two years later, in June, 1909, unanimous resolutions were passed, honoring Miss Nightingale and declaring that her work was the beginning of the Red Cross activities.

Then look at her influence in America! When our terrible Civil War broke out we were almost as unprepared in this matter of sanitation and nursing as the British had been at Scutari. Fortunately there were some women who lent their aid at once, and these were inspired by the example of Miss Nightingale. They were women of the same type. Let me read you the names of some of them. One, at least, is present here tonight, and I do not know but there are more. Dr. Elizabeth Blackwell, the intimate friend of

Miss Nightingale is, I believe, still living in England, one year younger than Miss Nightingale herself; Miss Louisa Lee Schuyler, Miss Dorothea L. Dix, Miss Collins, and Mrs. Griffin. What did they do? Why they were responsible, really, for our great sanitary commission, and they formed the woman's branch of that great humanitarian enterprise, which did so much to save our sick and wounded in that protracted and terrible war. They acknowledged their allegiance to Miss Nightingale, and were in constant correspondence with her. Dr. Blackwell had known absolutely all her methods, her principles, and her whole plan of nursing, and it was on those principles and those lines that our noble women worked.

Then, ten years afterwards, there came the foundation of this work in America, I might almost say, the foundation of the training school for nurses—at Bellevue Hospital. And there you find several of the same women again: Miss Schuyler, Miss Collins, Mrs. William Preston Griffin, and leading them was Mrs. Joseph Hobson, afterwards president of one of the committees; and there was the mother of our present chairman, that woman of sainted memory, Mrs. William H. Osborn, who led their activities in the creation of that great school. It is a splendid thing that he should be here to-night to represent one who gave so much of her heart, her soul, her life and her treasure, to the building up of that school. Miss Nightingale was immediately approached by the founders of that school, and gave them full written instructions as to how they ought to proceed.

Her letter ought to be read by everybody; it is full, explicit, and detailed, and she is as much entitled to the credit of the creation of this school in America as even those ladies of whom I have spoken.

Now, I close as I began. Do not let us separate to-night without authorizing our chairman to send, on behalf of all the nurses and all the people of America, a word of greeting and of gratitude to this noble woman.

### A. G. Gardiner (essay date 1914)

SOURCE: "Florence Nightingale," in *Prophets, Priests, & Kings,* E. P. Dutton & Co., 1914, pp. 114-20.

[*In the following essay, Gardiner offers a sketch of Nightingale's life and an assessment of her influence on nursing.*]

Lying before me is a manuscript. It is written on large sheets of stout paper which have turned yellow with the years. The writing, that of a woman, is bold and free, as of one accustomed to the pen; but the fashion of the letters belongs to a long-past time. It is an obituary notice of Florence Nightingale, written for the *Daily News* fifty-one years ago, when the most famous of Englishwomen was at the point of death. The faded manuscript has lain in its envelope for half a century unused. The busy pen that wrote it fell for ever from the hand of the writer more than thirty years ago, for that writer was Harriet Martineau. The subject of the memoir still lives, the most honoured and loved of all the subjects of the Sovereign.

There are tears in that old manuscript, the generous, almost passionate, tears of a great soul stricken by a sore bereavement. Miss Martineau was writing within three years of the Crimean war, when the name of Florence Nightingale still throbbed with memories vivid as last night's dream, and when her heroism had the dew of the dawn upon it. To-day that name is like a melody of a far-off time—a melody we heard in the remotest days of childhood. Florence Nightingale!

> It comes o'er the ear like the sweet South,
> Stealing and giving odour.

It has perfumed the years with the fragrance of gracious deeds. I have sometimes idly speculated on the strange fortuity of names, on the perfect echo of the name to the deed—Shakespeare, Milton, Wordsworth, Tennyson! Why is it that the world's singers come heralded with these significant names? Why is it that the infinite families of the Smiths and the Robinsons and the Joneses never sing? And Oliver Cromwell and John Churchill and Horatio Nelson! Why, there is the roar of guns and the thunder of great deeds in the very accents of their names. And so with the heroines of history, the Grace Darlings and the Florence Nightingales. One almost sees in the latter case events carefully avoiding the commonplace and shaping a lustrous name for the wearer. For her mother was named Smith, the daughter of that William Smith, the famous philanthropist, and member for Norwich, who fought the battle of the Dissenters in Parliament, and was one of the leaders of the anti-slavery movement. And her father was named Shore, and only assumed the name of Nightingale with the estates that made him a wealthy man. "A rose by any other name," no doubt. But the world is grateful for the happy accident that gave it "Florence Nightingale."

It is a name full of a delicate reminiscence, like the smell of lavender in a drawer, calling up memories of those from whose lips we first heard the story of "The Lady with the Lamp." It suggests not a personality, but an influence; not a presence, but a pervasive spirit. For since that tremendous time, when the eyes of the whole world were turned upon the gentle figure that moved like a benediction through the horrors of the hospitals of Scutari, Miss Nightingale's life has had something of the quiet of the cloister. It is not merely that her health was finally broken by her unexampled labours: it is that, combined with the courage of the chivalrous world into which she was born, she has the reticence of a temperament that shrinks from publicity with mingled scorn and humility.

This rare union of courage and modesty is illustrated by her whole career. When, after a girlhood spent in her native Italy—for she was born in Florence, as her only sister, afterwards Lady Verney, was born in Naples—

and in wanderings in many lands, she decided on her life work of nursing, she returned from her hard apprenticeship in many institutions, and especially in the Kaiserswerth Institution on the Rhine—the first Protestant nursing home in Germany—to take the management of the Sanatorium for Sick Ladies in Harley Street. In those days of our grandmothers, woman was still in the mediæval state of development. She was a pretty ornament of the drawing-room, subject to all the proprieties expressed in "prunes and prisms." She had no duty except the duty of being pretty and proper, no part in the work of the world except the task higher than that of seeing that her overlord's slippers were in the right place.

The advent of Florence Nightingale into Harley Street was like a challenge to all that was feminine and Early Victorian. A woman, a lady of birth and culture, as manager of an institution! The thing was impossible. The polite world thrilled with indignation at the outrage. "It was related at the time"—I quote from the yellow manuscript before me—"that if she had forged a bill, or eloped, or betted her father's fortune away at Newmarket, she could not have provoked a more virulent hue and cry than she did by settling herself to a useful work." And it was not society alone that assailed her now and later. "From the formalists at home, who were shocked at her handling keys and keeping accounts, to the jealous and quizzing doctors abroad, who would have suppressed her altogether, and the vulgar among the nurses, who whispered that she ate the jams and the jellies in a corner, she had all the hostility to encounter which the great may always expect from those who are too small to apprehend their mind and ways." But she had a dominating will and a dear purpose in all the acts of her life. She was indifferent to the judgment of the world. She saw the path, and trod it with fearless steps wherever it led.

Within her sphere she was an autocrat. Lord Stanmore, in his *Memoir of Sidney Herbert*—the War Minister whose letter inviting Miss Nightingale to go to the Crimea crossed her letter offering to go—has criticised her severe tongue and defiance of authority. But in the presence of the appalling problem of humanity that faced her and her band of thirty-eight nurses, what were red tape and authority? As she passed down through those four miles of beds, eighteen inches apart, each bearing its burden of pain and suffering, her passion of pity turned to a passion of indignation at the wanton neglect of the poor instruments of government, and she turned and rent the authors of the wrong. The hospital was chaos. There were neither hospital accessories, nor medical appliances, nor changes of clothing, nor proper food. It was a time for bitter speech and defiance of authority. And Florence Nightingale, her sight seared and her ears ringing with the infinite agony, thundered at the War Office until the crime was undone and her own powerful control was set up over all the hospitals of the East.

And now the war is over, the long avenue of death and suffering that has been her home has vanished, and she sets sail for England. The world is ringing with her deeds. England awaits her with demonstrations of national gratitude unparalleled in history. She takes an assumed name, steals back by an unexpected route, and escapes, exhausted and unrecognised, to the peace of her father's house at Lea Hurst, in the quiet valley of the Derwent. And when later the nation expresses its thanks by raising a fund of £50,000 for her benefit, she quietly hands it over to found the institution for training nurses at St. Thomas's Hospital. And with that act of radiant unselfishness she establishes the great modern movement of nursing. Mrs. Gamp flees for ever before the lady with the lamp.

For Florence Nightingale is not a mere figure of romance. It is beautiful to think of the ministering angel moving with her lamp down the long lanes of pain at Scutari, to hear those pathetic stories of the devotion of the rough soldiers all writing down her name as the name they loved, of the dying boy who wanted to see her pass because he could kiss her shadow as it moved across the pillow. But there have been many noble and self-sacrificing nurses, many who had as great a passion for suffering humanity as hers. To think of her only as a heroine in the romance of life is to mistake her place in history as well as to offend her deepest feelings.

She is much more than a heroine of romance. She is the greatest woman of action this nation produced in the last century—perhaps the greatest woman of action this country has ever produced. She is the type of the pioneer—one of those rare personalities who reshape the contours of life. She was not simply the lady with the lamp; she was the lady with the brain and the tyrannic will, and in her we may discover the first clear promise of that woman's revolution which plays so large a part in the world to-day. The hand that smoothed the hot pillow of the sufferer was the same hand that rent the red tape and broke, defiant of officialism, the locked door to get at the bedding within. Nursing to her was not a pastime or an occupation: it was a revelation. The child, whose dolls were always sick and being wooed back to life, who doctored the shepherd's dog in the valley of the Derwent, and bound up her boy cousin's sudden wound, was born with the fever of revolution in her as truly as a Danton or a Mazzini. She saw the world full of suffering, and beside the pillow—ignorance and Sarah Gamp. Her soul revolted against the grim spectacle, and she gave herself with single-eyed devotion to the task of reform.

There is about her something of the sleepless fury of the fanatic; but she differs from the fanatic in this, that her mighty indignation is controlled by her powerful understanding and by her cold, almost icy common sense. She has been the subject of more sentimental writing than any one of her time; but she is the least sentimental of women, and has probably dissolved fewer emotions in

tears than any of her contemporaries. She has had something better to do with her emotions than waste them in easy lamentations. She has turned them to iron and used them mercilessly to break down the stupidities that encompass the world of physical suffering and to crush the opposition of ignorance and professional interest. All who have come in conflict with her have, like Sidney Herbert, had to bow to her despotic will, and to-day, old and lonely, forgotten by the great world that ebbs and flows by her home near Hyde Park corner, she works with the same governed passion and concentration that she revealed in the great tragedy of sixty years ago.

Truly seen, therefore, the Crimean episode is only an incident in her career. Her title to rank among the great figures of history would have been as unchallengeable without that tremendous chapter. For her work was not incidental, but fundamental; not passing, but permanent. She, too, divides the crown with "Old Timotheus"—

> He raised a mortal to the skies,
> She brought an angel down.

When good Pastor Fleidner, the head of the Kaiserswerth Institution, laid his hands at parting on her bowed head, she went forth to work a revolution; and to-day every nurse that sits through the dim hours by the restless bed of pain is in a real sense the gracious product of that revolution.

She has made nursing a science. She has given it laws; she has revealed the psychology of suffering. How true, for example, is this:

> I have seen in fevers the most acute suffering produced from the patient in a hut not being able to see out of a window. . . . I remember in my own case a nosegay of wild flowers being sent me, and from that moment recovery becoming more rapid. People say it is the effect on the patient's mind. It is no such thing; it is on the patient's body, too. . . . Volumes are now written and spoken about the effect of the mind on the body. . . . I wish more was thought of the effect of the body on the mind.

She has moved mountains, but her ideal is still far off. For she wants not merely a profession of nurses, but a nation of nurses—every mother a health nurse and every nurse "an atom in the hierarchy of the Ministers of the Highest." It is a noble dream, and she has brought it within the grasp of the realities of that future which, as she says, "I shall not see, for I am old."

·  ·  ·  ·  ·

I put the yellow manuscript back into the envelope where it has lain for half a century. Sixteen hundred articles did Harriet Martineau write for the *Daily News*. They are buried in the bound volumes of the issues of long ago. One still remains unpublished, the last word happily still unwritten.

**Lytton Strachey (essay date 1918)**

SOURCE: Chapter III, *Eminent Victorians,* Garden City Publishing Co., Inc., 1918, pp. 164-87.

*[In the following excerpt, Strachey recounts Nightingale's reform efforts in England, undertaken after her return from the Crimean War.]*

The name of Florence Nightingale lives in the memory of the world by virtue of the lurid and heroic adventure of the Crimea. Had she died—as she nearly did—upon her return to England, her reputation would hardly have been different; her legend would have come down to us almost as we know it to-day—that gentle vision of female virtue which first took shape before the adoring eyes of the sick soldiers at Scutari. Yet, as a matter of fact, she lived for more than half a century after the Crimean War; and during the greater part of that long period all the energy and all the devotion of her extraordinary nature were working at their highest pitch. What she accomplished in those years of unknown labour could, indeed, hardly have been more glorious than her Crimean triumphs; but it was certainly more important. The true history was far stranger even than the myth. In Miss Nightingale's own eyes the adventure of the Crimea was a mere incident—scarcely more than a useful stepping-stone in her career. It was the fulcrum with which she hoped to move the world; but it was only the fulcrum. For more than a generation she was to sit in secret, working her lever: and her real life began at the very moment when, in the popular imagination, it had ended.

She arrived in England in a shattered state of health. The hardships and the ceaseless effort of the last two years had undermined her nervous system; her heart was pronounced to be affected; she suffered constantly from fainting-fits and terrible attacks of utter physical prostration. The doctors declared that one thing alone would save her—a complete and prolonged rest. But that was also the one thing with which she would have nothing to do. She had never been in the habit of resting; why should she begin now? Now, when her opportunity had come at last; now, when the iron was hot, and it was time to strike? No; she had work to do; and, come what might, she would do it. The doctors protested in vain; in vain her family lamented and entreated, in vain her friends pointed out to her the madness of such a course. Madness? Mad—possessed—perhaps she was. A demoniac frenzy had seized upon her. As she lay upon her sofa, gasping, she devoured blue-books, dictated letters, and, in the intervals of her palpitations, cracked her febrile jokes. For months at a stretch she never left her bed. For years she was in daily expectation of Death. But she would not rest. At this rate, the doctors assured her, even if she did not die, she would become an invalid for life. She could not help that; there was the work to be done; and, as for rest, very likely she might rest . . . when she had done it.

Wherever she went, in London or in the country, in the hills of Derbyshire, or among the rhododendrons at Embley, she was haunted by a ghost. It was the spectre of Scutari—the hideous vision of the organisation of a military hospital. She would lay that phantom, or she would perish. The whole system of the Army Medical Department, the education of the Medical Officer, the regulations of hospital procedure . . . *rest?* How could she rest while these things were as they were, while, if the like necessity were to arise again, the like results would follow? And, even in peace and at home, what was the sanitary condition of the Army? The mortality in the barracks was, she found, nearly double the mortality in civil life. "You might as well take 1100 men every year out upon Salisbury Plain and shoot them," she said. After inspecting the hospitals at Chatham, she smiled grimly. "Yes, this is one more symptom of the system which, in the Crimea, put to death 16,000 men." Scutari had given her knowledge; and it had given her power too: her enormous reputation was at her back—an incalculable force. Other work, other duties, might lie before her; but the most urgent, the most obvious of all was to look to the health of the Army.

One of her very first steps was to take advantage of the invitation which Queen Victoria had sent her to the Crimea, together with the commemorative brooch. Within a few weeks of her return, she visited Balmoral, and had several interviews both with the Queen and the Prince Consort. "She put before us," wrote the Prince in his diary, "all the defects of our present military hospital system and the reforms that are needed." She related the whole story of her experiences in the East; and, in addition, she managed to have some long and confidential talks with His Royal Highness on metaphysics and religion. The impression which she created was excellent. "Sie gefällt uns sehr," noted the Prince, "ist sehr bescheiden." Her Majesty's comment was different— "Such a *head!* I wish we had her at the War Office."

But Miss Nightingale was not at the War Office, and for a very simple reason: she was a woman. Lord Panmure, however, *was* (though indeed the reason for that was not quite so simple); and it was upon Lord Panmure that the issue of Miss Nightingale's efforts for reform must primarily depend. That burly Scottish nobleman had not, in spite of his most earnest endeavours, had a very easy time of it as Secretary of State for War. He had come into office in the middle of the Sebastopol campaign, and had felt himself very well fitted for the position, since he had acquired in former days an inside knowledge of the Army—as a Captain of Hussars. It was this inside knowledge which had enabled him to inform Miss Nightingale with such authority that "the British soldier is not a remitting animal." And perhaps it was this same consciousness of a command of his subject which had impelled him to write a dispatch to Lord Raglan, blandly informing the Commander-in-Chief in the Field just how he was neglecting his duties, and pointing out to him that if he would only try he really might do a little better next time. Lord Raglan's reply, calculated as it was to make its recipient sink into the earth, did not quite have that effect upon Lord Panmure, who, whatever might have been his faults, had never been accused of being super-sensitive. However, he allowed the matter to drop; and a little later Lord Raglan died—worn out, some people said, by work and anxiety. He was succeeded by an excellent red-nosed old gentleman, General Simpson, whom nobody has ever heard of, and who took Sebastopol. But Lord Panmure's relations with him were hardly more satisfactory than his relations with Lord Raglan; for, while Lord Raglan had been too independent, poor General Simpson erred in the opposite direction, perpetually asked advice, suffered from lumbago, doubted, his nose growing daily redder and redder, whether he was fit for his post, and, by alternate mails, sent in and withdrew his resignation. Then, too, both the General and the Minister suffered acutely from that distressingly useful new invention, the electric telegraph. On one occasion General Simpson felt obliged actually to expostulate.

> I think, my Lord [he wrote], that some telegraphic messages reach us that cannot be sent under due authority, and are perhaps unknown to you, although under the protection of your Lordship's name. For instance, I was called up last night, a dragoon having come express with a telegraphic message in these words, "Lord Panmure to General Simpson—Captain Jarvis has been bitten by a centipede. How is he now?"

General Simpson might have put up with this, though to be sure it did seem "rather too trifling an affair to call for a dragoon to ride a couple of miles in the dark that he may knock up the Commander of the Army out of the very small allowance of sleep permitted him"; but what was really more than he could bear was to find "upon sending in the morning another mounted dragoon to inquire after Captain Jarvis, four miles off, that he never has been bitten at all, but has had a boil, from which he is fast recovering." But Lord Panmure had troubles of his own. His favourite nephew, Captain Dowbiggin, was at the front, and to one of his telegrams to the Commander-in-Chief the Minister had taken occasion to append the following carefully qualified sentence—"I recommend Dowbiggin to your notice, should you have a vacancy, and if he is fit." Unfortunately, in those early days, it was left to the discretion of the telegraphist to compress the messages which passed through his hands; so that the result was that Lord Panmure's delicate appeal reached its destination in the laconic form of "Look after Dowb." The Headquarters Staff were at first extremely puzzled; they were at last extremely amused. The story spread; and "Look after Dowb" remained for many yearsthe familiar formula for describing official hints in favour of deserving nephews.

And now that all this was over, now that Sebastopol had been, somehow or another, taken, now that peace was, somehow or another, made, now that the troubles of office might surely be expected to be at an end at last—here was Miss Nightingale breaking in upon the scene, with her talk about the state of the hospitals and the necessity for sanitary reform. It was most irksome; and Lord Panmure almost began to wish that he was engaged upon some more congenial occupation—discussing, perhaps, the constitution of the Free Church of Scotland—a question in which he was profoundly interested. But no; duty was paramount; and he set himself, with a sigh of resignation, to the task of doing as little of it as he possibly could.

"The Bison" his friends called him; and the name fitted both his physical demeanour and his habit of mind. That large low head seemed to have been created for butting rather than for anything else. There he stood, foursquare and menacing, in the doorway of reform; and it remained to be seen whether the bulky mass, upon whose solid hide even the barbed arrows of Lord Raglan's scorn had made no mark, would prove amenable to the pressure of Miss Nightingale. Nor was he alone in the doorway. There loomed behind him the whole phalanx of professional conservatism, the stubborn supporters of the out-of-date, the worshippers and the victims of War Office routine. Among these it was only natural that Dr. Andrew Smith, the head of the Army Medical Department, should have been pre-eminent—Dr. Andrew Smith, who has assured Miss Nightingale before she left England that "nothing was wanted at Scutari." Such were her opponents; but she too was not without allies. She had gained the ear of Royalty—which was something; at any moment that she pleased she could gain the ear of the public—which was a great deal. She had a host of admirers and friends; and—to say nothing of her personal qualities—her knowledge, her tenacity, her tact—she possessed, too, one advantage which then, far more even than now, carried an immense weight—she belonged to the highest circle of society. She moved naturally among Peers and Cabinet Ministers—she was one of their own set; and in those days their set was a very narrow one. What kind of attention would such persons have paid to some middle-class woman with whom they were not acquainted, who possessed great experience of army nursing and had decided views upon hospital reform? They would have politely ignored her; but it was impossible to ignore Flo Nightingale. When she spoke, they were obliged to listen; and, when they had once begun to do that—what might not follow? She knew her power, and she used it. She supported her weightiest minutes with familiar witty little notes. The Bison began to look grave. It might be difficult—it might be damned difficult—to put down one's head against the white hand of a lady.

Of Miss Nightingale's friends, the most important was Sidney Herbert. He was a man upon whom the good fairies seemed to have showered, as he lay in his cradle, all their most enviable gifts. Well born, handsome, rich, the master of Wilton—one of those great country-houses, clothed with the glamour of a historic past, which are the peculiar glory of England—he possessed, besides all these advantages, so charming, so lively, so gentle a disposition that no one who had once come near him could ever be his enemy. He was, in fact, a man of whom it was difficult not to say that he was a perfect English gentleman. For his virtues were equal even to his good fortune. He was religious—deeply religious: "I am more and more convinced every day," he wrote, when he had been for some years a Cabinet Minister, "that in politics, as in everything else, nothing can be right which is not in accordance with the spirit of the Gospel." No one was more unselfish; he was charitable and benevolent to a remarkable degree; and he devoted the whole of his life with an unwavering conscientiousness to the public service. With such a character, with such opportunities, what high hopes must have danced before him, what radiant visions of accomplished duties, of ever-increasing usefulness, of beneficent power, of the consciousness of disinterested success! Some of those hopes and visions were, indeed, realised; but, in the end, the career of Sidney Herbert seemed to show that, with all their generosity, there was some gift or other—what was it?—some essential gift—which the good fairies had withheld, and that even the qualities of a perfect English gentleman may be no safeguard against anguish, humiliation, and defeat.

That career would certainly have been very different if he had never known Miss Nightingale. The alliance between them, which had begun with her appointment to Scutari, which had grown closer and closer while the war lasted, developed, after her return, into one of the most extraordinary of friendships. It was the friendship of a man and a woman intimately bound together by their devotion to a public cause; mutual affection, of course, played a part in it, but it was an incidental part; the whole soul of the relationship was a community of work. Perhaps out of England such an intimacy could hardly have existed—an intimacy so utterly untinctured not only by passion itself but by the suspicion of it. For years Sidney Herbert saw Miss Nightingale almost daily, for long hours together, corresponding with her incessantly when they were apart; and the tongue of scandal was silent; and one of the most devoted of her admirers was his wife. But what made the connection still more remarkable was the way in which the parts that were played in it were divided between the two. The man who acts, decides, and achieves; the woman who encourages, applauds, and—from a distance—inspires:—the combination is common enough; but Miss Nightingale was neither an Aspasia nor an Egeria. In her case it is almost true to say that the rôles were reversed; the qualities of pliáncy and sympathy fell to the man, those of command and initiative to the woman. There was one thing only which Miss Nightingale lacked in her equipment for public life; she had not—she never could have—the public power and authority which belong to the successful politician. That power and authority Sidney Herbert possessed; the fact was obvious, and the conclusion no less so: it was through the man that the woman must work her will. She took hold of him, taught him, shaped him, absorbed him, dominated him through and through. He did not resist—he did not wish to resist; his natural inclination lay along the same path

as hers; only that terrific personality swept him forward at her own fierce pace and with her own relentless stride. Swept him—where to? Ah! Why had he ever known Miss Nightingale? If Lord Panmure was a bison, Sidney Herbert, no doubt, was a stag—a comely, gallant creature springing through the forest; but the forest is a dangerous place. One has the image of those wide eyes fascinated suddenly by something feline, something strong; there is a pause; and then the tigress has her claws in the quivering haunches; and then——!

Besides Sidney Herbert, she had other friends who, in a more restricted sphere, were hardly less essential to her. If, in her condition of bodily collapse, she were to accomplish what she was determined that she should accomplish, the attentions and the services of others would be absolutely indispensable. Helpers and servers she must have; and accordingly there was soon formed about her a little group of devoted disciples upon whose affections and energies she could implicitly rely. Devoted, indeed, these disciples were, in no ordinary sense of the term; for certainly she was no light task-mistress, and he who set out to be of use to Miss Nightingale was apt to find, before he had gone very far, that he was in truth being made use of in good earnest—to the very limit of his endurance and his capacity. Perhaps, even beyond those limits; why not? Was she asking of others more than she was giving herself? Let them look at her lying there pale and breathless on the couch; could it be said that she spared herself? Why, then, should she spare others? And it was not for her own sake that she made these claims. For her own sake, indeed! No! They all knew it! it was for the sake of the work. And so the little band, bound body and soul in that strange servitude, laboured on ungrudgingly. Among the most faithful was her "Aunt Mai," her father's sister, who from the earliest days had stood beside her, who had helped her to escape from the thraldom of family life, who had been with her at Scutari, and who now acted almost the part of a mother to her, watching over her with infinite care in all the movements and uncertainties which her state of health involved. Another constant attendant was her brother-in-law, Sir Harry Verney, whom she found particularly valuable in parliamentary affairs. Arthur Clough, the poet, also a connection by marriage, she used in other ways. Ever since he had lost his faith at the time of the Oxford Movement, Clough had passed his life in a condition of considerable uneasiness, which was increased rather than diminished by the practice of poetry. Unable to decide upon the purpose of an existence whose savour had fled together with his belief in the Resurrection, his spirits lowered still further by ill-health, and his income not all that it should be, he had determined to seek the solution of his difficulties in the United States of America. But, even there, the solution was not forthcoming; and when, a little later, he was offered a post in a government department at home, he accepted it, came to live in London, and immediately fell under the influence of Miss Nightingale. Though the purpose of existence might be still uncertain and its nature still unsavoury, here, at any rate, under the eye of this inspired woman, was something real, something earnest: his only doubt was—could he be of any use? Certainly he could. There were a great number of miscellaneous little jobs which there was nobody handy to do. For instance, when Miss Nightingale was travelling, there were the railway-tickets to be taken; and there were proof-sheets to be corrected; and then there were parcels to be done up in brown paper, and carried to the post. Certainly he could be useful. And so, upon such occupations as these, Arthur Clough was set to work. "This that I see, is not all," he comforted himself by reflecting, "and this that I do is but little; nevertheless it is good, though there is better than it."

As time went on, her "Cabinet," as she called it, grew larger. Officials with whom her work brought her into touch and who sympathised with her objects, were pressed into her service; and old friends of the Crimean days gathered round her when they returned to England. Among these the most indefatigable was Dr. Sutherland, a sanitary expert, who for more than thirty years acted as her confidential private secretary, and surrendered to her purposes literally the whole of his life. Thus sustained and assisted, thus slaved for and adored, she prepared to beard the Bison.

Two facts soon emerged, and all that followed turned upon them. It became clear, in the first place, that that imposing mass was not immovable, and, in the second, that its movement, when it did move, would be exceeding slow. The Bison was no match for the Lady. It was in vain that he put down his head and planted his feet in the earth; he could not withstand her; the white hand forced him back. But the process was an extraordinarily gradual one. Dr. Andrew Smith and all his War Office phalanx stood behind, blocking the way; the poor Bison groaned inwardly, and cast a wistful eye towards the happy pastures of the Free Church of Scotland; then slowly, with infinite reluctance, step by step, he retreated, disputing every inch of the ground.

The first great measure, which, supported as it was by the Queen, the Cabinet, and the united opinion of the country, it was impossible to resist, was the appointment of a Royal Commission to report upon the health of the Army. The question of the composition of the Commission then immediately arose; and it was over this matter that the first hand-to-hand encounter between Lord Panmure and Miss Nightingale took place. They met, and Miss Nightingale was victorious; Sidney Herbert was appointed Chairman; and, in the end the only member of the commission opposed to her views was Dr. Andrew Smith. During the interview, Miss Nightingale made an important discovery: she found that "the Bison was bullyable"—the hide was the hide of a Mexican buffalo, but the spirit was the spirit of an Alderney calf. And there was one thing above all others which the huge creature dreaded—an appeal to public opinion. The faintest hint of such a terrible eventuality made his heart dissolve within him; he would agree to anything—he would cut short his grouse-shooting—he would make

a speech in the House of Lords—he would even overrule Dr. Andrew Smith—rather than that. Miss Nightingale held the fearful threat in reserve—she would speak out what she knew; she would publish the truth to the whole world, and let the whole world judge between them. With supreme skill, she kept this sword of Damocles poised above the Bison's head, and more than once she was actually on the point of really dropping it. For his recalcitrancy grew and grew. The *personnel* of the Commission once determined upon, there was a struggle, which lasted for six months, over the nature of its powers. Was it to be an efficient body, armed with the right of full inquiry and wide examination, or was it to be a polite official contrivance for exonerating Dr. Andrew Smith? The War Office phalanx closed its ranks, and fought tooth and nail; but it was defeated: the Bison was bullyable.

> Three months from this day [Miss Nightingale had written at last] I publish my experience of the Crimean Campaign, and my suggestions for improvement, unless there has been a fair and tangible pledge by that time for reform.

Who could face that?

And, if the need came, she meant to be as good as her word. For she had now determined, whatever might be the fate of the Commission, to draw up her own report upon the questions at issue. The labour involved was enormous; her health was almost desperate; but she did not flinch, and after six months of incredible industry she had put together and written with her own hand her "Notes affecting the Health, Efficiency, and Hospital Administration of the British Army." This extraordinary composition, filling more than eight hundred closely printed pages, laying down vast principles of far-reaching reform, discussing the minutest details of a multitude of controversial subjects, containing an enormous mass of information of the most varied kinds—military, statistical, sanitary, architectural—was never given to the public, for the need never came; but it formed the basis of the Report of the Royal Commission; and it remains to this day the leading authority on the medical administration of armies.

Before it had been completed the struggle over the powers of the Commission had been brought to a victorious close. Lord Panmure had given way once more; he had immediately hurried to the Queen to obtain her consent; and only then, when her Majesty's initials had been irrevocably affixed to the fatal document, did he dare to tell Dr. Andrew Smith what he had done. The Commission met, and another immense load fell upon Miss Nightingale's shoulders. To-day she would, of course, have been one of the Commission herself; but at that time the idea of a woman appearing in such a capacity was unheard of; and no one even suggested the possibility of Miss Nightingale's doing so. The result was that she was obliged to remain behind the scenes throughout, to coach Sidney Herbert in private at every important juncture, and to convey to him and to her other friends upon the Commission the vast funds of her expert knowledge—so essential in the examination of witnesses—by means of innumerable consultations, letters, and memoranda. It was even doubtful whether the proprieties would admit of her giving evidence; and at last, as a compromise, her modesty only allowed her to do so in the form of written answers to written questions. At length the grand affair was finished. The Commission's Report, embodying almost word for word the suggestions of Miss Nightingale, was drawn up by Sidney Herbert. Only one question remained to be answered—would anything, after all, be done? Or would the Royal Commission, like so many other Royal Commissions before and since, turn out to have achieved nothing but the concoction of a very fat blue-book on a very high shelf?

And so the last and the deadliest struggle with the Bison began. Six months had been spent in coercing him into granting the Commission effective powers; six more months were occupied by the work of the Commission; and now yet another six were to pass in extorting from him the means whereby the recommendations of the Commission might be actually carried out. But, in the end, the thing was done. Miss Nightingale seemed indeed, during these months, to be upon the very brink of death. Accompanied by the faithful Aunt Mai, she moved from place to place—to Hampstead, to Highgate, to Derbyshire, to Malvern—in what appeared to be a last desperate effort to find health somewhere; but she carried that with her which made health impossible. Her desire for work could now scarcely be distinguished from mania. At one moment she was writing a "last letter" to Sidney Herbert; at the next she was offering to go out to India to nurse the sufferers in the Mutiny. When Dr. Sutherland wrote, imploring her to take a holiday, she raved. Rest!—

> I am lying without my head, without my claws, and you all peck at me. It is *de rigueur, d'obligation,* like the saying something to one's hat, when one goes into church, to say to me all that has been said to me 110 times a day during the last three months. It is the *obbligato* on the violin, and the twelve violins all practise it together, like the clocks striking 12 o'clock at night all over London, till I say like Xavier de Maistre, *Assez, je le sais, je ne le sais que trop.* I am not a penitent; but you are like the R. C. confessor, who says what is *de rigueur.* . . .

Her wits began to turn, and there was no holding her. She worked like a slave in a mine. She began to believe, as she had begun to believe at Scutari, that none of her fellow-workers had their hearts in the business; if they had, why did they not work as she did? She could only see slackness and stupidity around her. Dr. Sutherland, of course, was grotesquely muddle-headed; and Arthur Clough incurably lazy. Even Sidney Herbert . . . oh yes, he had simplicity and candour and quickness of perception, no doubt; but he was an eclectic; and what could one hope for from a man who went away to fish in Ireland just when the Bison most needed bullying? As for the Bison himself he had fled to Scotland, where he

remained buried for many months. The fate of the vital recommendation in the Commission's Report—the appointment of four Sub-Commissions charged with the duty of determining upon the details of the proposed reforms and of putting them into execution—still hung in the balance. The Bison consented to everything; and then, on a flying visit to London, withdrew his consent and hastily returned to Scotland. Then for many weeks all business was suspended; he had gout—gout in the hands, so that he could not write. "His gout was always handy," remarked Miss Nightingale. But eventually it was clear even to the Bison that the game was up, and the inevitable surrender came.

There was, however, one point in which he triumphed over Miss Nightingale. The building of Netley Hospital had been begun, under his orders, before her return to England. Soon after her arrival she examined the plans, and found that they reproduced all the worst faults of an out-of-date and mischievous system of hospital construction. She therefore urged that the matter should be reconsidered, and in the meantime building stopped. But the Bison was obdurate; it would be very expensive, and in any case it was too late. Unable to make any impression on him, and convinced of the extreme importance of the question, she determined to appeal to a higher authority. Lord Palmerston was Prime Minister; she had known him from her childhood; he was a near neighbour of her father's in the New Forest. She went down to the New Forest, armed with the plans of the proposed hospital and all the relevant information, stayed the night at Lord Palmerston's house, and convinced him of the necessity of rebuilding Netley.

> It seems to me [Lord Palmerston wrote to Lord Panmure] that at Netley all consideration of what would best tend to the comfort and recovery of the patients has been sacrificed to the vanity of the architect, whose sole object has been to make a building which should cut a dash when looked at from the Southampton river. . . . Pray, therefore, stop all further progress in the work until the matter can be duly considered.

But the Bison was not to be moved by one peremptory letter, even if it was from the Prime Minister. He put forth all his powers of procrastination, Lord Palmerston lost interest in the subject, and so the chief military hospital in England was triumphantly completed on unsanitary principles, with unventilated rooms, and with all the patients' windows facing northeast.

But now the time had come when the Bison was to trouble and to be troubled no more. A vote in the House of Commons brought about the fall of Lord Palmerston's Government, and Lord Panmure found himself at liberty to devote the rest of his life to the Free Church of Scotland. After a brief interval, Sidney Herbert became Secretary of State for War. Great was the jubilation in the Nightingale Cabinet; the day of achievement had dawned at last. The next two and a half years (1859-61) saw the introduction of the whole system of reforms for which Miss Nightingale had been struggling so fiercely—reforms which make Sidney Herbert's tenure of power at the War Office an important epoch in the history of the British Army. The four Sub-Commissions, firmly established under the immediate control of the Minister, and urged forward by the relentless perseverance of Miss Nightingale, set to work with a will. The barracks and the hospitals were remodelled; they were properly ventilated and warmed and lighted for the first time; they were given a water supply which actually supplied water, and kitchens where, strange to say, it was possible to cook. Then the great question of the Purveyor—that portentous functionary whose powers and whose lack of powers had weighed like a nightmare upon Scutari—was taken in hand, and new regulations were laid down, accurately defining his responsibilities and his duties. One Sub-Commission reorganised the medical statistics of the Army. Another established—in spite of the last convulsive efforts of the Department—an Army Medical School. Finally the Army Medical Department itself was completely reorganised; an administrative code was drawn up; and the great and novel principle was established that it was as much a part of the duty of the authorities to look after the soldier's health as to look after his sickness. Besides this, it was at last officially admitted that he had a moral and intellectual side. Coffee-rooms and reading-rooms, gymnasiums and workshops were instituted. A new era did in truth appear to have begun. Already by 1861 the mortality in the Army had decreased by one half since the days of the Crimea. It was no wonder that even vaster possibilities began now to open out before Miss Nightingale. One thing was still needed to complete and to assure her triumphs. The Army Medical Department was indeed reorganised; but the great central machine was still untouched. The War Office itself—!—If she could remould *that* nearer to her heart's desire—there indeed would be a victory! And until that final act was accomplished, how could she be certain that all the rest of her achievements might not, by some capricious turn of Fortune's wheel—a change of Ministry, perhaps, replacing Sidney Herbert by some puppet of the permanent official gang—be swept to limbo in a moment?

Meanwhile, still ravenous for more and yet more work, her activities had branched out into new directions. The army in India claimed her attention. A Sanitary Commission, appointed at her suggestion, and working under her auspices, did for our troops there what the four Sub-Commissions were doing for those at home. At the same time, these very years which saw her laying the foundations of the whole modern system of medical work in the army, saw her also beginning to bring her knowledge, her influence, and her activity into the service of the country at large. Her *Notes on Hospitals* (1859) revolutionised the theory of hospital construction and hospital management. She was immediately recognised as the leading expert upon all the questions involved; her advice flowed unceasingly and in all directions, so that there is no great hospital today which does not bear upon it the impress of her mind. Nor was this all. With the opening of the Nightingale Training School for Nurses at St. Thomas's Hospital (1860), she became the founder of modern nursing.

But a terrible crisis was now fast approaching. Sidney Herbert had consented to undertake the root and branch reform of the War Office. He had sallied forth into that tropical jungle of festooned obstructiveness, of intertwisted irresponsibilities, of crouching prejudices, of abuses grown stiff and rigid with antiquity, which for so many years to come was destined to lure reforming ministers to their doom.

> The War Office [said Miss Nightingale] is a very slow office, an enormously expensive office, and one in which the Minister's intentions can be entirely negatived by all his sub-departments, and those of each of the sub-departments by every other.

It was true; and, of course, at the first rumour of a change, the old phalanx of reaction was bristling with its accustomed spears. At its head stood no longer Dr. Andrew Smith, who, some time since, had followed the Bison into outer darkness, but a yet more formidable figure, the permanent Under-Secretary himself, Sir Benjamin Hawes—Ben Hawes the Nightingale Cabinet irreverently dubbed him—a man remarkable even among civil servants for adroitness in baffling inconvenient inquiries, resource in raising false issues, and, in short, a consummate command of all the arts of officially sticking in the mud. "Our scheme will probably result in Ben Hawes's resignation," Miss Nightingale said; "and that is another of its advantages." Ben Hawes himself, however, did not quite see it in that light. He set himself to resist the wishes of the Minister by every means in his power. The struggle was long and desperate; and, as it proceeded, it gradually became evident to Miss Nightingale that something was the matter with Sidney Herbert. What was it? His health, never very strong, was, he said, in danger of collapsing under the strain of his work. But, after all, what is illness, when there is a War Office to be reorganised? Then he began to talk of retiring altogether from public life. The doctors were consulted, and declared that, above all things, what was necessary was rest. Rest! She grew seriously alarmed. Was it possible that, at the last moment, the crowning wreath of victory was to be snatched from her grasp? She was not to be put aside by doctors; they were talking nonsense; the necessary thing was not rest but the reform of the War Office; and, besides, she knew very well from her own case what one could do even when one was on the point of death. She expostulated vehemently, passionately: the goal was so near, so very near; he could not turn back now! At any rate, he could not resist Miss Nightingale. A compromise was arranged. Very reluctantly, he exchanged the turmoil of the House of Commons for the dignity of the House of Lords, and he remained at the War Office. She was delighted. "One fight more, the best and the last," she said.

For several more months the fight did indeed go on. But the strain upon him was greater even than she perhaps could realise. Besides the intestine war in his office, he had to face a constant battle in the Cabinet with Mr. Gladstone—a more redoubtable antagonist even than Ben Hawes—over the estimates. His health grew worse and worse. He was attacked by fainting-fits; and there were some days when he could only just keep himself going by gulps of brandy. Miss Nightingale spurred him forward with her encouragements and her admonitions, her zeal and her example. But at last his spirit began to sink as well as his body. He could no longer hope; he could no longer desire; it was useless, all useless; it was utterly impossible. He had failed. The dreadful moment came when the truth was forced upon him: he would never be able to reform the War Office. But a yet more dreadful moment lay behind; he must go to Miss Nightingale and tell her that he was a failure, a beaten man.

Blessed are the merciful! What strange ironic prescience had led Prince Albert, in the simplicity of his heart, to choose that motto for the Crimean brooch? The words hold a double lesson; and, alas! when she brought herself to realise at length what was indeed the fact and what there was no helping, it was not in mercy that she turned upon her old friend.

> Beaten! [she exclaimed]. Can't you see that you've simply thrown away the game? And with all the winning cards in your hands! And so noble a game! Sidney Herbert beaten! And beaten by Ben Hawes! It is a worse disgrace.... [her full rage burst out at last] ... a worse disgrace than the hospitals at Scutari.

He dragged himself away from her, dragged himself to Spa, hoping vainly for a return of health, and then, despairing, back again to England, to Wilton, to the majestic house standing there resplendent in the summer sunshine, among the great cedars which had lent their shade to Sir Philip Sidney, and all those familiar, darling haunts of beauty which he loved, each one of them, "as if they were persons"; and at Wilton he died. After having received the Eucharist he had become perfectly calm; then, almost unconscious, his lips were seen to be moving. Those about him bent down. "Poor Florence! Poor Florence!" they just caught. " . . . Our joint work . . . unfinished . . . tried to do . . ." and they could hear no more.

When the onward rush of a powerful spirit sweeps a weaker one to its destruction, the commonplaces of the moral judgment are better left unmade. If Miss Nightingale had been less ruthless, Sidney Herbert would not have perished; but then, she would not have been Miss Nightingale. The force that created was the force that destroyed. It was her Demon that was responsible. When the fatal news reached her, she was overcome by agony. In the revulsion of her feelings, she made a worship of the dead man's memory; and the facile instrument which had broken in her hand she spoke of for ever after as her "Master." Then, almost at the same moment,

another blow fell upon her. Arthur Clough, worn out by labours very different from those of Sidney Herbert, died too: never more would he tie up her parcels. And yet a third disaster followed. The faithful Aunt Mai did not, to be sure, die; no, she did something almost worse: she left Miss Nightingale. She was growing old, and she felt that she had closer and more imperative duties with her own family. Her niece could hardly forgive her. She poured out, in one of her enormous letters, a passionate diatribe upon the faithlessness, the lack of sympathy, the stupidity, the ineptitude of women. Her doctrines had taken no hold among them; she had never known one who had *appris à apprendre;* she could not even get a woman secretary; "they don't know the names of the Cabinet Ministers—they don't know which of the Churches has Bishops and which not." As for the spirit of self-sacrifice, well—Sidney Herbert and Arthur Clough were men, and they indeed had shown their devotion; but women—! She would mount three widow's caps "for a sign." The first two would be for Clough and for her Master; but the third, "the biggest widow's cap of all"—would be for Aunt Mai. She did well to be angry; she was deserted in her hour of need; and, after all, could she be sure that even the male sex was so impeccable? There was Dr. Sutherland, bungling as usual. Perhaps even he intended to go off, one of these days, too? She gave him a look, and he shivered in his shoes. No!—she grinned sardonically; she would always have Dr. Sutherland. And then she reflected that there was one thing more that she would always have—her work.

### Laurence Housman (essay date 1932)

SOURCE: "Florence Nightingale, 1820-1910," in *The Great Victorians,* edited by H. J. Massingham and Hugh Massingham, Doubleday, Doran & Company, Inc., 1932, pp. 319-30.

[*In the following essay, Housman considers Nightingale's exploits within the context of women's traditional roles in the Victorian age.*]

An iridescent medallion under glass, of a red cross surmounted by a crowned monogram of crystals, in a bed of lilies, and encircled by a blue band bearing the words "Blessed are the merciful," drew me in early years to the name—already sacred in legend—of Florence Nightingale. This medallion, the central ornament of a drawing-room table, formed the chief and most attractive art object of my young days. It combined in its gaudy setting—a brass tazza of florid scrollwork—beauty, religion, and patriotic sentiment; it also had the flavour of royalty, for the Prince Consort himself had designed it.

The original, then made popular by reproduction, symbolized the heroic service of a woman (still living, I was told) whose name struck me as more beautiful even than the design.

Has there, indeed, ever been a name more sweetly compounded for the lavishing of sentiment than the name of Florence Nightingale? Theosophists tell us that, when the soul reincarnates, it chooses its own time, name, and parentage. If that be true, Florence Nightingale chose her name wisely and well. It may have conveyed little of her character, but as a means of peaceful penetration for the pioneer work she was to accomplish, it could hardly have been bettered.

Another name, as felicitously chosen for the life it was to fit—the name Victoria—had come to its small beginning just a year earlier. And these two lives, so closely contemporary and so fortunately named, were destined to become symbolic and outstanding examples, in the era which followed, of the opposing forces through whose help or hindrance that great social revolution which is called the Woman's Movement, took shape and grew strong, producing results which, for the present generation, have made the conditions of those days (so little remote in time) seem unbelievably far off and strange.

But though, in aim and temperament, these two, Queen and Commoner, were so widely divided, each alike had a power of set purpose and initiative which produced revolutionary results. Victoria, within a decade of her accession, had revolutionized the social standards of the Regency and had made society decent.

This left Florence Nightingale a harder nut to crack; her revolution took longer; the decency of Victorianism (or what it regarded as such) took more than fifty years to undermine. The upheaval, begun by Miss Nightingale, did not reach its culmination till Queen Victoria's reign had prosperously ended. For to the Queen must be conceded that ponderous marking of time which bears her name; for fifty years she, more than any other woman, moulded the social history of England. But while she gave to the age a static expression by becoming the embodiment of its conventions, Florence Nightingale, by her own more forceful example, sowed those seeds of revolutionary change which have made Victorian woman a thing of the past.

Yet Florence was herself a very Victorian character. Her exceptional powers of body and brain, and the abnormal driving force which lay behind them, merely served to give anticipatory expression to a problem which already stirred uneasily beneath the surface in thousands of homes.

We do not consider it necessary to say of certain great men, however exceptional their powers, that they did not belong to their age; it is often far more true that by the exercise of those exceptional powers they brought out the latent qualities that were in it—that, through them, the age found itself. It is quite true that the women of the Victorian age took a long time to find themselves along the lines laid down by Florence Nightingale; but it was not because they lacked the strength of character. Strength of character made them obstinately possessive of the little world over which they bore rule; and a very strong little world it was—so strong that it survived absurdly into the twentieth century, and put up quite a good fight for itself when all the conditions on which it was based had become obsolete.

Some years ago I showed to a friend a set of photographs, taken when photography was young, of women who had come to maturity in mid-Victorian days. His comment, "What tremendous characters!" was a just summary. Strength of character was the salient feature, beauty and fashion the adjuncts. And yet, outside the domestic circle, those women had not made any mark on the world—they were unknown, unheard of. They were women who, supporting rigorously the conventions of their day, had gloried in the limitations of their sex, and imposed them censoriously on others. Convention formed, indeed, a part of their religion. And yet—as my mind browses up and down the records of those past lives—I am convinced that they accepted convention mainly because they believed that it gave them power. Victorian womanhood was an army, well drilled and well organized; yet it was all so quiet and underground, or so domestically within doors, that one wonders where the organization came in. Was it the "afternoon call," or was it—the power of prayer? "Leave then thy sister when she prays," said Tennyson. Had he spelt the word with an "e," it would have been more to the point. The religious views of our Victorian sisters needed no cockering, and no protection from the assaults of "honest doubt"; inflexible in quality and predatory in operation, they had a devastating effect upon the intellectual progress of the rising generations they controlled. Even to-day the pulpit has not quite rid itself of the influence of its Victorian mother's knee.

Florence Nightingale herself had, in those early days, strange views about prayer, and prayed, not according to the sinner's need, but according to how she liked him. "I could not," she owned, "pray for George IV. I thought people very good who prayed for him, and wondered if he could have been much worse if he had not been prayed for. William IV I prayed for a little. But when Victoria came to the throne, I prayed for her in a rapture of feeling, and my thoughts never wandered."

In that case one can only surmise that women of less advanced views were also praying for her, with equal rapture, and, judging by results, with more success.

Florence Nightingale found it hard to believe that in prayer thoughts could wander. "When you ask for what you want," she said, "your thoughts *don't* wander." But the reform of George IV's character lay outside the range of her desires. Evil, she believed, was a necessary ingredient in the creative scheme; God put it there to teach men what to avoid; it was educative. Law and order were the appointed means for bringing His Kingdom to earth; and God Himself was a Law-giver who believed in corporal punishment.

All of which goes to show that, though she was one of its most tremendous characters, Florence Nightingale belonged to her age; and it was as much her religion as anything which, in spite of great mental misery, kept her within the confines of the home till her thirty-fourth year. And from that long imprisonment of a body and mind so restless, so resolute, so energetic, we may measure the strength of the bondage she had to break. Her mother, not her father, was the main obstacle. It was from its women that the convention took its strength. In spite of their confined lives of narrow outlook and poor, scrappy education, they had as much force of character and power of will as the generations of women who have come after; and whether they put down their foot to maintain convention or to break it, it was with an equal will of their own that they did so.

Queen Victoria and Florence Nightingale were both masterful characters; and it was perhaps by a mere accident of circumstance that the one stood for the old order (with a difference), while the other stood for the new. Victoria became her own mistress at seventeen, Florence not till she was twice that age. It made a difference. Seventeen years of continuous contact with the "sleeping ignorance," which the social conditions of her day imposed on women, had caused the iron to enter into her soul. After she had made her escape into a life of active service, she wrote—but did not publish—a bitter commentary on the case as she then saw it. Under the subtitle "Cassandra," it strangely forms part of an appeal to the artisans of England for the recovery of "religious truth," at a time when the falling away from faith of the working class was becoming noticeable.

> "Why [she asks in her first paragraph] have woman passion, intellect, moral activity—these three—and a place in society where no one of these can be exercised? . . . Men are angry with misery. They are irritated with women for not being happy. They take it as a personal offense. . . . In the conventional society (which men have made for women, and women have accepted) 'women must have no passions.' They must act the farce of hypocrisy [and teach it, she goes on to say, to their daughters]. Society forbids. . . . The family uses people for what it wants them for—for its own uses. The system dooms some minds to incurable infancy, others to silent misery. . . . In society men and women meet to be idle. Is it extraordinary that they do not know each other, and that in their mutual ignorance they form no surer friendships? Did they meet to *do* something together, they might form some real tie. . . . The woman who has sold herself for an establishment, in what is she superior to those one may not name?"

An interesting sentence that—combining the new woman's revolt against the expedient of respectable marriage, with acceptance of the Victorian convention that the prostitute must not be named—not even when the actual parallel was being drawn.

> "And marriage being [she goes on] their only outlet in life, many women spend their lives in asking men to marry them, in a refined way."

Of the "philanthropy" which women were allowed to practise, she remarks scornfully:

> "Were the physician to set to work at his trade as the philanthropist does at his, how many bodies would he not spoil before he cured one? . . . Women long for an education to *teach* them to teach, to teach them the laws of the mind and how to apply them. . . . They long for experience, not patchwork experience, but experience followed up and systematized to enable them to know what they are about, and where they are casting their bread, and whether it *is bread* or a stone. . . . If we have no food for the body, how we do cry out, how all the world hears of it, how all the newspapers talk of it with a paragraph headed in great capital letters, 'DEATH FROM STARVATION!' But suppose one were to put a paragraph in *The Times,* 'DEATH OF THOUGHT FROM STARVATION,' or 'DEATH OF MORAL ACTIVITY FROM STARVATION,' how people would stare, how they would laugh and wonder! One would think that we have no heads nor hearts, by the total indifference of the public towards them. Our bodies are the only things of consequence. . . . With what labour women have toiled to break down all individual and independent life, in order to fit themselves for this social and domestic existence, thinking it right. And when they have killed themselves to do it, they have awakened (too late) to think it wrong."

This cry of distress was written by a woman who, five years earlier, had achieved an astounding success in the public service, and a popularity greater than that of the Queen herself. She was famous and powerful, and was still carrying on, with quiet efficiency, her work of public usefulness. She did not write it for herself, but for others. Of her two literary advisers, one, John Stuart Mill, wished her to publish it; the other, Benjamin Jowett, advised that she should not. She accepted Jowett's advice; one wonders why.

It was symptomatic of the sincerity of her character that she concentrated her attack, not on what was merely old-fashioned and narrow in the lives of the women of her day—their religion—for that was fairly sincere; but on that which was damnably false—their social and their sex relations. It is now almost unbelievable how false, root and branch, those relations were; and they were false, for the degrading reason that it was what men were supposed to like. Perhaps they did, from having known nothing better. The exhibitionism, called Modesty, which women assiduously practised in those days, was their main stock-in-trade for escape from the home of their parents to a home of their own, where, in a certain measure, they could become themselves. They spent their lives, as Florence put it, "in asking men to marry them, in a refined way"; and intellect being looked at askance and passion forbidden, they laid their modesty on with a trowel. It required a lot of doing and a lot of living-up to. I am inclined to think sometimes that it was sheer force of character and self-discipline which enabled women to faint, when—according to the conventions they worshipped—they were expected to faint; and that, had they been weaker characters, they could not with such unfailing regularity have performed the task required of them.

But the whole thing was a sham. Early Victorianism was an age of moral cosmetics; and women who would have regarded the lipstick as lascivious did not scruple to lard themselves with all the weaknesses which were supposed to appeal to man's taste for mastery. In the social entertainments of the day they sang love songs to themselves, and to each other without the slightest sapphic intent. Mrs. Norton's *Juanita,* and Adelaide Proctor's *Message* were set for the female voice; and with these aphrodisiacs the male heart was to be softened. One of the most popular songs of the day, pursuing femininity to the depth, told of a certain sweet Alice, "who wept with delight when you gave her a smile, and trembled with fear at your frown." In the last verse "sweet Alice," happily disposed of, "lies under the stone." Even as recently as fifty years ago, that song could be sung without being laughed at; that could not happen now.

Florence Nightingale was too sick and angry to laugh. She was a practical genius; and the wasting of woman's qualities enraged her. No doubt, in stating the woman's case, it was often her own past that she remembered, and, in certain passages, her own character and capabilities which she described in those vivid and bitter phrases.

> "Some women [she writes] have an attention like a battering-ram, which, slowly brought to bear, can work upon a subject for any length of time. They can work for ten hours just as well as two upon the same thing. . . . What these suffer— even physically—for the want of such work no one can tell. The accumulation of nervous energy, which has had nothing to do during the day, makes them feel, every night when they go to bed, as if they were going mad; and they are obliged to lie long in bed in the morning to let it evaporate and keep it down."

"Like a battering-ram": here undoubtedly we have self-portraiture; and for seventeen years the battering-ram adopted the device of lying late in bed as a means of escaping from its own consuming energy.

The device failed; at the age of thirty-four, tentatively at first, while out of sight on holiday abroad—then resolutely and completely—she broke the home ties and took up the practice of nursing. It was a more shocking thing to do than we can now well realize: hospital nurses were improper characters, they drank, they were suspected of illicit relations with the medical staff and the students, and had no training or qualifications worth talking about. And what they were then, to the Victorian mind,

they must always continue to be. Into this state of affairs the "battering-ram" entered. Her first act of organization was to set up a hospital—for women—in Harley Street: a fairly decent thing to do. Her committee decided to exclude Roman Catholics; she presented her resignation, and the decision was reversed. But honest, direct action like this was not always, she found, possible; intrigue and roundabout methods which, at the start, she had determined to avoid, were necessary for getting anything done. She presented her decisions to the committee as though they came from the medical staff; while with the medical staff she talked things out as man to man, and as though such things as committees did not exist. Within less than two years she had acquired a proficiency which would have taken others ten. And then, in the nick of time, came the call to action, in a great national crisis, which for the rest of her long life gave her the fame and power necessary for the practical and efficient employment, not so much of her great heart as of her great mind.

Her offense—for offense it had been—against the conventions of gentility was transformed by national need and by popular applause into heroic virtue, at the very moment when it took the jump from the comparative decency of the nursing of carefully selected gentlewomen (though it did include Roman Catholics) to the organization of an overcrowded military hospital where decency, sanitation, and system were all equally lacking. The happy accident of a nation badly and blunderingly at war was her opportunity; and the pretense that a modest woman must not look upon the body of any man but her own husband was blown sky-high in the patriotic fervour of the moment—never quite to return. Military and ministerial inefficiency had begun to make war dangerously unpopular; and while Tennyson wrote a famous poem to reconcile the public mind to one blunder, she, by the wiping out of another, almost restored to the war its popularity and saved the life of the government. On that figure of revolt, not knowing what they did, the Church, the Crown, and the public laid consecrating hands. The "public" in more senses than one. Florence Nightingale became, not merely the heroine of the nation, but the talk of the taverns; and it was approving talk. Tipplers toasted her and, damning the government and the War Office, went home drunk in her honour. Queen Victoria was herself temporarily weaned from her prejudice against the entry of women into public life, and though jealous of Florence's popularity, wished she could have "such a head" at the War Office. Two decades later the royal mind reverted to type, and declared that Lady Somebody-or-other, who wanted the vote, also "wanted whipping."

It was inevitable, under the circumstances, that an emotional interpretation should be given to the great work of rescue which Florence Nightingale accomplished, that heart should be put before head, and the "Commander of Genius," with her calm powers of organization and discipline (subduing even blockheads and fools), should be hailed as an "Angel of Mercy," with pity as her prevailing motive. But had she been asked to choose her own motto, it would not have been "Blessed are the merciful," with its corresponding reward, but far more probably "Blessed are the masterful, for they shall obtain mastery." Mercy she had in abundance, but it was not the incentive and mainspring of her action; her motive force was a passion which she was able to put unerringly into practice, for method as against muddle. The legendary "Angel of Mercy" could not have accomplished the task which the "battering-ram" was able to perform; and if there was in her character something hard and inflexible and quietly ruthless—to friends as well as to foes—let us take off our hats to it and thank God that it was so.

The mastery which she secured in that time of crisis she never let go. Her later career, through thirty more years of activity and over fifty of life, was amazing both in its methods and in its results. Broken in health, housebound, almost bed-ridden, she invented an economy of technique suited to her condition, by which it is quite likely that she got more work done than had she remained a vigorous and active member of Committees where so many wordy battles have to be fought and so much time lost. Without any diminution of industry or abatement of mental energy, the fiery reformer became a recluse; and we have the astonishing spectacle of this frail invalid exercising, through her own small band of workers, and sick-room interviews with selected persons, a greater and more persistent influence on royal commissions, Ministers, and the departmental acts of government than any other person of unofficial standing that one could name. To one after another of the departments of public service— hospitals, nursing, barracks, sanitation—she gave her great gifts of organization and common sense; wherever she directed her efforts, she brought health and saved life. Sometimes, as the result of reforms which she inculcated, the fall in the death rate was as great as that which she had brought about in the hospitals at Scutari. In the barracks and military hospitals in India the diminution of mortality was enormous; and it was mainly her doing.

She did not spare the dull officials, with whom she came in contact, the sharpness of her tongue. In spite of her feeble state of health, she went down to inspect the hospitals at Chatham, and commenting on what she found there, remarked: "Another symptom of the system which in the Crimea put to death 16,000 men. You might as well take 1,100 every year out into Salisbury Plain and shoot them."

And so it is not to be wondered at that with the old military type of mind (slow to move) she was never popular—was regarded, rather, as something which should not have been allowed. Many years after the Crimea, certain retired colonels and generals, who had perhaps tried a fall with her and had failed, spoke of her as "a damned nuisance"; the drop in the death rate at Scutari, from 42 to 2 per cent, not seeming to them sufficient compensation for that unwarrantable intrusion of a woman into the affairs of men.

During the quiet labour of her latter years she became almost a voluminous writer. In the drawing-up of schemes, the compiling of reports, and in contributions to blue-books, her handiwork—though anonymous—is constantly to be found. A royal commission, set up at her instigation in 1859, and making its report on lines which she laid down, was still the main basis of government action fifty years later. In the report of the Commission on the Health of the British Army in India, her own contribution formed the most readable part: it was reprinted and sold by the thousand. When a condensed version of the whole report was required for public consumption, finding the official synopsis unsatisfactory, she rewrote it, and published it at her own expense. Her record and her abilities combined placed her above criticism, almost above opposition. At the age of seventy-two we still find her a driving force—one whose policy was always to be ahead of what those in authority were willing to do. "We must create," she wrote, "a public opinion which will drive the government." And driving governments was, in fact, her life's work.

Her name became so valuable that, when she ceased to subscribe to a certain Society, the Society refused to take her name from its lists—her name being worth so much more than her subscription. And so far as the Woman's Movement was concerned, she stood, as a power and as an example, almost alone.

During the last long Suffrage Campaign which secured women the vote, two names of legendary preëminence were constantly invoked by the opposing forces—Queen Victoria and Florence Nightingale. Florence Nightingale was in favour of the vote, Queen Victoria was against it; but the approval of the former far outweighed the disapproval of the latter. People smiled when the old Queen's disapprobation was quoted—for had she not already so much more power than any vote could confer? Florence Nightingale, on the other hand, had discovered, not only for herself, but for women in general, the crying need for some public means of striking a balance against the incompetence and indifference of men in certain departments of life which to woman mattered considerably. After Florence Nightingale had come Josephine Butler; and whereas the one had achieved success through great popularity, the other—fighting a longer and harder battle—had won her victory, only after many defeats, through bitter opposition, reproach, and scorn.

Florence Nightingale stands curiously isolated—the one popular figure in a movement which incurred so much unpopularity before it became the accepted thing. But though her popularity greatly lightened her task and made much that she did possible which might otherwise have remained impossible, it is still probably true that hers was the most towering ability, as it was surely the most unusual in kind, of all those great and varying abilities which, from the sleep of the Victorian age, awoke the Woman's Movement into life and strength.

## Gamaliel Bradford (essay date 1933)

SOURCE: "Florence Nightingale," in *Portraits and Personalities,* edited by Mabel A. Bessey, Houghton Mifflin Company, 1933, pp. 116-32.

[*In the following essay, Bradford details the difficulties Nightingale encountered and overcame in her career as a reformer.*]

If there was ever a human being who was possessed by an Ideal that drove her, and whipped and scourged her into the arena, to fight and to struggle for it gallantly until she died, that human being was Florence Nightingale.

Florence was born in the city of that name, the City of Flowers, on May 12, 1820. She was brought up in aristocratic surroundings, with all the comfort and luxury that wealth could supply, so that even in girlhood her analytical temper was driven to cry, "Can reasonable people want all this? Is all that china, linen, glass necessary to make man a progressive animal?" From childhood she traveled widely, saw the habits and manners of mankind, and observed and compared them. Her education was varied and admirable, if somewhat desultory. She read and spoke several languages, was familiar with the classics and all the greater modern authors, and was interested in science and philosophy. Perhaps she had no profound knowledge of any of these things, but she was keenly sensitive to all of them.

With all the luxury and all the comfort and all the gay social life and activities about her, she was restless and discontented. Her family life did not at all satisfy her. Her father was a cultured, unoccupied, immensely busy English country gentleman. Her mother was an equally busy, practical, sensible, conventional English matron, of the Victorian type. Her sister had a passion for art. None of these things satisfied Florence. She wanted that scourging Ideal, if only she could find it: and until she found it, the humdrum doings of every day could bring her no satisfaction. What did she want? What could she do? How could she make her life fruitful, intense, significant, vital; give it the wide bearing of reality which was the only thing that could make it worth living at all? There was no one to tell her, no one to answer her passionate questions, nothing but futile waste of pointless, purposeless, idle talk—what Emily Dickinson calls, "the haggard necessities of parlor conversation." "Oh, how am I to get through this day—to talk through all this day!" she cried. And there were moments when the bitterness of it made life an agony—something to be fled from and escaped. "In my thirty-first year I see nothing desirable but death."

It might be thought that the best remedy for such restlessness would be love and marriage. Florence sometimes thought so herself and in one instance was sorely tempted. There was a cousin who meant a great deal to her and was very close to her, and there were minutes, days, almost years——. But somehow that scourging

Ideal was not quite satisfied with the prospect of a life devoted merely to society and domestic arrangements. So in those earlier, developing years, "the evil of dreaming" encroached upon her, involved her, threatened to absorb her completely: "The habit of living not in the present but in a future of dreams is gradually spreading over my whole existence. It is rapidly approaching the state of madness when dreams become realities."

Yet all the time she felt that the dream world was not natural to her, she did not breathe freely in it, and she was determined to escape from it. The means of escape for her was action—to do, to live, to accomplish something, to stand for something. Instinctively, from a very early period, action, for her, meant doing something for others, and very concretely relieving human suffering and misery. There has perhaps been a little exaggerated emphasis upon her early care for pets, her sympathy with their distresses, and her endeavor to relieve them, but this may have been little more than the quick tenderness of any sensitive child. The instinct, nevertheless, was real and grew upon her steadily, until, as she came gradually into womanhood, the desire to care for the unhappy became overpowering and irresistible: "Oh, God," she wrote in one of her early diaries, "Thou puttest into my heart this great desire to devote myself to the sick and sorrowful. I offer it to Thee." For in her strange blending of action and dreams a profoundly religious element and stimulus was always present and active.

But then she had the battle with family prejudice which so many ardent reformers have to go through. Public nursing? The idea was horrible, to the mother especially. A well-bred, modest English young lady think of such a career as that? It was simply out of the question. The battle was so strenuous that even Florence's energy at times seemed hardly equal to it and she was tempted to settle back into dreams—and death. But she would not, she never could, being a creature of magnificent will. Besides, there was always that Ideal with its relentless scourge driving her on. So even before she was permitted to make a business of nursing, she studied it in all its details, wherever she had the opportunity. She knew just how it was done and where it was done—the methods, the sublime possibilities, the tragic defects. Then, gradually, the family opposition was overcome, beaten down, and worn away. In 1850, when she was thirty, she managed to get some experience in a German nursing establishment at Kaiserswerth. A little later she served a short apprenticeship in a hospital run by the Sisters of Charity in Paris; and in August, 1853, she became Superintendent of an "Establishment for Gentlewomen during Illness," situated at No. 1, Harley Street, London.

The busy, useful, and permanently constructive labors in Harley Street were soon interrupted by the outbreak of the Crimean War, in which England and France, in conjunction with Turkey, endeavored to bring Russia to what they considered a reasonable settlement of the always turbulent Eastern Question. With the war, nursing, which had been of such absorbing personal interest to Florence Nightingale, became a matter of general and most pressing national concern.

To understand the wide and fundamental reforms in the business of nursing, which Miss Nightingale more than anyone else initiated, it is necessary to appreciate how crude, forlorn, and really tragic were the conditions in earlier times. Of course there never has been a time when human tenderness and sympathy did not go out to illness and suffering. Kind-hearted men and sensitive women had often given the best of their lives to relieving the misery about them, as far as they could. But organized, systematic, intelligent effort to relieve that misery, especially in the lives of the poor, had been woefully lacking, and without organization the most energetic individual effort is likely to go very little way.

Hospital arrangements, even in civilized countries, were almost as bad as prison arrangements. Anæsthetics were unknown. Consequently surgery was lamentably hasty and inefficient. Sanitary precautions were of the crudest order. Fresh air was lacking, proper food was lacking, above all cleanliness was lacking, and without cleanliness, the conquering of disease becomes a hopeless business.

In general, methods of caring for the sick were no more satisfactory than was the hospital equipment. Nursing, especially among the poor, was performed by neighbors in the most perfunctory manner, and even those who were able to hire assistance could, for the most part, secure only the most inefficient help. Nursing was largely in the hands of old women, who took little interest and had no sort of training. Their reputations were often unsavory and they had a strong propensity for drinking. In short, Dickens's Mrs. Gamp is no bad representative of the class.

But all these difficulties, which attended even civilian nursing, were greatly augmented when it came to the care of sick and wounded soldiers in the field. To appreciate these at their worst one may turn to the story of the American Revolution and see what the men had to suffer. When it was impossible to provide food, or clothing, or warmth for even the fighting men, it can easily be imagined how wretched were the wounded, with no comforts and very little care. Neither in the Revolution nor in any other war up to the time of Florence Nightingale had women nurses been seen in military hospitals. Common soldiers were detailed to take care of their suffering comrades, and even when good will was present, both experience and necessary means were usually wanting. If you were wounded or fell ill, a good constitution might pull you through. The chances were, you died, and those who died most quickly were the most fortunate. Miss Nightingale's own description of the conditions she found in the Crimea is by no means the most ghastly, but it is distressing enough: "The supply of bedsteads was inadequate. The commonest utensils for decency as well as for comfort, were lacking.

The sheets were of canvas, and so coarse that the wounded men begged to be left in their blankets. There was no bedroom furniture of any kind, and only empty beer or wine bottles for candle-sticks."

Rumors of such a state of things quickly aroused public sentiment in England, and Miss Nightingale, conscious as she was of the imperfection of nursing under the best conditions, at once began to feel that in the ranks of suffering soldiers she would find her place. As it happened, she was on intimate terms with Sidney Herbert, the Secretary of War, and his wife, and in October, 1854, she wrote to Mrs. Herbert, offering her services for nursing in any way that might be useful. Curiously enough, this letter crossed one from Herbert himself, in which he laid the whole situation before her and implored her to undertake exactly the task she was yearning for. This association with the energetic war secretary is of importance, because from this time on he and Florence worked hand in hand, sometimes with friendly criticism and difference, but always with devoted co-operation and sympathetic understanding.

But the task she had undertaken was a terrific one, perhaps more terrific than even her wide imagination had conceived. She hastily gathered about her as efficient a band of helpers as she could, and arrived in the Crimea just when she was needed most. The Battle of the Alma had been fought in September, 1854, that of Balaclava in October, and Inkerman took place in November, shortly after her arrival. She found the hospitals crowded, choked with poor wretches who needed attention of every kind, and they continued to pour in upon her in a stream utterly beyond any means that could be provided for taking proper care of them.

It is here that the peculiar, the extraordinary genius of the woman shines out. She was not only a nurse as most people interpret the term; she had the elements of a great organizer as well. People think of her chiefly as a ministrant at a bedside of agony. She was that when necessary, but she accomplished many other and perhaps more important tasks. To begin with, she went to the root of matters and tried to find out just where she stood. All her life she had had a passion for statistics. She wanted to know the facts. Napoleon felt that the great secret of his success lay in studying military reports before he made his plans. In like manner, Florence Nightingale was determined first to find out what conditions she had to deal with. She wanted to know what the needs were and what the possibilities were; for until she had such knowledge she could not act intelligently. And she had a lightning-like speed in getting the knowledge in the most unlikely places.

When she had the facts, she acted, with magnificent swiftness and magnificent efficiency. She had an excellent capacity for labor at all times, could work with tireless, well-directed zeal not only when she was fresh but when she was apparently exhausted. And she had the instinct of system without which so much labor is thrown away. The logical, intelligent method, which was closely connected with her love of statistics, made every stroke of labor tell.

The task that met her when she landed in the Crimea in the autumn of 1854 was one to tax all these qualities of action to the utmost. She was at once plunged into a chaos of disease, dirt, disorder, inefficiency, incompetence, and above all the most distracting official and officious red-tape. She wanted cleanliness, she wanted better equipment, she wanted better service. She wanted these things and she was determined to have them. In seeking them she could show extraordinary tact and extraordinary patience when the occasion called for them. She could wheedle the high authorities; she could reason with them gently till she brought them to her point of view. But also, when she saw that it was necessary, this quiet, ladylike person could bully and domineer, could be fierce and even bitter, if the good of the cause, the good of the suffering soldiers, the good of England required it. She could even write to her devoted friend, Herbert, "You have sacrificed the cause so near my heart, you have sacrificed me, a matter of small importance now; you have sacrificed your own written word to a popular cry." By one method or another, she was bound to get things done, and she did. Abraham Lincoln said quietly to his recalcitrant secretary, who refused to execute an order, "Mr. Secretary, I think you'll have to execute that order." So, when the doctors said to Miss Nightingale that something could not be done, she replied calmly, "It must be done." And it was.

The same gift of understanding and of handling human nature was shown within her nursing organization as well as without. She knew the virtue of obedience, was willing to apply it to herself, and insisted upon it from those who worked for her. She writes to one of her nurses: "Do you think I should have succeeded in doing anything if I had kicked and resisted and resented?" She wanted things done as she directed, done patiently, courageously, cheerfully, and she saw that they were so done. She proposed to have an efficient, capable, willing corps of helpers, and in the end she got them. But by far the most fruitful means of getting them was her own example, her own patience, her own courage, her own cheerfulness, and here, as in dealing with difficult officials who were outside her control, she fell back upon her wide interest in human nature and her profound and sympathetic understanding of it. Her brief notes on some of the nurses show how varied and how shrewd this interest was. Everywhere in this human dealing there was the same priceless, mysterious gift and power of putting herself in another's place, of understanding another's troubles and drawbacks and difficulties and of giving advice about meeting them.

One concrete difficulty that Miss Nightingale always had to encounter was that of getting necessary hospital supplies. Sometimes these were long in coming, sometimes they were delayed by vexatious routine, sometimes they never came at all. But her power of getting them by patient, persistent effort was so remarkable that at times it almost seemed as if she created them out of nothing. They were never all she wanted, or just what she wanted, but she got them somehow, till the regular officials were often dumb with astonishment.

All this tremendous efficiency might seem to obscure the tenderer, more feminine qualities that are usually associated with nursing. It is needless to say that Miss Nightingale had these qualities, that they formed the real basis of her passion for the work. But it was the more practical, organizing faculty that gave them their richest usefulness. Sympathy she unquestionably had in large measure. She could be strict, she could be even austere, when she felt that a patient needed it, but she had infinite fun, gayety, cheerfulness, confidence, and hope. She had not a trace of that long-faced dreariness which makes the gloom of a sick-chamber gloomier yet. She would devote herself with passionate forgetfulness of hours and food to the very worst cases and linger over them to the loss of her own comfort and even health. The effect of all this on the suffering soldiers themselves is best shown in the remark of one of them: "If the Queen came for to die, they ought to make *her* queen and I think they would." As her biographer says, "The men idolized her. They kissed her shadow, and they saluted her as she passed down their wounded ranks."

Miss Nightingale threw herself into her task with all the energy of her nature and with her whole soul. It absorbed all her thoughts and drained all her vitality. It made her utterly indifferent to the ordinary timidities of women and even of men. She did not hesitate to fight big rats in the hospitals when they bothered her and to dispose of them with her own hand. When it was necessary to study the actual conditions of the battlefield, she did not hesitate here either. To a young sentry who ventured to warn her of danger, she quietly said: "My good young man, more dead and wounded have passed through my hands than I hope you will ever see in the battlefield during the whole course of your military career: believe me, I have no fear of death." She was equally indifferent to the peril of infectious diseases, of course taking reasonable precautions, but going always where she was needed, no matter what the conditions were. As a consequence, she became dangerously ill with fever, and all England was alarmed about her. But she stuck to her post, and as soon as she was able, went about her work again. What wonder, when she was so exacting with regard to herself, that she was equally exacting with regard to others? She pushed and drove and urged everyone to the limit of his strength and beyond. But she got things done, and she accomplished invaluable service to her country and indirectly to the world.

The Crimean nightmare was over in the spring of 1856 and in July Miss Nightingale returned to England. History undoubtedly identifies her largely with her heroic service in the Crimean War. But it should never be forgotten that she lived on for over fifty years, dying

August 13, 1910, at the age of ninety. Although during all that time she was more or less of an invalid, her naturally delicate constitution broken by the Crimean strain, every day of those years was given to passionate thought for the causes she had at heart and to intense labor to bring those causes to triumph. Her external life was of course somewhat eclipsed by illness. She could not go to the world, but the world came to her. Honors were showered upon her; great personages visited her. She had her own interests and pleasures. She turned naturally to the world of dreams and thoughts, as she had always done, and wrote extensively upon philosophical and religious subjects. She enjoyed many friendships. One of the most notable of these was that with Benjamin Jowett, the great Oxford scholar and translator of Plato, who admired Miss Nightingale's work and perhaps even more, her character. With him she carried on an extensive correspondence dealing with most things in heaven and earth. And then she had her family, whom she loved, and who loved her, only they were different, or perhaps in some respects too much the same. In one of her letters to Jowett, she writes: "We are a great many too strong characters, and very different, all pulling different ways. And we are so dreadfully serious. Oh, how much good it does us to have some one to laugh at us."

And all the time, the perpetual, colossal, incessant work went on, right straight through, almost to the end of the fifty years. Her labors during all these later years may be summed up under three heads. She worked for the soldiers; she worked for India; she worked to improve nursing conditions for the whole world. Her work for the army was simply a logical continuation of her Crimean labors. For long years she had to battle with the same old official red tape, to improve conditions in hospitals and sanitation, to introduce the means of educational advancement and of wholesome amusement of every kind. In all this work she found the greatest assistance and support in her friend, Sidney Herbert, and his death in 1861 was a severe blow to her.

The work in India was an extension of that with the army. As her biographer expresses it, Miss Nightingale might be described as a Health Missionary for India. At any rate she labored untiringly to improve conditions in that difficult and suffering country, and while neither she nor anyone could overcome the enormous obstacles, the results of her efforts were substantial and enduring.

But undoubtedly Florence Nightingale's name will be most permanently associated with all that she effected in the ideals and the practice of nursing, a work which can hardly be appreciated except by one who has some familiarity with the crude and blundering methods of an earlier day. Miss Nightingale made nursing a profession of dignity and respect. According to her view, it was something to be learned with patience and humility and practiced with pride. Her nurses were taught to feel that there was always something that they could learn, ought to learn, must learn, always

something that would make their work better, more useful, more worthy of the high ideal for which they were striving. As her biographer puts it: "In the history of modern nursing the Sixteenth of May, 1865, is a date only less memorable than the Twenty-fourth of June, 1860. On the earlier day the Nightingale Training School was opened at St. Thomas's; on the latter, twelve Nightingale nurses began work in the Liverpool Infirmary, and instituted the reform of workhouse nursing. In other words, through Miss Nightingale's efforts modern hospitals and modern nurses began to develop into the beneficent institutions which they have continued increasingly to become."

So the long years wore on till 1910, filled often with weariness and pain, but always with usefulness and variety. What impresses one above all in such a life is the sense of immense value and profit in it. Miss Nightingale, with the charming frankness that always distinguished her, said in a moment of petulance: 'Now I see that no man would have put up with what I have put up with for ten years, to do even the little I have done—which is about a hundredth part of what I have tried for." Certainly few men in history have achieved more for humanity than she. The great conquerors have won glory by destroying; the great statesmen, who have tried to make over the world, have too often mixed personal considerations with their effort; and the same is true of the great artists. No one will deny that even in Florence Nightingale the ego was there. She liked to do big things and to feel that Florence Nightingale had done them. But where these considerations are merged, absorbed in such immense benefit to suffering mankind, one overlooks them altogether. And perhaps the key to all Miss Nightingale's achievement is to be found in her own significant words: "I attribute my success to this:— *I never gave or took an excuse.*"

## Elmer C. Adams and Warren Dunham Foster (essay date 1935)

SOURCE: "Florence Nightingale," in *Heroines of Modern Progress,* The Macmillan Company, 1935, pp. 120-46.

[*In the following essay, Adams and Foster examine Nightingale's life and character.*]

Florence Nightingale, when a child, had a large family of dolls. One day when she was entertaining them at a garden party on her father's estate in Derbyshire, her dog seized one in his teeth and scurried away for a romp with it. Florence rescued the doll a few minutes later. Sawdust was pouring out of a large rip in the side. But she did not mourn over the mishap; nor did she throw the tattered playmate away and ask her parents for another to fill its place. She stuffed fresh sawdust into the doll, until it was as plump as ever, and then bound her handkerchief neatly over the hole. And thereafter this doll, from all the large family, was the girl's favorite.

This was in Derbyshire, England, a hundred years ago. The shire was then a picturesque country devoted mainly to grazing. The shepherd population, in their thatch-roofed cottages, lived quiet and often solitary lives. Their condition varied from well-off to poor,—there were a good many poor—and, with the minimum education, they were generally much simpler than country folk of our own day.

In the midst of such a countryside was born Florence Nightingale, in the year 1820. She was not precisely in it, however, but above it. Her father, William Shore Nightingale, was a wealthy land owner and a country gentleman of the old style, known as "squire." His summer residence at Lea Hurst comprised a fine manorial house and estate, in which money had been spent without stint to produce comfort and elegance. Both parents, moreover, were cultured and refined. So, Florence Nightingale was born into riches and position, and refinement. She was born a lady, in fact. Every avenue to social eminence was open to her. And even the simplicity and poverty round about might easily have set her up in a narrow class pride, and made her all the more a "lady."

She seems to have profited well by her heritage in the way of personal comforts and education. As a very young girl she took her pleasures with dolls, in the manner described above. A little later she learned to ride horseback, and galloped daily over the downs in company with her father, or her father's friend, the vicar. Her education in modern languages went on, meanwhile, under the charge of a governess. Her father instructed her in mathematics and classic literature; and from her mother she learned to play, to draw and to sew. But this was the conventional training for a squire's daughter of the period. And if Florence Nightingale had been limited to it, she might never have been heard of, any more than a thousand other squire's daughters who were growing up in England at the time.

Squire Nightingale and his wife were people of singularly broad, sympathetic minds. Riding over the downs one day, the father noticed a peculiar flower blossoming among the weeds. He dismounted, with the girl, to examine it. He pronounced it a species very rare in Derbyshire, and suggested that Florence transplant it to her own garden. She did so, and by careful tending soon had a bed of the strange plants growing near the manor house. From this incident and others like it, the girl developed a curious interest in all kinds of plants that were having a hard time to live. In her garden at home she had raised peonies, pansies, forget-me-nots and mignonette. These were easily grown, and they flowered as beautifully as the girl could desire. But one day her father saw her going into the meadow and followed her. She stooped by a bunch of cowslips and began to dig up the weeds that choked its growth. Then she found a marigold that had been bruised by a passing cart wheel; this she reset in a safe place farther from the road. Finally she uprooted a wild lily plant, wrapped it in

paper, and set off for home with it. The squire saw that his daughter was a born gardener, but of a peculiar stamp: her concern was not in the garden so much as in the flowers that needed a garden's protection. That trait pleased the squire, and he did everything he could to foster it.

The same trait revealed itself in the child's care of animals. She had her squirrels, of course, and her pony and her dog, and she never tired of playing with them. But her keenest interest in these was awakened when they met with an accident. At least one may infer as much from one incident.

Florence was riding home with the vicar to tea. On the way they passed a herd of sheep, in wild commotion. The old shepherd, Roger, could do nothing to control them.

"What is the matter, Roger?" called the vicar, "where is your dog?"

"The boys have been throwing stones at him, sir," replied the shepherd. "They have broken his leg, and he will never be good for anything again. I shall have to take a bit of cord and put an end to his misery."

"Oh!" cried Florence, who overheard the story. "Poor Cap! Are you sure his leg is broken?"

"Yes, miss, it's broke sure enough. He hasn't set foot to the ground since, and no one can't go nigh him. Best put him out of his pains, I says."

But the vicar and the girl knew Cap. He was an intelligent and useful dog, and they were sorry to think of his dying. Riding on, they stopped at the cottage where he lay. Florence petted the cringing beast while the clergyman examined his injury. "Is it broken?" she called anxiously.

"No," said the vicar. "No bones are broken. There is no reason why Cap should not recover; all he needs is care and nursing."

"What shall I do first?" asked the girl quickly, accepting the duty as hers.

The vicar—he had studied medicine in his day—prescribed a hot compress. The fire was lighted, and the kettle put over. But no cloth was to be found until, looking all about the room, Florence saw the shepherd's extra smock hanging on the wall.

"This will do!" she cried. "Mamma will give him another."

So she tore the smock into strips, and bathed the dog's limb until the inflammation was gone. The injury healed, and the dog served his master many a year afterward. But that was not the only result of the incident, nor the main one. It first disclosed to the girl what her natural tastes were, and determined her to follow them.

It is not wise to emphasize the incident over much, however, for there were plenty of others that would turn her mind in the same direction. If her father was interested in flowers, he was more interested in people. There were a good many middle class and poor around him, as was said, and he, with his wealth and culture, took their welfare to heart. Often he flung open the gates of his estate and gave the village children food and presents and let them dance on his lawn. He had a benevolent care, too, for families that came upon hard times due to sickness or the failure of crops. To these he sent food and clothing and medicine; and often it was Florence who conveyed the gift, riding on her pony. Thus the child, so favored personally by fortune, grew familiar with the wants of others less fortunate.

Many of her errands were done in company with the vicar. He spoke words of cheer to the sick and bereaved, advised them as to the use of the foods and medicines the girl brought, and dropped a few hints about nursing and hygiene. So the girl learned how to do the most practical good to people in need, how to lessen suffering not alone by gifts and personal sympathy, but by the means a physician uses. She was daily welcomed in some poor cottage. Slight, graceful, with a fine, oval, delicate face, gray-blue eyes, and smoothly parted brown hair, she must have exercised a remarkable charm upon the sick rooms she entered. She read to the patients, measured out their medicine, prepared dainty foods, and turned her hand to any useful task. People called her a little "Angel of Mercy." And they spoke better than they knew. For in these visits with the vicar the strongest bent was given to the girl's nature. And the name bestowed by her simple admirers was also a prophecy.

As Florence grew to young womanhood, her character as the daughter of an opulent English squire continued to expand in a normal way.

She still rode horseback, in a habit that swept the ground, and a large hat trimmed with ostrich plumes; or performed social duties in a stylish frock with full skirts and sleeves and a collar of lace; or visited in a full plaited jacket with a belt and a "coal scuttle" bonnet. She "entered society," and played a conspicuous part in the parties, dances and other country gayeties. Moreover, she went to London for the "season" as a lady of her rank must, was presented to Queen Victoria, and shone among the best in court circles. She traveled on the continent, too, explored the galleries of Germany, France and Italy, and acquired a facile speaking knowledge of the languages of those countries.

From all this, however, her interest carried her back to the sick and the poor about Lea Hurst and Embly. She still ministered to these, and with such growing intelligence that she was nothing less than an unpaid country doctor. At seventeen, too, she conducted a Bible class at Lea Hurst for the girls employed in the hosiery mills. In short, with all her education and social success she could not forget the dependent people around her

childhood home; and, whatever might be her amusement, it was her earnest vocation to make the lives of those people easier and brighter.

Then, somewhere in this period, the realization came to her that she was unfit for so great a task. She had not strength to do so much alone; there were cases of sickness where she did not know what to prescribe; and the untrained mothers and daughters of the shire, who helped her, were too dull and awkward to carry out what small behests she gave. Such facts were true of Lea Hurst and Embly Park, and it saddened the young woman to think of them. But then she discovered that what was true of her home was equally true of all England.

In London she had seen the slum people poorer and sicker than they ever could be in rural Derbyshire. She looked about to see what help they had, corresponding to that she had volunteered for her own people; and she found, precisely—nothing. Or worse than nothing!

In the homes the most barbaric ignorance prevailed as to the simple matters of ventilation, cleanliness, light and food. This was a great shock to one who knew that every woman is a nurse, at some time in her life "has charge of the personal health of somebody," and ought to know the essentials of every day sanitation and nursing. On top of that there was no one to go about and dispense free medicine and advice as she had done at home. And, as the key to the whole tale of neglect and misery—there was no place where competent nurses could be trained.

Many of those sick with contagious diseases were gathered into great public hospitals and there tended by professional nurses. These invalids, Miss Nightingale thought, ought to be treated in a model way; and the treatment of them ought to provide a model training for a nurse. But the very opposite was true. The hospitals of London were as dirty and unsanitary as the slum homes. Nursing, as she says, "was largely in the hands of the coarsest type of women, not only untrained, but callous in feeling," and often of low character. People believed "that it requires nothing but a disappointment in love, the want of an object, a general disgust or incapacity for other things to turn a woman into a good nurse." "This reminds one of the parish where a stupid old man was set to be schoolmaster because he was past keeping the pigs."

The hospital nurses did, in fact, keep their patients "like pigs." And therein Florence Nightingale perceived the root of all the sick misery of England. And she determined—just where or how can never be known—to see what could be done to reform the hospitals. That was to be her life work. She was about twenty-one years old when she definitely settled upon it.

The decision required courage. Nursing was a base profession, not much above that of barmaid; and Florence Nightingale was a lady born and a lady bred. She had to have the confidence that she could preserve herself from contamination while she elevated the profession. And it was a prodigious undertaking. But she was not without inspiring examples. She laid her case before Elizabeth Fry, who had renovated the prisons of Europe, and was, of course, encouraged to go ahead. Then the Catholic hospitals on the Continent were sensibly constructed and the Sisters of Mercy in charge were generally capable women. Yet her strongest inducement was not these examples, but her knowledge of the shocking need for intelligent nursing. It was, above all, her own leaning toward that humane occupation. For that was the woman's natural bent—she who had healed Cap, and read consolation to her rheumatic neighbors. She did not lack the courage.

So for thirteen years more she was most of the time under the roofs of hospitals. She visited, apparently, every such institution in England, from the great wards of London to the county infirmaries; all the hospitals of Paris, where she studied with the Sisters of Charity; and those of Berlin, Brussels, Rome, Constantinople and Alexandria; and the war hospitals of the French and Sardinians.

Most of her study on the Continent was with the Catholic sisters, who were so far ahead of their time. Miss Nightingale well knew, however, that they and their system could never be transferred to Protestant England. If she was to produce nurses in England, they must be Protestant nurses. Hence when she discovered a solitary Lutheran deaconess hospital at Kaiserwerth on the Rhine, she attached herself to it for serious study. There she was thoroughly drilled in every department of nursing. "Never," she says, "have I met with a higher love and a purer devotion than there." And a sister nurse said of her, "She was only a few months there, but they so long to see her again. Such a loving and lovely womanly character, hers must be."

From Germany, finally, she came home, and, after nearly twelve years, her preparation was finished. Twelve years is rather a long period for study, modern graduate nurses may think. But she had to pick up the science in little bits, here and there, and the hardest part was not learning the facts, but separating the false from the true. And then, even for a twelve-year student, she was exceptionally well prepared—as will soon appear.

Miss Nightingale had not been long at home when an occasion came to apply her learning. A hospital for poor, broken down governesses in London was in straits. The management had failed, the philanthropic supporters had withdrawn their funds, and the home was about to be closed. That would have been a great calamity, as great as if an old soldiers' home were on short notice to turn all its boarders out of doors. In this crisis, Miss Nightingale was called to be superintendent of the Harley Street Home.

Probably here was forced upon the young woman the real test of her life. Heretofore she had been a student; now she was to face realities. The question now was—

would she *work* in hospitals, would she give her *life* to them? Was she willing at the crucial time to relinquish her place as a lady and actually dwell among the poor and the sick to serve them?

Florence Nightingale was willing. She took up residence on Harley Street among a swarm of ailing and despondent women, when she might have been attending balls at Buckingham Palace. She gave money. She encouraged old friends and new to subscribe. With her own hands she swept and made beds and spooned out medicine for these invalids whom she had never seen and for whom no one in the world cared a stiver. It was an obscure and a humble assignment. Few but her friends knew she was doing it, and many of them disapproved. But her work finally showed that she wanted not only to study nursing, but to nurse. She had chosen her career and she was fairly launched upon it.

She toiled so hard at Harley Street that she herself fell ill, and retired to her home for a rest. It was there, while still pondering the problems of her quiet London task, that she was suddenly summoned to another task, as spectacular and momentous as had ever been thrown into the hands of a woman.

The Crimean war was in progress, France and England being allied to defend Turkey against Russian aggression. The British army had sailed to a strange climate with shamefully poor commissary and medical staffs. The weather was stormy and the soldiers had little shelter against it. Said a correspondent of the *London Times,* "It is now pouring rain, the skies are black as ink, the wind is howling over the staggering tents, the trenches are turned into dykes; in the tents the water is sometimes a foot deep; our men have not either warm or waterproof clothing; they are out for twelve hours at a me in the trenches"—and so on without end.

Plenty of food and clothing had been shipped from England, but they never reached their destination. Some vessels were delayed; in some the stores were packed at the bottom of the hold and could not be raised; some hove in with the wrong goods at the wrong port—and, on one, the consignment of boots proved to be all for the left foot! But the most criminal point of mismanagement was this: food, clothing and medicine might be stored in a warehouse within easy reach of the army; but the official with authority to deal them out would be absent, and, so stringent were the army rules that no one dared so much as point at them! The rigid system was infinitely worse than no system. And the soldiers were starving in the midst of plenty, and freezing under the shadow of mountains of good woolen clothing.

Now, to come at once to the worst, imagine these conditions transferred to the military hospitals. In the great Barrack Hospital at Scutari lay two thousand sorely wounded men, and hundreds more were coming in every day. The wards were crowded to twice their capacity—the sick lay side by side on mattresses that touched each other. The floors and walls and ceilings were wet and filthy. There was no ventilation. Rats and vermin swarmed everywhere. The men lay "in their uniforms, stiff with gore and covered with filth to a degree and of a kind no one could write about." It was a "dreadful den of dirt, pestilence and death."

This might have been remedied by an adequate medical staff. But the doctors were few. They were hampered in their professional duties by administrative ones. And they had to trust the actual nursing to orderlies who had never seen sickness in their lives. Then, there was the same lack of supplies due to mismanagement. There "were no vessels for water or utensils of any kind; no soap, towels or cloths, no hospital clothes." "The sheets were of canvas and so coarse that the wounded men begged to be left in their blankets. There was no bedroom furniture of any kind, and only beer or wine bottles for candlesticks!" It is difficult to imagine a scene of worse disorder and misery. The proportion of deaths to the whole army, from disease alone—malaria and cholera—was sixty per cent. Seventy died in the hospital in one night. There was danger that the entire army would be wiped out,—most of it without ever receiving a scratch from the enemy's weapons.

It was in this extremity that the British nation appealed to Florence Nightingale to save the sick and wounded men,—an army of twenty-eight thousand as helpless as children before the ravages of disease—and to save the war. Was ever a bigger task put upon a woman?

And was ever a bigger honor? Female nurses had never before been admitted to English military hospitals, because English nurses anywhere had been something of a nuisance. This woman must have proved that she was not a nuisance. For the minister of war requested her to organize a band of nurses for Scutari and gave her power to draw upon the government to any extent.

Miss Nightingale at the time was thirty-four years old. An acquaintance described her thus: "Simple, intellectual, sweet, full of love and benevolence, she is a fascinating and perfect woman. She is tall and pale. Her face is exceedingly lovely. But better than all is the soul's glory that shines through every feature so exultingly. Nothing can be sweeter than her smile. It is like a sunny day in summer." Again, "young (about the age of our Queen) graceful, feminine, rich, popular, she holds a singularly gentle and persuasive influence over all with whom she comes in contact. Her friends and acquaintances are of all classes and persuasions, but her happiest place is at home in the center of a very large band of accomplished relatives, and in simplest obedience to her admiring parents."

Nevertheless Scutari needed her. She was ready for Scutari. It was that for which she had been unconsciously preparing since a girl. She was ready, and she went.

Within six days from the time she accepted the post, Miss Nightingale had selected thirty-eight nurses, and departed for the seat of war. She arrived at Scutari November 4, 1854, and walked the length of the barracks, viewing her two miles of patients. And next day before she could form any plans, the fresh victims of another battle began to arrive. There was not space for them within the walls and hundreds had to repose, with what comfort they could, in the mud outside. One of the nurses wrote, "Many died immediately after being brought in—their moans would pierce the heart—and the look of agony on those poor dying faces will never leave my heart." A terrible situation to face; and all England depending on her!

But the nurse did not hesitate. She ordered the patients brought in, and directed where to lay them, and what attention they should have. She was up and around twenty hours that day, and as many the next, until a place had been found for every man, even in the corridors and on the landings of the stair. As leader of the nurses she might have confined herself to administrative tasks—of which there were enough for any woman—and stayed in the office. But no. She shrank from the sight of no operation. Many men, indeed, whose cases the surgeons thought hopeless, she nursed back to health. A visitor saw her one morning at two o'clock at the bedside of a dying soldier, lamp in hand. She was writing down his last message to the home folks; and for them, too, she took in charge his watch and trinkets—and then soothed him in his last moments. And this was but one case in thousands. "She is a ministering angel, without any exaggeration, in these hospitals," wrote a correspondent of the *London Times,* "and as the slender form glides quietly along each corridor, every poor fellow's face softens with gratitude at the sight of her. When all the medical officers have retired for the night, and silence and darkness have settled down upon the miles of prostrate sick, she may be observed alone, with lamp in hand, making her solitary rounds."

One soldier said, "I can't help crying when I see them. Only think of Englishwomen coming out here to nurse us; it is so homely and comfortable." He probably did not cry alone. And one wrote to his people, "She would speak to one and another and nod and smile to many more; but she could not do it to all, you know, for we lay there by hundreds; but we could kiss her shadow as it fell, and lay our heads on our pillows again content!" It was of this incident that Longfellow wrote in his "Lady with the lamp":

> And slow, as in a dream of bliss,
> The speechless sufferer turns to kiss
> Her shadow as it falls
> Upon the darkening walls.

In a place like Scutari, however, this kind of feminine tenderness alone would avail little. Science was needed; the most perfect skill in scientific nursing. The windows were few, and the few were mostly locked; and where one was opened the odors of decaying animals came in to pollute still more the foul air of the wards.

The food for the whole hospital—for those sick of fever, cholera, wounds and what not, as well as for those in health—was cooked, like an "Irish stew," in big kettles. Vegetables and meats were dumped in together, and when any one felt hungry he could dip for himself. Naturally some got food overdone, and some got it raw; the luckiest got a mess that was scarcely palatable; and the sick could generally not eat at all. As for other matters, it has been shown how unclean the barrack wards were, how "only seven shirts" had been laundered in all those wretched weeks, and how the infected bed linen of all classes of patients was thrown, unsorted, into one general wash.

But Florence Nightingale had spent twelve years in the hospitals of Europe to learn how to conquer just such situations as this. She had the waste and pollution outside the walls cleared away. Then she threw up the windows, and set a carpenter to make more. Within ten days she had established a diet kitchen and was feeding the men each on the food his particular case demanded. She set up a laundry, too, where the garments of the sick could be cleansed in a sanitary way. All this was the easier to do because with wise foresight she had brought the necessary articles with her on the *Victus* from England. The ship gave up chicken, jelly, and all manner of delicacies; and, on a single day, "a thousand shirts, besides other clothing." In two weeks that "dreadful den of dirt, pestilence and death" had vanished; and in its place stood a building, light and well aired throughout, where patients lay on spotless cots, ate appetizing food from clean dishes, had their baths and their medicine at regular intervals, and never for an hour lacked any attention that would help their recovery.

But after all is said of Florence Nightingale's sympathy and her science, she owed her final triumph in the Crimea to a rarer talent, that of tactful organizing and executive power. Why was she not tethered by the system and the red tape that rendered ineffectual the best efforts of the medical men? Most things needful were in store not far from the barracks hospital. But the regular physicians could not get at them. Why could she?

In the first place she had tact enough not to offend the system. The minister of war had warned her, "a number of sentimental enthusiastic ladies turned loose into the hospital at Scutari would probably after a few days be *'mises á la porte'* by those whose business they would interrupt and whose authority they would dispute." Florence Nightingale did not at first interrupt or dispute anybody. She began by doing the neglected minor things, the things that no one else had time for. She opened windows. She scrubbed floors and walls. She laundered shirts. She peeled potatoes and boiled soup. She bathed the patients, dosed them with medicine while the worn-out surgeons were asleep, read to them, and wrote letters for them. In these activities she asked not even supplies from the system, but procured them from her own ship.

The hidebound officials were even then slow to concur. Perhaps they were jealous to see their own incompetence exposed. And there was one case,—just one—where she came to blows with them. The hospital inmates were in desperate want, and the articles for their relief were nearby in a warehouse, but the stores could not be disturbed until after inspection. Miss Nightingale tried to hasten the inspection. Failing of that, she tried to get them distributed without inspection. That also failed. "My soldiers are dying," she said. "I must have those stores." Whereupon, she called two soldiers, marched them to the warehouse, and bade them burst open the doors!

That was the kind of firm hand she could use. More often, though, she attained her ends in a peaceful way. Only a little feminine tact was necessary to bring together the dilatory members of a board and get them to unlock a storehouse. She was soon able to lay her hands on an abundance of anything the situation demanded. Then, besides her own small band of nurses, a large number of orderlies and common soldiers were, after a time, detailed to work under her direction. "Never," she says, "came from them one word or one look which a gentleman would not have used;" and many of them became attached to her with an almost slavish affection. More than that, she was, for the English at home, the one commanding figure, and her hospital office, the headquarters of the Crimean campaign. *The Times* collected a big fund and placed it at her disposal. And all over England women were making clothing—shiploads of it—which they addressed to the soldiers in her care. "The English Nobility must have emptied their wardrobes and linen stores," said a nurse, "to send out bandages for the wounded. There was the most beautiful underclothing and the finest cambric sheets, with merely a scissors run here and there through them to insure their being used for no other purpose, some from the Queen's palace, with the royal monogram beautifully worked."

In a word, Florence Nightingale became, through her wonderful executive talent, the trusted agent of the whole British people, as powerful in the work of nursing as the commander-in-chief of the army was in fighting. Some one called her the lady-in-chief. There is perhaps not a better designation.

And the result of her efforts justified this faith. When she arrived the death rate was sixty per cent. She reduced it in a few weeks to one per cent. Nine of her nurses died on duty; others were invalided home; she herself was long fever sick and near to death. But for two years she battled against disease, always in a winning fight. She conquered disease. And it is not too much to say that she conquered the Russian army, and saved the war for the allies. No wonder England welcomed her home as one of the greatest heroines in all her history.

Florence Nightingale returned home in 1856. It was soon noised about that she was not only the heroine but the martyr of Crimea. The strain of those terrible years and the fever had broken her health, and she was to live, thereafter, a house-ridden invalid. Although still a young woman, it might be assumed that her usefulness was ended. On the contrary, during the fifty odd years that remained to her, she carried on from her London home a great reform. To mankind and the world in general that reform is, in fact, so great that the Scutari experience becomes a mere incident in its history.

The English people had desired to present her some testimonial on her return. Rich and poor all over the kingdom eagerly subscribed—every soldier in the service giving a day's pay—and fifty thousand pounds were raised. But the woman who had modestly slipped home by a secret route to avoid bell ringing and processions in her honor would be not likely to care for a gift of money. Her heart was still in her work. She had learned much at Scutari that she wished to preserve. So she accepted the money on condition that she might use it to found a hospital!

The St. Thomas Hospital in London was accordingly opened. This was nothing more or less than a high-class school for nurses. A student had to bring a good character and a fair education. She was taught habits of punctuality, quietness, and personal neatness; how to dress wounds, and apply bandages; how to make beds and cook for, move and feed, and observe the symptoms of patients. Some might think this knowledge intuitive in women, said Miss Nightingale in the prospectus. "Send us as many such geniuses as you can, for we are sorely in need of them."

She knew the knowledge was not intuitive. Had it been so, she need never have toiled at Harley Street, never doctored and fed her poor neighbors at home. This school was the reply to the ignorance she had seen in those places. It was the goal of her study in the Kaiserwerth and the Catholic hospitals. It was the thing she had aimed at from the first and would, perhaps, have realized sooner or later. But the accidental call to Crimea gave her, in a brief time, prestige and ripe experience and money. And these she hastened to use for the project that had been simmering in her mind since a girl. Now at last she had her desire. She would reform the hospitals of England. She would fill them with nurses who brought something more to their calling than a "disappointment in love."

But this was not all. The hospitals were mostly reserved for contagious cases. And in the London slums were thousands of sick, in their homes, who could pay very little for a doctor's service, and who did not know the bare essentials of nursing. There were many such all over England. Yes, even at Lea Hurst! Had not their presence at Lea Hurst been the thing that first set her to thinking on the whole subject of hospitals and nurses? Well, then, she must do something for those sick poor at home!

In 1861 a training school for nurses was, at her suggestion, opened at Liverpool. The graduates of this school nursed the neglected sick in pauper institutions. Then in 1874 the National Nursing Association announced that it was ready to provide skilled nurses for the sick poor in their own homes. These, said Miss Nightingale, would keep families from pauperism by charming the bread winners back to life. And they would so "raise the homes that they would never fall back again into dirt and disorder." That this result might be the more certain, the school was at first recruited only from "gentlewomen" who would have a refining influence over the homes. With Miss Nightingale's example, women of the better class were quick to enroll. They went into the slums of London, wherever sickness was reported, and nursed the sick, and taught both the sick and the well. In 1877 the jubilee fund of seventy thousand pounds was set aside to extend the work. It quickly spread all over England. In her later years Miss Nightingale had the satisfaction of seeing set right the conditions that had first aroused her sympathy. And the half playful pastime of her childhood had become a skilled profession, known as "district nursing."

Miss Nightingale also wrote books of great value to her profession. ***Notes on Nursing*** is a little classic—as packed with common sense and science as it is with inspiration—which any woman or man can read with pleasure. By these means—by directing her own hospital, by agitating for others, by scattering knowledge broadcast in her books,—Florence Nightingale turned her Crimean experience into a general reform. Now there are hospitals perfectly equipped in every city— private hospitals for the rich, public hospitals where one may pay much, or little, according to his means. District nurses go everywhere, tending the sick, and showing the well how to keep well by clean and temperate living. Nurses examine children in the schools. They are ready for service in the great stores. Scarce a country doctor anywhere attempts a case of typhoid without calling a school-trained woman to assist him. And these nurses not only have skill—which Florence Nightingale proved necessary; they rightly enjoy the respect and admiration of every other class—for Florence Nightingale made nursing the fashion. All this is of infinitely more importance than the two years' labor when she healed a few thousand soldiers. For thousands are healed now every day in all walks of life. She affected all modern history,—but just because her influence was so wide her history cannot here be written.

She lived until August 13, 1910. She was always very retiring, and details of her private life are very scant. As with the testimonial, she always avoided public honors. Nevertheless, she had a greater honor than any monument, in that she was revered every day in the year by all who knew her name. This pleasing anecdote is told of a regiment that had suffered at Scutari. The officer heard of a bust just completed by a sculptor. He obtained permission to march his squad into the studio—they not knowing why. When the bust was unveiled, the men instantly broke out in a cry "Miss Nightingale," and with hats off cheered loud and long the image of their nurse. Another time a vote was taken at a banquet on who of the Crimean workers would be longest remembered. And every slip read Florence Nightingale.

She accomplished one of the greatest and most characteristic reforms of modern times. It is well that she was recognized and honored for it. And some will say that she deserved all the more glory because she did it as a woman. But this she herself denied. With her the work was the main thing. She would take no honor for herself and she would take none for her sex. Where work is to be done she would efface all distinctions among those who may do it.

"Surely," she said, "woman should bring the best she has, whatever that is, to the work of God's world, without attending to either of these cries. It does not make a thing good that it is remarkable that a woman should have been able to do it, neither does it make a thing bad, which would have been good had a man done it, that it has been done by a woman." "O, leave these jargons and go your way straight to God's work, in simplicity and singleness of heart!" She herself had gone in singleness of heart. For the work was indeed to her "God's work." "Nursing," she said, "is an art; and if it is to be made an art requires as exclusive a devotion as any painter's or sculptor's work: for what is the having to do with dead canvas or cold marble compared with having to do with the living body, the temple of God's spirit? Nursing is one of the fine arts; I had almost said the finest of the fine arts."

## Richard Rees (essay date 1958)

SOURCE: "Florence Nightingale and Simone Weil: Two Women Mystics," in *The Twentieth Century*, Vol. 164, No. 978, August, 1958, pp. 101-12.

[*In the following essay, Rees compares the philosophical thought of Nightingale—as expressed in her* Suggestions for Thought—*and that of Simone Weil.*]

The pages which follow are extracts from a study of Florence Nightingale's philosophical work, **Suggestions for Thought** (1860). Readers of the admirable biographies by Sir Edward Cook and Mrs Woodham-Smith already know that Florence Nightingale was a woman of wide culture and learning and that she had a strong, though usually repressed, philosophical and religious bent. It was inevitable, of course, that her titanic administrative and organizing activities after the Crimean War should leave her no time or energy for working at her philosophical treatise, which she used to refer to as 'the stuff' and which, when she could bring herself to look through it, she declared to be unreadable. Both Jowett and J. S. Mill read it carefully, however, and urged her to find the time to revise it for publication. Instead, she had it printed without revision for private circulation; and although it is indeed very difficult to read, it proves that she had a powerful mind and a strong mystical tendency of a type remarkably similar to that of the twentieth-century mystic, Simone Weil.

The lives of these two extraordinary women were in some ways almost as different as they could be, and yet the similarities between their minds are striking. It is noteworthy that neither of them appears to have had a specifically feminine point of view on any subject and neither of them showed any interest in 'women's problems' as distinguished from human problems in general. It may indeed be the case that Florence Nightingale knew how to use her feminine charm as an asset for her work, but this charm cannot have been a sexual weapon in any narrow or literal sense of the term, because it was as effective with women as with men and it enabled her to enlist the enthusiastic support of the wives of the men who collaborated with her. It is true, too, that she wrote scathingly and sometimes hysterically about the useless lives led by 'well-brought-up' girls of her generation. But it was not so much women's rights as women's duties that interested her, and she could not be described as a feminist in the same sense as Ibsen or Shaw.

. . . . .

In the course of her criticism of Comte, Florence Nightingale asserts that we know 'by experience' that every human being, born into the world with the ordinary human faculties, has capabilities for a divine nature. 'Where sin and selfishness prevail, can we not trace the maltreatment of nature whence they have sprung?' A few pages later, she to some extent disarms our criticism that her spirituality is tainted with scientific progressivism by stating that 'every *true* interpreter of the past and present will discover the invariable eternal existence, in every present, of provision for the greatest, truest wellbeing for all that is'; and this is followed by one of the profoundest of all her religious insights:

> . . . we may have, in some degree, experience of what a wise love is, in ourselves and each other. The very want of it, from which we suffer in ourselves and each other, teaches us what a wise love is, and this wise love—sometimes partially recognized, sometimes feelingly wanted, in ourselves—we recognize as existing not in ourselves. And this is our comprehension of God.

Since Florence Nightingale's death there can have existed very few human beings of comparable moral genius, but the one who in many ways most resembles her is another woman, Simone Weil. Even if we knew nothing about the lives of either of them and had only their written words to judge by, the number of exact parallels in their thinking would be sufficient to establish this. Not that there can be any comparison between their actual writings. Florence Nightingale had no pretension to being a professional philosopher. Her book was a by-product of her active life as a pioneer of hospital and nursing reform and of progress in sanitation. Simone Weil, on the other hand, was primarily a thinker, and her practical activities were the translation into act of her moral intuitions. In their opinions, too, there was all the difference between the intellectual climate of 1820-1910 and 1909-43, which are their respective dates. Put crudely, this means that Florence Nightingale was an optimist and Simone Weil a pessimist about the immediate future of civilization. But the similarity between the passage from Florence Nightingale which we have just quoted and Simone Weil's continual emphasis upon the truth that 'He whom we must love is absent' is so striking that it seems worth while to make this digression in order to insist upon it. 'God,' says Simone Weil, 'can only be present in Creation under the form of absence' and:

> Nothing which exists is absolutely worthy of love.
>
> We must therefore love that which does not exist.
>
> This non-existent object of love is not a fiction, however, for our fictions cannot be any more worthy of love than we are ourselves, and we are not worthy of it.

With a difference of nuance, which is easily accounted for by the different moral and intellectual climates in which they lived, this is almost exactly the same thought as Florence Nightingale's:

> . . . the very want of [a wise love] from which we suffer in ourselves and each other, teaches us what a wise love is, and this wise love—sometimes partially recognized, sometimes feelingly wanted, in ourselves—we recognize as existing not in ourselves. And this is our comprehension of God.

. . . . .

Florence Nightingale faces with spirit the age-old dilemma that God can be conceived as omnipotent *or* as benevolent, but not as both together (because if He is omnipotent he could dispense with pain and cruelty, and if He is benevolent He would wish to dispense with them; and yet pain and cruelty persist). Her solution is not unfamiliar. It is as follows. 'God's thought is truth, God's feeling is happiness, God's will is wisdom', and He wants to *share* His happiness. How will He manage this? He will create man and give him

> a will, an identity, a freedom of his own—and yet so arrange that his will shall become freely one with the will of God . . . for the will of God being the will of perfect love and wisdom, is the only will that can lead to perfect happiness. The will of man, therefore, in order to attain happiness must be the same as the will of God.

She returns again and again to this problem in one form or another. For example: a Perfect Being would will happiness to other than itself, therefore we cannot conceive a Perfect Being in isolation; there must be something other (e.g. man) for it to bestow happiness upon. The Perfect Being, willing only good, leaves evil in the world solely in order to stimulate human faculties by an unremitting struggle against evil.

When she discussed this hypothesis with Mill, he told her that he had formerly entertained it but had later felt

obliged to abandon it. Postponing for the moment any argument on the point, we will merely note here that the conclusion it leads to—that man's happiness consists in identifying his will with God's will—is not unlike Dante's. I am not aware that any philosopher who has tried to formulate a solution for this problem (probably one of those which, according to Wittgenstein, can be 'shown' but not expressed or formulated) has found a very different or a better way of dealing with it.

. . . . .

The truth is, of course, that no one has ever succeeded in justifying the ways of God to man in the language of science, or in the language of common sense. 'Scientists must try to find a reason for everything,' said D. H. Lawrence, 'and there is no reason for the religious impulse.' Scientists, therefore, can make nothing of it. Its existence simply has to be accepted.

'We feel that even if *all possible* scientific questions be answered, the problems of life have still not been touched at all,' said Wittgenstein. He also said: 'The solution of the riddle of life in space and time lies *outside* space and time.' And Simone Weil says almost exactly the same when, having expressed her belief in 'a reality beyond the world, outside space and time', she adds that one manifestation of this reality lies in 'the absurdities of paradox and the insoluble contradictions which are always the terminus of human thought when it moves exclusively in this world.' Human thought, using the tools, that is to say, the language, 'of this world', is inevitably sooner or later brought up against some such dilemma as Florence Nightingale's when she asks: 'Does God, then, in some sense, *divide* Himself?' and proceeds to wrestle with the problem in these words:

> . . . if you say that the being would not be perfect who willed limited [as opposed to perfect] happiness, then you assert that a Being would not be perfect who willed other nature than his own; in other words, that either there is no Perfect Being, or, being perfect, there is no other; that is, that only God can be consistently with God, and that if God only is, God would not be. For that would not be perfect benevolence who willed only His own being—who, possessing omnipotence, did not will other nature than His own to which to communicate His happiness.

Simone Weil, too, found herself obliged to think that God gives man an individuality, a personality, an 'I', in order that man may voluntarily give it back to God. These paradoxical thoughts may be obscure, but they never appear ridiculous when we find them in their context in the work of a writer of the quality of Florence Nightingale or Simone Weil. They do, however, help to explain what Wittgenstein meant when he said: 'Everything that can be thought at all can be thought clearly. Everything that can be said at all can be said clearly. But not everything that can be thought can be said.'

And here again it is interesting to note that Simone Weil said almost exactly the same thing:

> At the very best, a mind enclosed in language is in prison. It is limited to the number of relations that can be presented to it simultaneously; and remains in ignorance of thoughts which involve a greater number of relations.
>
> These thoughts are outside language, they are unformulable, although they are perfectly and rigorously clear and although every one of the relations they include is capable of precise expression in words. So the mind moves in an enclosed space of partial truth, which may be larger or smaller, without ever being able so much as to glance at what is outside.

(When Florence Nightingale opined that 'the carpenter's son' would have had 'a still truer conception of deity' if He had known all that Laplace could have told Him, she was perhaps confusing the enlargement of 'an enclosed space of partial truth' with a conception of deity, whereas in fact the enclosed space can never conceivably be enlarged to the point of giving even a glimpse of such a conception.) But because the mind 'enclosed in language' is unable to glance outside its prison, it does not follow that the mind, pure and simple, cannot do so. Wittgenstein himself, as Bertrand Russell points out in his introduction to the *Tractatus Logico-philosophicus,* manages to convey quite a lot of information about his ethical opinions without infringing his veto on 'ethical propositions'. (His conclusion that 'ethics and aesthetics are one' was anticipated, in the same number of words, by Keats, when he wrote: 'Beauty is Truth, Truth Beauty'.) Moreover, as Father Coplestone has observed, one should not allow oneself to be paralysed by Wittgenstein's dictum that 'what can be said at all can be said clearly'. One is not compelled to choose between absolute clarity on the one hand and silence on the other. Language cannot be expected to work less imperfectly than other human tools, and in any case it has more than one function. It can be used to 'draw attention to'. Florence Nightingale, in spite of her impatience and lack of method as a writer, certainly succeeds in drawing attention to a great many of the ethical truths which were 'shown' or embodied in her practical activities.

Wittgenstein believed that things which cannot be said can nevertheless be 'shown', and this belief is relevant in two ways to the phenomenon of mysticism. According to Wittgenstein's view, says Bertrand Russell,

> we could only say things about the world as a whole if we could get outside the world, if, that is to say, it ceased to be for us the whole world. Our world may be bounded for some superior being who can survey it from above, but for us, however finite it may be, it cannot have a boundary, since it has nothing outside it. . . . The metaphysical subject does not belong to the world but is a boundary of the world.

And Wittgenstein himself says: 'The feeling of the world as a bounded whole is the mystical feeling.'

Does not the claim of all the mystics throughout the ages amount to this—that the world as a whole has been 'shown' to them, as seen from 'outside the world'? And do not their paradoxical accounts of the revelation confirm Wittgenstein's dicta that 'not everything that can be thought can be said' and 'what *can* be shown *cannot* be said'? And further, do not the lives of the saints, and of many of the great mystics, *show* to the rest of the world the truths which were shown to them in their visions and which are inexpressible in language?

Equally important and interesting are the observations of mystics upon the non-visionary state of mind which is so familiar to the rest of us. Wittgenstein's maxim: 'Propositions cannot express anything higher', is the logical analogue of Simone Weil's psychological maxim: 'No imaginary perfection can draw me upwards even by the fraction of an inch. For an imaginary perfection is mathematically at the same level as I am who imagine it—neither higher nor lower.' Wittgenstein's conclusion is: 'It is clear that ethics cannot be expressed. Ethics are transcendental. (Ethics and aesthetics are one.)' Simone Weil deduces an 'experimental ontological proof' of the existence of God:

> I have not the principle of rising in me. I cannot climb to heaven through the air. It is only by directing my thoughts toward something better than myself that I am drawn upwards by this something. If I am really drawn up, this something which draws me is real. . . . For an imaginary perfection is mathematically at the same level as I am who imagine it. . . . What draws one up is directing one's thoughts toward a veritable perfection.

And this recalls a statement of Florence Nightingale's to which we shall return later:

> I am conscious of a voice that I can hear, telling me more truth and good than I *am*. As I rise to *be* more truly and more rightly, this voice is ever beyond and above me, calling to more and more good.

. . . . .

Was Florence Nightingale a mystic? She herself seems to deny it in the following passage:

> Is it not fact, revealed by experience and no mysticism, that, if man takes appropriate means, wisdom, goodness, benevolence, love, righteousness, become himself: those very attributes, the very same which he recognizes in God's laws, in the manifestations of God, in the communications with God? The spiritual and sincere Roman Catholic *did* receive these attributes, in receiving, as he supposed, the 'body and blood' of the manifestation of the Perfect, for he raised his nature to think, not of the body and blood, but

of the spirit. Let us try to enlarge and purify our conception, to remember our privilege of being invited *always* to this sacrament, to partake, to receive, to become one with the Perfect.

Mrs Woodham-Smith's view is that she was a mystic, though not a contemplative. Certainly her psychology was more Martha's than Mary's, yet in her twenties she was subject to trance-like states, and she was conscious on four occasions in her life, the last of them in her forty-first year, of a voice from God speaking to her. In the following passage, when she speaks of 'a voice that I can hear', it is almost certain that she means it quite literally:

> But God does not refuse to answer the longing, devoted spirit, which says Speak, Lord, for thy loving child heareth. He hears as the Father; He answers as the Son, and as the Holy Spirit. I could not understand God, if He were to speak to me. But the Holy Spirit, the Divine in me, tells me what I am to do. I am conscious of a voice that I can hear, telling me more truth and good than I *am*. As I rise to *be* more truly and more rightly, this voice is ever beyond and above me, calling to more and more good.
>
> But you have to invent what it says.
>
> We believe that each man has his Holy Ghost; that is, the best part of himself inspired by God. But whether it is I who speak, or whether it is God speaking to me, I do not know.

This is a very strange passage, and I do not know how to interpret it. The most probable interpretation seems to be that she believed she had a hallucination in which her own conscience appeared to be speaking to her with an audible voice. There is another comparable passage in which she undermines one of her own favourite arguments—namely, that the laws or uniformities of nature being God's thoughts, our moral progress depends upon our studying them. 'It may be said,' she writes, 'that it is reasoning in a circle to attribute the uniformities in question to a moral nature, because in them we find some satisfaction to our own moral nature, and then to seek to enlighten our own moral nature by means of them'; and she continues, without attempting to meet the objection: 'Yet thus we obtain our best glimpses of truth, our best conceptions of right, our best means of realizing it. And these being our objects, is not this the appropriate course?'

She certainly believes, however, that the human conscience is in touch with a real and not an imaginary 'higher Being':

> We believe, from experience, that man is capable of living always, as it were, in a state of reference to that higher Being—that, as the world's ways improve, far as we are from it now, man's intercourse with man will be regulated so as to help this higher intercourse, to keep it unbroken, whereas now it is almost impossible not to break it as soon as man is with his kind.

It is impossible to doubt that she was one of those rare individuals who differ from other people in much the same way that the Copernican theory differs from the Ptolemaic theory. It *seems* self-evident that the centre, the identity of each one of us is somehow identified with and inseparable from our physical body; but these rare individuals seem not merely to know but to be able, sometimes or often, to *feel* that their true centre is outside themselves, in much the same way that the centre of the solar system is outside the earth. It seems obvious to me personally that the whole of me is at a point in time between the past and the future and at a point in space where other objects (furniture, people, continents, stars) are at various measurable distances from me. 'From my point of view', therefore, I am at the centre. But 'from my point of view' it seems that the sun moves across the sky from east to west and that the earth is stationary. What Florence Nightingale apparently means by 'being always in reference to a higher Being' is the constant awareness that one's true centre is 'outside the world'. I find it as easy to believe she is right as to believe the Copernican theory. But I find it as impossible to *feel* it as to feel that I am on a star whirling through space. My theory is theocentric, but my practice is egocentric. If to *feel* the truth of theocentricity is the sign of a mystic, we can certainly describe Florence Nightingale and Simone Weil, and probably also Wittgenstein, as mystics. When Wittgenstein wrote that 'the feeling of the world as a bounded whole is the mystical feeling', it seems very probable that he was speaking from experience. All Wittgenstein's statements about ethics imply that there can be a consciousness which surveys the world from outside the world—for which, therefore, the world is not the centre. And the mystics in every age have proclaimed that there is a link between this consciousness and the human consciousness. To the extent that they feel this link, their consciousness becomes theocentric instead of egocentric, and they differ from other people in much the same way that the heliocentric theory differs from the geocentric.

But this kind of theorizing is inexcusable if it is merely a form of philosophical pipe-dream or armchair religion. My excuse for it here is that it justifies and explains the importance I attach to Florence Nightingale's religious and ethical opinions. Although long passages of her book are monotonously repetitive and carelessly written, there is always a chance on every page of finding some thought which bears the stamp of the authentic visionary.

. . . . .

We find again and again that ideas which are touched on by Florence Nightingale reappear lucidly ordered in the writings of Simone Weil. Thus, for example, Florence Nightingale writes: 'The word "matter" invariably implies *limit*. The study of matter is the study of various kinds and degrees of limit, and of their development towards the unlimited'. This leads on to a not very enlightening comment on the providential intermingling of pleasure and pain ('the feeling of vigour after a cold bath', etc.). But in Simone Weil we find this:

> Brute force is not sovereign in this world. It is by nature blind and indeterminate. What is sovereign in this world is determinateness, limit. Eternal Wisdom imprisons this universe in a network, a web of determinations. The universe accepts passively. The brute force of matter, which appears to us sovereign, is nothing else in reality but perfect obedience.

Florence Nightingale writes: 'I believe that there is a Perfect Being, of whose thought the universe in eternity is the incarnation', and 'With regard to matter, it is probably impossible for natures like ours ever to prove that it exists at all.' And once again we find the same thought expanded and made lucid by Simone Weil:

> Matter, blind force are not the object of science. Thought is incapable of reaching out to them; they fly ahead of it. The savant's thought is never able to reach beyond relations in which matter and force are knit into an invisible, impalpable and unalterable pattern of order and harmony. 'Heaven's net is vast,' says Lao-Tse; 'its meshes are wide; yet nothing gets through.'
>
> How should human thought ever have any other object but thought? That is so well known a difficulty in the theory of knowledge that one gives up trying to fathom it, leaving it on one side as an accepted fact. But there is an answer. It is that the object of human thought is itself thought. The savant's true aim is the union of his own mind with the mysterious wisdom eternally inscribed in the universe. That being so, how should there be any opposition or even separation between the spirit of science and that of religion? Scientific investigation is simply a form of religious contemplation. (*The Need for Roots*, p. 250)

—and a little further on: 'This universe around us is made up of mind materially present in our flesh' (*ibid.*, p. 279).

Once again, it is obvious that Florence Nightingale would have subscribed to every word. In many ways these two extraordinary and heroic women were as like as two sisters; but if Martha and Mary come to mind, it is with considerable reservations. Florence Nightingale was busied over many things, but she found time for a great deal of thought; and although Simone Weil wrote that 'a single thought of love, lifted up to God in truthfulness, is more useful, even for this world, than the most splendid action', she nevertheless lectured and taught, and worked in a factory and on the land, and enlisted with the Anarchist militia in Spain. The most striking difference between them is the difference between the confidence of the nineteenth century and the anxiety of the twentieth. Simone Weil wrote in *Intimations of Christianity among the Ancient Greeks*:

> So long as we think in the first person, we see necessity from below, from inside; it encloses us on all sides as the surface of the earth and the arc of the sky. From the time we renounce thinking in the first person, by consent to necessity, we see it from outside, beneath us, for we have passed to God's side. The side which it turned to us before, and still presents to almost the whole of our being, the natural part of ourselves, is brute domination. The side which it presents after this operation, to the fragment of our mind which has passed to the other side, is pure obedience. We have become sons of the home, and we love the docility of this slave, necessity, which at first we took for a master

—and this might be an echo of Florence Nightingale. But Simone Weil continues:

> . . . the possibility of such a change in point of view is inconceivable without experience. At the moment when we are resolved to consent to necessity, we cannot foresee the fruits of this consent. This consent is truly in the first place pure absurdity.

And by absurdity she means also anguish, despair, and dereliction. Whether, or how far, Florence Nightingale would have agreed, is difficult to determine. There are many indications of great unhappiness in her writings, but the longer she lived, the more her energy and optimism seem to have prevailed. It is true that at the age of sixty-four she spoke of General Gordon's death as 'the triumph of failure, the triumph of the Cross'; but it is doubtful if the Cross was a tragic symbol to her in the same sense that it was to Simone Weil. As a very old lady in her eighties, when someone spoke of a dead friend as being 'at rest', she countered immediately: 'Oh *no!* I am sure it is an *immense* activity.'

But, whatever their temperamental differences, the affinities of thought between 'the Lady with the Lamp' and the young Lycée professor are undeniable; and one can imagine how much Simone Weil, who once printed the story of the *Antigone* in a factory magazine, would have appreciated the splendid original full title of Florence Nightingale's book: ***Suggestions for Thought to Searchers after Truth among the Artizans of England.***

### Donald R. Allen (essay date 1975)

SOURCE: "Florence Nightingale: Toward Psychohistorical Interpretation," in *Journal of Interdisciplinary History*, Vol. VI, No. i, Summer, 1975, pp. 23-45.

[*In the following essay, Allen provides a psychoanalytic interpretation of Nightingale.*]

Florence Nightingale's life and career pose one demanding question above all else: How did a woman in mid- and late Victorian England achieve such formidable power and influence in so many areas of public administration? History is in large part the story of change, and the changes effected in this "age of reform" in public and private sanitation, in nursing, in the care and provisioning of the military, in the construction of hospitals, in the mighty War Office, and in the administration of India—to name only Florence Nightingale's major preoccupations—were often due directly to her efforts. Her public life, and a good part of her private life, have long been open to the public gaze; indeed, it would be difficult to find another woman in modern times about whom more has been written.[1] Yet, it seems that Florence Nightingale's success has never been adequately explained.

The present investigation makes no pretense of supplanting the major studies of Florence Nightingale's life and career.[2] Rather, it is an attempt to supplement these works by applying to them some of the concepts of psychoanalytic psychology. In this way it serves as a response to White's complaint that in an age when rationality, insight, and creative social invention are in urgent demand, little has been provided in the way of systematic case records of great fortitude, rare heroism, or special success in grasping and solving important social issues.[3] His complaint has special validity concerning women. The main theme of this study is that Florence Nightingale achieved greatness through her efforts to control the basic conflicts of her personality which affected her finding her niche in society. Her success in accomplishing this objective was only reached at high cost in each of the stages of her life, but the result was a unique and personally satisfying contribution of no small measure.

An understanding of Florence Nightingale's personality first requires a brief outline of her family constellation, of the attitude toward women in early and mid-Victorian society, and of the prevailing attitudes toward nursing as a profession, especially for women of high station. She was born on 12 May 1820, the younger daughter of William E. and Frances Smith Nightingale. The birth of the Nightingales' only children, two daughters, came during a long sojourn in Italy, and both were named after their birthplaces. The elder, born in Naples in 1819, was named Frances Parthenope, Frances after her mother and Parthenope after the old Greek settlement on the site of Naples.

Both families in the Nightingale marriage belonged to the moneyed and propertied Whig gentry. William Nightingale came from the old Derbyshire family of Shore of Tapton and changed his name in 1815 to Nightingale on succeeding to the property of his mother's uncle, Peter Nightingale of Lea. He was educated at Edinburgh University and Trinity College, Cambridge, and was fond of travel, having made the grand tour of the Continent shortly after the Napoleonic wars. As an active supporter of parliamentary reform, he was a follower of Bentham and, later, Lord Palmerston, who was a neighbor in the country. At his wife's urging he stood for a seat in the House of Commons in 1835, and lost. His idealism bruised, he then refused to take any further active role in politics, indulging instead his

preference for country life, local affairs, long solitary rides in the New Forest, speculation along religious and philosophical lines, and the education of his daughters.

The marriage was not a particularly happy one, although William Nightingale had been deeply in love with his new wife, six years his senior and the elder sister of one of his school friends.[4] To his daughters he appeared as a rather warm and sympathetic figure, though not as a particularly strong one. Later an alliance system developed which found William Nightingale siding with Florence, his prize pupil, against her mother and Parthe, especially over the question of Florence's independence. Yet in Florence's eyes, he was only mildly supportive in this role as in others: *"Effleurez, n'appuyez pas* has been not the rule but the habit of his life," she later wrote.[5] It would appear, however, that the lightness of the father's touch was made up for by the heaviness of the mother's.

Frances (Fanny) Smith had married William Nightingale only a year after falling in love with a younger son of the Earl of Caithness, a match rejected by her father because of the suitor's lack of an adequate income or expectations. Although she did not marry until age 29, Fanny was considered the beauty of a large, rich, and socially prominent family. Her father, William Smith, sat in Parliament for forty-six years as a champion of abolition, factory workers, dissenters, and Jews.[6] His ten children did not take up these interests but concentrated on their social talents and activities. Fanny's ambition was to become a great hostess, to mold her husband into one of the prosperous, cultivated, and liberal-minded country gentlemen, like her father, who played an important part in English public life. When this plan misfired in the elections of 1835, having no sons, she transferred her social ambitions to her daughters. In the family constellation Fanny became allied with her elder daughter against her husband and Florence; the lines were clearly discernible by the time of Florence's adolescence. Florence Nightingale's greatest agony concerned her inability to accept her mother's irreducible ideas of the kind of life which she should lead and the unhappiness and vexation this inability caused her mother.

Parthe was the elder (by one year), the plainer, the less gifted, in all, the less remarkable daughter. The relationship between the sisters was marked by a strong sibling rivalry which played a role in blocking full personality development for both of them. At age 48 Florence still referred to Parthe as "always, as she always had been, the spoilt child."[7] Florence early emerged as the leader and Parthe followed resentfully. Parthe fluctuated between passionate attachment to Florence and extreme vexation with her, enough so that their parents thought it prudent to send the two children to different branches of the family for holidays. While Florence responded well to her father's educating endeavors, Parthe reacted with boredom and a growing sense of distance between her father and herself. By age 16 she had joined with her mother in strictly feminine interests in the drawing-room and the garden, and later aided in her mother's decades-long efforts—with hysterics and illness—to make Florence "stay at home" and give up her dreams of a career in nursing. Parthe relinquished her hold on her younger sister only after her own marriage at age 39. Up to this point the more attractive suitors, the better looks, the more brilliant conversations, and the fame had largely belonged to her sister. Florence and Parthe became fully reconciled and returned to their childhood intimacy only after their parents' death and when Parthe was almost hopelessly crippled by arthritis. She died in 1890 at age 71, some twenty years before the death of Florence.

The Nightingale family constellation was marked, therefore, by several disturbing features: an ambitious and domineering mother who soon became estranged from her difficult younger daughter, a relatively weak father, an enduring alliance system, and intense sibling rivalry. These features alone would be serious enough to affect Florence's psychosexual and psychosocial development; joined with Victorian attitudes toward women, they amounted to a formidable barrier to the achievement of the goal for which she felt herself fated.

Today the lot of the Victorian middle-class woman would seem essentially unhappy, if, as in the case of Florence Nightingale, she rebelled against the standards of the time. The woman's world was strictly confined to the interests of home and family, and the only truly acceptable roles were, progressively, those of dutiful daughter, obedient wife, and protective mother. A spinster might be accommodated as a kind of higher-level servant at the beck and call of a thousand family needs. In fact, many women in upper stations did not marry, but it was in few ways a desirable situation. The rigidly defined parameters for the "perfect lady" were most fully developed in the upper middle class, where her upbringing combined total sexual innocence, conspicuous consumption, and the worship of the family hearth.[8] When she married, the perfect lady simply transferred her loyalties and values from her father's home to that of her husband.

That home life held no attraction for Florence Nightingale is perfectly clear from her writings; her indictment of life in a Victorian family, for all of the warmth and affection to be found there, is probably unsurpassed in its depth and feeling:

> O weary days—oh evenings that seem never to end—and for how many years have I watched that drawing-room clock and thought it never would reach ten! and for twenty, thirty years more to do this!

> 'Butchered to make a Roman Holiday.' Women don't consider themselves as human beings at all. There is absolutely no God, no country, no duty to them at all except family. . . . I have known a good deal of convents. And of course everyone has talked of the petty grinding tyrannies supposed to be exercised there. But I know

nothing like the petty grinding tyranny of a good English family. And the only alleviation is that the tyrannized submits with a heart full of affection.[9]

For Florence Nightingale the alternative to oppressive home life was nursing; yet that choice presented even further problems. Southwood Smith's remark in the 1840s that "the generality of nurses in hospitals are not such as the medical men can place much confidence in" was surely a discreet understatement for a deplorable situation.[10] Nursing in the mid-Victorian period was associated with menial domestic work and in no way considered a profession suited to "respectable" women. It was ill-paid, no high standard of efficiency was expected, and formal training was virtually non-existent. Low morality and a wanton life-style were other characteristics associated with nursing. A doctor in the North wrote in answer to a circular concerning the use of nurses, "If I can but obtain a sober set, it is as much as I can hope for." Florence Nightingale herself, after many observations, stated that hospitals were "a school . . . for immorality and impropriety—inevitable where women of bad character are admitted as nurses, to become worse by their contact with male patients and young surgeons."[11] In light of such evidence, and the fact that it was unthinkable for upperclass Victorian women to go "out to work," the hostile reaction of Florence Nightingale's family to her desire for a career in nursing is not surprising; nor is it surprising that the dutiful daughter took eight years of tremendous mental anguish to break her family bonds and realize her ambitions.

Five periods in Florence Nightingale's life call for special attention, for in each of these periods one can recognize a turning point, marked by an internal crisis, that led to a new stage in her development. Chronologically they are: her childhood development to about age 7; the "call from God" which she experienced at age 16; her decision, following a long moratorium at home, to renounce marriage and her family to pursue an independent course, a decision which resolved her long crisis of identity; her alliance with Sidney Herbert following her return from the Crimean War, which gave her access to power and defined her work style for her most productive and creative period; and, finally, the death of her parents and sister, which freed her from a lifelong conflict and permitted her to enter a long period at the end of her life when, her fury abated, she enjoyed the fruits of her labors and contributions.

Florence Nightingale's entire life carried the strain of conflict with her mother who ever opposed her finding her own identity. Florence, in turn, was torn between love for her mother, which she felt was never recognized, and desire for her own life. The attachment to her mother ended early. Florence was an unhappy child, not naughty, but strange, obstinate, and ready to attach herself passionately to any other female—to Miss Christie (her governess), to Aunt Mai (Mrs. Samuel Smith, her father's younger sister), to a beautiful older cousin.

When they left, "the violence of her feelings made her physically ill."[12] To her parents she seemed an unhappy child who was difficult to understand, a girl who had consciously rebelled against her life since age 6. Her mother was especially perplexed by the attitude of this "wild swan we have hatched," and her father wrote when she was twelve: "Ask Flo if she has lost her intellect. If not, why does she grumble at troubles which she cannot remedy by grumbling?"[13]

In a significant, private autobiographical note later in life, Florence Nightingale recalled the pain and difficulty of her childhood years. Writing of the time when she was about six years old she revealed that she had an obsession that she was some kind of "monster," different from other people and frightened that they might find out her "secret." The prospect of seeing a new face was agony, and she refused to dine downstairs with the rest of the family because "I had a morbid terror of not using my knives and forks like other people when I should come out." There was also a great fear of meeting children, "because I was sure I should not please them."[14] Not surprisingly, she often escaped into "dreaming," and for long hours at a time she transferred herself completely to a dream world where she saw herself in the role of a heroine, a habit that stayed with her through her early adult life.

The argument can be made that the sense of basic trust which Erikson posits as the fundamental prerequisite for mental vitality and which depends on the quality of the maternal relationship was somehow aborted in Florence Nightingale. Erikson points out that the guilt aroused by childhood moralism leads to consequences that often do not appear until much later "when conflicts over initiative may find expression in a self-restriction." This may keep an individual from living up to his inner capacities or "to the powers of his imagination and feeling (if not [resulting] in relative sexual impotence or frigidity)." In turn, the individual may overcompensate and show "tireless initiative," a "go-at-it-iveness at all cost."[15] Florence's early unhappiness and childhood moralism were reflected in her adult life along the lines suggested by Erikson. Her family had to be held at bay lest they interfere with her work; her relationship with her closest friend, Mary Clarke Mohl, worked only because Mme. Mohl lived in Paris and they saw each other infrequently; a self-restricted sexuality was irrevocably determined by her final rejection of Richard Monckton Milnes' long devotion and proposal of marriage in 1849—she had already rejected other proposals—despite her assertion that she loved him and that he was acceptable in every way;[16] and, as we shall see, she consistently experienced deep feelings of failure in spite of and even at the apex of her greatest achievements. In short, a discrepancy existed between her low self-esteem and high ego ideal. Her attempts to deal with this discrepancy took the direction of fantasy and, increasingly, action.

The development of Florence's sense of autonomy also seems to have been impaired, which may explain in part her heightened sense of shame as a child. There is some evidence that Florence's lifelong estrangement from her

mother might have been involved with her sexual development. Certainly Fanny saw her younger daughter's later rebellion in sexual terms. When Florence announced in 1845 that she wished to be trained as a nurse, her mother reacted with a terror that quickly turned to rage as she accused Florence of having "an attachment of which she was ashamed," a secret love life with some "low vulgar surgeon."[17] As Florence wrote to her cousin,

> . . . I thought something like a Protestant Sisterhood, without vows, for women of educated feelings, might be established. But there have been difficulties about my very first step, which terrified Mama. I do not mean the physically revolting parts of a hospital, but things about the surgeons and nurses which you may guess.[18]

A few years later when she rejected Milnes' proposal of marriage her mother accused her of "godless ingratitude, perversity, and conceit," extremely strong comments which revealed the depth of Fanny's feelings.[19]

Another reason for the conflict between mother and daughter—and for Florence's feeling of rejection and acquisition of "masculine" characteristics—may lie in Fanny's wish for a son. A son was especially desired by the Nightingales because a good part of the fortune of William Nightingale would pass on his death to his younger sister and then to her son if William did not have a direct male heir. That Florence accepted a man's education from her father was perhaps partly a wish to satisfy her mother. In a happier moment she even wrote an imaginary speech to her mother in which she begged to be regarded as a son, a masculine self-image that persisted in her work relationships throughout life. "You must look at me as your vagabond son," she wrote, "Remember, I should have cost you a great deal more if I had been married or a son. You were willing enough to part with me to be married."[20]

The estrangement from her mother led Florence to form strong attachments not only to surrogate mothers but also, quite naturally, to her father. At the same time, Parthe retained her own intimate tie with Fanny and began a lifelong relationship with Florence that alternated between Parthe's passionate over-attachment and long estrangement between the sisters. Florence suffered intensely from what she saw as a rejection brought on by her own willfulness: "I thought I would go up to the Eumenides Cave," she wrote poignantly in Greece in 1850, "and ask God there to explain to me what were these Eumenides which pursued me. I would not ask to be relieved of them—welcome, Eumenides—but to be delivered from doing further wrong. Orestes himself did not go on murdering."[21] The strong mixture of narcissism and masochism engendered by family conflict and reflected here accounts in part for the aggressive nature of her work style later on.

The alliance between Florence and her father intensified as her education came under his supervision. As a liberal Unitarian and Whig, William Nightingale held advanced ideas on the education of women and felt that no tutor could provide his daughters with the kind of education that he thought was necessary in the new age of enlightened liberalism. In fact, however, it might be suggested that his educational endeavors with his daughters constituted in large part a working out of his desire for a son. They were, in effect, given a thoroughly "modern" and "masculine" education which included instruction in French, German, Italian, history, philosophy, and classical Greek and Latin. Florence responded well to the rigorous hours and taxing schedule; Parthe, although bright, rebelled and escaped to her mother. By the time Florence was sixteen the lines were drawn: Florence and her father in the library, Parthe and her mother in the drawing room.[22]

The close relationship between father and younger daughter proved extremely advantageous to Florence when she made her decision to pursue a career in nursing. Although not pleased with her intention, he did not oppose it with the vehemence and force of Fanny and Parthe, and when in 1851 her first opportunity for employment presented itself in the form of the superintendency of the Institution for the Care of Sick Gentlewomen in Distressed Circumstances, William Nightingale quickly and quietly provided Florence with an allowance of £500 a year which secured her personal independence. He also told her to write to him privately at his club in order to circumvent the Nightingale family practice of passing around all letters. When Florence later took up her philosophical and religious speculations in a serious way, William again became her confidant and "sat at her feet and sympathized in her searches after truth."[23] Yet, this was not enough for Florence, who did not regard her father as sufficiently supportive; but then, nobody was. "My father," she wrote just before gaining her independence, "is a man who has never known what struggle is. Good impulses from his childhood up, and always remaining perfectly in a natural state, acting always from impulse—and never having by circumstances been forced to look into a thing, to carry it out."[24]

This picture of Florence Nightingale's psychosexual and psychosocial development in her childhood years corresponds rather closely to certain characteristics and personality traits described by Deutsch in her treatment of feminine masochism and the "masculinity complex" in the "active woman." Deutsch points out that although it is normal for the girl to turn away from the mother and childhood dependencies in favor of active adjustment to reality as represented by the father, this adjustment, or reaction formation, entails negative feelings of hostility toward the mother (to overcome fear of losing her), which in favorable cases ends with a positive, tender, and forgiving relation with the mother. Such a relation is one of the most important prerequisites for psychological harmony in later femininity. In certain cases, however, a split may occur at a very early age. The girl's active sublimating tendencies become attached to the father, while her sexual fantasies "assume an extraordinarily passive and masochistic character," which characterizes

her later sexual behavior; this type of woman either remains erotically isolated, avoiding all dangers—like Florence Nightingale—or falls victim to brutal men. In this situation "the feminine erotic component remains on the level of infantile masochism," the woman's attitude toward life may be very active and masculine, and "[she] may display particular resistance and aggressiveness in the struggle for life."[25] Feminine masochism may also be reflected in the willingness to serve a cause or a human being with love and abnegation—the kind of activity Florence undertook at an early age with sick relatives and with her mother among the poor and sick villagers of the neighborhood. Later it assumed massive proportions in her love for the British soldier, her disdain for her personal health and safety in the Crimea, her lifelong dedication to her cause, and her scorn for public acclaim. Here a compromise is effected between masochism and narcissism, between self-injury and self-love, "just like the erotic type of woman in her more normal manner."[26]

That a strong masochistic strain existed in Florence Nightingale, which helped her to choose and pursue a career in nursing, seems clear. The failure to resolve her conflict with her mother; the "inhibiting" education by her father along the lines then associated with boys; the strong and sometimes secret alliance with her father which may have prevented her from successfully completing her psychosexual development; her unhappiness as a child with escapes to a dreamworld and a morbid fear of being "found out"; the failure to achieve true personal erotic intimacy—all converged in a renewed aspiration, laden with masochistic elements, to go forward aggressively. This aspiration was funneled into an all-consuming passion to enter nursing and by so doing to create a unique identity and life style that would calm the conflicts within her.

Florence Nightingale's choice of nursing as a career brings us to the second turning point in her psychosocial and psychosexual development: a religious crisis in which she experienced a "call from God" directing her to a special destiny. This crisis began her long search for a career, which was partly resolved in her decision to pursue nursing, and culminated, in her early 30s, in an "identity crisis" whereupon she rejected marriage, won independence from her family, and began her productive life. This period served as a kind of moratorium when destructive and constructive forces battled within her and regressive and progressive alternatives presented themselves. Two questions call for special attention in this stage: What was the nature of her call and how did her religious ideas fit in with her overall development? And why did this religious experience direct her toward nursing?

In a private note to herself written in 1867, Florence Nightingale revealed that just before she turned seventeen, she underwent a religious experience akin to that of Joan of Arc: "on February 7th, 1837, God spoke to me and called me to His service."[27] This was not an inward revelation but an "objective" voice, outside of herself, speaking to her in human words. She later stated that her "voices" had spoken to her on four occasions: On the date of her call at Embley; once in 1853 before going to her first position at the hospital for poor gentlewomen in Harley Street; once before her departure for the Crimea in 1854; and once after the death of Sidney Herbert, her closest collaborator, in 1861.[28] All of these experiences with "voices" occurred after periods of extremely intense emotional and psychological stress marked by personal disappointment, strong feelings of self-doubt, deep depression, and a sense of failure. In turn, all were followed by a strong desire to accomplish something, a devotion to work, and some kind of fulfillment.

Florence Nightingale's religious ideas and writings deserve a chapter in their own right; not only are the private and published materials quite extensive, but they are also revealing in the sense of being the product of an intensely introspective and spiritual figure with a high degree of intelligence and unflagging energy.[29] Although there is no place here for any detailed treatment of her religious ideas, several elements should be noted because they relate to an understanding of her psychological makeup. First, there was a distinct "mystical" element as seen in her proclivity for introspection, in her conversion at age 16, and in her three subsequent experiences with "voices." Second, there was an overwhelming emotional and psychological need, sanctioned by and seen in terms of religious impulse, to devote her life to the care of the sick, which by age 24 had culminated in a decision to follow a nursing career at all cost. Third, in all of her religious thinking and writing there is little particular interest in doctrine or dogma, but rather a nearly exclusive concentration on "works" as the only criteria for the validity and purpose of religion, i.e., the testing of religious doctrine by practical results. As she once remarked to Richard Monckton Milnes, "It will never do unless we have a Church of which the terms of membership shall be works, not doctrines."[30] Fourth, she suffered from a profound sense of guilt, expressed in terms of sin, which plagued her for most of her life. "Bless me, too, as poor Esau said," she wrote to Harriet Nicholson on Christmas Eve 1845. "I have *so* felt with him and cried with an exceeding bitter cry 'Bless me, even me also, Oh my father,' but He never has yet and I have not deserved that He should."[31] One final aspect of her religious thought concerns her conception of the nature of God. She was not drawn to the figure of Jesus or the doctrines of salvation, redemption, and the incarnation of Christ. Rather she looked to God the Father, who wished his children to follow His absolute moral laws and do His work for the relief of misery. This primary alliance with God alone provided her with the sense of strength to unlock the chains which bound her, and it became the source of her tremendous tenacity and willpower.

The religious impulses moving Florence during these years formed but a part, albeit an important one, of the

decisive stage in her life when she came to grips with her identity and definitively mapped her future course in life. Her crisis of identity opened with her "call" at age 16 and closed—in the sense of her having defined her adult psychosocial and psychosexual style and being able to go on to her most creative and productive period—between her thirtieth and thirty-second years. By its end, she had come to believe totally in the uniqueness of her particular role in life; she had settled upon nursing as her profession; she had renounced marriage as a way of life acceptable to her (or to her nurses); and she had resolved to break the restraints imposed on her by her parents and sister.

In other ways, of course, her identity crisis was not "closed" at all, for problems which seemed momentarily solved reappeared later in new or familiar guises or had far-reaching results. Florence Nightingale failed, for example, to achieve true intimacy—either sexually or, in Erikson's words, as "a true and mutual psychosocial intimacy with another person, be it in a friendship, in erotic encounters, or in joint inspiration."[32] There were, indeed, close personal relationships and collaborations, such as those with Selina Bracebridge, who helped pry Florence loose from her mother and later accompanied her to the Crimea; with her closest partner in reform after the Crimean experience, Secretary of State for War Sidney Herbert; and with Benjamin Jowett, the Oxford classicist who became a great source of inspiration and consolation to her. But just as in childhood with her surrogate mothers, she could brook no hint in these intense relationships of "betrayal" or abandonment.

Two examples will suffice to show the extent of her insecurity. With her gift to command loyalty and devotion she literally worked her closest collaborator, Sidney Herbert, to death, while at the same time castigating the dying man unmercifully. When he was forced to resign from the War Office in 1861 because of a breakdown in health, Florence would have none of it. "No man in my day has thrown away so noble a game with all the winning cards in his hands," she wrote, although two months later Herbert was dead.[33] Another example occurred in 1860 with her oldest and dearest friend, "Aunt Mai," who, after having left her own family for four years (1857-1860) to live with and care for Florence, decided she must go home; her husband had become virtually a stranger and her second daughter was to be married. The bitterness that her departure provoked in Florence was intense and unreasonable. When she realized that Aunt Mai was leaving, Florence refused to speak to or see her, nor would she forgive her for twenty years, during which time they never met and the correspondence between them ceased.[34] There can be little doubt that the total blocking of her natural sex drives, finalized by her refusal of Monckton Milnes' marriage proposal but reaching back to her childhood experiences, could only prevent her from arriving at that true interpersonal intimacy in adult life described by Erikson as crucial to a "vital" personality.

The danger of the identity crisis stage is that of identity confusion or role confusion, which most often centers on the inability to choose an occupational identity:

> A state of acute identity confusion usually becomes manifest at a time when the young individual finds himself exposed to a combination of experiences which demand his simultaneous commitment to physical intimacy (not by any means always overtly sexual), to decisive occupational choice, to energetic competition, and to psychosocial self-definition. Whether or not the ensuing tension will lead to paralysis now depends primarily on the regressive pull exerted by a latent illness. . . . The social functioning of the state of paralysis which ensues is that of maintaining a state of minimal actual choice and commitment.[35]

Florence Nightingale experienced an extended moratorium marked by deep depressive states. Her "call" came in 1837, but it did not say what to do. Eight years passed until she decided what her vocation was, and the interval between the decision in 1844 to devote her life to nursing and her gaining freedom to pursue it lasted another eight years. The exciting trip to the continent and the enduring friendship with Mary Clarke Mohl, the tempting and brilliant series of balls and parties back in England, the flattering attentions of attractive suitors, all quickly paled in the face of her sense of frustration, confusion, and the lack of power to affect her own destiny. The personal notes poured out her increasing bitterness and despair in tens of thousands of works: "This morning I felt as if my soul would pass away in tears, in utter loneliness in a bitter passion of tears and agony of solitude." "I cannot live—forgive me, oh Lord, and let me die, this day let me die."[36] These statements date from 1845, just after the realization that her future life lay in nursing and while she was still playing the role of the faithful "daughter at home." They mark the profoundest depth of her depression and emanate from her parents' refusal to permit her to go to a hospital for training. Having plumbed these depths, however, she began the long upward struggle. It was often marked by disappointment and frustration, but by 1853 she found the strength to reintegrate the strands of her identity, make the decisions to break with family and suitor, and funnel her energies into productive and satisfying work.

The ties that bound Florence Nightingale during these years could have been broken only at immense emotional cost. Her failure to make the break points up the kind of severe identity confusion that Erikson describes, the characteristics of which in Florence Nightingale included an acute self-consciousness, the strain of tentative engagement with others, a severe upset in the sense of workmanship, and scornful hostility toward the roles offered by her family and society as proper and desirable. Her difficulty in stabilizing her ego identity, largely due to the conflict connected with the freeing of personal relationships, constituted a severe blockage in her development—in some ways, permanent—and is best revealed in her attitude toward her mother and sister.[37]

As the "daughter at home" or in the presence of Fanny and Parthe, Florence was always a child, until she finally succeeded in banishing them from her presence in London in 1858 by means of a manipulated "illness." Only then was she free to pursue her interests unimpeded by their well-meaning but stifling and inconsiderate overprotectiveness. The blockage was not entirely removed until Fanny, and later Parthe, old and in ill health, became entirely dependent on Florence, at which point she assumed supervision of their households and their care. Moreover, although the choice at age 24 of a career in nursing and its subsequent realization may have contributed to the stabilization of Florence's ego identity to the point of permitting her to break her family bonds, it was not sufficient to give her complete mental and emotional peace. Nursing as a profession, with its masochistic overtones, probably served as an important sponge to absorb her fury, but it did not totally obliterate her hatred nor completely resolve her conflict. That state of peace required the unraveling—by their dependence and death—of the ties which bound her to her mother and sister. Before dealing with the later stages of her life, however, it is necessary to survey the workings of her professional life, which carried in it the strains of her previous personal development.

When she returned from the Crimean War in 1856 Florence Nightingale was obsessed by a sense of failure. In the eyes of the world hers was the greatest of triumphs for a woman in modern times, but she saw none of it. The obstructions placed in her path by an offended military officialdom—the enduring of petty recriminations, false accusations, and impossible conditions—and the attacks of cholera, dysentery, and rheumatism, united to weaken her both physically and emotionally. What especially haunted her was the realization that the same system that had slaughtered soldiers by the thousands in the Crimea—the health administration of the British Army—continued to do so around the world. She also realized, in an almost desperate way, that to effect reform of the system meant immediate action. Yet she was so ill, "it seemed madness to contemplate work. She found difficulty in breathing, suffered from palpitations, and was overcome by nausea at the sight of food."[38] She fully expected to die shortly, a belief that remained constant for more than twenty years. Therefore her need was to find somebody to carry on the work: a man who would be acceptable to the official world, who would carry weight in high circles, yet who would be ready to submit to and be taught by her.

Florence Nightingale found her ideal collaborator in Sidney Herbert—except that the mantle was never passed on because she outlived him by more than fifty years. As Secretary of State at War during the Crimean War, Herbert was responsible for the provisioning and equipping of the British forces and had chosen Florence for the Scutari mission. He was an acquaintance of several years, came from the same social background, and was as well connected as anybody in public life. Moreover, he was a partisan of reform. Sidney Herbert formed part of that small band of men whose lives and careers became enmeshed with Florence Nightingale's cause, and whose devotion was illustrated by their total subjection to their acknowledged leader. The work style of Florence Nightingale is therefore elucidated by two factors: her illness, and her power to attract talented and powerful collaborators totally committed to her personally and to her cause.

In spite of her illness, an invitation from Queen Victoria to meet privately impelled Florence Nightingale to a burst of activity. She met with Lord Panmure, the Secretary for War, who agreed to set up a Royal Commission. The weakness and nausea continued, but Florence was able to work night and day preparing material for her interviews as *éminence grise* of the Commission, while in her few free hours she visited and inspected barracks, hospitals, and other institutions.[39] The inner circle for preparation of the Royal Commission to Enquire into the Sanitary Condition of the Army consisted of Florence Nightingale (whom the others called the Commander-in-Chief), Sidney Herbert, and Dr. John Sutherland. She was able to make these men, as well as their wives, her willing slaves through a combination of incredible charm, totally unreasonable demands, and her health. When Dr. Sutherland was late with a report one evening, for example, he consented at her insistence to stay and complete it. After reading it she was not satisfied and sent a message to his home in Highgate demanding his immediate return for rewriting. When he lost his temper and refused, she collapsed into an "agitated half-fainting state." The call went out again to Highgate, since Dr. Sutherland was also her physician, and he came immediately expressing "great sorrow and penitence."[40] Moreover, while constantly stressing her own maladies, she had contempt for the illnesses of those working closely with her. She pressed hard on Dr. Sutherland and even harder on the dying Sidney Herbert. To her their complaints were "fancies."

In 1857 her health gave way from overwork and she collapsed. She refused to go home to Embley or to be nursed—dependency was no longer acceptable—but instead insisted on taking a cure at Malvern, alone except for one footman. She was generally thought to be dying: Harriet Martineau even brought up to date her obituary notice for the *Daily Mail*. This collapse in August 1857 marked the beginning of Florence Nightingale's retirement into invalidism; she now began to use her illness as protection against her family and any unwanted attention. During that year her mother and sister had moved into the Burlington Hotel, where Florence had rooms, and they completely disrupted her life. When Parthe proposed coming to London in the winter as well, and Aunt Mai's letters could not prevent it, Florence had an "attack" consisting of "excessive hurried breathing with pain in the head and the heart"; this kept Parthe away. Another attempt in 1858 met with the same response. Aunt Mai successfully argued that while Florence's life "hung by a thread" it was too much for the family to expect to see her; they must stay away.[41]

By the summer of 1858 Parthe was engaged and abandoned her siege, as did Fanny. Florence was now left alone, her privacy guarded by Aunt Mai and Arthur Hugh Clough, Aunt Mai's son-in-law. Although Florence only ventured from her rooms twice in 1858, she continued to receive eminent visitors, especially if they could be of use, such as the Queen of Holland, the Crown Princess of Prussia, and the Duke of Cambridge.

Sidney Herbert's health gave way in 1858 but Florence refused to take notice. As she saw it, her function was to drive him on, and she was able to enlist Mrs. Herbert in the endeavor as well. Despite his declining health, Herbert accepted an appointment as Minister for War in 1859 in Palmerston's government, and he and Florence Nightingale together undertook to reform the War Office, an immensely laborious job. She approached this task almost with despair, dwelling on her self-sacrifice, her suffering, and the inadequacies of her collaborators. Never was there any expression of concern for Herbert's suffering, or even the realization that it could be serious. It is curious and even ironic that a woman whose name is most closely connected with the alleviation of human suffering, and who seemingly required great personal suffering in order to work at peak efficiency, had so little understanding of the pain and misery of those close to her.

After a long and arduous battle with kidney disease, Sidney Herbert died in 1861. According to his wife, his last words were "Poor Florence, poor Florence, our joint work unfinished."[42] When she received the news, grief, anger, frustration, and guilt all combined in Florence to cause another collapse which lasted four weeks. Yet her reaction had as its primary focus not the personal loss of a dear and devoted friend whom she had seen almost daily for years, but what that loss entailed for her work. "My work, the object of my life, the means to do it, all in one depart with him." Even God was in part to blame: It would have been "but to set aside a few trifling physical laws to save him."[43] She never blamed herself for the debilitating effect of her anger on him; nor did she admit that she had worked him—and others—to death. Yet, a remarkable transformation took place in her. With the death of Herbert their positions became reversed: She, who had always been the teacher, the leader, now became the faithful disciple, the servant who only loved him; he, the student, the instrument, now became her "Master," the object of love and praise. "I loved and served him as no one else," she wrote to Sir John McNeill, one of their collaborators.[44]

Her work, however, was far from over. She returned to activity, although now her isolation was practically complete. She soon undertook her greatest task, the peak of her working life—the Royal Commission on the Health of the Army in India. The tons of materials that she gathered and analyzed for the project filled two vans when she moved. She achieved great success, though any hint of failure or defeat brought back the symptoms of her illness. By 1865 she would see nobody not directly connected with her work, not even her oldest and dearest friend, Mary Clarke Mohl, or the Queen of Holland. Only her spiritual advisor, the Oxford classicist Benjamin Jowett, was allowed to call, and he was seldom in London.

From the experiences related above, a close connection between Florence Nightingale's work style and her illness can be inferred. The latter was most likely psychoneurotic, a defense mechanism tied both to her vexed relations with her family and to her consuming struggle for professional success. Her illness was at once a means of warding off the emotional conflict engendered by the interference of her mother and sister, and at the same time a mechanism which allowed her to become the object of their solicitous attention, and thus to overcome her childhood feeling of rejection. A consuming struggle for success, as White has pointed out, sometimes carries "the latent meaning of a vital personal vindication, a denial of inferiorities that had produced rage and panic in childhood."[45] That this element had a role in Florence Nightingale's career can be seen both in her extreme vulnerability to even the smallest hint that her success was incomplete and in her relentless drive to make her triumph perfect. The achievement of her aspirations brought only temporary relief from her physical and emotional pain. No matter how great her success, whenever it was threatened or in any way diluted she reverted to despair, and the symptoms of her illness became aggravated. A willingness to accept less than complete victory in a project, and to gain relative satisfaction, came to her only late in life after her family conflict was resolved and her old collaborators were all dead.

In her sixties a significant change came over Florence Nightingale as the final definition of her personality took form, and it lasted until her death at the age of ninety. Her parents were now both dead, and her lifelong depressions seemed to pass. She became completely reconciled with Parthe, who was ill and required looking after, and the pervading benevolence that had often marked her young womanhood returned. Failure weighed less heavily and the self-reproaches ceased. "I cannot remember the time," she wrote to her friend Clarkey (Mary Clarke Mohl) in 1881,

> when I have not longed for death. After Sidney Herbert's death and [Arthur Hugh] Clough's death in 1861, 20 years ago, for years and years I used to watch for death as no sick man ever watched for the morning. It is strange that now bereft of all, I crave for it less. I want to do a little work, a little better, before I die.[46]

Although opportunities presented themselves in both the War Office and the government of India, and she continued to work, it was no longer in a rage. When the tide turned against her now, as it did within a few years, it bothered her little. As she accepted old age, tolerance replaced the lifelong drive for perfection. Although her mind remained keen and her energy remarkable, she was no longer driven, and the last twenty years of her life were marked by warm relations with young relatives and student nurses of the Nightingale Training School, and by serenity and contentment. The last thirty years of her life were thus relatively happy. She was finally freed from the conflicts of her past, she enjoyed good health, and she was able to look back on her accomplishments with a sense of quiet pleasure and satisfaction.

Although Florence Nightingale was no ordinary person, as her achievements attest, the problems which she encountered were, for the most part, the same faced by any Victorian woman of her station who wished to create an independent and productive life outside of the prescribed progression of family, marriage, children, and discreet private charity: hostility, lack of understanding, and the realization of being out of tune with one's times. Moreover, the choice of nursing as the means to administrative power involved its own peculiar difficulties.

To understand Florence Nightingale's choice of nursing as a career and her development in accumulating and exercising power requires a recognition of the importance of conflict in her personality. The key to her conflict is her lifelong struggle with shame, or as she termed it, her "pride," a struggle which was probably the primary force for her drive toward accomplishment. When thirty she wrote, "Tomorrow will be Sacrament Sunday. I have read over all my history, a history of miserable woe, mistakes and blinding vanity, of seeking great things for myself."[47] The theme was repeated over and over again in her private writings, reflecting the conflict between "doing for myself" and "doing for others in God's name." As a career, nursing was admirably suited to control and direct this conflict, even though it did not remove it—indeed, to remove it would have been to remove the driving force itself. By choosing nursing, with all of its outer-directed and masochistic implications, she could absorb her fury, satisfy her drive for power, and at the same time placate the demands of her extremely strong superego by directing her efforts to the aid of others "in God's name." The need for power was itself rooted in her conflict with her mother and sister, which influenced every stage of her psychosocial and psychosexual development.

Florence Nightingale's career choice was not primarily directed toward producing pleasure by providing a channel for the unconscious investment of libidinal and aggressive emotional energy. "My work: an idol, a Molloch to me," she wrote in 1877 in another oft-repeated sentiment.[48] Rather than a source of pleasure, her work was more a shield against discomfort, an external support to her defenses, which helped to control internal conflict and anxiety by deflecting energy from fantasy to action. Her attempts to control the basic conflict that permeated her personality and stymied her effort to find a niche in society were successful only at great emotional cost in each of the stages of her life cycle, but one doubts that the happy old woman would have chosen any other way.

It should be obvious to the reader that this article represents but the first leg of a long journey on the road to a full understanding of the psychological forces that permitted Florence Nightingale to achieve such extraordinary power and influence. In this study we have relied chiefly on the signposts set out by Freud, Erikson, and Deutsch, i.e., the oedipal approach, which has been extremely useful in pointing the way. In the stages that lie ahead, however, other road maps will have to be used. Since, for example, in this first investigation a severely vulnerable narcissism has emerged as a primary characteristic of Florence Nightingale's personality, it will be necessary to apply the newer theories on narcissism such as are found in the works of Kohut.[49]

Some of the way can already be charted. Florence Nightingale had a strong need for revenge, for righting wrongs, for undoing a hurt by whatever means, and an unrelenting compulsion to pursue these aims until she was able to blot out the offense against her.[50] The matrix of her narcissistic rage is probably to be found in her sense of abandonment. Her traumatic reactions as a child when "abandoned" by the females to whom she had been passionately attached—such as her nurse, Miss Christie, or Aunt Mai—coupled with her reactions all through life to any hint of desertion and her lack of empathy toward the offender lead one to surmise that she blamed her family, and particularly her mother, first for abandoning her to her nurse, and second for the subsequent desertions by the nurse and other females to whom she became attached. Nobody else would ever be able to come so close to her, including her unsuccessful suitors. She could therefore protect herself against further abandonment while at the same time use the weapon that she so feared against others. Thus, with anything even remotely resembling desertion, as when Aunt Mai quite naturally returned to her family after years of sacrifice to Florence, her rage was unbounded and irrational. The degree which such rage could reach is best seen in her remarkable reaction to Sidney Herbert's death—she blamed Herbert and God for Herbert's "desertion" of her. Only in old age was this narcissistic anger blunted because all of those who could injure her by abandonment were dead. Thus, her shame subsided, and with it, her rage.

Future research on a psychohistorical study of Florence Nightingale will have to include not only the best observations emanating from psychoanalysis but also new information on her pregenital and adolescent development, which has not yet come to light either in the previously published biographies or in the main corpus of her own writings and papers. Only then will we be able to present a complete psychohistorical interpretation of this fascinating, and captivating, woman.

NOTES

[1] The most complete bibliography is that of W. J. Bishop and Sue Goldie, *A Bio-Bibliography of Florence Nightingale* (London, 1962).

[2] The most complete work remains the study of Edward Tyas Cook, *The Life of Florence Nightingale* (London, 1913), 2v. The most recent study and the best informed is Cecil Woodham-Smith, *Florence Nightingale* (New York, 1951).

[3] Robert W. White, *Lives in Progress* (New York, 1966; 2nd ed.), 2-3.

[4] Woodham-Smith, *Florence Nightingale*, 2, 4.

[5] Private note, 1851, Nightingale Papers, X.

[6] Richard W. Davis, *Dissent in Politics 1780-1830: The Political Life of William Smith, MP* (London, 1971), 54, 250.

[7] Woodham-Smith, *Florence Nightingale*, 326.

[8] Martha Vicinus (ed.), *Suffer and Be Still: Women in the Victorian Age* (Bloomington, 1972), ix-x; Constance Rover, *Love, Morals, and the Feminists* (London, 1970), 50.

[9] Private notes, 1851, 1852, Nightingale Papers, X; *Cassandra*, quoted in Woodham-Smith, *Florence Nightingale*, 62-63.

[10] Quoted in W. J. Reader, *Life in Victorian England* (New York, 1967), 160.

[11] Anon. [Mary Stanley], *Hospitals and Sisterhoods* (London, 1854), quoted in Cook, *Life*, I, 443; Anon. [Florence Nightingale], *The Institution of Kaiserswerth* (London, 1851), 15.

[12] Woodham-Smith, *Florence Nightingale*, 6.

[13] Quoted in Cook, *Life*, I, 12.

[14] Woodham-Smith, *Florence Nightingale*, 6.

[15] Erik H. Erikson, "Identity and the Life Cycle," *Psychological Issues*, I (1959), 80-81.

[16] Woodham-Smith, *Florence Nightingale*, 52.

[17] Quoted in *ibid.,* 38.

[18] Florence Nightingale to Hilary Bonham-Carter, 11 Dec. 1845, in Cook, *Life*, I, 44.

[19] Quoted in Woodham-Smith, *Florence Nightingale*, 46.

[20] Private note, 7 Dec. 1851, Nightingale Papers, X.

[21] Entry of 4 June, 1850, Diary, Nightingale Papers, CVIII.

[22] Woodham-Smith, *Florence Nightingale*, 3-5, 7-8; Cook, *Life*, I, 5-6, 12-13.

[23] *Ibid*, I, 138; II, 236. There is in fact a long correspondence between Florence and her father on her religious ideas. She often used him for a sounding board and he responded in lengthy and thoughtful letters.

[24] Private note, 1851, Nightingale Papers, X.

[25] Helene Deutsch, *The Psychology of Women* (New York, 1944), I, 243-247.

[26] *Ibid.*, I, 215.

[27] Quoted in Woodham-Smith, *Florence Nightingale*, 12. Cook states that there are later notes which still fix that day as the "dawn of her true life" (*Life*, I, 15).

[28] Woodham-Smith, *Florence Nightingale*, 13.

[29] Cook has provided an introduction; see, esp. I, Part I, ch. III; Part II, ch. VIII; Part IV, ch. V; II, Part VII, chs. II, VIII. Her own writings include *Suggestions for Thought to the Searchers after Truth among the Artizans of England* (London, 1860), 3v., "A Note of Interrogation," *Fraser's Magazine*, LXXXVIII (May 1873), 567-577; "A Sub-Note of Interrogation; What Will Our Religion Be in 1999?" *ibid.*, (July 1873), 25-36.

[30] Quoted in T. Wemyss Reid, *Life of Lord Houghton* (London, 1890), I, 524. Roman Catholicism's emphasis on works as well as faith, especially as regards the nursing and teaching orders of nuns, made it attractive to Florence Nightingale. Furthermore, she was much drawn to the works of the mystics, such as St. Catherine of Siena and St. Teresa of Ávila, and she prepared with Benjamin Jowett's encouragement a volume of writings entitled "Notes from Devotional Authors of the Middle Ages, Collected, Chosen, and Freely Translated by Florence Nightingale," but it was never completed.

[31] Quoted in Woodham-Smith, *Florence Nightingale*, 53-54.

[32] Erik H. Erikson, *Identity: Youth and Crisis* (New York, 1968), 135.

[33] Quoted in Woodham-Smith, *Florence Nightingale*, 247.

[34] *Ibid.*, 240.

[35] Erikson, *Identity*, 166-167.

[36] Quoted in Woodham-Smith, *Florence Nightingale*, 42.

[37] See Erikson, *Identity*, 165ff. For an observation on elements affecting natural growth during young adulthood, see White, *Lives in Progress*, 374-390.

[38] Woodham-Smith, *Florence Nightingale*, 182.

[39] *Ibid.*, 182-187.

[40] Quoted in *ibid.*, 201.

[41] *Ibid.*, 209

[42] Quoted in *ibid.*, 247.

[43] Quoted in *ibid.*, 248.

[44] Quoted in *ibid.*, 249.

[45] White, *Lives in Progress*, 12.

[46] Quoted in Woodham-Smith, *Florence Nightingale*, 341.

[47] Diary, 1850, Nightingale Papers, CVIII.

[48] Autobiographical note, Nightingale Papers, CIX.

[49] See, esp., Heinz Kohut, *The Analysis of the Self: A Systematic Approach to the Psychoanalytic Treatment of Narcissistic Personality Disorders* (New York, 1971); *idem*, "Thoughts on Narcissism and Narcissistic Rage," in Ruth Eissler, Anna Freud, Marianne Kris, and Albert J. Solnit (eds.), *The Psychoanalytic Study of the Child* (New York, 1973), XXVII, 360-400.

[50] Kohut, "Thoughts on Narcissism," 380-387. His description of the vulnerably narcissistic personality sheds considerable light on many of Florence Nightingale's actions.

**Elaine Showalter (essay date 1981)**

SOURCE: "Florence Nightingale's Feminist Complaint: Women, Religion, and *Suggestions for Thought*," in *Signs: Journal of Women in Culture and Society*, Vol. 6, No. 3, Spring, 1981, pp. 395-412.

[*In the following essay, Showalter investigates Nightingale's relationship to nineteenth-century feminism, using both psychological evidence and that of Nightingale's* Suggestions for Thought to Searchers after Religious Truth.]

Historians have often had to admit sadly that Florence Nightingale could not be counted among the great English feminists, saying, as historian Ray Strachey does, that she had "only an incomplete and easily exhausted sympathy with the organized Women's Movement."[1] Nightingale vehemently refused to join John Stuart Mill's women's suffrage committee; she was notoriously critical of female ignorance, laziness, incompetence, and lack of moral purpose.[2] And yet the new women's history, which in many ways has made our definitions of feminism more rigorous and exacting, has also expanded our sympathy with the varieties of nineteenth-century feminist experience. Looking afresh at Nightingale's life, and making use of the vast collection of her manuscripts in the British Library, especially her privately printed, three-volume work of feminist and theological speculation,

*Suggestions for Thought to Searchers after Religious Truth,* we ought to be able to reach some new conclusions about the nature of her relation to the feminism of her era and ours.[3]

In such an endeavor, however, it is best to concede at once that Nightingale's feminism has some defects. Even in Victorian terms, she was relentlessly upper class in her reliance on money, privilege, and personal connections. She was intellectually arrogant in her rejection of the emotions and values of ordinary women. She despised her mother and sister and never entirely forgave them for having fought against her efforts to train as a nurse. Her own life was deeply scarred by the need to resist the suffocating encroachments of her family. After her triumphant return from the Crimea she retreated into a strategic invalidism, emerging only after her mother's death when she herself was in her sixties. Yet if she seems a victim of familial and social values, Nightingale also dared to question the fundamental organization of family life, to scoff at the inflated virtues of motherhood and daughterhood, and to criticize the sexism of the English church. The institutions she attacked were even more formidable than Parliament, and more resistant to change. The suppression of *Suggestions for Thought,* which included her best-known feminist essay, *Cassandra,* is one of the most unfortunate sagas of Victorian censorship of female anger, protest, and passion. The continued neglect of the work today deprives us not only of a major document of Victorian religious thought, which should be studied alongside Newman's *Apologia Pro Vita Sua,* but also of a major text of English feminism, a link between Wollstonecraft and Woolf.

In order to understand the genesis of Nightingale's peculiar feminism we must look first at her turbulent relationship with her mother, Fanny, and her older sister, Parthenope. Although she was beautiful, brilliant, and accomplished, Florence from earliest childhood was miserable in the role of "daughter at home" in a rich upper-class family. As her mother lamented to Elizabeth Gaskell, "We are ducks who have hatched a wild swan."[4] From the age of six, Nightingale had experienced herself not as a superior being but as a shameful anomaly in her family. In a private autobiographical note she recorded "that as a very young child she had an obsession that she was not like other people. She was a monster, that was her secret which might at any moment be found out. Strangers must be avoided, especially children. She worked herself into an agony at the prospect of seeing a new face, and to be looked at was torture. She doubted her capacity to behave like other people and refused to dine downstairs, convinced that she would betray herself by doing something extraordinary with her knife and fork."[5] In Nightingale's case, as in so many lives described in women's literature and memoir, the image of monstrosity was related to her anger and discontent with the female role, to the need to disguise her drives for knowledge, mastery, and power.[6]

Fanny and Parthenope were extremely conventional women of their class: socially ambitious, intellectually lazy, and emotionally infantile. Yet they too were victims of the Victorian expectation that women would fulfill themselves through love and the achievements of others. When William Nightingale, after a defeat in a Parliamentary election, refused to compete further in public life, Fanny transferred her social ambition from her husband to her daughters; in a family without sons they had to bear the brunt of her frustrations and longings. Parthenope, a year older than Florence, reacted to her sister's superiority in beauty, intelligence, and character with jealousy disguised as passionate devotion. Only after her marriage at thirty-nine was Parthenope secure enough to relinquish her neurotic attachment to Florence and also to develop some of her own talents as a productive (though never distinguished) novelist and historical essayist.

William Nightingale undertook the education of both girls in Greek, Latin, German, French, Italian, history, and philosophy. However, by Florence's sixteenth birthday, the family had formed clear spatial and psychological divisions: she was her father's companion in the library, Parthenope was her mother's companion in the drawing room. The life of the drawing room, the indolent feminine life of chatting, reading aloud, sketching, singing, and gardening that pleased Fanny and Parthenope and contented her twelve aunts and twenty-seven cousins, bored and irritated Florence to despair. Like other gifted women of her generation, she translated intellectual and vocational drives into the language of religion, the only system that could justify them. Just before her seventeenth birthday, she experienced the first of four religious revelations during her lifetime: "On February 7, 1837, God spoke to me and called me to his service."[7]

Having divine (and masculine) sanction for her ambitions was some solace, but God did not make clear to her how she was to serve. Through years of desperate and often suicidal unhappiness, Nightingale worked out the details of her commitment to the profession of nursing and struggled to establish an ideology that would give her the fortitude to sacrifice marriage and break with her family. Fanny and Parthenope opposed her efforts with all the emotional weapons at their command. The next fifteen years were characterized by intense family conflict as Florence wearily carried out the duties of young-ladyhood, while each of her plans for autonomy was wrecked by her mother or sister. In 1845 she dreamed of establishing an informal religious community to train nurses; but when she asked her parents simply to allow her to go a few miles away to study nursing for three months at Salisbury Infirmary, Fanny was shocked and outraged, accusing Florence of having a love affair with some "low vulgar surgeon."[8] On a European trip a few years later, Florence made a crucial visit to Kaiserswerth in Germany where a model hospital was run by a Protestant religious order. When she returned, Parthenope had hysterics. Because Florence had been traveling for a year, her parents decided that she owed the next six months entirely to her sister; they must walk together, read together, gather posies in the garden, sing, and draw little sketches.

During this period of sibling slavery, Florence further scandalized her family by refusing an offer of marriage from a man she respected and loved—Richard Monckton Milnes, a wealthy philanthropist, intellectual, and social reformer. She had painfully determined that, while marriage would fulfill her intellectual and sexual needs, it would obstruct her need for purposeful and important work:

> I have an intellectual nature which requires satisfaction and that would find it in him. I have a passionate nature which requires satisfaction and that would find it in him. I have a moral, and an active, nature which requires satisfaction, and that would not find it in his life. Sometimes I think I will satisfy my passional nature at all events, because that will at least secure me from the evil of dreaming. But would it? I could be satisfied to spend a life with him in combining our different powers in some great object. I could not satisfy this nature by spending a life with him in making society and arranging domestic things.[9]

Yet as she saw all her efforts to undergo serious training as a nurse undermined and prevented by the combined emotional despotism of mother and sister, Nightingale became terrified that in refusing Milnes she had abandoned her only chance for even partial happiness. Her father would not intervene to help her leave; he would not make her financially independent. Her diary for these years shows her in the grip of repeated near-suicidal depressions: "My present life is suicide; In my 31st year I see nothing desirable but death; What am I that their life is not good enough for me? O God what am I? The thoughts and feelings that I have now I can remember since I was six years old. It was not I that made them. . . . But why, oh my God, cannot I be satisfied with the life that satisfies so many people?"[10]

During this period of bitter despair, Nightingale began to write *Suggestions for Thought.* Her plan was ambitious; she would do nothing less than justify the laws of God to men—especially working men—and, most important, to women. The first volume was dedicated to the "Artisans" of England and was to be the outline of a new philosophic religion that would combat atheism. The second volume, originally called "A Short Account of God's Dealings with the Author" and later "Practical Deductions," was to contain a sort of empirical research into religious psychology. The third volume would discuss divine law and moral right. There was also to have been a novel, and early drafts of volume 2 contain sections of an epistolary problem-novel about women and the memoir that eventually became *Cassandra.*[11]

Writing was both a burden and a therapy for her; working on the book helped her to work through her psychic turmoil. By 1851 she had surmounted this terrible depression. She saw clearly that she must not expect support from her family but must mother and support herself: "I must *take* some things . . . they will not be given to me."[12] She announced that she must return to Kaiserswerth Hospital.

Once again there were terrible arguments with Fanny and Parthenope; on the eve of her departure, Nightingale wrote, "The scene . . . was so violent that I fainted."[13]

When she returned from Germany, Fanny and Parthenope were furious and treated her like a criminal. In despair over her inability to break away, Nightingale seriously considered converting to Roman Catholicism and joining a convent. To Cardinal Manning she confided: "If you knew what a home the Catholic Church would be to me! All that I want I should find in her. All my difficulties would be removed."[14] Manning wisely discouraged her conversion, but he did make arrangements for her to work in two Catholic hospitals run by nursing orders, the Sisters of Mercy in Dublin and the Sisters of Charity in Paris. The announcement precipitated the most severe crisis in the Nightingale family, one which finally freed Florence from her bondage to her sister's neurotic demands. In 1852 Parthenope, who had declared that she was dying as a result of Florence's unnatural and unsisterly behavior, had a complete nervous breakdown. Sir James Clark, the Queen's physician, told the Nightingales that Parthenope showed total absorption in herself and that her only chance for a normal life was to be forced to become independent of Florence. As Nightingale ironically recounted, the "sister who was being Devoured" was told "that she might leave home in order that the Devouree might recover health and balance which had been lost in the process of devouring."[15] William Nightingale was sufficiently alarmed by the diagnosis to grant Florence a permanent allowance of £500 a year. The bonds were finally severed; she was free at last.

Just before her thirty-second birthday, on May 7, 1852, Nightingale experienced her second divine revelation, "a call from God to be a savior."[16] Within a year she left home to take an appointment as superintendent of an "Establishment for Gentlewomen during Illness" in Harley Street, London. She never went back to her former life, and in October 1854 she left with a party of thirty-eight nurses for Scutari in the Crimea. All her literary works were put aside for the life of action which took up most of the decade; indeed, as it turned out, Nightingale would never again equal the heroic intensity of action which she was able to achieve in the 1850s.

Even then, however, Nightingale's struggles were not entirely over. Parthenope and Fanny never visited her in Harley Street. Even after the Crimean War, when she was an idolized heroine, Nightingale was harassed by her mother and sister who were as flighty and demanding as before. They insisted on her time and company, lounged on sofas in her hotel suite, and interrupted her work. Finally Nightingale turned their own weapons against them, suffering "attacks" when they announced a visit and insisting that she was too sick to see them. Only long after her sister's belated marriage, when Fanny was senile and Parthenope crippled by arthritis, was Florence able to reestablish an intimate relationship with both women.[17]

This lifelong contest with her mother and sister scarred Nightingale psychologically, and it certainly limited the terms of her feminism. During the past decade, many of us have adopted a model of feminist consciousness based on the premise that full reconciliation with one's own mother and sisters is fundamental to personal and political authenticity. But in Nightingale's experience, and in her analysis of the Victorian family, the mother was the chief obstacle to the daughter's self-realization. The mother stood in the way of disciplined study, genuine self-improvement, and serious training. Whereas Carroll Smith-Rosenberg, in her study of female networks in nineteenth-century America, found a virtual absence of discord between mothers and daughters, Nightingale saw a society in which mother-daughter conflict was inevitable, in which each woman was enslaved to the other in a relationship of mutual incompatibility and incomprehension.[18] "Do you know one family," she demands in *Suggestions for Thought,* "where the mother has what may truly be called a beautiful relationship with the daughter?"[19] In *Cassandra,* she pointedly remarks that the real attraction of novels is that the heroine "has *generally* no family ties (almost *invariably* no mother)."[20] Nightingale's anger against repressive mothering was so strong that she believed that all children should be brought up in "a well-managed creche."[21] Her own maternal drives, she maintained, had been fully and effectively realized in her work: "For every one of my 18,000 children . . . I have expended more motherly feeling and action in a week than my mother has expended for me in thirty-seven years."[22]

Donald Allen argues that Nightingale's psychological and psychosexual development was permanently formed by the conflicts with her mother and sister. She totally sacrificed love and intimacy with others to ever more demanding work. Allen suggests that "by choosing nursing, with all of its outer-directed and masochistic implications, she could absorb her fury, satisfy her drive for power, and at the same time placate her extremely strong superego by directing her efforts to the aid of others 'in God's name.'"[23] But in her religious faith Nightingale was not attracted to the androgynous figure of Jesus or to the doctrines of salvation and redemption. She saw herself instead as the agent of a strong, masculine God who commanded her to be a savior and who justified her rebellion against the feminine morality of domestic duty and humble self-sacrifice.

Nightingale's struggles to define her profession took place against the background of intense mid-nineteenth-century debate over the position, rights, and potential of women in the Church of England. These controversies challenged the most basic institutions of Victorian life: the place and duty of women in the family, the need for female professions, the plight of the unmarried woman, and the rights of women to participate in the ministry of a patriarchal church. Women were demanding more meaningful roles in church ritual and more serious work than the embroidery of altar cloths. Despite centuries of superstition and calumny against nunneries, religious

sisterhoods and Anglican convents had a Victorian revival. According to the religious historian Michael Hill, sisterhoods "are the first signs of incipient feminism among women in the middle class," and the agitation for female religious communities began in England in the 1840s, before the agitation for women's rights. In 1845 the first Anglican sisterhood, Park Village, was formed.[24] Sisterhoods were associated with the Oxford Movement, and it became customary for advanced young clergymen to sponsor them along with other elements of the Anglo-Catholic revival. By 1873 there were forty-three Anglican sisterhoods in operation.

The concept of the female religious community was widely discussed in England during the period when Nightingale was agonizing over the direction of her own life, and many other High Church women of her generation, such as Christina and Maria Rossetti, were equally drawn to consider it. Although the sisterhood seemed to promise a life of purpose and a degree of autonomy, its conditions and costs disturbed both men and women at all levels of the English church. The traditional image of the Catholic convent, as a community of celibate women subjected to the spiritual authority of a male priesthood but otherwise independently directing its own course, alarmed many High Churchmen who feared that Anglican sisterhoods would follow a similar course. In 1854 Bishop Wilberforce wrote to the Tractarian T. T. Carter, "If Sisterhoods cannot be maintained except upon a semi-Romanist scheme, with its *direction,* with its development of self-conscious and morbid religious affection, with its exaltation of the contemplative life, its perpetual Confession, and its un-English tone, I am perfectly convinced that we had better have no Sisterhoods."[25] Low Churchmen opposed sisterhoods altogether and supported the revival of deaconesses, who, they argued, had been recognized by the primitive church and ought to be the "one existing ordained ministry for women."[26] In 1858 the Convocation of Canterbury Report recognized deaconesses as a form of women's work in the church, and in 1860 the Mildmay Deaconesses group was formed. Among dissenting groups, women's ministry had long been informally recognized; female Methodist preachers such as those George Eliot describes in *Adam Bede* (1857) were not uncommon. The evangelical energy of Catherine Booth found an outlet in the Salvation Army, which insisted on sex equality within its ranks and substituted military titles for "Miss" and "Mrs." In the 1860s Booth conducted prayer meetings for women only, which became immensely popular.[27]

Male supporters of the sisterhood movement often argued that it was expedient for the Church of England to provide a place for women of religious vocation who might otherwise convert to Catholicism and that the surplus population of unmarried women needed solace and occupation. Pusey feared a second Wesleyan exodus, of women this time, if the Church could not respond to the demand for sisterhoods. The problems of apostolic authority and scriptural legitimation, he declared, were of no interest to women, only the need for service: "Women are guided not by controversial arguments, but by intuitive feeling. Controversy they leave to us. But every religious woman whom God draws to more devoted service will obey that call, and if a veto is put upon [her] longing to lead the religious life . . . she will seek it elsewhere."[28] Some churchmen and laymen saw the sisterhood as an alternative to the wretchedness of a single life, and one archdeacon went so far as to detect a providential connection between the appearance of a female surplus and the emergence of sisterhoods which would employ the women in God's work.[29] Such a vision was confirmed in essays like Dinah Mulock Craik's "On Sisterhoods," which emphasized the femininity and the Protestantism of the Anglican convents and praised them as a refuge for failures and incompetents: "An institution which would absorb the waifs and strays of . . . gentlewomanhood—ladies of limited income and equally limited capacity, yet very good women so far as they go; which could take possession of them, income and all, saving and utilizing both it and themselves—would be a real boon to society."[30]

But feminists disputed the idea that hopeless spinsters with no other option would be the mainstay of the sisterhoods. Margaret Goodman, author of *Experiences of an English Sister of Mercy* (1862), protested, "It would appear from the writings of some persons, who urge the multiplication of sisterhoods, that they think them desirable because calculated to prove a blessing to women who have nothing to do: a mode of existence for ladies who, after every effort on their part, from the supply not equalling the demand, are unable to find husbands; or a refuge for the woe-worn, weary and disappointed. For neither of these three classes will a sisterhood prove a home. The work is far too real to be performed by lagging hands."[31] Similarly, the women's rights activist Barbara Leigh Bodichon argued in her pamphlet *Women and Work* that women were drawn to the Catholic church "because she gives work to her children."[32] Nina Auerbach has commented on the gap between male and female Victorian perceptions of the need for a sisterhood. For sympathetic men it "offers a restoration of the old relation of wife, mother, sister, a simulation of women's relative role within the family." For aspiring women "it offers the blessed work which promised many a release from love and family."[33]

Such was certainly the attraction of the sisterhood for Florence Nightingale, and for many years it seemed to her that the Roman Catholic church and the convent offered the only real opportunities for the training and hard work she craved. The Church of England offered only homilies, as Nightingale heatedly wrote: "I would have given her my head, my heart, my hand. She would not have them. She did not know what to do with them. She told me to go back and do crochet in my mother's sewing-room; or, if I were tired of that, to marry and look well at the head of my husband's table. You may go to the Sunday School, if you like it, she said. But she gave me no training even for that. She gave me neither work to do for her, nor education for it."[34]

This passage suggests what other comments by Nightingale make even more obvious—that she identified the Church of England with motherhood and specifically with her own mother. In *Suggestions for Thought*, Nightingale asks, "Why are mothers like the Church of England?" "Because their power declines when it becomes moral," she answers herself—that is, when it becomes open to question and debate.[35] Yet the Roman Catholic church too reminded her of a mother: "The Church of England is expected to be an over-idle mother, who lets her children entirely alone, because those made her who had found the Church of Rome an over-busy mother. *She* imprisoned us; she read our letters; she penetrated our thoughts; she regulated what we were to do every hour; she asked us what we had been doing and thinking; she burnt us if we had been thinking wrong."[36]

It is inconceivable that a woman like Nightingale, whose life had been shaped by the struggle to escape from the family community ruled by her mother and sister, could ever have lived contentedly in a sisterhood. Never having resolved the dreadful ambiguities of love, guilt, and anger that bound her to Fanny and Parthenope, she could not have endured the constant companionship of women or established working relationships with them. Her personal experiences with the sisterhood were disastrous; she alludes in her journal to some terrible lesson taught her by the Sisters of Mercy in Dublin. After such a battle to be free, she could not submit to the will of others; as she declared, "It is *not* the thought of God that we should be like a 'dead body' surrendering up the whole being to the superior."[37]

Throughout her life, her powerful individualistic feminism was interrupted by feverish outbursts against the women she knew. Unable genuinely to trust another woman, she was forced increasingly to work with, and through, men. A succession of male agents, most of them famous and distinguished, presented her plans and carried out her projects: Arthur Hugh Clough, Sidney Herbert, Sir John Sutherland, and Sir Harry Verney.

It is typical of Nightingale's ambivalence toward women, her feeling that even exceptional women would not understand her philosophy or her anger, that when she returned from the Crimea and set to revising the manuscript of *Suggestions for Thought* in the summer of 1859, she did not share her work with any of the distinguished literary women she knew, such as Harriet Martineau, Elizabeth Gaskell, or George Eliot. All of these writers would have responded to her critique of the limitations of family life more sympathetically than the male readers Nightingale consulted, and would have shared more deeply her feelings on the failure of the English church to offer women activities other than marriage and crochet. Ironically, Martineau, Gaskell, and Eliot, who were very close to Nightingale in age, were also close to her in their distrust of a women's rights movement and represented a "feminine" generation which had internalized many of the precepts of the

Victorian sexual code. But within their self-imposed boundaries, all of these women were courageous and effective supporters of women's emancipation. All were admirers of Nightingale's heroism during the war and of her pamphlets on nursing and hospital administration. Nightingale had sent Martineau a copy of her privately printed *Notes on Matters Affecting the Health, Efficiency, and Hospital Administration of the British Army* (1855), warning her to keep it private and not to exploit it in the women's cause, and writing about women in the metaphors of the Inquisition: "I have a great horror of its being made use of after my death by Women's Missionaries and those kinds of people. I am brutally indifferent to the wrongs or the rights of my sex. And I should have been equally so to any controversy as to whether women ought not to do what I have done for the Army; though a woman, having the opportunity and *not* doing it, ought, I think, to be burnt alive."[38] Although Martineau respected Nightingale's wishes about the *Notes,* and though they continued to correspond on political issues for many years, there is no indication that Martineau (well known for her atheism) ever saw the text of *Suggestions for Thought.* Gaskell too had been an enthusiastic follower of Nightingale's work, and Nightingale was rereading *Ruth* in September 1859; yet she did not select Gaskell (the wife of a Unitarian minister) as a confidante.

The most unlucky of these missed connections was George Eliot. The two women had met in 1852, while Eliot (then known as Marian Evans) was editing the *Westminster Review.* Although they had much in common—they were exactly the same age and Eliot too had made a difficult break with her family and with the Church of England in order to lead an independent and productive life—the anonymity and the secrecy of Victorian feminine ideology kept them from understanding each other. It is sadly ironic that just as Nightingale was having *Suggestions for Thought* printed in 1859, Eliot was sending *The Mill on the Floss,* which passionately dramatizes the protests of another "Cassandra," to her publishers. Yet Nightingale did not know that Marian Evans was the novelist George Eliot, and Eliot would never know that Nightingale had written a book about woman's spiritual crisis, about the tension between the "duty of obedience" and the "duty of resistance" which became one of the novelist's own major themes.[39]

Instead of turning to women, Nightingale submitted her writing to the most celebrated male intellectuals and scholars of her day. Some she knew personally, like Richard Milnes and Arthur Hugh Clough, but John Stuart Mill, Benjamin Jowett, and the historian J. A. Froude were strangers. Mill encouraged her to publish *Suggestions for Thought.* But Mill's enthusiasm counted less with Nightingale than the negative vote of her other senior reader, Benjamin Jowett, Regius Professor of Greek at Oxford. Jowett was deeply struck by the manuscript—"It seemed to me as if I had received the impress of a new mind," he wrote to Clough—and his annotations are copiously detailed and argumentative.[40]

The exchange was the beginning of a lifelong friendship between the two, a friendship which Jowett, apparently, would have liked to elevate into a romance. But there could have been few readers less likely to sympathize with Nightingale's originality of religious thought, pungent forthrightness of expression, and explicit angry feminism. Jowett represented an Oxford and classical patriarchal tradition as entrenched as the Church; much as he respected and admired Nightingale, he could not support the passionate and rebellious tone of *Suggestions for Thought.* Thus his advice was all in terms of modifying, subduing, and muting her message. He argued for a more disciplined and orderly arrangement of the text, for cutting and reorganization, and especially for the elimination of her anger: "[I] traced some degree of irritation in the tone, the book appears to me full of antagonisms—perhaps these could be softened."[41] Jowett's minute annotations were flattering but also discouraging; he wanted a degree of revision and censorship that Nightingale was not prepared to carry out. In a sense, he appropriated *Suggestions for Thought* and made Nightingale his pupil, a role she reluctantly accepted. A few copies of the book were privately printed in 1860, and that was the end. In an early will of 1862, she expressed a wish to have the book "revised and arranged according to the hints of Mr. Jowett and Mr. Mill, but without altering the spirit according to their principles with which I entirely disagree."[42] In 1865 she asked Jowett if he wished to do the editing for her, but he refused. In later years they conducted an enormous correspondence on philosophic and theological problems, and Jowett consulted her on his revised translations of Plato. But she did not return to the rewriting of her book.

It is tempting, but too simple, however, to blame Jowett for the loss of *Suggestions for Thought.* By 1860 Nightingale was no longer an apprentice; she was a confident and powerful woman. I suspect that the reason she did not revise and publish was that the book had achieved its purpose for her. Writing this work in 1851-52 had allowed her to define her personal philosophy. It was the handbook by which she transformed herself from the ineffectual and tragic Cassandra into the indomitable heroine of the Crimea. By 1860 the book was no longer important as the instrument of her emancipation, and she was unwilling to commit herself to it again. Such an investment would have seemed regressive.

*Suggestions for Thought,* as we turn to the text, is the most personal and instrumental of Florence Nightingale's literary works, the record of her struggle toward the possession of her own power. It provides both a critique of Roman Catholic and Anglican church doctrine regarding women and a daring vision of a feminist Messiah. By any conventional religious standards Nightingale was a heretic, but her personal ethos was even more heretical than her religion. Freeing herself from the demands of her own family and from the temptation to submerge her individuality in the collective purpose of a Catholic or Protestant sisterhood, Nightingale strenuously evolved her own religious code of self-fulfillment, concluding that God wishes us not to sacrifice ourselves to duty but to develop our own strengths and abilities for the sake of humanity.

Her God is a Being who leaves evil in the world in order to help people perfect themselves by struggling against it. Therefore each individual, woman as well as man, should be given the freedom to make the best of herself. God did not mean us to practice self-denial but to "do what we like, first learning to like the right."[43] Two things were necessary for human perfection and joy, Nightingale argued, "that we should come into free communication with mankind, so as to give us room for our sympathies to find a response, *and* that we should have all our powers called into the highest exercise."[44] Without all those powers employed, there could be no harmony or repose in human existence; with employment or exercise of those powers, "repose may be found in a hell, in a hospital of wounds and pain, and operations and death."[45]

In presenting such a doctrine she was subverting the Protestant ideology of humility and submission, especially as applied to women. Nightingale refused to glorify "the prison which is called a family."[46] Women of the upper classes, she wrote, were in solitary confinement, enslaved to their mothers, their lives "consumed by *ennui* as by a cancer."[47] Only marriage allowed them to leave, and marriage was risky when women could know so little about their potential husbands. Nightingale urged that women be made financially independent by their parents when they came of age and that they be encouraged to train for a vocation. The new family she envisioned was a commune where people "who liked to work for the same object, met to do so."[48] Once it was understood that the role of the family was to love and support the growth of its members, "all ages and both sexes really living and working for each other," her complaints could be seen as constructive: "We want to extend the family, not annihilate it. We want 'not to destroy, but to fulfill' the hopes it holds out. . . . We would not take away *anything*, we would enlarge and multiply."[49]

The only section of *Suggestions for Thought* that became available to the public, however, was *Cassandra,* and it was not published until long after her death. In her original manuscript, *Cassandra* was to have been a novel, the story of Nofriani, as recounted after her death at the age of thirty by her brother Fariseo. In successive revisions Nightingale eliminated the narrative framework and substituted the third for the first person. Many of the abrupt transitions and obscure allusions of the published text are due to her exclusion of personal narrative. But Nightingale's gifts as a novelist, it must be admitted, were not great. The characters talk endlessly to each other or to themselves. Her settings, inspired by memories of her own residences in England, Rome, and Paris, are lushly romantic. The oddly named Nofriani, with her "long hair of the golden tint which the Venetian

painter delighted to honour" and her melodramatic soliloquies, is too often stagy and unreal.[50] Yet sometimes her speeches have an intensity that suggests the Brontës:

> And I who dreamed of institutions to show women their work and to train them how to do it—to give them an object and to incline their wills to follow it—I, in whom thoughts of this kind put aside the thought of marriage, who sacrificed my individual future for great hopes, glimpses of a great general future, I have fallen so low that I can look back with a sigh even after the conventional dignity of a married woman . . . and say with a sigh, "such might have been mine if I had chosen."[51]

Nightingale had identified herself as "poor Cassandra" in a letter to a cousin, and the section is obviously autobiographical.[52] Her choice of the Cassandra myth as the frame for her narrative is revealing. Cassandra was the Trojan princess captured by Agamemnon, whose curse of futile prophecy came about because she had rejected the love of Apollo. The myth suggests that women who refuse sexuality and love are denied a voice, indeed can be driven mad by their society. Nightingale tormented herself that, in refusing to marry Milnes, she had doomed herself to an ineffectual life. Furthermore, Cassandra was killed by Clytemnestra, as Nightingale felt she was being destroyed by other women.

The image of the prophetess or evangelist was important for Nightingale, who believed that women must be shocked into an awareness of their own anger and frustration, an experience that must inevitably be painful. For Nightingale, painful discomfort is the initial and essential step in breaking away from childish bondage to the family. Experiencing one's discontent to its fullest, suffering all its pangs, is the price of adulthood, a "privilege" that may lead to action. To deny, suppress, and stupefy these emotions leads to paralysis and spiritual death, the atrophying of intellect and will Nightingale saw everywhere in the lives of well-to-do English women. Nightingale's insistence that women must risk pain in order to grow contradicted the liberalism of such nineteenth-century thinkers as Mill, who argued that human happiness requires the avoidance of pain. Out of her conviction came the most powerful and original passage of *Cassandra,* the defiant invocation at the beginning of section 2 in which Nightingale demands in women's behalf, not money or votes or even work, but the restoration of pain: "Give us back our suffering, we cry to heaven in our hearts—suffering rather than indifferentism; for out of nothing comes nothing. But out of suffering may come the cure. Better have pain than paralysis! A hundred struggle and drown in the breakers. One discovers the new world. But rather, ten times rather, die in the surf, heralding the way to that new world, than stand idly on the shore!"[53] We are uncannily reminded of those doomed heroines of women's fiction in the nineteenth century who are unable to endure the pain of awakening consciousness. Like *The Mill on the Floss, The Awakening,* and *The House of Mirth, Cassandra* ends in the heroine's death. Cassandra too becomes one who perishes in the breakers, "who can neither find happiness in life, nor alter it."[54] Yet her death is presented as a martyrdom, which may yet save the women's cause. Nightingale predicted the coming of a female savior: "The next Christ will be perhaps a female Christ," "a woman who will resume, in her own soul, all the sufferings of her race."[55] This woman would rouse her slumbering sisters with her cry: "Awake, ye women, all ye that sleep, awake!"[56]

Complaint is thus her special medium, essential to her concept of women's vital struggle. Repeatedly in *Cassandra,* Nightingale reverts to the theme of complaint and discontent. Women must channel their grievance through the medium of religion, to depersonalize it, she writes, because "men are angry with misery. They are irritated with women for not being happy. . . . To God alone may women complain, without insulting Him!"[57] Complaint was in the tradition of the great prophets and saints, who all had "a most deep and ingrained sense, a continual gnawing feeling of the miseries and wrongs of the world."[58] What terrified Nightingale was that women were Cassandras rendered so impotent by their society that they could rail and rave but never act. In a brilliant insight, Nightingale observes that unheeded altruism sours and turns to hate: "The great reformers of the world turn into the great misanthropists, if circumstances or organizations do not permit them to act. Christ, if he had been a woman, might have been nothing but a great complainer."[59]

How, finally, can we place Nightingale in the context of nineteenth-century feminism? Was she a great leader or merely a great complainer? Making use of the important definitions put forward by Gerda Lerner, we can say that Nightingale was a believer in women's emancipation, though not in women's rights. As Lerner explains:

> *Woman's emancipation* means: freedom from oppressive restrictions imposed by sex; self-determination; autonomy. Freedom from oppressive restrictions imposed by sex means freedom from biological and societal restrictions. Self-determination means being free to decide one's own destiny; being free to define one's own social role; having the freedom to make decisions concerning one's own body. Autonomy means earning one's own status, not being born into it nor marrying it; it means financial and cultural independence; freedom to choose one's own lifestyle and sexual preference, all of which implies a radical transformation of existing institutions, values, and theories.[60]

If *Cassandra* and *Suggestions for Thought* had been published when they were written, they might have been inspirations to the thousands of Victorian women who shared Nightingale's predicament but lacked her genius and her ferocious energy. Nightingale never became a feminist leader in her own time. But she has much to say to our time, especially about the development of women who burn themselves out in the struggle against mothers and sisters and who demand freedom from

women's culture as much as from women's sphere. Florence Nightingale's life is an example of the psychic cost of matrophobia, but it is also an example of courage and power. If we fail to respond to Nightingale, we betray a Cassandra whose complaint came from a female experience as authentic and profoundly felt as that of any of our cherished heroines.

NOTES

[1] Ray Strachey, *The Cause: A Short History of the Women's Movement in Great Britain* (London: Virago, Ltd., 1978), p. 24.

[2] The standard biographies of Nightingale which discuss in detail her attitudes toward women are Edward T. Cook, *The Life of Florence Nightingale,* 2 vols. (London: Macmillan & Co., 1913), and Cecil Woodham-Smith, *Florence Nightingale 1820-1910* (New York: McGraw-Hill Book Co., 1951). A helpful unpublished, photocopied study is Evelyn L. Pugh, "Florence Nightingale and J. S. Mill Debate Women's Rights" (History Department, George Mason College, Fairfax, Virginia). See also Strachey, pp. 23-29.

[3] Florence Nightingale, *Suggestions for Thought to Searchers after Religious Truth,* 3 vols., was privately printed by the London firm of Eyre & Spottiswoode in 1860. There are copies in the British Library, the London Library, the New York Public Library, and the Yale Medical School Library. Since a privately printed work that was not offered to the public is considered unpublished under British copyright law, all quotations from *Suggestions for Thought* are by permission of the Henry Bonham-Carter Will Trust. Manuscripts and drafts of these works are part of the Nightingale Papers in the British Library (Add. MSS 45837, 45838, and 45839); quotations are by permission of the British Library Department of Manuscripts and the Henry Bonham-Carter Will Trust.

[4] Woodham-Smith, p. 81.

[5] Ibid., p. 6.

[6] For an analysis of these images of monstrosity, see Ellen Moers, "Female Gothic," in *Literary Women* (New York: Doubleday & Co., 1976). Nightingale's writing is saturated with the characteristic imagery of the female literary tradition; *Cassandra* especially emphasizes images of madness, sickness, and starvation (see Sandra Gilbert and Susan Gubar, *The Madwoman in the Attic* [New Haven, Conn.: Yale University Press, 1979], chaps. 1-3).

[7] Cook, 1:15. Obviously, several different interpretations of Nightingale's mystical experiences are possible. Donald R. Allen points out that "all of these experiences with 'voices' occurred after periods of extremely intense emotional and psychological stress marked by personal disappointment, strong feelings of self-doubt,

deep depression, and a sense of failure" ("Florence Nightingale: Toward a Psychohistorical Explanation," *Journal of Interdisciplinary History* 8 [Summer 1975]: 33). Peter T. Cominos sees the phenomenon of female religious ecstasy as the outlet for repressed sexuality, a view shared by many Victorian psychiatric physicians ("Innocent Femina Sensualis in Unconscious Conflict," in *Suffer and Be Still* [Bloomington: Indiana University Press, 1972], pp. 163-64).

[8] Woodham-Smith, p. 38. Allen points out that "Fanny saw her younger daughter's later rebellion in sexual terms" and that her shocked reactions probably impeded Florence's sexual development (Allen, pp. 29-30).

[9] Woodham-Smith, p. 51. Nightingale's reasoned rejection of marriage is virtually unique among nineteenth-century English women.

[10] Ibid., pp. 58-59.

[11] Each volume is prefaced by a "digest" of the divisions and subdivisions of the contents, and running titles and marginal glosses highlight the arguments throughout. Sections of vol. 1 were first written as a dialogue. The epistolary novel in vol. 2 is an exchange of letters between four "daughters"—Fluquentia, Portia, Colomba, and Mary—who appear to represent different aspects of Nightingale's beliefs. For a description of the privately printed edition, see W. J. Bishop and Sue Goldie, *A Bio-Bibliography of Florence Nightingale* (London: William Dawsons & Sons, 1962), pp. 119-21. *Cassandra* was published as an appendix to Ray Strachey's *The Cause* in 1928, but Strachey omitted the running titles and long marginal glosses of the printed text. The recent edition of *Cassandra*, edited by Myra Stark and published by the Feminist Press, follows the text of the Strachey edition.

[12] Woodham-Smith, p. 60.

[13] Ibid.

[14] Ibid., p. 98.

[15] Ibid., p. 66.

[16] Cook, 1:43.

[17] She nursed both mother and sister when they were helpless and took charge of their households. George Pickering interprets Nightingale's illness as "psychoneurosis with a purpose" (*Creative Malady* [New York: Dell Publishing Co., 1976], esp. pp. 165-77). Allen describes her illness as "at once a means of warding off the emotional conflict engendered by the interference of her mother and sister, and at the same time a mechanism which allowed her to become the object of their solicitous attention, and thus to overcome her childhood feeling of rejection" (p. 41).

[18] See Carroll Smith-Rosenberg, "The Female World of Love and Ritual: Relations between Women in Nineteenth-Century America," *Signs: Journal of Women in Culture and Society* 1, no. 1 (1975): 1-29. Recently Smith-Rosenberg has recognized a more conflicted relationship between mothers and daughters beginning in the 1870s and 1880s, as role options expanded for daughters: "Mothers and other older women frequently acted to thwart their daughters' new role aspirations" ("Politics and Culture in Women's History," *Feminist Studies* 6 [Spring 1980]: 59).

[19] Nightingale, *Suggestions for Thought*, 2:65.

[20] The quotation is from the most easily available American edition of *Cassandra*, ed. Myra Stark (Old Westbury, N.Y.: Feminist Press, 1979), p. 28.

[21] Woodham-Smith, p. 81.

[22] Quoted in Pickering, p. 131.

[23] Allen, p. 43.

[24] Michael Hill, *The Religious Order* (London: Heinemann Educational Books, Ltd., 1973), p. 10. A sisterhood was defined by Rev. T. T. Carter, at Oxford Church Congress in 1862, as "a community of women, living a single life, in obedience to a fixed rule, with a common fund, seeking to advance the glory of God by the culture of their spiritual life, in closest union with Christ, and engaged in prayer or in works of mercy" (Hill, p. 142).

[25] Ibid., p. 182.

[26] Ibid., p. 142.

[27] See F. de L. Booth Tucker, *Catherine Booth* (London: Butler & Tanner, 1893), pp. 147, 163. There are fascinating parallels between the personalities and lives of Nightingale and Booth, and a comparative study would illuminate many aspects of Victorian feminism.

[28] Hill, p. 259.

[29] This was Archdeacon Harris at the Church Congress of 1866. See Hill, pp. 302-3.

[30] Dinah Mulock Craik, "On Sisterhoods," in *About Money and Other Things* (New York: Harper & Bros., 1887), pp. 159-60.

[31] Margaret Goodman, *Sisterhoods in the Church of England* (London: Smith, Elder, 1863), p. 268.

[32] Barbara Leigh Bodichon, *Women and Work* (London: Bosworth & Harrison, 1857), p. 9.

[33] Nina Auerbach, *Communities of Women* (Cambridge, Mass.: Harvard University Press, 1978), p. 195, n. 21.

[34] Cook, 1:57.

[35] Nightingale, *Suggestions for Thought*, 2:239-40.

[36] Ibid., p. 246.

[37] Ibid., p. 152. According to Woodham-Smith, "She craved an opportunity to use her powers, but she was very far from submission; indeed, she had no conception of submission in the Catholic sense—it was an idea utterly foreign to her" (p. 100).

[38] Cook, 1:285.

[39] See George Eliot, *Romola,* chap. 23.

[40] Cook, 1:471.

[41] Woodham-Smith, p. 350.

[42] Cook, 1:477.

[43] *Suggestions for Thought,* 2:64.

[44] Ibid., p. 227.

[45] Ibid., p. 214.

[46] Ibid., p. 197.

[47] Ibid., p. 59.

[48] Ibid., p. 225.

[49] Ibid., pp. 228, 276.

[50] *Cassandra,* Add. MS 45839, Nightingale Papers, British Library.

[51] Ibid.

[52] Cook, 1:116. Curiously, the heroine of Parthenope Nightingale Verney's first novel *Stone Edge* (1867) is also "Cassandra."

[53] Stark, ed., *Cassandra,* p. 29.

[54] Marginal gloss in *Cassandra, Suggestions for Thought,* 2:410.

[55] Stark, ed., *Cassandra,* pp. 53, 50.

[56] Ibid., p. 52.

[57] Ibid., p. 26.

[58] Ibid., p. 53.

[59] Ibid.

[60] Gerda Lerner, "Politics and Culture in Women's History: A Symposium," *Feminist Studies* 6 (Spring 1980): 50.

## Evelyn L. Pugh (essay date 1982)

SOURCE: "Florence Nightingale and J.S. Mill Debate Women's Rights," in *The Journal of British Studies,* Vol. XXI, No. 2, Spring, 1982, pp. 118-38.

[*In the following essay, Pugh discusses the correspondence of Nightingale and John Stuart Mill as it reveals the thoughts of both individuals on the subject of women's rights.*]

In Florence Nightingale's correspondence a series of letters to and from J.S. Mill treat a different subject than her usual correspondence with government officials, health and sanitation reformers, and hospital administrators in many parts of the world. Although it was never her intention when she initiated the exchange of letters, she and Mill quickly became involved in a controversy concerning the role of women.

Interwoven with some religious and philosophical matters, the Nightingale-Mill correspondence which falls into two periods, 1860 and 1867, is essentially a debate on women's rights. One debate concerns terminology and hinges on the entire validity of the question of publicity for the women's movement, then in its infancy, as well as the opening of the medical profession to women. The other focuses on differing perceptions of the role of women in political action. The exchange never became public during the lifetime of the participants, emerging with little notice only in the twentieth century with the complete publication of their correspondence in the journal *Hospitals* in 1936.[1]

J.S. Mill's views on women's rights were public knowledge in his own day and have continued to be studied exhaustively.[2] Florence Nightingale has been studied as the remarkable woman responsible for opening a respected profession for women.[3] The point is often made that she refused to sign the women's petition Mill presented to the House of Commons in 1866 and would not at first become a member of the London National Society for Women's Suffrage. Since this is usually the only connection made between the two, their letters have not received the attention warranted either by the historical prominence of the correspondents or by the value of the subject matter.

An analysis of the Nightingale-Mill correspondence illustrates vividly the dichotomy of thought between the pragmatic reformer of nursing and the theoretician of feminism. Within that context it becomes more understandable why Miss Nightingale, despite her enormously influential practical work in elevating the status of women, failed to become allied with Mill in the initial stages of the women's emancipation movement. Even more importantly, the correspondence brought to Mill's attention her then unpublished feminist tract, **"Cassandra,"** which provided him with insight into the life style of upper class women, examples of which emerged later in the *Subjection of Women.* There is the distinct possibility that Mill was perhaps more indebted to her for reinforcing the validity of some of his own preconceptions than has been previously realized. It was the acquaintance with Florence Nightingale as "Cassandra" rather than as the world famous "Lady of the Crimea" which was of more interest and of more significance to Mill. He had much to learn from "Cassandra" and he could share sympathetically and appreciate the concerns of a gifted individual thwarted by social conventions delineated by sex. On the other hand, he could only hope to persuade the "Lady of the Crimea" to join a women's suffrage organization.

Miss Nightingale had long admired Mill, had read his *Logic* three times and found it useful in her own studies, but had no personal acquaintance with him. She approached him in 1860 through the intermediary of Edwin Chadwick who paved the way by sending Mill a copy of her recently published *Notes on Nursing*. Mill assured Chadwick he would read the book although he had not had an illness which required nursing. Furthermore, he shared fully in the "admiration which is felt toward her more universally, I should think, than toward any other living person."[4]

To have Mill read *Notes on Nursing* was not, however, her immediate purpose in opening the correspondence. She was eager to have his criticism of her spiritual and philosophical speculations, *Suggestions for Thought to Seekers After Religious Truth,* written primarily in 1852. Making some revisions and additions after her return from the Crimea, she had a few copies of the three-volume, 829-page work privately printed in 1860. Specifically she wanted Mill's opinion as to whether the volumes should be published, the same question she addressed to Benjamin Jowett.

Mill, rather than Miss Nightingale, caused the correspondence to take a different direction than she had anticipated. As a result of reading her *Notes on Nursing,* he commented on one section of the little volume to Chadwick who passed his remarks on to her. Always sensitive to any reference to women's rights, he could hardly fail to notice her strictures on the subject which appeared at the conclusion in a paragraph too conspicuous to be missed, set in smaller type than the text. Earnestly advising her sisters to avoid two kinds of current jargon, she explained that the first was the

> rights of women which urges women to do all men do, including the medical and other professions, merely because men do it, and without regard to whether this *is* the best women can do.[5]

Secondly there was the jargon which admonished women to avoid everything men did

> merely because they are women, and should be "recalled to a sense of their duty," and because "this is women's work," and "that is men's" and "there are things which women should not do," which is all assertion and nothing more. Surely

> any woman should bring the best she has, *whatever* that is, to the work of God's world, without attending to either of these cries.[6]

In what amounted to a lecture on conduct, Miss Nightingale reminded her sisters of their obligation to perform good deeds without, however, paying any attention to talk about suitability of such acts since deeds were to be judged on merit alone. She trusted they would "leave these jargons, and go your own way straight to God's work in simplicity and singleness of heart."[7]

That Miss Nightingale's statements on women's rights might be accepted with the same authority as her advice on nursing was of genuine concern to Mill. *Notes on Nursing* was immensely popular, 15,000 copies of the first edition selling within a month of publication.[8] The book was in such demand that between the time Mill first read the troublesome passage and mentioned it to Chadwick Miss Nightingale published a revised and enlarged version. Describing the little book as "a work of genius according to the conscious or unconscious testimony of a miscellaneous multitude of readers," Harriet Martineau publicized it further in thirty pages of praise and summary in the *Quarterly Review*.[9] She remarked upon the section which bothered Mill and commended the author of *Notes of Nursing* for throwing a "strong light" on the "follies of the times."[10]

The author sent Mill a copy of the new edition and he noticed immediately that she had retained the lecture on jargon. He wrote Chadwick that he wished it had been omitted. To him its inclusion meant that Miss Nightingale gave the prestige of her name

> to the attempt to run down those who are contending that the only way in which either women or men can find out what they can and cannot do, is by being allowed to try; and that it is a gross injustice to women that men should pass sentence in the matter beforehand, by peremptorily excluding them from anything.[11]

Hearing of his comment, Miss Nightingale claimed that Mill had misunderstood what she had written. Pleased that she had not intended to give the impression her words actually conveyed, Mill wrote her that he thought this was the case since she also "seemed to imply that women should not be excluded by law or usage from the liberty of trying any mode of existence open to men, at their own risk in case of failure."[12] Unable to let the matter rest, he went on to tell her that this was exactly the contention of women's rights advocates who actually made too many concessions to the idea that women were unsuited for some occupations. Furthermore, he refused to believe women's rights advocates "can justly be accused of jargon, nor of contending that women ought to do certain things merely because men do them."[13]

Part of the differences between them was resolved when Miss Nightingale conceded that "from so great a master of language as yourself" she accepted Mill's interpretation of the passage in *Notes on Nursing.* Nevertheless, she was unwilling to admit he was right about her use of the term jargon. Protesting against his "assertion, that there is no such class as the one I designate as talking a 'jargon'," she reminded Mill tartly that she knew more about women than he did. He had never been as she had, "a 'scratting' female . . . among a world of 'scratting' females (and some very odd ones too)."[14]

Each approached the problem of women's rights in an entirely different fashion. Just as Miss Nightingale did, Mill's critics sometimes complained that he knew nothing about women. His approach to women's rights was highly abstract and intellectualized, based on concepts of legal and political equality. Her approach was intensely personal and based on wide experience with many women of different creeds and nationalities. Disappointed with that experience, discouraged by lack of progress in nursing and the little help she received in her crusade to reform the health of the British Army, she sometimes poured out her despair in letters to intimate friends, most of them women, in a more forthright manner than she ever did to Mill. In fact, there is more than a hint of disdain and contempt for women in some of her letters. To Madame Julius Mohl she wrote in 1861 that it was men who had helped her and that despite her work, her "doctrines have taken no hold among women." In short, she had "never found one woman who has altered her life by one iota for me or my opinions." The reason for this, she concluded, was that women lacked sympathy whereas she had found many men willing to help her out of sympathy. Consequently, "it makes me mad, the Women's Rights talk about 'the want of a field' for them . . ."[15] She said she would gladly pay five hundred pounds a year if she could find a woman secretary but it was impossible to get one.

Highly annoyed about the entire women's rights agitation, she referred from time to time in private correspondence, to the "enormous *jaw,* the infinite female ink which England pours forth on 'Woman's work!' It used to be said that people gave their *blood* to their country. Now they give their *ink.*"[16] Miss Nightingale had no patience with talk and writing about a field for women when she had opened one for them. In the second edition of *Notes on Nursing* she inserted a new section: a "Note upon Employment of Women." Contending that there were more employment opportunities for women than applicants, she cited her own experience in receiving hundreds of requests for nurses which had to remain unfilled. Blasting "female writers" who wrote about women's employment and their right to a field with adequate pay, she recommended that such writers should each train ten women for a demand already in existence.[17]

Her dislike of female writers on women's rights amounted to an obsession. Hearing that a book called *Impressions de Femme* was being published in Paris, she inquired of friends whether men published *Impressions d'Homme.* Unfortunately, she wrote, both men and women regarded women "as a great curiosity—a peculiar strange race, like the Aztecs; or rather like Dr. Howe's Idiots, whom, after the 'unremitting exertions of two years,' he 'actually taught to eat with a spoon.'"[18]

Yet despite these observations about women writers, she did maintain a friendly relationship, primarily through correspondence, with Harriet Martineau who as an editorial writer for the *Daily News* consistently advocated opening wider fields of employment to women. As early as 1854 she had called for opening the medical profession to women. Florence Nightingale often appeared in her columns as an example of a woman who had made nursing a respectable profession and in doing so had elevated the entire role of working women. She found Harriet Martineau a valuable ally as a means of influencing public opinion without attracting any particular attention to herself. In 1858 she sent her a copy of her *Notes on Matters Affecting the Health, Efficiency and Hospital Administration of the British Army,* warning, however, that it was not a public report. That information enabled Harriet Martineau to prepare a series of articles for the *Daily News* and to publish in book form in 1859 an exposé of the horrors of the Crimean War called *England and Her Soldiers.*[19] Since Miss Nightingale always insisted she was going to die momentarily, she wrote Miss Martineau that she had "a great horror" of the report being used after her death "by *Women's Missionaries* and those kinds of people." Additionally, she made it clear that she was "brutally indifferent to the wrongs or rights of my sex" just as she was equally indifferent to any "controversy as to whether women ought or ought not to do what I have done for the Army." Nevertheless any woman who refused to take advantage of such an opportunity should "be burnt alive."[20]

Indeed there seemed to be few things about women which suited Miss Nightingale. In private correspondence she complained that women knew little of the world. Not only were they ignorant of the names of cabinet ministers or the offices at the Horse Guard, they neither knew who was dead or alive nor even which churches had bishops.[21] She lectured on jargon and women's rights publicly in *Notes on Nursing,* and scattered throughout the text numerous comments about women's activities. They were criticized for giving unauthorized medicine to their friends, for being unobservant and unable to follow directions. Novelists were censured for their disservice to the nursing profession when they entertained the public with sentimental portrayals of "ladies disappointed in love . . . turning into the war hospitals to find their wounded lovers" and then abandoning the hospital for the lover.[22] Justly critical of the current state of nursing she digressed in the midst of a discussion of the noise problem in the sickroom to complain about dress and about women writers. It was, she wrote, peculiarly alarming that so many "female ink-bottles" were busy telling the world about women's "particular worth and general missionariness" at a time when their dress made them unsuited for anything useful at all, let alone a mission. The fashionable crinoline and starched petticoats that rustled and disturbed patients she regarded not only as a fire hazard but also as an affront to decency. When a woman wearing a crinoline leaned forward, Miss Nightingale said that she exposed just as much of herself as an opera dancer.[23] In fact, she quite agreed with Lord Melbourne's declaration that he preferred men around rather than women when he was sick since "it requires very strong health to put up with a woman."[24]

Perhaps because of these public pronouncements about writers on women's rights, Miss Nightingale hastened to assure Mill that when she talked about jargon she was not referring to anything he had written on the subject. Praising his work, she emphasized that "to every word of an article, called by your name on this subject, I heartily subscribe and defer." Clearly placing Mill in a distinctly different category from the "female ink-bottles" she wanted him to understand that "*this* is not the 'jargon' I mean."[25] Given her penchant for downgrading women writers on the subject perhaps her praise would have been considerably more restrained had she known that the 1851 *Westminster Review* essay, "Enfranchisement of Women," was more the work of Harriet Taylor than of Mill.[26]

When Miss Nightingale finally identified to Mill the perpetrators of jargon, they turned out to be the contingent of American women doctors led by Dr. Elizabeth Blackwell, the first woman doctor on the English Medical Register, who in 1859 gave a series of lectures in London, Manchester, Birmingham, and Liverpool, advocating the entry of women into the medical profession.[27] It was at that first London lecture, personally encouraged by Dr. Blackwell, that Elizabeth Garrett, later the celebrated Mrs. Garrett Anderson, made plans to study medicine.[28] Dr. Blackwell's novel activities were widely publicized, especially in the pages of the *Englishwoman's Journal* founded in 1858 to promote women's employment opportunities. The editors, Barbara Smith Bodichon and Bessie Rayner Parkes, aware of Dr. Blackwell's work in America, printed a lengthy biographical sketch of her in the first number of the *Journal,* helped prepare for her London lectures and in the 1860s included numerous articles and letters on the issue of women in medicine.[29] One such article written by a male physician announced that it was Miss Nightingale herself who provided the rationale for women doctors since probably there would no longer be any objection "to this new profession for ladies on the ground of its being unfeminine and indelicate, after the high and well deserved reputation achieved by Miss Florence Nightingale as a nurse."[30] Nursing exposed women to "far more repulsive and painful duties" than would be encountered in examining and prescribing for women and children.

From what Miss Nightingale communicated to Mill it would appear that only Dr. Blackwell and her followers were guilty of jargon, not the English women writers she denounced to her friends. She reasserted firmly that "Dr. Blackwell's world talks a 'jargon' and a very mischievous one—that their female M.D.'s have

taken up the worst part of a male M.D. ship of 30 years ago . . ."[31] In an effort not to attack Dr. Blackwell personally, she acknowledged to Mill that she was a good friend and that at one time she had hoped to work closely with her. In Miss Nightingale's appraisal of women in medicine as "third rate men" who "will fail in doing good" there was an apparent unwillingness either to accept women in the profession or to accept the same standard of accomplishment for them as for men. Because of her experiences in the Crimea she was, of course, unimpressed with the entire medical profession. If women were going to be doctors, she asserted, they should reform medicine not merely earn a living like the overwhelming majority of their male colleagues.[32] At the time she expressed her views to Mill no woman practiced medicine in England and none had yet been admitted to a medical school.[33] In the United States there were some 200 women doctors in a profession numbering about 555,000, few of whom were reformers of the Blackwell type.[34]

Mill's opinion of the medical profession was no higher than hers but he did point out that she could hardly expect the first few medical women to be of such high caliber as to make much of an improvement in the profession since first rate minds were, after all, very rare. He explained to her that women had a moral right to become doctors independent of their ability to reform the profession.[35] Despite her reluctant admission to Mill about women in medicine, "let all women try," Miss Nightingale never actually recommended that women study medicine. In a letter to "Dear Sisters" attached to her *Introductory Notes on Lying-In Institutions* (1871) she wrote that there was "a better thing for women to be than 'medical men,' and that is to be medical women."[36] By medical women she meant nurses and midwives and called upon educated women to pursue midwifery as a career.

Neither she nor Mill ever convinced the other about their differing views of the "jargon" of women's rights or the right of women to be in the medical profession. Yet despite such differences there were some areas of fundamental agreement about the social role of women. Mill recognized this when he read her *Practical Deductions,* the second volume of *Suggestions for Thought;* she sent the work in installments, fearful that he would not read all of it if three volumes arrived at once. Although she would never have called herself a feminist, there was one time in Miss Nightingale's life, consumed with pent-up anger and frustration, when she wrote one of the most moving and profoundly feminist statements in existence; a composition of furious intensity outlining concepts of religious thought combined with a penetratingly painful analysis of the experience of dutiful daughters in well-to-do households.

That fragment, called **"Cassandra,"** described the stultifying life exacted from women by the merciless restrictions of "conventional society, which men have made for women, and women have accepted . . ."[37] Women's lives were consumed by a dreary round of calls, of looking at pictures, of desultory reading aloud, of embroidery, and endless dinners. They were permitted no outlet for their passions, intellects, or moral activities which could not be satisfied in a "cold and oppressive conventional atmosphere."[38] Unable to deal with all the complexities of the subject, which would be nothing less than "the whole history of society, of the present state of civilization," Miss Nightingale still presented, in a few pages, a scathing indictment of a society which reduced women to spiritually and mentally impoverished creatures with no control over their lives. In examining the "poor lives" women led she concluded that the wonder was not that women were so bad but that they were so good.

Her most telling indictment of society and probably her most significant contribution was her explanation of the difference in the utilization of time by men and women. She painted a devastating picture of the laughter of society at a group of men sitting around a table in a drawing room all the morning looking at pictures and doing worsted work. But why was it perfectly acceptable for women to engage in such idle pursuits? She inquired whether a man's time was more valuable than a woman's or was the difference "that woman has confessedly nothing to do?" According to society

> women are never supposed to have occupation of sufficient importance *not* to be interrupted, except "suckling their fools"; and women themselves have accepted this, have written books to support it, and have trained themselves so as to consider whatever they do *not* of such value to the world or to others, but that they can throw it up at the first claim of social life . . . [39]

Consequently, women played through life and were robbed of their time because "it is laid down, that our time is of no value." Unable to control their own lives and their time women were taught that "it is wrong, ill-tempered, and a misunderstanding of 'woman's mission' (with a great M) if they do not allow themselves willingly to be interrupted at all hours."[40]

Having no patience with domestic life, **"Cassandra"** denounced the family as "too narrow a field for the development of an immortal spirit, be that spirit male or female." The family devoured people and was a system which "dooms some minds to incurable infancy, others to silent misery."[41] The "sacred hearth" was simply an institution from which sons escaped as soon as they were old enough and daughters left as soon as they could be married. The time had come for women to do something else rather than envelope themselves in the cocoon of that "sacred hearth" of domesticity.

Noticeably more impressed with the second volume of **Suggestions for Thought,** Mill wrote her that he had "seldom felt less inclined to criticism than in reading this book." Obviously referring to **"Cassandra,"** without, however, using the name, he complimented her on her presentation of life among the well-to-do classes. Her account was "so earnestly and feelingly and many parts of it so forcibly done" that it was "a testimony that ought not to be lost." Furthermore it was "an appeal of an unusually telling kind on a subject which it is very difficult to induce people to open their eyes to."[42] Mentioning that her reflections "were evidently the result of personal observation" Mill assumed, quite accurately, that she was "Cassandra."

At the time his correspondence with Miss Nightingale was in progress, Mill was working on the *Subjection of Women.* He noted in his *Autobiography* that the book was written during 1860 and 1861. As early as 1913 Sir Edward Cook, the official Nightingale biographer, asserted in a one sentence note without any supporting data that "a good deal of Mill's treatment of this branch of his subject recalls Miss Nightingale's *Suggestions.*"[43] An examination of **"Cassandra"** and Mill's treatise on women reinforces that opinion: that she had already anticipated in 1852 some of the arguments which appeared in his 1869 *Subjection of Women.* Admittedly, in any two compositions by thoughtful, perceptive individuals on the general condition of women similarities are almost inevitable. Yet in the discussion of certain themes, particularly the question of women's time and its relationship to their scholarly contributions, the similarities are too striking to be ignored.

**"Cassandra"** insisted that women's intellect remained unsatisfied because the "stimulus, the training, the time, are all wanting to us; or, in other words, the means and inducements are not there."[44] Attempting to answer the perennial question of why women had not made major contributions in literature, the arts, and the sciences, Mill listed the lack of opportunity to pursue systematic training and study which left women amateurs. He presented his elaboration of reasons for disparity in intellectual attainment in a two-dimensional framework of time: the problem of the individual woman's time as well as an historical discussion of the comparative lateness, about three generations previously, of women's endeavours in serious fields of study. It was questionable, he thought, whether sufficient time had yet elapsed for women to be expected to produce great works of originality. Furthermore, few women had time for scholarly pursuits which "may seem a paradox; yet it is an undoubted social fact."[45] His catalogue of a woman's daily routine—the care of a family and a household, her role in society, and necessary attention to dress—emphasized the ever present expectation that her time was at the command of everybody else.

Recognizing that the management of time was sex-related, Mill asked the same question as **"Cassandra"** when he inquired: "Are a woman's occupations, especially her chosen and voluntary ones, ever regarded as excusing her from any of what are termed the calls of society?"[46] His observation that it required an illness in the family or some other extraordinary development to enable a woman to devote any attention to her own affairs was almost a paraphrase of Miss Nightingale's plaint that "a married woman was heard to wish that she could break a limb that she might have a little time to herself."[47]

Women were denied useful work and yet their time was consumed with the trivialities of conventional idleness, as Miss Nightingale called the life-style of women in her circles. Mill listed the same activities: "the dinner parties, concerts, evening parties, morning visits, letter writing, and all that goes with them."[48] The physical strain of that life, **"Cassandra"** said, resulted in an "accumulation of nervous energy, which has had nothing to do during the day; makes them feel every night, when they go to bed, as if they were going mad; and they are obliged to lie long in bed in the morning to let it evaporate and keep it down."[49] Examining that problem Mill reasoned that women's "nervous susceptibility" which allegedly made them unsuited for anything other than domestic functions was one of the principal objections to their participation in the higher echelon of serious work. All the characteristics associated with that nervous susceptibility, he decided, were nothing more than the "mere overflow of nervous energy run to waste and would cease when the energy was directed to a definite end."[50] Women who worked, Mill said, exhibited none of the "morbid characteristics" associated with upper class women brought up like "hot house plants."[51] That nervous temperament which the professional and political world held against women was not, however, solely a feminine characteristic since "the most brilliant examples of success are continually given by the men of high nervous sensibility." Mill believed that people who possessed such a temperament or sustained spirit were especially suited for the "executive department of the leadership of mankind." They were the ones who had "the material of great orators, great preachers, impressive diffusers of moral influence."[52]

For several pages in the *Subjection of Women,* Mill was, in effect, describing Miss Nightingale's life during her "Cassandra" phase. He must have had her in mind when he wrote that if a woman "has a study or a pursuit, she must snatch any short interval which accidentally occurs to be employed in it."[53] Referring directly to her, he acknowledged that "a celebrated woman, in a work which I hope will some day be published, remarks truly that everything a woman does is done at odd times."[54]

Both regarded family as an instrument of tyranny. He called it a "school of despotism" but also said that properly constituted it could be the "real school of the virtues of freedom."[55] With a philosopher's more comprehensive view, his indictment of the family in the *Subjection of Women* was even more severe than hers as well as more generalized in its social effects. Identifying the family as the culprit in the continuing subordination of women to men, Mill claimed that women's "disabilities elsewhere are only clung to in order to maintain their subordination in domestic life; because the generality of the male sex cannot yet tolerate the idea of living with an equal."[56] She wrote from first hand experience of the tediousness and "tyrannous trifling" of her own family life. Without carrying it to the same point Mill did, there are indications that she had come to, or with further study might have arrived at, approximately the same conclusions. Writing of the unhappy woman who was asked whether she would abolish domestic life, "Cassandra" replied: "Men are afraid that their houses will not be so comfortable, that their wives will make themselves 'remarkable' women, that they will make themselves distasteful to men."[57] As a result women tried to convince themselves that the domestic sphere was their life. The *Subjection of Women* was the culmination of his years of reflection on the condition of women.[58] Her **"Cassandra"** was written in a period of intense desperation in 1852 at the family estate where her principal occupations were supervising the stillroom, counting silver and linen, passing the time in conventional idleness, and at odd moments writing *Suggestions for Thought.*

His last letter in 1860 encouraging Miss Nightingale to publish *Suggestions for Thought* remained unanswered, seven years elapsing before the correspondence was resumed at his initiative. By then women's rights had ceased to be merely the agitation of a few "female inkbottles" and had become a political movement with Mill's introduction on May 20, 1867 of a women's suffrage amendment on the Second Reform Bill.[59] Aware that she had refused to sign the first women's suffrage petition which he presented to the House of Commons in 1866, he made a point of writing to notify her about the London National Society for Women's Suffrage and to solicit her support for it. Explaining that many people, especially women, did not seem to realize the power of the political process which "is by far the greatest that it is possible to wield for human happiness," he told her that the new organization hoped to strike at the very evils she recognized as having such a harmful effect upon the character of women.[60] In what amounted to a challenge to a woman who lived in such retirement that it was often supposed she was no longer alive, Mill expressed disapproval both of women who refused to accept political responsibility and of men who tried to prevent them from having any such power. He further announced his conviction that until women directly and openly began to use political power the "evils" of which she was "peculiarly aware can never be satisfactorily dealt with."[61]

Conceding to Mill that women should have the vote and that it was important for married women to be persons and to control their own property, Miss Nightingale still believed that greater "evils" afflicted women than the lack of a vote. Furthermore, it would be years before he would be able to obtain women's votes. She made it clear to Mill that she had never suffered any personal deprivation because of that disability, asserting proudly that she could not have had more administrative influence than she had wielded in her eleven years of activity in government offices than if she "had been a borough returning two M.P.'s."[62] Politely agreeing with him that women should be open and direct about political power she explained that her personal preference was to work behind the scenes, believing that indirect method the most effective for her.

In launching a new social and political movement it was important to Mill that he persuade Miss Nightingale of the necessity for women of her caliber to become active participants.[63] Deploring her insistence on keeping her own work publicly unknown, his greatest regret was that most women seemed to share that characteristic. He thought it would have a salutary effect for the world to know "how much of all its important work is and always has been done by women."[64] Going to considerable pains to answer all her questions, his lengthy reply was literally a lecture on the fundamental principles of political liberty much of which can be read in *Considerations on Representative Government.* Unlike Miss Nightingale, he did not believe that legislative altruism would ever eliminate the present women's disabilities without their having the franchise. He told her that ruling bodies considered such questions urgently only when they were confronted with the possibility of the ruled obtaining political power. Even if present disabilities were swept away there was no guarantee that new ones might not arise the next day. The only way he saw of ensuring the justice of future legislation was to "either make men perfect or give women an equal voice in their own affairs."[65] He left her to decide which was the easiest.

Mill argued that women's enfranchisement would be more readily obtained than any of the other reforms for women which would, he thought, "inevitably follow from it."[66] To work for other measures first he compared to simply cutting branches away and leaving the tree trunk standing. This was always Mill's optimistic position on women's rights: once women had the franchise their political power would be sufficient to remedy other problems. He further assured Miss Nightingale, who had worried that enfranchisement would arouse political partisanship between men and women, that he did not foresee that the results would be any worse than at present. The possession of political power, he was convinced, "is the only security against every form of oppression" and would cause men to regard women with more respect since they presently looked upon women "as a few dearly loved pre-eminently worthy and charming persons and a great number of helpless fools."[67]

Mill's plea for political activism left Miss Nightingale unmoved. Even his arguments of a moral duty toward society to work toward the fulfillment of deeply held convictions had no effect. In terms of active commitment it is undeniable that Florence Nightingale did little for the cause Mill championed. Eventually she became a member of the National Society for Women's Suffrage, contributed money, but refused to give her time. However, it must have been a source of gratification to Mill to have her name head the list of the 50,000-signature petition for women's suffrage he presented to the House of Commons in 1868. In 1878 she relented sufficiently to write a brief paragraph for the leaflet "Opinions of Women

on Women's Suffrage." Claiming she had no reasons for the suffrage she proceeded to give the basic one: the axiom of taxation and representation.[68] Her declaration had a long life and was still being referred to as late as 1915.[69] Yet her most explicit statement about women's franchise indicated her lack of faith in the process. She added the caveat that she expected little from it.

Miss Nightingale never agreed with Mill's faith in the efficacy of the franchise. She once wrote Benjamin Jowett that "if women were to get the vote immediately Mr. Mill would be disappointed with the result." She wondered if the starving wives and daughters of workhouse paupers would be helped and whether "Mr. Mill really believes that the giving of any woman a vote will lead to the removal of even the least of these evils?"[70] He pinned his hopes on the active political process as a prerequisite for other social goals. She retained her skepticism about the franchise while simultaneously admitting that without representation there could be no freedom or progress.

Their correspondence ended in 1867 still without any personal acquaintance. Hearing of Mill's death in 1873 she expressed her shock to a friend, recalling how he had urged her to publish her work. Absorbed in other projects she had no time to revise *Suggestions for Thought* for publication although she did publish some portions on religion as articles in *Fraser's Magazine.*[71] Women's rights, in the political sense, remained low on her list of priorities. Her lifetime work was health and sanitation. Characteristically after Mill's death she wrote his friend Edwin Chadwick inquiring about the sanitation of Mill's house in Avignon. Chadwick could only tell her he knew nothing about it and had never been invited there.[72]

To a degree the Nightingale-Mill debate on women's rights mirrors the public debate which went on for years in newspapers, periodicals, and the House of Commons which regularly defeated bills for women's suffrage until 1918. Yet Mill's effort to convert Miss Nightingale to his mode of thought and political activism was not a debate with someone who refused to believe in the vote for women but with a woman who simply regarded it as of minor importance. In her own experience she did not see that legal restrictions had hampered her activities. Cushioned by wealth and social position she had no necessity to earn her own living in a day when thousands of women took any ill-paid job they could find. As a single woman she could control her own property, although for years her father gave her an allowance for five hundred pounds per year which she always overspent.

Eager for women to be involved in socially useful work she nonetheless expected that work to be done quietly and without fanfare. Despite the fact that few individuals knew more from firsthand experience of the tyranny of social conventions than she did, there was still little recognition on her part that such barriers had to be breached before more than a small number of women could enlarge their roles to lead the useful lives she envisioned. She had broken through and provided an example for other women. Her inability to perceive that her own situation had been truly unique and her lack of this perception in relation to the problem of the masses of women is at the heart of her lack of comprehension of Mill's viewpoint. Consequently she refused to acknowledge that reformers such as Dr. Blackwell and the "female ink bottles" were performing a vitally necessary educational function. Her own idiosyncratic hatred of publicity and her extreme retreat from the world, her method of controlling her own life, led her to regard such women as little more than publicity seekers. Furthermore they did not fit her definition of a good woman whom she characterized in 1881 in one of her many letters to nurses as having the attributes of "quietness, gentleness, patience, endurance, forbearance."[73] It is ironic that a woman of genius, demonic energy, iron will, and a profoundly manipulative spirit, listed precisely the characteristics of the idealized Victorian woman. Such a code of behavior did not lend itself either to polemical writing about women's rights or to political activism.

It was the prison of upper class social conventions, not legal restrictions, that had stifled Miss Nightingale in her younger years. **"Cassandra"** was a cry for freedom and time to engage in useful work and for women to control their own lives. In it was not so much as a hint of concern with either the vote or women's property rights. The basic issue of legal equality was ignored.[74] A woman of thirty-two when she wrote it, she was still unfree to follow her calling which to her was the same as a religious vocation. Once she began to escape, and she finally escaped through a war that brought her international fame and prestige, the document and its sentiments apparently ceased to have the same importance to her. It is significant that Miss Nightingale never made any reference to **"Cassandra"** in her correspondence with Mill.

Yet it was her second volume of *Suggestions for Thought* containing **"Cassandra"** which fully convinced him that her work should be published. Appreciating the value of her reflections, he wrote her that "few books have a better chance than this of doing some good" especially if she published it under her own name:

> Indeed, the mere fact that these are the opinions of such a woman as all the world knows you to be, is a fact which it would be of as much use to the world to know, as almost anything which could at this time be told to it.[75]

Despite such praise there was never any effort on her part to publish it. During her lifetime and for almost a generation after her death it remained buried in *Suggestions for Thought* until Rachel Strachey rescued it from oblivion and published it in *The Cause* in 1928.[76] Had she published her *Suggestions for Thought*, **"Cassandra"** might well have taken its rightful place at the time, without waiting for twentieth-century recognition, in the list of significant nineteenth-century feminist manifestoes. That fragment, in some respects, corresponds to the kind of work Mill described in the *Subjection of Women*. In terms of speculative thought he wrote of the person who "has by natural sagacity a happy intuition, which he can suggest, but cannot prove, which yet when matured, may be an important addition to knowledge."[77] Women often had ideas which were lost to the world either because of lack of help in bringing them forward in an acceptable manner within the context of existing knowledge, or because help received made their ideas appear as someone else's contribution. Consequently, no one could say how many original concepts, credited to men, actually belonged to women. Using his own case as an example, Mill said it was "a very large proportion indeed."[78] In the end she listened to Benjamin Jowett who advised against publication rather than to Mill, probably the only sympathetic reader of **"Cassandra"** during her lifetime. Jowett's advice is a poignant reminder that Mill had explained in the *Subjection of Women* that "few women writers dare tell anything which men, on whom their literary success depends, are unwilling to hear."[79]

The correspondence was more valuable to Mill than it was to her. When she read his *Subjection of Women* she said he had "quoted" her "stuff" as she called it and declared he should not have done it.[80] Actually Mill had not quoted anything from **"Cassandra"** in any formal sense of the word but had relied upon it for elaboration and verification of the life-style of a class of women whom she knew well from practical experience while his knowledge was primarily theoretical. Reading **"Cassandra"** enabled him to present more vivid, concrete examples of the activities of upper class women and their problems with time, without however, altering in any degree the central argument of the *Subjection of Women*—the equality of the sexes, an argument which does not appear in her work. Although early in their correspondence she assured Mill that she agreed with every word in the "Enfranchisement of Women," that declaration was obviously one of her tactful, diplomatic statements which did not necessarily coincide with her own personal views. She was, after all, attempting to gain a favorable opinion from him about her own writing. Little in her activities would indicate that she approved of the course of action recommended in the 1851 Taylor-Mill essay which was one of the early declarations of the rights of women to be admitted to full participation in political life, the professions, and other employment, as well as a denunciation of the traditional feminine spheres of activity. Neither the essay, her correspondence with Mill, the female "ink bottles," nor the *Subjection of Women* change her own frame of reference. Relying solely on her own experiences, Miss Nightingale's pragmatic impulses emerged in a narrow definition of the role of women in the professions. She would enlarge their role only to the minimum extent possible to encompass nursing and midwifery, old traditional spheres of female activity fallen into disrepute to be made newly respectable by the force of her own example and prestige.

Once she was in a position to control her own time and life, which she did with systematic ruthlessness, it was as if she had never written **"Cassandra,"** and bewailed the lack of opportunity for women to follow their own goals. Some of that earlier understanding of and sympathy with the general condition of women, however imperfect and class biased it may have been, seemed to evaporate. Her reaction to women in medicine is a case in point. It is revealing to note that Dr. Blackwell found it impossible to work with Miss Nightingale in her proposed school for nurses when she was told that her own private practice would be incompatible with the project.[81] In 1860 women in medicine were "third rate men." In 1852 "Cassandra" had written that women sometimes longed to enter "some man's profession where they will find direction, competition (or rather opportunity of measuring intellect with others) and, above all time."[82] In later years she softened slightly towards the women's rights movement and in 1896 inquired of a friend how the vote would help women: "I am afraid I have been too much enraged by vociferous ladies talking on things they know nothing at all about to think of the rank and file."[83] She was eighty in 1900 and in a letter to her nurses she indicated an awareness that the status of women had changed for the better: "Woman was the home drudge. Now she is the teacher." But she warned that women should not lose this new position "by being the Arrogant—the 'Equal with men.' She does not forfeit it by being the help 'meet'."[84] Yet in her old age she did select a well known woman doctor, May Thorne, as her personal physician.[85]

The areas of divergence between Mill and Miss Nightingale emerge most clearly in their application of theory to social action. To her the solution depended upon individual action; women could solve their problems by perseverance and hard work. Aside from his sympathy with the struggles of individual women, Mill saw the larger social problem to be solved by making women equal political partners with men so as to gain control of their lives and to share in the political process. Life had equipped Miss Nightingale with little understanding of the legal basis of society and the democratic process, while that process was at the heart of Mill's argument. Depending upon personal and elitist influence to accomplish her objectives, her methods were, after all, the time-honored ones of the upper classes of England. Her influence was granted only on the basis of her prestige and personal relationships rather than on the basis of any legally constituted power. A suffrage speaker commented in 1870 on the curious situation of women like Florence Nightingale who were consulted by men on political questions and whose views influenced masses of people. That kind of power was perfectly acceptable but such women were prohibited from voting for members of parliament and exerting their influence in an open, natural fashion.[86] As a practical matter, which she undoubtedly realized, she could only have such influence if she did not insist it was due as a matter of political principle. In approaching the women's problem, Miss Nightingale would chop the branches off the tree while Mill attacked the trunk.

NOTES

[1] "Florence Nightingale as a Leader in the Religious and Civic thought of her Times," *Hospitals*, X (July, 1936), 78-84. There are a total of ten letters, five from each, in the correspondence. Three of Mill's letters to Nightingale, with some omissions and two of them identified only as "To a Correspondent," were published in Hugh S. R. Elliot, *Letters of John Stuart Mill*, (London, 1910). Some of her letters to him with portions of his replies were published in Sir Edward Cook's official biography, *Life of Florence Nightingale*, (London, 1913). (The edition of Cook used in this essay is the 1914 printing).

[2] The clearest expression of Mill's views on women appears in his 1869 *Subjection of Women*, Comments on the women's question are scattered throughout earlier works including his "Periodical Literature: Edinburgh Review," *Westminster Review*, I (April, 1824), 505-41: "Rationale of Political Representation," *Ibid*, XXIX (July, 1835), 341-71. Of particular interest is his discussion in the *Principles of Political Economy* on the social independence of women, the question of women and wages and the population problem. See John M. Robson (ed.), *Principles of Political Economy*, (Toronto, 1965) in John M. Robson (gen. ed.), *Collected Works of John Stuart Mill* (Toronto, 1963—), II, 372-73, 393-96; III, 952-53. The special legislative interest of women is referred to in "Thoughts on Parliamentary Reform," (1859) in Gertrude Himmelfarb, *Essays on Politics and Culture by John Stuart Mill*, (New York, 1963), p. 328. See also the discussion of women and the suffrage in F.A. Hayek (ed.), *Considerations on Representative Government*, (Chicago, 1962), pp. 187-92. For recent commentaries see Gertrude Himmelfarb, *On Liberty and Liberalism: The Case of John Stuart Mill* (New York, 1974), especially pp. 169-275, and the chapter on Mill in Susan Moller Okin, *Women in Western Political Thought* (Princeton, 1979), pp. 197-230.

[3] Only a selection of the numerous studies are mentioned here. Aside from the standard Cook biography (1913) and Cecil Woodham-Smith's *Florence Nightingale* (New York, 1951) see also Lytton Strachey's acerbic portrait of her in his *Eminent Victorians* (London, 1918), pp. 135-200 and Rachel Strachey's sympathetic account in *The Cause: A Short History of the Women's Movement in Great Britain* (London, 1928), pp. 18-29. Other accounts include Sarah Tooley, *Life of Florence Nightingale* (London, 1913); Ida B. O'Malley, *Florence Nightingale: A Study of Her Life Down to the End of the Crimean War* (London, 1931) and Margaret Goldsmith, *Florence Nightingale: the Woman and the Legend* (London, 1937). For the nursing profession see Lucy Seymer, *Florence Nightingale's Nurses: The Nightingale Training School, 1860-1960* (London, 1960); Barbara Harmelink, *Florence Nightingale: Founder of*

*Modern Nursing* (New York, 1965); Brian Abel-Smith, *A History of the Nursing Profession* (London, 1960) and Vern L. and Bonnie Bullough, *The Care of the Sick: the Emergence of Modern Nursing* (New York, 1978). See also F.L. Berry, "Florence Nightingale's Influence on Military Medicine," *Bulletin of the New York Academy of Medicine*, XXXII (1957), 451-553. Her own writings as well as some accounts by others are extensively annotated in William John Bishop and Sue Goldie, *A Bio-Bibliography of Florence Nightingale* (London, 1962).

[4] Mill to Edwin Chadwick, Feb. 7, 1860, in Francis E. Mineka and Dwight W. Lindley (eds.), *The Later Letters of John Stuart Mill* (Toronto, 1972), in Robson (ed.) (hereafter *Later Letters: Collected Works), Collected Works of John Stuart Mill, XVII, 2009*. An account of Mill's life is in Michael St. John Packe, *The Life of John Stuart Mill* (New York, 1954). For Mill's long friendship with Chadwick see Samuel E. Finer, *The Life and Times of Sir Edwin Chadwick* (1952; rpt. New York, 1970). See also R. A. Lewis, *Edwin Chadwick and the Public Health Movement, 1832-1854* (London, 1952). Chadwick along with Nassau W. Senior drafted the report which became the Poor Law of 1834 and was secretary to the Poor Law Commissioners. He was later Commissioner of the Board of Health, 1848-54, Miss Nightingale's ally in health reform, and was consulted on details of the Crimean Sanitary Commission.

[5] Florence Nightingale, *Notes on Nursing: What it is and What it is Not* (London, 1859), p. 79.

[6] *Ibid.*

[7] *Ibid.*

[8] Florence Nightingale, *Notes on Nursing*, foreword by Virginia Dunbar (1860; rpt. New York, 1969), p. xviii. By 1946 the book had been printed at least fifty times.

[9] Harriet Martineau, "Miss Nightingale's 'Notes on Nursing,'" *Quarterly Review*, LVII (April, 1860), 392-422. See also "A Reverie after Reading Miss Nightingale's Notes on Nursing," *Fraser's Magazine*, CXI (June, 1860), 753-57.

[10] *Ibid.*, p. 412.

[11] Mill to Chadwick, Aug. 27, 1860 in *Later Letters: Collected Works*, XVII, 2010.

[12] Mill to Nightingale, Sept. 10, 1860 in *Hospitals*, X, 79; *Later Letters: Collected Works*, XV, 706-07.

[13] *Ibid.*

[14] Nightingale to Mill, Sept. 12, 1860 in *Hospitals*, X, 79.

[15] Cook, *Life of Nightingale*, II, 14.

[16] *Ibid.*, p. 142.

[17] Florence Nightingale, *Notes on Nursing: What it is and What it is Not* (rev. ed., London, 1860), pp. 219-20.

[18] Cook, *Life of Nightingale*, II, 315.

[19] Robert K. Webb, *Harriet Martineau: A Radical Victorian* (London, 1960), p. 353. For her articles in the *Daily News* on women see Webb's *Handlist of Contributions to the Daily News by Harriet Martineau* (Typescript, Library of Congress, 1959). See also Valerie Kossew Pichanick, "An Abominable Submission: Harriet Martineau's Views on the Role and Place of Women," *Women's Studies*, V (1977), 13-32.

[20] Cook, *Life of Nightingale*, I, 285.

[21] Strachey, *The Cause*, p. 25.

[22] Nightingale, *Notes* (rev. ed., 1860), p. 192.

[23] *Ibid.*, pp. 66-68.

[24] *Ibid.* p. 67.

[25] Nightingale to Mill, Sept. 12, 1860, in *Hospitals*, X, 79.

[26] The precise authorship of the article originally published in the *Westminster Review*, LV (July 1851), 289-311, is still questioned. Mill did not acknowledge publicly Harriet Taylor's authorship until after her death when he reprinted the essay in his *Dissertations and Discussions* (1859). This question is part of the complex problem of her influence on Mill about which an extensive literature has developed. See F. A. Hayek, *John Stuart Mill and Harriet Taylor: Their Friendship and Subsequent Marriage* (Chicago, 1951); R. P. Anschutz, "J.S. Mill, Carlyle and Mrs. Taylor," *Political Science*, VII (March, 1955), 65-75; H.O. Pappe, "The Mills and Harriet Taylor," *Ibid.*, (March, 1956), 19-30; H.O. Pappe, *John Stuart Mill and the Harriet Taylor Myth* (Melbourne, 1960); F.E. Mineka, "The Autobiography and the Lady," *University of Toronto Quarterly*, XXXII (April, 1963), 301-06; J.M. Robson, "Harriet Taylor and John Stuart Mill: Artist and Scientist, "Queen's Quarterly LXXIII (Summer, 1966), 167-86, and Glenn K.S. Man," John Stuart Mill and Harriet Taylor," *Antigonish Review*, XIV (Summer, 1973), 43-50. For an analysis of the question see John M. Robson, *The Improvement of Mankind: The Social and Political Thought of John Stuart Mill* (Toronto, 1968), pp. 50-68. The essay is reprinted in Alice Rossi, *Essays on Sex Equality* (Chicago, 1970) with an introduction which credits Taylor rather than Mill with the authorship of the article.

[27] For a brief account of these lectures see Elizabeth Blackwell, *Opening the Medical Profession to Women* (London, 1895), pp. 216-19. For Dr. Blackwell see Mary St. John Fancout, *They Dared to be Doctors: Elizabeth Blackwell and Elizabeth Garrett Andreson* (London, 1965); Carol Lopate, *Women in Medicine* (Baltimore, 1968), and Geoffrey Marks and William K. Beatty, *Women in White* (New York, 1972).

[28] See the accounts of Mrs. Anderson by her daughter Louisa Garrett Anderson, *Elizabeth Garrett Anderson, 1836-1917* (London, 1939) and Jo Manton, *Elizabeth Garrett, M.D.* (London, 1960).

[29] Anna Blackwell, "Elizabeth Blackwell," *English-woman's Journal,* I (April, 1858), 80-100; Elizabeth and Emily Blackwell, "Medicine as a Profession for Women," *Ibid.,* V (May 1, 1860), 145-60; Elizabeth Blackwell, "Letter to Young Ladies Desirous of Studying Medicine," *Ibid.,"* IV (Jan., 1860) 329-32; "Harriot K. Hunt: A Sanitary Reformer," *Ibid.,* (Feb., 1860) 375-86; By a Physician of Twenty Years Standing, "Female Physicians," *Ibid.,* IX (April, 1862), 138-41; "Letters of Female Physicians," *Ibid.,* IX (May, 1862), 195-200.

[30] By a Physician, "Medical Education for Ladies," *Ibid.,* V (July, 1860), 320.

[31] Nightingale to Mill, Sept. 12, 1860 in *Hospitals,* X, 79.

[32] *Ibid.* A more favorable view of her attitude toward the medical profession as well as a discussion of her friendship with Dr. Blackwell is given in Sir Zachary Cope, *Florence Nightingale and the Doctors* (London, 1958).

[33] For the development of the movement in Great Britain to admit women to the medical profession see Elizabeth Garrett Anderson, "The History of a Movement," *Fortnightly Review,* LIX (March, 1893), 404-17; Sophia Jex-Blake, "Medical Women," *Nineteenth Century,* XXII (Nov., 1877), 692-707; Florence F. Miller, "Pioneer Medical Women: A Record and Remembrance," *Fortnightly Review,* CXX (Nov., 1924) 692-706; Martha Wallstein, *History of Women in Medicine* (London, 1908); Margaret Todd, *Life of Sophia Jex-Blake* (London, 1918) and Enid Bell, *Storming the Citadel: Rise of the Woman Doctor* (London, 1953).

[34] See statistical data drawn primarily from Virginia Penny, *The Employment of Women: A Cyclopedia of Woman's Work* (Boston, 1863) and U.S. Bureau of Census in Mary Rath Walsh, *"Doctors Wanted No Women Need Apply": Sexual Barriers in the Medical Profession* (New Haven, 1977), p. 186.

[35] Mill to Nightingale, Sept. 23, 1860 in *Hospitals,* X, 80; *Later Letters: Collected Works,* XV, 708-11.

[36] Quoted in Woodham-Smith, *Nightingale,* p. 305. For a discussion of the problems associated with establishment of schools for midwives see Jean Donnison, "Medical Women and Lady Midwives: A Case Study in Medical and Feminist Politics," *Women's Studies,* III (1976, 229-50, and her *Midwives and Medical Men: A History of the Inter-Professional Rivalries and Women's Rights* (New York, 1977).

[37] Nightingale, "Cassandra," in Strachey, *The Cause,* p. 396.

[38] *Ibid.,* p. 398.

[39] *Ibid.,* p. 401.

[40] *Ibid.,* p. 403.

[41] *Ibid.,* p. 404.

[42] Mill to Nightingale, Oct. 4, 1860 in *Hospitals,* X, 81; *Later Letters: Collected Works,* XV, 711-12.

[43] Cook, *Life of Nightingale,* I, 471.

[44] "Cassandra," p. 399.

[45] J.S. Mill, *The Subjection of Women* (New York, 1870), p. 136.

[46] *Ibid.,* p. 139.

[47] *Ibid.,* "Cassandra," p. 402.

[48] *Ibid.,* p. 137.

[49] "Cassandra," p. 408.

[50] Mill, *Subjection,* p. 111.

[51] *Ibid.*

[52] *Ibid.,* p. 114.

[53] *Ibid.,* p. 139.

[54] *Ibid.*

[55] *Ibid.,* p. 81.

[56] *Ibid.,* p. 91.

[57] "Cassandra," p. 415.

[58] For the *Subjection of Women see* Anne Tatalovich, "John Stuart Mill—The Subjection of Women: An Analysis," *Southern Quarterly Review,* XII (Oct., 1973), 87-105; Susan M. Okin, "John Stuart Mill's Feminism: The Subjection of Women and the Improvement of Mankind," *New Zealand Journal of History,* VII (Oct., 1973), 105-27; Jacques Kornberg, "Feminism and the Liberal Dialectic: John Stuart Mill on Women's Rights," *Historical Papers, 1974* (Canadian Historical Association, 1974), 37-63; and Julia Annas, "Mill and the Subjection of Women," *Philosophy,* LII (April, 1977), 179-94.

[59] See Barbara Caine, "John Stuart Mill and the English Women's Movement," *Historical Studies: Australia and New Zealand,* XIX (April, 1978), 52-67 and Evelyn L. Pugh, "John Stuart Mill and the Women's Question in Parliament, 1865-1868," *The Historian,* XLII (May, 1980), 399-418.

[60] Mill to Nightingale, August 9, 1867 in *Hospitals,* X, 82; *Later Letters: Collected Works,* XVI, 1302-03.

[61] *Ibid.*

[62] Nightingale to Mill, August 11, 1867, *ibid.*

[63] Cf. Mill's letters of August 4, 1867 to Mary Thompson and August 9, 1867 to Mary Carpenter in *Later Letters Collected Works,* XVI, 1300; 1302. In letters to influential men of his acquaintance he usually asked the support of their wives for the new Society. For an account of the early years of that organization see A.P.W. Robson, "The Founding of the National Society for Women's Suffrage, 1866-1867," *Canadian Journal of History,* XIII (March, 1973), 1-23.

[64] Mill to Nightingale, December 31, 1867 in *Hospitals,* X, 83; *Later Letters: Collected Works,* XVI, 1343-46. Contemporaries noticed how difficult it was to find out about her work but one commentator said that her "toils must be known in due time." See "Something of What Florence Nightingale Has Done and Is Doing," *St. James Magazine,* I (April, 1861), 22-40. Her secretiveness in keeping her work hidden for which she seldom received credit is discussed in both the Cook and Woodham-Smith biographies. As only one example, Woodham-Smith, *Nightingale,* p. 266 notes that her system of cost-accounting for the Army Medical Services remained in effect until after World War II.

[65] *Ibid.* See similar statements on this question in *Subjection of Women,* p. 144.

[66] *Ibid.*

[67] *Ibid.*

[68] Text of her opinion printed in Bishop and Goldie, *Bio-Bibliography,* p. 110.

[69] Susan B. Anthony and Elizabeth Cady Stanton et al., *History of Woman Suffrage* (1881-1922, rpt., New York, 1969), V., 461. See resolution of 1915 convention of North American Woman's Suffrage Association.

[70] Quoted in Woodham-Smith, *Nightingale,* p. 312. For her friendship with Jowett see Geoffrey C. Faber, *Jowett: A Portrait with Background* (London, 1959), pp. 306-13; 332-36.

[71] Two of the articles were published: "A 'Note' of Interrogation," *Fraser's Magazine,* n.s. VII (May, 1873), 567-77; "A Sub-note of Interrogation: What Will Our Religion be in 1999?" *Ibid.* n.s. VIII (July, 1873), 25-36. The third one, "On What Government Night will Mr. Lowe Bring Out Our New Moral Budget? Another Sub-Note of Interrogation," was rejected by Froude and never published. See Bishop and Goldie, *A Bio-Bibliography,* pp. 121-22.

[72] Cook, *Nightingale,* II, 222.

[73] Quoted in Bishop and Goldie, *Bio-Bibliography,* p. 43. Some of her letters to nurses are in Roaslind Nash (ed.), *Florence Nightingale to her Nurses: A Selection from Miss Nightingale's Addresses to Probationers and Nurses of the Nightingale School at St. Thomas's Hospital* (London, 1914).

[74] Elaine Showalter reveals that the copy of "Cassandra" which was printed in *Suggestions for Thought* and published in Strachey's *The Cause* was a considerably truncated version of a manuscript originally designed as a novel which went through a great many changes and revisions. Her examination of the different versions of the manuscript indicates that even after the plan of the novel was abandoned it was ruthlessly cut in a number of places and that some of Miss Nightingale's strongest feminist pronouncements do not appear in the printed volume. She says that the "suppression of *Suggestions for Thought* which included her best-known feminist essay, *Cassandra,* is one of the most unfortunate sagas of Victorian censorship of female anger, protest, and passion." Showalter, "Florence Nightingale," *Signs,* VI, 396. My own comments on "Cassandra" are based solely on the version Miss Nightingale sent to Mill in *Suggestions for Thought* as it appeared in Strachey's *The Cause.*

[75] Mill to Nightingale, October 4, 1860 in *Hospitals,* X, 81; *Later Letters: Collected Works,* XV, 711-12.

[76] It has recently been reprinted with an introduction by Myra Stark, *Florence Nightingale's Cassandra* (Old Westbury, N.Y., 1979).

[77] Mill, *Subjection,* p. 131.

[78] *Ibid.,* p. 132.

[79] *Ibid.,* p. 49.

[80] Cook, *Nightingale,* II, 221.

[81] *Blackwell, Opening the Medical Profession to Women,* p. 218.

[82] "Cassandra," p. 400.

[83] Quoted in Woodham-Smith, *Nightingale,* p. 32.

[84] Quoted in Bishop and Goldie, *Bio-Bibliography,* p. 47.

[85] Cope, *Nightingale and the Doctors,* p. 147. May Thorne was the daughter of Mrs. Isabel Thorne who along with Sophia Jex-Blake and three other women first attended the Medical School of the University of Edinburgh. She continued her mother's tradition of long association with the London School of Medicine for Women. See Isabel Thorne, *A Sketch of the Foundation*

*of the London Medical School for Women* (London, 1905) and Edythe Lutzker, *Women Gain a Place in Medicine* (New York, 1969).

[86] Speech of Jacob Bright to *Annual Meeting [1870] of Edinburgh Branch of the National Society for Women's Suffrage* (Edinburgh, 1870), p. 15.

## Barbara T. Gates (essay date 1987)

SOURCE: "Not Choosing Not To Be: Victorian Literary Responses to Suicide," in *Literature and Medicine,* Vol. 6, edited by D. Heyward Brock, The Johns Hopkins University Press, 1987, pp. 77-91.

[*In the following excerpt, Gates examines Nightingale's struggle with thoughts of suicide prompted by her early role as an idle, upper middle-class Victorian woman.*]

I have written elsewhere about Victorian medical opinion on suicide and about its relationship to English law and Victorian social and intellectual history.[1] Briefly, throughout the Victorian era, suicide was illegal, considered "self-murder" by the courts; until 1870 the goods and chattels of a suicide were legally forfeited to the Crown. But by the 1830s, coroner's juries had begun heavily to utilize a loophole in the law: they found more and more suicides "temporarily insane," a verdict which negated forfeiture and thus saved already aggrieved families the further ignominy of poverty. There were a number of ramifications of this particular move toward tolerance. For one thing, physicians were consulted to aid in determining cases of "temporary insanity" and then found themselves embroiled in a controversy over the connection between suicide and insanity. In order to clarify their thinking, they pioneered in scientific studies of insanity and helped establish "mental science" as a province of medicine.

From 1830 to 1900 in Britain, medical opinion of suicide itself underwent significant changes. In the 1830s and 1840s physicians, like most of the rest of the populace, saw suicide as a legal and moral question. However, with increased use of medical testimony in questions of suicide, alienists were forced to refine their view of what was still termed "self-murder." By the 1850s and 1860s such refinement continued, with emphasis falling on categorization and physiology, while the 1870s and 1880s saw far more attention paid to the social factors determining suicide. Statistics became more reliable, and, increasingly, prevention and compassion were urged by a number of prominent practitioners. By the end of the century, earlier attitudes, particularly as to the criminal implications of suicide, were reviewed and mainly discarded. Emphasis was now placed on diagnosis and on the social significance of suicide.

In the current essay, my concerns lie elsewhere. Throughout the Victorian period—but particularly at its dawn and in its early years (the 1820s to 1840s)—there was both a reverence for self-healing and an aversion to suicide as a misuse of the will. Victorians hoped to use willpower as an instrument to excise their own self-doubt and depression and hoped to stay free of the medical men by looking for healthy models of how to live courageously. Writers of the past offered keys to this kind of living, and writing itself seemed to provide an antidote for suicide. Thus men like Thomas Carlyle and John Stuart Mill and women like Florence Nightingale found it efficacious to write autobiographical literature about self-destruction, in the meantime saving themselves from that fate and ultimately instructing others in how to survive. This essay analyzes the literary responses of these three eminent Victorians to the threat of suicide. . . .

Mill and Carlyle both found in work—writing, reforming, and teaching—ways to overcome "the stage in a young man's life when the grimness of the general human situation first comes clear."[2] A young woman's life offered few such outlets. Half a generation later than Mill, Florence Nightingale would confront depression and suicide from a female vantage point. A mother, not a father, was her bête noire, and enforced idleness, not purposeful work, seemed her future. As a lady and member of a wealthy, upper-class family, Nightingale was expected to marry, to visit, and to entertain. She was accorded a role to play, not a vocation to live for; and, detesting that role, she tried for years to break free from it. Throughout the 1840s, the decade of her twenties, she suffered intolerable frustration. By 1844 she had already settled on a métier—nursing—but she was barred access to it. Gentlewomen were not to put themselves in the way of dangers like exposure to dirt and disease, let alone warfare, nor were they to put aside Victorian modesty with regard to the human body. Nursing was a job for lower-class women or dedicated nuns. Nightingale's family strongly objected to her choice of nursing on such grounds and on the grounds that Florence might also be exposed to the flirtations and lechery of doctors. Nightingale's mother, Fanny, said as much and counseled marriage and travel as antidotes for Florence's "nursing fever."

Fanny's effect on her daughter was profound. Caught between her sense of duty to family and her desire for work, Nightingale fell victim to severe bouts of depression. Even recreational trips to the Continent inflamed her thwarted need to work. Throughout 1850 and 1851 she experienced her worst frustration. An unpublished diary for 1850 and an "autobiography" and memoranda for 1850-51 self-document two years of awesome hopelessness and yearning for death.[3] In May of 1850 Nightingale read Cowper and identified with his "deep despondency." In Greece by June 7, she determined to go to the Eumenides cave to exorcise her Furies. Unlike Carlyle's devils, her demons resembled the women in her family. Nightingale felt guilty and sinful toward her mother and conformist sister, Parthe, and angry at what felt like their vengeful, fury-like pursuit of her. Unfortunately, the cave was of no help to her. Alone inside, she still felt pursued and wondered, "who shall deliver me from the body of this death?" No Wordsworth, no Goethe came to her aid, only Richard Monkton Milnes, intellectual and philanthropist, who would ask for her hand in marriage in 1850. Much to her family's dismay, Nightingale refused. She thought her "active moral nature" would have been compromised even by this match. By Christmas eve, she lamented that "in my thirty first year, I can see nothing desirable but death. . . . I cannot understand it. I am ashamed to understand it" (BL, MS. 43402, fol. 53).

For a year and a half, Nightingale had tried to crucify her daydreams and to prepare for a life of action, but she had failed. What she did not realize was that those dreams were in fact her salvation, since her life was already like death. She had confused the literal with the symbolic: she really wanted metaphorically to kill her old life in order to assume a new one, but she thought she simply wanted to die. Her diary entries are full of such confusion:

> voluntarily to put it out of my power ever to be able to seize the chance of forming myself a . . . rich life would seem to me like suicide.
>
> And yet my present life is suicide. (BL, MS. 43402, fol. 54)

Eventually, the diaries focus on a metaphor that more clearly expresses Nightingale's state. Florence Nightingale is starving to death for want of work. Her suppressed rebellion against her family has left her a kind of emotional anorexic. She sees in her current state an equivalent to murder: she is being starved by others' expectations.

> I am perishing for want of food. And what prospect have I of better? While I am in this position, I can expect nothing else. Therefore I spend my day in dreams of other situations which will afford me food. (BL, MS. 43402, fol. 55)

Hers, then, is a death-in-life, but she does not really want to die, only to die to idleness and to live through work:

> Starvation does not lead a man to action—it only weakens him. Oh weary days—oh evenings that seem never to end—for how many years I have watched that drawing room clock . . . it is not the misery, the unhappiness that I feel is so insupportable, but I feel this habit, this disease gaining ground upon me and no hope, no help. This is the sting of death.
>
> Why do I wish to leave this world? God knows I do not suspect a heaven beyond—but that He will set me down in St. Giles, at a Kaiserswerth, there to find my work. (BL, MS. 43402, fol. 55)

Once Nightingale really understands the nature of her problem, her diary entries alter. She has converted herself, although she is not yet fully aware of this. A kind of religious meditation follows on an overleaf of the last letter of 1850. In it she opens a casement and feels the night wind blow over her. Unlike the early English Romantics for whom such wind was beneficial, a corresponding breeze answering the breaths of their voices, Nightingale experiences several winds from different directions. If some are benign, others are hostile, yet they indicate conflicting but invigorating movements in Nightingale's life and thought by the end of 1850.

After this meditation come a new form of self-discipline and a new form of self-address in Nightingale's papers. She begins to command herself; her voice is imperative:

> Let me not try to disguise these two facts from myself, Spirit of Truth, but let me honestly and with simplicity of purpose set to work not to complain, but to find the means to live. (BL, MS. 43402, fol. 67)

She asks to do God's will but determines to regiment her own. She must place intercourse with her family on a new footing; she must grow up; she must refuse to be treated as a child; she must give over the thoughts of real death; she must quit trying to be understood by her parents. She must also take the food she has been perishing for, "a nourishing life—that is happiness." Nightingale must feed herself in order not to become like the suicidal self-starvers of George Burrows's classic nineteenth-century work on insanity.[4] Such people show either a disgust for food or an obstinate rejection of it, whereas Nightingale wants to relieve her starvation.

By 1851, Nightingale turns more directly to the question of happiness. Once in her life she had been happy, at Kaiserswerth in Germany, where in 1848 she spent a fortnight at a model hospital staffed by Protestant religious. In the summer of 1851 she would return there and experience similar happiness. To Fanny she wrote: "I find the deepest interest in everything here and am so well in body and mind. . . . I really should be sorry now to leave life. I know you will be glad to hear, dearest mother, this" (BL, MS. 43402, fol. 137). Nightingale did not, however, live happily ever after. Her depressions recurred, and her troubles with Fanny and Parthe were never really resolved until her mother's and sister's final illnesses when Florence gained absolute control over her two weakened Furies. Maybe by then she realized that she herself was a Fury in their eyes, that they were all three the avengers.

Throughout her life, Nightingale would continue to hunger for death. To Mary Clarke Mohl in 1881 she wrote:

> "I cannot remember the time when I have not longed for death. After Sidney Herbert's death and Clough's death in 1861, 20 years ago, for years and years I used to watch for death as no sick man ever watched for the morning. It is strange that now I am bereft of all, I crave for it less."[5]

Throughout her life, too, she put herself in the way of death and disease merely by exercising her profession. When she was not directly in touch with danger, she had or contrived prolonged periods of invalidism when she controlled her mother, sister, and male associates like Herbert by letter and directive sent out from her bedroom. These illnesses were both forms of self-destruction and a means of survival. Yet Nightingale, like Carlyle and Mill, had one major suicidal crisis. When it passed she, too, wrote offering others directives on how not to die. Still in her thirty-first year, she received a call from God to be a "saviour" and produced *Suggestions for Thought to Searchers After Religious Truth.* A lumbering work in three volumes, *Suggestions* aims at an audience of artisans, purporting to give them a theology to live by. Newly in contact with the working classes, Nightingale was appalled at their lack of religion. Her message for them would be her diary's message to herself: individuals must use their own wills for human betterment and thus help to accomplish God's will on earth. "Many," she would say, "long intensely to die, to go to another world, which could not be worse and might be better than this. But is there any better world *there* to go into?" (BL, MS. 45840, fol. 178). Mill would be amused by Nightingale's missionary zeal in exhorting the working class to live and work on in God's service. The copy of *Suggestions* that Nightingale sent to him in 1860 includes this notation:

> Nightingale: . . . But He is too good a Father to put it into His children's power to refuse it. If He were to do this, timid spirits would resign at once. According to the theory of responsibility, suicide would be justified. For a man may put an end to his service, if dissatisfied with it.
>
> Mill: not if he has taken his wages.[6]

Nightingale, however, was utterly serious about her mission. In the notes for *Suggestions* she asks herself, "Can I will what I wish? Can I do what I will?" (BL, MS. 45837, fol. 28). What she would will in 1852 was to rewrite her diary in the service of humanity, careful to include not just working-class but also female humanity. In this light, the section of Volume Two called **"Cassandra"** bears re-examination. Like Nightingale, middle-class women are starving for work. They sit down daily to large meals of food but lack spiritual and mental sustenance. Idleness and marriage stifle them to the point that "Some are only deterred from suicide because it is the most distinct manner to say to an indifferent God: 'I will not, I will not do as Thou wouldst have me,' and because it is 'no use'" (BL, MS. 45848, fol. 239). And yet these women wait on for a palpable deliverer. Nightingale concludes this section of *Suggestions* with symbols and ambivalences. "The next Christ will perhaps be a female Christ," she hopes, and yet she queries, "do we see one woman who looks like a female Christ? or even like the messenger before her 'face,' to go before her and prepare the hearts and minds for her?" (BL, MS. 45848, fol. 240). Her answer to these questions is only implied: no, there is no such Christ unless she herself is to be one. There is only Cassandra, the dying and unheeded prophetess whose real death has already taken place in her earlier, thwarted talent, not in her ultimate physical end.

*Suggestions* was revised in 1859 and privately printed in 1860, after Florence Nightingale's return from Crimea. By then, Nightingale's personal and vocational crises had passed, and she had become less dedicated to philosophical and literary pursuits. Her mission lay elsewhere, in physically ministering to other lives. In doing so, she became both a literal savior and a legendary figure: the "Lady with the Lamp," a living female counterpart of Holman Hunt's portrait of Christ as "Light of the World."[7] With no Goethes, nor Wordsworths, nor even James Mills to show her the way, she transformed herself into her own and others' source of salvation from death—if not a kind of female Christ, then surely a kind of Virgin Florence. Unlike Carlyle and Mill and the women who left fathers only to marry, Nightingale did not want a change of masters. Instead she became one of the first Victorian women to point the way toward self-mastery as a road to female salvation.

Despite differences in temperament and sex, the sage of Ecclefechan, the great utilitarian and apostle of liberty, and the Lady with the Lamp all warred with suicidal despair in similar ways. Each had to metamorphose: to convert himself or herself from youthful despair and desire for death to useful adulthood. All three had to grow up. For Carlyle, self-denial, itself a kind of suicide, paradoxically offered the way. For Mill and Nightingale self-denial was hardly liberating but rather a kind of self-starvation. Yet each of these three eminent Victorians, who represented archetypal Victorian virtues and schools of thought, had metaphorically to kill a parent or bogey—a former self of sorts—in order to emerge rather than to die. And because each had a mission, each had to write and then rewrite his or her story, shifting from the private world of letters, notebooks, and journals to a public voice in more formal prose. Thus personal crisis became public narrative for the greater good of community, so that their literature is strongly marked by morality and didacticism. All three girded themselves in perseverance, willpower, and work and battled their own suicidal despair. In doing so they became apostles of self-transformation and endurance, evidence that upper- and middle-class Victorian Britain seemed determined not to be a "classic land of suicide." They laid legal issues and implications of insecurity aside, confronting suicide as a personal moral choice. Hard as it might seem, it was simply better to be than not to be. Like Gerard Manley Hopkins later in their century, they could "not choose not to be."[8]

NOTES

[1] Barbara T. Gates, "Suicide and the Victorian Physicians," *Journal of the History of the Behavioral Sciences* 16 (April 1980): 164-74.

[2] Thomas Hardy, *The Return of the Native,* ed. James Gindin (New York: Norton, 1969), 149.

[3] Florence Nightingale, autobiography and other memoranda, 1845-60, BL, MS. 43402. This and other

manuscripts referred to are from the Nightingale papers in the British Library and are quoted here by permission of the Department of Manuscripts of the Library. Subsequent citations are given parenthetically in the text as BL, followed by the manuscript and folio numbers.

[4] George Man Burrows, *Commentaries on the Causes, Forms, Symptoms, and Treatment, Moral and Medical, of Insanity* (London: Thomas and George Underwood, 1828), 426.

[5] Quoted in Cecil Woodham-Smith, *Florence Nightingale 1820-1910* (New York: Grosset & Dunlap, 1951), 341.

[6] Quoted in F. B. Smith, *Florence Nightingale: Reputation and Power* (London: Croom Helm, 1982), 187.

[7] Holman Hunt was said to have used a female model, Annie Miller, for his Christ.

[8] Gerard Manley Hopkins, "Carrion Comfort," line 4, in *The Poems of Gerard Manley Hopkins,* ed. W. H. Gardner and N. H. Mackenzie (London: Oxford University Press, 1967), 99.

## Mary Poovey (essay date 1988)

SOURCE: "A Housewifely Woman: The Social Construction of Florence Nightingale," in Uneven Developments: *The Ideological Work of Gender in Mid-Victorian England,* The University of Chicago Press, 1988, pp. 164-98.

[*In the following excerpt, Poovey explores Nightingale's conceptualization of nursing as contained in* Notes on Nursing *and other writings by Nightingale, examining her views in relation to the Victorian womanly ideal of domesticity.*]

Florence Nightingale's publications on nursing are extremely heterogeneous. They range from her most popular work—*Notes on Nursing* (1859), which was written for a general audience and sold fifteen thousand copies in just one month—to a series of reports written for Royal Commissions, which were only publicly available in the extremely limited numbers Nightingale had privately printed. That Nightingale's observations on nursing are so various and unsystematic partially reflects the lack of public or official interest in this subject at midcentury: even within the medical community, there was no consensus about what good nursing entailed, and no educated woman who was not called to a religious vocation was likely to take an interest in the subject. Through her writings, Nightingale therefore had to create an interested and sympathetic audience for nursing (including a body of potential recruits) as well as to answer to the bureaucratic specifications and political crosscurrents of the official groups she often addressed.

The material conditions in which Nightingale organized her first nursing corps also indelibly marked her conceptualization of nursing. By definition, shepherding thirty-eight variously trained women into a military hospital in a war zone for the first time in English history constituted a unique opportunity, but it also meant that Nightingale had to accommodate her ideas to the organizations that preceded her. The administrative inefficiency she encountered at Scutari impressed on Nightingale the necessity for a clearly specified, rigidly enforced chain of command in her nursing corps, just as the rigor and lapses of army discipline turned her attention to strict regimentation, discipline, and unflagging surveillance. Given her experience with the army medical corps, it is not surprising that the militaristic strain she emphasized focused not on the career of heroism so much as on the administrative prowess the good housekeeper could perfect. The organizing concepts of Nightingale's vision are discipline, subordination, surveillance, punishment, training, and regimentation; her favorite story chronicled the transformation of the raw recruit into an efficient nursing machine.

These things—and not medical training—preoccupied Nightingale in her first treatment of nursing. In an essay entitled **"Subsidiary Notes as to the Introduction of Female Nursing into Military Hospitals,"** appended to her long report for the 1857 Royal Commission on the Sanitary Conditions of the Army, Nightingale set out the qualifications any hospital nurse must learn to value; notably, her list entails a set of deferential attitudes rather than medical skills: "obedience, discipline, self-control, work understood as work, hospital service as implying masters, civil and medical, and a mistress, what service means, and abnegation of self.[1] To inculcate these attitudes, Nightingale argued that a two-part approach was necessary: the respectable character of working-class women must be ensured by "leavening" the mass of nurses with "ladies," and the entire operation must be well governed and closely watched.[2] "Rule, system, and superintendence"—these principles and not religious vows bind the Nightingale nurse. If these principles are strictly observed, she suggests, her nursing corps could effectively combat not only disease but also what emerges as an equally dangerous enemy—the moral infection that breeds where people "congregate" promiscuously.

In so far as disease is the enemy that must be treated in a hospital, Nightingale's solution was to allow the patients plenty of space and clean air.[3] Her insistence on the importance of adequate ventilation reflects her belief in Dr. William Farr's theory of "zymotic" disease: the theory, roughly speaking, that disease breeds as yeast ferments and that it is spread through the patient's inhalation of the "noxious matter" his own or another nearby body has excreted.[4] "As it is a law," she states, "that all excretions are injurious to health if reintroduced into the system it is easy to understand how the . . . reintroduction of excrementitious matter into the blood through the functions of respiration will tend to produce disease.

This will be still more the case in sick wards overcrowded with sick, the exhalations from whom are always highly morbid and dangerous, as they are nature's method of eliminating noxious matter from the body, in order that it may recover health" (SN 65). The zymotic disease theory was antithetical to the germ theory, which Nightingale resisted throughout her life, despite increasing medical acceptance. Instead of seeing diseases as discrete entities (as proponents of the germ theory did), she conceptualized the human body as an organism so attuned to and dependent on its environment that a disorder in the latter produced a disease in the former as surely as heat made mercury rise. The nurse's job was therefore simply to monitor the patient and his environment to ensure, as far as possible, that "morbid matter" was rapidly carried away.

A large squad of disciplined nurses, presumably, emptying bedpans and changing sheets, could effectively combat zymotic disease in a large, airy ward. But the problem Nightingale saw with military hospitals was not just that they lacked such wards, but also that if these wards were built, they would require more nurses and more superintendence. After considering various architectural schemes, Nightingale advocated the "Vincennes modification of the Pavilion plan" because of "the greater facility of supervision it affords." Her description of this system suggests that her supervisors were involved in an elaborate counterespionage scheme rather than the work of healing. In this design, she writes approvingly,

> the Military Superior, the Surgeon, the Matron, can at any instant pop in upon any ward of a Hospital. . . . Each pavilion may, unless the matter be specially considered with a view to providing this effectual supervision, perceive the approach of the inspector. The system of secrets, watch, alarm, is well understood in many hundred wards, whose patients would be puzzled to give the things names. Remember that Ward-Masters, Orderlies, and Nurses require inspection as well as patients. (SN 75)

Nightingale's concern here is with misconduct in the wards—most explicitly, with drinking: "remember," she writes, "there is such a thing as quiet drinking, as well as noisy drinking" (SN 106). But here, as in many nineteenth-century texts, alcohol consumption is metonymically connected to an unnameable (sexual) indulgence, which Nightingale suspects in every unlit hospital corner and from every inmate of the ward. "The orderly must never enter the Nurse's room," she insists twice in one paragraph. "Guard against too many closets, sinks, &c., &c., &c.," she writes; "endeavour to prevent the system of holes and corners. It is best that the Nurse's door should command the view of those who come in or out of the lavatory, and in and out of the water-closet. This whole section," Nightingale grimly concludes, "is both ugly and important" (SN 47, 92, 94).

These passages suggest that the unnameable activities include masturbation and homosexuality as well as heterosexual liaisons. To Nightingale, all such permutations of immorality are conceivable because the patients—as soldiers—are not moral beings. Despite the popular image of Nightingale championing the common man, her own writings reveal a distrust of soldiers bordering on scorn. "In contemplating a Military Hospital," she comments, "we contemplate a place through which, one year with another, all characters, including a few of the vilest, pass" (SN 92). As a consequence,

> a Military Hospital must, and should ever remain, essentially different from a Civil Hospital; both different in discipline and detail, and altogether a rougher and ruder place. It should never for a moment be forgotten that the soldier is a very peculiar individual, old and stern as is his trade. A regiment, if one thinks *into* it, is a curious thing. . . . The moral standard of the patients of the Military Hospital, their readiness to obey, their good feeling to each other, are strikingly higher than in the Civil Hospital; but the soldier is what, amidst all his faults, he has been made by the habit and spirit of discipline, which has become an instinct and a second nature, and which ennobles his own. Relax discipline, and in proportion as you do so, there remains of the soldier a being with as much or more of the brute than the man. (SN 37)

In many ways, Nightingale aspired to make her little squadron of nurses into a regiment—obedient and loyal, with discipline an "instinct and a second nature." But, as this quotation suggests, discipline was always in danger of breaking down; given the sexuality implicit in the domestic ideal, the "brute" was nearly as likely to materialize in a woman as a man. Nightingale, in her distrust of every unsupervised encounter, betrays her sensitivity to the sexuality contemporaries feared in women. Do not let nurses "congregate" with the orderlies *or* each other, she writes: "associating the nurses in large dormitories tends to corrupt the good, and make the bad worse." "Give the Nurse plenty to do" so that mischief will not tempt her. Keep the number of nurses as low as possible; "the fewer women are about an Army Hospital the better," Nightingale curtly remarks (SN 11, 81, 73). Above all, never let vigilance cease. Nightingale stopped just short of advocating spying, but this was with palpable regret. "Nurses trusted to do their duty in wards," she begrudgingly admits, "must be trusted to walk out alone if they choose, and I would not attempt to restrict it, though the Superintendent must see to this, so far as she can without doing or encouraging spywork, a thing which has many advantages, and is often done in various, very various ways, but which in the long run brings no blessing, and *pro tanto,* degrades all who are concerned with it" (SN 115-16).

Nightingale's caution is understandable from many points of view. Given the contemporary ambivalence toward female nature and the prejudice against introducing women into military hospitals in particular, it was imperative for her to protect her charges from suspicions about their characters. Moreover, given the administrative inefficiency at Scutari, the competing and complex chains of command, and the practice of employing convalescent soldiers as orderlies, Nightingale had to overcome hospital laxity as well as to accustom her own nurses to difficult and tiring labor. Then, too, those soldiers recovering from wounds were often hospitalized for several months, some weeks of which they were sufficiently ambulatory (and bored) to test hospital rules. But above and beyond these practical considerations, Nightingale's conceptualization of the problem also reflects the contradictions inherent in her own middle-class assumptions, as well as the difficulties these assumptions posed for the nursing squad she wanted to organize.

The problem that conceptualizing sexuality as both pernicious and pervasive constituted for nursing was that it not only implied but institutionalized a constantly circulating, ungovernable mistrust: in such a system there could be no effective government because no individual could be free of the system that reproduced what it was designed to police. Thus, as Nightingale explores the solutions, the problems simply proliferate: if the superior spies on her nurses, then everyone is degraded; if she does not, "congregation" or worse goes unchecked; if one increases the size of wards, ventilation is improved but supervision becomes more difficult; if one reduces the number of nurses, women's morality is protected, but the patients go unwatched; if one locks the nurses in a common room at night, orderlies can be kept out, but all the dangers of female congregation creep in again. Ultimately, the solution Nightingale institutionalized for these problems was a training program in which discipline could be ceaselessly monitored and indiscretions effectively punished; this was the system instituted in the Nightingale Training School at St. Thomas's Hospital (established 1860), where nurses were evaluated weekly in twenty-one subjects (from enema giving to sobriety and punctuality).[5] In 1858, however, and in a military hospital in Turkey, no such systematic discipline was possible. In its absence, Nightingale simply relinquished the entire dilemma to a higher authority—even though this admitted religious sisterhoods, which she wanted to exclude, back into the wards. "Let the female service obtain, please God," she writes, and then she opens this long, torturously qualified parenthesis:

> (I do not write these words *pro forma,*—if possible, I feel every day more intensely how solely it is to Him we must trust in this difficult work,—the more so that, if possible, I feel every day more intensely the importance of, if He grants it success, improving secular Hospital nursing, leaving the English Sisterhoods, which will always have great advantages, and, I believe, great disadvantages, with reference to Hospital nursing, to take their share of this great field, which has plenty of room for both), let, I say, the female service obtain a firm footing in the Army Hospitals, and with it, by cautious degrees, sundry ameliorations will creep in insensibly as to decorum among other things. (SN 118)

What Nightingale's early conceptualization lacks, quite obviously, is any morally reliable figure to superintend the other inmates. The source of this problem is that, in foregrounding only one side of the domestic ideal, she has collapsed the difference between men and women and therefore the possibility that sexual appetite will submit to control. Nightingale's halting reference to the "sundry ameliorations" that will "creep in" with women suggests how she will soon solve this problem: by emphasizing the other side of the domestic ideal, she will capitalize on the assumption that, no matter how debauched some nurses may currently be, all women are more capable of moral improvement than any man. To stabilize this representation, Nightingale subordinates her preoccupation with class to a more resolute focus on gender and on women's maternal nature in particular. This reorientation accompanies Nightingale's turn from wartime nursing to private nursing in the home.

Taking up the subject of nursing in the home enabled Nightingale to solve the problems endemic to the military hospital because it let her displace what she assumed to be the locus of those problems: the lower-class status of the patients and nurses she supervised at Scutari. The basis of this rhetorical displacement is at least partly material: because private nursing was typical of *middle-class* care, setting her discussion in the home implies that the patient and nurse are governed by middle-class standards of morality. The patient in *Notes on Nursing* is no "brute," but a tractable, silent man too preoccupied with the enemy of ill health to cause trouble himself.[6] "Remember," Nightingale remarks of this patient, "he is face to face with his enemy all the time, internally wrestling with him, having long, imaginary conversations with him" (*N* 38). The relationship between such a patient and his caretaker is also transformed by the domestic setting. What had been a volatile, ungovernable relation between two sexual (and always potentially immoral) beings now becomes a familial relationship, in which the difference between the sexes holds sway because the nurse can be represented as a literal or a metaphorical (middle-class) mother. Once more, this revision alludes to the stereotypical image of domesticity, which Nightingale reinforces in the opening to her slender volume: "Every woman," Nightingale proclaims, "or at least almost every woman, in England has, at one time or another of her life, charge of the personal health of somebody, whether child or invalid—in other words, every woman is a nurse" (N 3).

While the dismissal of class that I am describing had a material basis in the actual differences between private nursing and nursing in a military hospital, it derived its cultural appeal from the assumptions about female morality that the domestic narrative mobilized. These assumptions were so powerful partly because they cloaked a controversial set of assumptions about class beneath the less controversial set of assumptions about gender: the feminine path to glory epitomized in Agnes Wickfield's self-fulfilling self-denial and inscribed in the domestic narrative *assumed* a middle-class family and middle-class values while concentrating on the difference between the sexes. When the apparent classlessness of this narrative was further enhanced by the classlessness conferred on Nightingale by images of divinity and royalty, the domestic narrative seemed to underwrite a tension-free society, imperceptibly governed by moral influence, where everyone was happy in his or her allotted place. So effective did this narrative and the national image it supported prove as a symbolic solution to the problems of creating a nursing corps that Nightingale retained it, and the revision it implied, in all her subsequent nursing schemes—even though the literal setting of these schemes was never again a middle-class home.

If invoking the asexual, apparently classless image of woman by which her own exploits were publicly represented enabled Nightingale to solve rhetorically most of the problems introduced by her original conceptualization of nursing, it added one new difficulty. If "every woman is a nurse," then why should nurses earn money for what ought to be a labor of love? Because of its implicit middle-class bias and its position within the symbolic economy of separate spheres, the domestic ideal and the narrative that accompanied it were positioned outside of the system of waged labor, professional commitment, and the "public"; yet to accede to that exclusion would have been ruinous to any attempts to make nursing training systematic. Nightingale acknowledged this dilemma when she adamantly rejected attempts by popular novelists to blur the boundary between middle-class domestic life and nursing work. "It seems a commonly received idea among men and even among women themselves," she complains,

> that it requires nothing but a disappointment in love, the want of an object, a general disgust, or incapacity for other things, to turn a woman into a good nurse. Popular novelists of recent days have invented ladies disappointed in love or fresh out of the drawing-room turning into the war-hospitals to find their wounded lovers, and when found, forthwith abandoning their sick-ward for their lover, as might be expected. Yet in the estimation of the authors, these ladies were none the worse for that, but on the contrary were heroines of nursing. (N 134)

Nightingale's scorn for the lovelorn girl, whose susceptibility made visible the sexuality implicit in the domestic ideal, was equaled by her insistence that the nurse not err in the opposite direction—that she not be too manly, as strong-minded women were. So intent was Nightingale on reinforcing the difference between the sexes that she ends *Notes on Nursing* with a long note commanding the nurse to resist that "jargon . . . about the 'rights' of women, which urges women to do all that men do, including the medical and other professions, merely because men do it, and without regard to whether this *is* the best that women can do" (*N* 135n). Her solution to avoiding both of these extremes was to reproduce the ideological separation of spheres that

supposedly characterized society as a whole within medicine and to insist on the autonomy of each sphere. Within the separate sphere of their expertise, women would address problems of sanitation and hygiene (and midwifery), not medicine or surgery; establishing this separate sphere would therefore eliminate the risk of competition with medical men.[7] As Nightingale developed this idea, it becomes clear that, despite her mollifying rhetoric, she had launched a territorial campaign—one that would eventually eliminate altogether the need for medical men and expand nursing's domain outside the middle-class home. Nightingale justified the ambitiousness of this campaign by invoking the militaristic component of the domestic ideal, for the assertiveness sanctioned in the middle-class housewife not only accorded with the disciplined training Nightingale required for her nursing corps, but also rhetorically sanctioned her territorial design.

Nightingale elaborated the domestic and militaristic sides of the domestic ideal by aligning her nurse with a representation of the middle-class wife as commander in chief of a servant army. In the home, surveillance could be conceptualized as educative observation; discipline could be linked to cleanliness and hence to cure; and the military system of subordination and command could be represented as what Nightingale calls "petty management"—the art of household administration. "All the results of good nursing, as detailed in these notes," she cautions, "may be spoiled or utterly negatived by one defect, viz.: in petty management, or in other words, by not knowing how to manage that what you do when you are there, shall be done when you are not there" (*N* 35).

Nightingale's emphasis on domestic management makes clear that the militant strain implicit in the domestic ideology derived its authority from the morality that maternal instinct was assumed to bestow on all women: because it represented all women as middle class and invested them with commensurate moral power, the domestic ideology elevated every woman over every man. In *Notes on Nursing,* the patient is the first man to be dwarfed by this power. Representing the patient as a silent, immobile man obviously appealed to Nightingale's female readers, who bought the book in large numbers. One reviewer found the weakness Nightingale wrote into the patient so flattering that she further embroidered his emaciation and wistfulness, as if to enhance her own health, her prestige, and her rightful power. "Always before you," she remarks, describing the source of her fascination with the book, "there is the hero of the tale, an emaciated being, with sad wistful eyes, who depends upon good nursing as his best, perhaps his only chance of life."[8]

Medical men are also dwarfed in this representation of domestic authority. In one sense, they are simply redundant: "Did Nature intend mothers to be always accompanied by doctors?" Nightingale rhetorically asks (N 11). In another sense, as mere visitors to the domestic sphere, doctors are ineffective. "Now the medical man who sees the patient only once a day or even only once or twice a week, cannot possibly tell [how the patient is] without the assistance of the patient himself, or of those who are in constant observation on the patient. The utmost the medical man can tell is whether the patient is weaker or stronger at this visit than he was at the last visit" (N 75). Given Nightingale's definition of disease as a "reparative process," medical expertise is less relevant to cure than good housekeeping: it is the nurse cum commander who transports noxious exhalations away from the patient, the nurse who protects an environment conducive to repair. Nightingale is outspoken on this point:

> It is often thought that medicine is the curative process. It is no such thing; medicine is the surgery of functions, as surgery proper is that of limbs and organs. Neither can do anything but remove obstructions; neither can cure; nature alone cures. Surgery removes the bullet out of the limb, which is an obstruction to cure, but nature heals the wound. So it is with medicine; the function of an organ becomes obstructed; medicine, so far as we know, assists nature to remove the obstruction, but does nothing more. And what nursing has to do in either case, is to put the patient in the best condition for nature to act upon him. . . . You think fresh air, and quiet and cleanliness extravagant, perhaps dangerous, luxuries, which should be given to the patient only when quite convenient, and medicine the *sine qua non,* the panacea. If I have succeeded in any measure in dispelling this illusion, and in showing what true nursing is, and what it is not, my object will have been answered. (N 133)

If Nightingale's exploitation of the militancy inherent in the domestic ideal helped authorize the supremacy of nursing, it also aligned her vision of the nurse with another enterprise gaining momentum at midcentury. To appreciate the connection between these two campaigns, it is helpful to cast Nightingale's project in terms only slightly more militaristic than the ones she provided. If we view her campaign for nursing as an imperialistic program, we can see that it had two related fronts. The first was the "domestic" front within medicine; in this battle, Nightingale's opponents were medical men; her object was to carve out an autonomous—and ultimately superior—realm for female nursing. The second front was the "foreign" front of class; in this skirmish, her enemies were the "dirt, drink, diet, damp, draughts, drains" that made lower-class homes unsanitary; her object here was to bring the poor and their environment under the salutary sway of their middle-class betters.[9] Nightingale's strategy was to foreground the second campaign, which was a project shared by middle-class men, to mask the subversive character of the first, domestic campaign, which decidedly was not. But the rhetoric in which this strategy was accomplished made Nightingale's vision of nursing particularly amenable to appropriation by English politicians and imperialists, who had their own foreign front to conquer. The texts that chronicle this development go beyond the specific years of my study, for they were all written after the founding of the Nightingale Training

School in 1860. Enlarging the scope of my subject is important at this point, however, because it enables me to suggest the almost limitless potential the domestic ideology contained to authorize aggressive projects that far exceeded the boundaries of the home and even of England itself. The texts I draw on include Nightingale's report to the 1859 Royal Commission appointed to inquire into the sanitary state of the army in India (*Suggestions on a System of Nursing for Hospitals in India,* 1865); another paper prepared for a government committee, her 1867 *Suggestions on the Subject of Providing, Training, and Organizing Nurses for the Sick Poor in Workhouse Infirmaries;* the pamphlet entitled **"On Trained Nursing for the Sick Poor"** (1876), which was originally published as a letter to the *Times;* two entries to Sir Robert Quain's *A Dictionary of Medicine,* published in 1882 (**"Nurses, Training of"** and **"Nursing the Sick"**); and the paper Nightingale prepared for the 1893 Chicago Exhibition, later published in *Woman's Mission,* entitled **"Sick-Nursing and Health-Nursing."**

In her works written after 1860, Nightingale continued to emphasize discipline, but because the problematic aspects of class had disappeared from her representation of nursing, the object—and nature—of this discipline has changed. Discipline is no longer necessary to control the crafty, lascivious "brute"; as an aspect of moral training, discipline now more closely resembles female self-regulation, or even Christian resignation, than punitive or cautionary regimentation. Here, for example, is Nightingale's 1882 description of discipline. *"Discipline,"* Nightingale writes, "is the essence of training."

> People connect discipline with the idea of drill, standing at attention—some with flagellating themselves, some with flagellating boys. A lady who has, perhaps, more experience in training than anyone else, says: "It is education, instruction, training—all that in fact goes to the full development of our faculties, moral, physical, and spiritual, not only for this life, but looking on this life as the training-ground for the future and higher life. Then discipline embraces order, method, and, as we gain some knowledge of the laws of nature ('God's laws'), we not only see order, method, a place for everything, each its own work, but we find no waste of material or force or space; we find, too, no hurry; and we learn to have patience with our circumstances and ourselves; and so, as we go on learning, we become more disciplined, more content to work where we are placed, more anxious to fill our appointed work than to see the result thereof; and so God, no doubt, gives us the required patience and steadfastness to continue on our 'blessed drudgery,' which is the discipline He sees best for most of us."[10]

Nightingale's earlier nightmare of a hospital filled with immoral inmates lingers in the first sentence of this passage. But under the influence of her nameless "lady" authority, this nightmare gives way to a vision of a world where efficient government perfectly reconciles the needs of the governed with the plan of a benevolent, watchful God. The implicit model for this world is the orderly, happy, middle-class home. This model becomes explicit when Nightingale institutionalizes discipline in a training home for nurses.

Nightingale first elaborates her scheme for nursing homes in 1876, in her letter to the *Times*. Initially, she has in mind literal dwelling places—homes to which district (or "visiting") nurses can return after their day's work. These homes obviously carry the metaphorical valence of the domestic ideology, but they also retain militant connotations. As Nightingale elaborates her scheme, the home becomes the command post for a holy war against the "dirt and fever nests" that she now defines as the enemies. "The beginning has been made," she proclaims triumphantly,

> the first crusade has been fought and won, to bring a truly "national" undertaking—real nursing, trained nursing—to the bedsides of cases wanting real nursing among the London sick poor; and this is by providing a real home, within reach of their work, for the nurses to live in—a home which gives what real family homes are supposed to give—materially, a bedroom for each, dining and sitting-rooms in common, all meals prepared and eaten in the home; morally, direction, support, sympathy in a common work; further training and instruction in it; proper rest and recreation; and a head of the home, who is also and pre-eminently trained and skilled head of the nursing; in short, a home where any good mother, of whatever class, would be willing to let her daughter, however attractive or highly educated, live.[11]

The head of this domesticated command post is the matron-mother, who combines training with love so as to nurture her daughter-nurses into medical expertise. The matron, Nightingale writes, must exercise "a constant, motherly, intangible supervision" in the home. "She must know how to make it a real 'home,' with constant supply of all wants and constant *sympathy,* which must be taught by example and precept." "The probationers must really be the matron's children," Nightingale continues. "A training school without a mother is worse than children without parents" (NT 329, 330). This home does have a nominal father—the medical instructor from the hospital staff—but his presence is intermittent and his influence indirect (NT 332). In fact, despite Nightingale's nod to this figure, the home she envisions is really run by and for women. Like a religious sisterhood, it avoids male interference, domination, and competition. But because its metaphorical basis is familial, it is politically and religiously neutral—a bulwark of secular society instead of a potential threat to national unity, as all religious orders were thought to be.

The crusade that Nightingale originated in this autonomous, middle-class, female home was explicitly colonial: its aim was to "reform and re-create . . . the homes of the sick poor" in its own image. With the complacency of an imperialist, Nightingale assumed that bourgeois domesticity and cleanliness were universally desired. As a consequence, victory was assumed to be easy, and the "glory" of good nursing was promised to every young recruit. "Every home she has thus cleaned has always been kept so. This is her glory. She found it a pig-sty; she left it a tidy, airy room" (SP 312). In this image we see the stages of what, by the late 1870s, Nightingale explicitly represented as nursing's territorial expansion. From the patient's body, the nurse turns her attention to the room in which he lies: the nurse, Nightingale proclaims, must "nurse the room as well as the patient." The next step for the nurse is to monitor the alleyways of crowded slums, the narrow streets where sewage runs, entire neighborhoods and urban districts so that she can bring "such sanitary defects as produce sickness and death . . . to the notice of the public officer whom it concerns" (SP 314).

As monitor of the poor family's home environment, the nurse therefore becomes a public agent of moral reform. Just as Martineau represented Nightingale coaxing soldiers from "poisonous drinks and mischief," so Nightingale represents her nurses luring wayward men away from gin shops and public houses, back to the home where morality begins, back into the sphere of women's influence. "What efforts such a man will make *not* to drink, when his wife is sick, if you help him to help himself and her; to maintain his independence—and if you make his home by cleanliness and care less intolerable" (SP 315). As caretaker, sanitary warden, and moral reformer, the nurse deploys the cultural authority granted to (middle-class) women in the service of the reform middle-class men also wanted to effect. But Nightingale did not stop here. Because hers was also a domestic war against medical men, she yoked the conquest of the poor to the nurse's gradual usurpation of the doctor's authority. In her representation, the nurse becomes a complete medical staff—apparently from necessity: "she has not the doctor always at hand. . . . She is his staff of clinical clerks, dressers, and nurses" (SP 316). But necessity generates opportunity; from her position as helpmaid, the nurse can launch a social and medical revolution: after this revolution, all homes will be like the orderly, middle-class home she describes in *Notes on Nursing;* hospitals will completely disappear (except as training schools for nurses); and nurses will become the agents of health and morality in all classes, in all parts of the civilized world. "Hospitals are but an intermediate stage of civilization," she writes. "The ultimate object is to nurse all sick at home" (SP 317).

Nightingale's vision of a classless, hospital-less society is actually a vision of society as a network of middle-class families dominated if not run by women, penetrated and linked by nurses who emanate from the central hospital-homes where they are disciplined and trained. This panoptical plan, which is the Nightingale Nursing School writ large, reaches its logical conclusion in Nightingale's scheme of "health missioners," which she set out in 1893. The work of these health missioners undermines the doctor's hegemony within medicine precisely by doing what women do best—tidying up the homes and superintending the morals of the poor. In focusing on society's health, not individuals' diseases, the health missioner dispenses with the diagnosis as a means for determining who needs medical care, and she eliminates the present system that brings only some people under the doctor's supervision. In Nightingale's scheme, everyone comes under the health missioners' jurisdiction: "the art of health," she writes, "is an art which concerns every family in the world" (SH 355). Within this family, not surprisingly, the mother rules: "upon womankind," Nightingale declares, "the national health, as far as the household goes, depends" (SH 356). At least as an idea, Nightingale's health missioners therefore complete the "peaceful revolution" she inaugurated in the Crimea.[12] In their work, women's domestic labors of love are translated into nationwide housekeeping: in this vision, class tension and immorality can both be conquered through woman's aggressive domestic work, not just by the example she passively sets.

Paradoxically, given her emphasis on women's work, Nightingale vehemently opposed the campaign to professionalize nursing that was launched in the 1880s and 1890s. Nightingale rejected state nursing registration on the grounds that nursing was a calling that registration would debase.[13] Nightingale's increasingly insistent deployment of familial metaphors and the vocabulary of altruism that went with them was partly aimed at bolstering her arguments against professionalization: in a family, after all, responsibilities and rewards follow from love, not contracts or certificates. This is the positive sense in which the domestic sphere lies outside the marketplace; according to Nightingale, the true nurse nurses not for money but for some higher, abstract ideal—"to satisfy the high idea of what is the *right,* the *best*" (SH 363). For this, no certification will serve: "You might as well register mothers as nurses," she proclaims (SH 367). Above all, Nightingale wanted nursing to remain aloof from that motor of free enterprise—competition.

> Competition, or each man for himself, and the devil against us all, may be necessary, we are told, but it is the enemy of health. Combination is the antidote—combined interests, recreation, combination to secure the best air, the best food, and all that makes life useful, healthy, and happy. There is no such thing as independence. As far as we are successful, our success lies in combination. (SH 367)

Nightingale's deployment of familial metaphors and her fierce antipathy to both nursing registration and competition were part of her effort to displace the domestic struggle in which her nurses were actually engaged by foregrounding what I have called the "foreign" conflict—the moralization of the poor, here idealized as the working class's "combination" with their middle-class advisers. That is, Nightingale disavowed

competition between nurses and medical men for the same reason that she resisted nursing registration: she wanted to preserve an autonomous sphere for nursing, a sphere whose superiority was proved by women's greater efficacy with the poor. Furthermore, the domestic metaphors that underwrote both her domestic and foreign campaigns disguised the implications of Nightingale's own insistence that nurses be paid a fair market wage for their labor. If she were not rhetorically disentangled from the specter of the professional woman, the paid nurse could have jeopardized the existence of a separate sphere of (womanly) altruism, the idea of which was critical to Nightingale's elevation of female nurses over medical men.

NOTES

[1] "Subsidiary Notes as to the Introduction of Female Nursing into Military Hospitals," reprinted in *Selected Writings of Florence Nightingale,* ed. Lucy Ridgely Seymer (New York: Macmillan, 1954), p. 8. Hereafter cited as SN.

[2] Ibid., esp. pp. 5-6, 23, 33.

[3] Most of the men who were treated (and died) at Scutari were suffering from cholera, not wounds.

[4] The best discussion of Florence Nightingale's theory of disease is Charles E. Rosenberg, "Florence Nightingale on Contagion: The Hospital as Moral Universe," in Charles E. Rosenberg, ed., *Healing and History* (New York: Dawson, 1979), pp. 116-36. Sandra Holton also discusses this in "Feminine Authority," pp. 60-61.

[5] Nightingale explains the procedures and government of the Nightingale Training School in her report to the Royal Commission appointed to investigate the sanitary conditions of the army in India. See "Suggestions on a System of Nursing for Hospitals in India," in *Selected Writings,* pp. 237-43. The training school at St. Thomas's was financed by the Nightingale Fund, a scheme to honor Nightingale inaugurated by the duke of Cambridge on 29 November 1855. A good measure of the universality of Nightingale's popularity is the fact that Englishmen from all classes contributed to this fund, in sums ranging from six pence to several hundred pounds. The fund eventually raised over £44,000. See Lucy Seymer, *Florence Nightingale's Nurses: The Nightingale Training School, 1860-1960* (London: Pitman Medical Publishing, 1960), chap. 1.

[6] Florence Nightingale, *Notes on Nursing: What It Is and What It Is Not* (New York: Dover, 1969), p. 38. Hereafter cited as *N.* Occasionally in this text, Nightingale does refer to the patient as a female, but these references are all to her own experiences as a patient.

[7] In her 1871 text on midwifery, *Introductory Notes on Lying-in Institutions,* Nightingale makes it clear

that her argument for excluding women from some medical practices is one facet of her attempt to sidestep competition with medical men. "Why," she asks here, "(in the great movement there is now to make women into medical men) should not this branch, midwifery, which they will find no one to contest against them— not at least in the estimation of the patients—be the first ambition of cultivated women? . . . There is a better thing than making women into medical men, and that is making them into medical *women*." Nightingale, *Introductory Notes on Lying-in Institutions* (London: Longmans, Green, 1871), p. 106.

[8] "A Reverie after Reading Miss Nightingale's *Notes on Nursing*," *Fraser's Magazine* 61 (June 1860): p. 753. Other early reviews include [Harriet Martineau], "Miss Nightingale's *Notes on Nursing*," *Quarterly Review* 107 (April 1860): pp. 392-422; and "Something of What Florence Nightingale Has Done."

[9] This phrase comes from Nightingale's "Sick-Nursing and Health-Nursing," in *Selected Writings,* p. 362. Hereafter cited as SH.

[10] "Nurses, Training of," in *Selected Writings,* p. 334. Hereafter cited as NT. This definition also appears in SH, where Nightingale inserts the word "moral": "What is discipline?" she asks. "Discipline is the essence of moral training" (SH 358).

[11] "Suggestions on the Subject of Providing, Training, and Organizing Nurses for the Sick Poor in Workhouse Infirmaries," in *Selected Writings,* p. 311. Hereafter cited as SP.

[12] The phrase comes from "Something of What Florence Nightingale Has Done," p. 229.

[13] The campaign for state registration was led by Ethel Bedford Fenwick. Nightingale spelled out the basis of her resistance to registration in a letter to Dr. Henry Acland in 1869: "nursing and medicine must never be mixed up. It spoils both. If the enemy wished to ruin our nurses in training at St. Thomas's it would be by persuading me to accept your noble offer of a female special certificate (or any degree) for them. (and I can say quite unaffectedly that it is a noble and generous offer). If I were not afraid of being misunderstood I would almost say—the less knowledge of medicine a hospital matron has the better (1) because it does not improve her sanitary practice, (2) because it would make her miserable or intolerable to the doctors." A few years later Nightingale continued her argument: "Nursing does not come within the category of those arts (or sciences) which may be usefully 'examined' or 'certified' by the agency proposed. . . . Nursing is not only an art but a character, and how can that be arrived at by examination?" Quoted in Cope, *Florence Nightingale and the Doctors,* pp. 121, 122.

## George P. Landow (essay date 1990)

SOURCE: "Aggressive (Re)interpretations of the Female Sage: Florence Nightingale's 'Cassandra'," in *Victorian Sages and Cultural Discourse: Renegotiating Gender and Power,* edited by Thaïs E. Morgan, Rutgers University Press, 1990, pp. 32-45.

[*In the following essay, Landow studies Nightingale's "Cassandra" as an example of feminine "sagewriting"— a gendered version of a prose style that borrows its techniques from Old Testament prophecy.*]

Were there any female Victorian sages? Were there any women who wrote the kind of aggressive prose created by Thomas Carlyle and John Ruskin, a prose modeled on that of Jeremiah and Daniel? Florence Nightingale offers an interesting test case. Certainly, her *Cassandra* (1852) makes use of many techniques that characterize the writings of the Victorian sage in England and America, and in doing so it raises interesting questions about the relation, particularly during the nineteenth century, of gender and genre.

Like the writings of the Victorian sages and the Old Testament prophets from whom they derived many of their strategies, *Cassandra* positions the sage's voice outside society and in opposition to the audience. In other words, unlike the wisdom speaker or Augustan satirist, both of whom speak and write as if they confidently embody their culture's accepted wisdom, the sage aggressively stands apart from others. One reason for this strategy involves the prophetic claim that whereas the speaker has continued to follow the laws of God and nature, his listeners have not. The speaker's aggressive positioning of himself in opposition to his listeners and readers, then, plays a part in his claim to higher moral vision.

Like Old Testament prophets, Victorian sages chiefly concerned themselves with the present and not the future. As a modern authority on the Old Testament has stated this opposition, Jeremiah and other prophets were essentially *forthspeakers* about present events rather than *forespeakers* (or predictors) of future ones.[1] Both prophetic writings and sage writings, therefore, exist as records of public voices speaking forth on contemporary issues of interest to all in society. These public voices have almost always been male, and both Old Testament and Victorian prophecy have been essentially male genres with strong patriarchal associations. The question arises: What accommodations does a woman have to make to employ—and appropriate—sage writing?

Before examining Nightingale's modifications of this historically male genre, I propose to set forth a working definition of sage writing and then look at several ways in which *Cassandra* fulfills it. Then I shall suggest that Nightingale employs the sage's characteristic acts of interpretation and reinterpretation to extend the form and take possession of it as a female sage. Finally, I shall suggest some reasons why more Victorian women did not employ sage writing, which, despite its origins, seems so obviously suited to feminist as to other controversial concerns.

Sage writing is a form of postromantic nonfictional prose characterized by a congeries of techniques borrowed, usually quite self-consciously, from Old Testament prophecy, particularly as it was understood in the nineteenth century.[2] I should point out here at the beginning of our examination of Nightingale's relation to the male tradition of sage writing that I distinguish this literary form from two others that share a few of its techniques: wisdom writing, an essentially noncontentious genre that purports to record a culture's received wisdom, and the novel, a narrative genre, some instances of which create credibility for a wisdom-speaking narrator.[3] The writings of Ralph Waldo Emerson and many British Victorian essayists exemplify the wisdom tradition in discursive prose, and the novels of George Eliot exemplify its appearance in fiction.

In contrast to these other two genres, sage writing, which is an essentially hermeneutic form, takes a far more aggressive attitude towards the audience and its beliefs, something possible in part because of biblical precedent. Carlyle, who essentially invents sage writing, and the other sages all employ a four-part prophetic structure that derives from the Old Testament.

In the first part of this structure, the sage points to some sign of the times, which is often a general condition, such as the joblessness of English workers (in Carlyle's *Chartism*), or an apparently trivial phenomenon, such as the design of a pub railing (Ruskin's "Traffic") or advertisements for London hatters (Carlyle's *Past and Present*). *Cassandra*'s third paragraph states the general issue in the form of a question: "Why have women passion, intellect, moral activity . . . and a place in society where no one of the three can be exercised?" (25).[4]

In the second part of the pattern, the sage interprets the indicated phenomenon as a symptom of a falling away from the paths of God and nature. *Cassandra*, for instance, describes the way women, when denied the opportunity to exercise their natural passion, intellect, and moral ability, live in dreamworlds of erotic reverie and erotic renunciation. Nightingale then concludes with the standard prophetic denunciation of the audience's abandonment of the ways of God and nature: "But the laws of God for moral well-being are not thus to be obeyed" (27).

Third, the sage warns his contemporaries of coming disaster if they pursue their present course. In *Cassandra* this part of the pattern is least apparent but appears in Nightingale's portrayal of a continuing state of death-in-life when she describes British women of the middle and upper classes living useless lives "wearied out" and with "the springs of will broken" (37).

Finally, the sage offers the audience a vision of future bliss if it returns to the ways it has forgotten, or else the sage calls stirringly for that change in the language of visionary awakening. Thus, near the close of *Cassandra*, Nightingale makes the characteristic call—"Awake, ye women, awake . . . all ye that sleep, awake!"—after which she offers the consolatory and inspirational promise, however qualified, of a better future when she tells her reader, "the time is come when women must do something more than the 'domestic hearth'" (52).

This quadripartite structure combines with a set of other techniques. As we have already observed, in addition to employing this kind of structure, the sages again follow the Old Testament prophets by self-consciously setting themselves in opposition to contemporary society, especially to its rulers or priests, and thus speak from off-center or in a deliberately eccentric manner. Furthermore, sage writing employs grotesque analogies and various forms of redefinition and satiric definition of key terms.

Episodic (or discontinuous) structure further characterizes sage writing, and this quality in turn relates to its aggressive confrontations with the audience. Sage writing is a high-risk form: like few other genres and modes, it attacks the audience, and in so doing it risks alienating it. One reason for sage writing's episodic or discontinuous structure lies in its risk-taking. Since attacking the audience and its beliefs demands that the audience make a leap of faith, thereby shifting its emotional and intellectual allegiances, the sage will not always succeed. Therefore, a form that permits repeated separate attempts at moving the audience has a greater chance of succeeding than does a more tightly unified one.

Arguing from unpopular positions, the sage employs all his techniques to transfer the allegiance of his audience from popular or received opinions to him. All the sage's techniques serve to create an ideal speaker who makes unusual and even controversial points, but who, in the end, turns out to be more believable and more worthy of trust than those who represent conventional wisdom. The final argument of all sage writing, in other words, is what Aristotle and rhetoricians after him termed *ethos*, or the appeal to credibility. *The Rhetoric* (1356a) explains three modes of argumentation: *logos*, the appeal to logic or reason that includes use of evidence, statistics, appeals to authority, and the like; *pathos*, the appeal to emotions; and *ethos*, or the appeal to the speaker's credibility. As Aristotle points out, in matters like politics where no preponderance of clearcut evidence exists, the appeal to credibility carries the day.[5]

The sage's definitions provide one way of establishing credibility. Like Carlyle, Thoreau, Ruskin, and Arnold, Nightingale commandeers the discourse at crucial points by taking control of key words and phrases, as when she explains that "true marriage—that noble union, by which a man and a woman become together the one perfect being—probably does not exist at present on earth" (44). By defining a commonly accepted, important word (she would probably claim that for most women "marriage" was unfortunately their most important one), Nightingale both controls the direction of the argument and proves the sage's often implicit point, that the audience, which has been corrupted by those in authority, has fallen away from the true meaning of things and needs the restorative help of the sage.

The sage uses definition as a means of convincing his audience that he deserves its attention despite the oddness or unpopularity of his views. The sage's claims to understand words better than others do contains an implicit argument for moral and spiritual superiority, since he suggests that the true meaning of words has been lost in a corrupt society, and that only he can restore language to its authenticity and truth. By redefining key words in his discourse, the sage obviously seizes control of it and asserts his claim to provide a truth necessary to the well-being of the audience.

The sage's satiric definitions, which Nightingale also uses, have the additional effect of providing a convenient means of attacking society while continuing to establish the sage's own credibility. Thus, Nightingale satirically redefines those ideals given to women by patriarchal Victorian society when they are taught to "idealize 'the sacred hearth.' Sacred it is indeed. Sacred from the touch of their sons almost as soon as they are out of the touch of childhood—from its dullness and its tyrannous trifling *these* recoil. Sacred from the grasp of their daughters' affections, upon which it has so light a hold that they seize the first opportunity of marriage, *their* only chance of emancipation." (52). Again, as in more straightforward definition, this satirical form has the effect of undermining the opposing ideas that enslave the audience. Furthermore, as with her definition of "true marriage," Nightingale, like the male sages, also combines definitions of key terms with a commonplace opposition between true and false that derives, ultimately, from Samuel Wilberforce's immensely popular *Practical Christianity* (1819).[6] Like Ruskin, Carlyle, and Thoreau, she mocks those who follow the forms of religion without the spirit: "People talk about imitating Christ, and imitate Him in the little trifling formal things, such as washing the feet, saying his prayer, and so on; but if any one attempts the real imitation of Him, there are no bounds to the outcry with which the presumption of that person is condemned" (54). Definition here combines with an assertion that the speaker has finer moral and spiritual faculties than those she opposes, for part of the sage's strategy, which Nightingale here adopts, involves building her own credibility.

Another result of such aggressive uses of definition is to point out that religion itself, which one expects to be a source of inspiration and spirituality, has become corrupt. Pointing out that "insanity, sensuality, and monstrous fraud have constantly assumed to be 'the Christ,'" Nightingale argues that such "blasphemy" is not "very dangerous to the cause of true religion in general, any more than forgery is very dangerous to commerce in general. It is the universal dishonesty in religion, as in trade, which is really dangerous" (53n). Her assertions position the sage outside and against her audience. As Nightingale points out, in the present state of affairs, "religious men are and must be heretics now—for we must not pray, except in a 'form' of words, made beforehand—or think of God but with a prearranged idea" (45). Nightingale, in other words, creates herself in the presence of the reader as one who thinks with authentic, rather than with "prearranged," ideas. As *Cassandra* continues, she reveals that these authentic, radically new ideas include a female reconception of the deity.

Another version of this emphasis upon authentic faith appears when Nightingale claims with satiric bite that "dinner is the great sacred ceremony of this day, the great sacrament" (30). Like Ruskin in "Traffic" (1869), she implies that whatever her contemporaries might claim to be their religion, they in fact worship something very earthly. Ruskin argues that despite his contemporaries' energetic professions of Christianity on Sunday, they actually devote sixth-sevenths of their time to working in the service of their true religion—the service of Mammon, or the Goddess-of-Getting-on.[7] Nightingale similarly implies that her contemporaries in fact worship an idol—Society and social success. Much of *Cassandra* argues that this idol worship requires just as cruel human sacrifice as did Nebuchadnezzar's Babylon and as does Ruskin's Manchester, Bradford, and London: "Look at the poor lives which we lead. It is a wonder that we are so good as we are, not that we are so bad (30). . . . See how society fritters away the intellects of those committed to her charge! (33). . . . What wonder if, wearied out, sick at heart with hope deferred, the springs of will broken, not seeing clearly *where* her duty lies, she abandons intellect . . . ? . . . This system dooms some minds to incurable infancy, others to silent misery" (37).

Nightingale uses other techniques of the sage, including a characteristic organization of argument and structure by means of grotesque emblems and analogies. Her grotesques, like those of Carlyle, Thoreau, and Ruskin, take two basic forms. The first is the kind found in contemporary reality, such as the child murders cited by Carlyle and Arnold, the public railing in Ruskin's *The Crown of Wild Olive,* and the "happy unconscious" (25) state of Victorian women in Nightingale.

The second form of the grotesque, which the sage creates out of whole cloth, appears as an elaborate analogy or fable, such as that of the enchanted glass dome that imprisons English workers in Carlyle, Britannia of the Market (or the Goddess-of-Getting-on) in Ruskin, and the chained statue in Nightingale. She argues with fine bitter wit by means of a set piece that draws upon a range of conceits, including those of love poetry that put women on a pedestal. Whatever may be woman's potential, "now she is like the Archangel Michael as he stands upon Saint Angelo at Rome. She has an immense provision of wings, which seem as if they would bear her over earth and heaven; but when she tries to use them, she is petrified into stone, her feet are grown into the earth, chained to the bronze pedestal" (50).

A second use of such a satirical grotesque occurs earlier when Nightingale mentions that the modern British woman, trained to do nothing, is "like the Chinese woman, who could not make use of her feet, if she were brought into European life" (42). The symbolical grotesque receives much of its power from the way it combines a fresh perception about social reality with a perverse mixture of states and conditions that appear appropriate to that reality. Nightingale's uses of this form of polemical analogy derive their power specifically from the fact that they reveal the unnatural ways in which societies distort and contort women's nature, thus rendering the natural unnatural.

In addition to thus employing the sage's grotesques, Nightingale uses other thematized techniques, or literary techniques that merge so completely with themes that separating them becomes difficult. For example, like the male sages, she attacks the present by comparing it to the past, and like them, she criticizes the present in part because it has no heroes to emulate and makes no use of contemporary capacity for heroism (36). Then, having attacked the present, she points towards the future—thereby creating a literary structure that alternates satire with visionary promise.

Nightingale's main points also recall those of the Victorian sages. Like them, she reminds the members of her audience that they have abandoned the ways of God and nature, and like them, she points out how a corrupt, unnatural language and culture reinforce each other's worst tendencies, thereby creating a downward spiral toward inevitable disaster. One of her main themes, whatever the ostensible subject, always turns out to be the loss of health and happiness—the death, in short, of the pleasures of mind and imagination that make us, finally, fully human. "To have no food for our heads, no food for our hearts, no food for our activity, is that nothing?" (41). This sounds like Ruskin on the way factory owners starve the minds and spirits of English workers, but it is Nightingale.

All these similarities between *Cassandra* and the writings of the Victorian sages raise interesting and fundamental questions about the nature of genre in general and that of sage writing in particular. Although traditions of biblical hermeneutics, classical rhetoric, neoclassical satire, Romantic vision, and the English sermon all contribute to the formation of sage writing, this genre derives primarily from Old Testament prophecy, and that source produces problems for the modern reader of such prose. Without the close acquaintance with the Bible and its interpretative tradition that the Victorians had, we miss many allusive gestures toward scripture that not only provide so much of Victorian imagery, even in works of patent nonbelievers like Swinburne, but also serve as genre signals that tell us how to read.

One message this genre conveys immediately, whether or not one recognizes its roots in Jeremiah and Isaiah, is that it concerns matters of public, not private, interest. Although the sages frequently draw upon private experience, their speech is essentially public. I might point out that sage writing, like the Victorian novel, is paradigmatically Victorian just because it makes objective, public, political use of subjective, personal, private thought and experience.[8] In keeping with the sage's purpose, all the genre's techniques contribute toward creating an idealized public self and public voice.

But Victorian women were not supposed to have public voices, were not supposed to speak in public, were not supposed to speak forth at all, and those that did, like Dickens's Mrs. Jellyby, were savagely *spoken about,* since if a woman spoke forth and entered the public sphere, she obviously had abandoned domestic duties with the seemingly inevitable result that those closest to her suffered. "Suffer and be still," or speak out and make those nearest and dearest suffer. As Nightingale explains or complains (and *Cassandra* is largely about women's right to complain), we do not "see a woman making a *study* of what she does. Married women cannot; for a man would think, if his wife undertook any great work with the intention of carrying it out,—of making anything but a sham of it—that she would 'suckle his fools' and 'chronicle his small beer' less well for it,—that he would not have so good a dinner—that she would destroy, as it is called, his domestic life" (44).

Nonetheless, women did speak out. In fact, they did so to such an extent that the rule that women should have no public voice was frequently honored as much in the breach as in the observance, though often at great cost to the women themselves. Women, for example, may not have been *supposed* to comment on public issues or to make statements about men's actions and writings, but they did, publishing anonymously in intellectual periodicals, such as *The Westminster Review,* in which all authorship, male and female, was cloaked or hidden.[9] Similarly, they published novels anonymously and pseudonymously, and they published widely in forms, such as poetry, devotional works, and children's literature, through which (even more than novels), they could speak and even gain a reputation. But to speak thus publicly, women writers had to make accommodations that ranged from choosing less prestigious literary forms to disguising—that is, denying—the fact of their female identity.

Sage writing, however, presented an even more fundamentally difficult problem for Victorian women because it derived so importantly from one particular emphasis of Old Testament prophecy, the speaker's interpretations. The sage, like the prophet, presents himself as an interpreter, an exegete of the real, for he begins by pointing to some contemporary phenomenon, which he then reads for the members of his audience, thereby revealing some truth or warning that they need in order to survive. In both Old Testament prophecy and sage writing, these acts of interpretation depend heavily on the techniques of biblical interpretation—typology, allegory, and apocalyptics—that women were not supposed to apply or to which they were not supposed to have access. As Linda H. Peterson has shown, such prohibitions created major difficulties for women autobiographers since both nineteenth-century spiritual and secular autobiography borrowed structuring patterns from scripture.[10] In the first place, almost all the relevant role models were male, and in the second, the application of these biblical figures to one's own life required interpreting the Bible, something women were not supposed to do any more than they were supposed to preach—a rule made especially clear by the Methodist prohibition against female preachers that brought the sect into conformity with all other Christian denominations. Women did, however, write autobiography, poetry (Rossetti's "Easter Sunday"), and fiction (Brontë's *Jane Eyre*) that seized male exegetical prerogatives, but to do so they often made accommodations.[11] As Peterson, Mary W. Carpenter, and Janet L. Larson have shown, during the Victorian years female authors increasingly created their own, often subversive, readings of scripture.[12]

What subversive or female readings, then, did Nightingale make in order to write and speak the interpretations of a female sage? She denies societal restrictions on female interpretation by making such interpretations in the first place, and she makes them specifically those of the female sage by aggressively reinterpreting the commonplaces of male-centered biblical and classical interpretation. I must emphasize the importance of Nightingale's reinterpretations of male-centered tradition. In historical terms, *Cassandra* marks the point at which the historian of British prose no longer writes "the sage, he" but must write "the sage, she *or* he." With *Cassandra,* sage writing becomes a genre that is no longer gender-determined. The prophetic tradition had always been fundamentally aggressive—and fundamentally patriarchal. By writing as a female sage, Nightingale in one stroke makes the sage's aggressiveness no longer the sole property of men.

The female sage's aggressive style of reinterpretation appears in the first words of *Cassandra* that the reader encounters—Nightingale's title and the epigraphs that follow. Her title, *Cassandra,* alludes to the figure from the Trojan wars who sees all but is not believed—an embodiment of the fate of the woman who tries to speak forth and save others. The title, which becomes an image of what Nightingale, as female sage, fears she is or may become, simultaneously places her in opposition to her audience and, in the manner of the male sages, curries favor with that audience by a kind of implicit self-deprecation.

In thus entitling her work, Nightingale also aligns herself with a mythic figure who blends the Old Testament prophet and a Victorian woman's version of the experience of privileged but suffering isolation. Cassandra, we recall, had access to divine knowledge of the future but bore the curse that no one would believe her in the present. In Greek myth, she received both her prophetic gift and its associated punishment from Apollo, and both gift and punishment involve her status as a woman and relations of sexual power: Apollo gave her the seer's vision of the future in order to obtain her sexual favors, and he then punished her when she refused to grant them. From a conventional male perspective, her actions can be seen either as a dishonest breaking of her word or else as a blasphemous betrayal of the divine; from a female point of view, on the other hand, her actions may appear as a doomed attempt to obtain independent vision and see truth for herself. Nightingale has chosen a female image that bears a heavy freight of mythical allusion, and in so doing she has found something in ancient texts that speaks directly to the experience of women in the power of men. Cassandra's combination of prophetic vision, alienation, and ambiguity well embodies the position of the woman who seeks to be a Victorian sage. It also exemplifies the female sage's mode of taking a social phenomenon, treating it as a text, offering a nonconventional reading, and then using this unexpected intonation to enhance her credibility.

Similarly, Nightingale's reinterpretation of commonplace texts, images, and narratives, all of which we encounter in the way she uses the figure of Cassandra, exemplifies characteristically female intonations of sage writing. This reinterpretation of cultural commonplaces, which provides an obvious and effective means of communicating a woman's perspective, permeates British women's poetry, fiction, and nonfiction during the nineteenth century.

This Principle of Reinterpretation appears early in *Cassandra,* for not only the title but also the epigraph embodies it. Whereas the title proposes woman's subversive view of Greek myth, the epigraph does the same for the Bible. Like a sermon or a religious tract—in part the models for *Cassandra*—Nightingale's tract takes as its point of departure a passage from scripture, the mention of John the Baptist that appears in three of the Gospels: "The voice of one crying in the crowd, 'Prepare ye the way of the Lord.'" In Matthew 3:3, Mark 1:2, and Luke 3:4, the voice cries "in the wilderness," not "in the crowd," and Nightingale's careful use of quotation marks emphasizes that she expects her audience both to recognize the original source and her deviation from it. Once again, she has co-opted a male text, taking it out of its usual context (and understanding) and placing it in another. She uses biblical allusion to accomplish two things: first, to claim for herself the position of a female John the Baptist preparing the way for a female Christ, and, second, to reinterpret that martyred seer as a person isolated within the crowd rather than by a spatial removal from it. In other words, Nightingale has doubly feminized the commonplace figure to make it fit better with her own experience. By claiming a role analogous to that of John the Baptist, she shows that there is apparently no limit to the outrageousness (as judged by conventional standards) of her rewriting of tradition and of the discourse that presents it. In reinterpreting John the Baptist's isolation, however, she makes a different point—that the sensitive woman always exists alone in the crowd.

Having implicitly claimed the prophet's isolation in her title and epigraph, Nightingale immediately emphasizes it in her opening sentence, in which she states that "One often comes to be thus wandering alone in the bitterness of life without" (25). Such a lonely one, she explains, "longs to replunge into the happy unconscious sleep of the rest of the race! they slumber in one another's arms—they are not yet awake" (25). Like the male Victorian sages and their Old Testament models, Nightingale claims, by such portrayal of herself as a sage-speaker, greater spiritual and moral knowledge than that possessed by her contemporaries.

Nightingale's most powerful act of reinterpretation comes at the climax of *Cassandra* when she cites one of Christ's parables from the Gospels:

> Christ was saying something to the people one day, which interested Him very much, and interested them very much; and Mary and his brothers came in the middle of it, and wanted to interrupt him, and take Him home to dinner, very likely—(how natural that story is! Does it not speak more home than any historic evidence of the Gospel's reality?), and He, instead of being angry with their interruptions of Him in such an important work for some trifling thing, answers, "Who is my mother? and who are my brethren? Whosoever shall do the will of my Father which is in heaven, the same is my brother and sister and mother." But if *we* were to say that, we should be accused of "destroying the family tie," of diminishing the obligation of the home duties. (54)

In her citation of Matthew 14:48, Nightingale aggressively shows that as a woman, she feels free to interpret the scriptures, choosing those passages that she wishes to ground her argument. In fact, having again just made her distinction between true and false religion, she emphasizes the difference between true and false "talk" about religion in order to prepare for her radically literal reading of the Gospels. Nightingale, who is in the process of arguing that women should not be entirely enslaved by family considerations, urges upon her listeners a particularly subversive form of *imitatio cristi.*

The question arises: why did not more Victorian women write as sages? Since women readily adopted and then adapted other literary forms, including that of the devotional tract and novel as well as the poem and autobiography, one might expect that many of them would have appropriated this male form as well. At least four factors seem to have prevented more Victorian women writers from employing sage writing. First of all, it is a public form that places extraordinary emphasis upon creating a public self in an age when women were not supposed to have public selves. Second, the genre derives from a patriarchal form that emphasized the speaker's original acts of interpretation, and in the nineteenth century women were conventionally barred from making such interpretations. Third, sage writing, however radically subversive, nonetheless retained its association with a religion that confined women. Finally, the emphasis upon eccentricity and the irrational that characterizes sage writing may well have proved repugnant to many women who were anxious to appear rational and logical.

Having already discussed the first two factors, I must emphasize why some women shied away from this genre because of its associations with religion. Whereas some female believers might have hesitated to work in a form in which women almost automatically risked committing blasphemy, others avoided it, one may guess, precisely because using it would suggest too much commitment to Christianity. As Frank M. Turner has pointed out, writers like Frances Power Cobb, Olive Schreiner, and George Eliot abandoned Christianity in large part because of its associations with home, family, and women's role.[13] Male authors like Carlyle, Ruskin, Arnold, and Thoreau, none of whom had orthodox Christian beliefs, could easily use the form because they found support in its patriarchal origins, from which they adopted a range of literary devices. For women, who experienced Christianity as a means of their oppression, however, the religious origins of the form had become repugnant. Few were able to do what Nightingale did when she used the sage form to argue for a female Christ and a woman's right to speak out—to use the sage's devices to attack the religion that had engendered these devices.

A more fundamental reason that few women adopted sage writing for feminist and other topics lies, I suspect, in the potentially irrational nature of the form itself. Sage writing not only demands that authors foreground themselves by a range of aggressively individualistic techniques, all of which contribute to their ethos, but it also radically challenges conventional wisdom and conventional notions of rationality. As a result, those who write as sages frequently risk being accused of irrationality, inability to reason logically, and even insanity. Carlyle, Ruskin, and others encountered such charges. Since women and members of ethnic or racial minorities are often marginalized by claims that they are less rational than those in power, they are highly unlikely to employ a literary form that patently courts charges of irrationality. Mary Wollstonecraft and W.E.B. DuBois, for example, both strive to demonstrate that, even when judged by conventional standards, they are more rational than those whom they argue against. In contrast, Ruskin, who rejects the premises of classical economics, and Thoreau, who rejects the premises of democracy, explicitly refuse to think in conventional terms that are accepted as defining the rational. Those who belong to already marginalized groups cannot risk being considered irrational, since they may find it—or believe they may find it—doubly difficult to convince the audience that reason in fact lies with them.

NOTES

[1] Robert Gordis, "The Social Background of Wisdom Literature," in his *Poets, Prophets, and Sages: Essays in Biblical Interpretation* (Bloomington: Indiana University Press, 1971), 162.

[2] George P. Landow, *Elegant Jeremiahs: The Sage from Carlyle to Mailer* (Ithaca: Cornell University Press, 1986). Since I there make use of abundant quotation from nineteenth- and twentieth-century sages, I shall here generally avoid quoting from authors other than Nightingale for the sake of brevity.

[3] Like my emphasis on individual techniques other than imagery, this distinction between sage writing and wisdom literature distinguishes my approach from John Holloway's pioneering work, *The Victorian Sage: Studies in Argument* (London: Macmillan, 1953). For a more detailed discussion of wisdom literature, see my *Elegant Jeremiahs*, 22-24.

[4] Florence Nightingale, *Cassandra*, ed. Myra Stark (London: Feminist Press, n.d.), 44. Hereafter cited in text.

[5] See my *Elegant Jeremiahs*, 154-188, which compares the use of ethos in fiction and in sage writing and examines a range of techniques sages use to ingratiate themselves with readers. These devices include citing autobiographical experience and admitting the speaker's weakness.

[6] William Wilberforce's *Practical View of the Prevailing System of Professed Christians, in the Higher and Middle Classes in This Country, Contrasted with Real Christianity* (1819), commonly known as *Practical Christianity*, which went through dozens of editions, made popular the evangelical distinction between real and nominal faiths.

[7] John Ruskin, "Traffic," in *Works*, ed. E. T. Cook and Alexander Waterborne, 39 vols. (London: George Allen, 1903-1912), 18: 447-448.

[8] For the classic statement of this quality of Victorianism, see E. D. H. Johnson, *The Alien Vision of Victorian Poetry: Sources of the Poetic Imagination in Tennyson, Browning, and Arnold* (Princeton: Princeton University Press, 1952).

[9] Martha Wastewater's *The Wilson Sisters: A Biographical Study of Upper-Class Victorian Life* (Athens: Ohio University Press, 1984), provides examples of women reviewing anonymously for *The Economist*.

[10] Linda H. Peterson, *Victorian Autobiography* (New Haven: Yale University Press, 1986).

[11] For Rossetti, see George P. Landow, *Victorian Types, Victorian Shadows: Biblical Typology in Victorian Literature, Art, and Thought* (Boston: Routledge & Kegan Paul, 1980), 87-88; for Brontë, see 97-100.

[12] Peterson, *Victorian Autobiography;* Mary W. Carpenter, *George Eliot and the Landscape of Time: Narrative Form and Protestant Apocalyptic History* (Chapel Hill: University of North Carolina Press, 1986); Janet L. Larson, who is working on women writers and the Bible during the last two centuries, promises to create a much-needed overview of this problem in relation to fiction.

[13] Frank M. Turner made these observations during the course of an NEH seminar for college teachers at Yale University, Summer 1988.

**Katherine V. Snyder (essay date 1993)**

SOURCE: "From Novel to Essay: Gender and Revision in Florence Nightingale's 'Cassandra'," in *The Politics of the Essay: Feminist Perspectives*, edited by Ruth-Ellen Boetcher Joeres and Elizabeth Mittman, Indiana University Press, 1993, pp. 23-40.

[*In the following essay, Snyder investigates the literary and cultural significance of Nightingale's transformation of "Cassandra" from a novel written from a feminine point of view to an anonymously-narrated essay.*]

"About Cassandra I see that I was mistaken. I did not exactly take Cassandra for yourself, but I thought that it represented more of your own feeling about the world than could have been the case."[1] Thus wrote Benjamin Jowett, Regius Professor of Greek at Oxford, in a letter to Florence Nightingale sometime between May and July of 1861. Their correspondence had begun the previous summer when Arthur Hugh Clough, Nightingale's secretary and an undergraduate contemporary of Jowett's, asked Jowett to comment on a three-volume work by Nightingale which included her essay, **"Cassandra."** Although the letters immediately preceding Jowett's polite retraction no longer survive, we can deduce that in them Jowett mistook Nightingale for the subject of her essay and Nightingale rebuked him for this misapprehension. In assigning the identity of Cassandra to Nightingale herself, Jowett may have been responding to the fact that there *is* no Cassandra, after the title, in the essay that he read.[2] However, in an earlier, novelistic version of the manuscript, there *was* a Cassandra or at least a character who rhetorically renames herself after the cursed prophetess of ancient myth:

> "Oh! Call me no more Nofriani, call me Cassandra. For I have preached & prophesied in vain. I have gone about crying all these many years, Wo to the People! And no one has listened or believed. And now I cry, Wo to myself! For upon me the destruction has come." [Add. MS 45839, f. 269][3]

Cassandra and Nofriani are absent from the essay as it was eventually published; Nightingale's dismissal of both figures occurred in the course of revising the manuscript several years after its composition. Her editorial decisions, more process than strategy, resulted in a significantly altered text. The first phase of the novel's development had featured a heroine who told her own tragic life-story; a later but still novelistic recension made its world available through the agency of a masculine narrator; the final transformation of **"Cassandra"** is an authoritative, anonymously narrated, essayistic account of the tragic situation of all women in society. The temporary intervention of a masculine "interpreter" distanced the narrative voice from the feminine subjectivity at issue in Nightingale's social critique. This transitional regendering of the narrative persona marked what was ultimately a generic transformation of the text: from autobiographical novel to non-fictional essay.

The shift from feminine to masculine subjectivity does not reflect an essential gendering of these prose genres but rather the literary and social history behind them. Nightingale wrote first in, and then against, a novelistic tradition whose linkage to the needs and resources of middle-class women was apparent as early as the mid-nineteenth century.[4] Despite the publication of such influential Victorian women essayists as Harriet Martineau and Mary Russell Mitford, the essay was understood almost exclusively in terms of its masculine lineage. Indeed, the nineteenth century's endorsement of what Joel Haefner has termed the "dual father theory" of the essay's origins was heartfelt. Alexander Smith's popular 1863 essay, "On the Writing of Essays," for example, focuses almost exclusively on the dual heritage of Montaigne's familiar essay and Bacon's rational essay; some forty years earlier, William Hazlitt "extended the *mythos* of two generic giants by pinpointing Addison and Steele as literary 'sons' of the father, Montaigne" [Haefner, 261]. The location of the essay's "proper" origins—determining where and to whom it "belongs"—in this polarized yet complementary patrilineage effectively eliminates the need for a challenging myth of an essayistic mother. Because it subsumes the usual role of the personal/familiar/feminine other within its own self-division, the two-father system displaces the feminine altogether, contributing to the historical neglect of women's essays and the devaluing of "feminine" style in essayistic practice.

Taxonomical distinctions between personal and rational notwithstanding, nineteenth-century readers of both of these essayistic kinds took the immediate presence of the author and his consciousness as a preeminent and uniting generic feature. From this perspective, the essay is nonfiction and mimetic—it is an expression of the writer's actual experience and essential self. However, the terms "fiction" and "non-fiction" do not map precisely onto "novel" and "essay." Just as the label "autobiographical novel" already breaks down any pure or exclusionary opposition between fiction and non-fiction, the essay occupies an indeterminate discursive space between fiction and non-fiction. That is to say, the essay, whether familiar or formal, constructs a writerly self who resembles the author's historical self but whose verisimilitude in this area as in others—Montaigne's

inaccurate quoting from sources is the recurrent example—is not beyond question.[5] Late twentieth-century language-based theories, citing "the Death of the Author" [Barthes], encourage us to read essays as purely linguistic constructions, whose free-playing signifiers construct an "author" who does not otherwise already exist in the "world." Celeste Schenck articulates the political bind that this theoretical bias presents to the burgeoning field of women's autobiography, but its relevance for theorizing the essay should be readily apparent: "A feminist reading of women's writing would argue . . . that women, never having achieved the self-possession of post-Cartesian subjects, do not have the luxury of 'flirting with the escape from identity,' which the deconstructed subject may enjoy" [288]. If we focus exclusively on language and "absence" in our attention to essayistic subjectivity, we risk sacrificing the experience of historical women authors and we risk losing gender as a category of significance.

Importantly, the status of the author and her own experience concerned Nightingale's audience and Nightingale in her revisions. For the writer and for her readers, the appropriateness of the genre of **"Cassandra"** was intimately connected to the gender of its writer. By denovelizing **"Cassandra,"** Nightingale was attempting to distance herself from her heroine's story and problems, but her revisions generated an uneasy proximity of a different kind. Without the mediation of the novel's characters, the essay's unveiled account of women's confinement within the bounds of proper society seemed to her contemporary male readers like indecent exposure. Nightingale's revisions may have been a bid for authority or even a sign that she had attained it, but the essay that they yielded found no welcoming reception from Nightingale's contemporaries.

**"Cassandra"** comes at the end of the second volume (subheaded "Practical Deductions") of Nightingale's ***Suggestions for Thought to Searchers after Religious Truth.*** Nightingale wrote this theological tome in 1850 and 1851, a period during which she was profoundly, even suicidally, depressed; her despair was largely a response to her family's seemingly insurmountable resistance to her desire for active public work.[6] However, in 1853 Nightingale received from her father an independence of £500 per year, and several months later she accepted a post as the Superintendent of an Institution for the Care of Sick Gentlewomen in Distressed Circumstances at 1 Upper Harley Street in London. In 1854 she left for the Crimean War and the nursing work that was to make her an international legend.

When Nightingale returned from the Crimea, she set about revising the manuscript of ***Suggestions,*** including the section called **"Cassandra."** She went on, in late 1859 and 1860, to have the extensively revised manuscript privately printed up in a three-volume review edition, with wide margins for annotations. The six copies in this edition were sent to her father, her uncle Samuel Smith, Richard Monckton Milnes, Sir John

McNeill, John Stuart Mill, and Benjamin Jowett.[7] Nightingale undertook no further revisions of "The Stuff," as she customarily called it. An unknown number of copies, probably very few, were printed in 1860; these books were identical to the review copies but without the wide margins.[8] *Suggestions for Thought* never became publicly available, but **"Cassandra"** was reprinted in 1928 as the appendix to Ray Strachey's *The Cause* and reprinted again as a monograph by the Feminist Press in 1979. **"Cassandra"** has reached readers only in its heavily revised form.

In its early incarnation as a fictionalized autobiographical novel, **"Cassandra"** begins (following an epigraph retained in the revised version) this way:

> The night was mild & dark & cloudy. Nofriani was walking to & fro before the beautiful facade of a Palladian palace. All was still. Not one light shining through the window betrayed the existence of any life stirring within. "I, I alone am wandering in the bitterness of life without," she said. She went down where on the glassy dark pond the long shadows of the girdle of pines the tops of which seemed to touch heaven, were lying. The swans were sleeping on their little island. Even the Muscovy ducks were not yet awake. But she had suffered so much that she had outlived even the desire to die. [Add. MS 45839, f. 237].[9]

Reentering the palace and throwing herself down on her balcony, Nofriani "start[s] up, like the dying lioness who fronts her hunters," then bemoans the way society stifles women's moral and intellectual energy and the way women respond by withdrawing into a fantasy world. She puts it bluntly: "In the conventional society, which men have made for women, & women have accepted, women must have no passions, they must act the farce of hypocrisy, the lie that they are without Passion" [MS 239]. But then, in a more fanciful vein, she calls upon the "young maidens of the 'higher toned classes'" to speak, thereby causing phantasms to appear,

> the phantasms, the larvae of the most beautiful race of the world, the maidens of the ranks, whose white hands have never been made hard by toil. Graceful & lovely, pure & etherial they floated by & their thoughts and fancies took shape & form at the word of the Magician [Nofriani]. With each maiden there was a Phantom one! There were two, three, twenties, hundreds, ever varying, ever changing, but *never* was she *alone*. With the Phantom companion of her fancy, she talked, not love, she was too innocent, too pure, too full of genius and imagination & high toned feeling for that, but she talked, in fancy of that which interested her most . . . or if not that, if not absorbed in endless conversations, she saw herself engaged with him in stirring events, circumstances which called out the interest wanting to her. [Add. MS 45839, f. 239-40].[10]

The chapter concludes with an atmospheric, spiritual, and artistic crescendo in which the narrator likens the effect of "fleecy clouds" veiling the moon's "flood of radiance" to "the wings of the Almighty overshadowing suddenly the world, as in that inspired representation of Him in Michael Angelo's Sistine Chapel" [MS 244].

In the next chapter, Nofriani pursues her theme of the mental and emotional deprivation of women by society, but here she reclines beside a fountain on a fiercely hot day with her brother, Fariseo, as her audience. This discussion, a kind of dramatic dialogue, continues through the next five chapters, apparently over some time since chapter three takes place during a snowstorm. It encompasses a critique of the family and marriage, a contrast between ideal and actual life, and the possibility of the coming of a female Christ. The piece ends with Nofriani on her deathbed at the age of thirty, with Fariseo among the mourners recounting her last requests and her final words: "Free, free, oh! divine Freedom, art thou come at last? Welcome, beautiful Death!" [Add. MS 45839, f. 287].

These final words are virtually the only ones retained as indirect discourse in the essayistic version; in that later version, however, they are attributed to some unspecified "dying woman to her mourners." Elsewhere in the essay, Nightingale removed Nofriani's speeches from their quotation marks and changed "I" of her first-person singular narration to the first-person plural—women as "we"—or to the more generalized third-person plural—women as "they." With these changes in the personal pronoun comes a shift in tense—the historical past of one woman's life is transposed to the present condition of women in general. One paragraph, for example, originally read:

> *Thus I lived for over seven years dreaming always, never accomplishing—too much ashamed of my dreams, which I thought were "romantic," to tell them where I knew that they would be laughed at, if not considered wrong. So I lived, till my heart was broken. I am now an old woman at thirty . . .*

Nightingale then revised it to read:

> Dreaming always, never accomplishing, thus women live—too much ashamed of their dreams, which they think "romantic," to tell them to be laughed at, if not considered wrong. [Add. MS 45839, f. 263][11]

In this example, the shift in person and tense coincides with certain other alterations. These alterations, which characterize the revision of the manuscript as a whole, can be grouped into two categories. First, she cut or disguised autobiographical details, such as "at thirty," Cassandra's age at death and Nightingale's age when she first wrote **"Cassandra."** At the same time, she excised stylistic details that may have seemed overly fanciful, or "romantic," such as "till my heart was broken." In fact, the two categories of revised or excised material tend to overlap because Nightingale fictionalized many details of her life by framing them in fanciful (or sometimes highly spiritualized) language and settings.

Nightingale's revisions resemble the self-censorship described in the passage from **"Cassandra"**; that is, women's concealment of their "romantic" dreams suggests a paradigm for Nightingale's own censorship of "romantic" or "dreamy" passages in her manuscript. This censorship eliminated the exotic settings and atmospheric effects of the original version, including those that open and close the first chapter; it even foreshortened accounts of women's compensatory fantasy life that were themselves particularly fanciful, like the description of Nofriani conjuring up the phantasmic maidens. By eliminating the descriptions themselves, the essay actually enacts the censorship that the novel describes.

In an earlier, pre-Crimean journal entry, Nightingale articulated the threat of fantasy and the necessity for regulating it through concealment: "Every different kind of suffering is ranged under the one comprehensive word: Fancy, & disposed of with the one comprehensive remedy: Concealment or Self-Command which is the same thing" [Add. MS 43402, f. 35].[12] But despite Nightingale's indictment of fantasy as the source of all suffering, we may infer that such "fancies" were important to her early imagining of **"Cassandra"** as a novel written for her eyes only. They were a way for her to acknowledge the problem of these consuming daydreams for women while indulging in them at the same time. In other words, the fancies involved in the writing of **"Cassandra"** as an autobiographical novel were both a symptom of and a form of therapy for what ailed Nightingale.

However, in reimagining **"Cassandra"** as a public text for a male audience, Nightingale distanced the subjectivity of her authorial voice from the problematics of feminine subjectivity that it treats. By toning down the fancifulness of her text, she made the authorial consciousness of her essay seem immune to the very fantasies that the piece exposes. The genre of the essay thereby resolves the seeming paradox of Nightingale's equation of "self-command" with "concealment"; the generic transformation that reallocated her own experience to other women not only reflects Nightingale's assumed or achieved distance from fantasy but may have actually been a way for her to attain this emotional distance.

Both the novel and the essay versions of **"Cassandra"** involve what I have been calling distancing, although by different means and with different implications.[13] Cecil Woodham-Smith's biography of Nightingale, for example, gives this account, unfortunately without attribution, of an episode from Nightingale's own life that reappears in the novelistic and essayistic incarnations of **"Cassandra"**:

> In the spring of 1851 she unexpectedly met Richard Monckton Milnes at a party given in London by Lady Parthenope [Nightingale's sister]. She had not seen him since the day she refused

him, and she was shaken. He came across to her and said lightly: "The noise of this room is like a cotton mill." She was deeply wounded—how could he speak as if she were an ordinary acquaintance?[14]

In **"Cassandra"** the novel, Nofriani finishes her discussion with Fariseo about marriage thus:

> "Oh! How cruel are the revulsions which women suffer! I remember, on the ruins of Palmyra, amid the wrecks of worlds & palaces & temples, thinking of one I had loved, in connection with great deeds, noble thoughts, devoted feelings. I saw him again. It was at one of those crowded parties of Civilization which we call Society. His words were, 'the buzz tonight is like a manufactory.' Yet that man loved me still.
>
> And now, I have soon done with this world. The life of it has departed from me." [Add. MS 45839, f. 278]

The essay **"Cassandra"** renders the anecdote this way:

> How cruel are the revulsions which high-minded women suffer! There was one who loved, in connection with great deeds, noble thoughts, devoted feelings. They met after an interval. It was at one of those crowded parties of Civilization which we call Society. His only careless passing remark was, "the buzz tonight is like a manufactory." Yet he loved her. [Add. MS 45839, f. 278]

Nightingale's earlier, novelized version of the encounter is marked by several features. For one, Nofriani's sorrowful apostrophe, "Oh!", and her "end is nigh" refrain (repeated with variations throughout the chapter) signify the relevance of the anecdote to the suffering of the first-person speaker. Another important feature of the novelized version is the defamiliarized geographical and historical setting. The exoticism and belatedness of "the ruins of Palmyra, amid the wrecks of worlds & palaces & temples" set up a disjunction with the mundane contemporaneity of "Society" and the "manufactory." This disjunction characterizes the novelistic version as a whole, with its Italianate and aristocratic characters in their timeless Romance world discussing specifically mid-nineteenth century, English, and upper middle-class pursuits like "the Opera, the Exhibitions, the debate in the House of Commons & the caricature in Punch" [MS 243]. The romantic characters and scenery disguise the "real" writing subject and her Victorian milieu, but the artificial literariness and the jarring inconsistency of the romantic trappings constantly give themselves away. They are finally less a disguise than the self-conscious construction of a different world and a different self.

When Nightingale excised the components that contributed to the novelistic world of **"Cassandra,"** she established an essayistic world that appeared more realistic and objective: more realistic because of the familiar frame of reference within bourgeois Victorian society, and more objective because the narrator is not the subject of the narrated anecdote. The essayistic anecdote, with its disinterested, rational teller and its recognizable, plausible context, would tend to appear authoritative to an upper-class male Victorian reader. In short, the essayistic anecdote makes a truth claim of a kind that the novelistic anecdote does not. However, the process of transformation in the above sequence underlines the point that both autobiographical novel and essay are mediated forms that depend on generic expectations for their effect. Both the novelistic and the essayistic versions use the anecdotal device and the figure of the representative individual to epitomize the problems of women as a whole. The "other woman" of the essay bears an unmistakable resemblance to the "other woman" in the novelistic version who is Nofriani. Moreover, both Nofriani and the "one" who meets her former lover are distinct from the author; both figures are part of the narrative strategies by which Nightingale distanced her own experience.

One crucial difference is that the novel has Nofriani narrating her own life story while the essay imagines some "one" other than its writing self as the object of its speculation.[15] While retaining the romantic theme of the clash between transcendent love and conventional society, the rational voice of the essay poses the anecdote of thwarted love as somebody else's problem. The essayistic anecdote is no longer part of the sequence of a self-told life history but a block of evidence used to build the case against conventional society. Yet the essay condemns conventional society in a voice that allies itself (at least in part) with just that social convention which excludes "great deeds, noble thoughts, devoted feelings" from everyday life and contains them in fiction. I qualify my assertion about the alliance of Nightingale's essayistic voice with social (male) authority because of her sympathy, however distanced, for the female victims whose cause she promotes. It is conceivable that the essayistic voice betrays a kind of hybridization of the emotional investment of the Nofriani narrator and the cool disinterest of the anonymous third-person narrator, but to me this dialogism betokens not a heteroglossic vitality (my vocabulary here is, of course, Bakhtinian) but a conflicted self-division. Rather than having it both ways, Nightingale experiences a double bind: masculine privilege is both the object of her social critique and the ultimate source from which she seeks discursive authority.

The denovelization of **"Cassandra"** was facilitated by a transitional defeminization of its narrative voice and identity. Nightingale began **"Cassandra"** as a novel using a third-person omniscient narrator, but one whose voice is largely subordinate to the speaking "I" who is Nofriani. By the final stage of the essay's revision, there is still an omniscient narrator but no Nofriani; her subjectivity is repressed by this authoritative, writing persona.

There was, however, an intermediate stage somewhere between novel and essay that featured a masculine first-person narrator. As soon as Nofriani has an audience, the male audience of her brother, some ambivalence over the relations between audience and speaker surfaces. This ambivalence expresses itself in the form of pronoun trouble. When her brother first appears in chapter two, his comments are marked with "said Fariseo" or "he said." But several pages into the chapter, a question he puts to Nofriani is marked with "I said," which is crossed out and replaced by "said Fariseo." For his next speech, the text sticks with "said I" with an explanatory "I am Fariseo" in parentheses. The oscillation between "he said" and "I said" continues, but in the following chapters the use of the first-person voice for Fariseo's speech stabilizes. And in the last chapter, the voice telling the story announces its identity:

> Before I go on, I had better tell who "I" am. My name is Fariseo. I am one of those, who are called the Cynics of the age, who openly confess their own selfishness, admit the wants of the times, & preach that we should bear with them, making this confession not with sorrow of heart, nor well-trained resignation, but without shame & without difficulty, as, on the whole, the best state of mind. I am the brother of poor Nofriani, & I tell her story as she told it me, one day when I blamed her for not finding her happiness in life as I & her contemporaries have done, & she answered that I did not know whether her life had been such that she could either find happiness in it or alter it. I made some few notes of our conversation, for it occurred a short time only before her death. My poor sister! She died at 30 wearied of life, in which she could do nothing & having ceased to live the intellectual life long before she was deserted by the physical life. I saw her on her death-bed, & giving way to the tears and exclamations natural on such occasions, was answered by her. [Add. MS 45839, f. 286]

None of the intermediary oscillation between first and third person is apparent in the final printed version since both characters were ultimately excised, leaving only the words of Nofriani, initially transmitted through a third-person narrator and then reported by Fariseo, finally in the form of direct, written descriptions of the general plight of women.

The regendering of the narrative persona can be read as part of Nightingale's bid for the approval of her selected audience of male readers.[16] However, an unspoken but nevertheless stringent critique of Fariseo's masculine point of view complicated her design. The unspoken critique is palpable, for example, in the longest passage that was cut from the manuscript, a passage that occurs in the same chapter as the pronominal oscillation that ultimately alters Fariseo's status. Nofriani has been trying to answer Fariseo's uncomprehending questions about her despair by using a variety of anecdotes and arguments. Finally, she turns her attention to the fountain, with its "beautiful solitary spire of water," beside which they are sitting:

> "See, it struggles up towards heaven again. And this time it will succeed. Behold, it scales Infinity. It is rising higher and higher. That mighty heart will climb to heaven. Now it has conquered Earth.

It is out of the sphere of its attraction. Oh! it is rising now! It has ascended up on high. It is leading Gravitation captive. The earth cannot reach it to pull it down again. Shoot up, brave spirit, brave spirit, soar higher! Thou hast mastered matter. Be of good cheer, thou hast over come the world. . . .

Alas! where is it now? Its impulse is exhausted; its strength is at an end; its life is blasted; its struggles done; its hope destroyed. And it falls lifeless on the grass—it, which had so lately been striving to heaven. For it is dead. . . .

The ungrateful ground had been fertilized by it. It struggled to the skies—& it watered a weed. It thought to scale Infinity—& it made verdant a blade of grass." [Add. MS 45839, f. 253-55]

In response, Fariseo tries to "improvise a 'Ballata' for her benefit, to shew [sic] her that her sick fancies were not those of all the world":

"See, how the infant founts spring & gambol & dance in the sun-beams! There is one! He is shooting with his tiny arrow at the sun. He stands, the mimic Apollo, erect & fearless & laughing sends the missile at the mark. And when the harmless arrow falls playful at his foot, he runs, with joyous laughter, back, & hides his merry face in his mother-fountain, while he tells her how the sun held out his noble hand to catch the infant spear, & could not. . . .

There, pouring his joyous soul in song, he waves his little lance on high. Glad morning vision of *light* and merry *life* as brothers! Not long does he remain there, but eager to rejoin his Mother Earth, down he springs—& his sister fount welcomes him back with her glad eyes. In loving triumph, she holds up her watery mirror, while he, the daring little soarer, successful Icarus, admires his scatheless wings. [Add. MS 45839, f. 255-57]

The chapter ends with Fariseo's words; no commentary is necessary (or possible, since he has become the narrator) to criticize his version of the *paysage moralisé*. Nofriani's eloquent silence censures his sketch, a family drama that uncritically contrasts the unrestrained, phallic activity of the water-baby brothers with the passive mirroring of the "mother-fountain," "Mother Earth," and "sister fount." He doesn't get it, but we get it and so, implicitly, does Nofriani. His translation of Nofriani's interpretation unwittingly reveals the limitations of his masculine perspective and vindicates Nofriani's complaint.

In this intermediate phase between novel and essay, the text reveals a man's failure to understand a woman's suffering through the uncomprehending words of a man himself, hardly a flattering reflection on male editors, real or within the text. The irresolvable dilemma of a masculine perspective that is authoritative yet obtuse dramatizes the conflicted nature of Nightingale's transformation of **"Cassandra"** into an essay. She revised her writing to impress male figures of authority in her personal life and in the intellectual community, but these readers were affiliated with the conventional social authority that she criticizes in "Cassandra." Her relation to her readers thus motivated but also constricted Nightingale's revisions. The gaps that remain in her essay, evident in the manuscript's palimpsestic traces of the novel, bear witness to Nightingale's sense of the irreconcilable demands posed by her male audience.

Nightingale's revisions transformed *Suggestions* from private writing—her concealed response to the emotional and intellectual privations of enforced domesticity—to public writing intended for an audience wider than one. But while the revisions prepared her writing for publication, what publication meant for Nightingale is not entirely clear. It may well have been unclear, or at least conflicted, for Nightingale herself. In a letter to Sir John McNeill, Nightingale claimed that she wrote the first volume, entitled *Suggestions for Thought to Searchers after Religious Truth among the Artisans of England,* with the artisans in mind:

Eight years ago I had a large and very curious acquaintance among the Operatives of the North of England, and among those of what are called Holyoake's party in London. The most thinking and conscientious of our enormous artisan population appeared to me to have no religion at all.

I then wrote the first part of what I have ventured to send you, without the least idea of publishing it. And it was read in MS by some of them. . . .

Till this last spring I never thought for a moment of printing it. But just now I have had six copies done of which I send you one. No one knows of it. And, till after my death, I would never have it published, certainly not with my name.

My reason for sending it you is to ask you, should the subject interest you enough, to be so good as to say *at your leisure* whether you think it would be after my death at all useful among the "Atheist" Operatives, as they are called. [Add. MS 45768, f. 112][17]

The complexities within this single letter confound any simple bifurcation between private and public writing. Nightingale could write for a particular audience and purpose, and even show the manuscript to that audience, without having "the least idea of publishing." Moreover, she claimed that any publishing would have to be both posthumous and pseudonymous. But in the letter that accompanied the copy of *Suggestions* she sent to John Stuart Mill, Nightingale wrote that "I never intended to print it *as it was*. But my health broke down. I shall never now write out the original plan. I have therefore printed the ill S.S. [Suggestions to Searchers?] as they were, mainly in order to invite your criticism, if you can be induced to give it" [Add. MS 45787, f. 1].[18] To McNeill she disavowed any premeditated aim to publish, but to Mill she only denied that she premeditated printing it in its present state.

The inconsistencies in Nightingale's different accounts of her intentions suggest her ambivalence toward further revising and publishing *Suggestions*.[19] The problem of self-publicity was standard for Victorian women autobiographers. It was scandalous for a Victorian woman to publish her memoirs during her lifetime; a respectable woman let her family, usually her children, publish her memoirs posthumously, typically in a small, privately-printed edition for distribution to family members only.[20] Our understanding of Nightingale's ambivalence over publishing is further informed by a frequent theme in her private journals and correspondence during the post-Crimean years: the annoyance and dangers of publicity. Soon after returning from the Crimea, she condemned the popular attention her work had received:

> [T]he publicity & talk there have been about this work have injured it more than anything else—and in no way, I am determined, will I contribute to making a show of myself. On this ground I have determined to sit for no one as a public character unless the Queen desire it. I desire privacy for the reason that I consider publicity to have injured what is nearest to my heart. [Add. MS 43402, f. 162]

In a private note from the same period, Nightingale connected the exploitative superficiality of publicity to her troubled relation with her family:

> What have mothers & sisters ever done for me? They like my glory—they like my pretty things. Is there anything else they like in me? I was the same person who went to Harley St and who went to the Crimea. There was nothing different except my popularity. Yet the one who went to Harley St [illegible: "that"?] person was to be cursed, & the other to be blessed. The popularity does not signify much one way or other. It has hurt me less in the Crimea and vantaged me less at home than I expected. Good Public! It knew nothing what I was really doing in the Crimea. Good Public! It had known nothing of what I wanted to do, & have done, since I came home. . . . Yet, this adventitious, this false popularity based on ignorance has made all the difference in the feeling of my "family" towards me. [Add. MS 43402, f. 179]

Nancy Boyd makes the point that while Nightingale may have protested against publicity, she nevertheless used her public image as the saintly and maternal "lady with the lamp" to promote her work [188].[21] And, in fact, during this period Nightingale published *Notes on Nursing,* which fed the Nightingale legend and thereby facilitated her work on army sanitary reform. Nightingale's preoccupation with other projects following her return from the Crimea also helps to explain her decision not to continue work on *Suggestions.*

The feedback from Nightingale's selected readers did not influence her accomplished revisions since their responses came only *after* the printing of the review copies. However, their commentary may have dissuaded her from continuing to revise. The quantity as well as the nature of their suggested revisions were daunting—only Mill suggested minor changes, whereas both Jowett and McNeill advised substantive changes that would actually undo the revisions she had already made. Jowett explicitly advocated back-tracking—"[S]uppose you were to publish the novel & imaginary conversations as they stood originally" [Quinn and Prest, 8]—as well as numerous other changes. A reversion to novelistic form was implicit in McNeill's critique as well:

> [I]t is through the imagination rather than through the reason that the masses are influenced especially in matters of religion and . . . without appeals to the imagination and a certain romance of mystery it would at this time be impossible to produce any considerable impression. [Add. MS 45768, f. 122]

McNeill's remarks link genre to class. The workers, implicitly childlike or even childish in their dependence on fiction, might be induced to accept the bitter pill of religious truth if it were sugar-coated with "a certain romance of mystery." His evaluation of the capacities of the working classes "at this time" indicates the paternalism, however benevolent or visionary, underlying his class bias; if fiction controls the masses, McNeill seems to reason, then it can be used to exert control over them. McNeill's advice combines a species of social Darwinism—a theory of "human kinds" that locates the working classes low on the evolutionary ladder—with an evolutionary theory of literary kinds in which primitive genres like fiction forerun more advanced forms of rational discourse.[22]

One connection between these parallel theories of human kinds and of literary kinds—class and genre—is the category of gender. If the way to a worker's intellect is through his imagination, then the ideal explorer of these uncharted territories would be the upper middle-class woman. As a woman, she would be sympathetically childlike yet instinctively maternal. She would share the workers' primitive tendency towards fiction, and she would be suited to "raise" the intellectual young of society. Moreover, as upper middle-class she would be morally obliged to share the imperialist burden of spiritual and social instruction. Nightingale envisioned herself in this multi-faceted role in a letter to Jowett from this period: "If I were what I was 8 years ago, I would have a Working Men's Children's School . . . to teach them all the laws of Nature (known) upon this principle, that it is a religious act to clean out a gutter and to prevent cholera" [Quinn and Prest, 17-18]. Her association of working men with their children and her sense of herself as a maternal, spiritual teacher cum head nurse support the view of class and gender relations suggested by McNeill's comments on literary form.[23]

Both McNeill and Jowett emphasized the issue of audience (possibly to deflect their criticisms from the writer onto her readers and thereby to soften the blow), but their responses as readers are not, as my comments above indicate, separable from their feelings about

Nightingale as a woman. Jowett's initial response to *Suggestions,* directed to Clough since he had not yet been introduced to Nightingale, took the writer's situation into account:

> In a few places there appeared to me a trace of passion (shall I say?) which weakened the form of what was said. Feeling there should be, for feeling is the only language which everyone understands. But I thought that here and there I traced some degree of irritation in the tone. I hardly like to notice it, for it is probably only the unavoidable weakness of illness which always impairs the power of expression much more than [the] power of mind and thought. [Add. MS 45795, f. 19]

He interpreted the "weakened . . . form" as a product of the "weakness of illness," linking physical and literary weakness to uncontrolled "passion." In a later letter to Nightingale that comments explicitly on **"Cassandra,"** Jowett's concern with "weakness" resurfaced:

> But I think it would add to the effect of what is said . . . if the difficulties of the subject were more considered e.g., the extremely small number of women (or indeed of men) who are capable of fulfilling an ideal or carrying out an original walk of life;—the weakness which is often found precisely in the character most likely to form a sentimental idea;—the dangers which women must incur unless they could be supposed to be quite impassible. [Quinn and Prest, 4]

While he included men in a conciliatory parenthetical gesture, for him weakness was an attribute of illness and of passion, and therefore especially of women, those who are most susceptible to a "sentimental idea."

Despite his agreement with Nightingale that the "value" of her papers depends on "their being a record of your own experience" [Quinn and Prest, 8], Jowett repeatedly objected to just this feature of her writing:

> it would add to the effect of what is said . . . if the reflection on the family took less the form of individual experience; this appears to me to lessen the weight of what is said & may, perhaps, lead to painful remarks. [Quinn and Prest, 4]

> The difficulty I should find would be to separate the part which expresses your own feelings & thoughts from those which belong to other characters. [Quinn and Prest, 9]

Even in its revised essayistic form, **"Cassandra"** was still too emotional and too personal for Jowett's sense of decorum. Apparently, it seemed even more personal and emotional than a fully novelized version might have because no characters interpose between writer and reader; as nonfiction, it displays undisguised the feelings and experience of the author. To Jowett, the non-fiction essay left the woman writer indecently exposed, whereas fictionalized, novelistic trappings would provide fittingly modest attire for **"Cassandra"** and for Nightingale's life.

Whereas Nightingale's male readers saw the essayistic version of **"Cassandra"** as too revealing, I see it as a cover-up. Having witnessed the fragmentation and cancellations of the manuscript, I regard Nightingale's essay as inhibited and concealing, a form of protective self-censorship rather than liberated self-empowerment. While I grant that Nightingale's revisions reflect a new control over her fantasy life and may even have helped her to gain that control, it is a control that comes at a heavy price. Aligning herself with the masculine authority that was the subject of her critique may have enabled Nightingale to accomplish the social reforms that were her goals, but it played havoc with the voice of **"Cassandra."** The gaps and other structural and tonal peculiarities that characterize the essay testify to Nightingale's gendered and generic predicament, yet at least one recent critic has seen in them a subversive feminist poetics.[24]

The combination of defeat and resistance, of co-optation and subversion, in Nightingale's **"Cassandra"** resonates in the response of an early reader and feminist essayist in her own right. Virginia Woolf's landmark essay, "A Room of One's Own," published in the year following the belated public appearance of **"Cassandra"** in *The Cause* (1928), alludes several times to Nightingale's essay. Distinguishing her own essayistic style from that of **"Cassandra"** in which "Florence Nightingale shrieked aloud in agony," Woolf nevertheless partly derives her feminist poetics from the practice of Nightingale as an essayistic foremother. Thus, Woolf's prediction of the second coming of Judith Shakespeare echoes yet modifies the prophesy in **"Cassandra"** of a female savior. The belated reception that Nightingale's essay found in Woolf does not indicate that **"Cassandra"** was ahead of its time, but rather that Nightingale was entrenched in her historical moment.

NOTES

An earlier version of this article was presented at a 1989 MLA special session, "Illuminating the Lady with the Lamp: Writings by and about Florence Nightingale." I would like to thank the participants in that session, Linda Peterson, Nancy Armstrong, and the editors of this volume for helping to guide this essay along its way.

[1] Jowett-Nightingale correspondence, Balliol College Library, Oxford University. An abridged version of this letter is reproduced in Quinn and Prest, 8.

[2] Although Nightingale may have reproved Jowett's identification of her as Cassandra, she refers to herself as "poor Cassandra" in a letter to a cousin; see Cook, 1913, 1:116. Furthermore, many years after his retraction, in the established intimacy of their correspondence, Jowett could playfully address Nightingale: "My dear Cassandra, Are you really 'Cassandra,' as I suspect when I see the title of Mr. Grant Duff's article in the 'Contemporary Review'? I thought that Cassandra prophesied what was true but that nobody believed her. I am afraid that he may give you the labour of preparing an

answer." According to Quinn and Prest, 264, "Rocks ahead; or the Warnings of Cassandra," by W. R. Greg appeared in the *Contemporary Review* in 1874.

[3] "Cassandra," Add. MS 45839, f. 269, Nightingale Papers, British Library.

[4] Christ documents the link in nineteenth-century literary criticism (as well as in nineteenth-century literary production) between heroic masculinity and non-fiction prose, exploring the sexual politics implicit in the gendered and generic Victorian stereotyping of "lady novelists," "feminine poets," and "men of letters."

[5] The dialogue between fiction and nonfiction and the patching-together of quotations are two features of the essay which have encouraged its recent reconceptualization along the lines of Bakhtinian novel theory. But despite the "intergeneric" [Haefner], a-generic, or anti-generic [Bensmaïa] heteroglossia of both the novel and essay genres, the historical importance to Nightingale and her contemporary readers of an organic/evolutionary model, positing the family relation as well as the taxonomic distinction between novel and essay, warrants our attention here.

[6] For accounts of Nightingale's emotional and intellectual outlook during this period and after her return from the Crimea, see the standard biographies by Cook and Woodham-Smith. See also Showalter, 1981.

[7] This list of recipients is from Quinn and Prest, xii. Neither Woodham-Smith nor Showalter mentions Nightingale's father or uncle, although Showalter [1981, 407] includes historian J. A. Froude among Nightingale's selected readers of *Suggestions*.

[8] Copies of the narrow-margin book are in the British Library and in the Florence Nightingale Museum.

[9] To preserve Nightingale's voice, I have left her distinctive orthography—her ampersands and her underlinings—intact.

[10] These phantoms resemble the ones in an 1847 letter Nightingale wrote to her friend, Mary Clarke Mohl ("Clarkey") soon after her marriage:

> We must all take Sappho's leap, one way or other, before we attain to her repose—though some take it to death and some to marriage and some again to a new life even in this world. Which of them is the better part, God only knows. Popular prejudice gives it in favor of marriage. . . . In single life, the Stage of the Present and the Outward world is so filled with Phantoms, the phantoms, not unreal tho' intangible, of Vague Remorse, tears, dwelling on the threshold of everything we undertake alone, Dissatisfaction with what is, and Restless Yearnings for what is not . . . love laying to sleep those phantoms (by assuring us of a love

so great that we may lay aside all care for our own happiness . . . because it is of so much consequence to another. [Woodham-Smith, 45]

[11] The printed edition varies slightly from the revised manuscript here—"to tell them where they will be laughed at, even if not considered wrong" [Stark, 39]—and elsewhere in "Cassandra." These differences indicate that Nightingale made further revisions in proofs which are no longer extant. Most of these late revisions are minor. Several changes, however, are more substantive, including two discursive footnotes added in the proof stage which can be read in Stark, 50 and 53. Another substantive revision in proof tones down a scathing analogy comparing marriage to prostitution. The passage originally read:

> And now they are married. . . . The woman is as often a prostitute as a wife. She prostitutes herself, if she has sold her person for an establishment, as much as if she had sold it in the streets. She prostitutes herself, if, knowing so little of her husband as she does, she begins immediately, without further acquaintance, to allow him the rights of a husband over her person. She prostitutes herself, later, if, against her own desire, she allows herself to be made the blind instrument of producing involuntary children. It will be said, & truly, that, when she marries, her husband understands all these privileges as granted, & that she would drive him mad & deceive his understood expectation, if she did not grant them. But how is she to ascertain her husband's opinion on these points before marriage? [Add. MS 45839, f. 277]

Only the sentence about allowing "the rights of a husband over her person" was excised from the manuscript initially, but the entire passage was further abbreviated in proof to read: "And now they are married. . . . The woman who has sold herself for an establishment, in what is she superior to those we may not name?" [Stark, 48].

[12] Many critics have commented upon Nightingale's pre-Crimean struggles against day-dreaming, a habit which she compares to "gin-drinking" [Add. MS 43402, f. 54]; see especially Stark's introduction to "Cassandra," 8. Like the strategic invalidism of her later years, Nightingale's early brushes with madness can be interpreted as a response to social and domestic demands which were both overwhelming and confining; see Pickering, 1976, 165-177 and also Showalter, 1985, especially 62-66.

[13] "Distancing" is a useful paradigm for describing the activity of Nightingale's different generic discourses, but it is nevertheless problematic, not because it implies that there is a "real" historical experience to which the narrative refers, but because the essayistic and novelistic representations achieve proximity and connection with her experience as much as distance and separation. The important point here is that neither essay nor novel is intrinsically "closer" to Nightingale's actual experience but that each achieves its relative distance (or closeness) through a different generic code.

[14] Woodham-Smith, 70. It is worth reiterating here that Monckton Milnes was one of the recipients of the limited editions of *Suggestions* which included the fictionalized sketch of their encounter cited here as well as Nightingale's comments on the sketchiness of modern poets which mention Monckton Milnes along with Tennyson, one of his intimates, and Mrs. Browning. While we cannot know precisely what Nightingale meant to achieve by communicating her views of their thwarted love and his poetic skill in this manner, it certainly complicates our understanding of Nightingale's preparation of "Cassandra" for her male audience.

[15] Sidonie Smith holds that "[t]he doubling of the 'self' into a narrating 'I' and a narrated 'I' and, further, the fracturing of the narrated 'I' into multiple speaking postures mark the autobiographical process as rhetorical artifact and the authorial signature as mythography" [47]. My reading of Nightingale's imagining of Nofriani as the speaking self in her fictionalized autobiography implicitly accepts this position, although here I explicitly emphasize the alterity of the "one" who is the non-speaking object of the essayistic discourse.

[16] It is possible that what I have identified here as a stage of revision between novel and essay (in which Fariseo serves as the first-person narrator) may actually have occurred as part of Nightingale's pre-Crimean writing of the novel. If the shift did occur in the course of her early "private" writing (for her eyes only), its significance would have more to do with her writing as an early symptom and therapy than as a later bid for authority.

[17] This letter is marked "30, Old Burlington Street, London W. May 17/60." Nightingale sent McNeill the portion containing "Cassandra" about three months later (in a letter marked "August 29/60"): "I send you the Parts Second and Third of the religious 'stuff' (confidential) of which I sent you the first part some time ago" [Add. MS 45768, f. 118].

[18] The letter is on lined paper in a school-girl hand: either a copied letter or Nightingale assuming the ingénue. Nightingale writes of sending the second and third parts to Mill on Sept 28, 1860 [Add. MS 45787, f. 23].

[19] In his iconoclastic and essentially hostile study, F. B. Smith uses the discrepancies between the letters to her different readers to argue that Nightingale was self-aggrandizing and manipulative. He also casts doubt on Nightingale's relation to the artisans, citing the lack of evidence for Nightingale's relation to the working-class secularist G. J. Holyoake or to the Northern artisans. However, Smith weakens his argument when he suggests that Jowett humored Nightingale but "dodged her repeated requests to edit the work," and that "[o]nly good, grave John Stuart Mill . . . directly annotated Miss Nightingale's text" [185-86]. The voluminous Jowett-Nightingale correspondence which spans over 33 years evinces, to the contrary of Smith's animadversions, deep mutual respect. Moreover, Cook's biography reports that Jowett annotated *Suggestions* in detail: "The proof copy of 'The Stuff,' with Mr. Jowett's annotations, was one of Miss Nightingale's most cherished possessions" [1:472]. Unfortunately, Cook does not cite the location of this artifact, and I have been unable to discover it.

[20] I am grateful to Linda Peterson for this information about autobiographical publishing practice and for her insight into its parallels with Nightingale's declared intentions and ultimate distribution of *Suggestions* to her coterie of male readers. For more on permissible genres for Victorian women's autobiographies, see Peterson's chapter, "Martineau's *Autobiography:* The Feminine Debate over Self-Interpretation."

[21] Mary Poovey also argues that Nightingale participated in her own popular misrepresentation as a "saving angel" in her chapter, "A Housewifely Woman: The Social Construction of Florence Nightingale."

[22] The idea that fiction gratifies a primitive urge is shared by post-Darwinian genre critics well into the twentieth century, including the classic formulation in E. M. Forster's *Aspects of the Novel:* "For the more we look at the story (the story that is a story, mind), the more we disentangle it from the finer growths that it supports, the less shall we find to admire. It runs like a backbone—or may I say a tapeworm, for its beginning and end are arbitrary. It is immensely old—goes back to neolithic times, perhaps to paleolithic. Neanderthal man listened to stories, if one may judge by the shape of his skull" [26].

[23] My analysis of class and gender interactions is influenced by Mary Poovey's discussion of Nightingale's participation in British imperialism at home and abroad; she illuminates the gendered and classed implications of Nightingale's post-Crimean "campaign for nursing": "as an imperialistic program, we can see that it had two related fronts. The first was the 'domestic' front within medicine . . . her object was to carve out an autonomous—and ultimately superior—realm for female nursing. The second front was the 'foreign' front of class . . . her object here was to bring the poor and their environment under the salutary sway of their middle-class betters" [188].

[24] In a 1989 MLA paper, Elaine Showalter suggested that the structural peculiarities of Nightingale's "Cassandra," like those of Margaret Fuller's "Woman in the Nineteenth Century," present a political challenge to conventional masculine rhetoric.

WORKS CITED

Bakhtin, Mikhail M. *The Dialogic Imagination: Four Essays.* Edited by Michael Holquist; translated by Caryl Emerson and Michael Holquist. Austin: University of Texas Press, 1981.

Barthes, Roland. "The Death of the Author." In *Image, Music, Text/Roland Barthes: essays selected and translated by Stephen Heath.* New York: Hill and Wang, 1977.

Bensmaïa, Réda. *The Barthes Effect: The Essay as Reflective Text.* Translated by Pat Fedkiew. Minneapolis: University of Minnesota Press, 1987.

Boyd, Nancy. *Josephine Butler, Octavia Hill, Florence Nightingale: Three Victorian Women Who Changed Their World.* London: Macmillan, 1982.

Christ, Carol. "'The Hero as Man of Letters': Masculinity and Victorian Nonfiction Prose." *Victorian Sages and Cultural Discourse: Renegotiating Gender and Power.* Edited by Thaïs E. Morgan. New Brunswick: Rutgers University Press, 1990.

Cook, Edward T. *The Life of Florence Nightingale.* 2 vols. London: Macmillan, 1913.

Forster, E. M. *Aspects of the Novel.* San Diego: Harcourt Brace Jovanovich, 1927.

Haefner, Joel. "Unfathering the Essay: Resistance and Intergenreality in the Essay Genre." *Prose Studies: History, Theory, Criticism* 12 (3) 1989: 258-73.

Jowett, Benjamin. Jowett-Nightingale Correspondence. Balliol College Library. Oxford University.

———. Letter to Clough. Additional Manuscript 45795. Nightingale Papers. British Library.

Nightingale, Florence. *Cassandra: An Essay.* Edited by Myra Stark. Old Westbury, N.Y.: Feminist Press, 1979.

———. *Notes on Nursing; What It Is, and What It Is Not.* Boston: W. Carter, 1860.

———. *Suggestions for Thought to Searchers after Religious Truth.* 3 vols. Privately printed. London: Eyre & Spottiswoode, 1860.

———. Private papers. Additional Manuscript 43402. Nightingale Papers. British Library.

———. Letter to McNeill. Additional Manuscript 45768. Nightingale Papers. British Museum.

———. Letter to Mill. Additional Manuscript 45787. Nightingale Papers. British Museum.

———. "Cassandra." Additional Manuscript 45839. Nightingale Papers. British Museum.

Peterson, Linda. *Victorian Autobiography: The Tradition of Self-Interpretation.* New Haven: Yale University Press, 1986.

Pickering, George. *Creative Malady.* New York: Dell, 1976.

Poovey, Mary. *Uneven Developments: The Ideological Work of Gender in Mid-Victorian England.* Chicago: University of Chicago Press, 1988.

Quinn, Vincent, and John Prest, eds. *Dear Miss Nightingale: A Selection of Benjamin Jowett's Letters to Florence Nightingale, 1860-1893.* Oxford: Clarendon, 1987.

Schenck, Celeste. "All of a Piece: Women's Poetry and Autobiography." In *Life/Lines: Theorizing Women's Autobiography.* Edited by Bella Brodski and Schenck. Ithaca: Cornell University Press, 1988.

Showalter, Elaine. *The Female Malady: Women, Madness and English Culture, 1830-1980.* New York: Pantheon, 1985.

———. "Florence Nightingale's Feminist Complaint: Women, Religion, and *Suggestions for Thought.*" *Signs* 6 (1981): 395-412.

Smith, Alexander. *Dreamthorp; A Book of Essays Written in the Country.* London: Stratham, 1863.

Smith, F. B. *Florence Nightingale: Reputation and Power.* London: Croom Helm, 1982.

Smith, Sidonie. *A Poetics of Women's Autobiography; Marginality and the Fictions of Self-Representation.* Bloomington and Indianapolis: Indiana University Press, 1987.

Strachey, Ray. *The Cause: A Short History of the Women's Movement in Great Britain.* London: Virago, 1978.

Woodham-Smith, Cecil. *Florence Nightingale 1820-1910.* New York: McGraw-Hill, 1951.

Woolf, Virginia. *A Room of One's Own.* New York: Harcourt Brace Jovanovich, 1929.

## Michael D. Calabria and Janet A. Macrae (essay date 1994)

SOURCE: An introduction to *Suggestions for Thought by Florence Nightingale: Selections and Commentaries,* edited by Michael D. Calabria and Janet A. Macrae, University of Pennsylvania Press, 1994, pp. ix-xxxv.

[*In the following excerpted introduction to* Suggestions for Thought, *Calabria and Macrae detail the sources of Nightingale's ideas on religion.*]

> Many years ago, I had a large and very curious acquaintance among the artisans of the North of England and of London. I learned that they were without any religion whatever—though diligently seeking after one, principally in Comte and his school. Any return to what is called Christianity appeared impossible. It is for them this book was written.[1]

"This book," *Suggestions for Thought to the Searchers after Truth among the Artizans of England,* was an 829-page work in three volumes that Florence Nightingale had privately printed in 1860. She affectionately referred to it as her "Stuff." Her motivation for writing her "Stuff" was to offer the artisans, or working class people of England, an alternative to atheism. Disillusioned with conventional religion and weary of ungrounded metaphysical speculation, many were turning to the positivist philosophy of Auguste Comte,[2] in which all valid knowledge is based on verifiable propositions. Nightingale was also an empiricist, but, instead of abolishing the concept of God as did Comte, she sought to unify science and religion in a way that would bring order, meaning, and purpose to human life. Sir Edward Cook, Nightingale's early and still most authoritative biographer, wrote that *Suggestions for Thought* has conspicuous merits along with equally conspicuous defects:

> The merits are of the substance; the defects are of form and arrangement; but Miss Nightingale never found time or strength or inclination—I know not which or how many of the three were wanting—to remove the defects by recasting the book. Unpublished, therefore, it is likely, I suppose, to remain. But as it stands it is a remarkable work. No one, indeed, could read it without being impressed by the powerful mind, the spiritual force, and (with some qualifications) the literary ability of the writer. If she had not during her more active years been absorbed in practical affairs, or if at a later time her energy or inclination had not been impaired by ill health, Miss Nightingale might have attained a place among the philosophical writers of the nineteenth century.[3]

Although Nightingale was best known for her writings on nursing practice, she also wrote extensively on the subjects of nursing education and administration, hospital construction and administration, sanitation, statistics, social reform, the health of the British soldier, and the improvement of the farming systems of India. Most of her writings were in the form of privately printed reports, papers published in conference proceedings, and newspaper and journal articles.[4] The context or basis for all her work, however, is found in *Suggestions for Thought.* Although Nightingale expressed her opinions on spiritual matters in diary entries and in letters to family and friends, *Suggestions for Thought,* together with two 1873 articles in *Fraser's Magazine,*[5] are the only works exclusively devoted to the explication of her spiritual philosophy.

Nightingale, who lived for ninety years (1820-1910), wrote *Suggestions for Thought* when she was in her thirties. The work is thus a product of the young Florence Nightingale, and should be understood within the context of her intellectual and emotional life at that time. Accordingly, this introduction, rather than being a chronologically ordered biography, is a summary of some of the major influences—philosophies, persons, and events—that helped shape her thinking at an early age and thus form the background to *Suggestions for Thought.* . . .

THE PASSIONATE STATISTICIAN

Named for the Italian city in which she was born, Florence was the younger of two daughters born to William Edward and Frances ("Fanny") Smith Nightingale. Both parents came from wealthy British backgrounds: her father, the heir to an estate, and her mother, the daughter of a philanthropic Member of Parliament.

William Edward Nightingale, or W.E.N., as he was called, personally supervised the education of his daughters. A graduate of Cambridge and a liberal-minded Unitarian, his views on the education of women were much in advance of his time. He taught Florence and her older sister Parthenope history, philosophy, French, Italian, German, Latin, and classical Greek. A member of the British Association for the Advancement of Science, W.E.N. took the family to its meetings and, on at least one occasion, entertained a number of the scientists at the Nightingales' estate.[6] A "commonplace" book in which Florence kept lesson notes during her adolescence indicates that her education included rudiments of chemistry, geography, physics, and astronomy.[7] Florence was much more interested in mathematics than was her father, however, and she had to pursue the subject on her own because W.E.N. was reluctant to engage an instructor.[8]

Because of Nightingale's natural predilection for collecting and analyzing data, her interest in mathematics turned into a passion for statistics. She enjoyed reading statistical tables, particularly those dealing with nursing and public health, as most people enjoy reading novels. While in the Crimea (November 1854 to July 1856) she not only cared for the wounded, served as an auxiliary purveyor, and instituted sanitary reforms, but also systematized the careless record keeping practices of the military hospitals. In a lengthy report entitled *Notes on Matters Affecting the Health, Efficiency and Hospital Administration of the British Army* (1858), she pioneered the graphical representation of statistics, illustrating with charts and diagrams how improved sanitation decreased the rate of mortality.[9] This report served as the blueprint for a large scale system of reforms introduced by her friend Sidney Herbert, the Secretary at War, during the years 1859-1861.

Nightingale was deeply influenced by the work of Lambert-Adolph-Jacques Quetelet (1796-1874), the Belgian astronomer and natural scientist who is generally regarded as the founder of modern social statistics. In 1841 Quetelet organized the Commission Central de Statistique, which became the central agency for the collection of statistics in Belgium and set the standard for similar organizations throughout Europe. His efforts to achieve international cooperation in statistics led to the founding of the International Statistical Congress in 1853. Nightingale was a member of this organization and met with Quetelet when he traveled to England in 1860.[10]

Quetelet applied the statistical method to social dynamics (most notably the yearly crime rates in various groups) illustrating regularities in human behavior. He felt, as did Nightingale, that these regularities were caused by the social conditions of these groups and that legislation which improved social conditions would also improve human behavior. Unlike many of their contemporaries, who were committed to the doctrines of free will and individual responsibility, Quetelet and Nightingale felt that human will is subject to law, as is everything else in the universe. "If we could entirely know the character and circumstances of a man," Nightingale wrote, "we might predict his future conduct with mathematical precision."[11]

Nightingale was not only a "passionate statistician,"[12] as Cook described her, but also a "reverent statistician." In her view, God is the Divine Mind who organizes the universe through scientific laws. These laws or organizing principles are discovered through the study of statistical patterns. Statistics is thus a sacred science that allows one to transcend one's narrow, individual experience and read the thoughts of God.

## THE WESTERN MYSTICAL TRADITION

By the time she was in her teens, Nightingale had mastered the elements of classical Greek and had translated portions of Plato's *Phaedo, Crito,* and *Apology.*[13] Plato's metaphysical philosophy greatly appealed to her and influenced her view of the world. Some of the main concepts in *Suggestions for Thought,* for example, the material world as the imperfect expression of a transcendent reality, can be traced back to Plato. In her later years, she helped her friend Benjamin Jowett, the classical scholar and Master of Balliol College at Oxford, revise his translation of the *Dialogues of Plato* (published in 1875). She annotated his summaries and introductions, and at his request sent him copious suggestions for revision. He referred to her as a "first-rate Critic" who kept him up to a higher standard:

> I cannot be too grateful to you for criticizing Plato. . . . I have adopted nearly all your hints as far as I have gone (however many hints I might give you, my belief is that you would never adopt any of them).[14]

It is perhaps from the study of Plato that Nightingale became deeply interested in the Christian mystics. She mentioned to Jowett that there were "curious analogies" between the writings of Plato and those of medieval mystics such as Francis of Assisi and John of the Cross. With great interest she read Thomas à Kempis's *The Imitation of Christ,* copiously marking and annotating her copy with personal reflections.[15] Her attraction to the mystics was, she wrote, a result of the fact that they were "not for Church but *for* God," and that they threw overboard "all that mechanism & lived for God alone."[16]

During the years 1873-74 she worked on a book of extracts from various mystical writings which was to be entitled *Notes from Devotional Authors of the Middle Ages, Collected, Chosen, and Freely Translated by Florence Nightingale.* The book was unfortunately never completed, but Sir Edward Cook was able to reconstruct the preface from her various notes and rough drafts. In the following passages, she presents her view of mysticism and the spiritual life.

> For what is Mysticism? Is it not the attempt to draw near to God, not by rites or ceremonies, but by inward disposition? Is it not merely a hard word for "The Kingdom of Heaven is within"? Heaven is neither a place nor a time. There might be a Heaven not only *here* but *now* . . .
>
> That Religion is not devotion, but work and suffering for love of God; this is the true doctrine of Mystics—as is more particularly set forth in a definition of the 16th century: "True religion is to have no other will but God's."
>
> Christ Himself was the first true Mystic. "My meat is to do the will of Him that sent me and to finish His work." What is this but putting in fervent and the most striking words the foundation of all real Mystical Religion?—which is that for all our actions, all our words, all our thoughts, the food upon which they are to live and have their being is to be the indwelling Presence of God, the union with God; that is, with the Spirit of Goodness and Wisdom.
>
> Where shall I find God? In myself. That is the true Mystical Doctrine. But then I myself must be in a state for Him to come and dwell in me. This is the whole aim of the Mystical Life; and all Mystical Rules in all times and countries have been laid down for putting the soul into such a state.[17]

In spite of her emphasis on Christian mysticism, Nightingale argued that "you must go to Mahometanism, to Buddhism, to the East, to the Sufis & Fakirs, to Pantheism, for the right growth of mysticism."[18] As will be shown subsequently, Nightingale became well versed in the spiritual traditions of the east.

Thus at the center of Nightingale's spiritual philosophy is a concept that undergirds all the mystical traditions: that the universe is the incarnation or embodiment of a transcendent God, and that human beings, through a change in consciousness, are able to experience the underlying divinity of themselves and their world.[19] In Nightingale's view, all phenomena are regulated by law, and thus mystical union with God can be knowledgeably facilitated by creating the appropriate circumstances. Society should be organized, she thought, in a way that would help each individual attain physical and spiritual health, "for putting the soul into such a state" for the indwelling of the divine life. She found conventional society, including the Church of England of which she was a nominal member, sadly lacking.

She was particularly interested in the Roman Catholic religious orders, especially those devoted to serving the poor, because they represented an attempt to organize life around a spiritual purpose. During a six-month visit to Rome when she was twenty-seven years old, she went on a ten-day retreat at the convent of the Trinità de Monte. There she met Madre Santa Colomba, who had such a profound effect on her that two years later, while traveling in Egypt, she still felt the influence of her "madre" (see below). Although she attended mass and was received by the Pope, she tried to reassure her parents that she was not converting:

> Are you afraid that I am becoming a Roman Catholic? I might perhaps, if there had been anything in me for Roman Catholicism to lay hold of, but I was not a Protestant before. . . . Can either of these two [churches] be true? Can the "word" be pinned down to either one period or one church? All churches are, of course, only more or less unsuccessful attempts to represent the unseen to the mind.[20]

Despite these remarks to her family, Nightingale was indeed tempted to convert to Roman Catholicism, because she felt it offered more opportunities for women than did the Church of England. She discussed the issue with her friend the Rev. Henry Edward Manning,[21] a recent convert to Catholicism, who was working with the poor in the East End of London:

> But you do know now, with all its faults, what a home the Catholic Church is. And yet what is she to you compared with what she would be to me? No one can tell, no man can tell what she is to women—their training, their discipline, their hope, their home—to women because they are left wholly uneducated by the Church of England, almost wholly uncared-for—while men are not. For what training is there compared to that of the Catholic nun? . . . There is nothing like the training (in these days) which the Sacred Heart or the Order of St. Vincent gives to women.[22]

In the summer of 1852, while Nightingale was considering converting to Roman Catholicism, she was also preparing a 65-page proof of *Suggestions for Thought*. The content of the proof (much of which was included in the expanded work) centered on the lawful universe, a concept inconsistent with many widely held beliefs, such as God's forgiveness of sins, Christ's atonement, and the verity of miracles as recorded in the Bible. After reading her work, Manning prudently advised her *not* to convert as her views were far too radical. Although it would appear contradictory of Nightingale to consider converting to a church which "insists peremptorily upon my believing what I cannot believe,"[23] it illustrates her deep need to be part of an organization or institution through which she could channel her talent and energy, and which would help her give outward form to her inner life.

## THE FOUNDER OF MODERN NURSING

It was somewhat of an exaggeration for Nightingale to write that the Church of England left women "almost wholly uncared-for." The Anglo-Catholic revival represented by Tractarianism (see commentary in Chapter 1, "On the Concept of God") in the 1840s had stimulated the growth of women's religious orders modeled on Roman Catholic sisterhoods.[24] Edward Bouverie Pusey (1800-1882), the High Church reformer, influenced the founding of the Sisterhood of the Holy Cross in 1845, and his friend Priscilla Lydia Sellon established the Sisterhood of Mercy of Devonport and Plymouth in 1848. The first nursing sisterhood of the Church of England, the Training Institution for Nurses, St. John's House, was also founded in 1848. Nightingale showed little interest in these groups, and did not refer to them in *Suggestions for Thought*. The reasons for her lack of interest are unclear, but she did not support the Tractarian movement with which the Anglican sisterhoods were affiliated, and this position likely influenced her opinion of the sisterhoods themselves.

Nightingale spent a short time at the hospital of the Sisters of Charity in Paris in 1853 and three months at the Institution for Deaconesses at Kaiserswerth, Germany in 1851. The Institution had been founded in 1833 by Theodore Fliedner (1800-1864), an Evangelical pastor and philanthropist, and his wife as a refuge for women recently discharged from prison, but grew to include a hospital, nursery school, and orphanage. Years after her apprenticeship at Kaiserswerth, Nightingale wrote: " . . . never have I met with a higher tone, a purer devotion than there. There was no neglect." And yet: "the hospital was certainly the worst part of Kaiserswerth. I took all the training that was to be had—there was none to be had in England, but Kaiserswerth was far from having trained me."[25]

Nightingale was thus largely self-taught in the area of nursing. For years, she got up before dawn to study hospital and public health reports, making her own statistical analyses; she inspected hospitals all over England and abroad; and she took every opportunity to care personally for the ill, both within her own extended family and among the poor in the villages near her country estate. Nightingale acquired her nursing knowledge (that is, "knowledge of the laws of health") through observation and experience. Health is not an arbitrary gift of God, she concluded, but a state human beings must achieve for themselves. "With regard to health or sickness," she wrote in *Suggestions for Thought,* "these are not 'sent' to try us, but are the results of keeping, or not keeping, the laws of God; and, therefore, it would be 'conformable to the will of God' to keep His laws, so that you *would* have health."[26]

Her classic text, *Notes on Nursing* (1860), can be viewed as a practical application of the central concepts in *Suggestions for Thought*. Healing, like all physical phenomena, is a lawful process. It is regulated by nature, that is, the expression or manifestation of God. Through careful observation, nursing must discover the laws of healing, such as the need for proper nourishment, ventilation, cleanliness, and quiet, and thus be able to cooperate consciously in the restorative process. "Nature alone cures," she wrote, "and what nursing has to do . . . is to put the patient in the best condition for nature to act upon him."[27]

Unfortunately, at the time of the Crimean War (1853-56), not only were "the very elements of nursing . . . all but unknown,"[28] but secular hospital nursing was considered menial work for which little training was required. Nurses were often recruited from the ranks of street women, among whom alcoholism and sexual promiscuity were common. Charles Dickens caricaturized the nurse of the day in his portrayal of Sairey Gamp in *Martin Chuzzlewit*. Because hospital nursing had such a bad reputation, most parents (including the Nightingales) were horrified if their daughters evinced an interest in this type of work, and thus nursing lost a great many intelligent and compassionate women. Indeed, when Nightingale was asked by the government to select a group of nurses to work in the military hospitals in the Crimea, she had a difficult time finding qualified applicants.[29] It was not only to help relieve the suffering of the soldiers, therefore, that she accepted this challenge:

> The consideration of overwhelming importance was the opportunity offered to advance the cause of nursing. Were nurses capable of being employed with success to nurse men under such conditions? The eyes of the nation were fixed upon Scutari. If the nurses acquitted themselves creditably, never again would they be despised. "If this succeeds," Sidney Herbert had written, "an enormous amount of good will have been done now . . . a prejudice will have been broken through and a precedent established which will multiply the good to all time."[30]

Toward the end of the war, a Nightingale Fund was established as a thank offering from the people of England. The fund was used to establish the first non-sectarian nursing school, the Nightingale Training School at St. Thomas's Hospital in London.

THE STRUGGLE FOR FULFILLMENT

For Nightingale, service to God is service to Humanity. Mystical union with God is not an end in itself, but the source of strength and guidance for doing one's work in the world. The aim of human life, she wrote, is to create heaven—here and now—on the earth: "The 'kingdom of heaven is within,' indeed, but we must also create one without, because we are *intended* to act upon our circumstances."[31]

Unfortunately, however, Nightingale's sense of vocation created a great deal of friction in her family life. Bored and frustrated by the leisured life of an upper class young woman, Florence wrote: "I craved for some regular occupation, for something worth doing instead of frittering time away on useless trifles."[32] Fanny Nightingale had high social expectations for her attractive and charming daughter, and a bitter conflict arose when Florence insisted on devoting her life to nursing.

W.E.N., with his liberal views, was inclined to let Florence have her ways; his character was less forceful than his wife's, however, and in the end he chose the path of least resistance. It was only after years of struggle, disappointment, and unhappiness for all concerned that Florence was given permission to study nursing at the hospital of the Sisters of Charity and at the Institution for Deaconesses in Kaiserswerth.

The frustration Nightingale felt over the lack of opportunity for women is partly responsible for the tone of discontent that pervades much of *Suggestions for Thought*. Harsh criticisms of conventional society are found throughout the second volume of her work. "There appears to be now no relation to God in anything we do," she wrote, "no reference to Him in any of our modes of life. Among the rich the reference is to how much of material enjoyment they can crowd in; among the poor, how not to starve."[33] The structure of family life came under her attack, particularly with respect to the role and position of daughters. She was infuriated by the assumption that an unmarried woman would stay at home, cater to the whims of the family, and follow her own interests at "odd moments."

> The maxim of doing things at "odd moments" is a most dangerous one. Would not a painter spoil his picture by working on it "at odd moments?" If it be a picture worth painting at all, and if he be a man of genius, he must have the whole of his picture in his head every time he touches it, and this requires great concentration, and this concentration cannot be obtained at "odd moments," and if he works without it he will spoil his work. Can we fancy Michael Angelo running up and putting on a touch to his Sistine ceiling at "odd moments"?[34]

John Stuart Mill, one of the few people who received a copy of *Suggestions for Thought* when it was first printed in 1860, was particularly struck by Nightingale's social criticisms. In *The Subjection of Women*, written in 1861 and published in 1869, Mill directly alluded to her work:

> . . . if he [a man] has a pursuit, he offends nobody by devoting his time to it; occupation is received as a valid excuse for his not answering to every casual demand which may be made on him. Are a woman's occupations, especially her chosen and voluntary ones, ever regarded as excusing her from any of what are termed the calls of society? . . . She must always be at the beck and call of somebody, generally of everybody. If she has a study or a pursuit, she must snatch any short interval which accidently occurs to be employed in it. *A celebrated woman, in a work which I hope will some day be published, remarks truly that everything a woman does is done at odd*

*times.* Is it wonderful, then, if she does not attain the highest eminence in things which require consecutive attention, and the concentration on them of the chief interest of life?[35]

Years later, Virginia Woolf referred to these same social criticisms of Nightingale's in *A Room of One's Own* (1929), her classic book about women and fiction:

> If a woman wrote, she would have to write in the common sitting-room. And, as Miss Nightingale was so vehemently to complain,—"women never have an half hour . . . that they can call their own"—she was always interrupted. Still it would be easier to write prose and fiction there than to write poetry or a play. Less concentration is required. Jane Austen wrote like that to the end of her days.[36]

Woolf's footnote indicates that the quotation was taken from **"Cassandra,"** an essay (or "novel" as Nightingale called it) on the confined life of a woman in upper class British society. Nightingale had written the essay in 1852 and then appended it to the second volume of *Suggestions for Thought.* **"Cassandra"** was published separately in 1928 as an appendix to Ray Strachey's *The Cause: A Short History of the Women's Movement in Great Britain;*[37] Woolf indicated that it was Strachey's edition from which she was working. It is evident that Nightingale's words were on Woolf's mind when she was writing *A Room of One's Own.* She referred to Nightingale several times and many of her ideas are similar to those in **"Cassandra"** and other sections of *Suggestions for Thought:* the importance of one's state of mind for creative work; the necessity of money, time, and privacy for achieving that state of mind; and the creative process as an evolutionary phenomenon unfolding throughout history.

*Suggestions for Thought* is an excellent illustration of Virginia Woolf's thesis in *A Room of One's Own.* Tracing the history of women and fiction, she observes that, with a few notable exceptions such as Jane Austen, who had in some way made peace with the narrowness of her circumstances, the artistry of women's work has been distorted by bitterness and frustration:

> The reason perhaps why we know so little of Shakespeare . . . is that his grudges and spites and antipathies are hidden from us. We are not held up by some "revelation" which reminds us of the writer. All desire to protest, to preach, to proclaim an injury, to pay off a score, to make the world the witness of some hardship or grievance was fired out of him and consumed. Therefore his poetry flows from him free and unimpeded. If ever a human being got his work expressed completely, it was Shakespeare. If ever a mind was incandescent, unimpeded . . . it was Shakespeare's mind . . .

> . . . and when people compare Shakespeare and Jane Austen they may mean that the minds of both had consumed all impediments; and for that reason we do not know Jane Austen and we do not know Shakespeare, and for that reason Jane Austen pervades every word that she wrote, and so does Shakespeare.[38]

Unfortunately, Nightingale's mind, with all its greatness, was not "incandescent." As Woolf comments, "Florence Nightingale shrieked aloud in her agony."[39] Scathing criticisms of the "prison" of family life in which the daughters are being "murdered" crept into the second volume of *Suggestions for Thought,* taking the reader by surprise and disrupting the flow of the philosophical discussion. To strengthen the integrity of the work, we had planned to organize this material into an appendix, but later decided to give it a chapter of its own within the text. This is truer to the original work and also to Florence Nightingale herself, for the painful struggle to achieve fulfillment as a brilliant woman in nineteenth-century England was, indeed, an integral part of her life.

UNITARIANISM

Because Nightingale had been raised in the Anglican church and was deeply attracted to the religious orders of the Roman Catholic church, it comes as no surprise that most of her comments on organized religion in *Suggestions for Thought* focus on these two churches. It has been noted previously, however, that she may also have been influenced by Unitarian ideas because both parents came from Unitarian backgrounds. (Fanny Nightingale chose to rear her daughters in the Church of England probably for reasons of prestige.[40]) Nightingale's maternal grandfather, William Smith (1756-1835), was a prominent Unitarian Member of Parliament dedicated to securing rights for "dissenters" (non-Anglican Protestants) as well as Catholics. Smith convinced Parliament in 1813 to pass the Unitarian Toleration Act, which made denying the divinity of Christ no longer a crime.[41] Smith was also a supporter of Joseph Priestley (1733-1804), an outspoken Unitarian theologian and scientist (he discovered oxygen) whose radical opinions on religion and politics incited a riot in 1791, compelling him to flee to America. Nightingale recorded in a letter (ca. 1840) that her Uncle Sam (Samuel Smith, her mother's brother) read Dr. Priestley to the family.[42] That Nightingale was familiar with Priestley's work is also evident from her remarks in *Suggestions for Thought.*

Unitarians were distinguished by their rejection of the Trinity and of the divinity of Christ. They also disputed such beliefs as original sin, predestination, the atonement, the last judgement, and eternal damnation. Although initially Unitarians based their beliefs on scripture, under the growing influence of German biblical criticism (see below) and the leadership of James Martineau (1805-1900),[43] a more liberal faction developed whose adherents looked for solace in human reason and conscience rather than in the scriptures or church. Social causes such as prison reform, education, temperance, and women's rights became increasingly central to the work of the Unitarian community.

Although Nightingale held many beliefs in common with Unitarians, and like them was concerned with "deeds not creeds," if we can judge from the few remarks in *Suggestions for Thought,* Unitarianism on the whole does not seem to have impressed her. She referred to it as "dull" because, like Judaism, it was "pure Monotheism," and noted that while Unitarians had eliminated Christ and the Holy Ghost as objects of worship they had not succeeded in making God "more loved or more loveable."[44] She clearly spoke in terms of the Trinity, and believed that all people, like Christ, are "incarnations of God"—ideas that are contrary to Unitarian beliefs.

THE INFLUENCE FROM GERMANY AND THE EAST

Because dissenters were barred from attending Oxford and Cambridge Universities until 1854 and 1856 respectively, many Unitarians went abroad to study and thereby became familiar with German theology, which had a decidedly liberal bent. By the nineteenth century, Germany was far more advanced than England in the areas of theology, biblical criticism, and historical scholarship. At the end of the previous century, the German theologian Friedrich Schleiermacher (1768-1834) had addressed his remarks in *Religion: Speeches to Its Cultured Despisers* (1799) to the "sons of Germany," maintaining that they alone were capable and worthy of having awakened "the sense for holy and divine things," while the English knew "nothing of religion."[45] This sentiment was later corroborated in England by Mark Pattison, rector of Lincoln College, who noted that "It is now in Germany alone that the vital questions of Religion are discussed with the full and free application of all the resources of learning and criticism which our age has at its command."[46] This development can perhaps be traced back to the reign of Frederick II, the "Great" (1712-86), King of Prussia (1740-1786), who advocated religious toleration among his subjects. Although a number of socio-political factors contributed to religious unrest in the Victorian Church, the influence of German scholarship on English freethinkers should not be underestimated. Writers Samuel Coleridge and Thomas Carlyle did much to introduce German intellectualism into England, as did George Eliot,[47] who in 1846 undertook a translation of David Friedrich Strauss's *Das Leben Jesu.* Strauss's highly controversial work (with which Nightingale was familiar[48]) argued for a mythological interpretation of the New Testament, thereby denying the divinity of Jesus, his incarnation, miracles, and resurrection.

By age twenty, Florence Nightingale too was studying German, and reading the works of the German orientalist and theologian Heinrich Ewald (1803-1875).[49] In a letter to her parents from Paris in 1853, Nightingale listed "German Metaphysics" among her principal reading interests (along with "Catholic Rules" and the French philosophers Auguste Comte and Victor Cousin),[50] and she herself noted on several occasions that Germany was more advanced than England in terms of religion and philosophy.[51] She had ample opportunity to explore

German scholarship through her friendships with the German orientalists Julius von Mohl (1800-1876) and Christian Carl Josias von Bunsen (1791-1860). Through her friendships with these men, the young Florence Nightingale became familiar with the works of leading German theologians and historians, and became conversant in the spiritual legacy of the Near and Far East. This is evidenced by her letters and personal notes, which contain discussions of ancient Egyptian religion, Islam, Zoroastrianism, Hinduism, and Buddhism.[52]

Known primarily for his translation of the Persian epic *Shah Nameh* ("Book of Kings") by Firdausi, Julius von Mohl was the husband of Mary Clarke, a close friend of Nightingale's, whose home in Paris was a popular gathering place of intellectuals. Nightingale corresponded with Mohl on politics, literature, philosophy, and religion, and on several occasions pressed him for his opinion on gnosticism,[53] a religious and philosophical movement of the Hellenistic and early Christian world that combined elements from Judaism, Christianity, and other sources and emphasized secret knowledge. She was probably interested in the Gnostics because, like her, they sought spiritual truth through their own inner development rather than through the intercession of the Church. According to Cook, Mohl had great admiration for Nightingale's intellect, and she "regarded his studies in eastern religion as a real contribution to 'theodike,' one of her principal preoccupations."[54] Nightingale's confidence in Mohl's intellectual abilities was such that she considered him the ideal person to edit *Suggestions for Thought.*[55]

The German diplomat and scholar Christian Carl Josias von Bunsen, Prussian ambassador to the Court of St. James from 1842 to 1854, also proved to be of considerable importance to Florence Nightingale's intellectual and spiritual development. Nightingale frequented Bunsen's home in London, which had become a center of scholarly activity, and sought his advice on matters of both a personal and academic nature. He introduced her to the works of the great German philosophers, historians, and theologians of the day, such as Arthur Schopenhauer (1788-1860), Barthold Niebuhr (see below), and Friedrich Schleiermacher,[56] as well as the prominent English intellectuals and clergymen who comprised the "Broad Church" movement (see below). By means of her association with Bunsen and his colleagues, Nightingale was exposed to the spiritual traditions of the East as well as to elements of heterodox theology seen clearly in *Suggestions for Thought.*

The Baroness Bunsen indicates that the friendship between Nightingale and her husband commenced in 1842, when Florence was twenty-two years of age, and that he

> from the first valued her, on a few occasions, when nothing occurred peculiarly to rouse and reveal the soul which subsisted in her, in the fullness of its energy, or the powers which only waited for an opportunity to be developed; but

her calm dignity of deportment, self-conscious without either shyness or presumption, and the few words indicating deep reflection, just views, and clear perceptions of life and its obligations, and the trifling acts showing forgetfulness of self and devotedness to others, were of sufficient force to bring conviction to the observer, even before it had been proved by all outward experience, that she was possessed of all that moral greatness which her subsequent course of action, suffering, and of influential power, has displayed.[57]

Bunsen's significance goes much beyond his personal influence of Nightingale and her work, however, for, as R. A. D. Owen wrote in his study of Bunsen, "Certainly few men of foreign birth ever played so prominent a part in the religious discussions of the nation [i.e., England], certainly, none in the nineteenth century."[58]

Despite his career as a diplomat, Bunsen was primarily a scholar of ancient and oriental languages and mythology, as well as a theologian.[59] In addition to Latin, Greek, and Hebrew, Bunsen studied ancient Egyptian, Chinese, Persian, and Arabic, and for some time considered a journey to India to perform linguistic research. He described his scholarly objectives as follows:

> I remain firm, and strive after my earliest purpose in life, more felt, perhaps, than already discerned,—namely, to bring over into my own knowledge and into my own Fatherland the language and the spirit of the solemn and distant East. I would for the accomplishment of this object even quit Europe, in order to draw out of the ancient well that which I found not elsewhere.[60]

Bunsen applied his philological and historical knowledge to the study of scripture as means of enhancing religion—not threatening it as conservatives feared. He studied Jewish, Christian, Islamic, and Hindu scriptures, and the works of authors as diverse as the "heretic" Giordano Bruno (see below) and the Persian mystic Jalal ud-Din Rumi.[61] Like Nightingale, he was interested in the works of Plato and the Christian mystics.

In 1817, Bunsen entered diplomatic service in Rome under the tutelage of his mentor Barthold Niebuhr (1776-1831), a noted historian and the Prussian ambassador to the Vatican, whom he succeeded as Counsellor of the Legation in 1823. While in Rome, Bunsen formed enduring friendships with English intellectuals such as Connop Thirlwall, Julius Charles Hare, and Thomas Arnold,[62] all of whom were later subjected to criticism by religious authorities in England on account of their unorthodox views. Their interest in German scholarship in history and theology, such as Niebuhr's *History of Rome* and Schleiermacher's essay on St. Luke, which contradicted Church teachings on the chronology and origin of Scripture, provided the foundation for the "Broad Church" movement in England,[63] which will be discussed subsequently in relation to Nightingale's work. During his years in Rome, Bunsen also made the acquaintance of Richard Monckton Milnes, a student of

Connop Thirlwall's who was later to become a serious contender for the hand of Florence Nightingale.[64]

Bunsen's activities were not confined to the scholarly, but extended to humanitarian endeavors. In Rome he established a Protestant infirmary where people of that faith could receive medical care without being subjected to Catholic proselytizing. Later he would also establish a hospital in London to serve the large German-speaking population there. This facility proved to be of great benefit to all community residents regardless of nationality. Bunsen's work with hospitals undoubtedly influenced Nightingale, who for a short time before going to the Crimea (1853-54) served as superintendent of the Institution for the Care of Sick Gentlewomen in Distressed Circumstances. There she worked to secularize the institution, in order that women of all faiths might be admitted and their clergymen free to attend them. Prior to Nightingale's appointment, only Anglican patients and their priests were admitted to the facilities.

Bunsen left his diplomatic post in Rome in 1838 and served briefly as envoy to the Swiss Republic from 1839-40, during which time he befriended another controversial British theologian, Frederick Denison Maurice. (Some years later Maurice would be dismissed from his position at King's College on account of his *Theological Essays,* in which he argued against the doctrine of eternal damnation, as would Nightingale in *Suggestions for Thought.*)

In 1841 Bunsen was appointed envoy to England, and met the young Florence Nightingale the following year. In addition to her intellectual interests, Nightingale sought out Bunsen's advice on matters of spirituality, asking of him, "What can an individual do, towards lifting the load of suffering from the helpless and the miserable?"[65] She was to find the answer to her query in the Institution of Deaconesses at Kaiserswerth. Bunsen was familiar with the Institution because he had gone there himself in 1844 to find qualified nurses for the German Hospital in London. Nightingale mentioned in a letter that, finding it to be "an admirable institution," he considered sending one of his daughters there.[66] Shortly after Bunsen sent Nightingale the Institution's yearbook in 1846, she noted: "There is my home, there are my brothers and sisters all at work. There my heart is and there, I trust, will one day be my body."[67]

Before leaving on an extended voyage to Egypt in November 1849, Nightingale visited with Bunsen, who provided her with the "*dernier mot* on Egyptology," according to Nightingale's sister Parthenope.[68] Her trip to Egypt proved to be something of a spiritual catharsis as she struggled to realize her ambitions. Beginning in February 1850, she made frequent references in her diary to God calling or speaking to her. On several occasions God revealed His will to her in the words of her "madre," Santa Columba of the Convent Trinità de Monti in Rome. In early March she wrote that she had "settled the question with God,"—undoubtedly referring to her decision to dedicate her life to nursing.[69] Within a month after leaving Egypt, on her thirtieth birthday (May 12), she noted:

> To day I am 30—the age Xt began his Mission. Now no more childish things, no more vain things, no more love, no more marriage. Now Lord, let me only think of Thy will, what Thou willest me to do. O, Lord, Thy will, Thy will.[70]

Before returning to England in August 1850, she visited the hospital at Kaiserswerth, returning the following year for a three month sojourn.

The letters she wrote to her family from Egypt are also indicative of her spiritual state and contain remarkable discussions of religion, both ancient and modern. Her comments on ancient Egyptian religion are noteworthy because Egyptian hieroglyphs had only been deciphered as recently as 1822 by the French Egyptologist Jean Francois Champollion (1790-1832), a friend of Bunsen's. As evidenced by these letters from Egypt, Nightingale was familiar with hermetic writings.[71] The term "hermetic" is used to designate a body of Latin and Greek texts dating from the second and third centuries A.D. Esoteric in content and character, they are attributed to Hermes Trismegistus, the Greek counterpart of Thoth, the Egyptian god of wisdom, called "the thrice great." Although Platonic and Stoic influences are conspicuous in these writings, the texts also seem to incorporate elements of Egyptian theology. A central theme of the *Hermetica* is the emphasis on the acquisition of divine knowledge as the means for achieving an ultimate union with or absorption in God.[72] Undoubtedly Nightingale would have been attracted to this mystical component. During the Renaissance hermetic writings became known to the west primarily through the works of the philosophers Marsilio Ficino (1433-99) and Giordano Bruno. Burned as a heretic in part for espousing the virtues of ancient Egyptian occultism as related in the Hermetica, Bruno was of particular interest to Bunsen[73] and may have also influenced Nightingale's spiritual philosophy (see Chapter 4, "On Sin and Evil").

Many of the issues Nightingale would subsequently address in *Suggestions for Thought,* such as the benevolent nature of God and universal law, are discussed in her letters from Egypt in 1849-50. Universal Law, as an expression of Divine Will, occupies a prominent place in the personal philosophies of both Bunsen and Nightingale. Bunsen wrote that "whatever emanates from the spirit is a revelation of the Divine, unfolding itself according to eternal laws."[74] Later, Nightingale would speak of an "All-Ordering Power" whose thoughts are manifest as law, so that "everything, down to the minutest particular, is so governed, 'by laws which can be seen in their effects,' that not the most trifling action or feeling is left to chance . . ."[75]

Despite the fact that Bunsen's historical and philological investigations had revealed inaccuracies in the literal interpretation of scripture, he, as did Nightingale, nonetheless believed that Christianity provided a moral framework for life. In a letter to the Sanskrit scholar Friedrich Max Müller (see below), Bunsen commented on the gospels and the works of the German mystic Meister Eckhart (c.1260-c.1328):

> I am delighted that you are absorbed in Eckhart [sic] . . . there is nothing better, except for the Gospel of St. John. For there stands still more clearly than in the other gospel writings, that the object of life in this world is to *found the Kingdom of God on earth* . . . [76]

Nightingale too communicated this idea in her work, writing: "The 'Kingdom of heaven is within,' but we must also make it *without.*"[77] She was also greatly influenced by the Gospel of John, and wrote: "For myself the mystical or spiritual religion as laid down by St. John's Gospel, however, imperfectly I have lived up to it, was and is enough."[78]

As will become apparent, the spiritual philosophy espoused by Florence Nightingale in *Suggestions for Thought* contains elements not typical of either Anglican or Unitarian thought of her day, notably the evolution of consciousness, in which the individual progressively realizes his or her unity with the Divine. This concept can be found in Eckhart and Bruno, and is consistent with the writings of Teresa of Avila, with which Nightingale was familiar, but it became popular in nineteenth-century western thought primarily through the discovery of the far-eastern spiritual traditions and the study of Sanskrit and comparative religion.

In addition to her associations with Mohl and Bunsen, Nightingale may have become familiar with the fundamentals of the eastern spiritual tradition through the works of Friedrich Max Müller (1823-1900) and Rowland Williams (1817-1870).

Friedrich Max Müller, a German student of Sanskrit who was to become one of the most renowned scholars of Indian languages and literatures, came to London in 1846 to consult manuscripts in the library of the East India Company. Bunsen promptly befriended the young scholar, assisting him financially and professionally. It was Bunsen who persuaded the East India Company to publish Müller's translation of the *Rigveda* (1849), pointing out that "it would be a disgrace if some other country than England published this edition of the Sacred Books of the Brahmans."[79]

Although Nightingale would not meet Müller until late in life, it is likely that she was familiar with his work through Bunsen and other friends they had in common, such as Julius and Mary von Mohl.[80] Bunsen introduced Müller to the scholarly community at Oxford, where he would eventually become Professor of Comparative Philology. At Oxford, Müller met and became friends with Benjamin Jowett, the classical scholar and liberal theologian who would later figure largely in Nightingale's life, and James Anthony Froude

(1818-1894), a controversial historian and novelist. When Froude was forced to resign his fellowship at Exeter College over his *Nemesis of Faith* (1849),[81] Bunsen secured for him a position in Germany, which he nevertheless declined. More than ten years after the private printing of *Suggestions for Thought,* Nightingale sent a copy of the manuscript to Froude, whose opinion was unfavorable due to its "want of focus and form." As editor of *Fraser's Magazine,* Froude did publish two of her articles in May and June 1873, "A 'Note' of Interrogation" and "A Sub-'Note' of Interrogation." Written with the encouragement of Benjamin Jowett, the articles reiterate some of the issues developed at length in *Suggestions For Thought.* The articles were widely noticed and brought her many letters, both supportive and critical. Some individuals, shocked at her views, told Nightingale that they would pray daily for her conversion!

In the late 1850s, while revising and expanding her draft of *Suggestions for Thought,* it is possible that Nightingale became familiar with a comparative study of Christianity and Hinduism by Rowland Williams entitled *A Dialogue of the Knowledge of the Supreme Lord, in Which are Compared the Claims of Christianity and Hinduism.* On reading the book, Bunsen lauded Williams as "one of the deepest scholars and philosophical minds of the age."[82] Addressing both Buddhist and Hindu systems of belief, Williams discusses concepts such as the unity of mankind, the one supreme soul (God) which is particularized in the various forms of life, the idea that natural laws imply an ordering Mind, the existence of suprasensual knowledge beyond that of the body, that one's will is dependent on one's condition, reincarnation, the cyclic nature of existence, and that evil is a part of the divine plan and remedial in purpose. Many of these ideas are also discussed by Nightingale in *Suggestions for Thought.*

### NIGHTINGALE AND THE "BROAD CHURCH"

Among Bunsen's English friends and acquaintances were a number of liberal Anglicans including Benjamin Jowett, Thomas Arnold, Arthur Penrhyn Stanley,[83] Rowland Williams, Julius Charles Hare, Connop Thirlwall, and Frederick Denison Maurice. Because their opinions on theological matters were neither those of the "Low Church" (or Evangelical), which emphasized scripture and personal religious experience, nor those of the "High Church," which stressed the Church's authority in matters of doctrine, they were regarded as part of the "Broad Church." This term, according to Jowett, was coined by the poet Arthur Hugh Clough (1819-61), a classmate of both Jowett and Froude and later Nightingale's secretary.[84] Although many so-called "Broad Churchmen" differed on specific theological issues, the term generally designated a group of liberal Anglicans who were united by their critical approach to both doctrine and scripture and by their belief in the freedom of inquiry. Like Unitarians, the individuals comprising the Broad Church sought to emphasize the ethical component of Christianity rather than its doctrines

as represented by the Thirty-Nine Articles and the Book of Common Prayer. They took issue with some church tenets, such as original sin, eternal punishment, and atonement, and questioned whether the Bible was divinely inspired.[85] Broad Churchmen generally held that divine revelation had been imparted to mankind over the course of human history, and was therefore not exclusive to Christianity:

> . . . the moment we examine fairly the religions of India and of Arabia, or even those of primaeval Hellas and Latium, we find they appealed to the better side of our nature, and their essential strength lay in the elements of good will which they contained, rather than in any Satanic corruption.[86]

Similarly, Florence Nightingale wrote:

> To know God we must study Him in the Pagan and Jewish dispensations as in the Christian . . . this gives unity to the whole—one continuous thread of interest to all these pearls.[87]

Common to Broad Churchmen was their familiarity with German theology, philosophy, and historical scholarship, particularly the works of Schleiermacher and Niebuhr. Having been friends of both, Bunsen played a pivotal role in the Broad Church movement in England. Bunsen himself was the subject of an essay written by Rowland Williams in the highly controversial work of the Broad Churchmen entitled *Essays and Reviews.* The Broad Church movement culminated in the publication of this work, which appeared in print in 1860, the same year as *Suggestions for Thought.* Common to all the discussions in *Essays and Reviews*[88] was the demand on behalf of the clergy for freedom of inquiry in matters of theology and scripture. Noting the ever-widening abyss between official Church positions and those of its more educated members, Benjamin Jowett remarked in his essay "On the Interpretation of Scripture" that "the healthy tone of religion among the poor depends upon freedom of thought and inquiry among the educated."[89] The essayists concluded that theology must be subject to the same rigorous critical analysis as other academic disciplines, and that philosophical, scientific, and historical investigations must be admitted into discussions of theology. To this effect, essayist Frederick Temple remarked: "There are more things in heaven and earth than were dreamt of in patristic theology."[90]

The responses to *Essays and Reviews* were copious and unrelenting: over one hundred responses in print were elicited from members of the Church.[91] With the publication of Darwin's *Origin of Species* just three months prior to that of *Essays and Reviews,* the Church obviously sensed that its teachings were under attack and acted accordingly. Essayists H. B. Wilson and Rowland Williams were tried and found guilty of heresy before the ecclesiastical Court of Arches in 1862. (The Church was dealt a serious blow when they were later acquitted by the Judicial Committee of the Privy Council, a state rather than church body.) In 1863 Benjamin Jowett was tried before the vice-chancellor's court at Oxford. Although the charges were eventually dropped, Jowett was denied an increase in his stipend until 1865. In addition, his appointment as Master of Balliol College was blocked until 1870.[92] Ten years after the publication of *Essays and Reviews,* the theological climate was still such that Frederick Temple was forced to withdraw his essay from subsequent editions, following his appointment as Bishop of Exeter.

The Church and its institutions did not take criticisms from this constituency lightly: blatant rejection of Church doctrine by clergy and academics would cost many their reputations and offices. When F. D. Maurice expressed doubts on the Church's doctrine of eternal punishment in his *Theological Essays* (1853), the Council of King's College, London dismissed him, deeming his opinions to be of "dangerous tendency, and likely to unsettle the minds of the theological students."[93] Thomas Arnold and A. P. Stanley were never to receive bishoprics. Max Müller probably lost the election to the chair of Sanskrit at Oxford because of his association with Bunsen and the Broad Churchmen, and thus decided against contributing to *Essays and Reviews.*

Although both *Essays and Reviews* and **Suggestions for Thought** addressed such issues as the critical evaluation of scripture, the implausibility of miracles in a lawful universe, and the doctrine of eternal damnation, only *Essays and Reviews* garnered the wrath of ecclesiastical authorities because the unpublished **Suggestions for Thought** remained discreetly in the hands of a select few. To a great extent the controversy surrounding *Essays and Reviews* was due to the fact that six of the seven essayists were ordained clergymen in the Anglican Church, some of whom had previously aroused suspicion because of their unconventional views. Benjamin Jowett, for example, had been asked by the vice-chancellor of Oxford to renew his pledge to uphold orthodox Church doctrine as expressed in the Thirty-Nine Articles as a result of the views he expressed in his edition of the Epistles of St. Paul (1855).

Nightingale had much in common with the people who comprised the Broad Church: like them she wanted religion held to the same critical standards as science, philosophy, and history, and like them she had been influenced by German theology. She too challenged belief in the atonement, incarnation, eternal damnation, baptismal regeneration, and miracles. In addition to her friendship with Bunsen, her social and intellectual circle included several prominent Broad Churchmen and liberal Anglicans, including Frederick Temple, F. D. Maurice, A. P. Stanley, and later Benjamin Jowett.

Nightingale had known Temple (also a friend of Jowett, Arthur Hugh Clough, and Stanley), as early as 1852.[94] She probably met Maurice through his sister Mary, who served on the governing committee of the Institution for Sick Gentlewomen in Distressed Circumstances where Nightingale worked as superintendent in 1853.[95]

Nightingale was keenly interested in Maurice's quarrel with the Church, and Maurice himself visited her on at least one occasion in 1855.[96] She became acquainted with Arthur P. Stanley through his sister Mary, whom she had met in Rome, and who was also interested in hospital work and later served in the Crimea.

In addition to her friendships with the above, Nightingale was also familiar with the works of Baden Powell and Mark Pattison, two well-known Broad Churchmen who contributed to *Essays and Reviews* and whom she cites in *Suggestions for Thought.* Yet, despite her associations with these individuals and her familiarity with German theology, the vast literature on the Anglican Church in the nineteenth century nowhere mentions Nightingale in the Broad Church context. The opinions expressed in *Suggestions for Thought* will show, however, that she should be regarded as part of this movement, and that she was commenting on some of the most hotly disputed issues facing the Anglican Church in the nineteenth century. In many instances, her remarks parallel or anticipate those made by prominent theologians like Jowett, Stanley, and Maurice, although it cannot be determined what influence, if any, she had on these individuals.

Nightingale's comments on questions of theology should not be taken lightly. As we have seen, one's religious affiliation and opinions were serious matters in Victorian England. "Dissenters" and Catholics were prevented from holding public office until the repeal of the Test and Corporation acts (1828) and the Catholic Emancipation Act (1829), and Jews were barred from Parliament until 1858. Undergraduates matriculating at Oxford were required to subscribe to the Thirty-Nine Articles of the Church of England, and Cambridge required a declaration of membership in the Church of England as a condition for taking a degree. Connop Thirlwall was promptly dismissed from his tutorship at Cambridge in 1834 for writing a pamphlet in which he advocated the admission of dissenters to the university. The University of London, chartered in 1836, was open to all men "without distinction," but dissenters were finally admitted to Oxford and Cambridge only in 1854 and 1856 respectively,[97] and it was not until the Universities' Test Act of 1871 that the universities of Oxford, Cambridge, and Durham were opened to all men regardless of religion. (Degrees at London were not open to women until 1878, nor at Oxford and Cambridge until 1920 and 1921 respectively.[98])

Theological debates continued to rack the Anglican Church as it struggled to preserve its traditions in the face of scientific and historical investigations and political reforms. By the end of the nineteenth century progressive ideas had gained some ground, and "the opinions of the authors of *Essays and Reviews,* or most of them, became acceptable as well as legal."[99] Because *Suggestions for Thought* remained unpublished, Nightingale's spiritual and philosophical writings, however notable and unique, went virtually unnoticed, unlike her achievements in nursing and public health. In his book on science and religion in the Victorian Age, Basil Willey named "three great explosions . . . which rocked the fabric of Christendom and sent believers scuttling for shelter": Darwin's *Origin of Species,* the Broad Church's *Essays and Reviews,* and John Colenso's 1862 *Pentateuch and Book of Joshua Critically Examined*[100]. If **Suggestions for Thought** had been more widely known, undoubtedly it would have been the fourth.

NOTES

[1] Letter to John Stuart Mill (Sept. 5, 1860). The correspondence between Nightingale and Mill on the subject of *Suggestions for Thought* is contained in "Florence Nightingale as a Leader in the Religious and Civic Thought of Her Time."

[2] For Nightingale's views on positivism, see Chapter 2, "On Universal Law."

[3] Sir Edward Cook, *Life of Florence Nightingale,* vol. 1, p. 470.

[4] See Bishop and Goldie, *A Bio-Bibliography of Florence Nightingale.*

[5] "A 'Note' of Interrogation"; "A Sub-'Note' of Interrogation."

[6] Goldie, *A Calendar of the Letters of Florence Nightingale,* microfiche 2.A11,288.

[7] BM Add. MSS. 45848.

[8] Woodham-Smith, *Florence Nightingale, 1820-1910,* pp. 26-28.

[9] Some of her diagrams have been reproduced in Cohen, "Florence Nightingale."

[10] *Calendar of Letters,* 7.A14,345.

[11] *Suggestions for Thought,* vol. 1, p. 153. Unless otherwise noted, all quotations attributed to Nightingale in the introduction and commentary are from the original three volumes.

[12] Cook, *Life of Florence Nightingale,* vol. 1, p. 435.

[13] Cook, *Life of Florence Nightingale,* vol. 1, p. 13.

[14] 30 April 1874. Quinn and Prest, *Dear Miss Nightingale,* p. 257.

[15] In the collection of the Florence Nightingale Museum, London.

[16] BM Add. MSS. 47735.f226.

[17] Cited in Cook, *Life of Florence Nightingale,* vol. 2, p. 233.

[18] Letter dated 2 March [1853], Claydon Collection (*Calendar of Letters,* 3.C14,659).

[19] Aldous Huxley, *The Perennial Philosophy.* This work is an anthology such as Nightingale had planned to organize, but broader because it contains excerpts from a number of writings of eastern mystics that were not readily available in Nightingale's time.

[20] Quoted in Keele, ed., *Florence Nightingale in Rome: Letters Written by Florence Nightingale in Rome in the Winter of 1847-1848,* p. 155.

[21] He later became the famous Cardinal Manning, whose biography, as well as Florence Nightingale's, is included in Strachey's *Eminent Victorians.* See also Robert Gray, *Cardinal Manning: A Biography.*

[22] Letter to Henry Manning, 15 July 1852. Vicinus and Nergaard, *Ever Yours, Florence Nightingale: Selected Letters,* p. 59. Ellipsis in original. The Order of St. Vincent is discussed below, pp. 92, 142; the Sacred Heart community cannot be identified with certainty.

[23] Letter to Henry Manning, 15 July 1852.

[24] A discussion of the economic and social factors associated with the revival of the non-Catholic sisterhoods can be found in Anne Summer, "Ministering Angels." See also A. M. Allchin, *The Silent Rebellion: Anglican Religious Communities, 1845-1900;* Michael Hill, *The Religious Order: A Study of Virtuoso Religion and Its Legitimation in the Nineteenth-Century Church of England;* and Gail Malmgreen, ed., *Religion in the Lives of English Women: 1760-1930.*

[25] Quoted in Cook, *Life of Florence Nightingale,* vol. 1, pp. 111, 113; see also Vicinus and Nergaard, *Ever Yours, Florence Nightingale,* pp. 53, 433.

[26] *Suggestions for Thought,* vol. 2, p. 119.

[27] *Notes on Nursing: What It Is, and What It Is Not,* p. 133.

[28] *Notes on Nursing,* p. 8.

[29] Of the original group of thirty-eight, ten were Roman Catholic nuns; fourteen were Anglican Sisters (eight from Miss Sellon's sisterhood and six from St. John's House); the remainder were from various hospitals.

[30] 15 October, 1854, quoted in Cook, *Life of Florence Nightingale,* vol. 1, p. 153. Ellipsis in original.

[31] *Suggestions for Thought,* vol. 2, p. 205.

[32] Quoted in Woodham-Smith, *Florence Nightingale, 1820-1910,* p. 9. This biography details the family conflict over Florence's choice of a career.

[33] *Suggestions for Thought,* vol. 2, p. 105.

[34] *Suggestions for Thought,* vol. 2, pp. 65-66.

[35] John Stuart Mill, *The Subjection of Women,* p. 75. Emphasis added.

[36] Virginia Woolf, *A Room of One's Own,* pp. 69-70.

[37] "Cassandra" was later published as a separate volume by the Feminist Press (1980), and again in Mary Poovey's *Cassandra and Suggestions for Thought* (1990).

[38] *A Room of One's Own,* pp. 58, 71.

[39] *A Room of One's Own,* pp. 57-58.

[40] Widerquist, "The Spirituality of Florence Nightingale."

[41] Edwards, *Christian England,* vol. 3, *From the 18th Century to the First World War,* p. III. See Also "Smith, William" entry in the *Dictionary of National Biography.*

[42] *Calendar of Letters,* 1. D14,120. Priestley's writings include the two-volume *General History of the Christian Church to the Fall of the Western Empire.*

[43] James Martineau upheld the theist position (see below) against the negations of the physical sciences. He was the brother of the writer and anti-slavery advocate Harriet Martineau (1802-76), with whom Nightingale corresponded for many years. Nightingale records in a letter (ca. 1853) that her Aunt Mai went to hear James Martineau preach (*Calendar of Letters,* 3. D5,677).

[44] *Suggestions for Thought,* vol. 2, p. 308.

[45] *Religion: Speeches to Its Cultured Despisers* (1958 ed.), p. 9.

[46] Pattison, "Present State of Theology in Germany." Mark Pattison (1813-1884), rector of Lincoln College, was raised an Evangelical and was later influenced by J. H. Newman and Pusey; he came to hold liberal opinions on religion, however, becoming a Broad Churchman and contributing to *Essays and Reviews.*

[47] George Eliot was an acquaintance of Nightingale's and had many friends in common with her, including Benjamin Jowett, J. A. Froude, Max Müller, and Frederick Denison Maurice (see below). Eliot wrote of Nightingale: "There is a loftiness of mind about her which is well expressed by her form and manner" (*Life of George Eliot as Related in Her Letters and Journals,* p. 145).

[48] BM Add. MSS. 45845.f25.

[49] *Calendar of Letters,* 1.E1,124ff; 2.E6,433. Ewald also authored a Hebrew grammar Nightingale may have used in her studies of that language (2.F14,502).

[50] *Calendar of Letters,* 3.E3,717

[51] *Calendar of Letters,* 3.D11,697; 17.C4,87.

[52] BM Add. MSS. 45845.f137; 45793.f75; letter to Parthenope, 10 March [1853]; letter to her parents, [Paris, 1853], Claydon Collection (*Calendar of Letters,* 3.C14,659; 3.D9,692).

[53] BM Add. MSS. 46385.ff15-17.

[54] Cook, *Life of Florence Nightingale,* vol. 2, p. 317. *Theodike* or theodicy, a term coined by the philosopher Gottfried Liebniz (1646-1716), is a compound of the Greek words for God (*theos*) and justice (*dike*), and refers to the attempt to reconcile the benevolence, omnipotence, and justice of God with the existence of evil. Nightingale's theodicy is explicated in Chapter 4, "On Sin and Evil."

[55] BM Add. MSS. 45790.f248.

[56] Schleiermacher published translations of Plato; Platonic philosophy was crucial to the development of his spiritual views as for Nightingale's.

[57] *Memoirs of Baron Bunsen,* vol. 2, pp. 12-13.

[58] R. A. D. Owen, *Christian Bunsen and Liberal English Theology,* p. 83.

[59] English translations of his works include *The Church of the Future* (1847), *Egypt's Place in Universal History* (5 vols., 1848-60), *Hippolytus and His Age* (2 vols., 1852), *Christianity and Mankind* (7 vols., 1854), *Signs of the Times* (1856), and *God in History* (3 vols., 1868-70).

[60] Quoted by F. Max Müller in *Chips from a German Workshop,* vol. 3, p. 349.

[61] Jalal ud-Din Rumi (1207-73) was a Sufi poet best known for his poetic exposition of Sufism, the *Mathnawi.*

[62] Connop Thirlwall (1797-1875), classical historian and bishop (St. David's, Wales); Julius Charles Hare (1795-1855), archdeacon of Lewes; Thomas Arnold (1795-1842), educator and historian, headmaster at Rugby (1828-1842), father of the poet Matthew Arnold.

[63] R. A. D. Owen, *Christian Bunsen and Liberal English Theology;* Robert Preyer, "Bunsen and the Anglo-American Literary Community in Rome."

[64] Richard Moncton Milnes (1809-85), 1st Baron Houghton, was a poet and an active member of Parliament. He met Nightingale in 1842 and proposed marriage, but after a courtship of several years she refused him. They nevertheless remained lifelong friends and he became a trustee of the Nightingale Fund.

[65] Frances Baroness Bunsen, *Memoirs of Baron Bunsen,* vol. 2, p. 13.

[66] Letter to Fanny Nightingale from Kaiserswerth, 16 July 1851. Quoted in Vicinus and Nergaard, *Ever Yours,*

*Florence Nightingale*, p. 52. This is perhaps this same daughter, Frances, who prepared the German translation of Nightingale's *Notes on Nursing;* cf. Bishop and Goldie, *Bio-Bibliography of Florence Nightingale*, p. 20; *Calendar of Letters*, 6.G12,293.

[67] Private note, 7 October 1846; quoted in Woodham-Smith, *Florence Nightingale*, p. 44.

[68] Quoted by Anthony Sattin in Florence Nightingale's *Letters from Egypt: A Journey on the Nile, 1849-1850*, p. 12.

[69] BM Add. MSS. 45846.

[70] BM Add. MSS. 45846.

[71] The original edition of Nightingale's *Letters from Egypt*, which Parthenope had privately printed in 1854, contains more references to hermetic philosophy than does Anthony Sattin's edition.

[72] Walter Scott, *Hermetica: The Ancient Greek and Latin Writings Which Contain Religious or Philosophic Teachings Ascribed to Hermes Trismegistus.*

[73] In 1850, the year of Nightingale's Egyptian voyage, Bunsen wrote: "I too have studied Giordano Bruno in late years with peculiar interest and deep sympathy" (*Memoirs of Baron Bunsen*, vol. 2, p. 169).

[74] Frances Baroness Bunsen, *Christian Carl Josias freiherr von Bunsen aus seinem Briefen und nach eigener Erinnerung geschildert*, von seiner Witwe, vol. I, p. 81. Translation by the present editors; the passage is not included in the English translation of the *Memoirs.*

[75] "A Sub-'Note' of Interrogation," p. 25.

[76] F. Max Müller, *Chips from a German Workshop*, vol. 3, p. 487.

[77] "A Sub-'Note' of Interrogation," p. 32.

[78] Letter to Benjamin Jowett, 1899. Quoted in Cook, *Life of Florence Nightingale*, vol. 2, p. 366.

[79] F. Max Müller, *Life and Letters of the Right Honourable Friedrich Max Müller*, vol. 1, p. 61.

[80] M. C. M. Simpson, *Letters and Recollections of Julius and Mary Mohl*, p. 223.

[81] Froude's *Nemesis of Faith* is a novel about a divinity student who gives up his ministry because he cannot reconcile himself to various tenets held by the Church of England, including the Incarnation and Atonement. The book was publicly burned at Exeter College when Sub-Rector William Sewell discovered it in the possession of a student (Basil Willey, *More Nineteenth Century Studies: A Group of Honest Doubters*).

[82] Müller, *Life and Letters*, vol. 1, p. 311. Some years later Williams's discussion of Bunsen's biblical researches for *Essays and Reviews*, which refuted traditional interpretations of scripture, resulted in Williams's indictment on charges of heresy (see below).

[83] Arthur Penrhyn Stanley (1815-81) became Dean of Westminster in 1864 and was criticized for his introduction of Broad Church policies.

[84] Charles Richard Sanders, *Coleridge and the Broad Church Movement*, p. 7. Although some, such as Jowett, Maurice, and Thirlwall, objected to being classed under the term "Broad Church," most agreed on freedom of inquiry and the right to express their opinions on matters of theology.

[85] Dennis G. Wigmore-Beddoes, *Yesterday's Radicals: A Study of the Affinity Between Unitarianism and Broad Church Anglicanism in the Nineteenth Century.*

[86] Rowland Williams, "Bunsen's Biblical Researches," in *Essays and Reviews*, p. 51.

[87] Quoted in Cook, *Life of Florence Nightingale*, vol. 1, p. 74.

[88] Contributors included C. W. Goodwin, Benjamin Jowett, Mark Pattison, Baden Powell (1796-1860), Frederick Temple (1821-1902, Headmaster of Rugby, later Archbishop of Canterbury), Rowland Williams, and Henry Bristow Wilson.

[89] *Essays and Reviews*, p. 373.

[90] "The Education of the World," *Essays and Reviews*, p. 44.

[91] Josef L. Altholz, "The Mind of Victorian Orthodoxy: Anglican Responses to 'Essays and Reviews,' 1860-1864."

[92] Peter Hinchliff, *Benjamin Jowett and the Christian Religion*, pp. 62ff.

[93] Frederick Denison Maurice, *The Word "Eternal," and the Punishment of the Wicked*, p. vii.

[94] *Calendar of Letters*, 3.A7,554.

[95] *Calendar of Letters*, 3.E4,720.

[96] Parthenope Nightingale to Florence, 8 December 1855. Quoted in Cook, *Life of Florence Nightingale*, vol. 1, p. 266.

[97] Owen Chadwick, *The Victorian Church*, vol. 1, p. 480.

[98] Joan N. Burstyn, *Victorian Education and the Ideal Womanhood.*

[99] Chadwick, *The Victorian Church*, vol. 2, p. 106.

[100] Basil Willey, *Darwin and Butler: Two Versions of Evolution*, p. 9.

**Ruth Y. Jenkins (essay date 1995)**

SOURCE: "Florence Nightingale's Revisionist Theology: 'That Woman Will Be the Saviour of Her Race'," in *Reclaiming Myths of Power: Women Writers and the Victorian Crisis*, Bucknell University Press, 1995, pp. 30-63.

[*In the following essay, Jenkins probes Nightingale's theological thought, which, she argues, attempts to reclaim God's ethics for the marginalized feminine.*]

> [Florence Nightingale] seems as completely led by God as Joan of Arc. . . . it makes one feel the livingness of God more than ever to think how straight He is sending his spirit down into her, as into the prophets & saints of old.
>
> —Elizabeth Gaskell

In 1852 Florence Nightingale wrote that "Women [have] passion, intellect, moral activity . . . and a place in society where no one of the three can be exercised," that the "unity between the woman as inwardly developed and outwardly manifested" no longer exists.[1] Locating the cause for this discrepancy—between women's talents and social opportunities to articulate that talent—Nightingale identifies culture, not nature, as the oppressive force. That is, if, as she believed, God had endowed women with natural capacities that cannot be tapped or acknowledged in her patriarchal community due to gender-distinct roles, Nightingale concludes that it is man who prevents their development; in short, society interferes with divine design rather than enhances it. Thus, with this premise of cultural limitations, Nightingale deduces a conflict not only between women and their society, but also between that patriarchal society and God.

Although she perceives a spiritual conflict between her community and her God, and, consequently, experiences one herself, Nightingale does not participate in the spiritual *disillusionment* that has been traditionally ascribed to the Victorian period. In fact, while many of her contemporaries struggled with religious doubt, Florence Nightingale never questioned God's presence; her spiritual crisis did not involve the loss of faith at all. Instead, she structured her life around trying to work actively in His service, and it is the conflict already identified between Nightingale's desires and the limited opportunities to fulfill them that produced the crisis she experienced. Her spiritually driven life, however, must be clarified, and the competing forces of her faith and her community's institutionalized religion, which had to be reconciled before she could enact her beliefs, must be considered. Although Nightingale embraced her God, she rejected her culture's organized religion, differentiating between their missions and their directives. Functioning as an established institution, the Church, she believed, no longer attempted to advance God's word; instead, the Church reinforced doctrine and advanced dictates that sustained itself, rejecting and excommunicating voices that would challenge its dogma.

Believing in God but disbelieving in organized religion's efficacy or accuracy in interpreting His word, Nightingale found her spirituality at the heart of her conflict with her culture when she attempted to enact her faith. Because she was female, her nation's Church offered Nightingale no sanctioned vocation other than serving God by serving family, father, or husband.[2] To work for God *through* someone else, however, did not fulfill her spiritual needs; she felt compelled to serve God directly. Just as the Reformation had rejected mediators between God and man, Nightingale rejected mediators between God and woman—no longer should women's access to God be circumscribed by their husbands. That is, Nightingale rejected the popular Victorian borrowing of Milton's phrase "He for God only, she for God in him" to determine women's lives. But before she could serve God directly, Nightingale had to gain opportunity and authority to challenge the complicitous forces of her Church and state.

She obtained neither easily because of her social position and religious upbringing; consequently, a consideration of Nightingale's family history and its impact on her can provide context for both her frustrations and actions. As upper middle class and Anglican, Nightingale may have lived within authoritative communities, but because of her gender, she remained powerless. Born into a wealthy family, Nightingale experienced the fruits of privilege, but female, she could never wield its power or shape its course. Raised in the Church of England, Nightingale witnessed its sanctioned doctrines, but female, she could never participate as more than an observer. Her religious heritage further exaggerated this twin marginality, the dynamics of which instigated the split she would define as that between her God and her culture. Unitarian by descent, Fanny Smith Nightingale raised her daughters in the Church of England. Even though Florence's maternal grandfather was influential in the repeal of the Corporation and Test Acts, giving Unitarians religious freedom for the first time in English history, her mother accepted the dominant religious viewpoint of her day, conforming to the Church of England. In contrast, Florence's father, William Nightingale, retained his dissenting beliefs and attempted to educate his daughters from that liberal perspective.[3]

This schism between Established Church and Unitarianism, really between mother (and mother-church) and father (and Spiritual Father), reveals competing influences in Nightingale's life. She saw her mother as oppressive, too much concerned with society's opinions and too little concerned with her daughter's desires. While Fanny Nightingale relentlessly endeavored to train her daughter properly in the functions and obligations associated with their position, Nightingale resisted these gender-distinct duties. Consequently, she and her mother could never agree on the proper sphere for female, specifically Nightingale's, activity; in concert with her culture's patriarchal values, her mother continually attempted to socialize her into those same values.[4]

Just as Nightingale saw her mother as an agent of patriarchal values, she saw her also as representative of another, just as oppressive, social force—the Established Church. In this way, Nightingale's mother represented the two cultural forces which restricted and imprisoned her—patriarchy and institutionalized religion, both repressing, rather than reinforcing, what she believed to be her God-given talents. Because of this, Nightingale stood in contention with not just her mother (as complicitous with patriarchy) but also the culture and church she represented.

In contrast to the oppressive force that Nightingale attributed to her mother, she saw a degree of liberatory potential in her father. From a very early age, she aligned herself with him, rejecting the role of petite angel-in-the-house that her sister embraced. Instead of accepting her culture's prescriptions for women, she preferred to study Greek and Latin under her father's tutelage. And it was he who eventually enabled Nightingale's independence, bestowing upon her an annual maintenance of fifty pounds, even though his wife protested.[5] Throughout Nightingale's life, her father remained an important confidant as she agonized over her ethical beliefs and inability to enact them: there exists extensive correspondence between them about her religious ideas in which she would use him for a sounding board; in turn, he responded with long, thoughtful letters.[6]

Significantly, this childhood preference for father over mother—for intellectual enterprise and action over selfless private servitude, for opposition to the Established Church over complicity in its androcentric agenda—continued throughout Nightingale's life. This history of their relationship suggests that in her father, as in God-the-Father, Nightingale found what her culture denied her. In him, with his rejection of the Established Church as well as its conservative social vision, Nightingale recognized a possible model for confronting the forces, including her mother and the mother-church, that restricted her. As a daughter of her class, however, even with her father's model, she had only a limited number of preordained alternatives for her life, and those she found stifling.

These family dynamics frustrated Nightingale, precipitating intense suffering for her. Until she liberated herself from the need to answer cultural expectations, a freedom from even tacit approval, she could only fantasize about God's plan for her. Sir Edward Cook writes in his biography of Nightingale that "The constant burden

of her self-examination . . . was that she was forever 'dreaming' and never 'doing.'"[7] Lytton Strachey, reflecting on her rejection of a marriage proposal, writes that "She would think of nothing but how to satisfy that singular craving of hers to be *doing* something."[8] For nearly sixteen years, until she was thirty-three, Nightingale had to repress her dreams and silently plan and consider her future.[9]

Her passion to do this became an obsession; she could no longer be content simply to reject her culture's sanctioned roles for women. More than resist her "heretical" world, a resistance of somewhat mute articulation since it could be interpreted as displaying the passive behavior culturally sanctioned for women, Nightingale wanted, needed, to enact her faith. She felt compelled to work actively and directly for God in part because she believed that He had spoken to her at four different times during her life.[10] The first of these divine revelations occurred just before Nightingale's seventeenth birthday, marking what she would call "the dawn of her true life."[11] Recording this event in her journal, Nightingale wrote: "On February 7, 1837, God spoke to me and called me to His service."[12] Some eight years later, in an attempt to follow His call, Nightingale envisioned a religious community in which nurses would be trained; but, when she asked her parents to allow her to study nursing for three months at Salisbury Infirmary only a few miles away, Nightingale's mother and sister were shocked and appalled, accusing her of having an affair with some "low vulgar surgeon."[13] Nightingale details both this rejection of her plan by her mother and the subsequent despair she experienced in a letter to her cousin Hilary Bonham Carter, which explains the intended project and includes one of the many allusions that parallels her life to Christ's:

> I thought something like a Protestant Sisterhood, without vows, for women of educated feeling, might be established. I wonder if our saviour were to walk the earth again, and I were to go to Him and ask, whether He would send me back to live this life again, which crushes me into vanity and deceit. Oh for some strong thing to sweep this loathsome life into the past.[14]

The six years following Nightingale's first call from God fed and starved her dreams. God's initial call inchoate to her, Nightingale suffered under self-imposed patience until she would interpret her call as the reform of nursing. While traveling abroad, she visited a hospital run by a Protestant religious order in Kaiserswerth, Germany, which confirmed Nightingale's belief that nursing could be a moral, even religious profession. But however enticed by what she saw in Germany, Nightingale still could not act upon her vision if she wanted support and approval from her family; quite simply, they forbade it. Rather than encourage or even allow her to study nursing upon returning to England, Nightingale's mother insisted that she embrace the very role of dedicated daughter and devoted sister that she sought to escape. This continued resistance to her desires became harder for Nightingale to bear—precisely because she not only now knew what her spiritual vocation was to be but had seen the possibility in the Kaiserswerth order.

During this period of deep despair and near suicidal depression, Nightingale wrote her three-volume *Suggestions for Thought to Searchers After Religious Truth,* which contains embedded within it "Cassandra."[15] Here, Nightingale details her rejection of organized religion, identifying its failings and appropriations, the resulting harm to the individual believer who wants to seek actively after a better relationship with God (especially if that individual is a woman in Victorian society), and an alternative vision of women's relationship to the divine. Writing this theological discourse proved to be a crucial step in gaining her independence—both in earthly and spiritual terms. *Suggestions* became not only a working out of her personal beliefs but also the authority to act on those same ideas.

The theological struggle and liberating effect contained in *Suggestions* (both marked by rich autobiographical allusions) underscore Nightingale's complex and difficult life, illuminating her own struggle for religious and social independence. Analyzed in conjunction with this text, Nightingale's own life reads as a narrative—the story of one Victorian woman struggling to escape from her culture's oppression. Reclaiming God from a patriarchal appropriation, Nightingale uses Him to empower her desires and fantasies, to authorize her rejection of cultural values, and to revitalize His place in her world.

A closer analysis of *Suggestions* will clarify both how the document functioned to enable Nightingale and how she perceived her relationship to God as well as her culture. Here, she exposes what she believes to be at the heart of this conflict: although claiming divine design, patriarchal culture enlists the family and organized religion to serve as its agents for its agenda. In contrast to these conventional forces, Nightingale delineates what she believes to be the appropriate role of the individual in relationship to the divine—a personal, almost mystical relationship with God, which taps the talents He has given. In this way, *Suggestions* not only describes the conflicting forces the individual must face but also envisions her subsequent rejection of patriarchy's appropriation of God.

*Suggestions* reveals these tensions—between the individual believer and her culture—both in its style and content. Although the work can be roughly summarized by volume (volumes 1 and 3 explain and define her more abstract beliefs as they relate to the working class and natural laws, and volume 2 applies these theories specifically to daughters in Victorian culture), Nightingale's manner of developing these ideas defies a traditional, linear argument. Acknowledging her work's layered and circumlocutious rhetoric, Nightingale begins the second volume with the following note to her readers:

In the hope of reaching different minds, the same subjects have been differently (and not always consecutively) dealt with in the several portions of this book. A feeling of their extreme importance has dictated, and it is hoped will excuse, this course, which has rendered repetition, even to the frequent use of the same phraseology, unavoidable. (*ST,* 2)

Fulfilling this promise, Nightingale reiterates her observations about women in her Victorian culture in the semi-autobiographical **"Cassandra"** at the end of volume 2. Identifying herself as "poor Cassandra" in a letter to her cousin, Nightingale reveals the personal history which saturates this angry and frustrated narrative.[16] Just past the midpoint of the work, this focused energy completes the inward movement of perspective—from society, to families, to daughters, to one daughter in particular, before shifting the focus back to more generalized abstractions of her culture. With the narrowed focus of **"Cassandra"** comes a powerful refinement of the ideas Nightingale has considered elsewhere in *Suggestions.* Here she fuses the frustration of a specific daughter to the frustration of any individual trying to answer God's call, exposing with her greatest passion the appropriation of women's talents by patriarchy, significantly, within a sacred context.

The style in which Nightingale presents her ideas— nonlinear, recapitulative, and fragmented—evidences another aspect of *Suggestions'* subversive impact. Julia Kristeva's semiotic approach to language provides a useful theoretical method from which to analyze the revolutionary potential present in the articulation of Nightingale's ideas. Building upon Lacan's division of language into the symbolic (that which operates within the conventions of grammar and syntax, which he labels the Name-of-the-Father) and the imaginary (that which operates outside these rules), Kristeva redefines Lacan's "imaginary" as "semiotic," emphasizing its tie to the presymbolic language of the preoedipal period. Because of established conventions for communication, after the speaker enters into symbolic discourse, she must repress the semiotic or else risk psychotic behavior; the suppression of this earlier language produces a split between psychological processes and social constraints.[17] Since the semiotic must be suppressed to realize symbolic conventions, it becomes, by definition, marginal to the dominant language system, just as female is marginal to male in patriarchal culture.[18] Any discourse which allows the semiotic to erupt, then, becomes revolutionary in that it defies the conventional rules which should suppress it. In this way the revolutionary writer, while operating within the symbolic, transforms that "symbolic order of orthodox society from the inside."[19]

For Nightingale, engaging in the traditionally male domain of theological speculation—the symbolic rendering of the primary symbol—represents both an attempt to participate in that exclusionary vocation as well as to revise it.[20] This is especially evident in her desire and efforts to publish *Suggestions,* which would transform her ideas from a personal exploration of faith into a public articulation of her word, her gospel; that is, publication becomes prophecy, investing those ideas with a spiritual authority and making her efforts analogous to Christ's. After many years, her manuscripts for this work had been read by only a few friends; it was not until 1858 and 1859 that she returned to the manuscripts. Cook writes that Arthur Hugh Clough (who was a cousin by marriage) encouraged the resumption of Nightingale's religious speculations.[21] She sent manuscripts of *Suggestions* to both John Stuart Mill and Benjamin Jowett for their opinions. Mill loved the book and urged publication, but Jowett argued against publication and for "moderation, conciliation, and suavity."[22] Although Nightingale never revised the manuscripts after they were privately printed, Cook notes that in her testamentary instructions (made in early 1862) she asked that this work be revised according to Jowett's and Mill's suggestions, but because Clough was then dead, she did not know who would be able to do it. In April of 1865 she asked Jowett to edit *Suggestions* for her, but he still insisted that it was "rather the preparation or materials of a book than a book itself."[23]

Nightingale's style in *Suggestions,* which Jowett interpreted as unpolished, reveals her double motive of participation in and revision of theological doctrine. Such conflicting energies mark her discourse with expressions of a kind of semiotic articulation interwoven in the symbolic representation of her beliefs and experiences. While Nightingale's discourse never breaks down to a pure semiotic level, by which I mean a nearly incommunicable degree of nonconventional syntactic or grammatical aberrations, it can reveal her marginal position to the conventions of theology; instead, the eruption of the nonlinear, fragmented **"Cassandra"** in the treatise's center, framed on either side by more traditional discourse, indicates the tensions inherent in her enterprise.[24] In Nightingale's discourse the semiotic impulse takes the form of a shift in genre, rhetoric, and coherence, each of which underscores the revolutionary perspective voiced most sharply in **"Cassandra."** And, while much of the whole of *Suggestions* contrasts in its presentation to the rigorous, logical rhythm of most theological enterprises because of its circumlocution and digressions, **"Cassandra"** provides the most striking example of a cacophonous counterbeat. Here in this shift from abstract to concrete in the history of Cassandra, the discourse proceeds with marked breaches of continuity; nearly impressionistic in its presentation of scenes or moments that are left to the reader to deduce not only their controlling idea but also their connection to juxtaposed sections, the narrative of **"Cassandra"** seems nearly devoid of transitions, developed not by causal or traditionally logical relationships, but by the association of accumulated fragments. Although the parabolic style has a rich history of association with Christian teaching, Nightingale is not just interpreting canonical stories, she is writing one: Nightingale's voice echoes earlier, sacred ones by articulating this new parable of women in patriarchal culture. In this way, Nightingale conflates the position of concrete and abstract: at the core of her

treatise reverberates the impulses of the oppressed woman in patriarchy, not the symbolic delineation of God's word; she provides experiential illustration, not protracted, logical reasoning. In short, Nightingale not only interprets the world around her but also produces new parables to be interpreted. Thus with the act of writing and the manner in which she does write *Suggestions,* Nightingale challenges her culture at its most phallocentric: she challenges the Law-of-the-Father as her culture constructs it by representing the relationship between the believer and her God not just as that of the Word in need of interpretation but also as that of experience and feeling. (This revolutionary aspect present in *Suggestions* is clarified by a closer analysis of **"Cassandra,"** which I turn to later.) In creating an alternative text to reveal the position of believers in her world, Nightingale elaborates her criticism of orthodox beliefs by revising its doctrines to account for women's experiences; radically subverting traditional maxims, she rewrites, in **"Cassandra,"** the incarnation myth to envision a female Christ. With this provocative revision, Nightingale challenges patriarchy's exclusive position in sacred myth and subsequently its appropriation of Judeo-Christian religion. Thus, she revises, rather than completely rejects, the orthodox religious myth, both explaining women's powerlessness and identifying ways to regain greater power.

Before Nightingale rewrites the incarnation myth, however, she establishes the necessity for her revisionist theology: she exposes the complicity of organized religion and the state in suppressing God's gifts—both in workers and women—and details the prevailing sexual double-standard, regardless of class. By clarifying her culture's androcentric agenda, she gains some degree of authority to challenge that ideology, for she disagrees not with God but a heretical community, and, consequently, her challenge of patriarchal edicts is transformed from a personal to a spiritual dimension.

Nightingale reached these conclusions when, finding the Church of England inadequate for her needs, she undertook an analysis of Western religions in search of one that would empower her. For some time, Nightingale even flirted with Catholicism because she perceived in that faith two virtues absent in Protestantism—first, the continued recognition of a sacred vocation for women and, second, the continuing belief in a mystical relationship with God.[25] What she discovered, however, by this analysis was the overall inefficacy of organized religion, beginning with its inability to accurately represent the divine. "The perfect God," she writes, "is so unlike that of the Protestants and Roman Catholics" (*ST,* 2:40), who, she believed, distort His true character. In contrast to the institutionalized anthropomorphization, Nightingale envisions that:

> He is such an entirely different being, that we too may almost feel as if we were doing Him good service when we laugh at "their gods." At all events, there is such an absolute separation

between them, such an opposition of natures, that we are no more laughing at Him,—Him the infinite wisdom, the perfect love, than when we speak of Jupiter and Juno, or of Egyptian cats. (*ST,* 2:40)

By categorizing modern Christianity with so-called pagan religions, Nightingale demystifies the power of sacred institutions and introduces both historical context and a sense of Christian duty to reject their precepts: the established churches of her day are no closer to the Truth than if they still worshipped Jupiter, Juno, or cats. Nightingale uses this technique of juxtaposing "Christian" beliefs with "pagan" ones to reinforce what she saw as the antiquated status of organized religion and the necessity of a Christianity that evolves as its believers progress, remaining true to God, but reflecting the impact of growth and time. Later in *Suggestions,* Nightingale would return to this technique when she evokes Greek myth. Titling her narrative **"Cassandra,"** she underscores the image of that ancient, prophetic woman. The story of Cassandra becomes a powerful symbol for women, whose silenced voices could also hold truths. Like the mythical Cassandra, who is punished with the gift of unbelieved prophecy for rejecting Apollo, women whose words may be ignored still serve their cause—and God's—as prophets of the Truth. Strikingly, Nightingale reclaims one aspect of these "defunct" beliefs—Cassandra as prophet—to inform and clarify her revisionist Christianity. Through this allusion to Greek myth, like the earlier allusions to Juno and Jupiter, Nightingale inverts the traditional view of religious progress by paralleling the contemporary Church's devaluation of women with now defunct beliefs. In other words, the Truth has evolved beyond what the Church preaches, and, subsequently, true believers should challenge these edicts.

In effect, Nightingale points to what she believes to be the stagnation of organized religion: the Church, self-assured that it holds the Truth in its laws, no longer seeks a higher truth; satisfied with the security of an institutionalized position, it no longer seeks confrontation with worldly values. Nightingale boldly asserts that "The Church of England is no training-ground for a discoverer of religious truth" (*ST,* 2:83). Rather, the Church restricts those who question its customs and provides no educational mechanism for a serious pursuit of the interpretation of God's word; instead, the Church retains that privilege for its select few. With a metaphor of Church as mother, Nightingale explains the impetus of this shortcoming by suggesting that it is a reaction against the "over-busy mother" of the Catholic church; that, in contrast, "the Church of England is expected to be an over-idle mother, who lets her children entirely alone" (*ST,* 2:96-97). This provocative analogy reveals a great deal about Nightingale's perception of the forces that limit her desires, basic tensions that would operate through much of her life, and ironic, paradoxical inversions that complicate any analysis of her life and faith. Not only does this analogy imply greater spiritual opportunity for the member of the Catholic church precisely

because of its "interference" in the believer's life, challenging the ideal of the Protestant Reformation, but it exposes the significant presence of the mother in her life.

Nightingale perceived the Church as resting on its ordained laurels rather than revitalizing humanity's spirituality. In this way, then, Victorian religion, Nightingale believed, had become the perfect mouthpiece for a conservative and patriarchal ideology. As a voice for her androcentric culture, the doctrine espoused by institutionalized Christianity not only endorsed but also encouraged the marginalization of women and, even more significantly, that of God. Simply put, the adherence to radical Christian ethics—those that embraced individual needs and desires and those that Nightingale sought—would stifle the industrial energy and the competitive spirit upon which an increasingly market-driven economy would depend. As Barbara Taylor explains, the nineteenth century "domesticated Christianity," freeing man and mammon to rule the workplace.[26] Still, even if in this domestication the traditional patriarchal ideals dismissed Christian values of compassion and community and relegated them to the private (now predominantly female) sphere, religious power remained with men: the authoritative, rule-giving Church hierarchy never included women, and only in the earliest days of the Evangelical movement did women preach.[27] The Church, then, no longer serving God, not even really including women, appropriated His word but nonetheless claimed the history of divine authority for a patriarchal agenda.

As a result, Nightingale believes that nothing resembles the true essence of Christ—regardless of the number of relics or chapels—because humanity has long since given up searching after His truths. Unlike the sciences, which continually seek to advance more factual data from that held by previous generations, religion, she asserts, has stagnated with half-truths and outdated dogma. Troubled by this absence of any real spiritual inquiry, Nightingale would return to this in **"A Sub-Note of Interrogation: What Will Be Our Religion in 1999?"** where she considers the state of religion in future generations. Framing her inquiry by the solar eclipse of 1873, she wonders what the state of religion will be for the next total eclipse, in 1999:

> Will religion consist then, as now, not in whether a man is "just, true, and merciful"; whether the man seeks to know God, and what He is, and what He wishes us to do; whether the man seeks to be a fellow-worker with God, and for this purpose to find out God's plans; but whether the man "had believed what he was told to believe?" had gone to church "for what he called prayers," and "had duly paid the fees to the temple?"[28]

Victorian religion, then, it seems to her, depends not on scholars dedicating their lives to advancing theological truths but on docile believers obeying the status quo. Although her culture possesses the potential to better ascertain God's laws than any previous generation, theological scholarship has become retarded, even rigid, petrifying and enshrining now outdated and primitive values. She asks:

> What is morality to be referred to? Is it not to our sense of right? But we have referred it to a book, which book makes many contradictory assertions. Discoveries are being made every day in physical science; but in the most important science of all no discoveries are made or can be made. Why? because [the Bible] is final. Supposing Moses had written a book about mechanics, and this book was regarded as the ultimatum, we should have made no progress in mechanics. Aristotle was supposed to have written such a book, and for 1,800 years people disbelieved their own actual experience before their eyes, because they could quote chapter and verse of Aristotle to a contrary effect. Yes, with the sound of two weights falling simultaneously in their ears, they maintained that the weight which was ten times heavier than the other fell in one-tenth of the time of the other, because *Aristotle had said-so*. Is not this an exactly parallel case? (*ST,* 2:24)

Using Aristotle as the source to which early scientists clung unquestioningly, Nightingale evokes an interesting analogy—especially given her non-Aristotelian development and presentation of spiritual beliefs—to suggest the foolishness of organized religion holding fast to an equally outdated dogma. Christian rules may indeed be inscribed in stone, but, she argues, humanity's understanding of them is far from sufficient or complete: the longer organized religion clings to these primitive values, the more difficult it becomes to supplant those outdated beliefs with more accurate ones, with beliefs closer to the Truth. Established as *the* Truth and implicitly sanctioned by heaven, these archaic values, which Nightingale ascribes to the Church, continue to shape organized religion and dictate people's lives. With the absence of a living ethic, present-day believers can only passively act on their faith; instead of developing an individual understanding and relationship with God, these followers become circumscribed by ancient interpretations. Too often used as a pacifier of the oppressed, religion has ignored issues of poverty, imperialism, education, and legal reforms (*ST,* 2:29). No longer a medium through which to achieve a more compassionate world, organized religion becomes both a tool for the powerful to justify their desires and to exclude individualistic participation in shaping its creed. And while Nightingale was not naive enough to believe that atrocities had not occurred before in the name of God, she would not condone complacency in those shortcomings; failing to advance, Victorian religion not only vindicated systemic problems but also perpetuated them.

This travesty of religion becomes mirrored, she believes, in the dynamics of the Victorian family. Early in *Suggestions,* Nightingale establishes this connection, writing that "The two questions concerning the relation [of the individual] to God and the relation to the parent are one. You cannot separate the inquiry about religion and

about the family" (*ST,* 2:245). Just as her culture replicates Western religion's hierarchical structure, the family recreates the same, with father as lord (or, in Nightingale's case, with her mother representing patriarchy, as I have already argued). The power of God becomes implicitly transferred to the domestic ruler, and, because of this, the family, Nightingale insists, is the Protestant form of idolatry (*ST,* 2:179): children and wives serve the father, nearly worship the sons. She develops this analogy between the family and the church by pointing to their shared desire for uniformity among its members. Just as the Church rejects dissenting and nonconforming members, so does the family. In contrast, Nightingale suggests that rather than be threatened by challenging voices, the Church and the family should grow strong by the diversity of these members: "The parent, like the Church," she asserts, "must allow for varieties of character, *whilst* he retains his absolute authority"; otherwise, the parent "will turn out John Wesley," or a Florence Nightingale, "instead of being strengthened by his earnestness and zeal" (*ST,* 2:239-40). Regardless, then, of the child's dreams or even of God's plans, the family appropriates its members' talents for self-serving goals (*ST,* 2:198): "The family uses people, *not* for what they are, not for what they are intended to be, but for what it wants them for—its own uses. It thinks of them not as what God has made them, but as something which *it* arranged that they shall be" (*ST,* 2:389).

The family, Nightingale believes, has "Too narrow a field for the development of an immortal spirit, be that spirit male or female. The chances are a thousand to one that, in the small sphere, the task for which that immortal spirit is destined by the qualities and the gifts which its Creator has placed within it, will not be found" (*ST,* 2:388-89). Declaring that the family limits both male and female individualization, Nightingale extends the criticism of her culture beyond just the oppression of women's gifts to the oppression of God's gifts. She asks, "What is [the family's usurpation of the individual] but throwing the gifts of God aside as worthless and substituting for them those of the world?" (*ST,* 2:389).

With organized religion exposed as flawed and the family indicted through parallel failings, Nightingale considers the place of women and especially daughters, in both. In the family:

> It is vaguely taken for granted by women that it is to be their first object to please and obey their parents till they are married. But the times are totally changed since those patriarchal days. Man (and woman too) has a soul to unfold, a part to play in God's great world. (*ST,* 2:219)

Like outdated religions, this antiquated pattern must be changed; but, just as theology, in her opinion, failed to evolve with humanity, the position allowed women in patriarchal society has shown little progression. "Jesus Christ," she insists, "raised women above the condition of mere slaves, mere ministers of God. He gave them moral activity" (*ST,* 2:404). Really asking what women have done that society should make them slaves, Nightingale inverts the issue, querying "What has 'society' done for us?" (*ST*, 2:209).[29] "What has mankind done for us?" she continues, this time providing an answer: "It has created wants which not only it does not afford us the opportunity of satisfying, but which it compels us to disguise and deny" (*ST*, 2:210-11). Rather than encourage women to develop their capacities, her culture, Nightingale contends, has instead offered them the role of slave, or, at best, that of prisoner. "The prison which is called a family, will its rules ever be relaxed, its doors ever be opened? What is it, especially to the woman? The man may escape, and does" (*ST*, 2:198). In contrast, the woman's sentence, she believes, is stricter, her pardon more circumscript:

> Daughters are now their mothers' slaves . . . they are considered their parents' property; they are to have no other pursuit, nor power, nor independent life, unless they marry; they are to be entirely dependent upon their parents—white slaves in the family, from which marriage alone can emancipate them. (*ST*, 2:224)

"There is no tyranny," she concludes, "like that of the family, for it extends over the thoughts" (*ST*, 2:200).[30]

And, because her class and culture sanction no profession for women, only one option for escaping familial domination exists—marriage—and, echoing her earlier complaints, Nightingale sees in her state religion no viable alternative. "To the woman," she writes, "Protestantism offers nothing but marriage; she may leave home to marry, but for nothing else. . . . To justify herself she must take a husband" (*ST*, 2:180). So according to Nightingale's observation, daughters have but two options: to be married or to be forever a daughter (*ST*, 2:229). Neither, for Nightingale, offers anything appealing: "It is the hardest slavery, either to take the chance of a man whom she knows *so little,* or to vegetate at home, her life consumed by *ennui* as by a cancer" (*ST*, 2:59). Yet, she wonders, is marriage—especially as her culture defined it—really what God would intend for His daughters? God instituted marriage as a choice, Nightingale believes, not a mandate, for Jesus never married (*ST*, 2:284). And it would be unnatural to serve one man when one could serve humanity through God's works: "it is unnatural, and the most selfish of all ties *if* the tie is to be, as Milton has put it, 'He, thy God, thou mine,' if they are to serve and divinify one another" (*ST*, 2:44).

Nightingale acknowledges, however, that many women do choose marriage over remaining in their fathers' homes. She reflects upon their motivation: "three things on which marriage is generally founded—a good opinion of a person, a desire to love and be loved, and a wish to escape dissatisfaction at home" (*ST*, 2:230). And regardless which of the three foundations a marriage is based on, the woman receives little more freedom as wife than what she had as daughter. "A woman doesn't really gain independence with marriage; she only becomes 'property' of her husband, who gets all

her wealth" (*ST*, 2:278). For the man, who becomes the secular lord, the family life revolves around him and his activities. He acts; he controls; he masters. In contrast, a wife from Nightingale's social station produces nothing except perhaps children—and even they will be raised by their nanny, taught by their governess. Nightingale concludes that "A married woman's life consists in superintending what she does not know how to do": she orders dinner, rather than prepares it; she inspects the larder and store room, rather than supplies it; she visits the poor rather than acts to alleviate poverty (*ST*, 2:291). And all the while the daughter suffers, parents "hope that if [daughters] don't marry, they will at least be quiet" (*ST*, 2:59-60). Again assigning the suffering of Victorian daughters' sacred status, Nightingale hypothesizes whether "Christ, if He had been a woman might have been nothing but a great complainer" (*ST*, 2:408); and, doing so, she points to the fact that in her culture gender, not action, determines rights. As a man, Christ could detach himself from his earthly family's demands and follow his God-given mission; a woman, Nightingale believes, who would follow hers is accused of "destroying the family tie" and "obligation of home duties" (*ST*, 2:409). Implicit in this desire by parents for acquiescence is the view of daughters as worthless in themselves—the daughter is seen as a burden because parents refuse to (or cannot) see their daughters as productive members of the family or society. The work they do perform is undervalued, the work they might do lost. This point of difference between daughters and sons signals to her not only the incongruity between God's will and man's interpretation of it but also the subsequent impossibility for women to develop their talents in a patriarchal society.

In contrast to this exploitation, Nightingale presents an alternative for women. "Unmarried women," she claims, "should have every facility given them by parents to spend their time and faculties upon any exercise of their nature for which it has an attraction, which can be pursued in harmony with God, which can answer, in short, any good purpose" (*ST*, 2:256). The reality of women's lives, however, is that their "life is spent in pastime, men's in business. Women's business is supposed to be to find something to 'pass' the 'time'" (*ST*, 2:213). Nightingale elaborates:

> The maxim of doing things at "odd moments" is a most dangerous one. Would not the painter spoil his picture by working at it "at odd moments?" If it be a picture worth painting at all, and if he be a man of genius, he must have the whole of his picture in his head every time he touches it, and this requires great concentration, and this concentration cannot be obtained at "odd moments." (*ST*, 2:65-66)

This, she adds, is as ridiculous as telling people not to take regular meals, but to eat at odd times (*ST*, 2:66). Given only "odd moments" to develop their talents, women's abilities will never be realized, and the woman, when finally free to pursue her own desires, "will be too wasted to employ herself" (*ST*, 2:69).

Nightingale's own life illustrates the degree to which she did not want to work at odd moments or expend her primary energy tending to others' needs. Rather than become complicit in what she perceived as a cultural devaluation of God's plan for her, Nightingale rejected the acceptable patterns of behavior for a woman of her position. She refused what would have been considered a suitable marriage proposal from Richard Monckton Milnes, explaining:

> I have an intellectual nature which requires satisfaction, and that would find it in him. I have a passionate nature which requires satisfaction, and that would find it in him. I have a moral, an active nature which requires satisfaction, and that would not find it in his life. Sometimes I think I will satisfy my passional nature at all events, because that will at least secure me from the evil of dreaming. But would it? I could be satisfied to spend a life with him in combining our different powers in some great object. I could not satisfy this nature by spending a life with him making society and arranging domestic things.[31]

This reasoned rejection to Milnes's marriage proposal, which privileges her "active nature" even above passion or familial escape, is echoed by many passages in her journals concerning women and marriage. At the end of one of these entries, she pledges to make a better life for women.[32] This "better life" meant the opportunity for women to determine for themselves the course of their own life, to find avenues to satisfy their active natures and their untapped talents—independent of marriage. So when faced with what appeared to her to be the choice to either defy her God or her family, Nightingale boldly defied the latter by refusing to marry. This meant, however, that she would need to identify and pursue another channel for fulfilling her vision of God's plan.

Nightingale bolsters her argument by suggesting patriarchal edicts oppress not only women but also men who feel called in nontraditional ways, thus preventing the appearance of a purely personal agenda. She establishes this by analyzing the extent to which her culture suppresses the individual's God-given talents among the working class; in fact, she even dedicates the first volume of her *Suggestions for Thought* to "The Artisans of England." Their needs unmet or unaccounted for by a religion complicit in the capitalistic doctrines of industrialization, many working class men and women rejected orthodox beliefs and, in doing so, proved threatening to their economic superiors, who would have benefited from a meek acceptance by the workers of hard conditions softened by capitalistic interpretations of the doctrine of work.[33] This lack of "faith" appeared to the upper classes to be a complete abandonment of morality and God—and not incidentally a recognition of their place. Nightingale, herself dissatisfied by her place both in culture and in traditional religion, attempted to clarify this apparent atheism in a way that suggests a projection of her own beliefs onto these workers: "What the most conscientious among our working men seem to be doing now, is renouncing religious error, not announcing

religious truth; they seem not to be seeking after light, but giving up darkness" (*ST*, 2:39). The working class, Nightingale believed, was not rejecting God, but rejecting the dark state of religion, just as she was. Explaining the workers' apparent atheism in this way, Nightingale contextualizes her criticism of her culture's treatment of women.

Middle-class daughters and workers, she would contend, held positions analogous to each other in society. Just as capitalism and industry demanded obedience and uniformity, so, too, the family expected loyalty and devotion. While daughters like Nightingale did not face the real threats of poverty or the physical exploitation that the workers did, they still suffered from their culture's self-serving agenda, which had appropriated religious doctrine for authority. Just as many workers had turned away from organized religion—not because they were atheists but because they recognized the Church's failings—so, too, must daughters like Nightingale, who found neither comfort nor support in its oppressive preachments. Equating women's suppressed talents (and workers' exploited ones) with God's, Nightingale not only builds her case by revealing the widespread exploitation of believers but also by citing divine authority for their emancipation. Criticizing patriarchy in this way, she undercuts any easy authority from secular to sacred parallels; while patriarchal hierarchy may appear to replicate the paradigm of the traditional Judeo-Christian myth with God as father, it merely replicates the pattern, not the divine intent or sacred mission; consequently, she diagnoses female subjection, not as woman's proper role, but the result of a clerical misreading of God and a cultural appropriation of the associated power. Elevating her suffering as a daughter of patriarchy to sacred dimensions, Nightingale acquires not only the power to challenge that subjection but also the authority to voice alternative social and spiritual dynamics.

After exposing and detailing this cultural, as opposed to divine, subjection of women, Nightingale produces an alternative doctrine: she creates a revisionist incarnation story that accounts for women's pain and struggle, and she calls for female prophets to dedicate their lives to advancing this vision. Nightingale begins **"Cassandra"**:

> One often comes to be thus wandering alone in the bitterness of life without. It might be that such an one might be tempted to seek an escape in hope of a more congenial sphere. Yet, perhaps, if prematurely we dismiss ourselves from this world, all may even have to be suffered through again—the premature birth may not contribute to the production of another being, which must be begun from the beginning. (*ST*, 2:374)

Using the impersonal pronoun rather than "I" or "you," she rejects simple autobiography and instead creates a mythic, universal quality for **"Cassandra,"** allowing identification with this female prophet by all women. Borrowing from the Judeo-Christian myth, she sees the necessity of prophets and martyrs to serve as precursors for her revised incarnation. Through images of premature births, which she identifies as potential prophets who commit suicide, she notes that suicide's appeal masks the importance of female suffering as well as aborts female advancement by eliminating precursors and consequently delaying the new Christ's arrival.

In her discussion of Milton, Christine Froula has described basic differences in male and female authority. There she distinguishes these two models as: male respect and female questioning of an invisible authority; patriarchal anagogy of history, which invests spiritual authority only in a few; the image of a male creator, which subordinates the visible to the invisible, experience to mediated knowledge, and silence to the word. Froula's paradigm can be applied to Nightingale's revisionist discourse to illuminate the central, defining differences from canonical doctrine as she rewrites Christian doctrine, replacing patriarchal values with feminist ones.[34]

In arguing her theological beliefs, Nightingale points to concrete evidence in the visible world to challenge invisible patriarchal abstractions. This is especially evident in **"Cassandra."** There she asks: "What *do* we see? . . . We see girls and boys of seventeen, before whose noble ambitions, heroic dreams, and rich endowments we bow our heads, as before *God incarnate in the flesh.* But, ere they are thirty, they are withered, paralyzed, extinguished" (*ST,* 2:387). By comparing seventeen-year-old boys and girls to "God incarnate in the flesh," she empowers "ordinary" people, not an elite group of individuals. Asserting that the "'dreams of youth' have become a proverb" (*ST,* 2:387), she again links human dreams with divine truths and suggests that with the initiation into society, the young lose their spiritual connections and find, instead, a corrupt world. By labeling these repressed dreams proverbs in this way, Nightingale authorizes the dreams, not patriarchal suppression of them. Thus infusing a sacred identity in the seen and experienced as opposed to the invisible and the abstracted, Nightingale extends spiritual authority from a limited segment of believers to virtually all of humanity.

**"Cassandra"** continues to subvert patriarchal hierarchies, which limit power to a very few, by announcing that prophets were, and can be, abundant in every age. Asserting "it is a privilege to suffer for your race—a privilege not reserved to the Redeemer and martyrs alone, but one enjoyed by numbers in every age" (*ST,* 2:379)—Nightingale associates any who choose to struggle for their race with the Redeemer.[35] Doing so, she extends sacred power to anyone choosing to suffer for spiritual beliefs, contrasting sharply the limits of authority that institutionalized religion demands. Significantly, it is to suffer for this faith, and not to suffer under the restraints of her society, that empowers the individual. With this distinction, Nightingale challenges those who would explain, even condone, oppression in a Christian context: that believers who suffer in the physical world gain their rewards in the next. Instead, while

she also recognizes the sacred tradition of suffering, she transfers the spiritual dimension to women and workers; rather than see their suffering as God's plan for them, this revision asserts that they suffer because their exploiters seek to deter God's mission and that the suffering reveals the conflict between worldly and sacred values.

Through this privileged suffering, again linking the common to the sacred, Nightingale raises speech above silence. Recognizing patriarchal culture's ability to silence those under its power, realizing that such enforced silence perpetuates its agenda, Nightingale pleads with women to regain a heightened sensitivity to their suffering: made numb from years of oppression and repressed passion, women become mute; consequently, Nightingale cries for intensified pain. With the epigraph to the second section of **"Cassandra,"** she calls for this resensitivity to oppression's pain: "Yet I would spare no pang, / Would wish no torture less, / The more that anguish racks, / The earlier it will bless" (*ST,* 2:378). Invoking voice-giving pain to replace silent desensitization, Nightingale claims the martyrs' strength from suffering and rewrites the Christian martyr as female in patriarchal society. Thus she unites female oppression with that of the traditional Christian martyrs and encourages women to find strength, if not authority, through the pain. At the very least, she sees pain as the powerful reminder of their position, one that should help women resist a hegemonic culture.

Nightingale rewrites the Judeo-Christian myth's narrative of prophetic lineage with a feminist version. Using the epigraph "'The Voice of one crying in the' crowd, / 'Prepare ye the way of the Lord'" to begin **"Cassandra"** (*ST,* 2:374), Nightingale unites the mythologized "one" with a prophet heralding God's eventual incarnation. She continues to examine women's myopic pleasure in suicide, arguing that the pain and suffering women endure reveal that they are indeed furthering God's intended plan: "Some are only deterred from suicide because it is in the most distinct manner to say to God: 'I will not, I will not do as thou wouldst have me do,' and because it is 'no use'" (*ST,* 2:394). Rather than fight against worldly values, the suicide victim retreats from the struggle. In charging women to resist suicide, Nightingale extends the traditional view of the sacrilege of suicide: she equates it with female complicity in the patriarchal misreading of God.

Nightingale equates patriarchal suppression of women with the earlier Roman suppression of Christians by pointing to the struggle of women who serve as the necessary prophets of female incarnation. She reminds women of their duty to become those prophets and resist the temptations of silence and suicide, which would make them complicit in patriarchal interpretations of God's plan. She believes that unless women resensitize themselves to their oppression's pain, the new Christ will never be born. Each suffering woman, then, like the unbelieved Cassandras, becomes the new missing "messenger" and quickens the female incarnation.

In this context, Nightingale boldly asserts: "The next Christ will perhaps be a female Christ. But do we see one woman who looks like a female Christ? or even like 'the messenger before' her 'face,' to go before her and prepare the hearts and minds for her?" (*ST*, 2:408). How, then, will women finally be emancipated from their patriarchal prisons? Who will lead them out of their moral wilderness? These become the crucial questions for Nightingale. Who indeed? Women, like organized religion, need saviors, but again like the Church, "they have no *type* before them," no one to validate their desires (*ST*, 2:62).[36] The missing saviors, for the Church and for women, would serve the same function—emancipate religion from its antiquated codes and divest patriarchy of its power over women.

Nightingale would return to this belief that Victorian England boasted no prophets or saviors in **"A Note of Interrogation"**—a distillation of her ideas published in *Fraser's Magazine*—where she asks "Who is to be the founder, who the Bacon, of a method of enquiry into moral service?"[37] Like Carlyle searching for his heroes, Nightingale searches for saviors able to lead the people out of their moral wilderness. Although she admits that most people believe that the "time is past for *individual* saviours (male or female)," Nightingale insists that "the world cannot be saved, except through saviours, at present," and adds, "A saviour means one who saves from error" (*ST*, 2:201).

By foregrounding in her text the literal meaning of "saviour," Nightingale heightens her readers' consciousness of the corrective element of religion. A savior should be more than an icon for worship that suggests that all evils have been eradicated; instead, a savior should lead the on-going struggle to establish spiritual, as opposed to worldly, values. Nightingale extends this vision of the needed savior beyond the Church and its doctrines to encompass cultural dynamics as well; she adds that "there must be saviours from social, from moral error" (*ST*, 2:202). By including the secular world in her analysis of moral deterioration, Nightingale forces religion out of cathedrals and cloisters to what she sees as its rightful domain—society at large. Just as she believes God wants humanity to serve Him, not lay prostrate before Him, she believes the true motives of religion should be transferred from worship to life. No longer should humanity's morals be divided between secular and religious codes; each individual should shape his or her life with spirituality, as Nightingale believes she will do.

But with society in need of correction and saviors wanting, Nightingale can only lament the current condition: "There is so little religion now that we do not even feel the want of [a Savior]; we need a Saviour now as much as [the Greeks, Romans, and Egyptians] did then" (*ST*, 2:38). "What a hopeless state," she continues, "till some saviour strikes a cord which reveals to man what *is* his proper food by giving him a taste of it, or a consciousness of what that taste should be; for, by God's law, it is the appetite which is to lead to food, to determine *what* food" (*ST*, 2:286). But until a savior comes along to whet humanity's appetite for proper spiritual food, Nightingale fears that savior would be unrecognized. And as she pleads for a savior to herald the coming of God, she, somewhat ironically, becomes that prophet. To her readers Nightingale prophesizes: "Oh! that again someone would cry, in a voice that might reach the human heart, 'Prepare ye the way of the Lord!'" (*ST*, 2:370).

By rewriting the incarnation myth, Nightingale demystifies her patriarchal culture and reenfranchises women into their rightful spirituality. Nightingale subverts the fundamental Western myth—that of God's incarnation as man—by suggesting God's incarnation as woman. Doing so, Nightingale rejects patriarchy as divinely inspired and creates a new model, not matriarchal, but one enfranchising all who use their God-given talents. In this context, her reformed model of nursing, from training to hospital administration, can be understood as an extension of a spiritual vocation: the nurse that Nightingale envisions serves as a type of missionary, spreading a new gospel, a new ethic of care.

Much upon which Nightingale based her reconstructed theology can be found in her own life; because of this, a further examination of her struggle to enact what she believed to be God's plan will help to illuminate her revisionist spirituality. Nightingale's beliefs were shaped by years of suffering, years of tempering her desires while trying to make herself worthier to answer God's calls.[38] During this time, Nightingale read and thought extensively in her attempt to understand those calls. Finding no sanctioned time in her over-orchestrated day to pursue her ethical deliberations, Nightingale established a strict regimen for her "odd moments," studying mathematics, digesting hospital blue books, and recording her thoughts before her "real" day began.[39]

The exhaustion of this schedule and the apparently unswaying attitude of her family propelled Nightingale into a period of deep despair. Her diary for these years reveals her repeated near-suicidal depressions:

> My present life is suicide; in my 31st year I see nothing desirable but death; What am I that their life is not good enough for me? Oh God what am I? The thoughts and feelings that I have now I can remember since I was six years old. It was not I that made them. . . . But why, oh my God, cannot I be satisfied with the life that satisfies so many people?[40]

The frustration so evident here appears in other private writings from the time as well. In her 1847-49 notebook, she laments the need to suppress the thriving desires she cannot ignore:

> There are Private Martyrs as well as burnt or drowned ones. Society . . . does not know them; and the family cannot, because our position to one another in our families is . . . like that of the Moon to the Earth. The Moon revolves around

her, moves with her, never leaves her. Yet the Earth never sees but one side of her; the other side remains for ever unknown.[41]

In one of her journals, she writes of her desire for anonymity and hard work to enhance her God-given talents and enable them to "ripen" for "the Glory of His Name."[42] This agony of Nightingale's—caught between her culture's expectations for her and what she believed to be God's—could be neither easily overcome nor dismissed. The unbearable agony of this conflict must have seemed unending as she writes:

> The thoughts and feelings that I have now . . . I can remember since I was six years old. A profession, a trade, a necessary occupation, something to fill and employ all my faculties, I have always felt essential to me, I have always longed for. The first thought I can remember, and last, was nursing work; and in the absence of this, education work, but more the education of the bad than of the young. . . . Everything has been tried, foreign travel, kind friends, everything. My God! What is to become of me?[43]

And, in an 1850 diary entry, Nightingale claims a significant parallel between her life and Christ's, reflecting: "I am 30 . . . the age of which Christ began His mission. No more childish things, no more vain things, no more love, no more marriage. Now, Lord, let me only think of Thy will."[44] By associating her own life with Christ's, by presuming such a parallel, she reveals the important aspect of identification with the divine central to her revisionist theology: rather than operate from a position of deferential worship that would limit her access to sacred authority, she proceeds from a belief in her own sacred authority through this association.

As this entry also suggests, Nightingale's own life reveals a striking example of the oppressive position in which Victorian culture and religion placed nontraditional women, especially Nightingale, who believed God had called her into His service but found every opportunity to do so denied her—by family, culture, and organized religion.[45] So with a marriage rejected and a profession denied, Nightingale nearly suffocated in her mother's home. She "strove to say to God, 'Behold the handmaid of the Lord! *not* Behold the handmaid of correspondence, or of music, or of metaphysics!'"[46] At this point in her life, however, Nightingale had yet to apply to herself the strategies that she would eventually recommend to other women: suffering redirected into advancing God's work. Eventually, she would redirect her pain into the writing of *Suggestions.*

One significant issue in this analysis of Nightingale's spiritual crisis remains: where did she find the authority to rewrite established doctrine and then to enact her beliefs? Initially, her extensive reading exposed her to what she believed to be scientific approaches that could facilitate discerning and deciphering God's laws. Specifically her reading of John Stuart Mill, Edgar Quinet, and Adolphe Quetelet helped to codify her religious beliefs and translate them into the theories that *Suggestions* delineates.[47] Mill's logical assertions, Quinet's radical theological beliefs, and Quetelet's applied statistics provided the foundation for Nightingale's religion, a religion which thrived, rather than suffered, from contemporaneous scientific advances. The discovery of natural laws only confirmed Nightingale's beliefs; for if there are laws, she reasoned, then there must be a lawgiver.[48] She wrote that "Law [was] the basis of [her] new theology" (*ST,* 1:178) since law is the "volition of God" (*ST,* 3:6). Believing that natural laws—not the Church's preachments—evidenced God's essence, Nightingale, in her first *Fraser's Magazine* article, charged theologians to pursue religious studies with the rigorous inquiry that marked the sciences; they should try to figure out "what *are* the laws that govern the moral world."[49] Experience, research, and analysis, not blind adherence to traditional beliefs, would reveal His moral codes; "His *essence* might remain a mystery," but "the *character* of God was ascertainable" by this careful study.[50]

Applying the statistical methods she learned from Quetelet to discover patterns and correlations of disease and living conditions, Nightingale charged humanity to observe these laws of God, both to ascertain and follow them. The resulting patterns, when carefully studied and understood, could reveal a more advanced understanding of God's will. "In laws," she contended, "are found the means by which man may advance and approximate towards that absolute and perfect moral nature" (*ST,* 3:29). Nightingale's theology professed, then, that from careful study of the world's natural laws, one would discover God's laws, and by understanding His laws one could ascertain the Truth. In this way, she provides access to sacred truths to any who sought after them, any who observed natural patterns, not man-made rules.

The great need for humanity to seek these truths pervades her three volumes. She even concludes *Suggestions:*

> Man has attained much; but as yet man knows not God; man knows not man; man knows not his real satisfaction, though it be essential to him to seek it; man, while unconscious of the depth of his ignorance, is alike unconscious of the height of his ability. (*ST,* 3:126)

Nightingale spends much of the three volumes exposing this moral ignorance by observing its manifestations in her culture. Early in the second volume she asks, "In the last 300 years much has been gained politically, but what has been done for religion? . . . [only] denying and not constructing" (*ST,* 2:189). "Criticism," she asserts, "has stripped Religion of many superstitions. . . . but has it advanced us one step nearer in the study of God's real character, the character which makes us love? . . . May it not rather have killed Religion with the cure of superstition?" (*ST,* 2:36). And although she, like Carlyle, believes Victorian religion is in dire need of revision, Nightingale wants to revitalize it, but not by looking for saviors (or heroes) in traditional, established patterns. She asks: "If religion is lost, what is to become of England? unless one comes to raise up another religion" (*ST,* 2:40). And this, she laments, is unlikely since "there appears to be scarcely anything in England now which bears any resemblance to Christ" (*ST,* 2:189).

Believing that "The spirit of Truth will be our authority, if we will faithfully seek Him" (*ST,* 1:2), Nightingale extends the parameters of sacred authority, limited only by the degree to which the individual desires Truth; doing so, she claims a tremendous amount of authority for herself since, after all, she has dedicated her life to this pursuit. With desire for Truth the only prerequisite for authority, *anyone* can unearth the essence of God's laws, not just theologians, not just leaders of religious communities, not just men. Rather than look heavenward for dictates and rules, Nightingale looks earthward for evidence of God; rather than sanction authority by decree, she turns to experience and motivation.

By investing spiritual authority in any who faithfully seek God, Nightingale lays the groundwork for her mystical spirituality. To demonstrate the need for individual relationships with God rather than salvation through organized religion, Nightingale depicts the life of an individual in the decayed and self-serving society she has already exposed. Frustrated by what organized religion fails to achieve, she puts her faith in the individual member of that community; if sanctioned men of God do not (or will not) work to accomplish God's plan, she believes the individual, through heightened communion with Him, can. In a passage which echoes her own calls from God, Nightingale writes:

> But God does not refuse to answer the longing, devoted spirit, which says, Speak, Lord, for thy loving child heareth. He hears as the Father; He answers as the Son, and as the Holy Spirit. I could not understand God, if He were to speak to me. But the Holy Spirit, the Divine in me, tells me what I am to do. I am conscious of a voice that I can hear, telling me more truth and good than I *am.* As I rise to *be* more truly and more rightly, this voice is ever beyond and above me, calling to more and more good. (*ST,* 2:32)

Nightingale's intense belief in a personal God echoes the earlier Greek and Christian mystics.[51] Significantly, Nightingale's spiritual design also echoes aspects of the Gnostic Gospels. Elaine Pagels's important work on these suppressed texts reveals key parallels: direct access to God, the presence of the divine in the individual believer, and the importance of intuitive insight and the experience of knowing rather than the final knowledge.[52] For Nightingale, the personal connection with God that mysticism provided thoroughly entranced her; here existed a medium through which an individual could better understand God and his or her service to Him. Even if her family and culture prevented one from actively serving God, as was the case with Nightingale, the individual could still develop this personal relationship. In *Suggestions,* Nightingale defines mysticism as

the ability to focus on the "unseen" and to "endeavour to partake of the divine nature; that is, of Holiness."[53] Rejecting the notion that mysticism fails to serve community needs because it encourages personal ones, Nightingale believed that a community of believers charged by their own relationship with God would be far more productive than one populated by those told what to do or say by an outdated and misdirected Church. What mysticism offered the faithful, then, she believed, was direct access to God and, subsequently, His truths; mysticism encouraged the individual to serve, to experience, and to understand God, not simply to worship Him. Significantly, mysticism operates between the individual and God in much the same way as that of the semiotic language Kristeva identifies—not as a symbolically systematized abstraction taught or learned, but as a language or form of communication not included in conventional, symbolic constructs. In this, Nightingale reveals another aspect of the revolutionary potential of her revisionist theology: this spirituality would build from experience and connection independent of the exegetical interpretation of symbol enshrined as the foundation of patriarchal Christianity. And, although the Judeo-Christian religion includes a long history of early mystics who would ratify the appropriated religious belief, the authority by which they voiced their faith remained outside the established, hierarchical structure of even the early Church; that is, although incorporated into the myth of Christianity, mystics represented an alternative, independent manner of communicating between their God and fellow believers. Nightingale writes that God desires that we should be "one with Him, not prostrate before Him" (*ST,* 2:22), and thus charges her readers to "Organize then your life to act out your religion" (*ST,* 2:318). In this way, like the earlier Gnostic Gospels, Nightingale's revisionist theology proves extremely threatening to the patriarchal state and its religion; by building its truths upon individual experience and expanding access to the divine to all, these revolutionary tracts stand diametrically opposed to the foundations of the exclusivity of patriarchal authority.

The final section of **"Cassandra"** reveals the extent to which Nightingale subverts the conventions of her culture by representing a noncomplicitous woman in the dying Cassandra. Although many could read the joy at death as counterproductive to her desires for freedom (as Nightingale herself cautioned against the pleasure of suicide earlier in **"Cassandra"**), this conscious joy at death must be considered in the contexts of power and powerlessness. In this final section, Nightingale's Cassandra declares: "Let neither name nor date be placed on her grave, still less the expression of regret or of admiration; but simply the words, 'I believe in God'" (*ST,* 2:411). *This* dying woman, finding neither joy in this life nor a way to alter that fact, shocks her family by her exhilaration at death. She, and others brave enough to recognize patriarchal oppression of her talents, become messengers announcing the eventual birth of a female Christ, replacing the Judeo-Christian prophets of the male incarnation as new prophets of the female incarnation. And, as prophets, these women find divine authority to challenge their culture, regardless of their position in that culture. This Cassandra gains power—regains control over her life (or in this case, death)—by choosing death. Not motivated by complicity in her own subjection, this death refuses even to participate in the patriarchal options life would offer her, refuses even implicitly to validate those choices.[54]

Writing *Suggestions,* Elaine Showalter asserts, was a kind of therapy for Florence Nightingale; this lengthy discourse on religious vision and responsibility "helped her to work through her psychic turmoil."[55] Gaining power and control as author—although temporarily—Nightingale could create specific examples of the world as she envisioned it and she believed it could be.[56] With her movement from theory to practice in *Suggestions,* from theological abstractions to Cassandra's story, she produced possibilities for her own life—from fictional confrontations to sacrificial deaths.

The writing of *Suggestions,* however, was more than a therapeutic exercise to emancipate Nightingale; "Cassandra," especially, operated theologically as well.[57] Nightingale gained authority—divine authority—through Cassandra's death. Her culture with its outdated, stagnated religion crucified and martyred the victimized Cassandra, and Nightingale symbolically became the resurrected "saviour." Thus, by observing God's laws and recording man's misappropriation of them by society, Nightingale was reborn. In Cassandra's death, Nightingale also triumphed over her mother's power (as cultural socializer)—Cassandra (as surrogate for Nightingale) will not participate in her own subjection, and seeing no other alternative completely refuses to live dominated by patriarchal design. This victorious death must be seen in contrast to the seductive attraction Nightingale has earlier condemned: unlike that death which gives up the fight for the sacred truths Nightingale pursues, this death is the culmination of a life victimized by patriarchal oppression. Appropriate for this rejection of patriarchal social codes, Nightingale's production of text parallels that rejection; absent transitions, incomplete sentences, and layered voices mark the final fragment of "Cassandra" in a dialogue with mourners. Here, Nightingale rejects conventional patterns of behavior: celebrating death ("Welcome, beautiful death!" [*ST,* 2:411]) and calling for "wedding clothes instead of mourning" (*ST,* 2:411) for this quintessentially Christian interpretation of death as "divine freedom" from the chains of an earthly life (*ST,* 2:411). Seeing her life as thwarted by cultural restrictions on her talents, a sacrifice causing "a death . . . taken place some years ago" (*ST,* 2:411), Cassandra becomes a new kind of Christian prophet (identified as such in Nightingale's marginalia)—female in a world ordered not by her God or Christ, but by a patriarchal appropriation of the Judeo-Christian myth.

Earlier in *Suggestions,* Nightingale writes that "Disappointment often costs the woman her life—if by life is meant all spirit, energy, vitality" (*ST,* 2:214); here, Cassandra has been emotionally, spiritually, and intellectually killed, sacrificed by a patriarchally defined culture. This crucified woman, this female Christ, begins a revolutionary spirituality. In this section, Nightingale—vicariously through Cassandra's death—conquers what has become, in her life, the most restrictive and conservative forces—mother (and "woman's estate" [*ST,* 2:411]) and mother-church. Again through the association with Christ's crucifixion as well as her previous suggestion that the next Christ will be female, Cassandra's death empowers Nightingale through this symbolic resurrection in her creator.

*Suggestions* serves still another function for Nightingale. This discourse, especially volume 2 and "Cassandra," revises predominant religious beliefs of her time to include female experience. Elaine Showalter writes that "like other gifted women of her generation, she translated intellectual and vocational drives into the language of religion, the only system that could justify them."[58] In this way, *Suggestions* reveals the theological and cultural issues that Nightingale grappled with—not simply to validate her own desires, but also to reappropriate a religion which shaped her culture's values. That Nightingale chose to frame her own ambitions in a spiritual context, that she empowers herself through a fictive crucifixion and resurrection, cannot be ignored. Although female in a world dominated by men, she can argue and assert with equal, even higher authority. When her culture cites a divine plan to keep her a slave in her parents' home, wasting her talents as a handmaiden to an earthly lord, she can cite divine authority to free herself from that bondage. When her culture quotes scriptures to justify women's oppression, she can cite God's call. She becomes not just a woman critical of her androcentric culture, but a prophet of God.

Through her revisionist theology, Nightingale reappropriates the power associated with religion. Her theological discourse, infused with feminist vision, reveals a doctrine dependent upon women's active participation. By rejecting a patriarchally misconstrued God, Nightingale can challenge her society's controls over women without challenging God. By seeing each woman who struggles as the predecessor to the female incarnation, Nightingale invokes a God who embraces both male *and* female to authorize her criticism of a society that distorts His vision as exclusively male.

By asserting that "The next Christ will perhaps be a female Christ," she radically revises women's place in society. Not only does Nightingale's concept of a female Christ redefine martyr and prophet as female in patriarchal society, but that female divinity also subverts traditional values and images of power. This divinely sanctioned power, harnessed by resisting complicity, celebrating a resensitizing pain, and bearing witness to a greater Truth, shifts the locale of power. This power—both conservative and revolutionary—*returns* to God for authority while simultaneously revising organized religion and orthodox beliefs.[59] This double power mirrors the two strains of Nightingale's agenda—to participate in theological discourse and revise it. In this way, Nightingale's reclaims for women and other marginalized people what she believes to be true religious values and rejects self-serving patriarchal ones that rest on misinterpreted edicts. In asserting the misinterpretation of God's word, Nightingale further conflates the traditional power of the symbolic, the power upon which her culture builds its conventions. Rather than accurately communicate God's word, patriarchal representations distort and misconstrue His meanings and intentions.

Nightingale's revisionist theology, which rejects mother and mother-church and embraces a mystical relationship with God, confounds the gendered associations of God as word/symbol and revises that communication as more like the preverbal that finds parallels in the symbolic and semiotic language distinctions of Kristeva's theory. In Nightingale's discourse, mother and mother-church represent the socializing symbolic; the semiotic, in contrast, is represented by God, traditionally imagined male. Nightingale's mystical relationship with God, however, can be described more like that of the language of the semiotic—associative, fragmented, and representative of a not fully symbolized communication. In this way, Nightingale's spirituality demonstrates the extent to which her Victorian culture has displaced God from their society and religions: if God becomes associated with the nonconventional semiotic even if He has been imagined male, He (or aspects of Him) have become marginalized. The symbolic representation of His word has become too distant, too removed from what it signifies. In addition, God, for Nightingale, is not in concert with patriarchy, is not phallocentric.

Nightingale further conflates the traditional gender distinctions; her next Christ, after all, is female. She is female because women, in her culture, are those in need of a liberating theology. Similarly, she recreates for women a benevolent, nurturing God who sympathizes with women even while men threaten them with His wrath for subversive behavior: "Men say that God punishes for complaining. . . . They take it as a personal offense. To God alone may women complain, without insulting Him" (*ST*, 2:374). Women can complain because their quarrel is not with God but with man's injustice. In the end, Nightingale turns to God to authorize her desires, not because He is imagined male, but because He can provide her with the necessary authority as God, imagined to have called her to serve. She sees Him rejected even though His name is claimed, and so, even though He may in reality be marginalized, His word still evokes authority, if only, and ironically, because patriarchy has appropriated it.

The impact of these revisionist beliefs in empowering Nightingale can be clarified by returning to her life and considering the events immediately following the completion of *Suggestions.* After writing this theological treatise and just before her thirty-second birthday,

Nightingale received her second call from God, specifically, a "call from God to be a saviour."[60] With her years of waiting and theorizing behind her, Nightingale would act, and act decisively; she would be able to convince her father that she should be financially independent. With her revisionist theology and symbolic resurrection empowering her to act, Nightingale could now become one of those missing types she had looked for; she could attempt to save humanity from its erring ways.

Freed from family dependence, she accepted a job as superintendent of an Establishment for Gentlewomen during Illness, and within two years, she went to the Crimea with her nurses. While the war may have immortalized Nightingale, Strachey, in his biographical sketch of her, describes this experience as only "the fulcrum with which she hoped to move the world. . . . For more than a generation she was to sit in secret, working her lever: her real life began at the very moment when, in the popular imagination, [it] ended."[61] After the Crimean War, Nightingale proceeded to evoke sanitary and poor law reform as well as instigate military reforms by working through Sidney Herbert as commander-in-chief of the little War Office.[62]

Although the popular imagination will remember her as the founder of modern nursing, Nightingale's vision of nursing was not so much that of reforming a profession as answering a sacred call. In a letter to Jowett in 1889, she writes:

> the two thoughts which God has given me all my whole life have been—First, to infuse the mystical religion into the forms of others. . . . especially among women, to make them the "handmaidens of the Lord." Secondly, to give them an organization for their activity in which they could be trained to be the "handmaidens of the Lord". . . . When very many years ago I planned a future, my one idea was not organizing a Hospital, but organizing a Religion.[63]

Nightingale founded her "religion"—a feminist rewriting of the individual's place in her culture—through nursing, not the Church. Abandoning her culture's religious superstructure, she transposed her conception of God and His will into the secular sphere. In her revision, nursing could possibly become the force that would subvert a patriarchal misappropriation of God. A twentieth-century perspective makes it difficult to recognize the polemical impact caused by Nightingale's locating God in nursing: during the Victorian period, nursing was considered a vulgar occupation; nurses, intemperate and immoral women. Because of this, before Nightingale's reform, few respectable women would support themselves in this manner. Nightingale, however, recognized the fundamentally humanitarian, if not, by her vision, Christian, foundation of nursing. From this perspective, she sought to transform this occupation into a respectable and laudable profession.

Stripped of its clerical robes, Nightingale's religion infused what she believed to be God's ethics into the secular world; based on interpersonal care and the alleviation of suffering, this revisionist theology embraced those traditionally marginalized. Even if she rejected organized religion, Nightingale never abandoned her belief in God. For Nightingale, the spiritual crisis of the Victorian era was neither the disappearance of God nor an amoral universe, but rather the patriarchal appropriation of His word that imprisoned women's spirituality. Envisioning herself as a modern prophet of God, Nightingale reclaimed the power of religious myth and wrote her own liberation theology.

NOTES

J. A. V. Chapple and Arthur Pollard, eds. *The Letters of Mrs. Gaskell* (Cambridge: Harvard University Press, 1967), 307. Subsequent quotations from this work are cited in the text as *LG*.

[1] Florence Nightingale, *Suggestions for Thought to Searchers After Religious Truth* (London: Eyre and Spottiswoode, 1860), 2:374, 405. Subsequent quotations from this work are cited in the text as *ST*.

[2] Although the Anglican church did provide a limited number of Protestant convents for women, Nightingale felt her calling was to serve God in a public, less cloistered domain.

[3] Sir Edward Cook, *The Life of Florence Nightingale* (New York: Macmillan, 1942), 1:5, 7, 246; William George Tarrant, *Florence Nightingale as a Religious Thinker* (London: British and Foreign Unitarian Association, 1917), 8, 9. L. E. Elliott-Binns provides a useful explanation of the limited rights of Unitarians as well as the effects of the repeal of the Corporation and Test Acts (*Religion in the Victorian Era* [1936; reprint, London: Lutterworth Press, 1964], 31).

[4] Significantly these tensions between Nightingale and her mother continued throughout her life. Even after she returned from the Crimea a national figure, Florence felt so oppressed by her mother's influence that she developed an invalidism that enabled an escape from social obligations. These debilitating bouts lasted until her mother's death at which time she rose from bed cured.

[5] Cook, *Life of Nightingale* 1:6, 13, 122-23, 130.

[6] Donald R. Allen, "Florence Nightingale: Toward a Psychohistorical Interpretation," *Journal of Interdisciplinary History* 6, no. 1 (1975): 31.

[7] Cook, *Life of Nightingale* 1:14.

[8] Lytton Strachey, *Eminent Victorians: Cardinal Manning, Florence Nightingale, Dr. Arnold, and General Gordon* (New York: Capricorn, 1963), 131. Despite the fact that enforced passivity nearly drove Nightingale insane, Benjamin Jowett, who for years acted as her spiritual advisor, told her, "I sometimes think . . . that

you ought seriously to consider how your work may be carried on, not with less energy, but in a calmer spirit" (Strachey, 190).

[9] The forced patience and the passing of time is one of the extraordinary features that Cecil Woodham-Smith notes about Nightingale's life; eight years would pass between her first call from God and Nightingale's knowledge that nursing was to be her vocation, another eight years before she could pursue her work. "Sixteen years in all, sixteen years during which the eager susceptible girl was slowly hammered into the steely powerful woman of genius. The last eight years . . . were years in which suffering piled on suffering, frustration followed frustration, until she was brought to the verge of madness" (*Florence Nightingale* [New York: McGraw-Hill, 1951], 42).

[10] Woodham-Smith lists these four occasions: 7 February 1837; in 1853 prior to working at the Hospital for Poor Gentlewomen in Harley Street; in 1854 before going to the Crimea; and in 1861 after the death of Sidney Herbert (*Florence Nightingale,* 13). Nightingale believed that these calls were not "inward revelation" but an actual, external voice like that heard by Joan of Arc (12). In "Florence Nightingale: Toward a Psychohistorical Interpretation," Donald R. Allen asserts that "All of these experiences with 'voices' occurred after periods marked by personal disappointment, strong feelings of self-doubt, deep depression, and a sense of failure. In turn, all were followed by a strong desire to accomplish something, a devotion to work, and some kind of fulfillment" (33).

[11] Cook, *Life of Nightingale* 1:14.

[12] Ibid., 1:15.

[13] Woodham-Smith, *Florence Nightingale,* 42. From our modern perspective, nursing is not considered an immoral profession, nor is the only qualification to be a woman, but our sense of nursing is largely the result of Nightingale's reform. In fact, ironically, nursing has become synonymous with "good" female characteristics; this results partly because the popular imagination remembers Florence Nightingale not as the "Commander-in-Chief" of the "little War Office," but as the "Lady with the lamp." For a detailed analysis of this, see my manuscript "The Lady with the Lamp Refracted by Patriarchy: The Image of Florence Nightingale in Popular Consciousness and Historical Memory." It is also significant that what most worried Fanny Nightingale was the fear that her daughter was involved in a questionable relationship with a surgeon. Her concern reflects in a significant way just how radical Nightingale's desires were and the extent to which patriarchally prescribed heterosexuality saturates women's lives: an interclass liaison, while feared and frowned upon, would nonetheless be more comprehensible than a woman challenging cultural values for her own needs. The assumption presumes women act in relation to men, not independently. That Nightingale's desires existed outside this paradigm

made them both more threatening and less understandable to those operating within it.

[14] Cook, *Life of Nightingale* 1:44-45. Mary Poovey also notes analogies between Nightingale and Christ (*Uneven Developments: The Ideological Work of Gender in Mid-Victorian England* [Chicago: University of Chicago Press, 1988], 239). See also Martha Vicinus's *Independent Women: Work and Community for Single Women, 1850-1920* (Chicago: University of Chicago Press, 1985), esp. "Church Communities: Sisterhoods and Deaconesses' Houses" (46-84), for a useful analysis of the role religious communities played in Victorian women's spirituality.

[15] Elaine Showalter describes Nightingale's three-volume discourse as an attempt to "justify the laws of God to men—especially working men—and, most important, to women" ("Florence Nightingale's Feminist Complaint: Women, Religion, and *Suggestions for Thought*," *Signs* 6 [1981]: 399). Cook describes the three-volume work as "ostensibly one of Reconstruction; it was in fact very largely one of Revolt" (*Life of Nightingale* 1:475). See also Mary Poovey's insightful "Introduction" to her recent edition of *Cassandra and Other Selections from Suggestions for Thought* (New York: New York University Press, 1992) for a consideration of Nightingale's desire to write *Suggestions*.

[16] Showalter, "Nightingale's Feminist Complaint," 400.

[17] Kristeva, *Desire in Language*, 6.

[18] Toril Moi, *Sexual/Textual Politics: Feminist Literary Theory* (London: Methuen, 1985), 166.

[19] Ibid., 170, 11. In her analysis of Kristeva's revolutionary subject, Moi raises important questions about the relationship between agency and subversion. See pages 170-71 for an expanded discussion of Kristeva in a political context.

[20] Although *Suggestions* was only printed privately, the religious speculation that Nightingale pursued in it eventually reached the public forum through two articles—"A Note of Interrogation" (*Fraser's Magazine*, n.s., 7 [1873]: 567-77) and "A Sub-Note of Interrogation: What Will Be Our Religion in 1999?" (*Fraser's Magazine*, n.s., 8 [1873]: 25-36). Revising her ideas for these publications—focusing primarily on loss of faith and inadequate religious inquiry—Nightingale diluted the potency of the original text. With the militant challenges to patriarchy removed, the ideas become lost in the many voices of religious debate prevalent during the Victorian period. These two articles, however diluted, did elicit response: Carlyle described her second article as "a lost sheep bleating on the mountain," and Cook records that many prayed for Nightingale's conversion (*Life of Nightingale*, 1:219). *Suggestions* is available on microfiche as part of the Adelaide Nutting Historical Nursing Collection, and selections from the three-volume treatise have been published in

Mary Poovey's recent edition, *Cassandra and other Selections from Suggestions for Thought*.

[21] Cook, *Life of Nightingale* 1:469.

[22] Ibid. 1:472, 475.

[23] Ibid. 1:477.

[24] The structure that Nightingale uses in *Suggestions*, framing her most radical discourse with more traditional analysis (and that Brontë reproduces in *Shirley* to a lesser degree), anticipates that of Irigaray's *Speculum of the Other Woman*.

[25] Nightingale's decision not to convert was not entirely her own. On the brink of converting to Catholicism, Nightingale gave Cardinal Manning, then a priest, the manuscript of *Suggestions*; when he read her manuscript, Manning concluded that she was not in the "requisite state of mind for admission into the Church of Rome" (Woodham-Smith, *Florence Nightingale*, 65).

[26] Taylor, *Eve and the New Jerusalem*, 126.

[27] For an informative study of the interrelationship between religious and capitalistic politics in the shaping of Victorian values, see Taylor's *Eve and the New Jerusalem*.

[28] Nightingale, "Sub-Note," 28.

[29] In considering what society has done for women, Nightingale deliberately includes "fallen" women in her question; society treats these women, she contends, as if they are beyond redemption, with no claims to humanity (*ST*, 2:209). Like Gaskell, Nightingale sees the systemic cause of these women's problems, and in "Cassandra" she goes so far as to suggest that women who marry are just another kind of prostitute.

[30] Nightingale expands on this in a private note written in 1851: "Women don't consider themselves as human beings at all. There is absolutely no God, no country, no duty to them at all, except family. . . . I have known a good deal of convents. And of course everyone has talked of the petty grinding tyrannies supposed to be exercised there. But I know nothing like the petty grinding tyranny of a good English family. And the only alleviation is that the tyrannized submits with a heart full of affection" (Woodham-Smith, *Florence Nightingale*, 62).

[31] Woodham-Smith, *Florence Nightingale*, 51.

[32] Cook, *Life of Nightingale* 1:102.

[33] Taylor, *Eve and the New Jerusalem*, 126, 137.

[34] Froula, "When Eve Reads Milton," 321-47.

[35] In a 26 September 1863 letter to her father, Nightingale wrote: "*God* does hang on the Cross *every day* in *every one* of us" (Cook, *Life of Nightingale*, 1:485).

[36] She does add, however, that "it is perhaps incorrect to say that they have no type, England has the type of making money" (*ST*, 2:73). With this assertion, she once again echoes Carlyle's belief that their culture's values had shifted from spiritual to materialistic ones.

[37] Nightingale, "Note," 577.

[38] Woodham-Smith notes that at the end of 1845 Nightingale "spent her nights sleepless, wrestling with her soul, seeking with tears and prayers to make herself worthy to receive the kindness of God; she spent her days performing the duties of the daughter at home" (*Florence Nightingale*, 42).

[39] Nightingale began studying blue books and hospital reports at Lord Ashley's suggestion; just a few years earlier the first of these government reports dealing with public health had been published (Woodham-Smith, *Florence Nightingale*, 43).

[40] Showalter, "Nightingale's Feminist Complaint," 399.

[41] Cook, *Life of Nightingale* 1:59.

[42] Ibid., 1:43.

[43] Strachey, *Eminent Victorians*, 134-35.

[44] Cook, *Life of Nightingale*, 1:101.

[45] Allen divides Nightingale's life into five periods, which he identifies as turning points, each "marked by an internal crisis, that led to a new stage in her development." In chronological order they are: her childhood to around age 7; her call from God that she experienced when 16; her decision to reject marriage and follow what she believed to be God's call, a decision which Allen asserts "resolved her long crisis of identity"; her political alliance with Sidney Herbert after the Crimean War; and, finally, the death of her parents and sister, which, Allen contends, "freed her from a lifelong conflict and permitted her to enter a long period at the end of her life when, her fury abated, she enjoyed the fruits of her labors and contributions" ("Florence Nightingale," 28).

[46] Cook, *Life of Nightingale* 1:94.

[47] According to Clough, Nightingale regarded Quinet and Mill as "the two men who had the true belief about God's laws. She referred in particular to two chapters in Mill's *Logic* about Free Will and Necessity, which seemed to her to be the beginning of the true religious belief" (Cook, *Life of Nightingale* 1:469).

[48] Tarrant, *Florence Nightingale*, 18.

[49] Nightingale, "Note," 577.

[50] Cook, *Life of Nightingale* 1:480.

[51] Ibid., xv.

[52] Pagels, *Gnostic Gospels*, 27, 95, xix.

[53] Cook, *Life of Nightingale* 1:480.

[54] See Barbara Bellow Watson's extremely useful "On Power and the Literary Text" (*Signs* 1 [1975]: 111-18) for an examination of these issues in Chopin, Woolf, and Lessing. See also Elaine Showalter's *The Female Malady*, where she asserts, "The ending of *Cassandra* dramatizes the despair Nightingale could imagine as her own fate: Cassandra dies at the age of thirty, 'withered, paralyzed, extinguished.' In her youth she had 'dreamed of Institutions to show women their work and to train them how to do it' and had 'sacrificed my individual future' of marriage for 'glimpses of a great general future'" (64). Although Showalter's study is extremely useful in reconstructing the complete history of Nightingale, I believe that this reading of Cassandra's death oversimplifies what Nightingale achieves in "Cassandra."

[55] Showalter, "Nightingale's Feminist Complaint," 399.

[56] Watson, "On Power and the Literary Text," 112.

[57] Throughout her life, writing performed an important role in maintaining Nightingale's mental health. As with *Suggestions for Thought*, writing became a conduit to channel unsatiated energies that her forced passivity could not quench. After her first tenure in the Crimea, Nightingale, suffering from Crimean fever, was instructed simply to rest; but in "her delirium [Nightingale] was constantly writing. It was found impossible to keep her quiet unless she wrote, so she was given pen and paper" (Woodham-Smith, *Florence Nightingale*, 152). A few years earlier, at thirty, Nightingale had considered the possible directions for her life, writing "I had 3 paths among which to choose . . . I might have been a married woman, or a literary woman, or a hospital sister" (Woodham-Smith, *Florence Nightingale*, 55); but writing, while crucial to her stability and development, was always only a poor second for living. Nightingale explains this in her response to Mary Clarke's suggestion that she focus on expressing herself through writing: "You ask me why I do not write something. . . . I had so much rather live than write—writing is only a substitute for living. . . . I think one's feelings waste themselves in words, they ought all to be distilled into actions and actions which bring results" (Woodham-Smith, *Florence Nightingale*, 36).

[58] Showalter, "Nightingale's Feminist Complaint," 397-98.

[59] Jane P. Tompkins provides an important reevaluation of literary power in "Sentimental Power: *Uncle Tom's Cabin* and the Politics of Literary History," in *The New Feminist Criticism: Essays on Women, Literature, and Theory*, ed. Elaine Showalter (New York: Pantheon, 1985): 81-104.

[60] Showalter, "Nightingale's Feminist Complaint," 400.

[61] Strachey, *Eminent Victorians,* 158.

[62] Woodham-Smith, *Florence Nightingale,* 199. In the end it is ironic that Nightingale, who so strongly rejected marriage, resisting the common practice of working "through" one's husband, would ultimately "work through" Sidney Herbert in the War Office. With Herbert, however, she retained a power and independence that would have been most likely lost legally, if not practically, in marriage at that time.

[63] Cook, *Life of Nightingale* 2:366-67.

---

# FURTHER READING

## Biography

Andrews, Mary Raymond Shipman. *A Lost Commander: Florence Nightingale.* Garden City, N.Y.: Doubleday, Doran & Company, 1929, 299 p.
Laudatory biography of Nightingale.

Cook, Sir Edward. *The Life of Florence Nightingale.* New York: The Macmillan Company, 1942, 510 p.
Comprehensive and authoritative biography.

Goldie, Sue M., ed. *"I Have Done My Duty": Florence Nightingale in the Crimean War, 1854-56.* Manchester: Manchester University Press, 1987, 326 p.
Study of Nightingale's experience as a war nurse which features a large selection of correspondence from that period of her life.

Huxley, Elspeth. *Florence Nightingale.* London: Weidenfeld and Nicolson, 1975, 254 p.
Generously illustrated popular biography.

Smith, F. B. *Florence Nightingale: Reputation and Power.* New York: St. Martin's Press, 1982, 216 p.
Evaluation of Nightingale's life as a reformer that makes use of previously unavailable manuscripts.

Woodham-Smith, Cecil. *Florence Nightingale, 1820-1910.* New York: McGraw-Hill, 1951, 382 p.
Extensive popular biography of Nightingale which is indebted to the work of Sir Edward Cook.

## Criticism

Baly, Monica E. *Florence Nightingale and the Nursing Legacy.* London: Croom Helm, 1986, 237 p.
Discusses the influence of Nightingale and her schools on the field of nursing.

Boyd, Nancy. "Florence Nightingale." In *Three Victorian Women Who Changed Their World: Josephine Butler, Octavia Hill, Florence Nightingale,* pp. 167-234. Oxford: Oxford University Press, 1982.
Evaluation of Nightingale's work as a social reformer directed by faith.

Bullough, Vern, Bonnie Bullough, and Marietta P. Stanton, eds. *Florence Nightingale and Her Era: A Collection of New Scholarship.* New York: Garland Publishing, 1990, 365 p.
Collection of modern Nightingale scholarship, in which the editors endeavor to present a multidimensional view of their subject.

Forster, Margaret. "Florence Nightingale, 1820-1910." In *Significant Sisters: The Grassroots of Active Feminism, 1839-1939,* pp. 93-129. London: Secker & Warburg, 1984.
Explores Nightingale's efforts to open the field of medicine to women.

Pickering, George. "Florence Nightingale . . ." and "Miss Nightingale's Illness." In *Creative Malady: Illness in the Lives and Minds of Charles Darwin, Florence Nightingale, Mary Baker Eddy, Sigmund Freud, Marcel Proust, and Elizabeth Barrett Browning,* pp. 99-177. London: George Allen& Unwin, 1974.
Traces Nightingale's desire to reform the British War Office to a psychological illness that prompted her "to avenge her murdered children, the British soldiers who had died in the Crimea."

Rosenberg, Charles E. "Florence Nightingale on Contagion: The Hospital as Moral Universe." In *Explaining Epidemics and Other Studies in the History of Medicine,* pp. 90-108. Cambridge: Cambridge University Press, 1992.
Probes Nightingale's metaphorical understanding of disease.

Seymer, Lucy Ridgely, ed. *Selected Writings of Florence Nightingale.* New York: The Macmillan Company, 1954, 397 p.
Collection of Nightingale's most significant writings on nursing preceded by a brief introduction.

West, Anthony. "Florence Nightingale." In *Principles and Persuasions: The Literary Essays of Anthony West,* pp. 70-76. New York: Harcourt, Brace, 1957.
Attempts to correct some of the simplified and sentimental stereotypes promulgated by several of Nightingale's biographers.

---

The following source published by Gale includes further information on the life and work of Florence Nightingale: *Dictionary of Literary Biography,* Vol. 166.

# Rudolf Otto

## 1869-1937

(Born Louis Karl Rudolf Otto) German philosopher of religion.

## INTRODUCTION

Otto gained international renown as a philosopher of theology and religion with the 1917 publication of his book *Das Heilige* (*The Idea of the Holy*). Positing that religious experience is emotional and intuitive rather than rational and intellectual, Otto appealed to the sensibilities of those disillusioned by the horrific events of World War I. Additionally, Otto's studies of Eastern religions attempted to find common ground between East and West, a goal that was well illustrated by his foundation of the international Religious League of Mankind and of a museum of comparative religion in Marburg, Germany.

## Biographical Information

Otto was born in Peine, Germany, in 1869 to Wilhelm, a manufacturer, and Katherine Otto. The twelfth of thirteen children, Otto was raised in a strict evangelical Lutheran environment. In 1880 the family moved to Hildesheim, where Otto's father owned several factories; shortly thereafter, his father died. Even as a child, Otto was fascinated by religious study and would argue with young friends over Darwinism and biblical creation stories. In 1888 Otto entered the Friedrich-Alexander University in Erlangen, hoping to receive an education in theology that would validate his conservative religious beliefs. But while spending the summer of 1889 with friends at the University of Göttingen, Otto was exposed to more liberal views; he later asserted that the experience began a new phase in both his religious thinking and his personal life. Otto returned for another semester at Erlangen before going to study in Bavaria from late 1889 to 1891. In the summer of 1891 he enrolled again at the University of Göttingen, where he remained until 1899. Otto spent the years from 1891 to 1898 broadening his academic interests and focusing on a wider range of liberal arts studies rather than exclusively on religion. In 1895, inspired by his studies of Arabic and Aramaic, he traveled to Egypt, Palestine, and Greece. There he had his first direct experiences with Coptic Orthodoxy and Islam. When he returned to Göttingen, Otto received his Licentiate of Theology with the publication of his first major work, *Die Anschauung vom heiligen Geiste bei Luther* (*Luther's Conception of the Holy Spirit*). In 1899 Otto was made a *Privatdozent* (lecturer) at the University of Göttingen, but because of objections within the Lutheran church to his liberal theology, Otto was not made a full professor until he joined the staff of the University of Breslau in 1915. At one point he came close to a nervous breakdown and considered giving up theological study to become a pastor or a missionary to China. From 1911 to 1912 Otto traveled to Africa, India, and the Far East, where he first encountered Hinduism in India and Zen Buddhism in Japan. On this trip Otto first conceived of forming an international league of religions as well as a museum of comparative religion. In 1914 Otto was made an associate professor at Göttingen, and in 1915 he moved to the University of Breslau, where he was made a full professor. Between 1920 and 1924 Otto devoted much of his time to the Religious League of Mankind. Believing that, despite differences of ritual and expression, world religions shared the fundamental goals of battling superstition and immorality, Otto held the first successful meeting of his League in 1922. By 1933, however, interest had dwindled, and the League's activities were terminated. Otto, however, remained strongly interested in world religions, towards which the focus of his later work is directed. From 1917 to 1929 Otto was a professor at the University of Marburg, and in 1927 and 1928 he traveled again through Asia Minor, the Balkans, India, Palestine, and Ceylon. Otto had suffered from bouts of depression most of his life, and in 1936 he climbed to a tower in Staufenberg, from which he fell sixty feet. Whether or not this was a suicide attempt remains unclear, but in 1937 he checked into a psychiatric hospital to overcome a morphine addiction that had begun while he was recovering from his fall. He died of pneumonia eight days after entering the hospital.

## Major Works

While Otto published numerous works and translations, the book that made the strongest and most lasting impression on the academic and intellectual community was *The Idea of the Holy*. The most influential and widely read theological book of the early twentieth century, *The Idea of the Holy* rejected the notion of religious experience as rooted in objectivity and intellect and instead posited the idea that religion is a subjective, intuitive experience. But because Otto believed that the "Holy" in all world religions was a mysterious but ultimately objective reality, various religions were not at odds despite the subjectivity of their respective worshipers; rather, according to Otto, believers in every religion experienced a similar apprehension of the Holy, or numinous, as Otto defined it. This term–"numinous"– was introduced by Otto to mean the entity that at once inspired fear, awe, and attraction in worshipers. Otto thus rejected the idea held by Ludwig Feuerbach and Sigmund Freud that religion is illusory. In his later works–most notably *West-Östliche Mystik (Mysticism East and West)* and *Die Gnadenreligion Indiens und das Christentum (India's Religion of Grace and Christianity Compared and Contrasted)*–Otto further explored similarities in world religions, especially Christianity and Hinduism, for which he had developed a strong admiration while on his travels and while translating numerous Hindu religious texts. In his last work, *Reich Gottes und Menschensohn (The Kingdom of God and the Son of Man)*, Otto examined primitive Christianity and particularly the figure of Jesus and what Otto believed to be the Iranian influence on the teachings of Jesus.

## Critical Reception

The popularity of *The Idea of the Holy* overshadowed much of Otto's other work. The notion of spirituality as an emotional rather than an intellectual experience profoundly affected a generation of thinkers and scholars who had lived through World War I–at the time considered the most shocking and devastating event in human history–and who had developed a bitter cynicism about religion's ability to help them make sense of the political and social chaos of war. Otto was not without detractors, however. He was criticized for presenting too narrow a definition of religious experience, excluding as he did the social and abstract aspects of it. Others disapproved of his choice of Sanskrit texts for translation, believing him to be biased toward certain works that he concluded best illustrated the fundamentals of Hinduism. Nonetheless, Otto's works continue to be studied by theologians and religious historians for their adept studies in comparative religion and for Otto's discerning notion of the numinous.

# PRINCIPAL WORKS

*Die Anschauung vom Heiligen Geiste bei Luther: Eine historisch-dogmatisch Untersuchung* (nonfiction) 1898

*Leben und Werken Jesu nach historisch-kritischer Auggassung* [*The Life and Ministry of Jesus According to the Historical and Critical Method*] (nonfiction) 1902

*Naturalistische und religiöse Weltansicht* [*Naturalism and Religion*] (nonfiction) 1904

*Goethe und Darwin; Darwinismus und Religion* (nonfiction) 1909

*Kantisch-Fries'sche Religionsphilosophie und ihre Anwendung auf die Theologie* [*The Philosophy of Religion, Based on Kant and Fries*] (nonfiction) 1909

*Das Heilige: Über das Irrationale in der Idee des Göttlichen und sein Verhältnis zum Rationalen* [*The Idea of the Holy: An Inquiry into the Non-rational Factor in the Idea of the Divine and Its Relation to the Rational*] (nonfiction) 1917

*Aufsätze, das Numinose betreffend* (nonfiction) 1923; also published as *Sünde und Urschuld*, 1932 and as *Dar Gefühl des Überweltlichen (Sensus Numinis)*, 1932; selections published as *Religious Essays: A Supplement to "The Idea of the Holy,"* 1931

*Zur Erneuerung und Ausgestaltung des Gottesdienstes* (nonfiction) 1925

*West-Östliche Mystik: Vergleich und Unterscheifung zur Wesensdeutung* [*Mysticism East and West: A Comparative Analysis of the Nature of Mysticism*] (nonfiction) 1926

*Die Gnadenreligion Indiens und das Christentum* [*India's Religion of Grace and Christianity Compared and Contrasted*] (nonfiction) 1930

*Reich Gottes und Menschensohn: Ein religionsgeschichtlicher Versuch* [*The Kingdom of God and the Son of Man*] (nonfiction) 1934

*Freiheit und Notwendigkeit: Ein Gespräch mit Nikolai Hartmann über Antonomie und Theonomie der Werte* (nonfiction) 1940

*Verantwortliche Lebensgestaltung: Gespräch mit Rudolf Otto über Fragen der Ethik* [edited by Karl Küssner] (nonfiction) 1943

# CRITICISM

## Leo Strauss (essay date 1922)

SOURCE: "*The Idea of the Holy* (Rudolf Otto)," in *The Jew: Essays From Martin Buber's Journal, Der Jude, 1916-1928*, edited by Arthur A. Cohen, The University of Alabama Press, 1980, pp. 232-6.

[*In the following essay originally published in 1922 in the Martin Buber journal* Der Jude, *Strauss relates Otto's* The Idea of the Holy *to European Judaism.*]

It often happens in the Zionist youth movement that our young students take philosophical, sociological, and historical theories they have learned at university and apply them, in our periodicals, to our own problems, often without heeding the dubious aspects of such an application. This phenomenon, initially comical, springing as it does from a touching lack of reflection, has a serious background. Ultimately, it mirrors the overall spiritual situation of German Jews. Isn't that what all theologians of German Judaism have done? Haven't they all projected the German milieu, its predominant values and viewpoints, onto judgment and consideration of things Jewish? However legitimate such a projection may be (this legitimacy can be considered the cardinal problem of our spiritual situation), there are two instances where it apparently cannot be questioned by a doubting spirit. In one case, an ideologist of Judaism has taken a creative part in shaping German thought, so that through him Jewish energy, in the form of cultural elements, has entered the German world. Thus, his projection of German attitudes into Jewish things was preceded by his assimilating the minds of both nations. Only the man who has bridged the span himself (and not everyone who availed himself of the bridge) can truly judge the nature of the banks, the width and depth of the chasm, or the difficulty of bridging. The most venerable example of this case is the work of Hermann Cohen.

No less impressive is the second instance, when the German spirit, turning to Jewish tendencies, makes them alive within itself, especially if the tendencies in question are those whose effectiveness is restricted or repressed within the Jewish nation because of its untoward destiny. Such is the Protestant science of the Old Testament, a discipline shedding light on the real background of prophecy. It occurs in Nietzsche's critique of civilization, a critique striking to the pre-"Christian" depths of both the Jewish and the Hellenic-European spirit. And it occurs, last but not least, in Rudolf Otto's theological investigation, to which we shall return shortly.

The importance of Otto's work lies in the viewpoint he suggests for orienting the history of theology (and thereby positioning his own theological enterprise in intellectual history). To what extent can that orientation be applied to the science of Judaism? Earlier theology (whose most essential form for us was the doctrine of attributes during the age of Spanish Jewry) had the task of helping the "rational" elements in religion win out over the primitive and irrational elements. Today, after an all-too-complete performance of that task, theology has the opposite duty. It must leave the realm of the rational and, by means of a conscientious, scientifically irreproachable emphasis on the irrational, proceed to construct a system befitting the matter. Once upon a time, in a world filled with the irrational in religion, theologians had to achieve recognition for the right of *ratio.* Today, however, in a spiritual reality dominated by *ratio,* theology has the function of making "the irrational in the idea of the divine" alive through the medium of theoretical consciousness. Earlier theology speculated in a religiously closed vault—modern theology lives under an open sky and has to exert its own strength to help rebuild the vault. In the past the primary fact was God. Today it is the world, man, religious experience.

Formulating the task this way, we can recognize the question and the results of the doctrine of attributes without having to regard this doctrine as closed. Otto's categories permit the entire doctrine of attributes to enter the greater framework of a new theology. We cannot help thinking that it is not the idea of "attribute" in and of itself, but the hackneyed emptiness of the attributes of omnipotence, universal goodness, etc., that makes for the popular discrediting of the doctrine of attributes. Today, as a rule, people cite the "living fullness of experience," in opposition to the emptiness of the "attributes." Otto's investigation shows that one need not deviate from the straight, linear view of the religious object in order to grasp theoretically the objectiveness of religious life. In the object itself, the rational and the irrational elements are distinguished. The irrational in the religious object is the "bearer," the *substance* of the rational predicates, of the "attributes." The irrationality meant by religion is to be found not in the depth of the subject, but in the depth of the object. Hence we have no need for romantic "religious philosophy." This vouchsafes a connection to the tradition of the Bible and our worship on the one hand, and to the

tradition of our theology on the other hand. The latter teaches us the general position of the Jewish theologian and offers us the results of analyzing rational "attributes." The former makes available the most perfect expression that the substance of the religious object could find "in human speech." It is thus no coincidence that Otto derives his substantial categories not least of all from the Old Testament and Jewish liturgy (cf. *Yom Kippur Prayers,* p. 37 f. *Melekh 'Elyon,* translated by Otto, pp. 238 ff.).

Yet at times Otto very keenly stresses the contrast between religion and theology, siding with religion *against* theology. This emphasis is justified in order to establish, from a religious viewpoint, the secondary character of theology. Otherwise, it need not bind us, since Otto, as especially his citations indicate, is strongly influenced here by Lutheran tendencies that cannot be determining for us as Jews, for whom that peculiarly Protestant subjectivism has to be quite remote.

Even so, it is still possible to consider *The Idea of the Holy* as a work of "religious philosophy." But what distinguishes Otto's analysis from the usual kind of religious philosophy is that it turns directly to religious consciousness without undertaking a naturalistic explanation or a transcendental "constitution" of this consciousness.

The great significance of Otto's book is its restriction of the rational element of religion not primarily and not exclusively by citing the irrationality of "experience." Rather, it makes the transcendence of the religious object the self-evident starting-point of the investigation. However justified our skepticism towards the doctrine of attributes, our sympathy may still go out to this type of theology: the very formulation of its task already makes fundamental subjectivism impossible. One would have to *demand* a theology as a doctrine of attributes even if it were simply impracticable—merely in order to have the notion of God's transcendence as a keynote from the very outset. A deeper understanding of the meaning of "transcendence" within a religious context is, if not the intention, then certainly the consequence of Otto's investigation. Transcendence receives a distinction:

(1) as the *experiential* otherworldliness of God, i.e., of God's primacy in regard to religion. If God exists in and of Himself, an entity independent of human experience, and if we know of this being from what is revealed in the Torah and the Prophets, then the theoretical presentation of what we know is basically possible, i.e., theology. Theology is very much the expression of plain, straightforward piety.

(2) as the *living* otherworldliness of God. It is experienced in the "creature feeling" of man, in his "being earth, ashes, and nothing," also and precisely in that of the *nation,* as evidenced in Isaiah 6. It is identical with the completely "nonnatural" character of "God's wrath," and no less with the character of "sacredness" as a "numinous value."

(3) as the *ideal* otherworldliness of God. The final characteristic of the preceding could mislead one to "idealize" God. This danger is abolished by the reference to the character of the "energetic," to the "vitality" of God.

## Robert F. Davidson (essay date 1947)

SOURCE: "Introduction: Rudolf Otto and *The Idea of the Holy*," in *Rudolf Otto's Interpretation of Religion*, Princeton University Press, No. 1947, pp. 1-18.

[*In the following essay, Davidson examines the influence of* The Idea of the Holy *and several of Otto's other major works on modern religious studies.*]

The leadership of German thought has been well established in Protestant theological circles since the time of the Reformation and Rudolf Otto stands out among those men who have helped to perpetuate it into our own day. There are at present, of course, unmistakable indications that this intellectual preeminence of Germany has been at least temporarily brought to an end. The crisis in the German Church itself, the policies of the German government for the past decade or more, and the inevitable consequences of a tragic period of post-war reconstruction, all make continued German leadership in the theological thought of the Western World highly improbable.

In his discerning study of *Contemporary English Theology* Walter Horton recently suggested that the intellectual leadership of Western Christendom was passing to England. It may well be, as critics of Horton's study insisted, that American theology is now prepared to assert its independence of all foreign domination and develop an original and characteristic theological position of its own. But certainly as yet no British or American influence has been exerted upon contemporary religious thought comparable in significance or permanence to that emanating from Germany. Indeed Horton himself hastens to point this out in his own later work, *Contemporary Continental Theology.*

The viewpoint of Protestant Christianity during the past two decades has been largely shaped by the theology of Karl Barth and by Rudolf Otto's philosophy of religion—in Europe to a marked degree, in America to a much more limited but increasing extent. Whatever the theoretical validity of their positions may prove to be, both these men have apprehended and formulated in striking fashion something of the inner spirit of the present age. The thought of both must be ranked among the formative influences in the theological development of our generation. Numerous studies of the Barthian theology have appeared in English, but Otto's books, although widely commented upon, have been left in the main to speak for themselves.

I

Few books indeed have made such large and immediate impact upon the religious world as Otto's major work,

*The Idea of the Holy.* Published in 1917, its appeal was unquestionably enhanced by the widespread spirit of disillusionment engendered at that time by the first World War. Acute need was felt for some interpretation of man's life and destiny more satisfying than the secular and purely rational outlook prevalent in the years preceding the war. Otto's *Idea of the Holy* as definitely as Barth's *Commentary on Romans* provided a reorientation of life upon a distinctly religious basis, emphasizing a "dimension of depth" in experience which "liberal" Protestant theology had too largely lost from view. As a result both Otto and Barth at once commanded general attention.

An indication of the appeal and, to some extent, the importance of Otto's thought is to be found in the attention his book attracted. In Germany *Das Heilige* has gone through twenty-five editions (the latest in 1936) and has been published also in cheaper form for student use during a period hardly favorable for the wide circulation of scholarly studies. Within twelve years after its initial appearance it was translated into seven other languages (into English in 1923, Swedish in 1924, Spanish in 1925, Italian in 1926, Japanese in 1927, Dutch in 1928, and French in 1929). The English translation, *The Idea of the Holy,* has itself been reprinted six times and was included recently (1936) in a cheaper edition on the Oxford Book shelf. Otto's position has occasioned comment in almost every important theological work in Germany since the date of its publication and in Great Britain since its translation. To the widespread interest aroused by *The Idea of the Holy* may likewise be attributed the rapid translation into English of Otto's later works, which in the main are but historical or theological amplifications of its cardinal tenets.

The significance of Otto's book is not due, however, merely to its timeliness. Not only its discerning portrayal of religious experience but also its truly remarkable synthesis of the major tendencies of modern German theology mark it as one of the great books of our day. A typical comment is that of Charles A. Bennett: "In recent years the most striking and original attempt to distill the essence of religion is, beyond all question, that of Professor Otto in his book, *Das Heilige.*"[1]

The publication of *Das Heilige* established Otto almost immediately as one of Germany's foremost theologians. Prior to that time he had been professor of systematic theology at Göttingen (1904-1914) and at Breslau (1914-1917). In 1917 he was appointed to the same position at Marburg. The influence of his *Hauptwerk* was so great indeed that he was later offered the highly esteemed chairs in this field at the University of Halle and the University of Berlin. He was soon invited, largely for the same reason, to important lectureships throughout the English-speaking world. In 1924 he visited the United States, giving the Haskell Lectures at Oberlin College and speaking at other leading American Universities. Some years thereafter he was chosen to give the University of Calcutta Lectures on Comparative

Religion, and was also selected to deliver the Gifford Lectures at Aberdeen. Unfortunately, however, because of failing health he was not able finally to fill either of the latter appointments.

Otto's fame as a theologian, the inspirational quality of his teaching, and more perhaps than anything else, the depth of his own spiritual life, drew students from all the world to the beautiful university town of Marburg, where he chose to remain until his death in 1937, despite tempting offers of other posts that came to him. In increasing numbers during the nineteen-twenties aspiring young theologians from England and America met with those of Germany to find deepened insight and enlarged appreciation of religion in his Marburg seminars. A common path led visitors from the Orient and from the Occident to his study door. All were impressed by the catholicity of his spirit and understanding as well as by the genuineness of his interest in the issues discussed with him.[2]

The breadth of Otto's interest and the depth of his spiritual insight is well evidenced by his important contribution to the devotional life of the Lutheran Church. In addition to numerous articles and a volume devoted directly to discussion of improved method in public worship (*Zur Erneuerung und Ausgestaltung des Gottesdienstes,* 1925), he collaborated for a number of years in the publication of such devotional materials as orders of service for special occasions, prayers for use in church, school and home, and general liturgical aids for ministers.

Nor was he content to write of worship simply from the viewpoint of a theological professor. Instead, in more concrete experimental fashion, he undertook in a chapel near Marburg to develop a more vital and dynamic worship experience, thus infusing into institutional religion something of the mystical spirit and insight that his theological studies manifest so clearly.[3] Combining a practical with an historical purpose Otto also established and promoted zealously the *Marburger religionskundliche Sammlung,* a fine collection of ritualistic symbols of all sorts, primitive, Oriental and Christian.

In the same practical fashion he gave enthusiastic support to the missionary activity of his own Communion, taking a place of leadership in that endeavor without endorsing a narrow or sectarian evangelistic program. Indeed he united with his missionary interest not only a wholehearted advocacy of the more effective unity of Protestantism throughout the world, but likewise a deep and genuine appreciation of the great non-Christian faiths. From such breadth of vision the missionary enterprise itself could not but profit. It is no exaggeration to say that throughout his life Otto was concerned primarily with religion that was vital and inspiring rather than with a theory of religion that was logical and consistent. This concern brought a richness and penetration to his own philosophy of religion not to be found in many interpretations that perhaps exhibit greater theoretical and systematic precision.

## II

Every tendency of importance in recent German theology left its impress upon Otto's thought, and he made the spirit and the enduring insight of each in a very real sense his own. Lutheran piety and faith quite naturally condition his approach to religion and his point of view in general. Nurtured in the Lutheran Communion and in the theology of Luther, he never seriously questioned its position that religion is essentially a matter of inner spiritual experience. The first work he published was a study of Luther's idea of the Holy Spirit (*Die Anschauung vom heiligen Geiste bei Luther,* 1898). With this background it was inevitable that certain dominant aspects of Luther's religious life and thought should continually force themselves upon Otto's attention and shape his own conception of religion. He remained an enthusiastic disciple of Luther as long as he lived, reenforcing his own position again and again by appeal to the authority of the Great Reformer.

At the Universities of Erlangen and Göttingen, where he was educated during the last decade of the nineteenth century, Otto was greatly impressed also by the dominant Ritschlian theology and Kantian critical philosophy. His mature interpretation of religion rests largely upon this early Kantian-Ritschlian foundation. But further studies of Schleiermacher and a growing interest in the Neo-Friesian movement initiated by Leonard Nelson at Göttingen soon modified both his Ritschlian and his Kantian outlook. A centennial edition of Schleiermacher's *Addresses on Religion* which he brought out in 1899, together with several articles published immediately thereafter, reveal clearly the extent of Schleiermacher's influence. Nor was the allegiance professed at this time to the methodology and general viewpoint of the *Addresses* ever relinquished. Something of Schleiermacher's spirit is to be found in all of Otto's later work.

During the next ten years, however, he was increasingly attracted by the philosophy of Jakob Friedrich Fries, an early nineteenth century disciple of Kant who sought to develop the Kantian critique of reason along more definitely idealistic lines. Although Fries is much less important in the judgment of conventional histories of modern philosophy than his contemporaries, Hegel, Fichte or Schelling, he had again been given a place of prominence in German philosophical circles by Leonard Nelson's able advocacy of his position. Otto, a colleague of Nelson's at Göttingen during the first decade of the present century, became a leading member of the Neo-Friesian school established there. His *Kantisch-Friessche Religionsphilosophie,* written in 1909 and translated as *The Philosophy of Religion* (1931), was one of the more important publications of the Neo-Friesian movement. In that work Otto undertook to do for the philosophy of religion what Nelson had already done so forcefully in the realm of epistemology; that is, to present in effective fashion the position outlined by Fries, removing any defects or inconsistencies in its original statement and developing constructively the valid insight contained therein.

Yet a systematic philosophy of religion was never of primary interest to Otto. The empirical approach to theology adopted by Ernst Troeltsch and the German "religio-historical" school had quite as much effect upon him during his years at Göttingen as did the Neo-Friesian philosophy. Indeed one of his former students there has recently maintained that the Friesian idealism was merely a "foil" for Otto's religio-historical method of interpretation.[4] Such an assertion fails to recognize adequately the influence of Fries upon Otto's thought, but it does suggest his greater concern for empirical religion than for philosophical theory. And it reveals clearly the sort of impression his teaching was making at that time. The idealism of Fries interested him, Otto himself points out, largely because it afforded sound philosophical foundation for a more concrete "science of religion" *(Religionswissenschaft).* [5] With the religio-historical school he accepted as the task of theology the accurate psychological and historical ("scientific") analysis of man's religious consciousness. This conception of theology shaped his *Idea of the Holy* as definitely as it did his later studies of religion.

Actually it was Wilhelm Wundt's influential work on *Folk Psychology* that stirred Otto to undertake the formulation of his mature theory of religion. He was impelled to this by the very persuasiveness of Wundt's statement of a position so completely antithetical to that gradually taking shape in his own mind. In 1910 he published an article attacking Wundt's position in detail (**"Mythus und Religion in Wundts Völkerpsychologie"),** and this controversy launched him upon a careful analysis of religious experience which eventually paved the way for his *Idea of the Holy* (1917). Otto himself in a later study attributes the origin of his masterpiece to a more specific theological concern—the desire to provide an adequate interpretation of the doctrine of the atonement.[6] But the historico-psychological portrayal of religion, which has occasioned such general interest in *The Idea of the Holy,* is a direct development of the viewpoint adopted in his article on Wundt.

The controversy with Wundt likewise fixed Otto's attention upon "primitive" religion. A trip to North Africa, India and Japan in 1911-12 provided opportunity for more direct observation of religion in its cruder stages; it also gave Otto a new and abiding appreciation of the great Oriental faiths. Numerous studies and translations from the complex religious thought of India grew out of that trip, and these studies established Otto as one of the most discerning Western interpreters of Hinduism. Indeed the last monographs completed prior to his death were German translations and analyses of the Bhagavad-Gita and the Katha-Upanishad (1934-36). As a result of this contact with the East something of the mystical spirit of India permeated Otto's own religious life,

deepening and broadening his Lutheran heritage. Its effect is already to be seen in *The Idea of the Holy,* is much more apparent in two later volumes, *Mysticism East and West* (1926) and *India's Religion of Grace and Christianity* (1930), and is quite evident also in his final major work, *The Kingdom of God and the Son of Man* (1934).

Christian theology, however, was Otto's principal and enduring interest. History, psychology and philosophy were for him simply "handmaidens of theology." That such was the case in his masterpiece, he himself several times went out of his way to point out. "Our line of inquiry in *The Idea of the Holy,*" he wrote, "was directed toward Christian theology and not towards religious history or the psychology of religion." "This book had its origin in efforts to provide in my lectures for myself and my pupils an approach to the profoundest of all Christian intuitions which I perceived to be both indicated and concealed in the Orthodox constructions of the doctrine of 'reconciliation,' and which did not seem to me to have been found in the essays of Ritschl on *Justification and Reconciliation.*"[7]

Theological issues are equally basic in Otto's other important studies and translations of religious thought. Of the large number of essays that were added to later German editions of *Das Heilige* the more significant were selected and published separately in 1932 under the title, *Sin and Original Guilt.* (Most of these are included in the English volume of Otto's *Religious Essays.*) His volume on mysticism and his comparison of Christianity with religion in India are both devoted primarily to the meaning of salvation. Even his earlier work on the philosophy of Fries is motivated, as already suggested, by a predominantly theological purpose. This is quite explicitly indicated in the second half of its title and in its subtitle, neither of which are included in the English translation.[8]

In every instance, however, theology for Otto is primarily an historico-psychological "science of religion," designed to provide understanding of concrete religious experience; it is not a dogmatic or systematic exposition of Christian faith. As a result there is large similarity between his approach and that adopted by the contemporary phenomenological school in Germany. Indeed his own enduring contribution to modern theology may perhaps best be seen as a penetrating and highly suggestive "phenomenology of religion."

### III

Otto's work as a whole, whether practical or theoretical, devotional or theological, historical or philosophical, is dominated by one unifying principle—an almost passionate insistence upon the autonomy of religion. In his interpretation of this dominant principle Otto draws together and reformulates in original terms the cardinal insights of the greatest figures in modern German theology. Luther and Kant, Schleiermacher and Ritschl,

Fries and Troeltsch, all contribute essential elements to his mature conception of religion.

Already in Otto's early study of Luther, *Die Anschauung vom heiligen Geiste bei Luther,* there is clear recognition of a specific type of experience, characteristically religious in nature, existing in its own right alongside moral and aesthetic experience, and possessing its own claim to validity over against the rational, scientific interpretation of reality. "Whether one accounts for the religious experience as one aspect of feeling in general, or as a special capacity for the supersensible," he wrote at that time; "in any case that which we call religious experience comes into being as soon as the religious object is consciously perceived, in accord with exactly the same compulsion of psychological motivation through which our moral or aesthetic experience arises when a corresponding object comes into consciousness." "The religious feeling has rightful claim to its own scope, unimpaired and unobstructed. It should not allow itself to be curtailed or eliminated in favor of other plausible trains of thought; and it might well be the task of theology to reexamine that crushing chain of empirical relationships until it can find place for an answer to the question how religion is possible—and possible, moreover, in uncurtailed form."[9] The influence here of Schleiermacher as well as of Luther is obvious. And in an essay published a few years later, **"How Schleiermacher Rediscovered Religion"** (1903), Otto insists again in vigorous fashion upon the uniqueness and independence of the religious consciousness that Schleiermacher had so appealingly depicted.[10]

Recognizing clearly that the rising prestige of the natural sciences offered a serious challenge to the autonomy of religion, Otto soon turned his attention to the conflict between the two. In 1904 he published a study of *Naturalism and Religion (Naturalistische und religiöse Weltansicht)* which Sir J. Arthur Thomson translated into English in 1907 as an important contribution to the subject. The claims of religious faith are here defended largely through the medium of a spirited attack upon naturalism itself. A careful analysis of scientific thought at the turn of the century convinced Otto that scientific naturalism left the more significant and meaningful aspects of life and human personality entirely unaccounted for. The roots of religion he found in depths of spiritual experience that completely escape the grasp of natural science.[11]

This early attempt to validate religious faith increased Otto's interest in the Friesian idealism which Leonard Nelson was just then reviving at Göttingen. In the philosophy of Fries he discovered a convincing, logical and systematic development of the position colorfully suggested but left in romantic ambiguity in Schleiermacher's *Adresses on Religion.*[12] For a time, therefore, he gave enthusiastic support to the Neo-Friesian movement inaugurated by Nelson. But gradually the broad historical and psychological analysis of religious experience which he undertook in his later studies forced Otto to modify the Friesian idealism adopted so unreservedly in his early *Philosophy of Religion.* He came to see that Fries, while presenting effectively the rational and moral foundation of religion, had missed the uniquely religious element therein. Influenced at this time also by the thought of Ernst Troeltsch, Otto accordingly in *The Idea of the Holy* substitutes an autonomous religious *Apriori* for the rational *Apriori* upon which Fries had based religious faith.

The concept of religious autonomy, as formulated in *The Idea of the Holy* and developed in Otto's later studies, constitutes his original and enduring contribution to modern theology. Here Schleiermacher's notion of piety, Ritschl's independent religious value-judgment, and Troeltsch's religious *Apriori,* are synthesized in such fashion as to provide an interpretation of religion more discerning and comprehensive than that of any of Otto's predecessors. Only in terms of this principle of religious autonomy, moreover, can the underlying unity and originality of Otto's mature position be appreciated. As depicted in his able historical and psychological analysis there are three essential components of the religious moment of experience: (1) a unique emotional quality of religion in immediate personal experience, by which the specifically religious is unmistakably identified and set a part from moral, aesthetic or intellectual interests; (2) an autonomous religious valuation and interpretation of human life and destiny, similar to our moral and aesthetic judgments of value and equally ultimate and objective in human consciousness; and (3) an intuitive awareness in religious experience of the eternal nature of things, independent of and more basic than the rational scientific description of the universe. The emotional, valuational and cognitive elements which he distinguishes in the religious consciousness are interpreted by Otto as separate but essential aspects of an *a priori* religious category of meaning and value. In the sense of the *numinous,* as he so graphically portrays it, this autonomous religious interpretation and valuation finds immediate emotional expression. In the category of the *holy,* it is given more developed but mediate axiological formulation; religious myth or *ideogram* provides conceptual but necessarily symbolic statement of its cognitive content.

IV

When related to contemporary theological tendencies in Germany, Great Britain and the United States, the timeliness as well as the importance of Otto's interpretation of religion becomes apparent. Humanism has almost completely disappeared from the American theological scene. The semi-humanistic gospel, which for a time seemed destined to become the orthodox dogma of liberal Protestantism, is now hard put to find enthusiastic disciples, and true liberalism in religion has itself been imperiled because of its recent willingness in the garb of "modernism" to make common cause with humanism.

Theologically, humanism was the inevitable outcome of the complete domestication of religion within the limits of human reason. The humanist frankly based his only hope for man's salvation upon human reason, the scientific method, and the "democratic way of life." With Max C. Otto he might insist upon an "affirmative atheism," or with John Dewey he might make some compromise with traditional terminology in the vain hope of achieving *A Common Faith.* But there was no place to be found in his thoroughly rationalistic creed for any sort of supernaturalism or for an autonomous religious experience. The hypothesis of God seemed to be rendered practically unnecessary by the new richness and meaningfulness of life which democracy and industrialism made possible, as well as theoretically untenable by the advance of science. Or so at least the humanist argued, and insisted that the sooner this was generally recognized the better for all concerned.

Now that the social structure upon which the appeal of humanism really depended has collapsed, its spiritual inadequacy stands clearly revealed. It was not a faith capable of weathering the storms of life, and as a religious phenomenon humanism retains today primarily an historical interest. The economic and political crises of our day have effectively revealed the inadequacy not only of the rationalistic theology of the past decades but likewise of the optimistic social gospel which gave it moral dynamic. The social gospel as well as the rationalistic theology of liberal Protestantism in our country must undergo significant modification before it can provide a vital and inspiring faith for the rising generation. Ours is an age disillusioned by a growing awareness of the coercion and brutality inherent in the relations of race to race, nation to nation, and class to class. It cannot recapture the glowing confidence in reason and science which motivated the liberal social gospel, nor find an answer to its deeper spiritual needs in a semi-humanistic faith.

Humanity in the grip of social forces such as those operating in the world today demands of religion something much more significant than a rational program of social reform. Human reason alone will lead only to resignation and despair; man desperately needs a suprarational (supernatural) faith to give purpose and meaning to life in the face of the irrational social destiny with which he is confronted. On every hand evidence is to be seen of the profound effect of the social upheaval of our day upon religious thought. A new supernaturalism is being fashioned to meet the spiritual needs thus revealed just as surely as the appeal of the militant humanism of two decades ago has been destroyed.

The more profound expressions of the new supernaturalism have an obvious social motivation. This is clearly to be seen in the thought of Reinhold Niebuhr. The suprarationalistic faith ably advocated in his *Interpretation of Christian Ethics* and defended in his *The Nature and Destiny of Man* is definitely a response to the demands of the tragic irrationality of our social life so convincingly depicted in his *Moral Man and Immoral Society.* The discerning portrayal of the faith of the modern mystic in Nicolas Berdyaev's *Freedom and the Spirit* is similarly conditioned. Human history, as Berdyaev analyses it in *The Meaning of History,* reveals inescapable frustration as man's only social destiny, a frustration from which religious faith, to be of genuine spiritual significance, must provide salvation in a transhistorical goal.

There are undoubtedly times of crisis in the life of nations and of individuals that throw into bold relief the deeper needs of the human spirit and make available a more penetrating insight into that eternal order of things upon which human destiny depends. Ours is surely such a time and Rudolf Otto's interpretation of religion contains such an insight. Moreover, Otto's discerning portrayal of the autonomy of religion has a contribution and needed corrective to make to the new supernaturalism gradually taking shape in British and American theological circles. The ablest exponents of this new supernaturalism, men like Reinhold and Richard Niebuhr, Nicholas Berdyaev, Paul Tillich, John Oman, B. H. Streeter and Charles A. Bennett, all build in some sense upon an autonomous religious consciousness of meaning and value, yet none have defined and validated the autonomy of religion with Otto's precision and comprehensiveness.

The theology of Karl Barth and his followers has had large influence, of course, upon British and American thought in recent years. The emphasis of the Barthian theologians upon the determinative place of crisis in empirical religion and their moving description of the encounter of the presence and power of God in time of crisis has given their thought an appeal and vitality that is understandable in the light of contemporary events. Yet the unwillingness or inability of Barth and his disciples to define the character of the supernatural in convincing philosophical fashion has left their theology without adequate intellectual foundation. It is certainly true that religious faith must have its own independent foundation in human experience. But it is equally true that, without endangering the very independence that it is concerned to maintain, religion cannot scorn the service of reason in establishing its rightful claim upon the human spirit.

Otto's concrete and definitive formulation of the autonomy of religion not only provides a foundation for the new supernaturalism now gaining wide influence in our country. It likewise distinguishes his interpretation of religion effectively from that of Barth and reveals the unmistakable superiority of Otto's position. As a matter of fact the Barthian theologians, when identifying the divine initiative in the crises of human life, or the word of God in the Bible, covertly introduce as their criterion of meaning and value just such an autonomous religious category as that recognized and defined by Otto. Until this fact is taken into account and its implications made clear, the "theocentric" theology of Barth must continue to derive its impetus largely from its undefined prophetic quality or from the social distress of his hearers.

It can have but limited appeal for those in a position to exercise a less disturbed critical intelligence. On the other hand the influences now at work in British and American theology, enhanced by the stimulus that recent translations of Kierkegaard provide, will certainly themselves lead to greater appreciation of Otto's interpretation of religion and to further clarification of his cardinal insights.

NOTES

[1] "Religion and the Idea of the Holy." *Journal of Philosophy,* August 19, 1926, p. 461.

[2] cf. J. S. Bixler, "Rudolf Otto as a Religious Teacher." *The Christian Century,* July 17, 1929.

[3] An interesting description of Otto's chapel and the work there is given by B. E. Meland, *Modern Man's Worship* (Harpers, 1934) Ch. IV.

[4] Fr. Delekat, "Rudolf Otto und das Methodenproblem in der heutigen systematischen Theologie." *Die Christliche Welt,* Nr. 1, 1930.

[5] *Kantisch-Friessche Religionsphilosophie,* p. 2.

[6] *India's Religion of Grace and Christianity,* p. 105n.

[7] *Religious Essays,* p. 30; *India's Religion of Grace and Christianity,* p. 105n.

[8] *Kantisch-Friessche Religionsphilosophie und ihre Anwendung auf die Theologie.* Zur Einleitung in die Glaubenslehre für Studenten der Theologie.

[9] *Die Anschuung vom heiligen Geiste,* pp. 48, 96.

[10] *Religious Essays,* Essay VIII.

[11] cf. *Naturalism and Religion,* pp. 43-65, 295-350.

[12] cf. *The Philosophy of Religion,* pp. 15, 23.

**Joachim Wach (essay date 1951)**

SOURCE: "Rudolf Otto and *The Idea of the Holy,*" in *Types of Religious Experience Christian and Non-Christian,* The University of Chicago Press, 1951, pp. 209-27.

[*In the following essay, Wach presents an overview of Otto's life, works, and impact on modern European theology.*]

Two theological books profoundly impressed the generation of students which populated the German universities after the First World War: the *Commentary on the Epistle to the Romans* by Karl Barth and *The Idea of the Holy* by Rudolf Otto. It is not without significance that these were both books which made considerable demands on their readers. The effect of the work of Barth might be called sensational. This, however, did not prevent it from being not only a widespread but also a profound one, as the last three decades have demonstrated. While there was, even shortly after its publication, much talk of 'Barthians', and a Barthian 'Orthodoxy' began to develop, not always necessarily with the blessing of the master, there were never really any 'Ottonians.' But laymen and theologians, theologians of very different schools and denominations throughout the last thirty years, have read *The Idea of the Holy,* and have confessed to having been deeply stirred and influenced by that work. Both thinkers have found echoes far beyond the borders of Germany, especially in the Anglo-Saxon countries.

Why did a school of Barth begin to assemble so rapidly, while the permeation of theology with the thought of Otto did not result in producing such a 'school'? Different answers might be given to this question. There is, first, a notable difference in the 'concern' of both scholars, as well as in the goal towards which they worked and in the means which they employed to achieve it, but there is also, and more important, the difference in their personalities.

While innumerable books, articles and reviews have been devoted to Karl Barth and his theology, very few monographs or studies have been dedicated to Rudolf Otto and his teachings. The first full-length American treatment was published only in 1947.

It is difficult to convey to those who did not know him personally a picture of the unusual personality of the author of *The Idea of the Holy.* Rudolf Otto was possessed of an imposing appearance. He held himself straight and upright. His movements were measured. The sharply-cut countenance kept a grave expression which did not change much even when jesting. The colour of his skin was yellowish-white and betrayed past illness. Otto had contracted a tropical sickness in India which forced him ever after to husband his strength strictly. His hair was white and clipped, except in his last years, when it formed a crowning mane over his high forehead. A small white moustache covered his upper lip. His most fascinating features were his steel-blue eyes. There was a rigidity in his glance, and one would have the impression that he was 'seeing' something, as he spoke, to which his interlocutor had no access. I can remember him, stretched in his chaise-longue, on which he had to rest as much as possible, his shoulders covered with a shawl because he easily took cold, with a tom-cat perched on him which he admonished occasionally when it grew restless, without interrupting the serious conversation. No other background for him could be imagined than the many books heaped up in his study all around him. But I also recollect Rudolf Otto in a different environment which fitted him no less than his quiet study. I see him, wrapped in his cape, as we strolled in the neighbourhood of Marburg, his eyes fixed on the hilly scene, a *viator indefessus.* Nobody who knew him will expect that a biography of the author of **The Idea of the Holy** will ever be written, least of all one which would aim at bringing its hero 'close to the people.' An air of genuine mystery surrounded Otto. Familiarity was the last thing which a visitor would have expected of the great scholar or which he himself would have encouraged. The students who followed his lectures tensely and with awe called him the Saint ('Der Heilige,' an allusion to the title of his *magnum opus*). In the sense in which he himself used this term, not in its modern sentimentalized or moralizing meaning, this designation was singularly appropriate. Neither before nor since my meeting Otto have I known a person who impressed one more genuinely as a true mystic. There was something about him of the solitude into which an intimate communion with the Divine has frequently led those who were favoured in this way. In the eulogy on Rudolf Otto by Theodor Siegfried, one of his Marburg colleagues, someone is quoted as characterizing him: 'After all, he was something of a king ['ein Herrscher']; yet a king who did not lack humility.' 'He was,' someone else averred, 'the prophet of an inexorable God who in his inexorable way visited him and called him home.' Siegfried grasped it well: 'The inexplorability of the love of God remained for Otto the last of revelations and the profoundest of mysteries.'

The most important dates of his life are quickly mentioned. He was born September 25, 1869, in Peine (Hanover), was, from 1904, instructor and professor of systematic theology at Göttingen, taught in Breslau from 1914, and at the University of Marburg from 1917. There, as the most outstanding theologian at that school so rich in theological tradition, he taught until his retirement in 1928. From 1913 to 1918 Rudolf Otto was a member of the Prussian diet. He travelled extensively in the Mohammedan countries, in India and the United States. Oberlin College has the distinction of having invited him as a visiting professor. As his fame grew, professors and students came to Marburg from all parts of the world, to visit him, to study under him, and to learn from him.

His first publication appeared in 1898. From this distance—now nearly half a century has passed—we can reconstruct better than would have been possible a few decades ago the tendencies which prevailed in the intellectual life of Germany at the turn of the century. Three powerful movements had exerted their influence in succession, leaving no single sector of her cultural life untouched: the Enlightenment, Romanticism and Naturalistic Materialism. The history of the after-effects of the Enlightenment, the philosophy of which has been so brilliantly analysed in a well-known treatise by Ernst Troeltsch, has not yet been written. During the second half of the nineteenth century, motives which reflected its rationalistic temper penetrated with characteristic simplification into the thought-world of the masses, and

prepared the way for the philosophy of naturalistic materialism. The counter-movement against the Enlightenment which in the early nineteenth century assembled the most gifted of the intellectual élite of Germany under the Romantic banner, and was to determine the attitudes and the creative work of at least two generations, remained limited to the circles of the intellectuals. Romantic motives had long ceased to exert their lure by the turn of the century, and began to become effective again only with the neo-romantic school and the youth movement of the second decade of the twentieth century. Materialistic naturalism, relentlessly advancing from the eighteen-fifties to the end of the century, became the philosophical creed of the victoriously advancing natural sciences and of the Marxist social teaching with its mass-appeal. Only recently have we begun to understand how great a tribute the Enlightenment exacted from German Protestantism, especially its academic leaders. While at the intellectual centres many of the academic theologians tried to adapt their message to the philosophy of the Enlightenment, the ecclesiastical communities, especially in the north, west, and south of Germany, preserved the religious substance of the Protestant tradition of the Christian faith. The romantic school, primarily a movement of aesthetic character, though not lacking from its start an affinity to religion, endeavoured to develop, from its presuppositions, a new understanding of Christianity or, more exactly, of certain Christian motives. The two great Protestant theologians of the first half of the nineteenth century, Schleiermacher and Kierkegaard, both owe much to Romanticist inspiration. The pietism of the *ecclesiolae* ('Gemeinschaften') and Romanticism, though deeply at variance in their basic attitudes, determined—with the philosophy of Kant—the world-view of the young Schleiermacher and of his famous discourses on religion addressed to the educated among the contemptuous. These discourses were re-edited by the same Rudolf Otto who, as Siegfried reports, called himself in his farewell lecture to his students in 1928 a 'pietistic Lutheran.'

In what sense was Otto a Lutheran? The title of his first treatise gives us a hint: 'The Concept of the Holy Spirit in Luther' (originally: 'Geist und Wort nach Luther'). The young magister here shows how Luther's teaching has to be interpreted with a double front in mind: against Catholic sacramentalism and against the Anabaptists ('Schwärmer'). As against the former, the *intus docere* of the divine Spirit is emphasized; as against the latter the objectivity of the Word of the Scriptures, of preaching as brotherly admonition. Mere historical faith *(fides historica)* has to be excluded, as well as claims to subjective illumination. Otto quotes Luther: 'God first has to preach of his Son through the Spirit, so that it falls into our ears and then sinks into our heart, so that we hear and believe' ('Gott muss anheben und predigen durch seinen Geist vom Sohn, so schlägt dir's in die Ohren und her nach sinkt wieder in unser Herz, dass wir es hören und gläuben'). The author of **The Idea of the Holy** was not one of the conventional traditionalists among the latter-day Lutherans. The numinous experience of Luther, the personality of the mighty prophet-like promulgator of the notion of the hidden and yet mercifully revealing God, fascinated and deeply influenced Otto throughout his life. Yet did he not dwell with more than a purely historical interest on the study of the fathers of Lutheran orthodoxy, such as Hollaz, Quenstedt, and Chemnitz? Not much has been said in this regard by his eulogists. I should like to hazard the guess that, besides the great systematic talent to which their dogmatic works witness, it was the substance of Christian, reformatory faith revealed in their theology which was sensed and admired by Otto. Does that make him a narrow denominationalist? We shall see that this genuinely liberal theologian cannot be designated thus. But he was repelled by the semi-rationalistic theology of his day, by the superficiality with which the nature of religion and the nature of Christianity were frequently defined. As against an ossified intellectualism on the part of many contemporary theologians Otto had to stand by the word of the Apostle that the letter killeth but the spirit giveth life. It was by no accident that the doctrine of the Holy Spirit was a field neglected by the official theologians of the day.

A second great teacher, besides Luther, who deeply influenced the thought of Otto was Kant, who himself had his roots in the Enlightenment; the Königsberg philosopher who excluded metaphysics and religion from the realm of the scientifically ('wissenschaftlich') explorable had yet allowed for a satisfaction of the demand for demonstration of evidence for religious judgements. He had, in his way, safeguarded the domain of religious experience. But the important task of determining the nature of the latter had not been satisfactorily concluded. Four thinkers who were influenced by Kant and tried to find such a solution are important for Otto's theory of religion. Besides Schleiermacher, already mentioned, they are the less-known philosopher Fries, the theologian Albrecht Ritschl, and the theologian and philosopher Ernst Troeltsch. Fries postulated a faculty which he called 'Ahndung' (intuition), by means of which we become aware of the numen. Otto had a high regard for this thinker, whose ideas Leonard Nelson propagated with zeal among his colleagues at Göttingen, as we learn from Otto's treatise on Kant and Fries' philosophy of religion (1904). Albrecht Ritschl, without doubt the most influential Protestant theologian of the second half of the nineteenth century, followed Kant and Schleiermacher in his attempt to demonstrate the existence of a realm of religious experience which he thought was constituted by characteristic value-judgments. In this way Kant's moralistic concept of religion as well as its psychological foundation in feeling which Schleiermacher had proposed could be corrected. In the analysis of Christian consciousness which Ritschl undertakes in his comprehensive studies in the Christian doctrines of justification and reconciliation, the specific character of the Christian experience of redemption is sharply accentuated. However, the exclusiveness with which religion and Christianity are here identified, motivated the protest of Ritschl's most outstanding pupil, Ernst Troeltsch. He

did not see much difference between this solution and the old type of apologetics which tried to vindicate the absolute character of Christianity. We may assume that the problem of the religious *a priori* which occupied the mind of Troeltsch especially after 1895, was discussed between him, Rudolf Otto, and his colleague at the University of Göttingen. What is it that constitutes religious experience? While Troeltsch in far-reaching epistemological and philosophical studies—gathered in the second volume of his *Collected Writings*—continued the attempt to determine the nature of religion without reaching a result wholly satisfactory to himself or to others, Otto preserved silence for a number of years, to issue, in 1917, his book **The Idea of the Holy,** in which a new solution of the problem of the religious *a priori* is suggested. It is not without significance that Troeltsch, who recognized more clearly than any of his theological contemporaries the fundamental import for theology of the study of Non-Christian religions, was not really familiar with any of the non-Christian faiths.

We should be glad to know when and how Rudolf Otto came to study Sanskrit, the sacred language of India, and when and how he acquired his profound and thorough knowledge of the various great religions of the world. As a theologian he was, of course, intimately acquainted with Hebrew and early Christian religion. But it was something of an exception for a liberal Protestant theologian who was not a church historian to indicate his thorough acquaintance with patristic literature by well-chosen quotations from the texts. Of the Non-Christian religions it was Hinduism which attracted Otto most strongly. He devoted to this theme a series of basic, and in part pioneer studies (including valuable translations from the Sanskrit). In 1916 he published his rendering of the *Dīpikā* of Nivāsa with the sub-title: 'A Hindu Doctrine of Salvation.' In 1923 this was followed by *Vishnu-Nārāyana*, texts for the study of Hindu mysticism. In the same year he issued the first German version of the *Siddhānta* (text) of the great medieval theologian Rāmānuja. A work as important for its methodology as for its content was a comparison of the teachings of Meister Eckhardt and of Shankara, who is regarded by the Vedanta School as the greatest thinker of India, under the title **Western and Eastern Mysticism** (1926). A fundamental study followed in 1930 on the similarities and differences in the teachings on **Grace in Christianity and Hinduism,** and in 1930 an inquiry into the Indo-European Pantheon **(Gott und Gottheiten der Arier).** Not much later the author of **The Idea of the Holy** turned to the study of the ancient sacred literature of India. Two publications were devoted to the *Bhagavadgita,* and his German rendering of the *Katha-Upanishad,* one of the shorter philosophical treatises of Brahmanism, is a model translation.

All these studies not only bespeak an intimate acquaintance with the texts and the philological problems involved in their interpretation, not only a comprehensive knowledge of the theological and philosophical systems of India and of the outstanding Hindu thinkers and teachers, but also a deep understanding of Indian devotion. In contrast to many German Indologists Otto was attracted not only to the more ancient forms of it, but especially to its medieval expressions, which had hitherto hardly been studied in his home country. In his last great work on *The Kingdom of God and the Son of Man,* the author of *The Idea of the Holy* displayed also a considerable familiarity with the religions of ancient Iran. His extensive travels, especially in North Africa, had given him the opportunity of studying Islam at first hand. Though the East Asiatic religions were furthest removed from his special field of interest, Otto occupied himself especially with the mystical teachings of China and Japan, and refers to them in various passages in his chef-d'œuvre. He helped us markedly, though not an expert in anthropology, in our understanding of 'primitive' religions by analysing the notions of visions, of power, and of holiness, and thus continued the work of Marett, Söderblom and others.

It would be easy to overlook, amid all these detailed achievements, the results which have accrued from them to the concern for methodological reflection and theological principles. So it will not be amiss to summarize briefly some of the important results for the study of religions. Even in his early essay on naturalistic and religious outlooks (1904) Otto had criticized the naturalistic world-view. In a highly significant review of Wilhelm Wundt's *Social Psychology (Volkerpsychologie)* he took exception to that writer's highly schematic construction of development, and demonstrated the impossibility of reducing qualitative changes which occur in the life of nature and of the mind to quantitative differences. Religion does not 'develop' by itself from something that is not yet religion and the profounder insights of the higher religions are not simply the result of gradual evolution. Not only evolutionism but psychologism also came under Otto's attack. Feuerbach and Freud had drawn subjectivistic conclusions from the psychological principle underlying Schleiermacher's theory of religion, declaring religion to be an illusion. The Marxist interpretation had proceeded likewise. As against these 'explanations' Otto was not satisfied to show philosophically their methodological shortcomings, a task which was simultaneously undertaken by Husserl in his *Logische Untersuchungen,* by the Austrian philosophy of values, and, later, by Scheler in his critique of Kant. He attempted, in one of the profoundest analyses of religious experience which have ever been made, to indicate the objective character, the 'meaning' of religion. In the numinous experience man confronts the Wholly Other. This, according to Otto, is not self-deception but rather awareness of ultimate reality. Anthropologists and historians of religion debated around the turn of the century as to how similarities in religious notions and customs occurring in different parts of the world and in different cultural contexts were to be explained. One school favoured the theory of spontaneous origin ('Elementargedanken'), while the other, leaning towards an historical interpretation, postulated *one* centre of diffusion, with different members seeking the original home of the primordial ('Ur-') civilization and religion in different regions (Egypt, Babylonia, Central Asia, China, Europe). Otto submitted his solution of the problem in a treatise on *The Law of Parallels in the History of Religions* which is a methodological paradigm. His theory culminates in the notion of the convergence of types. Examples chosen from various areas show convincingly how similar are the expressions which religious experience has created in divers places, and how parallel forms become in turn qualified by the genius of the individual religion. The task of the historian of religions, requiring much sensitivity, is to weigh carefully both similarities *and* differences.

Before we can discuss Rudolf Otto's solutions of the problem of the religious *a priori,* a problem which had baffled his predecessors, and that of the relation of Christianity to the non-Christian religions, we must look more closely at his two main works, *The Idea of the Holy* and *The Kingdom of God and the Son of Man.*

The former book was published in 1917 and reprinted many times (twenty-five printings in 1936). We have already referred to the profound effect which it created. Translations into various languages—seven of them in 1934: English, Swedish, Spanish, Italian, French, Dutch and Japanese—followed each other rapidly. There can be little doubt that it is not elegance of style or presentation that is responsible for a popularity such as has rarely been accorded to a theological volume. The style not only of this but of all of Otto's books is very concise and crisp, always original. No time is wasted by the author in introductory or embellishing remarks. Several of his books, including *The Idea of the Holy* and its companion volume, are collections of relatively independent essays. In some of them he employed a peculiar orthography—no capitals for German substantives, special type-faces, etc.—which he wished to popularise. Very noteworthy always are Otto's quotations, which testify both to his vast information and his fine taste. It is not without significance that aesthetic considerations are by no means overlooked by this great scholar, whose efforts were so unflinchingly directed towards understanding the specifically religious element in human experience. But then this keen investigator of religious systems and theological opinions was one of those not too numerous students of religion who see its very heart in worship. In all the religions he studied he paid the greatest attention to the cultus, and the reform of worship in contemporary Protestantism was one of his most urgent concerns.

From all this it can be seen that Rudolf Otto was well equipped theologically for the execution of his plan to analyse the nature of religious experience. He stood in a philosophical tradition which was devoted to the solution of the great epistemological problem: What constitutes experience? With his teachers he was convinced of the specific character of religious experience, the categories of which he set out to define. To this task he brought, besides a gift for conceptual analysis, an unusual depth and intensity of religious feeling. It may be said that even if Otto had not been possessed of the talents of a historian and a systematic thinker, he would have contributed greatly to the history of devotion by the very expression of his own personal religious experience. It is, after all, a very mysterious fact that in the history of successive generations one or another individual personality, raised under the same conditions and influences as his contemporaries, reacts to the common tradition not only receptively but creatively, that he is stimulated to new and deepened experiences and a productive interpretation of them. Because our fellowmen are prone to provide anything which deviates from established norms, anything unusual, with a handy label, Rudolf Otto on the publication of his chief work was labelled a mystic. What do we mean by this ambiguous term? Do we want to subsume under this heading the uncommon and bizarre phenomena which the text-books on the psychology of religion have often treated as typical of religious experience, or are there reasons for assuming that all genuine and deep religion possesses a mystical element? Be that as it may, the author of *The Idea of the Holy* has succeeded not only in interpreting meaningfully innumerable religious notions, usages, and institutions by pointing out the religious principles which they illustrate, but also in determining clearly the central experience which is at the bottom of all manifestations of the religious spirit. The third presupposition which enabled Otto to do this was his intimate acquaintance with the variety of forms in which religious life is expressed: his mastery of the history of religions.

Without entering into a detailed discussion of the many fine and searching analyses which are found in Otto's chief work, we shall be satisfied with summing up its main results. Religious experience differs from other kinds, moral, aesthetic, etc., though it appears in interrelation with them. It is a specific category ('Bewertungs-Kategorie'), for which he conceived the term *numinous,* derived from the Latin word *numen.* The religious realm is the realm of the Holy. This statement is not, as one might think, tautological. However, it is not the final word. Some mistakes might have been avoided if the author had started, even more decidedly than he does, with the demonstration of the objective quality of the reality of which we become aware in religious experience. Some of his critics have objected to the fact that Otto prefaces this demonstration with an analysis of a psychological reaction (the feeling of creatureliness, the consciousness of sin ('numinos unwert'). However, I remember the emphasis with which in his lectures on Old Lutheran dogmatics he stressed the fact that they start, without fail, with the *locus de Deo.* The first proposition in *The Idea of the Holy* is that the Holy is mystery *(mysterium)*—an objective quality. The further description of it as that which inspires awe *(tremendum)* and yet attracts *(fascinosum)* seems to lead back to an analysis of subjective states. But it seems so only because the former reaction is explained as a response to an—objective—powerful reality ('energy') and the latter which blends with the former into a characteristic 'har-

mony of contrast' as an effect of the august nature of ultimate reality. We find the theological formulation of these definitions within and outside of Christianity in the doctrines of the attributes, especially of the 'wrath' and the 'grace' of God. Confronting God man experiences his creatureliness. 'Sin,' according to Otto, is consciousness of one's deficiency in value ('Unwert'). He has treated the question 'What is sin?' in a series of essays which are meant to supplement his main work. The numinous experience of our lack of value points to an 'infinite' value: holiness ('Tu solus es sanctus'). In the last period of his life Rudolf Otto attempted, in the context of his investigation of ethical problems, to outline systematically his theory of values. He developed a phenomenological axiology in his study: *Wert, Würde, Recht* (1931).

How do we have to explain religious experience as characterized by the fundamental categories outlined above? At the time of the publication of *The Idea of the Holy*— as to a great extent even now—the disciplines devoted to the study of the lower and higher religions, anthropology and the history of religions, were dominated by the proponents of the reductionist theory of epigeneticism. The higher was to be 'explained' by the lower. There was little provision made in this unqualified evolutionism for creative spontaneity. In his discussion with Wundt, Rudolf Otto asked humorously if milk, because it may turn into cheese, is to be called the 'same' thing as cheese. From nothing nothing can come. The religious *nisus* which Otto ascribes to man is irreducible. This proclivity and 'predestination' for religion may become a religious quest which will not rest until it rests in God. In a few brilliantly terse chapters the author of *The Idea of the Holy* conducts us through the whole religious history of man and illustrates the articulation of this numinous experience on different cultural and religious levels. His critics have chastised Otto for isolating religious experience from other modes of apprehending values. Though he tries to put in relief the specific nature ('Eigenart') of religion, he does not do so without considering the relationships that obtain between the numinous experience which he defines as irrational and other kinds. It does become united with the rational. Genuine religiosity is characterized by the avoidance of both extremes of rationalism and fanaticism. We shall have to say a word on other ways of blending the religious presently. But there can be no doubt that only 'that which is its core, the idea of the holy itself, and the degree to which a historical religion lives up to it, can be the standard by which the value of a religion can be measured.' What is in common to all as a disposition develops and becomes articulate in prophet and saint. The culmination of this process Otto sees in the figure of Him who has the plenitude of the Spirit, in whose person and work we are able to 'divine' in an incomparable degree the Holy. The last sentence of the book points to Him as 'the Son.'

The last two decades of his life the author of *The Idea of the Holy* devoted to two difficult problems, one of a philosophical, the other of a theological nature. Both resulted from the study of the nature and the manifestation of the 'Holy' in life and in history. The first of these is the question of the relation of religion and morality. We have in this actually a special application of the more general problem of the relation between the experience of the numinous and other kinds of experience. But this special query became a major concern of Otto's in the last years of his life as the fundamental problem of the foundation of ethics. We have seen previously that aesthetic considerations did not play a minor part in his thinking, and therefore it may be asked why the problem of the relationship obtaining between religion and other value-experiences did not lead him to an inquiry into aesthetics rather than ethics. The reason may quite possibly be found in the personality of the thinker to whom the formula of the categorical imperative was so congenial. Nearly all critics agree that the weakest point in Otto's analysis of religious experience is his concept of schematism ('Gefühlsgesellung'). The word he took from Kant, but he changed its meaning. Religious experience becomes schematized in entering into relationships with other modes of experience or of judgement. The central religious notions of sin and of redemption, even that of the Holy, have moral associations. A phenomenological demonstration of the foundation of moral values was the aim of the last endeavours of Rudolf Otto. He planned to include the content of five essays which were dedicated to the topic and had appeared in different journals in a volume to be entitled *Moral Law and the Will of God.* They were to have been the Gifford Lectures which he had been invited to deliver. His death intervened.

The first two treatises: **'Value, Dignity and the Just'** (**'Wert, Würde, Recht'**) and **'The Law of Value and Autonomy'** (**'Wertgesetz und Autonomie'**) indicate the influence of the Austrian school which had concentrated on the demonstration of the objective validity of values, and that of the phenomenology of Max Scheler and Nicolai Hartmann. The Kantian starting-point is not abandoned but is more strongly qualified than in Otto's main work. The same mastery is displayed in the analysis of subjective reaction to moral values as is found in the investigation of numinous experience. The specific nature and the inexorability of the demands of morality are more clearly stated than the nature of the mysterious value of the Holy. 'The moral law,' Otto says, in the last sentence of the first essay, 'to the extent that it is categorical, is not actually a law but a commandment' ('nicht "Gesetz", sondern "Gebot"'). It is not 'handed down' but discovered ('nicht "gegeben", sondern "ergibt sich" '), as founded in value and justice. To act in accordance with it confers the dignity of good will. The analysis of the basic moral value of freedom offered in the study **'On the Sense of Responsibility,'** leads the author back into the realm of religion and metaphysics, to the idea of 'creative making' ('schöpferisches Urheben'). In the sense of responsibility we have, 'per aenigma' (in a mysterious form) 'ein vestigium,' a non-conceptual awareness of the coincidence of necessity and contingency.

We have now to turn to the second, the great theological problem, which had commanded Otto's attention not for the first nor for the last time when he wrote his *The Idea of the Holy.* It is the question: What think you of Christ? In the same year (1902) in which Otto's small popular pamphlet on *The Life and Work of Jesus* was published, Ernst Troeltsch, in his famous essay on the incomparability of Christianity *(Die Absolutheit des Christentums),* had asked the question how, in view of the enormous increase in our knowledge, especially of the non-Christian religions, the old claim to absolute validity could be maintained. His answer was that no religion possesses absolute truth, not even the Christian. Only God, to enter into communion with whom and to be redeemed by whom we mortal men are striving, only God is 'absolute.' Christianity, like the other religions, is a historical phenomenon. This understanding need not imply relativistic consequences. History does not exclude norms, they are rather history's greatest discovery. So the Christian has no reason to despair. Yet the criterion for the evaluation of those religions which compete for the highest prize—their number is not great—cannot be an *a priori* but has to be 'produced in the free struggle of ideas.' Troeltsch himself has spoken in warm, convinced and convincing terms of the imcomparable character of Jesus.

Otto's early essay on *The Life and Work of Jesus* is rather conventional. Yet the way in which he portrays the new devotion of Jesus as against Old Testament piety already betrays the characteristic orientation of his theology. 'Here too,' he says, 'God is the Holy One, the embodiment of the moral law that severely puts us strictly under obligation.' And he adds: 'This new religion of Jesus does not grow out of reflection and thinking, out of speculation and philosophy; it is not artfully construed or demonstrated. It breaks forth from the mysterious depth of the individuality of this religious genius.' It centres—this early tract already stresses the fact—in the preaching of the Kingdom of God. To this cardinal notion the second of Rudolf Otto's major works was to be devoted. We have seen that the earlier one closes with a hint at the highest level of 'divination' where 'the Spirit dwells in its plenitude.' He who dwells there is more than a prophet; He is *The Son.*

*The Kingdom of God and the Son of Man* is the title of the second work, which does not seem to have become quite as widely known as it deserves. The modest but telling sub-title: *An Essay in the History of Religions,* would hardly make us suppose that this book actually represents one of the major contributions of the last decade to the understanding of New Testament theology and especially to Christological thought. The consequences of the situation which Ernst Troeltsch had characterized so convincingly in his treatise on the absolute nature of Christianity and the history of religions are fully drawn by the author, who had had an opportunity, at Göttingen, to enter into personal contact with leaders of the 'religionsgeschichtliche Schule,' especially with Wilhelm Bousset. Whereas other scholars had elucidated the special contributions to the formation of Christianity of the Jewish, Hellenistic, Egyptian, Mesopotamian and Syrian religions, Otto discussed at much greater length, as had been done before, the influence of Iranian notions upon the concept which played so central a rôle in the *Kerygma* of Jesus, the idea of the Kingdom of God. However, it is improbable from the start that the author of *The Idea of the Holy* would have been satisfied to add just one more proof of the thesis that the Christian message could be explained as an assemblage of foreign influences and nothing more. He could object to such a procedure according to his own methodological principles. Besides the interpretation of the 'religionsgeschichtliche Schule' another exegesis of the *Kerygma* of Jesus had had a considerable influence upon New Testament scholars in the first decade of the twentieth century; Albert Schweitzer's eschatological explanation. Otto also sees in Jesus a 'consistent eschatologist' as John the Baptist had been before him. But he contrasts the new message with that of the Forerunner. 'The Kingdom of Heaven is at hand' is not the same as 'The judgement day is approaching.' The place of the Johannine eschatological sacrament of baptism by water is taken by the announcement, later overshadowed, of the spiritual *dynamis* (power) of the Eschaton in the already-here ('schon-anbruch') of the Kingdom. That we have to comprehend if we wish to understand the 'meaning of Christ,' that he lives, notwithstanding his conviction that the kingdom of God is the future shape of the end of time, in its already apparent glory and power, and that he communicates by word and deed to those who follow him, on the basis of a charisma different from that of the Baptist, the effect of this 'miracle of transcendence' as his gift.

Otto has called his book *The Kingdom of God and the Son of Man.* In the beginning of the second part he discusses the much debated problem of the messianic titles of Jesus, and poses and sets forth a thesis which is characteristic of him as the theologian and historian of religions. The answer to the question: Was Jesus the Christ sent by God? can only be decided by faith, and thus does not fall within the competence of history. We are concerned here with a religious judgement referring to numinous reality, a judgement of a type which is analysed in *The Idea of the Holy.* As far as the messianic consciousness ('das Sendungsbewusstsein') of Jesus is concerned, it is expressed in images, the history of whose meaning might well be illuminated by the work of the historian of religion. Otto has devoted to these concepts, especially to the late Jewish messianic speculations, some analyses which are among the best things he has ever written. Otto shows from Christ's own pronouncements that he knew his own communion with God to be 'unique and incomparable.' His very passion and his glorification are anticipated by Jesus in the interpretation of Jeremiah liii as necessary stages in the coming of the Kingdom. We cannot dwell in this context on Otto's interpretation of the Last Supper as the initiation of the disciples ('Jüngerweihe') into the Kingdom of God which he develops in that part of his book.

His discussion on the nature of the Eucharist demonstrates anew his mastery of the exegetical and historical material, and proves the fruitfulness of an eschatological interpretation of the sacrament (which is treated all too frequently without such context), as a symbolic expression of the messianic consciousness of Christ. Otto had discussed previously in two pamphlets the best methods of a dignified celebration of the Eucharist. They are entitled: *The Sacrament as Manifestation of the Holy* ('als Ereignis des Heiligen') and *The Celebration of the Lord's Supper.*

The last section of *The Kingdom* leads back to the question at the beginning of the book: What think you of Christ? Here the interests of the theologian and the sociologist of religion coalesce. According to Otto, we have to see Jesus in the context of notions of charisma and of power as a charismatic: 'If one wants to say what Jesus was, one has to think of the exorcist, the charismatic.' 'Only from his person and its meaning can we derive the meaning of his message concerning the Kingdom.' For the theologian, an understanding of the charisma of Jesus is indispensable; in the words of Rudolf Otto: 'as an anticipated *eschaton* it becomes the foundation of a community which sees itself as the Church of the Nazarene.'

In the foregoing pages we have tried to do justice to the scholar and thinker. We have now to add a few words on Rudolf Otto as a citizen and leader of the academic community in which he lived, as a son of his people and, finally, as a citizen of the world. His inaugural address as Rector of the University of Marburg, on *The Meaning and the Task of a Modern University* (1927) develops the notion of the community of those who teach and those who learn as an ever-changing and ever-growing one, and treats of the work of the mind dedicated to the investigation of truth. Otto points out how it is necessary to integrate into a new idea of the *universitas* elements of truth from three successive movements, idealism, realism and a modern philosophy of life. Rudolf Otto was a good German. As a good German he was also a true cosmopolitan. He documents it in his scholarship and his programmes for a Religious League of Mankind which goes far beyond the ecumenical notion of a union of Protestants. The idea that a devout Christian, a devout Jew, a devout Moslem or Hindu possess something in common which could become the foundation of such a league appeared to many at the time fantastic or even ridiculous. It was overlooked that the author of *The Idea of the Holy* did not advocate an indiscriminate unification in ignorance of the profound differences which separate the great religious communities of the world. It turned out that in spite of his idealism, or very possibly because of it, Rudolf Otto has been the greater realist. To-day, under the violent onslaught of powers hostile to religion everywhere, the recognition begins to spread that in no religious community can there be room for the lukewarm. In all of them men search for a profounder understanding of the essentials in doctrine and in worship. New fronts begin to replace old divisions. Smaller cells begin to be formed, here and there, which draw spiritual nourishment from a common experience of the Holy and hence should be willing and able to understand each other. In such signs Rudolf Otto saw hope for the future of Christianity, of religion and of the world.


## Ninian Smart (essay date 1959)

SOURCE: "Numen, Nirvana, and the Definition of Religion," in *Concept and Empathy: Essays in the Study of Religion,* edited by Donald Wiebe, Macmillan, 1986, pp. 40-48.

[*In the following essay, originally published in 1959 in* The Church Quarterly Review, *Smart contends that Otto misunderstood the notion of nirvana, thus throwing into confusion his notion of the numinous in religious experience.*]

Despite Rudolf Otto's remarkable contributions to the philosophy and comparative study of religion, there is a defect in his treatment of spiritual experience—namely, his relative neglect of, and partial misinterpretation of, Buddhist nirvana.[1] This hinders a fully satisfactory analysis of mysticism and militates against a correct description of the nature of religion. What I wish to show here is, briefly, as follows. Given Otto's analysis of his own illuminating expression 'numinous', nirvana is not, strictly speaking, numinous; but nirvana is the key concept of (at least Lesser Vehicle) Buddhist doctrine and practice; hence it is unsatisfactory to define religion by reference to the numinous or analogous notions. Further, however, by appeal to the idea of 'family resemblance', we can avoid the embarrassment we might feel at not discovering some essence of all religion. Finally I attempt to indicate how a sharp differentiation between agnostic mysticism and theism (together with pantheism and other forms of characteristically numinous religion) can lead to new insights into the structure of religious doctrine and experience.


### I

Let us first examine one of Otto's rare and scattered remarks about nirvana: 'It exercises a "fascination" by which its votaries are as much carried away as are the Hindu or the Christian by the corresponding objects of their worship'.[2] It is surely clear that the use of the expression 'votaries' and the implication contained in the phrase 'corresponding objects of worship' accord *nirvana* a status it never possessed in Theravada Buddhism and almost certainly did not explicitly possess in the earliest form of the religion.[3] Gods and god-like entities can have votaries and be objects of worship: but the serenity of *nirvana* is no god, nor is it even the peace of God. It is interesting to note that Otto writes, in his foreword to **Mysticism East and West,** that we must combat the

erroneous assumption that mysticism is 'one and ever the same'. Only thus is it possible to comprehend such great spiritual phenomena as, for instance, the German Meister Eckhart, the Indian ankara, the Greek Plotinus, the mystics of the Buddhist Mahayana school, in all their characteristic individuality, instead of allowing them to disappear into the shadowy night of 'general mysticism'. The nature of mysticism only becomes clear in the fullness of its possible manifestations.[4]

The Hinayana is left out, even though it has produced such a striking handbook of mystical meditation as the *Visuddhimagga* and despite the accounts of the Buddha's Enlightenment. Further, Hinayana mysticism exhibits a greater divagation from theistic mysticism than does even the soul-mysticism of Yoga and Jainism.

Before listing rather briefly a few reasons for denying that nirvana, is, in the strict sense, numinous, it is perhaps as well to counter the criticism of unfairness: 'Surely we owe the term "numinous" to Otto, and if he uses it of nirvana, are we not to say that he knows best?' But once a term is introduced it becomes public property: I am not arguing against the use of 'numinous', for Otto's coining has been of great service—it is only that on certain occasions he is loose or inconsistent in his employment of it.

(i) The elements in the numinous discriminated by Otto are, it will be recalled, those of awefulness, overpoweringness, energy, and 'fascination'. Now these certainly depict admirably objects of worship, such as gods and God. To some extent also they define many ghostly and 'spooky' phenomena which Otto uses as examples. But a state such as nirvana hardly possesses all these characteristics: only, perhaps, 'fascination'. Now it may be replied that each of the elements should be regarded rather as a mark; that is to say, each by itself tends to or would establish the numinousness of whatever possesses it. But apart from the undesirable looseness that this interpretation would confer upon the term, Otto analysed the numinous in the way that he did because all the elements are usually or always found in genuine objects of worship.

(ii) Experiences cannot easily be understood in isolation, but are best seen in their whole setting—in the attitude and behaviour which surround them; in particular, religious experience must be viewed in the context of the spiritual practices associated with it or expressing it. Thus characteristically experiences of awe, of an overpowering and energetic presence, are associated with and expressed by such activities as worship and sacrifice. Now altogether it is true that the mystical Path towards some inner realisation as we find it in the Christian setting is integrated with activities such as the worship of and prayer to a personal God, in the Lesser Vehicle there is not merely formal agnosticism, but the religion of sacrifice and worship associated with a divine Being or beings is ignored as being irrelevant to salvation. Moreover, such attention as is paid to numinous entities such as *nats* and *devas* is merely peripheral, springing from non-Buddhist sources; while the veneration of relics such as the Sacred Tooth is moderated severely by the denial of Gotama's divinity.[5]

(iii) Otto, in criticising the subjectivism of Schleiermacher's account of creature-feeling, remarked: 'The numinous . . . is felt as objective and outside the self.'[6] This indeed is a correct description of how a *numen praesens* strikes the religious man; note that not merely is the *numen* in some way 'objective', but there is even a dualism continually being expressed in religious language between the worshipper and the object of awe. But nirvana could hardly be counted a *numen praesens;* and it is only in a rather peculiar sense 'outside the self'. Admittedly we here run into complications, on account both of the fact that in certain spiritual contexts there is the notion of a Self set over against the 'empirical self' and of the peculiarly Buddhist *anatta* (non-self) doctrine. But first, the *numen praesens* is usually thought of as nearby in some spatial or quasi-spatial way. And second, even those who would interpret nirvana as a kind of beatified persistence beyond death[7] not unlike Christian immortality (though without God there) give an account inconsistent with nirvana's being conceived as an object of worship. Also, whatever may be said—and quite a lot can be—in defence of the notion of mystical experience as 'other' than ordinary experience (thus generating the concept of an 'other' Self, etc., realisable through mystical endeavour, as in some of the *Upanisads*), quite clearly there is a difference between the sense in which the Atman is 'beyond' the empirical self and that in which God is 'beyond' the visible world and so is that mysterious Other. The difference is indicated by that tension which we find in theistic mysticism and which was well expressed by Rabindranath Tagore when he said: 'What we want is to worship God. But if the worshipper and the Object of Worship are one, how can there be any worship?' Nevertheless, despite the difference, it is the genius of certain religions to fuse together different insights into a single doctrinal scheme—so that, for example, realising the Atman is becoming Brahman and that the cloud of unknowing is the dwelling place of that God who appeared in a very different sort of cloud to Job: this commingling of strands of religious language, experience, and practice (for the three go together) will be further considered below.

(iv) Nirvana, however, is given certain epithets which might lead one to think of it as something like Ultimate Reality—and this in turn is sometimes an impersonal way of describing God.[8] And hence we get such statements as this: '*Nirvana* . . . is not stated in such a way that it can be identified with God, but it may be said to be feeling after an expression of the same truth'.[9] Thus *nirvana* is called 'deathless' *(amata),* 'unconditioned' *(asankhata),* 'permanent' *(nicca, dhuva),* etc. Now even if these epithets may be held to assimilate nirvana in some degree, though certainly in a loose manner, to God, they reveal themselves upon inspection to be typically applicable to a mystical state in this life just as much as to a genuinely transcendent Being. Thus nirvana is *amata* because it is (to quote another epithet) *akutobhaya,* 'with nothing to fear from anywhere', for in attaining it in this life one loses the fear of death—and not merely because of the doctrine that there will then be no rebirth hereafter,[10] but through the great peacefulness and serenity of it. And also it is *amata* because the mystical experience at its highest level is, in being without perceptions, likewise without time.[11] Again, it is permanent partly at least by contrast with the world of compound things, which are transitory and fleeting: for though early Buddhism denied the soul or *ātman,* the distinction between the spiritual state and the world of ordinary experience is, naturally enough, retained. Similarly with 'unconditioned'.[12] And nirvana transcends the impermanent world by being, so to speak, other-worldly—an otherworldliness defined by the training laid down in the Noble Eightfold Path, and because it is *yogakkhema anuttara,* 'unsurpassed peace', of transcendent value. That is to say, then, the epithets are understandably applicable even to nirvana in this existence,[13] without our bringing in that final nirvana accruing upon death and negatively expressed by saying that there is no rebirth.

(v) Otto elsewhere says: 'The salvation sought in nirvana, like that sought in Yoga, is magical and numinous. It is the utterly supra-rational, of which only silence can speak. It is a blessedness which fascinates. It is only to be achieved by way of negation—the inexpressible wonder.'[14] Here, to put it briefly, Otto's main ground for declaring nirvana to be numinous is that it is utterly non-rational. But that a thing is non-rational does not entail that it is numinous, though the converse may perhaps hold. Otto elsewhere gives an account of what he means by 'non-rational': while on the one hand we may experience deep joy, which on introspection can be 'identified in precise conceptual terms', it is otherwise with religious 'bliss': not even the most concentrated attention can elucidate the object to which it refers—it is purely a felt experience, only to be indicated symbolically.[15] But it is perhaps odd to say that in all non-religious contexts we can if pressed express our feelings 'in precise conceptual terms'. Nevertheless, there are certainly occasions upon which we can say why we are overjoyed, etc., and this clearly has something to do with 'the object to which the state of mind refers'. This understanding, however, is impossible with regard to a genuine mystical state for a different reason from that which makes it impossible with regard to a feeling of 'bliss' at the fascination of the numinous. For a feeling of supreme exaltation in the context of worship or worshipping meditation is connected with God: for God is that at which, so to speak, attention is directed; and God is mysterious and overwhelming and so not to be described adequately. On the other hand, in agnostic mysticism (and we find analogies in all mysticism) the state of mind is quite empty and rapt and there is in the nature of the case nothing 'to which the state of mind refers'. A different sort of 'non-rationality' is connected with reaction to the holy from that association with mystical liberation, though the two become fused in religions such as Brahmanism and Christianity. A second and most important point here that there is some danger in overemphasising the 'non-rational' character of such spiritual experiences. This can be illustrated from the fact that Otto, in discussing the difference between agnostic soul-mysticism (such as agnostic Yoga) and the Brahman-mysticism exemplified in Śankara, remarks that the difference between their contents is itself non-rational and only to be comprehended in mystical experience itself.[16] This despairing statement hardly does justice to Otto's own achievement in discriminating the two types; but it is connected with his belief that religious concepts are merely symbolical. The danger in regarding doctrines and religious terminology as 'only symbols' is that they can easily this way become distorted, by being viewed as somehow pointing to the same Reality. And to say this last thing is to utter at best a half-truth. For we must distinguish between (a) describing one religious view in terms of another, (b) describing it in its own terms, and (c) exhibiting analogies. Now, as for (a), a Christian or a Hindu might wish to say that the two religions are, in certain of their doctrines, pointing to the same truth; but because each would prefer or insist on using one set of symbols rather than another to depict this truth, they would in effect be interpreting the other religion in terms of their own. Similarly we may, as apologists, interpret nirvana in theistic terms, but this is emphatically not what the Buddha said, and to treat nirvana in Hinayana terms we have to retain the agnosticism. As to (c), it is certainly illuminating to trace the respects in which attaining nirvana may be like attaining the unitive life of Western mysticism: it is doubtless on such analogies that an interpretation of nirvana in a loosely theistic sense would have to be based. The differences too are important: but Otto in his extreme emphasis on non-rationality is in difficulty over characterising them.

(vi) Finally, with regard to the interpretation of final nirvana as a transcendent state 'beyond space and time', this indeed is a vexed and complicated subject. But even if we grant that the Buddha's negations leave room for the belief that there is some kind of entity persisting in a non-empirical state after death, the nearest model we have for picturing such a condition is the sheer tranquility of the yogic mystic in his highest self-realisation; and the points that have been made above about the pure mystical state as not necessarily having anything to do with the numinous will hold again in this context.

Briefly, then: although Otto's analysis of the numinous fits very well gods and god-like entities and well describes men's reactions to these in experience—although, that is, it is successful in regard to those beings who are typically addressed in worship and negotiated with in sacrifice—it hardly holds in regard to those states and entities that are encountered along the yogic path. But this point is sometimes obscured because, in the circle of theistic religion (and this is what we are most accustomed to in the West), it is common to associate the beatific nirvana-like state with God; nevertheless,

though it may in fact be true that the mystical vision is a vision of the numinous Deity, it is not self-evident, it is not analytically true. We must recognise the possibility of mysticism without worship, just as all along we have recognised the phases of religious history where there is worship, prayer, and sacrifice without any yogic or mystical path; but there is no genuine concept of god or God without worship, and conversely. The importance of nirvana is that it is a purer example of the mystical goal even than the soul-mysticism of Yoga that Otto studied, for in Buddhism there is not even the *atman,* and it is perhaps a sign of the Buddha's rigid determination to evolve a 'pure' mysticism without any theistic or pantheistic complications that he excluded the concept of an eternal soul, which in being capable of separate existence and in being described substantivally is already too much adaptable to numinous concepts—as both the Vedanta and theistic Yoga demonstrate.

II

The question arises here as to how we are to define 'religion' in such a way that the term will cover not only polytheism and theism (i.e. religions which are suffused with numinousness), together with not too dissimilar pantheistic faiths, but also agnostic and transtheistic Buddhism and Jainism. Of course the problem has exercised many before now, and for this or similar reasons Buddhism has often been regarded as a 'crux' in the comparative study of religion. One way of trying to produce an old-fashioned definition is to point to some 'essence' of religious phenomena; but a result of this is to distort the agnostic faiths by interpreting their negations as a type of theological agnosticism, so as to have an essential content in all religions. Another way is to place heavy emphasis on some essential spirit in all religions, such as their numinosity. In this way religions will have a common form: but again this is to distort, for instance, the numinous aspects of popular Buddhism in the Hinayana which are merely peripheral—it is not *nats* and spirits that make it a living faith, but the call to nirvana. Again, one may try to avoid these pit-falls by escape into empty generality, as with Tillich's definition in terms of 'man's ultimate concern'[17]—to give this content it is necessary to define these terms themselves, which leads back to a definition of the first type; and here we are in even subtler danger of interpreting another faith in terms, albeit vague, of one's own. But all this is unnecessary, once we abandon the old-fashioned notion of definition and throw off the fascination of essences. It is a commonplace in contemporary analytic philosophy that many general words apply to a wide variety of things in virtue, not of some common property, but of 'family resemblance', and so are not capable of an essentialist definition.[18] To give a crude scheme of family resemblance: suppose A has properties a, b, and c; while B has b, c, and d; and C has c, d and e; while D has d, e and f. Although A has nothing in common with D, it is sufficiently like B for them both to have the same name—and likewise with B and C and with C and D. Of course in actual examples the situation is a much richer one, with subtle and overlapping similarities, as with the word 'game'—though patience and hockey have no common item of content, or at least none which would help to define 'game', they are both called games. To call something a game is to place it in a family rather than to ascribe it some complex essence. Similarly, perhaps, with 'religion'—we can place both early Buddhism and early Islam in the same family, even though they have nothing obvious or important in common. Thus appeal to the notion of 'family resemblance' has at least the following two advantages. First, and negatively, it discourages attempts to define 'religion' in an essentialist manner, which leads to misinterpretations accruing upon trying to formulate some common insight in all faiths—there may be different sorts of spiritual insights. Second, and positively, it allows for a sort of disjunctive account of religion: thus, for instance (and crudely), the activities and doctrines associated with worship, sacrifice, *bhakti*, etc., on the one hand, and those associated with the yogic endeavour towards inner enlightenment and with other similar endeavours on the other hand, are two centrally important items in a number of major religions; but we need not insist on the central presence of both or of any particular one of these items for something to count as a religion.

Finally, by reserving the term 'numinous' for describing entities and experiences which inspire worship, awe, dread, etc., as well as those objects, places, etc., intimately associated with these, we can take a new look at mysticism. First, *à propos* of Otto, we avoid a mistaken mode of classification: for because of his conviction that the 'soul' is a numinous entity and that numinousness is central to religion, he was led to say that every higher faith includes in some way a belief in the soul.[19] This means that Buddhism, despite its *anattā* (non-soul) doctrine, has to be subsumed under the heading of 'soul-mysticism'. Second, more importantly, by taking agnostic mysticism as the 'typical' or 'pure' variety, in the sense explained before, one is faced by a number of interesting and fruitful questions. Why should it seem natural to take this kind of experience as intimately connected with the numinous object of worship? And on the doctrinal level, why should concepts seemingly arrived at in different ways (such as Brahman and Atman) be said in some way to coalesce? It is not sufficient to yield to the ever-present temptation in discussing these matters to say that concepts are not important in themselves, but point to something beyond. For it is at least a *prima facie* difficulty that a concept pointing towards a Power beyond, and sustaining, the visible world should be so closely related to one which points towards a mystical 'inner' experience. Nevertheless, we have already observed that there is a loose resemblance—though not so loose that the plasticity of religious language cannot absorb it—between some of the epithets of nirvana and some of those ascribed to God. Thus a theistic interpretation of mysticism is possible, though it is not absolutely forced on one. We may put the point another way, by reference to a classic example, by saying

that though it may be a deep insight that Brahman and Atman are one, this is not an analytic or necessary truth, since the concepts are arrived at along different paths and are connected with different sorts of spiritual activity: it is a welding together of initially different insights. The varying weights upon the activities and insights of different sects and faiths, moreover, goes a long way towards explaining doctrinal differences—once the types of doctrine associated with each are discriminated. Otto has done much here in his ***Mysticism East and West*** and elsewhere; but his somewhat wavering treatment of 'soul-mysticism' and his comparative neglect of nirvana militated against a successful chemistry of mystical, theistic, and mixed doctrines, for one element was not first isolated in its pure form.

NOTES

[1] Hereafter I use 'nirvana' by itself to stand for Buddhist *nirvana*.

[2] *The Idea of the Holy*, trans. J. W. Harvey, 2nd Edition, London (1950), p. 39.

[3] Nirvana does, however, undergo some transformation in the Mahayana schools. For instance, on the Madhyamika view, the Absolute *(tattva, śūnya)* is the same as *prajñā* (wisdom, i.e., non-dualistic insight, *jñānam advayam*) (Madh. Karika, XXV, 19-20). This in turn is identified with the *dharmakāya* or Truth-Body of the Buddhas. Now the knowledge of the Absolute is nirvana (ibid. xviii, 5); and thus there is, *via* the Three-Body doctrine, a fairly close relation between nirvana as the attainment of non-dualistic insight and the numinous as displayed in the *sambhogakāya* and *nirmānakāya* of the Buddhas—in these forms the Buddhas come to be objects of worship.

[4] Trans. B. L. Bruce and R. C. Payne, London (1932), p.v.

[5] On contemporary feeling about this, see R. L. Slater, *Paradox and Nirvana,* Chicago (1951), p. 31.

[6] *The Idea of the Holy*, p. 11.

[7] E.g. U. Agga in Shwe Zan Aung's 'Dialogue on Nibbana', *Journal of the Burmese Research Society,* VIII, Pt. iii (1918), quoted in Slater, op. cit., pp. 54ff, where survival is of 'one's own mind purged from corruption'.

[8] Such concepts as 'Ultimate Reality', 'Being', etc., often have a specifically religious, not just philosophical, function, and are frequently found in close connection, though also a state of tension, with notions of a personal divinity: e.g., *nirgunam* and *sagunam* Brahman and the chain of identities in the Mahayanist Three-Body doctrine. See Otto, *Mysticism East and West,* pp. 5 ff, and my article 'Being and the Bible', *Review of Metaphysics,* Vol. IX, no. 4 (June 1956).

[9] E. J. Thomas, *The Life of Buddha as Legend and History,* London (1927), p. 20f.

[10] More precisely the Buddha used the more comprehensive four-fold (catuskotika) negation: the arhat is not reborn, nor is he not reborn, nor is he both reborn and not reborn, nor is he neither reborn nor not reborn (Majjhima Nikaya, i. 426ff and elsewhere). As to survival, however, it would be better for the ordinary uninstructed man to mistake the body for the self (Samyutta Nikāya, ii. 95).

[11] E.g. the last stage of meditation (jhāna) is where one is 'beyond the sphere of neither perception nor non-perception' in which there is a cessation of both perception and sensation.

[12] I.e., it is not caused in any ordinary sense, though the way to it has been pointed out by the Buddha (Milinda-Pañha, IV. 7. 14).

[13] The usual Pali term is sa-upādisesa as opposed to anupādisesa nibbāna (nirvana with and without substrate: see Buddhaghosa in Dhammapada Commentary, ii. 163—sa-upādisesa n. is equivalent to kilesa-vattassa khepitatta, 'destruction of the cycle of impurity').

[14] Mysticism East and West, p. 143.

[15] The Idea of the Holy, pp. 58-9.

[16] Mysticism East and West, p. 143.

[17] Systematic Theology, Vol. I, London (1951), p. 15.

[18] See L. Wittgenstein's Philosophical Investigations, trans. G. E. M. Anscombe, Oxford, (1953), p. 32e.

[19] Mysticism East and West, p. 143.

## S. L. Varnado (essay date 1974)

SOURCE: "The Idea of the Numinous in Gothic Literature," in The Gothic Imagination: Essays in Dark Romanticism, edited by G. R. Thompson, Washington State University Press, 1974, pp. 11-21.

[In the following essay, Varnado examines the place of the numinous experience in Gothic literature.]

One of the engaging aspects of modern literary criticism has been the enthusiastic acceptance of aid from nonliterary disciplines. Psychoanalysis, anthropology, sociology, and semantics have undoubtedly enriched our understanding and influenced our critical response to literature.[1] One suspects, however, that such methodologies are best applied to works which are more or less subjective in nature. The Gothic tradition in British and American literature, for instance, offers itself as a prime candidate. Critical appraisal of Gothic literature has sometimes been marked by an ambiguity, as though

critics found difficulty in coming to terms with the material. In a well-known pronouncement on Edgar Allan Poe, T. S. Eliot has stated a common attitude toward Gothic fiction: "The forms which his lively curiosity takes are those in which a preadolescent mentality delights: wonders of nature and of mechanics and of the supernatural, cryptograms and cyphers, puzzles and labyrinths, mechanical chess-players, and wild flights of speculation. . . . There is just that lacking which gives dignity to the mature man: a consistent view of life. . . . "[2] The Gothic elements in Poe's writings seem to be at the root of Eliot's rejection. On the other hand, a writer whom Eliot admires, Charles Baudelaire, takes a different view toward this same sort of material. For Baudelaire, "what will always make him [Poe] worthy of praise is his preoccupation with all the truly important subjects and those which are alone worthy of the attention of a spiritual man: probabilities, mental illnesses, scientific hypotheses, hopes and considerations about a future life, analysis of the eccentrics and pariahs of this world. . . . "[3]

Such an antinomy raises, in fact, the central question about the Gothic spirit as it is reflected in the work of early novelists such as Horace Walpole, Ann Radcliffe, and Mary Shelley, as well as later writers like Charlotte Brontë, Edgar Allan Poe, Algernon Blackwood, and Franz Kafka. What, precisely, is the common denominator of a literary tradition that includes such a diverse company, and that has attracted, at least for a time, such dissimilar minds as those of Charles Dickens, Henry James, Joseph Conrad, and William Faulkner? The answer, as suggested, demands in part an analysis by way of non-literary disciplines, since it is evident that the literary powers of such writers are not in question.

The particular nonliterary discipline that I propose for analyzing the Gothic tradition consists of the impressive body of work left by the late German theologian and philosopher Rudolf Otto (1869-1937). In his major work, The Idea of the Holy (1917), Otto attempted to analyze religious experience by means of what he termed the numinous. His central concern in the book is indicated by its subtitle: "The nonrational factor in the idea of the divine and its relation to the rational." The numinous, the word he coined to represent this nonrational factor, is man's underlying sense of supernatural fear, wonder, and delight when he is confronted by the divine. Although the several elements in numinous feeling may be analyzed, the numinous is essentially nonrational—that is, not able to be fully understood conceptually. It is a "feeling" but a feeling that has innate connections with the intellect. The numinous, which in its more primitive forms gives rise to the belief in ghosts and other supernatural fantasies, is still present in purified form in the higher manifestations of religion. This experience, with its associated forms and connections, its dichotomies between "sacred and profane," between "natural and supernatural," "rational and non-rational," and its often fragile but sometimes strong relations to the human sense of the "holy" is, I believe, the essential goal of the Gothic writer, and so far as it is achieved, his central distinction.

Otto's terminology and some of his ideas have appeared in works of literary criticism. There is, for instance, a very sound discussion of Otto's works in Maud Bodkin's *Archetypal Patterns in Poetry.* Both G. Wilson Knight and Walter Kaufman have used Otto's terminology in exploring certain aspects of Shakespeare.[4] But even if the legitimacy of the numinous as a literary concept is granted, the question of relating it to the Gothic tale may appear doubtful. In what sense, it will be asked, does the preternatural element in Gothic fiction enter into the psychology of religious experience? Indeed, it will appear almost paradoxical to attempt to relate the two, since the more evident varieties of religious experience—prayer, contemplation, and mysticism—whether orthodox or otherwise, seem remote from the Gothic experience of Romantic literature.

It is in answer to this problem that the insights of Rudolf Otto are applicable. For Otto was certain that the area of religious experience which he termed the numinous is, in its early stages, closely associated with the preternatural; and that while some religions in their more advanced stages outgrow this association, they still retain vestiges of it. In fact, Otto was convinced that the preternatural as a condition of human consciousness is intimately connected with the whole phenomena of religion.

Otto begins *The Idea of the Holy* by distinguishing conceptual from non-conceptual statements about religion. Theistic religion, he believes, characterizes God by various conceptual statements about his nature, for example, his spirituality, power, and unity. Such conceptual statements Otto terms rational, and he makes it clear that they are of first importance in religious discussion. On the other hand, the nature of God is such that these rational attributes do not fully comprehend Him. "For so far are these 'rational' attributes from exhausting the idea of deity, that they in fact imply a non-rational or suprarational Subject of which they are predicates." This nonrational element, however, must be apprehended in some way "else absolutely speaking nothing could be asserted of it."[5]

To characterize this nonrational element or "unnamed Something" as he calls it, Otto coins the word *numinous,* from the Latin *numen* (a god or power). "I shall speak, then, of a unique 'numinous' category of value and of a definitely 'numinous' state of mind, which is always found wherever the category is applied. This mental state is perfectly *sui generis* and irreducible to any other; and therefore, like every absolutely primary and elementary datum, while it admits of being discussed, it cannot be strictly defined" (p. 7). But if the numinous cannot be defined it can, nevertheless, be suggested. "We must once again endeavour, by adducing feelings akin to them for the purpose of analogy or contrast and by the use of metaphor and symbolic expressions, to make the states of mind we are investigating ring out, as it were, of themselves" (p. 12).

In attempting to suggest these numinous states of mind, Otto uses as an ideogram the Latin phrase *mysterium tremendum.* "Conceptually *mysterium* is merely that which is hidden and esoteric, that which is beyond conception or understanding, extraordinary and unfamiliar. The term does not define the object more positively in its qualitative character. But though what is enunciated in the word is negative, what is meant is something absolutely and intensely positive. This pure positive we can experience in feelings, feelings which our discussion can help make clear to us, in so far as it arouses them actually in our hearts" (p. 13).

A number of distinct "notes" or feeling-states enter into Otto's analysis of the phrase *mysterium tremendum. Tremor,* for example, is the Latin word for the familiar experience of the natural emotion of fear. However, Otto uses it to suggest "a quite specific kind of emotional response, wholly distinct from that of being afraid. . . . There are in some languages special expressions which denote, either exclusively or in the first instance, this 'fear' that is more than fear proper. The Hebrew *Hiqdīsh* (hallow) is an example. To 'keep a thing holy in the heart' means to mark it off by a feeling of peculiar dread, not to be mistaken for any ordinary dread, that is, to appraise it by the category of the numinous" (p. 13).

The subtle, but distinct, qualitative difference between this feeling and ordinary human fear is suggested by an analysis of the physical reactions that accompany these states.

> We say: 'my blood ran icy cold,' and 'my flesh crept.' The 'cold blood' feeling may be a symptom of ordinary, natural fear, but there is something non-natural or supernatural about the symptom of 'creeping flesh.' And any one who is capable of more precise introspection must recognize that the distinction between such a 'dread' and natural fear is not simply one of degree and intensity. The awe or 'dread' *may* indeed be so overwhelmingly great that it seems to penetrate to the very marrow, making the man's hair bristle and his limbs quake. But it may also steal upon him almost unobserved as the gentlest of agitations, a mere fleeting shadow passing across his mood. It has therefore nothing to do with intensity, and no natural fear passes over into it merely by being intensified. (p. 16)

The accuracy of Otto's description is attested to by a number of passages from Gothic fiction. Cold blood and creeping flesh are, in fact, staples of Gothic literature, but it is the exceptional reader who has distinguished between "ordinary human fear" and the numinous emotions. A passage from Algernon Blackwood's short story "The Willows" suggests some remarkable parallels with what Otto has to say about numinous awe. In this tale, the narrator and a companion proceed by canoe into the upper reaches of the Danube where, amidst the loneliness of the primitive forest and a rising windstorm, they come upon a remote island entirely covered by small willow trees. They make camp, and as night falls the narrator attempts to analyze the alien emotions aroused in him by the island.

> Great revelations of nature, of course, never fail to impress in one way or another, and I was no stranger to moods of the kind. Mountains overawe and oceans terrify, while the mystery of great forests exercises a spell peculiarly its own. But all these, at one point or another, somewhere link on intimately with human life and human experience. They stir comprehensible, even if alarming, emotions. They tend on the whole to exalt.
>
> With this multitude of willows, however, it was something far different, I felt. Some essence emanated from them that besieged the heart. A sense of awe awakened, true, but of awe touched somewhere by a vague terror. Their serried ranks, growing everywhere darker about me as the shadows deepened, moving furiously yet softly in the wind, woke in me the curious and unwelcome suggestion that we had trespassed here upon the borders of an alien world, a world where we were intruders, a world where we were not wanted or invited to remain—where we ran grave risks perhaps![6]

This sense of the "uncanny" or "awesome" does not, however, exhaust the feeling states aroused by the ideogram *tremendum*. Otto perceives another element in it, namely the sense of "might," "power," "absolute overpoweringness," to which he gives the name of *majestas*.

> This second element of majesty may continue to be vividly preserved, where the first, that of unapproachability, recedes and dies away, as may be seen for example in mysticism. It is especially in relation to this element of majesty or absolute overpoweringness that the creature-consciousness, of which we have already spoken, comes upon the scene, as a sort of shadow or subjective reflection of it. Thus, in contrast to the 'overpowering' of which we are conscious, as an object over against the self, there is the feeling of one's own submergence, of being but 'dust and ashes' and nothingness. And this forms the numinous raw material for the feeling of religious humility. (p. 20)

Otto's representation of *majestas* must not be confused with the sense of "natural" majesty, although such awareness may be its starting point. This fugitive feeling-state is hard to depict in a single passage of literature. It generally finds its context in a cumulative series of narrations, as in the final chapters of *Moby-Dick*. The emotion does seem well focussed, however, in the description of the first sight of the numinous and nearly supernal whale.

> A gentle joyousness—a mighty mildness of repose in swiftness, invested the gliding whale. Not the white bull Jupiter swimming away with ravished Europa clinging to his graceful horns; his lovely, leering eyes sideways intent upon the maid; with smooth bewitching fleetness, rippling straight for the nuptial bower in Crete; not Jove, not that great majesty Supreme! did surpass the glorified White Whale as he so divinely swam.
>
> On each soft side—coincident with the parted swell, that but once leaving him, then flowed so wide away—on each bright side, the whale shed off enticings. No wonder there had been some among the hunters who namelessly transported and allured by all this serenity, had ventured to assail it; but had fatally found that quietude but the vesture of tornadoes. Yet calm, enticing calm, oh, whale! thou glidest on, to all who for the first time eye thee, no matter how many in that same way thou may'st have bejuggled and destroyed before.[7]

A final element suggested by the ideogram *tremendum* is termed by Otto the "urgency" or "energy" of the numinous object. This element is sometimes projected symbolically as the "wrath of God," and in qualities of vitality, passion, emotional temper, will-force, movement, excitement, activity, and impetus. Such a feeling, Otto tells us, makes its appearance in mysticism, especially "voluntaristic" mysticism and "the mysticism of love." It appears in Fichte's speculations on the Absolute as the gigantic, never-resting, active world-stress, and in Schopenhauer's daemonic "Will." In Goethe, too, the same note is sounded in his strange description of the "daemonic."[8] The quality isolated here is prominent in Gothic fiction. Some of it enters into the characterization of Mr. Rochester in *Jane Eyre,* and of the monster in Mary Shelley's *Frankenstein.* It appears in rather melodramatic form in the final chapter of *The Monk* when the fiend carries Ambrosio out of the dungeon and across the mountain peaks. And it certainly contributes to the character of Captain Ahab, the "grand ungodly god-like man" of *Moby-Dick.*

Thus Otto distinguishes three distinct, but related, moments suggested by the ideogram *tremendum:* awfulness, majesty, and energy. He now proceeds to an analysis of the substantive *mysterium,* which stands as the form of the numinous experience. The mental reaction to this "moment" in the numinous consciousness is best described analogically by the word "stupor." "Stupor is plainly a different thing from *tremor;* it signifies blank wonder, an astonishment that strikes us dumb, amazement absolute." Its objective concomitant, the *mysterium,* suggests that which is "wholly other" (*anyad, alienum*) or in other words "that which is quite beyond the sphere of the usual, the intelligible, and the familiar, which therefore falls quite outside the limits of the 'canny' and is contrasted with it, filling the mind with blank wonder and astonishment" (p. 26).

To suggest this sense of the "wholly other" Otto undertakes an analysis of the fear of ghosts—a subject obviously quite germane to the Gothic.

> The ghost's real attraction . . . consists in this, that of itself and in an uncommon degree it entices the imagination, awakening strong interest and

curiosity; it is the weird thing itself that allures the fancy. But it does this, not because it is 'something long and white' (as someone once defined a ghost) nor yet through any of the positive conceptual attributes which fancies about ghosts have invented, but because it is a thing that 'doesn't really exist at all,' the 'wholly other,' something which has no place in our scheme of reality but belongs to an absolutely different one and which at the same time arouses an irrepressible interest in the mind. (pp. 28-29)

The accuracy of Rudolf Otto's analysis of such ghostly matters is attested to by a great deal of literature of the supernatural, but no better paradigm is available than Henry James' classic ghost story "The Jolly Corner." The description of Spencer Brydon's encounter with his horrific doppelgänger clearly depicts both the "wholly other" character of the spirit as well as the sense of blank wonder and stupor.

> The hands, as he looked, began to move, to open; then, as if deciding in a flash, dropped from the face and left it uncovered and presented. Horror, with the sight, had leaped into Brydon's throat, gasping there in a sound he couldn't utter; for the bared identity was too hideous as *his,* and his glare was the passion of his protest. The face, *that* face, Spencer Brydon's?—he searched it still, but looking away from it in dismay and denial, falling straight from his height of sublimity. It was unknown, inconceivable, awful, disconnected from any possibility—! He had been "sold," he inwardly moaned, stalking such game as this: the presence before him was a presence, the horror within him a horror, but the waste of his nights had been only grotesque and the success of his adventure an irony. Such an identity fitted his at *no* point, made its alternative monstrous. A thousand times yes, as it came upon him nearer now—the face was the face of a stranger. It came upon him nearer now, quite as one of those expanding fantastic images projected by the magic lantern of childhood; for the stranger, whoever he might be, evil, odious, blatant, vulgar, had advanced as for aggression, and he knew himself give ground . . . he felt the whole vision turn to darkness and his very feet give way. His head went round; he was going; he had gone.[9]

In this passage, as in the entire story, the *mysterium* is transformed into and partakes of James' private universe, with all its exquisite values and peculiar defects. No writer could be further, in some ways, from the "average Gothic," and yet the numinous qualities provide a link. The apparition is "unknown, inconceivable, awful, disconnected from any possibility—!" which one takes to be a Jamesian rendition of the "wholly other." In fact, as James himself attests in several of his prefaces, the supernatural tale fascinated him.

It is the sense of fascination that forms the final strand in Otto's analysis of numinous feeling. Having analyzed what might be termed the daunting aspect of the numinous *(mysterium tremendum),* Otto discusses another

element that stands at the opposite pole. This element Otto designates by the term *fascinans,* a kind of fascination, attraction, or allurement in the numinous. This *fascinans* is "a bliss which embraces all those blessings that are indicated or suggested in a positive fashion by any 'doctrine of salvation,' and it quickens all of them through and through; but these do not exhaust it. Rather by its all pervading, penetrating glow it makes of these very blessings more than the intellect can conceive in them or affirm of them" (pp. 33-34).

Thus, Otto groups in what he calls a "harmony of contrasts" the various moments in the numinous experience; and these he indicates by the phrase (or ideogram as he terms it) *mysterium tremendum et fascinosum.*

> These two qualities, the daunting and the fascinating, now combine in a strange harmony of contrasts, and the resultant dual character of the numinous consciousness, to which the entire religious development bears witness, at any rate from the level of the 'daemonic dread' onwards, is at once the strangest and the most noteworthy phenomenon in the whole history of religion. The daemonic-divine object may appear to the mind an object of horror and dread, but at the same time it is no less something that allures with a potent charm, and the creature who trembles before it, utterly cowed and cast down, has always at the same time the impulse to turn to it, nay even to make it somehow his own. The 'mystery' is for him not merely something to be wondered at but something that entrances him; and beside that in it which bewilders and confounds, he feels a something that captivates and transports him with a strange ravishment, rising often enough to the pitch of intoxication: it is the Dionysiac-element in the numen. (p. 31)

The peculiar "harmony of contrasts" is a prominent feature in the work of Edgar Allan Poe, who certainly had an intuitive grasp of the numinous consciousness as Otto expounds it, and explains, to some degree, Poe's puzzling ideas concerning "perversity" ("The Imp of the Perverse"), ideas which interested Baudelaire. But on a higher plane this daunting-attracting quality of the numinous infuses most of Poe's tales and poems. A striking example is his tale "A Descent Into the Maelström." As the protagonist finds himself drawn into the immense and terrifying depths of the maelström, his reflections vary from awe and terror before this nearly preternatural manifestation to a strange sense of fascination.

> "It may look like boasting—but what I tell you is truth—I began to reflect how magnificent a thing it was to die in such a manner, and how foolish it was in me to think of so paltry a consideration as my own individual life, in view of so wonderful a manifestation of God's power. I do believe that I blushed with shame when this idea crossed my mind. After a little while I became possessed with the keenest curiosity about the whirl itself. I positively felt a *wish* to explore its depths, even at the sacrifice I was going to make; and my

principal grief was that I should never be able to tell my old companions on shore about the mysteries I should see."[10]

Throughout his book, Otto continually emphasizes that the numinous is not identical with the fully developed sense of the Holy. The concept of Holiness must of necessity include theological and moral elements. The numinous may thus be seen as bearing intrinsic relationship with and even providing a definition for a number of works, both literary and artistic, which might not generally be termed religious. For what else is one to say of the castles and mountain crags of Mrs. Radcliffe's novels, the glaciers, ice-floes, and desolate Scottish islands of *Frankenstein,* or the spectral sea-scapes of *The Narrative of Arthur Gordon Pym* but that they summon up many of the moods and tones that Otto has analyzed? Thus, by making use of Otto's insights, one is able to sense a new and more profound note in some very good literature of this kind that has sometimes been looked at with bewilderment if not downright condescension by certain critics.

Another fruitful link between the numinous and the Gothic tradition is to be found in Otto's remarks about preternatural events and magic. Preternaturalism has, of course, been a source of annoyance to some critics of the Gothic; and it does, indeed, require a strong palate to accept all the bleeding portraits, animated skeletons, lycanthropes, rattling chains, and vampires that infest Gothic literature, especially the older novels. But the artistic incorporation of the preternatural into literature should not, in itself, form a barrier to critical appreciation. It is on this point that Otto supplies a strong apologetic. "Now the magical," he says, "is nothing but a suppressed and dimmed form of the numinous, a crude form of it which great art purifies and ennobles." He adds, "To us of the West the Gothic appears as the most numinous of all types of art. This is due in the first place to its sublimity; but Worringer in his *Problem der Ghotik* has done a real service in showing that the peculiar impressiveness of Gothic does not consist in its sublimity alone, but draws upon a strain inherited from primitive magic, of which he tries to show the historical derivation" (pp. 67-68).

The magical or preternatural event, then, if introduced artistically may serve to reinforce the numinous quality of the work. Nathaniel Hawthorne, who was sparing in his use of the preternatural, seems to achieve the proper effect in a passage from *The Marble Faun.* Donatello, Miriam, and Kenyon approach the open bier of a dead monk who lies in the Church of the Capuchins in Rome.

> And now occurred a circumstance that would seem too fantastic to be told, if it had not actually happened, precisely as we set it down. As the three friends stood by the bier, they saw that a little stream of blood had begun to ooze from the dead monk's nostrils; it crept slowly towards the thicket of his beard, where, in the course of a moment or two, it hid itself.

> "How strange!" ejaculated Kenyon. "The monk died of apoplexy, I suppose, or by some sudden accident, and the blood has not yet congealed."

> "Do you consider that a sufficient explanation?" asked Miriam, with a smile from which the sculptor involuntarily turned away his eyes. "Does it satisfy you?"

> "And why not?" he inquired.

> "Of course, you know the old superstition about this phenomenon of blood flowing from a dead body," she rejoined. "How can we tell but that the murderer of this monk (or, possibly, it may be only that privileged murderer, his physician) may have just entered the church?"[11]

*The Idea of the Holy* contains chapters, of special interest to the literary critic, on the means of arousing the numinous consciousness by artistic works. "Of directer methods our Western art has only two," Otto says, "and they are in a noteworthy way negative, viz. *darkness* and *silence.*" His discussion of the artistic use of darkness conjures up many images of the "haunted castle" theme so dear to the tale of terror: "The semi-darkness that glimmers in vaulted halls, or beneath the branches of a lofty forest glade, strangely quickened and stirred by the mysterious play of half-lights, has always spoken eloquently to the soul, and the builders of temples, mosques and churches have made full use of it" (p. 68). Silence is "what corresponds to this in the language of musical sounds. . . . It is a spontaneous reaction to the feeling of the actual *numen praesens*" (pp. 68-69). Both of these "artistic means" are native to Western art; but Oriental art makes continual use of a third, namely, empty distance and emptiness. "Empty distance, remote vacancy, is, as it were, the sublime in the horizontal. The wide-stretching desert, the boundless uniformity of the steppe, have a real sublimity, and even in us Westerners they set vibrating chords of the numinous along with the note of the sublime, according to the principle of the association of feelings" (p. 69).

Perhaps Otto is right in concluding that most Western art has generally failed to make consistent use of emptiness, but the Gothic literary tradition has, indeed, effectively utilized this method as a means to register a sense of the numinous. The vacant loneliness associated with sea, desert, mountain prospects, or the night sky is a constant theme. This characteristic is especially true of Coleridge's *Ancient Mariner* ("Alone, alone, all, all alone/ Alone on a wide wide sea!") and Poe's *Narrative of Arthur Gordon Pym,* as well as of several of Joseph Conrad's novels in which brooding descriptions of the sea stimulate the numinous sense of emptiness and silence. In *Victory,* for instance, a work which contains certain strong numinous elements, the lonely protagonist Heyst is a man who feels this numinous call of the sea.

> Like most dreamers, to whom it is given sometimes to hear the music of the spheres, Heyst, the wanderer of the Archipelago, had a taste for

silence which he had been able to gratify for years. The islands are very quiet. One sees them lying about, clothed in their dark garments of leaves, in a great hush of silver and azure, where the sea without murmurs meets the sky in a ring of magic stillness. A sort of smiling somnolence broods over them; the very voices of their people are soft and subdued, as if afraid to break some protecting spell.[12]

Thus, it seems clear that Otto's work provides many insights into the spirit of Gothic literature. The mountain gloom, lonely castles, phantom ships, violent storms, and the vastness of sea and polar regions correspond closely with Otto's description of the numinous. Likewise, the preternatural machinery of Gothicism, whether magical lore, apparitions, ghouls, vampires, or revenants, finds its explanation not in an over-ripe fantasy, but in an effort to instill a sense of the numinous.

We have seen several ways in which the numinous plays a part both in background and event in the Gothic tale. But the numinous is not confined to ontological reality; Otto contends that it also has an axiological character. This is to say, the numinous exists as a category of value within its own right; and as a consequence it can be used in analyzing character and moral value.

According to Otto, the numinous experience in itself is not an ethical manifestation and may exist without any relation to morality, as for instance in the case of certain primitive religions. When the numinous is commingled with moral and rational elements it becomes something different—namely *The Holy*. On the other hand, the numinous in its pure form, and without moral connotations, is still permeated by certain axiological elements. The numinous "object" produces in the percipient a sense of "creature feelings"; in fact, this result is one of the essential ways in which it impinges upon the individual consciousness. Out of such a feeling grows the sense of numinous value and of numinous disvalue. In opposition to this sense of "disvalue" or the profane stands the sacred. "This sanctus is not merely 'perfect' or 'beautiful' or 'sublime' or 'good,' though, being like these concepts also a value, objective and ultimate, it has a definite, perceptible analogy with them. It is the positive numinous value or worth, and to it corresponds on the side of the creature a numinous disvalue or 'unworth'" (Otto, p. 51).

The sense of numinous value, the sacred, is recognized as standing outside the sphere of morality as such. "In every highly-developed religion the appreciation of moral obligation and duty, ranking as a claim of the deity upon man, has been developed side by side with the religious feeling itself. Nonetheless, a profoundly humble and heartfelt recognition of 'the holy' may occur in particular experiences without being always definitely charged or infused with the sense of moral demands. The 'holy' will then be recognized as that which commands our respect, as that whose real value is to be acknowledged inwardly" (p. 51). Likewise, the opposite

pole, the numinous "disvalue" or sense of the profane, is not intrinsically a moral category. "Mere 'unlawfulness' only becomes 'sin,' 'impiety,' 'sacrilege,' when the character of *numinous unworthiness or disvalue* goes on to be transferred to and centered in moral delinquency . . ." (p. 52).

Otto's explanation of numinous value and disvalue, if viewed as a phenomenological description, applies with equal force to many Gothic works which might otherwise appear to be morally neutral and therefore, at best, mere entertainment. There are, it is true, certain patent moral lessons attached to Mary Shelley's *Frankenstein*, but the categories of the sacred and profane, if applied to the hero's unholy experiments, add a new dimension to the story.

To explore this interpretation briefly, we must remember that the story projects a feeling of horror and evil that is disproportionate to the moral framework out of which Mary Shelley worked. The crimes of the monster and the ultimate ruin of his creator Frankenstein are the results of an experiment begun, perhaps, in good conscience. Mary Shelley suggests, in fact, that some of the evil nature of the monster is the result of economic and moral dislocations in society. Then, too, as a rationalist and liberal who followed the views of her father, she would have rejected a belief in the innate evil of man. What then is responsible for the brooding sense of profanity and unhallowed occupation that characterizes the inception of the monster?

> Who shall conceive the horrors of my secret toil, as I dabbled among the unhallowed damps of the grave, or tortured the living animal to animate the lifeless clay? My limbs now tremble and my eyes swim with the remembrance; but then a resistless, and almost frantic, impulse urged me forward; I seemed to have lost all soul or sensation but for this one pursuit. . . . I collected bones from charnel-houses, and disturbed, with profane fingers, the tremendous secrets of the human frame. In a solitary chamber, or rather cell, at the top of the house, and separated from all the other apartments by a gallery and staircase, I kept my workshop of filthy creation: my eye-balls were starting from their sockets in attending to the details of my employment.[13]

There is really no "rational" explanation for such feelings, given the moral views of Frankenstein. He feels, rather, the sense of numinous "disvalue" attendant upon his profane experiments, a feeling that Mary Shelley shared despite her liberal and utopian sentiments to the contrary. The famous description of the animation of the monster heightens this sense of profanity.

> It was already one in the morning; the rain pattered dismally against the panes, and my candle was nearly burnt out, when, by the glimmer of the half-extinguished light, I saw the dull yellow eye of the creature open; it breathed hard, and a convulsive motion agitated its limbs.

How can I describe my emotions at this catastrophe, or how delineate the wretch whom with such infinite pains and care I had endeavoured to form? His limbs were in proportion, and I had selected his features as beautiful. Beautiful!— Great God! His yellow skin scarcely covered the work of muscles and arteries beneath; his hair was of a lustrous black, and flowing; his teeth of a pearly whiteness; but these luxuriances only formed a more horrid contrast with his watery eyes, that seemed almost of the same colour as the dun white sockets in which they were set, his shrivelled complexion and straight black lips. (p. 51)

The question of Frankenstein's guilt in tampering with the well-springs of life is not treated directly. The consequent crimes and atrocities perpetrated by the monster are the results of "man's inhumanity to man," the evils of society and, to a certain extent, mere chance. Even at the last, Frankenstein absolves himself of direct guilt: "During these last days I have been occupied in examining my past conduct; nor do I find it blameable. In a fit of enthusiastic madness I created a rational creature, and was bound towards him, to assure, as far as was in my power, his happiness and well-being. This was my duty; but there was another still paramount to that. My duties towards the beings of my own species had greater claims to my attention, because they included a greater proportion of happiness or misery" (p. 235). Thus, on the merely rational level, *Frankenstein* expounds some rather patent moral truths which are perhaps most interesting from a historical standpoint. But in a deeper sense, the book portrays the mysterious sense of "profanity" and numinous disvalue which, according to Otto, is part of man's spiritual life.

It is upon such a system of thought, profound and original, that a new survey of Gothic literature may be conducted. Otto's description of the numinous, self-authenticating and convincing, suggests a new dimension to the literature of the preternatural.

[1] See Stanley Edgar Hyman, *The Armed Vision, A Study in the Methods of Modern Literary Criticism* (New York: Vintage Books, 1948), p. 3.

[2] "From Poe to Valéry," *Hudson Review,* 2 (1949), 335.

[3] *Baudelaire on Poe,* trans. and ed. Lois and Francis E. Hyslop, Jr. (State College, Pa.: Bald Eagle Press, 1952), p. 151.

[4] See Maud Bodkin, *Archetypal Patterns in Poetry* (London: Oxford Univ. Press, 1934), pp. 223, 241; Walter Kaufman, *From Shakespeare to Existentialism* (Boston: Beacon Press, 1949), p. 37; G. Wilson Knight, *The Crown of Life* (London: Methuen, 1947), p. 128.

[5] Rudolf Otto, *The Idea of the Holy,* trans. John W. Harvey (New York: Oxford Univ. Press, 1958), p. 2.

[6] Algernon Blackwood, *Tales of Terror and the Unknown* (New York: E. P. Dutton & Co., 1965), pp. 20-21.

[7] Herman Melville, *Moby-Dick,* ed. Charles Feidelson, Jr. (Indianapolis: The Bobbs-Merrill Company, Inc., 1964), p. 690.

[8] As described by Otto, pp. 23-24.

[9] Henry James, *Ghostly Tales of Henry James,* ed. Leon Edel (New York: Grosset & Dunlap, 1963), pp. 427-28.

[10] Edgar Allan Poe, *The Complete Works of Edgar Allan Poe,* ed. James A. Harrison (New York: Thomas Y. Crowell & Co., 1902), II, 240.

[11] Nathaniel Hawthorne, *The Writings of Nathaniel Hawthorne* (Boston: Houghton Mifflin and Company, 1903), IX, 263.

[12] Joseph Conrad, *Victory* (New York: The Modern Library, 1921), p. 64.

[13] Mary W. Shelley, *Frankenstein* (London: Everyman's Library, 1963), p. 48.

## David Bastow (essay date 1976)

SOURCE: "Otto and Numinous Experience," in *Religious Studies,* Vol. 12, No. 2, June, 1976, pp. 159-67.

[*In the following essay, Bastow examines the phenomenological aspects of Otto's religious theory.*]

The basic position of Otto in ***The Idea of the Holy***[2] may be stated as follows:

All religions involve and rest on experience of the numinous, which affords a positive knowledge of the central object of religion—God. This position is what may be called a Theory of Religion: like Freud's explanation of religion in terms of father figures, and Durkheim's claim that religion is society's celebration of itself, it claims to give an explanation of the phenomenon of religion—the fact that men belong to religions etc. Unlike some of its rivals, this Theory of Religion does not explain religion away; the explanation is intended to be compatible with religious belief; the explanatory concepts are supposed to be concepts from within religion. If Otto had just argued that religion was, or some religions were, true, his claims would have been only of theological interest. But what makes his writings especially important is that he looks at religion not merely as a theologian, but also as a phenomenologist; he is concerned to explain religion and religions as they are; even to explain the diversity of religions (with a version of evolutionism). It would be over-simple, but not entirely wide of the truth, to say that he first looks at religions in the sensitive but neutral manner of the phenomenologist, to decide what are the central phenomena of religion; and then puts forward a theological explanation of these phenomena. At least, this is what for much of his book he aims to do.

It is further the case that he aims to support this phenomenological—theological link by means of a philosophy of religion, a metaphysical system. This is not made as clear as it might be in **The Idea of the Holy,** though the words of the Foreword are very forceful: 'I feel that no-one ought to concern himself with the *Numen ineffabile* who has not already devoted assiduous and serious study to the *Ratio Aeterna*'. But I hope to show that a full understanding of **The Idea of the Holy** is impossible unless one understands the philosophical system taken over from Fries and expounded in **The Philosophy of Religion.**[3] I do not in what follows discuss the truth of Fries's philosophical system; nor do I commit myself to any phenomenological theses, though I do sometimes make suggestions about the plausibility or otherwise of such theses. Finally I do not discuss, as a theologian might, the truth of the claim that all religions have the truth in them, although often obscurely and confusedly. My main concern is with the coherence of the whole structure; with the boldness of attempting to unite in one movement of thought, theses of three distinct types, from the disciplines of philosophy, phenomenology of religion, and theology; and thereby, by implication, of grappling with the problems of the relations between the types of judgement made in these disciplines. It should be said that Otto does not in general bother to make explicit the differences in the character of his various theses; in particular he did not especially aim at a phenomenological neutrality anything like as sophisticated and carefully delimited as that of recent phenomenologists.[4] So my discussion treats Otto to some extent in terms of concepts which he did not acknowledge. (In **'In the Sphere of the Holy'**, *Hibbert Journal,* XXXI, 1932-3, Otto discusses and rejects the approach to religion of what he calls 'phenomenalists'. But he seems to think that their aim is the reduction of religious to non-religious categories.) But his concept of the numinous has been very widely used in modern intellectual contexts: and one of my aims is to see whether the concept can be so 'lifted', and put to modern uses. That is, if one tries to make sense of Otto's Theory by re-expressing it in modern terminology, is the Theory coherent, and if so, is it plausible; and therefore is the concept of the numinous fit for modern use—the concept which lies at the heart of the Theory, and may almost be said to be an encapsulation of it?

I wish first to describe in outline the theses within the three disciplines, and the links between them—i.e. the theses which when put together constitute the Theory, and the theses which accomplish this putting together. When the general plan has been made clear, I shall go on to describe and discuss the individual theses in more detail.

(1) *Philosophical Thesis*

By means of a Critique of Reason on Kantian lines, Otto, following Fries, claims that knowledge of absolute reality, with absolute value, is possible for man. Reflective conceptual but negative knowledge is possible—this Fries calls faith; but also positive knowledge is possible; this is by means of a kind of feeling, which Fries calls *Ahnung* or intimation; it is non-conceptual, ineffable. These possibilities of knowledge are not merely inborn in all men, but are a consequence of their most essential nature.

(2) *Phenomenological Theses*

*(a)* All religions are grounded on religious experience.

*(b)* This experience is basically similar in all religions, and is of a *Mysterium Tremendum Fascinans et Augustum.*

(3) *Theological Thesis*

In so far as religions clearly base themselves on this experience, they are true; Christianity supremely so.

The linking theses are:

(4) *Philosophical—Theological*

Knowledge of absolute reality is identified with religious knowledge.

(5) *Philosophical—Phenomenological*

The feeling-experience *Ahung* is identified with the experience of the numinous.

There are also supplementary theses, which sketch out accounts in terms of the Philosophical Thesis of the phenomenological fact of the diversity of religions. Before I can discuss these various theses and their relations to each other, I must attempt a summary account of the philosophical position which Otto took over from Fries.[5]

Fries's philosophy is a development and modification of Kant. In Kant's system, experience is the product of the given (which has for us the subjective form of the pure intuitions, space and time), and the original unity of apperception. This unity is imposed on intuitions, via the pure intuitions, by the understanding. Of course the understanding must operate in accordance with the categories, but it is otherwise free; we choose to divide our world up into chairs and tables, etc., but if our interests were different, other classifications would do as well. The original unity though, and its articulation in the categories, does not itself derive from the intellect or understanding; it is completely formal and *a priori,* its application to human experience is universal and necessary.

For Kant, the apriority of this original unity is sufficient to prove its subjectivity; but here Fries disagrees. He prepares his position by putting forward a general theory of the justification of judgements. All judgements either derive from other judgements, or do not. In the case of perception there must be 'basic judgements', which derive not from other judgements but from our confrontation with the object. They cannot be proved; their only possible justification is not by proof but by showing them to correspond to a perception, i.e. to immediate knowledge. The only question about immediate knowledge is whether we have it—there is no possibility of defending alleged immediate knowledge by comparing it with the object—for such a comparison would require one somehow to get behind the object as known to the object independent of knowledge. So *(a)* we must have immediate knowledge, *(b)* it requires no justification.

It is a commonplace that empirical judgements involve more than simple sense-reports; they involve classification and combination. Assumptions about the general rules governing this combination thus lie behind empirical judgements. The rules are general in the sense of being universal and necessary. (This Kantian position is supported in normal Kantian ways.) But what possible explanation could there be, of our having knowledge of necessary truths? Is this knowledge explicable in Humean psychological terms? But association psychology cannot explain the idea of objective combination. Neither can this idea (or the necessary judgements which specify it) come from perception, or from the understanding, which is itself purely a faculty of choice, not of independent knowledge. So there must be another kind of immediate knowledge, besides that of perception; though this second kind is immediate in the sense of being the grounding of basic judgements, but not in the sense of being immediately clear to consciousness, as is the immediate knowledge of perception. In fact we can make it explicit only by the hesitant and contingent process of abstraction. Of course, justification of this knowledge by proof is out of the question; we can only ascertain, as it were empirically, that we have it.

What then is the content of this knowledge, which we can speak of as produced by pure reason? It is the 'basic notion of the objective synthetic unity of all the manifold given in sense'. This notion underlies all particular notions of objective unity which we may have—such particular notions are partial representations and modifications, mediated by the understanding, of the original all-embracing product of pure reason. 'Formal apperception' is the name given to the notion of the unity of all immediate knowledge. The whole itself, formal unity plus what it unifies, is both subjectively and objectively a unity; its objectivity as a whole makes it appropriate to call it 'transcendental apperception'. The immediate knowledge which lies behind perception, the *content* of transcendental apperception, Fries calls 'material apperception'.

Transcendental apperception then is the whole of immediate knowledge of reality; but because the whole is a necessary and absolute unity, we in our limited human spatio-temporal circumstances cannot know it as a whole. Nevertheless, if it has been shown that reason has its own *immediate* knowledge, i.e. formal apperception, this is sufficient to destroy Kant's Formal Idealism—his view that our knowledge of the necessary rules of the form of experience has only subjective validity. So this formal knowledge is according to Fries objective; it tells us about reality. The articulation of what it tells us starts with the Deduction of the Categories.

In this Deduction (the detailed arguments of which cannot be given in summary; and which I find the least convincing part of Fries's argument) the fundamental idea of unity, which we know to be both objective and formal—i.e. knowledge about our knowledge—is applied to, worked out in terms of, the basic structures which govern all our knowledge—namely that it depends on the given, and on reflection, and on the synthesis of the given, producing unity in multiplicity. By considering all possible types of judgement, Fries arrives at twelve kinds of unity, the twelve categories as listed by Kant. All objects of knowledge must be unified in these ways; and it must therefore follow that each of the twelve provides a principle, an item of *a priori* knowledge. Three of the twelve in particular, the categories of relation, deal with the formal rules of synthesis as they are brought to our awareness by thought; that is, with the principles of metaphysics.

The categories thus produced—the principle of unity as applied to the necessary structure of our knowledge—are pure categories, true of knowledge in general. They become pure concepts of nature, providing principles for empirical knowledge, when schematized by time. Because of the infinity of time and space, empirical knowledge is always incomplete, it is always possible to add to it. So empirical knowledge always falls short of transcendental apperception, the whole of immediate knowledge.

Kant of course argues that we can have no real knowledge outside the temporally schematized categories; but Fries's system is not thus restricted. The Ideas of Reason, which are for Kant transcendental illusion, for Fries provide the principles of immediate formal knowledge such as reason itself demands; that is of a unity which is absolute, necessary and complete. Intuitive knowledge is incompletable; the Ideas are deduced by negating this incompletability, applying a schematism of completeness, of completed infinity. (Our knowledge of the Ideas thus derives from our knowledge of the temporally schematized categories.) Thus Ideally schematized, the metaphysical categories of Substance, Cause and Reciprocity become the Ideas of the Soul, Freedom, and Divinity or the principle of absolute community.

Being a negation of what was itself a limitation or negation, this second schematization gives us real knowledge of things as they are. Thus the categories, Ideally schematized, give us knowledge of the absolute. In fact this second schematization is no more than an undoing of the temporal one, and so makes clear to us the objective knowledge provided by the pure categories.

Transcendental apperception is a unity, but its content is material apperception, i.e. the immediate knowledge which is fundamental to sense-perception. Judgements of sense experience do not directly reveal the relation of material to transcendental apperception; as Kant shows, they involve rather the relation between intuition and concept. But Fries asserts that we can *feel* this relationship, between those objects the immediate knowledge of which is basic to sense perception, and the whole of absolute reality. Fries characterizes the feeling as aesthetic judgement. Aesthetic judgement cannot be conceptualized; nevertheless it claims objective validity. It represents objects as necessary, really real—whereas for science the existence of objects is contingent. This feeling will constitute, for anyone who has it, a realization of the reality of the relation between formal and material apperception; and thus a realization that the Ideas are not merely formal and empty but have content, and so can be said to be valid. It does not seem that *having* the feeling can be necessary to following Fries's arguments for his metaphysics; if the arguments are valid, they convince on their own. It is not clear to me what Fries himself thought on this matter; the point is not without importance for my later comments on Otto.

It will be seen how this aesthetic judging of nature may be thought to have a religious significance. Our interest in the beautiful is based, according to Fries, on our recognition in the beautiful phenomenon of the reality of the Ideas in nature; in the feeling which Fries calls *Ahnung*, intimation, the objects of empirical knowledge are subordinated to the objects of faith, the Ideas.

It is thought by Otto, and rather vaguely by Fries himself, that this philosophical system can provide the basis of an account of religion in general. The dogmas of religion, of all religion, i.e. what in religion can be claimed as categorically known, reduce to the Ideas, and thus derive from reason which is common to all men. To this extent, all religions are the same. But the Ideas are purely formal, and indeed negative, being known only by a process of negation. The positive doctrines of religions can only be symbolic; the differences between positive religions are merely differences of symbolism; what they symbolize remains the same. But underlying the whole, for religion, is the experience of *Ahnung*, which provides genuine though non-conceptual knowledge of the reality of the Ideas.

It should be added that the full description of these Ideas brings out the fact that the unity of reason embraces practical reason; and the basic principles of the philosophy of religion are the development of the Ideas as already described, in terms of the Idea of absolute worth. Thus these principles are of the absolute worth of the independent soul, of absolute good and radical evil, and of absolute being as being absolute good—divinity as the cause of everything that is intrinsically real, and

therefore eternally good. But these phrases do not constitute positive knowledge; they are just fillings-out of negations; the outlines of mysteries. Positive knowledge of the ideas as thus schematized practically comes as before only through feeling, *Ahnung* and therefore cannot be conceptualized. In sum, Otto's philosophical position, following Fries, is that although we cannot say what God is—except negatively, by denying of him the limitations of earthly life—we can in *Ahnung* feel what he is.

The most obvious way of taking *The Idea of the Holy* is as a work of phenomenology—as a description in very general terms of religious phenomena and their structure. In *The Idea of the Holy* Otto does not present his or Fries's philosophy of religion, which of course is not phenomenology; but there are good grounds for saying that his theses rely on it; it comes into the open in several places, but never as a complete structure, and never backed up by philosophical arguments. To see what Otto's phenomenological claims are, and whether they are plausible, we have to disentangle them if possible from this submerged philosophy.

The book is presented as an investigation of the concept of the holy. Otto says (*The Idea of the Holy* chapter II) that 'holy' is a category of interpretation peculiar to religion; and this can be accepted as a mere matter of definition. But he further claims that it or rather an abstraction from it is fundamental to all religions, as their 'innermost core'. This is a very strong claim: could it be phenomenology? He is not merely saying that the concept is inter-religious, and so can be used in a typology of religious phenomena, like 'prayer', 'sacrifice', etc.; but that the structural description of every religion must contain it, and must indeed be based on it. One explanation of the strength of this claim would be that it is again a matter of definition that a religious person just is a person who is willing to call something holy (i.e. not merely that anyone who calls something holy must be religious). Otto might be willing to accept this; but he would think of it as a *real* definition, one which throws light on the (necessary) structure of all religion. To say that structural descriptions of religions should be based on this phenomenon of attributing holiness to something, is to say that all important religious activities and beliefs can be explained in terms of it. (Whether such *explanations* could themselves be phenomenological is a matter of controversy within the phenomenology of religion itself. It is at least clear that no explanatory thesis can be allowed within the phenomenology of religion which threatens its neutrality. It might be argued that the exploration of possible *justifications* of one type of religious phenomenology in terms of another is a philosophical task.) What then does Otto say about this central religious phenomenon of the attribution of holiness? As everybody knows, he describes it in terms of an experience, an experience of the numinous. My term 'description in terms of' is intentionally vague; to eliminate the vagueness one must ask: what is the relation between the attribution of holiness and the numinous experience? It is in answering this question that *The Idea of the Holy* is most elusive.

I should like for a moment to consider holiness independently of Otto. A simple phenomenological hypothesis would be that two kinds of things are called holy; gods, and earthly things like church buildings. This view runs into difficulties, for it is by no means unknown for earthly things to be thought of as gods; one possible reformulation of the hypothesis would distinguish between gods and non-gods; another would distinguish between earthly things and non-earthly things. To take the second pair; an obvious difference between calling an earthly thing holy and calling a non-earthly thing holy, is that in the first case the existence of the thing can be known in the ordinary way, by sense perception etc. Calling it holy is not involved in establishing its existence. This is obviously the case with Jesus, an Indian guru, a church building. But in the other case there must be some special way of knowing of the thing's existence. It may also be noted that in at least some cases the attribution of holiness to some such non-earthly thing is intimately related to the question of its existence. There could be no question of first deciding on the Christian God's existence, and then deciding that he was holy—or of deciding that he existed, and then deciding that he was God.

To return to Otto; it may be argued that he was not explicitly aware of these distinctions, but that one of the reasons why he linked the attribution of holiness to numinous experience, one of the jobs he wanted the experience to do, was to explain people's belief in the *existence* of non-earthly gods. So it often seems that the numinous experience is thought of on a quasi-perceptual model. Especially towards the beginning of the book Otto speaks of a sense of presence. 'The numinous is thus felt as objective and outside the self' (p. 11). Taken as a phenomenological thesis, this implies that every attribution of holiness rests on some kind of meeting with the numen. But would, for example, all Christians say they believed in God because they had met him? Otto's reply in effect is that Christians rely on the authority of the prophets, who did meet God. It seems to me that Otto has here allowed himself to be forced into an unpleasantly tight corner. He is adopting a simple model of religious belief which describes it on analogy with empirical beliefs. As a phenomenologist he is, quite rightly, dissatisfied with a purely *a priori* defence of this position, such as, for example, 'people must have some kind of meeting with gods or God, else why should they believe in them?' He attempts to give the position some phenomenological backing by giving instances of religious experience which do readily fit into the quasi-perceptual model. Besides prophets he refers to shamans—who are thought of as being possessed by a deity—and mystics. But these instances are far from adequate to establish the general position that *all* religious belief rests on some quasi-perceptual experience, some 'sense of presence'. It seems, e.g. at least equally plausible to say that for most theists belief in God does not rest on any straightforward kind of meeting, even a vicarious one; it involves *thinking* of many of their earthly experiences *as* meeting with God (going to Church, taking

part in the sacraments) but this is very different from the 'sense of presence' which mystics and shamans experience; and the difference is not one the phenomenologist should gloss over.[6]

The reason why Otto does not argue sufficiently for, or sufficiently realize the implausibility of, this phenomenological thesis about a quasi-perceptual experience, is that it is entangled in his argument with a much more plausible one. This is that religious belief, ascription of holiness, involves certain basic emotional reactions. Again what is asserted is a relation between calling something holy and having an experience, and again there is a problem about the nature of this relation. Otto states his position thus:

First, the concept of holiness as used at present has a rational or moral element, and a non-rational element. This latter he calls the numinous. Whenever the category of the numinous is applied, there is always to be found a 'definitely numinous state of mind' (p. 7). This state of mind is *sui generis:* it cannot be described directly but only by analogies. (The term 'state of mind' is too vague to give us as yet any indication of what is being claimed.) Otto then proceeds, indirectly of course, to describe the state of mind. It involves a sense of presence (this we have already briefly discussed); but what can be described is not the being or numen itself, but man's reactions to it; or, rather, the only possible description of the numen is in terms of man's emotional reactions to it. We find that these reactions are such as lead to the description of a *Mysterium, Tremendum Fascinans et Augustum;* our reactions are of incomprehension or stupor, dread, yearning, recognition of absolute goodness. Otto justifies these claims partly by asking those of his readers who have had deeply-felt religious experiences to confirm what he says by introspection; and partly by giving examples from several religions of the expression of these emotions.

It is striking that Otto should be so confident that these methods will yield the same result—and indeed that anyone's deeply felt religious experience will be fundamentally the same as anyone else's. One might suspect that behind the confidence lies another analytic relationship, that holy, or numinous, just means *Mysterium, Tremendum Fascinans et Augustum,* and that since a religious experience is necessarily some kind of awareness of a divinity, it must involve these emotional elements. But this is *prima facie* unlikely, and Otto certainly does not argue as if it were so; rather he speaks of his thesis as of a phenomenological, i.e. empirical, discovery. He says that if we sympathetically consider the widest range of instances of 'the deepest and most fundamental element in all strong and sincerely felt religious emotion', 'we shall find that we are dealing with something for which there is only one appropriate expression, *"Mysterium Tremendum"'* (*The Idea of the Holy,* p. 12). Does he assume, or does the consideration of examples lead him to the conclusion that, all religious emotion is basically the same? It is tempting to suggest that he makes the assumption because of the philosophical background of his phenomenology. He believes (cf. pp. 163 and 164) that every man has within him the ability to know the Real, by *Ahnen,* and assumes (with what justification will be discussed below) that many men, in fact all religious men, do realize the ability, attain the knowledge. This knowledge cannot be conceptualized, but it might not seem out of the question that an indirect description could be given, and that although the context of myth and symbol would of course vary widely, the basic features of even the indirect description would be common to all such experiences. And indeed it might be expected that the surrounding positive religion of myth and symbol should reflect these basic features, while also being partially determined by purely contingent historical, geographical and social matters. Otto does not argue in *The Idea of the Holy* for this link between his philosophy and his phenomenology, but the validity of the link is for us a question of central importance. What are the possible relationships between a comprehensive philosophical system such as Otto took over from Fries, and the work of a phenomenologist of religious experience? According to the philosophy, men are capable of feeling-experiences which provide contact with an absolute reality, which can otherwise be described only negatively. Should the work of a phenomenologist who accepts this philosophy be affected by his acceptance; does such a philosophy have phenomenological implications?

It seems clear to me that there is no straightforward logical implication from Fries's philosophical thesis to any phenomenological thesis. For if the philosophical thesis confines itself to stating that men have the *ability* to feel the reality of the Ideas, this leaves quite open the possibility that no men in fact realize this ability; and *a fortiori* leaves open the possibility that no religious organization incorporates its realization, that nothing which might be called a *religious* experience, i.e. one which takes place or is interpreted in a religious context, is identifiable with *Ahnung.* So it certainly does not follow from Fries's metaphysics that *all* religions are based on the same fundamental experience; all the philosophical theses are of possibilities. This is what seems to me to be the true nature of the relationship between Fries's philosophy, his concept of *Ahnung,* and Otto's phenomenological thesis. But I must admit that the whole matter is puzzling and obscure. It is certainly not necessary, on Fries's system, that every man should have the experience of *Ahnung;* and strictly speaking it seems to be possible that no man has it, though certainly every man has the ability to have it. I cannot see that there are philosophical grounds for any estimate about the actual incidence of the experience. If we nevertheless assume that some or many men have the experience, we still have no justification for concluding that it lies behind any religion; and Fries's philosophy cannot be adduced in justification of the bold claim that the same experience lies behind all (true) religions. So in this case at least acceptance of a philosophical position should not predetermine any phenomenological positions.

Would it be justifiable to generalize from this case; or could there be philosophical positions which did make particular phenomenological findings necessary? I do not know the answer to the most general question; but it would seem that attempts to predict *a priori* the nature of religious experience would always have difficulty in dealing with the fact that for any type of actual religious experience, there are some people who have it, and some or many who do not.

It does seem though that Otto's phenomenology is (illegitimately) influenced by his philosophy. In the final chapter of *The Philosophy of Religion* there is an attempt to defend his position on this matter. Otto summarizes Fries's philosophy, and says 'in all these respects this philosophy reveals the disposition to religion in the spirit of man in general, the hidden source of all its manifestations in history, the ground for its claim to be true, to be indeed the supreme and ultimate Truth' (*The Philosophy of Religion,* p. 223). He goes on to describe the true Science of Religion, which will have 'two separate starting-points and will follow two paths, at first different, which, however, lead to each other and must meet at last' (*The Philosophy of Religion,* p. 224). The first of these paths is the 'empirico-inductive' investigation of religions which will secure a 'conception of the properties, character, and real nature of Religion as a whole'. The focal point in this investigation will be Religious Experience, and this at its highest level, namely that of Conversion. The other path is the Critique of Reason leading to a metaphysic of religion. But how can Otto claim to know that the paths will meet? My suggestion is that this is only because he builds assumptions taken from his philosophical position into his supposedly empirico-inductive investigation, i.e. he *assumes* a phenomenological unity based on religious experience, and considers that he merely has to find out its nature. In summary, to share Otto's confidence about the fundamental unity of all religious experience and hence basically of all religion, we must first adopt his Friesian metaphysics, and second provide the argument Otto omits, to show that the paths must meet. Only then could we justify the identification of Friesian knowledge of the absolute with the historical phenomena of religious experience.

What remains if we do not allow ourselves these supports? What we have is a phenomenological hypothesis, which needs but does not in *The Idea of the Holy* get thorough empirico-inductive support: that all religions as a matter of fact importantly involve not quasi-perceptual experiences but the emotions of dread, stupor etc. To show that these emotions occur in all religions would not be too difficult, but according to the hypothesis they occur importantly, i.e. many religious phenomena can be explained by reference to them. Otto's method, at least as presented in *The Idea of the Holy* is first to ascertain what the basic emotions are, and then to confirm the hypothesis by looking for examples in some religions. Of course looking for positive instances is a completely inadequate way of testing a hypothesis.

I am sure that one of the reasons why Otto's work has been so influential is that the hypothesis is a good one—and, in so far as it refers to the emotion of dread, is novel and striking. The best hypotheses are not necessarily those which turn out to be true, but may be those which lead to important new research. It does seem to throw new light on some religions to acknowledge that the divinity is seen as aweful as well as benevolent. But this provides us with no reason to believe that religions necessarily contain these elements. It should also be clearly understood that the numinous experience here referred to is one of emotion; i.e. of reaction to one's situation as one understands it. It leaves quite open the problem of explaining how people come to believe that their situation is awe-inspiring etc. In some cases this belief may derive from an overwhelming experience of the actual presence of God, as in examples given by William James: *The Varieties of Religious Experience,* Lectures 3 and 8 to 10 (see *The Idea of the Holy,* p. 38); its origin in other cases is a matter for phenomenological research i.e. research into institutionalized reasons for belief. (If reference is made to conversion, surely the idea of conversion as a decision, a God-given change of heart, is at least as widespread as the type of conversion exemplified by Paul's vision on the Damascus road.)

If the Phenomenological Theses, as now distinguished and described, are thus separated from any built-in philosophical assumptions, what can be said about their relation to the Philosophical Thesis? I have already discussed the difficulty of inferring from a philosophical position such as Fries's to particular theses in the phenomenology of religious experience; and it seems obvious on the other hand that whatever the phenomenologist may find about religious experience, this can have no effect on a philosophical position established by *a priori* arguments. (But see on this the discussion below about the holy as an *a priori* category.) But it does seem likely that phenomenological findings could reflect on the Link Thesis, identifying philosophical with phenomenological concepts, and in our present case *Ahnung* with religious experience. For the plausibility of any Link Thesis must surely rest on some kind of formal similarity to the two concepts to be linked. Does this formal similarity exist in the present case? The important question for Fries is whether there is a formal similarity between *Ahnung* as he describes it, and religious experience as it actually is. But an answer to this question must wait on the production of a comprehensive and well-grounded phenomenology of religious experience, such as we do not get from Otto. If we are concerned though with coherence of Otto's Theory, we must ask about the relation between Fries's *Ahnung* and Otto's experience of the numinous. The general description of *Ahnung* is as an aesthetic experience; a feeling which unites material and formal apperception, immediate knowledge of the world of phenomena and that immediate knowledge which is the province of reason. Thus the world is seen as one, and as necessary. On this description, *Ahnung* may well seem similar to a mystical experience, in which the classifications and contingencies of

the phenomenal world disappear. This realization of the unity of transcendental apperception as a whole would be quite distinct from experience of a numen, separated by an infinite and aweful gulf from the earthly being who experience him.

Fries also offers, though, a more detailed description of *Ahnung.* As formal apperception is described in terms of the categories, schematized absolutely and according to the Idea of absolute worth (see pp. 163 and 164), so there can be said to be three basic types of *Ahnung,* or religious emotion, corresponding to the three basic principles of the philosophy of religion (p. 164). The three emotions are enthusiasm at one's place as a free agent in the world, submission to one's fate in the world, and trust in or devotion to eternal goodness as being the ultimate law of reality. Could these emotional reactions to the world seen as a whole be identified with numinous experience? Again I think one must say that they do not reflect the 'dualism' of numinous experience as Otto describes it; the sense of, or emotional reaction to belief in, the numen as a distinct entity. It may be remembered that Divinity was introduced into Fries's system as the Ideal schematization of the metaphysical category of reciprocity; and as such was described as the 'principle of absolute community'. This is one possible interpretation of the real meaning of theism, but it is surely not to such an interpretation that one would be led by numinous experience.

I do not wish to place too much reliance on my interpretation of the subtleties of Fries's position; but if I am right it would seem that Otto exaggerated the suitability of Fries's philosophy for his purposes. I have already argued that Fries's system is not such that phenomenological theses about religious experience can be *derived* from it; it now seems that it does not even lend itself to the weaker relation of formal similarity with Otto's phenomenology of religious experience. It may be said that Otto obviously realized this when writing *The Idea of the Holy,* and this is why that book contains so few explicit references to Fries. But in that case, if the work assumes no philosophical position, it is the more obvious that the grounding for its phenomenological theses is quite inadequate. I am myself in little doubt that Otto took for granted, in writing *The Idea of the Holy,* what he conceived to be the main outlines of Fries's system.

A further aspect of the relation between philosophy and phenomenology in Otto's thought comes out in chapters 14 to 17 of *The Idea of the Holy,* where he argues that the holy is an *a priori* category. He has already argued that in the process of historical development the numinous emotions tend to become rationalized; developed and expressed in metaphysical and moral terms. (The concept of the holy contains both the non-rational numinous and its rationalizations.) This distinction is a clear reference to the relation in Fries between the conceptual but purely negative Ideas, i.e. the categories schematized according to the principle of completed infinity, and further the principle of absolute worth; and the non-conceptual experience of *Ahnung.* In the chapters now under consideration Otto states that both the rational and non-rational components of the category of the holy are *a priori.* In the case of the rational element, the meaning is that the Ideas have their origin in the pure reason. But Otto claims that something similar can be said of the numinous; 'It issues from the deepest foundation of cognitive apprehension that the soul possesses' (p. 117). 'The proof that in the numinous we have to deal with purely *a priori* cognitive elements is to be reached by introspection and a critical examination of reason such as Kant instituted' *(ibid.).* The last phrase obviously refers to Fries's philosophy; Otto is asserting the identification of *Ahnung* and numinous experience, implying that numinous experience provides a kind of knowledge of absolute and necessary reality. But the reference to introspection suggests that the claim has a phenomenological significance. 'We find . . . involved in the numinous experience, beliefs and feelings qualitatively different from anything that "natural" sense perception is capable of giving us' *(ibid.).* The wording is not entirely clear, but it seems very probable that this 'finding' is an empirical, that is a phenomenological, finding. Taken in this way, Otto's claim is certainly and perhaps obviously true. But Otto wishes to argue from this phenomenological premiss to the philosophical thesis that the numinous experience is *a priori:* hence some philosophical system which allows for this, as Fries's does, must be true; and, further, some non-reductive *explanation* of numinous experience must be accepted. It is because of this last claim that it has sometimes been argued that Otto's phenomenological discoveries establish the 'autonomy' of religion; this presumably means that religion cannot be explained away, accounted for in non-religious terms. (See for example Jan de Vries's comments on Otto in his *The Study of Religion* (New York, 1967).) Statements about the autonomy of religion would seem to be in the field of Theories of Religion, as I explained that term at the beginning of this paper. It would be untrue to say that Otto allows the whole argument for his Theory of Religion to rest on his concept of numinous experience taken as a phenomenological discovery; but he certainly wants it to bear some of the weight in *The Idea of the Holy,* where his reliance on Fries's philosophy does not come into the open. This theme appears in chapters 16 and 17 of *The Idea of the Holy;* in the primitive phases of religion we can distinguish between what is not yet real religion, and can be given a purely natural explanation, and real religion, which bears at least in part the characteristics of the numinous, and cannot be so explained, but bears witness to an *a priori* predisposition in man. Also in chapter 5 of *The Idea of the Holy,* where Otto argues against any kind of evolutionism which explains religion in terms of its non-religious origins, saying that the one 'evolved out of' the other. 'It is just the same with the feeling of the numinous as with that of moral obligation. It too is not to be derived from any other feeling, and is in this sense "unevolvable". It is a content of feeling that is qualitatively *sui generis*' (p. 45). The numinous, and therefore religion, is 'non-natural' (to use a term from

moral philosophy). A further argument in this direction, which Otto hints at but does not develop, is that the terms used to describe religious emotions are *sui generis,* and therefore cannot be reduced to terms for analogous but natural emotions, cannot indeed be understood by people who have not experienced the emotions. Such a person cannot for example understand the fundamental difference between 'religious dread' and 'fear'. That is, as a matter of observable fact, some words are comprehensible only to a certain class of people, those who have experienced the religious emotions. Therefore these emotions cannot be reduced to, explained in terms of, experiences which are available to anyone. Therefore these special emotions cannot have an explanation in terms of wholly non-religious categories. The proponent of such an argument would find it difficult to substantiate its original premiss. If a non-believer said he did understand the religious terms, and a believer denied that this was possible for the non-believer, it seems that the result of any test of understanding could be open to the same double interpretation. On the more general issue, it seems likely that it is only the phenomena under a certain description, i.e. a theory-laden description, which compel a certain type of explanation; if the reporting is done by a phenomenologist, which it is *ex hypothesi* in this argument, he should be able to find some other description not so laden. So if Otto's claim is to argue *a priori* from a phenomenological thesis to a Theory of Religion—i.e. that religious experience must be explained by reference to some non-natural entity—then his original thesis was not phenomenological, because not neutral. The issue then retreats to 'Is phenomenology, i.e., the neutral description of religious phenomena, always possible?' This is not an issue I know how to deal with at present. (These large questions are not raised if the inference from the phenomena to the level of Theory of Religion does not claim to be *a priori.* Thus one might for example assess the adequacy of a psycho-analytic explanation of religion in the normal scientific way, seeing whether it was sufficiently powerful, comprehensive, detailed, led to fruitful new hypotheses etc. If this is possible, one might argue that it was possible to assess in the same kind of way the Theory-hypothesis that religious phenomena are due to the action of some Transcendent being; numinous experiences are explained as being a meeting with a numen. But of course the question of the possibility of such an enterprise, testing scientifically the adequacy of what would amount to theological claims, is another large and difficult issue, beyond the scope of this paper.)

I have said that in the first part of *The Idea of the Holy* Otto puts forward two phenomenological theses; one that numinous experience is the universal way of coming to believe in (which is equal to or at least involves coming to believe in the existence of) divinities; and the other, more plausible, that people who do believe in gods always find them *Mysterium, Tremendum Fascinans et Augustum,* i.e. they *react* to their belief with the emotions of dread etc. In his chapter 'Manifestations of the "Holy" and the faculty of "Divination" ' Otto discusses what I have called earthly gods. Here the question is not whether they exist, but whether they are divine. Otto's second thesis extends easily to these cases; the first thesis, discussed above as it applies to belief in gods thought to be incorporeal, beyond normal experience, must be modified before it can apply to belief in gods who can be seen and touched in the normal way. One may bring the two types of case together, by saying that behind every earthly god stands a non-earthly one. This is one of the views Otto holds, but he also makes some use of a more sophisticated thesis, that the attribution of holiness to earthly beings is a kind of interpretative evaluation or judgement. This second view, which seems on the surface to accord with the Friesian talk of *Ahnung* as an aesthetic judgement, whereby some earthly phenomenon is seen as partaking in the unity of absolute reality, does raise problems about the status of numinous experience. If attributing divinity to an earthly being is the result of evaluative judgement on our part, this is something we do; but if it is the result of a numinous experience this would seem to be something that happens to us—analogous to the case of the shaman who is possessed by the deity. Also, to assert that a hill is beautiful is not to assert the existence of anything apart from the hill; whereas, as we have seen, a numinous experience typically does bring the experiencer to belief in an extra being. Does Otto's emphasis on the analogy with aesthetics constitute a tentative adoption of the view that to see an earthly being as holy is really a matter of according it paradigmatic significance? This would give a straightforward sense to his talk of 'evaluation'. I think that Otto is in two minds about whether to allow the possibility that a man can make up his mind to attribute holiness to an earthly being. He does very often use the analogy of aesthetic judgement; and extends the analogy to the history of religion, which he describes as like the development or maturation of aesthetic taste. In both the aesthetic and the religious contexts, Otto takes what may be called an intuitionist line; but a sophisticated one, which allows for the possibility of disagreement. At primitive stages of their development, people, and peoples (Otto here adheres to the recapitulation theory) can mistake the ugly for the beautiful, the merely frightening or incomprehensible for the aweful and mysterious. But as their taste matures, people's views, in both spheres, aesthetic and religious, will tend more and more to coincide. One can see these various theses coming together in examples Otto gives of the attribution of holiness to the earthly. Thus e.g. the recognition of Jesus as holy arises from the contemplation of the history of Israel leading up to the Incarnation, and of the life-work of Jesus. Whoever contemplates the history 'must feel the stirrings of an intimation that something Eternal is there . . . The impression is simply irresistible' (*The Idea of the Holy,* p. 174). Again 'whoever goes on to consider all this [the life and death of Jesus] must inevitably conclude "That is godlike and divine; that is verily Holiness" ' *(ibid.).* Such passages can bear more than one interpretation:

(1) that standing behind the earthly events is a God 'out there', who is indirectly experienced through the events;

(2) that the events themselves are holy—God is known in, not merely through his actions—he is identified as the god of Abraham, etc.; this is close to saying that the stories have the significance of myths.

My analysis of Otto's situation here is this; Fries's philosophy does provide, in *Ahnung,* an aesthetic-type judgement which is also a knowledge of reality, of what Fries refers to as transcendental apperception. But as we have seen, if this thesis is to be translated into religious terms, it fits best a mystical religion, in which the theology is basically negative. Positive religion is allowed in only as attempts, guided not by reason but by good taste, to express the inexpressible. This does not really support the phenomenology of the first part of the book, for it cannot explain the great emphasis placed on the emotions of dread, etc.; but Fries's transcendental idealism, the view that the earthly world is but an appearance, behind which stands true reality, does accord, although only superficially, with the view that in numinous experience man can come into contact with a numen, beyond the reach of normal perceptual experience. In the chapters I have just been considering Otto has to deal with a type of religion in which stories about earthly particularities are of central importance—are taken as paradigmatic, as telling of the true structure of life etc. It is natural to say that a man who sees a story in this way is evaluating it, making a judgement about it. But any relation between this judgement and Fries's aesthetic judgement is only superficial; Fries's philosophy does not fit a religion in which the details of earthly events are of the most profound religious significance. Otto half realizes this, and does sensitively describe the appropriate type of religious judgement; but at the same time he wishes to hold on to the transcendentalism of the first part of his book. Once more, his initial philosophical commitment enforces a phenomenological uniformity which is not supported by true phenomenological investigation.

It remains to make explicit the second Link Thesis; that philosophical truth, metaphysical reality as described by Fries, can be identified with the truth of religion. This is closely related to Otto's views about the evolution of religion; taken together with his other theses it implies that religions approach the truth—i.e. are true as religions—in so far as they clearly obey the promptings of the numinous experience (identified with *Ahnung*). As I have mentioned, Otto speaks also of a related path to truth, that of the rationalization of the elements of numinous experience; their translation into metaphysical and moral conceptual structures. The highest religion is that which is furthest developed in both these respects, i.e. Christianity. The philosophical backing for the idea of rationalization is the deduction by the intellect of the categories, schematized according to completed infinity and absolute worth. This commitment to statements about religious truth does not of course follow from Otto's phenomenological theses, which must be neutral. Nor is it implied by his acceptance of evolutionism as such; the term does not imply that any particular religion is true, it just means that one stage in the history of religion is determined by the previous one. But if we accepted Fries's philosophy, and were able to accept the truth of Otto's phenomenological claims and their alleged links with the philosophy, would we thereby have accepted his statements about religious truth? The question is a special case of the problem about the relation between the god of the philosophers and the god of religions. The relation between metaphysical and religious truth obviously depends on the nature of religion. Otto has attempted, though perhaps with only limited success, to describe religion in such a way that it can be seen to accord with, have the same structure as, and therefore be identifiable with, Fries's metaphysics. He could therefore not consistently refrain from identifying religious with metaphysical truth. But there are many cracks in Otto's structure; it is by no means clear, from what can be rescued from his phenomenology, that it is proper to see the history of religion as a groping towards this kind of truth. Indeed if one abandons evolutionism there is little reason to assume that all religions are alike in this matter—some may properly be seen on a metaphysical model, others as moral systems; others again as celebrations of social structure. If this pluralism were true, Theories of Religion would have to be much smaller and less courageous affairs than Otto's enterprise.

I have been mainly concerned with the relation between philosophy and phenomenology in Otto's work. I have argued that his phenomenological hypotheses are no more than hypotheses; he gives them a higher status because he wrongly thinks they can be derived, at least in their broad outlines, from the philosophical system he takes over from Fries. He also, on occasion (in the chapters on the numinous as an *a priori* category) argues from phenomenology to philosophy; this is equally illegitimate. It seems to me further that Fries's *Ahnung* and Otto's numinous experience are not sufficiently similar for them to be plausibly identified in a Link Thesis. I have also argued that when Otto's phenomenology of religious experience is, as it should be, disentangled from his philosophy of religion, it does not as phenomenology have the unity he imputes to it; it consists rather of several separable theses. Taken as hypotheses, these are in varying degrees plausible and fruitful. The best of them are very much worth pursuing; but none can be taken as having been established by Otto.

NOTES

[1] I am much indebted to my colleagues in the Department of Philosophy, University of Dundee, for their comments on the first draft of this paper.

[2] *The Idea of the Holy,* trans. J. W. Harvey (O.U.P. third impression, 1925).

[3] *The Philosophy of Religion Based on Kant and Fries,* trans. E. B. Dicker (London, 1931).

[4] See for example Ninian Smart, *The Phenomenon of Religion* (London, 1973) and Michael Pye, *Comparative Religion* (Newton Abbot, 1972).

[5] I am afraid that my knowledge of Fries comes not from his own writings, none of which has, as far as I know, been translated into English, but from Otto's *The Philosophy of Religion* and, much more importantly, from Leonard Nelson, *Progress and Regress in Philosophy,* trans. Humphrey Palmer (Oxford, 1971). The following account will be obscure to readers who are not acquainted with Kant's first *Critique,* but seems to me to be necessary to a proper understanding of Otto.

[6] The phrase 'sense of presence' is unfortunately ambiguous in a relevant way; it may mean a quasi-perceptual feeling that God is present, or merely a *belief,* of indeterminate origin, that God is present.

## Donald S. Lopez, Jr. (essay date 1979)

SOURCE: "Approaching the Numinous: Rudolf Otto and Tibetan Tantra," in *Philosophy East and West,* Vol. 29, No. 4, October, 1979, pp. 467-76.

[*In the following essay, Lopez compares Otto's idea of the numinous with that of Tibetan Buddhist scholars, particularly the "mysterium tremendum."*]

In Oriental art there may be no more evocative portrayal of what Rudolf Otto calls the *mysterium tremendum* than the wrathful deities of Tibetan Tantric Buddhism. Fearful in form, wreathed in flames, adorned with garlands of human heads, and brandishing dagger and skull-cup, their painted images conjure the feelings of dread and fascination which Otto describes in *The Idea of the Holy.* In this seminal work, he sets out to describe the central element of religious experience such that there is "no religion in which it does not live as the real innermost core, and without it no religion would be worthy of the name."[1]

This article will be an inquiry into whether the holy, described as *mysterium tremendum,* does indeed stand as the core of the tantric path of Tibetan Buddhism and will be a comparison of the methods of approaching the holy or "numinous" as set forth by Otto and Tibetan scholars. The presentation of tantra given here will follow that of the Gelukba order of Tibetan Buddhism, relying especially on the writings of Tsong-ka-pa (1357-1419), its founder.

In *The Idea of the Holy* Otto rejects the views held by many psychologists, historians of religion, philosophers, and anthropologists that religion "is a fact in nature and, to be understood, must be seen as a product of the same laws of nature that determine other natural phenomena."[2] Nor does he see religion, as does Clifford Geertz, as a system of conceptions formulated by man in response to ignorance, pain, and injustice.[3]

Rather, Otto sees religion as a *sui generis* category, which stands above all natural processes and whose essence is irreducible and unevolvable. He writes that "if there is any single domain of human experience that presents us with something unmistakably specific and unique, peculiar to itself, assuredly it is that of religious life."[4] This essence he calls the "numinous," which is the object of religious experience, and which "we cannot but feel"[5] for "it eludes the conceptual way of thinking."[6]

Throughout Otto draws sharp distinctions between the natural and the supernatural and between the rational and the nonrational. The "numinous" is not a natural phenomenon and our knowledge of it cannot be gained empirically; instead, "it issues from the deepest foundation of cognitive apprehension that the soul possesses, and though it of course comes into being in and amid sensory data and empirical material of the natural world and cannot anticipate or dispense with those, yet it does not arise *out of* them, but only *by their means*."[7] Further, the numinous is nonrational and "completely eludes apprehension in terms of concepts"[8] and "can only be suggested by means of the special way in which it is reflected in the mind in terms of feeling."[9]

It is Otto's view that religion cannot be fully understood through reason and rational thought. To support his claim, he looks not to scripture or theological treatise, but instead finds his affinity in the words of the mystics, Weber's "religious virtuosos," because they stress "the non-rational or suprarational elements in religion."[10]

The numinous cannot be known through ratiocination; awareness of it comes only through the feelings it evokes. Consequently, Otto devotes a great part of *The Idea of the Holy* to a description of these feelings, the first of which centers in the subject's sense of creature-consciousness, "the emotion of a creature, submerged and overwhelmed by its own nothingness in contrast to that which is supreme above all creatures."[11] It is a recognition of one's insignificance in the face of the absolute, exemplified by Arjuna's response to the theophany in the eleventh chapter of the *Bhagavad-gītā.*

Next Otto considers the experience of the *mysterium tremendum,* which carries with it a complex of feelings, with *mysterium* denoting "that which is hidden and esoteric, that which is beyond conception or understanding, extraordinary and unfamiliar."[12] *Tremendum* evokes a "peculiar dread" of something uncanny, aweful, weird, eerie, and absolutely unapproachable, causing the flesh to creep. Throughout his description, Otto stresses that although these feelings may have analogs among "natural" moments of consciousness, there is a qualitative difference between them. For example, he characterizes the dread of the

*tremendum* as something other than natural fear, "a terror fraught with an inward shuddering such as not even the most menacing and overpowering created thing can instil."[13] As the object of these feelings, the numinous is endowed with might, power, transcendence, absolute overpoweringness, majesty, and a "plenitude of being" surpassing any created thing. It has urgency, energy, passion, and emotional temper. Because it is that "which is quite beyond the sphere of the usual, the intelligible, and the familiar,"[14] it is called "the wholly other" which brings forth feelings of wonder, amazement, and astonishment. The numinous produces a captivating attraction in one sensitive to it—the element of fascination. Otto finds these feeling-responses to be common to all forms of mysticism.

Not only does he enumerate these various reactions to the numinous, he also emphatically contends that these feelings are the only media through which the numinous, or reality, can be known. Words, concepts, reasoning, and rational thought are incapable of producing true experience of the wholly other, which can only be "firmly grasped, thoroughly understood, and profoundly appreciated, purely in, with, and from the feeling itself."[15]

Otto traces these experiences of the numinous to the most primitive religious consciousness, where the feeling-response was one of "daemonic dread." This crude consciousness of the numinous evolved over the centuries to a more elevated and noble experience. Throughout this process of religious evolution, however, the object of these feelings remains the nonrational numinous, and the element of dread felt by the primitive savage, though superseded by other responses, "does not disappear on the highest level of all, where the worship of God is at its purest."[16] And although this process of evolution has occurred in all the great religions, it has reached its culmination in Christianity, which "stands out in complete superiority over its sister religions."[17] Thus, against all those who would see the rise of religion emanating from any number of "natural" factors, Otto holds the numinous to be "the basic factor and basic impulse underlying the entire process of religious evolution."[18]

Although Otto discounts reason as having any relation to the numinous whatsoever, he discovers a close relationship between the feeling of the numinous and aesthetic experience. He finds the feelings of the sublime, the beautiful, and the experience of music to be nonconceptual, nonrational, and wholly other, much like that of the numinous.

Weber also notes such a similarity between religion and art. However, Weber observes that for the mystic "the indubitable psychological affinity of profoundly shaking experience in art and religion can only be a symptom of the diabolical nature of art."[19] The mystic is seeking to transcend all form in order to achieve union with a reality that is beyond form. Weber perceives a contradiction between religion and art, with the result that "the more religion has emphasized either the supra-worldliness of its God or the other-worldliness of salvation, the more harshly has art been refuted."[20]

Otto on the other hand, far from refuting art, suggests that aesthetic feelings reveal the transcendent reality, that "in great art the point is reached at which we may no longer speak of the 'magical,' but rather are confronted with the numinous itself, with all its impelling power, transcending reason, expressed in sweeping lines and rhythm."[21]

Nonetheless, the numinous is a purely a priori category, underivable and irreducible. It cannot be explained but only presupposed. This numinous undergoes a process of development whereby it becomes "moralized," gaining ethical meaning through being endowed with rational qualities of absoluteness, completeness, morality, purpose, justice, goodness, and love. The wholly other numinous, having become "completely permeated and saturated" by these rational qualities, becomes what Otto calls "the holy." He finds these rational qualities also to be a priori and "not to be 'evolved' from any sort of sense perception."[22] Further, the connection of the numinous to these ethical qualities, the relation of the nonrational to the rational, is not to be derived from reasoning, but is also a priori.[23]

Finally, our capacity for experience of the numinous is a priori as well. The object of religious experience is the numinous, of which we are aware through numinous feelings. Objectively, the numinous seems to act as a stimulus for these feelings. However, from the subject's side there exists an a priori potency which allows the numinous to be experienced. This Otto calls "a hidden, substantive source, from which the religious ideas and feelings are formed, which lies in the mind independently of sense-experience."[24] It is a "primal element of our psychical nature that needs to be grasped in its uniqueness and cannot itself be explained by anything else."[25]

Despite philosophical problems that may inhere in such a wholesale attribution of the a priori category to all things religious,[26] it is important to consider Otto's purpose at this point. *The Idea of the Holy* is not intended as a philosophical treatise proving the existence of the numinous; rather it is an apology for the intuitive element of religious experience. Otto does not intend to persuade the unconvinced with his arguments. His words are offered only to kindred spirits, those whose innate capacity for the numinous has been awakened, for whom he eloquently verbalizes the experience of the holy, "the feeling which remains where the concept fails."[27] At the very outset, Otto invites the reader "to direct his mind to a moment of deeply-felt religious experience, as little as possible qualified by other forms of consciousness. Whoever cannot do this, whoever knows no such moments in his experience, is requested to read no further."[28] It is his purpose then, to "suggest this unnamed Something to the reader as far as we may, so that he may himself feel it."[29]

Thus, having stressed the intuitive aspect of religious experience, having presented numinous feeling for the sake of awakening that feeling, Otto in the end makes his appeal to feeling. The numinous is "something which the 'natural' man cannot, as such, know or even imagine,"[30] and no "intellectual, dialectical dissection or justification of such intuition is possible, nor indeed should any be attempted, for the essence most peculiar to it would be destroyed thereby."[31] Rather, the numinous must be directly experienced to be understood.

Once experienced, there need not be doubt concerning the validity of these numinous feelings for they are a priori by which Otto means that "as soon as an assertion has been clearly expressed and understood, knowledge of its truth comes into the mind with the certitude of first-hand insight."[32] In short, religious experience is autonomous, self-validating, and infallible. When the numinous feelings that Otto describes are experienced, there is immediate certainty that this is a realization of the deepest truth; religious experience "represents a perception which provides its own evidence."[33]

It is Otto's contention that the numinous and the feelings it evokes are common to all religions. To test this claim in the case of Tibetan tantra, it is first necessary to identify the numinous element in Buddhism.

According to the Prāsangika-Mādhyamika school, the highest system of tenets in Tibet, every object of knowledge, permanent or impermanent, is a phenomenon (*dharma*). Even the highest nature of an object, its emptiness, is a phenomenon. Taking phenomena in this sense, there are no noumena apart from phenomena in Buddhism, and our inquiry is cut short.

However, if we take the view found in Western metaphysics that phenomena refer to sense objects and that "behind the phenomena which present themselves in everyday experience, there lie realities whose existence and properties can be established only by the use of the intellect and which can hence be described as noumena,"[34] we then have a distinction between noumena and phenomena that can be applied to the Prāsangika-Mādhyamika view. That is, impermanent things or products (*samskrta*), the appearing objects of direct perception (*pratyaksa*), are phenomena and those objects which initially must be known through relying on inference (*anumāna*) are noumena.[35] For the purpose of comparison with Otto, we may consider only the most important of such objects—emptinesses (*śūnyatā*)—the ultimate truths (*paramārthasatya*) of the Prāsangika-Mādhyamika system, the realization of which leads to liberation from cyclic existence (*samsāra*). Otto identifies emptiness as the numinous element in Buddhism, writing that "the 'void' [emptiness] of the eastern, like the 'nothing' of the western, mystic is a numinous ideogram of the 'wholly other.'"[36]

An emptiness, according to Prāsangika, is an object's lack of inherent existence (*svabhāva-siddhi);* and when it is realized "what appears to the mind is a clear vacuity accompanied by the mere thought, 'These concrete things as they now appear to our minds do not exist at all.'"[37] In the direct realization of emptiness, the mind and emptiness are said to be mixed like fresh water poured into fresh water.[38]

Since Buddhism is an atheistic religion in the sense that it denies the existence of a preexistent creator deity, the experience of the numinous does not carry with it the feeling of creature-consciousness which Otto describes.[39] Emptiness is a mere negative, a lack of a falsely conceived predicate of existence.[40]

Reference is made in Prāsaṅgika to a fear which arises in the practice of emptiness. It is said that a person with a slight understanding of emptiness becomes fearful because "the phenomenon suddenly appears to his mind as not existing at all."[41] When emptiness is realized directly, however, all fear is dispelled because the source of fear—the conception of true existence—has disappeared. This fear bears little resemblance to the dread and terror that Otto describes which produces creeping flesh and which never disappears, even at the highest level of mystical experience.

Emptiness is neither shrouded in mystery, nor is it a "numinous ideogram of the wholly other."[42] An emptiness is not other than the phenomenon it qualifies in that they are of the same entity. Through the practice of the path, emptiness can be realized in a direct, nonconceptual, nondualistic experience free of doubt and mystery.[43]

Otto holds the mysterious to be an essential attribute of religious experience and for support points to a "mode of manifestation that in every religion occupies a foremost and extraordinary place,"[44] namely, miracle. Although the settings and circumstances of many Buddhist *sūtras,* especially in the Mahāyāna, may be termed magical or miraculous, miracles are not a central teaching technique of Buddha.

> Buddhas neither wash sins away with water
> Nor remove beings' suffering with their hands
> Nor transfer their realizations to others; beings
> Are freed through the teaching of the truth, the
> 　nature of things.[45]

Regarding miracles, it is noteworthy to compare the reactions of Christ and Buddha in a similar situation—being request to restore the life of a dead child. Christ resurrected Jairus' daughter,[46] while Buddha, in the Parable of the Mustard Seed,[47] used the opportunity to teach the mother of the child the all-pervasive nature of suffering. In both cases, it can be assumed that one result was that witnesses were inspired to follow the teaching, although the techniques of the two teachers were quite different.

Weber notes a more general difference in the style of teaching of Buddha as compared to those of Jesus and Muhammad:

Neither the short parable, the ironic dismissal, or the pathetic penitential sermon of the Galilean prophet, nor the address resting on visions of the Arabic holy leader find any sort of parallels to the lectures and conversations which seem to have constituted the true form of Buddha's activity. They address themselves purely to the intellect and affected the quiet, sober judgement detached from all internal excitement; their factual manner exhausts the topic always in systematic dialectical fashion.[48]

The emphasis on reason and analysis which Weber observes in the Theravāda *suttas* is also an essential element in the tantric path. In Tsong-kha-pa's major work on tantra, *The Great Exposition of Secret Mantra,* he explains that before beginning practice one must have firm conviction that the system one has chosen to follow is correct. A choice between two systems is not an act of partisanship but should be based on reasoned analysis. Specifically, "the scriptures of the two systems are what are to be analysed to find which does or does not bear the truth; thus, it would not be suitable to cite them as proof (of their own truth). Only reason distinguishes what is or is not true."[49]

Citation of scripture, mere belief, or respect are not suitable bases for strong conviction in a system of practice, as is evident in this quotation from the Buddha:

> Monks and scholars should
> Well analyze my words,
> Like gold (to be tested) through melting, cutting,
> 　and polishing,
> And then adopt them, but not for the sake of
> 　showing me respect.[50]

Reasoning is also essential to the practice of emptiness, through which the wisdom is generated which bestows liberation from suffering. According to Tsong-kha-pa's Ge-lug-pa order, it is a basic tenet of all three Buddhist vehicles—Hīnayāna, Perfection, and Mantra (or Tantra)—that direct realization of emptiness is gained through an initial acquaintance with an inferential realization of emptiness gained through reasoning, the basis of which is empirical. The fourteenth Dalai Lama, the current leader of the Gelukba order, states that the generation of a conceptual consciousness realizing emptiness "must depend solely on a correct reasoning. Fundamentally, therefore, the process traces back solely to a reasoning, which itself must fundamentally trace back to valid experiences common to ourselves and others."[51] Such reasonings are those set forth by Nāgārjuna in his *Treatise on the Middle Way (Madhyamakaśāstra).*

According to Ge-lug-pa, the many reasonings presented by Nāgārjuna are explicitly intended for the purpose of destroying the conception of inherent existence, the root cause of suffering. As far as this false conception forms the basis of philosophical systems, it can be said that Nāgārjuna's arguments refute the positions of those systems. Nevertheless, the fundamental purpose of reasoning in Prāsangika-Mādhyamika is to generate the wisdom which eradicates suffering and its causes. Refutations of opposing tenet systems are subsidiary.

A number of differences are thus evident between Otto and the Buddhist Ge-lug-pa position regarding the numinous element of religious experience. Otto's observations are astute when applied to the Abrahamic religions and theistic Hinduism. Yet the strength of his argument often relies on the existence of a creator deity endowed with the qualities of transcendence, majesty, and power, from whom man seeks atonement, which Otto sees as "a longing to transcend this sundering unworthiness, given with the self's existence as 'creature' and profane natural being."[52]

It is difficult to construe a parallel with Buddhism, which lacks such a creator god of whom we are creatures. The religious impulsion in Buddhism is not a priori, but a "natural" reaction to suffering and the practice of a prescribed set of teachings to escape that suffering, for the sake of oneself in Hīnayāna, for others in Mahāyāna.[53] The *dharma* is not an end in itself but, like a raft, is to be discarded upon reaching the further shore.[54]

According to Malinowski's distinction between magic and religion, one is then forced to assign Buddhism to the category of magic, which he defines as "a practical art consisting of acts which are only means to a definite end expected to follow later on"[55] and which are not ends in themselves. This is not to suggest that Buddhism is indeed magic, but rather to point out the difficulty, also encountered in Otto, in making general statements which are intended to hold true for all religions.

Returning to Otto, the more important point, however, is his contention that reasoning has no part in religious experience, where "coercion by proof and demonstration and the mistaken application of logical and juridical processes should be excluded."[56] For him, "the absolute exceeds our power to comprehend; the mysterious wholly eludes."[57] The nonconceptual, non-rational numinous cannot be approached with conceptuality and reason; "mysticism has nothing to do with 'reason' and 'rationality.'"[58]

According to the Ge-lug-pa position, the direct experience of emptiness, in both the *sūtra* and tantra systems, is nonconceptual. Yet without relying on reasoning and analysis, such an experience is impossible. In answer to how analysis and thought can serve as a cause for nonconceptuality, the fifth Dalai Lama (1617-1682) cites the *Kāśyapa Chapter Sūtra (Kāśyapa-parivarta):* "Kāshyapa, it is thus: For example, fire arises when the wind rubs two branches together. Once the fire has arisen, the two branches are burned. Just so Kāshyapa, if you have the correct analytical intellect, a superior's faculty of wisdom is generated. Through its generation,

the correct analytical intellect is consumed."[59] That is, conceptual thought can lead to experience of the nonconceptual, that which is beyond thought.

Reasoning alone, however, is not sufficient; the process of insight is not merely an intellectual exercise. Reasoning is an essential element of wisdom, the third element in the triad of ethics *(śīla),* meditative stabilization *(samādhi),* and wisdom *(prajñā),* all of which are necessary for realization of emptiness. For example, a *bodhisattva* of the *sūtra* system must engage in limitless forms of the six perfections *(pāramitā)*—giving, ethics, patience, effort, concentration, and wisdom—over many aeons in order to accumulate the merit which will empower his mind to penetrate emptiness and eventually overcome all obstructions.[60] In the tantra system, a special technique—deity yoga—is taught which allows this accumulation of merit to proceed more quickly.[61] Thus, the process of reasoning must be conjoined with ethical and meditative practices to yield realization of emptiness.

Reasoning must be used because emptiness is a hidden phenomenon *(parokṣa),* unable to appear to direct perception without initially depending on reasoning.[62] For Otto too, the numinous is hidden in the sense that it is something "which has no place in our scheme of reality but belongs to an absolutely different one, and which at the same time arouses an irrepressible interest in the mind."[63] For him, reasoning cannot be the key to the experience of the numinous because "our knowledge has certain irremovable limits."[64]

We find then, two different approaches to this hidden numinous, inaccessible to ordinary sense perception. For the Ge-lug-pas, the process of reasoning and analysis leads to the experience of reality. For Rudolf Otto, reasoning must be discarded, for reality—the holy—is only to be known through feeling.

NOTES

[1] Rudolf Otto, *The Idea of the Holy,* trans. John W. Harvey (London: Oxford University Press, 1976), p. 6.

[2] Anthony F. C. Wallace, *Religion: An Anthropological View* (New York: Random House, 1966), p. vi.

[3] Clifford Geertz, "Religion as a Cultural System," in *Reader in Comparative Religion: An Anthropological Approach,* ed. William A. Lessa and Evon Z. Vogt, 3d ed. (New York: Harper and Row, 1972), pp. 171-174.

[4] Otto, p. 4.

[5] Ibid., p. 5.

[6] Ibid., p. 2.

[7] Ibid., p. 113.

[8] Ibid., p. 5.

[9] Ibid., p. 12.

[10] Ibid., p. 22.

[11] Ibid., p. 10.

[12] Ibid., p. 13.

[13] Ibid., p. 14.

[14] Ibid., p. 26.

[15] Ibid., p. 34.

[16] Ibid., p. 17.

[17] Ibid., p. 142.

[18] Ibid., p. 15.

[19] Max Weber, "Religious Rejections of the World and their Directions," in *From Max Weber: Essays in Sociology,* ed. and trans. Hans H. Gerth and C. Wright Mills (New York: Oxford University Press, 1976), p. 342.

[20] Ibid., p. 343.

[21] Otto, p. 67.

[22] Ibid., p. 112.

[23] Wach notes that critics have found this to be the weakest element in Otto's presentation. See Joachim Wach, *Types of Religious Experience Christian and Non-Christian* (Chicago, Illinois: University of Chicago Press, 1951), p. 222. For an analysis of this relationship between the numinous and morality and of the process of "schematization" whereby the numinous becomes endowed with rational qualities see John P. Reeder, "The Relation of the Moral and the Numinous in Otto's Notion of the Holy," in *Religion and Morality: A Collection of Essays,* ed. Gene Outka and John P. Reeder, Jr. (Garden City, N.Y.: Anchor Books, 1973), pp. 255-292.

[24] Ibid., p. 114.

[25] Ibid., p. 124.

[26] *The Encyclopedia of Philosophy,* s.v. "Otto, Rudolf," by William J. Wainwright.

[27] Ibid., p. xxi.

[28] Ibid., p. 8.

[29] Ibid., p. 6.

[30] Ibid., p. 51.

[31] Ibid., p. 147.

[32] Ibid., p. 137.

[33] Joachim Wach, *Understanding and Believing: Essays by Joachim Wach,* edited with an Introduction by Joseph M. Kitagawa (Boston, Massachusetts: Harper and Row, 1968), p. 8.

[34] *The Encyclopedia of Philosophy,* s.v. "Metaphysics, Nature of," by W. H. Walsh.

[35] Geshe Lhundup Sopa and Jeffrey Hopkins, *Practice and Theory of Tibetan Buddhism* (Rider: London, 1976), p. 134.

[36] Otto, p. 30.

[37] Tenzin Gyatso, *The Buddhism of Tibet and the Key to the Middle Way* (New York: Harper and Row, 1975), p. 77.

[38] Tsong-ka-pa, *Tantra in Tibet: The Great Exposition of Secret Mantra* (London: Allen and Unwin, 1978), p. 191.

[39] Ninian Smart criticizes Otto on this point using the example of Therav da Buddhism. See Ninian Smart, *Philosophers and Religious Truth* (London: SCM Press Ltd., 1969), p. 113.

[40] Tenzin Gyatso, p. 77.

[41] Ten-dar-hla-ram-pa (bsTan-dar-lha-ram-pa), *A Presentation of the Lack of One and Many, an Elimination of Error Collected from the Ocean of Good Explanations (Geig du bral gyi rnam gzhag legs bshad rgya mtsho las btus pa'i 'khrul spong bdud rtsi'i gzegs ma)* (Lhasa: Great Press at the base of the Potala, Fire Dog Male year of the sixteenth cycle), blockprint of 43 folios, pp. 3a-3b.

[42] Otto, p. 30.

[43] Tsong-kha-pa, pp. 191-192.

[44] Otto, p. 63.

[45] Kensur Lekden, *Meditations of a Tibetan Tantric Abbot,* trans. and ed. Jeffrey Hopkins (Dharamsala, India: Library of Tibetan Works and Archives, 1974), p. 109.

[46] Mark 5:21-43.

[47] *Sutta Nipāta,* trans. V. Fausböll, in *Sacred Books of the East* (Oxford, 1881), Vol. 10, pt. 2, pp. 11-15.

[48] Max Weber, *The Religion of India: The Sociology of Hinduism and Buddhism,* trans. and ed. Hans H. Gerth and Don Martindale (New York: The Free Press, 1967), p. 225.

[49] Tsong-kha-po, p. 87.

[50] Tenzin Gyatso, p. 55.

[51] Ibid., pp. 55-56.

[52] Otto, p. 55.

[53] Tenzin Gyatso, pp. 28-29.

[54] *Middle Length Sayings (Majjhima-Nikāya),* trans. I. B. Horner, Pali Text Society Translation Series, No. 29 (London: The Pali Text Society, 1976), 1:173-74.

[55] Bronislaw Malinowski, *Magic, Science and Religion and Other Essays* (New York: Anchor Books, 1954), p. 88.

[56] Otto, p. 145.

[57] Ibid., p. 141.

[58] Ibid., p. 4.

[59] The Fifth Salai Lama, *The Practice of Emptiness,* trans. Jeffrey Hopkins (Dharamsala, India: Library of Tibetan Works and Archives, 1974), p. 21.

[60] Na-wang-pel-den (Ngag-dbang-dpal-ldan), *Presentation of the Grounds and Paths of the Four Great Secret Tantra Sets (gSang chen rgyud sde bzhi'i sa lam gyi rnam gzhag rgyud gzhung gsal byed)* (modern blockprint, rGyud smad par khang, date and place of publication not given), pp. 7a3-8a1.

[61] Tsong-kha-pa, p. 60.

[62] Ibid., p. 32.

[63] Otto, p. 29.

[64] Ibid., p. 59.

**Philip C. Almond (essay date 1984)**

SOURCE: "The Context of Otto's Thought," in *Rudolf Otto: An Introduction to His Philosophical Theology,* The University of North Carolina Press, No. 1984, pp. 26-54.

[*In the following essay, Almond explains major influences on Otto's thought.*]

*THE RATIONAL AND THE NONRATIONAL*

In Otto's mature philosophy, religions are viewed as consisting of both rational and nonrational elements. While religions have to do with theoretical and moral ideas, they are not finally dependent on these. Rather, these rational components are ultimately referrable to an object or "subject" that can only be apprehended in a nonrational "unique original feeling-response"[1] that is the core of all religions. Otto, standing squarely within the nineteenth-century tradition of the quest for the essence of religion, finds it partly in a nonrational core, and this is constituted by a specific and unique kind of experience: the numinous experience. We shall return to what Otto means by "nonrational," "original feeling-response," "numinous," and so on. For the moment, it suffices to note that the clarification of the core of religion, and of its connection to religion's rational factors, is the overall aim of *Das Heilige,* and indeed, of Otto's work as a whole.[2]

Those who see Otto as an irrationalist are mistaken for two reasons. First, he certainly recognizes the place and validity of rational thought in religion, but (and this is crucial) *only* insofar as this is related to religion's nonrational core, and insofar as this is recognized as deriving from it. For example: "we count this the very mark and criterion of a religion's high rank and superior value—that it should have no lack of *conceptions* about God; that it should admit knowledge—the knowledge that comes by faith—of the transcendent in terms of conceptual thought."[3] The harmony between rational and nonrational factors in religions is the central means by which their relative rank may be determined.

Second, for Otto, the rational defense of religion is a necessary prelude to any consideration of its nonrational essence. In the foreword to the English edition of *Das Heilige* he remarks, with reference to his *Naturalism and Religion* and *The Philosophy of Religion,* "And I feel that no one ought to concern himself with the 'Numen ineffabile' who has not already devoted assiduous and serious study to the 'Ratio aeterna.'"[4] Already in 1909, foreshadowing his work yet to come, Otto points out that the focus for a science of religion is religious experience, *and* that the philosophy of Jakob Fries is the key to its interpretation: "Our foundation in the philosophy of religion gives us a general method of interpreting this strange phenomenon, the true center of religious experience: it is the obscure knowledge of the Eternal in general and of the eternal determination of Existence, which comes to life in feeling."[5]

In short, the rational is by no means despised by Otto. The rational elements within religion are seen as significant; also, the relations of its rational and nonrational elements (and therefore religion as a whole) are illuminated by a rational metaphysical system, albeit one with an important place reserved for feeling.

Even at this point it is worth forewarning the reader that Otto's attempt to do justice to both elements in religion is a complex one, and his determination of the nature of religion in terms of a rational metaphysics is problematic. Be that as it may, Otto's attempt to effect a viable synthesis of these factors clearly arises from the various theological and philosophical influences upon this development. My primary concern in this chapter is to clarify these. Whether Otto effectively synthesizes a multiplicity of diverse currents or merely reflects willy-nilly the various spirits of his time is a question whose answer can only be broached at the conclusion of this study. Did he, *could* he, weld into a whole the concerns of those movements and individuals from which he derived his materials? This question must be kept in mind as we proceed.

### THE NONRATIONAL IN CHRISTIAN HISTORY

Otto certainly does not claim that his emphasis on the non-rational core of religion is original. Rather, he sees himself as part of a tradition which has stressed the nonrational since the beginning of Christianity, although he recognizes that this is a constant yet always threatened tradition. According to Otto, Christianity (and other religions) developed a continuing bias toward rationalization and intellectualization at the expense of the nonrational core. Orthodox Christianity, for example, in its failure to recognize the value of the nonrational, "gave to the idea of God a one-sidedly intellectualistic and rationalistic interpretation."[6] This bias occurs not only in Catholicism from the time of the great medieval scholastics, but also in Protestantism from the time of the Lutheran scholastic Johann Gerhardt (1582-1637) onward.[7]

For Otto, this interplay—even conflict—between rational and nonrational elements in religion has shown itself throughout Christian history: in the conflict between the God of the philosophers and the biblical God; in the contest between the Stoic idea of the divine impassibility and Lactantius's assertion of the incomprehensibility, majesty, and wrath of God; in Duns Scotus's emphasis on love and the will, as opposed to the Thomist stress on knowledge and reason. But it is above all in the Platonic tradition as a whole, mediated through Chrysostom, Gregory of Nyssa, Plotinus, Augustine, Pseudo-Dionysius, and Meister Eckhart, that Otto sees the continuity of tradition insuring the survival of the nonrational, at least until the time of the eighteenth-century Enlightenment. This continuity of tradition is, for Otto, grounded in Plato, who "grasps the object of religion by quite different means than those of conceptual thinking, viz. by the 'ideograms' of myth, by 'enthusiasm' or inspiration, 'eros' or love, 'mania' or the divine frenzy. He abandons the attempt to bring the object of religion into one system of knowledge with the objects of 'science' ($\epsilon\pi\iota\sigma\tau\eta\mu\eta$), i.e., reason, and it becomes something not less but greater thereby."[8]

Otto finds the nonrational essence of religion reflected especially in the life and writings of Martin Luther. If we take Otto at his word, his work on Luther brought him to a recognition of the nonrational in religion and enabled him to see Luther as part of a tradition reaching back through the German mystics[9] to the neo-Platonists and to Plato himself: "Indeed, I grew to understand the numinous and its difference from the rational in Luther's *De Servo Arbitrio* long before I identified it in the *qādôsh* of the Old Testament and in the elements of 'religious awe' in the history of religion in general."[10] Evidence for this claim can certainly be found in Otto's work on Luther, **Die Anschauung vom heiligen Geiste**

**bei Luther.** If the substantive conclusions of Otto's later works are only to be found in embryonic form here, the framework of much of his later work is nevertheless substantially in evidence. First, in spite of the Ritschlian flavor of the work, it goes beyond Ritschlianism in its assertion of the essentially nonrational depths of religion, and in its view of "Spirit" in Luther as the "bearer and creator of *religious* capacities."[11] Thus there is already in this work a clear sense of the autonomy of religion. Moreover, there is a recognition of a specific type of experience that is of its essence religious in nature,[12] and, allied with this, the claim that such experience points beyond itself to its object and is therefore in itself "experience of the grace of God."[13] That the study of religion and theology needs to be grounded in analysis of the religious consciousness—the pivotal issue in Otto's theory of religion—has its origin in this, Otto's first work: "The religious feeling has rightful claim to its own scope, unimpaired and unobstructed. It should not allow itself to be curtailed or eliminated in favor of other plausible trains of thought; and it may well be the task of theology to reexamine that crushing chain of empirical relationships until it can find place for an answer to the question how religion is possible— and possible, moreover, in uncurtailed form."[14]

Otto wants to maintain that, despite Luther's own experience and despite emphasis on the nonrational, this numinous depth was lost in later Lutheranism: "More and more it deprived the forms of worship of the genuinely contemplative and specifically 'devotional' elements in them. The conceptual and doctrinal—the ideal of orthodoxy—began to preponderate over the inexpressible, whose only life is in the conscious mental attitude of the devout soul."[15] This is not to say that the nonrational aspect of Christianity was extinguished after the Reformation. Rather, it continued alongside and in interplay with its rationalist alternative, making its presence felt in both Catholicism and Protestantism, particularly in their more mystical expressions.

Protestant nonrationalism in the period between the Reformation and the Enlightenment is exemplified for Otto in a number of individuals, all of whom were in conflict with the orthodoxy of their respective times and who therefore were more in tune with the inner spirit of Luther's teaching. Despite the rationalism of his theosophy, Otto maintains that in the Protestant mystic Jakob Böhme (1575-1624), for example, "The consciousness of the numinous was astir and alive as an element of genuine value: so that herein Böhme was an heir of Luther, preserving what in Luther's own school came to be overlooked and disregarded."[16] Mention is also made of the Lutheran theologian and mystical writer Johann Arndt (1555-1621), of the theologian and translator of mystical texts Gottfried Arnold (1666-97), and of Philipp Jakob Spener (1635-1705), the founder of Pietism. Undoubtedly what Otto found attractive in all of these men was their "pietistic" stance. Their attention was focussed on the *felt* character of religion, on inner conviction, on intensity of feeling; on the affective and the emotional elements of religion, as opposed to the vacuous rationalism of an intellectualist orthodoxy.

It is consequently somewhat surprising that, in *Das Heilige,* no mention is made of Count Nicholas von Zinzendorf (1700-1760), the leader of the Moravian Pietists at Herrnhut in Saxony. The count is only mentioned twice in any of Otto's previously published works, specifically in the epilogue to his edition of Schleiermacher's *Speeches on Religion.* Zinzendorf is a central figure in the history of pietistic movements, as Albrecht Ritschl made clear in the third volume of his *History of Pietism* (1886).[17] Although Otto was aware of the connection between Schleiermacher and Moravian Pietism as early as 1899,[18] and of the fact that Fries was brought up as a Moravian Pietist by 1908,[19] he seems not to have realized the importance of Zinzendorf both for his own theory of religion and for the influence upon Schleiermacher until much later.[20]

In 1919 an article appeared which (for Otto, at any rate) threw new light on Zinzendorf's account of religion.[21] It was especially concerned to present an address to be given by Zinzendorf to a synod of his community in 1745, and it prompted Otto to produce a paper entitled "Zinzendorf über den 'Sensus numinis.'"[22] In this article Otto points to intimations of his own account of religion in several aspects of Zinzendorf's writing. Zinzendorf sees *Scheu* (dread) and *Entsetzen* (horror) as uniquely determinative of religious feeling, affections which are quite analogous to Otto's delineation of the moment of *tremendum* in numinous experience. In addition, in Zinzendorf's use and explanation of the term *sensus numinis* Otto finds a close parallel to his own view. The relevant passage from Zinzendorf is as follows: "What is given above is simply to prove that in all human creatures there is a Sensus Numinis which indeed lies often very deep, but which the smallest contact from outside makes sensible to the subject himself and palpable to him who experiences it."[23]

This discovery of Zinzendorf later led Otto to see Schleiermacher as much more heavily dependent on Moravian Pietism than he had previously thought. In a revised version of his earlier paper on Zinzendorf, significantly retitled "Zinzendorf as Discoverer of the Sensus Numinis,"[24] Otto remarks that Zinzendorf was concerned not with dogmatics or theology, but with the essence of all religion: "It is an attempt at . . . as we would say, a 'phenomenology of religion' which seeks for the basic and essential moments of religious feeling, and is to this extent a forerunner of the writings of another 'Herrnhuter,' namely Schleiermacher, and of his *Speeches on Religion* and the introductory sections of his later *The Christian Faith.*"[25] Otto further maintains that the origin of Schleiermacher's use of the term *Gefühl* (feeling) may be seen in this address, and that the notion of *Ahndung* is used in the same sense by Zinzendorf as by Schleiermacher and, more especially, by Fries:

The connection which Schleiermacher later sets up in his second and fifth *Speeches on Religion* between general experience of the transcendent and the Christian idea of redemption, and then in the introduction to his *The Christian Faith* between the general feeling of dependence (an obvious transformation of the general *sensus numinis*) and religious feelings of Christian determination, is so similar to these assertions of Zinzendorf that one would like to posit a direct line of transmission between these two *Herrnhuter.*[26]

Early in his career, when he was most inclined to see Schleiermacher as the savior of modern theology, Otto did overstress the intellectualism and rationalism of eighteenth-century cultural life and consequently tended to ignore those powerful pietistic currents which were also present. Indeed, he went so far as to imply that Pietism was virtually nonexistent in the eighteenth century.[27] For Otto, the philosophy of the Enlightenment was intensely one sided: "It valued man essentially as a being thinking according to the laws of intelligence and acting according to the laws of morality, as the creature of 'theoretic' and 'practical' reason. It was blind to that wealth of human nature which lies outside the scope of these capacities, to the rich profundities of immediate experience of life, and nature, and history, which lie beyond rationalistic analysis and moralistic considerations."[28] Of the enlightened person's attitude toward religion he writes: "One did not hate religion but one somehow held it in contempt like something for which one no longer had any use. One was cultured and full of ideals; one was aesthetic, and one was moral, but one was no longer religious."[29]

This is not to be taken as suggesting that religion was under any sort of virulent attack in eighteenth-century Germany. German thought had resisted the onslaught of French materialism and atheism, as exemplified for Otto in d'Holbach (1723-89) and De la Mettrie (1705-51).[30] Indeed, the Enlightenment, says Otto, "prided itself on having overcome 'atheism,'"[31] although only by the subjection of religion to rational criticism. Still, the *sensus numinis* had been lost, and religion's "essential spirit which, as any pious person feels, is something quite different from the intellectual perception of some metaphysical things or the observance of ordinances, had escaped."[32]

Otto was subsequently to see the Enlightenment in a somewhat more positive light. But considering the above-quoted kind of judgment of it, and his underplaying of the Pietistic tradition of the period, it is clear why Schleiermacher could appear to the early Otto as the revitalizer of the nonrational Christian tradition that had, in Otto's view, been dormant for most of the eighteenth century. Schleiermacher, according to Otto, "opened for his age a new door to old and forgotten ideas: to divine marvel instead of supernatural miracle, to living revelation instead of instilled doctrine, to the manifestation of the divinely infinite in event, person, and history, and especially to a new understanding and valuation of biblical history as divine revelation."[33]

Before considering the significance of Schleiermacher for nineteenth-century religious thought, and for Otto, it is necessary to give a brief account of the philosophy of Immanuel Kant (1724-1804). Neither Schleiermacher nor Fries nor Otto can be understood apart from his relation to Kantianism. In 1781 the first of Kant's three critiques, the *Critique of Pure Reason,* appeared. While epitomizing eighteenth-century thought, it signaled the beginning of a new era in philosophy. As Karl Barth has aptly put it, "It was in this man and in this work that the eighteenth century saw, understood and affirmed itself in its own limitations. Itself—in its limitations."[34] The validity of this statement derives from Kant's unique blending of two separate streams of eighteenth-century thought—rationalism and empiricism—in his attempt to subject reason itself to rational criticism.[35]

Steeped in the rationalist tradition mediated to him from Leibniz via his teacher Christian Wolff, Kant nonetheless rejected the rationalist claim that pure thinking could generate knowledge of absolute reality. Having been awoken from his dogmatic slumbers (as he rather rhetorically put it) by the empiricism of David Hume, he asserted that knowledge had to be related to the tough givenness of experience. Theoretical knowledge is thereby limited to the phenomenal realm (the realm of things as they appear to us) and does not extend to the noumenal realm (the realm of the "thing-in-itself"). God, freedom, and immortality are by definition "parts" of the noumenal realm and are not possible objects of theoretical knowledge.

Still, Kant remains sufficiently wedded to rationalism to maintain that empiricism is misguided in supposing that *all* knowledge derives from experience, even if it originates there. "For it may well be," he writes, "that our empirical knowledge is made up of what we receive through impressions and of what our own faculty of knowledge (sensible impressions serving merely as the occasion) supplies from itself."[36] Moreover, if all knowledge were dependent on experience alone, there could be no certain knowledge; because experience can only give us generalizations from fact, these are always open to the possibility of refutation in the next moment by a contrary experience. What is learned from experience alone, therefore, does not bear the hallmarks of certain knowledge, namely, *universality* and *necessity.*

Kant's central aim is to show that we do have a priori (that is, universal and necessary) knowledge of things and, further, that such knowledge can only be explained if the character of things as known is determined by the way in which our minds know them. This means that we can never know things as they really are. Rather, we only know things as they appear to us by virtue of the constitutive and determinative powers of our minds.

In that section of the first *Critique* entitled "Transcendental Aesthetic," Kant argues that space and time are not conceptions that can be dependent on experience for their origin. Our intuitions of space and time are a priori because they are the universal and necessary conditions of the possibility of experience. That is to say, insofar as any object is given directly to us in experience, it will be in a spatiotemporal form. As a consequence, space and time are transcendentally ideal—they cannot be supposed to exist independently of our perceptions. They are merely the a priori forms of intuiting what is given to experience through the manifold of sense.

In "Transcendental Analytic," Kant argues that conceptual a prioris match the perceptual ones of space and time. As the "Aesthetic" gave us the pure intuitions of space and time, so the "Analytic" is intended to give us pure concepts or categories under which any and every possible object of knowledge must necessarily be thought.

In Kant's view, we possess one intellectual faculty which has a twofold task: a general task in logic, and a more specific one in making judgments about objects. Kant reasons that, if we want to discover pure concepts or categories of understanding, we can do so by derivation from the concepts of general logic, specifically, the forms of judgment. Because the forms of judgment are the universal and necessary modes of thinking, any and every object of experience can *only* be thought under *all* these necessary and universal forms of judgment. Hence the forms of judgment are necessarily the source of the pure categories of the understanding. In a passage popularly known as the Metaphysical Deduction of the Categories, Kant lists the various forms of judgment under four headings, each containing three divisions and a corresponding list of categories. The categories under the heading *quantity* are unity, plurality, totality; under the head *quality,* reality, negation, limitation; under the head *relation,* subsistence and inherence (*substantia* and *accidens*), causality and dependence (cause and effect), community (interaction between agent and patient); and finally, under the heading *modality,* possibility and impossibility, being and not-being, necessity and contingency. Of these, the most important for Fries, and for Otto, are those under the heading *relation.*

It is crucial to our later discussion that we now take up the distinction between pure and schematized categories. A pure category may be defined as the concept of a particular form of judgment which is able to characterize all things without exception. H. J. Paton points out that "Kant never varies . . . in his belief that the pure categories when we abstract from all reference to time and space, must be regarded as concepts, not of an *object* in general, but of a *thing* in general, that is, of things as they are in themselves. Indeed, so far as we can think of things-in-themselves at all, we must do so by means of the pure categories, for all thinking contains the forms of judgement."[37] But for Kant, the categories can only *legitimately* be applied to the extent that they can be, so to say, cashed in in terms of sense experiences (which have been brought under the a priori forms of intuition). That is, the categories have objective validity only when they are *schematized,* interpreted under the form of time (and space). The categories listed above refer to the categories *as schematized,* not to the pure categories. Indeed, although Kant believes that the pure categories are obtained when time (and space) are abstracted from the categories thus schematized, they cannot really be defined, since they contain no clear property by means of which the object to which they refer can be recognized. "The pure concepts," writes Kant, "can find no object and so can acquire no meaning which might yield a concept of some object."[38] As we shall see, in contrast to Kant, Jakob Fries attempts to derive knowledge of absolute reality by removing the temporal schema. Otto, in his account of the rational side of the Holy, is dependent on the Friesian method.

According to the *Critique of Pure Reason,* the world of actual and possible experience can be known by combining a priori elements contributed by the mind with sense experiences. Space and time do not characterize the noumenal realm and are only applicable to the realm of appearances. The categories of understanding, too, in their schematized form, are only applicable to the phenomenal world. The noumenal realm is outside the bounds of possible knowledge, and those ideas essential to religion—God, freedom, and immortality—are beyond possible knowledge, although within the bounds of faith.

Kant had not said all he wanted to say about reason in the first *Critique,* for reason has also to do with responsible human action. According to the *Critique of Practical Reason,* persons are bound, insofar as they are rational beings, by the moral law—by the necessity of acting out of reverence for lawfulness in general, by the categorical imperative to act only on that maxim through which it can at the same time be willed that it should become a universal law, and by the will for the highest good.

The necessity laid upon us by virtue of our practical reason has, according to Kant, a number of necessary consequences. First, the rational obligation to act morally implies that we *can* do so. Freedom is a universal and necessary precondition of morality, and its reality must consequently be postulated, albeit as pertaining to our actions noumenally and not phenomenally. (Phenomenally, all our actions are causally determined.) Second, the will for the highest good—the conjunction of moral perfection and complete happiness—requires two further postulates of practical reason: the immortality of the soul to provide the necessary time for the self to approach the highest good, and the existence of God to bring about the necessary relationship between virtue and happiness, duty and desire. In the Kantian scheme God is demoted from his position as an object of knowledge but reinstated as a reasonable postulate of practical faith. The obligation that man ought to act so as to achieve the highest good is an obligation conceivable only on the presupposition that God exists.

*SCHLEIERMACHER AND FEELING*

This then was the situation when, in 1799, Friedrich Schleiermacher (1772-1834) published his *Speeches on Religion* at the behest of the young Romantic circle with which he had become intimately involved a few years previously. Schleiermacher makes it quite clear that he, like the cultured despisers of religion to whom he writes, scorns the God of speculative reason deposed by the Kantian critique and the ethically dependent Kantian deity. For Schleiermacher, "belief must be something different from a mixture of opinions about God and the world, and of precepts for one life or for two. Piety cannot be an instinct craving for a mess of metaphysical and ethical crumbs."[39]

Although religion may contain metaphysical and moral conceptions, its essence is to be found not in knowledge or action, but in the nonrational and passive affections of feeling, intuition, taste, sense, and so on. Otto writes that for Schleiermacher

> There is a third relationship to the world: this is not science of the world, neither is it action upon the world; it is *experience* of this world in its profundity, the realization of its eternal content by the feeling of a contemplative and devout mind. This is not science or metaphysics; nor is it ethics or individual effort and directive activity. It is *religion:* the immediate appraisal of the universe as the one and the whole, transcending the mere parts which science may grasp, and at the same time the profound spiritual experience of its underlying ideal essence.[40]

According to Schleiermacher, this third mode of relation to the world consists in the consciousness of the existence of all finite things in and through the infinite, and of all temporal things in and through the eternal: "It is a life in the infinite nature of the whole, in the One and in the All, in God, having and possessing all things in God and God in all. . . . In itself it is an affection and revelation of the Infinite in the finite, God being seen in it and it in God."[41]

Although Otto recognizes that Schleiermacher's account of religion is conditioned by the intellectual situation of the time, certain aspects of Schleiermacher's analysis appear to have a direct influence on Otto's own understanding of religion. First, both Schleiermacher and Otto affirm that religion ultimately depends not on rational factors, but on a nonrational core, and both agree that religion accordingly has its own province in the mind. Second, and in consequence, both agree that all religious discourse, all theological ideas and principles, are or ought to be relatable to affections of the religious consciousness.[42]

Schleiermacher and Otto both argue that any attempt to determine a *rational* universal religion at the core of the world's historical religious traditions is misconceived. Consequently, both find the plurality of religions a necessary and desirable result of religion's universal *nonrational* essence. Opposing the efforts of the Enlightenment to construct a universal religion acceptable to all rational persons, Schleiermacher writes:

> You must abandon the vain and foolish wish that there should be only one religion; you must lay aside all repugnance to its multiplicity; as candidly as possible you must approach everything that has ever, in the changing shapes of humanity, been developed in its advancing career, from the ever fruitful bosom of the spiritual life. . . . The whole of religion is nothing but the sum of all relations of man to God, apprehended in all the possible ways in which any man can be immediately conscious in his life. . . . You are wrong, therefore, with your universal religion that is natural to all, for no one will have his own true and right religion, if it is the same for all.[43]

Otto similarly stresses the unique value of each religion. His argument for the necessity of recognizing the unique value of specific religions is directed not only against rationalism's attempt to formulate a universal religion, but also against what he calls "traditionalism's" attempt to do the same and, in so doing, invariably to assign the role to its own tradition.[44]

For "traditionalism" we might read "Ritschlianism," for there was an incipient tendency in Ritschl's theology as a whole to see religion in exclusively christocentric, bibliocentric, and, one might say, reformationistic terms. Moreover, Ritschl was criticized around the turn of this century by members of the so-called history-of-religions school (Wilhelm Bousset, Wilhelm Heitmüller, Hermann Gunkel, and Ernst Troeltsch) for rejecting Schleiermacher's pluralism in favor of Christian exclusivism. During his time at Göttingen, Otto was prominently associated with both Troeltsch and Bousset. Be that as it may, Otto writes very much in a Romantic spirit reminiscent of Schleiermacher:

> And we would urge the individual not to be led astray by universalizing analogies and resemblances between religions, but first of all to concentrate upon that which is central and individual in his own religion. We do not mean by this that he should restore the paraphernalia of tradition or the apparatus of an effete dogmatism. . . . We are concerned not to mend old clothes, but to ascertain in its truth and subtlety the individual *spirit* itself of a religion, and thus to set a value upon the particular, the essence of the ideals, sentiments, life and conduct which it produces, to liberate these and give them a new and appropriate form.[45]

Further, it is interesting to note that, although both affirm the desirability of religious pluralism, they nonetheless tend to view Christianity as the end point of the religious process.[46] Neither Schleiermacher nor Otto is able to substantiate this view satisfactorily.

Finally, both Otto and Schleiermacher see religious experience as having a cognitive status. Indeed, Otto is the first in a line of modern commentators upon Schleiermacher who point to the undeniably objective character (for him) of religious consciousness,[47] and thereby stand opposed to that tradition of Schleiermacher interpretation which, from Hegel and Feuerbach to Barth and Brunner, saw Schleiermacher as one enmeshed in inescapable subjectivism. Otto's view of Schleiermacher is quite clear in *Das Heilige,* but it is also present as early as 1899 in Otto's introduction to his edition of the *Speeches on Religion:*

> He [Schleiermacher] wished to show that man is not wholly confined to [scientific] knowledge [*Wissen*] and action, that the relationship of men to their environment—the world, being, mankind, events—is not exhausted in the mere perception or shaping of it. He sought to prove that if one experienced the environing world in a state of deep emotion, as intuition and feeling, and that if one were deeply affected by a sense of its eternal and abiding essence to the point where one was moved to feelings of devotion, awe, and reverence—then such an affective state was worth more than knowledge and action put together.[48]

Otto finds his own later commitment to the notion of a religious a priori in human consciousness outlined in Schleiermacher's work: "As Kant inquires after and examines the faculty of perception, of the power of judgment, of understanding, of reason, of theoretical and practical reason in order to find the essence of knowledge, of moral action, and of aesthetic taste, so Schleiermacher seeks the faculty of the mind out of which religion arises."[49]

### THE TURN TO IDEALISM

All this is not to suggest that Otto's relation to the writings of Schleiermacher was an uncritical one. Already in the introduction to his edition of the *Speeches on Religion* he complains that Schleiermacher neglects the *critical* examination of the autonomous nature of the religious life, a failure in Schleiermacher which was later to be a decisive one for Otto. Still, in 1899 Otto is very much a disciple of the first edition of the *Speeches on Religion.* He is critical of the later revised and edited versions: "the fresh, youthful and original effusion, which had produced the first direct effects, could no longer be recognized in them."[50] And certainly Schleiermacher gave his later versions fewer rhetorical flourishes and related them much more closely to his formal dogmatics. Otto also prefers the *Speeches on Religion* to any of Schleiermacher's later works (especially *The Christian Faith*), since many of these latter "forfeited the original meaning, richness and impact in the interests of a stricter and more systematic treatment."[51] Five years later, although he was already coming under the influence of the Friesian philosophy, Otto still maintains that Schleiermacher is superior to Fries in his breadth of ideas, even if less incisive in his expressions of them.[52]

By 1909, however, Otto has become a fervent disciple of Fries, and his position vis-à-vis Schleiermacher has changed. In the introduction to *The Philosophy of Religion* he writes:

Historians of the philosophy of religion have pointed to a certain affinity between Fries and Schleiermacher in their treatment of the theory of religious "feeling," but they have assumed that Schleiermacher's was the more original and comprehensive intellect. Really, however, in the philosophy of religion, the points of contact between Fries and Schleiermacher are less important than their points of difference; and when their views agree, Fries is quite original, and closer study proves him to be superior in comprehensiveness, thoroughness, and solidity.[53]

This shift from Schleiermacher to Fries entails also a revision of Otto's views on Kant, for only as a result of Fries's development of the Kantian philosophy does the philosophy of religion gain a solid philosophical foundation. By contrast, Schleiermacher offers "primarily a kind of inspired guesswork . . . and often enough in the *Discourses* [*Speeches*] the arbitrary decree of genius replaces the solid reasoning from philosophy and history."[54] In short, in Friesian philosophy Otto was to find the rational foundation for and the guarantee of his sympathy with Schleiermacher's position.

Otto's desire for a philosophical framework upon which to ground the study of religion was also motivated by the burgeoning of the natural sciences in the late nineteenth century, and the consequent devaluation of a religious worldview in the light of the materialistic and naturalistic philosophies which were thus fostered. Schleiermacher's account of religion was of little help in defending religion against this sort of attack. The overall aim of Otto's *Naturalism and Religion* was to defend the religious conception of the world by a vigorous assertion of its autonomous validity, since "the natural sciences, in association with other convictions and aims, tend readily to unite into a distinctive and independent system of world interpretation, which, if it were valid and sufficient, would drive the religious view into difficulties, or make it impossible."[55]

Otto does not want to defend the religious conception of the world by means of a natural theology based on evidences in nature, for he recognizes that such attempts too often ignore the "multitudinous enigmas," the many instances of what seems "unmeaning and purposeless, confused and dark."[56] Nor is he interested in arguing for any form of supernaturalism in which the cause of one part of any event is ascribed to natural causes and that of another part of the same event to the divine, for this conflicts with both the demands of science and the nature of religion. Rather, his aim is to show that what religion demands is compatible with a properly construed philosophy of science:

> It may, for instance, be possible that the mathematical-mechanical interpretation of things, even if it be sufficient within its own domain, does not take away from nature the characters which religion seeks and requires in it, namely, purpose, dependence, and mystery. Or it may be that nature itself does not correspond at all

to this ideal of mathematical explicability, that this ideal may well be enough as a guide for investigation, but that it is not a fundamental clue really applying to nature as a whole and in its essence. . . . And this suggests another possibility, namely, that the naturalistic method of interpretation cannot be applied throughout the whole territory of nature . . . and, finally, that it is distinctly interrupted and held in abeyance at particular points by the incommensurable which breaks forth spontaneously out of the depths of phenomena revealing a depth which is not to be explained away.[57]

Dependence, mystery, purpose—these are the three elements of human experience and existence with which, according to Otto, religion uniquely concerns itself, and which cannot be accounted for in a naturalistic conception of the world. One passage may suffice to indicate the direction of Otto's argument. He writes that in religion we find

> first, the interest, never to be relinquished, of experiencing and acknowledging the world and existence to be a mystery, and regarding all that is known and manifested in things merely as the thin crust which separates us from the uncomprehended and inexpressible. Secondly, there is the desire on the part of religion to bring ourselves and all creatures into the "feeling of absolute dependence". . . . Finally, there is the interest in a theological interpretation of the world as opposed to the purely causal interpretation of natural science.[58]

Just as Otto saw German idealism as a bulwark against the French materialism of the eighteenth century, so also he views Kantian idealism as the means whereby autonomy may be accorded to both religion and science in the nineteenth and twentieth centuries. While science deals with the phenomenal realm, the distinction between it and the noumenal allows for the possible reality of those "objects" to which religion avers. This is not to suggest that Otto adopts Kantianism outright, for he is quite aware, on the one hand, that Kant had placed religion outside the realm of knowledge, and, on the other, that even if religion had remained within the bounds of knowledge as defined by Kant, this would not satisfy the demands of religion: "Now for a student of natural science it may perhaps be of no importance whether the category he applies in his investigation . . . is only a form of the world of his ideas, or whether the world of reality corresponds to it and is obedient to it: for the religious man it is not a matter of indifference. Nay, rather for him everything is absolutely dependent on the valency of religious ideas apart from his own conception of them."[59]

Otto turned to Fries in order to resolve the problem of the validity of religion inherent within the Kantian scheme. Why to the philosophy of Fries rather than, say, to the neo-Kantianism of Hermann Lotze which had been (loosely) woven by Ritschl into his theology? Partly because of the efforts of the neo-Friesians to recruit Otto to their cause. And despite Otto's suggestion to the contrary, it can also be partly attributed to the similarities between Fries and Schleiermacher in their mutual emphasis on "feeling" as the basis of religion. (To be sure, Fries was more influenced by Kant's third critique, the *Critique of Judgment,* than by Romanticism.[60])

Troeltsch's negative judgment upon Ritschl's alliance with the neo-Kantianism of Lotze may also have been indirectly significant in Otto's becoming a Friesian. Certainly, anti-Ritschlianism was being aired in Göttingen, and from the beginning of his academic career Troeltsch had consistently rejected Ritschl's use of Kant's distinction between faith and knowledge to ground religion in value judgments.[61] For example, Troeltsch writes, "By placing all the emphasis upon the separation of theoretical and practical reason and stressing only the practical necessity of the values claimed by religion, they [the value-judgment theorists] lose the necessity of the object to which these values are attached and plunge into the abyss of a theology based on human desires and illusions."[62] Troeltsch himself may be criticized here for undervaluing the cognitive import of the notion of value judgments, and for thereby providing grist for the anti-Ritschlian mill. Still, the point remains that the philosophical foundations of Ritschlianism were seen as unviable. Moreover, Otto may have been more positively influenced by Troeltsch by virtue of the latter's own commitment to a form of neo-Kantianism without which, Troeltsch remarks, "one is tied down in advance to the impossibility of an epistemological or cognitive value in religion."[63]

I do not intend to suggest that Otto was able to or even wanted to cast off all vestiges of Ritschl's thought. Ritschlianism was dominant and very pervasive, and elements of it do appear in *Das Heilige.* Nevertheless, its insufficiency in providing Otto with an adequate philosophical grounding for religion probably played a role in his adoption of the philosophy of Fries.

### OTTO AND FRIES

We have seen that, for Kant, experience is the product of the given of experience (which has for us a spatiotemporal form) and the a priori categories of the understanding. For Kant, the a priori nature of the forms of intuition and the categories is sufficient to disprove their objective validity. Jakob Fries (1773-1843), although an avowed disciple of Kant's philosophy, disagrees on this point. He maintains that knowledge of reality in itself is possible—in the negative knowledge of rational faith, and in the positive knowledge afforded by intuitive feeling. In Fries's view, human understanding may be divided in a threefold way: scientific knowledge *(Wissen),* rational faith *(Glaube),* and religio-aesthetic intuition *(Ahndung)*—independent but interrelated forms of knowledge, with the latter two being higher forms.[64]

The foundation for Fries's argument is laid in his discussion of the nature of truth.[65] In an idealist system such as Kant's, truth cannot be defined as the agreement of an idea with its object, for, on the one hand, there is no means by which we can compare the object as known with the object independent of knowledge. (Apart from perception and cognition themselves, there are no checking procedures.[66]) We must have *immediate* knowledge that there is a world independent of our perceptions. On the other hand, truth as customarily defined cannot explain our knowledge of necessary truths, that is, truths independent of experience. To account for our knowledge of their validity, we must have *immediate* knowledge of them also. Truth expressed in rational judgments finally depends, therefore, upon "the agreement of the judgment with the immediate knowledge of reason on which it is based."[67] Although this immediate knowledge of reason can only be laid bare by the empirical examination of our mental processes, that is, in an *anthropologische Kritik* (anthropological critique), it possesses its own criterion of truth, a *Wahrheitsgefühl* (feeling of truth) which is inescapable and irreducible. Otto explains,

> The fact that we really *know* something in our sense perceptions, i.e., that we conceive an object which really exists and conceive it according to its being, is solely based on Reason's natural self-confidence that it is capable of truth and knowledge. . . . This applies with no less force—rather with more—to a priori kinds of real knowledge than to such as depend on sense perception. Those "self-evident" truths, which every child grasps at once, are valid for Reason, as laws for the objective world itself. . . . the condition in which immediate knowledge shows itself as active, even before light has penetrated to its primal obscurity is the *Feeling of Truth.*[68]

As Otto indicates in this passage, the content of this immediate knowledge of Reason is that of the objective reality of Being and existence in general. Furthermore, in this immediate knowledge is revealed the unity and necessity of that which is given to sense perception: "Each and everything in general is a *synthetic unity,* i.e., constitutes a whole, in the complete connection of its elements, a coherent world of Being and Happening. Not a hotch-potch of disparate and disconnected phenomena, of which there could be no experience, no observation, no science, which would be blind and senseless, a mere 'rhapsody of perceptions'; not this but an association of thorough and coherent interdependence."[69] Moreover, not a synthetic unity which has occurred by chance, but one which is necessarily so.

According to Fries, the a priori categories of understanding articulate the only possible forms of this immediate knowledge of reason—the idea of universal unity and necessity. Therefore the categories give us knowledge of objective reality, of the noumenal realm. According to Kant, we can have no real knowledge by means of the *pure* a priori categories, but only by means of these when schematized by the a priori forms of intuition. In contrast to this, according to Fries, the categories lose their absolute validity and are limited and restricted as a result of this schematizing. Our knowledge of the world through the schematized categories is incomplete and imperfect, in comparison to the purely rational interpretation of reality embedded in our immediate knowledge of Reason and expressed in the *pure* categories of the understanding.

Fries argues that, in the Ideas of Reason—God, the soul, and freedom—which for Kant are at most regulative ideals in the pursuit of scientific knowledge, we have a completely rational knowledge of reality, and that the realm of scientific knowledge *(Wissen)* allows transitions to this pure rational knowledge *(Glaube).* By applying to the incomplete and imperfect temporally schematized categories, especially those under the head of *relation,* an ideal schematism by which the categories are *completed,* the *Ideas* of Reason are able to be deduced directly. As R. F. Davidson comments, "the restriction and limitation imposed by the data of sense-experience upon the conceptual knowledge of the phenomenal world is removed and an ideal view of reality as a completely intelligible world of rational being is achieved."[70]

More specifically, the Ideas of the soul, freedom, and God are derived from the ideal schematism of the categories of subsistence and inherence (substance and accident), causality and dependence (cause and effect), and community (interaction between agent and patient), respectively. The removal of temporal schematism from the first of the above categories entails the disappearance of the quantitative aspects of material objects (extension, motion, change of motion and position) but the retention of their qualitative attributes—both outer qualities (color, sound, odor, warmth, hardness, etc.) and their inner correlates (pleasure, feeling, volition, desire, anger, hate, etc.). Otto writes, "In the individual (personal) mind with its 'inner qualities' do we alone know with certitude and clearness what substances are. By way of analogy to it we interpret that which is, then, as a world of spiritual being and life, of spiritual substances in general."[71] This, according to Otto, is the meaning contained in the notion of soul. So also with the category of cause and effect: when ideal schematism is applied, causation is no longer restricted to temporal succession, and there is the possibility of a cause which is not the result of another cause: "the category of causality becomes the Idea of the Free Will of spiritual Substances."[72] Finally, the category of community (that objects constitute a system the parts of which mutually exclude and mutually determine each other), when ideally schematized, points to "the operation of one unified, essential, necessary, extramundane cause of all in general"[73] which orders things in accord with final purpose, that is, God.

By negating or completing the temporally schematized categories (which are themselves negations or limitations of the pure categories), we gain that knowledge which is articulated in the pure categories, namely, knowledge of the "thing-in-itself." Although for Fries this purely rational knowledge is higher than that

gained by means of the operation of the schematized categories, since the Ideas of Reason arise by *negation,* we have *no positive* knowledge of them. We know *that* they are, but not *what* they are. All we can do is deny that the limitations of empirical existence apply to them.[74]

Kant found that God, freedom, and immortality arose as necessary postulates of the demands of practical reason. According to Fries, however, religious faith is not an outcome of the demands of the moral law. Rather, moral consciousness is itself conditioned by the immediate knowledge of reason, and therefore by the Ideas of Reason. The categorical imperative is itself determined by the existence of an absolute objective value which is reflected in all finite valuing. Otto writes:

> All the values of our existence as appearing in Time can be high, very high; they can never be absolutely high. To all finite value we oppose the absolutely completed value in the word "Dignity" [*Würde*]. It is applicable to that which, under the Idea, was conceived absolutely as Substance: the spirit of the person in its independence and freedom from the machinery of Nature as a whole. "Dignity of the Person" is the ideal principle under which we judge every man, as the appearance of an eternal and personal spirit.[75]

Moreover—and this becomes especially important for Otto's work on ethics toward the end of his life—in the dignity of the person is manifested an eternal worth and purpose, not only of the individual, but of the world as a whole:

> Ethics has given us the values and the purposes, which are possible for men as individuals, for humanity as a whole in the course of its history. . . . In the forms of ideal knowledge, however . . . it becomes the faith in the absolute value of Being in itself, in the *objective purpose* and the objective purposiveness of the real universe itself, which, on account of its holy and all powerful cause, the Godhead, dwells in man and by means of this becomes for him the "Highest Good."[76]

For Fries, religion is to be aware of this eternal purpose, and to live in accord with it.

Like God, the soul, and freedom, the objective purposiveness of the universe remains as negative knowledge in the realm of *Glaube.* What, then, of the relationship between that which is negatively known in *Glaube* about objective reality and that which is known through *Wissen* of the same objective reality that merely appears to us through the manifold senses? For Fries, the connection is provided through feeling: "knowledge of the Eternal in the finite is only possible through pure feeling."[77] Through *Ahndung,* which (like logical judgments) is characterized by an immediate feeling of truth, it is revealed that the world of scientific knowledge is really ordered in agreement with the principles of rational faith.[78] Otto remarks:

> Feeling, with Knowledge and Faith, gives a third kind of real knowledge, one which combines and

unifies both of these—"Ahnen." Obscure sentiments of the beautiful and sublime in all its phases, in the natural and spiritual life, have us in their power: and so we understand without any medium the Eternal in the Temporal, and the Temporal as an appearance of the Eternal. Intelligibly enough, positively, although beyond our powers of expression, the world of Faith here manifests itself in the world of Knowledge by means of "Ahnung."[79]

Neither *Glaube* nor *Ahndung* can be positively expressed, but the latter can be positively felt. As we shall see later, neither the rational nor the nonrational sides of the divine can be spoken of positively, though the nonrational is positively felt.

It is through *Ahndung* that religion arises,[80] for piety may be identified (according to Fries) with the enthusiasm, devotion, and self-surrender to God which result from it, and the consciousness of eternal destiny, of good and evil, of sin and responsibility that are inescapably connected with it. And, most important for Otto's later account of religious knowledge, all statements which derive from it are mere approximations, since *Ahndung* "is utterly incapable of being analyzed and is absolutely proof against presentation in conceptual form."[81]

We shall later see the extent of Otto's dependence on Fries in his mature philosophy of religion. For the moment, suffice it to say that in Fries's idealism Otto finds a rational framework for his conviction that religion is in its essence nonrational. The experience of its nonrational essence is formally identical with the experience of *Ahndung,* and the connection between *Glaube* and *Ahndung* later provides Otto with a model of the connection between the rational and nonrational elements of religion, and of our objective knowledge of these. All of these depend, in the final analysis, on the fact that in Friesianism Otto found a philosophical scheme which guaranteed the autonomy of religion and provided a defense against the onslaught of materialistic and naturalistic reductions of it.

There was one point at which Otto went beyond the Friesian position, even at the time of *The Philosophy of Religion.* Otto sees the possibility of *Ahndung* including the realization of the operation of the eternal in history. While Schleiermacher was his primary influence here, the Friesian theologian Wilhelm de Wette (1780-1849) was undoubtedly also important, for it was he who specifically attempted to apply the Friesian concept of *Ahndung* to the historical realm, a use to which Otto was to put the concept in *Das Heilige.*[82]

In the conclusion to *The Philosophy of Religion* Otto foreshadows his future work. He maintains that the science of religion will have "two separate starting points and will follow two paths, at first different, which, however, lead to each other and must meet at last."[83] The first of these is an empirical examination of religion which will "secure by induction an empirical conception of the properties, character, and real nature of Religion

as a whole."[84] The starting point for this will be religious experience. The other path will follow the work of the *Critique of Reason* as a whole which finds its completion, and the means for the interpretation of religious experience, in *Ahndung.*

The former path finds its culmination in *Das Heilige;* the latter is already well developed in *The Philosophy of Religion.* Surprisingly, in Otto's subsequent works there are few clear indications of the conjunction of these two paths. Indeed, references to Friesian philosophy are few and far between. For the moment, it is sufficient to note that Otto's psychological analysis of the contents of the religious consciousness is not compatible with the content of *Ahndung;* his commitment to the specifics of Friesianism becomes less forthright as a result. This is not to imply that Friesianism is of no importance in Otto's later philosophical theology; on the contrary, it continues to provide the philosophical substructure, in method if not in content. But it is not overtly present, and therefore it needs to be discerned beneath the surface of Otto's method and language.

NOTES

[1] Rudolf Otto, *The Idea of the Holy* (Oxford: Oxford University Press, 1958), p. 6.

[2] Ibid., p. 4.

[3] Ibid., p. 1.

[4] Ibid., p. xxi. See also Otto's notes on the English translation of *Kantisch-Fries'sche Religionsphilosophie* in Hans-Walter Schütte, *Religion und Christentum in der Theologie Rudolf Ottos.* (Berlin: de Gruyter, 1969), p. 123: *"On no account* do I wish to be considered a 'non-rationalist.' In all religion, and in my own religion, I indeed recognize the profundity of the nonrational factor; but this deepens my conviction that it is the duty of serious theology to win as much ground as it can for *Ratio* in this realm."

[5] Rudolf Otto, *The Philosophy of Religion* (London: Williams and Norgate, 1931), p. 229.

[6] Otto, *The Idea of the Holy,* p. 3.

[7] His *Loci Theologici* (1610-22) are regarded as the epitome of Lutheran dogmatic theology.

[8] Otto, *The Idea of the Holy,* p. 95. Otto buttresses this claim with passages from Plato's *Timaeus* (28c) and *Seventh Letter* (341c).

[9] On Luther and the mystical tradition, see Otto, *The Idea of the Holy,* pp. 104, 204-7; also "Mystische und gläubige Frömmigkeit," in *Aufsätze das Numinose betreffend,* (Stuttgart/Gotha: Verlag Friedrich Andreas Perthes, 1923), pp. 71-107, and "Rettung aus Verlorenheit nach Luther.

Justificatio per Fidem," in *Sünde und Urschuld* (München: C. H. Beck, 1932), pp. 43-60.

[10] Otto, *The Idea of the Holy*, pp. 99-100. See also pp. 23-24.

[11] Rudolf Otto, *Die Anschauung vom Heiligen Geiste bei Luther* (Göttingen: Vandenhoeck und Ruprecht, 1898), p. 15.

[12] Ibid., p. 48.

[13] Ibid., p. 53.

[14] Ibid., p. 96.

[15] Otto, *The Idea of the Holy*, p. 108. In Otto's own writings on liturgy and liturgical reform he stresses the desirability of a more contemplative form of worship in which the "real presence" of God may be fully and deeply experienced through a collective meditative silence. See, e.g., "Towards a Liturgical Reform,' in his *Religious Essays* (London: Oxford University Press, 1931), pp. 53-67, and "Schweigender Dienst," in *Aufsätze*, pp. 171-78.

[16] Otto, *The Idea of the Holy*, p. 108.

[17] Albrecht Ritschl, *Geschichte des Pietismus* (Bonn: Adolph Marcus, 1866), III, 195-438.

[18] See, e.g., the epilogue, to F. D. E. Schleiermacher, *Über die Religion: Reden an die Gebildeten unter ihren Verächtern* (Göttingen: Vandenhoeck und Ruprecht, 1899), p. xxxii. Or perhaps earlier, for Otto himself possessed a copy of the first edition of Wilhelm Dilthey's *Leben Schleiermachers*, a gift from Dilthey.

[19] Otto's review of Jakob Fries, *Wissen, Glaube und Ahndung*, ed. Leonard Nelson (Göttingen: Offentliches Leben, 1905), in *Die christliche Welt* 22 (1908): 819.

[20] In his review of Otto's *Kantisch-Fries'sche Religionsphilosophie*, in *Theologische Rundschau* 12 (1909): 424, Wilhelm Bousset remarks that Otto ought to have made more of Fries's connection to Moravian Pietism. He goes on to say that Fries's second wife was a member of the Brethren, as were his sisters.

[21] Otto Uttendörfer, "Die Entwürfe Zinzendorfs zu seiner Religions-schrift," *Zeitschrift für Brüdergeschichte* 13 (1919): 64-98.

[22] Rudolf Otto, "Zinzendorf über den 'Sensus Numinis,'" in *Aufsätze*, pp. 51-55.

[23] Uttendörfer, "Die Entwürfe Zinzendorfs," p. 73. Cf. Otto, *The Idea of the Holy*, p. 113.

[24] Rudolf Otto, "Zinzendorf als Entdecker des Sensus Numinis," in *Das Gefühl des Überweltlichen (Sensus Numinis)* (München: C. H. Beck, 1932), pp. 4-10. A revised version of his earlier essay on Schleiermacher's rediscovery of religion appears later in Otto, *Sünde und Urschuld*, pp. 123-39, under the (significantly) less emphatic title, "Der neue Aufbruch des Sensus Numinis bei Schleiermacher."

[25] Otto, "Zinzendorf als Entdecker," pp. 5-6.

[26] Ibid., pp. 9-10. See also Otto, *Sünde und Urschuld*, p. 139.

[27] Otto, *Religious Essays*, pp. 68-69.

[28] Ibid., p. 70.

[29] Rudolf Otto, introduction to F. D. E. Schleiermacher, *On Religion: Speeches to Its Cultured Despisers* (New York: Harper & Row, 1958), p. ix. This is an abbreviated version of Otto's introduction to his 1899 edition of the *Reden*.

[30] Ibid., p. viii.

[31] Otto, *Religious Essays*, p. 71.

[32] Ibid., p. 71.

[33] Ibid., p. 77.

[34] Karl Barth, *Protestant Theology in the Nineteenth Century* (London: S.C.M. Press, 1972), p. 266.

[35] In much of what follows, I am especially indebted to Herbert J. Paton, *Kant's Metaphysics of Experience* (London: Allen and Unwin, 1936).

[36] Norman Kemp Smith, *Immanuel Kant's Critique of Pure Reason* (London: Macmillan, 1964), pp. 41-42.

[37] Paton, *Kant's Metaphysics*, I, 304.

[38] Smith, *Immanuel Kant's Critique*, pp. 186-87.

[39] Schleiermacher, *On Religion*, p. 31.

[40] Otto, *Religious Essays*, p. 75. See also the introduction to Schleiermacher, *On Religion*, pp. 18-19.

[41] Schleiermacher, *On Religion*, p. 36.

[42] Ibid., p. 48. See also Otto, *The Idea of the Holy*, pp. 146, 171-72.

[43] Schleiermacher, *On Religion*, pp. 214-17. See also Otto, *Sünde und Urschuld*, p. 135.

[44] See Otto, *Religious Essays*, p. 112. Cf. Schleiermacher, *On Religion*, pp. 237-38.

[45] Otto, *Religious Essays*, pp. 115-16. See also the epilogue to Schleiermacher, *Über die Religion*, pp. xxix.

[46] See Schleiermacher, *On Religion*, pp. 241ff., epilogue to Schleiermacher, *Über die Religion*, pp. xxxi-xxxii, and Otto, *The Idea of the Holy*, pp. 177-78.

[47] See, e.g., Paul Tillich, *Systematic Theology* (Herts: Nisbet, 1968), I, 47; Richard R. Niebuhr, *Schleiermacher on Christ and Religion* (London: S.C.M. Press, 1964), pp. 116-17; Robert R. Williams, *Schleiermacher the Theologian* (Philadelphia: Fortress Press, 1978).

[48] Introduction to Schleiermacher, *On Religion*, p. xix. See also epilogue to Schleiermacher, *Über die Religion*, pp. xxxii-xxxiii.

[49] Epilogue to Schleiermacher, *Über die Religion*, p. xviii. See also Schleiermacher, *On Religion*, pp. 21, 71, 278.

[50] Introduction to Schleiermacher, *On Religion*, p. xix.

[51] Ibid., p. xii. See also Otto, *The Philosophy of Religion*, p. 23.

[52] Rudolf Otto, *Naturalism and Religion* (London: Williams and Norgate, 1907), p. 76.

[53] Otto, *The Philosophy of Religion*, p. 15.

[54] Ibid., p. 23.

[55] Otto, *Naturalism and Religion*, pp. 5-6.

[56] Ibid., p. 7.

[57] Ibid., p. 42.

[58] Ibid., p. 41. On dependence, see also pp. 64-65, 55, 58; Otto, *Religious Essays*, p. 137; and cf. Otto, *The Idea of the Holy*, pp. 9-10, 20, 108. On mystery, see Otto, *Naturalism and Religion*, p. 53, and, on purpose, pp. 151, 80, 82, 129.

[59] Otto, *The Philosophy of Religion*, p. 49.

[60] It is interesting to note that Schleiermacher voted for Hegel rather than for Fries to replace Johann G. Fichte in the chair of philosophy at Berlin. At the least, then, Schleiermacher did not see Fries as the best speculative philosopher available, despite the compatibility of their ideas, and much to the annoyance of Fries's disciple and Schleiermacher's friend and colleague Wilhelm de Wette. See Richard Crouter, "Hegel and Schleiermacher at Berlin: A Many-Sided Debate," *Journal of the American Academy of Religion* 48 (1980): 27-29. I am grateful to Dr. John Clayton for this reference. See also Otto, *The Philosophy of Religion*, pp. 26-27.

[61] See Robert Morgan, *Ernst Troeltsch: Writings on Theology and Religion* (London: Duckworth, 1977), p. 13.

[62] Ibid., p. 13.

[63] Ibid., p. 87.

[64] Jakob F. Fries, *Wissen, Glaube und Ahndung* (Göttingen: Öffentliches Leben, 1931), pp. 63-64.

[65] Ibid., pp. 19-30.

[66] See ibid., p. 35.

[67] Ibid., p. 29.

[68] Otto, *The Philosophy of Religion*, pp. 53, 58-59.

[69] Ibid., p. 78.

[70] Robert F. Davidson, *Rudolf Otto's Interpretation of Religion* (Princeton: Princeton University Press, 1947), p. 144. See also Otto, *The Philosophy of Religion*, pp. 66-67, 81.

[71] Otto, *The Philosophy of Religion*, pp. 84-85.

[72] Ibid., p. 85.

[73] Ibid., p. 87.

[74] See ibid., pp. 99-100. See also Fries, *Wissen, Glaube und Ahndung*, p. 122.

[75] Otto, *The Philosophy of Religion*, p. 115.

[76] Ibid., pp. 123-24. See also Fries, *Wissen, Glaube und Ahndung*, pp. 143-47.

[77] Fries, *Wissen, Glaube und Ahndung*, p. 175.

[78] *Ahndung* is somewhat archaic for what was in Otto's time and is today rendered by *Ahnung*; similarly with the verbal cognates *ahnden* and *ahnen*. In *The Philosophy of Religion* Otto uses *Ahnung* and its cognate. In *Das Heilige* and *Mysticism East and West*, for example, he reverts to *Ahndung*.

[79] Otto, *The Philosophy of Religion*, pp. 100-101. See also pp. 141-44.

[80] Fries, *Wissen, Glaube und Ahndung*, p. 235.

[81] Otto, *The Philosophy of Religion*, p. 133.

[82] See Otto, *The Idea of the Holy*, pp. 145-47.

[83] Otto, *The Philosophy of Religion*, p. 224.

[84] Ibid., p. 224.

**Michael Lattke (essay date 1985)**

SOURCE: "Rudolf Bultmann on Rudolf Otto," in *Harvard Theological Review,* Vol. 78, No. 1-2, January/April 1985, pp. 353-60.

*[In the following essay, Lattke discusses Otto's friendship with and intellectual split from Rudolf Bultmann at the University at Marburg.]*

Rudolf Otto (1869-1937),[1] well known for his book *The Idea of the Holy,*[2] and Rudolf Bultmann (1884-1976),[3] even more famous for his hermeneutical programs of demythologization and existential interpretation, had, according to Bultmann himself, "been friends at Breslau."[4] Although Bultmann admitted in 1969 with incorruptible fairness that "the calling of the systematic theologian Rudolf Otto was a great gain for the theological faculty at Marburg," he also had to state that "Otto and I grew so far apart that our students, too, were aware of the antithesis between his work and mine."[5] Already ten years earlier, in his first autobiographical draft of 1959, Bultmann mentioned "tensions with R. Otto, Hermann's successor," which "led to lively discussions"[6] among the students at Marburg. Those tensions date back at least to the early twenties, as two letters of Bultmann to Karl Barth reveal. In the first letter, written at the end of 1922, Bultmann stigmatizes the notes of Otto to F. Schleiermacher's *Reden, Über die Religion,* as "totally misleading."[7] In a letter written in April 1927 Bultmann expresses the hope that the opposition at Marburg to the Swiss theologian Eduard Thurneysen might be overcome "in six months, when Otto will be in India."[8] Thurneysen belonged to the new movement of so-called Dialectical Theology.[9]

In his most recent studies on Rudolf Otto, P. C. Almond, my colleague at the University of Queensland, clearly demonstrates that "the predominance of Dialectical Theology curtailed Otto's influence on the development of German theology during the first half of the twentieth century," and, "when Dialectical Theology became the vogue, from 1921 onward, there developed a rift within the (Marburg) theology faculty. Students flocked to hear Bultmann, and therefore Martin Heidegger also, leaving Otto with fewer and fewer."[10] However, as to Otto's late work *The Kingdom of God and the Son of Man* (1938), Almond mentions in a note only that his book "was harshly treated by Rudolf Bultmann," which "was in part, undoubtedly, because of the polemical stance taken by Otto against Bultmann's own position."[11]

Before looking at Bultmann's detailed but rather neglected review article "Reich Gottes und Menschensohn,"[12] published in the year of Rudolf Otto's death (1937), a few recent publications by or about Rudolf Bultmann should be investigated under the aspect of this research report.

In his major books[13] Bultmann neither polemizes against Otto, nor does he indicate that he has been influenced by him. Bultmann's important four-volume collection of hermeneutic and systematic essays, *Glauben und Verstehen,* contains only one short critical reference from 1924 to Otto's book *The Idea of the Holy.* He parallels Otto's emphasis on the wholly other[14] with the theological protest of Karl Barth and Friedrich Gogarten, but holds at the same time that their respective solutions are opposed to each other.

> Above all, R. Otto's book "The Idea of the Holy" grew out of the same theological situation as the protest of Barth, Gogarten and their circle. It is quite characteristic therefore that Otto calls God the wholly other, and stresses creaturely feeling as an essential factor in piety. The intention at the root of his concept of the Holy is the characterization of the essence of the divine as lying beyond the sphere of the rational and the ethical. Similarly, his stress on the inner connectedness of the aspects of the *tremendum* and *fascinosum* is an analogy, by no means superficial, to the doctrine of the inner unity of the knowledge of judgement and of grace. But, of course, the theological solution which Otto attempts to offer in this situation leads into the opposite direction.[15]

Bultmann's view of the reality of religion as the wholly other is, with respect to Rudolf Otto, still underlined by B. Jaspert[16] and M. Evang[17] in *Rudolf Bultmanns Werk und Wirkung,* published on the occasion of the centenary of his birth (20 August 1984). Evang's article also analyzes Bultmann's letter of 6 April 1918 to Otto on *The Idea of the Holy,*[18] a friendly letter, although it raises critical questions as to whether Otto's definition of the essence of religion is any more than a description of psychological phenomena appearing in the history of religions.[19] Against Otto's concept of an absolute feeling, Bultmann appeals to Schleiermacher's category of an absolute dependence.[20]

This reproach, that Otto has completely misunderstood Schleiermacher, appears in Bultmann's lecture notes for his *Theologische Enzyklopädie,* read five times between 1926 and 1936, and only recently published for the first time.[21] These lectures give us an idea of Bultmann's *public* remarks on Otto at the University of Marburg. Bultmann attacks Otto's confusion of God with the irrational, and declares the true *numinosum,* with its elements of the *tremendum* and *fascinosum,* to be the awareness of the enigma of our existence:

> An escape from the modern-liberal combination of romanticism and liberalism is attempted by the theological (and generally religious) current which, in sharp contrast to rationalism, understands the *irrational* as divine revelation. In contrast to Schleiermacherian romanticism, however, the experience of revelation is not the esthetic contemplation of the universe, but the realization of the uncanny and mysterious and at the same time captivating and attractive within which we stand. The awe before the numinous . . . feeling oneself as a creature, and yet the feeling that one is grasped by God and drawn to him, this is the experience of revelation . . . The negative aspect of this view

is correct, namely, that reason cannot say anything about that which lies beyond the limits of the human person, that it cannot portray a beyond. But it is false to mistake the irrational for God and to think one is speaking of God when one is speaking of the irrational. If "numinous" means more than the riddle of our existence, then "not having" is declared to be "having" and the devil is mistaken for God. In the numinous, human beings do not become aware of God, but of themselves; and they deceive themselves when they pretend the uncanny is God. This leads them not to take the riddle of their existence fully seriously.[22]

In his lecture on mysticism and faith[23] Bultmann points out examples of Otto's speculative and enthusiastic interpretation of religion.[24] The misdirections of mysticism,[25] culminating in the contempt of historicity and the negation of bodily existence, are shown to be the framework in which Otto's irrational elements of religion find their place.

> Of course, mysticism must not be defined as the "maximum tension or overstraining of the irrational aspects in religion" (Rudolf Otto . . . ) for, (1) what is the concept of the irrational and (2) what is overstraining? What is the point at which mysticism begins? The criterion which makes mysticism mysticism is not expressed in this statement.[26]

The true beyond of the human is, as Bultmann says, her or his personal and actual future.

> For just as "the human" is not something formal, but in every sense the concrete human being in a concrete historical situation, so also our beyond is only that which points us into the here. A beyond is always our concrete beyond, it is not the undefined, but the non-disposable, that which has disposition over us and bestows its gifts on us. . . . It is in the deed that God's beyond is affirmed.[27]

There is another important essay of Bultmann "which has never been published before, even in German."[28] In "Theology as Science" (1941)[29] Bultmann "reflects on the nature of theology itself as in its own way properly a science, thereby clarifying the methodological foundations of his whole theological approach."[30] With regard to Otto, Bultmann states that

> in the course of the nineteenth century and by the beginning of the twentieth, theology became essentially the science of religion. The biblical sciences became branches of the history of religion, and the same was true of church history insofar as it did not become simply profane history. Systematic theology became the philosophy or psychology of religion (Ernst Troeltsch and Rudolf Otto), and practical theology was now simply religious folklore, psychology of religion, and education.[31]

In answer to the question, "How can such a science of religion legitimate itself as Christian theology?",[32] Bultmann refers again to Schleiermacher's "feeling of absolute dependence"[33] and, more critically in his following remarks, to Otto's "numinous feeling, or creature feeling, that becomes aware of the *tremendum* and the *fascinosum* of deity."[34]

The publication of Bultmann's extensive answer to Otto's *The Kingdom of God and the Son of Man* tragically coincided with the death of Rudolf Otto "on March 6, 1937."[35] Contrary to the favorable review by "Otto's successor at Marburg,"[36] Heinrich Frick,[37] Bultmann's article criticizes Otto's exegetical methodology as well as his comparative interpretation.[38] Bultmann rightly confirms that the central synoptic Jewish term greek $\beta\alpha\sigma\iota\lambda\epsilon\iota\alpha$ $\tau\sigma\hat{\upsilon}$ $\theta\epsilon\sigma\hat{\upsilon}$ has to be translated by the reign or kingship of God and does not mean a numinous *mirum*.[39] There is nothing irrational[40] in the proclamation of God's gracious reign and challenging will, since the acceptance and realization of this liberating *kerygma* constitutes the human in her or his existential authenticity.[41] Bultmann demonstrates that Otto's broad approach cannot grasp the specific phenomenon of Jesus' $\epsilon\dot{\upsilon}\alpha\gamma\gamma\epsilon\lambda\iota\sigma\nu$ with its eschatological relation of present and future.[42]

With regard to Otto's interpretation of the $\upsilon\iota\dot{\sigma}\varsigma$ $\tau\sigma\hat{\upsilon}$ $\dot{\alpha}\nu\theta\rho\dot{\omega}\pi\sigma\nu$, one of the most difficult problems of biblical research, Bultmann shows that the reconstruction of Jesus' self-understanding out of the apocalyptic tradition of the Ethiopic Book of Enoch is a total illusion.[43] Otto's "Son of Man"—Jesus as ideally preexistent *"Messias designatus"*[44]—is merely a product of Otto's own fantasy,[45] without any critical stocktaking and analysis of the synoptic Son of Man sayings.[46] Otto's far-reaching thesis that the combination of the apocalyptic Son of Man (from Enoch) with the suffering servant of God (from Isaiah 53) was Jesus' original self-concept is indeed built on dubious evidence such as Mark 9:12 and 10:45.[47]

Rudolf Otto's chapter on the kingdom of God and charisma[48] deserves the most severe criticism,[49] because of his identification of Jesus with the charismatic figure of the holy man.[50] Historically, the literary genre of the New Testament sources is neither "hagiology" nor the "life" ($\beta\iota\sigma\varsigma$) of a $\theta\epsilon\hat{\iota}\sigma\varsigma$ $\dot{\alpha}\nu\dot{\eta}\rho$.[51] Theologically, one must carry on Bultmann's rejection of Otto's numinous "life of Jesus."[52] One must also radicalize Bultmann's call for an existential interpretation. Translated into a non-religious, even atheistic, theology, the criticism of religion[53] by Jesus and Paul can still be a guide: their protest against the dualism of holy and profane; their verbal and practical message of the justification of the ungodly; their realism as to individual and social life; their offer of freedom from all determining powers reflected by the new, eschatological, self-understanding of $\pi\iota\sigma\tau\iota\varsigma$, faith, which is open to the realization of human responsibility today.

[1] See G. Wünsch, "Otto, Rudolf," *RGG* (3d ed.; 1960) 4. cols. 1749-50.

[2] R. Otto, *The Idea of the Holy: An Inquiry into the Non-rational Factor in the Idea of the Divine and Its*

*Relation to the Rational* (trans. John W. Harvey; London: Oxford University Press, 1923; 2d ed. 1950; paperback ed. 1958 = reprint 1970). The first edition of *Das Heilige* was published in 1917, the year in which Otto moved from Breslau to Marburg. There is a great confusion in the numerous later editions of this study, subtitled *Über das Irrationale in der Idee des Göttlichen und sein Verhältnis zum Rationalen.*

[3] See Walter Schmithals, "Bultmann, Rudolf," *Theologische Realenzyklopädie* (1981) 7. 387-96; in this comprehensive article the name of R. Otto is not even mentioned.

[4] Cf. the longer version of his autobiographical "account of his relations with the city and university of Marburg," in Geoffrey W. Bromiley, trans. and ed., *Karl Barth - Rudolf Bultmann Letters: 1922-1966: Edited by Bernd Jaspert* (Grand Rapids: Eerdmans, 1981) 161-62.

[5] Ibid., 162; Bernd Jaspert, ed., *Karl Barth - Rudolf Bultmann Briefwechsel 1922-1966* (Zürich: Theologischer Verlag, 1971) 323: "A great gain for the Marburg theological faculty was the appointment of the systematician Rudolf Otto. Although we had once been friends in Breslau, we had become estranged from each other to such an extent that even our students felt the opposition between his and my work." (Ein grosser Gewinn für die Marburger theologische Fakultät war die Berufung des Systematikers Rudolf Otto. Wir waren, obwohl wir uns einst in Breslau angefreundet hatten, einander doch so fremd geworden, dass auch unsere Studenten den Gegensatz zwischen seiner und meiner Arbeit empfanden.)

[6] Cf. Bromiley, *Letters*, 159; Jaspert, *Briefwechsel*, 317: "In those days the theological faculty was by no means unanimous, and the various conflicts in it, especially the tensions between myself and Rudolf Otto, the successor of Wilhelm Herrmann, moved even the students and led to lively discussions." (Die theologische Fakultät war in jenen Tagen keineswegs einmütig, und die verschiedenen Auseinandersetzungen in ihr, vor allem die Spannung zwischen mir und Rudolf Otto, dem Nachfolger Wilhelm Herrmanns, bewegten sogar die Studenten und führten zu lebhaften Diskussionen.)

[7] Letter of 31 December 1922, in Bromiley, *Letters*, 6; Jaspert, *Briefwechsel*, 12: "Reden in der Ausgabe Ottos mit ihren m. E. gänzlich irre führenden Anmerkungen."

[8] Letter of 21 April 1927, in Bromiley, *Letters*, 31; Jaspert, *Briefwechsel*, 68.

[9] See Wilfried Härle, "Dialektische Theologie," *Theologische Realenzyklopädie* 8. 683-96.

[10] See Philip C. Almond, *Rudolf Otto: An Introduction to His Philosophical Theology* (Chapel Hill/London: University of North Carolina Press 1984) 5-6; see also 141 n. 7.

[11] Ibid., 125, 164 n. 51. The first edition of Otto's *Reich Gottes und Menschensohn: ein religionsgeschichtlicher Versuch* (München: Beck, 1934) contains 348 pages, whereas the *verbesserte* second one of 1940 (München: Beck) has only 326 pages. Unfortunately there is no synopsis of pagination.

[12] Rudolf Bultmann, "Reich Gottes und Menschensohn," *ThR* n.s. 9 (1937) 1-35.

[13] See the bibliography in Schmithals, "Bultmann," 396, and Rudolf Bultmann, *Exegetica: Aufsätze zur Erforschung des Neuen Testaments* (ed. Erich Dinkler; Tübingen: Mohr-Siebeck, 1967) 483-507.

[14] For *"das ganz Andere"* see also Almond, 68, 154 n. 39.

[15] Vor allem ist *R. Ottos* Buch "Das Heilige" aus der gleichen theologischen Situation erwachsen wie der Protest von Barth, Gogarten und ihrem Kreis. Seine Bezeichnung Gottes als des Ganz-Anderen, seine Betonung des Kreaturgefühls als wesentlichen Moments der Frömmigkeit sind dafür charakteristisch. Und wie seiner Fassung des "Heiligen" die Absicht zugrunde liegt, das Wesen des Göttlichen als jenseits der Sphäre des Rationalen und Ethischen liegend zu bestimmen, so ist seine Betonung der inneren Verbundenheit der Momente des Tremendum und Fascinosum im Numinosen eine nicht nur äusserliche Analogie zu jenem Satz von der inneren Zusammengehörigkeit der Erkenntnis des Gerichtes und der Gnade. Aber freilich führt die theologische Lösung, die Otto in dieser Situation zu geben versucht, in die entgegengesetzte Richtung. Rudolf Bultmann, "Dieliberale Theologie und die jüngste theologische Bewegung," in idem, *Glauben und Verstehen* (1933; 5th ed.; Tübingen: Mohr-Siebeck, 1964) 1. 22; cf. M. Lattke, *Register zu Rudolf Bultmanns Glauben und Verstehen, Band I-IV* (Tübingen: Mohr-Siebeck, 1984) 39. This index, published in the 4th ed. of vol. 4 of *Glauben und Verstehen* (Tübingen, Mohr-Siebeck, 1984) as well as Schubert M. Ogden, ed., *Rudolf Bultmann, New Testament and Mythology and Other Writings* (Philadelphia: Fortress, !984) should be added to the article of Hans Hübner, "Rückblick auf das Bultmann-Gedenkjahr 1984," *TLZ* 110 (1985) cols. 641-52.

[16] Bernd Jaspert, "Von der liberalen zur dialektischen Theologie," in idem, ed., *Rudolf Bultmanns Werk und Wirkung* (Darmstadt: Wissenschaftliche Buchgesellschaft, 1984) 25-43, esp. 39: "Wirklichkeit der Religion," als "das 'Ganz andere.'"

[17] Martin Evang, "Rudolf Bultmanns Berufung auf Friedrich Scheiermacher vor und um 1920," in Jaspert (ed.), *Werk und Wirkung*, 3-24, esp. 19: "die Welt des Jenseits, des 'ganz anderen.'"

[18] Cf. Almond, *Otto*, 141 n. 7.

[19] Cf. Evang, "Bultmann's Berufung," 6.

[20] Cf. ibid., 13: "Otto redet von einem schlechthinnigen *Gefühl* statt von schlechthinniger *Abhängigkeit.*" See also pp. 17-21 and Ogden, *Bultmann,* 51.

[21] Rudolf Bultmann, *Theologische Enzyklopädie* (ed. Eberhard Jüngel and Klaus W. Müller; Tübingen: Mohr-Siebeck, 1984) 24 n. 33.

[22] Der modern-liberalen Verbindung von Romantik und Liberalismus versucht die theologische (und allgemein religiöse) Richtung zu entgehen, die im Gegensatz zum Rationalismus das *Irrationale* als göttliche Offenbarung fasst. Im Gegensatz zur Schleiermacherschen Romantik ist aber das Erlebnis der Offenbarung nicht die ästhetische Anschauung des Universums, sondern das Innewerden des Unheimlichen und Rätselhaften und zugleich Bestrickenden und Anziehenden, in dem wir stehen. Die Scheu vor dem Numinosen, . . . das Sich-als-Kreatur-Fühlen und doch von Gott ergriffen und zu ihm gezogen Fühlen ist das Erlebnis der Offenbarung. . . . Daran ist das Negative richtig, dass die Ratio nichts über das, was jenseits der Grenzen des Menschen ist, aussagen kann, kein Jenseits entwerfen kann. Aber falsch ist es, das Irrationale mit Gott zu verwechseln und zu meinen, dass man von Gott redet, wenn man vom Irrationalen redet. Soll mit dem Numinosen mehr bezeichnet werden als eben das Innewerden des Rätsels unserer Existenz, so ist das Nichthaben zum Haben erklärt und Gott mit dem Teufel verwechselt worden. Im Numinosen wird der Mensch nicht Gottes, sondern seiner selbst inne; und er betrügt sich, wenn er das Unheimliche für Gott ausgibt; er nimmt das Rätsel seiner Existenz dann gar nicht ernst. Ibid., 81; cf. also 53.

[23] Ibid., 115-29: "Mystik und Glaube."

[24] Ibid., 120 n. 30.

[25] On mysticism cf. P. C. Almond, *Mystical Experience and Religious Doctrine: An Investigation of the Study of Mysticism in World Religions* (Berlin: Mouton, 1982).

[26] Natürlich darf Mystik aber nicht definiert werden als "Höchst- und Überspannung der irrationalen Momente in der Religion" (Rudolf Otto . . . ), denn 1. fragt es sich nach dem Begriff des Irrationalen überhaupt, und 2. was heisst "Überspannung"? Von wann ab beginnt die Mystik? Das Kriterium, das die Mystik zur Mystik macht, ist dabei gerade nicht genannt! (Bultmann, *Enzyklopädie,* 116-17)

[27] Denn wie "der Mensch" nichts Formales ist, sondern jeweils der bestimmte Mensch in einer konkreten geschichtlichen Situation, so ist auch sein Janseits nur das, was ihn ins Diesseits weist. Ein Jenseits ist immer sein konkretes Janseits; es ist nicht das Bestimmungslose, sondern das Unverfügbare, das über ihn Verfügende, ihn Beschenkende. . . . Gerade in der Tat wird Gottes Jenseitigkeit bejaht. Ibid., 129 n. 66: "Sein wirkliches Jenseits ist je seine Zukunft."

[28] Ogden, *Bultmann,* viii.

[29] Ibid., 45-67. Cf. now also R. Bultmann, "Theologie als Wissenschaft," *ZThK* 81 (1984) 447-69.

[30] Ibid., viii. For Bultmann on Schubert M. Ogden, the meritorious editor and translator of these and other writings of Bultmann, see Lattke, *Register,* 39.

[31] Ogden, *Bultmann,* 51.

[32] Ibid.

[33] Ibid.

[34] Ibid., 52.

[35] Almond, *Otto,* 24.

[36] Ibid., 164 n. 51.

[37] H. Frick, "Wider die Skepsis in der Leben-Jesu-Forschung: R. Ottos Jesus-Buch," *ZThK* 43 = 16 (1935) 1-20.

[38] Bultmann, "Reich Gottes," 6: "die Interpretation der synoptischen Texte mit Hilfe der Religionswissenschaft, speziell der Religionsvergleichung."

[39] Ibid., 8-9, 14-16, 21 ("Gottesherrschaft" versus "Wunderding"). See also M. Lattke, "On the Jewish Background of the Synoptic Concept 'The Kingdom of God,'" in Bruce Chilton, ed., *The Kingdom of God in the Teaching of Jesus* (Philadelphia: Fortress; London: SPCK, 1984) 72-91.

[40] Bultmann, "Reich Gottes," 12: "irrational ist hier nichts."

[41] Ibid., 13-14: "Eigentlichkeit."

[42] Ibid., 14-19; idem, *Jesus and the Word* (trans. L. Pettibone Smith and E. Huntress Landero; New York: Scribner's, 1958) 51-56.

[43] Ibid., "Reich Gottles," 22-24, esp. 22: "eine völlige Illusion."

[44] Ibid, 20.

[45] Ibid., 24.

[46] Ibid., 25-26.

[47] Ibid., 29-30. See also the criticism of Otto by Howard Clark Kee, "Messiah and the People of God," in J. T. Butler, E. W. Conrad, B. C. Ollenburger, eds., *Understanding the Word: Essays in Honor of Bernhard W. Anderson* (Sheffield: JSOT, 1985) 341-58, esp. 346.

[48] "Gottesreich und Charisma:" 1st ed., 1934, pp. 283-327; 2d ed., 1940, pp. 267-309.

[49] Bultmann, "Reich Gottes," 30-35.

[50] Ibid., 30: "Gestalt eines 'Heiligen'." See also M. Lattke, "Heiligkeit III. Neues Testament," *Theologische Realenzyklopädie* (1985,) 14. 703-8; idem, "Holiness and Sanctification in the New Testament," in E. G. Newing and E. W. Conrad, eds., *Perspectives on Language and text: Essays and Poems in Honor of Francis I. Andersen's Sixtieth Birthday July 28, 1985* (Winona Lake, IN: Eisenbrauns, 1986).

[51] Bultmann, "Reich Gottes," 31-34.

[52] Ibid., 34. As to the historical quest of Jesus, see M. Lattke, "Neue Aspekte der Frage nach dem historischen Jesus," *Kairos* 21 (1979) 288-99; H. Leroy, *Jesus: Überlieferung und Deutung* (Darmstadt: Wissenschaftliche Buchgesellschaft) 1978.

[53] Cf. M. Franzmann and M. Lattke, "Theological Anthropology and the Criticism of Religion(s)," *East Asia Journal of Theology* 4 (1986).

## Bruce W. Ballard (essay date 1988)

SOURCE: "Heidegger, Otto, & The Phenomenology of Awe," in *Philosophy Today,* Vol. 32, No. 1, Spring, 1988, pp. 62-74.

[*In the following essay, Ballard examines Otto's phenomenology of the numinous and Heidegger's "ontological inquiry" as set out in his* Being and Time.]

In what follows I work out some of the signal implications of Heidegger's philosophy of mood for a reinterpretation of Rudolf Otto's phenomenology of religious feeling. I further argue that Otto's investigation of numinous feeling makes better sense than Heidegger's account of anxiety in elaborating the most primary human questioning. Consequently, Otto's phenomenology more completely meets the criteria Heidegger sets out in *Being and Time* for thorough ontological inquiry, namely, that it keep the whole phenomenon (man's existence) in view and grasp it in the unity of its structures. Otto does not, however, work out an adequate philosophical anthropology and therefore does not grasp the unity of human existence explicitly. Hence, Heidegger's explanation of the relation between situatedness (the capacity for feelings, the affect) and understanding, along with the temporal interpretation of these existentials (basic structures of existence) is needed to ground Otto's insights. The synthesis I effect between Heidegger's existential ontology of the affect and Otto's phenomenology of awe expresses what I take to be among the more important possibilities of each.

### OTTO'S SHORTFALL: THE RATIONAL & IRRATIONAL

In his Introduction to the Phenomenology of Religion course of 1920-1921, Heidegger refers to Otto's chief distinction in the analysis of religious awe, namely, the distinction between rational and non-rational elements in the divine. Heidegger calls for a clarification of this distinction before it can be of real service. The problem with this pre-grasp of religion is evident: "To place religious phenomena in the category of the irrational, no matter how broadly one characterizes this, is to explain nothing, precisely because the contrast lives off the meaning of the "rational," which itself goes unquestioned or unclarified."[1] Heidegger himself provided the outline of a theory which would clarify Otto's distinction and, consequently, augment the study of awe which Otto undertakes in *The Idea of the Holy (Das Heilige).* At the same time, it is impossible simply to reinterpret Otto's work along Heideggerian lines. Though Heidegger repeatedly urges that his own work is pre-theological, his consciously this-worldly analysis of Dasein (in, e.g. *BT*) and his insistence in the later writings (cf. "Letter on Humanism") that Being cannot be identified with God, along with a number of other indications, put his philosophy at points in tension with Otto's Christianity. I will not suppress this tension but instead argue that Heidegger's teleology is inadequate at points in a way which Otto's surpasses. The affinity between Heidegger and Otto is due, in no small part, to the debt which Heidegger owes both to Paul and to Kierkegaard for some of his most fundamental concepts. Because, to my knowledge, Heidegger says nothing more explicitly about Otto's work as phenomenology and because Heidegger's philosophy is closely related to Husserl's, it is worthwhile listening to Husserl's interpretation of Otto's work.

In a letter to Otto of March 5, 1919, Husserl remarks:

> Through Heidegger and Oxner . . . I became aware last summer of your book, *Das Heilige,* and it has had a strong effect on me as hardly no other book in years. Allow me to express my impressions in this way: it is a first beginning for a phenomenology of religion, at least with regard to everything that does not go beyond a pure description and analysis of the phenomena themselves. To put it succinctly: I cannot share in the additional philosophical theorizing; and it is quite non-essential for the specific task and particular subject matter of this book, and it would be better left out. It seems to me that a great deal more progress would have to be made in the study of the phenomena and their eidetic analysis before a theory of religious consciousness, as a philosophical theory, could arise . . . One would need a systematic eidetic typification of the levels of religious data, indeed in their eidetically necessary development. It seems to me that the metaphysician (theologian) in Herr Otto has carried away on his wings Otto the phenomenologist. . . . But be that as it may, this book will hold an *abiding* place in the history of genuine philosophy of religion or phenomenology of religion. It is a beginning and its

significance is that it goes back to the "beginnings," the "origins," and thus, in the most beautiful sense of the word, is "original." And our age yearns for nothing so much as that the true origins might finally come to word and then, in the higher sense, come to their Word, to the Logos.[2]

Here in more detail Husserl anticipates Heidegger's call for a greater development of Otto's phenomenological categories, as well as expressing the esteem which both obviously had for *Das Heilige* as phenomenology.

As we have observed, Heidegger's complaint is that Otto never sufficiently clarified *the rational* upon which *the irrational* must be parasitic. What was Otto's conception of the rational? One description runs: "Now all these attributes [spirit, reason, purpose, good will, supreme power, unity, selfhood] can be grasped by the intellect; they can be analysed by thought; they admit of definition. An object that can thus be thought conceptually may be termed *rational*."[3] Hence, the rational is that which is susceptible of complete conceptual determination or definition. Otto's contrast in the definition of the Holy, however, is not between the rational and the irrational, but between rational and non-rational aspects of the divine. We suspect that the non-rational will simply be that which is not capable of complete conceptual determination or definition. This is true for Otto but there is more to it. He describes the non-rational in the following passage:

> beneath this sphere of clarity [the rational] and lucidity lies a hidden depth, inaccessible to our conceptual thought, which we in so far call the "non-rational." The meaning of the two contrasted terms may be made plainer by an illustration. A deep joy may fill our minds without any clear realization upon our part of its source and the object to which it refers, though some such objective reference there must always be. But as attention is directed to it the obscure object becomes clearly identified in precise conceptual terms. Such an object cannot, then, be called in our sense of the word, "non-rational." But it is quite otherwise with religious "bliss" and its essentially numinous aspect, the *fascinans*. Not the most concentrated attention can elucidate the object to which this state of mind refers, bringing it out of the impenetrable obscurity of feeling into the domain of the conceptual understanding. It remains purely a felt experience, only to be indicated symbolically by "ideograms." That is what we mean by saying it is non-rational . . . The object of *religious* awe or reverence—the *tremendum* and *augustum*, cannot be fully determined conceptually.[4]

What is the relation between the rational and the non-rational here? It is not *simply* the case that the so-called non-rational affect is the beginning of an understanding which culminates in an intellectual determination—Hegel's career of Spirit notwithstanding. The point Otto wants to make in the first chapter of *Das Heilige* is that the final intellectual "product" is not identical with, and

is only a partial determination of, the felt experience. So though Otto's distinction between the rational and the non-rational is not precisely that of Heidegger's understanding and situatedness, there is this similarity: in both cases, the affect gives us access to aspects of experience prior to and beyond the range of cognition. We recall that for Heidegger cognition is but one mode of understanding, and not the most basic. Cognition is the Heideggerian parallel to Otto's "rational." If we keep this similarity in mind it will not be so difficult to fill in the ontological blanks in Otto's phenomenology with Heidegger's development of Dasein. Again, while for Otto the relation between the non-rational and the rational is not *simply* epistemic inception to cognitive terminus, there is something of a hermeneutic structure to the affect running through his discussion.

In fact, Otto describes two hermeneutical and dialectical processes of development involving the affect. First, there is the permeation of the numinous with rational and moral elements. Second is the intrinsic development of the numinous.[25] Both processes illustrate the historically developed character of the category "Holy." We cannot translate "category" here as Heidegger's "existential" because though Otto's "Holy" contains an existential conception it is not a relation of Being-in-the-world such as Heidegger outlines. The Holy is a category which evolves. It does not, however, develop according to mere shifts of opinion among the populations of this world. Otto traces a conceptual development through the history of religion which he sees as a necessary outworking of numinous experience. The process first mentioned—permeation of the numinous with rational and moral elements—is parasitic on the second, sc. the *intrinsic* development of the numinous.

The so-called intrinsic development of the numinous begins with a non-conceptual grasp. Here Otto recognizes the necessity of a hermeneutic which begins in the affect. Of the essential, synthetic, rationally describable attributes of the divine, Otto remarks:

> We have to predicate them of a subject which they qualify, but which in its deeper essence is not, nor indeed can be, comprehended in them; which rather requires comprehension of a quite different kind. Yet, though it eludes the conceptual way of understanding, it must be in some way or other within our grasp, else absolutely nothing could be asserted of it.[6]

This remark adumbrates the more developed treatment of Heidegger's "dread" which eludes the conceptual determinations of scientific rationalism (cf. *What is Metaphysics?*).

Otto's point is made more perspicuous by Heidegger's discussion of the necessity for beginning with everyday existence in the analysis of human experience. The "they" is part of our existential structure—our social self—and our language is essentially its domain. If anything can be asserted about the Holy, we must start from its determination in our language, trace its history and get back to the original experiences from which it grew. About the coming to word of numinous experience Otto notes that our language prejudices us. Like Heidegger, Otto recognizes the need for, if not a new language, at least a new way of using the old forms, in order to stay in conformity with the phenomena. The prejudice goes as follows:

> All language, insofar as it consists of words, purports to convey ideas or concepts;—that is what language means—and the more clearly and unequivocally it does so, the better the language. And hence expositions of religious truth in language inevitably tend to stress the "rational" attributes of God.[7]

Not only does language prejudice our approach to experience in this way, but even the most thoughtful reflections or descriptions of religious experience do not express "directly" what is felt. In this connection Otto uses the term "ideogram." An ideogram is not "a genuine intellectual concept, but only . . . a sort of illustrative substitute for a concept."[8] Again, it is "an analogical notion taken from the natural sphere, illustrating, but incapable of exhaustively rendering, our real meaning."[9] This idea of course is not new with Otto. The scholastics commonly spoke of knowledge of God as analogous so that though the same terms might be used of men and God, they did not signify attributes in the same way. These were simply the best approximation for understanding an infinite being. A similar limitation is seen in the description of divine nature *via negativa*.

We have already noted Otto's claim that there is an intrinsic development of the numinous experience itself, apart from its rationalization and moralization. This claim is to be made out by investigating the a priori possibility of having such experience and the advances made with the conception historically. The historically necessary synthesis out of numinous feeling Otto describes in this way:

> It is . . . probable, that in the first stage of its development the religious consciousness started with only one of its poles—the 'daunting' aspect of the numen [the intentional objet of numinous experience]—and so first took shape only as "daemonic dread." But if this did not point to something beyond itself, if it were not but one "moment" of a completer experience, pressing up gradually into consciousness, then no transition would be possible to the feelings of positive self-surrender to the numen. It can never explain how it is that "the numinous" is the object of search and desire and yearning, and that too for its own sake and not only for the sake of the aid and backing that men expect from it in the natural sphere.[10]

Here Otto not only gets an explanation of the dramatic differences between religious primitive and civilized on the basis of a part-whole conception (rather than lumping every "religion" together under a genus which thereby becomes unintelligible), but is able to show intimations of this development in real examples.

One example of the numinous gaining a fuller affective determination runs as follows:

> Elements and strands are to be found in numerous mythologies and the stories of savage tribes, which reach altogether beyond the point they have otherwise attained in religious rites and usages. Notions of 'high gods' are adumbrated, with whom the savage has often hardly any relations in practice . . . if any at all, and in other mythological images, a value which may well accord with the divine in the highest sense.[11]

Otto wants to explain this progress out of a priori feeling which impels movement: "assuming the continual pressure and operation of an inward reasonable disposition to form certain ideas, these anticipations are not only no matter for surprise; they are . . . naturally to be expected."[12]

While I will not here retrace Otto's complete development of such a process, it is at least worth hearing his summary:

> Taking this non-rational process of development first, we have seen how the "daemonic dread," after itself passing, through various gradations, rises to the level of 'fear of the gods,' and thence to "fear of God." The daimonion or daemonic power becomes the Theion or divine power: 'dread' becomes worship; out of a confusion of inchoate emotions and bewildered palpitations of feeling grows *"religio,"* and out of "shudder" a holy awe. The feelings of dependence upon and beatitude in the numen, from being relative, become absolute. The false analogies and fortuitous associations are gradually dispelled or frankly rejected.[13]

With the dispelling or rejecting of false analogies and unnecessary associations, and through renewed numinous feeling, there is a dialectical progress within the historical hermeneutic movement. The process is as follows: I (or we) experience the Numen; I (or we) posit a certain construction of this experience; the next time the Numen is experienced under this construction and a sense of incongruity between my construction and my current experience is felt; whether from a mistaken or one-sided view, I am then led on to a new appreciation of the divine. Something very similar occurs in the development of a long-term relationship with another human being.

### BEYOND KANT TO PHENOMENOLOGY

Like the early Heidegger, Otto sees a need for an a priori structure of human Being which will explain the possibility of certain kinds of experience. This structure is claimed to be unchanging and, following Kant, transcendental. Otto follows Kant explicitly here, citing the *Critique of Pure Reason* on the a priori. He claims that knowledge of the numinous begins with experience but does not arise from it.[14] His argument for the a priori nature of the knowledge of the Holy runs:

> The proof . . . is to be reached by introspection and a critical examination of reason such as Kant instituted. We find, that is, involved in the numinous experience, beliefs and feelings qualitatively different from anything that "natural" sense-perception is capable of giving us. They are themselves not perceptions at all, but peculiar interpretations and valuations, at first of perceptual data, and then—at a higher level— of posited objects and entities, but are thought of as supplementing and transcending.[15]

Due to the uniqueness of their objects, these interpretations and valuations are said to have their source in "something still deeper than the 'pure reason'"[16]—both theoretical and practical. He reminds us of the "pure feeling" of respect for practical reason as law-giver (a feeling with no sensuous incitement or object) which is the subjective ground of the ultimate principle of morality. The new faculty he distinguishes is *spirit* or the ground of the soul.

Though we are now wary of a faculty psychology, it is not hard to see what motivates Otto's interpretation. Like Plato in the *Republic* (494e-441b), Otto is here distinguishing a special capacity of mind by virtue of its uniquely experienced function. Otto is ambivalent, however, on the nature of this ability. On one hand it is said to be "deeper" than pure or practical reason, on the other it is called a pure reason[17] which is nonetheless distinct from the two functions named. Whichever way Otto is interpreted, it is clear that Kant would have rejected these ideas respecting apprehension of the Holy. Otto's reply will be that a phenomenology of religion which stays close to religious experience.

> may be found fatal to the attempt to construct a "religion within the limits of pure reason," or "of humanity"; but, none the less, the matter is as we have described it, as far as concerns the psychological inquiry into religion, which asks, not what it is within the aforementioned limits, but what it is in its own essential nature.[18]

Here he refers of course to Kant's *Religion within the Limits of Reason Alone* which does in fact reduce Christianity to perfect morality. Kant also terms perfectly moral Being "holy" in the *Foundations of the Metaphysics of Morals*. Otto's objection is both phenomenological with respect to religious experience and directed against a dogmatic reduction of the possibilities for such experience in the conception of reason. It is phenomenological as an imperative to develop religious categories and (roughly) existentials *out of* the religious experience. It is also anti-reductionist (contra Kant): This "proceeding of constructing a 'humanity' prior to and apart from the most central and potent of human capacities is like nothing so much as the attempt to frame a standard idea of the human body after having previously cut off the head."[19]

It may be objected here that Otto overlooks Kant's discussion of the divine in the *Critique of Judgment*. The judgment is a faculty of knowledge operating with an a priori principle which discovers the sublimity of the divine.[20] In the third Critique, God serves as an instance of the sublime, i.e. "the absolutely great"[21] or "infinite".[22] This sublimity can never be found in nature since we can have no *presentation* of a natural infinity. But what is sublime here? For Kant, "instead of the object (of infinite magnitude), it is rather the cast of the mind in appreciating it that we have to estimate as sublime."[23]

In the sublime feeling of the infinite, it is precisely the struggle and failure of the imagination to give us a *picture* of the *idea* of infinity—which idea is given to our reason—that is sublime.[24] This struggle induces in us "a feeling of our possessing a pure and self-sufficient reason."[25]

Again, on Kant's account, the sublimity of nature and of God is the same in regard to infinity and to might. In both cases, what turns out to be sublime is neither nature nor God, but reason as having ideas beyond the power of imagination *and* as able to command right action despite external forces. For Kant the faculty of reflective judgment is able to estimate God as sublime as a form of the infinite or as the perfectly good. His position is summarily put as follows:

> Sublimity . . . does not reside in any of the things of nature, but only in our own mind, in so far as we may become conscious of our superiority over nature within, and thus also over nature without us (as exerting influence upon us). Everything that provokes this feeling in us, including the *might* of nature which challenges our strength, is then, though improperly, called sublime, and it is only under presupposition of this idea within us, and in relation to it, that we are capable of attaining to the idea of the sublimity of that Being which inspires deep respect in us, not by the mere display of its might in nature, but more by the faculty which is planted in us of estimating that might without fear, and of regarding our estate as exalted above it.[26]

These estimations fall short of the full grasp of the holy Otto wants for his faculty, spirit.

So far as numinous experience can be encompassed under the rubric of an existential, Otto may be said to have identified a basic situatedness (*Grundbefindlichkeit*). His treatment of the holy here is reminiscent of the transcendental generality Heidegger attributes to the basic existentials in *BT,* though Otto attempts to be more explicitly Kantian. Throughout this discussion we see Otto wrestling with the best account of knowledge and human faculties he knows, sc. Kant's, when the primordiality of the affect in the experience of the holy cries out for a different casting of the role of mood. This Heidegger accomplishes with the recognition of the equiprimordiality and, in fact, interdependence of the affect and the understanding. Though Otto struggles to get beyond Kant with his "spirit" he nonetheless seeks to incorporate this new faculty (if it is not an aspect of pure reason already) within the Kantian system. As he can expect no help from Kant's general thesis that the passional aspect of behavior is a kind of cause and effect relation, his best foothold within Kant for a more determinative affect is the feeling of respect for reason as legislative or in the feeling of the sublime made possible by the judgment. This is a beginning but does not reach the solution Heidegger achieves. Another obvious source for a fuller development of Otto's phenomenology of religious dread would be Heidegger's own discussion of dread.

OTTO & HEIDEGGER ON DREAD

There is a strong affinity between what Otto describes as alienation in the dread of the numen and Heidegger's encounter with the Nothing in dread. As we noted earlier, "awefulness" is an aspect of both major dimensions of the Numinous. As an aspect of the tremendum, dread (Otto prefers the English "awe" here) is to be distinguished from natural fear[27] and signifies the feeling of tremor before the completely awesome. A primitive form of this feeling Otto identifies is dread of the uncanny and of ghosts or demonic spirits. As an aspect of the Numen qua Mysterium, awe is something like stupor before the wholly other. Again Otto distinguishes this feeling of something mysterious from natural puzzlement.[28] Let us trace this feeling from the dread of ghosts to what is called an encounter with the Nothing.

Speaking of the attraction of ghost stories and horror tales, Otto asks what it is that draws us. He thinks we are drawn to ghost stories "because it (the ghost) is a thing that 'doesn't really exist at all,' the 'wholly other,' something which has no place in our scheme of reality but belongs to an absolutely different one, and which at the same time arouses an irrepressible interest in the mind."[29] This conception becomes more definite with further development in theism when

> the feeling of the "wholly other," is heightened and clarified, its higher modes of manifestation come into being, which set the numinous object in contrast not only to everything wonted and familiar (i.e. in the end, to nature in general), thereby turning it into the "supernatural," but finally to the world itself, and thereby exalt it to the "supramundane," that which is above the whole world-order.[30]

The development reaches its highest pitch in mysticism which concludes "by contrasting it [the Numen] with Being itself and all that 'is,' and finally actually calls it 'that which is nothing.'"[31]

In a conclusion to this discussion, Otto makes observations remarkably similar to Heidegger's a few years later in *What is Metaphysics?* Again, regarding the Nothing, Otto says:

> By this "nothing" is meant not only that of which nothing can be predicated, but that which is

absolutely and intrinsically other than and opposite of everything that is and can be thought. But while exaggerating to the point of paradox this *negation* and contrast—the only means open to conceptual thought to apprehend the *mysterium*—mysticism at the same time retains the *positive equality* of the "wholly other" as a very living factor in its overbrimming religious emotion.[32]

In Heidegger's description of the experience of nothing in dread,[33] he also marks the withdrawal of what-is-in-totality. Everything slips away and we with it. Hence, "it is not 'you' or 'I' that has the uncanny feeling, but 'one.'"[34] As with Otto, the nothing encountered in dread indicates an ontological difference between what-is-in-totality and what transcends it. Unlike Otto, Heidegger's thematic is the meaning of Being as such. Where Otto leaves Being and Nothing in traditional opposition, Heidegger recognizes the essential nihilating activity of the Nothing as an aspect or side of Being as such. Its nature is to repel and expel into what-is. Just as the significance of the world's connections is receding (even because of this) Dasein is oppressed by its continued Being-in-the-world absurdly. The experience of nothing shows the clearing where Being becomes manifest in beings through the Being of man. Hence, Nothing reveals the transcendental structure of Dasein. For Otto, however, there is something positive here for feeling, beyond simple direction for ontological research.

It may be thought that the same can be said of Heidegger since at the end of *What is Metaphysics?* he points to the fundamental affect "wonder" as directed toward the question of the meaning of Being based on this experience of Nothing. The feeling and its intentional object in Otto, however, point beyond man's Being. Again, Heidegger could say so much in *What is Metaphysics?* For him, experience of the Nothing directs us to the meaning of Being which is not man-made or subject to man's will. This is particularly clear in the later writings when he speaks of the destinies which are sent us by being—over which human will exercises no sway. What then is the crucial difference between Heidegger and Otto and how does this difference bear on the preferability of one account over the other so far as they diverge?

It may seem as though the two accounts, while bearing certain interesting affinities, are at last incomparable, that there can be no contest between them. This conclusion is reached by noting the distinctions Heidegger makes in the "Letter on Humanism," for example between Being and the Holy.[35] In the "Letter," the Holy is the "sphere of divinity" or the "dimension" for the gods and for God. Being—that which determines entities as entities—includes a determination of the Holy and the unholy alike. Another way of seeing the difference between the two accounts and especially the results derived from these experiences is by recognizing Otto's account of religious awe of the Nothing as only one aspect of a synthetic feeling-conception (i.e. the numinous). The object of dread for Otto is also the object of attractive mystery and later, goodness, mercy and love. For Otto, the incomparable object of awe is Holy Being. The synthetic notion of the numinous as the object of awe which reveals the Being of man in relation to Holy Being changes the meaning of authenticity in a way which sharply demarcates the two accounts.

We recall that for Heidegger the criterion of authentic living is the extent to which a manner of life renders Dasein's ontological structure transparent. This is particularly important with respect to the disclosure of the final horizon of interpretation for Being, time. In *BT,* the authentic understanding is anticipatory resoluteness coming out of the authentic mood, readiness for anxiety. This complex is claimed to show the three-fold nature of human temporality quite explicitly. To the degree that it does, it fulfills the requirements of an adequate ontological interpretation of man. I have also suggested, based on Heidegger's comments at the end of *What is Metaphysics?,* that wonder can be seen as the fundamental mood of human Being in Heidegger. It springs up in the experience of anxiety before the nothing which Heidegger uses in *BT* as well. The test of a basic situatedness *(Grundbefindlichkeit)* is the degree to which it allows for a far-reaching disclosure of Dasein. This should allow us to reach an ontological interpretation which (1) is in conformity with the phenomena under investigation, (2) grasps the whole of the phenomena in the initial grasp (fore-having), (3) grasps the unity of the structural items of the phenomena, and (4) reveals them in a simplified or elemental way. It is my closing contention that, far as Heidegger's existential analysis reaches, Otto provides the explication of a basic situatedness which reaches further in fulfilling the conditions which Heidegger sets for ontological investigation.

OTTO'S ADVANTAGE

Given that Heidegger never really answered the question of the meaning of Being as such, and because he does offer an existence-ethic even in *BT,* it is fair to ask whether the ethic he offered is supportable. On either of the following interpretations of his "ethics," Heidegger misses aspects of the existential structure of Dasein which are primary. One reading of Heidegger's prescriptive in *BT* and against technological absorption in other places is what I call an ontological ethics. On this reading, Heidegger's ethics are motivated or supported *only* to the degree to which they express underlying existential structures and reveal these in a way which will move along the investigation of the meaning of Being in general. This is the reading of any importance since the alternative is simply that Heidegger moralizes gratuitously throughout *BT.* Hence, I treat the former.

On this reading, Heidegger might be acquitted of prescriptivism or moralizing in any usual sense. Though it is doubtful that the prescriptions he seems to give in *BT* can be justified on the basis of their aid in the analysis of Dasein, I will not try to argue this. I do not argue the point because even if these prescriptions

were supportable as aids to ontology and even if Heidegger's metaphysics reflects the mood of wonder, it would still miss essential aspects of Dasein.

Who is to say which moods are the more essential? We have already noted the advantage for ontology which can be had out of an essential mood, but leave open the question of which moods *best* serve here. Unless one is willing to utterly reject what is commonly felt deeply as part of a pseudoconcrete life-world, it is impossible to ignore *certain* fundamental affects.

Heidegger's contention that wonder, in the way he describes it in *What is Metaphysics?,* is the fundamental affect is suspect. I do not deny that it may well serve for the type of investigation Heidegger had in mind, only that this investigation misses Dasein in the farthest reaching way. I am not forgetting here that Heidegger later rejected the voluntarism which is evident in 1928. The later authentic mood was *Gelassenheit* or releasement. As this also can be seen as a kind of wonder, however, there is no reason to treat it separately. The question "Why is there something, why not much rather nothing?" would not appear to be the most pressing of questions to most people, regardless of the supposedly implicit dependence of every other question upon its formulation. If we are thinking of the Being of man as Care, and as directed toward one's Being-at-issue (as Heidegger does), candidates for more fundamental affects would include the felt desire for intimacy, solidarity with one's fellows, a purpose in one's life. Certainly the experiences which Otto describes in *Das Heilige,* and the spiritual form of life Kierkegaard describes in almost all of his works come closer to these more pressing feelings (other than solidarity). The double conversion to Christianity and to Marxism described without a view to philosophical explication by Ernesto Cardenal and Guadalupe Carney *(To Be a Revolutionary)* might be taken as examples of sentiment laying hold of full relationship with the divine and entire solidarity with fellowmen. While it is too far from Otto for us to show how the revolutionary affect complex surpasses Heideggerian "wonder" as a revelation of the structure of human Being, it is certainly evident by now in historical examples that these sentiments reach deeper. Otto's advantage over Heidegger, though, is most clearly seen with respect to the question of purpose.

For Heidegger, our ultimate purpose is the "for the sake of which" of our activity. We act for the sake of some lived interpretation of ourselves, whether explicitly or not. The inauthentic person lives for the sake of pleasing others through conforming. What does the authentic person live for? The most Heidegger cares to say, or perhaps can say, is that he lives to fatefully repeat certain ways of life which have come down through our heritage and to live these possibilities with a view to his own death. This position is virtually indentical with the stoicism of, e.g. Epictetus, or more especially, Marcus Aurelius. There the will is all important in the conscious constitution of the meaning of every experience.

While it is true of Epictetus that he advocates living according to nature as well as toward the god(s), these apparent constraints are difficult to square with the all-constituting role of the will, that which is within one's absolute control. Though Heidegger also appears to have a limiting condition on resolute projection of one's ownmost possibilities, sc. that such a projection make your ontological nature apparent, his voluntarism is no more constrained in the early writings than that of Epictetus.

Dreyfus's remarks on the emptiness of role choices in Heidegger's conception of authenticity bring out the teleological ellipsis there: "The authentic Dasein who . . . in effect, has already sensed his non-being is not afraid of any threat to his projects, since they are a game anyway."[36] Again, "any role can be used to cover up or to face up."[37] The problem seems to be something like aborting a teleological chain of purposes before reaching any ultimate purpose. We are reminded of Aristotle here, from whom Heidegger appropriated much of his teleology. As he argues in the *Metaphysics,* it is difficult (Aristotle says impossible) to make sense of intermediate purposes without a final end in view. Heidegger abbreviates the order of purposes, stopping with one's own willed projection into the nothing. As we see in the enigmatic later writings, though, Heidegger does seem to recognize, if not imitation of the divine (which Aristotle saw as *the* final cause, not just of man but of what is in totality), at least the need to include god(s) in the "four-fold of Being." The abbreviation of the chain of purposes bears implications for the authentic disclosure of temporality.

The authentic present, the moment of vision Heidegger describes in *BT,* borrows both from Kierkegaard and from Paul. In relation to Paul's account (in the Introduction to the Phenomenology of Religion course of 1920-21), Heidegger tried to reduce the meaning of authentic religious life to a form of temporality which need not continue beyond this life. This interpretation misses essential moments in the Pauline writings and the same may be said of Heidegger's borrowing of the "moment of vision" in *BT.* Nothing limits or prevents the insight which might come in the Heideggarian moment of vision from bringing the most vicious treatment upon oneself or others. In a moment of vision which is unto-death, one batters his head against finitude to return with "sober joy" to stoic resoluteness. It is obvious from these borrowings as well as from the later writings on the "gods" that Heidegger is not even attempting to explicate a religious experience. Of course, nothing I have used from Otto purports to prove that the seeming knowledge got in such experiences is genuine. Whether or not showing this is even feasible I leave to others. For the moment, I want simply to note that in this type of experience with its correlative form of life, more far-reaching and searching feelings are discovered and expressed.

An example of the type of response which could be further developed from both the desire for meaningfulness and love and in terms of the form of religious life is found throughout Kierkegaard's writings. His affective-understanding dialectic of stages—from aesthetic through ethical to spiritual—is one such example. In *Works of Love* Kierkegaard also argues how, with our capacity for total (Hegel's "infinite") commitment, and given the objects possible for such commitment, none is adequate but the omnibenevolent changeless. This treatment too is based in a dialectic of the affect and will through human love to the divine. If one acknowledges the desire for such a commitment, two famous possibilities exist for its interpretation. Though not exactly alike, Camus and Kant both recognized an apparently profound absurdity. In Camus the conflict is expressed in this manner: "This world in itself is not reasonable, that is all that can be said. But what is absurd is the confrontation of this irrational and the wild longing for clarity whose call echoes in the human heart. The absurd depends as much on man as on the world . . ."[38] Camus's resolution of this tension is well-known—fist-shaking at the absent god(s). Kant, facing almost the identical paradox in the second *Critique,* adopts the second alternative. The problem for Kant is reconciling the way things go in the phenomenal world—i.e., by cause and effect, which includes corporal death for all—and the direction of reason in conduct. Reason as the moral director puts perfection up as the goal of moral life. This goal is unreachable under the conditions imposed on the will in the phenomenal world since, on Kant's construal, a being of finite powers would require an infinite amount of time in order to progress to a perfectly moral (holy) will. If death is the dissolution of persons, the goal of reason would be unattainable in principle. There is then, a lack of fit between the order of reason expressed in the phenomenal world and the order of reason in conduct. Unless reason is ultimately out of sync with itself, there must be a ground of the two worlds which dovetails nature and the moral order. Hence, the famous necessity to postulate the existence of God and an afterlife.

I do not think either Camus's or Kant's resolution of the question is determinative. Without the numinous experience Otto describes, the question of the ultimate significance of one's life is ever underdetermined for resolution. This does not establish the experience Otto relates as genuine but as much can be said of any experience which is affectually intentional. One can at best talk up to and around such feelings as hate, love, humor, appreciation or enjoyment of the beautiful—with those who acknowledge their possibility at least, but get the description without the experience out of which it is described. Otto often says the same about his own phenomenology of numinous experience in *Das Heilige.* The same might be said of Heidegger's description of the experience of the nothing in dread. It is bound to sound strange or ad hoc to the one who is without such personal experience. Though Otto's phenomenology of religious feeling is subject to the same limitation (depending on the experience of his reader), what he says there has received wide-scale acceptance among a variety of the religious as a description of their feelings and is also not wholly foreign to received concepts of religion among the wider secular language community.

NOTES

[1] As cited in Thomas Sheehan, "Heidegger's 'Introduction to the Phenomenology of Religion,' 1920-21," *The Personalist,* Vol. 60, No. 3, July 1979, p. 319.

[2] "Letter to Rudolf Otto," tr. Thomas Sheehan, *Heidegger: The Man and the Thinker* (Chicago, 1981), p. 25.

[3] Rudolf Otto, *The Idea of the Holy,* tr. John Harvey (New York, 1979), p. 1.

[4] Ibid., p. 1.

[5] For Otto, the Holy is a complex category with a fundamentally tripartite structure, sc. rational, moral and *numinous.* He notes that generally, theology and philosophy of religion have attended to rational and moral elements of the Holy. The numinous aspects is that which is non-rational and *felt.* The object of such feeling he breaks down into two major aspects: Mysterium and Tremendum. The three primary elements of the Tremendum are awefulness, majesty and urgency or energy. The three primary elements of the Mysterium aspect are again awefulness and majesty, but also the fascinans. The explication of these aspects comprises *The Idea of the Holy.*

[6] *The Idea of the Holy,* p. 2.

[7] Ibid., p. 2.

[8] Ibid., p. 19.

[9] Ibid., p. 26.

[10] Ibid., p. 32.

[11] Ibid., p. 129.

[12] Ibid., p. 130.

[13] Ibid., pp. 109-10.

[14] Ibid., p. 113.

[15] Ibid., p. 113.

[16] Ibid., p. 112.

[17] Ibid., p. 114.

[18] Ibid., p. 37.

[19] Ibid., p. 37.

[20] Kant, *The Critique of Judgment,* tr. James Creed Meredith (Oxford, 1982), pp. 4, 114.

[21] Ibid., p. 94.

[22] Ibid., p. 102.

[23] Ibid., p. 104.

[24] Ibid., p. 107.

[25] Ibid., p. 107.

[26] Ibid., p. 114.

[27] *The Idea of the Holy,* p. 13.

[28] Ibid., p. 27.

[29] Ibid., p. 29.

[30] Ibid., p. 29.

[31] Ibid., p. 29.

[32] Ibid., p. 29.

[33] Heidegger, *What is Metaphysics?,* tr. R.R.F. Hull and Alan Crick, *Science, Faith, and Man* (New York, 1968).

[34] Ibid., p. 117.

[35] Heidegger, "Letter on Humanism," tr. Frank Capuzzi and J. Glenn Gray, *Basic Writings* (Bloomington, 1962), p. 218.

[36] Hubert Dreyfus, *Commentary on Heidegger's Being and Time* (Berkeley, 1977), p. 71.

[37] Ibid., p. 71.

[38] Camus, *The Myth of Sisyphus,* tr. Justin O'Brien (New York, 1955), p. 16.

---

# FURTHER READING

**Criticism**

Almond, Philip C. *Rudolf Otto: An Introduction to His Philosophical Theology.* Chapel Hill: University of North Carolina Press, 1984, 172 p.

Includes detailed and extensive examinations of Otto's life and works and his theory of the numinous experience.

Martin, James Alfred, Jr. "Holiness and Beauty in Modern Theories of Religion." In *Beauty and Holiness. The Dialogue between Aesthetics and Religion,* pp. 65-103.

New Jersey: Princeton University Press, 1990.
> Includes Otto and his theories in a discussion of "the role of concepts and procedures analogous to concepts and procedures employed in aesthetics in . . . theories of religion" and "the religious significance of aesthetic phenomena.""

Reeder, John P., Jr. "The Relation of the Moral and the Numinous in Otto's Notion of the Holy." In *Religion and Morality: A Collection of Essays*, edited by Gene Outka and John P. Reeder, Jr., pp. 255-92. Garden City, N.Y.: Anchor Press/Doubleday, 1973.
> Examines the place of morality in Otto's theory of the numinous.

Varnado, S. L. "The Numinous." In *Haunted Presence: The Numinous in Gothic Fiction*, pp. 8-19. Tuscaloosa: University of Alabama Press, 1987.
> Discusses Otto's idea of the numinous and its place in nineteenth-century Gothic fiction.

Webster, Alexander, F. C. "Orthodox Mystical Tradition and the Comparative Study of Religion: An Experimental Synthesis." *Journal of Ecumenical Studies* 23, No. 4 (Fall 1986): 621-49.
> Attempts to "determine the parameters for a phenomenological description of 'religion' that might at once reflect and inform the Orthodox mystical tradition," using Otto's idea of the numinous.

# Allen Upward

## 1863-1926

(Also wrote under the pseudonyms Ebenezer Lobb and 20/1631) English novelist, nonfiction writer, and autobiographer

## INTRODUCTION

Allen Upward sought and expected to be recognized as a figure of genius, and to this purpose he wrote *The New Word,* in which he put himself forth as a candidate for the Nobel Prize. He failed to attain such recognition, either from the Swedish Academy or from posterity, and though in his time he was widely known for a series of popular novels, he has been generally forgotten in the years since his death. His chief interest to literary history lies in his friendship with Ezra Pound, a great admirer of Upward's *The Divine Mystery*, who published parts of Upward's *Scented Leaves from a Chinese Jar* in the journal *Des Imagistes*. Pound mentioned Upward often in letters, and refers to him five times in *The Cantos*.

### Biographical Information

Upward was born in Worcester in 1863, the son of a landowner and justice of the peace who belonged to the Plymouth Brethren. His family moved repeatedly, and Upward's early education was mixed. In 1873, when he was ten years old, the family settled in London. At the age of nineteen, in 1882, Upward enrolled at the Royal University of Ireland, where he first showed his gift for oratory when he won the O'Hagan gold medal. During the late 1880s, he published his first works, which were characteristic both of his high aspirations and of the limited success his "serious" writing would enjoy. The first was an anonymous pamphlet advocating Home Rule for Ireland, the second a volume of poetry (*Songs in Ziklag,* 1888) which by Upward's own account sold fewer than twenty copies. Having read law at the Inns of Court, where he won two first-class scholarships, Upward was called to the bar in Ireland in 1887, and in England two years later. In the early 1890s he worked in Cardiff, Wales, as a barrister, journalist, and politician. Upward was an enthusiastic participant in political affairs, advocating liberal and nationalist causes for the Welsh as he had for the Irish; but he failed to win election to Parliament when he ran in 1895. Under the pseudonym Ebenezer Lobb, he wrote a sardonic column in the *South Wales Echo,* and during the mid-1890s began to—in his own disdainful characterization— "grind romances" such as *The Queen against Owen* and *The Prince of Balkistan.* Upward wrote such books merely to earn money, and he seems to have been embarrassed when they did so in such abundance that his

lifestyle improved greatly during later decades. The romantic idealist remained strong within him, however, and in 1897 he fought as a volunteer on the side of Greece in the Greco-Turkish War. Upon his return to England, he joined L. Cranmer Byng in an attempt to found a society for unrecognized geniuses, as he considered himself. Byng introduced Upward to the discovery of James Legge's translations of Chinese poetry, which led Upward to a friendship with Pound, likewise an enthusiast of the works of Li Po and other ancient poets. In the late 1890s Upward lived in Torquay, near Plymouth in the southwest of England, where he served as a judge; in 1901, he went as proconsul to Nigeria. From this experience came the roots of *The Divine Mystery.* Upward contracted malaria and had to leave Africa after less than two years. Returning to England, he again joined forces with Byng, this time to establish a publishing house for "books of an idealist tendency," a scheme similar in principles to Alfred Nobel's endowment for the prize that bears his name. Upward's series of poems *Scented Leaves from a Chinese Jar* attracted the notice of Pound and other poets in the Imagist movement, yet Upward did not become a leading Imagist. Pound continued to admire Upward, and often referred to him sympathetically in letters. After Upward killed himself with a gunshot in the head on 12 November 1926, Pound attributed the suicide to despair over his lifelong lack of recognition as a serious writer and thinker.

### Major Works

Upward wrote countless novels that have long since been forgotten. Though he would later purport, in *The New Word* and in the publishing house he established with Byng, to promote "works of an idealist tendency," his more than two dozen novels tend toward a less than idealistic, sometimes bizarre, portrayal of the world. *High Treason* and *The Fourth Conquest of England,* for instance, depict the establishment of a theocratic Roman Catholic state in England, complete with a new Inquisition. *The Discovery of the Dead* is a science-fiction novel about a group of dead people, "necromorphs," who inhabit a vast city at the North Pole; and his last book, *The Venetian Key,* is straight detective fiction. Of particular interest is *Lord Alistair's Rebellion,* because it portrays a tragic genius-hero akin to Upward's apparent vision of himself. Upward's own real-life tragedy is evidenced by the tepid reception of *The New Word,* which as its subtitle makes clear, is a treatise "on the meaning of the word idealist." Despite its lack of success with the Swedish Academy to whom he addressed the book, his foray into anthropology and etymology in *The New Word* seems to have led to *The Divine Mystery,* a work of anthropology which Upward viewed as his magnum opus. Though Pound shared Upward's view of his work, particularly *The New Word* and *The Divine Mystery,* few others did, and Upward, writing under a particularly self-effacing pseudonym, the number 20/1631, lamented this lack of recognition in his autobiography, *Some Personalities.*

## PRINCIPAL WORKS

*Songs in Ziklag* (poetry)  1888
*The Queen against Owen* (novel)  1894
*The Prince of Balkistan* (novel)  1897
*High Treason* (novel)  1903
*The Fourth Conquest of England* (novel)  1904
*The New Word: An Open Letter Addressed to the Swedish Academy on the Meaning of the Word Idealist* (nonfiction)  1908
*Lord Alistair's Rebellion* (fiction)  1909
*The Discovery of the Dead* (novel)  1910
*The Divine Mystery: A Reading of the History of Christianity Down to the Time of Christ* (nonfiction)  1913
*Scented Leaves from a Chinese Jar* (poetry)  1913-14; published in the journal *Des Imagistes*
*Some Personalities* [as 20/1631] (autobiography)  1921
*The Venetian Key* (novel)  1927

## CRITICISM

### Ezra Pound (essay dates 1913-1914)

SOURCE: "The Divine Mystery," in *Selected Prose: 1909-1965,* edited by William Cookson, Faber and Faber, 1973, pp. 373-76.

[*In the following essays, two pieces published respectively in* The New Freewoman *in 1913 and* The New Age *in 1914, Pound extols the clarity and breadth of vision in* The Divine Mystery *and* The New Word.]

THE DIVINE MYSTERY

'I was sitting like Abraham in my tent door in the heat of the day, outside a Pagan city of Africa, when the lord of the thunder appeared before me, going on his way into the town to call down thunder from heaven upon it.

'He had on his wizard's robe, hung round with magical shells that rattled as he moved; and there walked behind him a young man carrying a lute. I gave the musician a piece of silver, and he danced before me the dance that draws down the thunder. After which he went his way into the town; and the people were gathered together in the courtyard of the king's house; and he danced before them all. Then it thundered for the first time in many days; and the king gave the thundermaker a black goat—the immemorial reward of the performing god.

'So begins the history of the Divine Man, and such is his rude nativity. The secret of genius is sensitiveness. The Genius of the Thunder who revealed himself to me could not call the thunder, but he could be called by it. He was more quick than other men to feel the changes of the atmosphere; perhaps he had rendered his nervous system more sensitive still by fasting or mental abstraction; and he had learned to read his own symptoms as we read a barometer. So, when he felt the storm gathering round his head, he put on his symbolical vestment, and marched forth to be its Word, the archetype of all Heroes in all Mysteries.'

So begins the most fascinating book on folk-lore that I have ever opened. [*The Divine Mystery.*] I can scarcely call it a book on 'folk-lore', it is a consummation. It is a history of the development of human intelligence. It is not a mass of theories, it is this history told in a series of vivid and precise illustrations, like the one I have chosen for quotation. It is not a philosophy, yet it manages to be an almost complete expression of philosophy. Mr. Upward has been 'resident' in Nigeria; he has had much at first hand, and in all his interpretation of documents he has never for an instant forgotten that documents are but the shadow of the fact. He has never forgotten the very real man inside the event or the history. It is this which distinguishes him from all the encyclopaedists who have written endlessly upon corn gods, etc.

Moreover, he thinks.

He thinks, *il pense.* He is intelligent. Good God! is it not a marvel that in the age of Cadbury and Northcliffe, and the 'Atlantic Monthly' and the present 'English Review', etc., etc., *ad nauseam,* is it not an overwhelming wonder that a thinking sentient being should still inhabit this planet and be allowed to publish a book!

Very well then. Mr. Upward is intelligent. He is cognizant of the forces of intelligence and has traced, in some measure, their influence. He has traced the growth of religion and superstition from the primitive type of the thunder-maker to the idea of the messiah. He has traced many of the detestable customs of modern life to their roots in superstition.

The first half of the book is planned, if it can be called so, on the slow recognition of the sun. That is to say, primitive man turns from his worship of the dead, and of the earth and of various fears, to a worship of the lifegiving Helios. The solar missionary says it is unnecessary to bury a man in the cornfield in order that crops shall rise by virtue of his spirit. The Aten disc is explained. The 'Dies Irae' turns out to be a relic of fire worship. The 'Divine Mystery' necessitates a new translation of the bible. And if the ecclesiastical mind were not ossified beyond all hope of revivification we should see the introductory notes above the chapters abandoned in favour of something related to truth.

Mr. Upward has left the charming pastoral figure of Jesus in a more acceptable light than have the advocates of 'That religion which the Nazarene has been accused of having founded.'

He has derived the word God from the word Goat, which will be a satisfaction to many. He has related prophecy to astrology, and has shown the new eras to be related to the ascent of the successive signs of the zodiac in which the sun appears, changing his mansion about once in each eight centuries.

The book itself is a summary, a leisured summary, that does not cut corners, or leave one with insufficient information. Still it contains so much and so much of vivid interest that it is very nearly impossible to review it.

It is a book full of suggestion for half a dozen sorts of specialist, at the same time it is legible and so clearly written that one has no need of specialised knowledge to read it.

I, personally, find in it clues and suggestions for the Provençal love customs of the Middle Ages—in the chapter on early marriage laws. Modern marriage is, apparently, derived from the laws of slave concubinage, not from the more honourable forms of primitive European marriage. So much for the upholders of 'Sacrament'.

It is great satisfaction to find a nice, logical book, where all the canting fools who have plagued one are— no, not 'abused', but where an author, writing in a gentle and reasonable tone, presenting simple fact after simple fact, undermines their position, and shows them naked in all their detestability, in all their unutterable silliness.

The lovely belief in a durable hot hell dates back to the Parsee who squatted over a naphtha volcano. And various other stupidities still prevalent are shown to be as little inspired by either divine or human intelligence. It is a great book for liberations.

Someday, when the circulationists are nearly forgotten, people will take note of Mr. Upward's work in fundamentals. His **The New Word** will be recognised, instead of being ranted about by a few enthusiasts.

He is wholly careless of certain matters; he is apparently quite willing that his work should be immortal in general belief, instead of being 'preserved' in specific works.

This author is a focus, that is to say he has a sense of major relations. The enlightenments of our era have come to him. He has seen how the things 'put together'.

It is pleasing to know that the ordinary native's hunt in Africa sets out with an ark of the covenant every whit as sacred as the junk box which the Israelites carried before them.

Especially if one has been 'reared in the Christian faith' and been forced to eat at the same table with ministers and members of the Y.M.C.A., it is pleasant to know for certain just what part of their conversation is pure buncomb.

I do not wish to lead anyone into the belief that this is an impious book. I believe Allen Upward to be one of the devoutest men of the age. He insists that the real God is neither a cad nor an imbecile, and that is, to my mind, a fairly good ground for religion.

'All that has been was right, and will be wrong.' He shows that even the crusades of the earlier and now detestable religions came in their own time as liberations.

It is a very difficult work to review. How Mr. Upward has managed to tell so many interesting facts in three hundred pages, is somewhat beyond me. It is, I must repeat, a clarifying book, it is not a set of facts very rigorously chosen in proportion to their interest. The idea of the goddess, the mother goddess, is analysed; queenship and kingship and the priesthood are treated. Mr. Upward is not only perspicacious, but his mind is balanced by nature and by a knowledge of the Chinese classics. He is nowhere content with a sham.

Speaking in moderation, I suppose one might call 'The Divine Mystery' a book indispensable to clergymen, legislators, students of folk-lore, and the more intelligent public.

I do not write this as a specialist; but judging by those points where Mr. Upward's *specialité* coincides with my own, I should say that he was led by a scholarship not only wide but precise. He shows remarkable powers of synthesis.

However correct or incorrect I may be in my estimate, of this at least I am certain: no sane man will be bored during the hours he gives to the reading of this book.

. . . . .

ALLEN UPWARD SERIOUS

'It is a curious thing about England'???? No, it is not a 'curious thing' about England or about anywhere else, it is a natural habit of il mal seme d' Adamo that they neglect the clear thinker in his own day. And if a man have done valuable work of one sort, and have, at the same time, done vendible work of another, the vendible work will kill him among the little clique who decide whether or no one is to be 'taken seriously'. So Mr. Upward is known for short stories of a sort, and not for two books, as interesting philosophically as any that have been written in our time.

Of course, any man who thinks is a bore. He will either make you think or he will despise, irritate and insult you if you don't, and all this is very distressing.

What for instance could be more distressing to a wooden-headed imbecile, fat with his own scholastic conceit, than such a clearly-written paragraph as that which follows?

> 'That old talk about the Gods, which is called mythology, is confused in many ways, partly because all language is confused, partly because it is a layer of many languages. When the talkers no longer used the beast as an idol they used it as a symbol, in short a word; when they no longer slew the real Christ at Easter they named the sun at Easter, Christ. Their language is tangled and twisted beyond our power wholly to unravel because it was beyond their power; because it began as a tangle when man's mind was still a blur, and he saw men as trees walking, and trees as men standing still. How hard the old cloistered scholarship to which the Nobels of a bygone age gave their endowments has toiled to understand the word glaukopis given to the goddess Athene. Did it mean blue-eyed or grey-eyed, or—by the aid of Sanskrit—merely glare-eyed? And all the time they had not only the word glaux staring them in the face, but they had the owl itself cut at the foot of every statue of Athene and stamped on every coin of Athens, to tell them that she was the owl-eyed goddess, the lightning that blinks like an owl. For what is characteristic of the owl's eyes is not that they glare, but that they suddenly leave off glaring like lighthouses whose light is shut off. We may see the shutter of the lightning in that mask that overhangs Athene's brow and hear its click in the word glaukos. And the leafage of the olive whose writhen trunk bears, as it were, the lightning's brand, does not glare but glitters, the pale under face of the leaves alternating with the dark upper face, and so the olive is Athene's tree and is called glaukos.[1] Why need we carry owls to Oxford?'

That is the sort of clarity and hard writing that one finds all through *The New Word*. Of course, it is very irritating: if you suggest to Mr. Upward that his mind is as clear as Bacon's, he will agree with you. If you suggest to Mr. Upward that his middles are less indefinite than Plato's, he will agree with you. If you suggest to him that one man who thinks is worth a dozen ambulating works of reference, he will agree with you; and all this is very annoying to the supporters of things at large, for our ambulating works of reference are far more numerous than our thinkers.

The writer of this present essay has suffered from a modern education; he has met a number of ambulating works of reference; his respect for the mnemonic mind has been lessened by contact, and by the presence in the modern world of the cinematograph and the gramophone.

Mr. Upward has taken up the cause of intelligence, of the perceptive man; it is the height of quixotism on his part.

If you refer to him as a thinker, if you say his mind is less messy than Bergson's, they tell you he writes detective stories. Yet if *The New Word* and *The Divine Mystery* had been written by a civil servant or a clerk in a dry goods shop, or by a broken-down parson, they would have been acclaimed as great works. They would have been patted on their covers by 'The Edinburgh', etc.

But there is something so degrading—at least, one would think that there were something so degrading in the practice of writing as a trade—that anyone who has once earned a livelihood, or part of it, obviously and openly, by popular writing, can never be seriously regarded by any great number of people. And then, of course, 'he does too much'. The populace, the reading populace, is like the fat critic in 'Fanny's First Play', it cannot conceive the same man doing two kinds of work, or at least it won't. It is perfectly logical. It is insanely logical.

On the other hand, one clear, hard paragraph like the one quoted is enough to queer a man's chances. 'How,' say the professors, 'is this man a classicist? Why does he not stick to his trade? Why does he expose our patent error? To hell with him!'

'How!' says the windy logomachist, who believes that if a thing is worth doing it is worth doing badly. 'Clear, hard, serious, specialised writing from a journalist. Damn him.'

And then of course, there's the church; nearly everybody has an uncle or a cousin who gets paid for believing, officially, in the established church. It won't do to think about religion too seriously or else we'll have to scrap the lot: all the established salaries. We must not treat this gentleman too gravely. Let us label him a brilliant superficial writer. So it goes.

Mr. Upward has taken up the cause of the sensitive; and the sensitives are too few and too indolent to support him, save in their slow and ultimately victorious manner.

Of course, what Mr. Upward says will be believed in another twenty or fifty or a hundred years, just as a lot of Voltaire's quiet thrusts are now a part of our gospel. Mr. Upward will be nicely buried and no living curate will be out of a job, so that will be all right.

Mr. Upward takes on the lot of 'em. If he were content to poke fun at one science . . . ah! But he says most scientists are stupid, or something of that sort: most of the rank and file—but what is the use of talking about mosts?

Let us search for Mr. Upward's dangerous and heretical doctrines. Most mild is their aspect. Thus:

> 'When, instead of thinking of men one by one you think of them all at once and call your thought humanity, you have merely added a new word to the dictionary and not a new thing to the contents of the universe.'

That ought to be fairly obvious.

> 'Altruism is the principle that mankind ought to serve those who are serving it, but not those who are not serving it.'

Ah!

> 'It used to be written . . ."All men are liars." . . ."It repented the Lord that he had made man." No one would dare to say such things about Humanity."

> 'The religion of Humanity is not the worship of the best man nor of the best in man. It is the worship of the middling man.'

This begins to look ugly.

And still he goes on. He draws an invidious comparison between science and 'scientology'. He propounds riddles. He asks: 'When is the good not good?' and answers, 'When it is an abstract noun.' Perplexing!

> 'In the beginning the Goat created heaven and earth.'

It is the astrological goat, but it gets the churchman's.

> 'The religion which that Idealist (i.e., Christ) has been accused of founding.'

> 'The ultimate nature of Materialism is the worship of fixity under a hundred names.'

> 'I think that no two men have ever had wholly the same religion, and I am sure no two men ought to.'

> 'Whatever is has been right and will be wrong.'

> 'The Churchmen had no doubt that Aquinas was a saint. They applied a simple test and found that, however impartial might be the summing up, the verdict was always in their favour.'

> 'Today this book (Aquinas), the greatest book of Catholic Theology, ranks as a curiosity rather than as literature. And that is not because, like the book of Copernicus it has done its work, but because no one any longer hopes that it can do any work.'

> 'The bloodiest iconoclasts the world has ever seen ought not to whine so miserably when their own idol is being washed.'

Of course, Mr. Upward should not assail the scientists, the philologists and the churchmen all in one book. What faction will come to his aid? What formed party will support him?

The clear-headed logician has lost sight of psychology, of crowd psychology. One should always compromise with fools, one should always be sure to please a majority of the dullards, if one desire immediate results.

What! Not desire immediate results? Do I suggest that any man is content to await the verdict of the future, or at least of the next generation?

Supposing I do?

Of course, I am not an impartial judge. I think all established churches an outrage, save in so far as they teach medicine and courage to the more obfuscated heathen, and they don't do such a lot of that.

But on the whole they are nearly as great a pest as were the 'fat bellies of the monks toward the end of the Middle Ages'; they sit in fat livings; they lead lives of intellectual sloth supported by subsidies originally intended, at least in part, for 'clerks', for clerics who were supposed to need a certain shelter wherein to conduct the intellectual life of the race. One demands purely and simply that people oust the parson from his feathered eyrie, and put in it some constructive person, some thinker, or artist, or scientific experimenter, or some teacher of something or other, which he can himself take seriously and which might conceivably be of some use to the race. They might take to reading Confucius . . . if it amused them. Or they might even talk seriously about their professed religion instead of playing the barrister. But this is a matter aside. It is one of the minute corollaries of Mr. Upward's work as I understand it. It is a part of what he calls 'Altruism'.

I recognise the danger of leaving Mr. Upward at large. Not an immediate peril! I recognise also the need of some sort of delayed book reviewing. I mean that the present advertising system provides that all books of whatever merit shall be praised by a certain number of people the instant they appear; that certain kinds of books, or certain particular books, shall be largely circulated; and that certain, practically all, books, save books of verse, go into desuetude within a year or so.

There should be a new sort of semi-critic, semi-reviewer, to go over the mess of books that are a few years old and pick out the few worth saving, the few that he still remembers. It is something of that sort that I am trying.

We all recognise the type of writer produced by present conditions, who keeps in the public eye by a continuous output of inferior work. He is known for his persistent ubiquity. Damn him! I want some more efficient machinery for the preservation of the sort of writer who only writes when he has something to say, who produces odd sorts of books in uncommercial sizes.

I think also that we should try to discriminate between the real man and his secondary emanations. Does it matter the least whether Mr. Upward plays golf or writes detective stories in the intervals between his serious work?

I present Mr. Upward's dicta rather jerkily, partly because I think the readers of *The New Age* are heartily sick of my writing, and partly because I believe they do not want their pabulum diluted, and that they are able to build up the intellectual consequences of a given theme. However, I cannot quote Mr. Upward entire, and I cannot adequately represent his trend in scattered quotations, so I must needs make a partial summary of certain things that he stands for, or that he appears to me to stand for; certain conclusions which I draw more or less from his books.

1. That a nation is civilised in so far as it recognises the special faculties of the individual, and makes use thereof. You do not weigh coals with the assayer's balance.

1*a*. Corollary. Syndicalism. A social order is well balanced when the community recognises the special aptitudes of groups of men and applies them.

2. That Mr. Upward's propaganda is for a syndicat of intelligence; of thinkers and authors and artists.

2*a*. That such a guild is perfectly in accord with Syndicalist doctrines. That it would take its place with the guilds of more highly skilled craftsmen.

3. That Mr. Upward 'sees further into a mile-stone, etc.', I mean that his propaganda is for the recognition of the man who can see the meaning of data, not necessarily as opposed to, but as supplementary to, the man who is only capable of assembling or memorising such data. NOTE.—This latter sort of man is the only sort now provided for by the American University system. I cannot speak for the English.

Aristotle said something about 'the swift perception of relations'. He said it was the hall mark of genius.

The *Century Magazine* wants to bring its fiction 'as near to truth, and make it as interpretive of life, as conditions allow' (*Century Magazine* for September, 1913, page 791, col. 2, lines 29 and 30). Mr. Upward has nothing to do with this spirit. 'As conditions allow'!!!!!! 'Let the bridge come as near to bearing the strain of traffic "as conditions allow".'

4. That since Christ's notable success—in gaining a reputation, I mean—a number of people have desired to 'save the world' without undergoing the inconvenience of crucifixion.

5. That Mr. Upward is a very capable thinker, and that he deserves more attention than he now gets.

¹ See Canto LXXIV . . .

## Bryant Knox (essay date 1974)

SOURCE: "Allen Upward and Ezra Pound," in *Paideuma: A Journal Devoted to Ezra Pound Scholarship*, Vol. 3, No. 1, Spring, 1974, pp. 71-83.

*[In the following excerpt, Knox offers an account of ideas shared between Pound and Upward, and lists the five references to Upward in Pound's* Cantos.]

Allen Upward (1863-1926) was a personal friend of Jerome K. Jerome and contributed to Jerome's *Idler*. He knew James Whistler and corresponded with Theodor Mommsen and Lloyd George; received letters from Augustus John; wrote to Samuel Clemens and T. H. Huxley for a brief time; and corresponded with the Sultan of Turkey and the Crown Prince of Greece. He came to know Gilbert Murray through the Royal Anthropological Institute of Great Britain of which both men were members. He was also a corresponding member of the Parnassus Philological Society, Athens. He was a good friend of G.R.S. Mead, editor of *The Quest,* a journal devoted to gnosticism and the pagan mystery religions, and especially of A.R. Orage, editor of the *New Age,* whom he first met in 1900. He knew T.E. Hulme, Amy Lowell and Harriet Monroe and all those of Pound's "circle" at that time. As Noel Stock points out, "Pound had always been a believer in the importance of the individual genius in the history of mankind, but his belief was greatly strengthened about 1913 when he began reading the works of Allen Upward."¹ Upward in fact founded the "Order of Genius" with his friend Lancelot Cranmer Byng and Byng's brother Hugh, "both men of genius."² The "Order," explains Upward, "is a society for the prevention of cruelty to the Son of Man, because He is the Servant of Man. It is an international society, because Genius is the Servant of all nations."³ Upward's *The New Word* (1907) and especially *The Divine Mystery* (1915) are books which establish the centrality of this idea in his thinking. The "Order," not a "religious" one in the usual sense of the word, was one which maintained that the "victim" was the key to all the existing pagan and religious cults of the past. Christ, the Son of Man (not of God), for instance, is such a "victim." "Not the priest but the victim" Pound states in Canto 78. This line has its root in Upward's "Order"—more of which later. But first, some biographical information.

Upward, born of Welsh parentage in the English city of Helstonleigh,⁴ entered grammar school before he was twelve; graduated from the Royal University of Ireland "without a serious effort" as he recalls; as a law student at the Inns of Court won the O'Hagan Gold Medal for Oratory and the Brooke Scholarship; became a barrister winning the highest prizes of both the Irish and the English Bars. He was called to the Irish Bar in 1887 and the English in 1889; joined the South Wales Circuit and settled as a local barrister in Cardiff for six years; was nominated for the Cardiff Town Council and helped organize and back the Labour Party (1905 campaigned for a seat for the Liberal Party); was made an Honourary Bard (his bardic name was Maenhir) of the National Gorsedd "after the Privilege and Ceremonial of the Bards of the Isle of Britain."⁵ In 1897 he ran the blockade of Crete set up by the League of Nations and made friends among the Greeks—many in high-ranking government posts. In 1901 Upward left for Africa. The chief Justice of Northern Nigeria had originally accepted him as legal assessor, but Upward soon found himself Resident of two Nigerian provinces. His experiences in Africa provided him with material for *The Divine Mystery.* In 1908 Upward was offered the position of local correspondent for the *Paris Daily Mail.* No sooner had he settled down in the job than he was off again to southeast Europe to help Macedonian Greeks fight Bulgarian plunderers, an adventure recorded in *The East End of Europe* (1908). In 1916 he became Head Master of Inverness College and during the First World War held the position of Scoutmaster for General Commanding.

An interesting point about *Some Personalities*[6] (the autobiography from which much of this information comes) is that Upward has refrained from signing his name as the author of the work; indeed, his name is nowhere mentioned in the text. "The Board of Education knew me as 20/1631,"[7] and that number appears on the title page with a quotation from Confucius: "I will not be grieved because men do not know me; I will be grieved because I do not know men." "The desire to stand on the stage, the desire of plaudits has nothing to do with serious art,"[8] Pound has remarked.

In 1900 Upward and Byng established a rather small printing firm in Fleet Street. Its original name was "The Yellow Press," later modified into "Primrose" and finally "Orient." Its most important publication was the "Wisdom of the East" series (still offered today) in which Upward contributed a volume of the "Sayings of Confucius" and Byng the Confucian "Odes."[9] In Dublin Upward contributed articles to the *United Ireland* under a nom-de-plume;[10] as a barrister in Cardiff conducted a column of legal answers in the *South Wales Daily News* and began the "Adventures of Ebenezer Lobb," a weekly sketch contributed to Cardiff's *South Wales Echo.* In London, 1905, he produced a serial for the *Daily Express,* later entrusting its sale to an agency which embezzled most of the proceeds. This blow, following many of the same nature, finally broke down his health and he spent the next three years recovering in France, Switzerland and Sweden. His first serious contributions of poetry were made to a review in Trinity College, Dublin which brought him in touch with W.B. Yeats.[11] His first book of poems, *Songs In Ziglag,* he published himself; his first volume, *The Truth About Ireland,* was published by Kegan Paul and *Secrets of the Courts of Europe* by *Pearson's Magazine.* He wrote *Lord Alistar's Rebellion,* one of his few serious novels, while recuperating in France. His plays were notable successes, though he had his share of problems. In 1892 Oscar Wilde's play *Lady Windemere's Fan* was being well received. This prompted Upward to write *A Flash in the Pan,* which became a hit in Dublin a few years later—Upward, however, had previously sold the rights. *Private Inquiry,* stolen due to his own naiveté, later became a hit under the name *Facing the Music; Slaves of Society* became successful as a novel; *Paradise Found* (1913) parodied Socialist "prophecies" (although he himself has been called a "socialist writer"[12]).

Around 1902 he began work on *The New Word,* Geneva, 1907; second edition New York, 1910. In 1907 A.R. Orage began publishing the *New Age* and asked Upward for contributions. "It was," Upward recalls, "his original proposal that I should develop my ideas on the subject of the Overman, in correction of Nietzsche, and I made a serious effort to obey the call. I contributed three articles under the heading 'The Order of the Seraphim'."[13] Other contributions to the *New Age* (many of them anonymous) dealt with philosophy and religion; history and politics; literature; marriage; the Labour Party and its leader Keir Hardie; and speculations on the nebular origins of life, as well as various letters to the editor. An autobiographical poem, **"The Discarded Imagist,"**[14] is important because it provides answers to certain references in *The Cantos* and establishes the date at which Upward was introduced to "immemorial China" (as the poem puts it). Pound was introduced to Upward in 1911, two years prior to his acquisition of Fenollosa's manuscripts—that the two men did not speak of China is unlikely.

About the time he began writing articles for the *New Age,* Upward set to work on *The Divine Mystery:*

> It is, I believe, the nearest approach to a sound general history of religion, and certainly the only outspoken one that has commanded general approval.[15]

> In the course of twenty years I had accumulated two thousand pages of MS. notes on the composition of the Gospels and the life of their Hero. I dredged deeper than the textual critic . . . I hadn't studied it only in the light of classical lexicons compiled from the writings of cultured Athenians in the fourth century before Christ . . . I had studied the text in the light of the Parsi and Buddhist scriptures; the history of religion in the Levant, including the history of Jerusalem; and the results of anthropological research, including my own research . . . I had brought to the work one qualification that the scribe can never possess—some insight into the mind and heart of genius . . . It seemed to me that I had made an advance towards the solution of the most difficult and momentous of all literary problems, and in doing so had recovered some genuine features of the central Figure of the world's history.[16]

Pound reviewed the book,[17] praising it highly. One of its main concerns is that "the secret of genius is sensitiveness."[18] That is, the Genius is more "sensitive" to changes and its relations than most, be they climatic shifts or the shifting process of thought. And Pound realized that as Upward probed, juxtaposed and ultimately related pieces of historical, philological and mythical evidence in favour of the Divine Man or Genius, he was, by that very process, establishing his own right as genius. Upward, being more sensitive to "relations," could put together those things of the past which had hitherto lain unconnected in the minds of others.

Pound says of Upward: "This author is a focus, that is to say he has a sense of major relations. . . . He has seen how the things put together."[19] This same concept structures the *Cantos*. The 'swift perception of relations is the hallmark of genius,' says Pound, quoting Aristotle.[20] As Noel Stock has stated, Pound found in Upward "a key with which to free those ideas and feelings about science and religion that had been forming in his mind without his being able to bring them into focus. Now he could employ them in his thought and work."[21]

*Canto References*[22]

To my knowledge, there are only five references to Upward in the *Cantos*. The first:

<blockquote>

          sd/ old Upward:<br>
"not the priest but the victim"<br>
   his seal Sitalkas, sd/ the old combattant: "victim,<br>
withstood them by Thames and by Niger with pistol by Niger<br>
   with a printing press by the Thomas bank"<br>
   until I end my song<br>
       and shot himself

                   (74/437:464)

</blockquote>

"Not the priest but the victim" comes from *The Divine Mystery,* where Upward traces the evolution of the Genius/Victim from the first pagan wizard to the coming of Christ. The entire book introduces the idea that the "victim" is the force behind all religions.[23]

> Many reasons make it likely that it was in the part of a barometer that the wizard revealed himself first. His name, both in its older forms, *witga* and *wicca,* and its newer one, has the same root as wisdom and vision; and the expression weather-wise suggests that the first prophet was a weather prophet.[24]

> Such is the wizard of the foreworld . . . a being having the outward form of man, subject to human infirmities, and vulnerable to mortal wounds; yet nevertheless something more than man, standing in some mysterious relation with forces and energies not understood by man, wielding strange powers whose limits have not been perceived, mighty if not almighty, wise if not all-knowing, *tapu* himself and able to make other men and things *tapu,* incomprehensible—in a word, divine.[25] Worship, in the form of awe and deprecation, is paid by primitive man to everything he fears, irrespective of any theory as to its nature. He worships the very beasts he chases and is chased by . . . He worships the lightning and the thunder, the earth that quakes beneath him, the flaming mountain and the burning bush. How, then, could the wizard escape worship as the Living God . . . The Divine Man, having passed through successive avatars, as wizard, priest and king, is now represented by the sacrificial Christ. The king is the hereditary Genius, the Christ is the fabricated Genius . . . The Christ may be defined as the sacrificial king, the king anointed not as ruler but as redeemer. The royal title clings to him still;

we shall find it written up over the head of the crucified Nazarene: 'This is the King of the Jews.' But it has lost its political significance. The christ-king is the representative of the nation before its offended God, the one man who dies for the people.[26]

It is not the priest but the victim who brings about the sun's amiability, the weather's benevolence, and conditions the powers of both celestial and earthly divinities. Osiris, Christ—they keep order; the world functions as a result of their "being." In 1911 (the year he met Upward) Pound published a series of articles in the *New Age* (30 November 1911—22 February 1912) entitled "I Gather the Limbs of Osiris."[27] Pound's ideas of Osiris and the metamorphic in general, are concentrated in the chthonic and the metempsychic.

> Kai MOIRAI' ADONIN

> The sea is streaked red with Adonis,<br>
> The lights flicker red in small jars.<br>
> Wheat shoots rise new by the altar,<br>
>    flower from the swift seed.

>                (47/236-37:246)

>       men rose out of $\chi\theta\grave{U}\nu o s$<br>
>           (77/465:494)

> How drawn, O GEA TERRA,<br>
>    what draws as thou drawest<br>
>       till one sink into thee by an arm's width<br>
> embracing thee. Drawest,<br>
>       truly thou drawest.<br>
> Wisdom lies next thee,<br>
>      simply, past metaphor.<br>
> Where I lie let the thyme rise<br>
>              and bassilicum<br>
>    let the herbs rise in April abundant[28]<br>
>           (82/526:561)

Pound and Upward both use the myth of Osiris and regeneration to exemplify the "process" of the victim:

> The attention of primitive man . . . could scarcely ignore the superior richness of the vegetation on soil which had been dug and manured by the process of burial . . . And it has been suggested further, that wild grains and berries buried with the corpse to serve it as food may have been observed rising again. We know that ears of wheat, peas and other food-stuffs have been found in Egyptian graves, and the monuments of Egypt afford two striking corroborations of the foregoing suggestions. One is the representation of a mummy with ears of corn sprouting from it, accompanied by the inscription: 'This is Osiris.' The other is a similar picture of a tree growing out of a sarcophagus, with the explanation: 'Osiris springs forth.'[29]

Pound's poems *The Tree* and *A Girl,* particularly, are interesting in light of the tree associated with Osiris as it springs from the sarcophagus. This is "metastrophe," states Upward, meaning not "metabolism" as archbishops have meant, but "growth turning into decay, and decay turning into growth . . . And I mean more than life; I mean also the expression of life. Metastrophe is a mood."[30] "The stone is alive in my hand, the crops will be thick in my death year" (6/21:26)

The metamorphic sense of the passage expands from the chthonic (or Dionysian) to the celestial (or Apollonian), as Pound focuses on Upward's seal Sitalkas.[31] The *Annotated Index* offers the following note regarding Sitalkas: "A Thracian king of the tribe Odrysae, d. 424 B.C." Originally, Sitalkas was the cult name given to Apollo at Delphi.[32] The word means "protector of grain" (sitos—"grain," alalkein—"to protect"). The relationship between Apollo and agriculture is obvious and, in his manifestation as an agricultural god, Apollo symbolizes the life-giving metamorphic cycle. Upward's "seal Sitalkas" may be a literal reference to a possession of Upward's, but it is also, most certainly, a metaphorical one. The "life-giving" process which Upward embodies (as Sitalkas) is the phenomenon of mental acumen and intellectual prognosis. And by extension, all the attributes and manifestations Pound admired in Apollo, from god of light and enemy of darkness (mental darkness) to the god of truth. Upward's "seal," his bearing, his "being" as a man, was as Sitalkas.

The "sd/ the old combattant" of Pound's next line has part of its source in Upward's military forays among the Greeks and Africans. In Nigeria, Upward was frequently sent out as a Judge for various crimes committed by the Nigerians of his Provinces. In one instance, he stood

> . . . on the height of the blood-stained stone of Semarika, with a revolver in his hand, and three human skulls at his feet, while an ogre, whose boast it is that he never has to strike more than one blow to cut off a human head, yells to his followers to deliver him out of the Judge's hand.[33]

Now, as Upward "withstood them by Niger," so too did he withstand the mediocre and perverted English taste in the arts by establishing a printing firm to combat the "howling, as of a hen-yard in a printing house, the clatter of presses" (14/61:66) which populate the Hell Cantos. Upward fights "clatter" with "wisdom" (it was with this particular printing press that Upward and Byng brought the "Wisdom of the East" to the west). But the old combattant lost—"until I end my song and shot himself." "Have always thought that poor old Upward shot himself in discouragement on reading of award to Shaw. Feeling of utter hopelessness in struggle for values," states Pound.[34] The entire passage invokes the tragedy of all genius victimized by circumjacent stupidity and evil. "The suicide is not serious from conviction," Pound states in *Rock-Drill*, but "From sheer physical depression, c'est autre chose" (93/625:658). "We, whose gift and doom it is to be more sensitive than other men"—Upward, speaking of Genius.[35] Those of the caliber of Plato and Bacon will always be the victims of society. Hence the second reference to Upward:

> "the mind of Plato . . . or that of Bacon" said Upward
> seeking parallel for his own
> (77/469:498)

In *The New Word,* Upward brings the best of Plato and Bacon together. "The comparison with Socrates was inevitable; the book contained a Platonic dialogue. I had challenged comparison with Bacon by the title."[36] Upward regarded Plato as the archetypal idealist, as the "father of all such as work in metaphysics, and patentee of the metaphysical *Idea.*"[37] In Upward's redefinition of the word "idealism," Plato, as idealist, is practical and reformist. Upward has thus moved Plato into Bacon's realm.

> Three hundred years ago a challenge was addressed by Bacon to the physical sciences, under the name of natural philosophy. His famous sub-stitution of inductive for deductive reasoning amounted to no more than this advice: learn from the things themselves, instead of from the words about the things.[38]

"You would think that anyone wanting to know about poetry would do one of two things or both. I.E. LOOK AT it or listen to it," states Pound.[39]

"I wrote *The New Word* in a fortnight. I had been composing it for twenty-five years."[40] That is, Upward had been living it—the collective knowledge and experience of an idealist who skillfully moved into the realm of the true prophet. The Platonic parallel becomes obvious. Bacon challenged the physical sciences, Upward challenges contemporary mankind—his book, by the very title (as he himself has alluded) is, in the Baconian sense, the thing itself, *The New Word!* "Words," to Upward, are root systems, the foundation contemporary man has lost. "Never change native Names; for there are Names in every nation, God-given, of unexplained power in the Mysteries," Upward offers in the Chaldean epigraph to *The New Word.* The entire book is one in which Upward digs to the root of words so that we see their original etymologies. Like Pound, Upward makes it new—he divests the original word of its accumulated garments. For example, the root meaning of religion or *religio,* is "re-ligare, to fast-bind, the bond or covenant between God and man."[41] Religion is a shared experience, not dogma.[42] One may *see* things more clearly if one *looks* for the root. "The words look and see contain between them the whole secret of metaphysics . . . Looking is the question, and sight the answer."[43] But to "see," of course, one needs light; hence light metaphysics and poetic vision in the *Cantos.* Upward, like Pound, felt the need to escape the confinement of Aryan etymology. They both talk of human experience, rather than Western experience—there is an expansion of interests.

Upward and Pound shared other opinions as well. Upward tells us

> The Religion of Humanity is not the worship of the best man, nor of the best in man. It is the worship of the middling man.[44]

> Who can patronize the Idealist, except some greater Idealist? England will always have fifteen thousand a year for some respectable clergyman; she will never have it for Shelley or Carlyle.[45]

"Some college presidents," as Pound observes, "have been chosen rather for their sycophantic talents than for their intellectual acumen or their desire to enliven and build intellectual life."[46] Another point of interest is Upward's statement that "Words are, like money, a medium of exchange."[47] The identity of words and money stems from the idea that they are both forms of communication.[48] Pound made this a central concern of the *Cantos*.

Upward, like Pound, believes "No two men have ever had wholly the same religion."[49] Pound's opinion of monotheism is well known—"someone, having to keep a troublesome rabble in order, invents and scares them with a disagreeable bogie, which he calls god."[50] Their views of Buddhism were similar. Upward states that Buddhism "is not Idealism. It is Nihilism."[51] In Canto 95/646:679 "Do not Hindoos lust after vacuity?" For both men Confucianism was the important Oriental philosophy. "Of K'ung the Master . . . it is recorded that one of the subjects which he never would discuss with his followers was the appointments of Heaven," Upward states.[52] Pound found this information worthy of inclusion in Canto 13/59:63. Note that both men spoke of Confucius as K'ung. In *The New Word*, p. 313, Upward brings up Mencius. Both he and Pound have the tendency to avoid using examples from Christianity when an earlier example can be found—they are not narrowly nationalistic.

"He who has watched the iron crumbs drawn into patterns by the magnet; or who in the frostwork on the window pane has apprehended the unknown beauty of the crystal's law, seems to me to have an idea more wholesome to our frail imaginings of the meaning of the Mystery of Life'.[53] "Hast 'ou seen the rose in the steel dust/(or swansdown ever?)/ so light is the urging, so ordered the dark petals of iron/ we who have passed over Lethe" (74/449:477). To use Hugh Kenner's phrase, both men adopted the structural approach of "patterned energies" in their work.

The third reference:

> Put down the slave trade, made the desert to yield
> and menaced the loan swine
>     Sitalkas, double Sitalkas
>     "not the priest but the victim"
> said Allen Upward
>
>                          (78/479:511)

I have been unable to locate any specific references concerning Upward's suppression of the slave trade. Upward was, however, involved in the Freed Slaves Home in Nigeria in the capacity of marriage-broker for the women of the Home. His signature was required on paper before any man was able to procure a wife from the house. It was Upward's responsibility to be sure of the "good character" of the men.[54] He aided the "freed" children in a similar way. Again, Upward's autobiography relates nothing which really substantiates Pound's reference about making the desert yield. What Upward does mention, is that under his Residentship "caravans began to arrive in town from all quarters. Merchants and others from distant regions came and settled in Lokoja to be under my rule; for such is the custom of Africa, where a strong man attracts subjects from far around."[55]

The fourth reference is one which we have already discussed:

> Allen Upward's seal showed Sitalkas
>                   (107/763:787)

And finally, the fifth:

> Bunting and Upward neglected,
>     all the registers blacked out,
> From time's wreckage shored,
>     these fragments shored against ruin
>                   (110/781)

"No classics, no American history, no centre, no general root" (85/549:585). "Libraries LACK work by, and comments on, Allan Upward and B. [asil] Bunting,"[56] Pound wrote Harry Meacham in 1958. Like Upward and Bunting, "All the resisters [are] blacked out."[57] And it is not only academia and the "enormous organized cowardice" (95/647:679) that censors intelligence, it is time, the wrecker. But, "From time's wreckage shored, these fragments shored against ruin." Pound's concern has always been to shore, not shelve fragments against ruin. The sense of the passage is rooted in it:

> The character is pivotal—its form holds the tension, the horizontal dash and vertical stroke on either side of the upright maintaining a tentative equilibrium—it is the point of rest, as much the place out of which new movement is born as the place into which past action settles. In the *Ta Hsio*, chih is the ground from whence virtuous action springs: 'The Great Learning . . . is rooted in coming to rest, being at ease in perfect equity.'[58]

In the post-war world there is no point of rest for old concepts as well as no point or base out of which new concepts may grow; there is no awareness of Bunting, nor of Upward, men who are roots. "The mind may be likened to a tree whose roots are feelings and whose leaves are words," Upward believes.[59] In some men, Pound states,

> Their thoughts are in them as the thought of the tree is in the seed, or in the grass, or the grain, or the blossom. And these minds are the more poetic, and they affect mind about them, and transmute it as the seed the earth. And this latter sort of mind is close on the vital universe.[60]

Upward, and all like him, are not only associated with it, but in one way or another with the many manifestations of the word "root" as it appears throughout the *Cantos*.

> The plan is in nature
>             rooted
> Coming from earth
>                   (99/709:738)

NOTES

[1] Noel Stock, *Poet In Exile: Ezra Pound* (Manchester: Manchester Univ., 1964), p. 145. It was at a meeting of G.R.S. Mead's Quest Society in 1911 that Pound first met Upward. Stock also points out, again in *Poet In Exile* (p. 226), that Pound may have gained a little knowledge of Chinese poetry from Upward in 1912. Hugh Kenner, *The Pound Era* (Berkeley and Los Angeles: Univ. of Calif., 1971), pp. 45, 505 and Herbert N. Schneidau, *Ezra Pound, The Image and the Real* (Baton Rouge: Louisiana State Univ., 1969), pp. 118-21, 126, 130, 133, 134, 145, among others, also acknowledge Upward's importance.

[2] 20/1631 [Allen Upward], *Some Personalities* (London: John Murray, 1921), p. 153.

[3] Ibid., p. 301.

[4] *Who Was Who 1916-1928*, Vol. II (London: Adam & Charles Black, 1962), however, lists his birthplace as Worcester.

[5] *Some Personalities*, p. 94.

[6] It was written in response to a request from an American publishing firm.

[7] *Some Personalities*, p. 187.

[8] Ezra Pound, *Literary Essays of Ezra Pound*, ed. T.S. Eliot, (New York: New Directions, 1968), p. 47.

[9] The firm's last important publication was Upward's story *Treason* (1903) which, among other things, informed the reader of a rival claimant to the British throne (apparently true—Mary III).

[10] He does not disclose it.

[11] Yeats, then into theosophical and psychical research, planned to communicate telepathically with Upward across Dublin—the attempt was unsuccessful.

[12] See Jane Lidderdale and Mary Nicholson, *Dear Miss Weaver* (New York: Viking, 1970), p. 73.

[13] *Some Personalities*, p. 242-43. I have not been able to get the *New Age* article to which Upward refers. But I imagine the concept of the Overman is a development of his ideas on genius.

[14] *Poetry,* VI (September 1915) 317-18.

[15] *Some Personalities*, p. 243.

[16] Ibid., p. 281-82.

[17] Pound [review of *The Divine Mystery*] *The New Freewoman*, I, No. XI 15 November 1913) 207-8.

[18] Allen Upward, *The Divine Mystery* (Boston and New York: Houghton Mifflin, 1915), p. 1.

[19] Pound [review of *The Divine Mystery*] p. 208.

[20] Ernest Fenollosa, *The Chinese Written Character As A Medium For Poetry,* ed. Ezra Pound, (San Francisco: City Lights, 1969), p. 22n.

[21] Noel Stock, *The Life of Ezra Pound* (New York: Pantheon, 1970), p. 143,

[22] I wish to thank Jamila Ismail for her help in the refining of certain points in this section.

[23] This parallels, somewhat, Pound's search for a denominator common to all religions. As Clark Emery points out in *Ideas Into Action* (Coral Gables: Univ. of Miami, 1958), p. 17, "In his search for the base of religious faith common to various cultures, Pound has discovered images that—for him, at least—possess . . . life and vitality. He has found them in Greek and Egyptian, Chinese and Japanese myth particularly, and he has made them his own."

[24] *Divine Mystery*, pp. 5-6.

[25] Ibid., p. 35.

[26] Ibid., p. 109.

[27] Hugh Kenner states in *The Pound Era*, pp. 150-51, that "The 'New Method" [Pound's new method in scholarship] began with his title, for as we learn from the *Oxford Companion to Classical Literature,* it was Osiris, 'the male productive principle in nature,' who became when his scattered limbs had been regathered the god of the dead (of Homer, of the Seafarer poet, of Arnaut Daniel), but also 'the source . . . of renewed life. The Greeks identified him with Dionysus.' The limbs' reunited energies assert themselves; Pound's book [the series of "Osiris" articles] by a young man at the threshold of great renovations, was about patterned energies."

[28] Of this passage Daniel Parlman in *The Barb of Time* (New York: Oxford Univ., 1969), p. 286, points out, "If we remember that . . . death implies new life, just as life implies death, we can have no difficulty in apprehending Pound's attitude towards physical death in the present Canto . . . When Pound says, 'Where I lie let the thyme rise,' the suggestion is stronger than ever of the punning use of *thyme* to mean organic time, that is, the process, which would constitute the atoms of Pound's corpse into new life through the vegetative cycle."

[29] *Divine Mystery*, p. 100.

[30] Allen Upward, *The New Word* (New York: Mitchell Kennerley, 1910), p. 204.

[31] I have been unable to find anything in Upward about Sitalkas.

[32] Pausanias states that there once existed a statue of Apollo at Delphi called Sitalces. See his *Description of Greece,* Vol. IV, trans. W.H.S. Jones, (Cambridge Harvard Univ., 1961), p. 449. It is also interesting to note that H.D., *Collected Poetry of H.D.* (New York: Boni and Liveright, 1940), p. 88, has written a poem entitled "Sitalkas."

[33] *Some Personalities,* p. 200.

[34] Ezra Pound, *The Selected Letters of Ezra Pound,* ed. D.D. Paige, (New York: New Directions, 1971), p. 284.

[35] *Some Personalities,* p. 236.

[36] Ibid., pp. 208-9. The Platonic dialogue of which Upward speaks occurs between himself and a friend on the meaning of "altruism" which was sparked by the search for the true meaning of the word "idealist. *The New Word* itself began as an attempt to define precisely the word "idealist," because the fourth bequest of Alfred Nobel's Peace Prizes was to go to "the person who shall have produced in the field of Literature the most distinguished work of an idealist tendency" (quoted in *The New Word,* p. 10).

[37] *New Word,* p. 70.

[38] Ibid., p. 21.

[39] Ezra Pound, *ABC of Reading* (New York: New Directions, 1960), p. 30.

[40] *Some Personalities,* p. 184.

[41] *New Word,* p. 252.

[42] See Pound's "Religio," *The New Freewoman,* I, No. IX (15 October 1913), 173-74.

[43] *New Word,* p. 58.

[44] Ibid., p. 100.

[45] Ibid., p. 293.

[46] *Literary Essays,* p. 62.

[47] *New Word,* p. 193.

[48] See also *ABC of Reading,* p. 25.

[49] *New Word,* p. 219.

[50] Ezra Pound, *The Spirit of Romance* (New York: New Directions, 1968), p. 95.

[51] *New Word,* p. 219.

[52] Ibid., p. 244.

[53] Ibid., p. 222.

[54] K'ung did the same thing; see Canto XIII.

[55] *Some Personalities,* 197.

[56] Harry M. Meacham, *The Caged Panther, Ezra Pound at Saint Elizabeths* (New York: Twayne, 1967), p. 170.

[57] Bunting resisted literally. As Pound recalled, "I think Bunting is the only man who did six months in jail as a conscientious objector during the armistice, i.e. after the war was over, on the principle that if there was a war he wouldn't go" (quoted in Noel Stock, *Life of Ezra Pound,* p. 283).

[58] Tom Grieve, *Annotations to the Chinese in the Rock-Drill Cantos of Ezra Pound* (Masters thesis in progress, Simon Fraser University, 1973). Chih[3] does not mean "root," but Pound clearly deals with this aspect of it.

[59] *New Word,* p. 54.

[60] *Spirit of Romance,* pp. 92-3.


## A. D. Moody (essay date 1975)

SOURCE: "Pound's Allen Upward," in *Paideuma: A Journal Devoted to Ezra Pound Scholarship,* Vol. 4, No. 1, Spring, 1975, pp. 55-70.

[*In the following excerpt, Moody examines in detail a variety of references to Upward in Pound's work, and chronicles Upward's involvement with the Imagists.*]

We can get some way further with 'Sitalkas' and the rest than Bryant Knox does (Vol. III, No. 1, pp. 71-83). Some of his information is helpful, but there are things he has missed which are essential to a full understanding of the Upward ideogram, both as to what it is in itself and as to how it fits into *The Pisan Cantos.* First its components must be recognized and brought into clear focus. Then it may become as a lens, bringing related material into order.

Anyone who wants to grasp the scope of Upward's presence in Pound's mind must read at least **The New Word** and **The Divine Mystery,** the importance of which Pound very strongly affirmed.[1] The acknowledgment is in *Thrones:*

> So that Dante's view is quite natural:
> this light
> as a river
> in Kung; in Ocellus, Coke, Agassiz
> ϱεῖ, the flowing
> this persistent awareness
> Three Ninas from Gaudier,
> Their mania is a lusting for farness
> Blind to the olive leaf,
> not seeing the oak's veins.

Wheat was in bread in the old days.
    (1.46 after midnight)
Alan Upward's seal showed Sitalkas.
Coin was in Ambracia;
The caelator's son, named Pythagora.
                (107/762:787)

Upward's place in this company is by virtue of more than his seal, coin of the mind though that is. Sitalkas is the divinity in the wheat; and more than that, as I shall show—there is reason, *ratio,* in the glance at Pound himself between the two lines. Again, in *The New Word* he had shown 'this persistent awareness', seeing the living waterspout in the oak's veins, and from the olive leaf how Athene is *glaukopis.*[2] The argument of that book is all of 'this light/ as a river . . . the flowing'. 'Mr. Upward is not only perspicacious, but his mind is balanced by nature and by a knowledge of the Chinese classics.'[3] There is all of that behind the Upward ideograms.

## I

We will want its context later, so I give it in context now. There is also 'so lay men in Circe's swine-sty', and 'Magna NUX animae'. (The italics are mine):

> *every bank of discount is downright iniquity*
>   *robbing the public for private individual's gain*
>   *nec benecomata Kirkê, mah!* χᾀκὰ φάργᾳκ᾽ ἔδωκεν
> *neither with lions nor leopards attended*
>     *but poison, veleno*
> *in all the veins of the commonweal*
> *if on high, will flow downward all through them*
>   *if on the forge at Predappio?* sd/ old Upward:
>     "not the priest but the victim"
>     his seal Sitalkas, sd/the old combatant: "victim,
> withstood them by Thames and by Niger with pistol by Niger
> with a printing press by the Thames bank"
>   until I end my song
>       and shot himself;
>         *for praise of intaglios*
> *Matteo and Pisanello out of Babylon*
>     *they are left us*
> *for roll or plain impact* .
>   *or cut square in the jade block*
>                 (74/437:464)

## HIS SEAL

'I have in my possession an ancient Greek gem that appears to represent "John Barleycorn" with a seed basket on his arm and three spikes rising from his cap,' wrote Upward in *The Divine Mystery.*[4] A footnote indicates that the seal stamped in gold on the cover of the volume is from this gem—it is also stamped on the cover of his 'autobiography,' *Some Personalities* (London, 1921). This figure holds a reaping knife in his advanced right hand, has a flail beneath his left arm, and in his left hand the seed basket. This last detail, however, could be identified as a winnowing-fan, 'the large open shovel-shaped basket . . . used by farmers to separate the grain from the chaff,' and one of the emblems of Dionysus 'conceived as a deity of agriculture

and the corn.'[5] In his note Upward adds: 'There may be further significance in the fact that the figure is engraved on a sardonyx or bloodstone, green with red spots. I bought it at Corfu.' The 'Genius of the Corn' has been also the sacrificial victim—Dionysus: Christ. He quotes Burns' 'Ballad of John Barleycorn' as an example of the persistence of the primitive mind, and the 'coincidence' of primitive and civilized religion. But his concern, as it became Pound's, was to dissociate the dionysiac from the christian, and to save the genius of things from death.

There is one mention of his seal in *The New Word.* 'I have . . . talked with the Black Men in their own land beside the Black River, in the oldest and most catholic speech, the language of signs. In a place where no White man had been before me, I found a Black King and his fold withheld by an old curse from planting a medicinal tree; and I broke the curse by showing to them a stone whereon a Greek long ago had carved the figure of his god.'[6] 'I know that he performed at least one "miracle" by means of a gnostic gem,' Pound wrote to Harriet Monroe in January 1914.[7]

## SITALKAS

So far as I know, Upward himself doesn't use this name. It's a fair guess that Pound takes it from H. D.'s poem, and that he had reason for associating the poem with the seal. The close friendship and collaboration of H.D. and Pound in 1912-13, the moment of Imagisme, is of course well known.

>   H. D. once said "serenitas"
>     (Atthis, etc.)
>   at Dieudonné's
>     in pre-history.
>               (113/787)

'Sitalkas' was first printed in *The New Freewoman* of 1 September 1913, on a page devoted to 'The Newer School,' and preceded by Aldington's version of Sappho's 'To Atthis.' Pound had just taken over the literary pages of the paper, and was presenting a preview of *Des Imagistes,* in which both poems appeared.

### SITALKAS

Thou art come at length
More beautiful
Than any cool god
In a chamber under
Lycia's far coast,
Than any high god
Who touches us not
Here in the seeded grass.
Aye, than Argestes
Scattering the broken leaves.

In the temple of his oracle at *Lycia* Apollo was supposed to pass the winter. *Argestes,* signifying clearing, brightening, was an epithet applied first to the south wind, but later to Zephyrus the West wind (cf. Shelley's *Ode*). The latter would complete a succession of seasons, and make central that of 'the seeded grass.' *Sitalkas* is corn + power, force, i.e., the genius of the corn. (Not its 'protector', as Mr. Knox suggests—but the life *in* it.)

If I were trying fiction, there would be a scene in Dieudonné's restaurant, near the British Museum, with H. D., Aldington, Upward, Pound, and the talk of the Imagiste programme, and of the appearance of *The Divine Mystery,* with Upward's seal *the* image. But Pound has done that, in his own way, and made far more of it.

## NOT THE PRIEST BUT THE VICTIM

This is the primary and controlling term. I haven't noticed the exact phrase in the three books of Upward's which I have read; but it does give the gist of his view of the fate of genius in history. Bryant Knox's gloss is precisely what Upward, and Pound, did not mean: 'It is not the priest but the victim who brings about the sun's amiability, the weather's benevolence, and conditions the powers of both celestial and earthly divinities. Osiris, Christ—they keep order; the world functions as a result of their "being." '[8] This is indeed what humanity has believed, in error, superstition, vanity, *against nature.*

Reviewing *The Divine Mystery* in *The New Freewoman* (15 November 1913) Pound observed:

> The first half of the book is planned, if it can be called so, on the slow recognition of the sun. That is to say, primitive man turns from his worship of the dead, and of the earth and of various fears, to a worship of the life-giving Helios. The solar missionary says it is unnecessary to bury a man in the cornfield in order that crops shall rise by virtue of his spirit.[9]

In his retrospective review of *The New Word* (*New Age,* 23 April 1914) he drew from Upward's work the conclusion

> That since Christ's notable success—in gaining a reputation, I mean—a number of people have desired to 'save the world' without undergoing the inconvenience of crucifixion.[10]

Upward had written:

> There were idealists in those days interpreting the ways of heaven by the heart of man. Did not that Bright One in the sun say by his prophets in Egypt and Syria and Asia and Greece:—'What are ye anointing a man at Easter, and slaying him and burying him in your cornfields, that his life may give life to the seed, and his flesh be your bread! Ye know not what ye do. It is I who give life to the seed, I who give you your daily bread . . . .'—preaching the Gospel of the Sun, and snatching the victim from the cross.[11]

Thus the rite, the *religio,* of the *Cantos*—in 36 and 39 and 47, and in the very death-cells of Pisa—refuses crucifixion, and celebrates the vital universe. *Glorious,*

*deathless of many names, Zeus aye ruling all things, founder of the inborn qualities of nature, by laws piloting all things.*[12] No man, whether as priest or as victim, brings about the sun's energy and orders the cosmos—

> Pull down thy vanity, it is not man
> Made courage, or made order, or made grace,
>    Pull down thy vanity, I say pull down.
> Learn of the green world what can be thy place . . .

The passage just quoted from Upward's *New Word* gives the point of view implicit in his story *Karos, the God,* published in *The New Freewoman* of 15 December 1913. It is an account of primitive ignorance and superstition, of a practice against nature. It should prevent such unthinking and unfeeling abstractions as that it is 'the victim who brings about the sun's amiability' etc. This is basic, it is fundamental. The following is an excerpt:

*Karos, a slave, runs away from 'the lighthouse of civilization' where his god Hermes has failed to protect him in theft, into a region of barbarians whose gods are unknown to him. This is the latter half of the story:*

> . . . A runaway slave, his clothing a few dirty rags, his body a mass of sores and bruises, his bones coming through his skin, sick, forlorn and desperate, he stood there for a few minutes, shrinking.
>
> Then he began to go down the mountain side.
>
> Between him and the village there were fields of wheat and millet, and another corn which was strange to Karos. The wheat was being cut in one of the fields by women who were unlike any one the slave had ever seen. They were stunted in shape, and dark-skinned with long, straight black hair. They wore woollen garments, and shoes that ended in a turned-up point. As the slave came toward them, they left off reaping and stood up to stare at him, and a man dressed in a sheepskin cloak, who had been ordering the work, gave a shout, and started off running toward the village.
>
> Karos' heart sank. He went forward slowly, dragging one swollen foot after the other. He had just got to the last field outside the village when he was astonished to see a troop coming out to meet him.
>
> At the head marched an old man, taller than the rest, whose long white beard and venerable aspect struck the slave with awe. He wore a fillet on his head which reminded Karos of the sacred fillet worn by the priest of Demeter, and in his hand he carried a garland of wheat-ears mixed with blue cornflowers, like the garlands bound round the horns of a bull about to be sacrificed. Next to the leader of the procession came boys and girls with their hands full of flowers, and after them young men playing on reeds and wooden cymbals, and then a crowd of villagers. As they came along they kept up a joyous chant like the sacred chorus of Dionusos.

Karos stood still, and waited: The old man, whom he supposed to be the village king or priest, came up to him and greeted him in a strange tongue, with a respect the slave could not account for. Next he bound the fillet on Karos' head, and as he did so the musicians clashed their cymbals, and the procession burst into a louder and more exciting chant. Than the priest took Karos by the hand and led him into the village, the children running in front and casting their flowers under his feet.

Karos was bewildered. He suffered himself to be led along, scarcely knowing what he did. The music made him drowsy, and he told himself that this was another dream like those which had come to him when he was climbing the hill.

The village was defended by a mud wall the height of a man's breast. Outside the gate they passed by a great oak, and beneath it there stood an enormous stone with a flat top like an altar; but Karos looked in vain for the god. The dwellings of the villagers were rude wigwams built of untrimmed boughs wattled together, the cracks being stopped up with mud, so that they looked to the Greek like birds' nests. But there was one house in the middle, better than the others, built round the trunk of a living tree that stood in an open space, and thatched over with fine straw. Into this house the priest led Karos.

The slave had to lower his head to pass through the doorway. The inside was dark at first, but after a time he saw a pile of skins, of some animal he had never met with, the fur of which was soft and brown. There were also some domestic furnishings, such as a platter and drinking cup, and a large flint stone, shaped like a hatchet-blade.

Karos sank down on the bed of skins. He was light-headed owing to extreme hunger, and did not yet feel sure that all this was real. But the venerable old man seemed to understand his condition. He spoke to the men who had followed them to the door, and they hurried away, returning quickly with milk and boiled chestnuts and small cakes of bread. The slave snatched the food from their hands, and devoured it. The chant was still going on outside, and the sounds reached his ears. A warm, soothing languor passed into him. He felt very happy, and went to sleep.

When Karos awoke he was alone. He arose and went to the door of the hut. He found a man squatting on the threshold, who stood up when he saw Karos, shaking his head and signing to him not to pass out. The runaway shrank back with a touch of fear. It seemed he was a prisoner.

During the time that followed Karos fared much the same. He saw that the villagers wanted to please him, but that they were careful to give him no chance of escape. They brought him the best of everything they had to eat and drink. After a few days they placed a young girl in his hut, and signified that she was given to him for a wife.

The girl fell on her knees to Karos, who was pleased that she should be afraid of him. This, and the reverence of his keepers, gave him boldness, and after a time he insisted on going out of doors, and walking about the village. That was permitted, but a close watch was kept on him, and whenever he tried to wander out into the fields he was turned back.

Meanwhile the venerable priest came day by day to visit Karos, and from him and from the girl the Greek began to pick up the speech of the barbarians. As soon as he could make himself any way understood he sought to learn the name of the village god.

All this time he had been wondering what was the worship of the place. He remembered that strange altar he had passed outside the village; but he had seen no sign of any god there, neither was there sign of temple or idol anywhere else. To Karos it was a fearful thing to live without the presence of some divine protection, for he had been taught that the gods resented and punished the neglect of men.

When he tried to question his wife about this she seemed afraid to answer, responding only by gestures that puzzled him. The old priest explained to him that there were many evil spirits whom the people kept off by means of magic signs and tokens. Some of these signs he offered to teach Karos, who found they were familiar to him already, being the same as the slaves used. At the same time the priest assured him that he need have no fear on his own account, as long as he remained indoors, inasmuch as the tree around which his dwelling-place had been constructed was itself possessed of magical properties, a powerful defence against the demons.

None of this lore was new to the Greek, but what puzzled him was the absence of those greater and more beneficent beings who were worshipped in the world from which he had fled. There were the Sun and Moon, for instance, Diana of the Ephesians and the great Phrygian Cybele—did these barbarous highlanders know nothing of such gods as those?

The old man shook his head. The sun and moon were too far off to be reached by their prayers; they hardly recognized them as divine.

Whom did they worship then?—for a village could not exist without a god.

"You are our god," the old priest answered, staring at him curiously.

The slave was struck dumb. As the light broke into his mind he found an explanation of all that had so bewildered him; the joy at his arrival, the religious march, the sacred fillet and flowers. Evidently these barbarians had mistaken him for a heavenly visitor, like Hermes or Apollo. The hut he was in was the village temple, the old man was his priest.

From that hour a great change came over Karos. In all his coming and goings he felt that the eyes of the villagers were fixed on him in awe, and he strove to act up to his divine part. His step grew stately, his mien severe and condescending. He spoke to the people rarely, and with much reserve. They on their part seemed to be prepared for this divine assumption, and to be gratified by it. Only his girl-companion shrank from him in his exalted mood and sometimes he found her weeping silently. Once when he was fingering the stone axe-head in the wigwam she snatched it from him, and hid it out of his reach. Karos beat her.

Upon a day in spring the divine slave heard outside his dwelling the joyous music that had welcomed him when he first came. The aged priest appeared, and bade him make ready for the great yearly festival of the seed. In Springtime all men sacrifice to their gods to gain a blessing on the fields, and Karos exulted at the thought that sacrifice should be offered up to him. The priest made him put on a new white robe and anointed him and gave him an intoxicating drink. Then they went out into the open space before the house, and found it filled with minstrels and singers, and children carrying willow branches that were bursting into bud, and a great crowd of men and women.

Karos was dizzy, but men on each side held him up, and led him along, following the joyful music, till they came to the tree outside the village wall, where stood the great stone altar. Karos noticed that the priest carried in one hand an axe with a flint head like that which his wife had hidden; and when they had reached the place of sacrifice he looked round for the dedicated calf or lamb, but could not see it. He became aware that the people were strangely excited, thronging round him, and laying their hands on his garment as if to snatch a blessing.

Then the music waxed louder and frantically loud, and the chant rose to a scream as the singers broke their ranks and whirled round him in a mad dance; and the divine slave's head whirled round with the dancers, and he swooned and found himself falling backwards on the altar, and saw the flint-edge above him taking a thousand years to reach his throat.

## SD/ THE OLD COMBATANT: 'VICTIM, . . . ' . . . AND SHOT HIMSELF

Upward was no believer in such sacrifices; no more was Pound. But it was Upward's conviction, based on his studies and on experience, that it was the fate of genius—i.e. the man who was a vortex of the vital universe[13]—to be crucified rather than honoured.

> The Idealist . . . knows what he has to expect of mankind. The crucifix set up at the entrance of every Catholic village, Lamartine has written, is Humanity's warning to the Idealist.[14]

—'a warning given in vain', he added, but that was before his new word had fallen upon closed minds. The tone is more bitter in his first contribution to *The New Freewoman* (15 July 1913):

> . . . The law permits attacks on me as a writer which it does not permit on me as a lawyer, or as a shareholder in a frozen meat company; but that is because the public which makes the law has been taught for 1913 years, more or less, that the sufferings of genius are for the benefit of humanity— an opinion I do not share.

> It is not my intention to review the new book of my friend Mr. Gerald Stanley Lee. *Crowds* is more than a book; it is a prophecy and a policy; and it includes as part of its vision and its purpose the protection of genius from the policy of crucifixion.

The main part of the article illustrates the contention that in England genius has always been prevented from serving the nation, and saving it: Carlyle, Dickens, General Gordon and Richard Burton, and Upward himself, who having been 'allowed to render practical services to the labouring people of South Wales,' was 're-jected in favour of a millionaire . . . who has since broken the back of the miners' organisation,' when he 'sought the privilege of rendering further help in Parliament'. '"There has been a curse on us ever since," ' he was told—

> That is the moral of *Crowds*. The class or the nation, the aristocracy or the democracy, that cannot tolerate its saviours places itself under a curse from which no one else can relieve it.

He was crucified by being disregarded, not taken seriously. On the title page of *Some Personalities* 'by 20/1631' (London, 1921) he set this saying of Confucius: 'I will not be grieved because men do not know me; I will be grieved because I do not know men.' In the introduction to his version of the *Sayings* Upward had presented K'ung the Master as 'a fount of moral energy', the man of genius whose ideas had gone into action: 'The real monument to K'ung the Master is not the literary canon associated with his name, but the Chinese Empire itself, the greatest and most enduring of human societies, under whose shelter nearly a third of the human race have lived in comparative civilisation and happiness from an age far antedating the foundation of Troy or the Exodus of the Hebrews, down to the present day, and which, during that vast period, has been known to those who inhabit it as the Heavenly Kingdom.'[15] Upward had dreamt of founding a civilisation upon genius—not *his* genius, but the genius of things—and knew only failure. Nor could he maintain the Confucian balance to which he aspired. The tone of the autobiography is that of a man sadly, even tragically, unbalanced; the wild hyperbole, forced levity and grim desperation all betraying the lacerated spirit. In this passage he is uncharacteristically sober:

> I have taken this opportunity of explaining to certain correspondents why it is that I have not been able to carry on the work begun in *The New*

*Word.* I meant it as a foreword, and as an advertisement. . . . Knowing full well what likelihood there was of my receiving Nobel's legacy, I felt bound to intimate that my going on must depend on the goodwill of my readers. Twenty years, perhaps the best twenty years of my life have now been lost to the world. I am still, what I always have been, one of the unemployed. Like Milton's angels, my part is to stand and wait. During an illusory respite shortly before the war I sat down to write *The Horoscope of Man.* Again my brain caught fire. Wonderful glimpses began opening on every side. Sometimes I had to lay down the pen in sheer amazement at the things which flowed from it, not at the dictation of the lying spirits of the dead, but of the Spirit which prompts every true work of an idealist tendency, the Muse of prophecy.

The respite proved illusory. I am again leading a double life. I have gone back to grinding lenses. My latest lenses have been those through which the future generation are being trained to look on life, the lens of the Latin grammar and the lens of Commercial Geography. I am now on the books of the Board of Education. But the Board of Education does not know me as the author of *The New Word.* It does not even know me by name. . . . Posterity may be interested in the state of education in England in this year of grace. It will learn a good deal in learning that the Board of Education knew me as 20/1631.[16]

The last words of the book are echoed in 'not the priest but the victim:' they are the personal form of the general truth.

That Temple [of the Living Spirit of God] is not mine to build. Like David, I have been a man of strife. Solomon's temple must be built by Solomon. My Instructions read that my part is not that of Founder, but of foundation-victim.[17]

Was that how Pound remembered and honoured him: not a founder of the *paradiso terrestre,* but one whose work could be built upon? The dissociation of the two aspects of Sitalkas, combatant/victim, is faithful to the spirit of what is best in that work. Yet to be thus divided is to be self-destroyed: 'Have always thought poor old Upward shot himself in discouragement on reading of [Nobel] award to Shaw. Feeling of utter hopelessness in struggle for values.'[18] His *name* is set against 'poison . . . in all the veins of the commonweal . . . downward;' he is recognised as a 'combatant,' one of the 'resisters' (110/781)—'a man of strife.' But he is seen too as the victim of what he opposed; with the implication possibly, in 'and shot himself,' of

nor shall diamond die in the avalanche
    be it torn from its setting
first must destroy himself ere others destroy him.
                             (74/430:457)

'"Non combaattere" said Giovanna', meaning (as it stands in the ideogram) don't try to force things, let them grow, naturally (83/531:567). Also

That I lost my centre
fighting the world.

But the cause of the imbalance, in Upward? He is remembered by his seal, an intaglio; and, self-confessedly, he lacked the skill 'to forge Achaia'. He wanted to bring genius into action. 'Genius', Pound wrote in *Jefferson &/or Mussolini,* 'is the capacity to see ten things where the ordinary man sees one, and where the man of talent sees two or three, PLUS the ability to register that multiple perception in the material of his art.'[19] The latter, indispensable ability, Upward lacked; or at least, he never found his natural form of action. He remained a thinker, and thwarted; not a Doer, not a maker. The memorial to his genius is his seal, not a Heavenly Kingdom in the mind and heart indestructible.

Yet there is 'praise of intaglios' that are left us, the work of *caelators.*

. . . . .

To fill in the documentary record here is Upward's verse letter which Pound was recalling. The previous number of *The Egoist* had featured the Imagists, Pound not contributing.

### THE DISCARDED IMAGIST

*To the Editor,* The Egoist.
MADAM,
    O thou unborn historian of literature—(if you ever
        mention my name spell it better than F. S. Flint,
        please!)
    Do not believe a single word
    That others have written about me.

    In the year nineteen hundred a poet named
        Cranmer Byng brought to my attic in Whitehall
        Gardens a book of Chinese Gems by Professor
        Giles,
    Eastern butterflies coming into my attic there beside
        the Stygian Thames,
    And read me one of them—willows, forsaken young
        wife, spring.

    Immediately my soul kissed the soul of immemorial
        China:
    I perceived that all we in the West were indeed
        barbarians and foreign devils.
    And that we knew scarcely anything about poetry.

    I set to work and wrote little poems
    Some of which I read to a scientific friend
    Who said,—"After all, what do they prove?"

    Then I hid them away for ten or twelve years,
    Scented leaves in a Chinese jar,
    While I went on composing the poem of life.

    I withstood the savages of the Niger with a revolver:
    I withstood the savages of the Thames with a
        printing-press:
    Byng and I we set up as publishers in Fleet Street,

and produced the "Odes of Confucius," and the
"Sayings."
My own poems I did not produce:
They were sent back to me by the *Spectator* and the
*English Review*.
I secretly grudged them to the Western devils.

After many years I sent them to Chicago, and they
    were printed by Harriet Monroe. (They also were
    printed in THE EGOIST.)
Thereupon Ezra Pound the generous rose up and
    called me an Imagist. (I had no idea what he
    meant.)
And he included me in an anthology of Imagists.
This was a very great honour.
But I was left out of the next anthology.
This was a very great shame.

And now I have read in a history of Imagism
That the movement was started in nineteen hundred
    and eight
By Edward Storer and T. E. Hulme.

(Poetry the crystal of language,
Passion frozen by art,
Fallen in love with its likeness!)

Evil is the advice of Horace
That poems should be given nine years to fix,
Evil in the day of swift movements—(for I hear that
    already Imagism is out of date.)

O thou divine soul of China
Brooding over millenniums of perfect art,
May you never be troubled by the impertinences of
    the West!

And thou unborn literary historian (if you ever
    mention my name)
Write me down as imitator of Po Li and Shakespeare
As well as of Edward Storer and T. E. Hulme.
                                        ALLEN UPWARD.[20]

Pound cared enough for Upward's prose poems to put
them into *The New Freewoman* (**'Scented Leaves from
a Chinese Jar'**) and *The Egoist* (**'Chinese Lanterns'**);
to include some in *Des Imagistes,* and others in *Catholic Anthology* (1915); and to give them a page in *Profile*
(Milan, 1932), 'a collection of poems which have stuck
in my memory and which may possibly define their
epoch, or at least rectify current ideas of it in respect to
at least one contour.' The poems belong now to 'prehis-
tory', if it is Pound we are interested in, though some
are memorable for their own sake. But it will have
struck the acute reader that Upward's K'ung the Master
is very nearly related to Pound's, and that his introduction to the *Sayings* might serve as well for the Chinese
cantos. There is evidence that Pound valued this effort
to civilise the savages of the Thames. Upward's version
was published in 1904, in the Wisdom of the East Series, Orient Press, London. By 1907 the series had been
taken over by John Murray; Upward had been succeeded
as co-editor by Dr. S.A. Kapadia; and his version had
been replaced by a new translation from the original by

Lionel Giles. That three selections from Upward's *Sayings,* together with his introduction, appeared in *The
New Freewoman* (1, 15 November, 1 December 1913),
is almost certainly to have been Pound's doing.

> "wherein is no responsible person
> having a front name, a hind name and an
>     address"
> "not a right but a duty"
>     those words still stand uncancelled,
> "Presente!"
>     and merrda for the monopolists
>         the bastardly lot of 'em
> Put down the slave trade, made the desert to
>     yield
> and menaced the loan swine
>     Sitalkas, double sitalkas
>     "not the priest but the victim"
>     said Allen Upward
> knew something was phoney, when he
>     (Pellegrini)
> sd/: the money is there.
>
>                              (78/479:510)

Here the gist or pith of the Upward ideogram becomes
a component of a Mussolini/ Italia *tradita* ideogram. The
link was implicit in 'if on the forge at Predappio? sd/ old
Upward': Mussolini was born at Predappio, son of a blacksmith. The first quotation is of course one of his aphorisms, attributed (in a variant form) near the end of *ABC
of Economics*. I associate 'and merrda for the monopolists
/ the bastardly lot of 'em' with the beginning of Canto XLI
("Ma qvesto" said the Boss *etc.*). Pellegrini held posts in
his Ministry of Finance, and was Minister of Finance in
the Saló Republic. A main theme in the canto as a whole
is Mussolini's effort to give Italy a new *forma mentis,* and
this passage has to be taken as part of the development of
the theme. "'It will not take uth 20 years to cwuth
Mussolini'". . . . 'il Programma di Verona . . . Foresteria,
Saló, Gardone / to dream the Republic'. And later—

> à la Wörgl. Sd/ one wd/ have to think about that
> but was hang'd dead by the heels before his thought in
>     proposito
>         came into action efficiently
> 'For a pig, Jepson said, 'for a woman.' For the infamies of
>     usura. . . .

There is a change of voice in 'Put down . . . the loan
swine', signalling a remove from Mussolini in particular to
the generic. These are the acts of responsible government
found equally in Confucian China, Jeffersonian America,
and Mussolini's effort. The words reach out in this way
through their associations. Jefferson was vehement against
negro slavery (65/367:386, and cf. 34/170:175); and
Acoetes' companions, wanting to sell Dionysus, were 'mad
for a little slave money' (2/7:11). The 'loan swine' are men
changed by the 'poison, veleno' of ' "robbing the public for
private individual's gain." ' The combination of Circe's
swine and slavers—with Jefferson the implicit per-
ceiver—occurred in the lines just before the Upward
ideogram (74/436:464). And Mussolini's resistance to
that poison was manifest in his 'Having drained off the

muck by Vada / From the marshes, by Circeo, where no one else wd. have drained it' (41/202:210).

Given all this, it seems to me unpromising to ask whether Upward had done these things. The only answer would be that he failed to carry his thought into action efficiently. That may be the subject-rhyme which brings him into this passage. But our attention is no longer upon Upward; and the function of the 'Sitalkas . . . Upward' inset is to apply that earlier ideogram to the Mussolini/Italia tradita elements, and to bring them into focus (Zagreus, with a difference). Mussolini, the man whose genius Pound affirmed in *Jefferson &/or Mussolini*, has been not followed but crucified, 'twice crucified' in fact. That was stated in the first lines of the *Pisan Cantos*. So too was the identification of Mussolini with Dionysus, which lies behind this linking with Upward's Sitalkas.

> The enormous tragedy of the dream in the
>     peasant's bent shoulders
> Manes! Manes was tanned and stuffed,
> Thus Ben and la Clara *a Milano*
>     by the heels at Milano
> That maggots shd/ eat the dead bullock
> DIGENES, διγενές, but the twice crucified
>     where in history will you find it?
> yet say this to the Possum: a bang, not a
>     whimper,
>   with a bang not with a whimper,
> To build the city of Dioce whose terraces are the
>     colour of stars.
>
>                                        (74/425:451)

" . . . language charged with meaning to the utmost possible degree;" and nothing random. My notes touch certain elements of the patterning, not the whole.

*Enormous*, strictly, means having departed from the rule, from order. *Tragedy*, the song of the (scape) goat. And the peasant bent as if himself beneath the yoke—for a painted paradise, is it? or to appease the dead, the Manes. The founder of the Manicheans (whose songs celebrated the illumination of love), was born in Ecbatan, city of Dioce, and was crucified there, his corpse being flayed. 'Tanned and stuffed' might connect his end with the flaying of the sacrificial ox in the Athenian *bouphonia*, as described by Frazer:

> the ox was skinned and all present partook of its flesh. Then the hide was stuffed with straw and sewed up; next the stuffed animal was set on its feet and yoked to a plough as if it were ploughing.[21]

The ox, Frazer explains, was being regarded as an incarnation of the corn-spirit. 'Thus Ben and la Clara . . . ' Even the names take on a colouring of myth, or will come to: *Ben*, not *bent*, but in Italian near to *bene*, *benito*—the good, the blessed one; as *la Clara* might be his light of love. But hung up by the heels, the dead bullock on a meat-hook.

When Pound called Il Duce 'the Boss' there was an under-sense of latin *bos*, the bull; but not of bossiness or bullying, as he explicitly stated in *Jefferson &/or Mussolini*, and not 'the will to power' as usually understood; rather of 'the will toward *order*' τὸ καλόν.[22] The Greek for will/power, *buleia*, can be heard in 'bull' and 'bullock.' (Why *bullock*, an ox or castrated bull? Is it because his will/power had gone from him before the end?) The connection with Dionysus is to be found in Frazer:

> there are indications, few but significant, that Dionysus was conceived as a deity of agriculture and the corn. He is spoken of as himself doing the work of a husbandman: he is reported to have been the first to yoke oxen to the plough, which before had been dragged by hand alone; and some people found in this tradition the clue to the bovine shape in which . . . the god was often supposed to present himself to his worshippers. . . .

> Like other gods of vegetation Dionysus was believed to have died a violent death, but to have been brought to life again; and his sufferings, death and resurrection were enacted in his sacred rites.

As told by Nonnus, his 'tragic story' ended with his being cut to pieces 'in the form of a bull . . . by the murderous knives of his enemies.'[23] *Digonos*, the twice-born, is an epithet of Dionysus. Pound actually wrote *digenes*, which the Faber text has kept thus far: might he have had in mind not only the 'correct' epithet, but genius, the power which generates?

' . . . but the twice crucified / where in history will you find it?' Mussolini was first shot at Lake Como, then hung up in Milan. 'That maggots shd/ eat the dead bullock.' The enormity of it, the derangement not only of the order of things perceived by the solar missionary, but even of human custom, that the life which was in the victim should be blankly dishonoured, in no way transmitted.

It will be apparent that what I have been finding in the opening lines corresponds very closely to what I found in the Upward ideogram. Upward's Sitalkas rhymes with Mussolini as genius/dead bullock. However, the later 'double Sitalkas' may do more than simply restate 'twice crucified': it may reinforce the sense of defeat and self-defeat. But the matter of Pound's view of Mussolini from Pisa is beyond my present scope. I must simply remark, having observed its most positive elements, that it is not only aware of the failure, but that the cause of failure must be his 'own fault for not understanding the universe.'[24] That is to say, 'if the prince have not order within him / He cannot put order in his dominions' (13/59:63). Nor do I find it suggested that Il Duce transmitted a precise definition, as others by seal, intaglio, Tempio, the constitution, or the city of Dioce in the mind indestructible. But this is only to open a question of some importance, to which I am far from having an answer.

. . . . .

A final observation, to suggest the bearing of Sitalkas upon the protagonist in Pisa. It is remarkable that neither in the opening lines nor in the Upward ideogram is there any elegiac sentiment; nor does Pound say anything of the life after death. Those attitudes he leaves to Eliot: 'with a bang not with a whimper,' 'until I end my song'.[25] His attitude, from the wreckage of Europe and from the death cells, has nothing to do with any end of the world feeling:

> I surrender neither the empire nor the temples
> 　　　　　　　　　　　　　　　plural
> nor the constitution nor yet the city of Dioce
> each one in his god's name
> as by Terracina rose from the sea Zephyr behind her
> 　　　and from her manner of walking
> 　　　　　　　　　　　　　as had Anchises
> till the shrine be again white with marble
> till the stone eyes look again seaward
> 　　　　　　　　　　　　　(74/434:461)

—in short, making a paradiso terrestre. Now that is the main drive, the life force of the *Pisan Cantos*. And it is a drive *against* Upward's end and Mussolini's; against Sitalkas so far as it signifies defeat and crucifixion. To be 'twice-born', to have no truck with death. Is it an achievement unique in English literature, this perfect transcendence of the usual elegiac mood which is self-enclosing and passive? He was then, and to the end of *The Cantos* '(1.46 after midnight)' the *caelator:* engraving the mandate of heaven, making new in himself the one life which flows through all things. The taint of the victim was not in him.

NOTES

[1] Pound reviewed *The Divine Mystery* upon publication, in *The New Freewoman* (15 November 1913), and *The New Word* (Geneva, 1907; London 1908)—retrospectively—in *The New Age* (23 April 1914). Both reviews are in *Selected Prose 1909-1965*, ed. William Cookson (1973).

[2] See *Selected Prose* p. 377.

[3] Ibid. p. 375

[4] *The Divine Mystery* (Letchworth, 1913) p. 105.

[5] Frazer, *The Golden Bough* (abridged ed., London 1954) pp. 387-8.

[6] *The New Word* (2nd ed., London, 1908) p. 29.

[7] *Letters* (London, 1951) p. 69—letter dated 20 January 1914.

[8] *Paideuma* III. 1, p. 76.

[9] *Selected Prose* p. 374.

[10] Ibid. p. 382.

[11] *The New Word* p. 233.

[12] 71/421:443—as translated in the Notes.

[13] The terms are as much Upward's as Pound's.

[14] *The New Word* p. 290.

[15] *The New Freewoman* (1 November 1913) p. 190.

[16] *Some Personalities* (London, 1921) pp. 186-7.

[17] Ibid. p. 302.

[18] *Letters* p. 374—to Eric Mesterton, December 1936.

[19] Op. cit. (New York, 1936, 1970) p. 88.

[20] *The Egoist* (1 June 1915) p. 98.

[21] *The Golden Bough* (ed, cit.) p. 466.

[22] *Jefferson &/or Mussolini* (New York, 1936, 1970) pp. 99, 128.

[23] *The Golden Bough* pp. 387-8. Frazer notices that Dionysus was represented also as a goat.

[24] Adapted from 'Laws for Maria' in Mary de Rachewiltz's *Discretions* (London, 1971) p. 69.

[25] Allusions to *The Hollow Men,* and *The Waste Land*—the latter apparently overlooked by *Annotated Index.*

**Paul Skinner (essay date 1988)**

SOURCE: "Of Owls and Waterspouts," in *Paideuma: A Journal Devoted to Ezra Pound Scholarship,* Vol. 17, No. 1, Spring, 1988, pp. 59-68.

[*In the following essay, Skinner discusses the respective influences of Ford Madox Ford and Allen Upward on the works of Ezra Pound.*]

In his stimulating short study of Ezra Pound, Donald Davie devotes considerable attention to the ideas of Allen Upward and their impact upon the evolution of Pound's mature aesthetic.[1] In the following pages, I want to examine two specific points that Davie discusses, and slightly augment the range of reference evoked by them thus far: firstly, Upward's inspection of the Greek word *glaukopis,* and secondly, his figure of the waterspout or double vortex.

In his habit of intense etymological scrutiny, Upward had, of course, both predecessors and successors, though the habit is rarer, perhaps, than it should be. For Pound himself, "reading" the ideogram, whether or not it was to be seen as "less an element of language than a mystical virtuous emblem to contemplate and get ideas from,"[2] came to serve as a paradigm for a particular kind of intelligent attention. Gaudier, he recalled, twenty years after reviewing Upward's *The New Word,* "accustomed to looking at the real shape of things, could read a certain amount of Chinese writing without ANY STUDY. He said, 'Of course, you can *see* it's a horse' (or a wing or whatever)."[3] And accurate identification of root, as against branch—"In every country idiots treat the branch as the root"[4]—became a central strategic element in Pound's investigations into past (and present) cultures.

But we also encounter such attention in the work of writers as varied as James Joyce, Thoreau and John Ruskin. And, in this instance, I merely chronicle another reader's attention. Charles Tomlinson mentioned to me that Ruskin had discussed the meaning of *glaukopis* in *The Queen of the Air* (1869): and so he does, in "Athena Keramitis,"[5] when writing of "confusion between light and colour in the word used for the blue of the eyes of Athena," a confusion brought about by "the intensity of the Greek sense that the heaven is light, more than that it is blue." *Glaukopis,* then:

> chiefly means grey-eyed; grey standing for a pale or luminous blue; but it only means "owl-eyed" in thought of the roundness and expansion, not from the colour . . .

Ruskin goes on to quote from a book by Payne Knight, entitled *Inquiry into the Symbolical Language of Ancient Art* (1818): "Before the human form was adopted, her [Athena's] proper symbol was the owl, a bird which seems to surpass all other creatures in acuteness of organic perception," and adds:

> I cannot find anywhere an account of the first known occurrence of the type; but, in the early ones on Attic coins, the wide round eyes are clearly the principal things to be made manifest.

Upward would also mention the owl stamped on Athenian coins, in the passage from *The New Word* quoted by Pound in "Allen Upward Serious," his *New Age* review of 23 April, 1914.[6] Ruskin does not allude to the tendency of the owl's eyes to glare and then to cease from glaring, which Upward went on to link with the leaves of the olive tree, but the essential point is certainly made.

Was Upward familiar with Ruskin's work? It would be surprising if he were not, considering the position Ruskin still held at the turn of the century. We know that Pound had read Ruskin, though his published references are sparse and often dismissive. Yet, once their works are brought into conjunction, the affinities between them (both generally and in particulars) are evident. A number of Pound-Ruskin connections have already been made and more work will surely follow on their extensive and often startling similarities.[7]

But my main business here is with the waterspout, and my alignment of selected details of the intellectual climate of 1913-1914 will, I hope, avoid infection by what

Hugh Kenner somewhere terms "the genetic fallacy." I am not seeking to pinpoint specific sources or "influences," rather stressing the wide-ranging nature of Pound's mind and interests, a mind, indeed, "from which, and through which, and into which" ideas were "constantly rushing."[8]

Pound had met Allen Upward in 1911 but his active interest seems to have awakened in the autumn of 1913. On 17 September, he wrote to Dorothy Shakespear, praising Upward's "Chinese things in 'Poetry'" which were, he considered, "worth the price of admission." In another letter of 23 September, he commented: "Upward of the chinese poems is quite an addition. . . . *Il pense* that IS an addition. He seems to [know] things that ain't in Frazer, at least he talked sense about sun-worship & the siege of Troy. . . . " On 2 October, Pound reported: "I would have writ before but I went to Ryde to visit Upward. *Il pense.* It is a rare phenomenon. He has just finished '**The Divine Mystery,**' digested golden bough with a lot more of his own intelligence stuck into it."[9]

The phrase "Il pense" recurs again in Pound's review of *The Divine Mystery*[10] and, in letters and reviews, his respect for Upward's clear thinking and intellectual independence is expressed in terms similar to those in which he would praise Eliot, de Gourmont and Frobenius.[11] But when did Pound read *The New Word* (reviewed retrospectively in April, 1914)? Writing to Michael Roberts in 1937, he remarked that Hulme had read "Upward's new work," and added: "I didn't till I knew Upward."[12] Not "met" but "knew." On 23 September 1913 (the same date as that of the letter to Dorothy quoted above), writing to Harriet Monroe about Upward's "**Chinese poems,**" Pound referred to Upward as "a very interesting chap."[13] The real excitement seems to emerge after the visit to Ryde in late September 1913, which must have afforded opportunities for extended and uninterrupted conversation, during that period when Pound was most often galvanized by *talk,* the living voice, whether that of Yeats, Wyndham Lewis or Ford Madox Ford.

In 1913-1914, while actively engaged with Upward and Lewis, with Yeats at Stone Cottage and in correspondence (from December 1913) with James Joyce in Trieste, Pound was also in close contact with Ford, discussing Ford's work with him and reading that work, often before publication. In August 1913, he read Ford's *Mr. Apollo* (1908, concerning a divine visitation to Earth): it had "decent spots in it."[14] In September, he and Ford were rearranging the latter's *Collected Poems* (November 1913) and they also "mucked about the preface" of Ford's *Henry James* (published 1 January, 1914).[15] In March 1914, Pound praised Ford's long poem "On Heaven" and commented that his new novel was "as far as it has gone—above his others."[16] If this means "as far as it has gone towards completion," Pound presumably referred to *The Good Soldier,* early chapters of which would appear in BLAST; if it means "as far as it represents a literary advance," Pound is alluding to *The Young Lovell,* published in October

1913. But Pound must have read this novel soon after publication (if not before) since he mentions it in his review of Ford's *Collected Poems* (in the *New Freewoman*, 15 December, 1913), where he also refers to two other novels by Ford, *Ladies Whose Bright Eyes* (1911) and *Mr. Fleight* (April 1913).[17]

Much of *The Young Lovell* was written in the spring of 1913. Ford and Violet Hunt were drifting around the south of France after the trail arising from Elsie Hueffer's libel suit against *The Throne*, a magazine which had referred to Violet Hunt as "Mrs. Hueffer" although Ford and Elsie were never divorced. The verdict went against *The Throne*, and the attendant publicity humiliated and distressed Ford immeasurably. But, as so often in discouraging circumstances, he continued to work prodigiously (writing "all day on the table in the study they had given him" at the hotel in Carcassonne—"the lid of the bath in the bathroom"),[18] and informed his agent of the novel's completion on 7 July 1913.[19]

*The Young Lovell* is a romance, set in the border country of Northumberland just after the accession of Henry VII. It is the last novel Ford wrote before beginning *The Good Soldier* and exhibits many familiar Fordian motifs and themes: the problematical status of the "real" world, courtly values, corruption by luxury and materialism, the inactive or seemingly paralysed hero, the adumbrations of cultural collapse. Like much of Ford's historical fiction, it is essentially "about" the time of its writing rather than that of its action—this was particularly the case after 1910-1911, when he began to develop the ability to correlate personal tensions with his quickening apprehension of England's decline.

More to my present purpose, however, is the novel's preoccupation with Venus (and the many allusions to Venice). Young Lovell (whose forename is Paris) is afflicted by visions as he keeps his self-imposed vigil prior to becoming a knight: among these are Helen of Troy and "a courtesan he had seen in Venice long ago."[20] Early in the novel, having just sworn "by the paps of Venus," Lovell encounters the woman who will entrance him:

> On a green hill there stood a pink temple, and the woman on the back of the white horse held a white falcon. She smiled at him with the mocking eyes of the naked woman that stood upon the shell, in the picture he had seen in Italy. (12)

Later, she is described as having "a crooked and voluptuous mouth," "mocking eyes of a shade of green" and a "figure of waves." Lovell "had never seen so bright a lady, no, not among the courtesans of Venice. His heart at the sight of her hair beat in great, stealthy pulses; his throat was dry and the flowers grew all about her." (47)

The woman/goddess appears to a number of other characters in the course of the novel, her aspect varying according to the observer. The Bishop Palatine, seeking to alert the monk Francis to the threat she poses, reviews the many sightings and concludes that "All those women were one woman." (234), an assertion curiously echoed in a note to a famous poem published nine years later.

At the climax of the novel, during the battle for Castle Lovell, which is built above the sea and has been seized by usurpers, the monk Francis and the Lady Margaret of Glororem (betrothed of the Young Lovell) wait by the chapel, set on a nearby hill, watching

> the dawn pointing over the sea, which came with the grey forms of waterspouts. They moved silently, here and there upon the horizon. So they saw the sun come up white and fiercely shining between those monstrous appearances. (299)

The Young Lovell stands on the coping of the white tower while enemy archers try to pick him off; their arrows glance off his armor "because of their slanting flight. He stood there looking down and behind him were the grey waterspouts." Then comes "one scream so high and dreadful that all men stood deaf and amazed" (300), a cry which "deprived them of the powers of motion," although some that heard it "said afterwards that it was no more than the voice of the elements."

Francis will believe "to the end of his life" that he has heard "the cry of fear of a false goddess." The Bishop Palatine tells him that the "false goddess" who is "the bane of all Christendom" had cried out when, "in the form of a cloud of mist or may be of a rainspout, she had hastened to the rescue of the hero Paris. That had been at the siege of a strong castle called Troy. That Paris of Troy she had carried away to the top of a high hill near the town," and kept safe until the battle was over. Francis is certain that he has heard "at least the cry of fear of a false goddess wailing for her love, and that in the waterspout that bore the Young Lovell away he had seen her twisting and writhing form." A terrible weight of water cascades over the battlements of Castle Lovell: "There was no man there could stand up against that torrent of rain twisting round. Four waterspouts struck that Castle one after the other. . . . " (302).

Known only to Francis, the earthly body of the Young Lovell is afterwards walled up in a hermit's kennel. The whereabouts of his spiritual form are revealed in the novel's closing pages:

> In a very high valley of Corsica the mistress of the world sate upon a throne of white marble in a little round temple. . . . A round roof it had, like a pie-dish, and little columns of white marble. (306)

In this valley the Young Lovell does battle with his Homeric counterpart; afterwards, they bathe "in the foam of the rapid stream" and their wounds are healed. They bask in paradisal sunlight, and in the favours of attendant nymphs. And

> Through the opening of that valley, the goddess showed them the blue sea with triremes upon it,

the white foam going away from their oars as they had fought at Actium. The galleys of Venice she showed them too. . . . (309)

In "Ford Madox (Hueffer) Ford; Obit" (1939), Ezra Pound wrote:

That Ford was an *hallucine* few of his intimates can doubt. He felt until it paralysed his efficient action, he saw quite distinctly the Venus immortal crossing the tram tracks.[21]

Is that choice of goddess significant?[22] Lovell (not alone among Fordian heroes) has indeed "felt until it paralysed his efficient action," and the frequent doubling of those heroes finds its divine analogue in the seductive and destructive goddess who is alluded to again in the novel Ford had probably begun by the time *The Young Lovell* was published. Dowell, in *The Good Soldier,* refers to "the ruin of my small household cockleshell," and describes Florence emerging from her room each morning "as fresh as Venus rising from any of the couches that are mentioned in Greek legends."[23]

The conjunction of the divine and the profoundly quotidian ("tramtracks") is certainly a notable one. Pound too, surely, was "an *hallucine*," his attention, though vociferously concentrated upon the terrestrial world in his middle years, by no means limited to it. As early as 1908, he had written to William Carlos Williams that "men think and feel certain things and see certain things not with the bodily vision."[24] The initial stages of the evolution of *The Cantos* present the story of Pound's struggle to develop a form capable of addressing both the urgently contemporary and his conviction that—as Ford had phrased it—"We are the heirs of all the ages."[25] The heirs, that is, not only of the products of past cultures but also of what aroused the emotions that went to their making: the recurrent, the enduring elements, purged of the accidental, the local in time or place. "Essence of religion is the *present* tense," Pound wrote to Ronald Duncan in 1940,[26] while a god (1913) is "an eternal state of mind."[27]

The importance to Pound of gods—and of Venus above almost all others ("Beyond civic order / l'AMOR," 94/634)—is irrefutable, and evident from *A Lume Spento* onwards. In 1915, he wrote:

> Are they gods behind me?
> How many worlds we have! If Botticelli
> Brings her ashore on that great cockle-shell—
> His Venus (Simonetta?),
> And Spring and Aufidus fill all the air
> With their clear-outlined blossoms?[28]

Canto I closes with Venus, adorned with copper (which the alchemists called "Venus"); Canto II concerns metamorphosis, the confluence of human and divine, Helen (who "moves like a goddess") and Eleanor, bringers of love and death; Dionysus, beneficent and destructive god; and Poseidon, screened by a wave:

> Twisted arms of the sea-god,
> Lithe sinews of water, gripping her, cross-hold,
> And the blue-gray glass of the wave tents them

and this canto (then the Eighth Canto) was the subject of a series of letters between Pound and Ford in 1922, though Ford's comments were largely confined to such matters as "zoological *questionabilities,*" repetitions and "compound words."[29] Ford would soon begin *Some Do Not . . .* (1924), whose Sylvia Tietjens, endeavouring to seduce her husband Christopher, hums "Venusberg music" as they dance together. "She said: 'You call the compounds where you keep the W.A.A.C.'s Venusbergs, don't you? Isn't it queer that Venus should be your own? . . .'"[30]

Pound's formulation of his "debt" to Ford remained remarkably consistent, from "The Prose Tradition in Verse" through to the 1962 *Paris Review* interview: freshness of language, registration of the writer's own times, the value of "the prose tradition," a language to think in and to write in. Pound was always generous in acknowledging such debts, and was almost alone among the major writers whom Ford championed in praising Ford in return.[31] Yet Pound's powerful sense of Ford's value as a critic, particularly of poetry and particularly *viva voce,* tended, I think, to obscure for him Ford's real achievements as a novelist. For the most part, Pound's critics have also assigned Ford an important but strictly delimited role in Pound's development. The Prose Tradition, 1911-1913. While not seeking to overturn this view in any major respect, I would suggest that Ford's importance to Pound was more general, of longer duration, more *miscellaneous.* The shared knowledge of Provencal language and literature, Anglo-Saxon, the classics and the modern European languages. Stray phrases, in conversation and on the page, names dropped, books mentioned, stances adopted. The ending of *The Young Lovell* may have been one of countless details noted and held, if not consciously, in the mind.

Because "the vortex" was, in many of its aspects, for others as well as for Pound, under the star of Venus. The Vorticist campaign was notable for its many quasi-military terms; but notable also for the many references to manliness, virility, fecundity. "Vortex. That is the right word, if I did find it myself," Pound wrote to John Quinn in March 1916. "Every kind of geyser from jism bursting up white as ivory, to hate or a storm at sea. Spermatozoon, enough to repopulate the island with active and vigorous animals."[32] And Gaudier wrote, of the African and Oceanic artists, "They pulled the sphere lengthways and made the cylinder, this is the VORTEX OF FECUNDITY, and it has left us the masterpieces that are known as love charms."[33]

"As we start to read the *Cantos,*" Donald Davie comments, "we float out upon a sea where we must be on the look-out for waterspouts. These, when they occur, are ideas, the only sort this poem is going to give us."[34] Upward's waterspout presents "Man and God as two interpenetrating strengths . . ."[35] and "the infant Gargantua," we recall, had been taught "to look 'up' and to be ready for the benefits of the gods, whether so whither they might come upon him."[36] Such a figure as Upward's wrestling of "whirl" and "swirl," of air and water, imaging in turn the earthly and the divine, would surely have made a dramatic impression on Pound in any case. But to have read the closing pages of Ford's novel, with that divine "bust through" into the quotidian, the mortal man rescued by the goddess—as Pound-Odyseus would be on more than one occasion—that collision between mythological and "real" time, with natural forms containing and expressing the divine, with *the* Poundian goddess at the radiant centre of it all, rising from that sea which is the *Cantos'* paradigmatic image of both flux *and* permanence,[37] must have enhanced that impression immeasurably.

NOTES

[1] *Pound* (London, 1975), Chapter 4, "Ideas in the Cantos."

[2] Dorothy Pound to Hugh Kenner: "D.P. Remembered," *Paideuma,* 2, 3 (Winter, 1973), 489.

[3] Pound, *ABC of Reading* (London, 1961), p. 21.

[4] "Mang Tsze," in *Selected Prose 1909-1965,* edited by William Cookson (London, 1973), p. 106, and see Bryant Knox, "Allen Upward and Ezra Pound," *Paideuma,* 3, 1 (1974), 82-83.

[5] Ruskin, *Works* (London, 1903-1912), Volume XIX: all quotations from p. 380-381.

[6] Pound, *Selected Prose,* p. 377.

[7] Hugh Witemeyer, "Ruskin and the Signed Capital in Canto 45," *Paideuma,* 4, 1 (Spring, 1975), 85-88; "'Of Kings' Treasuries': Pound's Allusion to Ruskin in *Hugh Selwyn Mauberley,*" *Paideuma,* 15, 1 (Spring, 1986), 23-31; Davie, *Ezra Pound: The Poet as Sculptor* (London, 1965); Kenner, *The Pound Era* (London, 1972); and, particularly, Guy Davenport, "The House that Jack Built" (1975), in *The Geography of the Imagination* (London, 1984), and *Cities on Hills* (Ann Arbor, Michigan, 1983). A chapter heading in the latter presumably provided the title for Robert Faulkner Casillo's *The Parallel Design in John Ruskin and Ezra Pound* (Ph.D., The Johns Hopkins University, 1978): I have not seen this thesis.

[8] Pound, "Vorticism" (1914), reprinted in *Gaudier-Brzeska* (New York, 1970), 92.

[9] *Ezra Pound and Dorothy Shakespear—Their Letters: 1909-1914,* edited by Omar Pound and A. Walton Litz (London, 1985), p. 256, 259, 264.

[10] *Selected Prose,* p. 374.

[11] See Pound to C.K. Ogden (28 January, 1935): "Intelligence is so . . . *rare* that when one, once in 10 years, finds traces of it, the fact shd. cause joy. Bruhl just a professor. Frobenius *thinks.*" *Selected Letters 1907-1941,* edited by D.D. Paige (New York, 1971), p. 266.

[12] Ibid, p. 296.

[13] Ibid, 22.

[14] Pound and Litz, op. cit., p. 238.

[15] Ibid, p. 256.

[16] Ibid, p. 316. Sometime in 1912-1913, Ford also read to Pound the manuscript of "Women and Men," "the best book Ford Madox Hueffer has written" (Pound, 1917). See "Editorial on Solicitous Doubt," *Little Review,* IV, 6 (October 1917), 20.

[17] See *Pound/Ford,* edited by Brita Lindberg-Seyersted (London, 1982), p. 13-15.

[18] Violet Hunt, *I Have This to Say* (1926; reprinted, New York, 1982), p. 235.

[19] See Arthur Mizener, *The Saddest Story* (London, 1972), p. 229-234, 603 n. 32.

[20] *The Young Lovell* (London, 1913), p. 2. Page references in text hereafter.

[21] Pound, *Selected Prose,* p. 431. I know that Donald Pearce reported Pound's assertion of an opposite view—see *Pound / Ford,* p. 180—but prefer to stress—what Ford admirer would not?—the earlier one.

[22] It is noted by Mizener, *The Saddest Story,* xiv, and by Thomas C. Moser, *The Life in the Fiction of Ford Madox Ford* (Princeton, 1980), p. 115.

[23] *The Good Soldier* (London, 1962), p. 56, 84, and noted by T.A. Hanzo, "Downward to Darkness," *Sewanee Review,* Vol. 74, No. 4 (Autumn, 1966), 832-855, who adds that Hermes and Aphrodite are the two pagan deities whose influence is made to dominate the novel's action.

[24] Pound, *Selected Letters,* p. 5.

[25] Ford, "Preface" to *Collected Poems* (London, 1914; actually 1913), p. 20.

[26] *Selected Letters,* p. 342.

[27] "Religio": see *Selected Prose,* p. 47. By 1918, "the great gods of the present" were "national qualities," "potent chemicals"—see *Literary Essays* (London, 1960), 300—as Ronald Bush noted: *The Genesis of Ezra Pound's Cantos* (Princeton, 1976), 290.

[28] "Three Cantos, I" (1917): conveniently reprinted, ibid, p. 59.

[29] See Lindberg-Seyersted, *Pound / Ford,* p. 63-67.

[30] *Parade's End* (New York, 1961), p. 422-443 (punctuation amended).

[31] As Ford noted: see *Return to Yesterday* (1931, reprint, New York, 1972), p. 391.

[32] The latter part of this passage, omitted from *Selected Letters,* is included by B.L. Reid, *The Man From New York: John Quinn and his Friends* (New York, 1968), p. 252.

[33] "Gaudier-Brzeska Vortex," in Pound, *Gaudier-Brzeska,* p. 23.

[34] Davie, *Pound,* p. 73.

[35] Bush, *The Genesis of Ezra Pound's Cantos,* p. 93.

[36] Pound, "Indiscretions," in *Pavannes and Divagations* (New York, 1974), p. 42.

[37] And evoked as image of the poem itself by Davie, *Pound,* p. 74.

**Donald Davie (essay date 1990)**

SOURCE: "The Mysterious Allen Upward," in *The American Scholar,* Vol. 59, 1990, pp. 53-65.

[*In the following essay, Davie explores the enigma of Upward's virtual disappearance from literary history, and discusses* The East End of Europe *in detail.*]

Allen Upward (b. 1863) remains a mystery man. I have no hope here of dispelling the mystery, not even of casting anything but very tentative light on it. My intention is only to emphasize that the mystery persists; that it is unaccountable; and that, so long as it persists, our pretensions to chart the intellectual history of our times, or the times of our grandfathers, are hollow. It is not after all as if we were dealing with a figure from the sixteenth century or earlier; Upward died by his own hand no longer ago than 1926. How can it be that a figure so historically recent, by no means a recluse but on the contrary gregarious and a prolific self-promoter, should have been consigned to oblivion so conclusively that, so far as I can make out, there exists not a single sketchy impression of him from those who knew him in life, and of his many books even the best libraries can muster only a few? This inquiry, therefore, if it can be dignified by that name, is an inquiry into the processes of cultural transmission or non-transmission. And if I may anticipate my conclusion, the case seems to prove that the period of Edward VII and George V, of Presidents Theodore Roosevelt and Woodrow Wilson, and since them the age of computerized information retrieval,

no more ensures the continuity of historical memory than did the times of Henry VIII or Edward VI. In fact, rather less so.

The mystery of Upward is encapsulated in an issue ten years old of that eccentric and unreliable but invaluable London magazine, *Agenda,* which in 1978-79 carried two essays about Upward, one by Kenneth Cox, the other by Michael Sheldon. How could the figure that emerges from Michael Sheldon's biographical researches—a flitting opportunist, scaremonger, and demagogue of municipal politics in England, Wales, and Ireland—have written a book, **The Divine Mystery,** which (Kenneth Cox decides) "stands in breadth of view, in novelty of ideas, in clarity of exposition and in brilliance of *obiter dicta* at least on a par with the work of Montesquieu"? And if Cox is right, as I'm sure he is (for the name of Montesquieu is not chosen at random), how can it be that such a book should never have been reprinted since its first publication in 1913 until 1976, and then in Santa Barbara, California? Somewhere here there is a scandal; and we cannot as intellectual historians look ourselves in the face until we have probed it.

With every month that passes, the chance of rescuing Upward from oblivion gets slimmer—not just because there can now be hardly anyone left among eyewitnesses who might testify, and not just because under imposed budgetary constraints British libraries at all levels are now shredding seldom-asked-for books from eighty or sixty years ago, but because we get further and further away from sympathizing with or understanding the world of speculation that Upward took for granted. Kenneth Cox is very good about this:

> Opportunities for self-instruction in his time were not bad: many books were cheap and some serious attempts were made to popularise science. Those were the days when educated men still thought it possible to discuss the latest theories, when you could still drop into the British Museum to do some reading and, if you wanted to know about the reformation of the zodiac in 700 B.C., write to the Astronomer Royal. . . .

> The mental world Upward inhabited was one where matter not divided into disciplines or bedevilled by politicians is subjected to independent and wide-ranging enquiry. He called himself a scientist and his subject "ontology, commonly called truth."

Nothing could be further from the assumptions and guidelines that govern nowadays the deliberations of bodies like the Royal Society and the British Academy and the Social Science Research Institute, where research proposals are, no doubt scrupulously, vetted by specialist committees and sub-committees. In such a context Upward would not have stood a chance—not of financial support (that would be out of the question), but of recognition in the sense of being taken seriously. The same goes of course for such a contemporary of his as H. G. Wells. The matter is aggravated by the fields (so we think of them, though Upward didn't) that Upward ranged over and ranged across. Cox cites them as: "mythology, comparative religion, anthropology, etymology, theoretical physics and the paranormal." And he pungently and prudently anticipates the objection:

> In these notorious areas amateurs soon lose their footing and proclaim as truth, or at least as plausible speculation, ideas others dismiss as moonshine. The literature of these studies is cluttered with the lucubrations of bookish old geezers not quite right in the head: not every Casaubon failed to write his *Key to all mythologies*. What makes Upward any different?

Kenneth Cox has his answer to that question, in two parts; and it is a very good answer. What is interesting is to ask why in Upward's lifetime no one asked the question, let alone answered it, except Ezra Pound and more dubiously A. R. Orage; and since Upward died the question has been asked (obliquely) and answered (partially) only by certain recent commentators on *The Cantos* of Ezra Pound.

These last, of whom I am one, deserve no great credit. Pound from first to last thrust Upward's name on our attention; and beyond a certain stage of sophistication in studies of Pound's poem, the instigation could not be ignored. But all that we Poundians made of Upward was as much of him as could be brought to bear on Pound's poetry. And this is not good enough. To begin with, among those, still a minority of the reading public, who are sure that Pound was a very great though manifestly imperfect poet, there is certainly no agreement that he was a coherent and consistent thinker; accordingly it is abundantly possible to admire Pound for making admirable poetry out of "the lucubrations of bookish old geezers not quite right in the head," Upward among them. In the second place, those of us who are professionally or semi-professionally students of poetry are ourselves infected by the domination of "specialisms." How can we fail to be, since most of us are required at some point to go cap in hand to an institution like the British Academy or its American equivalents like the Guggenheim Foundation? Accordingly there is insistent pressure, which most of us at some point accede to, to regard our concern with poetry as a specialized discipline on a par with other specialized concerns in, say, organic chemistry. It is certainly significant that only poetry has imposed on its students the necessity to take *some* notice of an otherwise obliterated thinker whose cast of mind wasn't fundamentally poetic or literary at all (for Upward's poems and stories are the least valuable of his writings). That attests to the stubborn determination of serious poetry to regard the exertions of the human mind as somewhere, at some level, all one. But because we who have specialized in the study of poetry have just for that reason neglected to consider how that study locks in with others, our consideration of Upward stops short of the point where he is most challenging: that is to say, the point where, as Cox shows, he requires us to rethink the whole map of intellectual

endeavor, challenging the accepted demarcations that split that endeavor into bureaucratically manageable fiefdoms.

Either that, or else when our studies force us to a frontier between poetic and other modes of thinking, we lunge across that frontier inconsiderately and foolishly. Thus thirteen years ago, carried beyond myself by excitement at Upward's *The New Word* (London, 1908, but possibly written as early as 1896), I quoted from it as follows:

> The story of the waterspout, as it is told in books, shows it to be a brief-lived tree. A cloud is whirling downwards, and thrusting out its whirlpoint towards the sea, like a sucking mouth. The sea below whirls upward, thrusting out its whirlpoint towards the cloud. The two ends meet, and the water swept up in the sea-whirl passes on into the cloud-whirl, and swirls up through it, as it were gain-saying it. . . .

> In the ideal waterspout, not only does the water swirl upward through the cloud-whirl, but the cloud swirls downward through the sea-whirl. . . .

> The ideal waterspout is not yet complete. The upper half must unfold like a fan, only it unfolds all around like a flower-cup; and it does not leave the cup empty, so that this flower is like a chrysanthemum. At the same time the lower half has unfolded in the same way, till there are two chrysanthemums back to back. . . .

> It is strength turning inside out. Such is the true beat of strength, the first beat, the one from which all others part, the beat which we feel in all things that come within our measure, in ourselves, and in our starry world.

Rashly (with a rashness that I must say I was half conscious of) I commented, "Upward of course did not live to see this inspired guess at 'the first beat' astonishingly confirmed experimentally, when the biophysicists Crick and Watson broke the genetic code to reveal 'the double helix' (that's to say, double-vortex)." I accept Cox's reprimand when he writes entertainingly that to see Upward's "inspired guess" thus "confirmed experimentally" is "a pleasant fancy differing only in degree from seeing the invention of the submarine predicted in the Rigveda." It is a true bill: a literary sensibility (mine) got itself carried away into an intellectual world I was not at home in, where for instance *proof* and *experiment* had meanings different from those I was used to.

And yet "a pleasant fancy" seems more dismissive than is called for. It doesn't measure up to the excitement, the heightened awareness, that Upward's sentences provoked in me (and do again, now that I re-read them), nor for the unforeseen analogy that that excitement provoked me to. The formula that Cox offers me is unexceptionable: "It is more sensible to admit that the verbal faculty, while capable at its heights of marvellous insights and syntheses, which may precede and even suggest discoveries (Heisenberg got ideas from Anaximander), produces formulations that as such cannot be proved or applied." And yet I am not clear in what sense the faculty in Upward that produced these sentences can be called precisely verbal; nor, while accepting that such formulations cannot as such be proved, am I sure that they cannot be applied. The important point to my mind is that in these sentences by Upward we experience a powerful mind thinking powerfully about the physical and the non-physical world; and it seems wrong and self-defeating for us to scout and ignore his apprehensions merely because we cannot securely label them under hydraulics or oceanography or botany or metaphysics. At this point the preservation of what I have called the historical memory seems involved with the current articulation of the world of learning, an articulation ever more minutely intricate according as, in Cox's sardonic words, more and more of our sciences "are both more exact and more uncertain." Each of us may be remembered *in our discipline;* woe, and in the worst cases oblivion, attend those who have no one discipline, or have one that they stray outside of; who detect what Upward was to call, and after him Pound, "rhymes" between disciplines—something more than analogies, yet less than equivalences.

And yet if we ask why Upward was ignored in his lifetime and has been largely ignored since, it will hardly do to suppose this was because his synthesizing intelligence flew in the face of a strong professional determination to compartmentalize. For there were other synthesizing popular educators—H. G. Wells has been mentioned—who in Upward's day received sufficient acclaim. G. K. Chesterton might be another instance. Yet if it isn't the intellectual climate that must bear the blame, on the other hand, as Michael Sheldon says, "it seems clear that the practical factors alone are not sufficient to explain the obscurity surrounding his life and works." By the time of *The Divine Mystery,* Upward was arguing that in all human cultures, including quite notably Christendom, the genius is doomed to the role of changeling and sacrificial scapegoat. And "genius" was surely, and rightly, how he characterized himself. Accordingly some have suggested that his suicide eleven years later was the logical outcome. But a man does not shoot himself to prove the rightness of a theory. Years before, Upward had advanced a much more mundane but more plausible explanation of why he was, as increasingly we must think he was, vindictively overlooked:

> The reputation, and even the livelihood, of a private man of letters is largely at the mercy of great organs of opinion like *The Daily News;* their grudges are often lasting, and they have the means of keeping up a vendetta long after the public has forgotten its origin; and the law of England does not afford that protection to assailed individuals which is afforded by the law of other countries, by requiring the signature of newspaper articles and the insertion of replies. In these circumstances I can only place myself in the hands of the public, and trust to its sense of fair play to protect me in the discharge of my duty to itself and to those who have appealed to it through me.

This is from *The East End of Europe* (1908), one of Upward's books that is nowadays little read and indeed seldom to be found. I have seen it described as "a travel-book" and also as "a war-correspondent's dispatches." Neither description is accurate. Better is the subtitle: "The Report of an Unofficial Mission to the European Provinces of Turkey on the Eve of the Revolution." The Revolution meant is the bloodless one of the Young Turks in 1908 against Abdul Hamid II. At once we see why *The East End of Europe* can never attract even such few readers as have lately been brought to *The Divine Mystery* (not to speak of *The New Word,* shamefully never reprinted to this day): where those books sail at a high and intoxicating level of abstraction, *The East End of Europe* is unremittingly concerned with the quotidian and the contingent—in a setting, moreover, the Balkan peninsula in the first decade of this century, than which few can seem more remote from the modern common reader's interests or frame of reference. And yet, whatever Upward may have distorted or suppressed (for instance, his mission was unofficial—who then financed it, and in whose interests?), *The East End of Europe* gives to his thought an extra dimension that we should not have dreamed of, after reading only *The Divine Mystery* and *The New Word.*

Here is Upward the historian; and in fact the first fifty pages of *The East End of Europe* are masterly in their concise clarity, making manageable sense of a conflict of languages and races so traditionally intractable that it has generated the baleful word *Balkanization.* As a traveler Upward is humorous and relaxed, urbane; and towards the schoolchildren whom he meets in their classrooms—Turkish, Greek, Bulgarian, and of mixed races—he is tender. Hardly ever does he fall back on that staple of travelers' tales—the lousiness or other disadvantages of his accommodation. And he eschews altogether, drawing attention to it himself, impressions of landscape; his concern is entirely with the inhabitants of those landscapes, and from that, their human and civic condition day by day, nothing is allowed to distract him. We get another surprising shaft of light onto him when he concludes his castigation of an English journalist who had preceded him: "I confess myself unable to understand how any writer could have imagined that he could help his argument by including such passages as those in a book intended to be read by English gentlemen." Was "English gentlemen" written straight faced or with tongue in cheek? Kenneth Cox seems to be right when he says that "irony was not one of Upward's weapons"; and so I infer that, disconcerting as it may be for modern readers, Upward's appeal to English gentlemen was made in all naïve sincerity.

Again, we may feel, Upward was extraordinarily ill-advised, or else unlucky, or else perverse. For who in seventy or eighty years has cared what "Rumelia" is, or was? It was what Upward chose to travel over, and to report on: that large Balkan territory which, as the Ottoman Empire found ever less energy to administer it, was becoming a power vacuum. Into that vacuum were rushing Bulgar, Serb and Greek, Rumanian and Albanian, each of them more or less manipulated by one of the Great Powers: Russia and Austria, Britain and France and Italy, covertly but effectively Germany—the powers which had created the vacuum in the first place, by harassing and humiliating the retreating Turk, under the seldom enunciated but always understood pretext of defending Christendom against Islam.

Upward presents the principal power struggle in the region as between Bulgar and Greek. He declares himself, firmly and indeed fervently, Hellenophile. Armed bands both Bulgarian and Greek were roaming the territory; and Upward claims to have found that the Greek bands were defensive and protective vigilantes, whereas the Bulgarian bands *(comitadji),* directly organized from Sofia, were "Bulgarizing" by terror. More surprisingly, he is strongly pro-Turk; at least, in one anecdote after another, he presents the Ottoman administration as thoroughly mild and humane, the Pashas' rule over their Christian subjects as by and large enlightened. Indeed, a strong undertow in the book, which we become more aware of the further we read, is that, whereas the Christian communities are murderous towards each other, the Mohammedan is evenhandedly compliant and considerate towards all of them. The cumulative effect is almost Swiftian. It challenges at every point the originally Gladstonian consensus that had for many years governed British policy on "the Eastern question":

> In our nurseries, if a child shows a boisterous and ungovernable disposition, we call him a "young Turk." A favourite figure in our nursery tales is that of the terrible Turk, with his big turban, and big beard, and baggy trousers, his curly moustache, curly slippers, and curly scimitar. The redoubtable Bluebeard, according to historians, was actually a French or Breton noble; but he is always pictured as a Turk. Such ideas, so early implanted, are never really effaced.

> For a hundred years past those Powers which hope to aggrandize themselves at the expense of Turkey, and those aspiring peoples which have desired foreign aid in overthrowing their old conquerors, have deluged Europe with denunciations of the Turk. The cause of Christianity, the cause of liberty, and the cause of territorial greed have found a common enemy in the Turk. In the year 1876 two of these causes found a champion in the most powerful popular orator since Demosthenes.

> Gladstone, a name which I have never heard mentioned by any Turk except in terms of sincere respect, had two supreme interests at heart—what he believed to be Christianity, and what he believed to be freedom. On many occasions in his life one of these interests pleaded against the other. Over the question of Bulgaria the two were united, and the result was tremendous.

> The great statesman then at the helm of the British empire trimmed his sails to the wind, and brought the ship into port. What was genuinely

Bulgarian territory was rendered independent; but the ambitions of Russia were repressed, Turkey was safeguarded, and the future was left open for Greece.

> This result could not satisfy Gladstone. The General Election of 1880 was one of the few ever fought in England on a question of foreign politics, and it resulted in an overwhelming condemnation of the Turk for the "Bulgarian atrocities"—a strangely prophetic phrase!

> That decision of the electorate was loyally accepted by the followers of Beaconsfield, and their new leader afterwards emulated Gladstone in his language about Turkey and her sovereign.

"Bulgarian atrocities" is said to be "a strangely prophetic phrase" because, whereas Gladstone meant by it atrocities allegedly committed by Turks in Bulgaria, Upward means by it atrocities that he alleges the Bulgarians have committed in Macedonia.

What is remarkable here is that, in his several fruitless attempts to enter parliamentary politics (Michael Sheldon gives us such details as we have), Upward himself seems to have campaigned on what we might now call the left wing of Gladstonian liberalism. Accordingly it may seem that in *The East End of Europe* we encounter, in the field of politics, what Kenneth Cox laboriously but valuably defines as a characteristic habit of Upward's mind:

> Upward had the kind of mind which, proceeding from a central sense of an ungraspable whole, what he called the "All-thing," advances to an outpost of opinion only to find itself associated with persons who have arrived there by some process of ratiocination, or who have stationed themselves there for motives of self-interest, and which thereupon retires to its centre, refreshes itself at its source and advances again in a different direction, sometimes to a position diametrically opposite to the first. His writing continually takes up new starting points, working round his main preoccupations, but breaking off before a definite conclusion can be identified and fixed.

It is rather important to see what Cox is here claiming for Upward. He is not saying that Upward "couldn't make up his mind"—which is an incapacity that, where we have encountered it, none of us is called on to condone. He isn't saying, either, that Upward rather often changed his mind and consistently claimed his right to do so—though that's a right that we ought to recognize, as much in intellectual endeavor as in politics, though we seldom do. Nor is Kenneth Cox, as I understand him, advancing a claim for "the free play of mind," where "free" means "irresponsible." Rather, if I read him right, he is making a plea for the provisional: that is to say, for assertions which, however trenchantly made (and why assert at all, if not trenchantly?), are corrigible in the light of further evidence, even of further reflection and extraneous opinion. What Cox is standing up for in fact, with Upward as prime instance, is the rights of the *speculative* intelligence.

That intelligence cannot be, in political or any other terms, partisan. And so politics, because it is of its nature partisan, cannot make use of, because it cannot trust, an intelligence like Upward's. The English electors were right therefore to deny Upward a parliamentary seat, whenever he asked for it. However there are intelligences (many more of them, indeed) that are at once keen and partisan. Such was Henry Noel Brailsford (1873-1958), the English journalist whose *Macedonia* had appeared in 1906, whom Upward girds at on page after page, and in footnote after footnote, of *The East End of Europe;* of whose retaliation in the *Daily News* Upward admits himself afraid. It would be worth someone's while to scan the columns of the *Daily News* through the relevant years to see if Upward's fears of retaliation were or were not well-founded. What is certain is that Brailsford went on to have a career, as opinion-maker, that is abundantly and even deferentially recorded; his books are still remembered, and (some of them) reprinted. Brailsford's principal publications are: *The Broom of the War-God* (a novel, 1898); *Shelley, Godwin and Their Circle* (1913); *The War of Steel and Gold* (1914); *Belgium and the Scrap of Paper* (1915); *A League of Nations* (1917); *The Russian Workers' Republic* (1921); *Socialism for Today* (1925); *How the Soviets Work* (1928); *Property or Peace?* (1934); *Voltaire* (1935); *Rebel India* (1931); and *Subject India* (1943). He earned a long and respectful entry in *The Twentieth Century Dictionary of National Biography,* from which Upward's name is, alas not conspicuously, absent.

And yet, for as long as Upward was alive, his career and Brailsford's seemed to run in parallel—with this difference: that Brailsford was consistent. Brailsford was, from first to last, a left-wing thinker; and though, like all such in his lifetime, he had to make tactical adjustments from time to time (now ardent about communist Russia, now keeping his distance from it), his bent is, whatever the subject he takes up, predictable. That surely is what we mean when we characterize such consistency as "admirable": we mean that on any given question we can be certain, within manageable limits, which way Brailsford will jump. There never was any such certainty about Upward. And to be radically unpredictable scares everybody—in the world of learning, as in other worlds.

A good case in point is Upward's attitude toward the Irish. Born in Worcester to a family attached to the Plymouth Brethren, Upward attended and graduated from the Royal University of Ireland, an institution particularly intended—largely on J. H. Newman's initiative—for Irish Roman Catholics. Why his alma mater should have been thus unlikely, not to say outlandish, is what no one offers to explain, unless he explains it himself in his pseudonymous autobiography, *Some Personalities* (1921), which I have not seen. (Robert Duncan, who has, did not trust it very far.) This is in itself an instance of how Upward, in his life as in his thinking, not so much eludes all categories as confounds them. We cannot even, in our ignorance of circumstances now probably irrecoverable, label the choice "quixotic." However that may be, it seems that Upward in his Irish years aligned himself, quite actively too, with certain Irish nationalists. Yet in *The East End of Europe* when Upward alludes to the Irish, as he does several times, his sympathies seem to lie quite elsewhere. Brailsford had argued, in support of the *comitadji,* that "a revolutionary organisation has as much right as a recognised Government to punish traitors, and to levy taxes by force." In one who was or would shortly be in touch with Lenin, the sentiment is not surprising. But Upward is appalled:

> The Bulgarian apologist can only excuse the atrocities of his clients by arguments which would be rejected with horror by the ordinary anarchist. According to him, if in any country a body of men, however contemptible in point of numbers, band themselves together to seize the government, they are thereby justified, not merely in employing assassination against the agents and supporters of the government in existence; they are justified in usurping authority over the ordinary peaceable inhabitants; they may rob and plunder them, they may murder those who complain, or torture those who hang back.

> If the anarchists of Europe should ever be tempted to act upon these principles, the world will become one great carnival of horror. And if anything could add to their wickedness it would be their extension to what is, in substance, a war of annexation waged, not against the Turkish Government, but against the Hellenist people. In order to understand the full bearing of this frightful reasoning, we must imagine Ireland an independent republic, and emissaries from Dublin landing in Liverpool to conquer that city. They will be received and sheltered in the Irish quarter; they will shirk encounters with the English police; but they will set about bringing over the Welsh citizens to their side by a campaign of savage terror.

There is no denying that this reads very quaintly in 1989. Has the I.R.A. in fact missed a trick by not terrorizing Welsh citizens of Liverpool? It is surely a comical notion. Yet Upward's only mistake was to pick on the wrong city; read "Belfast" for "Liverpool," and "Unionist" for "Welsh citizens," and his analogy not only holds up, it is an accurate prediction. Moreover, in the areas which it controls, the I.R.A., like other terrorist organizations, assumes just those "rights" that Brailsford asserts on behalf of his Bulgarians, acting in this on thoroughly Leninist principles. Should we react to Upward's "one great carnival of horror" by exclaiming, *o sancta simplicitas?* Or should we not give him credit for foreseeing, however incredulously, what has in fact come to pass since he died?

We may wonder, it seems we *ought* to wonder, whether Upward was not "blacked out" quite deliberately, for political reasons, by thinkers in the Leninist tradition of the Fabian Society, powerful in British public and intellectual life from Wells and Shaw and the youthful Brailsford through to Kingsley Martin, who wrote the hagiography of Brailsford for *The Twentieth Century D.N.B.* For of course even today to be, like Brailsford, an apologist for political terror is not held in Britain to disqualify anyone from esteem among the intellectual *élite,* nor even from public office. And yet to speculate along these lines is unthinkable. For to entertain such speculations is to subscribe in some measure to "the conspiracy theory of history." And that is unthinkable, because Ezra Pound is unavoidably part of the story, and once Pound is named we are in sight of such a monstrous product of conspiracy theory as *The Protocols of the Elders of Zion.* Yet most of us have seen in our own spheres of interest, including the world of learning, that plots *are* hatched, exclusions and blackballings *are* engineered, vendettas *are* maintained; that some persons who think themselves discriminated against are right to think so. The initiators of pogroms, up to and including the Nazi genocide, are still triumphing in our midst if, by their cynical manipulation of conspiracy theory, they blackmail us into refusing to acknowledge that in some circles and at some stages of recorded history conspiracies against certain individuals were hatched, were maintained, and were successful—to the point where, in the worst cases, the targeted individual was virtually written out of the historical record altogether.

Moreover, the world of professional scholarship cannot escape its share of the blame. For there is professional pride on the part of historians. Intellectual historians, like other kinds, have come to think it ignominious for them, even part of their time, to go about stooping to keyholes and listening at half-open doors or to backstairs gossip—which is what they are condemned to, if they accept that conspiracies sometimes happen. Where in such furtive researches are to be found the wide vistas, the uncoverings of dynamisms and laws operating through many eras, such as historians have felt themselves called to since Hegel if not before? For a not unreasonably ambitious historian, the trouble with a case like Upward's is that it is stubbornly particular. There is no law of history that he exemplifies, no generalization however modest or tentative that can be drawn from his life, so far as we know it. There is no way in which to make him representative. The late poet Robert Duncan, introducing the Californian reprint of *The Divine Mystery,* thought he could see one way in which Upward in his generation was a representative case:

> Allen Upward has to contend with . . . the gap that was beginning to appear between popularizing journalism and the high styles of personal expression, as he has to contend with his lower class Plymouth origins and his Grammar School Education, with his Grub Street ambitions and his job writing, with his careers in civil service, in an England where class consciousness and a literary elitism growing out of Oxford and Cambridge associations made for his cultural isolation.

Thus Duncan (though it's way off his main concern) finds a category that Upward can be slotted into: he was

"born the wrong side of the tracks." But it won't do. Upward lived in fact through a period when crossing from the wrong side of the tracks to the right side was, for persons of talent, comparatively easy and could be very profitable. Again, though many cases could be cited (Wells, Chesterton, Shaw), the best counter-example is Brailsford who, born ten years after Upward to a provincially nonconformist background like his, survived to write books still acclaimed as "minor classic" or "socialist classic." Even Brailsford's university, Glasgow, was neither more nor less provincial than the Royal University of Ireland, neither more nor less remote from "Oxford and Cambridge associations." Why then is Brailsford remembered and Upward not? It seems that the social historian's safety net is as little as any other able to catch Upward; he falls through it, plummet-like, as certainly as through any other of the nets that scholars have woven, of ever finer mesh, to ensure that the memorable is remembered. It doesn't happen; a maverick like Allen Upward is only very partially, and by accident, rescued from oblivion.

Kenneth Cox decided that Upward is best described as "a visionary." But that is the merest device, even (one might say) a cop-out. "Visionary" is a catch-all category devised to accommodate those—Swedenborg, Nietzsche, Upward (other names will come to mind)—whom none of the properly constituted committees and sub-committees will take on. It is good that such a category exists, to stop the committees and sub-committees from thinking that between them they have taken account of the entire range of intellectual endeavor. All the same, a cop-out is what it is. The sort of thinking that we agree to call "visionary" is, where it is not self-deluding and charlatan, a sort of thinking that the currently accepted map of human thought cannot, any more than earlier now discredited maps, find room for. But just suppose that this were a primal kind of thinking which secondary kinds, theology as much as philology or physics, can batten on. In that case its exclusion from the array or hierarchy of accredited disciplines would still be justified. And the sacrificial victimization of its exponents would be understandable, indeed almost a matter of course. But that would bear out Upward's thesis that the truly original thinker is at once scapegrace and scapegoat. It is a thesis that his own life and subsequent reputation may be thought to bear out, in a quite spectacular or exemplary fashion. Brailsford of course posed no such problems.

Upward died unmarried and childless. He fathered no spiritual children either, unless we count a maverick and half-crazy American poet. Whom therefore does it help, to have his teasing obscurity worried over? The history of the modern mind is complete enough without him. Those of us who feel a little worry and a little shame on this score must be, whether we know it or not, appealing to a principle metaphysical if not religious: the *lacuna* impugns our dignity and the dignity of the intellectual pursuit we conceive ourselves to be engaged in. That is an irrational conviction: metaphysical, at best speculative. Keeping the historical record full, or as full as possible, the keeping of faith with past generations—these tasks, which we tend to think of as obvious and practical necessities, are nothing of the sort. They rest, whether we know it or not, on somewhere an act of faith.

## Yuet May Ching (essay date 1995)

SOURCE: "From Priest to Victim: The Problem of a Sacrifice in Allen Upward and Ezra Pound," in *Paideuma: A Journal Devoted to Ezra Pound Scholarship,* Vol. 24, No. 1, Spring, 1995, pp. 53-69.

[*In the following excerpt, Ching provides a close study of* The Divine Mystery *as a means of shedding understanding on the symbol of blood sacrifice in Pound's work.*]

Sacrifice has long interested poets, long before anthropology supposedly tore the veil of mystery from the cruel rite, and after.[1] The blood sacrifice in Ezra Pound's canto 1 illustrates the magical spell of sacrifice, as a modern poet anchors the epic for and of his time in a primitive rite of killing. There is a conventional glorification of sacrifice, sanctioned by religious and primitivistic impulses, that cushions it from adverse criticism by poets, sometimes even distracting an anthropologist from his path of scientific inquiry. Literary criticism nowadays, however, refuses more and more to abide with conventions. The blood rite in canto 1, used by Pound and praised by critics as symbolic of the transference of energy,[2] is now discovered to be symptomatic of Pound's fascism and anti-semitism. This canto thus provides, curiously, occasion for one more slaughter, this time the condemnation of Pound, notably by Robert Casillo in *The Genealogy of Demons: Anti-Semitism, Fascism, and the Myths of Ezra Pound,* as racist, and as a hypocritic priest scapegoating the Jews for the failures of the modern world.

Casillo, however, refuses to acknowledge a crucial ambivalence or a change in Pound's attitude prompted by a near encounter with death. This failure of a full understanding becomes magnified in the criticism on Allen Upward, a minor writer admired by Pound but often cited by critics as a corollary, if not a source, for Pound's preference for sacrifice.[3] Upward protested against the sham and cruelty of sacrifice in *The Divine Mystery,* bringing out an interpretation that was not "poetic fancy" (*DM* 169), that even paralleled in certain ways the strong criticism of sacrifice by René Girard decades later. This protest, however, has been largely ignored both by Pound and by the critics, because in another book, *The New Word,* Upward seemed to favor metamorphic changes sanctioning sacrifice. But there is an inherent subtlety in Upward's theories about the universe and the human individual. His criticism of sacrifice, not so much as set forth in *The Divine Mystery* but as enacted in his life and in the very process of arguing about change and integrity in *The New Word,* set an example for Pound, who remembered him in *The*

*Pisan Cantos* and after. The near-death experience at Pisa made glorifications of sacrifice sound hollow and human existence precious though precarious. Against the world of change wherein the demise of individual man is inevitable, Upward and Pound assert the integrity of man, not by the principle of permanence, but by instigating still one more change, one more difference that distinguishes the human individual.

Beginning in the late nineteenth century, anthropological discussions placed sacrifice under the light of scientific inquiry, revealing its origins as human, not god-given. Religion yielded place to science, but the attraction of sacrifice remained, mainly due to a primitivistic desire closely associated with the fascination of the primitive and the natural recently exemplified so well in Romantic writings (Stocking). Sir James Frazer, revered both by anthropologists and by poets, managed to escape from a religious mystification of sacrifice, but he could not escape from a nostalgia for a primitive world where the bonding between man and nature was much stronger than in the modern wasteland of objectivity and science. Frazer analysed the origin of sacrifice as a magical rite used by primitive people who hoped to ensure spring's return after winter by killing their best man, their priest-king, in his prime and before the decline of his powers, so that his energy could be preserved and reborn. Calling his book a record of "human error and folly" (11:304), he nevertheless thought that the intention to "ensure the revival of nature in spring" was laudable (4:266). When he warned people against the primitiveness of sacrifice, he also showed a yearning for it:

> We may feel some natural regret at the disappearance of quaint customs and picturesque ceremonies, which have preserved to an age often deemed dull and prosaic something of the flavour and freshness of the olden time, some breath of the springtime of the world; yet our regret will be lessened when we remember that these pretty pageants, these now innocent diversions, had their origin in ignorance and superstition . . . and that for all their gay trappings—their flowers, their ribbons, and their music—they partake far more of tragedy than of farce. (4:269)

Despite his final emphasis on the cruelty of sacrifice, Frazer's opposition between a colorful past and a "prosaic" present and his nostalgia for the "springtime of the world" reveal a fascination with the rite in the name of poetry.

In *The Divine Mystery,* where Upward analyses the reasons for the practice of sacrifice and traces its development to the time of Christ, he acknowledges his debt to other anthropologists, the most notable of whom is Frazer. Yet he criticizes Frazer for disguising the cruelty of sacrifice by claims of its imitating nature. He objects that in the Osirian myth, Fraser sees only a "mythical way of expressing either the sowing or the winnowing of the grain."[4] This interpretation is just "poetical fancy" that tames savagery to suit the sensibility of the modern mind: "If the play of poetical fancy, trying to interpret savagery to a civilised conscience, is thus to be accepted as aboriginal theology, the *Golden Bough* itself has been written in vain" (*DM* 169). Though poetical fancy is not exactly poetry proper, the two may be perilously close to each other. John Vickery in *The Literary Impact of The Golden Bough* discusses how Frazer crystallized certain thoughts for writers and intellectuals of the twentieth century. It is no coincidence that some of the poets cited, notably Pound, Yeats, and Eliot, have been identified as having fascist or even Nazi tendencies. Jessie Weston's *From Ritual to Romance,* a book cited by Eliot as crucial for *The Waste Land,* emphasizes repeatedly the resurrection element of sacrifice in vegetation cults and downplays the part of death: "it is not the tragic death of Attis-Adonis which is of importance for these cults, but their subsequent restoration to life" (4). What Frazer has acknowledged as tragedy becomes a divine comedy. Poetical fancy yields to religious manipulation again, and Frazer's attempt at de-mystification leads to further mystification. The danger that Upward sees is real, and the question of poetry's and criticism's responsibility to society and historical truth has to be answered.

In contrast with Frazer, Upward allows no nostalgia, no excuse. He adopts an evolutionary point of view popular in his days, and aligns himself with science and objectivity. At first, primitive physics, the observation of energy transference in food ingestion and at burial grounds rich with vegetation, resulted in cannibalism, and in the killing of victims for burial to enrich the fields (*DM* 54-57). Then the people with their primitive political thinking tried to avoid having old and weak rulers by sacrificing them and replacing them with younger and stronger ones. When primitive people's religious sense developed, they found still one further excuse for sacrifice, as they attributed their king's weakness to god's anger (92). They also tried to appease malevolent gods—crocodiles and serpents—by offering them victims (112-13). Primitive reasoning was later supplemented by hypocrisy, as kings found substitutes to die for them (93-94). But evolution brought men out of the dark past; and the people's learning that the sun, not a dead corpse, caused the richness of crops (116) was a real advancement, with the added merit of symbolizing the enlightenment of mankind. With the advancement of scientific knowledge, political and religious knowledge also progressed, letting men know that heredity could not guarantee leadership abilities, thus eliminating one condition that kept on bringing weaklings to the throne, and letting them know also that gods are not necessarily violent (154-55).

Upward thus contrasts what he thinks is an objective, scientific interpretation of sacrifice with Frazer's subjective, "poetic" interpretation. He feels that his interpretation is closer to truth and more responsible to society while the other view hinders social enlightenment. However, the issue of objectivity and subjectivity in anthropology itself is a complex one. Franz Boas, a

seminal figure in American anthropology, distinguishes between two modes of inquiry, the objective and the subjective; and George W. Stocking Jr. expands the predecessor's point in his commentary on anthropological sensibilities. Both, however, finally question the distinction. For Boas, the so-called objective stance ultimately derives from the investigator's personal bias towards a certain type of reasoning (645). For Stocking, anthropology, being a cross-cultural study, necessarily makes subjectivity a cause for anxiety, and this anxiety underlies the opposition of the subjective and the objective (4-5, 267-68). The problem does not pertain to anthropology alone, for to see the ambiguity of the opposition is an insight into human experience. A one-sided argument against subjectivity is not necessarily convincing, as can be shown in Pound's case. Pound only pays lip service to Upward's argument against Frazer. There is, however, a subtle treatment of the opposition by Upward himself in an earlier work, *The New Word.* Upward's ideas in *The New Word,* of change, and of resistance argued for and enacted, make subjective and objective interpretations become relative terms that constantly change positions. Change is in fact the crux of *The New Word,* complicating critical interpretations of Upward and yet calling for a mode of action that suits the human condition in the sublunary world of change. Upward's ideas in *The New Word* became useful to Pound at the moment of drastic change in his life, the poet's imprisonment at Pisa.

From the beginning, Pound understands Upward's position on sacrifice and comments on it in both of his reviews on Upward. He particularly notes the progress from superstition to enlightenment when man recognized the sun as the bringer of crops: "The solar missionary says it is unnecessary to bury a man in the cornfield in order that crops shall rise by virtue of his spirit" (*SP* 404). He also notes Upward's view of Christ as a sacrificial victim undermining the superstition: "since Christ's notable success—in gaining a reputation, I mean—a number of people have desired to 'save the world' without undergoing the inconvenience of crucifixion" (*SP* 412). In "Degrees of Honesty in Occidental Religions," he laments the cruelty of sacrifice and compares it to a usurious, even to a democratic society:

> 'Pleasing to heaven,' etc. Various ideas of pleasing the spirits are all very well, but there could still be a lesson in animal sacrifice for any group that had evolved beyond primitive stages. Animals are killed now in abattoirs; the sight of a killing can remind us, in the midst of our normal semi-consciousness of all that goes on in our vile and degraded mercantilist ambience, that life exists by destruction of other life. The sight of one day's hecatomb might even cause thought in the midst of our democracy and usuriocracy. (*SP* 68)

Despite Pound's censure of sacrifice, the linking of sacrificial cruelty, democracy, and usuriocracy in the last quotation is unsettling, lending support to Casillo's criticism. Pound indeed has two different positions, his many affirmations of sacrifice contradicting his censure. In "Terra Italica," an essay whose title states his love for Italy, Pound tries to justify a beneficial kind of sacrifice. He distinguishes between Mithraism, which has "sadistic and masochistic tendencies" (*SP* 58) and Eleusis, which aims at union with god and nature. Both involve sacrifice, but Pound would raise one rite above the other, seeing Eleusis as privileged to hold the secret key to harmony. He translates Eleusis into the modern terminology of "'aim the union with nature'" [sic] or "'consciousness of the unity with nature'" (*SP* 59), ironically repeating what Upward objects to as the fault of poetic fancy.

On the importance of Persephone in the Eleusinian rite, Upward has written starkly: "In what may be called the maternal age, when the Virgin was the most obvious symbol of fruitfulness, her flesh may well have been esteemed the most efficacious charm" (*DM* 146). Critics like Leon Surette have emphasized the positive impact of Eleusis on Pound in general and on *The Cantos* in particular where a descent to Hades is followed by a "moment of metamorphosis, bust thru from quotidian into 'divine or permanent world.' Gods, etc." (*SL* 210). However, when juxtaposed with Upward's criticism, the Eleusinian rite reveals a sinister aspect, and knowing Pound's interest in Upward, we begin to see the anxiety in Pound's polarization of Eleusis and Mithraism. Somehow Pound knows he needs to justify the switch from his earlier position, "it is unnecessary to bury a man in the cornfield," to his position in "Terra Italica," "you find Frobenius' profoundly satisfactory account of the old chief who 'was so foine and so healthy' that he was convinced that his soul would go into the soil of Africa and enrich the crops at his death" (*SP* 60).

Thus Pound has two different positions on sacrifice, or rather, he splits the same rite into two different acts, one cruel and superstitious, the other beneficent and mystical. His distinction between the worship of Adonis as a fertility cult and that of Atys as asceticism—a distinction made by neither Frazer nor Upward—is one further proof of Pound's arbitrariness (*LE* 85). His knowledge of *The Divine Mystery* cannot prevent him from glorifying sacrifice, turning "poetic fancy" into a figment of his imagination. In the cantos before the Pisan experience, sacrifice is wholly of a beneficent nature, while the poet or his persona often plays the part of the priest, presiding over the sacrifice of other people or animals. He may even preside over his own sacrifice, making himself a willing victim, but he is never the unwilling victim who does not believe in the rite's efficacy. Odysseus/Pound in canto 1 descends into the underworld and sacrifices animals in order to gain the knowledge necessary for his return home. Himself a victim of Poseidon's wrath, the hero luckily escapes death because he is favored by other gods and goddesses who may be cruel to other mortals but not to him. While Aphrodite bears the ominous "golden bough of Argicida" (1/5) and Circe turns all his companions into pigs, Odysseus/Pound can proudly assert his privileged status: "Nec in harum ingressus sum" (39/194).[5] In canto 47, the descent of Odysseus/Pound into the realm of darkness, compounded with the death of Adonis, becomes a pleasurable self-sacrifice symbolic of the ecstatic surrender in sexual union and in union with nature. New life issues from this rite: "Wheat shoots rise new by the altar." The process is wholly natural: "The bull runs blind on the sword, *naturans*" (47/237).

When even in Frazer, nostalgia and painful fact interlace, Pound celebrates sacrifice. When in Frazer, the hapless fate of youths enamored of goddesses in Greek myths is admitted to originate from "a deeper philosophy of the relation of the life of man to the life of nature—a sad philosophy which gave birth to a tragic practice" (1:40), Pound celebrates such encounters. When in Frazer the succession of the kings of the woods at Nemi is explained as a series of human sacrifices, Pound enjoys the mask of Odysseus as priest. We perhaps do not need Upward to show Pound's "poetic fancy," which even exceeds Frazer's. Pound's isolated prose jottings about the cruelty of sacrifice become ironical. But a radical change comes at the beginning of the Pisan sequence. Odysseus/Pound will say "ac ego in harum" (74/436),[6] and another hero will appear, Apollonius, who preaches against sacrifice, human or animal. Concommittant with this change, Pound also begins to mention Upward in *The Cantos,* two of these references occurring at strategic places: the first of *The Pisan Cantos,* and the first of *Drafts and Fragments.* The first reference in canto 74 to Upward, "'not the priest but the victim'" (451) marks the essence of the reversal. We do need Upward to evaluate fully the change in Pound's attitude to sacrifice.

Despite its clear argument against sacrifice, *The Divine Mystery* does not seem to have really convinced Pound. An earlier book, however, debunks sacrifice in a subtle, undogmatic way. *The New Word,* first published in 1907, earnestly pursues a theory leading to the inevitable sanctioning of sacrifice, and then contradicts itself, causing much critical confusion and yet lending Pound an example of resistance against fixity, and a mode of action possible after his failure in the eyes of the world at the end of World War II. It is a book that demands adroitness of response from the reader. In the first half of his argument, Upward reconciles the issue of the dualism between energy and matter by a solution based on the scientific theory of the convertibility of matter and energy. The universe is made up of energy, and matter is no more than a formed patterning of the flow of energy. Two ways of energy meet and interlock to form matter, like the making of a knot, or, envisaged three-dimensionally, like two vortices whirling in and swirling out at the point of struggle. Energy whirls in to form matter, and swirls out again; and there is no difference in essence between the two, solving the issue of dualism between energy and matter (180-89).

However, this reconciliation has two major weaknesses. First, the solution is questionable because energy is privileged, energy being treated as the one essence in the universe while matter is only a structuring of it. Second, the theory of the convertibility of matter and energy has a shocking implication. If energy constantly changes into matter, and vice versa, if the world is in a constant state of flux and metamorphosis, then the life and death of man as an individual and the rise and fall of empires, of whole planetary systems even, should be viewed with nonchalance. The cyclical view confirms the efficacy of sacrifice, which Upward in *The Divine Mystery* explains as a primitive attempt to make energy pass from the victim to benefit others. It also supports the critical focus, represented by Bryant Knox, on Upward's view of a fluid universe wherein sacrifice facilitates metamorphic changes.[7]

Upward, however, does not stop at the convertibility of matter and energy, nor is he satisfied by what Ian Bell calls his implied transcendentalizing of matter in his preference for energy (227-28). The second half of his theory debunks what he has just established. Much has been written about the fluid double vortex and its analogues in nature, for example, the waterspout and the tree Yggdrasil; but the further development of this shape has seldom been noticed.[8] Upward does not see the whirl-swirl, the double vortex, as existing in a vacuum. He places it in the context of another greater double vortex, and defines the relationship between the two as constant interaction *and* resistance. Hence Upward maintains the individuality of a basic unit of existence while allowing for its contact with its environment, be it society, god, or nature. He describes the relationship between the two whirl-swirls thus:

> If both the inner and the outer whirl-swirls are of pure strength, and both keep the same time, shrinking and swelling together, then one will not feel the other. Where there is no resistance there is no existence, and so the two whirl-swirls will be one. And that is the demonstration of the Nirvana of the Buddhists.
>
> But both do not keep the same time, any more than the waves of the incoming tide all reach the same height upon the shore. The farthest wave, as it ebbs back, meets the next wave flowing forward; and so the outer strength, as it whirls inward from its longer period, meets the inner strength swirling outward, and resisting it. And that meeting is a real outline. The inner whirl-swirl is created. (200)

He further compares the inner whirl-swirl enclosed by a larger one to the situation of the human individual: "Suppose it is yourself" and "Suppose . . . the Body is a network woven between the tiny Strength Within and the greater Strength Without" (202). The obliteration of difference and of individual identity implied in his view of the universe as a constant flux now changes to an affirmation of this difference. He even applies the distinction between the two whirl-swirls to the relationship between man and god. Things as common as changes in weather make the primitive man know that an outer

strength exists. Man communicates with it. He need not, however, sacrifice himself for the communication.

Thus Upward marks out a mode of relationship between man and his environment, and a mode of action for the individual. A man exists in a larger context, ecological, political, and religious; he needs to interact with it, and yet the main reason for his continued existence is his ability to resist total absorption by his environment. A world of harmony changes to a warring state; and actually change is the crux, with change meaning not just metamorphic changes, but also differentiation, and a resistance against homogenization. Change adds a further twist to even the second half of Upward's argument, as he envisages not only two double vortices but a series of double vortices, one enclosing the other *ad infinitum*. Subjectivity is thus displaced, depending on the angle from which a certain unit is viewed, and individuality becomes problematic.

Upward himself demonstrates such displacements. In *The Divine Mystery* he makes use of Frazer's materials and yet opposes Frazer's poetic fancy. This disagreement with other people is a common instance of resistance but Upward also disagrees with himself, and fights against his own justification of sacrifice in *The New Word*. This inconsistency in fact enacts what Upward himself claims at the beginning of the book, that he is an idealist, whose focus is ever on the swirl, who fights against fixity. However, to become a thorough idealist ever watchful for change and activity means Upward cannot always maintain his one position as idealist. Upward is well aware of this paradox and accepts it. Rather than adhering to any fixed principle, he adheres to no principle, except for the principle of change and contradiction.

Though men are often paralysed by a fear of contradiction, the lack of a consistent principle constitutes for Upward the very ground for action. He thinks that he needs to keep on actively changing, to be different from what he was before and from his surroundings. Thus he not only writes about action and change, but also makes many reversals and efforts at resistance in his life. "Whatever is has been right and will be wrong": Pound quotes this from Upward (*NW* 223, qtd. in *SP* 410), and both writers in their different ways also experience the fate of Ixion, "unstill, ever turning" (113/790). Critics like Donald Davie, Kenneth Cox, and Michael Sheldon emphasize the importance of change in Upward, but the problem of inconsistency and resistance still has to be addressed. Born an Englishman, Upward nevertheless sought for light and reason in Northern Europe, East Asia, and sometimes Africa. Joining politics, he was at home with none of the political parties in England or in Europe. Trained as a barrister, he joked about legal jargon, and turned into a journalist and pop novel writer, while claiming to be a poet at heart. That he was first drilled in the legal profession and then flaunted this practice says much about his attitude to laws—legal, philosophical, or scientific. The law of consistency can neither be applied to *The New Word* itself nor to its relationship with *The Divine Mystery.* "I am a mass of contradictions" he declared in *Some Personalities* (162), an anti-autobiography in which he constantly cut the ground from under the reader as well as the author.[9] Despite his sense of social responsibility as shown in his advocacy of anthropology's ethical relevance, the idea of resistance inherent in his theorizing about sacrifice put him in a position antagonistic to his society. He envisioned himself as a genius ostracized from and scapegoated by society, while his final act of suicide protested against the cruelty of sacrifice and yet simultaneously confirmed its continued practice.

In Upward, we see the very earnestness and thoroughness with which he deals with change, and the burden of constant change when one does not only write about it, but earnestly lives with it. Upward's fame is much compromised by this lack of consistency. Even Davie, who treasures Upward's genius, admits that he is "at times like a proto-Nazi" (71). But Upward can also write lucidly against racism, for example, "In our own time we have seen what influence a brutalizing ethnological theory may exercise on the minds of statesmen and soldiers, and with what disastrous consequences."[10] Casillo interprets Upward as approbatory of sacrifice, but interestingly, Girard, the authority Casillo relies on, echoes Upward's attitude to sacrifice. Though Girard's theory of mimesis is not shared by Upward, both see through the sham of sacrifice as an excuse used by society to persecute a few in order to gain a semblance of order and harmony. Both claim that certain texts in the Old Testament and the whole spirit of the New Testament undermine sacrifice. Both urge the relevance of ethical issues for anthropology, making the chamber studies of antiquated or remote cultures answer the needs for social justice in the violent modern world. However, unlike Girard and unlike most other anthropologists, though Upward can be no authority to cite from, because he has no fixed position, he can be a source of inspiration and can provide a mode of action in times of change, when authority and fixed values are questioned.

At the end of World War II and of a fascist era, at the junction of historical change and of a personal reversal of fate, and imprisoned in a cage like a captive animal, Pound remembered Upward. Before, Pound had been self-righteous and he had thought he could distinguish a beneficent type of sacrifice, free from blame. But now he was judged as a fascist priest of darkness; and the myth of a beneficent sacrifice exploded when this priest saw himself being displaced by still other self-righteous priests, in the guise of judges and critics, all involved in a long succession of priest-victims as told in *The Golden Bough.* He may still be self-righteous in his new role as victim, in line with the isolationist poetics of the early modernists that Frank Kermode has commented on. Yet Pound's new attitude to sacrifice reevaluates sacrifice as a whole and the self in particular, complicating the very concepts of dark and self-righteousness.

The priest turns victim, and the subject lord of the sacrificial rite becomes the object of a cruel practice. Roles shift in a world of change, yet this same changeability compels a person to act, and this activeness characterizes a person and gives him a memorable identity, resisting nihilism and annihilation. In the cantos before Pisa, Pound has seen change as purely metamorphic. This kind of change is ultimately static; as Michael Bernstein has observed: "The most fundamental meaning of metamorphosis, a change in external form without a corresponding change in the inner essence, is, in itself, static" (93).

In Upward's case, though he admits the world to be metamorphic, he recognizes the need for a different kind of change, for a change that is characterized by differentiation, by an attempt to resist sameness and stasis. This idea is similar to the Derridean idea of difference where identity or meaning is always different and deferred; but it also differs from the post-structuralist displacement because the effort to maintain the significance and identity of a certain unit, while knowing full well these to be provisional and contextual, is strong. In Pound's case, his early predilection for metamorphic changes evolves into an effort to resist metamorphoses, and in doing so he gives place and significance to self, to human action, and to identity in the sublunary world.

Recognizing the importance of human action and identity, Pound in the cantos after Pisa conveys a view of sacrifice different from before. He still recognizes the importance of the relationship between man and his environment, using the Na-Khi people as example: "without ²Mùan ¹bpö, / no reality" (112/798). However, instead of focussing on their blood rite, which Joseph Rock in his study of the people describes in detail, he is interested in their vegetarian offerings and purificatory rites. He emphasizes the non-violence of the arcanum, presenting Apollonius as a direct contrast to Odysseus' way of seeking communion with the unknown: "'It was not by ditch-digging and sheep's-guts . . .'" (94/652), and, in *Drafts and Fragments,* "Milkweed the sustenance / as to enter arcanum" (817). Plants and incense suffice as a token of respect for the gods: "And after 500 years / still offered that shrub to the sea-gull" (102/742), and "Flowers, incense, in the temple enclosure, / no blood in that TEMENOS" (97/695). His line "no blood on the altar stone" (97/694) echoes Upward's "In those temples what fell rites, / Blood upon the altar screen" (*Some Personalities* 188). In short, Pound affirms the importance of maintaining integrity while allowing communication: "I am all for Verkehr without tyranny" (110/791).

In the cantos before Pisa, the gods and goddesses have often been tyrannical. However, as the relationship between man and god becomes non-violent, either the divinities in the cantos after Pisa become more benign, or the mortals escape from their oppressive hold. In canto 1, Aphrodite, though a goddess of love, has ominous "dark eyelids" and bears "the golden bough of Argicida" (5). In canto 2, Dionysus turns the disrespectful mortals into fish, and Poseidon rapes Tyro. In canto 4, Actaeon's glimpse of the arcanum, Diana's body, brings him death. In canto 30, the poet-persona addresses his complaint against pity to Artemis, the goddess of merciless hunt. He prefers clean killing to a rotten state fermented by bloodless pity. However, in the cantos after Pisa, the ironic force of the reference to the golden bough, unbeknownst to the poet before, becomes apparent. The molü which once protected Odysseus against all harm, reminiscent of the golden bough in Frazer, no longer graces the former priest. Pity now is needed, and one significant new goddess is Kuanon, the oriental goddess of mercy. Leucothea, the late cantos' compassionate goddess who rescues Odysseus, contrasts with the dark Aphrodite of the early cantos. Tyro is now free from the grasp of Poseidon, her ascent compared to the burning of incense: "bright flame now on the altar / the crystal funnel of air" (90/622). A civilized means of communication between man and god is represented by the use of incense, and the incense motif plays a significant part in three passages mentioning resistance:

> And that Leucothoe rose as an incense bush
> —Orchamus, Babylon—
> resisting Apollo.
>
> (98/699)

>                       Leucothoe
> rose as an incense bush,
>        resisting Apollo,
>             Orchamus, Babylon
>               (102/742)

> But with Leucothoe's mind in that incense
>       all Babylon could not hold it down.
>           (102/743-44)

In these passages, the hot pursuit of Leucothoe by Apollo is not welcome. Nor does the poet praise the beauty of metamorphosed beings as in canto 2 ("the coral face under wave-tinge" [9]). The focus is now on the mortal's resistance against Apollo. This god, together with Orchamus and Babylon, represent the aggressive force of the divine, the patriarchal, and the societal other. Unable to stop the fate of metamorphosis, Leucothoe nevertheless shows her irreconcilable spirit in the new form taken. This new form hints at a more civilized relationship between mortal and god, a relationship of mutual respect, not violation.

In the history of human development, men gradually shed their primitive past and, discarding violence, progress to a more civilized state. Apollonius represents an achievement over the blood-dimmed tide of the past, and the agriculturists overtake the "butchers of lesser cattle" (87/587). The development of Pound's attitude to sacrifice in *The Cantos* mirrors such progress. Progress, however, implies change, and since change is paradoxically the only constant in the sublunary world, even the idea of a permanently bloodless state is questionable.

The inner whirl-swirl cannot keep on resisting the outer whirl-swirl; it will collapse one day. Here one treads on very dangerous ground, remembering Girard's portrayal of how a society's priesthood pretends that sacrifice is inevitable and necessary for the society's well-being. But what distinguishes Upward's argument in *The New Word* from this pretense is a genuine appreciation of change which makes Upward compromise his own authorial and authoritative stance. And what distinguishes Pound's scanty references to blood sacrifice in the cantos after Pisa is not the triumphant note of the early cantos, but a note of resignation acknowledging the inevitable demise of individual life as dictated by change. [ . . . ]

Pound lauds Upward as an "old combattant" (74/451) and as one of the "resisters" (110/795). Still, Upward succumbed to the force of the outer whirl-swirl, and committed suicide at the age of 63, enacting a self-sacrifice to draw attention to what he saw as the society's neglect of geniuses. Pound understands that Upward's death is not due to a lapse of faith in change and resistance, but to fatigue: "The suicide is not serious from conviction /. . . . / From sheer physical depression, c'est autre chose" (93/639). Though Upward has succumbed to sheer exhaustion, Pound after his Pisan experience still has the spirit to fight, to resist annihilation.

Thus is it significant that at the nadir of his life, when death is imminent and activities confined to a cage's space, he re-discovers the importance of human action and of human identity. In the cantos before Pisa, Pound has used masks as one principle of construction, while the poetic self often retreats into the background, seemingly in command like god paring his fingernails, but increasingly given over to enumerating historical personages and acts, especially in the Chinese and American history cantos. In the cantos after Pisa, the poetic self often comes to the foreground, involved much with the time and place of the poet's own life (Bernstein 178-81). The change, propelled by actual events, shows the close connection between life and poetry. The objection against poetic fancy is now reinscribed in Pound's poetry, as shown in the changed attitude to sacrifice. The poet's self is also being reinstated, invigorated by the poet's responses to events in his life.

Man lives under Fortuna, but Pound sees the importance of human action to maintain integrity. Demise will come one day, yet man's part is not to anticipate demise but "time the thunder." Both Pound's and Upward's conception of change is double-faced, like Janus, recognizing the homogenizing effect of metamorphic changes while insisting that change is also differential, that one stage differs from another, that one entity has its own claim to integrity. Thus Pound and Upward do not replace change with permanence, nor fight the tyranny of totalitarian homogenization by using another totalitarian system. Instead, they respond to demands from the outside while marking out their intellectual and moral territory; and in this territory, they also mark out different stages of devlopment, giving each stage a significance and intensity of its own.

Seen in this light, even Pound's early affirmations of sacrifice may be related to his later development; but viewed in the same light, the difference between Pound's early and late attitudes to sacrifice also has to be maintained. As the writers have taken up the difficult task of fighting change with change, so has this paper taken up the risky task of charting a sea of change, using sacrifice as both example and explanation. It is only apt that this discussion of change should be conducted through a discussion of sacrifice, since the rite, in its various forms, crude as in primitive tribes or sophisticated as in modern scapegoating devices of racism, war, and punishment, threatens the very existence of mortal man.

WORKS CITED

Bell, Ian. *The Critic as Scientist: The Modern Poetics of Ezra Pound.* London: Methuen, 1981.

Bernstein, Michael André. *The Tale of the Tribe: Ezra Pound and the Modern Verse Epic.* Princeton: Princeton UP, 1980.

Berryman, Jo Brantley. *Circe's Craft: Ezra Pound's Hugh Selwyn Mauberley.* Ann Arbor: UMI Research P, 1983.

Boas, Franz. "The Study of Geography." *Race, Language, and Culture.* 1940. Chicago: U of Chicago P, 1982. 639-47.

Bourdillon, M. F. C., and Meyer Fortes. *Sacrifice.* London: Academic Press, 1980.

Bush, Ronald. *The Genesis of Ezra Pound's Cantos.* Princeton: Princeton UP, 1976.

Casillo, Robert. *The Genealogy of Demons: Anti-Semitism, Fascism, and the Myths of Ezra Pound.* Evanston: Northwestern UP, 1988.

Cox, Kenneth, "Allen Upward." *Agenda* 16.3-4 (1978/9): 87-107.

Davie, Donald. *Ezra Pound.* New York: Viking, 1975.

Frazer, Sir James. *The Golden Bough.* 3rd ed. 1911. 13 vols. London: Macmillan, 1955.

Girard, René. *The Scapegoat.* Baltimore: Johns Hopkins UP, 1986.———. *Violence and the Sacred.* Baltimore: Johns Hopkins UP, 1977.

Kenner, Hugh. "The Broken Mirrors and the Mirror of Memory." *Critics on Ezra Pound.* Ed. San Juan Jr. Coral Gables: U of Miami P, 1972. 56-64.

Kermode, Frank. *The Romantic Image.* London: Routledge, 1957.

Knox, Bryant. "Allen Upward and Ezra Pound." *Paideuma* 3.1 (1974): 71-83.

Moody, A. D. "Pound's Allen Upward." *Paideuma* 4.1 (1975): 55-70.

Pound, Ezra. *The Cantos of Ezra Pound.* London: Faber, 1987.

———. *Literary Essays of Ezra Pound.* Ed. T. S. Eliot. New York: New Directions, 1968.

———. *The Selected Letters of Ezra Pound, 1907-1941.* Ed. D. D. Paige. 1950. New York: New Directions, 1971.

———. *Selected Prose: 1909-1965.* Ed. William Cookson. New York: New Directions, 1975.

Rock, Joseph. "The ²Muan Bpö Ceremony, or the Sacrifice to Heaven as Practiced by the ¹Na-²Khi." *Monumenta Serica* 13 (1948): 1-160.

Schneidau, Herbert. *Ezra Pound: The Image and the Real.* Baton Rouge: Louisiana State UP, 1969.

Sheldon, Michael. "Allen Upward: Some Biographical Notes." *Agenda* 16.3-4 (1978/9): 108-21.

Stocking, George W. Jr., ed. *Romantic Motives: Essays on Anthropological Sensibilities.* Madison: U of Wisconsin P, 1989.

Surette, Leon. *A Light from Eleusis: A Study of Ezra Pound's Cantos.* Oxford: Clarendon P, 1979.

Terrell, Carroll F. *A Companion to the Cantos of Ezra Pound.* 2 vols. Berkeley: U of California P, 1980, 1984.

Upward, Allen. *The Divine Mystery.* 1915. Santa Barbara: Ross-Erikson, 1976. Intro. Robert Duncan. Appendix with Poems and Miscellaneous Articles.

———. *The New Word.* New York: Kennerley, 1910.

———. *Some Personalities.* London: Murray, 1921.

Vickery, John. *The Literary Impact of The Golden Bough.* Princeton: Princeton UP, 1973.

Weston, Jessie. *From Ritual to Romance.* New York: Doubleday, 1957.

Wilhelm, Hellmut. *Change: Eight Lectures on the I Ching.* Trans. Cary Baynes. Bollingen Series, 62. New York: Pantheon, 1960.

NOTES

[1] In the late nineteenth century, anthropological discussions of sacrifice bloomed, e.g., discussions by Sir Edward Tylor, Sir James Frazer, Robertson Smith, and H. Hubert

and M. Mauss. Bourdillon, commenting on Tylor, writes, "The early humanist anthropologists dismissed the rites of religion as based on logical error, and presumed that the rites were simply not efficacious" (7).

[2] E. g., Kenner 57.

[3] There are two different approaches to Upward, represented by Moody's debate with Knox. Berryman agrees with Moody, but most critics take a line similar to Knox's, and see Upward as approbatory of sacrifice: Schneidau 118-21, 126-34; Bush 100-02; Bell 225-29; Casillo 261-62, 397.

[4] Frazer 6:97, qtd. in *DM* 169.

[5] "Nor into the pigsty did I enter," (Terrell 1:161).

[6] "and I too in the pig-sty," (Terrell 2:376).

[7] See note 3.

[8] Bush almost detects the outer whirl-swirl by calling attention to the issue of man's relation to the universe in Upward. However, he explains this relationship only in terms of the waterspout and the double vortex, without referring to the greater double vortex (98).

[9] Duncan in his introduction to the reprint of *The Divine Mystery* rightly observes that the title of this autobiography refers not just to Upward's acquaintances, but to his various voices, one truly visionary, the others journalistic and purposefully banal. It is the purpose of this paper, however, to point out the importance of these marginal voices.

[10] From "The Nebular Origin of Life," collected in Duncan's reprint of *The Divine Mystery* and miscellaneous articles (365).

## FURTHER READING

### Criticism

Review of *The Discovery of the Dead. The Bookman* XXXVIII, No. 226 (July 1910): 173.
　　Very brief review of Upward's "weird, grotesquely imaginative fantasy."

Review of *The East End of Europe. The Nation* 89, No. 2301 (5 August 1909): 123-24.
　　Favorable review of Upward's report on the Greco-Bulgarian conflict over Macedonia that, despite its topicality at the time of publication, describes the book as "belated" because the Balkan conflict has gone into hiatus, and "when the conflict revives . .. it will bear a different character."

Eliot, T. S. Review of *The House of Sin. The New Criterion* V, No. 1 (January 1927): 137-43.
　　Eliot presents Upward's detective novel, along with numerous others, as a violator of several basic rules governing detective fiction.

Eliot, T. S. Review of *The Venetian Key. The New Criterion* V, No. 1 (January 1927): 354-62.
　　Eliot, in a review of numerous detective books, laments the passing of Upward's character Sir Frank Tarleton along with his recently deceased creator.

Payne, William Morton. Review of *Secrets of the Courts of Europe. The Dial* XXII, No. 253 (1 January 1897): 21-22.
　　Brief mention of Upward's "new romance of imaginary history" in a lengthy review of various books.

Saunders, John. "Poetry Chronicle." *Stand* (Autumn 1989): 77-83.
　　Reviews Upward's *Scented Leaves from a Chinese Jar.*

# Twentieth-Century Literary Criticism

Cumulative Indexes
Volumes 1-85

# How to Use This Index

### The main references

> **Calvino, Italo**
> 1923–1985 ....... CLC 5, 8, 11, 22, 33, 39,
> 73; SSC 3

**list all author entries in the following Gale Literary Criticism series:**

*BLC* = *Black Literature Criticism*
*CLC* = *Contemporary Literary Criticism*
*CLR* = *Children's Literature Review*
*CMLC* = *Classical and Medieval Literature Criticism*
*DA* = *DISCovering Authors*
*DAB* = *DISCovering Authors: British*
*DAC* = *DISCovering Authors: Canadian*
*DAM* = *DISCovering Authors: Modules*
      *DRAM*: *Dramatists Module*; *MST*: *Most-Studied Authors Module*;
      *MULT*: *Multicultural Authors Module*; *NOV*: *Novelists Module*;
      *POET*: *Poets Module*; *POP*: *Popular Fiction and Genre Authors Module*
*DC* = *Drama Criticism*
*HLC* = *Hispanic Literature Criticism*
*LC* = *Literature Criticism from 1400 to 1800*
*NCLC* = *Nineteenth-Century Literature Criticism*
*PC* = *Poetry Criticism*
*SSC* = *Short Story Criticism*
*TCLC* = *Twentieth-Century Literary Criticism*
*WLC* = *World Literature Criticism, 1500 to the Present*

### The cross-references

> See also CANR 23; CA 85-88;
>    obituary CA116

**list all author entries in the following Gale biographical and literary sources:**

*AAYA* = *Authors & Artists for Young Adults*
*AITN* = *Authors in the News*
*BEST* = *Bestsellers*
*BW* = *Black Writers*
*CA* = *Contemporary Authors*
*CAAS* = *Contemporary Authors Autobiography Series*
*CABS* = *Contemporary Authors Bibliographical Series*
*CANR* = *Contemporary Authors New Revision Series*
*CAP* = *Contemporary Authors Permanent Series*
*CDALB* = *Concise Dictionary of American Literary Biography*
*CDBLB* = *Concise Dictionary of British Literary Biography*
*DLB* = *Dictionary of Literary Biography*
*DLBD* = *Dictionary of Literary Biography Documentary Series*
*DLBY* = *Dictionary of Literary Biography Yearbook*
*HW* = *Hispanic Writers*
*JRDA* = *Junior DISCovering Authors*
*MAICYA* = *Major Authors and Illustrators for Children and Young Adults*
*MTCW* = *Major 20th-Century Writers*
*NNAL* = *Native North American Literature*
*SAAS* = *Something about the Author Autobiography Series*
*SATA* = *Something about the Author*
*YABC* = *Yesterday's Authors of Books for Children*

**20/1631**
   See Upward, Allen
**A/C Cross**
   See Lawrence, T(homas) E(dward)
**Abasiyanik, Sait Faik** 1906-1954
   See Sait Faik
   See also CA 123
**Abbey, Edward** 1927-1989 ......... **CLC 36, 59**
   See also CA 45-48; 128; CANR 2, 41
**Abbott, Lee K(ittredge)** 1947- ........... **CLC 48**
   See also CA 124; CANR 51; DLB 130
**Abe, Kobo** 1924-1993**CLC 8, 22, 53, 81; DAM NOV**
   See also CA 65-68; 140; CANR 24, 60; DLB 182; MTCW 1
**Abelard, Peter** c. 1079-c. 1142 ...... **CMLC 11**
   See also DLB 115
**Abell, Kjeld** 1901-1961 ...................... **CLC 15**
   See also CA 111
**Abish, Walter** 1931- ............................. **CLC 22**
   See also CA 101; CANR 37; DLB 130
**Abrahams, Peter (Henry)** 1919- ......... **CLC 4**
   See also BW 1; CA 57-60; CANR 26; DLB 117; MTCW 1
**Abrams, M(eyer) H(oward)** 1912- .... **CLC 24**
   See also CA 57-60; CANR 13, 33; DLB 67
**Abse, Dannie** 1923- . **CLC 7, 29; DAB; DAM POET**
   See also CA 53-56; CAAS 1; CANR 4, 46; DLB 27
**Achebe, (Albert) Chinua(lumogu)** 1930-**C L C 1, 3, 5, 7, 11, 26, 51, 75; BLC 1; DA; DAB; DAC; DAM MST, MULT, NOV; WLC**
   See also AAYA 15; BW 2; CA 1-4R; CANR 6, 26, 47; CLR 20; DLB 117; MAICYA; MTCW 1; SATA 40; SATA-Brief 38
**Acker, Kathy** 1948-1997 ............. **CLC 45, 111**
   See also CA 117; 122; 162; CANR 55
**Ackroyd, Peter** 1949-................... **CLC 34, 52**
   See also CA 123; 127; CANR 51; DLB 155; INT 127
**Acorn, Milton** 1923- ................ **CLC 15; DAC**
   See also CA 103; DLB 53; INT 103
**Adamov, Arthur** 1908-1970**CLC 4, 25; DAM DRAM**
   See also CA 17-18; 25-28R; CAP 2; MTCW 1
**Adams, Alice (Boyd)** 1926-**CLC 6, 13, 46; SSC 24**
   See also CA 81-84; CANR 26, 53; DLBY 86; INT CANR-26; MTCW 1
**Adams, Andy** 1859-1935 ................ **TCLC 56**
   See also YABC 1
**Adams, Brooks** 1848-1927 ............. **TCLC 80**
   See also CA 123; DLB 47
**Adams, Douglas (Noel)** 1952- .... **CLC 27, 60; DAM POP**
   See also AAYA 4; BEST 89:3; CA 106; CANR 34, 64; DLBY 83; JRDA
**Adams, Francis** 1862-1893 ............ **NCLC 33**
**Adams, Henry (Brooks)** 1838-1918 **TCLC 4, 52; DA; DAB; DAC; DAM MST**
   See also CA 104; 133; DLB 12, 47, 189

**Adams, Richard (George)** 1920-**CLC 4, 5, 18; DAM NOV**
   See also AAYA 16; AITN 1, 2; CA 49-52; CANR 3, 35; CLR 20; JRDA; MAICYA; MTCW 1; SATA 7, 69
**Adamson, Joy(-Friederike Victoria)** 1910-1980 **CLC 17**
   See also CA 69-72; 93-96; CANR 22; MTCW 1; SATA 11; SATA-Obit 22
**Adcock, Fleur** 1934- .......................... **CLC 41**
   See also CA 25-28R; CAAS 23; CANR 11, 34, 69; DLB 40
**Addams, Charles (Samuel)** 1912-1988**CLC 30**
   See also CA 61-64; 126; CANR 12
**Addams, Jane** 1860-1945 ................ **TCLC 76**
**Addison, Joseph** 1672-1719 ................. **LC 18**
   See also CDBLB 1660-1789; DLB 101
**Adler, Alfred (F.)** 1870-1937 ........... **TCLC 61**
   See also CA 119; 159
**Adler, C(arole) S(chwerdtfeger)** 1932- . **C L C 35**
   See also AAYA 4; CA 89-92; CANR 19, 40; JRDA; MAICYA; SAAS 15; SATA 26, 63, 102
**Adler, Renata** 1938- ........................ **CLC 8, 31**
   See also CA 49-52; CANR 5, 22, 52; MTCW 1
**Ady, Endre** 1877-1919 ..................... **TCLC 11**
   See also CA 107
**A.E.** 1867-1935 ............................. **TCLC 3, 10**
   See also Russell, George William
**Aeschylus** 525B.C.-456B.C. ..**CMLC 11; DA; DAB; DAC; DAM DRAM, MST; DC 8; WLCS**
   See also DLB 176
**Aesop** 620(?)B.C.-564(?)B.C. ......... **CMLC 24**
   See also CLR 14; MAICYA; SATA 64
**Affable Hawk**
   See MacCarthy, Sir(Charles Otto) Desmond
**Africa, Ben**
   See Bosman, Herman Charles
**Afton, Effie**
   See Harper, Frances Ellen Watkins
**Agapida, Fray Antonio**
   See Irving, Washington
**Agee, James (Rufus)** 1909-1955 **TCLC 1, 19; DAM NOV**
   See also AITN 1; CA 108; 148; CDALB 1941-1968; DLB 2, 26, 152
**Aghill, Gordon**
   See Silverberg, Robert
**Agnon, S(hmuel) Y(osef Halevi)** 1888-1970 **CLC 4, 8, 14; SSC 30**
   See also CA 17-18; 25-28R; CANR 60; CAP 2; MTCW 1
**Agrippa von Nettesheim, Henry Cornelius** 1486-1535 ....................................... **LC 27**
**Aherne, Owen**
   See Cassill, R(onald) V(erlin)
**Ai** 1947- ..................................... **CLC 4, 14, 69**
   See also CA 85-88; CAAS 13; CANR 70; DLB 120
**Aickman, Robert (Fordyce)** 1914-1981 **C L C**

**57**
   See also CA 5-8R; CANR 3, 72
**Aiken, Conrad (Potter)** 1889-1973**CLC 1, 3, 5, 10, 52; DAM NOV, POET; SSC 9**
   See also CA 5-8R; 45-48; CANR 4, 60; CDALB 1929-1941; DLB 9, 45, 102; MTCW 1; SATA 3, 30
**Aiken, Joan (Delano)** 1924- ............... **CLC 35**
   See also AAYA 1, 25; CA 9-12R; CANR 4, 23, 34, 64; CLR 1, 19; DLB 161; JRDA; MAICYA; MTCW 1; SAAS 1; SATA 2, 30, 73
**Ainsworth, William Harrison** 1805-1882 **NCLC 13**
   See also DLB 21; SATA 24
**Aitmatov, Chingiz (Torekulovich)** 1928-**C L C 71**
   See also CA 103; CANR 38; MTCW 1; SATA 56
**Akers, Floyd**
   See Baum, L(yman) Frank
**Akhmadulina, Bella Akhatovna** 1937-**CLC 53; DAM POET**
   See also CA 65-68
**Akhmatova, Anna** 1888-1966**CLC 11, 25, 64; DAM POET; PC 2**
   See also CA 19-20; 25-28R; CANR 35; CAP 1; MTCW 1
**Aksakov, Sergei Timofeyvich** 1791-1859 **NCLC 2**
   See also DLB 198
**Aksenov, Vassily**
   See Aksyonov, Vassily (Pavlovich)
**Akst, Daniel** 1956-............................**CLC 109**
   See also CA 161
**Aksyonov, Vassily (Pavlovich)** 1932-**CLC 22, 37, 101**
   See also CA 53-56; CANR 12, 48
**Akutagawa, Ryunosuke** 1892-1927 **TCLC 16**
   See also CA 117; 154
**Alain** 1868-1951 ............................... **TCLC 41**
   See also CA 163
**Alain-Fournier** ..................................... **TCLC 6**
   See also Fournier, Henri Alban
   See also DLB 65
**Alarcon, Pedro Antonio de** 1833-1891**NCLC 1**
**Alas (y Urena), Leopoldo (Enrique Garcia)** 1852-1901 ....................................................
**TCLC 29**
   See also CA 113; 131; HW
**Albee, Edward (Franklin III)** 1928-**CLC 1, 2, 3, 5, 9, 11, 13, 25, 53, 86, 113; DA; DAB; DAC; DAM DRAM, MST; WLC**
   See also AITN 1; CA 5-8R; CABS 3; CANR 8, 54; CDALB 1941-1968; DLB 7; INT CANR-8; MTCW 1
**Alberti, Rafael** 1902- ........................... **CLC 7**
   See also CA 85-88; DLB 108
**Albert the Great** 1200(?)-1280 ...... **CMLC 16**
   See also DLB 115
**Alcala-Galiano, Juan Valera y**
   See Valera y Alcala-Galiano, Juan

See Prado (Calvo), Pedro

**Angelique, Pierre**
See Bataille, Georges

**Angell, Roger** 1920- ............................ **CLC 26**
See also CA 57-60; CANR 13, 44, 70; DLB 171, 185

**Angelou, Maya** 1928-**CLC 12, 35, 64, 77; BLC 1; DA; DAB; DAC; DAM MST, MULT, POET, POP; WLCS**
See Johnson, Marguerite (Annie)
See also AAYA 7, 20; BW 2; CA 65-68; CANR 19, 42, 65; CLR 53; DLB 38; MTCW 1; SATA 49

**Anna Comnena** 1083-1153 .............. **CMLC 25**

**Annensky, Innokenty (Fyodorovich)** 1856-1909 **TCLC 14**
See also CA 110; 155

**Annunzio, Gabriele d'**
See D'Annunzio, Gabriele

**Anodos**
See Coleridge, Mary E(lizabeth)

**Anon, Charles Robert**
See Pessoa, Fernando (Antonio Nogueira)

**Anouilh, Jean (Marie Lucien Pierre)** 1910-1987 **CLC 1, 3, 8, 13, 40, 50; DAM DRAM; DC 8**
See also CA 17-20R; 123; CANR 32; MTCW 1

**Anthony, Florence**
See Ai

**Anthony, John**
See Ciardi, John (Anthony)

**Anthony, Peter**
See Shaffer, Anthony (Joshua); Shaffer, Peter (Levin)

**Anthony, Piers** 1934- .... **CLC 35; DAM POP**
See also AAYA 11; CA 21-24R; CANR 28, 56; DLB 8; MTCW 1; SAAS 22; SATA 84

**Anthony, Susan B(rownell)** 1916-1991 **T C L C 84**
See also CA 89-92; 134

**Antoine, Marc**
See Proust, (Valentin-Louis-George-Eugene-) Marcel

**Antoninus, Brother**
See Everson, William (Oliver)

**Antonioni, Michelangelo** 1912- ......... **CLC 20**
See also CA 73-76; CANR 45

**Antschel, Paul** 1920-1970
See Celan, Paul
See also CA 85-88; CANR 33, 61; MTCW 1

**Anwar, Chairil** 1922-1949 .............. **TCLC 22**
See also CA 121

**Apess, William** 1798-1839(?)**NCLC 73; DAM MULT**
See also DLB 175; NNAL

**Apollinaire, Guillaume** 1880-1918**TCLC 3, 8, 51; DAM POET; PC 7**
See also Kostrowitzki, Wilhelm Apollinaris de
See also CA 152

**Appelfeld, Aharon** 1932- ........... **CLC 23, 47**
See also CA 112; 133

**Apple, Max (Isaac)** 1941-............... **CLC 9, 33**
See also CA 81-84; CANR 19, 54; DLB 130

**Appleman, Philip (Dean)** 1926- ........ **CLC 51**
See also CA 13-16R; CAAS 18; CANR 6, 29, 56

**Appleton, Lawrence**
See Lovecraft, H(oward) P(hillips)

**Apteryx**
See Eliot, T(homas) S(tearns)

**Apuleius, (Lucius Madaurensis)** 125(?)-175(?) **CMLC 1**

**Aquin, Hubert** 1929-1977 ................. **CLC 15**
See also CA 105; DLB 53

**Aragon, Louis** 1897-1982.. **CLC 3, 22; DAM NOV, POET**
See also CA 69-72; 108; CANR 28, 71; DLB 72; MTCW 1

**Arany, Janos** 1817-1882 ................. **NCLC 34**

**Arbuthnot, John** 1667-1735 ................... **LC 1**
See also DLB 101

**Archer, Herbert Winslow**
See Mencken, H(enry) L(ouis)

**Archer, Jeffrey (Howard)** 1940- ..... **CLC 28; DAM POP**
See also AAYA 16; BEST 89:3; CA 77-80; CANR 22, 52; INT CANR-22

**Archer, Jules** 1915-............................. **CLC 12**
See also CA 9-12R; CANR 6, 69; SAAS 5; SATA 4, 85

**Archer, Lee**
See Ellison, Harlan (Jay)

**Arden, John** 1930-**CLC 6, 13, 15; DAM DRAM**
See also CA 13-16R; CAAS 4; CANR 31, 65, 67; DLB 13; MTCW 1

**Arenas, Reinaldo** 1943-1990 . **CLC 41; DAM MULT; HLC**
See also CA 124; 128; 133; DLB 145; HW

**Arendt, Hannah** 1906-1975 ........ **CLC 66, 98**
See also CA 17-20R; 61-64; CANR 26, 60; MTCW 1

**Aretino, Pietro** 1492-1556 ..................... **LC 12**

**Arghezi, Tudor** 1880-1967 ................. **CLC 80**
See also Theodorescu, Ion N.
See also CA 167

**Arguedas, Jose Maria** 1911-1969 **CLC 10, 18**
See also CA 89-92; DLB 113; HW

**Argueta, Manlio** 1936-....................... **CLC 31**
See also CA 131; DLB 145; HW

**Ariosto, Ludovico** 1474-1533 ................. **LC 6**

**Aristides**
See Epstein, Joseph

**Aristophanes** 450B.C.-385B.C.**CMLC 4; DA; DAB; DAC; DAM DRAM, MST; DC 2; WLCS**
See also DLB 176

**Arlt, Roberto (Godofredo Christophersen)** 1900-1942 ..................................................
**TCLC 29; DAM MULT; HLC**
See also CA 123; 131; CANR 67; HW

**Armah, Ayi Kwei** 1939- . **CLC 5, 33; BLC 1; DAM MULT, POET**
See also BW 1; CA 61-64; CANR 21, 64; DLB 117; MTCW 1

**Armatrading, Joan** 1950- ................. **CLC 17**
See also CA 114

**Arnette, Robert**
See Silverberg, Robert

**Arnim, Achim von (Ludwig Joachim von Arnim)** 1781-1831 ...... **NCLC 5; SSC 29**
See also DLB 90

**Arnim, Bettina von** 1785-1859 ....... **NCLC 38**
See also DLB 90

**Arnold, Matthew** 1822-1888**NCLC 6, 29; DA; DAB; DAC; DAM MST, POET; PC 5; WLC**
See also CDBLB 1832-1890; DLB 32, 57

**Arnold, Thomas** 1795-1842 ............ **NCLC 18**
See also DLB 55

**Arnow, Harriette (Louisa) Simpson** 1908-1986 **CLC 2, 7, 18**
See also CA 9-12R; 118; CANR 14; DLB 6; MTCW 1; SATA 42; SATA-Obit 47

**Arouet, Francois-Marie**
See Voltaire

**Arp, Hans**
See Arp, Jean

**Arp, Jean** 1887-1966 ........................... **CLC 5**
See also CA 81-84; 25-28R; CANR 42

**Arrabal**
See Arrabal, Fernando

**Arrabal, Fernando** 1932- .... **CLC 2, 9, 18, 58**
See also CA 9-12R; CANR 15

**Arrick, Fran** .......................................... **CLC 30**

See also Gaberman, Judie Angell

**Artaud, Antonin (Marie Joseph)** 1896-1948 **TCLC 3, 36; DAM DRAM**
See also CA 104; 149

**Arthur, Ruth M(abel)** 1905-1979 ...... **CLC 12**
See also CA 9-12R; 85-88; CANR 4; SATA 7, 26

**Artsybashev, Mikhail (Petrovich)** 1878-1927 **TCLC 31**

**Arundel, Honor (Morfydd)** 1919-1973**CLC 17**
See also CA 21-22; 41-44R; CAP 2; CLR 35; SATA 4; SATA-Obit 24

**Arzner, Dorothy** 1897-1979 .............. **CLC 98**

**Asch, Sholem** 1880-1957 .................. **TCLC 3**
See also CA 105

**Ash, Shalom**
See Asch, Sholem

**Ashbery, John (Lawrence)** 1927-**CLC 2, 3, 4, 6, 9, 13, 15, 25, 41, 77; DAM POET**
See also CA 5-8R; CANR 9, 37, 66; DLB 5, 165; DLBY 81; INT CANR-9; MTCW 1

**Ashdown, Clifford**
See Freeman, R(ichard) Austin

**Ashe, Gordon**
See Creasey, John

**Ashton-Warner, Sylvia (Constance)** 1908-1984 **CLC 19**
See also CA 69-72; 112; CANR 29; MTCW 1

**Asimov, Isaac** 1920-1992 **CLC 1, 3, 9, 19, 26, 76, 92; DAM POP**
See also AAYA 13; BEST 90:2; CA 1-4R; 137; CANR 2, 19, 36, 60; CLR 12; DLB 8; DLBY 92; INT CANR-19; JRDA; MAICYA; MTCW 1; SATA 1, 26, 74

**Assis, Joaquim Maria Machado de**
See Machado de Assis, Joaquim Maria

**Astley, Thea (Beatrice May)** 1925- ... **CLC 41**
See also CA 65-68; CANR 11, 43

**Aston, James**
See White, T(erence) H(anbury)

**Asturias, Miguel Angel** 1899-1974 **CLC 3, 8, 13; DAM MULT, NOV; HLC**
See also CA 25-28; 49-52; CANR 32; CAP 2; DLB 113; HW; MTCW 1

**Atares, Carlos Saura**
See Saura (Atares), Carlos

**Atheling, William**
See Pound, Ezra (Weston Loomis)

**Atheling, William, Jr.**
See Blish, James (Benjamin)

**Atherton, Gertrude (Franklin Horn)** 1857-1948 **TCLC 2**
See also CA 104; 155; DLB 9, 78, 186

**Atherton, Lucius**
See Masters, Edgar Lee

**Atkins, Jack**
See Harris, Mark

**Atkinson, Kate** ...................................... **CLC 99**
See also CA 166

**Attaway, William (Alexander)** 1911-1986 **CLC 92; BLC 1; DAM MULT**
See also BW 2; CA 143; DLB 76

**Atticus**
See Fleming, Ian (Lancaster); Wilson, (Thomas) Woodrow

**Atwood, Margaret (Eleanor)** 1939-**CLC 2, 3, 4, 8, 13, 15, 25, 44, 84; DA; DAB; DAC; DAM MST, NOV, POET; PC 8; SSC 2; WLC**
See also AAYA 12; BEST 89:2; CA 49-52; CANR 3, 24, 33, 59; DLB 53; INT CANR-24; MTCW 1; SATA 50

**Aubigny, Pierre d'**
See Mencken, H(enry) L(ouis)

**Aubin, Penelope** 1685-1731(?) .............. **LC 9**
See also DLB 39

**Auchincloss, Louis (Stanton)** 1917-**CLC 4, 6,**

9, 18, 45; DAM NOV; SSC 22
See also CA 1-4R; CANR 6, 29, 55; DLB 2;
DLBY 80; INT CANR-29; MTCW 1
**Auden, W(ystan) H(ugh)** 1907-1973 CLC 1, 2,
3, 4, 6, 9, 11, 14, 43; DA; DAB; DAC; DAM
DRAM, MST, POET; PC 1; WLC
See also AAYA 18; CA 9-12R; 45-48; CANR
5, 61; CDBLB 1914-1945; DLB 10, 20;
MTCW 1
**Audiberti, Jacques** 1900-1965 CLC 38; DAM
DRAM
See also CA 25-28R
**Audubon, John James** 1785-1851 .. NCLC 47
**Auel, Jean M(arie)** 1936- CLC 31, 107; DAM
POP
See also AAYA 7; BEST 90:4; CA 103; CANR
21, 64; INT CANR-21; SATA 91
**Auerbach, Erich** 1892-1957 .......... TCLC 43
See also CA 118; 155
**Augier, Emile** 1820-1889 ................ NCLC 31
See also DLB 192
**August, John**
See De Voto, Bernard (Augustine)
**Augustine, St.** 354-430 .......... CMLC 6; DAB
**Aurelius**
See Bourne, Randolph S(illiman)
**Aurobindo, Sri**
See Ghose, Aurabinda
**Austen, Jane** 1775-1817 NCLC 1, 13, 19, 33,
51; DA; DAB; DAC; DAM MST, NOV;
WLC
See also AAYA 19; CDBLB 1789-1832; DLB
116
**Auster, Paul** 1947- ............................. CLC 47
See also CA 69-72; CANR 23, 52
**Austin, Frank**
See Faust, Frederick (Schiller)
**Austin, Mary (Hunter)** 1868-1934 . TCLC 25
See also CA 109; DLB 9, 78
**Autran Dourado, Waldomiro**
See Dourado, (Waldomiro Freitas) Autran
**Averroes** 1126-1198 ........................... CMLC 7
See also DLB 115
**Avicenna** 980-1037 ......................... CMLC 16
See also DLB 115
**Avison, Margaret** 1918- CLC 2, 4, 97; DAC;
DAM POET
See also CA 17-20R; DLB 53; MTCW 1
**Axton, David**
See Koontz, Dean R(ay)
**Ayckbourn, Alan** 1939- CLC 5, 8, 18, 33, 74;
DAB; DAM DRAM
See also CA 21-24R; CANR 31, 59; DLB 13;
MTCW 1
**Aydy, Catherine**
See Tennant, Emma (Christina)
**Ayme, Marcel (Andre)** 1902-1967 .... CLC 11
See also CA 89-92; CANR 67; CLR 25; DLB
72; SATA 91
**Ayrton, Michael** 1921-1975 ................ CLC 7
See also CA 5-8R; 61-64; CANR 9, 21
**Azorin** ....................................................... CLC 11
See also Martinez Ruiz, Jose
**Azuela, Mariano** 1873-1952 . TCLC 3; DAM
MULT; HLC
See also CA 104; 131; HW; MTCW 1
**Baastad, Babbis Friis**
See Friis-Baastad, Babbis Ellinor
**Bab**
See Gilbert, W(illiam) S(chwenck)
**Babbis, Eleanor**
See Friis-Baastad, Babbis Ellinor
**Babel, Isaac**
See Babel, Isaak (Emmanuilovich)
**Babel, Isaak (Emmanuilovich)** 1894-1941(?)
TCLC 2, 13; SSC 16
See also CA 104; 155

**Babits, Mihaly** 1883-1941 ............... TCLC 14
See also CA 114
**Babur** 1483-1530 ..................................... LC 18
**Bacchelli, Riccardo** 1891-1985 ......... CLC 19
See also CA 29-32R; 117
**Bach, Richard (David)** 1936- CLC 14; DAM
NOV, POP
See also AITN 1; BEST 89:2; CA 9-12R; CANR
18; MTCW 1; SATA 13
**Bachman, Richard**
See King, Stephen (Edwin)
**Bachmann, Ingeborg** 1926-1973 ....... CLC 69
See also CA 93-96; 45-48; CANR 69; DLB 85
**Bacon, Francis** 1561-1626 ............. LC 18, 32
See also CDBLB Before 1660; DLB 151
**Bacon, Roger** 1214(?)-1292 ........... CMLC 14
See also DLB 115
**Bacovia, George** ................................. TCLC 24
See also Vasiliu, Gheorghe
**Badanes, Jerome** 1937- ...................... CLC 59
**Bagehot, Walter** 1826-1877 ............ NCLC 10
See also DLB 55
**Bagnold, Enid** 1889-1981 ...... CLC 25; DAM
DRAM
See also CA 5-8R; 103; CANR 5, 40; DLB 13,
160, 191; MAICYA; SATA 1, 25
**Bagritsky, Eduard** 1895-1934 ........ TCLC 60
**Bagrjana, Elisaveta**
See Belcheva, Elisaveta
**Bagryana, Elisaveta** ............................ CLC 10
See also Belcheva, Elisaveta
See also DLB 147
**Bailey, Paul** 1937- ................................ CLC 45
See also CA 21-24R; CANR 16, 62; DLB 14
**Baillie, Joanna** 1762-1851 .............. NCLC 71
See also DLB 93
**Bainbridge, Beryl (Margaret)** 1933- CLC 4, 5,
8, 10, 14, 18, 22, 62; DAM NOV
See also CA 21-24R; CANR 24, 55; DLB 14;
MTCW 1
**Baker, Elliott** 1922- .............................. CLC 8
See also CA 45-48; CANR 2, 63
**Baker, Jean H.** ................................ TCLC 3, 10
See also Russell, George William
**Baker, Nicholson** 1957- CLC 61; DAM POP
See also CA 135; CANR 63
**Baker, Ray Stannard** 1870-1946 .... TCLC 47
See also CA 118
**Baker, Russell (Wayne)** 1925- ........... CLC 31
See also BEST 89:4; CA 57-60; CANR 11, 41,
59; MTCW 1
**Bakhtin, M.**
See Bakhtin, Mikhail Mikhailovich
**Bakhtin, M. M.**
See Bakhtin, Mikhail Mikhailovich
**Bakhtin, Mikhail**
See Bakhtin, Mikhail Mikhailovich
**Bakhtin, Mikhail Mikhailovich** 1895-1975
CLC 83
See also CA 128; 113
**Bakshi, Ralph** 1938(?)- ...................... CLC 26
See also CA 112; 138
**Bakunin, Mikhail (Alexandrovich)** 1814-1876
NCLC 25, 58
**Baldwin, James (Arthur)** 1924-1987 CLC 1, 2,
3, 4, 5, 8, 13, 15, 17, 42, 50, 67, 90; BLC 1;
DA; DAB; DAC; DAM MST, MULT, NOV,
POP; DC 1; SSC 10; WLC
See also AAYA 4; BW 1; CA 1-4R; 124; CABS
1; CANR 3, 24; CDALB 1941-1968; DLB
2, 7, 33; DLBY 87; MTCW 1; SATA 9;
SATA-Obit 54
**Ballard, J(ames) G(raham)** 1930- CLC 3, 6, 14,
36; DAM NOV, POP; SSC 1
See also AAYA 3; CA 5-8R; CANR 15, 39, 65;
DLB 14; MTCW 1; SATA 93
**Balmont, Konstantin (Dmitriyevich)** 1867-1943

TCLC 11
See also CA 109; 155
**Balzac, Honore de** 1799-1850 NCLC 5, 35, 53;
DA; DAB; DAC; DAM MST, NOV; SSC
5; WLC
See also DLB 119
**Bambara, Toni Cade** 1939-1995 CLC 19, 88;
BLC 1; DA; DAC; DAM MST, MULT;
WLCS
See also AAYA 5; BW 2; CA 29-32R; 150;
CANR 24, 49; DLB 38; MTCW 1
**Bamdad, A.**
See Shamlu, Ahmad
**Banat, D. R.**
See Bradbury, Ray (Douglas)
**Bancroft, Laura**
See Baum, L(yman) Frank
**Banim, John** 1798-1842 ................... NCLC 13
See also DLB 116, 158, 159
**Banim, Michael** 1796-1874 ............. NCLC 13
See also DLB 158, 159
**Banjo, The**
See Paterson, A(ndrew) B(arton)
**Banks, Iain**
See Banks, Iain M(enzies)
**Banks, Iain M(enzies)** 1954- .............. CLC 34
See also CA 123; 128; CANR 61; DLB 194;
INT 128
**Banks, Lynne Reid** .............................. CLC 23
See also Reid Banks, Lynne
See also AAYA 6
**Banks, Russell** 1940- ..................... CLC 37, 72
See also CA 65-68; CAAS 15; CANR 19, 52;
DLB 130
**Banville, John** 1945- ............................ CLC 46
See also CA 117; 128; DLB 14; INT 128
**Banville, Theodore (Faullain) de** 1832-1891
NCLC 9
**Baraka, Amiri** 1934- CLC 1, 2, 3, 5, 10, 14, 33,
115; BLC 1; DA; DAC; DAM MST, MULT,
POET, POP; DC 6; PC 4; WLCS
See also Jones, LeRoi
See also BW 2; CA 21-24R; CABS 3; CANR
27, 38, 61; CDALB 1941-1968; DLB 5, 7,
16, 38; DLBD 8; MTCW 1
**Barbauld, Anna Laetitia** 1743-1825 NCLC 50
See also DLB 107, 109, 142, 158
**Barbellion, W. N. P.** ......................... TCLC 24
See also Cummings, Bruce F(rederick)
**Barbera, Jack (Vincent)** 1945- .......... CLC 44
See also CA 110; CANR 45
**Barbey d'Aurevilly, Jules Amedee** 1808-1889
NCLC 1; SSC 17
See also DLB 119
**Barbusse, Henri** 1873-1935 .............. TCLC 5
See also CA 105; 154; DLB 65
**Barclay, Bill**
See Moorcock, Michael (John)
**Barclay, William Ewert**
See Moorcock, Michael (John)
**Barea, Arturo** 1897-1957 ............... TCLC 14
See also CA 111
**Barfoot, Joan** 1946- ........................... CLC 18
See also CA 105
**Baring, Maurice** 1874-1945 ............. TCLC 8
See also CA 105; 168; DLB 34
**Barker, Clive** 1952- ....... CLC 52; DAM POP
See also AAYA 10; BEST 90:3; CA 121; 129;
CANR 71; INT 129; MTCW 1
**Barker, George Granville** 1913-1991 CLC 8,
48; DAM POET
See also CA 9-12R; 135; CANR 7, 38; DLB
20; MTCW 1
**Barker, Harley Granville**
See Granville-Barker, Harley
See also DLB 10
**Barker, Howard** 1946- ...................... CLC 37

Bickerstaff, Isaac
See Swift, Jonathan
Bidart, Frank 1939- ........................... **CLC 33**
See also CA 140
Bienek, Horst 1930- ...................... **CLC 7, 11**
See also CA 73-76; DLB 75
Bierce, Ambrose (Gwinett) 1842-1914(?)
**TCLC 1, 7, 44; DA; DAC; DAM MST; SSC 9; WLC**
See also CA 104; 139; CDALB 1865-1917; DLB 11, 12, 23, 71, 74, 186
Biggers, Earl Derr 1884-1933 ........ **TCLC 65**
See also CA 108; 153
Billings, Josh
See Shaw, Henry Wheeler
Billington, (Lady) Rachel (Mary) 1942- **C L C 43**
See also AITN 2; CA 33-36R; CANR 44
Binyon, T(imothy) J(ohn) 1936- ....... **CLC 34**
See also CA 111; CANR 28
Bioy Casares, Adolfo 1914-1984 **CLC 4, 8, 13, 88; DAM MULT; HLC; SSC 17**
See also CA 29-32R; CANR 19, 43, 66; DLB 113; HW; MTCW 1
Bird, Cordwainer
See Ellison, Harlan (Jay)
Bird, Robert Montgomery 1806-1854 **NCLC 1**
See also DLB 202
Birney, (Alfred) Earle 1904-1995 **CLC 1, 4, 6, 11; DAC; DAM MST, POET**
See also CA 1-4R; CANR 5, 20; DLB 88; MTCW 1
Bishop, Elizabeth 1911-1979 **CLC 1, 4, 9, 13, 15, 32; DA; DAC; DAM MST, POET; PC 3**
See also CA 5-8R; 89-92; CABS 2; CANR 26, 61; CDALB 1968-1988; DLB 5, 169; MTCW 1; SATA-Obit 24
Bishop, John 1935- ........................... **CLC 10**
See also CA 105
Bissett, Bill 1939- .................. **CLC 18; PC 14**
See also CA 69-72; CAAS 19; CANR 15; DLB 53; MTCW 1
Bitov, Andrei (Georgievich) 1937- ... **CLC 57**
See also CA 142
Biyidi, Alexandre 1932-
See Beti, Mongo
See also BW 1; CA 114; 124; MTCW 1
Bjarme, Brynjolf
See Ibsen, Henrik (Johan)
Bjoernson, Bjoernstjerne (Martinius) 1832-1910 ...................... **TCLC 7, 37**
See also CA 104
Black, Robert
See Holdstock, Robert P.
Blackburn, Paul 1926-1971 .......... **CLC 9, 43**
See also CA 81-84; 33-36R; CANR 34; DLB 16; DLBY 81
Black Elk 1863-1950 **TCLC 33; DAM MULT**
See also CA 144; NNAL
Black Hobart
See Sanders, (James) Ed(ward)
Blacklin, Malcolm
See Chambers, Aidan
Blackmore, R(ichard) D(oddridge) 1825-1900 **TCLC 27**
See also CA 120; DLB 18
Blackmur, R(ichard) P(almer) 1904-1965 **CLC 2, 24**
See also CA 11-12; 25-28R; CANR 71; CAP 1; DLB 63
Black Tarantula
See Acker, Kathy
Blackwood, Algernon (Henry) 1869-1951 **TCLC 5**
See also CA 105; 150; DLB 153, 156, 178
Blackwood, Caroline 1931-1996 **CLC 6, 9, 100**

See also CA 85-88; 151; CANR 32, 61, 65; DLB 14; MTCW 1
Blade, Alexander
See Hamilton, Edmond; Silverberg, Robert
Blaga, Lucian 1895-1961 .................. **CLC 75**
See also CA 157
Blair, Eric (Arthur) 1903-1950
See Orwell, George
See also CA 104; 132; DA; DAB; DAC; DAM MST, NOV; MTCW 1; SATA 29
Blais, Marie-Claire 1939- **CLC 2, 4, 6, 13, 22; DAC; DAM MST**
See also CA 21-24R; CAAS 4; CANR 38; DLB 53; MTCW 1
Blaise, Clark 1940- ........................... **CLC 29**
See also AITN 2; CA 53-56; CAAS 3; CANR 5, 66; DLB 53
Blake, Fairley
See De Voto, Bernard (Augustine)
Blake, Nicholas
See Day Lewis, C(ecil)
See also DLB 77
Blake, William 1757-1827 . **NCLC 13, 37, 57; DA; DAB; DAC; DAM MST, POET; PC 12; WLC**
See also CDBLB 1789-1832; CLR 52; DLB 93, 163; MAICYA; SATA 30
Blasco Ibanez, Vicente 1867-1928 **TCLC 12; DAM NOV**
See also CA 110; 131; HW; MTCW 1
Blatty, William Peter 1928- **CLC 2; DAM POP**
See also CA 5-8R; CANR 9
Bleeck, Oliver
See Thomas, Ross (Elmore)
Blessing, Lee 1949- ........................... **CLC 54**
Blish, James (Benjamin) 1921-1975 . **CLC 14**
See also CA 1-4R; 57-60; CANR 3; DLB 8; MTCW 1; SATA 66
Bliss, Reginald
See Wells, H(erbert) G(eorge)
Blixen, Karen (Christentze Dinesen) 1885-1962
See Dinesen, Isak
See also CA 25-28; CANR 22, 50; CAP 2; MTCW 1; SATA 44
Bloch, Robert (Albert) 1917-1994 .... **CLC 33**
See also CA 5-8R; 146; CAAS 20; CANR 5; DLB 44; INT CANR-5; SATA 12; SATA-Obit 82
Blok, Alexander (Alexandrovich) 1880-1921 **TCLC 5; PC 21**
See also CA 104
Blom, Jan
See Breytenbach, Breyten
Bloom, Harold 1930- ................. **CLC 24, 103**
See also CA 13-16R; CANR 39; DLB 67
Bloomfield, Aurelius
See Bourne, Randolph S(illiman)
Blount, Roy (Alton), Jr. 1941- ........... **CLC 38**
See also CA 53-56; CANR 10, 28, 61; INT CANR-28; MTCW 1
Bloy, Leon 1846-1917 ...................... **TCLC 22**
See also CA 121; DLB 123
Blume, Judy (Sussman) 1938- ... **CLC 12, 30; DAM NOV, POP**
See also AAYA 3, 26; CA 29-32R; CANR 13, 37, 66; CLR 2, 15; DLB 52; JRDA; MAICYA; MTCW 1; SATA 2, 31, 79
Blunden, Edmund (Charles) 1896-1974 **C L C 2, 56**
See also CA 17-18; 45-48; CANR 54; CAP 2; DLB 20, 100, 155; MTCW 1
Bly, Robert (Elwood) 1926- **CLC 1, 2, 5, 10, 15, 38; DAM POET**
See also CA 5-8R; CANR 41; DLB 5; MTCW 1
Boas, Franz 1858-1942 .................... **TCLC 56**
See also CA 115

Bobette
See Simenon, Georges (Jacques Christian)
Boccaccio, Giovanni 1313-1375 ... **CMLC 13; SSC 10**
Bochco, Steven 1943- ........................ **CLC 35**
See also AAYA 11; CA 124; 138
Bodel, Jean 1167(?)-1210 .............. **CMLC 28**
Bodenheim, Maxwell 1892-1954 .... **TCLC 44**
See also CA 110; DLB 9, 45
Bodker, Cecil 1927- ........................... **CLC 21**
See also CA 73-76; CANR 13, 44; CLR 23; MAICYA; SATA 14
Boell, Heinrich (Theodor) 1917-1985 **CLC 2, 3, 6, 9, 11, 15, 27, 32, 72; DA; DAB; DAC; DAM MST, NOV; SSC 23; WLC**
See also CA 21-24R; 116; CANR 24; DLB 69; DLBY 85; MTCW 1
Boerne, Alfred
See Doeblin, Alfred
Boethius 480(?)-524(?) .................... **CMLC 15**
See also DLB 115
Bogan, Louise 1897-1970 . **CLC 4, 39, 46, 93; DAM POET; PC 12**
See also CA 73-76; 25-28R; CANR 33; DLB 45, 169; MTCW 1
Bogarde, Dirk ................................... **CLC 19**
See also Van Den Bogarde, Derek Jules Gaspard Ulric Niven
See also DLB 14
Bogosian, Eric 1953- ........................ **CLC 45**
See also CA 138
Bograd, Larry 1953- ......................... **CLC 35**
See also CA 93-96; CANR 57; SAAS 21; SATA 33, 89
Boiardo, Matteo Maria 1441-1494 ........ **LC 6**
Boileau-Despreaux, Nicolas 1636-1711 . **LC 3**
Bojer, Johan 1872-1959 .................. **TCLC 64**
Boland, Eavan (Aisling) 1944- .. **CLC 40, 67, 113; DAM POET**
See also CA 143; CANR 61; DLB 40
Boll, Heinrich
See Boell, Heinrich (Theodor)
Bolt, Lee
See Faust, Frederick (Schiller)
Bolt, Robert (Oxton) 1924-1995 ..... **CLC 14; DAM DRAM**
See also CA 17-20R; 147; CANR 35, 67; DLB 13; MTCW 1
Bombet, Louis-Alexandre-Cesar
See Stendhal
Bomkauf
See Kaufman, Bob (Garnell)
Bonaventura ...................................... **NCLC 35**
See also DLB 90
Bond, Edward 1934- **CLC 4, 6, 13, 23; DAM DRAM**
See also CA 25-28R; CANR 38, 67; DLB 13; MTCW 1
Bonham, Frank 1914-1989 ............... **CLC 12**
See also AAYA 1; CA 9-12R; CANR 4, 36; JRDA; MAICYA; SAAS 3; SATA 1, 49; SATA-Obit 62
Bonnefoy, Yves 1923- ... **CLC 9, 15, 58; DAM MST, POET**
See also CA 85-88; CANR 33; MTCW 1
Bontemps, Arna(ud Wendell) 1902-1973 **C L C 1, 18; BLC 1; DAM MULT, NOV, POET**
See also BW 1; CA 1-4R; 41-44R; CANR 4, 35; CLR 6; DLB 48, 51; JRDA; MAICYA; MTCW 1; SATA 2, 44; SATA-Obit 24
Booth, Martin 1944- ......................... **CLC 13**
See also CA 93-96; CAAS 2
Booth, Philip 1925- ........................... **CLC 23**
See also CA 5-8R; CANR 5; DLBY 82
Booth, Wayne C(layson) 1921- ......... **CLC 24**
See also CA 1-4R; CAAS 5; CANR 3, 43; DLB 67

See also AITN 1; CA 41-44R; 151; CANR 37; DAM POET; MTCW 1

**Brodsky, Joseph** 1940-1996 CLC **4, 6, 13, 36, 100; PC 9**
See also Brodskii, Iosif; Brodsky, Iosif Alexandrovich

**Brodsky, Michael (Mark)** 1948- ........ CLC **19**
See also CA 102; CANR 18, 41, 58

**Bromell, Henry** 1947- ........................... CLC **5**
See also CA 53-56; CANR 9

**Bromfield, Louis (Brucker)** 1896-1956 T C L C **11**
See also CA 107; 155; DLB 4, 9, 86

**Broner, E(sther) M(asserman)** 1930- CLC **19**
See also CA 17-20R; CANR 8, 25, 72; DLB 28

**Bronk, William** 1918- ......................... CLC **10**
See also CA 89-92; CANR 23; DLB 165

**Bronstein, Lev Davidovich**
See Trotsky, Leon

**Bronte, Anne** 1820-1849 ................. NCLC **71**
See also DLB 21, 199

**Bronte, Charlotte** 1816-1855 NCLC **3, 8, 33, 58; DA; DAB; DAC; DAM MST, NOV; WLC**
See also AAYA 17; CDBLB 1832-1890; DLB 21, 159, 199

**Bronte, Emily (Jane)** 1818-1848 NCLC **16, 35; DA; DAB; DAC; DAM MST, NOV, POET; PC 8; WLC**
See also AAYA 17; CDBLB 1832-1890; DLB 21, 32, 199

**Brooke, Frances** 1724-1789 ................... LC **6**
See also DLB 39, 99

**Brooke, Henry** 1703(?)-1783 ................. LC **1**
See also DLB 39

**Brooke, Rupert (Chawner)** 1887-1915 T C L C **2, 7; DA; DAB; DAC; DAM MST, POET; PC 24; WLC**
See also CA 104; 132; CANR 61; CDBLB 1914-1945; DLB 19; MTCW 1

**Brooke-Haven, P.**
See Wodehouse, P(elham) G(renville)

**Brooke-Rose, Christine** 1926(?)- ....... CLC **40**
See also CA 13-16R; CANR 58; DLB 14

**Brookner, Anita** 1928- CLC **32, 34, 51; DAB; DAM POP**
See also CA 114; 120; CANR 37, 56; DLB 194; DLBY 87; MTCW 1

**Brooks, Cleanth** 1906-1994 CLC **24, 86, 110**
See also CA 17-20R; 145; CANR 33, 35; DLB 63; DLBY 94; INT CANR-35; MTCW 1

**Brooks, George**
See Baum, L(yman) Frank

**Brooks, Gwendolyn** 1917- CLC **1, 2, 4, 5, 15, 49; BLC 1; DA; DAC; DAM MST, MULT, POET; PC 7; WLC**
See also AAYA 20; BW 2; CA 1-4R; CANR 1, 27, 52; CDALB 1941-1968; CLR 27; DLB 5, 76, 165; MTCW 1; SATA 6

**Brooks, Mel** ......................................... CLC **12**
See also Kaminsky, Melvin
See also AAYA 13; DLB 26

**Brooks, Peter** 1938- ............................ CLC **34**
See also CA 45-48; CANR 1

**Brooks, Van Wyck** 1886-1963 ........... CLC **29**
See also CA 1-4R; CANR 6; DLB 45, 63, 103

**Brophy, Brigid (Antonia)** 1929-1995 CLC **6, 11, 29, 105**
See also CA 5-8R; 149; CAAS 4; CANR 25, 53; DLB 14; MTCW 1

**Brosman, Catharine Savage** 1934- ..... CLC **9**
See also CA 61-64; CANR 21, 46

**Brossard, Chandler** 1922-1993 ....... CLC **115**
See also CA 61-64; 142; CAAS 2; CANR 8, 56; DLB 16

**Brother Antoninus**
See Everson, William (Oliver)

**The Brothers Quay**
See Quay, Stephen; Quay, Timothy

**Broughton, T(homas) Alan** 1936- ..... CLC **19**
See also CA 45-48; CANR 2, 23, 48

**Broumas, Olga** 1949- ..................... CLC **10, 73**
See also CA 85-88; CANR 20, 69

**Brown, Alan** 1950- ............................. CLC **99**
See also CA 156

**Brown, Charles Brockden** 1771-1810 N C L C **22**
See also CDALB 1640-1865; DLB 37, 59, 73

**Brown, Christy** 1932-1981 ................. CLC **63**
See also CA 105; 104; CANR 72; DLB 14

**Brown, Claude** 1937- CLC **30; BLC 1; DAM MULT**
See also AAYA 7; BW 1; CA 73-76

**Brown, Dee (Alexander)** 1908-.. CLC **18, 47; DAM POP**
See also CA 13-16R; CAAS 6; CANR 11, 45, 60; DLBY 80; MTCW 1; SATA 5

**Brown, George**
See Wertmueller, Lina

**Brown, George Douglas** 1869-1902 TCLC **28**
See also CA 162

**Brown, George Mackay** 1921-1996 CLC **5, 48, 100**
See also CA 21-24R; 151; CAAS 6; CANR 12, 37, 67; DLB 14, 27, 139; MTCW 1; SATA 35

**Brown, (William) Larry** 1951- .......... CLC **73**
See also CA 130; 134; INT 133

**Brown, Moses**
See Barrett, William (Christopher)

**Brown, Rita Mae** 1944-CLC **18, 43, 79; DAM NOV, POP**
See also CA 45-48; CANR 2, 11, 35, 62; INT CANR-11; MTCW 1

**Brown, Roderick (Langmere) Haig-**
See Haig-Brown, Roderick (Langmere)

**Brown, Rosellen** 1939- ...................... CLC **32**
See also CA 77-80; CAAS 10; CANR 14, 44

**Brown, Sterling Allen** 1901-1989 CLC **1, 23, 59; BLC 1; DAM MULT, POET**
See also BW 1; CA 85-88; 127; CANR 26; DLB 48, 51, 63; MTCW 1

**Brown, Will**
See Ainsworth, William Harrison

**Brown, William Wells** 1813-1884 ...NCLC **2; BLC 1; DAM MULT; DC 1**
See also DLB 3, 50

**Browne, (Clyde) Jackson** 1948(?)- .... CLC **21**
See also CA 120

**Browning, Elizabeth Barrett** 1806-1861 NCLC **1, 16, 61, 66; DA; DAB; DAC; DAM MST, POET; PC 6; WLC**
See also CDBLB 1832-1890; DLB 32, 199

**Browning, Robert** 1812-1889 NCLC **19; DA; DAB; DAC; DAM MST, POET; PC 2; WLCS**
See also CDBLB 1832-1890; DLB 32, 163; YABC 1

**Browning, Tod** 1882-1962 ................. CLC **16**
See also CA 141; 117

**Brownson, Orestes Augustus** 1803-1876 NCLC **50**
See also DLB 1, 59, 73

**Bruccoli, Matthew J(oseph)** 1931- ... CLC **34**
See also CA 9-12R; CANR 7; DLB 103

**Bruce, Lenny** ................................... CLC **21**
See also Schneider, Leonard Alfred

**Bruin, John**
See Brutus, Dennis

**Brulard, Henri**
See Stendhal

**Brulls, Christian**
See Simenon, Georges (Jacques Christian)

**Brunner, John (Kilian Houston)** 1934-1995

CLC **8, 10; DAM POP**
See also CA 1-4R; 149; CAAS 8; CANR 2, 37; MTCW 1

**Bruno, Giordano** 1548-1600 ................ LC **27**

**Brutus, Dennis** 1924- CLC **43; BLC 1; DAM MULT, POET; PC 24**
See also BW 2; CA 49-52; CAAS 14; CANR 2, 27, 42; DLB 117

**Bryan, C(ourtlandt) D(ixon) B(arnes)** 1936-
CLC **29**
See also CA 73-76; CANR 13, 68; DLB 185; INT CANR-13

**Bryan, Michael**
See Moore, Brian

**Bryant, William Cullen** 1794-1878 . NCLC **6, 46; DA; DAB; DAC; DAM MST, POET; PC 20**
See also CDALB 1640-1865; DLB 3, 43, 59, 189

**Bryusov, Valery Yakovlevich** 1873-1924
TCLC **10**
See also CA 107; 155

**Buchan, John** 1875-1940 ..... TCLC **41; DAB; DAM POP**
See also CA 108; 145; DLB 34, 70, 156; YABC 2

**Buchanan, George** 1506-1582 ................ LC **4**
See also DLB 152

**Buchheim, Lothar-Guenther** 1918- .... CLC **6**
See also CA 85-88

**Buchner, (Karl) Georg** 1813-1837 . NCLC **26**

**Buchwald, Art(hur)** 1925- ................. CLC **33**
See also AITN 1; CA 5-8R; CANR 21, 67; MTCW 1; SATA 10

**Buck, Pearl S(ydenstricker)** 1892-1973 CLC **7, 11, 18; DA; DAB; DAC; DAM MST, NOV**
See also AITN 1; CA 1-4R; 41-44R; CANR 1, 34; DLB 9, 102; MTCW 1; SATA 1, 25

**Buckler, Ernest** 1908-1984 .... CLC **13; DAC; DAM MST**
See also CA 11-12; 114; CAP 1; DLB 68; SATA 47

**Buckley, Vincent (Thomas)** 1925-1988 CLC **57**
See also CA 101

**Buckley, William F(rank), Jr.** 1925-CLC **7, 18, 37; DAM POP**
See also AITN 1; CA 1-4R; CANR 1, 24, 53; DLB 137; DLBY 80; INT CANR-24; MTCW 1

**Buechner, (Carl) Frederick** 1926-CLC **2, 4, 6, 9; DAM NOV**
See also CA 13-16R; CANR 11, 39, 64; DLBY 80; INT CANR-11; MTCW 1

**Buell, John (Edward)** 1927- .............. CLC **10**
See also CA 1-4R; CANR 71; DLB 53

**Buero Vallejo, Antonio** 1916- ..... CLC **15, 46**
See also CA 106; CANR 24, 49; HW; MTCW 1

**Bufalino, Gesualdo** 1920(?)- ............. CLC **74**
See also DLB 196

**Bugayev, Boris Nikolayevich** 1880-1934
TCLC **7; PC 11**
See also Bely, Andrey
See also CA 104; 165

**Bukowski, Charles** 1920-1994 CLC **2, 5, 9, 41, 82, 108; DAM NOV, POET; PC 18**
See also CA 17-20R; 144; CANR 40, 62; DLB 5, 130, 169; MTCW 1

**Bulgakov, Mikhail (Afanas'evich)** 1891-1940
TCLC **2, 16; DAM DRAM, NOV; SSC 18**
See also CA 105; 152

**Bulgya, Alexander Alexandrovich** 1901-1956
TCLC **53**
See also Fadeyev, Alexander
See also CA 117

**Bullins, Ed** 1935- CLC **1, 5, 7; BLC 1; DAM DRAM, MULT; DC 6**

See also BW 2; CA 49-52; CAAS 16; CANR 24, 46; DLB 7, 38; MTCW 1

**Bulwer-Lytton, Edward (George Earle Lytton)** 1803-1873 .............................. **NCLC 1, 45**
See also DLB 21

**Bunin, Ivan Alexeyevich** 1870-1953 **TCLC 6; SSC 5**
See also CA 104

**Bunting, Basil** 1900-1985 ..... **CLC 10, 39, 47; DAM POET**
See also CA 53-56; 115; CANR 7; DLB 20

**Bunuel, Luis** 1900-1983 .. **CLC 16, 80; DAM MULT; HLC**
See also CA 101; 110; CANR 32; HW

**Bunyan, John** 1628-1688 ... **LC 4; DA; DAB; DAC; DAM MST; WLC**
See also CDBLB 1660-1789; DLB 39

**Burckhardt, Jacob (Christoph)** 1818-1897 **NCLC 49**

**Burford, Eleanor**
See Hibbert, Eleanor Alice Burford

**Burgess, Anthony** **CLC 1, 2, 4, 5, 8, 10, 13, 15, 22, 40, 62, 81, 94; DAB**
See also Wilson, John (Anthony) Burgess
See also AAYA 25; AITN 1; CDBLB 1960 to Present; DLB 14, 194

**Burke, Edmund** 1729(?)-1797 **LC 7, 36; DA; DAB; DAC; DAM MST; WLC**
See also DLB 104

**Burke, Kenneth (Duva)** 1897-1993 **CLC 2, 24**
See also CA 5-8R; 143; CANR 39; DLB 45, 63; MTCW 1

**Burke, Leda**
See Garnett, David

**Burke, Ralph**
See Silverberg, Robert

**Burke, Thomas** 1886-1945 .............. **TCLC 63**
See also CA 113; 155; DLB 197

**Burney, Fanny** 1752-1840 ......... **NCLC 12, 54**
See also DLB 39

**Burns, Robert** 1759-1796 ....................... **PC 6**
See also CDBLB 1789-1832; DA; DAB; DAC; DAM MST, POET; DLB 109; WLC

**Burns, Tex**
See L'Amour, Louis (Dearborn)

**Burnshaw, Stanley** 1906- ........ **CLC 3, 13, 44**
See also CA 9-12R; DLB 48; DLBY 97

**Burr, Anne** 1937- .................................. **CLC 6**
See also CA 25-28R

**Burroughs, Edgar Rice** 1875-1950 . **TCLC 2, 32; DAM NOV**
See also AAYA 11; CA 104; 132; DLB 8; MTCW 1; SATA 41

**Burroughs, William S(eward)** 1914-1997 **CLC 1, 2, 5, 15, 22, 42, 75, 109; DA; DAB; DAC; DAM MST, NOV, POP; WLC**
See also AITN 2; CA 9-12R; 160; CANR 20, 52; DLB 2, 8, 16, 152; DLBY 81, 97; MTCW 1

**Burton, Richard F.** 1821-1890 ....... **NCLC 42**
See also DLB 55, 184

**Busch, Frederick** 1941- ..... **CLC 7, 10, 18, 47**
See also CA 33-36R; CAAS 1; CANR 45; DLB 6

**Bush, Ronald** 1946- ............................ **CLC 34**
See also CA 136

**Bustos, F(rancisco)**
See Borges, Jorge Luis

**Bustos Domecq, H(onorio)**
See Bioy Casares, Adolfo; Borges, Jorge Luis

**Butler, Octavia E(stelle)** 1947- **CLC 38; BLCS; DAM MULT, POP**
See also AAYA 18; BW 2; CA 73-76; CANR 12, 24, 38; DLB 33; MTCW 1; SATA 84

**Butler, Robert Olen (Jr.)** 1945- **CLC 81; DAM POP**
See also CA 112; CANR 66; DLB 173; INT 112

**Butler, Samuel** 1612-1680 .............. **LC 16, 43**
See also DLB 101, 126

**Butler, Samuel** 1835-1902 . **TCLC 1, 33; DA; DAB; DAC; DAM MST, NOV; WLC**
See also CA 143; CDBLB 1890-1914; DLB 18, 57, 174

**Butler, Walter C.**
See Faust, Frederick (Schiller)

**Butor, Michel (Marie Francois)** 1926- **CLC 1, 3, 8, 11, 15**
See also CA 9-12R; CANR 33, 66; DLB 83; MTCW 1

**Butts, Mary** 1892(?)-1937 ............... **TCLC 77**
See also CA 148

**Buzo, Alexander (John)** 1944- .......... **CLC 61**
See also CA 97-100; CANR 17, 39, 69

**Buzzati, Dino** 1906-1972 ................... **CLC 36**
See also CA 160; 33-36R; DLB 177

**Byars, Betsy (Cromer)** 1928- ............. **CLC 35**
See also AAYA 19; CA 33-36R; CANR 18, 36, 57; CLR 1, 16; DLB 52; INT CANR-18; JRDA; MAICYA; MTCW 1; SAAS 1; SATA 4, 46, 80

**Byatt, A(ntonia) S(usan Drabble)** 1936- **C L C 19, 65; DAM NOV, POP**
See also CA 13-16R; CANR 13, 33, 50; DLB 14, 194; MTCW 1

**Byrne, David** 1952- .............................. **CLC 26**
See also CA 127

**Byrne, John Keyes** 1926-
See Leonard, Hugh
See also CA 102; INT 102

**Byron, George Gordon (Noel)** 1788-1824 **NCLC 2, 12; DA; DAB; DAC; DAM MST, POET; PC 16; WLC**
See also CDBLB 1789-1832; DLB 96, 110

**Byron, Robert** 1905-1941 ............... **TCLC 67**
See also CA 160; DLB 195

**C. 3. 3.**
See Wilde, Oscar (Fingal O'Flahertie Wills)

**Caballero, Fernan** 1796-1877 ........ **NCLC 10**

**Cabell, Branch**
See Cabell, James Branch

**Cabell, James Branch** 1879-1958 .... **TCLC 6**
See also CA 105; 152; DLB 9, 78

**Cable, George Washington** 1844-1925 **T C L C 4; SSC 4**
See also CA 104; 155; DLB 12, 74; DLBD 13

**Cabral de Melo Neto, Joao** 1920- ... **CLC 76; DAM MULT**
See also CA 151

**Cabrera Infante, G(uillermo)** 1929- **CLC 5, 25, 45; DAM MULT; HLC**
See also CA 85-88; CANR 29, 65; DLB 113; HW; MTCW 1

**Cade, Toni**
See Bambara, Toni Cade

**Cadmus and Harmonia**
See Buchan, John

**Caedmon** fl. 658-680 ........................ **CMLC 7**
See also DLB 146

**Caeiro, Alberto**
See Pessoa, Fernando (Antonio Nogueira)

**Cage, John (Milton, Jr.)** 1912-1992 .. **CLC 41**
See also CA 13-16R; CANR 9; DLB 193; INT CANR-9

**Cahan, Abraham** 1860-1951 .......... **TCLC 71**
See also CA 108; 154; DLB 9, 25, 28

**Cain, G.**
See Cabrera Infante, G(uillermo)

**Cain, Guillermo**
See Cabrera Infante, G(uillermo)

**Cain, James M(allahan)** 1892-1977 **CLC 3, 11, 28**
See also AITN 1; CA 17-20R; 73-76; CANR 8, 34, 61; MTCW 1

**Caine, Mark**

See Raphael, Frederic (Michael)

**Calasso, Roberto** 1941- ...................... **CLC 81**
See also CA 143

**Calderon de la Barca, Pedro** 1600-1681 .. **L C 23; DC 3**

**Caldwell, Erskine (Preston)** 1903-1987 **CLC 1, 8, 14, 50, 60; DAM NOV; SSC 19**
See also AITN 1; CA 1-4R; 121; CAAS 1; CANR 2, 33; DLB 9, 86; MTCW 1

**Caldwell, (Janet Miriam) Taylor (Holland)** 1900-1985 ......................................................... **CLC 2, 28, 39; DAM NOV, POP**
See also CA 5-8R; 116; CANR 5; DLBD 17

**Calhoun, John Caldwell** 1782-1850 **NCLC 15**
See also DLB 3

**Calisher, Hortense** 1911- **CLC 2, 4, 8, 38; DAM NOV; SSC 15**
See also CA 1-4R; CANR 1, 22, 67; DLB 2; INT CANR-22; MTCW 1

**Callaghan, Morley Edward** 1903-1990 **CLC 3, 14, 41, 65; DAC; DAM MST**
See also CA 9-12R; 132; CANR 33; DLB 68; MTCW 1

**Callimachus** c. 305B.C.-c. 240B.C. **CMLC 18**
See also DLB 176

**Calvin, John** 1509-1564 ....................... **LC 37**

**Calvino, Italo** 1923-1985 **CLC 5, 8, 11, 22, 33, 39, 73; DAM NOV; SSC 3**
See also CA 85-88; 116; CANR 23, 61; DLB 196; MTCW 1

**Cameron, Carey** 1952- ....................... **CLC 59**
See also CA 135

**Cameron, Peter** 1959- ......................... **CLC 44**
See also CA 125; CANR 50

**Campana, Dino** 1885-1932 ............. **TCLC 20**
See also CA 117; DLB 114

**Campanella, Tommaso** 1568-1639 ....... **LC 32**

**Campbell, John W(ood, Jr.)** 1910-1971 **C L C 32**
See also CA 21-22; 29-32R; CANR 34; CAP 2; DLB 8; MTCW 1

**Campbell, Joseph** 1904-1987 ............. **CLC 69**
See also AAYA 3; BEST 89:2; CA 1-4R; 124; CANR 3, 28, 61; MTCW 1

**Campbell, Maria** 1940- ........... **CLC 85; DAC**
See also CA 102; CANR 54; NNAL

**Campbell, (John) Ramsey** 1946- **CLC 42; SSC 19**
See also CA 57-60; CANR 7; INT CANR-7

**Campbell, (Ignatius) Roy (Dunnachie)** 1901-1957 ............................................................ **TCLC 5**
See also CA 104; 155; DLB 20

**Campbell, Thomas** 1777-1844 ........ **NCLC 19**
See also DLB 93; 144

**Campbell, Wilfred** ............................... **TCLC 9**
See also Campbell, William

**Campbell, William** 1858(?)-1918
See Campbell, Wilfred
See also CA 106; DLB 92

**Campion, Jane** ...................................... **CLC 95**
See also CA 138

**Campos, Alvaro de**
See Pessoa, Fernando (Antonio Nogueira)

**Camus, Albert** 1913-1960 **CLC 1, 2, 4, 9, 11, 14, 32, 63, 69; DA; DAB; DAC; DAM DRAM, MST, NOV; DC 2; SSC 9; WLC**
See also CA 89-92; DLB 72; MTCW 1

**Canby, Vincent** 1924- ......................... **CLC 13**
See also CA 81-84

**Cancale**
See Desnos, Robert

**Canetti, Elias** 1905-1994 **CLC 3, 14, 25, 75, 86**
See also CA 21-24R; 146; CANR 23, 61; DLB 85, 124; MTCW 1

**Canin, Ethan** 1960- ............................. **CLC 55**
See also CA 131; 135

**Cannon, Curt**

**Author Index**

Clancy, Thomas L., Jr.  1947-
See Clancy, Tom
See also CA 125; 131; CANR 62; INT 131;
MTCW 1
Clancy, Tom .. CLC 45, 112; DAM NOV, POP
See also Clancy, Thomas L., Jr.
See also AAYA 9; BEST 89:1, 90:1
Clare, John  1793-1864 NCLC 9; DAB; DAM
POET; PC 23
See also DLB 55, 96
Clarin
See Alas (y Urena), Leopoldo (Enrique Garcia)
Clark, Al C.
See Goines, Donald
Clark, (Robert) Brian  1932- ............... CLC 29
See also CA 41-44R; CANR 67
Clark, Curt
See Westlake, Donald E(dwin)
Clark, Eleanor  1913-1996 ............. CLC 5, 19
See also CA 9-12R; 151; CANR 41; DLB 6
Clark, J. P.
See Clark, John Pepper
See also DLB 117
Clark, John Pepper  1935-.. CLC 38; BLC 1;
DAM DRAM, MULT; DC 5
See also Clark, J. P.
See also BW 1; CA 65-68; CANR 16, 72
Clark, M. R.
See Clark, Mavis Thorpe
Clark, Mavis Thorpe  1909- ............... CLC 12
See also CA 57-60; CANR 8, 37; CLR 30;
MAICYA; SAAS 5; SATA 8, 74
Clark, Walter Van Tilburg  1909-1971CLC 28
See also CA 9-12R; 33-36R; CANR 63; DLB
9; SATA 8
Clark Bekederemo, J(ohnson) P(epper)
See Clark, John Pepper
Clarke, Arthur C(harles)  1917-CLC 1, 4, 13,
18, 35; DAM POP; SSC 3
See also AAYA 4; CA 1-4R; CANR 2, 28, 55;
JRDA; MAICYA; MTCW 1; SATA 13, 70
Clarke, Austin  1896-1974 .... CLC 6, 9; DAM
POET
See also CA 29-32; 49-52; CAP 2; DLB 10, 20
Clarke, Austin C(hesterfield)  1934-CLC 8, 53;
BLC 1; DAC; DAM MULT
See also BW 1; CA 25-28R; CAAS 16; CANR
14, 32, 68; DLB 53, 125
Clarke, Gillian  1937- ................... CLC 61
See also CA 106; DLB 40
Clarke, Marcus (Andrew Hislop)  1846-1881
NCLC 19
Clarke, Shirley  1925- ...................... CLC 16
Clash, The
See Headon, (Nicky) Topper; Jones, Mick;
Simonon, Paul; Strummer, Joe
Claudel, Paul (Louis Charles Marie)  1868-1955
TCLC 2, 10
See also CA 104; 165; DLB 192
Clavell, James (duMaresq)  1925-1994CLC 6,
25, 87; DAM NOV, POP
See also CA 25-28R; 146; CANR 26, 48;
MTCW 1
Cleaver, (Leroy) Eldridge  1935-1998CLC 30;
BLC 1; DAM MULT
See also BW 1; CA 21-24R; 167; CANR 16
Cleese, John (Marwood)  1939- ......... CLC 21
See also Monty Python
See also CA 112; 116; CANR 35; MTCW 1
Cleishbotham, Jebediah
See Scott, Walter
Cleland, John  1710-1789 ........................ LC 2
See also DLB 39
Clemens, Samuel Langhorne  1835-1910
See Twain, Mark
See also CA 104; 135; CDALB 1865-1917; DA;
DAB; DAC; DAM MST, NOV; DLB 11, 12,

23, 64, 74, 186, 189; JRDA; MAICYA; SATA
100; YABC 2
Cleophil
See Congreve, William
Clerihew, E.
See Bentley, E(dmund) C(lerihew)
Clerk, N. W.
See Lewis, C(live) S(taples)
Cliff, Jimmy ....................................... CLC 21
See also Chambers, James
Clifton, (Thelma) Lucille  1936- CLC 19, 66;
BLC 1; DAM MULT, POET; PC 17
See also BW 2; CA 49-52; CANR 2, 24, 42;
CLR 5; DLB 5, 41; MAICYA; MTCW 1;
SATA 20, 69
Clinton, Dirk
See Silverberg, Robert
Clough, Arthur Hugh  1819-1861 ... NCLC 27
See also DLB 32
Clutha, Janet Paterson Frame  1924-
See Frame, Janet
See also CA 1-4R; CANR 2, 36; MTCW 1
Clyne, Terence
See Blatty, William Peter
Cobalt, Martin
See Mayne, William (James Carter)
Cobb, Irvin S.  1876-1944 ................ TCLC 77
See also DLB 11, 25, 86
Cobbett, William  1763-1835 ........... NCLC 49
See also DLB 43, 107, 158
Coburn, D(onald) L(ee)  1938- ........... CLC 10
See also CA 89-92
Cocteau, Jean (Maurice Eugene Clement)  1889-
1963 .............................................................
CLC 1, 8, 15, 16, 43; DA; DAB; DAC; DAM
DRAM, MST, NOV; WLC
See also CA 25-28; CANR 40; CAP 2; DLB
65; MTCW 1
Codrescu, Andrei  1946-CLC 46; DAM POET
See also CA 33-36R; CAAS 19; CANR 13, 34,
53
Coe, Max
See Bourne, Randolph S(illiman)
Coe, Tucker
See Westlake, Donald E(dwin)
Coen, Ethan  1958- ........................... CLC 108
See also CA 126
Coen, Joel  1955- .............................. CLC 108
See also CA 126
The Coen Brothers
See Coen, Ethan; Coen, Joel
Coetzee, J(ohn) M(ichael)  1940- CLC 23, 33,
66; DAM NOV
See also CA 77-80; CANR 41, 54; MTCW 1
Coffey, Brian
See Koontz, Dean R(ay)
Cohan, George M(ichael)  1878-1942TCLC 60
See also CA 157
Cohen, Arthur A(llen)  1928-1986 . CLC 7, 31
See also CA 1-4R; 120; CANR 1, 17, 42; DLB
28
Cohen, Leonard (Norman)  1934- CLC 3, 38;
DAC; DAM MST
See also CA 21-24R; CANR 14, 69; DLB 53;
MTCW 1
Cohen, Matt  1942- .................... CLC 19; DAC
See also CA 61-64; CAAS 18; CANR 40; DLB
53
Cohen-Solal, Annie  19(?)- ................. CLC 50
Colegate, Isabel  1931- ...................... CLC 36
See also CA 17-20R; CANR 8, 22; DLB 14;
INT CANR-22; MTCW 1
Coleman, Emmett
See Reed, Ishmael
Coleridge, M. E.
See Coleridge, Mary E(lizabeth)
Coleridge, Mary E(lizabeth)  1861-1907TCLC

73
See also CA 116; 166; DLB 19, 98
Coleridge, Samuel Taylor  1772-1834NCLC 9,
54; DA; DAB; DAC; DAM MST, POET;
PC 11; WLC
See also CDBLB 1789-1832; DLB 93, 107
Coleridge, Sara  1802-1852 ............. NCLC 31
See also DLB 199
Coles, Don  1928- ............................... CLC 46
See also CA 115; CANR 38
Coles, Robert (Martin)  1929- .......... CLC 108
See also CA 45-48; CANR 3, 32, 66, 70; INT
CANR-32; SATA 23
Colette, (Sidonie-Gabrielle)  1873-1954T CL C
1, 5, 16; DAM NOV; SSC 10
See also CA 104; 131; DLB 65; MTCW 1
Collett, (Jacobine) Camilla (Wergeland)  1813-
1895 ................................................................
NCLC 22
Collier, Christopher  1930- ................. CLC 30
See also AAYA 13; CA 33-36R; CANR 13, 33;
JRDA; MAICYA; SATA 16, 70
Collier, James L(incoln)  1928-CLC 30; DAM
POP
See also AAYA 13; CA 9-12R; CANR 4, 33,
60; CLR 3; JRDA; MAICYA; SAAS 21;
SATA 8, 70
Collier, Jeremy  1650-1726 ..................... LC 6
Collier, John  1901-1980 ..................... SSC 19
See also CA 65-68; 97-100; CANR 10; DLB
77
Collingwood, R(obin) G(eorge)  1889(?)-1943
TCLC 67
See also CA 117; 155
Collins, Hunt
See Hunter, Evan
Collins, Linda  1931- .......................... CLC 44
See also CA 125
Collins, (William) Wilkie  1824-1889NCLC 1,
18
See also CDBLB 1832-1890; DLB 18, 70, 159
Collins, William  1721-1759 . LC 4, 40; DAM
POET
See also DLB 109
Collodi, Carlo  1826-1890 ................. NCLC 54
See also Lorenzini, Carlo
See also CLR 5
Colman, George  1732-1794
See Glassco, John
Colt, Winchester Remington
See Hubbard, L(afayette) Ron(ald)
Colter, Cyrus  1910- .......................... CLC 58
See also BW 1; CA 65-68; CANR 10, 66; DLB
33
Colton, James
See Hansen, Joseph
Colum, Padraic  1881-1972 ................ CLC 28
See also CA 73-76; 33-36R; CANR 35; CLR
36; MAICYA; MTCW 1; SATA 15
Colvin, James
See Moorcock, Michael (John)
Colwin, Laurie (E.)  1944-1992CLC 5, 13, 23,
84
See also CA 89-92; 139; CANR 20, 46; DLBY
80; MTCW 1
Comfort, Alex(ander)  1920-CLC 7; DAM POP
See also CA 1-4R; CANR 1, 45
Comfort, Montgomery
See Campbell, (John) Ramsey
Compton-Burnett, I(vy)  1884(?)-1969CLC 1,
3, 10, 15, 34; DAM NOV
See also CA 1-4R; 25-28R; CANR 4; DLB 36;
MTCW 1
Comstock, Anthony  1844-1915 ...... TCLC 13
See also CA 110
Comte, Auguste  1798-1857 ............. NCLC 54
Conan Doyle, Arthur

**Dove, Rita (Frances)** 1952-CLC 50, 81; BLCS; DAM MULT, POET; PC 6
   See also BW 2; CA 109; CAAS 19; CANR 27, 42, 68; DLB 120
**Doveglion**
   See Villa, Jose Garcia
**Dowell, Coleman** 1925-1985 ............. CLC 60
   See also CA 25-28R; 117; CANR 10; DLB 130
**Dowson, Ernest (Christopher)** 1867-1900 TCLC 4
   See also CA 105; 150; DLB 19, 135
**Doyle, A. Conan**
   See Doyle, Arthur Conan
**Doyle, Arthur Conan** 1859-1930TCLC 7; DA; DAB; DAC; DAM MST, NOV; SSC 12; WLC
   See also AAYA 14; CA 104; 122; CDBLB 1890-1914; DLB 18, 70, 156, 178; MTCW 1; SATA 24
**Doyle, Conan**
   See Doyle, Arthur Conan
**Doyle, John**
   See Graves, Robert (von Ranke)
**Doyle, Roddy** 1958(?)- ........................ CLC 81
   See also AAYA 14; CA 143; DLB 194
**Doyle, Sir A. Conan**
   See Doyle, Arthur Conan
**Doyle, Sir Arthur Conan**
   See Doyle, Arthur Conan
**Dr. A**
   See Asimov, Isaac; Silverstein, Alvin
**Drabble, Margaret** 1939-CLC 2, 3, 5, 8, 10, 22, 53; DAB; DAC; DAM MST, NOV, POP
   See also CA 13-16R; CANR 18, 35, 63; CDBLB 1960 to Present; DLB 14, 155; MTCW 1; SATA 48
**Drapier, M. B.**
   See Swift, Jonathan
**Drayham, James**
   See Mencken, H(enry) L(ouis)
**Drayton, Michael** 1563-1631 ...... LC 8; DAM POET
   See also DLB 121
**Dreadstone, Carl**
   See Campbell, (John) Ramsey
**Dreiser, Theodore (Herman Albert)** 1871-1945 TCLC 10, 18, 35, 83; DA; DAC; DAM MST, NOV; SSC 30
   See also CA 106; 132; CDALB 1865-1917; DLB 9, 12, 102, 137; DLBD 1; MTCW 1
**Drexler, Rosalyn** 1926- ..................... CLC 2, 6
   See also CA 81-84; CANR 68
**Dreyer, Carl Theodor** 1889-1968 ...... CLC 16
   See also CA 116
**Drieu la Rochelle, Pierre(-Eugene)** 1893-1945 TCLC 21
   See also CA 117; DLB 72
**Drinkwater, John** 1882-1937 .......... TCLC 57
   See also CA 109; 149; DLB 10, 19, 149
**Drop Shot**
   See Cable, George Washington
**Droste-Hulshoff, Annette Freiin von** 1797-1848 NCLC 3
   See also DLB 133
**Drummond, Walter**
   See Silverberg, Robert
**Drummond, William Henry** 1854-1907T CLC 25
   See also CA 160; DLB 92
**Drummond de Andrade, Carlos** 1902-1987 CLC 18
   See also Andrade, Carlos Drummond de
   See also CA 132; 123
**Drury, Allen (Stuart)** 1918- ............... CLC 37
   See also CA 57-60; CANR 18, 52; INT CANR-18
**Dryden, John** 1631-1700LC 3, 21; DA; DAB;

DAC; DAM DRAM, MST, POET; DC 3; WLC
   See also CDBLB 1660-1789; DLB 80, 101, 131
**Duberman, Martin (Bauml)** 1930- ..... CLC 8
   See also CA 1-4R; CANR 2, 63
**Dubie, Norman (Evans)** 1945- ........... CLC 36
   See also CA 69-72; CANR 12; DLB 120
**Du Bois, W(illiam) E(dward) B(urghardt)** 1868-1963 ......................................................
CLC 1, 2, 13, 64, 96; BLC 1; DA; DAC; DAM MST, MULT, NOV; WLC
   See also BW 1; CA 85-88; CANR 34; CDALB 1865-1917; DLB 47, 50, 91; MTCW 1; SATA 42
**Dubus, Andre** 1936- CLC 13, 36, 97; SSC 15
   See also CA 21-24R; CANR 17; DLB 130; INT CANR-17
**Duca Minimo**
   See D'Annunzio, Gabriele
**Ducharme, Rejean** 1941- ................... CLC 74
   See also CA 165; DLB 60
**Duclos, Charles Pinot** 1704-1772 ........... LC 1
**Dudek, Louis** 1918- ................... CLC 11, 19
   See also CA 45-48; CAAS 14; CANR 1; DLB 88
**Duerrenmatt, Friedrich** 1921-1990CLC 1, 4, 8, 11, 15, 43, 102; DAM DRAM
   See also CA 17-20R; CANR 33; DLB 69, 124; MTCW 1
**Duffy, Bruce** (?)- ................................ CLC 50
**Duffy, Maureen** 1933- ......................... CLC 37
   See also CA 25-28R; CANR 33, 68; DLB 14; MTCW 1
**Dugan, Alan** 1923- ............................. CLC 2, 6
   See also CA 81-84; DLB 5
**du Gard, Roger Martin**
   See Martin du Gard, Roger
**Duhamel, Georges** 1884-1966 ............. CLC 8
   See also CA 81-84; 25-28R; CANR 35; DLB 65; MTCW 1
**Dujardin, Edouard (Emile Louis)** 1861-1949 TCLC 13
   See also CA 109; DLB 123
**Dulles, John Foster** 1888-1959 ....... TCLC 72
   See also CA 115; 149
**Dumas, Alexandre (pere)**
   See Dumas, Alexandre (Davy de la Pailleterie)
**Dumas, Alexandre (Davy de la Pailleterie)** 1802-1870 ...................................................
NCLC 11; DA; DAB; DAC; DAM MST, NOV; WLC
   See also DLB 119, 192; SATA 18
**Dumas, Alexandre (fils)** 1824-1895NCLC 71; DC 1
   See also AAYA 22; DLB 192
**Dumas, Claudine**
   See Malzberg, Barry N(athaniel)
**Dumas, Henry L.** 1934-1968 ......... CLC 6, 62
   See also BW 1; CA 85-88; DLB 41
**du Maurier, Daphne** 1907-1989CLC 6, 11, 59; DAB; DAC; DAM MST, POP; SSC 18
   See also CA 5-8R; 128; CANR 6, 55; DLB 191; MTCW 1; SATA 27; SATA-Obit 60
**Dunbar, Paul Laurence** 1872-1906 . TCLC 2, 12; BLC 1; DA; DAC; DAM MST, MULT, POET; PC 5; SSC 8; WLC
   See also BW 1; CA 104; 124; CDALB 1865-1917; DLB 50, 54, 78; SATA 34
**Dunbar, William** 1460(?)-1530(?) ........ LC 20
   See also DLB 132, 146
**Duncan, Dora Angela**
   See Duncan, Isadora
**Duncan, Isadora** 1877(?)-1927 ....... TCLC 68
   See also CA 118; 149
**Duncan, Lois** 1934- ............................. CLC 26
   See also AAYA 4; CA 1-4R; CANR 2, 23, 36; CLR 29; JRDA; MAICYA; SAAS 2; SATA

1, 36, 75
**Duncan, Robert (Edward)** 1919-1988CLC 1, 2, 4, 7, 15, 41, 55; DAM POET; PC 2
   See also CA 9-12R; 124; CANR 28, 62; DLB 5, 16, 193; MTCW 1
**Duncan, Sara Jeannette** 1861-1922 TCLC 60
   See also CA 157; DLB 92
**Dunlap, William** 1766-1839 ............. NCLC 2
   See also DLB 30, 37, 59
**Dunn, Douglas (Eaglesham)** 1942- CLC 6, 40
   See also CA 45-48; CANR 2, 33; DLB 40; MTCW 1
**Dunn, Katherine (Karen)** 1945- ........ CLC 71
   See also CA 33-36R; CANR 72
**Dunn, Stephen** 1939- ......................... CLC 36
   See also CA 33-36R; CANR 12, 48, 53; DLB 105
**Dunne, Finley Peter** 1867-1936 ...... TCLC 28
   See also CA 108; DLB 11, 23
**Dunne, John Gregory** 1932- ............. CLC 28
   See also CA 25-28R; CANR 14, 50; DLBY 80
**Dunsany, Edward John Moreton Drax Plunkett** 1878-1957
   See Dunsany, Lord
   See also CA 104; 148; DLB 10
**Dunsany, Lord** ............................... TCLC 2, 59
   See also Dunsany, Edward John Moreton Drax Plunkett
   See also DLB 77, 153, 156
**du Perry, Jean**
   See Simenon, Georges (Jacques Christian)
**Durang, Christopher (Ferdinand)** 1949-C L C 27, 38
   See also CA 105; CANR 50
**Duras, Marguerite** 1914-1996CLC 3, 6, 11, 20, 34, 40, 68, 100
   See also CA 25-28R; 151; CANR 50; DLB 83; MTCW 1
**Durban, (Rosa) Pam** 1947- ................ CLC 39
   See also CA 123
**Durcan, Paul** 1944-CLC 43, 70; DAM POET
   See also CA 134
**Durkheim, Emile** 1858-1917 ........... TCLC 55
**Durrell, Lawrence (George)** 1912-1990 C L C 1, 4, 6, 8, 13, 27, 41; DAM NOV
   See also CA 9-12R; 132; CANR 40; CDBLB 1945-1960; DLB 15, 27; DLBY 90; MTCW 1
**Durrenmatt, Friedrich**
   See Duerrenmatt, Friedrich
**Dutt, Toru** 1856-1877 ...................... NCLC 29
**Dwight, Timothy** 1752-1817 ........... NCLC 13
   See also DLB 37
**Dworkin, Andrea** 1946- ..................... CLC 43
   See also CA 77-80; CAAS 21; CANR 16, 39; INT CANR-16; MTCW 1
**Dwyer, Deanna**
   See Koontz, Dean R(ay)
**Dwyer, K. R.**
   See Koontz, Dean R(ay)
**Dwyer, Thomas A.** 1923- ................. CLC 114
   See also CA 115
**Dye, Richard**
   See De Voto, Bernard (Augustine)
**Dylan, Bob** 1941- ............. CLC 3, 4, 6, 12, 77
   See also CA 41-44R; DLB 16
**Eagleton, Terence (Francis)** 1943-
   See Eagleton, Terry
   See also CA 57-60; CANR 7, 23, 68; MTCW 1
**Eagleton, Terry** ................................... CLC 63
   See also Eagleton, Terence (Francis)
**Early, Jack**
   See Scoppettone, Sandra
**East, Michael**
   See West, Morris L(anglo)
**Eastaway, Edward**
   See Thomas, (Philip) Edward

**Feldman, Irving (Mordecai)** 1928- ..... **CLC 7**
See also CA 1-4R; CANR 1; DLB 169
**Felix-Tchicaya, Gerald**
See Tchicaya, Gerald Felix
**Fellini, Federico** 1920-1993 ........ **CLC 16, 85**
See also CA 65-68; 143; CANR 33
**Felsen, Henry Gregor** 1916- .............. **CLC 17**
See also CA 1-4R; CANR 1; SAAS 2; SATA 1
**Fenno, Jack**
See Calisher, Hortense
**Fenton, James Martin** 1949- ............. **CLC 32**
See also CA 102; DLB 40
**Ferber, Edna** 1887-1968 .............. **CLC 18, 93**
See also AITN 1; CA 5-8R; 25-28R; CANR 68;
DLB 9, 28, 86; MTCW 1; SATA 7
**Ferguson, Helen**
See Kavan, Anna
**Ferguson, Samuel** 1810-1886 ......... **NCLC 33**
See also DLB 32
**Fergusson, Robert** 1750-1774 .............. **LC 29**
See also DLB 109
**Ferling, Lawrence**
See Ferlinghetti, Lawrence (Monsanto)
**Ferlinghetti, Lawrence (Monsanto)** 1919(?)-
**CLC 2, 6, 10, 27, 111; DAM POET; PC 1**
See also CA 5-8R; CANR 3, 41; CDALB 1941-
1968; DLB 5, 16; MTCW 1
**Fernandez, Vicente Garcia Huidobro**
See Huidobro Fernandez, Vicente Garcia
**Ferrer, Gabriel (Francisco Victor) Miro**
See Miro (Ferrer), Gabriel (Francisco Victor)
**Ferrier, Susan (Edmonstone)** 1782-1854
**NCLC 8**
See also DLB 116
**Ferrigno, Robert** 1948(?)- .................. **CLC 65**
See also CA 140
**Ferron, Jacques** 1921-1985 .... **CLC 94; DAC**
See also CA 117; 129; DLB 60
**Feuchtwanger, Lion** 1884-1958 ........ **TCLC 3**
See also CA 104; DLB 66
**Feuillet, Octave** 1821-1890 ............. **NCLC 45**
See also DLB 192
**Feydeau, Georges (Leon Jules Marie)** 1862-
1921 .................. **TCLC 22; DAM DRAM**
See also CA 113; 152; DLB 192
**Fichte, Johann Gottlieb** 1762-1814 **NCLC 62**
See also DLB 90
**Ficino, Marsilio** 1433-1499 .................. **LC 12**
**Fiedeler, Hans**
See Doeblin, Alfred
**Fiedler, Leslie A(aron)** 1917- . **CLC 4, 13, 24**
See also CA 9-12R; CANR 7, 63; DLB 28, 67;
MTCW 1
**Field, Andrew** 1938- ........................... **CLC 44**
See also CA 97-100; CANR 25
**Field, Eugene** 1850-1895 .................. **NCLC 3**
See also DLB 23, 42, 140; DLBD 13; MAICYA;
SATA 16
**Field, Gans T.**
See Wellman, Manly Wade
**Field, Michael** 1915-1971 ............... **TCLC 43**
See also CA 29-32R
**Field, Peter**
See Hobson, Laura Z(ametkin)
**Fielding, Henry** 1707-1754 **LC 1; DA; DAB;**
**DAC; DAM DRAM, MST, NOV; WLC**
See also CDBLB 1660-1789; DLB 39, 84, 101
**Fielding, Sarah** 1710-1768 .............. **LC 1, 44**
See also DLB 39
**Fields, W. C.** 1880-1946 .................. **TCLC 80**
See also DLB 44
**Fierstein, Harvey (Forbes)** 1954- ... **CLC 33;**
**DAM DRAM, POP**
See also CA 123; 129
**Figes, Eva** 1932- .................................. **CLC 31**
See also CA 53-56; CANR 4, 44; DLB 14
**Finch, Anne** 1661-1720 ............. **LC 3; PC 21**

See also DLB 95
**Finch, Robert (Duer Claydon)** 1900- **CLC 18**
See also CA 57-60; CANR 9, 24, 49; DLB 88
**Findley, Timothy** 1930- . **CLC 27, 102; DAC;**
**DAM MST**
See also CA 25-28R; CANR 12, 42, 69; DLB
53
**Fink, William**
See Mencken, H(enry) L(ouis)
**Firbank, Louis** 1942-
See Reed, Lou
See also CA 117
**Firbank, (Arthur Annesley) Ronald** 1886-1926
**TCLC 1**
See also CA 104; DLB 36
**Fisher, M(ary) F(rances) K(ennedy)** 1908-1992
**CLC 76, 87**
See also CA 77-80; 138; CANR 44
**Fisher, Roy** 1930- ............................... **CLC 25**
See also CA 81-84; CAAS 10; CANR 16; DLB
40
**Fisher, Rudolph** 1897-1934 **TCLC 11; BLC 2;**
**DAM MULT; SSC 25**
See also BW 1; CA 107; 124; DLB 51, 102
**Fisher, Vardis (Alvero)** 1895-1968 ...... **CLC 7**
See also CA 5-8R; 25-28R; CANR 68; DLB 9
**Fiske, Tarleton**
See Bloch, Robert (Albert)
**Fitch, Clarke**
See Sinclair, Upton (Beall)
**Fitch, John IV**
See Cormier, Robert (Edmund)
**Fitzgerald, Captain Hugh**
See Baum, L(yman) Frank
**FitzGerald, Edward** 1809-1883 ....... **NCLC 9**
See also DLB 32
**Fitzgerald, F(rancis) Scott (Key)** 1896-1940
**TCLC 1, 6, 14, 28, 55; DA; DAB; DAC;**
**DAM MST, NOV; SSC 6, 31; WLC**
See also AAYA 24; AITN 1; CA 110; 123;
CDALB 1917-1929; DLB 4, 9, 86; DLBD 1,
15, 16; DLBY 81, 96; MTCW 1
**Fitzgerald, Penelope** 1916- ... **CLC 19, 51, 61**
See also CA 85-88; CAAS 10; CANR 56; DLB
14, 194
**Fitzgerald, Robert (Stuart)** 1910-1985 **CLC 39**
See also CA 1-4R; 114; CANR 1; DLBY 80
**FitzGerald, Robert D(avid)** 1902-1987 **CLC 19**
See also CA 17-20R
**Fitzgerald, Zelda (Sayre)** 1900-1948 **TCLC 52**
See also CA 117; 126; DLBY 84
**Flanagan, Thomas (James Bonner)** 1923-
**CLC 25, 52**
See also CA 108; CANR 55; DLBY 80; INT
108; MTCW 1
**Flaubert, Gustave** 1821-1880 **NCLC 2, 10, 19,**
**62, 66; DA; DAB; DAC; DAM MST, NOV;**
**SSC 11; WLC**
See also DLB 119
**Flecker, Herman Elroy**
See Flecker, (Herman) James Elroy
**Flecker, (Herman) James Elroy** 1884-1915
**TCLC 43**
See also CA 109; 150; DLB 10, 19
**Fleming, Ian (Lancaster)** 1908-1964 . **CLC 3,**
**30; DAM POP**
See also AAYA 26; CA 5-8R; CANR 59;
CDBLB 1945-1960; DLB 87, 201; MTCW
1; SATA 9
**Fleming, Thomas (James)** 1927- ....... **CLC 37**
See also CA 5-8R; CANR 10; INT CANR-10;
SATA 8
**Fletcher, John** 1579-1625 .......... **LC 33; DC 6**
See also CDBLB Before 1660; DLB 58
**Fletcher, John Gould** 1886-1950 .... **TCLC 35**
See also CA 107; 167; DLB 4, 45
**Fleur, Paul**

See Pohl, Frederik
**Flooglebuckle, Al**
See Spiegelman, Art
**Flying Officer X**
See Bates, H(erbert) E(rnest)
**Fo, Dario** 1926- . **CLC 32, 109; DAM DRAM**
See also CA 116; 128; CANR 68; DLBY 97;
MTCW 1
**Fogarty, Jonathan Titulescu Esq.**
See Farrell, James T(homas)
**Folke, Will**
See Bloch, Robert (Albert)
**Follett, Ken(neth Martin)** 1949- ..... **CLC 18;**
**DAM NOV, POP**
See also AAYA 6; BEST 89:4; CA 81-84; CANR
13, 33, 54; DLB 87; DLBY 81; INT CANR-
33; MTCW 1
**Fontane, Theodor** 1819-1898 ......... **NCLC 26**
See also DLB 129
**Foote, Horton** 1916- **CLC 51, 91; DAM DRAM**
See also CA 73-76; CANR 34, 51; DLB 26; INT
CANR-34
**Foote, Shelby** 1916- **CLC 75; DAM NOV, POP**
See also CA 5-8R; CANR 3, 45; DLB 2, 17
**Forbes, Esther** 1891-1967 ................. **CLC 12**
See also AAYA 17; CA 13-14; 25-28R; CAP 1;
CLR 27; DLB 22; JRDA; MAICYA; SATA
2, 100
**Forche, Carolyn (Louise)** 1950- **CLC 25, 83,**
**86; DAM POET; PC 10**
See also CA 109; 117; CANR 50; DLB 5, 193;
INT 117
**Ford, Elbur**
See Hibbert, Eleanor Alice Burford
**Ford, Ford Madox** 1873-1939 **TCLC 1, 15, 39,**
**57; DAM NOV**
See also CA 104; 132; CDBLB 1914-1945;
DLB 162; MTCW 1
**Ford, Henry** 1863-1947 ................... **TCLC 73**
See also CA 115; 148
**Ford, John** 1586-(?) ............................... **DC 8**
See also CDBLB Before 1660; DAM DRAM;
DLB 58
**Ford, John** 1895-1973 ....................... **CLC 16**
See also CA 45-48
**Ford, Richard** 1944- .................... **CLC 46, 99**
See also CA 69-72; CANR 11, 47
**Ford, Webster**
See Masters, Edgar Lee
**Foreman, Richard** 1937- .................... **CLC 50**
See also CA 65-68; CANR 32, 63
**Forester, C(ecil) S(cott)** 1899-1966 ... **CLC 35**
See also CA 73-76; 25-28R; DLB 191; SATA
13
**Forez**
See Mauriac, Francois (Charles)
**Forman, James Douglas** 1932- .......... **CLC 21**
See also AAYA 17; CA 9-12R; CANR 4, 19,
42; JRDA; MAICYA; SATA 8, 70
**Fornes, Maria Irene** 1930- .......... **CLC 39, 61**
See also CA 25-28R; CANR 28; DLB 7; HW;
INT CANR-28; MTCW 1
**Forrest, Leon (Richard)** 1937-1997 .. **CLC 4;**
**BLCS**
See also BW 2; CA 89-92; 162; CAAS 7; CANR
25, 52; DLB 33
**Forster, E(dward) M(organ)** 1879-1970 **C L C**
**1, 2, 3, 4, 9, 10, 13, 15, 22, 45, 77; DA; DAB;**
**DAC; DAM MST, NOV; SSC 27; WLC**
See also AAYA 2; CA 13-14; 25-28R; CANR
45; CAP 1; CDBLB 1914-1945; DLB 34, 98,
162, 178, 195; DLBD 10; MTCW 1; SATA
57
**Forster, John** 1812-1876 ................. **NCLC 11**
See also DLB 144, 184
**Forsyth, Frederick** 1938- **CLC 2, 5, 36; DAM**
**NOV, POP**

See also BEST 89:4; CA 85-88; CANR 38, 62; DLB 87; MTCW 1

**Forten, Charlotte L.** ........... **TCLC 16; BLC 2**
See also Grimke, Charlotte L(ottie) Forten
See also DLB 50

**Foscolo, Ugo** 1778-1827 .................... **NCLC 8**

**Fosse, Bob** ........................... **CLC 20**
See also Fosse, Robert Louis

**Fosse, Robert Louis** 1927-1987
See Fosse, Bob
See also CA 110; 123

**Foster, Stephen Collins** 1826-1864 **NCLC 26**

**Foucault, Michel** 1926-1984 . **CLC 31, 34, 69**
See also CA 105; 113; CANR 34; MTCW 1

**Fouque, Friedrich (Heinrich Karl) de la Motte** 1777-1843 .................... **NCLC 2**
See also DLB 90

**Fourier, Charles** 1772-1837 ........... **NCLC 51**

**Fournier, Henri Alban** 1886-1914
See Alain-Fournier
See also CA 104

**Fournier, Pierre** 1916- ......................... **CLC 11**
See also Gascar, Pierre
See also CA 89-92; CANR 16, 40

**Fowles, John (Philip)** 1926- **CLC 1, 2, 3, 4, 6, 9, 10, 15, 33, 87; DAB; DAC; DAM MST**
See also CA 5-8R; CANR 25, 71; CDBLB 1960 to Present; DLB 14, 139; MTCW 1; SATA 22

**Fox, Paula** 1923- ............................... **CLC 2, 8**
See also AAYA 3; CA 73-76; CANR 20, 36, 62; CLR 1, 44; DLB 52; JRDA; MAICYA; MTCW 1; SATA 17, 60

**Fox, William Price (Jr.)** 1926- ........... **CLC 22**
See also CA 17-20R; CAAS 19; CANR 11; DLB 2; DLBY 81

**Foxe, John** 1516(?)-1587 ..................... **LC 14**
See also DLB 132

**Frame, Janet** 1924- **CLC 2, 3, 6, 22, 66, 96; SSC 29**
See also Clutha, Janet Paterson Frame

**France, Anatole** .................................. **TCLC 9**
See also Thibault, Jacques Anatole Francois
See also DLB 123

**Francis, Claude** 19(?)- ......................... **CLC 50**

**Francis, Dick** 1920- **CLC 2, 22, 42, 102; DAM POP**
See also AAYA 5, 21; BEST 89:3; CA 5-8R; CANR 9, 42, 68; CDBLB 1960 to Present; DLB 87; INT CANR-9; MTCW 1

**Francis, Robert (Churchill)** 1901-1987 **CLC 15**
See also CA 1-4R; 123; CANR 1

**Frank, Anne(lies Marie)** 1929-1945 **TCLC 17; DA; DAB; DAC; DAM MST; WLC**
See also AAYA 12; CA 113; 133; CANR 68; MTCW 1; SATA 87; SATA-Brief 42

**Frank, Bruno** 1887-1945 ................. **TCLC 81**
See also DLB 118

**Frank, Elizabeth** 1945- ...................... **CLC 39**
See also CA 121; 126; INT 126

**Frankl, Viktor E(mil)** 1905-1997 ...... **CLC 93**
See also CA 65-68; 161

**Franklin, Benjamin**
See Hasek, Jaroslav (Matej Frantisek)

**Franklin, Benjamin** 1706-1790 .. **LC 25; DA; DAB; DAC; DAM MST; WLCS**
See also CDALB 1640-1865; DLB 24, 43, 73

**Franklin, (Stella Maria Sarah) Miles (Lampe)** 1879-1954 .................................. **TCLC 7**
See also CA 104; 164

**Fraser, (Lady) Antonia (Pakenham)** 1932- **CLC 32, 107**
See also CA 85-88; CANR 44, 65; MTCW 1; SATA-Brief 32

**Fraser, George MacDonald** 1925- ...... **CLC 7**
See also CA 45-48; CANR 2, 48

**Fraser, Sylvia** 1935- ............................ **CLC 64**
See also CA 45-48; CANR 1, 16, 60

**Frayn, Michael** 1933- **CLC 3, 7, 31, 47; DAM DRAM, NOV**
See also CA 5-8R; CANR 30, 69; DLB 13, 14, 194; MTCW 1

**Fraze, Candida (Merrill)** 1945- ........ **CLC 50**
See also CA 126

**Frazer, J(ames) G(eorge)** 1854-1941 **TCLC 32**
See also CA 118

**Frazer, Robert Caine**
See Creasey, John

**Frazer, Sir James George**
See Frazer, J(ames) G(eorge)

**Frazier, Charles** 1950- ...................... **CLC 109**
See also CA 161

**Frazier, Ian** 1951- ............................... **CLC 46**
See also CA 130; CANR 54

**Frederic, Harold** 1856-1898 ........... **NCLC 10**
See also DLB 12, 23; DLBD 13

**Frederick, John**
See Faust, Frederick (Schiller)

**Frederick the Great** 1712-1786 ............. **LC 14**

**Fredro, Aleksander** 1793-1876 ........ **NCLC 8**

**Freeling, Nicolas** 1927- ...................... **CLC 38**
See also CA 49-52; CAAS 12; CANR 1, 17, 50; DLB 87

**Freeman, Douglas Southall** 1886-1953 **TCLC 11**
See also CA 109; DLB 17; DLBD 17

**Freeman, Judith** 1946- ....................... **CLC 55**
See also CA 148

**Freeman, Mary Eleanor Wilkins** 1852-1930 **TCLC 9; SSC 1**
See also CA 106; DLB 12, 78

**Freeman, R(ichard) Austin** 1862-1943 **TCLC 21**
See also CA 113; DLB 70

**French, Albert** 1943- .......................... **CLC 86**
See also CA 167

**French, Marilyn** 1929- **CLC 10, 18, 60; DAM DRAM, NOV, POP**
See also CA 69-72; CANR 3, 31; INT CANR-31; MTCW 1

**French, Paul**
See Asimov, Isaac

**Freneau, Philip Morin** 1752-1832 ... **NCLC 1**
See also DLB 37, 43

**Freud, Sigmund** 1856-1939 ............ **TCLC 52**
See also CA 115; 133; CANR 69; MTCW 1

**Friedan, Betty (Naomi)** 1921- ........... **CLC 74**
See also CA 65-68; CANR 18, 45; MTCW 1

**Friedlander, Saul** 1932- ..................... **CLC 90**
See also CA 117; 130; CANR 72

**Friedman, B(ernard) H(arper)** 1926- **CLC 7**
See also CA 1-4R; CANR 3, 48

**Friedman, Bruce Jay** 1930- ...... **CLC 3, 5, 56**
See also CA 9-12R; CANR 25, 52; DLB 2, 28; INT CANR-25

**Friel, Brian** 1929- **CLC 5, 42, 59, 115; DC 8**
See also CA 21-24R; CANR 33, 69; DLB 13; MTCW 1

**Friis-Baastad, Babbis Ellinor** 1921-1970 **CLC 12**
See also CA 17-20R; 134; SATA 7

**Frisch, Max (Rudolf)** 1911-1991 **CLC 3, 9, 14, 18, 32, 44; DAM DRAM, NOV**
See also CA 85-88; 134; CANR 32; DLB 69, 124; MTCW 1

**Fromentin, Eugene (Samuel Auguste)** 1820-1876 .......................................... **NCLC 10**
See also DLB 123

**Frost, Frederick**
See Faust, Frederick (Schiller)

**Frost, Robert (Lee)** 1874-1963 **CLC 1, 3, 4, 9, 10, 13, 15, 26, 34, 44; DA; DAB; DAC; DAM MST, POET; PC 1; WLC**

See also AAYA 21; CA 89-92; CANR 33; CDALB 1917-1929; DLB 54; DLBD 7; MTCW 1; SATA 14

**Froude, James Anthony** 1818-1894 **NCLC 43**
See also DLB 18, 57, 144

**Froy, Herald**
See Waterhouse, Keith (Spencer)

**Fry, Christopher** 1907- **CLC 2, 10, 14; DAM DRAM**
See also CA 17-20R; CAAS 23; CANR 9, 30; DLB 13; MTCW 1; SATA 66

**Frye, (Herman) Northrop** 1912-1991 **CLC 24, 70**
See also CA 5-8R; 133; CANR 8, 37; DLB 67, 68; MTCW 1

**Fuchs, Daniel** 1909-1993 ................. **CLC 8, 22**
See also CA 81-84; 142; CAAS 5; CANR 40; DLB 9, 26, 28; DLBY 93

**Fuchs, Daniel** 1934- ........................... **CLC 34**
See also CA 37-40R; CANR 14, 48

**Fuentes, Carlos** 1928- **CLC 3, 8, 10, 13, 22, 41, 60, 113; DA; DAB; DAC; DAM MST, MULT, NOV; HLC; SSC 24; WLC**
See also AAYA 4; AITN 2; CA 69-72; CANR 10, 32, 68; DLB 113; HW; MTCW 1

**Fuentes, Gregorio Lopez y**
See Lopez y Fuentes, Gregorio

**Fugard, (Harold) Athol** 1932- **CLC 5, 9, 14, 25, 40, 80; DAM DRAM; DC 3**
See also AAYA 17; CA 85-88; CANR 32, 54; MTCW 1

**Fugard, Sheila** 1932- .......................... **CLC 48**
See also CA 125

**Fuller, Charles (H., Jr.)** 1939- **CLC 25; BLC 2; DAM DRAM, MULT; DC 1**
See also BW 2; CA 108; 112; DLB 38; INT 112; MTCW 1

**Fuller, John (Leopold)** 1937- ............ **CLC 62**
See also CA 21-24R; CANR 9, 44; DLB 40

**Fuller, Margaret** ........................... **NCLC 5, 50**
See also Ossoli, Sarah Margaret (Fuller marchesa d')

**Fuller, Roy (Broadbent)** 1912-1991 **CLC 4, 28**
See also CA 5-8R; 135; CAAS 10; CANR 53; DLB 15, 20; SATA 87

**Fulton, Alice** 1952- ............................. **CLC 52**
See also CA 116; CANR 57; DLB 193

**Furphy, Joseph** 1843-1912 .............. **TCLC 25**
See also CA 163

**Fussell, Paul** 1924- ............................. **CLC 74**
See also BEST 90:1; CA 17-20R; CANR 8, 21, 35, 69; INT CANR-21; MTCW 1

**Futabatei, Shimei** 1864-1909 ......... **TCLC 44**
See also CA 162; DLB 180

**Futrelle, Jacques** 1875-1912 ........... **TCLC 19**
See also CA 113; 155

**Gaboriau, Emile** 1835-1873 ........... **NCLC 14**

**Gadda, Carlo Emilio** 1893-1973 ....... **CLC 11**
See also CA 89-92; DLB 177

**Gaddis, William** 1922- **CLC 1, 3, 6, 8, 10, 19, 43, 86**
See also CA 17-20R; CANR 21, 48; DLB 2; MTCW 1

**Gage, Walter**
See Inge, William (Motter)

**Gaines, Ernest J(ames)** 1933- **CLC 3, 11, 18, 86; BLC 2; DAM MULT**
See also AAYA 18; AITN 1; BW 2; CA 9-12R; CANR 6, 24, 42; CDALB 1968-1988; DLB 2, 33, 152; DLBY 80; MTCW 1; SATA 86

**Gaitskill, Mary** 1954- ........................ **CLC 69**
See also CA 128; CANR 61

**Galdos, Benito Perez**
See Perez Galdos, Benito

**Gale, Zona** 1874-1938 **TCLC 7; DAM DRAM**
See also CA 105; 153; DLB 9, 78

**Galeano, Eduardo (Hughes)** 1940- ... **CLC 72**

See also CA 29-32R; CANR 13, 32; HW
**Galiano, Juan Valera y Alcala**
  See Valera y Alcala-Galiano, Juan
**Galilei, Galileo** 1546-1642 .................... **LC 45**
**Gallagher, Tess** 1943- ...... **CLC 18, 63; DAM POET; PC 9**
  See also CA 106; DLB 120
**Gallant, Mavis** 1922- ... **CLC 7, 18, 38; DAC; DAM MST; SSC 5**
  See also CA 69-72; CANR 29, 69; DLB 53; MTCW 1
**Gallant, Roy A(rthur)** 1924- ............. **CLC 17**
  See also CA 5-8R; CANR 4, 29, 54; CLR 30; MAICYA; SATA 4, 68
**Gallico, Paul (William)** 1897-1976 ..... **CLC 2**
  See also AITN 1; CA 5-8R; 69-72; CANR 23; DLB 9, 171; MAICYA; SATA 13
**Gallo, Max Louis** 1932- ..................... **CLC 95**
  See also CA 85-88
**Gallois, Lucien**
  See Desnos, Robert
**Gallup, Ralph**
  See Whitemore, Hugh (John)
**Galsworthy, John** 1867-1933 **TCLC 1, 45; DA; DAB; DAC; DAM DRAM, MST, NOV; SSC 22; WLC 2**
  See also CA 104; 141; CDBLB 1890-1914; DLB 10, 34, 98, 162; DLBD 16
**Galt, John** 1779-1839 ...................... **NCLC 1**
  See also DLB 99, 116, 159
**Galvin, James** 1951- ........................... **CLC 38**
  See also CA 108; CANR 26
**Gamboa, Federico** 1864-1939 ........ **TCLC 36**
  See also CA 167
**Gandhi, M. K.**
  See Gandhi, Mohandas Karamchand
**Gandhi, Mahatma**
  See Gandhi, Mohandas Karamchand
**Gandhi, Mohandas Karamchand** 1869-1948 **TCLC 59; DAM MULT**
  See also CA 121; 132; MTCW 1
**Gann, Ernest Kellogg** 1910-1991 ...... **CLC 23**
  See also AITN 1; CA 1-4R; 136; CANR 1
**Garcia, Cristina** 1958- ...................... **CLC 76**
  See also CA 141
**Garcia Lorca, Federico** 1898-1936 **TCLC 1, 7, 49; DA; DAB; DAC; DAM DRAM, MST, MULT, POET; DC 2; HLC; PC 3; WLC**
  See also CA 104; 131; DLB 108; HW; MTCW 1
**Garcia Marquez, Gabriel (Jose)** 1928- **CLC 2, 3, 8, 10, 15, 27, 47, 55, 68; DA; DAB; DAC; DAM MST, MULT, NOV, POP; HLC; SSC 8; WLC**
  See also AAYA 3; BEST 89:1, 90:4; CA 33-36R; CANR 10, 28, 50; DLB 113; HW; MTCW 1
**Gard, Janice**
  See Latham, Jean Lee
**Gard, Roger Martin du**
  See Martin du Gard, Roger
**Gardam, Jane** 1928- ........................... **CLC 43**
  See also CA 49-52; CANR 2, 18, 33, 54; CLR 12; DLB 14, 161; MAICYA; MTCW 1; SAAS 9; SATA 39, 76; SATA-Brief 28
**Gardner, Herb(ert)** 1934- ................. **CLC 44**
  See also CA 149
**Gardner, John (Champlin), Jr.** 1933-1982 **CLC 2, 3, 5, 7, 8, 10, 18, 28, 34; DAM NOV, POP; SSC 7**
  See also AITN 1; CA 65-68; 107; CANR 33; DLB 2; DLBY 82; MTCW 1; SATA 40; SATA-Obit 31
**Gardner, John (Edmund)** 1926- **CLC 30; DAM POP**
  See also CA 103; CANR 15, 69; MTCW 1
**Gardner, Miriam**

See Bradley, Marion Zimmer
**Gardner, Noel**
  See Kuttner, Henry
**Gardons, S. S.**
  See Snodgrass, W(illiam) D(e Witt)
**Garfield, Leon** 1921-1996 .................. **CLC 12**
  See also AAYA 8; CA 17-20R; 152; CANR 38, 41; CLR 21; DLB 161; JRDA; MAICYA; SATA 1, 32, 76; SATA-Obit 90
**Garland, (Hannibal) Hamlin** 1860-1940 **TCLC 3; SSC 18**
  See also CA 104; DLB 12, 71, 78, 186
**Garneau, (Hector de) Saint-Denys** 1912-1943 **TCLC 13**
  See also CA 111; DLB 88
**Garner, Alan** 1934- **CLC 17; DAB; DAM POP**
  See also AAYA 18; CA 73-76; CANR 15, 64; CLR 20; DLB 161; MAICYA; MTCW 1; SATA 18, 69
**Garner, Hugh** 1913-1979 ................... **CLC 13**
  See also CA 69-72; CANR 31; DLB 68
**Garnett, David** 1892-1981 ................... **CLC 3**
  See also CA 5-8R; 103; CANR 17; DLB 34
**Garos, Stephanie**
  See Katz, Steve
**Garrett, George (Palmer)** 1929- **CLC 3, 11, 51; SSC 30**
  See also CA 1-4R; CAAS 5; CANR 1, 42, 67; DLB 2, 5, 130, 152; DLBY 83
**Garrick, David** 1717-1779 ........ **LC 15; DAM DRAM**
  See also DLB 84
**Garrigue, Jean** 1914-1972 ............. **CLC 2, 8**
  See also CA 5-8R; 37-40R; CANR 20
**Garrison, Frederick**
  See Sinclair, Upton (Beall)
**Garth, Will**
  See Hamilton, Edmond; Kuttner, Henry
**Garvey, Marcus (Moziah, Jr.)** 1887-1940 **TCLC 41; BLC 2; DAM MULT**
  See also BW 1; CA 120; 124
**Gary, Romain** ...................................... **CLC 25**
  See also Kacew, Romain
  See also DLB 83
**Gascar, Pierre** ...................................... **CLC 11**
  See also Fournier, Pierre
**Gascoyne, David (Emery)** 1916- ....... **CLC 45**
  See also CA 65-68; CANR 10, 28, 54; DLB 20; MTCW 1
**Gaskell, Elizabeth Cleghorn** 1810-1865 **NCLC 70; DAB; DAM MST; SSC 25**
  See also CDBLB 1832-1890; DLB 21, 144, 159
**Gass, William H(oward)** 1924- **CLC 1, 2, 8, 11, 15, 39; SSC 12**
  See also CA 17-20R; CANR 30, 71; DLB 2; MTCW 1
**Gasset, Jose Ortega y**
  See Ortega y Gasset, Jose
**Gates, Henry Louis, Jr.** 1950- **CLC 65; BLCS; DAM MULT**
  See also BW 2; CA 109; CANR 25, 53; DLB 67
**Gautier, Theophile** 1811-1872 .. **NCLC 1, 59; DAM POET; PC 18; SSC 20**
  See also DLB 119
**Gawsworth, John**
  See Bates, H(erbert) E(rnest)
**Gay, Oliver**
  See Gogarty, Oliver St. John
**Gaye, Marvin (Penze)** 1939-1984 ..... **CLC 26**
  See also CA 112
**Gebler, Carlo (Ernest)** 1954- ............ **CLC 39**
  See also CA 119; 133
**Gee, Maggie (Mary)** 1948- ............... **CLC 57**
  See also CA 130
**Gee, Maurice (Gough)** 1931- ............ **CLC 29**
  See also CA 97-100; CANR 67; SATA 46, 101

**Gelbart, Larry (Simon)** 1923- .... **CLC 21, 61**
  See also CA 73-76; CANR 45
**Gelber, Jack** 1932- ............ **CLC 1, 6, 14, 79**
  See also CA 1-4R; CANR 2; DLB 7
**Gellhorn, Martha (Ellis)** 1908-1998 **CLC 14, 60**
  See also CA 77-80; 164; CANR 44; DLBY 82
**Genet, Jean** 1910-1986 **CLC 1, 2, 5, 10, 14, 44, 46; DAM DRAM**
  See also CA 13-16R; CANR 18; DLB 72; DLBY 86; MTCW 1
**Gent, Peter** 1942- ............................... **CLC 29**
  See also AITN 1; CA 89-92; DLBY 82
**Gentlewoman in New England, A**
  See Bradstreet, Anne
**Gentlewoman in Those Parts, A**
  See Bradstreet, Anne
**George, Jean Craighead** 1919- ......... **CLC 35**
  See also AAYA 8; CA 5-8R; CANR 25; CLR 1; DLB 52; JRDA; MAICYA; SATA 2, 68
**George, Stefan (Anton)** 1868-1933 **TCLC 2, 14**
  See also CA 104
**Georges, Georges Martin**
  See Simenon, Georges (Jacques Christian)
**Gerhardi, William Alexander**
  See Gerhardie, William Alexander
**Gerhardie, William Alexander** 1895-1977 **CLC 5**
  See also CA 25-28R; 73-76; CANR 18; DLB 36
**Gerstler, Amy** 1956- .......................... **CLC 70**
  See also CA 146
**Gertler, T.** ........................................... **CLC 34**
  See also CA 116; 121; INT 121
**Ghalib** .................................................. **NCLC 39**
  See also Ghalib, Hsadullah Khan
**Ghalib, Hsadullah Khan** 1797-1869
  See Ghalib
  See also DAM POET
**Ghelderode, Michel de** 1898-1962 **CLC 6, 11; DAM DRAM**
  See also CA 85-88; CANR 40
**Ghiselin, Brewster** 1903- ................... **CLC 23**
  See also CA 13-16R; CAAS 10; CANR 13
**Ghose, Aurabinda** 1872-1950 ......... **TCLC 63**
  See also CA 163
**Ghose, Zulfikar** 1935- ........................ **CLC 42**
  See also CA 65-68; CANR 67
**Ghosh, Amitav** 1956- .......................... **CLC 44**
  See also CA 147
**Giacosa, Giuseppe** 1847-1906 .......... **TCLC 7**
  See also CA 104
**Gibb, Lee**
  See Waterhouse, Keith (Spencer)
**Gibbon, Lewis Grassic** ...................... **TCLC 4**
  See also Mitchell, James Leslie
**Gibbons, Kaye** 1960- **CLC 50, 88; DAM POP**
  See also CA 151
**Gibran, Kahlil** 1883-1931 . **TCLC 1, 9; DAM POET, POP; PC 9**
  See also CA 104; 150
**Gibran, Khalil**
  See Gibran, Kahlil
**Gibson, William** 1914- .. **CLC 23; DA; DAB; DAC; DAM DRAM, MST**
  See also CA 9-12R; CANR 9, 42; DLB 7; SATA 66
**Gibson, William (Ford)** 1948- ... **CLC 39, 63; DAM POP**
  See also AAYA 12; CA 126; 133; CANR 52
**Gide, Andre (Paul Guillaume)** 1869-1951 **TCLC 5, 12, 36; DA; DAB; DAC; DAM MST, NOV; SSC 13; WLC**
  See also CA 104; 124; DLB 65; MTCW 1
**Gifford, Barry (Colby)** 1946- ............ **CLC 34**
  See also CA 65-68; CANR 9, 30, 40
**Gilbert, Frank**

See Eluard, Paul
See also CA 104
**Grisham, John** 1955- .... **CLC 84; DAM POP**
See also AAYA 14; CA 138; CANR 47, 69
**Grossman, David** 1954- ..................... **CLC 67**
See also CA 138
**Grossman, Vasily (Semenovich)** 1905-1964
**CLC 41**
See also CA 124; 130; MTCW 1
**Grove, Frederick Philip** ..................... **TCLC 4**
See also Greve, Felix Paul (Berthold Friedrich)
See also DLB 92
**Grubb**
See Crumb, R(obert)
**Grumbach, Doris (Isaac)** 1918-**CLC 13, 22, 64**
See also CA 5-8R; CAAS 2; CANR 9, 42, 70;
INT CANR-9
**Grundtvig, Nicolai Frederik Severin** 1783-1872
**NCLC 1**
**Grunge**
See Crumb, R(obert)
**Grunwald, Lisa** 1959- ....................... **CLC 44**
See also CA 120
**Guare, John** 1938- . **CLC 8, 14, 29, 67; DAM
DRAM**
See also CA 73-76; CANR 21, 69; DLB 7;
MTCW 1
**Gudjonsson, Halldor Kiljan** 1902-1998
See Laxness, Halldor
See also CA 103; 164
**Guenter, Erich**
See Eich, Guenter
**Guest, Barbara** 1920- ........................ **CLC 34**
See also CA 25-28R; CANR 11, 44; DLB 5,
193
**Guest, Judith (Ann)** 1936- **CLC 8, 30; DAM
NOV, POP**
See also AAYA 7; CA 77-80; CANR 15; INT
CANR-15; MTCW 1
**Guevara, Che** .................... **CLC 87; HLC**
See also Guevara (Serna), Ernesto
**Guevara (Serna), Ernesto** 1928-1967
See Guevara, Che
See also CA 127; 111; CANR 56; DAM MULT;
HW
**Guild, Nicholas M.** 1944- ................... **CLC 33**
See also CA 93-96
**Guillemin, Jacques**
See Sartre, Jean-Paul
**Guillen, Jorge** 1893-1984 ....... **CLC 11; DAM
MULT, POET**
See also CA 89-92; 112; DLB 108; HW
**Guillen, Nicolas (Cristobal)** 1902-1989 **C L C
48, 79; BLC 2; DAM MST, MULT, POET;
HLC; PC 23**
See also BW 2; CA 116; 125; 129; HW
**Guillevic, (Eugene)** 1907- .................. **CLC 33**
See also CA 93-96
**Guillois**
See Desnos, Robert
**Guillois, Valentin**
See Desnos, Robert
**Guiney, Louise Imogen** 1861-1920 **TCLC 41**
See also CA 160; DLB 54
**Guiraldes, Ricardo (Guillermo)** 1886-1927
**TCLC 39**
See also CA 131; HW; MTCW 1
**Gumilev, Nikolai (Stepanovich)** 1886-1921
**TCLC 60**
See also CA 165
**Gunesekera, Romesh** 1954- .............. **CLC 91**
See also CA 159
**Gunn, Bill** .................................... **CLC 5**
See also Gunn, William Harrison
See also DLB 38
**Gunn, Thom(son William)** 1929-**CLC 3, 6, 18,
32, 81; DAM POET**

See also CA 17-20R; CANR 9, 33; CDBLB
1960 to Present; DLB 27; INT CANR-33;
MTCW 1
**Gunn, William Harrison** 1934(?)-1989
See Gunn, Bill
See also AITN 1; BW 1; CA 13-16R; 128;
CANR 12, 25
**Gunnars, Kristjana** 1948- .................. **CLC 69**
See also CA 113; DLB 60
**Gurdjieff, G(eorgei) I(vanovich)** 1877(?)-1949
**TCLC 71**
See also CA 157
**Gurganus, Allan** 1947- . **CLC 70; DAM POP**
See also BEST 90:1; CA 135
**Gurney, A(lbert) R(amsdell), Jr.** 1930- . **C L C
32, 50, 54; DAM DRAM**
See also CA 77-80; CANR 32, 64
**Gurney, Ivor (Bertie)** 1890-1937 ... **TCLC 33**
See also CA 167
**Gurney, Peter**
See Gurney, A(lbert) R(amsdell), Jr.
**Guro, Elena** 1877-1913 ................... **TCLC 56**
**Gustafson, James M(oody)** 1925- ...**CLC 100**
See also CA 25-28R; CANR 37
**Gustafson, Ralph (Barker)** 1909- ..... **CLC 36**
See also CA 21-24R; CANR 8, 45; DLB 88
**Gut, Gom**
See Simenon, Georges (Jacques Christian)
**Guterson, David** 1956- ..................... **CLC 91**
See also CA 132
**Guthrie, A(lfred) B(ertram), Jr.** 1901-1991
**CLC 23**
See also CA 57-60; 134; CANR 24; DLB 6;
SATA 62; SATA-Obit 67
**Guthrie, Isobel**
See Grieve, C(hristopher) M(urray)
**Guthrie, Woodrow Wilson** 1912-1967
See Guthrie, Woody
See also CA 113; 93-96
**Guthrie, Woody** ................................ **CLC 35**
See also Guthrie, Woodrow Wilson
**Guy, Rosa (Cuthbert)** 1928- .............. **CLC 26**
See also AAYA 4; BW 2; CA 17-20R; CANR
14, 34; CLR 13; DLB 33; JRDA; MAICYA;
SATA 14, 62
**Gwendolyn**
See Bennett, (Enoch) Arnold
**H. D.** ................ **CLC 3, 8, 14, 31, 34, 73; PC 5**
See also Doolittle, Hilda
**H. de V.**
See Buchan, John
**Haavikko, Paavo Juhani** 1931- .. **CLC 18, 34**
See also CA 106
**Habbema, Koos**
See Heijermans, Herman
**Habermas, Juergen** 1929- ................ **CLC 104**
See also CA 109
**Habermas, Jurgen**
See Habermas, Juergen
**Hacker, Marilyn** 1942- **CLC 5, 9, 23, 72, 91;
DAM POET**
See also CA 77-80; CANR 68; DLB 120
**Haeckel, Ernst Heinrich (Philipp August)** 1834-
1919 ................................................
**TCLC 83**
See also CA 157
**Haggard, H(enry) Rider** 1856-1925**TCLC 11**
See also CA 108; 148; DLB 70, 156, 174, 178;
SATA 16
**Hagiosy, L.**
See Larbaud, Valery (Nicolas)
**Hagiwara Sakutaro** 1886-1942**TCLC 60; PC
18**
**Haig, Fenil**
See Ford, Ford Madox
**Haig-Brown, Roderick (Langmere)** 1908-1976
**CLC 21**

See also CA 5-8R; 69-72; CANR 4, 38; CLR
31; DLB 88; MAICYA; SATA 12
**Hailey, Arthur** 1920-**CLC 5; DAM NOV, POP**
See also AITN 2; BEST 90:3; CA 1-4R; CANR
2, 36; DLB 88; DLBY 82; MTCW 1
**Hailey, Elizabeth Forsythe** 1938- ..... **CLC 40**
See also CA 93-96; CAAS 1; CANR 15, 48;
INT CANR-15
**Haines, John (Meade)** 1924- .............. **CLC 58**
See also CA 17-20R; CANR 13, 34; DLB 5
**Hakluyt, Richard** 1552-1616 ................ **LC 31**
**Haldeman, Joe (William)** 1943- ........ **CLC 61**
See also CA 53-56; CAAS 25; CANR 6, 70,
72; DLB 8; INT CANR-6
**Haley, Alex(ander Murray Palmer)** 1921-1992
**CLC 8, 12, 76; BLC 2; DA; DAB; DAC;
DAM MST, MULT, POP**
See also AAYA 26; BW 2; CA 77-80; 136;
CANR 61; DLB 38; MTCW 1
**Haliburton, Thomas Chandler** 1796-1865
**NCLC 15**
See also DLB 11, 99
**Hall, Donald (Andrew, Jr.)** 1928- **CLC 1, 13,
37, 59; DAM POET**
See also CA 5-8R; CAAS 7; CANR 2, 44, 64;
DLB 5; SATA 23, 97
**Hall, Frederic Sauser**
See Sauser-Hall, Frederic
**Hall, James**
See Kuttner, Henry
**Hall, James Norman** 1887-1951 ..... **TCLC 23**
See also CA 123; SATA 21
**Hall, (Marguerite) Radclyffe** 1886-1943
**TCLC 12**
See also CA 110; 150
**Hall, Rodney** 1935- ............................ **CLC 51**
See also CA 109; CANR 69
**Halleck, Fitz-Greene** 1790-1867 .... **NCLC 47**
See also DLB 3
**Halliday, Michael**
See Creasey, John
**Halpern, Daniel** 1945- ....................... **CLC 14**
See also CA 33-36R
**Hamburger, Michael (Peter Leopold)** 1924-
**CLC 5, 14**
See also CA 5-8R; CAAS 4; CANR 2, 47; DLB
27
**Hamill, Pete** 1935- ............................. **CLC 10**
See also CA 25-28R; CANR 18, 71
**Hamilton, Alexander** 1755(?)-1804 **NCLC 49**
See also DLB 37
**Hamilton, Clive**
See Lewis, C(live) S(taples)
**Hamilton, Edmond** 1904-1977 ............. **CLC 1**
See also CA 1-4R; CANR 3; DLB 8
**Hamilton, Eugene (Jacob) Lee**
See Lee-Hamilton, Eugene (Jacob)
**Hamilton, Franklin**
See Silverberg, Robert
**Hamilton, Gail**
See Corcoran, Barbara
**Hamilton, Mollie**
See Kaye, M(ary) M(argaret)
**Hamilton, (Anthony Walter) Patrick** 1904-1962
**CLC 51**
See also CA 113; DLB 10
**Hamilton, Virginia** 1936- ....... **CLC 26; DAM
MULT**
See also AAYA 2, 21; BW 2; CA 25-28R;
CANR 20, 37; CLR 1, 11, 40; DLB 33, 52;
INT CANR-20; JRDA; MAICYA; MTCW 1;
SATA 4, 56, 79
**Hammett, (Samuel) Dashiell** 1894-1961 **C L C
3, 5, 10, 19, 47; SSC 17**
See also AITN 1; CA 81-84; CANR 42; CDALB
1929-1941; DLBD 6; DLBY 96; MTCW 1
**Hammon, Jupiter** 1711(?)-1800(?) ..**NCLC 5;**

BLC 2; DAM MULT, POET; PC 16
See also DLB 31, 50

Hammond, Keith
See Kuttner, Henry

Hamner, Earl (Henry), Jr. 1923- ...... CLC 12
See also AITN 2; CA 73-76; DLB 6

Hampton, Christopher (James) 1946- CLC 4
See also CA 25-28R; DLB 13; MTCW 1

Hamsun, Knut ........................ TCLC 2, 14, 49
See also Pedersen, Knut

Handke, Peter 1942-CLC 5, 8, 10, 15, 38; DAM
DRAM, NOV
See also CA 77-80; CANR 33; DLB 85, 124;
MTCW 1

Hanley, James 1901-1985 ..... CLC 3, 5, 8, 13
See also CA 73-76; 117; CANR 36; DLB 191;
MTCW 1

Hannah, Barry 1942- ............ CLC 23, 38, 90
See also CA 108; 110; CANR 43, 68; DLB 6;
INT 110; MTCW 1

Hannon, Ezra
See Hunter, Evan

Hansberry, Lorraine (Vivian) 1930-1965CLC
17, 62; BLC 2; DA; DAB; DAC; DAM
DRAM, MST, MULT; DC 2
See also AAYA 25; BW 1; CA 109; 25-28R;
CABS 3; CANR 58; CDALB 1941-1968;
DLB 7, 38; MTCW 1

Hansen, Joseph 1923- ......................... CLC 38
See also CA 29-32R; CAAS 17; CANR 16, 44,
66; INT CANR-16

Hansen, Martin A(lfred) 1909-1955TCLC 32
See also CA 167

Hanson, Kenneth O(stlin) 1922- ....... CLC 13
See also CA 53-56; CANR 7

Hardwick, Elizabeth (Bruce) 1916- CLC 13;
DAM NOV
See also CA 5-8R; CANR 3, 32, 70; DLB 6;
MTCW 1

Hardy, Thomas 1840-1928TCLC 4, 10, 18, 32,
48, 53, 72; DA; DAB; DAC; DAM MST,
NOV, POET; PC 8; SSC 3; WLC
See also CA 104; 123; CDBLB 1890-1914;
DLB 18, 19, 135; MTCW 1

Hare, David 1947- ....................... CLC 29, 58
See also CA 97-100; CANR 39; DLB 13;
MTCW 1

Harewood, John
See Van Druten, John (William)

Harford, Henry
See Hudson, W(illiam) H(enry)

Hargrave, Leonie
See Disch, Thomas M(ichael)

Harjo, Joy 1951- ........ CLC 83; DAM MULT
See also CA 114; CANR 35, 67; DLB 120, 175;
NNAL

Harlan, Louis R(udolph) 1922- ........ CLC 34
See also CA 21-24R; CANR 25, 55

Harling, Robert 1951(?)- ................... CLC 53
See also CA 147

Harmon, William (Ruth) 1938- ........ CLC 38
See also CA 33-36R; CANR 14, 32, 35; SATA
65

Harper, Daniel
See Brossard, Chandler

Harper, F. E. W.
See Harper, Frances Ellen Watkins

Harper, Frances E. W.
See Harper, Frances Ellen Watkins

Harper, Frances E. Watkins
See Harper, Frances Ellen Watkins

Harper, Frances Ellen
See Harper, Frances Ellen Watkins

Harper, Frances Ellen Watkins 1825-1911
TCLC 14; BLC 2; DAM MULT, POET;
PC 21
See also BW 1; CA 111; 125; DLB 50

Harper, Michael S(teven) 1938- .... CLC 7, 22
See also BW 1; CA 33-36R; CANR 24; DLB
41

Harper, Mrs. F. E. W.
See Harper, Frances Ellen Watkins

Harris, Christie (Lucy) Irwin 1907- CLC 12
See also CA 5-8R; CANR 6; CLR 47; DLB 88;
JRDA; MAICYA; SAAS 10; SATA 6, 74

Harris, Frank 1856-1931 ................ TCLC 24
See also CA 109; 150; DLB 156, 197

Harris, George Washington 1814-1869NCLC
23
See also DLB 3, 11

Harris, Joel Chandler 1848-1908 ...TCLC 2;
SSC 19
See also CA 104; 137; CLR 49; DLB 11, 23,
42, 78, 91; MAICYA; SATA 100; YABC 1

Harris, John (Wyndham Parkes Lucas) Beynon
1903-1969
See Wyndham, John
See also CA 102; 89-92

Harris, MacDonald ............................. CLC 9
See also Heiney, Donald (William)

Harris, Mark 1922- ........................... CLC 19
See also CA 5-8R; CAAS 3; CANR 2, 55; DLB
2; DLBY 80

Harris, (Theodore) Wilson 1921- ..... CLC 25
See also BW 2; CA 65-68; CAAS 16; CANR
11, 27, 69; DLB 117; MTCW 1

Harrison, Elizabeth Cavanna 1909-
See Cavanna, Betty
See also CA 9-12R; CANR 6, 27

Harrison, Harry (Max) 1925- ........... CLC 42
See also CA 1-4R; CANR 5, 21; DLB 8; SATA
4

Harrison, James (Thomas) 1937- CLC 6, 14,
33, 66; SSC 19
See also CA 13-16R; CANR 8, 51; DLBY 82;
INT CANR-8

Harrison, Jim
See Harrison, James (Thomas)

Harrison, Kathryn 1961- .................. CLC 70
See also CA 144; CANR 68

Harrison, Tony 1937- ......................... CLC 43
See also CA 65-68; CANR 44; DLB 40; MTCW
1

Harriss, Will(ard Irvin) 1922- .......... CLC 34
See also CA 111

Harson, Sley
See Ellison, Harlan (Jay)

Hart, Ellis
See Ellison, Harlan (Jay)

Hart, Josephine 1942(?)-CLC 70; DAM POP
See also CA 138; CANR 70

Hart, Moss 1904-1961CLC 66; DAM DRAM
See also CA 109; 89-92; DLB 7

Harte, (Francis) Bret(t) 1836(?)-1902TCLC 1,
25; DA; DAC; DAM MST; SSC 8; WLC
See also CA 104; 140; CDALB 1865-1917;
DLB 12, 64, 74, 79, 186; SATA 26

Hartley, L(eslie) P(oles) 1895-1972CLC 2, 22
See also CA 45-48; 37-40R; CANR 33; DLB
15, 139; MTCW 1

Hartman, Geoffrey H. 1929- ............. CLC 27
See also CA 117; 125; DLB 67

Hartmann, Sadakichi 1867-1944 ... TCLC 73
See also CA 157; DLB 54

Hartmann von Aue c. 1160-c. 1205CMLC 15
See also DLB 138

Hartmann von Aue 1170-1210 ...... CMLC 15

Haruf, Kent 1943- ............................... CLC 34
See also CA 149

Harwood, Ronald 1934- ......... CLC 32; DAM
DRAM, MST
See also CA 1-4R; CANR 4, 55; DLB 13

Hasegawa Tatsunosuke
See Futabatei, Shimei

Hasek, Jaroslav (Matej Frantisek) 1883-1923
TCLC 4
See also CA 104; 129; MTCW 1

Hass, Robert 1941- ... CLC 18, 39, 99; PC 16
See also CA 111; CANR 30, 50, 71; DLB 105;
SATA 94

Hastings, Hudson
See Kuttner, Henry

Hastings, Selina .................................... CLC 44

Hathorne, John 1641-1717 ................... LC 38

Hatteras, Amelia
See Mencken, H(enry) L(ouis)

Hatteras, Owen ................................. TCLC 18
See also Mencken, H(enry) L(ouis); Nathan,
George Jean

Hauptmann, Gerhart (Johann Robert) 1862-
1946 ................... TCLC 4; DAM DRAM
See also CA 104; 153; DLB 66, 118

Havel, Vaclav 1936- ... CLC 25, 58, 65; DAM
DRAM; DC 6
See also CA 104; CANR 36, 63; MTCW 1

Haviaras, Stratis ............................... CLC 33
See also Chaviaras, Strates

Hawes, Stephen 1475(?)-1523(?) .......... LC 17
See also DLB 132

Hawkes, John (Clendennin Burne, Jr.) 1925-
1998 .. CLC 1, 2, 3, 4, 7, 9, 14, 15, 27, 49
See also CA 1-4R; 167; CANR 2, 47, 64; DLB
2, 7; DLBY 80; MTCW 1

Hawking, S. W.
See Hawking, Stephen W(illiam)

Hawking, Stephen W(illiam) 1942- .CLC 63,
105
See also AAYA 13; BEST 89:1; CA 126; 129;
CANR 48

Hawkins, Anthony Hope
See Hope, Anthony

Hawthorne, Julian 1846-1934 ........ TCLC 25
See also CA 165

Hawthorne, Nathaniel 1804-1864 NCLC 39;
DA; DAB; DAC; DAM MST, NOV; SSC
3, 29; WLC
See also AAYA 18; CDALB 1640-1865; DLB
1, 74; YABC 2

Haxton, Josephine Ayres 1921-
See Douglas, Ellen
See also CA 115; CANR 41

Hayaseca y Eizaguirre, Jorge
See Echegaray (y Eizaguirre), Jose (Maria
Waldo)

Hayashi, Fumiko 1904-1951 .......... TCLC 27
See also CA 161; DLB 180

Haycraft, Anna
See Ellis, Alice Thomas
See also CA 122

Hayden, Robert E(arl) 1913-1980 .CLC 5, 9,
14, 37; BLC 2; DA; DAC; DAM MST,
MULT, POET; PC 6
See also BW 1; CA 69-72; 97-100; CABS 2;
CANR 24; CDALB 1941-1968; DLB 5, 76;
MTCW 1; SATA 19; SATA-Obit 26

Hayford, J(oseph) E(phraim) Casely
See Casely-Hayford, J(oseph) E(phraim)

Hayman, Ronald 1932- ...................... CLC 44
See also CA 25-28R; CANR 18, 50; DLB 155

Haywood, Eliza 1693(?)-1756 .............. LC 44
See also DLB 39

Haywood, Eliza (Fowler) 1693(?)-1756 LC 1,
44

Hazlitt, William 1778-1830 ............ NCLC 29
See also DLB 110, 158

Hazzard, Shirley 1931- ...................... CLC 18
See also CA 9-12R; CANR 4, 70; DLBY 82;
MTCW 1

Head, Bessie 1937-1986 CLC 25, 67; BLC 2;
DAM MULT
See also BW 2; CA 29-32R; 119; CANR 25;

Ilf, Ilya .................................................. TCLC 21
   See also Fainzilberg, Ilya Arnoldovich
Illyes, Gyula 1902-1983 ......................... PC 16
   See also CA 114; 109
Immermann, Karl (Lebrecht) 1796-1840
   NCLC 4, 49
   See also DLB 133
Inchbald, Elizabeth 1753-1821 ...... NCLC 62
   See also DLB 39, 89
Inclan, Ramon (Maria) del Valle
   See Valle-Inclan, Ramon (Maria) del
Infante, G(uillermo) Cabrera
   See Cabrera Infante, G(uillermo)
Ingalls, Rachel (Holmes) 1940- ......... CLC 42
   See also CA 123; 127
Ingamells, Reginald Charles
   See Ingamells, Rex
Ingamells, Rex 1913-1955 .............. TCLC 35
   See also CA 167
Inge, William (Motter) 1913-1973 . CLC 1, 8,
   19; DAM DRAM
   See also CA 9-12R; CDALB 1941-1968; DLB
   7; MTCW 1
Ingelow, Jean 1820-1897 ................. NCLC 39
   See also DLB 35, 163; SATA 33
Ingram, Willis J.
   See Harris, Mark
Innaurato, Albert (F.) 1948(?)- .. CLC 21, 60
   See also CA 115; 122; INT 122
Innes, Michael
   See Stewart, J(ohn) I(nnes) M(ackintosh)
Innis, Harold Adams 1894-1952 .... TCLC 77
   See also DLB 88
Ionesco, Eugene 1909-1994CLC 1, 4, 6, 9, 11,
   15, 41, 86; DA; DAB; DAC; DAM DRAM,
   MST; WLC
   See also CA 9-12R; 144; CANR 55; MTCW 1;
   SATA 7; SATA-Obit 79
Iqbal, Muhammad 1873-1938 ........ TCLC 28
Ireland, Patrick
   See O'Doherty, Brian
Iron, Ralph
   See Schreiner, Olive (Emilie Albertina)
Irving, John (Winslow) 1942-CLC 13, 23, 38,
   112; DAM NOV, POP
   See also AAYA 8; BEST 89:3; CA 25-28R;
   CANR 28; DLB 6; DLBY 82; MTCW 1
Irving, Washington 1783-1859 . NCLC 2, 19;
   DA; DAB; DAM MST; SSC 2; WLC
   See also CDALB 1640-1865; DLB 3, 11, 30,
   59, 73, 74, 186; YABC 2
Irwin, P. K.
   See Page, P(atricia) K(athleen)
Isaacs, Jorge Ricardo 1837-1895 ... NCLC 70
Isaacs, Susan 1943- ....... CLC 32; DAM POP
   See also BEST 89:1; CA 89-92; CANR 20, 41,
   65; INT CANR-20; MTCW 1
Isherwood, Christopher (William Bradshaw)
   1904-1986 ................................................
   CLC 1, 9, 11, 14, 44; DAM DRAM, NOV
   See also CA 13-16R; 117; CANR 35; DLB 15,
   195; DLBY 86; MTCW 1
Ishiguro, Kazuo 1954- .. CLC 27, 56, 59, 110;
   DAM NOV
   See also BEST 90:2; CA 120; CANR 49; DLB
   194; MTCW 1
Ishikawa, Hakuhin
   See Ishikawa, Takuboku
Ishikawa, Takuboku 1886(?)-1912 TCLC 15;
   DAM POET; PC 10
   See also CA 113; 153
Iskander, Fazil 1929- ......................... CLC 47
   See also CA 102
Isler, Alan (David) 1934- ................... CLC 91
   See also CA 156
Ivan IV 1530-1584 ................................. LC 17
Ivanov, Vyacheslav Ivanovich 1866-1949

TCLC 33
   See also CA 122
Ivask, Ivar Vidrik 1927-1992 ............ CLC 14
   See also CA 37-40R; 139; CANR 24
Ives, Morgan
   See Bradley, Marion Zimmer
J. R. S.
   See Gogarty, Oliver St. John
Jabran, Kahlil
   See Gibran, Kahlil
Jabran, Khalil
   See Gibran, Kahlil
Jackson, Daniel
   See Wingrove, David (John)
Jackson, Jesse 1908-1983 ................... CLC 12
   See also BW 1; CA 25-28R; 109; CANR 27;
   CLR 28; MAICYA; SATA 2, 29; SATA-Obit
   48
Jackson, Laura (Riding) 1901-1991
   See Riding, Laura
   See also CA 65-68; 135; CANR 28; DLB 48
Jackson, Sam
   See Trumbo, Dalton
Jackson, Sara
   See Wingrove, David (John)
Jackson, Shirley 1919-1965 . CLC 11, 60, 87;
   DA; DAC; DAM MST; SSC 9; WLC
   See also AAYA 9; CA 1-4R; 25-28R; CANR 4,
   52; CDALB 1941-1968; DLB 6; SATA 2
Jacob, (Cyprien-)Max 1876-1944 .... TCLC 6
   See also CA 104
Jacobs, Harriet A(nn) 1813(?)-1897NCLC 67
Jacobs, Jim 1942- ............................... CLC 12
   See also CA 97-100; INT 97-100
Jacobs, W(illiam) W(ymark) 1863-1943
   TCLC 22
   See also CA 121; 167; DLB 135
Jacobsen, Jens Peter 1847-1885 .... NCLC 34
Jacobsen, Josephine 1908- ........ CLC 48, 102
   See also CA 33-36R; CAAS 18; CANR 23, 48
Jacobson, Dan 1929- ..................... CLC 4, 14
   See also CA 1-4R; CANR 2, 25, 66; DLB 14;
   MTCW 1
Jacqueline
   See Carpentier (y Valmont), Alejo
Jagger, Mick 1944- ............................. CLC 17
Jahiz, Al- c. 776-869 ........................ CMLC 25
Jahiz, al- c. 780-c. 869 ..................... CMLC 25
Jakes, John (William) 1932- .. CLC 29; DAM
   NOV, POP
   See also BEST 89:4; CA 57-60; CANR 10, 43,
   66; DLBY 83; INT CANR-10; MTCW 1;
   SATA 62
James, Andrew
   See Kirkup, James
James, C(yril) L(ionel) R(obert) 1901-1989
   CLC 33; BLCS
   See also BW 2; CA 117; 125; 128; CANR 62;
   DLB 125; MTCW 1
James, Daniel (Lewis) 1911-1988
   See Santiago, Danny
   See also CA 125
James, Dynely
   See Mayne, William (James Carter)
James, Henry Sr. 1811-1882 ........... NCLC 53
James, Henry 1843-1916 TCLC 2, 11, 24, 40,
   47, 64; DA; DAB; DAC; DAM MST, NOV;
   SSC 8, 32; WLC
   See also CA 104; 132; CDALB 1865-1917;
   DLB 12, 71, 74, 189; DLBD 13; MTCW 1
James, M. R.
   See James, Montague (Rhodes)
   See also DLB 156
James, Montague (Rhodes) 1862-1936T C L C
   6; SSC 16
   See also CA 104; DLB 201
James, P. D. 1920- ........................ CLC 18, 46

   See also White, Phyllis Dorothy James
   See also BEST 90:2; CDBLB 1960 to Present;
   DLB 87; DLBD 17
James, Philip
   See Moorcock, Michael (John)
James, William 1842-1910 ........ TCLC 15, 32
   See also CA 109
James I 1394-1437 .............................. LC 20
Jameson, Anna 1794-1860 .............. NCLC 43
   See also DLB 99, 166
Jami, Nur al-Din 'Abd al-Rahman 1414-1492
   LC 9
Jammes, Francis 1868-1938 .......... TCLC 75
Jandl, Ernst 1925- ............................. CLC 34
Janowitz, Tama 1957- .. CLC 43; DAM POP
   See also CA 106; CANR 52
Japrisot, Sebastien 1931- ................... CLC 90
Jarrell, Randall 1914-1965CLC 1, 2, 6, 9, 13,
   49; DAM POET
   See also CA 5-8R; 25-28R; CABS 2; CANR 6,
   34; CDALB 1941-1968; CLR 6; DLB 48, 52;
   MAICYA; MTCW 1; SATA 7
Jarry, Alfred 1873-1907 .. TCLC 2, 14; DAM
   DRAM; SSC 20
   See also CA 104; 153; DLB 192
Jarvis, E. K.
   See Bloch, Robert (Albert); Ellison, Harlan
   (Jay); Silverberg, Robert
Jeake, Samuel, Jr.
   See Aiken, Conrad (Potter)
Jean Paul 1763-1825 ........................... NCLC 7
Jefferies, (John) Richard 1848-1887NCLC 47
   See also DLB 98, 141; SATA 16
Jeffers, (John) Robinson 1887-1962CLC 2, 3,
   11, 15, 54; DA; DAC; DAM MST, POET;
   PC 17; WLC
   See also CA 85-88; CANR 35; CDALB 1917-
   1929; DLB 45; MTCW 1
Jefferson, Janet
   See Mencken, H(enry) L(ouis)
Jefferson, Thomas 1743-1826 ........ NCLC 11
   See also CDALB 1640-1865; DLB 31
Jeffrey, Francis 1773-1850 .............. NCLC 33
   See also DLB 107
Jelakowitch, Ivan
   See Heijermans, Herman
Jellicoe, (Patricia) Ann 1927- .......... CLC 27
   See also CA 85-88; DLB 13
Jen, Gish ............................................ CLC 70
   See also Jen, Lillian
Jen, Lillian 1956(?)-
   See Jen, Gish
   See also CA 135
Jenkins, (John) Robin 1912- ............. CLC 52
   See also CA 1-4R; CANR 1; DLB 14
Jennings, Elizabeth (Joan) 1926- . CLC 5, 14
   See also CA 61-64; CAAS 5; CANR 8, 39, 66;
   DLB 27; MTCW 1; SATA 66
Jennings, Waylon 1937- ..................... CLC 21
Jensen, Johannes V. 1873-1950 ...... TCLC 41
Jensen, Laura (Linnea) 1948- ........... CLC 37
   See also CA 103
Jerome, Jerome K(lapka) 1859-1927TCLC 23
   See also CA 119; DLB 10, 34, 135
Jerrold, Douglas William 1803-1857NCLC 2
   See also DLB 158, 159
Jewett, (Theodora) Sarah Orne 1849-1909
   TCLC 1, 22; SSC 6
   See also CA 108; 127; CANR 71; DLB 12, 74;
   SATA 15
Jewsbury, Geraldine (Endsor) 1812-1880
   NCLC 22
   See also DLB 21
Jhabvala, Ruth Prawer 1927-CLC 4, 8, 29, 94;
   DAB; DAM NOV
   See also CA 1-4R; CANR 2, 29, 51; DLB 139,
   194; INT CANR-29; MTCW 1

See also CA 134

**Kant, Immanuel** 1724-1804 ......**NCLC 27, 67**
See also DLB 94

**Kantor, MacKinlay** 1904-1977 ...........**CLC 7**
See also CA 61-64; 73-76; CANR 60, 63; DLB 9, 102

**Kaplan, David Michael** 1946- ..........**CLC 50**

**Kaplan, James** 1951- .........................**CLC 59**
See also CA 135

**Karageorge, Michael**
See Anderson, Poul (William)

**Karamzin, Nikolai Mikhailovich** 1766-1826
NCLC 3
See also DLB 150

**Karapanou, Margarita** 1946- ..........**CLC 13**
See also CA 101

**Karinthy, Frigyes** 1887-1938 ..........**TCLC 47**

**Karl, Frederick R(obert)** 1927- ........**CLC 34**
See also CA 5-8R; CANR 3, 44

**Kastel, Warren**
See Silverberg, Robert

**Kataev, Evgeny Petrovich** 1903-1942
See Petrov, Evgeny
See also CA 120

**Kataphusin**
See Ruskin, John

**Katz, Steve** 1935- ...............................**CLC 47**
See also CA 25-28R; CAAS 14, 64; CANR 12; DLBY 83

**Kauffman, Janet** 1945- .....................**CLC 42**
See also CA 117; CANR 43; DLBY 86

**Kaufman, Bob (Garnell)** 1925-1986 . **CLC 49**
See also BW 1; CA 41-44R; 118; CANR 22; DLB 16, 41

**Kaufman, George S.** 1889-1961**CLC 38; DAM DRAM**
See also CA 108; 93-96; DLB 7; INT 108

**Kaufman, Sue** .....................................**CLC 3, 8**
See also Barondess, Sue K(aufman)

**Kavafis, Konstantinos Petrou** 1863-1933
See Cavafy, C(onstantine) P(eter)
See also CA 104

**Kavan, Anna** 1901-1968 .........**CLC 5, 13, 82**
See also CA 5-8R; CANR 6, 57; MTCW 1

**Kavanagh, Dan**
See Barnes, Julian (Patrick)

**Kavanagh, Patrick (Joseph)** 1904-1967 **C L C 22**
See also CA 123; 25-28R; DLB 15, 20; MTCW 1

**Kawabata, Yasunari** 1899-1972 `CLC 2, 5, 9, 18, 107; DAM MULT; SSC 17`
See also CA 93-96; 33-36R; DLB 180

**Kaye, M(ary) M(argaret)** 1909- ........**CLC 28**
See also CA 89-92; CANR 24, 60; MTCW 1; SATA 62

**Kaye, Mollie**
See Kaye, M(ary) M(argaret)

**Kaye-Smith, Sheila** 1887-1956 .......**TCLC 20**
See also CA 118; DLB 36

**Kaymor, Patrice Maguilene**
See Senghor, Leopold Sedar

**Kazan, Elia** 1909- ....................**CLC 6, 16, 63**
See also CA 21-24R; CANR 32

**Kazantzakis, Nikos** 1883(?)-1957 **TCLC 2, 5, 33**
See also CA 105; 132; MTCW 1

**Kazin, Alfred** 1915- .....................**CLC 34, 38**
See also CA 1-4R; CAAS 7; CANR 1, 45; DLB 67

**Keane, Mary Nesta (Skrine)** 1904-1996
See Keane, Molly
See also CA 108; 114; 151

**Keane, Molly** ......................................**CLC 31**
See also Keane, Mary Nesta (Skrine)
See also INT 114

**Keates, Jonathan** 1946(?)- ..................**CLC 34**

See also CA 163

**Keaton, Buster** 1895-1966 .................**CLC 20**

**Keats, John** 1795-1821**NCLC 8, 73; DA; DAB; DAC; DAM MST, POET; PC 1; WLC**
See also CDBLB 1789-1832; DLB 96, 110

**Keene, Donald** 1922- ..........................**CLC 34**
See also CA 1-4R; CANR 5

**Keillor, Garrison** ........................**CLC 40, 115**
See also Keillor, Gary (Edward)
See also AAYA 2; BEST 89:3; DLBY 87; SATA 58

**Keillor, Gary (Edward)** 1942-
See Keillor, Garrison
See also CA 111; 117; CANR 36, 59; DAM POP; MTCW 1

**Keith, Michael**
See Hubbard, L(afayette) Ron(ald)

**Keller, Gottfried** 1819-1890**NCLC 2; SSC 26**
See also DLB 129

**Keller, Nora Okja** .............................**CLC 109**

**Kellerman, Jonathan** 1949- ... **CLC 44; DAM POP**
See also BEST 90:1; CA 106; CANR 29, 51; INT CANR-29

**Kelley, William Melvin** 1937- ............**CLC 22**
See also BW 1; CA 77-80; CANR 27; DLB 33

**Kellogg, Marjorie** 1922- .....................**CLC 2**
See also CA 81-84

**Kellow, Kathleen**
See Hibbert, Eleanor Alice Burford

**Kelly, M(ilton) T(erry)** 1947- ...........**CLC 55**
See also CA 97-100; CAAS 22; CANR 19, 43

**Kelman, James** 1946- ...................**CLC 58, 86**
See also CA 148; DLB 194

**Kemal, Yashar** 1923- ...................**CLC 14, 29**
See also CA 89-92; CANR 44

**Kemble, Fanny** 1809-1893 ..............**NCLC 18**
See also DLB 32

**Kemelman, Harry** 1908-1996 ..............**CLC 2**
See also AITN 1; CA 9-12R; 155; CANR 6, 71; DLB 28

**Kempe, Margery** 1373(?)-1440(?) ..........**LC 6**
See also DLB 146

**Kempis, Thomas a** 1380-1471 ..............**LC 11**

**Kendall, Henry** 1839-1882 .............**NCLC 12**

**Keneally, Thomas (Michael)** 1935- **CLC 5, 8, 10, 14, 19, 27, 43; DAM NOV**
See also CA 85-88; CANR 10, 50; MTCW 1

**Kennedy, Adrienne (Lita)** 1931-**CLC 66; BLC 2; DAM MULT; DC 5**
See also BW 2; CA 103; CAAS 20; CABS 3; CANR 26, 53; DLB 38

**Kennedy, John Pendleton** 1795-1870**NCLC 2**
See also DLB 3

**Kennedy, Joseph Charles** 1929-
See Kennedy, X. J.
See also CA 1-4R; CANR 4, 30, 40; SATA 14, 86

**Kennedy, William** 1928- ..**CLC 6, 28, 34, 53; DAM NOV**
See also AAYA 1; CA 85-88; CANR 14, 31; DLB 143; DLBY 85; INT CANR-31; MTCW 1; SATA 57

**Kennedy, X. J.** ...............................**CLC 8, 42**
See also Kennedy, Joseph Charles
See also CAAS 9; CLR 27; DLB 5; SAAS 22

**Kenny, Maurice (Francis)** 1929- .....**CLC 87; DAM MULT**
See also CA 144; CAAS 22; DLB 175; NNAL

**Kent, Kelvin**
See Kuttner, Henry

**Kenton, Maxwell**
See Southern, Terry

**Kenyon, Robert O.**
See Kuttner, Henry

**Kepler, Johannes** 1571-1630 ................**LC 45**

**Kerouac, Jack** ........ **CLC 1, 2, 3, 5, 14, 29, 61**

See also Kerouac, Jean-Louis Lebris de
See also AAYA 25; CDALB 1941-1968; DLB 2, 16; DLBD 3; DLBY 95

**Kerouac, Jean-Louis Lebris de** 1922-1969
See Kerouac, Jack
See also AITN 1; CA 5-8R; 25-28R; CANR 26, 54; DA; DAB; DAC; DAM MST, NOV, POET, POP; MTCW 1; WLC

**Kerr, Jean** 1923- ................................**CLC 22**
See also CA 5-8R; CANR 7; INT CANR-7

**Kerr, M. E.** ..................................**CLC 12, 35**
See also Meaker, Marijane (Agnes)
See also AAYA 2, 23; CLR 29; SAAS 1

**Kerr, Robert** ......................................**CLC 55**

**Kerrigan, (Thomas) Anthony** 1918-**CLC 4, 6**
See also CA 49-52; CAAS 11; CANR 4

**Kerry, Lois**
See Duncan, Lois

**Kesey, Ken (Elton)** 1935- **CLC 1, 3, 6, 11, 46, 64; DA; DAB; DAC; DAM MST, NOV, POP; WLC**
See also AAYA 25; CA 1-4R; CANR 22, 38, 66; CDALB 1968-1988; DLB 2, 16; MTCW 1; SATA 66

**Kesselring, Joseph (Otto)** 1902-1967**CLC 45; DAM DRAM, MST**
See also CA 150

**Kessler, Jascha (Frederick)** 1929- ......**CLC 4**
See also CA 17-20R; CANR 8, 48

**Kettelkamp, Larry (Dale)** 1933- .......**CLC 12**
See also CA 29-32R; CANR 16; SAAS 3; SATA 2

**Key, Ellen** 1849-1926 ......................**TCLC 65**

**Keyber, Conny**
See Fielding, Henry

**Keyes, Daniel** 1927-**CLC 80; DA; DAC; DAM MST, NOV**
See also AAYA 23; CA 17-20R; CANR 10, 26, 54; SATA 37

**Keynes, John Maynard** 1883-1946 **TCLC 64**
See also CA 114; 162, 163; DLBD 10

**Khanshendel, Chiron**
See Rose, Wendy

**Khayyam, Omar** 1048-1131**CMLC 11; DAM POET; PC 8**

**Kherdian, David** 1931- .....................**CLC 6, 9**
See also CA 21-24R; CAAS 2; CANR 39; CLR 24; JRDA; MAICYA; SATA 16, 74

**Khlebnikov, Velimir** ..........................**TCLC 20**
See also Khlebnikov, Viktor Vladimirovich

**Khlebnikov, Viktor Vladimirovich** 1885-1922
See Khlebnikov, Velimir
See also CA 117

**Khodasevich, Vladislav (Felitsianovich)** 1886-1939 ..........................................................
**TCLC 15**
See also CA 115

**Kielland, Alexander Lange** 1849-1906**T C L C 5**
See also CA 104

**Kiely, Benedict** 1919- ..................**CLC 23, 43**
See also CA 1-4R; CANR 2; DLB 15

**Kienzle, William X(avier)** 1928- .....**CLC 25; DAM POP**
See also CA 93-96; CAAS 1; CANR 9, 31, 59; INT CANR-31; MTCW 1

**Kierkegaard, Soren** 1813-1855 ......**NCLC 34**

**Killens, John Oliver** 1916-1987 ........**CLC 10**
See also BW 2; CA 77-80; 123; CAAS 2; CANR 26; DLB 33

**Killigrew, Anne** 1660-1685 ....................**LC 4**
See also DLB 131

**Kim**
See Simenon, Georges (Jacques Christian)

**Kincaid, Jamaica** 1949- **CLC 43, 68; BLC 2; DAM MULT, NOV**
See also AAYA 13; BW 2; CA 125; CANR 47,

MTCW 1
**Kroetz, Franz**
See Kroetz, Franz Xaver
**Kroetz, Franz Xaver** 1946- ................ **CLC 41**
See also CA 130
**Kroker, Arthur (W.)** 1945- ................ **CLC 77**
See also CA 161
**Kropotkin, Peter (Aleksieevich)** 1842-1921
**TCLC 36**
See also CA 119
**Krotkov, Yuri** 1917- ............................ **CLC 19**
See also CA 102
**Krumb**
See Crumb, R(obert)
**Krumgold, Joseph (Quincy)** 1908-1980 **C L C 12**
See also CA 9-12R; 101; CANR 7; MAICYA;
SATA 1, 48; SATA-Obit 23
**Krumwitz**
See Crumb, R(obert)
**Krutch, Joseph Wood** 1893-1970 ...... **CLC 24**
See also CA 1-4R; 25-28R; CANR 4; DLB 63
**Krutzch, Gus**
See Eliot, T(homas) S(tearns)
**Krylov, Ivan Andreevich** 1768(?)-1844 **N C L C 1**
See also DLB 150
**Kubin, Alfred (Leopold Isidor)** 1877-1959
**TCLC 23**
See also CA 112; 149; DLB 81
**Kubrick, Stanley** 1928- ...................... **CLC 16**
See also CA 81-84; CANR 33; DLB 26
**Kumin, Maxine (Winokur)** 1925- **CLC 5, 13, 28; DAM POET; PC 15**
See also AITN 2; CA 1-4R; CAAS 8; CANR 1,
21, 69; DLB 5; MTCW 1; SATA 12
**Kundera, Milan** 1929- .. **CLC 4, 9, 19, 32, 68, 115; DAM NOV; SSC 24**
See also AAYA 2; CA 85-88; CANR 19, 52;
MTCW 1
**Kunene, Mazisi (Raymond)** 1930- .... **CLC 85**
See also BW 1; CA 125; DLB 117
**Kunitz, Stanley (Jasspon)** 1905- **CLC 6, 11, 14; PC 19**
See also CA 41-44R; CANR 26, 57; DLB 48;
INT CANR-26; MTCW 1
**Kunze, Reiner** 1933- .......................... **CLC 10**
See also CA 93-96; DLB 75
**Kuprin, Aleksandr Ivanovich** 1870-1938
**TCLC 5**
See also CA 104
**Kureishi, Hanif** 1954(?)- .................... **CLC 64**
See also CA 139; DLB 194
**Kurosawa, Akira** 1910- **CLC 16; DAM MULT**
See also AAYA 11; CA 101; CANR 46
**Kushner, Tony** 1957(?)- **CLC 81; DAM DRAM**
See also CA 144
**Kuttner, Henry** 1915-1958 .............. **TCLC 10**
See also Vance, Jack
See also CA 107; 157; DLB 8
**Kuzma, Greg** 1944- .............................. **CLC 7**
See also CA 33-36R; CANR 70
**Kuzmin, Mikhail** 1872(?)-1936 ...... **TCLC 40**
**Kyd, Thomas** 1558-1594 **LC 22; DAM DRAM; DC 3**
See also DLB 62
**Kyprianos, Iossif**
See Samarakis, Antonis
**La Bruyere, Jean de** 1645-1696 .......... **LC 17**
**Lacan, Jacques (Marie Emile)** 1901-1981
**CLC 75**
See also CA 121; 104
**Laclos, Pierre Ambroise Francois Choderlos de**
1741-1803 .................................. **NCLC 4**
**Lacolere, Francois**
See Aragon, Louis
**La Colere, Francois**

See Aragon, Louis
**La Deshabilleuse**
See Simenon, Georges (Jacques Christian)
**Lady Gregory**
See Gregory, Isabella Augusta (Persse)
**Lady of Quality, A**
See Bagnold, Enid
**La Fayette, Marie (Madelaine Pioche de la Vergne Comtes** 1634-1693 ............ **LC 2**
**Lafayette, Rene**
See Hubbard, L(afayette) Ron(ald)
**Laforgue, Jules** 1860-1887 **NCLC 5, 53; PC 14; SSC 20**
**Lagerkvist, Paer (Fabian)** 1891-1974 **CLC 7, 10, 13, 54; DAM DRAM, NOV**
See also Lagerkvist, Par
See also CA 85-88; 49-52; MTCW 1
**Lagerkvist, Par** ...................................... **SSC 12**
See also Lagerkvist, Paer (Fabian)
**Lagerloef, Selma (Ottiliana Lovisa)** 1858-1940
**TCLC 4, 36**
See also Lagerlof, Selma (Ottiliana Lovisa)
See also CA 108; SATA 15
**Lagerlof, Selma (Ottiliana Lovisa)**
See Lagerloef, Selma (Ottiliana Lovisa)
See also CLR 7; SATA 15
**La Guma, (Justin) Alex(ander)** 1925-1985
**CLC 19; BLCS; DAM NOV**
See also BW 1; CA 49-52; 118; CANR 25; DLB
117; MTCW 1
**Laidlaw, A. K.**
See Grieve, C(hristopher) M(urray)
**Lainez, Manuel Mujica**
See Mujica Lainez, Manuel
See also HW
**Laing, R(onald) D(avid)** 1927-1989 . **CLC 95**
See also CA 107; 129; CANR 34; MTCW 1
**Lamartine, Alphonse (Marie Louis Prat) de**
1790-1869 ..............................................
**NCLC 11; DAM POET; PC 16**
**Lamb, Charles** 1775-1834 ..... **NCLC 10; DA; DAB; DAC; DAM MST; WLC**
See also CDBLB 1789-1832; DLB 93, 107, 163;
SATA 17
**Lamb, Lady Caroline** 1785-1828 ... **NCLC 38**
See also DLB 116
**Lamming, George (William)** 1927- **CLC 2, 4, 66; BLC 2; DAM MULT**
See also BW 2; CA 85-88; CANR 26; DLB 125;
MTCW 1
**L'Amour, Louis (Dearborn)** 1908-1988 **C L C 25, 55; DAM NOV, POP**
See also AAYA 16; AITN 2; BEST 89:2; CA 1-
4R; 125; CANR 3, 25, 40; DLBY 80; MTCW
1
**Lampedusa, Giuseppe (Tomasi) di** 1896-1957
**TCLC 13**
See also Tomasi di Lampedusa, Giuseppe
See also CA 164; DLB 177
**Lampman, Archibald** 1861-1899 ... **NCLC 25**
See also DLB 92
**Lancaster, Bruce** 1896-1963 ............. **CLC 36**
See also CA 9-10; CANR 70; CAP 1; SATA 9
**Lanchester, John** ................................. **CLC 99**
**Landau, Mark Alexandrovich**
See Aldanov, Mark (Alexandrovich)
**Landau-Aldanov, Mark Alexandrovich**
See Aldanov, Mark (Alexandrovich)
**Landis, Jerry**
See Simon, Paul (Frederick)
**Landis, John** 1950- ............................. **CLC 26**
See also CA 112; 122
**Landolfi, Tommaso** 1908-1979 .... **CLC 11, 49**
See also CA 127; 117; DLB 177
**Landon, Letitia Elizabeth** 1802-1838 **N C L C 15**
See also DLB 96

**Landor, Walter Savage** 1775-1864 **NCLC 14**
See also DLB 93, 107
**Landwirth, Heinz** 1927-
See Lind, Jakov
See also CA 9-12R; CANR 7
**Lane, Patrick** 1939- ... **CLC 25; DAM POET**
See also CA 97-100; CANR 54; DLB 53; INT
97-100
**Lang, Andrew** 1844-1912 .............. **TCLC 16**
See also CA 114; 137; DLB 98, 141, 184;
MAICYA; SATA 16
**Lang, Fritz** 1890-1976 .............. **CLC 20, 103**
See also CA 77-80; 69-72; CANR 30
**Lange, John**
See Crichton, (John) Michael
**Langer, Elinor** 1939- ......................... **CLC 34**
See also CA 121
**Langland, William** 1330(?)-1400(?) ... **LC 19; DA; DAB; DAC; DAM MST, POET**
See also DLB 146
**Langstaff, Launcelot**
See Irving, Washington
**Lanier, Sidney** 1842-1881 ..... **NCLC 6; DAM POET**
See also DLB 64; DLBD 13; MAICYA; SATA
18
**Lanyer, Aemilia** 1569-1645 .......... **LC 10, 30**
See also DLB 121
**Lao-Tzu**
See Lao Tzu
**Lao Tzu** fl. 6th cent. B.C.- ................ **CMLC 7**
**Lapine, James (Elliot)** 1949- ............. **CLC 39**
See also CA 123; 130; CANR 54; INT 130
**Larbaud, Valery (Nicolas)** 1881-1957 **TCLC 9**
See also CA 106; 152
**Lardner, Ring**
See Lardner, Ring(gold) W(ilmer)
**Lardner, Ring W., Jr.**
See Lardner, Ring(gold) W(ilmer)
**Lardner, Ring(gold) W(ilmer)** 1885-1933
**TCLC 2, 14; SSC 32**
See also CA 104; 131; CDALB 1917-1929;
DLB 11, 25, 86; DLBD 16; MTCW 1
**Laredo, Betty**
See Codrescu, Andrei
**Larkin, Maia**
See Wojciechowska, Maia (Teresa)
**Larkin, Philip (Arthur)** 1922-1985 **CLC 3, 5, 8, 9, 13, 18, 33, 39, 64; DAB; DAM MST, POET; PC 21**
See also CA 5-8R; 117; CANR 24, 62; CDBLB
1960 to Present; DLB 27; MTCW 1
**Larra (y Sanchez de Castro), Mariano Jose de**
1809-1837 .................................. **NCLC 17**
**Larsen, Eric** 1941- ............................. **CLC 55**
See also CA 132
**Larsen, Nella** 1891-1964 .... **CLC 37; BLC 2; DAM MULT**
See also BW 1; CA 125; DLB 51
**Larson, Charles R(aymond)** 1938- ... **CLC 31**
See also CA 53-56; CANR 4
**Larson, Jonathan** 1961-1996 ............. **CLC 99**
See also CA 156
**Las Casas, Bartolome de** 1474-1566 ... **LC 31**
**Lasch, Christopher** 1932-1994 ........ **CLC 102**
See also CA 73-76; 144; CANR 25; MTCW 1
**Lasker-Schueler, Else** 1869-1945 ... **TCLC 57**
See also DLB 66, 124
**Laski, Harold** 1893-1950 ................ **TCLC 79**
**Latham, Jean Lee** 1902-1995 ........... **CLC 12**
See also AITN 1; CA 5-8R; CANR 7; CLR 50;
MAICYA; SATA 2, 68
**Latham, Mavis**
See Clark, Mavis Thorpe
**Lathen, Emma** ...................................... **CLC 2**
See also Hennissart, Martha; Latsis, Mary J(ane)
**Lathrop, Francis**

See Slade, Bernard
See also CA 81-84; CANR 49; DAM DRAM
**Newby, P(ercy) H(oward)** 1918-1997 **CLC 2, 13; DAM NOV**
See also CA 5-8R; 161; CANR 32, 67; DLB 15; MTCW 1
**Newlove, Donald** 1928- .......................... **CLC 6**
See also CA 29-32R; CANR 25
**Newlove, John (Herbert)** 1938- ........ **CLC 14**
See also CA 21-24R; CANR 9, 25
**Newman, Charles** 1938- ................... **CLC 2, 8**
See also CA 21-24R
**Newman, Edwin (Harold)** 1919- ....... **CLC 14**
See also AITN 1; CA 69-72; CANR 5
**Newman, John Henry** 1801-1890 .. **NCLC 38**
See also DLB 18, 32, 55
**Newton, Suzanne** 1936- ...................... **CLC 35**
See also CA 41-44R; CANR 14; JRDA; SATA 5, 77
**Nexo, Martin Andersen** 1869-1954 **TCLC 43**
**Nezval, Vitezslav** 1900-1958 ........... **TCLC 44**
See also CA 123
**Ng, Fae Myenne** 1957(?)- ................... **CLC 81**
See also CA 146
**Ngema, Mbongeni** 1955- ..................... **CLC 57**
See also BW 2; CA 143
**Ngugi, James T(hiong'o)** ........... **CLC 3, 7, 13**
See also Ngugi wa Thiong'o
**Ngugi wa Thiong'o** 1938- .. **CLC 36; BLC 3; DAM MULT, NOV**
See also Ngugi, James T(hiong'o)
See also BW 2; CA 81-84; CANR 27, 58; DLB 125; MTCW 1
**Nichol, B(arrie) P(hillip)** 1944-1988 **CLC 18**
See also CA 53-56; DLB 53; SATA 66
**Nichols, John (Treadwell)** 1940- ....... **CLC 38**
See also CA 9-12R; CAAS 2; CANR 6, 70; DLBY 82
**Nichols, Leigh**
See Koontz, Dean R(ay)
**Nichols, Peter (Richard)** 1927- **CLC 5, 36, 65**
See also CA 104; CANR 33; DLB 13; MTCW 1
**Nicolas, F. R. E.**
See Freeling, Nicolas
**Niedecker, Lorine** 1903-1970 .... **CLC 10, 42; DAM POET**
See also CA 25-28; CAP 2; DLB 48
**Nietzsche, Friedrich (Wilhelm)** 1844-1900 **TCLC 10, 18, 55**
See also CA 107; 121; DLB 129
**Nievo, Ippolito** 1831-1861 ............... **NCLC 22**
**Nightingale, Anne Redmon** 1943-
See Redmon, Anne
See also CA 103
**Nightingale, Florence** 1820-1910 ... **TCLC 85**
See also DLB 166
**Nik. T. O.**
See Annensky, Innokenty (Fyodorovich)
**Nin, Anais** 1903-1977 **CLC 1, 4, 8, 11, 14, 60; DAM NOV, POP; SSC 10**
See also AITN 2; CA 13-16R; 69-72; CANR 22, 53; DLB 2, 4, 152; MTCW 1
**Nishida, Kitaro** 1870-1945 ............. **TCLC 83**
**Nishiwaki, Junzaburo** 1894-1982 ........ **PC 15**
See also CA 107
**Nissenson, Hugh** 1933- ...................... **CLC 4, 9**
See also CA 17-20R; CANR 27; DLB 28
**Niven, Larry** ............................................. **CLC 8**
See also Niven, Laurence Van Cott
See also AAYA 27; DLB 8
**Niven, Laurence Van Cott** 1938-
See Niven, Larry
See also CA 21-24R; CAAS 12; CANR 14, 44, 66; DAM POP; MTCW 1; SATA 95
**Nixon, Agnes Eckhardt** 1927- .......... **CLC 21**
See also CA 110

**Nizan, Paul** 1905-1940 ..................... **TCLC 40**
See also CA 161; DLB 72
**Nkosi, Lewis** 1936- .... **CLC 45; BLC 3; DAM MULT**
See also BW 1; CA 65-68; CANR 27; DLB 157
**Nodier, (Jean) Charles (Emmanuel)** 1780-1844 **NCLC 19**
See also DLB 119
**Noguchi, Yone** 1875-1947 ............... **TCLC 80**
**Nolan, Christopher** 1965- .................. **CLC 58**
See also CA 111
**Noon, Jeff** 1957- ................................. **CLC 91**
See also CA 148
**Norden, Charles**
See Durrell, Lawrence (George)
**Nordhoff, Charles (Bernard)** 1887-1947 **TCLC 23**
See also CA 108; DLB 9; SATA 23
**Norfolk, Lawrence** 1963- ................... **CLC 76**
See also CA 144
**Norman, Marsha** 1947- **CLC 28; DAM DRAM; DC 8**
See also CA 105; CABS 3; CANR 41; DLBY 84
**Normyx**
See Douglas, (George) Norman
**Norris, Frank** 1870-1902 ..................... **SSC 28**
See also Norris, (Benjamin) Frank(lin, Jr.)
See also CDALB 1865-1917; DLB 12, 71, 186
**Norris, (Benjamin) Frank(lin, Jr.)** 1870-1902 **TCLC 24**
See also Norris, Frank
See also CA 110; 160
**Norris, Leslie** 1921- ............................. **CLC 14**
See also CA 11-12; CANR 14; CAP 1; DLB 27
**North, Andrew**
See Norton, Andre
**North, Anthony**
See Koontz, Dean R(ay)
**North, Captain George**
See Stevenson, Robert Louis (Balfour)
**North, Milou**
See Erdrich, Louise
**Northrup, B. A.**
See Hubbard, L(afayette) Ron(ald)
**North Staffs**
See Hulme, T(homas) E(rnest)
**Norton, Alice Mary**
See Norton, Andre
See also MAICYA; SATA 1, 43
**Norton, Andre** 1912- ............................ **CLC 12**
See also Norton, Alice Mary
See also AAYA 14; CA 1-4R; CANR 68; CLR 50; DLB 8, 52; JRDA; MTCW 1; SATA 91
**Norton, Caroline** 1808-1877 ........... **NCLC 47**
See also DLB 21, 159, 199
**Norway, Nevil Shute** 1899-1960
See Shute, Nevil
See also CA 102; 93-96
**Norwid, Cyprian Kamil** 1821-1883 **NCLC 17**
**Nosille, Nabrah**
See Ellison, Harlan (Jay)
**Nossack, Hans Erich** 1901-1978 ........ **CLC 6**
See also CA 93-96; 85-88; DLB 69
**Nostradamus** 1503-1566 ...................... **LC 27**
**Nosu, Chuji**
See Ozu, Yasujiro
**Notenburg, Eleanora (Genrikhovna) von**
See Guro, Elena
**Nova, Craig** 1945- ........................... **CLC 7, 31**
See also CA 45-48; CANR 2, 53
**Novak, Joseph**
See Kosinski, Jerzy (Nikodem)
**Novalis** 1772-1801 ............................ **NCLC 13**
See also DLB 90
**Novis, Emile**
See Weil, Simone (Adolphine)

**Nowlan, Alden (Albert)** 1933-1983 **CLC 15; DAC; DAM MST**
See also CA 9-12R; CANR 5; DLB 53
**Noyes, Alfred** 1880-1958 ................... **TCLC 7**
See also CA 104; DLB 20
**Nunn, Kem** ........................................... **CLC 34**
See also CA 159
**Nye, Robert** 1939- .. **CLC 13, 42; DAM NOV**
See also CA 33-36R; CANR 29, 67; DLB 14; MTCW 1; SATA 6
**Nyro, Laura** 1947- ............................. **CLC 17**
**Oates, Joyce Carol** 1938-**CLC 1, 2, 3, 6, 9, 11, 15, 19, 33, 52, 108; DA; DAB; DAC; DAM MST, NOV, POP; SSC 6; WLC**
See also AAYA 15; AITN 1; BEST 89:2; CA 5-8R; CANR 25, 45; CDALB 1968-1988; DLB 2, 5, 130; DLBY 81; INT CANR-25; MTCW 1
**O'Brien, Darcy** 1939-1998 ................. **CLC 11**
See also CA 21-24R; 167; CANR 8, 59
**O'Brien, E. G.**
See Clarke, Arthur C(harles)
**O'Brien, Edna** 1936- **CLC 3, 5, 8, 13, 36, 65; DAM NOV; SSC 10**
See also CA 1-4R; CANR 6, 41, 65; CDBLB 1960 to Present; DLB 14; MTCW 1
**O'Brien, Fitz-James** 1828-1862 ..... **NCLC 21**
See also DLB 74
**O'Brien, Flann** .............. **CLC 1, 4, 5, 7, 10, 47**
See also O Nuallain, Brian
**O'Brien, Richard** 1942- ...................... **CLC 17**
See also CA 124
**O'Brien, (William) Tim(othy)** 1946- . **CLC 7, 19, 40, 103; DAM POP**
See also AAYA 16; CA 85-88; CANR 40, 58; DLB 152; DLBD 9; DLBY 80
**Obstfelder, Sigbjoern** 1866-1900 ... **TCLC 23**
See also CA 123
**O'Casey, Sean** 1880-1964**CLC 1, 5, 9, 11, 15, 88; DAB; DAC; DAM DRAM, MST; WLCS**
See also CA 89-92; CANR 62; CDBLB 1914-1945; DLB 10; MTCW 1
**O'Cathasaigh, Sean**
See O'Casey, Sean
**Ochs, Phil** 1940-1976 .......................... **CLC 17**
See also CA 65-68
**O'Connor, Edwin (Greene)** 1918-1968**CLC 14**
See also CA 93-96; 25-28R
**O'Connor, (Mary) Flannery** 1925-1964 **C L C 1, 2, 3, 6, 10, 13, 15, 21, 66, 104; DA; DAB; DAC; DAM MST, NOV; SSC 1, 23; WLC**
See also AAYA 7; CA 1-4R; CANR 3, 41; CDALB 1941-1968; DLB 2, 152; DLBD 12; DLBY 80; MTCW 1
**O'Connor, Frank** ..................... **CLC 23; SSC 5**
See also O'Donovan, Michael John
See also DLB 162
**O'Dell, Scott** 1898-1989 ..................... **CLC 30**
See also AAYA 3; CA 61-64; 129; CANR 12, 30; CLR 1, 16; DLB 52; JRDA; MAICYA; SATA 12, 60
**Odets, Clifford** 1906-1963**CLC 2, 28, 98; DAM DRAM; DC 6**
See also CA 85-88; CANR 62; DLB 7, 26; MTCW 1
**O'Doherty, Brian** 1934- ..................... **CLC 76**
See also CA 105
**O'Donnell, K. M.**
See Malzberg, Barry N(athaniel)
**O'Donnell, Lawrence**
See Kuttner, Henry
**O'Donovan, Michael John** 1903-1966**CLC 14**
See also O'Connor, Frank
See also CA 93-96
**Oe, Kenzaburo** 1935- **CLC 10, 36, 86; DAM NOV; SSC 20**

See also CA 97-100; CANR 36, 50; DLB 182;
DLBY 94; MTCW 1
**O'Faolain, Julia** 1932- .... **CLC 6, 19, 47, 108**
See also CA 81-84; CAAS 2; CANR 12, 61;
DLB 14; MTCW 1
**O'Faolain, Sean** 1900-1991 **CLC 1, 7, 14, 32,
70; SSC 13**
See also CA 61-64; 134; CANR 12, 66; DLB
15, 162; MTCW 1
**O'Flaherty, Liam** 1896-1984 **CLC 5, 34; SSC 6**
See also CA 101; 113; CANR 35; DLB 36, 162;
DLBY 84; MTCW 1
**Ogilvy, Gavin**
See Barrie, J(ames) M(atthew)
**O'Grady, Standish (James)** 1846-1928 **T C L C
5**
See also CA 104; 157
**O'Grady, Timothy** 1951- .................... **CLC 59**
See also CA 138
**O'Hara, Frank** 1926-1966 . **CLC 2, 5, 13, 78;
DAM POET**
See also CA 9-12R; 25-28R; CANR 33; DLB
5, 16, 193; MTCW 1
**O'Hara, John (Henry)** 1905-1970 **CLC 1, 2, 3,
6, 11, 42; DAM NOV; SSC 15**
See also CA 5-8R; 25-28R; CANR 31, 60;
CDALB 1929-1941; DLB 9, 86; DLBD 2;
MTCW 1
**O Hehir, Diana** 1922- ......................... **CLC 41**
See also CA 93-96
**Okigbo, Christopher (Ifenayichukwu)** 1932-
1967 . **CLC 25, 84; BLC 3; DAM MULT,
POET; PC 7**
See also BW 1; CA 77-80; DLB 125; MTCW 1
**Okri, Ben** 1959- ................................. **CLC 87**
See also BW 2; CA 130; 138; CANR 65; DLB
157; INT 138
**Olds, Sharon** 1942- .... **CLC 32, 39, 85; DAM
POET; PC 22**
See also CA 101; CANR 18, 41, 66; DLB 120
**Oldstyle, Jonathan**
See Irving, Washington
**Olesha, Yuri (Karlovich)** 1899-1960 .. **CLC 8**
See also CA 85-88
**Oliphant, Laurence** 1829(?)-1888 .. **NCLC 47**
See also DLB 18, 166
**Oliphant, Margaret (Oliphant Wilson)** 1828-
1897 ...................... **NCLC 11, 61; SSC 25**
See also DLB 18, 159, 190
**Oliver, Mary** 1935- ................ **CLC 19, 34, 98**
See also CA 21-24R; CANR 9, 43; DLB 5, 193
**Olivier, Laurence (Kerr)** 1907-1989 . **CLC 20**
See also CA 111; 150; 129
**Olsen, Tillie** 1913- **CLC 4, 13, 114; DA; DAB;
DAC; DAM MST; SSC 11**
See also CA 1-4R; CANR 1, 43; DLB 28; DLBY
80; MTCW 1
**Olson, Charles (John)** 1910-1970 **CLC 1, 2, 5,
6, 9, 11, 29; DAM POET; PC 19**
See also CA 13-16; 25-28R; CABS 2; CANR
35, 61; CAP 1; DLB 5, 16, 193; MTCW 1
**Olson, Toby** 1937- ............................... **CLC 28**
See also CA 65-68; CANR 9, 31
**Olyesha, Yuri**
See Olesha, Yuri (Karlovich)
**Ondaatje, (Philip) Michael** 1943- **CLC 14, 29,
51, 76; DAB; DAC; DAM MST**
See also CA 77-80; CANR 42; DLB 60
**Oneal, Elizabeth** 1934-
See Oneal, Zibby
See also CA 106; CANR 28; MAICYA; SATA
30, 82
**Oneal, Zibby** ...................................... **CLC 30**
See also Oneal, Elizabeth
See also AAYA 5; CLR 13; JRDA
**O'Neill, Eugene (Gladstone)** 1888-1953 **TCLC
1, 6, 27, 49; DA; DAB; DAC; DAM DRAM,**

MST; WLC
See also AITN 1; CA 110; 132; CDALB 1929-
1941; DLB 7; MTCW 1
**Onetti, Juan Carlos** 1909-1994 ... **CLC 7, 10;
DAM MULT, NOV; SSC 23**
See also CA 85-88; 145; CANR 32, 63; DLB
113; HW; MTCW 1
**O Nuallain, Brian** 1911-1966
See O'Brien, Flann
See also CA 21-22; 25-28R; CAP 2
**Ophuls, Max** 1902-1957 .................. **TCLC 79**
See also CA 113
**Opie, Amelia** 1769-1853 .................. **NCLC 65**
See also DLB 116, 159
**Oppen, George** 1908-1984 ...... **CLC 7, 13, 34**
See also CA 13-16R; 113; CANR 8; DLB 5,
165
**Oppenheim, E(dward) Phillips** 1866-1946
**TCLC 45**
See also CA 111; DLB 70
**Opuls, Max**
See Ophuls, Max
**Origen** c. 185-c. 254 ........................ **CMLC 19**
**Orlovitz, Gil** 1918-1973 .................... **CLC 22**
See also CA 77-80; 45-48; DLB 2, 5
**Orris**
See Ingelow, Jean
**Ortega y Gasset, Jose** 1883-1955 .... **TCLC 9;
DAM MULT; HLC**
See also CA 106; 130; HW; MTCW 1
**Ortese, Anna Maria** 1914- ................ **CLC 89**
See also DLB 177
**Ortiz, Simon J(oseph)** 1941- .. **CLC 45; DAM
MULT, POET; PC 17**
See also CA 134; CANR 69; DLB 120, 175;
NNAL
**Orton, Joe** ....................... **CLC 4, 13, 43; DC 3**
See also Orton, John Kingsley
See also CDBLB 1960 to Present; DLB 13
**Orton, John Kingsley** 1933-1967
See Orton, Joe
See also CA 85-88; CANR 35, 66; DAM
DRAM; MTCW 1
**Orwell, George** . **TCLC 2, 6, 15, 31, 51; DAB;
WLC**
See also Blair, Eric (Arthur)
See also CDBLB 1945-1960; DLB 15, 98, 195
**Osborne, David**
See Silverberg, Robert
**Osborne, George**
See Silverberg, Robert
**Osborne, John (James)** 1929-1994 **CLC 1, 2, 5,
11, 45; DA; DAB; DAC; DAM DRAM,
MST; WLC**
See also CA 13-16R; 147; CANR 21, 56;
CDBLB 1945-1960; DLB 13; MTCW 1
**Osborne, Lawrence** 1958- .................... **CLC 50**
**Oshima, Nagisa** 1932- ........................ **CLC 20**
See also CA 116; 121
**Oskison, John Milton** 1874-1947 .. **TCLC 35;
DAM MULT**
See also CA 144; DLB 175; NNAL
**Ossian** c. 3rd cent. - ........................ **CMLC 28**
See also Macpherson, James
**Ossoli, Sarah Margaret (Fuller marchesa d')**
1810-1850
See Fuller, Margaret
See also SATA 25
**Ostrovsky, Alexander** 1823-1886 **NCLC 30, 57**
**Otero, Blas de** 1916-1979 .................. **CLC 11**
See also CA 89-92; DLB 134
**Otto, Rudolf** 1869-1937 .................... **TCLC 85**
**Otto, Whitney** 1955- .......................... **CLC 70**
See also CA 140
**Ouida** ................................................ **TCLC 43**
See also De La Ramee, (Marie) Louise
See also DLB 18, 156

**Ousmane, Sembene** 1923- .... **CLC 66; BLC 3**
See also BW 1; CA 117; 125; MTCW 1
**Ovid** 43B.C.-18(?) **CMLC 7; DAM POET; PC
2**
**Owen, Hugh**
See Faust, Frederick (Schiller)
**Owen, Wilfred (Edward Salter)** 1893-1918
**TCLC 5, 27; DA; DAB; DAC; DAM MST,
POET; PC 19; WLC**
See also CA 104; 141; CDBLB 1914-1945;
DLB 20
**Owens, Rochelle** 1936- ......................... **CLC 8**
See also CA 17-20R; CAAS 2; CANR 39
**Oz, Amos** 1939- **CLC 5, 8, 11, 27, 33, 54; DAM
NOV**
See also CA 53-56; CANR 27, 47, 65; MTCW
1
**Ozick, Cynthia** 1928- **CLC 3, 7, 28, 62; DAM
NOV, POP; SSC 15**
See also BEST 90:1; CA 17-20R; CANR 23,
58; DLB 28, 152; DLBY 82; INT CANR-
23; MTCW 1
**Ozu, Yasujiro** 1903-1963 .................... **CLC 16**
See also CA 112
**Pacheco, C.**
See Pessoa, Fernando (Antonio Nogueira)
**Pa Chin** .............................................. **CLC 18**
See also Li Fei-kan
**Pack, Robert** 1929- .............................. **CLC 13**
See also CA 1-4R; CANR 3, 44; DLB 5
**Padgett, Lewis**
See Kuttner, Henry
**Padilla (Lorenzo), Heberto** 1932- ..... **CLC 38**
See also AITN 1; CA 123; 131; HW
**Page, Jimmy** 1944- .............................. **CLC 12**
**Page, Louise** 1955- .............................. **CLC 40**
See also CA 140
**Page, P(atricia) K(athleen)** 1916- **CLC 7, 18;
DAC; DAM MST; PC 12**
See also CA 53-56; CANR 4, 22, 65; DLB 68;
MTCW 1
**Page, Thomas Nelson** 1853-1922 ....... **SSC 23**
See also CA 118; DLB 12, 78; DLBD 13
**Pagels, Elaine Hiesey** 1943- ............. **CLC 104**
See also CA 45-48; CANR 2, 24, 51
**Paget, Violet** 1856-1935
See Lee, Vernon
See also CA 104; 166
**Paget-Lowe, Henry**
See Lovecraft, H(oward) P(hillips)
**Paglia, Camille (Anna)** 1947- ........... **CLC 68**
See also CA 140; CANR 72
**Paige, Richard**
See Koontz, Dean R(ay)
**Paine, Thomas** 1737-1809 .............. **NCLC 62**
See also CDALB 1640-1865; DLB 31, 43, 73,
158
**Pakenham, Antonia**
See Fraser, (Lady) Antonia (Pakenham)
**Palamas, Kostes** 1859-1943 .............. **TCLC 5**
See also CA 105
**Palazzeschi, Aldo** 1885-1974 ............. **CLC 11**
See also CA 89-92; 53-56; DLB 114
**Paley, Grace** 1922- **CLC 4, 6, 37; DAM POP;
SSC 8**
See also CA 25-28R; CANR 13, 46; DLB 28;
INT CANR-13; MTCW 1
**Palin, Michael (Edward)** 1943- ......... **CLC 21**
See also Monty Python
See also CA 107; CANR 35; SATA 67
**Palliser, Charles** 1947- ....................... **CLC 65**
See also CA 136
**Palma, Ricardo** 1833-1919 ............. **TCLC 29**
See also CA 168
**Pancake, Breece Dexter** 1952-1979
See Pancake, Breece D'J
See also CA 123; 109

13, 33
See also CA 85-88; DLB 40

**Porter, William Sydney** 1862-1910
See Henry, O.
See also CA 104; 131; CDALB 1865-1917; DA; DAB; DAC; DAM MST; DLB 12, 78, 79; MTCW 1; YABC 2

**Portillo (y Pacheco), Jose Lopez**
See Lopez Portillo (y Pacheco), Jose

**Post, Melville Davisson** 1869-1930 **TCLC 39**
See also CA 110

**Potok, Chaim** 1929- ... **CLC 2, 7, 14, 26, 112; DAM NOV**
See also AAYA 15; AITN 1, 2; CA 17-20R; CANR 19, 35, 64; DLB 28, 152; INT CANR-19; MTCW 1; SATA 33

**Potter, (Helen) Beatrix** 1866-1943
See Webb, (Martha) Beatrice (Potter)
See also MAICYA

**Potter, Dennis (Christopher George)** 1935-1994 **CLC 58, 86**
See also CA 107; 145; CANR 33, 61; MTCW 1

**Pound, Ezra (Weston Loomis)** 1885-1972 **CLC 1, 2, 3, 4, 5, 7, 10, 13, 18, 34, 48, 50, 112; DA; DAB; DAC; DAM MST, POET; PC 4; WLC**
See also CA 5-8R; 37-40R; CANR 40; CDALB 1917-1929; DLB 4, 45, 63; DLBD 15; MTCW 1

**Povod, Reinaldo** 1959-1994 .............. **CLC 44**
See also CA 136; 146

**Powell, Adam Clayton, Jr.** 1908-1972 **CLC 89; BLC 3; DAM MULT**
See also BW 1; CA 102; 33-36R

**Powell, Anthony (Dymoke)** 1905- **CLC 1, 3, 7, 9, 10, 31**
See also CA 1-4R; CANR 1, 32, 62; CDBLB 1945-1960; DLB 15; MTCW 1

**Powell, Dawn** 1897-1965 .................... **CLC 66**
See also CA 5-8R; DLBY 97

**Powell, Padgett** 1952- ......................... **CLC 34**
See also CA 126; CANR 63

**Power, Susan** 1961- ............................. **CLC 91**

**Powers, J(ames) F(arl)** 1917- **CLC 1, 4, 8, 57; SSC 4**
See also CA 1-4R; CANR 2, 61; DLB 130; MTCW 1

**Powers, John J(ames)** 1945-
See Powers, John R.
See also CA 69-72

**Powers, John R.** ................................ **CLC 66**
See also Powers, John J(ames)

**Powers, Richard (S.)** 1957- ................ **CLC 93**
See also CA 148

**Pownall, David** 1938- ......................... **CLC 10**
See also CA 89-92; CAAS 18; CANR 49; DLB 14

**Powys, John Cowper** 1872-1963 **CLC 7, 9, 15, 46**
See also CA 85-88; DLB 15; MTCW 1

**Powys, T(heodore) F(rancis)** 1875-1953 **TCLC 9**
See also CA 106; DLB 36, 162

**Prado (Calvo), Pedro** 1886-1952 ... **TCLC 75**
See also CA 131; HW

**Prager, Emily** 1952- ........................... **CLC 56**

**Pratt, E(dwin) J(ohn)** 1883(?)-1964 **CLC 19; DAC; DAM POET**
See also CA 141; 93-96; DLB 92

**Premchand** ........................................ **TCLC 21**
See also Srivastava, Dhanpat Rai

**Preussler, Otfried** 1923- ...................... **CLC 17**
See also CA 77-80; SATA 24

**Prevert, Jacques (Henri Marie)** 1900-1977 **CLC 15**
See also CA 77-80; 69-72; CANR 29, 61; MTCW 1; SATA-Obit 30

**Prevost, Abbe (Antoine Francois)** 1697-1763 **LC 1**

**Price, (Edward) Reynolds** 1933- **CLC 3, 6, 13, 43, 50, 63; DAM NOV; SSC 22**
See also CA 1-4R; CANR 1, 37, 57; DLB 2; INT CANR-37

**Price, Richard** 1949- ....................... **CLC 6, 12**
See also CA 49-52; CANR 3; DLBY 81

**Prichard, Katharine Susannah** 1883-1969 **CLC 46**
See also CA 11-12; CANR 33; CAP 1; MTCW 1; SATA 66

**Priestley, J(ohn) B(oynton)** 1894-1984 **CLC 2, 5, 9, 34; DAM DRAM, NOV**
See also CA 9-12R; 113; CANR 33; CDBLB 1914-1945; DLB 10, 34, 77, 100, 139; DLBY 84; MTCW 1

**Prince** 1958(?)- .................................. **CLC 35**

**Prince, F(rank) T(empleton)** 1912- .. **CLC 22**
See also CA 101; CANR 43; DLB 20

**Prince Kropotkin**
See Kropotkin, Peter (Alekseievich)

**Prior, Matthew** 1664-1721 ...................... **LC 4**
See also DLB 95

**Prishvin, Mikhail** 1873-1954 .......... **TCLC 75**

**Pritchard, William H(arrison)** 1932- **CLC 34**
See also CA 65-68; CANR 23; DLB 111

**Pritchett, V(ictor) S(awdon)** 1900-1997 **C L C 5, 13, 15, 41; DAM NOV; SSC 14**
See also CA 61-64; 157; CANR 31, 63; DLB 15, 139; MTCW 1

**Private 19022**
See Manning, Frederic

**Probst, Mark** 1925- ............................. **CLC 59**
See also CA 130

**Prokosch, Frederic** 1908-1989 ...... **CLC 4, 48**
See also CA 73-76; 128; DLB 48

**Prophet, The**
See Dreiser, Theodore (Herman Albert)

**Prose, Francine** 1947- ........................ **CLC 45**
See also CA 109; 112; CANR 46; SATA 101

**Proudhon**
See Cunha, Euclides (Rodrigues Pimenta) da

**Proulx, Annie**
See Proulx, E(dna) Annie

**Proulx, E(dna) Annie** 1935- ... **CLC 81; DAM POP**
See also CA 145; CANR 65

**Proust, (Valentin-Louis-George-Eugene-) Marcel** 1871-1922 **TCLC 7, 13, 33; DA; DAB; DAC; DAM MST, NOV; WLC**
See also CA 104; 120; DLB 65; MTCW 1

**Prowler, Harley**
See Masters, Edgar Lee

**Prus, Boleslaw** 1845-1912 .............. **TCLC 48**

**Pryor, Richard (Franklin Lenox Thomas)** 1940- **CLC 26**
See also CA 122

**Przybyszewski, Stanislaw** 1868-1927 **TCLC 36**
See also CA 160; DLB 66

**Pteleon**
See Grieve, C(hristopher) M(urray)
See also DAM POET

**Puckett, Lute**
See Masters, Edgar Lee

**Puig, Manuel** 1932-1990 **CLC 3, 5, 10, 28, 65; DAM MULT; HLC**
See also CA 45-48; CANR 2, 32, 63; DLB 113; HW; MTCW 1

**Pulitzer, Joseph** 1847-1911 ............. **TCLC 76**
See also CA 114; DLB 23

**Purdy, A(lfred) W(ellington)** 1918- **CLC 3, 6, 14, 50; DAC; DAM MST, POET**
See also CA 81-84; CAAS 17; CANR 42, 66; DLB 88

**Purdy, James (Amos)** 1923- **CLC 2, 4, 10, 28, 52**

See also CA 33-36R; CAAS 1; CANR 19, 51; DLB 2; INT CANR-19; MTCW 1

**Pure, Simon**
See Swinnerton, Frank Arthur

**Pushkin, Alexander (Sergeyevich)** 1799-1837 **NCLC 3, 27; DA; DAB; DAC; DAM DRAM, MST, POET; PC 10; SSC 27; WLC**
See also SATA 61

**P'u Sung-ling** 1640-1715 ......... **LC 3; SSC 31**

**Putnam, Arthur Lee**
See Alger, Horatio, Jr.

**Puzo, Mario** 1920- **CLC 1, 2, 6, 36, 107; DAM NOV, POP**
See also CA 65-68; CANR 4, 42, 65; DLB 6; MTCW 1

**Pygge, Edward**
See Barnes, Julian (Patrick)

**Pyle, Ernest Taylor** 1900-1945
See Pyle, Ernie
See also CA 115; 160

**Pyle, Ernie** 1900-1945 ..................... **TCLC 75**
See also Pyle, Ernest Taylor
See also DLB 29

**Pyle, Howard** 1853-1911 ................. **TCLC 81**
See also CA 109; 137; CLR 22; DLB 42, 188; DLBD 13; MAICYA; SATA 16, 100

**Pym, Barbara (Mary Crampton)** 1913-1980 **CLC 13, 19, 37, 111**
See also CA 13-14; 97-100; CANR 13, 34; CAP 1; DLB 14; DLBY 87; MTCW 1

**Pynchon, Thomas (Ruggles, Jr.)** 1937- **CLC 2, 3, 6, 9, 11, 18, 33, 62, 72; DA; DAB; DAC; DAM MST, NOV, POP; SSC 14; WLC**
See also BEST 90:2; CA 17-20R; CANR 22, 46; DLB 2, 173; MTCW 1

**Pythagoras** c. 570B.C.-c. 500B.C. . **CMLC 22**
See also DLB 176

**Q**
See Quiller-Couch, Sir Arthur (Thomas)

**Qian Zhongshu**
See Ch'ien Chung-shu

**Qroll**
See Dagerman, Stig (Halvard)

**Quarrington, Paul (Lewis)** 1953- ..... **CLC 65**
See also CA 129; CANR 62

**Quasimodo, Salvatore** 1901-1968 ..... **CLC 10**
See also CA 13-16; 25-28R; CAP 1; DLB 114; MTCW 1

**Quay, Stephen** 1947- ......................... **CLC 95**

**Quay, Timothy** 1947- ......................... **CLC 95**

**Queen, Ellery** .............................. **CLC 3, 11**
See also Dannay, Frederic; Davidson, Avram; Lee, Manfred B(ennington); Marlowe, Stephen; Sturgeon, Theodore (Hamilton); Vance, John Holbrook

**Queen, Ellery, Jr.**
See Dannay, Frederic; Lee, Manfred B(ennington)

**Queneau, Raymond** 1903-1976 **CLC 2, 5, 10, 42**
See also CA 77-80; 69-72; CANR 32; DLB 72; MTCW 1

**Quevedo, Francisco de** 1580-1645 ....... **LC 23**

**Quiller-Couch, Sir Arthur (Thomas)** 1863-1944 **TCLC 53**
See also CA 118; 166; DLB 135, 153, 190

**Quin, Ann (Marie)** 1936-1973 ............. **CLC 6**
See also CA 9-12R; 45-48; DLB 14

**Quinn, Martin**
See Smith, Martin Cruz

**Quinn, Peter** 1947- ............................. **CLC 91**

**Quinn, Simon**
See Smith, Martin Cruz

**Quiroga, Horacio (Sylvestre)** 1878-1937 **TCLC 20; DAM MULT; HLC**
See also CA 117; 131; HW; MTCW 1

51; DAM NOV; SSC 21
See also CA 25-28R; 85-88; CANR 35, 62;
CDBLB 1945-1960; DLB 36, 117, 162;
MTCW 1

**Ribeiro, Darcy** 1922-1997 ................. **CLC 34**
See also CA 33-36R; 156

**Ribeiro, Joao Ubaldo (Osorio Pimentel)** 1941-
**CLC 10, 67**
See also CA 81-84

**Ribman, Ronald (Burt)** 1932- ............. **CLC 7**
See also CA 21-24R; CANR 46

**Ricci, Nino** 1959-................................. **CLC 70**
See also CA 137

**Rice, Anne** 1941- ........... **CLC 41; DAM POP**
See also AAYA 9; BEST 89:2; CA 65-68; CANR
12, 36, 53

**Rice, Elmer (Leopold)** 1892-1967 **CLC 7, 49;
DAM DRAM**
See also CA 21-22; 25-28R; CAP 2; DLB 4, 7;
MTCW 1

**Rice, Tim(othy Miles Bindon)** 1944- **CLC 21**
See also CA 103; CANR 46

**Rich, Adrienne (Cecile)** 1929-**CLC 3, 6, 7, 11,
18, 36, 73, 76; DAM POET; PC 5**
See also CA 9-12R; CANR 20, 53; DLB 5, 67;
MTCW 1

**Rich, Barbara**
See Graves, Robert (von Ranke)

**Rich, Robert**
See Trumbo, Dalton

**Richard, Keith** ............................... **CLC 17**
See also Richards, Keith

**Richards, David Adams** 1950- **CLC 59; DAC**
See also CA 93-96; CANR 60; DLB 53

**Richards, I(vor) A(rmstrong)** 1893-1979**C L C
14, 24**
See also CA 41-44R; 89-92; CANR 34; DLB
27

**Richards, Keith** 1943-
See Richard, Keith
See also CA 107

**Richardson, Anne**
See Roiphe, Anne (Richardson)

**Richardson, Dorothy Miller** 1873-1957**TCLC
3**
See also CA 104; DLB 36

**Richardson, Ethel Florence (Lindesay)** 1870-
1946
See Richardson, Henry Handel
See also CA 105

**Richardson, Henry Handel** ............... **TCLC 4**
See also Richardson, Ethel Florence (Lindesay)
See also DLB 197

**Richardson, John** 1796-1852**NCLC 55; DAC**
See also DLB 99

**Richardson, Samuel** 1689-1761**LC 1, 44; DA;
DAB; DAC; DAM MST, NOV; WLC**
See also CDBLB 1660-1789; DLB 39

**Richler, Mordecai** 1931-**CLC 3, 5, 9, 13, 18, 46,
70; DAC; DAM MST, NOV**
See also AITN 1; CA 65-68; CANR 31, 62; CLR
17; DLB 53; MAICYA; MTCW 1; SATA 44,
98; SATA-Brief 27

**Richter, Conrad (Michael)** 1890-1968**CLC 30**
See also AAYA 21; CA 5-8R; 25-28R; CANR
23; DLB 9; MTCW 1; SATA 3

**Ricostranza, Tom**
See Ellis, Trey

**Riddell, Charlotte** 1832-1906 ......... **TCLC 40**
See also CA 165; DLB 156

**Riding, Laura** ..................................... **CLC 3, 7**
See also Jackson, Laura (Riding)

**Riefenstahl, Berta Helene Amalia** 1902-
See Riefenstahl, Leni
See also CA 108

**Riefenstahl, Leni** ............................... **CLC 16**
See also Riefenstahl, Berta Helene Amalia

**Riffe, Ernest**
See Bergman, (Ernst) Ingmar

**Riggs, (Rolla) Lynn** 1899-1954 ..... **TCLC 56;
DAM MULT**
See also CA 144; DLB 175; NNAL

**Riis, Jacob A(ugust)** 1849-1914 ..... **TCLC 80**
See also CA 113; 168; DLB 23

**Riley, James Whitcomb** 1849-1916**TCLC 51;
DAM POET**
See also CA 118; 137; MAICYA; SATA 17

**Riley, Tex**
See Creasey, John

**Rilke, Rainer Maria** 1875-1926**TCLC 1, 6, 19;
DAM POET; PC 2**
See also CA 104; 132; CANR 62; DLB 81;
MTCW 1

**Rimbaud, (Jean Nicolas) Arthur** 1854-1891
**NCLC 4, 35; DA; DAB; DAC; DAM MST,
POET; PC 3; WLC**

**Rinehart, Mary Roberts** 1876-1958**TCLC 52**
See also CA 108; 166

**Ringmaster, The**
See Mencken, H(enry) L(ouis)

**Ringwood, Gwen(dolyn Margaret) Pharis**
1910-1984 ................................... **CLC 48**
See also CA 148; 112; DLB 88

**Rio, Michel** 19(?)- ............................. **CLC 43**

**Ritsos, Giannes**
See Ritsos, Yannis

**Ritsos, Yannis** 1909-1990 ........ **CLC 6, 13, 31**
See also CA 77-80; 133; CANR 39, 61; MTCW
1

**Ritter, Erika** 1948(?)- ........................ **CLC 52**

**Rivera, Jose Eustasio** 1889-1928 ... **TCLC 35**
See also CA 162; HW

**Rivers, Conrad Kent** 1933-1968 ......... **CLC 1**
See also BW 1; CA 85-88; DLB 41

**Rivers, Elfrida**
See Bradley, Marion Zimmer

**Riverside, John**
See Heinlein, Robert A(nson)

**Rizal, Jose** 1861-1896 ...................... **NCLC 27**

**Roa Bastos, Augusto (Antonio)** 1917-**CLC 45;
DAM MULT; HLC**
See also CA 131; DLB 113; HW

**Robbe-Grillet, Alain** 1922-**CLC 1, 2, 4, 6, 8, 10,
14, 43**
See also CA 9-12R; CANR 33, 65; DLB 83;
MTCW 1

**Robbins, Harold** 1916-1997 ..... **CLC 5; DAM
NOV**
See also CA 73-76; 162; CANR 26, 54; MTCW
1

**Robbins, Thomas Eugene** 1936-
See Robbins, Tom
See also CA 81-84; CANR 29, 59; DAM NOV,
POP; MTCW 1

**Robbins, Tom** ............................ **CLC 9, 32, 64**
See also Robbins, Thomas Eugene
See also BEST 90:3; DLBY 80

**Robbins, Trina** 1938- ........................ **CLC 21**
See also CA 128

**Roberts, Charles G(eorge) D(ouglas)** 1860-1943
**TCLC 8**
See also CA 105; CLR 33; DLB 92; SATA 88;
SATA-Brief 29

**Roberts, Elizabeth Madox** 1886-1941 **T C L C
68**
See also CA 111; 166; DLB 9, 54, 102; SATA
33; SATA-Brief 27

**Roberts, Kate** 1891-1985 ................... **CLC 15**
See also CA 107; 116

**Roberts, Keith (John Kingston)** 1935-**CLC 14**
See also CA 25-28R; CANR 46

**Roberts, Kenneth (Lewis)** 1885-1957**TCLC 23**
See also CA 109; DLB 9

**Roberts, Michele (B.)** 1949-............... **CLC 48**

See also CA 115; CANR 58

**Robertson, Ellis**
See Ellison, Harlan (Jay); Silverberg, Robert

**Robertson, Thomas William** 1829-1871**NCLC
35; DAM DRAM**

**Robeson, Kenneth**
See Dent, Lester

**Robinson, Edwin Arlington** 1869-1935**TCLC
5; DA; DAC; DAM MST, POET; PC 1**
See also CA 104; 133; CDALB 1865-1917;
DLB 54; MTCW 1

**Robinson, Henry Crabb** 1775-1867**NCLC 15**
See also DLB 107

**Robinson, Jill** 1936-............................ **CLC 10**
See also CA 102; INT 102

**Robinson, Kim Stanley** 1952-........... **CLC 34**
See also AAYA 26; CA 126

**Robinson, Lloyd**
See Silverberg, Robert

**Robinson, Marilynne** 1944- ............... **CLC 25**
See also CA 116

**Robinson, Smokey** ............................... **CLC 21**
See also Robinson, William, Jr.

**Robinson, William, Jr.** 1940-
See Robinson, Smokey
See also CA 116

**Robison, Mary** 1949- ................... **CLC 42, 98**
See also CA 113; 116; DLB 130; INT 116

**Rod, Edouard** 1857-1910 ................ **TCLC 52**

**Roddenberry, Eugene Wesley** 1921-1991
See Roddenberry, Gene
See also CA 110; 135; CANR 37; SATA 45;
SATA-Obit 69

**Roddenberry, Gene** ............................ **CLC 17**
See also Roddenberry, Eugene Wesley
See also AAYA 5; SATA-Obit 69

**Rodgers, Mary** 1931-.......................... **CLC 12**
See also CA 49-52; CANR 8, 55; CLR 20; INT
CANR-8; JRDA; MAICYA; SATA 8

**Rodgers, W(illiam) R(obert)** 1909-1969**CLC 7**
See also CA 85-88; DLB 20

**Rodman, Eric**
See Silverberg, Robert

**Rodman, Howard** 1920(?)-1985 ........ **CLC 65**
See also CA 118

**Rodman, Maia**
See Wojciechowska, Maia (Teresa)

**Rodriguez, Claudio** 1934-................... **CLC 10**
See also DLB 134

**Roelvaag, O(le) E(dvart)** 1876-1931**TCLC 17**
See also CA 117; DLB 9

**Roethke, Theodore (Huebner)** 1908-1963**CLC
1, 3, 8, 11, 19, 46, 101; DAM POET; PC 15**
See also CA 81-84; CABS 2; CDALB 1941-
1968; DLB 5; MTCW 1

**Rogers, Samuel** 1763-1855 ............. **NCLC 69**
See also DLB 93

**Rogers, Thomas Hunton** 1927- ......... **CLC 57**
See also CA 89-92; INT 89-92

**Rogers, Will(iam Penn Adair)** 1879-1935
**TCLC 8, 71; DAM MULT**
See also CA 105; 144; DLB 11; NNAL

**Rogin, Gilbert** 1929-.......................... **CLC 18**
See also CA 65-68; CANR 15

**Rohan, Koda** ...................................... **TCLC 22**
See also Koda Shigeyuki

**Rohlfs, Anna Katharine Green**
See Green, Anna Katharine

**Rohmer, Eric** ...................................... **CLC 16**
See also Scherer, Jean-Marie Maurice

**Rohmer, Sax** ...................................... **TCLC 28**
See also Ward, Arthur Henry Sarsfield
See also DLB 70

**Roiphe, Anne (Richardson)** 1935- ..**CLC 3, 9**
See also CA 89-92; CANR 45; DLBY 80; INT
89-92

**Rojas, Fernando de** 1465-1541 ............**LC 23**

Sommer, Scott 1951- .......................... CLC 25
See also CA 106
Sondheim, Stephen (Joshua) 1930- . CLC 30, 39; DAM DRAM
See also AAYA 11; CA 103; CANR 47, 68
Song, Cathy 1955-................................. PC 21
See also CA 154; DLB 169
Sontag, Susan 1933-CLC 1, 2, 10, 13, 31, 105; DAM POP
See also CA 17-20R; CANR 25, 51; DLB 2, 67; MTCW 1
Sophocles 496(?)B.C.-406(?)B.C. ... CMLC 2; DA; DAB; DAC; DAM DRAM, MST; DC 1; WLCS
See also DLB 176
Sordello 1189-1269 ......................... CMLC 15
Sorel, Julia
See Drexler, Rosalyn
Sorrentino, Gilbert 1929-CLC 3, 7, 14, 22, 40
See also CA 77-80; CANR 14, 33; DLB 5, 173; DLBY 80; INT CANR-14
Soto, Gary 1952- CLC 32, 80; DAM MULT; HLC
See also AAYA 10; CA 119; 125; CANR 50; CLR 38; DLB 82; HW; INT 125; JRDA; SATA 80
Soupault, Philippe 1897-1990 ........... CLC 68
See also CA 116; 147; 131
Souster, (Holmes) Raymond 1921-CLC 5, 14; DAC; DAM POET
See also CA 13-16R; CAAS 14; CANR 13, 29, 53; DLB 88; SATA 63
Southern, Terry 1924(?)-1995 ............. CLC 7
See also CA 1-4R; 150; CANR 1, 55; DLB 2
Southey, Robert 1774-1843 ............... NCLC 8
See also DLB 93, 107, 142; SATA 54
Southworth, Emma Dorothy Eliza Nevitte 1819-1899 ................................................
NCLC 26
Souza, Ernest
See Scott, Evelyn
Soyinka, Wole 1934-CLC 3, 5, 14, 36, 44; BLC 3; DA; DAB; DAC; DAM DRAM, MST, MULT; DC 2; WLC
See also BW 2; CA 13-16R; CANR 27, 39; DLB 125; MTCW 1
Spackman, W(illiam) M(ode) 1905-1990CLC 46
See also CA 81-84; 132
Spacks, Barry (Bernard) 1931- ......... CLC 14
See also CA 154; CANR 33; DLB 105
Spanidou, Irini 1946- ........................ CLC 44
Spark, Muriel (Sarah) 1918-CLC 2, 3, 5, 8, 13, 18, 40, 94; DAB; DAC; DAM MST, NOV; SSC 10
See also CA 5-8R; CANR 12, 36; CDBLB 1945-1960; DLB 15, 139; INT CANR-12; MTCW 1
Spaulding, Douglas
See Bradbury, Ray (Douglas)
Spaulding, Leonard
See Bradbury, Ray (Douglas)
Spence, J. A. D.
See Eliot, T(homas) S(tearns)
Spencer, Elizabeth 1921- ................... CLC 22
See also CA 13-16R; CANR 32, 65; DLB 6; MTCW 1; SATA 14
Spencer, Leonard G.
See Silverberg, Robert
Spencer, Scott 1945- .......................... CLC 30
See also CA 113; CANR 51; DLBY 86
Spender, Stephen (Harold) 1909-1995CLC 1, 2, 5, 10, 41, 91; DAM POET
See also CA 9-12R; 149; CANR 31, 54; CDBLB 1945-1960; DLB 20; MTCW 1
Spengler, Oswald (Arnold Gottfried) 1880-1936 TCLC 25

See also CA 118
Spenser, Edmund 1552(?)-1599LC 5, 39; DA; DAB; DAC; DAM MST, POET; PC 8; WLC
See also CDBLB Before 1660; DLB 167
Spicer, Jack 1925-1965 CLC 8, 18, 72; DAM POET
See also CA 85-88; DLB 5, 16, 193
Spiegelman, Art 1948- ........................ CLC 76
See also AAYA 10; CA 125; CANR 41, 55
Spielberg, Peter 1929- ......................... CLC 6
See also CA 5-8R; CANR 4, 48; DLBY 81
Spielberg, Steven 1947-...................... CLC 20
See also AAYA 8, 24; CA 77-80; CANR 32; SATA 32
Spillane, Frank Morrison 1918-
See Spillane, Mickey
See also CA 25-28R; CANR 28, 63; MTCW 1; SATA 66
Spillane, Mickey ............................... CLC 3, 13
See also Spillane, Frank Morrison
Spinoza, Benedictus de 1632-1677 ........ LC 9
Spinrad, Norman (Richard) 1940- ... CLC 46
See also CA 37-40R; CAAS 19; CANR 20; DLB 8; INT CANR-20
Spitteler, Carl (Friedrich Georg) 1845-1924 TCLC 12
See also CA 109; DLB 129
Spivack, Kathleen (Romola Drucker) 1938-CLC 6
See also CA 49-52
Spoto, Donald 1941- .......................... CLC 39
See also CA 65-68; CANR 11, 57
Springsteen, Bruce (F.) 1949- ........... CLC 17
See also CA 111
Spurling, Hilary 1940- ....................... CLC 34
See also CA 104; CANR 25, 52
Spyker, John Howland
See Elman, Richard (Martin)
Squires, (James) Radcliffe 1917-1993CLC 51
See also CA 1-4R; 140; CANR 6, 21
Srivastava, Dhanpat Rai 1880(?)-1936
See Premchand
See also CA 118
Stacy, Donald
See Pohl, Frederik
Stael, Germaine de 1766-1817
See Stael-Holstein, Anne Louise Germaine Necker Baronn
See also DLB 119
Stael-Holstein, Anne Louise Germaine Necker Baronn 1766-1817 .................... NCLC 3
See also Stael, Germaine de
See also DLB 192
Stafford, Jean 1915-1979CLC 4, 7, 19, 68; SSC 26
See also CA 1-4R; 85-88; CANR 3, 65; DLB 2, 173; MTCW 1; SATA-Obit 22
Stafford, William (Edgar) 1914-1993 CLC 4, 7, 29; DAM POET
See also CA 5-8R; 142; CAAS 3; CANR 5, 22; DLB 5; INT CANR-22
Stagnelius, Eric Johan 1793-1823 . NCLC 61
Staines, Trevor
See Brunner, John (Kilian Houston)
Stairs, Gordon
See Austin, Mary (Hunter)
Stannard, Martin 1947- ..................... CLC 44
See also CA 142; DLB 155
Stanton, Elizabeth Cady 1815-1902TCLC 73
See also DLB 79
Stanton, Maura 1946- .......................... CLC 9
See also CA 89-92; CANR 15; DLB 120
Stanton, Schuyler
See Baum, L(yman) Frank
Stapledon, (William) Olaf 1886-1950 TCLC 22

See also CA 111; 162; DLB 15
Starbuck, George (Edwin) 1931-1996CLC 53; DAM POET
See also CA 21-24R; 153; CANR 23
Stark, Richard
See Westlake, Donald E(dwin)
Staunton, Schuyler
See Baum, L(yman) Frank
Stead, Christina (Ellen) 1902-1983 CLC 2, 5, 8, 32, 80
See also CA 13-16R; 109; CANR 33, 40; MTCW 1
Stead, William Thomas 1849-1912 TCLC 48
See also CA 167
Steele, Richard 1672-1729 ................... LC 18
See also CDBLB 1660-1789; DLB 84, 101
Steele, Timothy (Reid) 1948- ............. CLC 45
See also CA 93-96; CANR 16, 50; DLB 120
Steffens, (Joseph) Lincoln 1866-1936 T C L C 20
See also CA 117
Stegner, Wallace (Earle) 1909-1993CLC 9, 49, 81; DAM NOV; SSC 27
See also AITN 1; BEST 90:3; CA 1-4R; 141; CAAS 9; CANR 1, 21, 46; DLB 9; DLBY 93; MTCW 1
Stein, Gertrude 1874-1946TCLC 1, 6, 28, 48; DA; DAB; DAC; DAM MST, NOV, POET; PC 18; WLC
See also CA 104; 132; CDALB 1917-1929; DLB 4, 54, 86; DLBD 15; MTCW 1
Steinbeck, John (Ernst) 1902-1968 CLC 1, 5, 9, 13, 21, 34, 45, 75; DA; DAB; DAC; DAM DRAM, MST, NOV; SSC 11; WLC
See also AAYA 12; CA 1-4R; 25-28R; CANR 1, 35; CDALB 1929-1941; DLB 7, 9; DLBD 2; MTCW 1; SATA 9
Steinem, Gloria 1934- ........................ CLC 63
See also CA 53-56; CANR 28, 51; MTCW 1
Steiner, George 1929- ... CLC 24; DAM NOV
See also CA 73;76; CANR 31, 67; DLB 67; MTCW 1; SATA 62
Steiner, K. Leslie
See Delany, Samuel R(ay, Jr.)
Steiner, Rudolf 1861-1925 .............. TCLC 13
See also CA 107
Stendhal 1783-1842NCLC 23, 46; DA; DAB; DAC; DAM MST, NOV; SSC 27; WLC
See also DLB 119
Stephen, Adeline Virginia
See Woolf, (Adeline) Virginia
Stephen, SirLeslie 1832-1904 ......... TCLC 23
See also CA 123; DLB 57, 144, 190
Stephen, Sir Leslie
See Stephen, SirLeslie
Stephen, Virginia
See Woolf, (Adeline) Virginia
Stephens, James 1882(?)-1950 .......... TCLC 4
See also CA 104; DLB 19, 153, 162
Stephens, Reed
See Donaldson, Stephen R.
Steptoe, Lydia
See Barnes, Djuna
Sterchi, Beat 1949- ........................... CLC 65
Sterling, Brett
See Bradbury, Ray (Douglas); Hamilton, Edmond
Sterling, Bruce 1954- ........................ CLC 72
See also CA 119; CANR 44
Sterling, George 1869-1926 ........... TCLC 20
See also CA 117; 165; DLB 54
Stern, Gerald 1925- ..................... CLC 40, 100
See also CA 81-84; CANR 28; DLB 105
Stern, Richard (Gustave) 1928- ....CLC 4, 39
See also CA 1-4R; CANR 1, 25, 52; DLBY 87; INT CANR-25
Sternberg, Josef von 1894-1969 ........ CLC 20

See also CA 81-84

**Sterne, Laurence** 1713-1768 **LC 2; DA; DAB; DAC; DAM MST, NOV; WLC**
See also CDBLB 1660-1789; DLB 39

**Sternheim, (William Adolf) Carl** 1878-1942 **TCLC 8**
See also CA 105; DLB 56, 118

**Stevens, Mark** 1951- ............................ **CLC 34**
See also CA 122

**Stevens, Wallace** 1879-1955 **TCLC 3, 12, 45; DA; DAB; DAC; DAM MST, POET; PC 6; WLC**
See also CA 104; 124; CDALB 1929-1941; DLB 54; MTCW 1

**Stevenson, Anne (Katharine)** 1933- **CLC 7, 33**
See also CA 17-20R; CAAS 9; CANR 9, 33; DLB 40; MTCW 1

**Stevenson, Robert Louis (Balfour)** 1850-1894 **NCLC 5, 14, 63; DA; DAB; DAC; DAM MST, NOV; SSC 11; WLC**
See also AAYA 24; CDBLB 1890-1914; CLR 10, 11; DLB 18, 57, 141, 156, 174; DLBD 13; JRDA; MAICYA; SATA 100; YABC 2

**Stewart, J(ohn) I(nnes) M(ackintosh)** 1906-1994 .................................. **CLC 7, 14, 32**
See also CA 85-88; 147; CAAS 3; CANR 47; MTCW 1

**Stewart, Mary (Florence Elinor)** 1916- **CLC 7, 35; DAB**
See also CA 1-4R; CANR 1, 59; SATA 12

**Stewart, Mary Rainbow**
See Stewart, Mary (Florence Elinor)

**Stifle, June**
See Campbell, Maria

**Stifter, Adalbert** 1805-1868 **NCLC 41; SSC 28**
See also DLB 133

**Still, James** 1906- ............................... **CLC 49**
See also CA 65-68; CAAS 17; CANR 10, 26; DLB 9; SATA 29

**Sting** 1951-
See Sumner, Gordon Matthew
See also CA 167

**Stirling, Arthur**
See Sinclair, Upton (Beall)

**Stitt, Milan** 1941- ................................. **CLC 29**
See also CA 69-72

**Stockton, Francis Richard** 1834-1902
See Stockton, Frank R.
See also CA 108; 137; MAICYA; SATA 44

**Stockton, Frank R.** ............................ **TCLC 47**
See also Stockton, Francis Richard
See also DLB 42, 74; DLBD 13; SATA-Brief 32

**Stoddard, Charles**
See Kuttner, Henry

**Stoker, Abraham** 1847-1912
See Stoker, Bram
See also CA 105; 150; DA; DAC; DAM MST, NOV; SATA 29

**Stoker, Bram** 1847-1912 **TCLC 8; DAB; WLC**
See also Stoker, Abraham
See also AAYA 23; CDBLB 1890-1914; DLB 36, 70, 178

**Stolz, Mary (Slattery)** 1920- .............. **CLC 12**
See also AAYA 8; AITN 1; CA 5-8R; CANR 13, 41; JRDA; MAICYA; SAAS 3; SATA 10, 71

**Stone, Irving** 1903-1989 ..**CLC 7; DAM POP**
See also AITN 1; CA 1-4R; 129; CAAS 3; CANR 1, 23; INT CANR-23; MTCW 1; SATA 3; SATA-Obit 64

**Stone, Oliver (William)** 1946- ........... **CLC 73**
See also AAYA 15; CA 110; CANR 55

**Stone, Robert (Anthony)** 1937- **CLC 5, 23, 42**
See also CA 85-88; CANR 23, 66; DLB 152; INT CANR-23; MTCW 1

**Stone, Zachary**

See Follett, Ken(neth Martin)

**Stoppard, Tom** 1937- **CLC 1, 3, 4, 5, 8, 15, 29, 34, 63, 91; DA; DAB; DAC; DAM DRAM, MST; DC 6; WLC**
See also CA 81-84; CANR 39, 67; CDBLB 1960 to Present; DLB 13; DLBY 85; MTCW 1

**Storey, David (Malcolm)** 1933- **CLC 2, 4, 5, 8; DAM DRAM**
See also CA 81-84; CANR 36; DLB 13, 14; MTCW 1

**Storm, Hyemeyohsts** 1935- ...... **CLC 3; DAM MULT**
See also CA 81-84; CANR 45; NNAL

**Storm, (Hans) Theodor (Woldsen)** 1817-1888 **NCLC 1; SSC 27**
See also DLB 129

**Storni, Alfonsina** 1892-1938 . **TCLC 5; DAM MULT; HLC**
See also CA 104; 131; HW

**Stoughton, William** 1631-1701 ............. **LC 38**
See also DLB 24

**Stout, Rex (Todhunter)** 1886-1975 ..... **CLC 3**
See also AITN 2; CA 61-64; CANR 71

**Stow, (Julian) Randolph** 1935- .. **CLC 23, 48**
See also CA 13-16R; CANR 33; MTCW 1

**Stowe, Harriet (Elizabeth) Beecher** 1811-1896 **NCLC 3, 50; DA; DAB; DAC; DAM MST, NOV; WLC**
See also CDALB 1865-1917; DLB 1, 12, 42, 74, 189; JRDA; MAICYA; YABC 1

**Strachey, (Giles) Lytton** 1880-1932 **TCLC 12**
See also CA 110; DLB 149; DLBD 10

**Strand, Mark** 1934- **CLC 6, 18, 41, 71; DAM POET**
See also CA 21-24R; CANR 40, 65; DLB 5; SATA 41

**Straub, Peter (Francis)** 1943- . **CLC 28, 107; DAM POP**
See also BEST 89:1; CA 85-88; CANR 28, 65; DLBY 84; MTCW 1

**Strauss, Botho** 1944- .......................... **CLC 22**
See also CA 157; DLB 124

**Streatfeild, (Mary) Noel** 1895(?)-1986 **CLC 21**
See also CA 81-84; 120; CANR 31; CLR 17; DLB 160; MAICYA; SATA 20; SATA-Obit 48

**Stribling, T(homas) S(igismund)** 1881-1965 **CLC 23**
See also CA 107; DLB 9

**Strindberg, (Johan) August** 1849-1912 **TCLC 1, 8, 21, 47; DA; DAB; DAC; DAM DRAM, MST; WLC**
See also CA 104; 135

**Stringer, Arthur** 1874-1950 ............ **TCLC 37**
See also CA 161; DLB 92

**Stringer, David**
See Roberts, Keith (John Kingston)

**Stroheim, Erich von** 1885-1957 ..... **TCLC 71**

**Strugatskii, Arkadii (Natanovich)** 1925-1991 **CLC 27**
See also CA 106; 135

**Strugatskii, Boris (Natanovich)** 1933- **CLC 27**
See also CA 106

**Strummer, Joe** 1953(?)- ...................... **CLC 30**

**Stuart, Don A.**
See Campbell, John W(ood, Jr.)

**Stuart, Ian**
See MacLean, Alistair (Stuart)

**Stuart, Jesse (Hilton)** 1906-1984 **CLC 1, 8, 11, 14, 34; SSC 31**
See also CA 5-8R; 112; CANR 31; DLB 9, 48, 102; DLBY 84; SATA 2; SATA-Obit 36

**Sturgeon, Theodore (Hamilton)** 1918-1985 **CLC 22, 39**
See also Queen, Ellery
See also CA 81-84; 116; CANR 32; DLB 8;

DLBY 85; MTCW 1

**Sturges, Preston** 1898-1959 ............ **TCLC 48**
See also CA 114; 149; DLB 26

**Styron, William** 1925- **CLC 1, 3, 5, 11, 15, 60; DAM NOV, POP; SSC 25**
See also BEST 90:4; CA 5-8R; CANR 6, 33; CDALB 1968-1988; DLB 2, 143; DLBY 80; INT CANR-6; MTCW 1

**Su, Chien** 1884-1918
See Su Man-shu
See also CA 123

**Suarez Lynch, B.**
See Bioy Casares, Adolfo; Borges, Jorge Luis

**Suckow, Ruth** 1892-1960 ..................... **SSC 18**
See also CA 113; DLB 9, 102

**Sudermann, Hermann** 1857-1928 .. **TCLC 15**
See also CA 107; DLB 118

**Sue, Eugene** 1804-1857 ...................... **NCLC 1**
See also DLB 119

**Sueskind, Patrick** 1949- ...................... **CLC 44**
See also Suskind, Patrick

**Sukenick, Ronald** 1932- ........ **CLC 3, 4, 6, 48**
See also CA 25-28R; CAAS 8; CANR 32; DLB 173; DLBY 81

**Suknaski, Andrew** 1942- ..................... **CLC 19**
See also CA 101; DLB 53

**Sullivan, Vernon**
See Vian, Boris

**Sully Prudhomme** 1839-1907 ......... **TCLC 31**

**Su Man-shu** ....................................... **TCLC 24**
See also Su, Chien

**Summerforest, Ivy B.**
See Kirkup, James

**Summers, Andrew James** 1942- ........ **CLC 26**

**Summers, Andy**
See Summers, Andrew James

**Summers, Hollis (Spurgeon, Jr.)** 1916- **CLC 10**
See also CA 5-8R; CANR 3; DLB 6

**Summers, (Alphonsus Joseph-Mary Augustus) Montague** 1880-1948 .............. **TCLC 16**
See also CA 118; 163

**Sumner, Gordon Matthew** .................. **CLC 26**
See also Sting

**Surtees, Robert Smith** 1803-1864 .. **NCLC 14**
See also DLB 21

**Susann, Jacqueline** 1921-1974 ........... **CLC 3**
See also AITN 1; CA 65-68; 53-56; MTCW 1

**Su Shih** 1036-1101 ......................... **CMLC 15**

**Suskind, Patrick**
See Sueskind, Patrick
See also CA 145

**Sutcliff, Rosemary** 1920-1992 **CLC 26; DAB; DAC; DAM MST, POP**
See also AAYA 10; CA 5-8R; 139; CANR 37; CLR 1, 37; JRDA; MAICYA; SATA 6, 44, 78; SATA-Obit 73

**Sutro, Alfred** 1863-1933 ................... **TCLC 6**
See also CA 105; DLB 10

**Sutton, Henry**
See Slavitt, David R(ytman)

**Svevo, Italo** 1861-1928 . **TCLC 2, 35; SSC 25**
See also Schmitz, Aron Hector

**Swados, Elizabeth (A.)** 1951- ............ **CLC 12**
See also CA 97-100; CANR 49; INT 97-100

**Swados, Harvey** 1920-1972 ................. **CLC 5**
See also CA 5-8R; 37-40R; CANR 6; DLB 2

**Swan, Gladys** 1934- ........................... **CLC 69**
See also CA 101; CANR 17, 39

**Swarthout, Glendon (Fred)** 1918-1992 **CLC 35**
See also CA 1-4R; 139; CANR 1, 47; SATA 26

**Sweet, Sarah C.**
See Jewett, (Theodora) Sarah Orne

**Swenson, May** 1919-1989 **CLC 4, 14, 61, 106; DA; DAB; DAC; DAM MST, POET; PC 14**
See also CA 5-8R; 130; CANR 36, 61; DLB 5; MTCW 1; SATA 15

Thomas, (Philip) Edward 1878-1917 . **T C L C
10; DAM POET**
See also CA 106; 153; DLB 19

Thomas, Joyce Carol 1938- ............... **CLC 35**
See also AAYA 12; BW 2; CA 113; 116; CANR
48; CLR 19; DLB 33; INT 116; JRDA;
MAICYA; MTCW 1; SAAS 7; SATA 40, 78

Thomas, Lewis 1913-1993 ................. **CLC 35**
See also CA 85-88; 143; CANR 38, 60; MTCW
1

Thomas, Paul
See Mann, (Paul) Thomas

Thomas, Piri 1928- ............................. **CLC 17**
See also CA 73-76; HW

Thomas, R(onald) S(tuart) 1913- **CLC 6, 13,
48; DAB; DAM POET**
See also CA 89-92; CAAS 4; CANR 30;
CDBLB 1960 to Present; DLB 27; MTCW 1

Thomas, Ross (Elmore) 1926-1995 ... **CLC 39**
See also CA 33-36R; 150; CANR 22, 63

Thompson, Francis Clegg
See Mencken, H(enry) L(ouis)

Thompson, Francis Joseph 1859-1907**TCLC 4**
See also CA 104; CDBLB 1890-1914; DLB 19

Thompson, Hunter S(tockton) 1939- **CLC 9,
17, 40, 104; DAM POP**
See also BEST 89:1; CA 17-20R; CANR 23,
46; DLB 185; MTCW 1

Thompson, James Myers
See Thompson, Jim (Myers)

Thompson, Jim (Myers) 1906-1977(?)**CLC 69**
See also CA 140

Thompson, Judith ............................. **CLC 39**

Thomson, James 1700-1748 ...**LC 16, 29, 40;
DAM POET**
See also DLB 95

Thomson, James 1834-1882 **NCLC 18; DAM
POET**
See also DLB 35

Thoreau, Henry David 1817-1862**NCLC 7, 21,
61; DA; DAB; DAC; DAM MST; WLC**
See also CDALB 1640-1865; DLB 1

Thornton, Hall
See Silverberg, Robert

Thucydides c. 455B.C.-399B.C. ..... **CMLC 17**
See also DLB 176

Thurber, James (Grover) 1894-1961 . **CLC 5,
11, 25; DA; DAB; DAC; DAM DRAM,
MST, NOV; SSC 1**
See also CA 73-76; CANR 17, 39; CDALB
1929-1941; DLB 4, 11, 22, 102; MAICYA;
MTCW 1; SATA 13

Thurman, Wallace (Henry) 1902-1934**T C L C
6; BLC 3; DAM MULT**
See also BW 1; CA 104; 124; DLB 51

Ticheburn, Cheviot
See Ainsworth, William Harrison

Tieck, (Johann) Ludwig 1773-1853 **NCLC 5,
46; SSC 31**
See also DLB 90

Tiger, Derry
See Ellison, Harlan (Jay)

Tilghman, Christopher 1948(?)- ....... **CLC 65**
See also CA 159

Tillinghast, Richard (Williford) 1940-**CLC 29**
See also CA 29-32R; CAAS 23; CANR 26, 51

Timrod, Henry 1828-1867 ............. **NCLC 25**
See also DLB 3

Tindall, Gillian (Elizabeth) 1938- ...... **CLC 7**
See also CA 21-24R; CANR 11, 65

Tiptree, James, Jr. ........................ **CLC 48, 50**
See also Sheldon, Alice Hastings Bradley
See also DLB 8

Titmarsh, Michael Angelo
See Thackeray, William Makepeace

Tocqueville, Alexis (Charles Henri Maurice
Clerel Comte) 1805-1859 ...**NCLC 7, 63**

Tolkien, J(ohn) R(onald) R(euel) 1892-1973
**CLC 1, 2, 3, 8, 12, 38; DA; DAB; DAC;
DAM MST, NOV, POP; WLC**
See also AAYA 10; AITN 1; CA 17-18; 45-48;
CANR 36; CAP 2; CDBLB 1914-1945; DLB
15, 160; JRDA; MAICYA; MTCW 1; SATA
2, 32, 100; SATA-Obit 24

Toller, Ernst 1893-1939 ................... **TCLC 10**
See also CA 107; DLB 124

Tolson, M. B.
See Tolson, Melvin B(eaunorus)

Tolson, Melvin B(eaunorus) 1898(?)-1966
**CLC 36, 105; BLC 3; DAM MULT, POET**
See also BW 1; CA 124; 89-92; DLB 48, 76

Tolstoi, Aleksei Nikolaevich
See Tolstoy, Alexey Nikolaevich

Tolstoy, Alexey Nikolaevich 1882-1945**T C L C
18**
See also CA 107; 158

Tolstoy, Count Leo
See Tolstoy, Leo (Nikolaevich)

Tolstoy, Leo (Nikolaevich) 1828-1910**TCLC 4,
11, 17, 28, 44, 79; DA; DAB; DAC; DAM
MST, NOV; SSC 9, 30; WLC**
See also CA 104; 123; SATA 26

Tomasi di Lampedusa, Giuseppe 1896-1957
See Lampedusa, Giuseppe (Tomasi) di
See also CA 111

Tomlin, Lily ......................................... **CLC 17**
See also Tomlin, Mary Jean

Tomlin, Mary Jean 1939(?)-
See Tomlin, Lily
See also CA 117

Tomlinson, (Alfred) Charles 1927-**CLC 2, 4, 6,
13, 45; DAM POET; PC 17**
See also CA 5-8R; CANR 33; DLB 40

Tomlinson, H(enry) M(ajor) 1873-1958**TCLC
71**
See also CA 118; 161; DLB 36, 100, 195

Tonson, Jacob
See Bennett, (Enoch) Arnold

Toole, John Kennedy 1937-1969 **CLC 19, 64**
See also CA 104; DLBY 81

Toomer, Jean 1894-1967**CLC 1, 4, 13, 22; BLC
3; DAM MULT; PC 7; SSC 1; WLCS**
See also BW 1; CA 85-88; CDALB 1917-1929;
DLB 45, 51; MTCW 1

Torley, Luke
See Blish, James (Benjamin)

Tornimparte, Alessandra
See Ginzburg, Natalia

Torre, Raoul della
See Mencken, H(enry) L(ouis)

Torrey, E(dwin) Fuller 1937- ............ **CLC 34**
See also CA 119; CANR 71

Torsvan, Ben Traven
See Traven, B.

Torsvan, Benno Traven
See Traven, B.

Torsvan, Berick Traven
See Traven, B.

Torsvan, Berwick Traven
See Traven, B.

Torsvan, Bruno Traven
See Traven, B.

Torsvan, Traven
See Traven, B.

Tournier, Michel (Edouard) 1924-**CLC 6, 23,
36, 95**
See also CA 49-52; CANR 3, 36; DLB 83;
MTCW 1; SATA 23

Tournimparte, Alessandra
See Ginzburg, Natalia

Towers, Ivar
See Kornbluth, C(yril) M.

Towne, Robert (Burton) 1936(?)- ..... **CLC 87**
See also CA 108; DLB 44

Townsend, Sue ...................................... **CLC 61**
See also Townsend, Susan Elaine
See also SATA 55, 93; SATA-Brief 48

Townsend, Susan Elaine 1946-
See Townsend, Sue
See also CA 119; 127; CANR 65; DAB; DAC;
DAM MST

Townshend, Peter (Dennis Blandford) 1945-
**CLC 17, 42**
See also CA 107

Tozzi, Federigo 1883-1920 .............. **TCLC 31**
See also CA 160

Traill, Catharine Parr 1802-1899 ..**NCLC 31**
See also DLB 99

Trakl, Georg 1887-1914 ....... **TCLC 5; PC 20**
See also CA 104; 165

Transtroemer, Tomas (Goesta) 1931-**CLC 52,
65; DAM POET**
See also CA 117; 129; CAAS 17

Transtromer, Tomas Gosta
See Transtroemer, Tomas (Goesta)

Traven, B. (?)-1969 ................... **CLC 8, 11**
See also CA 19-20; 25-28R; CAP 2; DLB 9,
56; MTCW 1

Treitel, Jonathan 1959- ...................... **CLC 70**

Tremain, Rose 1943- ......................... **CLC 42**
See also CA 97-100; CANR 44; DLB 14

Tremblay, Michel 1942- **CLC 29, 102; DAC;
DAM MST**
See also CA 116; 128; DLB 60; MTCW 1

Trevanian ............................................. **CLC 29**
See also Whitaker, Rod(ney)

Trevor, Glen
See Hilton, James

Trevor, William 1928- . **CLC 7, 9, 14, 25, 71;
SSC 21**
See also Cox, William Trevor
See also DLB 14, 139

Trifonov, Yuri (Valentinovich) 1925-1981
**CLC 45**
See also CA 126; 103; MTCW 1

Trilling, Lionel 1905-1975 ...... **CLC 9, 11, 24**
See also CA 9-12R; 61-64; CANR 10; DLB 28,
63; INT CANR-10; MTCW 1

Trimball, W. H.
See Mencken, H(enry) L(ouis)

Tristan
See Gomez de la Serna, Ramon

Tristram
See Housman, A(lfred) E(dward)

Trogdon, William (Lewis) 1939-
See Heat-Moon, William Least
See also CA 115; 119; CANR 47; INT 119

Trollope, Anthony 1815-1882**NCLC 6, 33; DA;
DAB; DAC; DAM MST, NOV; SSC 28;
WLC**
See also CDBLB 1832-1890; DLB 21, 57, 159;
SATA 22

Trollope, Frances 1779-1863 .......... **NCLC 30**
See also DLB 21, 166

Trotsky, Leon 1879-1940 ............... **TCLC 22**
See also CA 118; 167

Trotter (Cockburn), Catharine 1679-1749**L C
8**
See also DLB 84

Trout, Kilgore
See Farmer, Philip Jose

Trow, George W. S. 1943- ................. **CLC 52**
See also CA 126

Troyat, Henri 1911- ........................... **CLC 23**
See also CA 45-48; CANR 2, 33, 67; MTCW 1

Trudeau, G(arretson) B(eekman) 1948-
See Trudeau, Garry B.
See also CA 81-84; CANR 31; SATA 35

Trudeau, Garry B. ............................... **CLC 12**
See also Trudeau, G(arretson) B(eekman)
See also AAYA 10; AITN 2

Wallace, Irving 1916-1990 **CLC 7, 13; DAM NOV, POP**
See also AITN 1; CA 1-4R; 132; CAAS 1; CANR 1, 27; INT CANR-27; MTCW 1

Wallant, Edward Lewis 1926-1962**CLC 5, 10**
See also CA 1-4R; CANR 22; DLB 2, 28, 143; MTCW 1

Walley, Byron
See Card, Orson Scott

Walpole, Horace 1717-1797 .................. **LC 2**
See also DLB 39, 104

Walpole, Hugh (Seymour) 1884-1941**TCLC 5**
See also CA 104; 165; DLB 34

Walser, Martin 1927- ......................... **CLC 27**
See also CA 57-60; CANR 8, 46; DLB 75, 124

Walser, Robert 1878-1956 **TCLC 18; SSC 20**
See also CA 118; 165; DLB 66

Walsh, Jill Paton ................................. **CLC 35**
See also Paton Walsh, Gillian
See also AAYA 11; CLR 2; DLB 161; SAAS 3

Walter, Villiam Christian
See Andersen, Hans Christian

Wambaugh, Joseph (Aloysius, Jr.) 1937-**CLC 3, 18; DAM NOV, POP**
See also AITN 1; BEST 89:3; CA 33-36R; CANR 42, 65; DLB 6; DLBY 83; MTCW 1

Wang Wei 699(?)-761(?) ........................ **PC 18**

Ward, Arthur Henry Sarsfield 1883-1959
See Rohmer, Sax
See also CA 108

Ward, Douglas Turner 1930- ............ **CLC 19**
See also BW 1; CA 81-84; CANR 27; DLB 7, 38

Ward, Mary Augusta
See Ward, Mrs. Humphry

Ward, Mrs. Humphry 1851-1920 .. **TCLC 55**
See also DLB 18

Ward, Peter
See Faust, Frederick (Schiller)

Warhol, Andy 1928(?)-1987 .............. **CLC 20**
See also AAYA 12; BEST 89:4; CA 89-92; 121; CANR 34

Warner, Francis (Robert le Plastrier) 1937-
**CLC 14**
See also CA 53-56; CANR 11

Warner, Marina 1946- ........................ **CLC 59**
See also CA 65-68; CANR 21, 55; DLB 194

Warner, Rex (Ernest) 1905-1986 ...... **CLC 45**
See also CA 89-92; 119; DLB 15

Warner, Susan (Bogert) 1819-1885 **NCLC 31**
See also DLB 3, 42

Warner, Sylvia (Constance) Ashton
See Ashton-Warner, Sylvia (Constance)

Warner, Sylvia Townsend 1893-1978 **CLC 7, 19; SSC 23**
See also CA 61-64; 77-80; CANR 16, 60; DLB 34, 139; MTCW 1

Warren, Mercy Otis 1728-1814 ..... **NCLC 13**
See also DLB 31, 200

Warren, Robert Penn 1905-1989**CLC 1, 4, 6, 8, 10, 13, 18, 39, 53, 59; DA; DAB; DAC; DAM MST, NOV, POET; SSC 4; WLC**
See also AITN 1; CA 13-16R; 129; CANR 10, 47; CDALB 1968-1988; DLB 2, 48, 152; DLBY 80, 89; INT CANR-10; MTCW 1; SATA 46; SATA-Obit 63

Warshofsky, Isaac
See Singer, Isaac Bashevis

Warton, Thomas 1728-1790 ..... **LC 15; DAM POET**
See also DLB 104, 109

Waruk, Kona
See Harris, (Theodore) Wilson

Warung, Price 1855-1911 ............... **TCLC 45**

Warwick, Jarvis
See Garner, Hugh

Washington, Alex

See Harris, Mark

Washington, Booker T(aliaferro) 1856-1915
**TCLC 10; BLC 3; DAM MULT**
See also BW 1; CA 114; 125; SATA 28

Washington, George 1732-1799 .......... **LC 25**
See also DLB 31

Wassermann, (Karl) Jakob 1873-1934**T C L C 6**
See also CA 104; DLB 66

Wasserstein, Wendy 1950- ... **CLC 32, 59, 90; DAM DRAM; DC 4**
See also CA 121; 129; CABS 3; CANR 53; INT 129; SATA 94

Waterhouse, Keith (Spencer) 1929- . **CLC 47**
See also CA 5-8R; CANR 38, 67; DLB 13, 15; MTCW 1

Waters, Frank (Joseph) 1902-1995 ..**CLC 88**
See also CA 5-8R; 149; CAAS 13; CANR 3, 18, 63; DLBY 86

Waters, Roger 1944- .......................... **CLC 35**

Watkins, Frances Ellen
See Harper, Frances Ellen Watkins

Watkins, Gerrold
See Malzberg, Barry N(athaniel)

Watkins, Gloria 1955(?)-
See hooks, bell
See also BW 2; CA 143

Watkins, Paul 1964- ........................... **CLC 55**
See also CA 132; CANR 62

Watkins, Vernon Phillips 1906-1967 **CLC 43**
See also CA 9-10; 25-28R; CAP 1; DLB 20

Watson, Irving S.
See Mencken, H(enry) L(ouis)

Watson, John H.
See Farmer, Philip Jose

Watson, Richard F.
See Silverberg, Robert

Waugh, Auberon (Alexander) 1939- .. **CLC 7**
See also CA 45-48; CANR 6, 22; DLB 14, 194

Waugh, Evelyn (Arthur St. John) 1903-1966
**CLC 1, 3, 8, 13, 19, 27, 44, 107; DA; DAB; DAC; DAM MST, NOV, POP; WLC**
See also CA 85-88; 25-28R; CANR 22; CDBLB 1914-1945; DLB 15, 162, 195; MTCW 1

Waugh, Harriet 1944- ......................... **CLC 6**
See also CA 85-88; CANR 22

Ways, C. R.
See Blount, Roy (Alton), Jr.

Waystaff, Simon
See Swift, Jonathan

Webb, (Martha) Beatrice (Potter) 1858-1943
**TCLC 22**
See also Potter, (Helen) Beatrix
See also CA 117

Webb, Charles (Richard) 1939- .......... **CLC 7**
See also CA 25-28R

Webb, James H(enry), Jr. 1946- ....... **CLC 22**
See also CA 81-84

Webb, Mary (Gladys Meredith) 1881-1927
**TCLC 24**
See also CA 123; DLB 34

Webb, Mrs. Sidney
See Webb, (Martha) Beatrice (Potter)

Webb, Phyllis 1927- ........................... **CLC 18**
See also CA 104; CANR 23; DLB 53

Webb, Sidney (James) 1859-1947 .. **TCLC 22**
See also CA 117; 163; DLB 190

Webber, Andrew Lloyd ...................... **CLC 21**
See also Lloyd Webber, Andrew

Weber, Lenora Mattingly 1895-1971 **CLC 12**
See also CA 19-20; 29-32R; CAP 1; SATA 2; SATA-Obit 26

Weber, Max 1864-1920 ................... **TCLC 69**
See also CA 109

Webster, John 1579(?)-1634(?) ... **LC 33; DA; DAB; DAC; DAM DRAM, MST; DC 2; WLC**

See also CDBLB Before 1660; DLB 58

Webster, Noah 1758-1843 ............... **NCLC 30**

Wedekind, (Benjamin) Frank(lin) 1864-1918
**TCLC 7; DAM DRAM**
See also CA 104; 153; DLB 118

Weidman, Jerome 1913- ..................... **CLC 7**
See also AITN 2; CA 1-4R; CANR 1; DLB 28

Weil, Simone (Adolphine) 1909-1943**TCLC 23**
See also CA 117; 159

Weininger, Otto 1880-1903 ............ **TCLC 84**

Weinstein, Nathan
See West, Nathanael

Weinstein, Nathan von Wallenstein
See West, Nathanael

Weir, Peter (Lindsay) 1944- ............. **CLC 20**
See also CA 113; 123

Weiss, Peter (Ulrich) 1916-1982**CLC 3, 15, 51; DAM DRAM**
See also CA 45-48; 106; CANR 3; DLB 69, 124

Weiss, Theodore (Russell) 1916-**CLC 3, 8, 14**
See also CA 9-12R; CAAS 2; CANR 46; DLB 5

Welch, (Maurice) Denton 1915-1948**TCLC 22**
See also CA 121; 148

Welch, James 1940- ..... **CLC 6, 14, 52; DAM MULT, POP**
See also CA 85-88; CANR 42, 66; DLB 175; NNAL

Weldon, Fay 1931- . **CLC 6, 9, 11, 19, 36, 59; DAM POP**
See also CA 21-24R; CANR 16, 46, 63; CDBLB 1960 to Present; DLB 14, 194; INT CANR-16; MTCW 1

Wellek, Rene 1903-1995 ..................... **CLC 28**
See also CA 5-8R; 150; CAAS 7; CANR 8; DLB 63; INT CANR-8

Weller, Michael 1942- ................... **CLC 10, 53**
See also CA 85-88

Weller, Paul 1958- ............................ **CLC 26**

Wellershoff, Dieter 1925- .................. **CLC 46**
See also CA 89-92; CANR 16, 37

Welles, (George) Orson 1915-1985**CLC 20, 80**
See also CA 93-96; 117

Wellman, John McDowell 1945-
See Wellman, Mac
See also CA 166

Wellman, Mac 1945- ........................... **CLC 65**
See also Wellman, John McDowell; Wellman, John McDowell

Wellman, Manly Wade 1903-1986 .... **CLC 49**
See also CA 1-4R; 118; CANR 6, 16, 44; SATA 6; SATA-Obit 47

Wells, Carolyn 1869(?)-1942 .......... **TCLC 35**
See also CA 113; DLB 11

Wells, H(erbert) G(eorge) 1866-1946**TCLC 6, 12, 19; DA; DAB; DAC; DAM MST, NOV; SSC 6; WLC**
See also AAYA 18; CA 110; 121; CDBLB 1914-1945; DLB 34, 70, 156, 178; MTCW 1; SATA 20

Wells, Rosemary 1943- ...................... **CLC 12**
See also AAYA 13; CA 85-88; CANR 48; CLR 16; MAICYA; SAAS 1; SATA 18, 69

Welty, Eudora 1909- **CLC 1, 2, 5, 14, 22, 33, 105; DA; DAB; DAC; DAM MST, NOV; SSC 1, 27; WLC**
See also CA 9-12R; CABS 1; CANR 32, 65; CDALB 1941-1968; DLB 2, 102, 143; DLBD 12; DLBY 87; MTCW 1

Wen I-to 1899-1946 ........................ **TCLC 28**

Wentworth, Robert
See Hamilton, Edmond

Werfel, Franz (Viktor) 1890-1945 ... **TCLC 8**
See also CA 104; 161; DLB 81, 124

Wergeland, Henrik Arnold 1808-1845**N C L C 5**

Wersba, Barbara 1932- ...................... **CLC 30**

See also AAYA 2; CA 29-32R; CANR 16, 38;
CLR 3; DLB 52; JRDA; MAICYA; SAAS 2;
SATA 1, 58
**Wertmueller, Lina** 1928- .................... **CLC 16**
See also CA 97-100; CANR 39
**Wescott, Glenway** 1901-1987 ............ **CLC 13**
See also CA 13-16R; 121; CANR 23, 70; DLB
4, 9, 102
**Wesker, Arnold** 1932- .... **CLC 3, 5, 42; DAB;**
**DAM DRAM**
See also CA 1-4R; CAAS 7; CANR 1, 33;
CDBLB 1960 to Present; DLB 13; MTCW 1
**Wesley, Richard (Errol)** 1945- ........... **CLC 7**
See also BW 1; CA 57-60; CANR 27; DLB 38
**Wessel, Johan Herman** 1742-1785 ......... **LC 7**
**West, Anthony (Panther)** 1914-1987 **CLC 50**
See also CA 45-48; 124; CANR 3, 19; DLB 15
**West, C. P.**
See Wodehouse, P(elham) G(renville)
**West, (Mary) Jessamyn** 1902-1984 **CLC 7, 17**
See also CA 9-12R; 112; CANR 27; DLB 6;
DLBY 84; MTCW 1; SATA-Obit 37
**West, Morris L(anglo)** 1916- ......... **CLC 6, 33**
See also CA 5-8R; CANR 24, 49, 64; MTCW 1
**West, Nathanael** 1903-1940 **TCLC 1, 14, 44;**
**SSC 16**
See also CA 104; 125; CDALB 1929-1941;
DLB 4, 9, 28; MTCW 1
**West, Owen**
See Koontz, Dean R(ay)
**West, Paul** 1930- ...................... **CLC 7, 14, 96**
See also CA 13-16R; CAAS 7; CANR 22, 53;
DLB 14; INT CANR-22
**West, Rebecca** 1892-1983 ... **CLC 7, 9, 31, 50**
See also CA 5-8R; 109; CANR 19; DLB 36;
DLBY 83; MTCW 1
**Westall, Robert (Atkinson)** 1929-1993 **CLC 17**
See also AAYA 12; CA 69-72; 141; CANR 18,
68; CLR 13; JRDA; MAICYA; SAAS 2;
SATA 23, 69; SATA-Obit 75
**Westlake, Donald E(dwin)** 1933- **CLC 7, 33;**
**DAM POP**
See also CA 17-20R; CAAS 13; CANR 16, 44,
65; INT CANR-16
**Westmacott, Mary**
See Christie, Agatha (Mary Clarissa)
**Weston, Allen**
See Norton, Andre
**Wetcheek, J. L.**
See Feuchtwanger, Lion
**Wetering, Janwillem van de**
See van de Wetering, Janwillem
**Wetherald, Agnes Ethelwyn** 1857-1940 **TCLC 81**
See also DLB 99
**Wetherell, Elizabeth**
See Warner, Susan (Bogert)
**Whale, James** 1889-1957 ................ **TCLC 63**
**Whalen, Philip** 1923- ..................... **CLC 6, 29**
See also CA 9-12R; CANR 5, 39; DLB 16
**Wharton, Edith (Newbold Jones)** 1862-1937
**TCLC 3, 9, 27, 53; DA; DAB; DAC; DAM**
**MST, NOV; SSC 6; WLC**
See also AAYA 25; CA 104; 132; CDALB 1865-
1917; DLB 4, 9, 12, 78, 189; DLBD 13;
MTCW 1
**Wharton, James**
See Mencken, H(enry) L(ouis)
**Wharton, William (a pseudonym) CLC 18, 37**
See also CA 93-96; DLBY 80; INT 93-96
**Wheatley (Peters), Phillis** 1754(?)-1784 **LC 3;**
**BLC 3; DA; DAC; DAM MST, MULT,**
**POET; PC 3; WLC**
See also CDALB 1640-1865; DLB 31, 50
**Wheelock, John Hall** 1886-1978 ....... **CLC 14**
See also CA 13-16R; 77-80; CANR 14; DLB
45

**White, E(lwyn) B(rooks)** 1899-1985 **CLC 10,**
**34, 39; DAM POP**
See also AITN 2; CA 13-16R; 116; CANR 16,
37; CLR 1, 21; DLB 11, 22; MAICYA;
MTCW 1; SATA 2, 29, 100; SATA-Obit 44
**White, Edmund (Valentine III)** 1940- **CLC 27,**
**110; DAM POP**
See also AAYA 7; CA 45-48; CANR 3, 19, 36,
62; MTCW 1
**White, Patrick (Victor Martindale)** 1912-1990
**CLC 3, 4, 5, 7, 9, 18, 65, 69**
See also CA 81-84; 132; CANR 43; MTCW 1
**White, Phyllis Dorothy James** 1920-
See James, P. D.
See also CA 21-24R; CANR 17, 43, 65; DAM
POP; MTCW 1
**White, T(erence) H(anbury)** 1906-1964 **C L C**
**30**
See also AAYA 22; CA 73-76; CANR 37; DLB
160; JRDA; MAICYA; SATA 12
**White, Terence de Vere** 1912-1994 ... **CLC 49**
See also CA 49-52; 145; CANR 3
**White, Walter F(rancis)** 1893-1955 **TCLC 15**
See also White, Walter
See also BW 1; CA 115; 124; DLB 51
**White, William Hale** 1831-1913
See Rutherford, Mark
See also CA 121
**Whitehead, E(dward) A(nthony)** 1933- **CLC 5**
See also CA 65-68; CANR 58
**Whitemore, Hugh (John)** 1936- ........ **CLC 37**
See also CA 132; INT 132
**Whitman, Sarah Helen (Power)** 1803-1878
**NCLC 19**
See also DLB 1
**Whitman, Walt(er)** 1819-1892 . **NCLC 4, 31;**
**DA; DAB; DAC; DAM MST, POET; PC**
**3; WLC**
See also CDALB 1640-1865; DLB 3, 64; SATA
20
**Whitney, Phyllis A(yame)** 1903- ..... **CLC 42;**
**DAM POP**
See also AITN 2; BEST 90:3; CA 1-4R; CANR
3, 25, 38, 60; JRDA; MAICYA; SATA 1, 30
**Whittemore, (Edward) Reed (Jr.)** 1919- **CLC 4**
See also CA 9-12R; CAAS 8; CANR 4; DLB 5
**Whittier, John Greenleaf** 1807-1892 **NCLC 8,**
**59**
See also DLB 1
**Whittlebot, Hernia**
See Coward, Noel (Peirce)
**Wicker, Thomas Grey** 1926-
See Wicker, Tom
See also CA 65-68; CANR 21, 46
**Wicker, Tom** ............................................. **CLC 7**
See also Wicker, Thomas Grey
**Wideman, John Edgar** 1941- **CLC 5, 34, 36,**
**67; BLC 3; DAM MULT**
See also BW 2; CA 85-88; CANR 14, 42, 67;
DLB 33, 143
**Wiebe, Rudy (Henry)** 1934- .. **CLC 6, 11, 14;**
**DAC; DAM MST**
See also CA 37-40R; CANR 42, 67; DLB 60
**Wieland, Christoph Martin** 1733-1813 **N C L C**
**17**
See also DLB 97
**Wiene, Robert** 1881-1938 ............... **TCLC 56**
**Wieners, John** 1934- ........................... **CLC 7**
See also CA 13-16R; DLB 16
**Wiesel, Elie(zer)** 1928- **CLC 3, 5, 11, 37; DA;**
**DAB; DAC; DAM MST, NOV; WLCS 2**
See also AAYA 7; AITN 1; CA 5-8R; CAAS 4;
CANR 8, 40, 65; DLB 83; DLBY 87; INT
CANR-8; MTCW 1; SATA 56
**Wiggins, Marianne** 1947- ................. **CLC 57**
See also BEST 89:3; CA 130; CANR 60
**Wight, James Alfred** 1916-1995

See Herriot, James
See also CA 77-80; SATA 55; SATA-Brief 44
**Wilbur, Richard (Purdy)** 1921- **CLC 3, 6, 9, 14,**
**53, 110; DA; DAB; DAC; DAM MST,**
**POET**
See also CA 1-4R; CABS 2; CANR 2, 29; DLB
5, 169; INT CANR-29; MTCW 1; SATA 9
**Wild, Peter** 1940- ................................. **CLC 14**
See also CA 37-40R; DLB 5
**Wilde, Oscar (Fingal O'Flahertie Wills)**
1854(?)-1900 ...........................................
**TCLC 1, 8, 23, 41; DA; DAB; DAC; DAM**
**DRAM, MST, NOV; SSC 11; WLC**
See also CA 104; 119; CDBLB 1890-1914;
DLB 10, 19, 34, 57, 141, 156, 190; SATA 24
**Wilder, Billy** ...................................... **CLC 20**
See also Wilder, Samuel
See also DLB 26
**Wilder, Samuel** 1906-
See Wilder, Billy
See also CA 89-92
**Wilder, Thornton (Niven)** 1897-1975 **CLC 1, 5,**
**6, 10, 15, 35, 82; DA; DAB; DAC; DAM**
**DRAM, MST, NOV; DC 1; WLC**
See also AITN 2; CA 13-16R; 61-64; CANR
40; DLB 4, 7, 9; DLBY 97; MTCW 1
**Wilding, Michael** 1942- ..................... **CLC 73**
See also CA 104; CANR 24, 49
**Wiley, Richard** 1944- ........................ **CLC 44**
See also CA 121; 129; CANR 71
**Wilhelm, Kate** ...................................... **CLC 7**
See also Wilhelm, Katie Gertrude
See also AAYA 20; CAAS 5; DLB 8; INT
CANR-17
**Wilhelm, Katie Gertrude** 1928-
See Wilhelm, Kate
See also CA 37-40R; CANR 17, 36, 60; MTCW
1
**Wilkins, Mary**
See Freeman, Mary Eleanor Wilkins
**Willard, Nancy** 1936- ..................... **CLC 7, 37**
See also CA 89-92; CANR 10, 39, 68; CLR 5;
DLB 5, 52; MAICYA; MTCW 1; SATA 37,
71; SATA-Brief 30
**Williams, C(harles) K(enneth)** 1936- **CLC 33,**
**56; DAM POET**
See also CA 37-40R; CAAS 26; CANR 57; DLB
5
**Williams, Charles**
See Collier, James L(incoln)
**Williams, Charles (Walter Stansby)** 1886-1945
**TCLC 1, 11**
See also CA 104; 163; DLB 100, 153
**Williams, (George) Emlyn** 1905-1987 **CLC 15;**
**DAM DRAM**
See also CA 104; 123; CANR 36; DLB 10, 77;
MTCW 1
**Williams, Hank** 1923-1953 ............. **TCLC 81**
**Williams, Hugo** 1942- ........................ **CLC 42**
See also CA 17-20R; CANR 45; DLB 40
**Williams, J. Walker**
See Wodehouse, P(elham) G(renville)
**Williams, John A(lfred)** 1925- **CLC 5, 13; BLC**
**3; DAM MULT**
See also BW 2; CA 53-56; CAAS 3; CANR 6,
26, 51; DLB 2, 33; INT CANR-6
**Williams, Jonathan (Chamberlain)** 1929-
**CLC 13**
See also CA 9-12R; CAAS 12; CANR 8; DLB
5
**Williams, Joy** 1944- .......................... **CLC 31**
See also CA 41-44R; CANR 22, 48
**Williams, Norman** 1952- ................... **CLC 39**
See also CA 118
**Williams, Sherley Anne** 1944- **CLC 89; BLC 3;**
**DAM MULT, POET**
See also BW 2; CA 73-76; CANR 25; DLB 41;

# Literary Criticism Series
# Cumulative Topic Index

This index lists all topic entries in Gale's *Classical and Medieval Literature Criticism, Contemporary Literary Criticism, Literature Criticism from 1400 to 1800, Nineteenth-Century Literature Criticism,* and *Twentieth-Century Literary Criticism.*

Topic Index

**Topic Index**

**Topic Index**

urban and rural life in the Victorian novel, 397-406

women in the Victorian novel, 406-25

Mudie's Circulating Library, 425-34

the late-Victorian novel, 434-51

**Vietnam War in Literature and Film** CLC 91: 383-437

overview, 384-8

prose, 388-412

film and drama, 412-24

poetry, 424-35

**Vorticism** TCLC 62: 330-426

Wyndham Lewis and Vorticism, 330-8

characteristics and principles of Vorticism, 338-65

Lewis and Pound, 365-82

Vorticist writing, 382-416

Vorticist painting, 416-26

**Women's Diaries, Nineteenth-Century** NCLC 48: 308-54

overview, 308-13

diary as history, 314-25

sociology of diaries, 325-34

diaries as psychological scholarship, 334-43

diary as autobiography, 343-8

diary as literature, 348-53

**Women Writers, Seventeenth-Century** LC 30: 2-58

overview, 2-15

women and education, 15-9

women and autobiography, 19-31

women's diaries, 31-9

early feminists, 39-58

**World War I Literature** TCLC 34: 392-486

overview, 393-403

English, 403-27

German, 427-50

American, 450-66

French, 466-74

and modern history, 474-82

**Yellow Journalism** NCLC 36: 383-456

overviews, 384-96

major figures, 396-413

**Young Playwrights Festival**

1988—CLC 55: 376-81

1989—CLC 59: 398-403

1990—CLC 65: 444-8

**Topic Index**

# Twentieth-Century Literary Criticism
## Cumulative Nationality Index

Hulme, T(homas) E(rnest)  21
Hunt, Violet  53
Jacobs, W(illiam) W(ymark)  22
James, Montague (Rhodes)  6
Jerome, Jerome K(lapka)  23
Johnson, Lionel (Pigot)  19
Kaye-Smith, Sheila  20
Keynes, John Maynard  64
Kipling, (Joseph) Rudyard  8, 17
Laski, Harold  79
Lawrence, D(avid) H(erbert Richards)  2, 9,
   16, 33, 48, 61
Lawrence, T(homas) E(dward)  18
Lee, Vernon  5
Lee-Hamilton, Eugene (Jacob)  22
Leverson, Ada  18
Lewis, (Percy) Wyndham  2, 9
Lindsay, David  15
Lowndes, Marie Adelaide (Belloc)  12
Lowry, (Clarence) Malcolm  6, 40
Lucas, E(dward) V(errall)  73
Macaulay, Rose  7, 44
MacCarthy, (Charles Otto) Desmond  36
Maitland, Frederic  65
Manning, Frederic  25
Meredith, George  17, 43
Mew, Charlotte (Mary)  8
Meynell, Alice (Christina Gertrude Thompson)
   6
Middleton, Richard (Barham)  56
Milne, A(lan) A(lexander)  6
Morrison, Arthur  72
Murry, John Middleton  16
Nightingale, Florence  85
Noyes, Alfred  7
Oppenheim, E(dward) Phillips  45
Orwell, George  2, 6, 15, 31, 51
Ouida  43
Owen, Wilfred (Edward Salter)  5, 27
Pinero, Arthur Wing  32
Powys, T(heodore) F(rancis)  9
Quiller-Couch, Arthur (Thomas)  53
Richardson, Dorothy Miller  3
Rohmer, Sax  28
Rolfe, Frederick (William Serafino Austin Lewis
   Mary)  12
Rosenberg, Isaac  12
Ruskin, John  20
Rutherford, Mark  25
Sabatini, Rafael  47
Saintsbury, George (Edward Bateman)  31
Saki  3
Sapper  44
Sayers, Dorothy L(eigh)  2, 15
Shiel, M(atthew) P(hipps)  8
Sinclair, May  3, 11
Stapledon, (William) Olaf  22
Stead, William Thomas  48
Stephen, Leslie  23
Strachey, (Giles) Lytton  12
Summers, (Alphonsus Joseph-Mary Augustus)
   Montague  16
Sutro, Alfred  6
Swinburne, Algernon Charles  8, 36
Symons, Arthur  11
Thomas, (Philip) Edward  10
Thompson, Francis Joseph  4
Tomlinson, H(enry) M(ajor)  71
Upward, Allen  85
Van Druten, John (William)  2
Wallace, (Richard Horatio) Edgar  57
Walpole, Hugh (Seymour)  5
Ward, Mrs. Humphry  55

Warung, Price  45
Webb, (Martha) Beatrice (Potter)  22
Webb, Mary (Gladys Meredith)  24
Webb, Sidney (James)  22
Welch, (Maurice) Denton  22
Wells, H(erbert) G(eorge)  6, 12, 19
Williams, Charles (Walter Stansby)  1, 11
Woolf, (Adeline) Virginia  1, 5, 20, 43, 56
Yonge, Charlotte (Mary)  48
Zangwill, Israel  16

## ESTONIAN
Tammsaare, A(nton) H(ansen)  27

## FINNISH
Leino, Eino  24
Soedergran, Edith (Irene)  31

## FRENCH
Alain  41
Alain-Fournier  6
Apollinaire, Guillaume  3, 8, 51
Artaud, Antonin (Marie Joseph)  3, 36
Barbusse, Henri  5
Barres, (Auguste-) Maurice  47
Benda, Julien  60
Bergson, Henri(-Louis)  32
Bernanos, (Paul Louis) Georges  3
Bernhardt, Sarah (Henriette Rosine)  75
Bloy, Leon  22
Bourget, Paul (Charles Joseph)  12
Claudel, Paul (Louis Charles Marie)  2, 10
Colette, (Sidonie-Gabrielle)  1, 5, 16
Coppee, Francois  25
Daumal, Rene  14
Desnos, Robert  22
Drieu la Rochelle, Pierre(-Eugene)  21
Dujardin, Edouard (Emile Louis)  13
Durkheim, Emile  55
Eluard, Paul  7, 41
Fargue, Leon-Paul  11
Feydeau, Georges (Leon Jules Marie)  22
France, Anatole  9
Gide, Andre (Paul Guillaume)  5, 12, 36
Giraudoux, (Hippolyte) Jean  2, 7
Gourmont, Remy (-Marie-Charles) de  17
Huysmans, Joris-Karl  7, 69
Jacob, (Cyprien-)Max  6
Jammes, Francis  75
Jarry, Alfred  2, 14
Larbaud, Valery (Nicolas)  9
Leautaud, Paul  83
Leblanc, Maurice (Marie Emile)  49
Leroux, Gaston  25
Loti, Pierre  11
Martin du Gard, Roger  24
Melies, Georges  81
Mirbeau, Octave  55
Mistral, Frederic  51
Moreas, Jean  18
Nizan, Paul  40
Peguy, Charles Pierre  10
Peret, Benjamin  20
Proust, (Valentin-Louis-George-Eugene-)
   Marcel  7, 13, 33
Rachilde  67
Radiguet, Raymond  29
Renard, Jules  17
Rolland, Romain  23
Rostand, Edmond (Eugene Alexis)  6, 37
Roussel, Raymond  20
Saint-Exupery, Antoine (Jean Baptiste Marie
   Roger) de  2, 56

Schwob, Marcel (Mayer Andre)  20
Sully Prudhomme  31
Teilhard de Chardin, (Marie Joseph) Pierre  9
Valery, (Ambroise) Paul (Toussaint Jules)  4,
   15
Verne, Jules (Gabriel)  6, 52
Vian, Boris  9
Weil, Simone (Adolphine)  23
Zola, Emile (Edouard Charles Antoine)  1, 6,
   21, 41

## GERMAN
Andreas-Salome, Lou  56
Auerbach, Erich  43
Barlach, Ernst  84
Benjamin, Walter  39
Benn, Gottfried  3
Borchert, Wolfgang  5
Brecht, (Eugen) Bertolt (Friedrich)  1, 6, 13,
   35
Carossa, Hans  48
Cassirer, Ernst  61
Doblin, Alfred  13
Doeblin, Alfred  13
Einstein, Albert  65
Ewers, Hanns Heinz  12
Feuchtwanger, Lion  3
Frank, Bruno  81
George, Stefan (Anton)  2, 14
Goebbels, (Paul) Joseph  68
Haeckel, Ernst Heinrich (Philipp August)  83
Hauptmann, Gerhart (Johann Robert)  4
Heym, Georg (Theodor Franz Arthur)  9
Heyse, Paul (Johann Ludwig von)  8
Hitler, Adolf  53
Horney, Karen (Clementine Theodore
   Danielsen)  71
Huch, Ricarda (Octavia)  13
Kaiser, Georg  9
Klabund  44
Kolmar, Gertrud  40
Lasker-Schueler, Else  57
Liliencron, (Friedrich Adolf Axel) Detlev von
   18
Luxemburg, Rosa  63
Mann, (Luiz) Heinrich  9
Mann, (Paul) Thomas  2, 8, 14, 21, 35, 44, 60
Mannheim, Karl  65
Morgenstern, Christian  8
Nietzsche, Friedrich (Wilhelm)  10, 18, 55
Ophuls, Max  79
Otto, Rudolf  85
Plumpe, Friedrich Wilhelm  53
Raabe, Wilhelm (Karl)  45
Rilke, Rainer Maria  1, 6, 19
Simmel, Georg  64
Spengler, Oswald (Arnold Gottfried)  25
Sternheim, (William Adolf) Carl  8
Sudermann, Hermann  15
Toller, Ernst  10
Vaihinger, Hans  71
Wassermann, (Karl) Jakob  6
Weber, Max  69
Wedekind, (Benjamin) Frank(lin)  7
Wiene, Robert  56

## GHANIAN
Casely-Hayford, J(oseph) E(phraim)  24

## GREEK
Cavafy, C(onstantine) P(eter)  2, 7
Kazantzakis, Nikos  2, 5, 33
Palamas, Kostes  5

Nationality Index